THE **OFFICIAL** GUIDE FOR

GMAT®

REVIEW

Prepared for the
Graduate Management Admission Council
by Educational Testing Service

Inquiries concerning this publication should be directed to Graduate and Professional Education,
Educational Testing Service, MS 61L, P.O. Box 6666, Princeton, NJ 08541-6666.

ETS Educational Testing Service

Graduate
Management
Admission
Council®

Creating Access to Graduate Business Education™

The Graduate Management Admission Council® (GMAC®), comprised of leading business schools worldwide, is a not-for-profit educational association dedicated to creating access to graduate management and professional education. GMAC provides products and services that add value to graduate business schools and their students, including:

- Graduate Management Admission Test® (GMAT®)
- MBA Forums®
- MBA LOANS℠
- POWERPREP® Software and *The Official Guide for GMAT® Review*
- The Essay Insight℠ Product
- Pre-MBA CD-ROM Series:
  Accounting Interactive®
  Finance Interactive®
  Quantitative Skills Interactive®
  Statistics Interactive®
- Web site, *www.mba.com*, offering in-depth information about the MBA—from selecting a program type and applying effectively to making the decision about which program to attend—as well as a searchable database of graduate management education programs

Contents

Contents

Introduction

The Official Guide for GMAT Review has been designed and written by the staff of Educational Testing Service (ETS), which prepares the Graduate Management Admission Test used by many graduate schools of business and management as one criterion in considering applications for admission to the schools' graduate programs. This book is intended to be a general guide to the kinds of questions likely to appear in the GMAT®. All questions used to illustrate the various types of verbal and mathematical multiple-choice questions are taken from actual administrations of the test.*

The questions that appear in this Guide are presented in the format used in the paper-based version of the *GMAT*. The *GMAT* is now administered as a computer-adaptive test (CAT) in most countries. The *GMAT* includes the question types found in this Guide, but the format and presentation of the questions is different on the computer.

- Only one question at a time is presented on the computer screen.
- The answer choices for the multiple-choice questions are preceded by ovals rather than by letters.
- You select your answer using the computer mouse.
- You must choose an answer and confirm your choice before moving on to the next question; you cannot skip any question, and you cannot return to a question or change your answer once you have confirmed your answer and moved on to the next question.
- The questions in this Guide are arranged by question type, whereas in the *GMAT* the multiple-choice quantitative

questions appear in one timed section and the multiple-choice verbal questions appear in another separately timed section; within these sections questions of different types may appear in any order.

- The two analytical writing sections are separately timed, and you write your responses for these sections using a word processor that is part of the computer-based test.

For more information about how you will respond to questions in the test, see chapter 2, Answering *GMAT* Questions.

The *GMAT* is not a test of knowledge in specific subjects — for example, it does not test knowledge specifically or uniquely acquired in accounting or economics courses. Rather, it is a test of certain skills and abilities that have been found to contribute to success in graduate programs in business and management. For this reason, it is useful to become familiar with the general types of questions likely to be found in *GMAT* and the reasoning skills, analytical writing skills, and problem-solving strategies that these types of questions demand. This book illustrates various types of questions that appear in the *GMAT* and explains in detail some of the most effective strategies for mastering these questions.

The most efficient and productive way to use this book is to read first through chapters 1 and 2. Each type of question is briefly described, the directions are given, and the skills each question type measures are outlined. You should pay particular attention to the directions for each question type. This is especially important for the data sufficiency questions, which have lengthy and complex directions, and for the Analytical Writing Assessment, which requires you to discuss the complexities of a given issue and to critique a

given argument. In chapter 2 you will learn how to respond to questions in the *GMAT*.

You may find it useful to read through all of chapter 3, Math Review, before working through chapters 4, Problem Solving, and 5, Data Sufficiency, or you may wish to use chapter 3 as a reference as you work on chapters 4 and 5. However, because chapter 3 is intended to provide you with a comprehensive review of the basic mathematical concepts used in the quantitative section of the *GMAT*, you may find it valuable to read through the chapter as a whole.

Chapters 4-9 provide detailed illustrations and explanations of individual question types. You will find the most advantageous way to use the book to study for the multiple-choice sections of the test is to choose a chapter on a particular multiple-choice question type; read the introductory material carefully; and then do the sample questions in that chapter. As you do the sample questions, follow the directions and try to work as quickly and efficiently as possible. Then review the questions and explanations, spending as much time as is necessary to familiarize yourself with the range of questions or problems presented.

The chapter on the Analytical Writing Assessment (chapter 9) is somewhat different from those on the multiple-choice questions. It presents writing tasks that may appear on the test as well as a selection of actual examinee responses to two questions. Each response is followed by an explanation of why it was awarded a particular score. You will also see the general scoring guides that readers use to score the responses. Chapter 9, Analytical Writing Assessment, provides all the information you need to familiarize yourself thoroughly with the kinds of writing tasks that you will see in the *GMAT* as well as with the standards that will be used in judging your responses.

Because a computer-adaptive test cannot be presented in paper form, practice versions of the GMAT® have been developed to allow you to experience the computer-adaptive test and gauge your preparedness for the *GMAT* before you actually take it. *Test Preparation for the GMAT : POWERPREP®* software is available for the personal computer and includes two *GMAT* tests as well as practice questions and information about the test. POWERPREP is now provided to all registrants for the *GMAT*, and is also available for download at www.mba.com.

NOTE: The tests in POWERPREP are made up of questions that appear in this Guide. If you are using the Guide and POWERPREP together, you may want to take the POWERPREP tests before reviewing the questions in this book. Prior familiarity with the questions you receive could make the POWERPREP tests easier for you than they would otherwise be and could artificially inflate your scores.

1 Description of the Graduate Management Admission Test

The Graduate Management Admission Test® (GMAT®) is designed to help graduate schools assess the qualifications of applicants for advanced study in business and management. The test can be used by both schools and students in evaluating verbal and mathematical skills as well as general knowledge and preparation for graduate study. Note, however, that *GMAT* scores should be considered as only one of several indicators of ability.

Format

The *GMAT* consists of four separately timed sections (see table below). Each of the first two sections contains a 30-minute writing task; the other two sections are 75 minutes each and contain multiple-choice questions. The first of these sections contains quantitative questions, and the second contains verbal questions.

Every test contains trial multiple-choice questions needed for pretesting for future use. These questions, however, are not identified and appear in varying locations within the test. You should therefore do your best on all questions. Answers to trial questions are not counted in the scoring of your test.

In a computer-adaptive test, questions are chosen from a very large pool of test questions categorized by content and difficulty. Only one question at a time is presented. The test is constantly trying to target your individual ability level; this means that the questions you are presented with depend on your answers to all previous questions. Consequently, you must enter an answer for each question and may not return to or change your answer to any previous question. If you answer a question incorrectly by mistake — or correctly by lucky guess — your answer to subsequent questions will lead you back to questions that are at the appropriate level of difficulty for you.

Your scores will depend on the statistical characteristics of the questions presented to you, including difficulty level; your answers to those questions; and the number of questions you answer. Adaptive test score calculations do not assign any differential credit to questions depending on where they appear in the test. The questions in an adaptive test are weighted according to their difficulty and other statistical properties, not according to their position in the test. However, because the test is adaptive, the responses provided to early questions do influence the selection of later questions.

Content

It is important to recognize that the *GMAT* evaluates skills and abilities that develop over relatively long periods of time. Although the sections are basically verbal or mathematical, the complete test provides one method of measuring overall ability. The *GMAT* does not test specific knowledge obtained in college course work, and it does not seek to measure achievements in any specific areas of study.

The Graduate Management Admission Council® recognizes that questions arise concerning techniques for taking standardized examinations such as the *GMAT*, and it is hoped that the descriptions, sample questions, and explanations given here will give you a practical familiarity with the concepts and techniques required by *GMAT* questions.

All of the multiple-choice questions in this book have appeared in the actual *GMAT*.

Format of the GMAT

	Questions	Timing
Analytical Writing		
Analysis of an Issue	1	30 min.
Analysis of an Argument	1	30 min.
Optional Break		5 min.
Quantitative	37	75 min
Problem Solving		
Data Sufficiency		
Optional Break		5 min.
Verbal	41	75 min.
Reading Comprehension		
Critical Reasoning		
Sentence Correction		
Total Time:		**4 hours (approx.)**

Quantitative Section

The quantitative section of the GMAT® measures basic mathematical skills and understanding of elementary concepts, and the ability to reason quantitatively, solve quantitative problems, and interpret graphic data.

Two types of multiple-choice questions are used in the quantitative section:

- problem solving
- data sufficiency

Problem solving and data sufficiency questions are intermingled throughout the section. Both types of questions require knowledge of

- arithmetic
- elementary algebra
- commonly known concepts of geometry

Problem Solving Questions

Problem solving questions are designed to test basic mathematical skills, understanding of elementary mathematical concepts, and the ability to reason quantitatively and to solve quantitative problems.

The directions for problem solving questions read as follows:

Solve the problem and indicate the best of the answer choices given.

Numbers: All numbers used are real numbers.

Figures: A figure accompanying a problem solving question is intended to provide information useful in solving the problem. Figures are drawn as accurately as possible EXCEPT when it is stated in a specific problem that its figure is not drawn to scale. Straight lines may sometimes appear jagged. All figures lie in a plane unless otherwise indicated.

Data Sufficiency Questions

Each data sufficiency question consists of a question, often accompanied by some initial information, and two statements, labeled (1) and (2), containing additional information. You must decide whether sufficient information to answer the question is given by either (1) or (2) individually or, if not, by both combined.

Data sufficiency questions are designed to measure your ability to analyze a quantitative problem, to recognize which information is relevant, and to determine at what point there is sufficient information to solve the problem.

These are the directions for data sufficiency questions. Read them carefully.

This data sufficiency problem consists of a question and two statements, labeled (1) and (2), in which certain data are given. You have to decide whether the data given in the statements are <u>sufficient</u> for answering the question. Using the data given in the statements <u>plus</u> your knowledge of mathematics and everyday facts (such as the number of days in July or the meaning of *counterclockwise*), you must indicate whether

- statement (1) ALONE is sufficient, but statement (2) alone is not sufficient to answer the question asked;
- statement (2) ALONE is sufficient, but statement (1) alone is not sufficient to answer the question asked;
- BOTH statements (1) and (2) TOGETHER are sufficient to answer the question asked, but NEITHER statement ALONE is sufficient;
- EACH statement ALONE is sufficient to answer the question asked;
- statements (1) and (2) TOGETHER are NOT sufficient to answer the question asked, and additional data specific to the problem are needed.

Numbers: All numbers used are real numbers.

Figures: A figure accompanying a data sufficiency problem will conform to the information given in the question, but will not necessarily conform to the additional information given in statements (1) and (2).

Lines shown as straight can be assumed to be straight and lines that appear jagged can also be assumed to be straight.

You may assume that the positions of points, angles, regions, etc., exist in the order shown and that angle measures are greater than zero.

All figures lie in a plane unless otherwise indicated.

Note: In data sufficiency problems that ask for the value of a quantity, the data given in the statements are sufficient only when it is possible to determine exactly one numerical value for the quantity.

Example:

In $\triangle PQR$, what is the value of x?

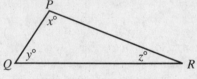

(1) $PQ = PR$
(2) $y = 40$

Explanation: According to statement (1), $PQ = PR$; therefore, $\triangle PQR$ is isosceles and $y = z$. Since $x + y + z = 180$, it follows that $x + 2y = 180$. Since statement (1) does not give a value for y, you cannot answer the question using statement (1) alone. According to statement (2), $y = 40$; therefore, $x + z = 140$. Since statement (2) does not give a value for z, you cannot answer the question using statement (2) alone. Using both statements together, since $x + 2y = 180$ and the value of y is given, you can find the value of x. Therefore, BOTH statements (1) and (2) TOGETHER are sufficient to answer the question, but NEITHER statement ALONE is sufficient.

Verbal Section

The verbal section of the GMAT® measures your ability to read and comprehend written material, to reason and evaluate arguments, and to correct written material to conform to standard written English.

Three types of multiple-choice questions are used in the verbal section of the *GMAT*:

- reading comprehension
- critical reasoning
- sentence correction

These question types are intermingled throughout the verbal section.

Reading Comprehension Questions

Reading comprehension passages are accompanied by interpretive, applicative, and inferential questions. The passages are up to 350 words long, and they discuss topics from the social sciences, the physical or biological sciences, and such business-related fields as marketing, economics, and human resource management. Because the verbal section of the *GMAT* includes passages from several different content areas, you may be generally familiar with some of the material; however, neither the passages nor the questions assume detailed knowledge of the topics discussed.

WHAT IS MEASURED

Reading comprehension questions measure your ability to understand, analyze, and apply information and concepts presented in written form. All questions are to be answered on the basis of what is stated or implied in the reading material, and no specific knowledge of the material is required.

Reading comprehension therefore evaluates your ability to

- understand words and statements in the reading passages (Questions of this type are not vocabulary questions. These questions test your understanding of and ability to comprehend terms used in the passage as well as your understanding of the English language. You may also find that questions of this type ask about the overall meaning of a passage.)
- understand the logical relationships between significant points and concepts in the reading passages (For example, such questions may ask you to determine the strong and weak points of an argument or to evaluate the importance of arguments and ideas in a passage.)
- draw inferences from facts and statements in the reading passages (The inference questions will ask you to consider factual statements or information and, on the basis of that information, reach a general conclusion.)
- understand and follow the development of quantitative concepts as they are presented in verbal material (This may involve the interpretation of numerical data or the use of simple arithmetic to reach conclusions about material in a passage.)

The directions for reading comprehension questions read as follows:

The questions in this group are based on the content of a passage. After reading the passage, choose the best answer to each question. Answer all questions following the passage on the basis of what is <u>stated</u> or <u>implied</u> in the passage.

Critical Reasoning Questions

Critical reasoning questions are designed to test the reasoning skills involved (1) in making arguments, (2) in evaluating arguments, and (3) in formulating or evaluating a plan of action. The materials on which questions are based are drawn from a variety of sources. No familiarity with the subject matter of those materials is presupposed.

WHAT IS MEASURED

Critical reasoning questions are designed to provide one measure of your ability to reason effectively in the areas of

- argument construction (Questions in this category may ask you to recognize such things as the basic structure of an argument; properly drawn conclusions; underlying assumptions; well-supported explanatory hypotheses; parallels between structurally similar arguments.)
- argument evaluation (Questions in this category may ask you to analyze a given argument and to recognize such things as factors that would strengthen, or weaken, the given argument; reasoning errors committed in making that argument; aspects of the method by which the argument proceeds.)
- formulating and evaluating a plan of action (Questions in this category may ask you to recognize such things as the relative appropriateness, effectiveness, or efficiency of different plans of action; factors that would strengthen, or weaken, the prospects of success for a proposed plan of action; assumptions underlying a proposed plan of action.)

The directions for critical reasoning questions read as follows:

For this question, select the best of the answer choices given.

Sentence Correction Questions

Sentence correction questions ask you which of the five choices best expresses an idea or relationship. The questions will require you to be familiar with the stylistic conventions and grammatical rules of standard written English and to demonstrate your ability to improve incorrect or ineffective expressions.

WHAT IS MEASURED

Sentence correction questions test two broad aspects of language proficiency:

1. *Correct expression.* A correct sentence is grammatically and structurally sound. It conforms to all the rules of standard written English (for example: noun-verb agreement, noun-pronoun agreement, pronoun consistency, pronoun case, and verb tense sequence). Further, a correct sentence will not have dangling, misplaced, or improperly formed modifiers, unidiomatic or inconsistent expressions, or faults in parallel construction.

2. *Effective expression.* An effective sentence expresses an idea or relationship clearly and concisely as well as grammatically. This does not mean that the choice with the fewest and simplest words is necessarily the best answer. It means that there are no superfluous words or needlessly complicated expressions in the best choice.

   In addition, an effective sentence uses proper diction. (Diction refers to the standard dictionary meanings of words and the appropriateness of words in context.) In evaluating the diction of a sentence, you must be able to recognize whether the words are well chosen, accurate, and suitable for the context.

The directions for sentence correction questions read as follows:

This question presents a sentence, part of which or all of which is underlined. Beneath the sentence you will find five ways of phrasing the underlined part. The first of these repeats the original; the other four are different. If you think the original is best, choose the first answer; otherwise choose one of the others.

This question tests correctness and effectiveness of expression. In choosing your answer, follow the requirements of standard written English; that is, pay attention to grammar, choice of words, and sentence construction. Choose the answer that produces the most effective sentence; this answer should be clear and exact, without awkwardness, ambiguity, redundancy, or grammatical error.

Analytical Writing Assessment

The Analytical Writing Assessment consists of two 30-minute writing tasks, "Analysis of an Issue" and "Analysis of an Argument." For the Analysis of an Issue task, you will need to analyze a given issue or opinion and then explain your point of view on the subject by citing relevant reasons and/or examples drawn from your experience, observations, or reading. For the Analysis of an Argument task, you will need to analyze the reasoning behind a given argument and then write a critique of that argument. You may, for example, consider what questionable assumptions underlie the thinking, what alternative explanations or counterexamples might weaken the conclusion, or what sort of evidence could help strengthen or refute the argument.

WHAT IS MEASURED

The Analytical Writing Assessment is designed as a direct measure of your ability to think critically and to communicate your ideas. More specifically, the Analysis of an Issue task tests your ability to explore the complexities of an issue or opinion and, if appropriate, to take a position informed by your understanding of those complexities. The Analysis of an Argument task tests your ability to formulate an appropriate and constructive critique of a specific conclusion based upon a specific line of thinking.

The issue and argument that you will find on the test concern topics of general interest, some related to business and some pertaining to a variety of other subjects. It is important to note, however, that none presupposes any specific knowledge of business or of other specific content areas: only your capacity to write analytically is being assessed.

College and university faculty members from various subject matter areas, including but not confined to management education, will evaluate how well you write. To qualify as GMAT® readers, they must first demonstrate their ability to evaluate a large number of sample responses accurately and reliably, according to *GMAT* standards and scoring criteria. Once qualified, readers will consider both the overall quality of your ideas about the issue and argument presented and your overall ability to organize, develop, and express those ideas; to provide relevant supporting reasons and examples; and to control the elements of standard written English. In addition, responses may be scored by e-rater™, an automated scoring program designed to reflect the judgment of expert readers. *

---

* In considering the elements of standard written English, readers are trained to be sensitive and fair in evaluating the responses of English as a Second Language [ESL] examinees.

The directions for the two writing tasks in the Analytical Writing Assessment read as follows:

ANALYSIS OF AN ISSUE

In this section, you will need to analyze the issue presented and explain your views on it. There is no "correct" answer. Instead, you should consider various perspectives as you develop your own position on the issue.

WRITING YOUR RESPONSE: Take a few minutes to think about the issue and plan a response before you begin writing. Be sure to organize your ideas and develop them fully, but leave time to reread your response and make any revisions that you think are necessary.

EVALUATION OF YOUR RESPONSE: College and university faculty members from various subject-matter areas, including management education, will evaluate the overall quality of your thinking and writing. They will consider how well you

- organize, develop, and express your ideas about the issue presented
- provide relevant supporting reasons and examples
- control the elements of standard written English

ANALYSIS OF AN ARGUMENT

In this section you will be asked to write a critique of the argument presented. *You are NOT being asked to present your own views on the subject.*

WRITING YOUR RESPONSE: Take a few minutes to evaluate the argument and plan a response before you begin writing. Be sure to organize your ideas and develop them fully, but leave time to reread your response and make any revisions that you think are necessary.

EVALUATION OF YOUR RESPONSE: College and university faculty members from various subject-matter areas, including management education, will evaluate the overall quality of your thinking and writing. They will consider how well you

- organize, develop, and express your ideas about the argument presented
- provide relevant supporting reasons and examples
- control the elements of standard written English

Examples of both types of writing tasks in the Analytical Writing Assessment can be found in chapter 9.

General Test-taking Suggestions

Specific test-taking strategies for individual question types are presented in chapters 4-9. The following are general suggestions to help you perform your best on the GMAT®.

1. Although the *GMAT* stresses accuracy more than speed, it is important to use the allotted time wisely. You will be able to do so if you are familiar with the mechanics of the test and the kinds of materials, questions, and directions in the test. Therefore, become familiar with the formats and requirements of each section of the test.

2. After you become generally familiar with all question types, use the individual chapters on each question type in this book (chapters 4-9), which include sample questions and detailed explanations, to prepare yourself for the actual *GMAT*.

3. Read all test directions carefully. The directions explain exactly what is required in order to answer each question type. If you read hastily, you may miss important instructions and seriously jeopardize your scores. To review directions during the test, click on the Help icon.

4. In the multiple-choice sections, it is important to try to answer all of the questions in the section. If a question is too difficult for you, do not waste time on it; eliminate as many answer choices as possible, select the best answer from among the remaining choices, and move on to the next question. **Keep moving through the test and try to finish each section. There is a chance that guessing at the end of the test can seriously lower your score. The best strategy is to pace yourself so that you have time to consider each test question, so you don't have to guess.**

5. The best way to approach the two writing tasks comprising the Analytical Writing Assessment is to take a few minutes to think about each question and plan a response before you begin writing. Take care to organize your ideas and develop them fully, but leave time to reread your response and make any revisions that you think would improve it.

6. On all sections of the test, make every effort to pace yourself. Consult the on-screen timer periodically and note the time remaining during your testing session. Work steadily and as rapidly as possible without being careless. It is not wise to spend too much time on one question if that causes you to neglect other questions. On the average, a verbal question takes about 1 3/4 minutes and a quantitative question takes about 2 minutes to answer. Give yourself enough time to answer every question. **If you do not finish in the allotted time, you will still get a score as long as you've worked on every section. However, your score will reflect the number of questions answered, and most test takers get higher scores when they finish each section.**

7. On all sections of the test, multiple-choice and writing, read each question carefully and thoroughly. Before answering a question,

determine exactly what is being asked. Never skim a question or, in the case of a multiple-choice question, the possible answers. Skimming may cause you to miss important information or nuances in the question.

8. Do not become upset if you have to guess at a question in a multiple-choice section. A person can do very well without answering every question correctly. No one is expected to get a perfect score.

Test Development Process

Educational Testing Service professional staff responsible for developing the verbal and writing measures of the GMAT® have backgrounds and advanced degrees in the humanities, in measurement, or in writing assessment. Those responsible for the quantitative portion have advanced degrees in mathematics or related fields.

Standardized procedures have been developed to guide the test-generation process, to assure high-quality test material, to avoid idiosyncratic questions, and to encourage development of test material that is widely appropriate.

An important part of the development of test material is the review process. Each question, whether writing task or multiple-choice question, as well as any stimulus material on which questions are based, must be reviewed by several independent critics. Questions are also reviewed by experts outside ETS who can bring fresh perspectives to bear on the questions in terms of actual content or in terms of sensitivity to minority and women's concerns.

After all the questions have been reviewed and revised as appropriate, the multiple-choice questions are assembled into clusters suitable for trial during actual administrations of the *GMAT*. In this manner, new questions are tried out, under standard testing conditions, by representative samples of *GMAT* examinees. Questions being tried out do not affect examinees' scores but are themselves evaluated: they are analyzed statistically for usefulness and weaknesses. The questions that perform satisfactorily are added to the pool of questions from which each computer-adaptive test is constructed; those that do not are rewritten to correct the flaws and tried out again — or discarded.

In contrast to the multiple-choice questions, the writing tasks are not tried out during actual administrations of the *GMAT*: this would be impractical. Instead, the writing tasks are pretested on first-year business school students — students who not so long ago were *GMAT* examinees themselves and who are therefore representative of the *GMAT* test-taking population. The responses are read at a pretest scoring session to determine which writing tasks are clear and accessible to examinees, which can be successfully completed within the allotted half-hour, and which discriminate fairly and reliably (i.e., they are not skewed in some way so as to disadvantage certain examinees, and they produce scores all along the scoring scale). Only those tasks that perform well in the pretest scoring sessions become part of the pool used in the *GMAT*.

2 Answering GMAT Questions

Before you arrive at the test center, it is very important that you familiarize yourself with the mechanics of taking a computer-adaptive test. Test tutorials have been developed for this purpose; they allow you to review the testing tools you will have for responding to the questions (both multiple-choice and writing) as well as gain experience using a mouse and scrolling. These tutorials are part of the GMAT® POWERPREP software, which is provided free to all test registrants; the tutorials can also be accessed by following the links provided at *www.ets.org/powerprep*.

The tutorials are divided into specific areas:

- How to Use a Mouse
- How to Answer
- How to Use the Testing Tools
- How to Scroll

This chapter highlights the "How to Use the Testing Tools" and "How to Answer" tutorial screens.

How to Use the Testing Tools

Click on the icon on the right to continue. ▶

**Or, click on the Exit icon to leave
this section of instructions.**

Below is a small version of the screen you will see when taking a test. The top part of the screen is the TITLE LINE, which will contain the following:

  • Center – the name and section of the test
  • Right Side – the question number on which you are currently working
       and the total number of questions in that section

The question will be located below the title line.

Click on one of the icons on the right. ◀ ▶

| Name of Test | 1 of 3 |

What is the capital of the United States of America?

SAMPLE

○ New York City

● Washington, D.C.

○ Seattle

○ Miami

Look at the TESTING TOOLS below the question. You will use them to tell the computer what to do. On the following screens each tool will be explained and you will have a chance to try it.

Note: You will not be able to answer the sample questions that will be shown during the next few screens. They are only there to help you understand how things work during the actual test.

Click on one of the icons on the right.

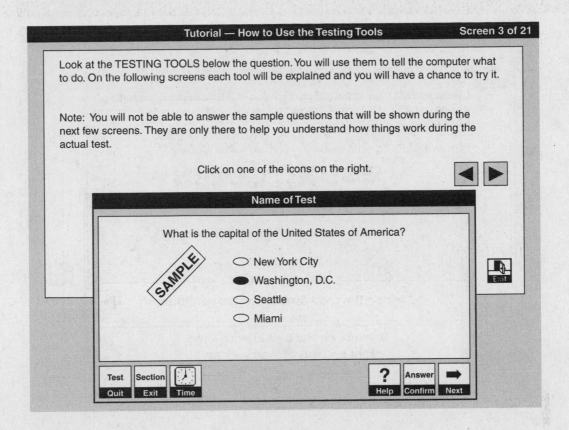

Look at the testing tools at the bottom of the screen – some are gray in color and one is dark. A gray tool will not work, so if you click on a gray tool, nothing will happen. During the test a tool may be gray on some screens and dark on others.

Remember: a gray tool won't work, AND
a dark tool will work.

Click on the dark tool (at the bottom).
Or, click on the icon on the right.

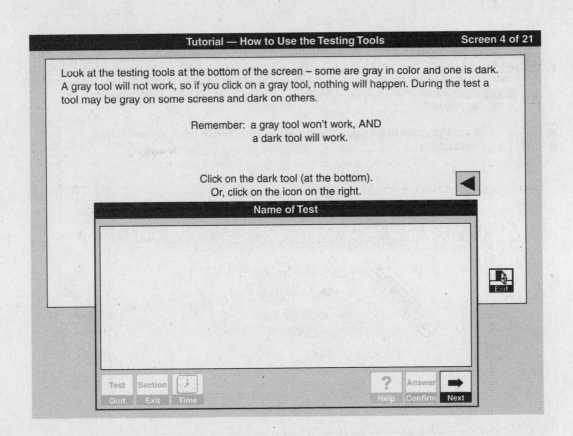

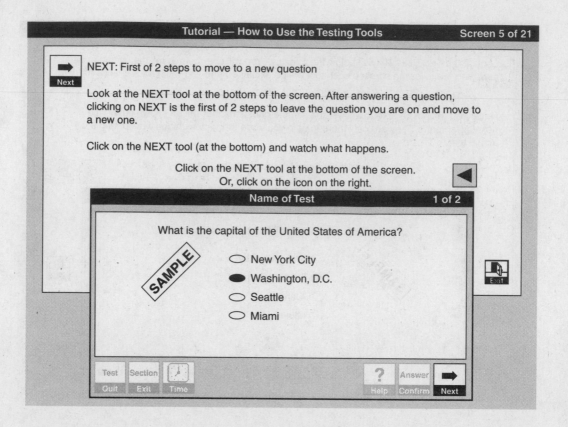

Next

NEXT: First of 2 steps to move to a new question

Look at the NEXT tool at the bottom of the screen. After answering a question, clicking on NEXT is the first of 2 steps to leave the question you are on and move to a new one.

Click on the NEXT tool (at the bottom) and watch what happens.

Click on the NEXT tool at the bottom of the screen.
Or, click on the icon on the right.

Name of Test   1 of 2

What is the capital of the United States of America?

SAMPLE

○ New York City
● Washington, D.C.
○ Seattle
○ Miami

Test Section [clock]   ? Answer →
Quit Exit Time   Help Confirm Next

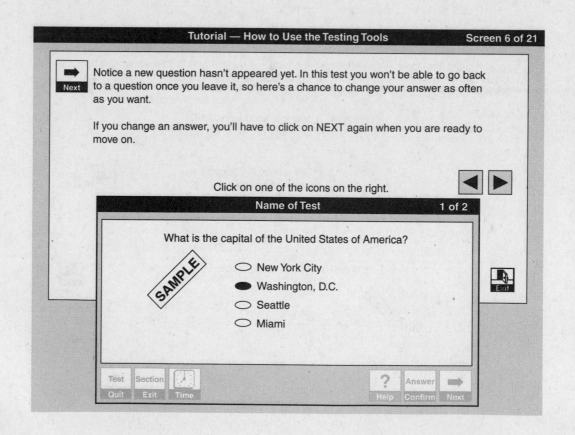

Next

Notice a new question hasn't appeared yet. In this test you won't be able to go back to a question once you leave it, so here's a chance to change your answer as often as you want.

If you change an answer, you'll have to click on NEXT again when you are ready to move on.

Click on one of the icons on the right.

Name of Test   1 of 2

What is the capital of the United States of America?

SAMPLE

○ New York City
● Washington, D.C.
○ Seattle
○ Miami

Test Section [clock]   ? Answer →
Quit Exit Time   Help Confirm Next

Answer Confirm CONFIRM ANSWER: Last of 2 steps to move to a new question

Clicking on NEXT causes the CONFIRM ANSWER icon to become dark.

When you click on CONFIRM ANSWER, your answer is saved, a new question appears, and you can't go back – try it.

Click on the CONFIRM ANSWER tool at the bottom of the screen.
Or, click on the icon on the right.

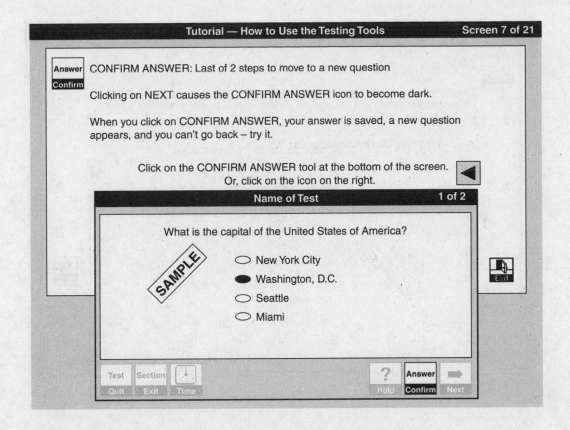

Answer Confirm Notice:

- a new question has appeared
- the question number in the title line has changed (2 of 2), AND
- the NEXT tool is now black – it won't work here, for explanation only.

Click on one of the icons on the right.

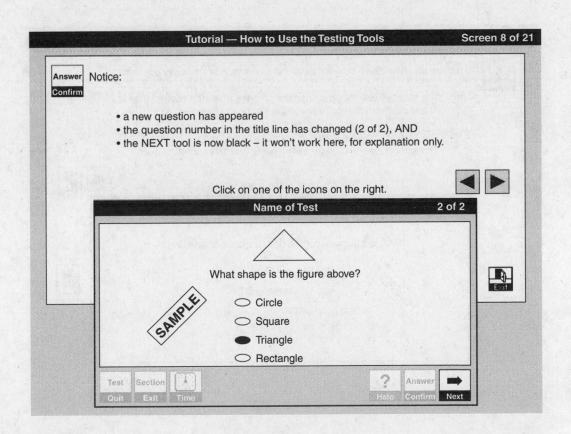

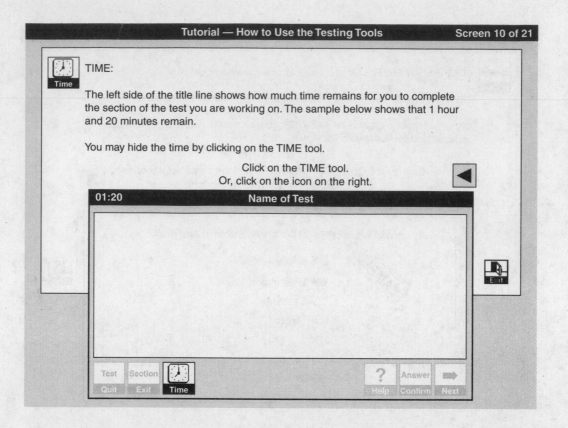

TIME:

The left side of the title line shows how much time remains for you to complete the section of the test you are working on. The sample below shows that 1 hour and 20 minutes remain.

You may hide the time by clicking on the TIME tool.

Click on the TIME tool.
Or, click on the icon on the right.

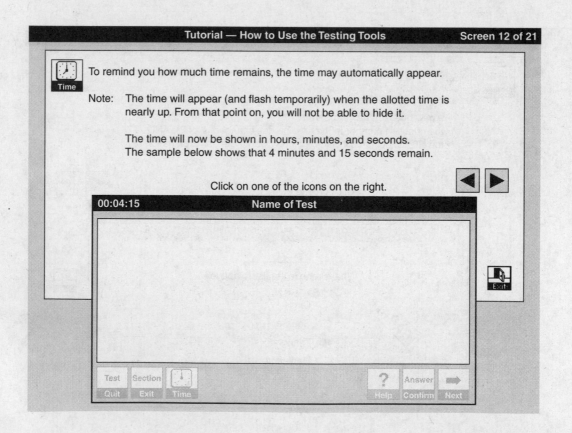

To remind you how much time remains, the time may automatically appear.

Note: The time will appear (and flash temporarily) when the allotted time is nearly up. From that point on, you will not be able to hide it.

The time will now be shown in hours, minutes, and seconds.
The sample below shows that 4 minutes and 15 seconds remain.

Click on one of the icons on the right.

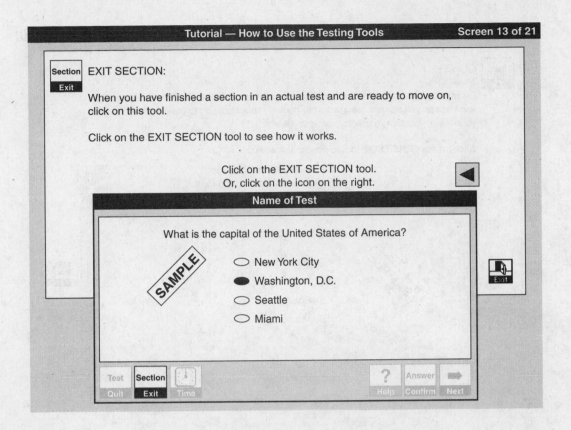

Section Exit EXIT SECTION:

When you have finished a section in an actual test and are ready to move on, click on this tool.

Click on the EXIT SECTION tool to see how it works.

Click on the EXIT SECTION tool.
Or, click on the icon on the right.

Name of Test

What is the capital of the United States of America?

SAMPLE

○ New York City
● Washington, D.C.
○ Seattle
○ Miami

Test Quit | Section Exit | Time | ? Help | Answer Confirm | Next

---

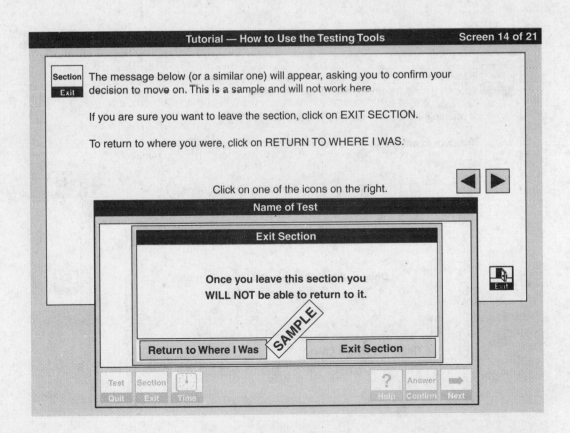

Section Exit The message below (or a similar one) will appear, asking you to confirm your decision to move on. This is a sample and will not work here.

If you are sure you want to leave the section, click on EXIT SECTION.

To return to where you were, click on RETURN TO WHERE I WAS.

Click on one of the icons on the right.

Name of Test

Exit Section

**Once you leave this section you
WILL NOT be able to return to it.**

SAMPLE

| **Return to Where I Was** | **Exit Section** |

Test Quit | Section Exit | Time | ? Help | Answer Confirm | Next

Test Quit   QUIT TEST:

During testing if you want to quit the entire test, click on the QUIT TEST tool. A message will appear asking you to confirm your decision to quit. If you change your mind, you can return to where you were.

Click on the QUIT TEST tool to see how it works.

Click on the QUIT TEST tool.
Or, click on the icon on the right.

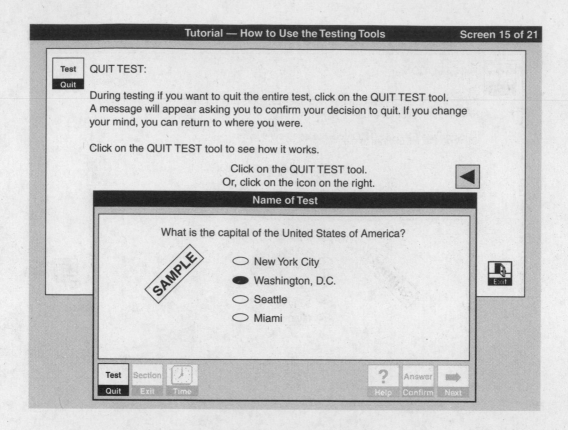

Test Quit   Notice the message below asking you to confirm your decision to quit the testing session. This is a sample and will not work here.

If you are sure you want to quit, click on QUIT TEST.

To return to where you were, click on RETURN TO WHERE I WAS.

Click on one of the icons on the right.

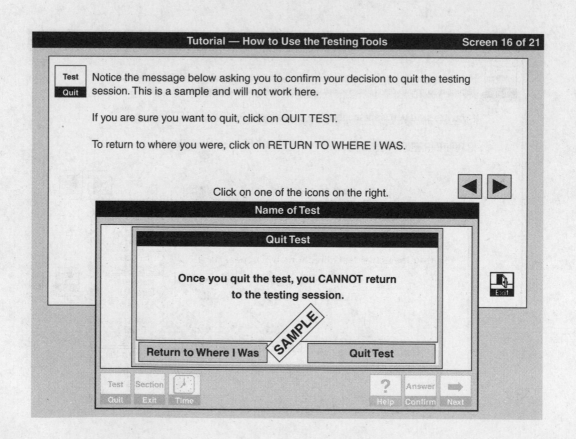

HELP:

If you want to recall the directions for the question or section you are working on, or want help in other areas, click on this tool.

Click on the HELP tool to see how it works.

Click on the HELP tool.
Or, click on the icon on the right.

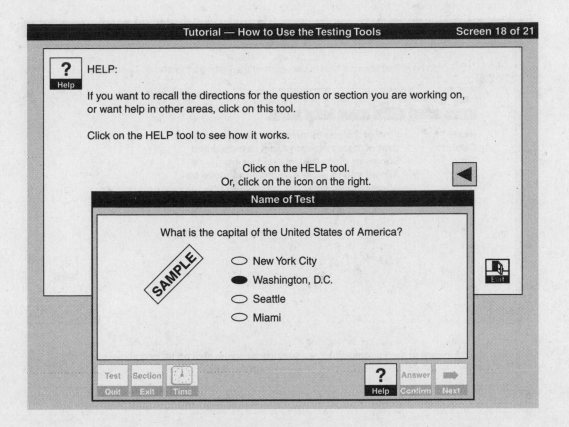

The screen below will appear. Directions for the question you are working on will be shown. Additional HELP icons will appear on the right.

For other information, click on the appropriate HELP icon.

To return to where you were in the test, click on RETURN TO WHERE I WAS.

Click on one of the icons on the right.

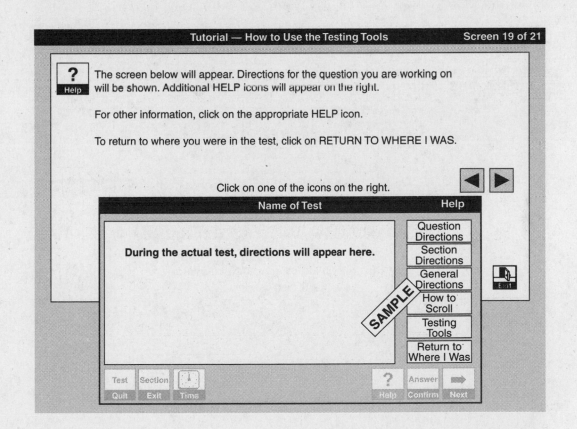

You have just learned how to use each of the testing tools shown below.

Next	First of 2 steps to move to a new question
Confirm	Last of 2 steps to move to a new question
Time	Shows or hides the time remaining
Exit	Allows you to leave a section and move on
Quit	Allows you to leave the entire test
Help	Recalls directions or provides help on how to take a test

To look at the information on any testing tool again, click on its icon above.
Or, click on the icon on the right.

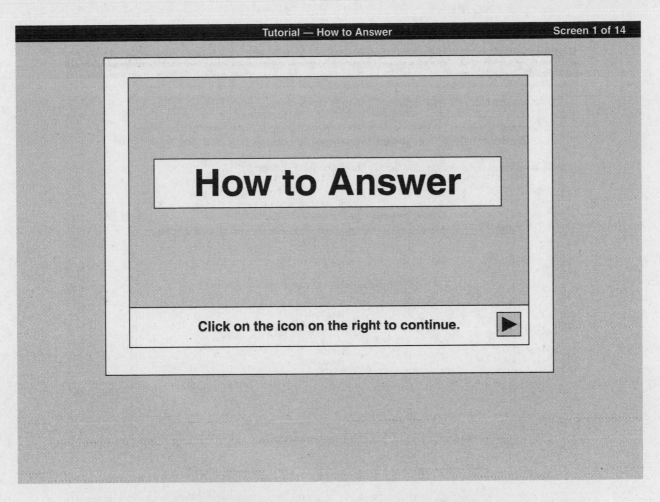

How to Answer

Click on the icon on the right to continue. ▶

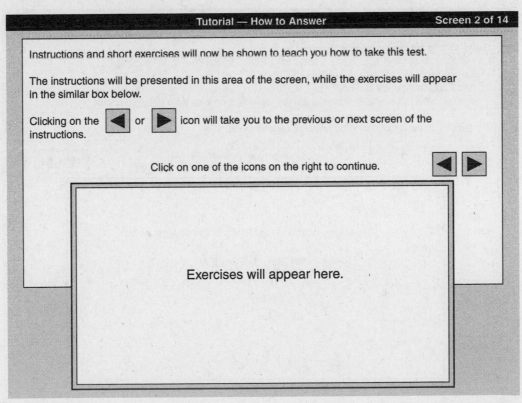

Instructions and short exercises will now be shown to teach you how to take this test.

The instructions will be presented in this area of the screen, while the exercises will appear in the similar box below.

Clicking on the ◀ or ▶ icon will take you to the previous or next screen of the instructions.

Click on one of the icons on the right to continue. ◀ ▶

Exercises will appear here.

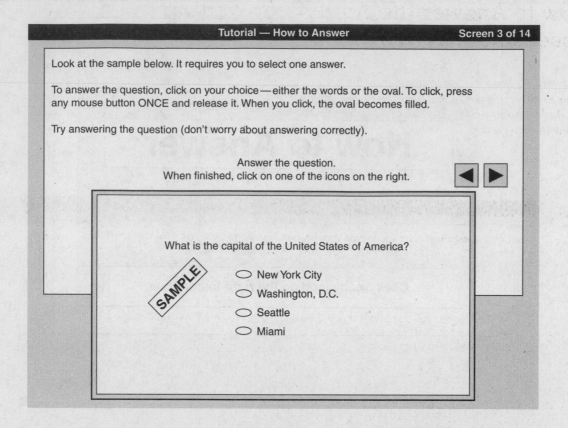

Look at the sample below. It requires you to select one answer.

To answer the question, click on your choice—either the words or the oval. To click, press any mouse button ONCE and release it. When you click, the oval becomes filled.

Try answering the question (don't worry about answering correctly).

Answer the question.
When finished, click on one of the icons on the right.

What is the capital of the United States of America?

SAMPLE

○ New York City

○ Washington, D.C.

○ Seattle

○ Miami

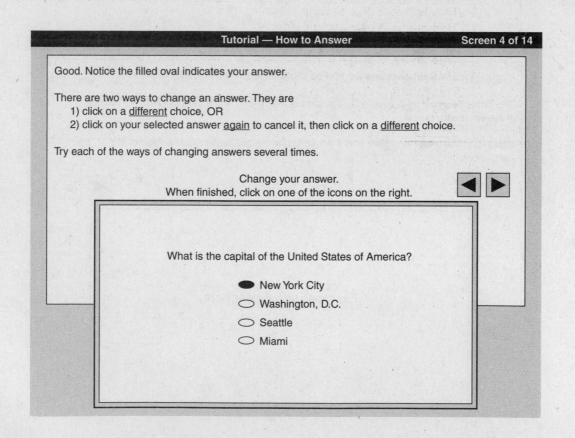

Good. Notice the filled oval indicates your answer.

There are two ways to change an answer. They are
  1) click on a different choice, OR
  2) click on your selected answer again to cancel it, then click on a different choice.

Try each of the ways of changing answers several times.

Change your answer.
When finished, click on one of the icons on the right.

What is the capital of the United States of America?

● New York City

○ Washington, D.C.

○ Seattle

○ Miami

How to Answer the Analytical Writing Assessment (AWA)

The following screens of information from the
"How to Answer" tutorial will help you to become familiar
with the word processing tools available for responding to
the AWA writing tasks.

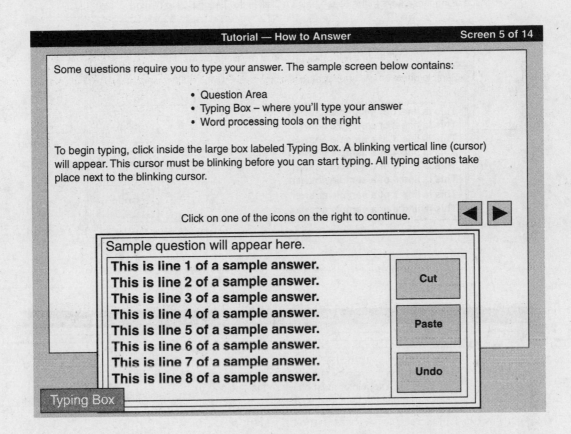

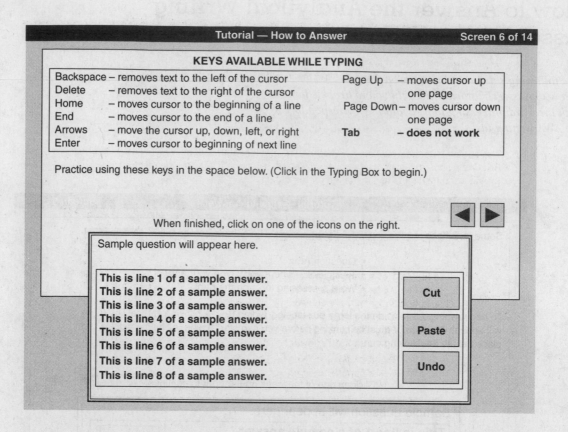

KEYS AVAILABLE WHILE TYPING

Backspace	– removes text to the left of the cursor	Page Up	– moves cursor up one page
Delete	– removes text to the right of the cursor		
Home	– moves cursor to the beginning of a line	Page Down	– moves cursor down one page
End	– moves cursor to the end of a line		
Arrows	– move the cursor up, down, left, or right	**Tab**	**– does not work**
Enter	– moves cursor to beginning of next line		

Practice using these keys in the space below. (Click in the Typing Box to begin.)

When finished, click on one of the icons on the right.

Sample question will appear here.

This is line 1 of a sample answer.
This is line 2 of a sample answer.
This is line 3 of a sample answer.
This is line 4 of a sample answer.
This is line 5 of a sample answer.
This is line 6 of a sample answer.
This is line 7 of a sample answer.
This is line 8 of a sample answer.

Cut

Paste

Undo

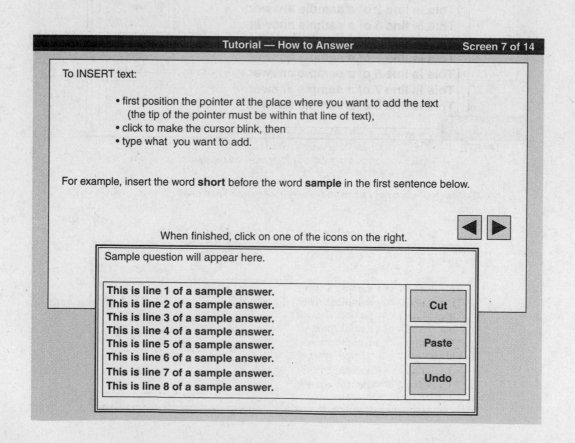

To INSERT text:

- first position the pointer at the place where you want to add the text (the tip of the pointer must be within that line of text),
- click to make the cursor blink, then
- type what you want to add.

For example, insert the word **short** before the word **sample** in the first sentence below.

When finished, click on one of the icons on the right.

Sample question will appear here.

This is line 1 of a sample answer.
This is line 2 of a sample answer.
This is line 3 of a sample answer.
This is line 4 of a sample answer.
This is line 5 of a sample answer.
This is line 6 of a sample answer.
This is line 7 of a sample answer.
This is line 8 of a sample answer.

Cut

Paste

Undo

You will need to HIGHLIGHT text to cut or paste it. To highlight:
- position the pointer directly before the first letter you want to highlight,
- press the mouse button down and while HOLDING it down, drag to the place you want to stop, then
- release the mouse button — the text will be highlighted.

To <u>un</u>highlight, click again anywhere within the Typing Box.

The tip of the pointer must stay in the MIDDLE of a line of text. If the tip moves ABOVE or BELOW a line, text from another line will also be highlighted. Moving the pointer to the left (or the right) highlights text to the left (or the right).

Try highlighting the words **sample answer** in a sentence below.
When finished, click on one of the icons on the right.

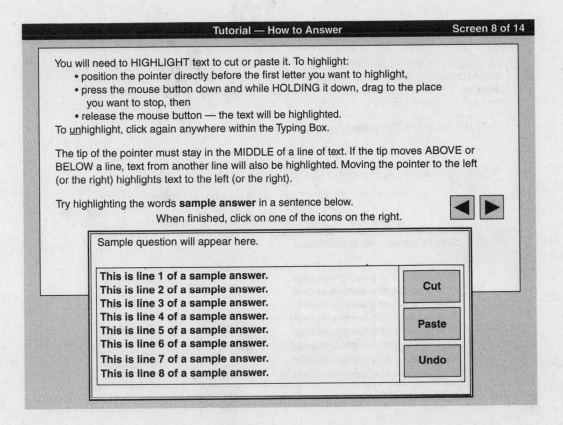

Sample question will appear here.

This is line 1 of a sample answer.
This is line 2 of a sample answer.
This is line 3 of a sample answer.
This is line 4 of a sample answer.
This is line 5 of a sample answer.
This is line 6 of a sample answer.
This is line 7 of a sample answer.
This is line 8 of a sample answer.

Cut

Paste

Undo

The CUT icon cuts (removes) a block of text and stores it in the computer's memory. The text remains in memory until you replace it with text from another cut.

To CUT:
- highlight the text, then
- click on the CUT icon.

The PASTE icon inserts the block of text that you previously cut.

To PASTE:
- first CUT the text you want to paste,
- click where you want the text to appear (to make the cursor blink), then
- click on the PASTE icon.

Try cutting the words **sample answer** in a sentence below. Then paste them at the beginning of a sentence.

When finished, click on one of the icons on the right.

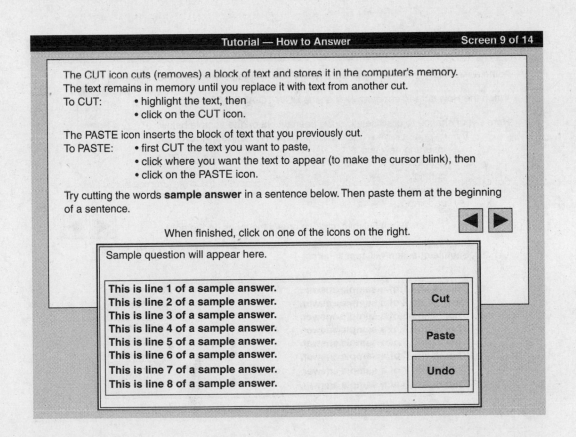

Sample question will appear here.

This is line 1 of a sample answer.
This is line 2 of a sample answer.
This is line 3 of a sample answer.
This is line 4 of a sample answer.
This is line 5 of a sample answer.
This is line 6 of a sample answer.
This is line 7 of a sample answer.
This is line 8 of a sample answer.

Cut

Paste

Undo

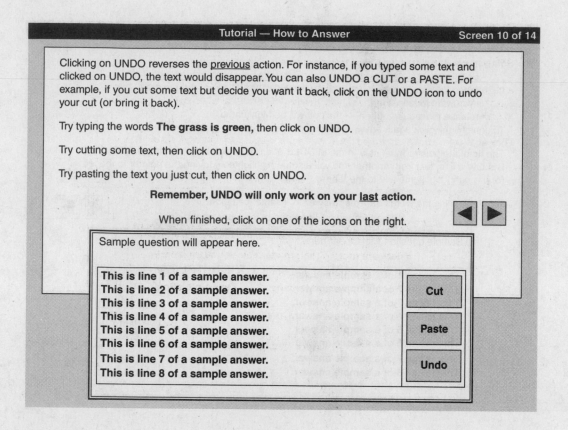

Clicking on UNDO reverses the <u>previous</u> action. For instance, if you typed some text and clicked on UNDO, the text would disappear. You can also UNDO a CUT or a PASTE. For example, if you cut some text but decide you want it back, click on the UNDO icon to undo your cut (or bring it back).

Try typing the words **The grass is green,** then click on UNDO.

Try cutting some text, then click on UNDO.

Try pasting the text you just cut, then click on UNDO.

Remember, UNDO will only work on your <u>last</u> action.

When finished, click on one of the icons on the right.

Sample question will appear here.

This is line 1 of a sample answer.
This is line 2 of a sample answer.
This is line 3 of a sample answer.
This is line 4 of a sample answer.
This is line 5 of a sample answer.
This is line 6 of a sample answer.
This is line 7 of a sample answer.
This is line 8 of a sample answer.

Cut

Paste

Undo

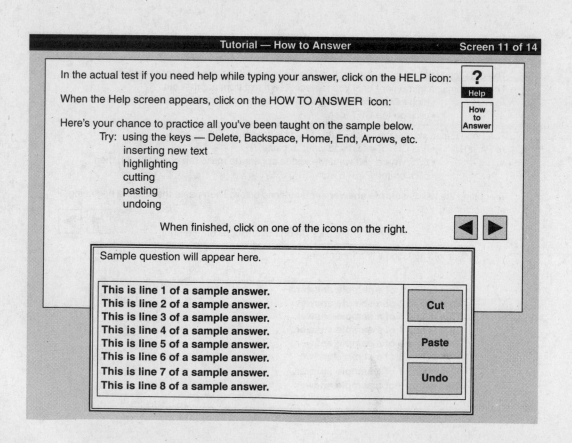

In the actual test if you need help while typing your answer, click on the HELP icon: **?** Help

When the Help screen appears, click on the HOW TO ANSWER icon: How to Answer

Here's your chance to practice all you've been taught on the sample below.
Try: using the keys — Delete, Backspace, Home, End, Arrows, etc.
     inserting new text
     highlighting
     cutting
     pasting
     undoing

When finished, click on one of the icons on the right.

Sample question will appear here.

This is line 1 of a sample answer.
This is line 2 of a sample answer.
This is line 3 of a sample answer.
This is line 4 of a sample answer.
This is line 5 of a sample answer.
This is line 6 of a sample answer.
This is line 7 of a sample answer.
This is line 8 of a sample answer.

Cut

Paste

Undo

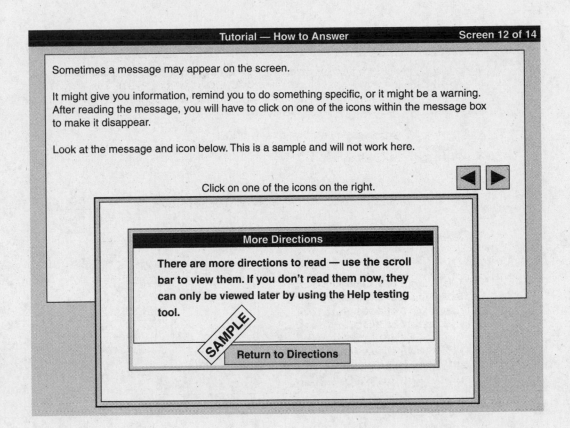

Sometimes a message may appear on the screen.

It might give you information, remind you to do something specific, or it might be a warning. After reading the message, you will have to click on one of the icons within the message box to make it disappear.

Look at the message and icon below. This is a sample and will not work here.

Click on one of the icons on the right.

More Directions

There are more directions to read — use the scroll bar to view them. If you don't read them now, they can only be viewed later by using the Help testing tool.

SAMPLE

Return to Directions

3 Math Review

Although this chapter provides a review of some of the mathematical concepts of arithmetic, algebra, and geometry, it is not intended to be a textbook. You should use this chapter to familiarize yourself with the kinds of topics that are tested in the GMAT®. You may wish to consult an arithmetic, algebra, or geometry book for a more detailed discussion of some of the topics.

The topics that are covered in Section A, arithmetic, include:

1. Properties of integers
2. Fractions
3. Decimals
4. Real numbers
5. Ratio and proportion
6. Percents
7. Powers and roots of numbers
8. Descriptive statistics
9. Sets
10. Counting methods
11. Discrete probability

The content of Section B, algebra, does not extend beyond what is usually covered in a first-year high school algebra course. The topics included are:

1. Simplifying algebraic expressions
2. Equations
3. Solving linear equations with one unknown
4. Solving two linear equations with two unknowns
5. Solving equations by factoring
6. Solving quadratic equations
7. Exponents
8. Inequalities
9. Absolute value
10. Functions

Section C, geometry, is limited primarily to measurement and intuitive geometry or spatial visualization. Extensive knowledge of theorems and the ability to construct proofs, skills that are usually developed in a formal geometry course, are not tested. The topics included in this section are:

1. Lines
2. Intersecting lines and angles
3. Perpendicular lines
4. Parallel lines
5. Polygons (convex)
6. Triangles
7. Quadrilaterals
8. Circles
9. Rectangular solids and cylinders
10. Coordinate geometry

Section D, word problems, presents examples of and solutions to the following types of word problems:

1. Rate
2. Work
3. Mixture
4. Interest
5. Discount
6. Profit
7. Sets
8. Geometry
9. Measurement
10. Data interpretation

A. Arithmetic

An *integer* is any number in the set $\{\ldots -3, -2, -1, 0, 1, 2, 3, \ldots\}$. If x and y are integers and $x \neq 0$, then x is a *divisor* (*factor*) of y provided that $y = xn$ for some integer n. In this case, y is also said to be *divisible* by x or to be a *multiple* of x. For example, 7 is a divisor or factor of 28 since $28 = (7)(4)$, but 8 is not a divisor of 28 since there is no integer n such that $28 = 8n$.

If x and y are positive integers, there exist unique integers q and r, called the *quotient* and *remainder*, respectively, such that $y = xq + r$ and $0 \leq r < x$. For example, when 28 is divided by 8, the quotient is 3 and the remainder is 4 since $28 = (8)(3) + 4$. Note that y is divisible by x if and only if the remainder r is 0; for example, 32 has a remainder of 0 when divided by 8 because 32 is divisible by 8. Also, note that when a smaller integer is divided by a larger integer, the quotient is 0 and the remainder is the smaller integer. For example, 5 divided by 7 has the quotient 0 and the remainder 5 since $5 = (7)(0) + 5$.

Any integer that is divisible by 2 is an *even integer*; the set of even integers is $\{\ldots -4, -2, 0, 2, 4, 6, 8, \ldots\}$. Integers that are not divisible by 2 are *odd integers*; $\{\ldots -3, -1, 1, 3, 5, \ldots\}$ is the set of odd integers.

If at least one factor of a product of integers is even, then the product is even; otherwise the product is odd. If two integers are both even or both odd, then their sum and their difference are even. Otherwise, their sum and their difference are odd.

A *prime* number is a positive integer that has exactly two different positive divisors, 1 and itself. For example, 2, 3, 5, 7, 11, and 13 are prime numbers, but 15 is not, since 15 has four different positive divisors, 1, 3, 5, and 15. The number 1 is not a prime number, since it has only one positive divisor. Every integer greater than 1 is either prime or can be uniquely expressed as a product of prime factors. For example, $14 = (2)(7)$, $81 = (3)(3)(3)(3)$, and $484 = (2)(2)(11)(11)$.

The numbers $-2, -1, 0, 1, 2, 3, 4, 5$ are *consecutive integers*. Consecutive integers can be represented by $n, n + 1, n + 2, n + 3, \ldots$, where n is an integer. The numbers $0, 2, 4, 6, 8$ are *consecutive even integers*, and $1, 3, 5, 7, 9$ are *consecutive odd integers*. Consecutive even integers can be represented by $2n, 2n + 2, 2n + 4, \ldots$, and consecutive odd integers can be represented by $2n + 1, 2n + 3, 2n + 5, \ldots$, where n is an integer.

Properties of the integer 1. If n is any number, then $1 \cdot n = n$, and for any number $n \neq 0$, $n \cdot \dfrac{1}{n} = 1$. The number 1 can be expressed in many ways; for example, $\dfrac{n}{n} = 1$ for any number $n \neq 0$. Multiplying or dividing an expression by 1, in any form, does not change the value of that expression.

Properties of the integer 0. The integer 0 is neither positive nor negative. If n is any number, then $n + 0 = n$ and $n \cdot 0 = 0$. Division by 0 is not defined.

2. FRACTIONS

In a fraction $\frac{n}{d}$, n is the *numerator* and d is the *denominator*. The denominator of a fraction can never be 0, because division by 0 is not defined.

Two fractions are said to be *equivalent* if they represent the same number. For example, $\frac{8}{36}$ and $\frac{14}{63}$ are equivalent since they both represent the number $\frac{2}{9}$. In each case, the fraction is reduced to lowest terms by dividing both numerator and denominator by their *greatest common divisor* (gcd). The gcd of 8 and 36 is 4 and the gcd of 14 and 63 is 7.

Addition and subtraction of fractions. Two fractions with the same denominator can be added or subtracted by performing the required operation with the numerators, leaving the denominators the same. For example, $\frac{3}{5} + \frac{4}{5} = \frac{3+4}{5} = \frac{7}{5}$, and $\frac{5}{7} - \frac{2}{7} = \frac{5-2}{7} = \frac{3}{7}$. If two fractions do not have the same denominator, express them as equivalent fractions with the same denominator. For example, to add $\frac{3}{5}$ and $\frac{4}{7}$, multiply the numerator and denominator of the first fraction by 7 and the numerator and denominator of the second fraction by 5, obtaining $\frac{21}{35}$ and $\frac{20}{35}$, respectively;

$$\frac{21}{35} + \frac{20}{35} = \frac{41}{35}.$$

For the new denominator, choosing the *least common multiple* (lcm) of the denominators usually lessens the work. For $\frac{2}{3} + \frac{1}{6}$, the lcm of 3 and 6 is 6 (not $3 \times 6 = 18$), so

$$\frac{2}{3} + \frac{1}{6} = \frac{2}{3} \times \frac{2}{2} + \frac{1}{6} = \frac{4}{6} + \frac{1}{6} = \frac{5}{6}.$$

Multiplication and division of fractions. To multiply two fractions, simply multiply the two numerators and multiply the two denominators. For example,

$$\frac{2}{3} \times \frac{4}{7} = \frac{2 \times 4}{3 \times 7} = \frac{8}{21}.$$

To divide by a fraction, invert the divisor (that is, find its *reciprocal*) and multiply. For example $\frac{2}{3} \div \frac{4}{7} = \frac{2}{3} \times \frac{7}{4} = \frac{14}{12} = \frac{7}{6}$.

In the problem above, the reciprocal of $\frac{4}{7}$ is $\frac{7}{4}$. In general, the reciprocal of a fraction $\frac{n}{d}$ is $\frac{d}{n}$ where n and d are not zero.

Mixed numbers. A number that consists of a whole number and a fraction, for example, $7\frac{2}{3}$, is a mixed number: $7\frac{2}{3}$ means $7+\frac{2}{3}$.

To change a mixed number into a fraction, multiply the whole number by the denominator of the fraction and add this number to the numerator of the fraction; then put the result over the denominator of the fraction. For example,

$$7\frac{2}{3} = \frac{(3\times 7)+2}{3} = \frac{23}{3}.$$

3. DECIMALS

In the decimal system, the position of the period or *decimal point* determines the place value of the digits. For example, the digits in the number 7,654.321 have the following place values:

Thousands	Hundreds	Tens	Ones or units	Tenths	Hundredths	Thousandths
7	6	5	4	3	2	1

Some examples of decimals follow.

$$0.321 = \frac{3}{10} + \frac{2}{100} + \frac{1}{1,000} = \frac{321}{1,000}$$

$$0.0321 = \frac{0}{10} + \frac{3}{100} + \frac{2}{1,000} + \frac{1}{10,000} = \frac{321}{10,000}$$

$$1.56 = 1 + \frac{5}{10} + \frac{6}{100} = \frac{156}{100}$$

Sometimes decimals are expressed as the product of a number with only one digit to the left of the decimal point and a power of 10. This is called *scientific notation*. For example, 231 can be written as 2.31×10^2 and 0.0231 can be written as 2.31×10^{-2}. When a number is expressed in scientific notation, the exponent of the 10 indicates the number of places that the decimal point is to be moved in the number that is to be multiplied by a power of 10 in order to obtain the product. The decimal point is moved to the right if the exponent is positive and to the left if the exponent is negative. For example, 20.13×10^3 is equal to 20,130 and 1.91×10^{-4} is equal to 0.000191.

Addition and subtraction of decimals. To add or subtract two decimals, the decimal points of both numbers should be lined up. If one of the numbers has fewer digits to the right of the decimal point than the other, zeros may be inserted to the right of the last digit. For example, to add 17.6512 and 653.27, set up the numbers in a column and add:

$$
\begin{array}{r}
17.6512 \\
+\ 653.2700 \\
\hline
670.9212
\end{array}
$$

Likewise for 653.27 minus 17.6512:

$$
\begin{array}{r}
653.2700 \\
-\ 17.6512 \\
\hline
635.6188
\end{array}
$$

Multiplication of decimals. To multiply decimals, multiply the numbers as if they were whole numbers and then insert the decimal point in the product so that the number of digits to the right of the decimal point is equal to the sum of the numbers of digits to the right of the decimal points in the numbers being multiplied. For example:

$$
\begin{array}{rl}
2.09 & \text{(2 digits to the right)} \\
\times\,1.3 & \text{(1 digit to the right)} \\
\hline
627 & \\
209 & \\
\hline
2.717 & \text{(2 + 1 = 3 digits to the right)}
\end{array}
$$

Division of decimals. To divide a number (the dividend) by a decimal (the divisor), move the decimal point of the divisor to the right until the divisor is a whole number. Then move the decimal point of the dividend the same number of places to the right, and divide as you would by a whole number. The decimal point in the quotient will be directly above the decimal point in the new dividend. For example, to divide 698.12 by 12.4:

$$12.4\overline{)698.12}$$

will be replaced by

$$124\overline{)6981.2}$$

and the division would proceed as follows:

$$
\begin{array}{r}
56.3 \\
124\overline{)6981.2} \\
\underline{620} \\
781 \\
\underline{744} \\
372 \\
\underline{372} \\
0
\end{array}
$$

4. REAL NUMBERS

All *real* numbers correspond to points on the number line and all points on the number line correspond to real numbers. All real numbers except zero are either positive or negative.

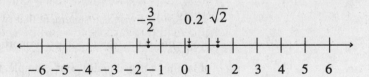

On a number line, numbers corresponding to points to the left of zero are negative and numbers corresponding to points to the right of zero are positive. For any two numbers on the number line, the number to the left is less than the number to the right; for example,

$$-4 < -3, \quad -\frac{3}{2} < -1, \text{ and } 1 < \sqrt{2} < 2.$$

To say that the number n is between 1 and 4 on the number line means that $n > 1$ and $n < 4$, that is, $1 < n < 4$. If n is "between 1 and 4, inclusive," then $1 \le n \le 4$.

The distance between a number and zero on the number line is called the *absolute value* of the number. Thus 3 and –3 have the same absolute value, 3, since they are both three units from zero. The absolute value of 3 is denoted $|3|$. Examples of absolute values of numbers are

$$|-5| = |5| = 5, \quad \left|-\frac{7}{2}\right| = \frac{7}{2}, \text{ and } |0| = 0$$

Note that the absolute value of any nonzero number is positive.

Here are some properties of real numbers that are used frequently. If x, y, and z are real numbers, then

(1) $x + y = y + x$ and $xy = yx$.

For example, $8 + 3 = 3 + 8 = 11$, and $(17)(5) = (5)(17) = 85$.

(2) $(x + y) + z = x + (y + z)$ and $(xy)z = x(yz)$.

For example, $(7 + 5) + 2 = 7 + (5 + 2) = 7 + (7) = 14$, and $(5\sqrt{3})(\sqrt{3}) = (5\sqrt{3}\,\sqrt{3}) = (5)(3) = 15$.

(3) $x(y + z) = xy + xz$.

For example, $718(36) + 718(64) = 718(36 + 64) = 718(100) = 71,800$.

(4) If x and y are both positive, then $x + y$ and xy are positive.

(5) If x and y are both negative, then $x + y$ is negative and xy is positive.

(6) If x is positive and y is negative, then xy is negative.

(7) If $xy = 0$, then $x = 0$ or $y = 0$. For example, $3y = 0$ implies $y = 0$.

(8) $|x + y| \le |x| + |y|$. For example, if $x = 10$ and $y = 2$, then $|x + y| = |12| = 12 = |x| + |y|$; and if $x = 10$ and $y = -2$, then $|x + y| = |8| = 8 < 12 = |x| + |y|$.

5. RATIO AND PROPORTION

The *ratio* of the number a to the number b ($b \ne 0$) is $\frac{a}{b}$.

A ratio may be expressed or represented in several ways. For example, the ratio of 2 to 3 can be written as 2 to 3, 2:3, or $\frac{2}{3}$. The order of the terms of a ratio is important. For example, the ratio of the number of months with exactly 30 days to the number with exactly 31 days is $\frac{4}{7}$, not $\frac{7}{4}$.

A *proportion* is a statement that two ratios are equal; for example, $\frac{2}{3} = \frac{8}{12}$ is a proportion. One way to solve a proportion involving an unknown is to cross multiply, obtaining a new equality. For example, to solve for n in the proportion $\frac{2}{3} = \frac{n}{12}$, cross multiply, obtaining $24 = 3n$; then divide both sides by 3, to get $n = 8$.

6. PERCENTS

Percent means *per hundred* or *number out of 100*. A percent can be represented as a fraction with a denominator of 100, or as a decimal. For example, $37\% = \frac{37}{100} = 0.37$.

To find a certain percent of a number, multiply the number by the percent expressed as a decimal or fraction. For example:

$$20\% \text{ of } 90 = 0.2 \times 90 = 18$$

or

$$20\% \text{ of } 90 = \frac{20}{100} \times 90 = \frac{1}{5} \times 90 = 18.$$

Percents greater than 100%. Percents greater than 100% are represented by numbers greater than 1. For example:

$$300\% = \frac{300}{100} = 3$$

$$250\% \text{ of } 80 = 2.5 \times 80 = 200.$$

Percents less than 1%. The percent 0.5% means $\frac{1}{2}$ of 1 percent. For example, 0.5% of 12 is equal to $0.005 \times 12 = 0.06$.

Percent change. Often a problem will ask for the percent increase or decrease from one quantity to another quantity. For example, "If the price of an item increases from $24 to $30, what is the percent increase in price?" To find the percent increase, first find the amount of the increase; then divide this increase by the original amount, and express this quotient as a percent. In the example above, the percent increase would be found in the following way: the amount of the increase is $(30 - 24) = 6$.

Therefore, the percent increase is $\frac{6}{24} = 0.25 = 25\%$.

Likewise, to find the percent decrease (for example, the price of an item is reduced from $30 to $24), first find the amount of the decrease; then divide this decrease by the original amount, and express this quotient as a percent. In the example above, the amount of decrease is $(30 - 24) = 6$. Therefore, the percent decrease is

$\frac{6}{30} = 0.20 = 20\%$.

Note that the percent increase from 24 to 30 is not the same as the percent decrease from 30 to 24.

In the following example, the increase is greater than 100 percent: If the cost of a certain house in 1983 was 300 percent of its cost in 1970, by what percent did the cost increase?

If n is the cost in 1970, then the percent increase is equal to $\frac{3n - n}{n} = \frac{2n}{n} = 2$, or 200 percent.

7. POWERS AND ROOTS OF NUMBERS

When a number k is to be used n times as a factor in a product, it can be expressed as k^n, which means the nth power of k. For example, $2^2 = 2 \times 2 = 4$ and $2^3 = 2 \times 2 \times 2 = 8$ are powers of 2.

Squaring a number that is greater than 1, or raising it to a higher power, results in a larger number; squaring a number between 0 and 1 results in a smaller number. For example:

$3^2 = 9$ $(9 > 3)$

$\left(\frac{1}{3}\right)^2 = \frac{1}{9}$ $\left(\frac{1}{9} < \frac{1}{3}\right)$

$(0.1)^2 = 0.01$ $(0.01 < 0.1)$

A *square root* of a number n is a number that, when squared, is equal to n. The square root of a negative number is not a real number. Every positive number n has two square roots, one positive and the other negative, but $\sqrt{n}$ denotes the positive number whose square is n. For example, $\sqrt{9}$ denotes 3. The two square roots of 9 are $\sqrt{9} = 3$ and $-\sqrt{9} = -3$.

Every real number r has exactly one real *cube root*, which is the number s such that $s^3 = r$. The real cube root of r is denoted by $\sqrt[3]{r}$. Since $2^3 = 8$, $\sqrt[3]{8} = 2$. Similarly, $\sqrt[3]{-8} = -2$, because $(-2)^3 = -8$.

8. DESCRIPTIVE STATISTICS

A list of numbers, or numerical data, can be described by various statistical measures. One of the most common of these measures is the *average*, or *(arithmetic) mean*, which locates a type of "center" for the data. The average of n numbers is defined as the sum of the n numbers divided by n. For example, the average of 6, 4, 7, 10, and 4 is $\dfrac{6+4+7+10+4}{5} = \dfrac{31}{5} = 6.2$.

The *median* is another type of center for a list of numbers. To calculate the median of n numbers, first order the numbers from least to greatest; if n is odd, the median is defined as the middle number, while if n is even, the median is defined as the average of the two middle numbers. In the example above, the numbers, in order, are 4, 4, 6, 7, 10, and the median is 6, the middle number. For the numbers 4, 6, 6, 8, 9, 12, the median is $\dfrac{6+8}{2} = 7$. Note that the mean of these numbers is 7.5. The median of a set of data can be less than, equal to, or greater than the mean. Note that for a large set of data (for example, the salaries of 800 company employees), it is often true that about half of the data is less than the median and about half of the data is greater than the median; but this is not always the case, as the following data show.

$$3, 5, 7, 7, 7, 7, 7, 7, 8, 9, 9, 9, 9, 10, 10$$

Here the median is 7, but only $\dfrac{2}{15}$ of the data is less than the median.

The *mode* of a list of numbers is the number that occurs most frequently in the list. For example, the mode of 1, 3, 6, 4, 3, 5 is 3. A list of numbers may have more than one mode. For example, the list 1, 2, 3, 3, 3, 5, 7, 10, 10, 10, 20 has two modes, 3 and 10.

The degree to which numerical data are spread out or dispersed can be measured in many ways. The simplest measure of dispersion is the *range*, which is defined as the greatest value in the numerical data minus the least value. For example, the range of 11, 10, 5, 13, 21 is $21 - 5 = 16$. Note how the range depends on only two values in the data.

One of the most common measures of dispersion is the *standard deviation*. Generally speaking, the greater the data are spread away from the mean, the greater the standard deviation. The standard deviation of n numbers can be calculated as follows: (1) find the arithmetic mean, (2) find the differences between the mean and each of the n numbers, (3) square each of the differences, (4) find the average of the squared differences, and (5) take the nonnegative square root of this average. Shown below is this calculation for the data 0, 7, 8, 10, 10, which have arithmetic mean 7.

x	$x - 7$	$(x - 7)^2$
0	−7	49
7	0	0
8	1	1
10	3	9
10	3	9
Total		68

Standard deviation: $\sqrt{\dfrac{68}{5}} \approx 3.7$

Notice that the standard deviation depends on every data value, although it depends most on values that are farthest from the mean. This is why a distribution with data grouped closely around the mean will have a smaller standard deviation than will data spread far from the mean. To illustrate this, compare the data 6, 6, 6.5, 7.5, 9, which also have mean 7. Note that the numbers in the second set of data seem to be grouped more closely around the mean of 7 than the numbers in the first set. This is reflected in the standard deviation, which is less for the second set (approximately 1.1) than for the first set (approximately 3.7).

There are many ways to display numerical data that show how the data are distributed. One simple way is with a *frequency distribution*, which is useful for data that have values occurring with varying frequencies. For example, the 20 numbers

$$
\begin{array}{cccccccccc}
-4 & 0 & 0 & -3 & -2 & -1 & -1 & 0 & -1 & -4 \\
-1 & -5 & 0 & -2 & 0 & -5 & -2 & 0 & 0 & -1
\end{array}
$$

are displayed below in a frequency distribution by listing each different value x and the frequency f with which x occurs.

Data Value x	Frequency f
−5	2
−4	2
−3	1
−2	3
−1	5
0	7
Total	20

From the frequency distribution, one can readily compute descriptive statistics:

Mean: $\dfrac{(-5)(2) + (-4)(2) + (-3)(1) + (-2)(3) + (-1)(5) + (0)(7)}{20} = -1.6$

Median: −1 (the average of the 10th and 11th numbers)

Mode: 0 (the number that occurs most frequently)

Range: $0 - (-5) = 5$

Standard deviation:

$$
\sqrt{\dfrac{(-5 + 1.6)^2(2) + (-4 + 1.6)^2(2) + \ldots + (0 + 1.6)^2(7)}{20}} \approx 1.7
$$

9. SETS

In mathematics a *set* is a collection of numbers or other objects. The objects are called the *elements* of the set. If S is a set having a finite number of elements, then the number of elements is denoted by $|S|$. Such a set is often defined by listing its elements; for example, $S = \{-5,0,1\}$ is a set with $|S| = 3$. The order in which the elements are listed in a set does not matter; thus $\{-5, 0, 1\} = \{0, 1, -5\}$. If all the elements of a set S are also elements of a set T, then S is a *subset* of T; for example, $S = \{-5, 0, 1\}$ is a subset of $T = \{-5, 0, 1, 4, 10\}$.

For any two sets A and B, the *union* of A and B is the set of all elements that are in A *or* in B or in both. The *intersection* of A and B is the set of all elements that are both in A *and* in B. The union is denoted by $A \cup B$ and the intersection is denoted by $A \cap B$. As an example, if $A = \{3, 4\}$ and $B = \{4, 5, 6\}$, then $A \cup B = \{3, 4, 5, 6\}$ and $A \cap B = \{4\}$. Two sets that have no elements in common are said to be *disjoint* or *mutually exclusive*.

The relationship between sets is often illustrated with a *Venn diagram* in which sets are represented by regions in a plane. For two sets S and T that are not disjoint and neither is a subset of the other, the intersection $S \cap T$ is represented by the shaded region of the diagram below.

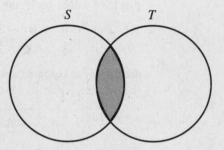

This diagram illustrates a fact about any two finite sets S and T: the number of elements in their union equals the sum of their individual numbers of elements minus the number of elements in their intersection (because the latter are counted twice in the sum); more concisely,

$$|S \cup T| = |S| + |T| - |S \cap T|.$$

This counting method is called the general addition rule for two sets. As a special case, if S and T are disjoint, then

$$|S \cup T| = |S| + |T|$$

since $|S \cap T| = 0$.

10. COUNTING METHODS

There are some useful methods for counting objects and sets of objects without actually listing the elements to be counted. The following principle of multiplication is fundamental to these methods.

If an object is to be chosen from a set of m objects and a second object is to be chosen from a different set of n objects, then there are mn ways of choosing both objects simultaneously.

As an example, suppose the objects are items on a menu. If a meal consists of one entree and one dessert and there are 5 entrees and 3 desserts on the menu, then there are $5 \times 3 = 15$ different meals that can be ordered from the menu. As another example, each time a coin is flipped, there are two possible outcomes, heads and tails. If an experiment consists of 8 consecutive coin flips, then the experiment has 2^8 possible outcomes, where each of these outcomes is a list of heads and tails in some order.

A symbol that is often used with the multiplication principle is the *factorial*. If n is an integer greater than 1, then n factorial, denoted by the symbol $n!$, is defined as the product of all the integers from 1 to n. Therefore,

$$2! = (1)(2) = 2,$$
$$3! = (1)(2)(3) = 6,$$
$$4! = (1)(2)(3)(4) = 24, \text{ etc.}$$

Also, by definition, $0! = 1! = 1$.

The factorial is useful for counting the number of ways that a set of objects can be ordered. If a set of n objects is to be ordered from 1st to nth, then there are n choices for the 1st object, $n-1$ choices for the 2nd object, $n-2$ choices for the 3rd object, and so on, until there is only 1 choice for the nth object. Thus, by the multiplication principle, the number of ways of ordering the n objects is

$$n(n-1)(n-2) \cdots (3)(2)(1) = n!.$$

For example, the number of ways of ordering the letters A, B, and C is 3!, or 6:

$$\text{ABC, ACB, BAC, BCA, CAB, and CBA.}$$

These orderings are called the *permutations* of the letters A, B, and C.

A permutation can be thought of as a selection process in which objects are selected one by one in a certain order. If the order of selection is not relevant and only k objects are to be selected from a larger set of n objects, a different counting method is employed. Specifically, consider a set of n objects from which a complete selection of k objects is to be made without regard to order, where $0 \leq k \leq n$. Then the number of possible complete selections of k objects is called the number of

combinations of n objects taken k at a time and is denoted by $\binom{n}{k}$. The value of $\binom{n}{k}$

is given by

$$\binom{n}{k} = \frac{n!}{k!(n-k)!}.$$

Note that $\binom{n}{k}$ is the number of k-element subsets of a set with n elements. For

example, if $S = \{A, B, C, D, E\}$, then the number of 2-element subsets of S, or the

number of combinations of 5 letters taken 2 at a time, is $\binom{5}{2} = \frac{5!}{2!3!} = \frac{120}{(2)(6)} = 10$.

The subsets are {A, B}, {A, C}, {A, D}, {A, E}, {B, C}, {B, D}, {B, E}, {C, D}, {C, E,}, and {D, E}. Note that $\binom{5}{2} = 10 = \binom{5}{3}$ since every 2-element subset chosen from a set of 5 elements corresponds to a unique 3-element subset consisting of the elements *not* chosen. In general,

$$\binom{n}{k} = \binom{n}{n-k}$$

11. DISCRETE PROBABILITY

Many of the ideas discussed in the preceding three topics are important to the study of discrete probability. Discrete probability is concerned with *experiments* that have a finite number of *outcomes*. Given such an experiment, an *event* is a particular set of outcomes. For example, rolling a number cube with faces numbered 1 to 6 (similar to a 6-sided die) is an experiment with 6 possible outcomes: 1, 2, 3, 4, 5, or 6. One event in this experiment is that the outcome is 4, denoted {4}; another event is that the outcome is an odd number: {1, 3, 5}.

The probability than an event E occurs, denoted by $P(E)$, is a number between 0 and 1, inclusive. If E has no outcomes, then E is *impossible* and $P(E) = 0$; if E is the set of all possible outcomes of the experiment, then E is *certain* to occur and $P(E) = 1$. Otherwise, E is possible but uncertain, and $0 < P(E) < 1$. If F is a subset of E, then $P(F) \leq P(E)$. In the example above, if the probability of each of the 6 outcomes is the same, then the probability of each outcome is $\frac{1}{6}$, and the outcomes are said to be *equally likely*. For experiments in which all of the individual outcomes are equally likely, the probability of an event E is

$$P(E) = \frac{\text{The number of outcomes in } E}{\text{The total number of possible outcomes}}.$$

In the example, the probability that the outcome is an odd number is

$$P(\{1,3,5\}) = \frac{|\{1,3,5\}|}{6} = \frac{3}{6}.$$

Given an experiment with events E and F, the following events are defined.

"*not E*" is the set of outcomes that are not outcomes in E;

"*E or F*" is the set of outcomes in E or F or both, that is, $E \cup F$;

"*E and F*" is the set of outcomes in both E and F, that is, $E \cap F$.

The probability that E does not occur is $P(\text{not } E) = 1 - P(E)$. The probability that "*E or F*" occurs is

$$P(E \text{ or } F) = P(E) + P(F) - P(E \text{ and } F),$$

using the general addition rule at the end of Section A.9. For the number cube, if E is the event that the outcome is an odd number, {1, 3, 5}, and F is the event that the outcome is a prime number, {2, 3, 5}, then $P(E \text{ and } F) = P(\{3,5\}) = \frac{2}{6}$, and so

$$P(E \text{ or } F) \ = \ P(E) + P(F) - P(E \text{ and } F) \ = \ \frac{3}{6} + \frac{3}{6} - \frac{2}{6} = \frac{4}{6}.$$

Note that the event "E or F" is $E \cup F = \{1, 2, 3, 5\}$, and hence $P(E \text{ or } F) = \frac{|\{1,2,3,5\}|}{6} = \frac{4}{6}$.

If the event "E and F" is impossible (that is, $E \cap F$ has no outcomes), then E and F are said to be *mutually exclusive* events, and $P(E \text{ and } F) = 0$. Then the general addition rule is reduced to

$$P(E \text{ or } F) = P(E) + P(F).$$

This is the special addition rule for the probability of two mutually exclusive events.

Two events A and B are said to be *independent* if the occurrence of either event does not alter the probability that the other event occurs. For one roll of the number cube, let $A = \{2, 4, 6\}$ and let $B = \{5, 6\}$. Then the probability that A occurs is $P(A) = \frac{|A|}{6} = \frac{3}{6} = \frac{1}{2}$, while, *presuming B occurs*, the probability that A occurs is

$$\frac{|A \cap B|}{|B|} = \frac{|\{6\}|}{|\{5,6\}|} = \frac{1}{2}.$$

Similarly, the probability that B occurs is $P(B) = \frac{|B|}{6} = \frac{2}{6} = \frac{1}{3}$, while, *presuming A occurs*, the probability that B occurs is

$$\frac{|B \cap A|}{|A|} = \frac{|\{6\}|}{|\{2,4,6\}|} = \frac{1}{3}.$$

Thus, the occurrence of either event does not affect the probability that the other event occurs. Therefore, A and B are independent.

The following multiplication rule holds for any independent events E and F:

$$P(E \text{ and } F) = P(E)P(F).$$

For the independent events A and B above,

$$P(A \text{ and } B) = P(A)P(B)$$

$$= \left(\frac{1}{2}\right)\left(\frac{1}{3}\right) = \left(\frac{1}{6}\right).$$

Note that the event "A and B" is $A \cap B = \{6\}$, and hence $P(A \text{ and } B) = P(\{6\}) = \frac{1}{6}$.

It follows from the general addition rule and the multiplication rule above that if E and F are independent, then

$$P(E \text{ or } F) = P(E) + P(F) - P(E)P(F).$$

For a final example of some of these rules, consider an experiment with events A, B, and C for which $P(A) = 0.23$, $P(B) = 0.40$, and $P(C) = 0.85$. Also, suppose that events A and B are mutually exclusive and events B and C are independent. Then

$$
\begin{aligned}
P(A \text{ or } B) &= P(A) + P(B) \quad \text{(since } A \text{ and } B \text{ are mutually exclusive)} \\
&= 0.23 + 0.40 \\
&= 0.63 \\
P(B \text{ or } C) &= P(B) + P(C) - P(B)P(C) \quad \text{(by independence)} \\
&= 0.40 + 0.85 - (0.40)(0.85) \\
&= 0.91
\end{aligned}
$$

Note that $P(A \text{ or } C)$ and $P(A \text{ and } C)$ cannot be determined using the information given. But it can be determined that A and C are *not* mutually exclusive since $P(A) + P(C) = 1.08$, which is greater than 1, and therefore cannot equal $P(A \text{ or } C)$; from this it follows that $P(A \text{ and } C) \geq 0.08$. One can also deduce that $P(A \text{ and } C) \leq P(A) = 0.23$, since $A \cap C$ is a subset of A, and that $P(A \text{ or } C) \geq P(C) = 0.85$ since C is a subset of $A \cup C$. Thus, one can conclude that $0.85 \leq P(A \text{ or } C) \leq 1$ and $0.08 \leq P(A \text{ and } C) \leq 0.23$.

B. Algebra

Algebra is based on the operations of arithmetic and on the concept of an *unknown quantity,* or *variable*. Letters such as x or n are used to represent unknown quantities. For example, suppose Pam has 5 more pencils than Fred. If F represents the number of pencils that Fred has, then the number of pencils that Pam has is $F + 5$. As another example, if Jim's present salary S is increased by 7%, then his new salary is $1.07S$. A combination of letters and arithmetic operations, such as $F + 5$, $\dfrac{3x^2}{2x-5}$, and $19x^2 - 6x + 3$, is called an *algebraic expression*.

The expression $19x^2 - 6x + 3$ consists of the *terms* $19x^2$, $-6x$, and 3, where 19 is the *coefficient* of x^2, -6 is the coefficient of x^1, and 3 is a *constant term* (or coefficient of $x^0 = 1$). Such an expression is called a *second degree* (or *quadratic*) *polynomial in x* since the highest power of x is 2. The expression $F + 5$ is a *first degree* (or *linear*) *polynomial in F* since the highest power of F is 1. The expression $\dfrac{3x^2}{2x-5}$ is not a polynomial because it is not a sum of terms that are each powers of x multiplied by coefficients.

1. SIMPLIFYING ALGEBRAIC EXPRESSIONS

Often when working with algebraic expressions, it is necessary to simplify them by factoring or combining *like* terms. For example, the expression $6x + 5x$ is equivalent to $(6 + 5)x$, or $11x$. In the expression $9x - 3y$, 3 is a factor common to both terms: $9x - 3y = 3(3x - y)$. In the expression $5x^2 + 6y$, there are no like terms and no common factors.

If there are common factors in the numerator and denominator of an expression, they can be divided out, provided that they are not equal to zero.

For example, if $x \neq 3$, then $\dfrac{x-3}{x-3}$ is equal to 1; therefore,

$$
\begin{aligned}
\frac{3xy - 9y}{x-3} &= \frac{3y(x-3)}{x-3} \\
&= (3y)(1) \\
&= 3y.
\end{aligned}
$$

To multiply two algebraic expressions, each term of one expression is multiplied by each term of the other expression. For example:

$$(3x - 4)(9y + x) = 3x(9y + x) - 4(9y + x)$$
$$= (3x)(9y) + (3x)(x) + (-4)(9y) + (-4)(x)$$
$$= 27xy + 3x^2 - 36y - 4x$$

An algebraic expression can be evaluated by substituting values of the unknowns in the expression. For example, if $x = 3$ and $y = -2$, then $3xy - x^2 + y$ can be evaluated as

$$3(3)(-2) - (3)^2 + (-2) = -18 - 9 - 2 = -29$$

2. EQUATIONS

A major focus of algebra is to solve equations involving algebraic expressions. Some examples of such equations are

$$5x - 2 = 9 - x \quad \text{(a linear equation with one unknown)}$$
$$3x + 1 = y - 2 \quad \text{(a linear equation with two unknowns)}$$
$$5x^2 + 3x - 2 = 7x \quad \text{(a quadratic equation with one unknown)}$$

$$\frac{x(x-3)(x^2+5)}{x-4} = 0$$

(an equation that is factored on one side with 0 on the other).

The *solutions* of an equation with one or more unknowns are those values that make the equation true, or "satisfy the equation," when they are substituted for the unknowns of the equation. An equation may have no solution or one or more solutions. If two or more equations are to be solved together, the solutions must satisfy all of the equations simultaneously.

Two equations having the same solution(s) are *equivalent equations*. For example, the equations

$$2 + x = 3$$
$$4 + 2x = 6$$

each have the unique solution $x = 1$. Note that the second equation is the first equation multiplied by 2. Similarly, the equations

$$3x - y = 6$$
$$6x - 2y = 12$$

have the same solutions, although in this case each equation has infinitely many solutions. If any value is assigned to x, then $3x - 6$ is a corresponding value for y that will satisfy both equations; for example, $x = 2$ and $y = 0$ is a solution to both equations, as is $x = 5$ and $y = 9$.

3. SOLVING LINEAR EQUATIONS WITH ONE UNKNOWN

To solve a linear equation with one unknown (that is, to find the value of the unknown that satisfies the equation), the unknown should be isolated on one side of the equation. This can be done by performing the same mathematical operations on both sides of the equation. Remember that if the same number is added to or subtracted from both sides of the equation, this does not change the equality; likewise, multiplying or dividing both sides by the same nonzero number does not change the equality. For example, to solve the equation $\frac{5x-6}{3} = 4$ for x, the variable x can be isolated using the following steps:

$$\frac{5x-6}{3} = 4$$

$$5x - 6 = 12 \quad \text{(multiplying by 3)}$$

$$5x = 12 + 6 = 18 \quad \text{(adding 6)}$$

$$x = \frac{18}{5} \quad \text{(dividing by 5)}$$

The solution, $\frac{18}{5}$, can be checked by substituting it for x in the original equation to determine whether it satisfies that equation:

$$\frac{5\left(\frac{18}{5}\right) - 6}{3} = \frac{18-6}{3} = \frac{12}{3} = 4.$$

Therefore, $x = \frac{18}{5}$ is the solution.

4. SOLVING TWO LINEAR EQUATIONS WITH TWO UNKNOWNS

For two linear equations with two unknowns, if the equations are equivalent, then there are infinitely many solutions to the equations, as illustrated at the end of Section B.2. If the equations are not equivalent, then they have either one unique solution or no solution. The latter case is illustrated by the two equations:

$$3x + 4y = 17$$
$$6x + 8y = 35$$

Note that $3x + 4y = 17$ implies $6x + 8y = 34$, which contradicts the second equation. Thus, no values of x and y can simultaneously satisfy both equations.

There are several methods of solving two linear equations in two unknowns. With any method, if a contradiction is reached, then the equations have no solution; if a trivial equation such as $0 = 0$ is reached, then the equations are equivalent and have infinitely many solutions. Otherwise, a unique solution can be found.

One way to solve for the two unknowns is to express one of the unknowns in terms of the other using one of the equations, and then substitute the expression into the remaining equation to obtain an equation with one unknown. This equation can be solved and the value of the unknown substituted into either of the original equations to find the value of the other unknown. For example, the following two equations can be solved for x and y.

$$(1) \quad 3x + 2y = 11$$
$$(2) \quad x - y = 2$$

In equation (2), $x = 2 + y$. Substitute $2 + y$ in equation (1) for x:

$$3(2 + y) + 2y = 11$$
$$6 + 3y + 2y = 11$$
$$6 + 5y = 11$$
$$5y = 5$$
$$y = 1$$

If $y = 1$, then $x = 2 + 1 = 3$.

There is another way to solve for x and y by eliminating one of the unknowns. This can be done by making the coefficients of one of the unknowns the same (disregarding the sign) in both equations and either adding the equations or subtracting one equation from the other. For example, to solve the equations

$$(1) \quad 6x + 5y = 29$$
$$(2) \quad 4x - 3y = -6$$

by this method, multiply equation (1) by 3 and equation (2) by 5 to get

$$18x + 15y = 87$$
$$20x - 15y = -30$$

Adding the two equations eliminates y, yielding $38x = 57$, or $x = \dfrac{3}{2}$. Finally, substituting $\dfrac{3}{2}$ for x in one of the equations gives $y = 4$. These answers can be checked by substituting both values into both of the original equations.

5. SOLVING EQUATIONS BY FACTORING

Some equations can be solved by factoring. To do this, first add or subtract expressions to bring all the expressions to one side of the equation, with 0 on the other side. Then try to factor the nonzero side into a product of expressions. If this is possible, then using property (7) in Section A.4 each of the factors can be set equal to 0, yielding several simpler equations that possibly can be solved. The solutions of the simpler equations will be solutions of the factored equation. As an example, consider the equation $x^3 - 2x^2 + x = -5 (x - 1)^2$:

$$x^3 - 2x^2 + x + 5 (x - 1)^2 = 0$$
$$x(x^2 - 2x + 1) + 5 (x - 1)^2 = 0$$
$$x(x - 1)^2 + 5 (x - 1)^2 = 0$$
$$(x + 5) (x - 1)^2 = 0$$
$$x + 5 = 0 \text{ or } (x - 1)^2 = 0$$
$$x = -5 \text{ or } x = 1.$$

For another example, consider $\dfrac{x(x-3)(x^2 + 5)}{x - 4} = 0$ A fraction equals 0 if and only if its numerator equals 0. Thus, $x(x - 3)(x^2 + 5) = 0$:

$$x = 0 \text{ or } x - 3 = 0 \text{ or } x^2 + 5 = 0$$
$$x = 0 \text{ or } x = 3 \text{ or } x^2 + 5 = 0.$$

But $x^2 + 5 = 0$ has no real solution since $x^2 + 5 > 0$ for every real number. Thus, the solutions are 0 and 3.

The solutions of an equation are also called the *roots* of the equation. These roots can be checked by substituting them into the original equation to determine whether they satisfy the equation.

6. SOLVING QUADRATIC EQUATIONS

The standard form for a *quadratic equation* is

$$ax^2 + bx + c = 0,$$

where a, b, and c are real numbers and $a \neq 0$; for example:

$$x^2 + 6x + 5 = 0,$$
$$3x^2 - 2x = 0, \text{ and}$$
$$x^2 + 4 = 0.$$

Some quadratic equations can easily be solved by factoring. For example:

(1) $x^2 + 6x + 5 = 0$

$(x + 5)(x + 1) = 0$

$x + 5 = 0$ or $x + 1 = 0$

$x = -5$ or $x = -1$

(2) $3x^2 - 3 = 8x$

$3x^2 - 8x - 3 = 0$

$(3x + 1)(x - 3) = 0$

$3x + 1 = 0$ or $x - 3 = 0$

$x = -\dfrac{1}{3}$ or $x = 3$

A quadratic equation has at most two real roots and may have just one or even no real root. For example, the equation $x^2 - 6x + 9 = 0$ can be expressed as $(x - 3)^2 = 0$, or $(x - 3)(x - 3) = 0$; thus the only root is 3. The equation $x^2 + 4 = 0$ has no real root; since the square of any real number is greater than or equal to zero, $x^2 + 4$ must be greater than zero.

An expression of the form $a^2 - b^2$ can be factored as $(a - b)(a + b)$.

For example, the quadratic equation $9x^2 - 25 = 0$ can be solved as follows.

$$(3x - 5)(3x + 5) = 0$$
$$3x - 5 = 0 \text{ or } 3x + 5 = 0$$
$$x = \frac{5}{3} \text{ or } x = -\frac{5}{3}$$

If a quadratic expression is not easily factored, then its roots can always be found using the *quadratic formula*: If $ax^2 + bx + c = 0$ $(a \neq 0)$, then the roots are

$$x = \frac{-b + \sqrt{b^2 - 4ac}}{2a} \text{ and } x = \frac{-b - \sqrt{b^2 - 4ac}}{2a}.$$

These are two distinct real numbers unless $b^2 - 4ac \leq 0$. If $b^2 - 4ac = 0$, then these two expressions for x are equal to $-\dfrac{b}{2a}$, and the equation has only one root. If $b^2 - 4ac < 0$, then $\sqrt{b^2 - 4ac}$ is not a real number and the equation has no real roots.

7. EXPONENTS

A positive integer exponent of a number or a variable indicates a product, and the positive integer is the number of times that the number or variable is a factor in the product. For example, x^5 means $(x)(x)(x)(x)(x)$; that is, x is a factor in the product 5 times.

Some rules about exponents follow.

Let x and y be any positive numbers, and let r and s be any positive integers.

(1) $(x^r)(x^s) = x^{(r+s)}$; for example, $(2^2)(2^3) = 2^{(2+3)} = 2^5 = 32$.

(2) $\dfrac{x^r}{x^s} = x^{r-s}$; for example, $\dfrac{4^5}{4^2} = 4^{5-2} = 4^3 = 64$.

(3) $(x^r)(y^r) = (xy)^r$; for example, $(3^3)(4^3) = 12^3 = 1{,}728$.

(4) $\left(\dfrac{x}{y}\right)^r = \dfrac{x^r}{y^r}$; for example, $\left(\dfrac{2}{3}\right)^3 = \dfrac{2^3}{3^3} = \dfrac{8}{27}$.

(5) $(x^r)^s = x^{rs} = (x^s)^r$; for example, $(x^3)^4 = x^{12} = (x^4)^3$.

(6) $x^{-r} = \dfrac{1}{x^r}$; for example, $3^{-2} = \dfrac{1}{3^2} = \dfrac{1}{9}$.

(7) $x^0 = 1$; for example, $6^0 = 1$.

(8) $x^{\frac{r}{s}} = \left(x^{\frac{1}{s}}\right)^r = \left(x^r\right)^{\frac{1}{s}} = \sqrt[s]{x^r}$; for example, $8^{\frac{2}{3}} = \left(8^{\frac{1}{3}}\right)^2 = \left(8^2\right)^{\frac{1}{3}} = \sqrt[3]{8^2} = \sqrt[3]{64}$

$= 4$ and $9^{\frac{1}{2}} = \sqrt{9} = 3$.

It can be shown that rules 1-6 also apply when r and s are not integers and are not positive, that is, when r and s are any real numbers.

8. INEQUALITIES

An *inequality* is a statement that uses one of the following symbols:

$\neq$	not equal to
$>$	greater than
$\geq$	greater than or equal to
$<$	less than
$\leq$	less than or equal to

Some examples of inequalities are $5x - 3 < 9$, $6x \geq y$, and $\frac{1}{2} < \frac{3}{4}$. Solving a linear inequality with one unknown is similar to solving an equation; the unknown is isolated on one side of the inequality. As in solving an equation, the same number can be added to or subtracted from both sides of the inequality, or both sides of an inequality can be multiplied or divided by a positive number without changing the truth of the inequality. However, multiplying or dividing an inequality by a negative number reverses the order of the inequality. For example, $6 > 2$, but $(-1)(6) < (-1)(2)$.

To solve the inequality $3x - 2 > 5$ for x, isolate x by using the following steps:

$$3x - 2 > 5$$

$$3x > 7 \quad \text{(adding 2 to both sides)}$$

$$x > \frac{7}{3} \quad \text{(dividing both sides by 3)}$$

To solve the inequality $\frac{5x - 1}{-2} < 3$ for x, isolate x by using the following steps:

$$\frac{5x - 1}{-2} < 3$$

$$5x - 1 > -6 \quad \text{(multiplying both sides by -2)}$$
$$5x > -5 \quad \text{(adding 1 to both sides)}$$
$$x > -1 \quad \text{(dividing both sides by 5)}$$

9. ABSOLUTE VALUE

The absolute value of x, denoted $|x|$, is defined to be x if $x \geq 0$ and $-x$ if $x < 0$. Note that $\sqrt{x^2}$ denotes the nonnegative square root of x^2, and so $\sqrt{x^2} = |x|$.

10. FUNCTIONS

An algebraic expression in one variable can be used to define a *function* of that variable. A function is denoted by a letter such as f or g along with the variable in the expression. For example, the expression $x^3 - 5x^2 + 2$ defines a function f that can be denoted by

$$f(x) = x^3 - 5x^2 + 2.$$

The expression $\frac{2z + 7}{\sqrt{z + 1}}$ defines a function g that can be denoted by

$$g(z) = \frac{2z + 7}{\sqrt{z + 1}}.$$

The symbols "$f(x)$" or "$g(z)$" do not represent products; each is merely the symbol for an expression, and is read "f of x" or "g of z."

Function notation provides a short way of writing the result of substituting a value for a variable. If $x = 1$ is substituted in the first expression, the result can be written $f(1) = -2$, and $f(1)$ is called the "value of f at $x = 1$." Similarly, if $z = 0$ is substituted in the second expression, then the value of g at $z = 0$ is $g(0) = 7$.

Once a function $f(x)$ is defined, it is useful to think of the variable x as an input and $f(x)$ as the corresponding output. In any function there can be no more than one output for a given input. However, more than one input can give the same output; for example, if $h(x) = |x + 3|$, then $h(-4) = 1 = h(-2)$.

The set of all allowable inputs for a function is called the *domain* of the function. For f and g defined above, the domain of f is the set of all real numbers and the domain of g is the set of all numbers greater than -1. The domain of any function can be arbitrarily specified, as in the function defined by "$h(x) = 9x - 5$ for $0 \leq x \leq 10$." Without such a restriction, the domain is assumed to be all values of x that result in a real number when substituted into the function.

The domain of a function can consist of only the positive integers and possibly 0. For example,

$$a(n) = n^2 + \frac{n}{5} \text{ for } n = 0, 1, 2, 3, \ldots.$$

Such a function is called a *sequence* and $a(n)$ is denoted by a_n. The value of the sequence a_n at $n = 3$ is $a_3 = 3^2 + \frac{3}{5} = 9.6$. As another example, consider the sequence defined by $b_n = (-1)^n(n!)$ for $n = 1, 2, 3, \ldots.$ A sequence like this is often indicated by listing its values in the order $b_1, b_2, b_3, \ldots, b_n, \ldots$ as follows:

$$-1, 2, -6, \ldots, (-1)^n(n!), \ldots,$$

and $(-1)^n(n!)$ is called the nth term of the sequence.

C. Geometry

1. LINES

In geometry, the word "line" refers to a straight line that extends without end in both directions.

The line above can be referred to as line PQ or line ℓ. The part of the line from P to Q is called a *line segment*. P and Q are the *endpoints* of the segment. The notation PQ is used to denote both the segment and the length of the segment. The intention of the notation can be determined from the context.

2. INTERSECTING LINES AND ANGLES

If two lines intersect, the opposite angles are called *vertical angles* and have the same measure. In the figure

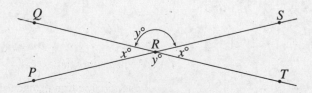

$\angle PRQ$ and $\angle SRT$ are vertical angles and $\angle QRS$ and $\angle PRT$ are vertical angles. Also, $x + y = 180$ since PRS is a straight line.

3. PERPENDICULAR LINES

An angle that has a measure of 90° is a *right angle*. If two lines intersect at right angles, the lines are *perpendicular*. For example:

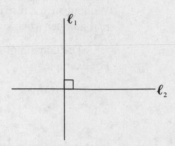

ℓ_1 and ℓ_2 above are perpendicular, denoted by $\ell_1 \perp \ell_2$. A right angle symbol in an angle of intersection indicates that the lines are perpendicular.

4. PARALLEL LINES

If two lines that are in the same plane do not intersect, the two lines are *parallel*. In the figure

lines ℓ_1 and ℓ_2 are parallel, denoted by $\ell_1 \parallel \ell_2$. If two parallel lines are intersected by a third line, as shown below, then the angle measures are related as indicated, where $x + y = 180$.

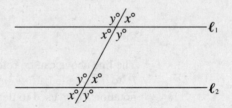

5. POLYGONS (CONVEX)

A *polygon* is a closed plane figure formed by three or more line segments, called the *sides* of the polygon. Each side intersects exactly two other sides at their endpoints. The points of intersection of the sides are *vertices*. The term "polygon" will be used to mean a convex polygon, that is, a polygon in which each interior angle has a measure of less than 180°.

The following figures are polygons:

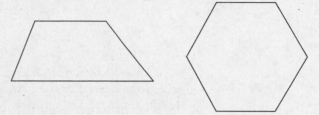

The following figures are not polygons:

A polygon with three sides is a *triangle*; with four sides, a *quadrilateral*; with five sides, a *pentagon*; and with six sides, a *hexagon*.

The sum of the interior angle measures of a triangle is 180°. In general, the sum of the interior angle measures of a polygon with n sides is equal to $(n-2)180°$. For example, this sum for a pentagon is $(5-2)180 = (3)180 = 540$ degrees.

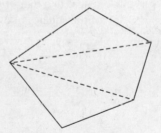

Note that a pentagon can be partitioned into three triangles and therefore the sum of the angle measures can be found by adding the sum of the angle measures of three triangles.

The *perimeter* of a polygon is the sum of the lengths of its sides.

The commonly used phrase "area of a triangle" (or any other plane figure) is used to mean the area of the region enclosed by that figure.

6. TRIANGLES

There are several special types of triangles with important properties. But one property that all triangles share is that the sum of the lengths of any two of the sides is greater than the length of the third side, as illustrated below.

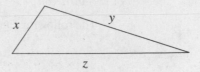

$$x + y > z, \quad x + z > y, \text{ and } y + z > x.$$

An *equilateral* triangle has all sides of equal length. All angles of an equilateral triangle have equal measure. An *isosceles* triangle has at least two sides of the same length. If two sides of a triangle have the same length, then the two angles opposite those sides have the same measure. Conversely, if two angles of a triangle have the same measure, then the sides opposite those angles have the same length. In isosceles triangle PQR below, $x = y$ since $PQ = QR$.

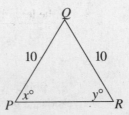

A triangle that has a right angle is a *right* triangle. In a right triangle, the side opposite the right angle is the *hypotenuse*, and the other two sides are the *legs*. An important theorem concerning right triangles is the *Pythagorean theorem*, which states: In a right triangle, the square of the length of the hypotenuse is equal to the sum of the squares of the lengths of the legs.

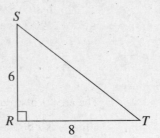

In the figure above, ΔRST is a right triangle, so $(RS)^2 + (RT)^2 = (ST)^2$. Here, $RS = 6$ and $RT = 8$, so $ST = 10$, since $6^2 + 8^2 = 36 + 64 = 100 = (ST)^2$ and $ST = \sqrt{100}$. Any triangle in which the lengths of the sides are in the ratio 3:4:5 is a right triangle. In general, if a, b, and c are the lengths of the sides of a triangle and $a^2 + b^2 = c^2$, then the triangle is a right triangle.

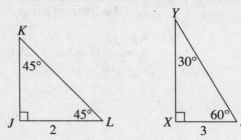

In 45°-45°-90° triangles, the lengths of the sides are in the ratio $1:1:\sqrt{2}$. For example, in $\triangle JKL$, if $JL = 2$, then $JK = 2$ and $KL = 2\sqrt{2}$. In 30°-60°-90° triangles, the lengths of the sides are in the ratio $1:\sqrt{3}:2$. For example, in $\triangle XYZ$, if $XZ = 3$, then $XY = 3\sqrt{3}$ and $YZ = 6$.

The *altitude* of a triangle is the segment drawn from a vertex perpendicular to the side opposite that vertex. Relative to that vertex and altitude, the opposite side is called the *base*.

The area of a triangle is equal to:

$$\frac{\text{(the length of the altitude)} \times \text{(the length of the base)}}{2}$$

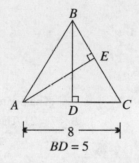

$$BD = 5$$

In $\triangle ABC$, BD is the altitude to base AC and AE is the altitude to base BC. The area of $\triangle ABC$ is equal to

$$\frac{BD \times AC}{2} = \frac{5 \times 8}{2} = 20.$$

The area is also equal to $\frac{AE \times BC}{2}$. If $\triangle ABC$ above is isosceles and $AB = BC$, then altitude BD bisects the base; that is, $AD = DC = 4$. Similarly, any altitude of an equilateral triangle bisects the side to which it is drawn.

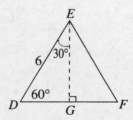

In equilateral triangle DEF, if $DE = 6$, then $DG = 3$ and $EG = 3\sqrt{3}$. The area of $\triangle DEF$ is equal to $\frac{3\sqrt{3} \times 6}{2} = 9\sqrt{3}$.

7. QUADRILATERALS

A polygon with four sides is a *quadrilateral*. A quadrilateral in which both pairs of opposite sides are parallel is a *parallelogram*. The opposite sides of a parallelogram also have equal length.

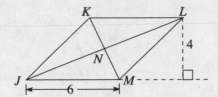

In parallelogram *JKLM*, *JK* ∥ *LM* and *JK* = *LM*; *KL* ∥ *JM* and *KL* = *JM*.

The diagonals of a parallelogram bisect each other (that is, *KN* = *NM* and *JN* = *NL*).

The area of a parallelogram is equal to

(the length of the altitude) × (the length of the base).

The area of *JKLM* is equal to 4 × 6 = 24.

A parallelogram with right angles is a *rectangle*, and a rectangle with all sides of equal length is a *square*.

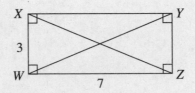

The perimeter of *WXYZ* = 2(3) + 2(7) = 20 and the area of *WXYZ* is equal to 3 × 7 = 21. The diagonals of a rectangle are equal; therefore $WY = XZ = \sqrt{9 + 49} = \sqrt{58}$.

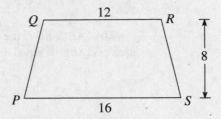

A quadrilateral with two sides that are parallel, as shown above, is a *trapezoid*. The area of trapezoid *PQRS* may be calculated as follows:

$$\frac{1}{2} \text{ (sum of bases)(height)} = \frac{1}{2}(QR + PS)(8) = \frac{1}{2}(28 \times 8) = 112.$$

8. CIRCLES

A *circle* is a set of points in a plane that are all located the same distance from a fixed point (the *center* of the circle).

A *chord* of a circle is a line segment that has its endpoints on the circle. A chord that passes through the center of the circle is a *diameter* of the circle. A *radius* of a circle is a segment from the center of the circle to a point on the circle. The words "diameter" and "radius" are also used to refer to the lengths of these segments.

The *circumference* of a circle is the distance around the circle. If r is the radius of the circle, then the circumference is equal to $2\pi r$, where π is approximately $\frac{22}{7}$ or 3.14. The *area* of a circle of radius r is equal to πr^2.

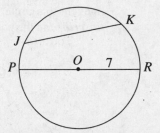

In the circle above, O is the center of the circle and JK and PR are chords. PR is a diameter and OR is a radius. If $OR = 7$, then the circumference of the circle is $2\pi(7) = 14\pi$ and the area of the circle is $\pi(7)^2 = 49\pi$.

The number of degrees of arc in a circle (or the number of degrees in a complete revolution) is 360.

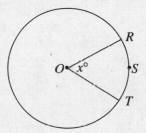

In the circle with center O above, the length of arc RST is $\frac{x}{360}$ of the circumference of the circle; for example, if $x = 60$, then arc RST has length $\frac{1}{6}$ of the circumference of the circle.

A line that has exactly one point in common with a circle is said to be *tangent* to the circle, and that common point is called the *point of tangency*. A radius or diameter with an endpoint at the point of tangency is perpendicular to the tangent line, and, conversely, a line that is perpendicular to a diameter at one of its endpoints is tangent to the circle at that endpoint.

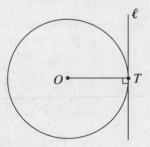

The line ℓ above is tangent to the circle and radius OT is perpendicular to ℓ.

If each vertex of a polygon lies on a circle, then the polygon is *inscribed* in the circle and the circle is *circumscribed* about the polygon. If each side of a polygon is tangent to a circle, then the polygon is *circumscribed* about the circle and the circle is *inscribed* in the polygon.

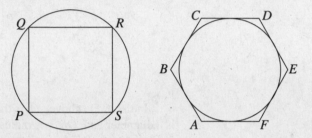

In the figure above, quadrilateral *PQRS* is inscribed in a circle and hexagon *ABCDEF* is circumscribed about a circle.

If a triangle is inscribed in a circle so that one of its sides is a diameter of the circle, then the triangle is a right triangle.

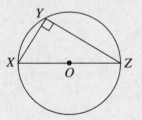

In the circle above, *XZ* is a diameter and the measure of $\angle XYZ$ is 90°.

9. RECTANGULAR SOLIDS AND CYLINDERS

A *rectangular solid* is a three-dimensional figure formed by six rectangular surfaces, as shown below. Each rectangular surface is a *face*. Each solid or dotted line segment is an *edge*, and each point at which the edges meet is a *vertex*. A rectangular solid has six faces, twelve edges, and eight vertices. Opposite faces are parallel rectangles that have the same dimensions. A rectangular solid in which all edges are of equal length is a *cube*.

The *surface area* of a rectangular solid is equal to the sum of the areas of all the faces. The *volume* is equal to

(length) × (width) × (height);
in other words, (area of base) × (height).

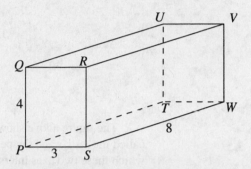

In the rectangular solid above, the dimensions are 3, 4, and 8. The surface area is equal to $2(3 \times 4) + 2(3 \times 8) + 2(4 \times 8) = 136$. The volume is equal to $3 \times 4 \times 8 = 96$.

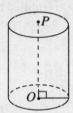

The figure above is a right circular *cylinder*. The two bases are circles of the same size with centers O and P, respectively, and altitude (height) OP is perpendicular to the bases. The surface area of a right circular cylinder with a base of radius r and height h is equal to $2(\pi r^2) + 2\pi rh$ (the sum of the areas of the two bases plus the area of the curved surface).

The volume of a cylinder is equal to $\pi r^2 h$, that is,

(area of base) × (height).

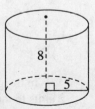

In the cylinder above, the surface area is equal to

$$2(25\pi) + 2\pi(5)(8) = 130\pi,$$

and the volume is equal to

$$25\pi(8) = 200\pi.$$

10. COORDINATE GEOMETRY

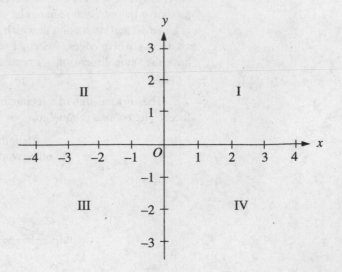

The figure above shows the (rectangular) *coordinate plane*. The horizontal line is called the *x-axis* and the perpendicular vertical line is called the *y-axis*. The point at which these two axes intersect, designated *O*, is called the *origin*. The axes divide the plane into four quadrants, I, II, III, and IV, as shown.

Each point in the plane has an *x-coordinate* and a *y-coordinate*. A point is identified by an ordered pair (x, y) of numbers in which the *x*-coordinate is the first number and the *y*-coordinate is the second number.

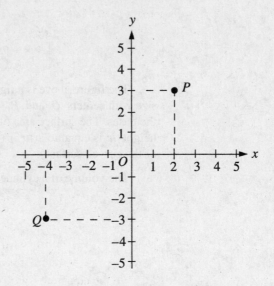

In the graph above, the (x, y) coordinates of point *P* are $(2, 3)$ since *P* is 2 units to the right of the *y*-axis (that is, $x = 2$) and 3 units above the *x*-axis (that is, $y = 3$). Similarly, the (x, y) coordinates of point *Q* are $(-4, -3)$. The origin *O* has coordinates $(0, 0)$.

One way to find the distance between two points in the coordinate plane is to use the Pythagorean theorem.

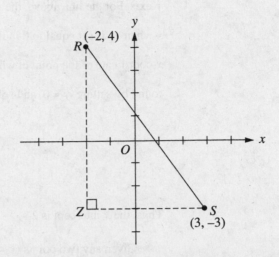

To find the distance between points R and S using the Pythagorean theorem, draw the triangle as shown. Note that Z has (x, y) coordinates $(-2, -3)$, $RZ = 7$, and $ZS = 5$. Therefore, the distance between R and S is equal to

$$\sqrt{7^2 + 5^2} = \sqrt{74}.$$

For a line in the coordinate plane, the coordinates of each point on the line satisfy a linear equation of the form $y = mx + b$ (or the form $x = a$ if the line is vertical).

For example, each point on the line below satisfies the equation $y = -\dfrac{1}{2}x + 1$. One can verify this for the points $(-2, 2)$, $(2, 0)$, and $(0, 1)$ by substituting the respective coordinates for x and y in the equation.

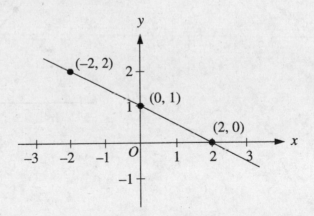

In the equation $y = mx + b$ of a line, the coefficient m is the *slope* of the line and the constant term b is the *y-intercept* of the line. For any two points on the line, the slope is defined to be the ratio of the difference in the y-coordinates to the difference in the x-coordinates. Using $(-2, 2)$ and $(2, 0)$ above, the slope is

$$\frac{\text{The difference in the y-coordinates}}{\text{The difference in the x-coordinates}} = \frac{0-2}{2-(-2)} = \frac{-2}{4} = -\frac{1}{2}.$$

The y-intercept is the y-coordinate of the point at which the line intersects the y-axis. For the line above, the y-intercept is 1, and this is the resulting value of y when x is set equal to 0 in the equation $y = -\frac{1}{2}x + 1$. The *x-intercept* is the x-coordinate of the point at which the line intersects the x-axis. The x-intercept can be found by setting $y = 0$ and solving for x. For the line $y = -\frac{1}{2}x + 1$, this gives

$$-\frac{1}{2}x + 1 = 0$$
$$-\frac{1}{2}x = -1$$
$$x = 2.$$

Thus, the x-intercept is 2.

Given any two points (x_1, y_1) and (x_2, y_2) with $x_1 \neq x_2$, the equation of the line passing through these points can be found by applying the definition of slope. Since the slope is $m = \frac{y_2 - y_1}{x_2 - x_1}$, then using a point known to be on the line, say (x_1, y_1), any point (x, y) on the line must satisfy $\frac{y - y_1}{x - x_1} = m$, or $y - y_1 = m(x - x_1)$. (Using (x_2, y_2) as the known point would yield an equivalent equation.) For example, consider the points $(-2, 4)$ and $(3, -3)$ on the line below.

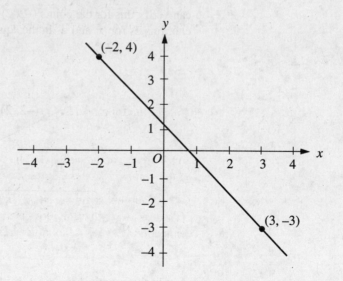

The slope of this line is $\frac{-3 - 4}{3 - (-2)} = \frac{-7}{5}$, so an equation of this line can be found using the point $(3, -3)$ as follows:

$$y - (-3) = -\frac{7}{5}(x - 3)$$
$$y + 3 = -\frac{7}{5}x + \frac{21}{5}$$
$$y = -\frac{7}{5}x + \frac{6}{5}.$$

The y-intercept is $\frac{6}{5}$. The *x-intercept* can be found as follows:

$$0 = -\frac{7}{5}x + \frac{6}{5}$$

$$\frac{7}{5}x = \frac{6}{5}$$

$$x = \frac{6}{7}.$$

Both of these intercepts can be seen on the graph.

If the slope of a line is negative, the line slants downward from left to right; if the slope is positive, the line slants upward. If the slope is 0, the line is horizontal; the equation of such a line is of the form $y = b$ since $m = 0$. For a vertical line, slope is not defined, and the equation is of the form $x = a$, where a is the x-intercept.

There is a connection between graphs of lines in the coordinate plane and solutions of two linear equations with two unknowns. If two linear equations with unknowns x and y have a unique solution, then the graphs of the equations are two lines that intersect in one point, which is the solution. If the equations are equivalent, then they represent the same line with infinitely many points or solutions. If the equations have no solution, then they represent parallel lines, which do not intersect.

There is also a connection between functions (see Section B.10) and the coordinate plane. If a function is graphed in the coordinate plane, the function can be understood in different and useful ways. Consider the function defined by

$$f(x) = -\frac{7}{5}x + \frac{6}{5}.$$

If the value of the function, $f(x)$, is equated with the variable y, then the graph of the function in the xy-coordinate plane is simply the graph of the equation

$$y = -\frac{7}{5}x + \frac{6}{5}.$$

shown above. Similarly, any function $f(x)$ can be graphed by equating y with the value of the function:

$$y = f(x).$$

So for any x in the domain of the function f, the point with coordinates $(x, f(x))$ is on the graph of f, and the graph consists entirely of these points.

As another example, consider a quadratic polynomial function defined by $f(x) = x^2 - 1$. One can plot several points $(x, f(x))$ on the graph to understand the connection between a function and its graph:

x	$f(x)$
–2	3
–1	0
0	–1
1	0
2	3

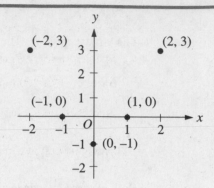

If all of the points were graphed for $-2 \leq x \leq 2$, then the graph would appear as follows.

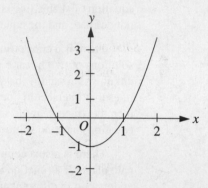

The graph of a quadratic function is called a *parabola* and always has the shape of the curve above, although it may be upside down or have a greater or lesser width. Note that the roots of the equation $f(x) = x^2 - 1 = 0$ are $x = 1$ and $x = -1$; these coincide with the x-intercepts since x-intercepts are found by setting $y = 0$ and solving for x. Also, the y-intercept is $f(0) = -1$ since this is the value of y corresponding to $x = 0$. For any function f, the x-intercepts are the solutions of the equation $f(x) = 0$ and the y-intercept is the value $f(0)$.

D. Word Problems

Many of the principles discussed in this chapter are used to solve word problems. The following discussion of word problems illustrates some of the techniques and concepts used in solving such problems.

1. RATE PROBLEMS

The distance that an object travels is equal to the product of the average speed at which it travels and the amount of time it takes to travel that distance, that is,

$$\text{Rate} \times \text{Time} = \text{Distance.}$$

Example 1: If a car travels at an average speed of 70 kilometers per hour for 4 hours, how many kilometers does it travel?

Solution: Since rate × time = distance, simply multiply 70 km/hour × 4 hours. Thus, the car travels 280 kilometers in 4 hours.

To determine the average rate at which an object travels, divide the total distance traveled by the total amount of traveling time.

Example 2: On a 400-mile trip, car X traveled half the distance at 40 miles per hour and the other half at 50 miles per hour. What was the average speed of car X?

Solution: First it is necessary to determine the amount of traveling time. During the first 200 miles, the car traveled at 40 mph; therefore, it took $\frac{200}{40} = 5$ hours to travel the first 200 miles. During the second 200 miles, the car traveled at 50 mph; therefore, it took $\frac{200}{50} = 4$ hours to travel the second 200 miles. Thus, the average speed of car X was $\frac{400}{9} = 44\frac{4}{9}$ mph. Note that the average speed is *not* $\frac{40+50}{2} = 45$.

Some rate problems can be solved by using ratios.

Example 3: If 5 shirts cost $44, then, at this rate, what is the cost of 8 shirts?

Solution: If c is the cost of the 8 shirts, then $\frac{5}{44} = \frac{8}{c}$. Cross multiplication results in the equation

$$5c = 8 \times 44 = 352$$

$$c = \frac{352}{5} = 70.40$$

The 8 shirts cost $70.40.

2. WORK PROBLEMS

In a work problem, the rates at which certain persons or machines work alone are usually given, and it is necessary to compute the rate at which they work together (or vice versa).

The basic formula for solving work problems is: $\frac{1}{r} + \frac{1}{s} = \frac{1}{h}$, where r and s are, for example, the number of hours it takes Rae and Sam, respectively, to complete a job when working alone, and h is the number of hours it takes Rae and Sam to do the job when working together. The reasoning is that in 1 hour Rae does $\frac{1}{r}$ of the job, Sam does $\frac{1}{s}$ of the job, and Rae and Sam together do $\frac{1}{h}$ of the job.

Example 1: If machine X can produce 1,000 bolts in 4 hours and machine Y can produce 1,000 bolts in 5 hours, in how many hours can machines X and Y, working together at these constant rates, produce 1,000 bolts?

Solution:
$$\frac{1}{4} + \frac{1}{5} = \frac{1}{h}$$
$$\frac{5}{20} + \frac{4}{20} = \frac{1}{h}$$
$$\frac{9}{20} = \frac{1}{h}$$
$$9h = 20$$
$$h = \frac{20}{9} = 2\frac{2}{9}$$

Working together, machines X and Y can produce 1,000 bolts in $2\frac{2}{9}$ hours.

Example 2: If Art and Rita can do a job in 4 hours when working together at their respective constant rates and Art can do the job alone in 6 hours, in how many hours can Rita do the job alone?

Solution:

$$\frac{1}{6} + \frac{1}{R} = \frac{1}{4}$$

$$\frac{R+6}{6R} = \frac{1}{4}$$

$$4R + 24 = 6R$$

$$24 = 2R$$

$$12 = R$$

Working alone, Rita can do the job in 12 hours.

3. MIXTURE PROBLEMS

In mixture problems, substances with different characteristics are combined, and it is necessary to determine the characteristics of the resulting mixture.

Example 1: If 6 pounds of nuts that cost $1.20 per pound are mixed with 2 pounds of nuts that cost $1.60 per pound, what is the cost per pound of the mixture?

Solution: The total cost of the 8 pounds of nuts is

$$6(\$1.20) + 2(\$1.60) = \$10.40.$$

The cost per pound is $\dfrac{\$10.40}{8} = \$1.30$.

Example 2: How many liters of a solution that is 15 percent salt must be added to 5 liters of a solution that is 8 percent salt so that the resulting solution is 10 percent salt?

Solution: Let *n* represent the number of liters of the 15% solution. The amount of salt in the 15% solution [$0.15n$] plus the amount of salt in the 8% solution [$(0.08)(5)$] must be equal to the amount of salt in the 10% mixture [$0.10\,(n + 5)$]. Therefore,

$$0.15n + 0.08(5) = 0.10(n + 5)$$

$$15n + 40 = 10n + 50$$

$$5n = 10$$

$$n = 2 \text{ liters.}$$

Two liters of the 15% salt solution must be added to the 8% solution to obtain the 10% solution.

4. INTEREST PROBLEMS

Interest can be computed in two basic ways. With simple annual interest, the interest is computed on the principal only and is equal to (principal) × (interest rate) × (time). If interest is compounded, then interest is computed on the principal as well as on any interest already earned.

Example 1: If $8,000 is invested at 6 percent simple annual interest, how much interest is earned after 3 months?

Solution: Since the annual interest rate is 6%, the interest for 1 year is

$(0.06)(\$8,000) = \$480$. The interest earned in 3 months is $\dfrac{3}{12}(\$480) = \$120$.

Example 2: If $10,000 is invested at 10 percent annual interest, compounded semiannually, what is the balance after 1 year?

Solution: The balance after the first 6 months would be

$10,000 + (10,000)(0.05) = 10,500$ dollars. The balance after one year would be $10,500 + (10,500)(0.05) = 11,025$ dollars.

Note that the interest rate for each 6-month period is 5%, which is half of the 10% annual rate. The balance after one year can also be expressed as

$$10,000 \left(1 + \frac{0.10}{2}\right)^2 \text{ dollars.}$$

5. DISCOUNT

If a price is discounted by n percent, then the price becomes $(100 - n)$ percent of the original price.

Example 1: A certain customer paid $24 for a dress. If that price represented a 25 percent discount on the original price of the dress, what was the original price of the dress?

Solution: If p is the original price of the dress, then $0.75p$ is the discounted price and $0.75p = \$24$, or $p = \$32$. The original price of the dress was $32.

Example 2: The price of an item is discounted by 20 percent and then this reduced price is discounted by an additional 30 percent. These two discounts are equal to an overall discount of what percent?

Solution: If p is the original price of the item, then $0.8p$ is the price after the first discount. The price after the second discount is $(0.7)(0.8)p = 0.56p$. This represents an overall discount of 44 percent (100% − 56%).

6. PROFIT

Gross profit is equal to revenues minus expenses, or selling price minus cost.

Example: A certain appliance costs a merchant $30. At what price should the merchant sell the appliance in order to make a gross profit of 50 percent of the cost of the appliance?

Solution: If s is the selling price of the appliance, then $s - 30 = (0.5)(30)$, or $s = \$45$. The merchant should sell the appliance for $45.

7. SETS

If S is the set of numbers 1, 2, 3, and 4, you can write $S = \{1, 2, 3, 4\}$. Sets can also be represented by Venn diagrams. That is, the relationship among the members of sets can be represented by circles.

Example 1: Each of 25 people is enrolled in history, mathematics, or both. If 20 are enrolled in history and 18 are enrolled in mathematics, how many are enrolled in both history and mathematics?

Solution: The 25 people can be divided into three sets: those who study history only, those who study mathematics only, and those who study history and mathematics. Thus a Venn diagram may be drawn as follows, where n is the number of people enrolled in both courses, $20 - n$ is the number enrolled in history only, and $18 - n$ is the number enrolled in mathematics only.

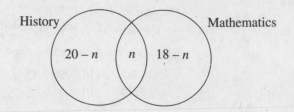

Since there is a total of 25 people, $(20 - n) + n + (18 - n) = 25$, or $n = 13$. Thirteen people are enrolled in both history and mathematics. Note that $20 + 18 - 13 = 25$, which is the general addition rule for two sets.
(See Section A.9.)

Example 2: In a certain production lot, 40 percent of the toys are red and the remaining toys are green. Half of the toys are small and half are large. If 10 percent of the toys are red and small, and 40 toys are green and large, how many of the toys are red and large?

Solution: For this kind of problem, it is helpful to organize the information in a table:

	Red	Green	Total
Small	10%		50%
Large			50%
Total	40%	60%	100%

The numbers in the table are the percents given. The following percents can be computed on the basis of what is given:

	Red	Green	Total
Small	10%	40%	50%
Large	30%	20%	50%
Total	40%	60%	100%

Since 20% of the number of toys (n) are green and large, $0.20n = 40$ (40 toys are green and large), or $n = 200$. Therefore, 30% of the 200 toys, or $(0.3)(200) = 60$, are red and large.

8. GEOMETRY PROBLEMS

The following is an example of a word problem involving geometry.

Example:

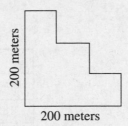

200 meters

The figure above shows an aerial view of a piece of land. If all angles shown are right angles, what is the perimeter of the piece of land?

Solution: For reference, label the figure as

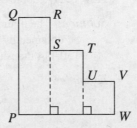

If all the angles are right angles, then $QR + ST + UV = PW$, and $RS + TU + VW = PQ$. Hence, the perimeter of the land is $2PW + 2PQ = 2 \times 200 + 2 \times 200 = 800$ meters.

9. MEASUREMENT PROBLEMS

Some questions on the GMAT® involve metric units of measure, whereas others involve English units of measure. However, except for units of time, if a question requires conversion from one unit of measure to another, the relationship between those units will be given.

Example: A train travels at a constant rate of 25 meters per second. How many kilometers does it travel in 5 minutes? (1 kilometer = 1,000 meters)

Solution: In 1 minute the train travels $(25)(60) = 1,500$ meters, so in 5 minutes it travels 7,500 meters. Since 1 kilometer = 1,000 meters, it follows that 7,500 meters equals $\frac{7,500}{1,000}$, or 7.5 kilometers.

10. DATA INTERPRETATION

Occasionally a question or set of questions will be based on data provided in a table or graph. Some examples of tables and graphs are given below.

Example 1:

POPULATION BY AGE GROUP
(in thousands)

Age	Population
17 years and under	63,376
18-44 years	86,738
45-64 years	43,845
65 years and over	24,054

How many people are 44 years old or younger?

Solution: The figures in the table are given in thousands. The answer in thousands can be obtained by adding 63,376 thousand and 86,738 thousand. The result is 150,114 thousand, which is 150,114,000.

Example 2:

AVERAGE TEMPERATURE AND PRECIPITATION IN CITY *X*

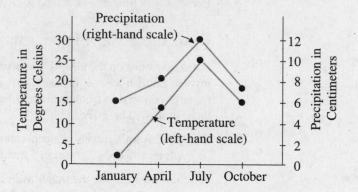

What are the average temperature and precipitation in City *X* during April?

Solution: Note that the scale on the left applies to the temperature line graph and the one on the right applies to the precipitation line graph. According to the graph, during April the average temperature is approximately 14° Celsius and the average precipitation is 8 centimeters.

Example 3:

DISTRIBUTION OF AL'S WEEKLY NET SALARY

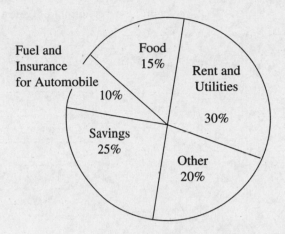

Weekly Net Salary: $350

To how many of the categories listed was at least $80 of Al's weekly net salary allocated?

Solution: In the circle graph, the relative sizes of the sectors are proportional to their corresponding values and the sum of the percents given is 100%. Note that $\frac{80}{350}$ is approximately 23%, so at least $80 was allocated to each of 2 categories — Rent and Utilities, and Savings — since their allocations are each greater than 23%.

4 Problem Solving

In these questions you are to solve each problem and select the best of the five answer choices given. The mathematics required to answer the questions does not extend beyond that assumed to be common to the mathematics background of all examinees.

The following pages include test-taking strategies, sample questions, and explanations for all the problems. These explanations present possible problem-solving strategies for the problems.

Test-taking Strategies for Problem Solving

1. Pacing yourself is very important. Consult the on-screen timer periodically. Work as carefully as possible, but do not spend valuable time checking answers or pondering over problems that you find difficult.

2. Scratchpaper is provided. Working a problem out in writing may help you avoid errors in solving the problem. If diagrams or figures are not presented, it may help if you draw your own.

3. Read each question carefully to determine what information is given and what is being asked. For word problems, take one step at a time, reading each sentence carefully and translating the information into equations or other useful mathematical representations.

4. Before attempting to answer a question, scan the answer choices; otherwise you may waste time putting answers in a form that is not given (for example, finding the answer in decimal form, such as 0.25, when the choices are given in fractional form, such as $\frac{1}{4}$).

5. For questions that require approximations, scan the answer choices to get some idea of the required closeness of approximation; otherwise, you may waste time on long computations where a short mental process would serve as well (for example, taking 48 percent of a number instead of half the number).

6. Don't waste time trying to solve a problem that is too difficult for you. Guess and move on to another question.

When finished reading directions click on the icon below

Dismiss

Directions

Solve the problem and indicate the best of the answer choices given.

Numbers: All numbers used are real numbers.

Figures: A figure accompanying a problem solving question is intended to provide information useful in solving the problem. Figures are drawn as accurately as possible EXCEPT when it is stated in a specific problem that its figure is not drawn to scale. Straight lines may some-times appear jagged. All figures lie in a plane unless otherwise indicated.

To review these directions for subsequent questions of this type, click on HELP.

Test	Section				?	Answer	➡
Quit	Exit	Time			Help	Confirm	Next

PROBLEM SOLVING SAMPLE QUESTIONS

1. If Mario was 32 years old 8 years ago, how old was he x years ago?

   (A) $x - 40$
   (B) $x - 24$
   (C) $40 - x$
   (D) $24 - x$
   (E) $24 + x$

2. Running at the same constant rate, 6 identical machines can produce a total of 270 bottles per minute. At this rate, how many bottles could 10 such machines produce in 4 minutes?

   (A)   648
   (B) 1,800
   (C) 2,700
   (D) 10,800
   (E) 64,800

3. Three business partners, Q, R, and S, agree to divide their total profit for a certain year in the ratios 2 : 5 : 8, respectively. If Q's share was $4,000, what was the total profit of the business partners for the year?

   (A) $26,000
   (B) $30,000
   (C) $52,000
   (D) $60,000
   (E) $300,000

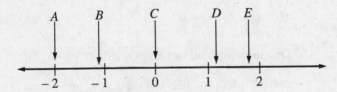

4. Of the five coordinates associated with points A, B, C, D, and E on the number line above, which has the greatest absolute value?

   (A) A
   (B) B
   (C) C
   (D) D
   (E) E

5. A restaurant meal cost $35.50 and there was no tax. If the tip was more than 10 percent but less than 15 percent of the cost of the meal, then the total amount paid must have been between

   (A) $40 and $42
   (B) $39 and $41
   (C) $38 and $40
   (D) $37 and $39
   (E) $36 and $37

6. Harriet wants to put up fencing around three sides of her rectangular yard and leave a side of 20 feet unfenced. If the yard has an area of 680 square feet, how many feet of fencing does she need?

   (A) 34
   (B) 40
   (C) 68
   (D) 88
   (E) 102

7. If $u > t$, $r > q$, $s > t$, and $t > r$, which of the following must be true?

   I. $u > s$
   II. $s > q$
   III. $u > r$

   (A) I only
   (B) II only
   (C) III only
   (D) I and II
   (E) II and III

8. Increasing the original price of an article by 15 percent and then increasing the new price by 15 percent is equivalent to increasing the original price by

   (A) 32.25%
   (B) 31.00%
   (C) 30.25%
   (D) 30.00%
   (E) 22.50%

9. If k is an integer and 0.0010101×10^k is greater than 1,000, what is the least possible value of k?

   (A) 2
   (B) 3
   (C) 4
   (D) 5
   (E) 6

10. If $(b-3)\left(4+\dfrac{2}{b}\right)=0$ and $b \neq 3$, then $b =$

(A) −8

(B) −2

(C) $-\dfrac{1}{2}$

(D) $\dfrac{1}{2}$

(E) 2

11. In a weight-lifting competition, the total weight of Joe's two lifts was 750 pounds. If twice the weight of his first lift was 300 pounds more than the weight of his second lift, what was the weight, in pounds, of his <u>first</u> lift?

(A) 225
(B) 275
(C) 325
(D) 350
(E) 400

12. One hour after Yolanda started walking from X to Y, a distance of 45 miles, Bob started walking along the same road from Y to X. If Yolanda's walking rate was 3 miles per hour and Bob's was 4 miles per hour, how many miles had Bob walked when they met?

(A) 24
(B) 23
(C) 22
(D) 21
(E) 19.5

13. The average (arithmetic mean) of 6 numbers is 8.5. When one number is discarded, the average of the remaining numbers becomes 7.2. What is the discarded number?

(A) 7.8
(B) 9.8
(C) 10.0
(D) 12.4
(E) 15.0

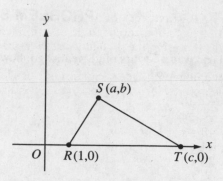

14. In the rectangular coordinate system above, the area of $\triangle RST$ is

(A) $\dfrac{bc}{2}$

(B) $\dfrac{b(c-1)}{2}$

(C) $\dfrac{c(b-1)}{2}$

(D) $\dfrac{a(c-1)}{2}$

(E) $\dfrac{c(a-1)}{2}$

15. Which of the following equations has a root in common with $x^2 - 6x + 5 = 0$?

(A) $x^2 + 1 = 0$
(B) $x^2 - x - 2 = 0$
(C) $x^2 - 10x - 5 = 0$
(D) $2x^2 - 2 = 0$
(E) $x^2 - 2x - 3 = 0$

16. One inlet pipe fills an empty tank in 5 hours. A second inlet pipe fills the same tank in 3 hours. If both pipes are used together, how long will it take to fill $\dfrac{2}{3}$ of the tank?

(A) $\dfrac{8}{15}$ hr

(B) $\dfrac{3}{4}$ hr

(C) $\dfrac{5}{4}$ hr

(D) $\dfrac{15}{8}$ hr

(E) $\dfrac{8}{3}$ hr

17. During the first week of September, a shoe retailer sold 10 pairs of a certain style of oxfords at $35.00 a pair. If, during the second week of September, 15 pairs were sold at the sale price of $27.50 a pair, by what amount did the revenue from weekly sales of these oxfords increase during the second week?

(A) $62.50
(B) $75.00
(C) $112.50
(D) $137.50
(E) $175.00

18. The number $2 - 0.5$ is how many times the number $1 - 0.5$?

(A) 2
(B) 2.5
(C) 3
(D) 3.5
(E) 4

19. If $x = -1$, then $-(x^4 + x^3 + x^2 + x) =$

(A) -10
(B) -4
(C) 0
(D) 4
(E) 10

20. Coins are dropped into a toll box so that the box is being filled at the rate of approximately 2 cubic feet per hour. If the empty rectangular box is 4 feet long, 4 feet wide, and 3 feet deep, approximately how many hours does it take to fill the box?

(A) 4
(B) 8
(C) 16
(D) 24
(E) 48

21. $\left(\dfrac{1}{5}\right)^2 - \left(\dfrac{1}{5}\right)\left(\dfrac{1}{4}\right) =$

(A) $-\dfrac{1}{20}$

(B) $-\dfrac{1}{100}$

(C) $\dfrac{1}{100}$

(D) $\dfrac{1}{20}$

(E) $\dfrac{1}{5}$

22. A club collected exactly $599 from its members. If each member contributed at least $12, what is the greatest number of members the club could have?

(A) 43
(B) 44
(C) 49
(D) 50
(E) 51

23. A union contract specifies a 6 percent salary increase plus a $450 bonus for each employee. For a certain employee, this is equivalent to an 8 percent salary increase. What was this employee's salary before the new contract?

(A) $21,500
(B) $22,500
(C) $23,500
(D) $24,300
(E) $25,000

24. If n is a positive integer and $k + 2 = 3^n$, which of the following could NOT be a value of k ?

(A) 1
(B) 4
(C) 7
(D) 25
(E) 79

25. Elena purchased brand X pens for $4.00 apiece and brand Y pens for $2.80 apiece. If Elena purchased a total of 12 of these pens for $42.00, how many brand X pens did she purchase?

(A) 4
(B) 5
(C) 6
(D) 7
(E) 8

26. If the length and width of a rectangular garden plot were each increased by 20 percent, what would be the percent increase in the area of the plot?

(A) 20%
(B) 24%
(C) 36%
(D) 40%
(E) 44%

27. The population of a bacteria culture doubles every 2 minutes. Approximately how many minutes will it take for the population to grow from 1,000 to 500,000 bacteria?

(A) 10
(B) 12
(C) 14
(D) 16
(E) 18

28. When 10 is divided by the positive integer n, the remainder is $n - 4$. Which of the following could be the value of n ?

(A) 3
(B) 4
(C) 7
(D) 8
(E) 12

29. For a light that has an intensity of 60 candles at its source, the intensity in candles, S, of the light at a point d feet from the source is given by the formula $S = \dfrac{60k}{d^2}$, where k is a constant. If the intensity of the light is 30 candles at a distance of 2 feet from the source, what is the intensity of the light at a distance of 20 feet from the source?

(A) $\dfrac{3}{10}$ candle

(B) $\dfrac{1}{2}$ candle

(C) $1\dfrac{1}{3}$ candles

(D) 2 candles

(E) 3 candles

30. If x and y are prime numbers, which of the following CANNOT be the sum of x and y ?

(A) 5
(B) 9
(C) 13
(D) 16
(E) 23

31. Of the 3,600 employees of Company X, $\dfrac{1}{3}$ are clerical. If the clerical staff were to be reduced by $\dfrac{1}{3}$, what percent of the total number of the remaining employees would then be clerical?

(A) 25%
(B) 22.2%
(C) 20%
(D) 12.5%
(E) 11.1%

32. In which of the following pairs are the two numbers reciprocals of each other?

I. 3 and $\dfrac{1}{3}$

II. $\dfrac{1}{17}$ and $\dfrac{-1}{17}$

III. $\sqrt{3}$ and $\dfrac{\sqrt{3}}{3}$

(A) I only
(B) II only
(C) I and II
(D) I and III
(E) II and III

33. What is 45 percent of $\dfrac{7}{12}$ of 240 ?

(A) 63
(B) 90
(C) 108
(D) 140
(E) 311

34. If x books cost $5 each and y books cost $8 each, then the average (arithmetic mean) cost, in dollars per book, is equal to

(A) $\dfrac{5x + 8y}{x + y}$

(B) $\dfrac{5x + 8y}{xy}$

(C) $\dfrac{5x + 8y}{13}$

(D) $\dfrac{40xy}{x + y}$

(E) $\dfrac{40xy}{13}$

35. If $\frac{1}{2}$ of the money in a certain trust fund was invested in stocks, $\frac{1}{4}$ in bonds, $\frac{1}{5}$ in a mutual fund, and the remaining $10,000 in a government certificate, what was the total amount of the trust fund?

(A) $100,000
(B) $150,000
(C) $200,000
(D) $500,000
(E) $2,000,000

36. Marion rented a car for $18.00 plus $0.10 per mile driven. Craig rented a car for $25.00 plus $0.05 per mile driven. If each drove d miles and each was charged exactly the same amount for the rental, then d equals

(A) 100
(B) 120
(C) 135
(D) 140
(E) 150

37. Machine A produces bolts at a uniform rate of 120 every 40 seconds, and machine B produces bolts at a uniform rate of 100 every 20 seconds. If the two machines run simultaneously, how many seconds will it take for them to produce a total of 200 bolts?

(A) 22
(B) 25
(C) 28
(D) 32
(E) 56

38. $\dfrac{3.003}{2.002} =$

(A) 1.05
(B) 1.50015
(C) 1.501
(D) 1.5015
(E) 1.5

Questions 39-41 refer to the following graph.

AVERAGE COSTS OF OPERATING SUBCOMPACT, COMPACT, AND MIDSIZE CARS IN THE UNITED STATES, 1982-1986

Cost per mile for cars bought new in the indicated year and driven 10,000 miles annually

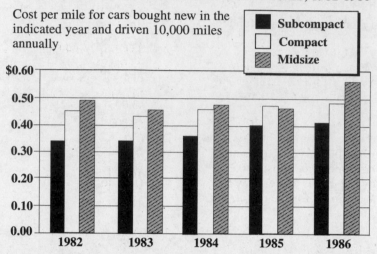

39. In 1982 the approximate average cost of operating a subcompact car for 10,000 miles was

(A) $360
(B) $3,400
(C) $4,100
(D) $4,500
(E) $4,900

40. In 1984 the average cost of operating a subcompact car was approximately what percent less than the average cost of operating a midsized car?

(A)   12%
(B)   20%
(C)   25%
(D)   33%
(E)   48%

41. For each of the years shown, the average cost per mile of operating a compact car minus the average cost per mile of operating a subcompact car was between

(A) $0.12 and $0.18
(B) $0.10 and $0.15
(C) $0.09 and $0.13
(D) $0.06 and $0.12
(E) $0.05 and $0.08

42. What is the decimal equivalent of $\left(\dfrac{1}{5}\right)^5$?

(A) 0.00032
(B) 0.0016
(C) 0.00625
(D) 0.008
(E) 0.03125

43. Two hundred gallons of fuel oil are purchased at $0.91 per gallon and are consumed at a rate of $0.70 worth of fuel per hour. At this rate, how many hours are required to consume the 200 gallons of fuel oil?

(A) 140
(B) 220
(C) 260
(D) 322
(E) 330

44. If $\dfrac{4-x}{2+x} = x$, what is the value of $x^2 + 3x - 4$?

(A) -4
(B) -1
(C) 0
(D) 1
(E) 2

45. If $b < 2$ and $2x - 3b = 0$, which of the following must be true?

(A) $x > -3$
(B) $x < 2$
(C) $x = 3$
(D) $x < 3$
(E) $x > 3$

46. The trapezoid shown in the figure above represents a cross section of the rudder of a ship. If the distance from A to B is 13 feet, what is the area of the cross section of the rudder in square feet?

(A) 39
(B) 40
(C) 42
(D) 45
(E) 46.5

47. $\dfrac{(-1.5)(1.2) - (4.5)(0.4)}{30} =$

(A) -1.2
(B) -0.12
(C) 0
(D) 0.12
(E) 1.2

48. If n is a positive integer, then $n(n + 1)(n + 2)$ is

(A) even only when n is even
(B) even only when n is odd
(C) odd whenever n is odd
(D) divisible by 3 only when n is odd
(E) divisible by 4 whenever n is even

-81-

49. If Jack had twice the amount of money that he has, he would have exactly the amount necessary to buy 3 hamburgers at $0.96 apiece and 2 milk shakes at $1.28 apiece. How much money does Jack have?

(A) $1.60
(B) $2.24
(C) $2.72
(D) $3.36
(E) $5.44

50. If a photocopier makes 2 copies in $\frac{1}{3}$ second, then, at the same rate, how many copies does it make in 4 minutes?

(A)   360
(B)   480
(C)   576
(D)   720
(E) 1,440

51. The price of a certain television set is discounted by 10 percent, and the reduced price is then discounted by 10 percent. This series of successive discounts is equivalent to a single discount of

(A) 20%
(B) 19%
(C) 18%
(D) 11%
(E) 10%

52. If $\dfrac{2}{1 + \dfrac{2}{y}} = 1$, then $y =$

(A) -2

(B) $-\dfrac{1}{2}$

(C) $\dfrac{1}{2}$

(D) 2

(E) 3

53. If a rectangular photograph that is 10 inches wide by 15 inches long is to be enlarged so that the width will be 22 inches and the ratio of width to length will be unchanged, then the length, in inches, of the enlarged photograph will be

(A) 33
(B) 32
(C) 30
(D) 27
(E) 25

54. If m is an integer such that $(-2)^{2m} = 2^{9-m}$, then $m =$

(A) 1
(B) 2
(C) 3
(D) 4
(E) 6

55. If $0 \le x \le 4$ and $y < 12$, which of the following CANNOT be the value of xy ?

(A) -2
(B) 0
(C) 6
(D) 24
(E) 48

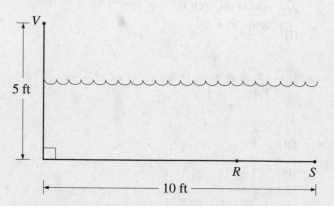

56. In the figure above, V represents an observation point at one end of a pool. From V, an object that is actually located on the bottom of the pool at point R appears to be at point S. If $VR = 10$ feet, what is the distance RS, in feet, between the actual position and the perceived position of the object?

(A) $10 - 5\sqrt{3}$

(B) $10 - 5\sqrt{2}$

(C) 2

(D) $2\dfrac{1}{2}$

(E) 4

57. If the total payroll expense of a certain business in year Y was \$84,000, which was 20 percent more than in year X, what was the total payroll expense in year X?

(A) \$70,000
(B) \$68,320
(C) \$64,000
(D) \$60,000
(E) \$52,320

58. If a, b, and c are consecutive positive integers and $a < b < c$, which of the following must be true?

 I. $c - a = 2$

 II. abc is an even integer.

 III. $\dfrac{a + b + c}{3}$ is an integer.

(A) I only
(B) II only
(C) I and II only
(D) II and III only
(E) I, II, and III

59. A straight pipe 1 yard in length was marked off in fourths and also in thirds. If the pipe was then cut into separate pieces at each of these markings, which of the following gives all the different lengths of the pieces, in fractions of a yard?

(A) $\dfrac{1}{6}$ and $\dfrac{1}{4}$ only

(B) $\dfrac{1}{4}$ and $\dfrac{1}{3}$ only

(C) $\dfrac{1}{6}, \dfrac{1}{4}$, and $\dfrac{1}{3}$

(D) $\dfrac{1}{12}, \dfrac{1}{6}$, and $\dfrac{1}{4}$

(E) $\dfrac{1}{12}, \dfrac{1}{6}$, and $\dfrac{1}{3}$

60. What is the least integer that is a sum of three different primes each greater than 20 ?

(A) 69
(B) 73
(C) 75
(D) 79
(E) 83

61. A tourist purchased a total of \$1,500 worth of traveler's checks in \$10 and \$50 denominations. During the trip the tourist cashed 7 checks and then lost all of the rest. If the number of \$10 checks cashed was one more or one less than the number of \$50 checks cashed, what is the minimum possible value of the checks that were lost?

(A) \$1,430
(B) \$1,310
(C) \$1,290
(D) \$1,270
(E) \$1,150

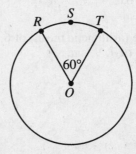

62. If the circle above has center O and circumference 18π, then the perimeter of sector $RSTO$ is

(A) $3\pi + 9$
(B) $3\pi + 18$
(C) $6\pi + 9$
(D) $6\pi + 18$
(E) $6\pi + 24$

63. If each of the following fractions were written as a repeating decimal, which would have the longest sequence of different digits?

(A) $\dfrac{2}{11}$

(B) $\dfrac{1}{3}$

(C) $\dfrac{41}{99}$

(D) $\dfrac{2}{3}$

(E) $\dfrac{23}{37}$

64. Today Rose is twice as old as Sam and Sam is 3 years younger than Tina. If Rose, Sam, and Tina are all alive 4 years from today, which of the following must be true on that day?

   I. Rose is twice as old as Sam.
  II. Sam is 3 years younger than Tina.
 III. Rose is older than Tina.

(A) I only
(B) II only
(C) III only
(D) I and II
(E) II and III

65. The average (arithmetic mean) of 6, 8, and 10 equals the average of 7, 9, and

(A) 5
(B) 7
(C) 8
(D) 9
(E) 11

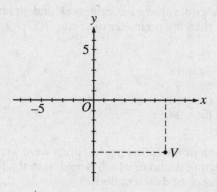

66. In the figure above, the coordinates of point V are

(A) $(-7, 5)$
(B) $(-5, 7)$
(C) $(5, 7)$
(D) $(7, 5)$
(E) $(7, -5)$

67. Tickets for all but 100 seats in a 10,000-seat stadium were sold. Of the tickets sold, 20 percent were sold at half price and the remaining tickets were sold at the full price of $2. What was the total revenue from ticket sales?

(A) $15,840
(B) $17,820
(C) $18,000
(D) $19,800
(E) $21,780

68. In a mayoral election, Candidate X received $\frac{1}{3}$ more votes than Candidate Y, and Candidate Y received $\frac{1}{4}$ fewer votes than Candidate Z. If Candidate Z received 24,000 votes, how many votes did Candidate X receive?

(A) 18,000
(B) 22,000
(C) 24,000
(D) 26,000
(E) 32,000

69. René earns $8.50 per hour on days other than Sundays and twice that rate on Sundays. Last week she worked a total of 40 hours, including 8 hours on Sunday. What were her earnings for the week?

(A) $272
(B) $340
(C) $398
(D) $408
(E) $476

70. In a shipment of 120 machine parts, 5 percent were defective. In a shipment of 80 machine parts, 10 percent were defective. For the two shipments combined, what percent of the machine parts were defective?

(A) 6.5%
(B) 7.0%
(C) 7.5%
(D) 8.0%
(E) 8.5%

71. $\dfrac{2\frac{3}{5} - 1\frac{2}{3}}{\frac{2}{3} - \frac{3}{5}} =$

(A) 16
(B) 14
(C) 3
(D) 1
(E) −1

72. If $x = -1$, then $\dfrac{x^4 - x^3 + x^2}{x - 1} =$

    (A) $-\dfrac{3}{2}$

    (B) $-\dfrac{1}{2}$

    (C) 0

    (D) $\dfrac{1}{2}$

    (E) $\dfrac{3}{2}$

73. Which of the following equations is NOT equivalent to $25x^2 = y^2 - 4$?

    (A) $25x^2 + 4 = y^2$

    (B) $75x^2 = 3y^2 - 12$

    (C) $25x^2 = (y + 2)(y - 2)$

    (D) $5x = y - 2$

    (E) $x^2 = \dfrac{y^2 - 4}{25}$

74. A toy store regularly sells all stock at a discount of 20 percent to 40 percent. If an additional 25 percent were deducted from the discount price during a special sale, what would be the lowest possible price of a toy costing $16 before any discount?

    (A) $5.60
    (B) $7.20
    (C) $8.80
    (D) $9.60
    (E) $15.20

75. If there are 664,579 prime numbers among the first 10 million positive integers, approximately what percent of the first 10 million positive integers are prime numbers?

    (A) 0.0066%
    (B) 0.066%
    (C) 0.66%
    (D) 6.6%
    (E) 66%

76. A bank customer borrowed $10,000, but received y dollars less than this due to discounting. If there was a separate $25 service charge, then, in terms of y, the service charge was what fraction of the amount that the customer received?

    (A) $\dfrac{25}{10,000 - y}$

    (B) $\dfrac{25}{10,000 - 25y}$

    (C) $\dfrac{25y}{10,000 - y}$

    (D) $\dfrac{y - 25}{10,000 - y}$

    (E) $\dfrac{25}{10,000 - (y - 25)}$

77. An airline passenger is planning a trip that involves three connecting flights that leave from Airports A, B, and C, respectively. The first flight leaves Airport A every hour, beginning at 8:00 a.m., and arrives at Airport B $2\dfrac{1}{2}$ hours later. The second flight leaves Airport B every 20 minutes, beginning at 8:00 a.m., and arrives at Airport C $1\dfrac{1}{6}$ hours later. The third flight leaves Airport C every hour, beginning at 8:45 a.m. What is the least total amount of time the passenger must spend between flights if all flights keep to their schedules?

    (A) 25 min
    (B) 1 hr 5 min
    (C) 1 hr 15 min
    (D) 2 hr 20 min
    (E) 3 hr 40 min

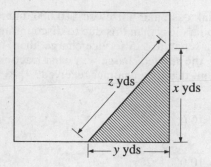

78. The shaded portion of the rectangular lot shown above represents a flower bed. If the area of the bed is 24 square yards and $x = y + 2$, then z equals

   (A) $\sqrt{13}$
   (B) $2\sqrt{13}$
   (C) 6
   (D) 8
   (E) 10

79. How many multiples of 4 are there between 12 and 96, inclusive?

   (A) 21
   (B) 22
   (C) 23
   (D) 24
   (E) 25

80. Jack is now 14 years older than Bill. If in 10 years Jack will be twice as old as Bill, how old will Jack be in 5 years?

   (A) 9
   (B) 19
   (C) 21
   (D) 23
   (E) 33

81. In Country X a returning tourist may import goods with a total value of $500 or less tax free, but must pay an 8 percent tax on the portion of the total value in excess of $500. What tax must be paid by a returning tourist who imports goods with a total value of $730 ?

   (A) $58.40
   (B) $40.00
   (C) $24.60
   (D) $18.40
   (E) $16.00

82. Which of the following is greater than $\frac{2}{3}$?

   (A) $\frac{33}{50}$

   (B) $\frac{8}{11}$

   (C) $\frac{3}{5}$

   (D) $\frac{13}{27}$

   (E) $\frac{5}{8}$

83. A rope 40 feet long is cut into two pieces. If one piece is 18 feet longer than the other, what is the length, in feet, of the shorter piece?

   (A) 9
   (B) 11
   (C) 18
   (D) 22
   (E) 29

84. If 60 percent of a rectangular floor is covered by a rectangular rug that is 9 feet by 12 feet, what is the area, in square feet, of the floor?

   (A) 65
   (B) 108
   (C) 180
   (D) 270
   (E) 300

85. The Earth travels around the Sun at a speed of approximately 18.5 miles per second. This approximate speed is how many miles per hour?

   (A)   1,080
   (B)   1,160
   (C)   64,800
   (D)   66,600
   (E) 3,996,000

86. A collection of books went on sale, and $\frac{2}{3}$ of them were sold for $2.50 each. If none of the 36 remaining books were sold, what was the total amount received for the books that were sold?

(A) $180
(B) $135
(C) $90
(D) $60
(E) $54

87. If "basis points" are defined so that 1 percent is equal to 100 basis points, then 82.5 percent is how many basis points greater than 62.5 percent?

(A)   0.02
(B)   0.2
(C)   20
(D)   200
(E) 2,000

88. The amounts of time that three secretaries worked on a special project are in the ratio of 1 to 2 to 5. If they worked a combined total of 112 hours, how many hours did the secretary who worked the longest spend on the project?

(A) 80
(B) 70
(C) 56
(D) 16
(E) 14

89. If the quotient $\frac{a}{b}$ is positive, which of the following must be true?

(A) $a > 0$
(B) $b > 0$
(C) $ab > 0$
(D) $a - b > 0$
(E) $a + b > 0$

90. If $8^{2x+3} = 2^{3x+6}$, then $x =$

(A) -3
(B) -1
(C) 0
(D) 1
(E) 3

91. Of the following, the closest approximation to

$$\sqrt{\frac{5.98(601.5)}{15.79}} \text{ is}$$

(A)   5
(B)   15
(C)   20
(D)   25
(E)   225

92. Which of the following CANNOT be the greatest common divisor of two positive integers x and y ?

(A) 1
(B) x
(C) y
(D) $x - y$
(E) $x + y$

93. An empty pool being filled with water at a constant rate takes 8 hours to fill to $\frac{3}{5}$ of its capacity. How much more time will it take to finish filling the pool?

(A) 5 hr 30 min
(B) 5 hr 20 min
(C) 4 hr 48 min
(D) 3 hr 12 min
(E) 2 hr 40 min

94. A positive number x is multiplied by 2, and this product is then divided by 3. If the positive square root of the result of these two operations equals x, what is the value of x ?

(A) $\frac{9}{4}$

(B) $\frac{3}{2}$

(C) $\frac{4}{3}$

(D) $\frac{2}{3}$

(E) $\frac{1}{2}$

95. A tank contains 10,000 gallons of a solution that is 5 percent sodium chloride by volume. If 2,500 gallons of water evaporate from the tank, the remaining solution will be approximately what percent sodium chloride?

(A) 1.25%
(B) 3.75%
(C) 6.25%
(D) 6.67%
(E) 11.7%

96. A certain grocery purchased x pounds of produce for p dollars per pound. If y pounds of the produce had to be discarded due to spoilage and the grocery sold the rest for s dollars per pound, which of the following represents the gross profit on the sale of the produce?

(A) $(x - y)s - xp$
(B) $(x - y)p - ys$
(C) $(s - p)y - xp$
(D) $xp - ys$
(E) $(x - y)(s - p)$

97. If $x + 5y = 16$ and $x = -3y$, then $y =$

(A) −24
(B) −8
(C) −2
(D) 2
(E) 8

98. An empty swimming pool with a capacity of 5,760 gallons is filled at the rate of 12 gallons per minute. How many hours does it take to fill the pool to capacity?

(A) 8
(B) 20
(C) 96
(D) 480
(E) 720

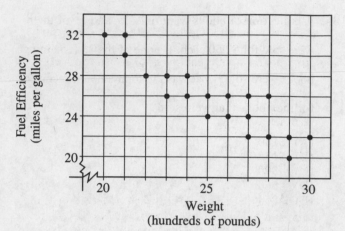

Weight
(hundreds of pounds)

99. The dots on the graph above indicate the weights and fuel efficiency ratings for 20 cars. How many of the cars weigh more than 2,500 pounds and also get more than 22 miles per gallon?

(A) Three
(B) Five
(C) Eight
(D) Ten
(E) Eleven

100. $\dfrac{90 - 8(20 \div 4)}{\frac{1}{2}} =$

(A) 25
(B) 50
(C) 100
(D) 116
(E) 170

101. If a, b, and c are nonzero numbers and $a + b = c$, which of the following is equal to 1 ?

(A) $\dfrac{a - b}{c}$

(B) $\dfrac{a - c}{b}$

(C) $\dfrac{b - c}{a}$

(D) $\dfrac{b - a}{c}$

(E) $\dfrac{c - b}{a}$

102. Bill's school is 10 miles from his home. He travels 4 miles from school to football practice, and then 2 miles to a friend's house. If he is then x miles from home, what is the range of possible values for x?

(A) $2 \leq x \leq 10$
(B) $4 \leq x \leq 10$
(C) $4 \leq x \leq 12$
(D) $4 \leq x \leq 16$
(E) $6 \leq x \leq 16$

103. Three machines, individually, can do a certain job in 4, 5, and 6 hours, respectively. What is the greatest part of the job that can be done in one hour by two of the machines working together at their respective rates?

(A) $\dfrac{11}{30}$

(B) $\dfrac{9}{20}$

(C) $\dfrac{3}{5}$

(D) $\dfrac{11}{15}$

(E) $\dfrac{5}{6}$

104. In 1985, 45 percent of a document storage facility's 60 customers were banks, and in 1987, 25 percent of its 144 customers were banks. What was the percent increase from 1985 to 1987 in the number of bank customers the facility had?

(A) 10.7%

(B) 20%

(C) 25%

(D) $33\dfrac{1}{3}\%$

(E) $58\dfrac{1}{3}\%$

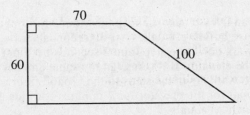

105. What is the perimeter of the figure above?

(A) 380
(B) 360
(C) 330
(D) 300
(E) 230

106. A committee is composed of w women and m men. If 3 women and 2 men are added to the committee, and if one person is selected at random from the enlarged committee, then the probability that a woman is selected can be represented by

(A) $\dfrac{w}{m}$

(B) $\dfrac{w}{w+m}$

(C) $\dfrac{w+3}{m+2}$

(D) $\dfrac{w+3}{w+m+3}$

(E) $\dfrac{w+3}{w+m+5}$

107. Last year Carlos saved 10 percent of his annual earnings. This year he earned 5 percent more than last year and he saved 12 percent of his annual earnings. The amount saved this year was what percent of the amount saved last year?

(A) 122%
(B) 124%
(C) 126%
(D) 128%
(E) 130%

108. Jan lives x floors above the ground floor of a high-rise building. It takes her 30 seconds per floor to walk down the steps and 2 seconds per floor to ride the elevator. If it takes Jan the same amount of time to walk down the steps to the ground floor as to wait for the elevator for 7 minutes and ride down, then x equals

(A) 4
(B) 7
(C) 14
(D) 15
(E) 16

109. A corporation that had $115.19 billion in profits for the year paid out $230.10 million in employee benefits. Approximately what percent of the profits were the employee benefits? (1 billion = 10^9)

(A) 50%
(B) 20%
(C) 5%
(D) 2%
(E) 0.2%

Questions 110-111 refer to the following definition.

For any positive integer n, $n > 1$, the "length" of n is the number of positive primes (not necessarily distinct) whose product is n. For example, the length of 50 is 3 since 50 = (2)(5)(5).

110. Which of the following integers has length 3 ?

(A)   3
(B)   15
(C)   60
(D)   64
(E) 105

111. What is the greatest possible length of a positive integer less than 1,000 ?

(A) 10
(B)   9
(C)   8
(D)   7
(E)   6

112. A dealer originally bought 100 identical batteries at a total cost of q dollars. If each battery was sold at 50 percent above the original cost per battery, then, in terms of q, for how many dollars was each battery sold?

(A) $\dfrac{3q}{200}$

(B) $\dfrac{3q}{2}$

(C) $150q$

(D) $\dfrac{q}{100} + 50$

(E) $\dfrac{150}{q}$

113. Two oil cans, X and Y, are right circular cylinders, and the height and the radius of Y are each twice those of X. If the oil in can X, which is filled to capacity, sells for $2, then at the same rate, how much does the oil in can Y sell for if Y is filled to only half its capacity?

(A) $1
(B) $2
(C) $3
(D) $4
(E) $8

114. If x, y, and z are positive integers such that x is a factor of y, and x is a multiple of z, which of the following is NOT necessarily an integer?

(A) $\dfrac{x+z}{z}$

(B) $\dfrac{y+z}{x}$

(C) $\dfrac{x+y}{z}$

(D) $\dfrac{xy}{z}$

(E) $\dfrac{yz}{x}$

115. If $x + y = 8z$, then which of the following represents the average (arithmetic mean) of x, y, and z, in terms of z ?

(A) $2z + 1$

(B) $3z$

(C) $5z$

(D) $\dfrac{z}{3}$

(E) $\dfrac{3z}{2}$

116. If the product of the integers $w, x, y,$ and z is 770, and if $1 < w < x < y < z$, what is the value of $w + z$?

(A) 10
(B) 13
(C) 16
(D) 18
(E) 21

117. If the population of a certain country increases at the rate of one person every 15 seconds, by how many persons does the population increase in 20 minutes?

(A) 80
(B) 100
(C) 150
(D) 240
(E) 300

118. The value of $-3 - (-10)$ is how much greater than the value of $-10 - (-3)$?

(A) 0
(B) 6
(C) 7
(D) 14
(E) 26

119. For an agricultural experiment, 300 seeds were planted in one plot and 200 were planted in a second plot. If exactly 25 percent of the seeds in the first plot germinated and exactly 35 percent of the seeds in the second plot germinated, what percent of the total number of seeds germinated?

(A) 12%
(B) 26%
(C) 29%
(D) 30%
(E) 60%

120. If $\dfrac{a}{b} = \dfrac{2}{3}$, which of the following is NOT true?

(A) $\dfrac{a+b}{b} = \dfrac{5}{3}$

(B) $\dfrac{b}{b-a} = 3$

(C) $\dfrac{a-b}{b} = \dfrac{1}{3}$

(D) $\dfrac{2a}{3b} = \dfrac{4}{9}$

(E) $\dfrac{a+3b}{a} = \dfrac{11}{2}$

121. On the number line, if $r < s$, if p is halfway between r and s, and if t is halfway between p and r, then $\dfrac{s-t}{t-r} =$

(A) $\dfrac{1}{4}$　(B) $\dfrac{1}{3}$　(C) $\dfrac{4}{3}$　(D) 3　(E) 4

122. Coins are to be put into 7 pockets so that each pocket contains at least one coin. At most 3 of the pockets are to contain the same number of coins, and no two of the remaining pockets are to contain an equal number of coins. What is the least possible number of coins needed for the pockets?

(A) 　7
(B) 　13
(C) 　17
(D) 　22
(E) 　28

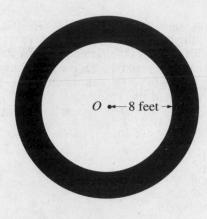

123. The figure above shows a circular flower bed, with its center at O, surrounded by a circular path that is 3 feet wide. What is the area of the path, in square feet?

(A) 25π　(B) 38π　(C) 55π　(D) 57π　(E) 64π

	Brand X	Brand Y
Miles per Gallon	40	36
Cost per Gallon	$0.80	$0.75

124. The table above gives the gasoline costs and consumption rates for a certain car driven at 50 miles per hour, using each of two brands of gasoline. How many miles farther can the car be driven at this speed on $12 worth of brand X gasoline than on $12 worth of brand Y gasoline?

(A) 20　(B) 24　(C) 84　(D) 100　(E) 104

125. If $1 were invested at 8 percent interest compounded annually, the total value of the investment, in dollars, at the end of 6 years would be

(A) $(1.8)^6$
(B) $(1.08)^6$
(C) $6(1.08)$
(D) $1 + (0.08)^6$
(E) $1 + 6(0.08)$

126. A furniture store sells only two models of desks, model A and model B. The selling price of model A is \$120, which is 30 percent of the selling price of model B. If the furniture store sells 2,000 desks, $\frac{3}{4}$ of which are model B, what is the furniture store's total revenue from the sale of desks?

(A) \$114,000
(B) \$186,000
(C) \$294,000
(D) \$380,000
(E) \$660,000

127. How many minutes does it take John to type y words if he types at the rate of x words per minute?

(A) $\frac{x}{y}$ (B) $\frac{y}{x}$ (C) xy (D) $\frac{60x}{y}$ (E) $\frac{y}{60x}$

128. The weights of four packages are 1, 3, 5, and 7 pounds, respectively. Which of the following CANNOT be the total weight, in pounds, of any combination of the packages?

(A) 9
(B) 10
(C) 12
(D) 13
(E) 14

129. $\sqrt{(16)(20)+(8)(32)} =$

(A) $4\sqrt{20}$
(B) 24
(C) 25
(D) $4\sqrt{20}+8\sqrt{2}$
(E) 32

130. The positive integer n is divisible by 25. If $\sqrt{n}$ is greater than 25, which of the following could be the value of $\frac{n}{25}$?

(A) 22
(B) 23
(C) 24
(D) 25
(E) 26

131. If x and y are different integers and $x^2 = xy$, which of the following must be true?

 I. $x = 0$
 II. $y = 0$
 III. $x = -y$

(A) I only
(B) II only
(C) III only
(D) I and III only
(E) I, II, and III

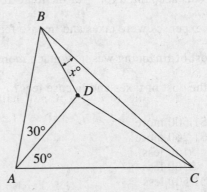

Note: Figure not drawn to scale.

132. In the figure above, $DA = DB = DC$. What is the value of x ?

(A) 10
(B) 20
(C) 30
(D) 40
(E) 50

133. If X and Y are sets of integers, $X \triangle Y$ denotes the set of integers that belong to set X or set Y, but not both. If X consists of 10 integers, Y consists of 18 integers, and 6 of the integers are in both X and Y, then $X \triangle Y$ consists of how many integers?

(A) 6
(B) 16
(C) 22
(D) 30
(E) 174

-93-

134. During the four years that Mrs. Lopez owned her car, she found that her total car expenses were $18,000. Fuel and maintenance costs accounted for $\frac{1}{3}$ of the total and depreciation accounted for $\frac{3}{5}$ of the remainder. The cost of insurance was 3 times the cost of financing, and together these two costs accounted for $\frac{1}{5}$ of the total. If the only other expenses were taxes and license fees, then the cost of financing was how much more or less than the cost of taxes and license fees?

(A) $1,500 more
(B) $1,200 more
(C) $100 less
(D) $300 less
(E) $1,500 less

135. A car travels from Mayville to Rome at an average speed of 30 miles per hour and returns immediately along the same route at an average speed of 40 miles per hour. Of the following, which is closest to the average speed, in miles per hour, for the round-trip?

(A) 32.0
(B) 33.0
(C) 34.3
(D) 35.5
(E) 36.5

136. If $\dfrac{0.0015 \times 10^{m}}{0.03 \times 10^{k}} = 5 \times 10^{7}$, then $m - k =$

(A) 9
(B) 8
(C) 7
(D) 6
(E) 5

		x
37	38	15
		y

137. In the figure above, the sum of the three numbers in the horizontal row equals the product of the three numbers in the vertical column. What is the value of xy ?

(A) 6
(B) 15
(C) 35
(D) 75
(E) 90

138. For telephone calls between two particular cities, a telephone company charges $0.40 per minute if the calls are placed between 5:00 a.m. and 9:00 p.m. and $0.25 per minute if the calls are placed between 9:00 p.m. and 5:00 a.m. If the charge for a call between the two cities placed at 1:00 p.m. was $10.00, how much would a call of the same duration have cost if it had been placed at 11:00 p.m. ?

(A) $3.75
(B) $6.25
(C) $9.85
(D) $10.00
(E) $16.00

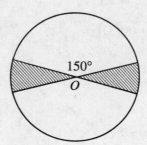

139. If O is the center of the circle above, what fraction of the circular region is shaded?

(A) $\dfrac{1}{12}$

(B) $\dfrac{1}{9}$

(C) $\dfrac{1}{6}$

(D) $\dfrac{1}{4}$

(E) $\dfrac{1}{3}$

140. If a compact disc that usually sells for $12.95 is on sale for $9.95, then the percent decrease in price is closest to

(A) 38%
(B) 31%
(C) 30%
(D) 29%
(E) 23%

141. $\dfrac{1}{1 + \dfrac{1}{2 + \dfrac{1}{3}}} =$

(A) $\dfrac{3}{10}$

(B) $\dfrac{7}{10}$

(C) $\dfrac{6}{7}$

(D) $\dfrac{10}{7}$

(E) $\dfrac{10}{3}$

142. A fruit-salad mixture consists of apples, peaches, and grapes in the ratio 6 : 5 : 2, respectively, by weight. If 39 pounds of the mixture is prepared, the mixture includes how many more pounds of apples than grapes?

(A) 15
(B) 12
(C) 9
(D) 6
(E) 4

143. If $\dfrac{3}{x} = 2$ and $\dfrac{y}{4} = 3$, then $\dfrac{3 + y}{x + 4} =$

(A) $\dfrac{10}{9}$

(B) $\dfrac{3}{2}$

(C) $\dfrac{20}{11}$

(D) $\dfrac{30}{11}$

(E) 5

144. $\left(1 + \sqrt{5}\right)\left(1 - \sqrt{5}\right) =$

(A) -4
(B) 2
(C) 6
(D) $-4 - 2\sqrt{5}$
(E) $6 - 2\sqrt{5}$

145. Starting from point O on a flat school playground, a child walks 10 yards due north, then 6 yards due east, and then 2 yards due south, arriving at point P. How far apart, in yards, are points O and P ?

(A) 18
(B) 16
(C) 14
(D) 12
(E) 10

146. A certain car increased its average speed by 5 miles per hour in each successive 5-minute interval after the first interval. If in the first 5-minute interval its average speed was 20 miles per hour, how many miles did the car travel in the third 5-minute interval?

(A) 1.0
(B) 1.5
(C) 2.0
(D) 2.5
(E) 3.0

147. Lois has x dollars more than Jim has, and together they have a total of y dollars. Which of the following represents the number of dollars that Jim has?

(A) $\dfrac{y - x}{2}$

(B) $y - \dfrac{x}{2}$

(C) $\dfrac{y}{2} - x$

(D) $2y - x$

(E) $y - 2x$

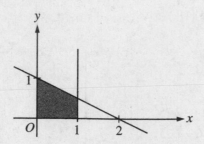

148. In the rectangular coordinate system above, the shaded region is bounded by straight lines. Which of the following is NOT an equation of one of the boundary lines?

(A) $x = 0$
(B) $y = 0$
(C) $x = 1$
(D) $x - y = 0$
(E) $x + 2y = 2$

149. A certain population of bacteria doubles every 10 minutes. If the number of bacteria in the population initially was 10^4, what was the number in the population 1 hour later?

(A) $2(10^4)$
(B) $6(10^4)$
(C) $(2^6)(10^4)$
(D) $(10^6)(10^4)$
(E) $(10^4)^6$

150. During a certain season, a team won 80 percent of its first 100 games and 50 percent of its remaining games. If the team won 70 percent of its games for the entire season, what was the total number of games that the team played?

(A) 180
(B) 170
(C) 156
(D) 150
(E) 105

151. If Juan takes 11 seconds to run y yards, how many seconds will it take him to run x yards at the same rate?

(A) $\dfrac{11x}{y}$

(B) $\dfrac{11y}{x}$

(C) $\dfrac{x}{11y}$

(D) $\dfrac{11}{xy}$

(E) $\dfrac{xy}{11}$

152. Which of the following fractions has the greatest value?

(A) $\dfrac{6}{(2^2)(5^2)}$

(B) $\dfrac{1}{(2^3)(5^2)}$

(C) $\dfrac{28}{(2^2)(5^3)}$

(D) $\dfrac{62}{(2^3)(5^3)}$

(E) $\dfrac{122}{(2^4)(5^3)}$

153. Of 30 applicants for a job, 14 had at least 4 years experience, 18 had degrees, and 3 had less than 4 years experience and did not have a degree. How many of the applicants had at least 4 years experience and a degree?

(A) 14
(B) 13
(C) 9
(D) 7
(E) 5

154. Which of the following CANNOT yield an integer when divided by 10?

(A) The sum of two odd integers
(B) An integer less than 10
(C) The product of two primes
(D) The sum of three consecutive integers
(E) An odd integer

155. A certain clock marks every hour by striking a number of times equal to the hour, and the time required for a stroke is exactly equal to the time interval between strokes. At 6:00 the time lapse between the beginning of the first stroke and the end of the last stroke is 22 seconds. At 12:00, how many seconds elapse between the beginning of the first stroke and the end of the last stroke?

(A) 72
(B) 50
(C) 48
(D) 46
(E) 44

156. If $k \neq 0$ and $k - \dfrac{3 - 2k^2}{k} = \dfrac{x}{k}$, then $x =$

(A) $-3 - k^2$
(B) $k^2 - 3$
(C) $3k^2 - 3$
(D) $k - 3 - 2k^2$
(E) $k - 3 + 2k^2$

157. $\dfrac{\dfrac{1}{2} + \dfrac{1}{3}}{\dfrac{1}{4}} =$

(A) $\dfrac{1}{12}$
(B) $\dfrac{5}{24}$
(C) $\dfrac{2}{3}$
(D) $\dfrac{9}{4}$
(E) $\dfrac{10}{3}$

158. John has 10 pairs of matched socks. If he loses 7 individual socks, what is the greatest number of pairs of matched socks he can have left?

(A) 7
(B) 6
(C) 5
(D) 4
(E) 3

159. Last year's receipts from the sale of candy on Valentine's Day totaled 385 million dollars, which represented 7 percent of total candy sales for the year. Candy sales for the year totaled how many million dollars?

(A) 55
(B) 550
(C) 2,695
(D) 5,500
(E) 26,950

160. How many minutes does it take to travel 120 miles at 400 miles per hour?

(A) 3
(B) $3\dfrac{1}{3}$
(C) $8\dfrac{2}{3}$
(D) 12
(E) 18

161. If $1 + \dfrac{1}{x} = 2 - \dfrac{2}{x}$, then $x =$

(A) -1
(B) $\dfrac{1}{3}$
(C) $\dfrac{2}{3}$
(D) 2
(E) 3

162. Last year, for every 100 million vehicles that traveled on a certain highway, 96 vehicles were involved in accidents. If 3 billion vehicles traveled on the highway last year, how many of those vehicles were involved in accidents? (1 billion = 1,000,000,000)

(A) 288
(B) 320
(C) 2,880
(D) 3,200
(E) 28,800

163. If the perimeter of a rectangular garden plot is 34 feet and its area is 60 square feet, what is the length of each of the longer sides?

(A) 5 ft
(B) 6 ft
(C) 10 ft
(D) 12 ft
(E) 15 ft

164. What is the least positive integer that is divisible by each of the integers 1 through 7, inclusive?

(A)   420
(B)   840
(C) 1,260
(D) 2,520
(E) 5,040

165. Thirty percent of the members of a swim club have passed the lifesaving test. Among the members who have not passed the test, 12 have taken the preparatory course and 30 have not taken the course. How many members are there in the swim club?

(A) 60
(B) 80
(C) 100
(D) 120
(E) 140

166. For all numbers s and t, the operation $*$ is defined by $s * t = (s - 1)(t + 1)$. If $(-2) * x = -12$, then $x =$

(A) 2
(B) 3
(C) 5
(D) 6
(E) 11

167. In an increasing sequence of 10 consecutive integers, the sum of the first 5 integers is 560. What is the sum of the last 5 integers in the sequence?

(A) 585
(B) 580
(C) 575
(D) 570
(E) 565

168. A certain manufacturer produces items for which the production costs consist of annual fixed costs totaling $130,000 and variable costs averaging $8 per item. If the manufacturer's selling price per item is $15, how many items must the manufacturer produce and sell to earn an annual profit of $150,000 ?

(A) 2,858
(B) 18,667
(C) 21,429
(D) 35,000
(E) 40,000

169. How many two-element subsets of $\{1, 2, 3, 4\}$ are there that do not contain the pair of elements 2 and 4 ?

(A) One
(B) Two
(C) Four
(D) Five
(E) Six

170. In a certain company, the ratio of the number of managers to the number of production-line workers is 5 to 72. If 8 additional production-line workers were to be hired, the ratio of the number of managers to the number of production-line workers would be 5 to 74. How many managers does the company have?

(A) 5
(B) 10
(C) 15
(D) 20
(E) 25

171. If $(x - 1)^2 = 400$, which of the following could be the value of $x - 5$?

(A) 15
(B) 14
(C) -24
(D) -25
(E) -26

172. Salesperson A's compensation for any week is $360 plus 6 percent of the portion of A's total sales above $1,000 for that week. Salesperson B's compensation for any week is 8 percent of B's total sales for that week. For what amount of total weekly sales would both salespeople earn the same compensation?

(A) $21,000
(B) $18,000
(C) $15,000
(D) $4,500
(E) $4,000

-98-

173. If a square region has area x, what is the length of its diagonal in terms of x ?

(A) $\sqrt{x}$

(B) $\sqrt{2x}$

(C) $2\sqrt{x}$

(D) $x\sqrt{2}$

(E) $2x$

174. In a certain class consisting of 36 students, some boys and some girls, exactly $\frac{1}{3}$ of the boys and exactly $\frac{1}{4}$ of the girls walk to school. What is the greatest possible number of students in this class who walk to school?

(A) 9
(B) 10
(C) 11
(D) 12
(E) 13

175. The sum of the ages of Doris and Fred is y years. If Doris is 12 years older than Fred, how many years old will Fred be y years from now, in terms of y ?

(A) $y - 6$

(B) $2y - 6$

(C) $\frac{y}{2} - 6$

(D) $\frac{3y}{2} - 6$

(E) $\frac{5y}{2} - 6$

1,234
1,243
1,324
. . . .
. . . .
+ 4,321

176. The addition problem above shows four of the 24 different integers that can be formed by using each of the digits 1, 2, 3, and 4 exactly once in each integer. What is the sum of these 24 integers?

(A) 24,000
(B) 26,664
(C) 40,440
(D) 60,000
(E) 66,660

177. If $x = -(2 - 5)$, then $x =$

(A) -7 (B) -3 (C) 3 (D) 7 (E) 10

178. What percent of 30 is 12 ?

(A) 2.5% (B) 3.6% (C) 25%

(D) 40% (E) 250%

179. On a 3-day fishing trip, 4 adults consumed food costing $60. For the same food costs per person per day, what would be the cost of food consumed by 7 adults during a 5-day fishing trip?

(A) $300
(B) $175
(C) $105
(D) $100
(E) $84

180. In a poll of 66,000 physicians, only 20 percent responded; of these, 10 percent disclosed their preference for pain reliever X. How many of the physicians who responded did not disclose a preference for pain reliever X ?

(A) 1,320
(B) 5,280
(C) 6,600
(D) 10,560
(E) 11,880

181. If $\dfrac{1.5}{0.2 + x} = 5$, then $x =$

    (A) – 3.7
    (B)   0.1
    (C)   0.3
    (D)   0.5
    (E)   2.8

182. If a basketball team scores an average (arithmetic mean) of x points per game for n games and then scores y points in its next game, what is the team's average score for the $n + 1$ games?

    (A) $\dfrac{nx + y}{n+1}$

    (B) $x + \dfrac{y}{n+1}$

    (C) $x + \dfrac{y}{n}$

    (D) $\dfrac{n(x + y)}{n+1}$

    (E) $\dfrac{x + ny}{n+1}$

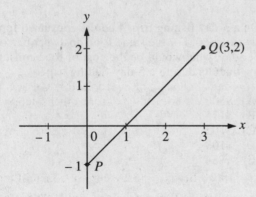

183. In the figure above, the point on segment PQ that is twice as far from P as from Q is

    (A) (3, 1)
    (B) (2, 1)
    (C) (2, – 1)
    (D) (1.5, 0.5)
    (E) (1, 0)

184. $\dfrac{3}{100} + \dfrac{5}{1,000} + \dfrac{7}{100,000} =$

    (A) 0.357
    (B) 0.3507
    (C) 0.35007
    (D) 0.0357
    (E) 0.03507

185. If the number n of calculators sold per week varies with the price p in dollars according to the equation $n = 300 - 20p$, what would be the total weekly revenue from the sale of \$10 calculators?

    (A) \$100 (B) \$300 (C) \$1,000

    (D) \$2,800 (E) \$3,000

186. Of the 65 cars on a car lot, 45 have air-conditioning, 30 have power windows, and 12 have both air-conditioning and power windows. How many of the cars on the lot have neither air-conditioning nor power windows?

    (A)   2
    (B)   8
    (C) 10
    (D) 15
    (E) 18

187. Of the following numbers, which one is third greatest?

    (A) $2\sqrt{2} - 1$ (B) $\sqrt{2} + 1$ (C) $1 - \sqrt{2}$

    (D) $\sqrt{2} - 1$ (E) $\sqrt{2}$

188. During the second quarter of 1984, a total of 2,976,000 domestic cars were sold. If this was 24 percent greater than the number sold during the first quarter of 1984, how many were sold during the first quarter?

    (A)   714,240
    (B) 2,261,760
    (C) 2,400,000
    (D) 3,690,240
    (E) 3,915,790

189. If a positive integer n is divisible by both 5 and 7, the n must also be divisible by which of the following?

   I. 12
   II. 35
   III. 70

   (A) None   (B) I only   (C) II only
   (D) I and II   (E) II and III

190. An author received $0.80 in royalties for each of the first 100,000 copies of her book sold, and $0.60 in royalties for each additional copy sold. If she received a total of $260,000 in royalties, how many copies of her book were sold?

   (A) 130,000
   (B) 300,000
   (C) 380,000
   (D) 400,000
   (E) 420,000

191. Starting from Town S, Fred rode his bicycle 8 miles due east, 3 miles due south, 2 miles due west, and 11 miles due north, finally stopping at Town T. If the entire region is flat, what is the straight-line distance, in miles, between Towns S and T?

   (A) 10

   (B) $8\sqrt{2}$

   (C) $\sqrt{157}$

   (D) 14

   (E) 24

192. Which of the following describes all values of x for which $1 - x^2 \geq 0$?

   (A) $x \geq 1$
   (B) $x \leq -1$
   (C) $0 \leq x \leq 1$
   (D) $x \leq -1$ or $x \geq 1$
   (E) $-1 \leq x \leq 1$

193. Four hours from now, the population of a colony of bacteria will reach 1.28×10^6. If the population of the colony doubles every 4 hours, what was the population 12 hours ago?

   (A) 6.4×10^2
   (B) 8.0×10^4
   (C) 1.6×10^5
   (D) 3.2×10^5
   (E) 8.0×10^6

194. At a certain pizzeria, $\dfrac{1}{8}$ of the pizzas sold in one week were mushroom and $\dfrac{1}{3}$ of the <u>remaining</u> pizzas sold were pepperoni. If n of the pizzas sold were pepperoni, how many were mushroom?

   (A) $\dfrac{3}{8}n$

   (B) $\dfrac{3}{7}n$

   (C) $\dfrac{7}{16}n$

   (D) $\dfrac{7}{8}n$

   (E) $3n$

195. If 4 is one solution of the equation $x^2 + 3x + k = 10$, where k is a constant, what is the other solution?

   (A) -7 (B) -4 (C) -3 (D) 1 (E) 6

196. The probability is $\dfrac{1}{2}$ that a certain coin will turn up heads on any given toss. If the coin is to be tossed three times, what is the probability that on at least one of the tosses the coin will turn up tails?

   (A) $\dfrac{1}{8}$ (B) $\dfrac{1}{2}$ (C) $\dfrac{3}{4}$ (D) $\dfrac{7}{8}$ (E) $\dfrac{15}{16}$

197. A caterer ordered 125 ice-cream bars and 125 sundaes. If the total price was $200.00 and the price of each ice-cream bar was $0.60, what was the price of each sundae?

(A) $0.60
(B) $0.80
(C) $1.00
(D) $1.20
(E) $1.60

198. Lloyd normally works 7.5 hours per day and earns $4.50 per hour. For each hour he works in excess of 7.5 hours on a given day, he is paid 1.5 times his regular rate. If Lloyd works 10.5 hours on a given day, how much does he earn for that day?

(A) $33.75
(B) $47.25
(C) $51.75
(D) $54.00
(E) $70.00

199. If $x = -3$, what is the value of $-3x^2$?

(A) –27   (B) –18   (C) 18   (D) 27   (E) 81

200. Of the final grades received by the students in a certain math course, $\frac{1}{5}$ are A's, $\frac{1}{4}$ are B's, $\frac{1}{2}$ are C's, and the remaining 10 grades are D's. What is the number of students in the course?

(A)   80
(B) 110
(C) 160
(D) 200
(E) 400

201. $\dfrac{29^2 + 29}{29} =$

(A) 870   (B) 841   (C) 58   (D) 31   (E) 30

202. Mr. Hernandez, who was a resident of State X for only 8 months last year, had a taxable income of $22,500 for the year. If the state tax rate were 4 percent of the year's taxable income prorated for the proportion of the year during which the taxpayer was a resident, what would be the amount of Mr. Hernandez's State X tax for last year?

(A) $900   (B) $720   (C) $600
(D) $300   (E) $60

203. If $x = 1 - 3t$ and $y = 2t - 1$, then for what value of t does $x = y$?

(A) $\dfrac{5}{2}$ (B) $\dfrac{3}{2}$ (C) $\dfrac{2}{3}$ (D) $\dfrac{2}{5}$ (E) 0

204. Which of the following fractions is equal to the decimal 0.0625 ?

(A) $\dfrac{5}{8}$ (B) $\dfrac{3}{8}$ (C) $\dfrac{1}{16}$ (D) $\dfrac{1}{18}$ (E) $\dfrac{3}{80}$

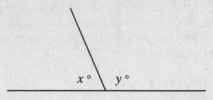

205. In the figure above, if $\dfrac{x}{x + y} = \dfrac{3}{8}$, then $x =$

(A)   60
(B)   67.5
(C)   72
(D)   108
(E)   112.5

206. The number of coronary-bypass operations performed in the United States increased from 13,000 in 1970 to 191,000 in 1983. What was the approximate percent increase in the number of coronary-bypass operations from 1970 to 1983 ?

(A)   90%
(B)   140%
(C)   150%
(D) 1,400%
(E) 1,600%

207. If positive integers x and y are not both odd, which of the following must be even?

(A) xy
(B) $x + y$
(C) $x - y$
(D) $x + y - 1$
(E) $2(x + y) - 1$

208. Two trains, X and Y, started simultaneously from opposite ends of a 100-mile route and traveled toward each other on parallel tracks. Train X, traveling at a constant rate, completed the 100-mile trip in 5 hours; train Y, traveling at a constant rate, completed the 100-mile trip in 3 hours. How many miles had train X traveled when it met train Y?

(A) 37.5   (B) 40.0   (C) 60.0
(D) 62.5   (E) 77.5

209. As x increases from 165 to 166, which of the following must increase?

   I. $2x - 5$

  II. $1 - \dfrac{1}{x}$

 III. $\dfrac{1}{x^2 - x}$

(A) I only
(B) III only
(C) I and II
(D) I and III
(E) II and III

210. If it is true that $x > -2$ and $x < 7$, which of the following must be true?

(A) $x > 2$
(B) $x > -7$
(C) $x < 2$
(D) $-7 < x < 2$
(E) None of the above

211. A club sold an average (arithmetic mean) of 92 raffle tickets per member. Among the female members, the average number sold was 84, and among the male members, the average number sold was 96. What was the ratio of the number of male members to the number of female members in the club?

(A) 1 : 1
(B) 1 : 2
(C) 1 : 3
(D) 2 : 1
(E) 3 : 1

212. How many bits of computer memory will be required to store the integer x, where $x = -\sqrt{810,000}$, if each digit requires 4 bits of memory and the sign of x requires 1 bit?

(A) 25   (B) 24   (C) 17   (D) 13   (E) 12

213. One week a certain truck rental lot had a total of 20 trucks, all of which were on the lot Monday morning. If 50 percent of the trucks that were rented out during the week were returned to the lot on or before Saturday morning of that week, and if there were at least 12 trucks on the lot that Saturday morning, what is the greatest number of different trucks that could have been rented out during the week?

(A) 18
(B) 16
(C) 12
(D) 8
(E) 4

214. Ms. Adams sold two properties, X and Y, for $30,000 each. She sold property X for 20 percent more than she paid for it and sold property Y for 20 percent less than she paid for it. If expenses are disregarded, what was her total net gain or loss, if any, on the two properties?

(A) Loss of $1,250
(B) Loss of $2,500
(C) Gain of $1,250
(D) Gain of $2,500
(E) There was neither a net gain nor a net loss.

215. A rectangular box is 10 inches wide, 10 inches long, and 5 inches high. What is the greatest possible (straight-line) distance, in inches, between any two points on the box?

(A) 15

(B) 20

(C) 25

(D) $10\sqrt{2}$

(E) $10\sqrt{3}$

216. How many positive integers less than 20 are either a multiple of 2, an odd multiple of 9, or the sum of a positive multiple of 2 and a positive multiple of 9?

(A) 19
(B) 18
(C) 17
(D) 16
(E) 15

217. On 3 sales John has received commissions of $240, $80, and $110, and he has 1 additional sale pending. If John is to receive an average (arithmetic mean) commission of exactly $150 on the 4 sales, then the 4th commission must be

(A) $164
(B) $170
(C) $175
(D) $182
(E) $185

218. $\sqrt{463}$ is between

(A) 21 and 22
(B) 22 and 23
(C) 23 and 24
(D) 24 and 25
(E) 25 and 26

219. The annual budget of a certain college is to be shown on a circle graph. If the size of each sector of the graph is to be proportional to the amount of the budget it represents, how many degrees of the circle should be used to represent an item that is 15 percent of the budget?

(A) $15°$
(B) $36°$
(C) $54°$
(D) $90°$
(E) $150°$

220. A company accountant estimates that airfares next year for business trips of a thousand miles or less will increase by 20 percent and airfares for all other business trips will increase by 10 percent. This year total airfares for business trips of a thousand miles or less were $9,900 and airfares for all other business trips were $13,000. According to the accountant's estimate, if the same business trips will be made next year as this year, how much will be spent for airfares next year?

(A) $22,930
(B) $26,180
(C) $26,330
(D) $26,490
(E) $29,770

221. What is the value of $2x^2 - 2.4x - 1.7$ for $x = 0.7$?

(A) -0.72
(B) -1.42
(C) -1.98
(D) -2.40
(E) -2.89

222. If $x * y = xy - 2(x + y)$ for all integers x and y, then $2 * (-3) =$

(A) -16
(B) -11
(C) -4
(D) 4
(E) 16

223. During a two-week period, the price of an ounce of silver increased by 25 percent by the end of the first week and then decreased by 20 percent of this new price by the end of the second week. If the price of silver was x dollars per ounce at the beginning of the two-week period, what was the price, in dollars per ounce, by the end of the period?

(A) $0.8x$
(B) $0.95x$
(C) x
(D) $1.05x$
(E) $1.25x$

224. If a cube has a volume of 64, what is its total surface area?

(A) 16
(B) 24
(C) 48
(D) 64
(E) 96

Club	Number of Students
Chess	40
Drama	30
Math	25

225. The table above shows the number of students in three clubs at McAuliffe School. Although no student is in all three clubs, 10 students are in both chess and drama, 5 students are in both chess and math, and 6 students are in both drama and math. How many different students are in the three clubs?

(A) 68
(B) 69
(C) 74
(D) 79
(E) 84

226. If s, u, and v are positive integers and $2^s = 2^u + 2^v$, which of the following must be true?

    I. $s = u$
    II. $u \neq v$
    III. $s > v$

(A) None
(B) I only
(C) II only
(D) III only
(E) II and III

227. In a nationwide poll, N people were interviewed. If $\frac{1}{4}$ of them answered "yes" to question 1, and of those, $\frac{1}{3}$ answered "yes" to question 2, which of the following expressions represents the number of people interviewed who did <u>not</u> answer "yes" to both questions?

(A) $\dfrac{N}{7}$

(B) $\dfrac{6N}{7}$

(C) $\dfrac{5N}{12}$

(D) $\dfrac{7N}{12}$

(E) $\dfrac{11N}{12}$

228. In a certain pond, 50 fish were caught, tagged, and returned to the pond. A few days later, 50 fish were caught again, of which 2 were found to have been tagged. If the percent of tagged fish in the second catch approximates the percent of tagged fish in the pond, what is the approximate number of fish in the pond?

(A)   400
(B)   625
(C) 1,250
(D) 2,500
(E) 10,000

229. The ratio of two quantities is 3 to 4. If each of the quantities is increased by 5, what is the ratio of these two new quantities?

(A) $\dfrac{3}{4}$

(B) $\dfrac{8}{9}$

(C) $\dfrac{18}{19}$

(D) $\dfrac{23}{24}$

(E) It cannot be determined from the information given.

230. In 1986 the book value of a certain car was $\frac{2}{3}$ of the original purchase price, and in 1988 its book value was $\frac{1}{2}$ of the original purchase price. By what percent did the book value of this car decrease from 1986 to 1988 ?

(A) $16\frac{2}{3}\%$

(B) 25%

(C) $33\frac{1}{3}\%$

(D) 50%

(E) 75%

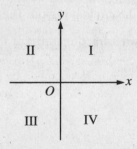

231. In the rectangular coordinate system shown above, which quadrant, if any, contains no point (x, y) that satisfies the inequality $2x - 3y \leq -6$?

(A) None
(B) I
(C) II
(D) III
(E) IV

232. A hiker walked for two days. On the second day the hiker walked 2 hours longer and at an average speed 1 mile per hour faster than he walked on the first day. If during the two days he walked a total of 64 miles and spent a total of 18 hours walking, what was his average speed on the first day?

(A) 2 mph
(B) 3 mph
(C) 4 mph
(D) 5 mph
(E) 6 mph

233. If a printer can print 2 pages of text per second, then, at this rate, approximately how many minutes will it take to print 5,000 pages of text?

(A)   4
(B)   25
(C)   42
(D) 250
(E) 417

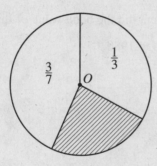

234. In the circular region with center O, shown above, the two unshaded sections comprise $\frac{3}{7}$ and $\frac{1}{3}$ of the area of the circular region. The shaded section comprises what fractional part of the area of the circular region?

(A) $\frac{3}{5}$

(B) $\frac{6}{7}$

(C) $\frac{2}{21}$

(D) $\frac{5}{21}$

(E) $\frac{16}{21}$

235. Envelopes can be purchased for $1.50 per pack of 100, $1.00 per pack of 50, or $0.03 each. What is the greatest number of envelopes that can be purchased for $7.30 ?

(A) 426
(B) 430
(C) 443
(D) 460
(E) 486

236. $\sqrt{16+16} =$

(A) $4\sqrt{2}$

(B) $8\sqrt{2}$

(C) $16\sqrt{2}$

(D) 8

(E) 16

237. An automobile's gasoline mileage varies, depending on the speed of the automobile, between 18.0 and 22.4 miles per gallon, inclusive. What is the maximum distance, in miles, that the automobile could be driven on 15 gallons of gasoline?

(A) 336
(B) 320
(C) 303
(D) 284
(E) 270

238. $\frac{(0.3)^5}{(0.3)^3} =$

(A) 0.001
(B) 0.01
(C) 0.09
(D) 0.9
(E) 1.0

239. In a horticultural experiment, 200 seeds were planted in plot I and 300 were planted in plot II. If 57 percent of the seeds in plot I germinated and 42 percent of the seeds in plot II germinated, what percent of the total number of planted seeds germinated?

(A) 45.5%
(B) 46.5%
(C) 48.0%
(D) 49.5%
(E) 51.0%

240. The organizers of a fair projected a 25 percent increase in attendance this year over that of last year, but attendance this year actually decreased by 20 percent. What percent of the projected attendance was the actual attendance?

(A) 45%
(B) 56%
(C) 64%
(D) 75%
(E) 80%

241. An optometrist charges $150 per pair for soft contact lenses and $85 per pair for hard contact lenses. Last week she sold 5 more pairs of soft lenses than hard lenses. If her total sales for pairs of contact lenses last week were $1,690, what was the total number of pairs of contact lenses that she sold?

(A) 11
(B) 13
(C) 15
(D) 17
(E) 19

242. What is the ratio of $\frac{3}{4}$ to the product $4\left(\frac{3}{4}\right)$?

(A) $\frac{1}{4}$

(B) $\frac{1}{3}$

(C) $\frac{4}{9}$

(D) $\frac{9}{4}$

(E) 4

243. The cost to rent a small bus for a trip is x dollars, which is to be shared equally among the people taking the trip. If 10 people take the trip rather than 16, how many more dollars, in terms of x, will it cost per person?

(A) $\frac{x}{6}$

(B) $\frac{x}{10}$

(C) $\frac{x}{16}$

(D) $\frac{3x}{40}$

(E) $\frac{3x}{80}$

244. If x is an integer and $y = 3x + 2$, which of the following CANNOT be a divisor of y?

(A) 4
(B) 5
(C) 6
(D) 7
(E) 8

245. The size of a television screen is given as the length of the screen's diagonal. If the screens were flat, then the area of a square 21-inch screen would be how many square inches greater than the area of a square 19-inch screen?

(A) 2
(B) 4
(C) 16
(D) 38
(E) 40

246. If the average (arithmetic mean) of x and y is 60 and the average (arithmetic mean) of y and z is 80, what is the value of $z - x$?

(A) 70
(B) 40
(C) 20
(D) 10
(E) It cannot be determined from the information given.

247. If 3 and 8 are the lengths of two sides of a triangular region, which of the following can be the length of the third side?

I.   5
II. 8
III. 11

(A) II only
(B) III only
(C) I and II only
(D) II and III only
(E) I, II, and III

248. One night a certain motel rented $\frac{3}{4}$ of its rooms, including $\frac{2}{3}$ of its air-conditioned rooms. If $\frac{3}{5}$ of its rooms were air-conditioned, what percent of the rooms that were <u>not</u> rented were air-conditioned?

(A) 20%

(B) $33\frac{1}{3}$%

(C) 35%

(D) 40%

(E) 80%

249. If $3 - x = 2x - 3$, then $4x =$

(A) -24
(B) -8
(C) 0
(D) 8
(E) 24

250. A certain electronic component is sold in boxes of 54 for $16.20 and in boxes of 27 for $13.20. A customer who needed only 54 components for a project had to buy 2 boxes of 27 because boxes of 54 were unavailable. Approximately how much more did the customer pay for each component due to the unavailability of the larger boxes?

(A) $0.33
(B) $0.19
(C) $0.11
(D) $0.06
(E) $0.03

251. On a certain street, there is an odd number of houses in a row. The houses in the row are painted alternately white and green, with the first house painted white. If n is the total number of houses in the row, how many of the houses are painted white?

(A) $\dfrac{n+1}{2}$

(B) $\dfrac{n-1}{2}$

(C) $\dfrac{n}{2}+1$

(D) $\dfrac{n}{2}-1$

(E) $\dfrac{n}{2}$

$$\begin{array}{r} \square\,\triangle \\ \times\ \triangle\,\square \\ \hline \end{array}$$

252. The product of the two-digit numbers above is the three-digit number $\square\,\diamond\,\square$, where $\square$, $\triangle$, and $\diamond$ are three different nonzero digits. If $\square \times \triangle < 10$, what is the two-digit number $\square\,\triangle$?

(A) 11
(B) 12
(C) 13
(D) 21
(E) 31

253. As a salesperson, Phyllis can choose one of two methods of annual payment: either an annual salary of $35,000 with no commission or an annual salary of $10,000 plus a 20 percent commission on her total annual sales. What must her total annual sales be to give her the same annual pay with either method?

(A) $100,000
(B) $120,000
(C) $125,000
(D) $130,000
(E) $132,000

254. A restaurant buys fruit in cans containing $3\frac{1}{2}$ cups of fruit each. If the restaurant uses $\frac{1}{2}$ cup of the fruit in each serving of its fruit compote, what is the least number of cans needed to prepare 60 servings of the compote?

(A) 7
(B) 8
(C) 9
(D) 10
(E) 12

255. If $x > 3,000$, then the value of $\frac{x}{2x+1}$ is closest to

(A) $\frac{1}{6}$

(B) $\frac{1}{3}$

(C) $\frac{10}{21}$

(D) $\frac{1}{2}$

(E) $\frac{3}{2}$

256. Machine A produces 100 parts twice as fast as machine B does. Machine B produces 100 parts in 40 minutes. If each machine produces parts at a constant rate, how many parts does machine A produce in 6 minutes?

(A) 30
(B) 25
(C) 20
(D) 15
(E) 7.5

257. If 18 is 15 percent of 30 percent of a certain number, what is the number?

(A) 9
(B) 36
(C) 40
(D) 81
(E) 400

258. A necklace is made by stringing N individual beads together in the repeating pattern red bead, green bead, white bead, blue bead, and yellow bead. If the necklace design begins with a red bead and ends with a white bead, then N could equal

(A) 16
(B) 32
(C) 41
(D) 54
(E) 68

259. If $x = (0.08)^2$, $y = \frac{1}{(0.08)^2}$, and $z = (1 - 0.08)^2 - 1$, which of the following is true?

(A) $x = y = z$
(B) $y < z < x$
(C) $z < x < y$
(D) $y < x$ and $x = z$.
(E) $x < y$ and $x = z$.

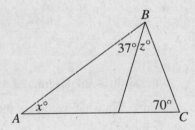

260. In $\triangle ABC$ above, what is x in terms of z ?

(A) $z + 73$
(B) $z - 73$
(C) $70 - z$
(D) $z - 70$
(E) $73 - z$

261. In 1990 a total of x earthquakes occurred worldwide, some but not all of which occurred in Asia. If m of these earthquakes occurred in Asia, which of the following represents the ratio of the number of earthquakes that occurred in Asia to the number that did not occur in Asia?

(A) $\dfrac{x}{m}$

(B) $\dfrac{m}{x}$

(C) $\dfrac{m}{x-m}$

(D) $\dfrac{x}{x-m}$

(E) $1-\dfrac{m}{x}$

262. If $\dfrac{x+y}{xy}=1$, then $y=$

(A) $\dfrac{x}{x-1}$

(B) $\dfrac{x}{x+1}$

(C) $\dfrac{x-1}{x}$

(D) $\dfrac{x+1}{x}$

(E) x

263. If $\dfrac{1}{2}$ of the air in a tank is removed with each stroke of a vacuum pump, what fraction of the original amount of air has been removed after 4 strokes?

(A) $\dfrac{15}{16}$

(B) $\dfrac{7}{8}$

(C) $\dfrac{1}{4}$

(D) $\dfrac{1}{8}$

(E) $\dfrac{1}{16}$

264. Last year Department Store X had a sales total for December that was 4 times the average (arithmetic mean) of the monthly sales totals for January through November. The sales total for December was what fraction of the sales total for the year?

(A) $\dfrac{1}{4}$

(B) $\dfrac{4}{15}$

(C) $\dfrac{1}{3}$

(D) $\dfrac{4}{11}$

(E) $\dfrac{4}{5}$

265. How many integers n are there such that $1 < 5n + 5 < 25$?

(A) Five
(B) Four
(C) Three
(D) Two
(E) One

266. If the two-digit integers M and N are positive and have the same digits, but in reverse order, which of the following CANNOT be the sum of M and N?

(A) 181
(B) 165
(C) 121
(D) 99
(E) 44

267. Working alone, printers $X, Y,$ and Z can do a certain printing job, consisting of a large number of pages, in 12, 15, and 18 hours, respectively. What is the ratio of the time it takes printer X to do the job, working alone at its rate, to the time it takes printers Y and Z to do the job, working together at their individual rates?

(A) $\dfrac{4}{11}$

(B) $\dfrac{1}{2}$

(C) $\dfrac{15}{22}$

(D) $\dfrac{22}{15}$

(E) $\dfrac{11}{4}$

268. In 1985 a company sold a brand of shoes to retailers for a fixed price per pair. In 1986 the number of pairs of the shoes that the company sold to retailers decreased by 20 percent, while the price per pair increased by 20 percent. If the company's revenue from the sales of the shoes in 1986 was $3.0 million, what was the approximate revenue from the sale of the shoes in 1985 ?

(A) $2.4 million
(B) $2.9 million
(C) $3.0 million
(D) $3.1 million
(E) $3.6 million

269. $\dfrac{(3)(0.072)}{0.54} =$

(A) 0.04
(B) 0.3
(C) 0.4
(D) 0.8
(E) 4.0

270. A car dealer sold x used cars and y new cars during May. If the number of used cars sold was 10 greater than the number of new cars sold, which of the following expresses this relationship?

(A) $x > 10y$
(B) $x > y + 10$
(C) $x > y - 10$
(D) $x = y + 10$
(E) $x = y - 10$

271. What is the maximum number of $1\frac{1}{4}$-foot pieces of wire that can be cut from a wire that is 24 feet long?

(A) 11
(B) 18
(C) 19
(D) 20
(E) 30

272. If each of the two lines ℓ_1 and ℓ_2 is parallel to line ℓ_3, which of the following must be true?

(A) Lines ℓ_1, ℓ_2, and ℓ_3 lie in the same plane.
(B) Lines ℓ_1, ℓ_2, and ℓ_3 lie in different planes.
(C) Line ℓ_1 is parallel to line ℓ_2.
(D) Line ℓ_1 is the same line as line ℓ_2.
(E) Line ℓ_1 is the same line as line ℓ_3.

$$\frac{61.24 \times (0.998)^2}{\sqrt{403}}$$

273. The expression above is approximately equal to

(A) 1
(B) 3
(C) 4
(D) 5
(E) 6

274. Car X and car Y traveled the same 80-mile route. If car X took 2 hours and car Y traveled at an average speed that was 50 percent faster than the average speed of car X, how many hours did it take car Y to travel the route?

(A) $\dfrac{2}{3}$

(B) 1

(C) $1\dfrac{1}{3}$

(D) $1\dfrac{3}{5}$

(E) 3

275. If the numbers $\dfrac{17}{24}$, $\dfrac{1}{2}$, $\dfrac{3}{8}$, $\dfrac{3}{4}$, and $\dfrac{9}{16}$ were ordered from greatest to least, the middle number of the resulting sequence would be

(A) $\dfrac{17}{24}$

(B) $\dfrac{1}{2}$

(C) $\dfrac{3}{8}$

(D) $\dfrac{3}{4}$

(E) $\dfrac{9}{16}$

276. If a 10 percent deposit that has been paid toward the purchase of a certain product is $110, how much more remains to be paid?

(A) $880
(B) $990
(C) $1,000
(D) $1,100
(E) $1,210

277. Kim purchased n items from a catalog for $8 each. Postage and handling charges consisted of $3 for the first item and $1 for each additional item. Which of the following gives the total dollar amount of Kim's purchase, including postage and handling, in terms of n ?

(A) $8n + 2$
(B) $8n + 4$
(C) $9n + 2$
(D) $9n + 3$
(E) $9n + 4$

278. $\left(\sqrt{7} + \sqrt{7}\right)^2 =$

(A) 98
(B) 49
(C) 28
(D) 21
(E) 14

279. If the average (arithmetic mean) of the four numbers K, $2K + 3$, $3K - 5$, and $5K + 1$ is 63, what is the value of K ?

(A) 11

(B) $15\dfrac{3}{4}$

(C) 22

(D) 23

(E) $25\dfrac{3}{10}$

280. A rabbit on a controlled diet is fed daily 300 grams of a mixture of two foods, food X and food Y. Food X contains 10 percent protein and food Y contains 15 percent protein. If the rabbit's diet provides exactly 38 grams of protein daily, how many grams of food X are in the mixture?

(A) 100
(B) 140
(C) 150
(D) 160
(E) 200

281. A company that ships boxes to a total of 12 distribution centers uses color coding to identify each center. If either a single color or a pair of two different colors is chosen to represent each center and if each center is uniquely represented by that choice of one or two colors, what is the minimum number of colors needed for the coding? (Assume that the order of the colors in a pair does not matter.)

(A) 4
(B) 5
(C) 6
(D) 12
(E) 24

282. If $x + y = a$ and $x - y = b$, then $2xy =$

(A) $\dfrac{a^2 - b^2}{2}$

(B) $\dfrac{b^2 - a^2}{2}$

(C) $\dfrac{a - b}{2}$

(D) $\dfrac{ab}{2}$

(E) $\dfrac{a^2 + b^2}{2}$

283. A rectangular circuit board is designed to have width w inches, perimeter p inches, and area k square inches. Which of the following equations must be true?

(A) $w^2 + pw + k = 0$
(B) $w^2 - pw + 2k = 0$
(C) $2w^2 + pw + 2k = 0$
(D) $2w^2 - pw - 2k = 0$
(E) $2w^2 - pw + 2k = 0$

284. On a certain road, 10 percent of the motorists exceed the posted speed limit and receive speeding tickets, but 20 percent of the motorists who exceed the posted speed limit do not receive speeding tickets. What percent of the motorists on that road exceed the posted speed limit?

(A) $10\dfrac{1}{2}\%$

(B) $12\dfrac{1}{2}\%$

(C) 15%

(D) 22%

(E) 30%

285. If p is an even integer and q is an odd integer, which of the following must be an odd integer?

(A) $\dfrac{p}{q}$

(B) pq

(C) $2p + q$

(D) $2(p + q)$

(E) $\dfrac{3p}{q}$

286. A certain college has a student-to-teacher ratio of 11 to 1. The average (arithmetic mean) annual salary for teachers is $26,000. If the college pays a total of $3,380,000 in annual salaries to its teachers, how many students does the college have?

(A) 130
(B) 169
(C) 1,300
(D) 1,430
(E) 1,560

287. Last year if 97 percent of the revenues of a company came from domestic sources and the remaining revenues, totaling $450,000, came from foreign sources, what was the total of the company's revenues?

(A) $1,350,000
(B) $1,500,000
(C) $4,500,000
(D) $15,000,000
(E) $150,000,000

288. Drum X is $\dfrac{1}{2}$ full of oil and drum Y, which has twice the capacity of drum X, is $\dfrac{2}{3}$ full of oil. If all of the oil in drum X is poured into drum Y, then drum Y will be filled to what fraction of its capacity?

(A) $\dfrac{3}{4}$

(B) $\dfrac{5}{6}$

(C) $\dfrac{11}{12}$

(D) $\dfrac{7}{6}$

(E) $\dfrac{11}{6}$

289. In a certain population, there are 3 times as many people aged twenty-one or under as there are people over twenty-one. The ratio of those twenty-one or under to the total population is

(A) 1 to 2
(B) 1 to 3
(C) 1 to 4
(D) 2 to 3
(E) 3 to 4

290. $\dfrac{2 + 2\sqrt{6}}{2} =$

(A) $\sqrt{6}$

(B) $2\sqrt{6}$

(C) $1 + \sqrt{6}$

(D) $1 + 2\sqrt{6}$

(E) $2 + \sqrt{6}$

291. A certain telescope increases the visual range at a particular location from 90 kilometers to 150 kilometers. By what percent is the visual range increased by using the telescope?

   (A) 30%

   (B) $33\frac{1}{2}\%$

   (C) 40%

   (D) 60%

   (E) $66\frac{2}{3}\%$

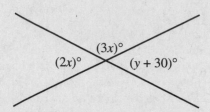

Note: Figure not drawn to scale.

292. In the figure above, the value of y is

   (A) 6
   (B) 12
   (C) 24
   (D) 36
   (E) 42

293. A part-time employee whose hourly wage was increased by 25 percent decided to reduce the number of hours worked per week so that the employee's total weekly income would remain unchanged. By what percent should the number of hours worked be reduced?

   (A) 12.5%
   (B) 20%
   (C) 25%
   (D) 50%
   (E) 75%

294. If $x > 0$, $\dfrac{x}{50} + \dfrac{x}{25}$ is what percent of x ?

   (A) 6%

   (B) 25%

   (C) $37\frac{1}{2}\%$

   (D) 60%

   (E) 75%

295. If the operation $\circledast$ is defined for all a and b by the equation $a \circledast b = \dfrac{a^2 b}{3}$, then $2 \circledast (3 \circledast -1) =$

   (A) 4

   (B) 2

   (C) $-\dfrac{4}{3}$

   (D) -2

   (E) -4

296. A factory that employs 1,000 assembly-line workers pays each of these workers $5 per hour for the first 40 hours worked during a week and $1\frac{1}{2}$ times that rate for hours worked in excess of 40. What was the total payroll for the assembly-line workers for a week in which 30 percent of them worked 20 hours, 50 percent worked 40 hours, and the rest worked 50 hours?

   (A) $180,000
   (B) $185,000
   (C) $190,000
   (D) $200,000
   (E) $205,000

297. If $x \neq 2$, then $\dfrac{3x^2(x-2) - x + 2}{x - 2} =$

   (A) $3x^2 - x + 2$

   (B) $3x^2 + 1$

   (C) $3x^2$

   (D) $3x^2 - 1$

   (E) $3x^2 - 2$

298. In a certain school, 40 more than $\frac{1}{3}$ of all the students are taking a science course and $\frac{1}{4}$ of those taking a science course are taking physics. If $\frac{1}{8}$ of all the students in the school are taking physics, how many students are in the school?

(A) 240
(B) 300
(C) 480
(D) 720
(E) 960

299. If $d > 0$ and $0 < 1 - \frac{c}{d} < 1$, which of the following must be true?

I. $c > 0$

II. $\frac{c}{d} < 1$

III. $c^2 + d^2 > 1$

(A) I only
(B) II only
(C) I and II only
(D) II and III only
(E) I, II, and III

300. The inside dimensions of a rectangular wooden box are 6 inches by 8 inches by 10 inches. A cylindrical cannister is to be placed inside the box so that it stands upright when the closed box rests on one of its six faces. Of all such cannisters that could be used, what is the radius, in inches, of the one that has maximum volume?

(A) 3
(B) 4
(C) 5
(D) 6
(E) 8

301. $\dfrac{\frac{1}{2}}{\frac{1}{4} + \frac{1}{6}} =$

(A) $\frac{6}{5}$

(B) $\frac{5}{6}$

(C) $\frac{5}{24}$

(D) $\frac{1}{5}$

(E) $\frac{1}{12}$

302. Kelly and Chris packed several boxes with books. If Chris packed 60 percent of the total number of boxes, what was the ratio of the number of boxes Kelly packed to the number of boxes Chris packed?

(A) 1 to 6
(B) 1 to 4
(C) 2 to 5
(D) 3 to 5
(E) 2 to 3

303. A train travels from New York City to Chicago, a distance of approximately 840 miles, at an average rate of 60 miles per hour and arrives in Chicago at 6:00 in the evening, Chicago time. At what hour in the morning, New York City time, did the train depart for Chicago? (Note: Chicago time is one hour earlier than New York City time.)

(A) 4:00
(B) 5:00
(C) 6:00
(D) 7:00
(E) 8:00

304. Of the following, which is the closest approximation of $\dfrac{50.2 \times 0.49}{199.8}$?

(A) $\dfrac{1}{10}$

(B) $\dfrac{1}{8}$

(C) $\dfrac{1}{4}$

(D) $\dfrac{5}{4}$

(E) $\dfrac{25}{2}$

305. Last year Manfred received 26 paychecks. Each of his first 6 paychecks was $750; each of his remaining paychecks was $30 more than each of his first 6 paychecks. To the nearest dollar, what was the average (arithmetic mean) amount of his paychecks for the year?

(A) $752
(B) $755
(C) $765
(D) $773
(E) $775

306. A certain pair of used shoes can be repaired for $12.50 and will last for 1 year. A pair of the same kind of shoes can be purchased new for $28.00 and will last for 2 years. The average cost per year of the new shoes is what percent greater than the cost of repairing the used shoes?

(A) 3%
(B) 5%
(C) 12%
(D) 15%
(E) 24%

307. In a certain brick wall, each row of bricks above the bottom row contains one less brick than the row just below it. If there are 5 rows in all and a total of 75 bricks in the wall, how many bricks does the bottom row contain?

(A) 14
(B) 15
(C) 16
(D) 17
(E) 18

308. If 25 percent of p is equal to 10 percent of q, and $pq \neq 0$, then p is what percent of q ?

(A) 2.5%
(B) 15%
(C) 20%
(D) 35%
(E) 40%

309. If the length of an edge of cube X is twice the length of an edge of cube Y, what is the ratio of the volume of cube Y to the volume of cube X ?

(A) $\dfrac{1}{2}$

(B) $\dfrac{1}{4}$

(C) $\dfrac{1}{6}$

(D) $\dfrac{1}{8}$

(E) $\dfrac{1}{27}$

310. $(\sqrt{2}+1)(\sqrt{2}-1)(\sqrt{3}+1)(\sqrt{3}-1) =$

(A) 2

(B) 3

(C) $2\sqrt{6}$

(D) 5

(E) 6

311. In a certain calculus class, the ratio of the number of mathematics majors to the number of students who are not mathematics majors is 2 to 5. If 2 more mathematics majors were to enter the class, the ratio would be 1 to 2. How many students are in the class?

(A) 10
(B) 12
(C) 21
(D) 28
(E) 35

312. Machines A and B always operate independently and at their respective constant rates. When working alone, machine A can fill a production lot in 5 hours, and machine B can fill the same lot in x hours. When the two machines operate simultaneously to fill the production lot, it takes them 2 hours to complete the job. What is the value of x?

(A) $3\frac{1}{3}$

(B) 3

(C) $2\frac{1}{2}$

(D) $2\frac{1}{3}$

(E) $1\frac{1}{2}$

313. In the xy-coordinate system, if (a, b) and $(a+3, b+k)$ are two points on the line defined by the equation $x = 3y - 7$, then $k =$

(A) 9

(B) 3

(C) $\frac{7}{3}$

(D) 1

(E) $\frac{1}{3}$

314. What is the units digit of $(13)^4 (17)^2 (29)^3$?

(A) 9
(B) 7
(C) 5
(D) 3
(E) 1

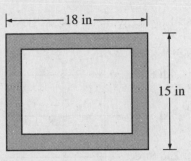

Note: Figure not drawn to scale.

315. The shaded region in the figure above represents a rectangular frame with length 18 inches and width 15 inches. The frame encloses a rectangular picture that has the same area as the frame itself. If the length and width of the picture have the same ratio as the length and width of the frame, what is the length of the picture, in inches?

(A) $9\sqrt{2}$

(B) $\frac{3}{2}$

(C) $\frac{9}{\sqrt{2}}$

(D) $15\left(1 - \frac{1}{\sqrt{2}}\right)$

(E) $\frac{9}{2}$

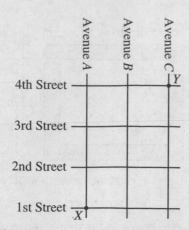

316. Pat will walk from intersection X to intersection Y along a route that is confined to the square grid of four streets and three avenues shown in the map above. How many routes from X to Y can Pat take that have the minimum possible length?

(A) Six
(B) Eight
(C) Ten
(D) Fourteen
(E) Sixteen

317. A certain fishing boat is chartered by 6 people who are to contribute equally to the total charter cost of $480. If each person contributes equally to a $150 down payment, how much of the charter cost will each person still owe?

(A) $80 (B) $66 (C) $55 (D) $50 (E) $45

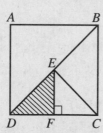

318. In square $ABCD$ above, if $DE = EB$ and $DF = FC$, then the area of the shaded region is what fraction of the area of square region $ABCD$?

(A) $\frac{1}{16}$ (B) $\frac{1}{8}$ (C) $\frac{1}{6}$ (D) $\frac{1}{4}$ (E) $\frac{1}{3}$

319. Craig sells major appliances. For each appliance he sells, Craig receives a commission of $50 plus 10 percent of the selling price. During one particular week Craig sold 6 appliances for selling prices totaling $3,620. What was the total of Craig's commissions for that week?

(A) $412 (B) $526 (C) $585
(D) $605 (E) $662

320. The average (arithmetic mean) of 10, 30, and 50 is 5 more than the average of 20, 40, and

(A) 15 (B) 25 (C) 35 (D) 45 (E) 55

321. What number when multiplied by $\frac{4}{7}$ yields $\frac{6}{7}$ as the result?

(A) $\frac{2}{7}$ (B) $\frac{2}{3}$ (C) $\frac{3}{2}$ (D) $\frac{24}{7}$ (E) $\frac{7}{2}$

322. If $y = 4 + (x - 3)^2$, then y is least when $x =$

(A) -4 (B) -3 (C) 0 (D) 3 (E) 4

323. If 3 pounds of dried apricots that cost x dollars per pound are mixed with 2 pounds of prunes that cost y dollars per pound, what is the cost, in dollars, per pound of the mixture?

(A) $\dfrac{3x + 2y}{5}$

(B) $\dfrac{3x + 2y}{x + y}$

(C) $\dfrac{3x + 2y}{xy}$

(D) $5(3x + 2y)$

(E) $3x + 2y$

324. A cashier mentally reversed the digits of one customer's correct amount of change and thus gave the customer an incorrect amount of change. If the cash register contained 45 cents more than it should have as a result of this error, which of the following could have been the correct amount of change in cents?

(A) 14 (B) 45 (C) 54 (D) 65 (E) 83

325. Which of the following is NOT equal to the square of an integer?

(A) $\sqrt{\sqrt{1}}$ (B) $\sqrt{4}$ (C) $\dfrac{18}{2}$

(D) $41 - 25$ (E) 36

326. An artist wishes to paint a circular region on a square poster that is 2 feet on a side. If the area of the circular region is to be $\dfrac{1}{2}$ the area of the poster, what must be the radius of the circular region in feet?

(A) $\dfrac{1}{\pi}$ (B) $\sqrt{\dfrac{2}{\pi}}$ (C) 1 (D) $\dfrac{2}{\sqrt{\pi}}$ (E) $\dfrac{\pi}{2}$

327. Which of the following must be equal to zero for all real numbers x ?

I. $-\dfrac{1}{x}$

II. $x + (-x)$

III. x^0

(A) I only
(B) II only
(C) I and III only
(D) II and III only
(E) I, II, and III

328. At the rate of m meters per s seconds, how many meters does a cyclist travel in x minutes?

(A) $\dfrac{m}{sx}$ (B) $\dfrac{mx}{s}$ (C) $\dfrac{60m}{sx}$

(D) $\dfrac{60ms}{x}$ (E) $\dfrac{60mx}{s}$

	City A	City B	City C	City D	City E	City F
City A						
City B						
City C						
City D						
City E						
City F						

329. In the table above, what is the least number of table entries that are needed to show the mileage between each city and each of the other five cities?

(A) 15 (B) 21 (C) 25 (D) 30 (E) 36

330. A certain tax rate is $0.82 per $100.00. What is this rate, expressed as a percent?

(A) 82% (B) 8.2% (C) 0.82%
(D) 0.082% (E) 0.0082%

331. Fermat primes are prime numbers that can be written in the form $2^k + 1$, where k is an integer and a power of 2. Which of the following is NOT a Fermat prime?

(A) 3 (B) 5 (C) 17 (D) 31 (E) 257

332. A shipment of 1,500 heads of cabbage, each of which was approximately the same size, was purchased for $600. The day the shipment arrived, $\dfrac{2}{3}$ of the heads were sold, each at 25 percent above the cost per head. The following day the rest were sold at a price per head equal to 10 percent less than the price each head sold for on the day before. What was the gross profit on this shipment?

(A) $100 (B) $115 (C) $125
(D) $130 (E) $135

333. If $(t - 8)$ is a factor of $t^2 - kt - 48$, then $k =$

(A) -6 (B) -2 (C) 2 (D) 6 (E) 14

334. If a is a positive integer, and if the units' digit of a^2 is 9 and the units' digit of $(a + 1)^2$ is 4, what is the units' digit of $(a + 2)^2$?

(A) 1 (B) 3 (C) 5 (D) 7 (E) 9

335. The ratio, by volume, of soap to alcohol to water in a certain solution is 2 : 50 : 100. The solution will be altered so that the ratio of soap to alcohol is doubled while the ratio of soap to water is halved. If the altered solution will contain 100 cubic centimeters of alcohol, how many cubic centimeters of water will it contain?

(A) 50 (B) 200 (C) 400 (D) 625 (E) 800

336. If 75 percent of a class answered the first question on a certain test correctly, 55 percent answered the second question on the test correctly, and 20 percent answered neither of the questions correctly, what percent answered both correctly?

(A) 10% (B) 20% (C) 30%
(D) 50% (E) 65%

337. $\dfrac{31}{125} =$

(A) 0.248
(B) 0.252
(C) 0.284
(D) 0.312
(E) 0.320

338. Members of a social club met to address 280 newsletters. If they addressed $\dfrac{1}{4}$ of the newsletters during the first hour and $\dfrac{2}{5}$ of the remaining newsletters during the second hour, how many newsletters did they address during the second hour?

(A) 28 (B) 42 (C) 63 (D) 84 (E) 112

339. If $x^2 = 2y^3$ and $2y = 4$, what is the value of $x^2 + y$?

(A) -14
(B) -2
(C) 3
(D) 6
(E) 18

340. If the cost of 12 eggs varies between $0.90 and $1.20, then the cost per egg varies between

(A) $0.06 and $0.08
(B) $0.065 and $0.085
(C) $0.07 and $0.09
(D) $0.075 and $0.10
(E) $0.08 and $0.105

341. $(\sqrt{3} + 2)(\sqrt{3} - 2) =$

(A) $\sqrt{3} - 4$ (B) $\sqrt{6} - 4$ (C) -1
(D) 1 (E) 2

342. A glucose solution contains 15 grams of glucose per 100 cubic centimeters of solution. If 45 cubic centimeters of the solution were poured into an empty container, how many grams of glucose would be in the container?

(A) 3.00
(B) 5.00
(C) 5.50
(D) 6.50
(E) 6.75

343. If Sam were twice as old as he is, he would be 40 years older than Jim. If Jim is 10 years younger than Sam, how old is Sam?

(A) 20
(B) 30
(C) 40
(D) 50
(E) 60

344. If $\frac{1}{2}+\frac{1}{3}+\frac{1}{4}=\frac{13}{x}$, which of the following must be an integer?

   I. $\frac{x}{8}$

   II. $\frac{x}{12}$

   III. $\frac{x}{24}$

   (A) I only   (B) II only   (C) I and III only
   (D) II and III only   (E) I, II, and III

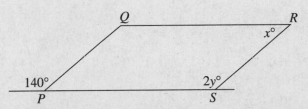

345. In the figure above, if $PQRS$ is a parallelogram, then $y - x =$

   (A) 30   (B) 35   (C) 40   (D) 70   (E) 100

346. The temperature in degrees Celsius (C) can be converted to temperature in degrees Fahrenheit (F) by the formula $F = \frac{9}{5}C + 32$. What is the temperature at which $F = C$?

   (A) 20°   (B) $\left(\frac{32}{5}\right)°$ (C) 0°
   (D) −20°   (E) −40°

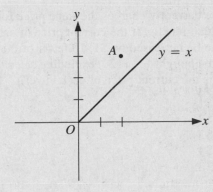

347. In the rectangular coordinate system above, the line $y = x$ is the perpendicular bisector of segment AB (not shown), and the x-axis is the perpendicular bisector of segment BC (not shown). If the coordinates of point A are (2, 3), what are the coordinates of point C ?

   (A) (−3, −2)
   (B) (−3, 2)
   (C) (2, −3)
   (D) (3, −2)
   (E) (2, 3)

348. If 1 kilometer is approximately 0.6 mile, which of the following best approximates the number of kilometers in 2 miles?

   (A) $\frac{10}{3}$ (B) 3   (C) $\frac{6}{5}$ (D) $\frac{1}{3}$ (E) $\frac{3}{10}$

349. A $500 investment and a $1,500 investment have a combined yearly return of 8.5 percent of the total of the two investments. If the $500 investment has a yearly return of 7 percent, what percent yearly return does the $1,500 investment have?

   (A) 9%

   (B) 10%

   (C) $10\frac{5}{8}$%

   (D) 11%

   (E) 12%

350. A store currently charges the same price for each towel that it sells. If the current price of each towel were to be increased by $1, 10 fewer of the towels could be bought for $120, excluding sales tax. What is the current price of each towel?

(A) $1
(B) $2
(C) $3
(D) $4
(E) $12

351. If the sum of n consecutive integers is 0, which of the following must be true?

I. n is an even number.
II. n is an odd number.
III. The average (arithmetic mean) of the n integers is 0.

(A) I only   (B) II only   (C) III only
(D) I and III   (E) II and III

352. In the formula $V = \dfrac{1}{(2r)^3}$, if r is halved, then V is multiplied by

(A) 64

(B) 8

(C) 1

(D) $\dfrac{1}{8}$

(E) $\dfrac{1}{64}$

353. For any integer n greater than 1, $\lfloor n$ denotes the product of all the integers from 1 to n, inclusive. How many prime numbers are there between $\lfloor 6 + 2$ and $\lfloor 6 + 6$, inclusive?

(A) None   (B) One   (C) Two
(D) Three   (E) Four

354. In how many arrangements can a teacher seat 3 girls and 3 boys in a row of 6 seats if the boys are to have the first, third, and fifth seats?

(A) 6   (B) 9   (C) 12   (D) 36   (E) 720

355. A circular rim 28 inches in diameter rotates the same number of inches per second as a circular rim 35 inches in diameter. If the smaller rim makes x revolutions per second, how many revolutions per minute does the larger rim make in terms of x ?

(A) $\dfrac{48\pi}{x}$

(B) $75x$

(C) $48x$

(D) $24x$

(E) $\dfrac{x}{75}$

356. The cost C of manufacturing a certain product can be estimated by the formula $C = 0.03rst^2$, where r and s are the amounts, in pounds, of the two major ingredients and t is the production time, in hours. If r is increased by 50 percent, s is increased by 20 percent, and t is decreased by 30 percent, by approximately what percent will the estimated cost of manufacturing the product change?

(A) 40% increase
(B) 12% increase
(C) 4% increase
(D) 12% decrease
(E) 24% decrease

357. Reggie purchased a car costing $8,700. As a down payment he used a $2,300 insurance settlement, and an amount from his savings equal to 15 percent of the difference between the cost of the car and the insurance settlement. If he borrowed the rest of the money needed to purchase the car, how much did he borrow?

(A) $6,400
(B) $6,055
(C) $5,440
(D) $5,095
(E) $3,260

MEMBERSHIP OF ORGANIZATION X, 1988

Honorary Members	78
Fellows	9,209
Members	35,509
Associate Members	27,909
Affiliates	2,372

358. According to the table above, the number of fellows was approximately what percent of the total membership of Organization X?

(A) 9%
(B) 12%
(C) 18%
(D) 25%
(E) 35%

359. The arithmetic mean and standard deviation of a certain normal distribution are 13.5 and 1.5, respectively. What value is exactly 2 standard deviations less than the mean?

(A) 10.5
(B) 11.0
(C) 11.5
(D) 12.0
(E) 12.5

360. Mark bought a set of 6 flower pots of different sizes at a total cost of $8.25. Each pot cost $0.25 more than the next one below it in size. What was the cost, in dollars, of the largest pot?

(A) $1.75
(B) $1.85
(C) $2.00
(D) $2.15
(E) $2.30

361. When N is divided by T, the quotient is S and the remainder is V. Which of the following expressions is equal to N?

(A) ST
(B) $S + V$
(C) $ST + V$
(D) $T(S + V)$
(E) $T(S - V)$

38, 69, 22, 73, 31, 47, 13, 82

362. Which of the following numbers is greater than three-fourths of the numbers but less than one-fourth of the numbers in the list above?

(A) 56
(B) 68
(C) 69
(D) 71
(E) 73

363. Lucy invested $10,000 in a new mutual fund account exactly three years ago. The value of the account increased by 10 percent during the first year, increased by 5 percent during the second year, and decreased by 10 percent during the third year. What is the value of the account today?

(A) $10,350
(B) $10,395
(C) $10,500
(D) $11,500
(E) $12,705

364. A certain bakery has 6 employees. It pays annual salaries of $14,000 to each of 2 employees, $16,000 to 1 employee, and $17,000 to each of the remaining 3 employees. The average (arithmetic mean) annual salary of these employees is closest to which of the following?

(A) $15,200
(B) $15,500
(C) $15,800
(D) $16,000
(E) $16,400

365. If x is equal to the sum of the even integers from 40 to 60, inclusive, and y is the number of even integers from 40 to 60, inclusive, what is the value of $x + y$?

(A) 550
(B) 551
(C) 560
(D) 561
(E) 572

366. If $\left(7^{\frac{3}{4}}\right)^n = 7$, what is the value of n ?

(A) $\dfrac{1}{3}$

(B) $\dfrac{2}{3}$

(C) $\dfrac{4}{3}$

(D) $\dfrac{5}{3}$

(E) $\dfrac{6}{3}$

367. Which of the following is equal to the average (arithmetic mean) of $(x+2)^2$ and $(x-2)^2$?

(A) x^2
(B) $x^2 + 2$
(C) $x^2 + 4$
(D) $x^2 + 2x$
(E) $x^2 + 4x$

368. If $x^4 + y^4 = 100$ then the greatest possible value of x is between

(A) 0 and 3
(B) 3 and 6
(C) 6 and 9
(D) 9 and 12
(E) 12 and 15

369. During a car trip, Maria stopped to rest after she traveled $\dfrac{1}{2}$ of the total distance to her destination. She stopped again after she traveled $\dfrac{1}{4}$ of the distance remaining between her first stop and her destination, and then she drove the remaining 120 miles to her destination. What was the total distance, in miles, from Maria's starting point to her destination?

(A) 280
(B) 320
(C) 360
(D) 420
(E) 480

NUMBER OF SOLID-COLORED MARBLES
IN THREE JARS

Jar	Number of Red Marbles	Number of Green Marbles	Total Number of Red and Green Marbles
P	x	y	80
Q	y	z	120
R	x	z	160

370. In the table above, what is the number of green marbles in jar R ?

(A) 70
(B) 80
(C) 90
(D) 100
(E) 110

371. The cost of picture frame M is $10.00 less than 3 times the cost of picture frame N. If the cost of frame M is $50.00, what is the cost of frame N ?

(A) $13.33
(B) $16.66
(C) $20.00
(D) $26.66
(E) $40.00

372. If x is to be chosen at random from the set $\{1, 2, 3, 4\}$ and y is to be chosen at random from the set $\{5, 6, 7\}$, what is the probability that xy will be even?

(A) $\dfrac{1}{6}$

(B) $\dfrac{1}{3}$

(C) $\dfrac{1}{2}$

(D) $\dfrac{2}{3}$

(E) $\dfrac{5}{6}$

373. If $S = \{0, 4, 5, 2, 11, 8\}$, how much greater than the median of the numbers in S is the mean of the numbers in S?

(A) 0.5
(B) 1.0
(C) 1.5
(D) 2.0
(E) 2.5

374. The value of $\sqrt[3]{-89}$ is

(A) between −9 and −10
(B) between −8 and −9
(C) between −4 and −5
(D) between −3 and −4
(E) undefined

Shipment	Number of Defective Chips in the Shipment	Total Number of Chips in the Shipment
S1	2	5,000
S2	5	12,000
S3	6	18,000
S4	4	16,000

375. A computer chip manufacturer expects the ratio of the number of defective chips to the total number of chips in all future shipments to equal the corresponding ratio for shipments S1, S2, S3, and S4 combined, as shown in the table above. What is the expected number of defective chips in a shipment of 60,000 chips?

(A) 14
(B) 20
(C) 22
(D) 24
(E) 25

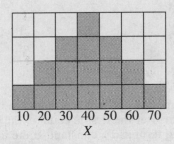

X

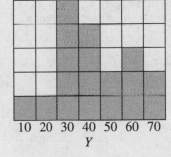

Y

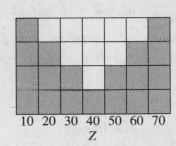

Z

376. If the variables, X, Y, and Z take on only the values 10, 20, 30, 40, 50, 60, or 70 with frequencies indicated by the shaded regions above, for which of the frequency distributions is the mean equal to the median?

(A) X only
(B) Y only
(C) Z only
(D) X and Y
(E) X and Z

377. In a certain furniture store, each week Nancy earns a salary of $240 plus 5 percent of the amount of her total sales that exceeds $800 for the week. If Nancy earned a total of $450 one week, what were her total sales that week?

(A) $2,200
(B) $3,450
(C) $4,200
(D) $4,250
(E) $5,000

$$A = \{2, 3, 4, 5\}$$
$$B = \{4, 5, 6, 7, 8\}$$

378. Two integers will be randomly selected from the sets above, one integer from set A and one integer from set B. What is the probability that the sum of the two integers will equal 9?

(A) 0.15
(B) 0.20
(C) 0.25
(D) 0.30
(E) 0.33

$$p, r, s, t, u$$

379. An arithmetic sequence is a sequence in which each term after the first is equal to the sum of the preceding term and a constant. If the list of numbers shown above is an arithmetic sequence, which of the following must also be an arithmetic sequence?

    I. $2p, 2r, 2s, 2t, 2u$
    II. $p - 3, r - 3, s - 3, t - 3, u - 3$
    III. p^2, r^2, s^2, t^2, u^2

(A) I only
(B) II only
(C) III only
(D) I and II
(E) II and III

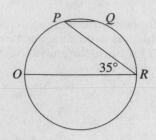

380. In the circle above, PQ is parallel to diameter OR, and OR has length 18. What is the length of minor arc PQ ?

(A) 2π

(B) $\dfrac{9\pi}{4}$

(C) $\dfrac{7\pi}{2}$

(D) $\dfrac{9\pi}{2}$

(E) 3π

381. Dick and Jane each saved $3,000 in 1989. In 1990 Dick saved 8 percent more than in 1989, and together he and Jane saved a total of $5,000. Approximately what percent less did Jane save in 1990 than in 1989 ?

(A) 8%
(B) 25%
(C) 41%
(D) 59%
(E) 70%

382. Of the following, which is least?

(A) $\dfrac{1}{0.2}$

(B) $(0.2)^2$

(C) 0.02

(D) $\dfrac{0.2}{2}$

(E) 0.2

383. S represents the sum of the weights of n fish in pounds. Which of the following represents the average (arithmetic mean) of the n weights in ounces? (1 pound = 16 ounces)

(A) $16nS$

(B) $\dfrac{16S}{n}$

(C) $\dfrac{16n}{S}$

(D) $\dfrac{nS}{16}$

(E) $\dfrac{S}{16n}$

NET INCOME BY SECTOR, SECOND QUARTER, 1996

Sector	Net Income (in billions)	Percent Change from First Quarter, 1996
Basic Materials	$4.83	−26%
Energy	7.46	+40
Industrial	5.00	−1
Utilities	8.57	+303
Conglomerates	2.07	+10

384. The table above represents the combined net income of all United States companies in each of five sectors for the second quarter of 1996. Which sector had the greatest net income during the first quarter of 1996 ?

(A) Basic Materials
(B) Energy
(C) Industrial
(D) Utilities
(E) Conglomerates

385. For how many integers n is $2^n = n^2$?

(A) None
(B) One
(C) Two
(D) Three
(E) More than three

386. The manager of a theater noted that for every 10 admission tickets sold, the theater sells 3 bags of popcorn at $2.25 each, 4 sodas at $1.50 each, and 2 candy bars at $1.00 each. To the nearest cent, what is the average (arithmetic mean) amount of these snack sales per ticket sold?

(A) $1.48
(B) $1.58
(C) $1.60
(D) $1.64
(E) $1.70

387. If $n = 4p$, where p is a prime number greater than 2, how many different positive <u>even</u> divisors does n have, including n ?

(A) Two
(B) Three
(C) Four
(D) Six
(E) Eight

388. S is a set containing 9 different numbers. T is a set containing 8 different numbers, all of which are members of S. Which of the following statements CANNOT be true?

(A) The mean of S is equal to the mean of T.
(B) The median of S is equal to the median of T.
(C) The range of S is equal to the range of T.
(D) The mean of S is greater than the mean of T.
(E) The range of S is less than the range of T.

389. In a recent election, James received 0.5 percent of the 2,000 votes cast. To win the election, a candidate needed to receive more than 50 percent of the vote. How many additional votes would James have needed to win the election?

(A) 901
(B) 989
(C) 990
(D) 991
(E) 1,001

390. The regular price per can of a certain brand of soda is $0.40. If the regular price per can is discounted 15 percent when the soda is purchased in 24-can cases, what is the price of 72 cans of this brand of soda purchased in 24-can cases?

(A) $16.32
(B) $18.00
(C) $21.60
(D) $24.48
(E) $28.80

391. If r and s are integers and $rs + r$ is odd, which of the following must be even?

(A) r
(B) s
(C) $r + s$
(D) $rs - r$
(E) $r^2 + s$

List I: 3, 6, 8, 19
List II: x, 3, 6, 8, 19

392. If the median of the numbers in list I above is equal to the median of the numbers in list II above, what is the value of x ?

(A) 6
(B) 7
(C) 8
(D) 9
(E) 10

393. If $d = 2.0453$ and $d*$ is the decimal obtained by rounding d to the nearest hundredth, what is the value of $d* - d$?

(A) −0.0053
(B) −0.0003
(C) 0.0007
(D) 0.0047
(E) 0.0153

394. Right triangle PQR is to be constructed in the xy-plane so that the right angle is at P and PR is parallel to the x-axis. The x- and y-coordinates of P, Q, and R are to be integers that satisfy the inequalities $-4 \le x \le 5$ and $6 \le y \le 16$. How many different triangles with these properties could be constructed?

(A) 110
(B) 1,100
(C) 9,900
(D) 10,000
(E) 12,100

395. A box contains 100 balls, numbered from 1 to 100. If three balls are selected at random and with replacement from the box, what is the probability that the sum of the three numbers on the balls selected from the box will be odd?

(A) $\dfrac{1}{4}$

(B) $\dfrac{3}{8}$

(C) $\dfrac{1}{2}$

(D) $\dfrac{5}{8}$

(E) $\dfrac{3}{4}$

396. How many different positive integers are factors of 441 ?

(A) 4
(B) 6
(C) 7
(D) 9
(E) 11

397. Company K's earnings were $12 million last year. If this year's earnings are projected to be 150 percent greater than last year's earnings, what are Company K's projected earnings this year?

(A) $13.5 million
(B) $15 million
(C) $18 million
(D) $27 million
(E) $30 million

2, 4, 6, 8, n, 3, 5, 7, 9

398. In the list above, if n is an integer between 1 and 10, inclusive, then the median must be

(A) either 4 or 5
(B) either 5 or 6
(C) either 6 or 7
(D) n
(E) 5.5

399. If $0 < x < 1$, which of the following inequalities must be true?

    I. $x^5 < x^3$
    II. $x^4 + x^5 < x^3 + x^2$
    III. $x^4 - x^5 < x^2 - x^3$

(A) None
(B) I only
(C) II only
(D) I and II only
(E) I, II, and III

400. If $(2^x)(2^y) = 8$ and $(9^x)(3^y) = 81$, then $(x, y) =$

(A) (1, 2)
(B) (2, 1)
(C) (1, 1)
(D) (2, 2)
(E) (1, 3)

401. If $a = 1$ and $\dfrac{a-b}{c} = 1$, which of the following is NOT a possible value of b ?

(A) −2
(B) −1
(C) 0
(D) 1
(E) 2

402. Which of the following is equal to x^{18} for all positive values of x ?

(A) $x^9 + x^9$
(B) $(x^2)^9$
(C) $(x^9)^9$
(D) $(x^3)^{15}$
(E) $\dfrac{x^4}{x^{22}}$

403. A television manufacturer produces 600 units of a certain model each month at a cost to the manufacturer of \$90 per unit and all of the produced units are sold each month. What is the minimum selling price per unit that will ensure that the monthly profit (revenue from sales minus the manufacturer's cost to produce) on the sales of these units will be at least \$42,000 ?

(A) \$110
(B) \$120
(C) \$140
(D) \$160
(E) \$180

404. A square countertop has a square tile inlay in the center, leaving an untiled strip of uniform width around the tile. If the ratio of the tiled area to the untiled area is 25 to 39, which of the following could be the width, in inches, of the strip?

    I. $1\dfrac{1}{2}$
    II. 3
    III. $4\dfrac{1}{2}$

(A) I only
(B) II only
(C) I and II only
(D) I and III only
(E) I, II, and III

$$\begin{array}{r} 4 \,\square\, 7 \\ \triangle\, 2\ 3 \\ +\ 1\ 6\ 2 \\ \hline 1,\ 2\ 2\ 2 \end{array}$$

405. If $\square$ and $\triangle$ represent single digits in the correctly worked computation above, what is the value of $\square + \triangle$?

(A) 7
(B) 9
(C) 10
(D) 11
(E) 13

THE KLEIN FAMILY'S ANNUAL INCOME, 1985-1995

406. Which of the following statements can be inferred from the data above?

I.   The Klein family's annual income more than doubled from 1985 to 1995.

II. The Klein family's annual income increased by a greater amount from 1985 to 1990 than from 1990 to 1995.

III. The Klein family's average (arithmetic mean) annual income for the period shown was greater than $40,000.

(A) I only
(B) II only
(C) I and III only
(D) II and III only
(E) I, II, and III

407. Anne bought a computer for $2,000 and then paid a 5 percent sales tax, and Henry bought a computer for $1,800 and then paid a 12 percent sales tax. The total amount that Henry paid, including sales tax, was what percent less than the total amount that Anne paid, including sales tax?

(A)   3%
(B)   4%
(C)   7%
(D) 10%
(E) 12%

408. If $\dfrac{x}{y} = \dfrac{2}{3}$, then $\dfrac{x-y}{x} =$

(A) $-\dfrac{1}{2}$

(B) $-\dfrac{1}{3}$

(C) $\dfrac{1}{3}$

(D) $\dfrac{1}{2}$

(E) $\dfrac{5}{2}$

409. If $4x + 3y = -2$ and $3x + 6 = 0$, what is the value of y ?

(A) $-3\dfrac{1}{3}$

(B) -2

(C) $-\dfrac{2}{3}$

(D) $\dfrac{2}{3}$

(E) 2

I.   72, 73, 74, 75, 76
II. 74, 74, 74, 74, 74
III. 62, 74, 74, 74, 89

410. The data sets I, II, and III above are ordered from greatest standard deviation to least standard deviation in which of the following?

(A) I, II, III
(B) I, III, II
(C) II, III, I
(D) III, I, II
(E) III, II, I

411. The contents of a certain box consist of 14 apples and 23 oranges. How many oranges must be removed from the box so that 70 percent of the pieces of fruit in the box will be apples?

(A)   3
(B)   6
(C) 14
(D) 17
(E) 20

412. If n is a positive integer and n^2 is divisible by 72, then the largest positive integer that must divide n is

(A) 6
(B) 12
(C) 24
(D) 36
(E) 48

413. If -3 is 6 more than x, what is the value of $\frac{x}{3}$?

(A) -9
(B) -6
(C) -3
(D) -1
(E) 1

$$r = 400\left(\frac{D+S-P}{P}\right)$$

414. If stock is sold three months after it is purchased, the formula above relates P, D, S, and r, where P is the purchase price of the stock, D is the amount of any dividend received, S is the selling price of the stock, and r is the yield of the investment as a percent. If Rose purchased $400 worth of stock, received a dividend of $5, and sold the stock for $420 three months after purchasing it, what was the yield of her investment according to the formula? (Assume that she paid no commissions.)

(A) 1.25%
(B) 5%
(C) 6.25%
(D) 20%
(E) 25%

415. An athlete runs R miles in H hours, then rides a bicycle Q miles in the same number of hours. Which of the following represents the athlete's average speed, in miles per hour, for these two activities combined?

(A) $\dfrac{R-Q}{H}$

(B) $\dfrac{R-Q}{2H}$

(C) $\dfrac{2(R+Q)}{H}$

(D) $\dfrac{2(R+Q)}{2H}$

(E) $\dfrac{R+Q}{2H}$

416. If a certain sample of data has a mean of 20.0 and a standard deviation of 3.0, which of the following values is more than 2.5 standard deviations from the mean?

(A) 12.0
(B) 13.5
(C) 17.0
(D) 23.5
(E) 26.5

417. Which of the following is the least positive integer that is divisible by 2, 3, 4, 5, 6, 7, 8, and 9 ?

(A) 15,120
(B) 3,024
(C) 2,520
(D) 1,890
(E) 1,680

418. Of the 50 researchers in a workgroup, 40 percent will be assigned to team A and the remaining 60 percent to team B. However, 70 percent of the researchers prefer team A and 30 percent prefer team B. What is the least possible number of researchers who will NOT be assigned to the team they prefer?

(A) 15
(B) 17
(C) 20
(D) 25
(E) 30

419. Last year, a certain public transportation system sold an average (arithmetic mean) of 41,000 tickets per day on weekdays (Monday through Friday) and an average of 18,000 tickets per day on Saturday and Sunday. Which of the following is closest to the total number of tickets sold last year?

(A)   1 million
(B)   1.25 million
(C)   10 million
(D)   12.5 million
(E) 125 million

County	Amount Recycled	Amount Disposed of
A	16,700	142,800
B	8,800	48,000
C	13,000	51,400
D	3,900	20,300
E	3,300	16,200

District	Number of Votes	Percent of Votes for Candidate P	Percent of Votes for Candidate Q
1	800	60	40
2	1,000	50	50
3	1,500	50	50
4	1,800	40	60
5	1,200	30	70

420. The table above shows the amount of waste material, in tons, recycled by each of five counties in a single year and the amount of waste material, also in tons, that was disposed of in landfills by the five counties in that year. Which county had the lowest ratio of waste material disposed of to waste material recycled in the year reported in the table?

(A) A
(B) B
(C) C
(D) D
(E) E

421. If a number between 0 and $\frac{1}{2}$ is selected at random, which of the following will the number most likely be between?

(A) 0 and $\frac{3}{20}$

(B) $\frac{3}{20}$ and $\frac{1}{5}$

(C) $\frac{1}{5}$ and $\frac{1}{4}$

(D) $\frac{1}{4}$ and $\frac{3}{10}$

(E) $\frac{3}{10}$ and $\frac{1}{2}$

422. The table above shows the results of a recent school board election in which the candidate with the higher total number of votes from the five districts was declared the winner. Which district had the greatest number of votes for the winner?

(A) 1
(B) 2
(C) 3
(D) 4
(E) 5

423. If m is the average (arithmetic mean) of the first 10 positive multiples of 5 and if M is the median of the first 10 positive multiples of 5, what is the value of $M - m$?

(A) -5
(B) 0
(C) 5
(D) 25
(E) 27.5

424. If n is a positive integer less than 200 and $\frac{14n}{60}$ is an integer, then n has how many different positive prime factors?

(A) Two
(B) Three
(C) Five
(D) Six
(E) Eight

Day	Change in Dollars
Monday	$+1\frac{1}{2}$
Tuesday	$-\frac{3}{4}$
Wednesday	0
Thursday	$-\frac{1}{8}$
Friday	$+2\frac{1}{4}$

425. The table above shows the daily change in the price of a certain stock last week. What was the net change in dollars in the price of the stock for the week?

(A) $-4\frac{5}{8}$

(B) $-2\frac{7}{8}$

(C) $+2\frac{7}{8}$

(D) $+3\frac{3}{4}$

(E) $+4\frac{5}{8}$

426. A group of store managers must assemble 280 displays for an upcoming sale. If they assemble 25 percent of the displays during the first hour and 40 percent of the remaining displays during the second hour, how many of the displays will <u>not</u> have been assembled by the end of the second hour?

(A) 70
(B) 98
(C) 126
(D) 168
(E) 182

427. The temperatures in degrees Celsius recorded at 6 in the morning in various parts of a certain country were 10°, 5°, –2°, –1°, –5°, and 15°. What is the median of these temperatures?

(A) –2°C
(B) –1°C
(C) 2°C
(D) 3°C
(E) 5°C

428. In the figure above, what is the value of x ?

(A) 55
(B) 60
(C) 65
(D) 70
(E) 75

1	2	3	4	5	6	7
–2	–4	–6	–8	–10	–12	14
3	6	9	12	15	18	21
–4	–8	–12	–16	–20	–24	–28
5	10	15	20	25	30	35
–6	–12	–18	–24	–30	–36	–42
7	14	21	28	35	42	49

429. What is the sum of the integers in the table above?

(A) 28
(B) 112
(C) 336
(D) 448
(E) 784

430. If $m > 0$ and x is m percent of y, then, in terms of m, y is what percent of x ?

(A) $100m$

(B) $\dfrac{1}{100m}$

(C) $\dfrac{1}{m}$

(D) $\dfrac{10}{m}$

(E) $\dfrac{10,000}{m}$

$$3, k, 2, 8, m, 3$$

431. The arithmetic mean of the list of numbers above is 4. If k and m are integers and $k \neq m$, what is the median of the list?

(A) 2
(B) 2.5
(C) 3
(D) 3.5
(E) 4

432. A certain junior class has 1,000 students and a certain senior class has 800 students. Among these students, there are 60 sibling pairs, each consisting of 1 junior and 1 senior. If 1 student is to be selected at random from each class, what is the probability that the 2 students selected will be a sibling pair?

(A) $\dfrac{3}{40,000}$

(B) $\dfrac{1}{3,600}$

(C) $\dfrac{9}{2,000}$

(D) $\dfrac{1}{60}$

(E) $\dfrac{1}{15}$

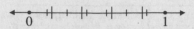

433. On the number line above, the segment from 0 to 1 has been divided into fifths, as indicated by the large tick marks, and also into sevenths, as indicated by the small tick marks. What is the least possible distance between any two of the tick marks?

(A) $\dfrac{1}{70}$

(B) $\dfrac{1}{35}$

(C) $\dfrac{2}{35}$

(D) $\dfrac{1}{12}$

(E) $\dfrac{1}{7}$

434. A certain musical scale has 13 notes, each having a different frequency, measured in cycles per second. In the scale, the notes are ordered by increasing frequency, and the highest frequency is twice the lowest. For each of the 12 lower frequencies, the ratio of a frequency to the next higher frequency is a fixed constant. If the lowest frequency is 440 cycles per second, then the frequency of the 7th note in the scale is how many cycles per second?

(A) $440\sqrt{2}$

(B) $440\sqrt{2^7}$

(C) $440\sqrt{2^{12}}$

(D) $440\sqrt[12]{2^7}$

(E) $440\sqrt[7]{2^{12}}$

435. If $a = 7$ and $b = -7$, what is the value of $2a - 2b + b^2$?

(A) -49
(B) 21
(C) 49
(D) 63
(E) 77

436. Equal amounts of water were poured into two empty jars of different capacities, which made one jar $\frac{1}{4}$ full and the other jar $\frac{1}{3}$ full. If the water in the jar with the lesser capacity is then poured into the jar with the greater capacity, what fraction of the larger jar will be filled with water?

(A) $\frac{1}{7}$

(B) $\frac{2}{7}$

(C) $\frac{1}{2}$

(D) $\frac{7}{12}$

(E) $\frac{2}{3}$

437. If Mel saved more than $10 by purchasing a sweater at a 15 percent discount, what is the smallest amount the original price of the sweater could be, to the nearest dollar?

(A) 45
(B) 67
(C) 75
(D) 83
(E) 150

438. Which of the following CANNOT be the median of the three positive integers x, y, and z ?

(A) x
(B) z
(C) $x + z$
(D) $\frac{x+z}{2}$
(E) $\frac{x+z}{3}$

439. $\dfrac{(8^2)(3^3)(2^4)}{96^2} =$

(A) 3
(B) 6
(C) 9
(D) 12
(E) 18

440. What is the 25th digit to the right of the decimal point in the decimal form of $\frac{6}{11}$?

(A) 3
(B) 4
(C) 5
(D) 6
(E) 7

441. Which of the following lists the number of points at which a circle can intersect a triangle?

(A) 2 and 6 only
(B) 2, 4, and 6 only
(C) 1, 2, 3, and 6 only
(D) 1, 2, 3, 4, and 6 only
(E) 1, 2, 3, 4, 5, and 6

Explanatory Material: Problem Solving

The following discussion is intended to familiarize you with the most efficient and effective approaches to the kinds of problems common to problem solving questions. The questions in this chapter are generally representative of the kinds of problems you will encounter in the GMAT®. Remember that it is the problem-solving strategy that is important, not the specific details of a particular problem.

1. If Mario was 32 years old 8 years ago, how old was he x years ago?

   (A) $x - 40$
   (B) $x - 24$
   (C) $40 - x$
   (D) $24 - x$
   (E) $24 + x$

Since Mario was 32 years old 8 years ago, his age now is $32 + 8 = 40$. x years ago, Mario was x years younger, so his age then was $40 - x$. Thus, the best answer is C.

2. Running at the same constant rate, 6 identical machines can produce a total of 270 bottles per minute. At this rate, how many bottles could 10 such machines produce in 4 minutes?

   (A)   648
   (B)   1,800
   (C)   2,700
   (D) 10,800
   (E) 64,800

The production rate of each machine is $\frac{270}{6} = 45$ bottles per minute. The production rate for 10 machines is $45(10) = 450$ bottles per minute. Therefore, the 10 machines can produce $450(4) = 1,800$ bottles in 4 minutes. The best answer is B.

3. Three business partners, Q, R, and S, agree to divide their total profit for a certain year in the ratios $2 : 5 : 8$, respectively. If Q's share was $4,000, what was the total profit of the business partners for the year?

   (A) $26,000
   (B) $30,000
   (C) $52,000
   (D) $60,000
   (E) $300,000

Based on the ratios $2 : 5 : 8$, the total profit T was divided as follows: $\frac{2}{15} T$ was given to Q, $\frac{5}{15} T$ was given to R, and $\frac{8}{15} T$ was given to S. Since $\frac{2}{15} T = \$4,000$, $T = \frac{15}{2} (4,000) = \$30,000$.

Therefore, the best answer is B.

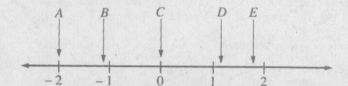

4. Of the five coordinates associated with points A, B, C, D, and E on the number line above, which has the greatest absolute value?

   (A) A
   (B) B
   (C) C
   (D) D
   (E) E

The absolute value of a number x may be thought of as the distance between x and 0 on the number line. By inspection of the five points, the coordinate of point A is farthest from 0 and thus has the greatest absolute value. Therefore, the best answer is A.

5. A restaurant meal cost $35.50 and there was no tax. If the tip was more than 10 percent but less than 15 percent of the cost of the meal, then the total amount paid must have been between

   (A) $40 and $42
   (B) $39 and $41
   (C) $38 and $40
   (D) $37 and $39
   (E) $36 and $37

If P is the total amount paid, then P must be greater than $35.50(1.1)$ but less than $35.50(1.15)$. That is, P is between $39.05 and $40.825. It follows that P must be between $39 and $41, which is choice B. Each of the other choices excludes a possible value of P. Thus, the best answer is B.

6. Harriet wants to put up fencing around three sides of her rectangular yard and leave a side of 20 feet unfenced. If the yard has an area of 680 square feet, how many feet of fencing does she need?

(A) 34
(B) 40
(C) 68
(D) 88
(E) 102

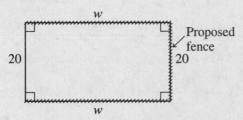

The diagram above shows the rectangular yard with the known dimension, 20 feet, and the unknown dimension, w feet. The area of the yard is $20w = 680$ square feet,

so $w = \dfrac{680}{20} = 34$ feet. The length of fencing needed is then

$34 + 20 + 34 = 88$ feet. Thus, the best answer is D.

7. If $u > t, r > q, s > t$, and $t > r$, which of the following must be true?

  I. $u > s$
  II. $s > q$
  III. $u > r$

(A) I only
(B) II only
(C) III only
(D) I and II
(E) II and III

The number line shown above is based on the given inequalities and may be helpful when I, II, and III are considered.

  I. It may be that $q = 0$, $r = 1$, $t = 2$, $u = 3$, and $s = 4$, so that $u > s$ is not necessarily true.

  II. Since $s > t$, $t > r$, and $r > q$, it follows that $s > q$.

  III. Since $u > t$ and $t > r$, it follows that $u > r$.

Since II and III must be true, the best answer is E.

8. Increasing the original price of an article by 15 percent and then increasing the new price by 15 percent is equivalent to increasing the original price by

(A) 32.25%
(B) 31.00%
(C) 30.25%
(D) 30.00%
(E) 22.50%

If p is the original price, then the 15 percent increase in price results in a price of $1.15p$. The next 15 percent increase in price results in a price of $1.15(1.15p)$, or $1.3225p$. Thus, the price increased by $1.3225p - p = 0.3225p$, or 32.25% of p. The best answer is A.

9. If k is an integer and 0.0010101×10^k is greater than 1,000, what is the least possible value of k ?

(A) 2
(B) 3
(C) 4
(D) 5
(E) 6

Since 0.0010101 is being multiplied by the kth power of 10, k is the number of decimal places that the decimal point in 0.0010101 will move to the right (if $k > 0$) in the product 0.0010101×10^k. By inspection, 6 is the least number of decimal places that the decimal point must move to the right in order for the product to be greater than 1,000. Thus, the best answer is E.

10. If $(b - 3)\left(4 + \dfrac{2}{b}\right) = 0$ and $b \neq 3$, then $b =$

(A) -8

(B) -2

(C) $-\dfrac{1}{2}$

(D) $\dfrac{1}{2}$

(E) 2

Since $(b - 3)\left(4 + \dfrac{2}{b}\right) = 0$, it follows that either $b - 3 = 0$ or

$4 + \dfrac{2}{b} = 0$. That is, either $b = 3$ or $b = -\dfrac{1}{2}$. But $b \neq 3$ is given,

so $b = -\dfrac{1}{2}$, and the best answer is C.

11. In a weight-lifting competition, the total weight of Joe's two lifts was 750 pounds. If twice the weight of his first lift was 300 pounds more than the weight of his second lift, what was the weight, in pounds, of his first lift?

(A) 225
(B) 275
(C) 325
(D) 350
(E) 400

Let F and S be the weights, in pounds, of Joe's first and second lifts, respectively. Then $F + S = 750$ and $2F = S + 300$. The second equation may be written as $S = 2F - 300$, and $2F - 300$ may be substituted for S in the first equation to get $F + (2F - 300) = 750$. Thus, $3F = 1,050$, or $F = 350$ pounds, and the best answer is D.

12. One hour after Yolanda started walking from X to Y, a distance of 45 miles, Bob started walking along the same road from Y to X. If Yolanda's walking rate was 3 miles per hour and Bob's was 4 miles per hour, how many miles had Bob walked when they met?

(A) 24
(B) 23
(C) 22
(D) 21
(E) 19.5

Let t be the number of hours that Bob had walked when he met Yolanda. Then, when they met, Bob had walked $4t$ miles and Yolanda had walked $3(t + 1)$ miles. These distances must sum to 45 miles, so $4t + 3(t + 1) = 45$, which may be solved for t as follows.
$$4t + 3(t + 1) = 45$$
$$4t + 3t + 3 = 45$$
$$7t = 42$$
$$t = 6 \text{ (hours)}$$

Therefore, Bob had walked $4t = 4(6) = 24$ miles when they met. The best answer is A.

13. The average (arithmetic mean) of 6 numbers is 8.5. When one number is discarded, the average of the remaining numbers becomes 7.2. What is the discarded number?

(A) 7.8
(B) 9.8
(C) 10.0
(D) 12.4
(E) 15.0

The sum of the 6 numbers is $6(8.5) = 51.0$; the sum of the 5 remaining numbers is $5(7.2) = 36.0$. Thus, the discarded number must be $51.0 - 36.0 = 15.0$, and the best answer is E.

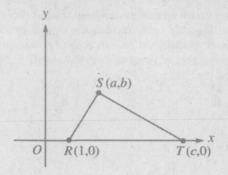

14. In the rectangular coordinate system above, the area of $\triangle RST$ is

(A) $\dfrac{bc}{2}$

(B) $\dfrac{b(c - 1)}{2}$

(C) $\dfrac{c(b - 1)}{2}$

(D) $\dfrac{a(c - 1)}{2}$

(E) $\dfrac{c(a - 1)}{2}$

If segment RT is chosen as the base of $\triangle RST$, then the height is b, the y-coordinate of point S. Since $RT = c - 1$ (the difference between the x-coordinates of R and T), the area of $\triangle RST$ is $\frac{1}{2}(RT)b = \frac{1}{2}(c - 1)b$, and the best answer is B.

15. Which of the following equations has a root in common with $x^2 - 6x + 5 = 0$?

(A) $x^2 + 1 = 0$
(B) $x^2 - x - 2 = 0$
(C) $x^2 - 10x - 5 = 0$
(D) $2x^2 - 2 = 0$
(E) $x^2 - 2x - 3 = 0$

Since $x^2 - 6x + 5 = (x - 5)(x - 1)$, the roots of $x^2 - 6x + 5 = 0$ are 1 and 5. When these two values are substituted in each of the five choices to determine whether or not they satisfy the equation, only in choice D does a value satisfy the equation, namely, $2(1)^2 - 2 = 0$. Thus, the best answer is D.

16. One inlet pipe fills an empty tank in 5 hours. A second inlet pipe fills the same tank in 3 hours. If both pipes are used together, how long will it take to fill $\frac{2}{3}$ of the tank?

(A) $\frac{8}{15}$ hr

(B) $\frac{3}{4}$ hr

(C) $\frac{5}{4}$ hr

(D) $\frac{15}{8}$ hr

(E) $\frac{8}{3}$ hr

Since the first pipe fills $\frac{1}{5}$ of the tank in one hour and the second pipe fills $\frac{1}{3}$ of the tank in one hour, together they fill $\frac{1}{5} + \frac{1}{3} = \frac{8}{15}$ of the tank in one hour. At this rate, if t is the number of hours needed to fill $\frac{2}{3}$ of the tank, then $\frac{8}{15}t = \frac{2}{3}$, or $t = \frac{2}{3}\left(\frac{15}{8}\right) = \frac{5}{4}$ hours. Thus, the best answer is C.

17. During the first week of September, a shoe retailer sold 10 pairs of a certain style of oxfords at $35.00 a pair. If, during the second week of September, 15 pairs were sold at the sale price of $27.50 a pair, by what amount did the revenue from weekly sales of these oxfords increase during the second week?

(A) $62.50
(B) $75.00
(C) $112.50
(D) $137.50
(E) $175.00

The total sales revenue from the oxfords during the first week was 10($35.00) = $350.00, and during the second week it was 15($27.50) = $412.50. Thus, the increase in sales revenue was $412.50 – $350.00 = $62.50, and the best answer is A.

18. The number 2 – 0.5 is how many times the number 1 – 0.5 ?

(A) 2
(B) 2.5
(C) 3
(D) 3.5
(E) 4

Since 2 – 0.5 = 1.5 and 1 – 0.5 = 0.5, the number 2 – 0.5 is $\frac{1.5}{0.5} = 3$ times the number 1 – 0.5. Thus, the best answer is C.

19. If $x = -1$, then $-(x^4 + x^3 + x^2 + x) =$

(A) –10
(B) –4
(C)   0
(D)   4
(E) 10

$-((-1)^4 + (-1)^3 + (-1)^2 + (-1)) = -(1 - 1 + 1 - 1) = -0 = 0$. The best answer is C.

20. Coins are dropped into a toll box so that the box is being filled at the rate of approximately 2 cubic feet per hour. If the empty rectangular box is 4 feet long, 4 feet wide, and 3 feet deep, approximately how many hours does it take to fill the box?

(A)   4
(B)   8
(C) 16
(D) 24
(E) 48

The volume of the toll box is (4)(4)(3) = 48 cubic feet. Since the box is filled at the rate of 2 cubic feet per hour, it takes $\frac{48}{2} = 24$ hours to fill the box. Thus, the best answer is D.

21. $\left(\dfrac{1}{5}\right)^2 - \left(\dfrac{1}{5}\right)\left(\dfrac{1}{4}\right) =$

(A) $-\dfrac{1}{20}$

(B) $-\dfrac{1}{100}$

(C) $\dfrac{1}{100}$

(D) $\dfrac{1}{20}$

(E) $\dfrac{1}{5}$

$\left(\dfrac{1}{5}\right)^2 - \left(\dfrac{1}{5}\right)\left(\dfrac{1}{4}\right) = \dfrac{1}{25} - \dfrac{1}{20} = \dfrac{4}{100} - \dfrac{5}{100} = -\dfrac{1}{100}$. Thus, the best answer is B.

22. A club collected exactly $599 from its members. If each member contributed at least $12, what is the greatest number of members the club could have?

(A) 43
(B) 44
(C) 49
(D) 50
(E) 51

If n is the number of members in the club, then at least $12n$ dollars, but perhaps more, was contributed. Thus, $12n \leq 599$, or $n \leq \dfrac{599}{12} = 49\dfrac{11}{12}$. Since n is a whole number, the greatest possible value of n is 49. Therefore, the best answer is C.

23. A union contract specifies a 6 percent salary increase plus a $450 bonus for each employee. For a certain employee, this is equivalent to an 8 percent salary increase. What was this employee's salary before the new contract?

(A) $21,500
(B) $22,500
(C) $23,500
(D) $24,300
(E) $25,000

If S is the employee's salary before the new contract, then the increase in the employee's earnings is $450 plus 6 percent of S, or $450 + 0.06S$. Since this increase is 8 percent of S, it follows that $450 + 0.06S = 0.08S$, or $0.02S = 450, so that $S = \dfrac{\$450}{0.02} = \$22,500$. Thus, the best answer is B.

24. If n is a positive integer and $k + 2 = 3^n$, which of the following could NOT be a value of k ?

(A) 1
(B) 4
(C) 7
(D) 25
(E) 79

As each of the choices is substituted for k, the sum $k + 2$ can be examined to determine whether or not it is a power of 3. The sums corresponding to A-E are 3, 6, 9, 27, and 81, respectively. Note that $3 = 3^1$, $9 = 3^2$, $27 = 3^3$, and $81 = 3^4$, but 6 is not a power of 3. So 4 cannot be a value of k, whereas 1, 7, 25, and 79 can be values of k. Thus, the best answer is B.

Alternatively, since any power of 3 must be odd, $k = 3^n - 2$ must also be odd and $k = 4$ is not possible.

25. Elena purchased brand X pens for $4.00 apiece and brand Y pens for $2.80 apiece. If Elena purchased a total of 12 of these pens for $42.00, how many brand X pens did she purchase?

(A) 4
(B) 5
(C) 6
(D) 7
(E) 8

Let x denote the number of brand X pens Elena purchased. Then the number of brand Y pens she purchased was $12 - x$ and the total cost of the pens was $4x + 2.80(12 - x) = 42.00$ dollars. This equation can be solved as follows.

$$4x + 2.80(12 - x) = 42.00$$
$$4x + 33.60 - 2.80x = 42.00$$
$$1.20x = 8.40$$
$$x = 7$$

Thus, the best answer is D.

26. If the length and width of a rectangular garden plot were each increased by 20 percent, what would be the percent increase in the area of the plot?

(A) 20%
(B) 24%
(C) 36%
(D) 40%
(E) 44%

If the length and width are L and W, respectively, then the increased length and width are $1.2L$ and $1.2W$, respectively. Thus, the increased area is $(1.2L)(1.2W) = 1.44LW$, and the percent increase in area is 44%. The best answer is therefore E.

27. The population of a bacteria culture doubles every 2 minutes. Approximately how many minutes will it take for the population to grow from 1,000 to 500,000 bacteria?

(A) 10
(B) 12
(C) 14
(D) 16
(E) 18

After each successive 2-minute period, the bacteria population is 2,000, 4,000, 8,000, 16,000, 32,000, 64,000, 128,000, 256,000, and then 512,000. Therefore, after eight 2-minute periods, or 16 minutes, the population is only 256,000; and after nine 2-minute periods, or 18 minutes, the population is just over 500,000. Thus, the best answer is E.

Alternatively, if n denotes the number of 2-minute periods it takes for the population to grow from 1,000 to 500,000, then $2^n(1,000) = 500,000$, or $2^n = 500$. Since $2^4 = 16$, $2^8 = 16^2 = 256$, and $2^9 = 2(256) = 512$, the value of n is approximately 9. Thus, the approximate time is $2(9) = 18$ minutes.

28. When 10 is divided by the positive integer n, the remainder is $n - 4$. Which of the following could be the value of n ?

(A) 3
(B) 4
(C) 7
(D) 8
(E) 12

One way to answer the question is to examine each option to see which one satisfies the specified divisibility conditions. A: If $n = 3$, then $n - 4 = -1$; but 10 divided by 3 has remainder 1. B: If $n = 4$, then $n - 4 = 0$; but 10 divided by 4 has remainder 2. C: If $n = 7$, then $n - 4 = 3$, which does equal the remainder when 10 is divided by 7. That neither D nor E gives a possible value of n can be shown in the manner used for A and B. Thus, the best answer is C.

An alternative solution, which does not involve extensive checking of each option, is to first write the divisibility condition as the equation $10 = nq + (n - 4)$, where q denotes the quotient. Then,
$$14 = nq + n = n(q + 1),$$
so n must be a divisor of 14. Also, $n - 4 \geq 0$, or $n \geq 4$. Thus, $n = 7$ or $n = 14$.

29. For a light that has an intensity of 60 candles at its source, the intensity in candles, S, of the light at a point d feet from the source is given by the formula $S = \dfrac{60k}{d^2}$, where k is a constant. If the intensity of the light is 30 candles at a distance of 2 feet from the source, what is the intensity of the light at a distance of 20 feet from the source?

(A) $\dfrac{3}{10}$ candle

(B) $\dfrac{1}{2}$ candle

(C) $1\dfrac{1}{3}$ candles

(D) 2 candles

(E) 3 candles

In order to compute $S = \dfrac{60k}{d^2}$ when $d = 20$, the value of the constant k must be determined. Since $S = 30$ candles when $d = 2$ feet, substituting these values into the formula yields $30 = \dfrac{60k}{2^2}$, or $k = 2$. Therefore, when $d = 20$ feet, the intensity is $S = \dfrac{60(2)}{20^2} = \dfrac{120}{400} = \dfrac{3}{10}$ candle. Thus, the best answer is A.

30. If x and y are prime numbers, which of the following CANNOT be the sum of x and y ?

(A) 5
(B) 9
(C) 13
(D) 16
(E) 23

Note that $5 = 2 + 3$, $9 = 2 + 7$, $13 = 2 + 11$, and $16 = 5 + 11$, so that each of choices A-D may be expressed as a sum of two prime numbers. However, if $23 = x + y$, then either x or y (but not both) must be even. Since 2 is the only even prime number, either $x = 2$ and $y = 21$, or $x = 21$ and $y = 2$. Since 21 is not prime, 23 cannot be expressed as the sum of two prime numbers, and the best answer is E.

31. Of the 3,600 employees of Company X, $\frac{1}{3}$ are clerical.

If the clerical staff were to be reduced by $\frac{1}{3}$, what percent of the total number of the remaining employees would then be clerical?

(A) 25%
(B) 22.2%
(C) 20%
(D) 12.5%
(E) 11.1%

The number of clerical employees is $\frac{1}{3}(3,600) = 1,200$. As a result of the proposed reduction, the number of clerical employees would be reduced by $\frac{1}{3}(1,200) = 400$ and consequently would equal $1,200 - 400 = 800$. The total number of employees would then be $3,600 - 400 = 3,200$. Hence, the percent of clerical employees would then be $\frac{800}{3,200} = \frac{1}{4} = 25\%$. Thus, the best answer is A.

32. In which of the following pairs are the two numbers reciprocals of each other?

I.   3 and $\frac{1}{3}$

II. $\frac{1}{17}$ and $\frac{-1}{17}$

III. $\sqrt{3}$ and $\frac{\sqrt{3}}{3}$

(A) I only
(B) II only
(C) I and II
(D) I and III
(E) II and III

Two numbers are reciprocals of each other if and only if their product is 1. Since $3\left(\frac{1}{3}\right) = 1$, $\left(\frac{1}{17}\right)\left(-\frac{1}{17}\right) = -\frac{1}{289} \neq 1$, and $\sqrt{3}\left(\frac{\sqrt{3}}{3}\right) = \frac{3}{3} = 1$, only in I and III are the two numbers reciprocals of each other. Thus, the best answer is D.

33. What is 45 percent of $\frac{7}{12}$ of 240 ?

(A) 63
(B) 90
(C) 108
(D) 140
(E) 311

Since 45 percent is $\frac{45}{100} = \frac{9}{20}$, 45 percent of $\frac{7}{12}$ of 240 is $\left(\frac{9}{20}\right)\left(\frac{7}{12}\right)(240) = 63$. The best answer is A.

34. If x books cost \$5 each and y books cost \$8 each, then the average (arithmetic mean) cost, in dollars per book, is equal to

(A) $\dfrac{5x + 8y}{x + y}$

(B) $\dfrac{5x + 8y}{xy}$

(C) $\dfrac{5x + 8y}{13}$

(D) $\dfrac{40xy}{x + y}$

(E) $\dfrac{40xy}{13}$

The total number of books is $x + y$, and their total cost is $5x + 8y$ dollars. Therefore, the average cost per book is $\dfrac{5x + 8y}{x + y}$ dollars. The best answer is A.

35. If $\frac{1}{2}$ of the money in a certain trust fund was invested in stocks, $\frac{1}{4}$ in bonds, $\frac{1}{5}$ in a mutual fund, and the remaining $10,000 in a government certificate, what was the total amount of the trust fund?

(A) $100,000
(B) $150,000
(C) $200,000
(D) $500,000
(E) $2,000,000

Since $\frac{1}{2} + \frac{1}{4} + \frac{1}{5} = \frac{19}{20}$, then $\frac{19}{20}$ of the trust fund was invested in stocks, bonds, and a mutual fund. Thus, if F is the dollar amount of the trust fund, the remaining $\frac{1}{20}$ of F is $10,000. That is, $\frac{1}{20}F = \$10,000$, or $F = \$200,000$. The best answer is therefore C.

36. Marion rented a car for $18.00 plus $0.10 per mile driven. Craig rented a car for $25.00 plus $0.05 per mile driven. If each drove d miles and each was charged exactly the same amount for the rental, then d equals

(A) 100
(B) 120
(C) 135
(D) 140
(E) 150

Marion's total rental charge was $18.00 + 0.10d$ dollars, and Craig's total rental charge was $25.00 + 0.05d$ dollars. Since these amounts are the same, $18.00 + 0.10d = 25.00 + 0.05d$, which implies $0.05d = 7.00$, or $d = \dfrac{7.00}{0.05} = 140$ miles. Thus, the best answer is D.

37. Machine A produces bolts at a uniform rate of 120 every 40 seconds, and machine B produces bolts at a uniform rate of 100 every 20 seconds. If the two machines run simultaneously, how many seconds will it take for them to produce a total of 200 bolts?

(A) 22
(B) 25
(C) 28
(D) 32
(E) 56

Machine A produces $\dfrac{120}{40} = 3$ bolts per second and machine B produces $\dfrac{100}{20} = 5$ bolts per second. Running simultaneously, they produce 8 bolts per second. At this rate, they will produce 200 bolts in $\dfrac{200}{8} = 25$ seconds. The best answer is therefore B.

38. $\dfrac{3.003}{2.002} =$

(A) 1.05
(B) 1.50015
(C) 1.501
(D) 1.5015
(E) 1.5

$\dfrac{3.003}{2.002} = \dfrac{3(1.001)}{2(1.001)} = \dfrac{3}{2} = 1.5$

The best answer is E.

Questions 39-41 refer to the following graph.

AVERAGE COSTS OF OPERATING SUBCOMPACT, COMPACT, AND MIDSIZE CARS IN THE UNITED STATES, 1982-1986

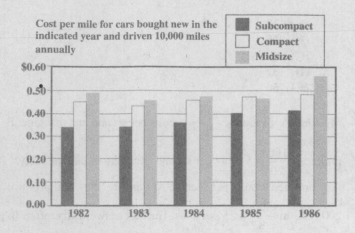

39. In 1982 the approximate average cost of operating a subcompact car for 10,000 miles was

(A) $360
(B) $3,400
(C) $4,100
(D) $4,500
(E) $4,900

According to the bar graph, the average cost per mile of operating a subcompact car in 1982 was about $0.34. Thus, the cost of operating the car for 10,000 miles was approximately $0.34(10,000) = $3,400. The best answer is B.

40. In 1984 the average cost of operating a subcompact car was approximately what percent less than the average cost of operating a midsized car?

(A)   12%
(B)   20%
(C)   25%
(D)   33%
(E)   48%

According to the bars shown for 1984, the average operating cost per mile for a subcompact car was approximately $0.36, or $0.12 less than the $0.48 per mile for a midsized car. Thus, in 1984 the operating cost for a subcompact car was approximately $\frac{0.12}{0.48} = 25\%$ less than the operating cost for a midsized car. The best answer is C.

41. For each of the years shown, the average cost per mile of operating a compact car minus the average cost per mile of operating a subcompact car was between

(A) $0.12 and $0.18
(B) $0.10 and $0.15
(C) $0.09 and $0.13
(D) $0.06 and $0.12
(E) $0.05 and $0.08

The differences in the average operating cost per mile between a subcompact car and a compact car may be estimated from the bar graph. For the consecutive years 1982-1986, the differences were approximately $0.11, $0.09, $0.10, $0.07, and $0.07, respectively. Only choice D gives a range that includes all of these amounts. Thus, the best answer is D.

Alternatively, inspection of the bar graph reveals that the largest difference was about $0.11 (in 1982) and the smallest difference was about $0.07 (in 1985 or 1986). Only choice D gives a range that includes these extreme values, and thus the differences for all five years.

42. What is the decimal equivalent of $\left(\frac{1}{5}\right)^5$?

(A)   0.00032
(B)   0.0016
(C)   0.00625
(D)   0.008
(E)   0.03125

$$\left(\frac{1}{5}\right)^5 = (0.2)^5 = (0.2)(0.2)(0.2)(0.2)(0.2) = 0.00032$$

The best answer is A.

43. Two hundred gallons of fuel oil are purchased at $0.91 per gallon and are consumed at a rate of $0.70 worth of fuel per hour. At this rate, how many hours are required to consume the 200 gallons of fuel oil?

(A)   140
(B)   220
(C)   260
(D)   322
(E)   330

The total worth of the 200 gallons of fuel oil is $0.91(200) = $182.00. The time required to consume the $182.00 worth of fuel at a rate of $0.70 worth of fuel per hour is $\frac{\$182.00}{\$0.70} = 260$ hours. Therefore, the best answer is C.

44. If $\dfrac{4-x}{2+x} = x$, what is the value of $x^2 + 3x - 4$?

(A) −4
(B) −1
(C) 0
(D) 1
(E) 2

Multiplying both sides of $\dfrac{4-x}{2+x} = x$ by $2 + x$ yields

$4 - x = x(2 + x) = 2x + x^2$, or $x^2 + 3x - 4 = 0$. Thus, the value of $x^2 + 3x - 4$ is 0, and the best answer is C.

45. If $b < 2$ and $2x - 3b = 0$, which of the following must be true?

(A) $x > -3$
(B) $x < 2$
(C) $x = 3$
(D) $x < 3$
(E) $x > 3$

It follows from $2x - 3b = 0$ that $b = \dfrac{2}{3}x$. So $b < 2$ implies

$\dfrac{2}{3}x < 2$, or $x < 2\left(\dfrac{3}{2}\right)$, which means $x < 3$ (choice D). Since none of the other choices must be true (although $x > -3$ and $x < 2$ could be true), the best answer is D.

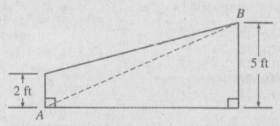

46. The trapezoid shown in the figure above represents a cross section of the rudder of a ship. If the distance from A to B is 13 feet, what is the area of the cross section of the rudder in square feet?

(A) 39
(B) 40
(C) 42
(D) 45
(E) 46.5

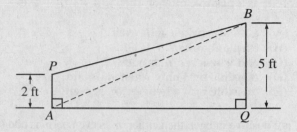

From the figure above, the area of the trapezoidal cross section is $\dfrac{1}{2}(AP + BQ)(AQ) = \dfrac{1}{2}(2 + 5)(AQ) = \dfrac{7}{2}(AQ)$. Since $AB = 13$ feet, using the Pythagorean theorem,

$AQ = \sqrt{13^2 - 5^2} = \sqrt{144} = 12$ feet. Thus, the area is

$\dfrac{7}{2}(12) = 42$ square feet, and the best answer is C.

Alternatively, the areas of the two triangles may be added together. If AP is taken as the base of $\triangle APB$ and BQ is taken as the base of $\triangle BQA$, then the height of both triangles is AQ. Thus, the area of the trapezoid is

$\dfrac{1}{2}(AP)(AQ) + \dfrac{1}{2}(BQ)(AQ) = \dfrac{1}{2}(2)(12) + \dfrac{1}{2}(5)(12) = 42$

square feet.

47. $\dfrac{(-1.5)(1.2) - (4.5)(0.4)}{30} =$

(A) −1.2
(B) −0.12
(C) 0
(D) 0.12
(E) 1.2

One way to reduce the expression is

$\dfrac{(-1.5)(1.2) - (4.5)(0.4)}{30} = \dfrac{-1.80 - 1.80}{30} = \dfrac{-3.60}{30} = -0.12$.

Another way is

$\dfrac{(-1.5)(1.2) - (4.5)(0.4)}{30} = -\dfrac{15(12) + 45(4)}{3,000} = -\dfrac{12 + 3(4)}{200}$

$= -\dfrac{24}{200} = -\dfrac{12}{100} = -0.12$

The best answer is B.

48. If n is a positive integer, then $n(n + 1)(n + 2)$ is

(A) even only when n is even
(B) even only when n is odd
(C) odd whenever n is odd
(D) divisible by 3 only when n is odd
(E) divisible by 4 whenever n is even

If n is a positive integer, then either n is even or n is odd (and thus $n + 1$ is even). In either case, the product $n(n + 1)(n + 2)$ is even. Thus, each of choices A, B, and C is false. Since $n(n + 1)(n + 2)$ is divisible by 3 when n is 6 (or any even multiple of 3), choice D is false. If n is even, then $n + 2$ is even as well; thus, $n(n + 1)(n + 2)$ is divisible by 4 since even numbers are divisible by 2. The best answer is therefore E.

49. If Jack had twice the amount of money that he has, he would have exactly the amount necessary to buy 3 hamburgers at $0.96 apiece and 2 milk shakes at $1.28 apiece. How much money does Jack have?

(A) $1.60
(B) $2.24
(C) $2.72
(D) $3.36
(E) $5.44

Let J be the amount of money Jack has. Then

$2J = 3(\$0.96) + 2(\$1.28) = \$5.44$. So $J = \dfrac{1}{2}(\$5.44) = \$2.72$,

and the best answer is C.

50. If a photocopier makes 2 copies in $\dfrac{1}{3}$ second, then, at the same rate, how many copies does it make in 4 minutes?

(A)   360
(B)   480
(C)   576
(D)   720
(E) 1,440

The photocopier makes copies at the rate of 2 copies in $\dfrac{1}{3}$ second, or 6 copies per second. Since 4 minutes equals 240 seconds, the photocopier makes $6(240) = 1,440$ copies in 4 minutes. Therefore, the best answer is E.

51. The price of a certain television set is discounted by 10 percent, and the reduced price is then discounted by 10 percent. This series of successive discounts is equivalent to a single discount of

(A) 20%
(B) 19%
(C) 18%
(D) 11%
(E) 10%

If P is the original price of the television set, then $0.9P$ is the price after the first discount, and $0.9(0.9P) = 0.81P$ is the price after the second discount. Thus, the original price is discounted by 19% $(100\% - 81\%)$, and the best answer is B.

52. If $\dfrac{2}{1 + \dfrac{2}{y}} = 1$, then $y =$

(A) -2

(B) $-\dfrac{1}{2}$

(C) $\dfrac{1}{2}$

(D) 2

(E) 3

Since $\dfrac{2}{1 + \dfrac{2}{y}} = 1$, $1 + \dfrac{2}{y} = 2$. Thus, $\dfrac{2}{y} = 1$, or $y = 2$, and the best answer is D.

53. If a rectangular photograph that is 10 inches wide by 15 inches long is to be enlarged so that the width will be 22 inches and the ratio of width to length will be unchanged, then the length, in inches, of the enlarged photograph will be

(A) 33
(B) 32
(C) 30
(D) 27
(E) 25

The ratio of width to length of the original photograph is

$\dfrac{10}{15} = \dfrac{2}{3}$. If x is the length of the enlarged photograph, in

inches, then $\dfrac{2}{3} = \dfrac{22}{x}$ since the ratio of width to length will be

unchanged. Thus, $x = 33$ inches, and the best answer is A.

54. If m is an integer such that $(-2)^{2m} = 2^{9-m}$, then $m =$

(A) 1
(B) 2
(C) 3
(D) 4
(E) 6

Since $(-2)^{2m} = ((-2)^2)^m = 4^m = 2^{2m}$, it follows that $2^{2m} = 2^{9-m}$. The exponents must be equal, so that $2m = 9 - m$, or $m = 3$. The best answer is therefore C.

55. If $0 \leq x \leq 4$ and $y < 12$, which of the following CANNOT be the value of xy ?

(A) -2
(B) 0
(C) 6
(D) 24
(E) 48

Each of choices A, B, and C can be a value of xy. For if $x = 1$, then $xy = y$, and each of these choices is less than 12. If $x = 4$ and $y = 6$, then $xy = 24$, so that choice D also gives a possible value of xy. In choice E, if $xy = 48$, then for all values of x such that $0 < x \leq 4$, it follows that $y \geq 12$, which contradicts $y < 12$. Thus, 48 cannot be the value of xy, and the best answer is E.

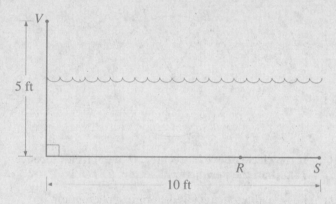

56. In the figure above, V represents an observation point at one end of a pool. From V, an object that is actually located on the bottom of the pool at point R appears to be at point S. If $VR = 10$ feet, what is the distance RS, in feet, between the actual position and the perceived position of the object?

(A) $10 - 5\sqrt{3}$

(B) $10 - 5\sqrt{2}$

(C) 2

(D) $2\frac{1}{2}$

(E) 4

Let P be the point 5 feet directly below V. P is the vertex of the right angle indicated in the figure, and $\triangle VPR$ is thus a right triangle. Then, by the Pythagorean theorem,

$$PR = \sqrt{10^2 - 5^2} = \sqrt{75} = 5\sqrt{3}. \text{ Thus,}$$

$RS = PS - PR = 10 - 5\sqrt{3}$, and the best answer is A.

57. If the total payroll expense of a certain business in year Y was \$84,000, which was 20 percent more than in year X, what was the total payroll expense in year X ?

(A) \$70,000
(B) \$68,320
(C) \$64,000
(D) \$60,000
(E) \$52,320

If p is the total payroll expense in year X, then $1.2p = \$84,000$,

so that $p = \dfrac{\$84,000}{1.2} = \$70,000$. Thus, the best answer is A.

58. If a, b, and c are consecutive positive integers and $a < b < c$, which of the following must be true?

I. $c - a = 2$

II. abc is an even integer.

III. $\dfrac{a + b + c}{3}$ is an integer.

(A) I only
(B) II only
(C) I and II only
(D) II and III only
(E) I, II, and III

Since a, b, and c are consecutive integers and $a < b < c$, it follows that $b = a + 1$ and $c = a + 2$. Statement I follows from $c = a + 2$. Concerning statement II, if a is even, then abc is even; if a is odd, then b is even so that abc is even. In either case, abc is even, so statement II must be true. In statement III,

$$\frac{a + b + c}{3} = \frac{a + (a + 1) + (a + 2)}{3} = \frac{3a + 3}{3} = a + 1 = b,$$

which is an integer. Therefore, statement III must be true, and the best answer is E.

59. A straight pipe 1 yard in length was marked off in fourths and also in thirds. If the pipe was then cut into separate pieces at each of these markings, which of the following gives all the different lengths of the pieces, in fractions of a yard?

(A) $\frac{1}{6}$ and $\frac{1}{4}$ only

(B) $\frac{1}{4}$ and $\frac{1}{3}$ only

(C) $\frac{1}{6}$, $\frac{1}{4}$, and $\frac{1}{3}$

(D) $\frac{1}{12}$, $\frac{1}{6}$, and $\frac{1}{4}$

(E) $\frac{1}{12}$, $\frac{1}{6}$, and $\frac{1}{3}$

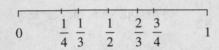

The number line above illustrates the markings on the pipe. Since the pipe is cut at the five markings, six pieces of pipe are produced having lengths, in yards,

$$\frac{1}{4} - 0 = \frac{1}{4}, \ \frac{1}{3} - \frac{1}{4} = \frac{1}{12}, \ \frac{1}{2} - \frac{1}{3} = \frac{1}{6}, \ \frac{2}{3} - \frac{1}{2} = \frac{1}{6},$$

$\frac{3}{4} - \frac{2}{3} = \frac{1}{12}$, and $1 - \frac{3}{4} = \frac{1}{4}$. The different lengths of the pieces are therefore $\frac{1}{12}$, $\frac{1}{6}$, and $\frac{1}{4}$ yard, and the best answer is D.

60. What is the least integer that is a sum of three different primes each greater than 20 ?

(A) 69
(B) 73
(C) 75
(D) 79
(E) 83

The three smallest primes that are each greater than 20 are 23, 29, and 31, and their sum is 83. Since any other set of three primes, each greater than 20, would include a prime greater than 31 but no prime less than 23, the corresponding sum would be greater than 83. Thus, 83 is the least such sum, and the best answer is E.

61. A tourist purchased a total of $1,500 worth of traveler's checks in $10 and $50 denominations. During the trip the tourist cashed 7 checks and then lost all of the rest. If the number of $10 checks cashed was one more or one less than the number of $50 checks cashed, what is the minimum possible value of the checks that were lost?

(A) $1,430
(B) $1,310
(C) $1,290
(D) $1,270
(E) $1,150

Let t be the number of $10 traveler's checks that were cashed and let f be the number of $50 traveler's checks that were cashed. Then $t + f = 7$, and either $t = f + 1$ or $t = f - 1$. Thus, either $t = 4$ and $f = 3$, or $t = 3$ and $f = 4$. In the first case, the value of the lost checks would have been $1,500 - t(\$10) - f(\$50) = \$1,500 - \$40 - \$150 = \$1,310$; whereas, in the second case, the value would have been $1,500 - \$30 - \$200 = \$1,270$. Since the lesser of these amounts is $1,270, the best answer is D.

Alternatively, note that the minimum possible value of the lost checks corresponds to the maximum possible value of the checks that were cashed. Thus, $t = 3$ and $f = 4$, and the minimum possible value of the lost checks is $1,500 - \$30 - \$200 = \$1,270$.

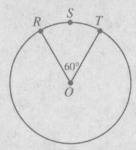

62. If the circle above has center O and circumference 18π, then the perimeter of sector $RSTO$ is

(A) $3\pi + 9$
(B) $3\pi + 18$
(C) $6\pi + 9$
(D) $6\pi + 18$
(E) $6\pi + 24$

If r is the radius of the circle, then the circumference is $2\pi r = 18\pi$, so that $r = 9$. The ratio of the length of arc RST to the circumference is the same as the ratio of $60°$ to $360°$. Thus, the length of arc RST is $\frac{60}{360}(18\pi) = 3\pi$, and, consequently, the perimeter of sector $RSTO$ is $3\pi + r + r = 3\pi + 18$. The best answer is therefore B.

63. If each of the following fractions were written as a repeating decimal, which would have the longest sequence of different digits?

(A) $\dfrac{2}{11}$

(B) $\dfrac{1}{3}$

(C) $\dfrac{41}{99}$

(D) $\dfrac{2}{3}$

(E) $\dfrac{23}{37}$

As repeating decimals, choices A-E are $\dfrac{2}{11} = 0.181818\ldots$, $\dfrac{1}{3} = 0.333\ldots$, $\dfrac{41}{99} = 0.414141\ldots$, $\dfrac{2}{3} = 0.666\ldots$, and $\dfrac{23}{37} = 0.621621621\ldots$, respectively. The longest sequence of different digits appears in the last decimal, so the best answer is E.

64. Today Rose is twice as old as Sam and Sam is 3 years younger than Tina. If Rose, Sam, and Tina are all alive 4 years from today, which of the following must be true on that day?

    I. Rose is twice as old as Sam.
   II. Sam is 3 years younger than Tina.
  III. Rose is older than Tina.

(A) I only
(B) II only
(C) III only
(D) I and II
(E) II and III

When considering the relationships between people's ages, it may be helpful to keep in mind the fact that the difference between two ages remains constant from one year to the next, but their ratio does not. Thus, statement I need not be true, whereas statement II must be true. For statement III, if R, S, and T denote the respective ages of Rose, Sam, and Tina today, then $R = 2S$ and $S = T - 3$, so that $R = 2(T - 3)$. Thus, $R > T$ if and only if $2(T - 3) > T$, or $T > 6$. Therefore, statement III need not be true, and the best answer is B.

65. The average (arithmetic mean) of 6, 8, and 10 equals the average of 7, 9, and

(A) 5
(B) 7
(C) 8
(D) 9
(E) 11

The average of 6, 8, and 10 is $\dfrac{6 + 8 + 10}{3} = 8$, which equals the average of 7, 9, and x. Thus, $\dfrac{7 + 9 + x}{3} = 8$, $16 + x = 24$, and $x = 8$. The best answer is therefore C.

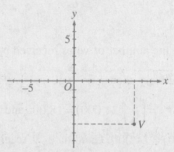

66. In the figure above, the coordinates of point V are

(A) $(-7, 5)$
(B) $(-5, 7)$
(C) $(5, 7)$
(D) $(7, 5)$
(E) $(7, -5)$

The x-coordinate of V is 7 and the y-coordinate of V is -5. Thus, the coordinates, (x, y), of V are $(7, -5)$, and the best answer is E. Alternatively, since point V lies in quadrant IV, the x-coordinate of V is positive, and the y-coordinate of V is negative. Only choice E meets these conditions and is, therefore, the best answer.

67. Tickets for all but 100 seats in a 10,000-seat stadium were sold. Of the tickets sold, 20 percent were sold at half price and the remaining tickets were sold at the full price of $2. What was the total revenue from ticket sales?

(A) $15,840
(B) $17,820
(C) $18,000
(D) $19,800
(E) $21,780

The number of tickets sold was $10,000 - 100 = 9,900$. If 20 percent of the tickets were sold at half price, then 80 percent were sold at full price. Total revenue was therefore $0.2(9,900)(\$1.00) + 0.8(9,900)(\$2.00) = \$17,820$. The best answer is B.

68. In a mayoral election, Candidate X received $\frac{1}{3}$ more votes than Candidate Y, and Candidate Y received $\frac{1}{4}$ fewer votes than Candidate Z. If Candidate Z received 24,000 votes, how many votes did Candidate X receive?

(A) 18,000
(B) 22,000
(C) 24,000
(D) 26,000
(E) 32,000

If x, y, and z are the number of votes received by Candidates X, Y, and Z, respectively, then $x = \frac{4}{3}\, y$, $y = \frac{3}{4}\, z$, and $z = 24{,}000$. By substitution, $y = \left(\frac{3}{4}\right)(24{,}000) = 18{,}000$ and $x = \left(\frac{4}{3}\right)(18{,}000) = 24{,}000$. Candidate X received a total of 24,000 votes, and the best answer is C. Alternatively, and more directly, $x = \left(\frac{4}{3}\right)\left(\frac{3}{4}\right)z = z = 24{,}000$.

69. René earns \$8.50 per hour on days other than Sundays and twice that rate on Sundays. Last week she worked a total of 40 hours, including 8 hours on Sunday. What were her earnings for the week?

(A) \$272
(B) \$340
(C) \$398
(D) \$408
(E) \$476

René worked a total of 32 hours at \$8.50 per hour during the week, and 8 hours on Sunday at \$17.00 per hour. Her total earnings for the week were $32(\$8.50) + 8(\$17) = \$408$. The best answer is D.

70. In a shipment of 120 machine parts, 5 percent were defective. In a shipment of 80 machine parts, 10 percent were defective. For the two shipments combined, what percent of the machine parts were defective?

(A) 6.5%
(B) 7.0%
(C) 7.5%
(D) 8.0%
(E) 8.5%

In the combined shipments, there was a total of 200 machine parts, of which $0.05(120) + 0.1(80) = 6 + 8 = 14$ were defective. The percent of machine parts that were defective in the two shipments combined was $\frac{14}{200} = \frac{7}{100} = 7\%$. The best answer is therefore B.

71. $\dfrac{2\frac{3}{5} - 1\frac{2}{3}}{\frac{2}{3} - \frac{3}{5}} =$

(A) 16
(B) 14
(C) 3
(D) 1
(E) −1

$$\frac{2\frac{3}{5} - 1\frac{2}{3}}{\frac{2}{3} - \frac{3}{5}} = \frac{\frac{13}{5} - \frac{5}{3}}{\frac{2}{3} - \frac{3}{5}} = \frac{\frac{39-25}{15}}{\frac{10-9}{15}} = \frac{\frac{14}{15}}{\frac{1}{15}} = \frac{14}{15} \times \frac{15}{1} = 14.$$

The best answer is B.

72. If $x = -1$, then $\dfrac{x^4 - x^3 + x^2}{x - 1} =$

(A) $-\dfrac{3}{2}$

(B) $-\dfrac{1}{2}$

(C) 0

(D) $\dfrac{1}{2}$

(E) $\dfrac{3}{2}$

Substituting the value -1 for x in the expression results in

$$\frac{(-1)^4 - (-1)^3 + (-1)^2}{-1-1} = \frac{1 - (-1) + 1}{-2} = -\frac{3}{2}.$$

The best answer is A.

73. Which of the following equations is NOT equivalent to $25x^2 = y^2 - 4$?

(A) $25x^2 + 4 = y^2$

(B) $75x^2 = 3y^2 - 12$

(C) $25x^2 = (y + 2)(y - 2)$

(D) $5x = y - 2$

(E) $x^2 = \dfrac{y^2 - 4}{25}$

Choice A is obtained by adding 4 to both sides of the equation $25x^2 = y^2 - 4$. Choice B is obtained by multiplying both sides of the original equation by 3, while choice C is equivalent because $y^2 - 4 = (y + 2)(y - 2)$. Choice E is obtained by dividing both sides of the original equation by 25. By the process of elimination, the answer must be D. Squaring both sides of $5x = y - 2$, choice D, gives $25x^2 = y^2 - 4y + 4$, which is NOT equivalent to the original equation. Therefore, the best answer is D.

74. A toy store regularly sells all stock at a discount of 20 percent to 40 percent. If an additional 25 percent were deducted from the discount price during a special sale, what would be the lowest possible price of a toy costing $16 before any discount?

(A) $5.60

(B) $7.20

(C) $8.80

(D) $9.60

(E) $15.20

The lowest possible price is paid when the maximum discount is received, so the lowest possible regular price is $16 - 0.40(\$16) = \$9.60$. With an additional 25 percent discount, the lowest possible price is $\$9.60 - 0.25(\$9.60) = \$7.20$. The best answer is B.

Alternatively, the lowest possible price to be paid for the item can be calculated by realizing that if you are being given a discount of 40 percent you are paying 60 percent of the listed price of the item. If an additional 25 percent discount is offered on the item, the price of the item becomes $(0.75)(0.60)(\$16) = \$7.20$.

75. If there are 664,579 prime numbers among the first 10 million positive integers, approximately what percent of the first 10 million positive integers are prime numbers?

(A) 0.0066%

(B) 0.066%

(C) 0.66%

(D) 6.6%

(E) 66%

The ratio of 664,579 to 10 million is approximately 660,000 to 10,000,000 or $\dfrac{66}{1,000} = 0.066 = 6.6\%$. The best answer is therefore D.

76. A bank customer borrowed $10,000, but received y dollars less than this due to discounting. If there was a separate $25 service charge, then, in terms of y, the service charge was what fraction of the amount that the customer received?

(A) $\dfrac{25}{10,000 - y}$

(B) $\dfrac{25}{10,000 - 25y}$

(C) $\dfrac{25y}{10,000 - y}$

(D) $\dfrac{y - 25}{10,000 - y}$

(E) $\dfrac{25}{10,000 - (y - 25)}$

The amount of money the customer received was $(10,000 - y)$ dollars. The $25 service charge as a fraction of the amount received was, therefore, $\dfrac{25}{10,000 - y}$. The best answer is A.

77. An airline passenger is planning a trip that involves three connecting flights that leave from Airports A, B, and C, respectively. The first flight leaves Airport A every hour, beginning at 8:00 a.m., and arrives at Airport B $2\frac{1}{2}$ hours later. The second flight leaves Airport B every 20 minutes, beginning at 8:00 a.m., and arrives at Airport C $1\frac{1}{6}$ hours later. The third flight leaves Airport C every hour, beginning at 8:45 a.m. What is the least total amount of time the passenger must spend between flights if all flights keep to their schedules?

(A) 25 min

(B) 1 hr 5 min

(C) 1 hr 15 min

(D) 2 hr 20 min

(E) 3 hr 40 min

Regardless of the time of departure from Airport A, arrival at Airport B will be at 30 minutes past the hour. Flights leave Airport B on the hour, and at either 20 or 40 minutes past the hour. Therefore, the earliest a passenger from Airport A could leave Airport B would be at 40 minutes past the hour with a 10-minute wait between flights. The flight from Airport B to Airport C takes $1\frac{1}{6}$ hours or 1 hour 10 minutes. A flight taken at 40 minutes past the hour would arrive at Airport C at 50 minutes past the hour, causing the passenger to have missed the flight from Airport C by 5 minutes. The passenger therefore has a 55-minute wait, and the least total amount of time the passenger must spend between flights is $10 + 55 = 65$ minutes, or 1 hour 5 minutes. The best answer is B.

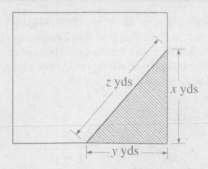

78. The shaded portion of the rectangular lot shown above represents a flower bed. If the area of the bed is 24 square yards and $x = y + 2$, then z equals

(A) $\sqrt{13}$

(B) $2\sqrt{13}$

(C) 6

(D) 8

(E) 10

The area of the triangular flower bed can be found by the formula $A = \dfrac{1}{2}$ (altitude)(base) or $24 = \dfrac{1}{2}(x)(y) = \dfrac{1}{2}(y + 2)(y)$. Thus, $y^2 + 2y = 48$ or $y^2 + 2y - 48 = 0$. Factoring yields $(y + 8)(y - 6) = 0$, and $y = 6$ since the length must be positive. The altitude x of the region is $6 + 2 = 8$, and the flower bed is a 6-8-10 right triangle. The hypotenuse, z, can be found by using the Pythagorean theorem. The best answer is therefore E.

79. How many multiples of 4 are there between 12 and 96, inclusive?

(A) 21

(B) 22

(C) 23

(D) 24

(E) 25

The most direct way to find the number of multiples of 4 between 12 and 96, inclusive, would be to write every multiple of 4 starting with 12 (i.e., 12, 16, 20, 24, . . . , 96), but this is very time-consuming and leaves many opportunities for error. Another approach would be to note that in each group of 4 consecutive integers there is one multiple of 4. Between 12 and 96, inclusive, there are 85 numbers that, when divided by 4, yield 21 groups of 4 with 1 number remaining that must be considered independently. In the 21 groups of 4, there are 21 multiples of 4 and the remaining number, 96, is also a multiple of 4. The total number of multiples of 4 between 12 and 96, inclusive, is thus $21 + 1 = 22$. The best answer is B.

Alternatively, since $12 = 3 \times 4$ and $96 = 24 \times 4$, the number of multiples of 4 between 12 and 96, inclusive, is the same as the number of integers between 3 and 24, inclusive, namely, 22.

80. Jack is now 14 years older than Bill. If in 10 years Jack will be twice as old as Bill, how old will Jack be in 5 years?

(A) 9

(B) 19

(C) 21

(D) 23

(E) 33

Let j and b be Jack's and Bill's current ages. Then $j = b + 14$ and $j + 10 = 2(b + 10)$. By substitution, $b + 14 + 10 = 2(b + 10)$, and $b + 24 = 2b + 20$. Therefore, $b = 4$ and $j = 18$, and Jack's age in 5 years is $18 + 5 = 23$. The best answer is D.

81. In Country X a returning tourist may import goods with a total value of $500 or less tax free, but must pay an 8 percent tax on the portion of the total value in excess of $500. What tax must be paid by a returning tourist who imports goods with a total value of $730 ?

(A) $58.40

(B) $40.00

(C) $24.60

(D) $18.40

(E) $16.00

The tourist must pay tax on $730 - $500 = $230. The amount of the tax is $0.08(\$230) = \$18.40$. The best answer is therefore D.

82. Which of the following is greater than $\dfrac{2}{3}$?

(A) $\dfrac{33}{50}$

(B) $\dfrac{8}{11}$

(C) $\dfrac{3}{5}$

(D) $\dfrac{13}{27}$

(E) $\dfrac{5}{8}$

One way to determine which of the options given is a value greater than $\dfrac{2}{3}$ is to establish equivalent fractions. In choice A, $\dfrac{33}{50} < \dfrac{2}{3}$ because $\dfrac{99}{150} < \dfrac{100}{150}$. In B, $\dfrac{8}{11} > \dfrac{2}{3}$ because $\dfrac{24}{33} > \dfrac{22}{33}$. In C, $\dfrac{3}{5} < \dfrac{2}{3}$ because $\dfrac{9}{15} < \dfrac{10}{15}$; in D, $\dfrac{13}{27} < \dfrac{2}{3}$ because $\dfrac{13}{27} < \dfrac{18}{27}$; and in E, $\dfrac{5}{8} < \dfrac{2}{3}$ because $\dfrac{15}{24} < \dfrac{16}{24}$. Therefore, the best answer is B.

Alternatively, convert the fractions to decimal form:

$\frac{2}{3} = 0.666666\ldots$, $\frac{33}{50} = 0.66$, $\frac{8}{11} = 0.727272\ldots$, $\frac{3}{5} = 0.6$,

$\frac{13}{27} = 0.481481\ldots$, and $\frac{5}{8} = 0.625$. Thus, by comparing

decimal equivalents, only $\frac{8}{11}$ is greater than $\frac{2}{3}$.

83. A rope 40 feet long is cut into two pieces. If one piece is 18 feet longer than the other, what is the length, in feet, of the shorter piece?

   (A)   9
   (B)   11
   (C)   18
   (D)   22
   (E)   29

Let x be the length of the shorter piece of rope, and let $x + 18$ be the length of the longer piece. Then $x + (x + 18) = 40$, which yields $2x + 18 = 40$, and $x = 11$. The best answer is B.

84. If 60 percent of a rectangular floor is covered by a rectangular rug that is 9 feet by 12 feet, what is the area, in square feet, of the floor?

   (A)   65
   (B)   108
   (C)   180
   (D)   270
   (E)   300

The area of the rug is $(9)(12) = 108$ square feet, which is 60 percent of x, the total area of the floor. Thus, $108 = 0.6x$, or

$x = \frac{108}{0.6} = 180$. The best answer is therefore C.

85. The Earth travels around the Sun at a speed of approximately 18.5 miles per second. This approximate speed is how many miles per hour?

   (A)   1,080
   (B)   1,160
   (C)   64,800
   (D)   66,600
   (E) 3,996,000

There are 60 seconds in one minute, and 60 minutes in one hour. In one hour the Earth travels $18.5 \times 60 \times 60 = 66,600$ miles, and the best answer is D.

86. A collection of books went on sale, and $\frac{2}{3}$ of them were sold for $2.50 each. If none of the 36 remaining books were sold, what was the total amount received for the books that were sold?

   (A) $180
   (B) $135
   (C) $90
   (D) $60
   (E) $54

Since $\frac{2}{3}$ of the books in the collection were sold, $\frac{1}{3}$ were not sold. The 36 unsold books represent $\frac{1}{3}$ of the total number of books in the collection, and $\frac{2}{3}$ of the total number of books equals $2(36)$ or 72. The total proceeds of the sale was $72(\$2.50)$ or $180. The best answer is therefore A.

87. If "basis points" are defined so that 1 percent is equal to 100 basis points, then 82.5 percent is how many basis points greater than 62.5 percent?

   (A)   0.02
   (B)   0.2
   (C)   20
   (D)   200
   (E)   2,000

There is a difference of 20 percent between 82.5 percent and 62.5 percent. If 1 percent equals 100 basis points, then 20 percent equals $20(100)$ or 2,000 basis points. The best answer is E.

88. The amounts of time that three secretaries worked on a special project are in the ratio of 1 to 2 to 5. If they worked a combined total of 112 hours, how many hours did the secretary who worked the longest spend on the project?

   (A)   80
   (B)   70
   (C)   56
   (D)   16
   (E)   14

Since the ratio of hours worked by the secretaries on the project is 1 to 2 to 5, the third secretary spent the longest time on the project, that is, $\frac{5}{8}(112)$ or 70 hours. The best answer is therefore B.

89. If the quotient $\frac{a}{b}$ is positive, which of the following must be true?

(A) $a > 0$
(B) $b > 0$
(C) $ab > 0$
(D) $a - b > 0$
(E) $a + b > 0$

If the quotient $\frac{a}{b}$ is positive, then either $a > 0$ and $b > 0$, or $a < 0$ and $b < 0$. It follows that answer choices A and B need not be true. Choice C must be true, because the product of two positive or two negative numbers is positive. Finally, $2 - 3 = -1$ and $-2 + (-1) = -3$ show that choices D and E, respectively, need not be true. The best answer is therefore C.

90. If $8^{2x+3} = 2^{3x+6}$, then $x =$

(A) -3
(B) -1
(C) 0
(D) 1
(E) 3

Since $8^{2x+3} = (2^3)^{2x+3} = 2^{6x+9}$, it follows, by equating exponents, that $6x + 9 = 3x + 6$, or $x = -1$. The best answer is therefore B.

91. Of the following, the closest approximation to

$$\sqrt{\frac{5.98(601.5)}{15.79}} \text{ is}$$

(A) 5
(B) 15
(C) 20
(D) 25
(E) 225

The value of the expression under the square root sign is approximately $\frac{6(600)}{16} = 225$. Since $225 = 15^2$, $\sqrt{225} = 15$, and the best answer is B.

92. Which of the following CANNOT be the greatest common divisor of two positive integers x and y?

(A) 1
(B) x
(C) y
(D) $x - y$
(E) $x + y$

Each answer choice except E can be the greatest common divisor (g.c.d.) of two positive integers. For example, if $x = 3$ and $y = 2$, then x and y have g.c.d. 1, which equals $x - y$, eliminating A and D. If the two numbers are 2 and 4, then the g.c.d. is 2, which can be x or y, eliminating B and C. However, the greatest common divisor of two positive integers cannot be greater than either one of the integers individually, so the best answer is E.

93. An empty pool being filled with water at a constant rate takes 8 hours to fill to $\frac{3}{5}$ of its capacity. How much more time will it take to finish filling the pool?

(A) 5 hr 30 min
(B) 5 hr 20 min
(C) 4 hr 48 min
(D) 3 hr 12 min
(E) 2 hr 40 min

If t is the total time required to fill the entire pool, then $\frac{3}{5}t = 8$.

Thus, $t = \frac{40}{3} = 13\frac{1}{3}$ hours, or 13 hours 20 minutes. It will therefore take 13 hours 20 minutes – 8 hours = 5 hours 20 minutes to finish filling the pool, and the best answer is B.

94. A positive number x is multiplied by 2, and this product is then divided by 3. If the positive square root of the result of these two operations equals x, what is the value of x?

(A) $\frac{9}{4}$

(B) $\frac{3}{2}$

(C) $\frac{4}{3}$

(D) $\frac{2}{3}$

(E) $\frac{1}{2}$

The value of x must satisfy the equation $x = \sqrt{\frac{2x}{3}}$. Squaring both sides of the equation and multiplying by 3 yields $2x = 3x^2$, and, since $x > 0$, it follows that $x = \frac{2}{3}$. The best answer is therefore D.

95. A tank contains 10,000 gallons of a solution that is 5 percent sodium chloride by volume. If 2,500 gallons of water evaporate from the tank, the remaining solution will be approximately what percent sodium chloride?

(A) 1.25%
(B) 3.75%
(C) 6.25%
(D) 6.67%
(E) 11.7%

The amount of sodium chloride in the tank is $0.05 \times 10,000$ or 500 gallons. After the evaporation of the water, the total amount of solution is $10,000 - 2,500 = 7,500$ gallons, and 500 gallons of sodium chloride remain. The percent of sodium chloride is thus $\dfrac{500}{7,500} = 6.67$ percent. The best answer is D.

Alternatively, this problem can be approached as an inverse proportion. The original solution contains 5 percent sodium chloride by volume in 10,000 gallons. As water evaporates from the tank, the concentration of sodium chloride in the solution will increase. If x is the fraction of sodium chloride in the remaining solution, then $\dfrac{10,000}{7,500} = \dfrac{x}{0.05}$. Solving for x gives $\dfrac{(0.05)(10,000)}{7,500} = 0.0667$, which equals 6.67 percent.

96. A certain grocery purchased x pounds of produce for p dollars per pound. If y pounds of the produce had to be discarded due to spoilage and the grocery sold the rest for s dollars per pound, which of the following represents the gross profit on the sale of the produce?

(A) $(x-y)s - xp$
(B) $(x-y)p - ys$
(C) $(s-p)y - xp$
(D) $xp - ys$
(E) $(x-y)(s-p)$

The grocery paid xp dollars for the produce. The grocery sold $(x - y)$ pounds of the produce for s dollars per pound, and so the total income was $(x - y)s$ dollars. The gross profit, or income minus cost, was therefore $(x - y)s - xp$. The best answer is A.

97. If $x + 5y = 16$ and $x = -3y$, then $y =$

(A) -24
(B) -8
(C) -2
(D) 2
(E) 8

Substituting the second equation into the first equation yields
$$(-3y) + 5y = 16$$
$$2y = 16$$
$$y = 8.$$
Thus, the best answer is E.

98. An empty swimming pool with a capacity of 5,760 gallons is filled at the rate of 12 gallons per minute. How many hours does it take to fill the pool to capacity?

(A) 8
(B) 20
(C) 96
(D) 480
(E) 720

Since the pool fills at the rate of 12 gallons per minute, the number of minutes required to fill the pool is $5760 \div 12 = 480$ minutes. The number of hours required to fill the pool is $\dfrac{480}{60}$, or 8. The best answer is A.

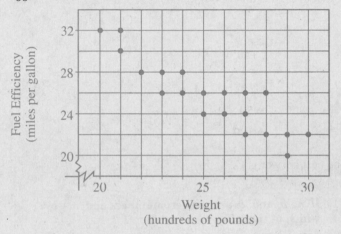

99. The dots on the graph above indicate the weights and fuel efficiency ratings for 20 cars. How many of the cars weigh more than 2,500 pounds and also get more than 22 miles per gallon?

(A) Three
(B) Five
(C) Eight
(D) Ten
(E) Eleven

Count the number of dots to the right of 25 and above 22 as shown on the graph below. The dots on the vertical line at 25 and those on the horizontal line at 22 are not included. Thus, the best answer is B.

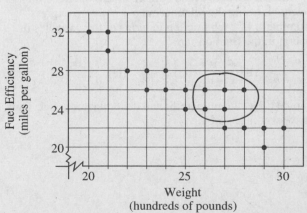

Weight
(hundreds of pounds)

-155-

100. $\dfrac{90 - 8(20 \div 4)}{\dfrac{1}{2}} =$

(A) 25
(B) 50
(C) 100
(D) 116
(E) 170

$$\frac{90 - 8(20 \div 4)}{\dfrac{1}{2}} = \frac{90 - 8(5)}{\dfrac{1}{2}}$$

$$= \frac{90 - 40}{\dfrac{1}{2}}$$

$$= \frac{50}{\dfrac{1}{2}}$$

$$= 50 \times 2$$

$$= 100$$

The best answer is C.

101. If a, b, and c are nonzero numbers and $a + b = c$, which of the following is equal to 1 ?

(A) $\dfrac{a-b}{c}$

(B) $\dfrac{a-c}{b}$

(C) $\dfrac{b-c}{a}$

(D) $\dfrac{b-a}{c}$

(E) $\dfrac{c-b}{a}$

For any fraction equal to 1, the numerator and the denominator must be equal. Using the relationship $a + b = c$ to express the denominator of each fraction in terms of the variables in the numerator, the fractions are

(A) $\dfrac{a-b}{a+b}$ (B) $\dfrac{a-c}{c-a}$ (C) $\dfrac{b-c}{c-b}$ (D) $\dfrac{b-a}{a+b}$ (E) $\dfrac{c-b}{c-b}$

Only choice E has the numerator and denominator equal. Thus, the best answer is E.

102. Bill's school is 10 miles from his home. He travels 4 miles from school to football practice, and then 2 miles to a friend's house. If he is then x miles from home, what is the range of possible values for x ?

(A) $2 \leq x \leq 10$
(B) $4 \leq x \leq 10$
(C) $4 \leq x \leq 12$
(D) $4 \leq x \leq 16$
(E) $6 \leq x \leq 16$

A diagram is helpful to solve this problem. The value of x will be greatest if Bill's home (H), school (S), football practice (P), and friend's house (F) are laid out as shown below in Figure 1 with $x = 10 + 4 + 2 = 16$ miles. The value of x will be least if Bill's home, school, football practice, and friend's house are situated as shown below in Figure 2 with $x = 10 - 6 = 4$ miles.

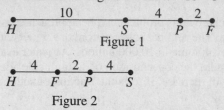

Figure 1

Figure 2

Thus, the best answer is D.

103. Three machines, individually, can do a certain job in 4, 5, and 6 hours, respectively. What is the greatest part of the job that can be done in one hour by two of the machines working together at their respective rates?

(A) $\dfrac{11}{30}$

(B) $\dfrac{9}{20}$

(C) $\dfrac{3}{5}$

(D) $\dfrac{11}{15}$

(E) $\dfrac{5}{6}$

In one hour these machines can do $\dfrac{1}{4}$, $\dfrac{1}{5}$, and $\dfrac{1}{6}$ of the job, respectively. Since the third machine does the smallest part of the job in one hour and only two machines are to be used, the third machine should be eliminated. Therefore, the first two machines will complete $\dfrac{1}{4} + \dfrac{1}{5} = \dfrac{9}{20}$ of the job in one hour.

The best answer is B.

104. In 1985, 45 percent of a document storage facility's 60 customers were banks, and in 1987, 25 percent of its 144 customers were banks. What was the percent increase from 1985 to 1987 in the number of bank customers the facility had?

(A) 10.7%
(B) 20%
(C) 25%
(D) $33\frac{1}{3}\%$
(E) $58\frac{1}{3}\%$

In 1985, the number of banks using the storage facility was $0.45(60) = 27$ banks. In 1987, the number of banks using the storage facility was $0.25(144) = 36$ banks. Between 1985 and 1987, the number of banks increased by 9. Since 27 was the number that was increased, the percent increase equals $\frac{9}{27} = \frac{1}{3}$, which is $33\frac{1}{3}\%$. Thus, the best answer is D.

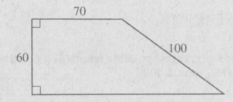

105. What is the perimeter of the figure above?

(A) 380
(B) 360
(C) 330
(D) 300
(E) 230

The figure below shows how the problem can be approached by partitioning the trapezoid into a rectangle and a triangle.

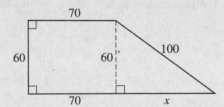

The two pieces of the lower horizontal line segment are 70 and x. From the Pythagorean theorem, $x^2 + 60^2 = 100^2$, $x^2 = 6,400$, and $x = 80$. The length of the lower horizontal line is $70 + 80 = 150$; therefore, the perimeter of the figure is $60 + 70 + 100 + 150 = 380$. The best answer is A.

106. A committee is composed of w women and m men. If 3 women and 2 men are added to the committee, and if one person is selected at random from the enlarged committee, then the probability that a woman is selected can be represented by

(A) $\dfrac{w}{m}$

(B) $\dfrac{w}{w+m}$

(C) $\dfrac{w+3}{m+2}$

(D) $\dfrac{w+3}{w+m+3}$

(E) $\dfrac{w+3}{w+m+5}$

With the additional people the committee has a total of $w + 3$ women and $m + 2$ men for a total of $w + m + 5$ people. The probability that a woman is selected is

$$\frac{\text{the number of women}}{\text{the total number of members}} = \frac{w+3}{w+m+5}$$

Thus, the best answer is E.

107. Last year Carlos saved 10 percent of his annual earnings. This year he earned 5 percent more than last year and he saved 12 percent of his annual earnings. The amount saved this year was what percent of the amount saved last year?

(A) 122%
(B) 124%
(C) 126%
(D) 128%
(E) 130%

If x represents the amount of Carlos' annual earnings last year, then $1.05x$ would represent his earnings this year. The amount Carlos saved last year was $0.10x$, and the amount saved this year is $0.12(1.05x) = 0.126x$. The amount saved this year as a percent of the amount saved last year is

$$\frac{0.126x}{0.1x} = 1.26 = 126\%$$

The best answer is C.

108. Jan lives x floors above the ground floor of a highrise building. It takes her 30 seconds per floor to walk down the steps and 2 seconds per floor to ride the elevator. If it takes Jan the same amount of time to walk down the steps to the ground floor as to wait for the elevator for 7 minutes and ride down, then x equals

   (A)   4
   (B)   7
   (C) 14
   (D) 15
   (E) 16

Since Jan lives x floors above the ground floor and it takes her 30 seconds per floor to walk and 2 seconds per floor to ride, it takes $30x$ seconds to walk down and $2x$ seconds to ride down after waiting 7 minutes (420 seconds) for the elevator. Thus, $30x = 2x + 420$; $x = 15$. The best answer is D.

109. A corporation that had $115.19 billion in profits for the year paid out $230.10 million in employee benefits. Approximately what percent of the profits were the employee benefits? (1 billion = 10^9)

   (A)   50%
   (B)   20%
   (C)   5%
   (D)   2%
   (E)   0.2%

The employee benefits as a fraction of profits is $\dfrac{230.10 \times 10^6}{115.19 \times 10^9}$,

which is approximately $\dfrac{230}{115 \times 10^3} = \dfrac{2}{1,000} = 0.2\%$. Thus, the

best answer is E.

Questions 110–111 refer to the following definition.

For any positive integer n, $n > 1$, the "length" of n is the number of positive primes (not necessarily distinct) whose product is n. For example, the length of 50 is 3 since $50 = (2)(5)(5)$.

110. Which of the following integers has length 3 ?

   (A)   3
   (B)   15
   (C)   60
   (D)   64
   (E)   105

To solve this problem it is necessary to factor each number into its primes and determine its "length" until the number of "length" 3 is found. It is obvious that 3 and 15 have lengths 1 and 2, respectively, and

   $60 = (5)(3)(2)(2)$ has length 4
   $64 = (2)(2)(2)(2)(2)(2)$ has length 6
   $105 = (5)(3)(7)$ has length 3

Therefore, the best answer is E.

111. What is the greatest possible length of a positive integer less than 1,000 ?

   (A) 10
   (B)   9
   (C)   8
   (D)   7
   (E)   6

A positive integer less than 1,000 with greatest possible "length" would be the positive number with the greatest number of prime factors with a product less than 1,000. The greatest number of factors can be obtained by using the smallest prime number, 2, as a factor as many times as possible. Since $2^9 = 512$ and $2^{10} = 1,024$, the greatest possible "length" is 9. The best answer is B.

112. A dealer originally bought 100 identical batteries at a total cost of q dollars. If each battery was sold at 50 percent above the original cost per battery, then, in terms of q, for how many dollars was each battery sold?

(A) $\dfrac{3q}{200}$

(B) $\dfrac{3q}{2}$

(C) $150q$

(D) $\dfrac{q}{100} + 50$

(E) $\dfrac{150}{q}$

The cost per battery (in dollars) is $\dfrac{q}{100}$. Since the selling price is 150% of the cost, each battery sells for $\dfrac{150}{100} \times \dfrac{q}{100} = \dfrac{3q}{200}$ dollars. The best answer is A.

113. Two oil cans, X and Y, are right circular cylinders, and the height and the radius of Y are each twice those of X. If the oil in can X, which is filled to capacity, sells for \$2, then at the same rate, how much does the oil in can Y sell for if Y is filled to only half its capacity?

(A) \$1
(B) \$2
(C) \$3
(D) \$4
(E) \$8

The volume of a right circular cylinder can be found by using the formula $V = \pi r^2 h$. If can X has radius r and height h, then can Y has radius $2r$ and height $2h$. Thus, the volume of can Y is $\pi(2r)^2(2h) = 8\pi r^2 h$, or 8 times that of can X. Since can Y is filled to only half its capacity, it contains 4 times as much oil as can X, so the cost of the oil in can Y is $4(\$2) = \$8$. The best answer is E.

114. If x, y, and z are positive integers such that x is a factor of y, and x is a multiple of z, which of the following is NOT necessarily an integer?

(A) $\dfrac{x+z}{z}$

(B) $\dfrac{y+z}{x}$

(C) $\dfrac{x+y}{z}$

(D) $\dfrac{xy}{z}$

(E) $\dfrac{yz}{x}$

If x is a factor of y and x is a multiple of z, then $y = kx$ and $x = cz$, where c and k are positive integers. Now each answer choice can be evaluated by substituting cz for x or kx for y into each expression until one is found that is not an integer. For example,

$$\frac{x+z}{z} = \frac{cz+z}{z} = \frac{(c+1)z}{z} = (c+1), \text{ where } c+1 \text{ is an integer;}$$

but, $\dfrac{y+z}{x} = \dfrac{y}{x} + \dfrac{z}{x} = \dfrac{kx}{x} + \dfrac{z}{cz} = k + \dfrac{1}{c}$, where $\dfrac{1}{c}$ is not

necessarily an integer. Therefore, the best answer is B.

Alternatively, since z is a factor of x and y, z is a factor of $x + y$, $x + z$ and xy; also, since x is a factor of y, x is a factor of yz. So choices A, C, D, and E must be integers. Choice B is an integer if and only if x is a factor of z, that is, $x = z$, which obviously need not be the case.

115. If $x + y = 8z$, then which of the following represents the average (arithmetic mean) of x, y, and z, in terms of z ?

(A) $2z + 1$
(B) $3z$
(C) $5z$

(D) $\dfrac{z}{3}$

(E) $\dfrac{3z}{2}$

The average of the three numbers is $\dfrac{x+y+z}{3}$. Since $x + y = 8z$,

substituting $8z$ for $x + y$ yields $\dfrac{8z+z}{3} = \dfrac{9z}{3} = 3z$. Therefore,

the best answer is B.

116. If the product of the integers w, x, y, and z is 770, and if $1 < w < x < y < z$, what is the value of $w + z$?

(A) 10
(B) 13
(C) 16
(D) 18
(E) 21

The prime factorization of 770 is $(2)(5)(7)(11)$. Since $1 < w < x < y < z$, the values for the variables must be $w = 2$, $x = 5$, $y = 7$, and $z = 11$, so $w + z = 2 + 11 = 13$. The best answer is B.

117. If the population of a certain country increases at the rate of one person every 15 seconds, by how many persons does the population increase in 20 minutes?

(A) 80
(B) 100
(C) 150
(D) 240
(E) 300

Since the population increases at the rate of 1 person every 15 seconds, it increases by 4 people every 60 seconds, that is, by 4 people every minute. Thus, in 20 minutes the population increases by $20 \times 4 = 80$ people. The best answer is A.

118. The value of $-3 - (-10)$ is how much greater than the value of $-10 - (-3)$?

(A) 0
(B) 6
(C) 7
(D) 14
(E) 26

The value of $-3 - (-10)$ is $-3 + 10 = 7$, and the value of $-10 - (-3)$ is $-10 + 3 = -7$. The difference is $7 - (-7) = 7 + 7 = 14$. Thus, the value of the first expression is 14 more than the value of the second. The best answer is D.

119. For an agricultural experiment, 300 seeds were planted in one plot and 200 were planted in a second plot. If exactly 25 percent of the seeds in the first plot germinated and exactly 35 percent of the seeds in the second plot germinated, what percent of the total number of seeds germinated?

(A) 12%
(B) 26%
(C) 29%
(D) 30%
(E) 60%

In the first plot 25% of 300 seeds germinated, so $0.25 \times 300 = 75$ seeds germinated. In the second plot, 35% of 200 seeds germinated, so $0.35 \times 200 = 70$ seeds germinated. Since $75 + 70 = 145$ seeds germinated out of a total of $300 + 200 = 500$ seeds, the percent of seeds that germinated is $\frac{145}{500} \times 100\%$, or 29%. Thus, the best answer is C.

120. If $\frac{a}{b} = \frac{2}{3}$, which of the following is NOT true?

(A) $\frac{a + b}{b} = \frac{5}{3}$

(B) $\frac{b}{b - a} = 3$

(C) $\frac{a - b}{b} = \frac{1}{3}$

(D) $\frac{2a}{3b} = \frac{4}{9}$

(E) $\frac{a + 3b}{a} = \frac{11}{2}$

One approach is to express the left side of each of the choices in terms of $\frac{a}{b}$. Thus, A is true since $\frac{a + b}{b} = \frac{a}{b} + 1 = \frac{2}{3} + 1 = \frac{5}{3}$. D and E can be shown to be true in a similar manner. One way to see that B is true is to first invert both sides, that is, show that $\frac{b - a}{b} = \frac{1}{3}$. This is true since $\frac{b - a}{b} = \frac{b}{b} - \frac{a}{b} = 1 - \frac{2}{3} = \frac{1}{3}$. Thus, B is true. On the other hand, C is not true since $\frac{a - b}{b} = \frac{a}{b} - \frac{b}{b} = \frac{2}{3} - 1 = -\frac{1}{3}$ not $\frac{1}{3}$.

121. On the number line, if $r < s$, if p is halfway between r and s, and if t is halfway between p and r, then $\frac{s - t}{t - r} = $

(A) $\frac{1}{4}$ (B) $\frac{1}{3}$ (C) $\frac{4}{3}$ (D) 3 (E) 4

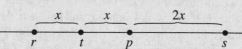

The figure above shows the relative positions of the numbers r, t, p, and s on the number line, where x denotes the length of the line segment from r to t. Thus, $\frac{s - t}{t - r} = \frac{x + 2x}{x} = \frac{3x}{x} = 3$.

The best answer is D.

122. Coins are to be put into 7 pockets so that each pocket contains at least one coin. At most 3 of the pockets are to contain the same number of coins, and no two of the remaining pockets are to contain an equal number of coins. What is the least possible number of coins needed for the pockets?

(A)   7
(B)   13
(C)   17
(D)   22
(E)   28

To determine the least possible number of coins needed, the smallest possible number of coins should be placed in each pocket, subject to the constraints of the problem. Thus, one coin should be put in three of the pockets, 2 coins in the fourth pocket, 3 coins in the fifth, 4 coins in the sixth, and 5 coins in the seventh. The least possible number of coins is therefore $1 + 1 + 1 + 2 + 3 + 4 + 5 = 17$, so the best answer is C.

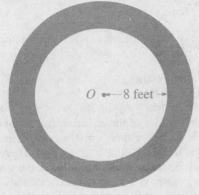

O ⊷—8 feet→

123. The figure above shows a circular flower bed, with its center at O, surrounded by a circular path that is 3 feet wide. What is the area of the path, in square feet?

(A) 25π (B) 38π (C) 55π (D) 57π (E) 64π

Since the path is 3 feet wide, its outer boundary forms a circle with a radius of $8 + 3 = 11$ feet. The area of the path can be found by finding the area of a circle with a radius of 11 feet and subtracting the area of a circle with a radius of 8 feet. The area of the path is therefore $\pi(11)^2 - \pi(8)^2 = (121 - 64)\pi = 57\pi$ square feet. Thus, the best answer is D.

	Brand X	Brand Y
Miles per Gallon	40	36
Cost per Gallon	$0.80	$0.75

124. The table above gives the gasoline costs and consumption rates for a certain car driven at 50 miles per hour, using each of two brands of gasoline. How many miles farther can the car be driven at this speed on $12 worth of brand X gasoline than on $12 worth of brand Y gasoline?

(A) 20   (B) 24   (C) 84   (D) 100   (E) 104

$12.00 worth of brand X gasoline is $\dfrac{12.00}{0.80} = 15$ gallons. Since the car gets 40 miles per gallon on brand X, the car would be able to go $(40)(15) = 600$ miles. On the other hand, $12.00 worth of brand Y gasoline is $\dfrac{12.00}{0.75} = 16$ gallons. Since the car gets 36 miles per gallon using brand Y, the car would be able to go $(36)(16) = 576$ miles. Therefore, the car would be able to go $600 - 576 = 24$ more miles with brand X. The best answer is B.

125. If $1 were invested at 8 percent interest compounded annually, the total value of the investment, in dollars, at the end of 6 years would be

(A) $(1.8)^6$
(B) $(1.08)^6$
(C) $6(1.08)$
(D) $1 + (0.08)^6$
(E) $1 + 6(0.08)$

Since the 8 percent interest is compounded annually, each year 0.08 times the investment is added to the investment. This is the same as multiplying the investment by 1.08. Therefore, after six years the initial investment of $1 is $(1)(1.08)^6 = (1.08)^6$ dollars. Thus, the best answer is B.

126. A furniture store sells only two models of desks, model A and model B. The selling price of model A is $120, which is 30 percent of the selling price of model B. If the furniture store sells 2,000 desks, $\dfrac{3}{4}$ of which are model B, what is the furniture store's total revenue from the sale of desks?

(A) $114,000
(B) $186,000
(C) $294,000
(D) $380,000
(E) $660,000

The number of model B desks sold was $\dfrac{3}{4}(2,000) = 1,500$, so the number of model A desks sold was $2,000 - 1,500 = 500$. Since the price of model A is $120 and this is 30 percent of the price of model B, the price of model B is $\dfrac{\$120}{0.3} = \$400$.

Thus, the total revenue from the sales of the desks is $500(\$120) + 1,500(\$400) = \$60,000 + \$600,000 = \$660,000$. The best answer is E.

127. How many minutes does it take John to type y words if he types at the rate of x words per minute?

(A) $\dfrac{x}{y}$ (B) $\dfrac{y}{x}$ (C) xy (D) $\dfrac{60x}{y}$ (E) $\dfrac{y}{60x}$

Let m represent the number of minutes John types. John types x words a minute for m minutes, so he would type a total of $xm = y$ words. Dividing both sides of the equation by x yields $m = y/x$. Thus, the best answer is B.

128. The weights of four packages are 1, 3, 5, and 7 pounds, respectively. Which of the following CANNOT be the total weight, in pounds, of any combination of the packages?

(A) 9
(B) 10
(C) 12
(D) 13
(E) 14

For each of choices A-D there is a combination of the packages that gives that total: (A) $9 = 1 + 3 + 5$, (B) $10 = 3 + 7$, (C) $12 = 5 + 7$, and (D) $13 = 1 + 5 + 7$. On the other hand, no combination of the packages weighs 14 pounds, since the total weight of the four packages is $1 + 3 + 5 + 7 = 16$ pounds, and there is no combination of packages weighing 2 pounds, whose removal would result in a combination weighing 14 pounds. The best answer is E.

129. $\sqrt{(16)(20) + (8)(32)} =$

(A) $4\sqrt{20}$

(B) 24

(C) 25

(D) $4\sqrt{20} + 8\sqrt{2}$

(E) 32

$\sqrt{(16)(20) + (8)(32)} = \sqrt{320 + 256} = \sqrt{576} = 24$
Thus, the best answer is B.
Alternatively, since $(16)(20) + (8)(32) = (16)(20) + (8)(2)(16)$
$$= (16)(20 + 16)$$
$$= (16)(36),$$
it follows that
$\sqrt{(16)(20) + (8)(32)} = \sqrt{(16)(36)} = (4)(6) = 24$.

130. The positive integer n is divisible by 25. If $\sqrt{n}$ is greater than 25, which of the following could be the value of $\dfrac{n}{25}$?

(A) 22
(B) 23
(C) 24
(D) 25
(E) 26

If $\sqrt{n} > 25$, then $n > 25^2$, so $n > 625$. Hence $\dfrac{n}{25} > \dfrac{625}{25} = 25$. Since only choice E is greater than 25, the best answer is E.

131. If x and y are different integers and $x^2 = xy$, which of the following must be true?

I. $x = 0$
II. $y = 0$
III. $x = -y$

(A) I only
(B) II only
(C) III only
(D) I and III only
(E) I, II, and III

If $x \neq 0$, then both sides of the equation can be divided by x, resulting in $x = y$. Thus, either $x = 0$ or $x = y$. Since it is given that $x \neq y$, it follows that x must be 0. Therefore, statement I must be true. On the other hand, the values $x = 0$ and $y = 3$ clearly satisfy $x^2 = xy$ but do not satisfy II or III, so II and III do not have to be true. Thus, the best answer is A.

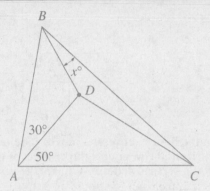

Note: Figure not drawn to scale.

132. In the figure above, $DA = DB = DC$. What is the value of x?

(A) 10 (B) 20 (C) 30 (D) 40 (E) 50

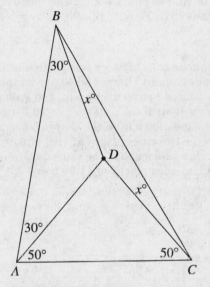

Since $DA = DB = DC$, the interior triangles are all isosceles, and thus the other angles of $\triangle ABC$ have degree measures as indicated in the figure above (drawn to scale). Since the measures of the three angles of a triangle always add up to $180°$, it follows that

$$80 + (30 + x) + (50 + x) = 180$$
$$160 + 2x = 180$$
$$2x = 20$$
$$x = 10.$$

Thus, the best answer is A.

133. If X and Y are sets of integers, $X \triangle Y$ denotes the set of integers that belong to set X or set Y, but not both. If X consists of 10 integers, Y consists of 18 integers, and 6 of the integers are in both X and Y, then $X \triangle Y$ consists of how many integers?

(A)   6
(B)   16
(C)   22
(D)   30
(E) 174

Since $X \triangle Y$ denotes the set of integers that belong to the set X or the set Y, but not both, the number of integers in $X \triangle Y$ is the number in the union of X and Y, minus the number in the intersection. The number of integers in the union is the number in X plus the number in Y, minus the number in the intersection, which is $10 + 18 - 6 = 22$, and thus the number in $X \triangle Y$ is $22 - 6 = 16$. Thus, the best answer is B.

Another way of seeing this is to look at the Venn diagram below. $X \triangle Y$ consists of those integers in X alone together with those in Y alone. Thus, $X \triangle Y = 4 + 12 = 16$.

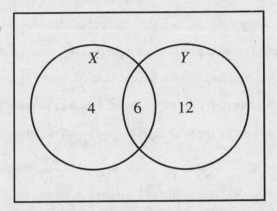

134. During the four years that Mrs. Lopez owned her car, she found that her total car expenses were $18,000. Fuel and maintenance costs accounted for $\frac{1}{3}$ of the total and depreciation accounted for $\frac{3}{5}$ of the remainder. The cost of insurance was 3 times the cost of financing, and together these two costs accounted for $\frac{1}{5}$ of the total. If the only other expenses were taxes and license fees, then the cost of financing was how much more or less than the cost of taxes and license fees?

(A) $1,500 more
(B) $1,200 more
(C) $100 less
(D) $300 less
(E) $1,500 less

The table below gives the distribution of the $18,000 in total costs.

fuel and maintenance:	$\frac{1}{3}$ ($18,000) = $6,000
depreciation: $\frac{3}{5}$($18,000 − $6,000) =	$\frac{3}{5}$ ($12,000) = $7,200
insurance plus financing:	$\frac{1}{5}$ ($18,000) = $3,600
	$16,800
taxes and license:	$18,000 − $16,800 = $1,200

Since insurance was 3 times the cost of financing, insurance came to $2,700 and financing came to $900 ($2,700 + $900 = $3,600). Thus, the cost of financing ($900) was $300 less than the cost of taxes and license fees ($1,200), and the best answer is D.

135. A car travels from Mayville to Rome at an average speed of 30 miles per hour and returns immediately along the same route at an average speed of 40 miles per hour. Of the following, which is closest to the average speed, in miles per hour, for the round-trip?

(A) 32.0
(B) 33.0
(C) 34.3
(D) 35.5
(E) 36.5

Let m represent the number of miles between Mayville and Rome. On the trip to Rome the car took $\frac{m}{30}$ hours, and on the trip back to Mayville the car took $\frac{m}{40}$ hours. Hence, the average speed for the trip is the total number of miles, or $2m$ divided by the total time, or $\frac{m}{30} + \frac{m}{40}$. Thus, the average speed is $\frac{2m}{\frac{m}{30} + \frac{m}{40}} = \frac{2}{\frac{1}{30} + \frac{1}{40}} = \frac{2}{\frac{70}{1,200}} = \frac{2,400}{70}$, which is approximately 34.3. The best answer is C.

136. If $\frac{0.0015 \times 10^m}{0.03 \times 10^k} = 5 \times 10^7$, then $m - k =$

(A) 9
(B) 8
(C) 7
(D) 6
(E) 5

$$\frac{0.0015 \times 10^m}{0.03 \times 10^k} = \frac{0.0015}{0.03} \times 10^{m-k} = 0.05 \times 10^{m-k}$$
$$= 5 \times 10^{-2} 10^{m-k} = (5)10^{m-k-2}$$

Since this must be equal to $(5)(10^7)$, $m - k - 2 = 7$, so $m - k = 9$. Thus, the best answer is A.

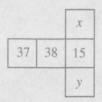

137. In the figure above, the sum of the three numbers in the horizontal row equals the product of the three numbers in the vertical column. What is the value of xy?

(A) 6
(B) 15
(C) 35
(D) 75
(E) 90

The sum of the three numbers in the horizontal row is $37 + 38 + 15$, or 90. The product of the three numbers in the vertical column is $15xy$. Thus, $15xy = 90$, or $xy = 6$, and the best answer is A.

138. For telephone calls between two particular cities, a telephone company charges $0.40 per minute if the calls are placed between 5:00 a.m. and 9:00 p.m. and $0.25 per minute if the calls are placed between 9:00 p.m. and 5:00 a.m. If the charge for a call between the two cities placed at 1:00 p.m. was $10.00, how much would a call of the same duration have cost if it had been placed at 11:00 p.m.?

(A) $3.75
(B) $6.25
(C) $9.85
(D) $10.00
(E) $16.00

The ratio of the charge per minute for a call placed at 11:00 p.m. to the charge per minute for a call placed at 1:00 p.m. is $\frac{\$0.25}{\$0.40}$, or $\frac{5}{8}$. Therefore, if the charge for a call placed at 1:00 p.m. is $10.00, the charge for a call of the same duration placed at 11:00 p.m. would be $\left(\frac{5}{8}\right)(\$10.00)$, or $6.25, and the best answer is B.

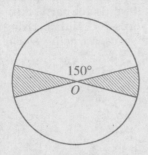

139. If O is the center of the circle above, what fraction of the circular region is shaded?

(A) $\dfrac{1}{12}$

(B) $\dfrac{1}{9}$

(C) $\dfrac{1}{6}$

(D) $\dfrac{1}{4}$

(E) $\dfrac{1}{3}$

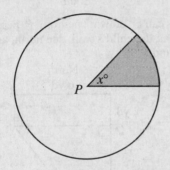

If P is the center of the circle above, then the fraction of the area of the circular region that is shaded is $\dfrac{x}{360}$. Since vertical angles are equal, the sum of the central angles of the two shaded regions is $360^{\circ} - 2(150)^{\circ}$, or 60°. Therefore, $\dfrac{60}{360} = \dfrac{1}{6}$ of the circular region is shaded, and the best answer is C.

140. If a compact disc that usually sells for $12.95 is on sale for $9.95, then the percent decrease in price is closest to

(A) 38%
(B) 31%
(C) 30%
(D) 29%
(E) 23%

The percent decrease in the price of an item =

$$\frac{\text{the decrease in the cost of the item}}{\text{the original price of the item}}.$$

Thus, the percent decrease in the price of a compact disc is $\dfrac{12.95 - 9.95}{12.95}$, or $\dfrac{3}{12.95}$, which is a little less than $\dfrac{30}{12.50}$, or 24 percent. Thus, the best answer is E.

141. $\dfrac{1}{1 + \dfrac{1}{2 + \dfrac{1}{3}}} =$

(A) $\dfrac{3}{10}$

(B) $\dfrac{7}{10}$

(C) $\dfrac{6}{7}$

(D) $\dfrac{10}{7}$

(E) $\dfrac{10}{3}$

$$\frac{1}{1 + \dfrac{1}{2 + \dfrac{1}{3}}} = \frac{1}{1 + \dfrac{1}{\dfrac{7}{3}}} = \frac{1}{1 + \dfrac{3}{7}} = \frac{1}{\dfrac{10}{7}} = \frac{7}{10}$$

Thus, the best answer is B.

142. A fruit-salad mixture consists of apples, peaches, and grapes in the ratio $6:5:2$, respectively, by weight. If 39 pounds of the mixture is prepared, the mixture includes how many more pounds of apples than grapes?

(A) 15
(B) 12
(C) 9
(D) 6
(E) 4

Since the ratio of apples to peaches to grapes is $6:5:2$, for each $6 + 5 + 2$ or 13 equal parts by weight of the mixture, 6 parts are apples and 2 parts are grapes. There are then $\dfrac{6}{13}(39) = 18$ pounds of apples and $\dfrac{2}{13}(39) = 6$ pounds of grapes. Therefore, there are $18 - 6 = 12$ more pounds of apples than grapes in 39 pounds of the mixture. The best answer is B.

143. If $\frac{3}{x} = 2$ and $\frac{y}{4} = 3$, then $\frac{3+y}{x+4} =$

(A) $\frac{10}{9}$

(B) $\frac{3}{2}$

(C) $\frac{20}{11}$

(D) $\frac{30}{11}$

(E) 5

Since $\frac{3}{x} = 2$ and $\frac{y}{4} = 3$, it follows that $x = \frac{3}{2}$ and $y = 12$.

Thus, $\frac{3+y}{x+4} = \frac{3+12}{\frac{3}{2}+4} = \frac{15}{\frac{11}{2}} = \frac{30}{11}$, and the best answer is D.

144. $\left(1 + \sqrt{5}\right)\left(1 - \sqrt{5}\right) =$

(A) -4
(B) 2
(C) 6
(D) $-4 - 2\sqrt{5}$
(E) $6 - 2\sqrt{5}$

$\left(1 + \sqrt{5}\right)\left(1 - \sqrt{5}\right) = 1^2 + \sqrt{5} - \sqrt{5} - \left(\sqrt{5}\right)^2$

$= 1^2 - \left(\sqrt{5}\right)^2 = 1 - 5 = -4$

Thus, the best answer is A.

145. Starting from point O on a flat school playground, a child walks 10 yards due north, then 6 yards due east, and then 2 yards due south, arriving at point P. How far apart, in yards, are points O and P?

(A) 18
(B) 16
(C) 14
(D) 12
(E) 10

The figure below represents the information given in the question.

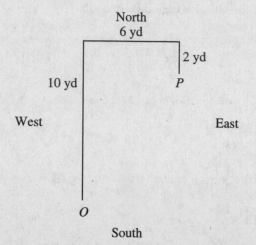

Next, two lines can be drawn; one from P perpendicular to the line representing the child's walk due north, and the other connecting O and P.

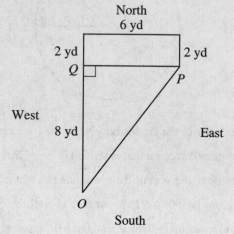

OPQ is a right triangle, $QP = 6$ yards, and $OQ = (10 - 2)$ yards $= 8$ yards. Thus, by the

Pythagorean theorem $OP = \sqrt{6^2 + 8^2} = \sqrt{100} = 10$ yards, and the best answer is E.

146. A certain car increased its average speed by 5 miles per hour in each successive 5-minute interval after the first interval. If in the first 5-minute interval its average speed was 20 miles per hour, how many miles did the car travel in the third 5-minute interval?

(A) 1.0
(B) 1.5
(C) 2.0
(D) 2.5
(E) 3.0

In the first 5-minute interval the car's average speed was 20 miles per hour, and the car's average speed increased by 5 miles per hour in each successive 5-minute interval. Thus, the average speed was 25 miles per hour in the second 5-minute interval and 30 miles per hour in the third 5-minute interval. Since 5 minutes is $\frac{1}{12}$ of an hour, the car traveled $\frac{1}{12}(30)$, or 2.5, miles in the third 5-minute interval, and the best answer is D.

147. Lois has x dollars more than Jim has, and together they have a total of y dollars. Which of the following represents the number of dollars that Jim has?

(A) $\dfrac{y-x}{2}$

(B) $y - \dfrac{x}{2}$

(C) $\dfrac{y}{2} - x$

(D) $2y - x$

(E) $y - 2x$

If J is the number of dollars that Jim has, then Lois has $J + x$ dollars. Thus, the amount, y, that they have together is $J + (J + x)$. So $y = J + (J + x) = 2J + x$, $J = \dfrac{y-x}{2}$, and the best answer is A.

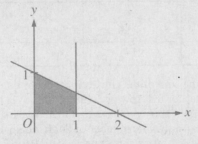

148. In the rectangular coordinate system above, the shaded region is bounded by straight lines. Which of the following is NOT an equation of one of the boundary lines?

(A) $x = 0$
(B) $y = 0$
(C) $x = 1$
(D) $x - y = 0$
(E) $x + 2y = 2$

The equation of the x-axis is $y = 0$. The equations of the y-axis and the line one unit to the right of the y-axis are $x = 0$ and $x = 1$, respectively. Thus, the answer key cannot be A, B, or C. The top boundary line passes through the point $(2, 0)$. To lie on a certain line the point $(2, 0)$ must satisfy the equation of that line. Substituting in D yields $2 - 0 = 0$, which is not a true statement. Thus, $x - y = 0$ is NOT an equation of one of the boundary lines and the best answer is D.

149. A certain population of bacteria doubles every 10 minutes. If the number of bacteria in the population initially was 10^4, what was the number in the population 1 hour later?

(A) $2(10^4)$
(B) $6(10^4)$
(C) $(2^6)(10^4)$
(D) $(10^6)(10^4)$
(E) $(10^4)^6$

If the population of bacteria doubles every 10 minutes, it doubles 6 times in an hour. The population after 10 minutes was $(2)(10^4)$ and after 20 minutes was $(2)(2)(10^4)$, or $(2^2)(10^4)$. Continuing to multiply by 2 each time the population doubles, it follows that the population after an hour is $(2^6)(10^4)$, and the best answer is C.

150. During a certain season, a team won 80 percent of its first 100 games and 50 percent of its remaining games. If the team won 70 percent of its games for the entire season, what was the total number of games that the team played?

(A) 180
(B) 170
(C) 156
(D) 150
(E) 105

Let G equal the number of games played by the team this season. Expressed algebraically, 80 percent of its first 100 games and 50 percent of its remaining games is $(0.80)(100) + 0.50(G - 100)$ and 70 percent of its games is $0.70G$. Thus,

$$0.70G = (0.80)(100) + 0.50(G - 100)$$
$$0.70G = 80 + 0.50G - 50$$
$$0.20G = 30$$
$$G = 150$$

Therefore, the team played 150 games and the best answer is D.

151. If Juan takes 11 seconds to run y yards, how many seconds will it take him to run x yards at the same rate?

(A) $\dfrac{11x}{y}$

(B) $\dfrac{11y}{x}$

(C) $\dfrac{x}{11y}$

(D) $\dfrac{11}{xy}$

(E) $\dfrac{xy}{11}$

If Juan takes 11 seconds to run y yards, it takes him

$\dfrac{11}{y}$ seconds to run 1 yard. Therefore, it takes him

$x\left(\dfrac{11}{y}\right) = \dfrac{11x}{y}$ seconds to run x yards and the best answer is A.

Alternatively, recall that rate $\times$ time = distance.

Therefore, if Juan takes 11 seconds to run y yards he runs

at a rate of $\dfrac{y}{11}$ yards per second. So, to run x yards he

takes $\dfrac{x}{\dfrac{y}{11}} = \dfrac{11x}{y}$ seconds.

152. Which of the following fractions has the greatest value?

(A) $\dfrac{6}{\left(2^2\right)\left(5^2\right)}$

(B) $\dfrac{1}{\left(2^3\right)\left(5^2\right)}$

(C) $\dfrac{28}{\left(2^2\right)\left(5^3\right)}$

(D) $\dfrac{62}{\left(2^3\right)\left(5^3\right)}$

(E) $\dfrac{122}{\left(2^4\right)\left(5^3\right)}$

Notice that $(2^2)(5^2)$ is a factor of the denominator of each of the answer choices. Factoring it out will make comparison of the sizes of the fractions easier.

(A) $\dfrac{6}{\left(2^2\right)\left(5^2\right)} = 6 \times \dfrac{1}{\left(2^2\right)\left(5^2\right)}$

(B) $\dfrac{1}{\left(2^3\right)\left(5^2\right)} = \dfrac{1}{2} \times \dfrac{1}{\left(2^2\right)\left(5^2\right)}$

(C) $\dfrac{28}{\left(2^2\right)\left(5^3\right)} = \dfrac{28}{5} \times \dfrac{1}{\left(2^2\right)\left(5^2\right)}$

(D) $\dfrac{62}{\left(2^3\right)\left(5^3\right)} = \dfrac{62}{(2)(5)} \times \dfrac{1}{\left(2^3\right)\left(5^2\right)} = \dfrac{31}{5} \times \dfrac{1}{\left(2^2\right)\left(5^2\right)}$

(E) $\dfrac{122}{\left(2^4\right)\left(5^3\right)} = \dfrac{122}{\left(2^2\right)(5)} \times \dfrac{1}{\left(2^2\right)\left(5^2\right)} = \dfrac{61}{10} \times \dfrac{1}{\left(2^2\right)\left(5^2\right)}$

Of these fractions, the one with the greatest factor preceding

$\dfrac{1}{\left(2^2\right)\left(5^2\right)}$ is $\dfrac{31}{5} \times \dfrac{1}{\left(2^2\right)\left(5^2\right)}$. Thus, the best answer is D.

153. Of 30 applicants for a job, 14 had at least 4 years experience, 18 had degrees, and 3 had less than 4 years experience and did not have a degree. How many of the applicants had at least 4 years experience and a degree?

(A) 14
(B) 13
(C) 9
(D) 7
(E) 5

The applicants for a job were classified in the problem by (1) whether they had more or less than 4 years experience and (2) whether they had a degree. The given information can be summarized in the following table:

	Experience		Total
	At least 4 years	Less than 4 years	
Degree			18
No Degree		3	
Total	14		30

Notice that the sum of the entries in a row or column must equal the total for that row or column. Thus, (1) the total number of applicants who have less than 4 years experience is $30 - 14$, or 16; (2) the number of applicants who have a degree and less than 4 years experience is $16 - 3$, or 13; and (3) the number of applicants who have at least 4 years experience and a degree is $18 - 13$, or 5. Therefore, the best answer is E.

154. Which of the following CANNOT yield an integer when divided by 10 ?

   (A) The sum of two odd integers
   (B) An integer less than 10
   (C) The product of two primes
   (D) The sum of three consecutive integers
   (E) An odd integer

To solve this problem, look at each option to see if there are integers that (1) satisfy the condition in the option and (2) yield an integer when divided by 10.

(A) 3 and 7 are both odd integers and $\frac{3+7}{10} = 1$.

(B) -10 is an integer that is less than 10 and $\frac{-10}{10} = -1$.

(C) 2 and 5 are primes and $\frac{(5)(2)}{10} = 1$.

(D) 9, 10, and 11 are three consecutive integers and $\frac{9+10+11}{10} = 3$.

(E) All multiples of 10 are even integers; therefore, an odd integer divided by 10 CANNOT yield an integer.

Thus, the best answer is E.

155. A certain clock marks every hour by striking a number of times equal to the hour, and the time required for a stroke is exactly equal to the time interval between strokes. At 6:00 the time lapse between the beginning of the first stroke and the end of the last stroke is 22 seconds. At 12:00, how many seconds elapse between the beginning of the first stroke and the end of the last stroke?

   (A) 72
   (B) 50
   (C) 48
   (D) 46
   (E) 44

At 6:00 there are 6 strokes and 5 intervals between strokes. Thus, there are 11 equal time intervals in the 22 seconds between the beginning of the first stroke and the end of the last stroke. Each time interval is $\frac{22}{11} = 2$ seconds long. At 12:00 there are 12 strokes and 11 intervals between strokes. Thus, there are 23 equal 2-second time intervals, or 46 seconds, between the beginning of the first stroke and the end of the last stroke. The best answer is D.

156. If $k \neq 0$ and $k - \frac{3 - 2k^2}{k} = \frac{x}{k}$, then $x =$

   (A) $-3 - k^2$
   (B) $k^2 - 3$
   (C) $3k^2 - 3$
   (D) $k - 3 - 2k^2$
   (E) $k - 3 + 2k^2$

Multiplying both sides of the equation $k - \frac{3 - 2k^2}{k} = \frac{x}{k}$ by k yields $k^2 - (3 - 2k^2) = x$, or $x = 3k^2 - 3$. Thus, the best answer is C.

157. $\dfrac{\frac{1}{2} + \frac{1}{3}}{\frac{1}{4}} =$

   (A) $\dfrac{1}{12}$

   (B) $\dfrac{5}{24}$

   (C) $\dfrac{2}{3}$

   (D) $\dfrac{9}{4}$

   (E) $\dfrac{10}{3}$

This complex fraction can be simplified by multiplying numerator and denominator by the lowest common denominator, 12.

$$\frac{\frac{1}{2} + \frac{1}{3}}{\frac{1}{4}} = \frac{\left(\frac{1}{2} + \frac{1}{3}\right) \times 12}{\frac{1}{4} \times 12} = \frac{6 + 4}{3} = \frac{10}{3}$$

Thus, the best answer is E.

158. John has 10 pairs of matched socks. If he loses 7 individual socks, what is the greatest number of pairs of matched socks he can have left?

   (A) 7
   (B) 6
   (C) 5
   (D) 4
   (E) 3

If John loses 7 individual socks, they could belong to either 4, 5, 6, or 7 different pairs. Therefore, the greatest possible number of pairs of matched socks is $10 - 4 = 6$. Thus, the best answer is B.

   Alternatively, since there were 20 socks altogether, there are $20 - 7 = 13$ socks left, which could be at most 6 pairs.

159. Last year's receipts from the sale of candy on Valentine's Day totaled 385 million dollars, which represented 7 percent of total candy sales for the year. Candy sales for the year totaled how many million dollars?

  (A)   55
  (B)   550
  (C)   2,695
  (D)   5,500
  (E)   26,950

Let x represent the number of millions of dollars spent on candy for the year. Since the Valentine's Day receipts are 7% of the year's receipts, $0.07x = 385$. Solving the equation yields 5,500 million dollars. The best answer is D.

160. How many minutes does it take to travel 120 miles at 400 miles per hour?

  (A)   3

  (B) $3\dfrac{1}{3}$

  (C) $8\dfrac{2}{3}$

  (D)   12

  (E)   18

The number of minutes it takes to travel 120 miles at 400 miles per hour can be found by completing the computation
$$\frac{120\text{ miles} \times 60\text{ minutes/hour}}{400\text{ miles/hour}} = 18\text{ minutes. Therefore, the}$$
best answer is E.

161. If $1 + \dfrac{1}{x} = 2 - \dfrac{2}{x}$, then $x =$

  (A) -1

  (B) $\dfrac{1}{3}$

  (C) $\dfrac{2}{3}$

  (D) 2

  (E) 3

Multiplying both sides of the equation by x yields $x + 1 = 2x - 2$; and combining like terms leaves $x = 3$. The best answer is E.

162. Last year, for every 100 million vehicles that traveled on a certain highway, 96 vehicles were involved in accidents. If 3 billion vehicles traveled on the highway last year, how many of those vehicles were involved in accidents? (1 billion = 1,000,000,000)

  (A)   288
  (B)   320
  (C)   2,880
  (D)   3,200
  (E)   28,800

The problem states that on a certain highway 96 vehicles out of each 100 million were involved in accidents. Since 3 billion vehicles is equivalent to 3,000 million, the number of vehicles that were involved in accidents last year was
$$\frac{96}{100\text{ million}} \times 3,000\text{ million} = 2,880\text{ vehicles. Thus, the}$$
best answer is C.

163. If the perimeter of a rectangular garden plot is 34 feet and its area is 60 square feet, what is the length of each of the longer sides?

  (A)   5 ft
  (B)   6 ft
  (C)   10 ft
  (D)   12 ft
  (E)   15 ft

Let x represent the width of the rectangular garden and y the length of the garden. Since the garden has perimeter 34 feet and area 60 square feet, it follows that $2x + 2y = 34$ and $xy = 60$. Dividing the first equation by 2 gives $x + y = 17$; thus, the problem reduces to finding two numbers whose product is 60 and whose sum is 17. It can be seen by inspection that the two numbers are 5 and 12, so $y = 12$. Therefore, the best answer is D.

164. What is the least positive integer that is divisible by each of the integers 1 through 7, inclusive?

  (A)   420
  (B)   840
  (C)   1,260
  (D)   2,520
  (E)   5,040

A number that is divisible by 1, 2, 3, 4, 5, 6, and 7 must contain 2, 3, 4, 5, 6, and 7 as factors. The least positive integer is achieved by assuring there is no duplication of factors. Since 2 and 3 are factors of 6, they are not included as factors of our least positive integer. Because 4 contains two factors of 2, and 6 contains only one factor of 2, the number must contain a second factor of 2. The number is $(2)(5)(6)(7) = 420$. Thus, the best answer is A.

165. Thirty percent of the members of a swim club have passed the lifesaving test. Among the members who have <u>not</u> passed the test, 12 have taken the preparatory course and 30 have not taken the course. How many members are there in the swim club?

(A) 60
(B) 80
(C) 100
(D) 120
(E) 140

If 30 percent of the members of the swim club have passed the lifesaving test, then 70 percent have not. Among the members who have not passed the test, 12 have taken the course and 30 have not, for a total of 42 members. If x represents the number of members in the swim club, $0.70x = 42$, so $x = 60$. The best answer is A.

166. For all numbers s and t, the operation $*$ is defined by $s * t = (s - 1)(t + 1)$. If $(-2) * x = -12$, then $x =$

(A) 2
(B) 3
(C) 5
(D) 6
(E) 11

Since $s * t = (s - 1)(t + 1)$ and $(-2) * x = (-12)$, $(-2) * x = (-2 - 1)(x + 1) = -12$. Solving $(-3)(x + 1) = -12$ for x yields $x = 3$. Therefore, the best answer is B.

167. In an increasing sequence of 10 consecutive integers, the sum of the first 5 integers is 560. What is the sum of the last 5 integers in the sequence?

(A) 585
(B) 580
(C) 575
(D) 570
(E) 565

If $x, x + 1, x + 2, x + 3$, and $x + 4$ are the first five consecutive integers and their sum is 560, then $5x + 10 = 560$, so $x = 110$. The sixth through tenth consecutive numbers are represented by $x + 5, x + 6, x + 7, x + 8$, and $x + 9$; so their sum is $5x + 35 = 5(110) + 35 = 585$. Thus, the best answer is A.

Alternatively, note that the sixth number is 5 more than the first, the seventh is 5 more than the second, and so on; so the sum of the last five integers is $5(5) = 25$ more than the sum of the first five consecutive integers. Therefore, the sum of the last 5 integers is $560 + 25 = 585$.

168. A certain manufacturer produces items for which the production costs consist of annual fixed costs totaling $130,000 and variable costs averaging $8 per item. If the manufacturer's selling price per item is $15, how many items must the manufacturer produce and sell to earn an annual profit of $150,000 ?

(A) 2,858
(B) 18,667
(C) 21,429
(D) 35,000
(E) 40,000

Let x represent the number of items produced. The manufacturer's profit, $P(x)$, is determined by subtracting cost from revenue, that is, $P(x) = R(x) - C(x)$. Since $R(x) = 15x$ dollars, $C(x) = 8x + 130,000$ dollars, and $P(x) = \$150,000$, $15x - (8x + 130,000) = 150,000$. Solving this equation yields $x = 40,000$. Therefore, the best answer is E.

169. How many two-element subsets of $\{1, 2, 3, 4\}$ are there that do <u>not</u> contain the pair of elements 2 and 4 ?

(A) One
(B) Two
(C) Four
(D) Five
(E) Six

This problem can be solved by finding the difference between the total number of two-element subsets and the number that contain both 2 and 4. There is only one two-element subset that contains both 2 and 4. The total number of two-element subsets is $\frac{(4)(3)}{2} = 6$; therefore, the difference is five. Thus, the best answer is D.

Alternatively, the two-element subsets of $\{1, 2, 3, 4\}$ are $\{1, 2\}, \{1, 3\}, \{1, 4\}, \{2, 3\}, \{2, 4\}$, and $\{3, 4\}$. There are 5 two-element subsets that do not contain both 2 and 4.

170. In a certain company, the ratio of the number of managers to the number of production-line workers is 5 to 72. If 8 additional production-line workers were to be hired, the ratio of the number of managers to the number of production-line workers would be 5 to 74. How many managers does the company have?

(A) 5
(B) 10
(C) 15
(D) 20
(E) 25

If m represents the number of managers and p represents the number of production-line workers, then the ratio of managers to production-line workers is $\dfrac{m}{p} = \dfrac{5}{72}$. With 8 additional production-line workers, $p + 8$ represents the new number of production-line workers and the new ratio is $\dfrac{m}{p+8} = \dfrac{5}{74}$. The two ratios form the system of two equations $5p - 72m = 0$ and $5p - 74m = -40$. Subtracting the two equations to eliminate p yields $m = 20$. Therefore, the best answer is D.

171. If $(x - 1)^2 = 400$, which of the following could be the value of $x - 5$?

   (A)   15
   (B)   14
   (C)   −24
   (D)   −25
   (E)   −26

Since $(x - 1)^2 = 400$, $(x - 1) = 20$ or -20; so $x = 21$ or -19. Thus, $x - 5 = 16$ or -24. The best answer is C.

172. Salesperson A's compensation for any week is $360 plus 6 percent of the portion of A's total sales above $1,000 for that week. Salesperson B's compensation for any week is 8 percent of B's total sales for that week. For what amount of total weekly sales would both salespeople earn the same compensation?

   (A) $21,000
   (B) $18,000
   (C) $15,000
   (D) $4,500
   (E) $4,000

Let x represent the total weekly sales amount at which both salespersons earn the same compensation. Salesperson B's compensation is represented by $0.08x$ and Salesperson A's compensation is represented by $360 + 0.06(x - 1,000)$. Solving the equation $0.08x = 360 + 0.06(x - 1,000)$ yields $x = 15,000$. Therefore, the best answer is C.

173. If a square region has area x, what is the length of its diagonal in terms of x ?

   (A) $\sqrt{x}$

   (B) $\sqrt{2x}$

   (C) $2\sqrt{x}$

   (D) $x\sqrt{2}$

   (E) $2x$

Since the area of the square region is x, $s^2 = x$, where $s = \sqrt{x}$ is the length of the side of the square. Because a diagonal divides the square into two right triangles as shown in the figure below, the Pythagorean theorem yields

$$d^2 = \left(\sqrt{x}\right)^2 + \left(\sqrt{x}\right)^2 = x + x = 2x, \text{ or } d = \sqrt{2x} .$$

Thus, the best answer is B.

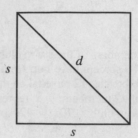

174. In a certain class consisting of 36 students, some boys and some girls, exactly $\dfrac{1}{3}$ of the boys and exactly $\dfrac{1}{4}$ of the girls walk to school. What is the greatest possible number of students in this class who walk to school?

   (A)   9
   (B)   10
   (C)   11
   (D)   12
   (E)   13

Let x represent the number of boys in the class and $36 - x$ the number of girls in the class. The numbers of boys and girls who walk to school are $\dfrac{1}{3}x$ and $\dfrac{1}{4}(36 - x)$, respectively. The greatest possible number of students who walk is the greatest number that $\dfrac{1}{3}x + \dfrac{1}{4}(36 - x) = 9 + \dfrac{1}{12}x$ can be. Since there are some girls in the class, x cannot equal 36, so $\dfrac{1}{12}x$ can be a maximum of 2. Hence, the best answer is C.

   Alternatively, if x boys and y girls ($x > 0$ and $y > 0$) walk to school, then $3x + 4y = 36$. Since $4y$ and 36 are divisible by 4, it follows that $3x$, and thus x, must be divisible by 4. The only pairs (x, y) that satisfy these conditions are $(4, 6)$ and $(8, 3)$, so the maximum value of $x + y$ is $8 + 3 = 11$.

175. The sum of the ages of Doris and Fred is y years. If Doris is 12 years older than Fred, how many years old will Fred be y years from now, in terms of y ?

(A) $y - 6$

(B) $2y - 6$

(C) $\dfrac{y}{2} - 6$

(D) $\dfrac{3y}{2} - 6$

(E) $\dfrac{5y}{2} - 6$

Let d represent the age of Doris and f represent the age of Fred. Since the sum of Doris' age and Fred's age is y years, $d + f = y$; and since Doris is 12 years older than Fred, $d = f + 12$. Substituting the second equation into the first

yields $(12 + f) + f = y$. Solving for f, $f = \dfrac{y - 12}{2} = \dfrac{y}{2} - 6$.

Fred's age after y years is $f + y = \dfrac{y}{2} - 6 + y = \dfrac{3y}{2} - 6$.

Therefore, the best answer is D.

$$
\begin{array}{r}
1,234 \\
1,243 \\
1,324 \\
\cdot\ \cdot\ \cdot\ \cdot \\
\cdot\ \cdot\ \cdot\ \cdot \\
+\ 4,321
\end{array}
$$

176. The addition problem above shows four of the 24 different integers that can be formed by using each of the digits 1, 2, 3, and 4 exactly once in each integer. What is the sum of these 24 integers?

(A) 24,000
(B) 26,664
(C) 40,440
(D) 60,000
(E) 66,660

Note that each column contains six 1's, six 2's, six 3's, and six 4's, whose sum is $6(1 + 2 + 3 + 4) = 6(10) = 60$. In the tens, hundreds, and thousands columns, the sum is 66 due to the 6 carried from the previous column. Therefore, the sum of these 24 integers is 66,660. Hence, the best answer is E.

177. If $x = -(2 - 5)$, then $x =$

(A) -7 (B) -3 (C) 3 (D) 7 (E) 10

Since $x = -(2 - 5)$, $x = -(-3) = 3$. The best answer is C.

178. What percent of 30 is 12 ?

(A) 2.5% (B) 3.6% (C) 25%
(D) 40% (E) 250%

$\dfrac{12}{30} = \dfrac{2}{5} = \dfrac{40}{100} = 40\%$. The best answer is D.

179. On a 3-day fishing trip, 4 adults consumed food costing \$60. For the same food costs per person per day, what would be the cost of food consumed by 7 adults during a 5-day fishing trip?

(A) \$300
(B) \$175
(C) \$105
(D) \$100
(E) \$84

On the 3-day fishing trip, each adult consumed an average of $\dfrac{\$60}{4}$ or \$15 worth of food. Thus, the cost of food per person per day was \$5. At the same rate, the cost of food consumed by 7 adults during a 5-day fishing trip would be $5(7)(\$5) = \$175$. The best answer is B.

180. In a poll of 66,000 physicians, only 20 percent responded; of these, 10 percent disclosed their preference for pain reliever X. How many of the physicians who responded did not disclose a preference for pain reliever X ?

(A) 1,320
(B) 5,280
(C) 6,600
(D) 10,560
(E) 11,880

The number of physicians who responded to the poll was $0.2\,(66,000)$ or 13,200. If 10 percent of the respondents disclosed a preference for X, then 90 percent did not disclose a preference for X. Thus, the best answer is $0.9\,(13,200)$ or choice E.

181. If $\dfrac{1.5}{0.2 + x} = 5$, then $x =$

    (A) -3.7
    (B) 0.1
    (C) 0.3
    (D) 0.5
    (E) 2.8

Multiplying both sides of the equation by $0.2 + x$ yields the equation $1.5 = 1 + 5x$, so that $5x = 0.5$ and $x = 0.1$. The best answer is B.

182. If a basketball team scores an average (arithmetic mean) of x points per game for n games and then scores y points in its next game, what is the team's average score for the $n + 1$ games?

    (A) $\dfrac{nx + y}{n + 1}$

    (B) $x + \dfrac{y}{n + 1}$

    (C) $x + \dfrac{y}{n}$

    (D) $\dfrac{n(x + y)}{n + 1}$

    (E) $\dfrac{x + ny}{n + 1}$

For the first n games, the team has scored a total of nx points; and for the $n + 1$ games, the team has scored a total of $nx + y$ points. Thus, the average score for the $n + 1$ games is $\dfrac{nx + y}{n + 1}$. The best answer is A.

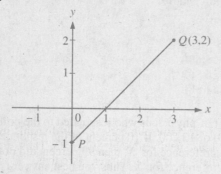

183. In the figure above, the point on segment PQ that is twice as far from P as from Q is

    (A) $(3, 1)$
    (B) $(2, 1)$
    (C) $(2, -1)$
    (D) $(1.5, 0.5)$
    (E) $(1, 0)$

Since the slope of PQ is 1 and the y–intercept is -1, the points $(0, -1)$, $(1, 0)$, $(2, 1)$, and $(3, 2)$ are on segment PQ and divide the segment into three intervals of equal length as shown in the figure below.

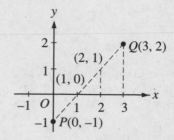

Note that the point $(2, 1)$ is twice as far from $P(0, -1)$ as from $Q(3, 2)$, and the best answer is B.

Alternatively, to solve this problem we need to find a point, X, on segment PQ such that $PX = 2QX$. Since the slope and y-intercept of PQ are 1 and -1, respectively, the coordinates for X are of the form $(x, x - 1)$. Therefore,

$$PX = \sqrt{(x - 0)^2 + ((x - 1) + 1)^2} = \sqrt{2x^2} = \sqrt{2}\,x \quad \text{and}$$

$$QX = \sqrt{(3 - x)^2 + (2 - (x - 1))^2} = \sqrt{2(3 - x)^2} = \sqrt{2}\,(3 - x).$$

So since $PX = 2QX$, it follows that $\sqrt{2}\,x = 2\sqrt{2}\,(3 - x)$, or $x = 2(3 - x)$, or $x = 2$. Thus, X has coordinates $(2, 1)$ and the best answer is B.

184. $\dfrac{3}{100} + \dfrac{5}{1,000} + \dfrac{7}{100,000} =$

    (A) 0.357
    (B) 0.3507
    (C) 0.35007
    (D) 0.0357
    (E) 0.03507

If each fraction is written in decimal form, the sum to be found is

$$\begin{array}{r} 0.03 \\ 0.005 \\ \underline{0.00007} \\ 0.03507 \end{array}$$

Thus, the best answer is E.

185. If the number n of calculators sold per week varies with the price p in dollars according to the equation $n = 300 - 20p$, what would be the total weekly revenue from the sale of $10 calculators?

(A) $100 (B) $300 (C) $1,000

(D) $2,800 (E) $3,000

If the price of a calculator is $10, then the number n of calculators that would be sold is $n = 300 - 20(10) = 100$. Thus, the total revenue from the sale of 100 calculators at $10 each would be $1,000, and the best answer is C.

186. Of the 65 cars on a car lot, 45 have air-conditioning, 30 have power windows, and 12 have both air-conditioning and power windows. How many of the cars on the lot have neither air-conditioning nor power windows?

(A)   2
(B)   8
(C) 10
(D) 15
(E) 18

One way to solve problems of this type is to construct a Venn diagram and to assign values to the nonoverlapping regions. For example,

45 cars that have air-conditioning
30 cars that have power windows

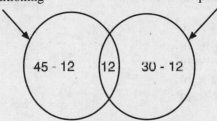

If there were 65 cars in all, then the number of cars that have neither air-conditioning nor power windows is $65 - (33 + 12 + 18) = 2$. Thus, the best answer is A.

187. Of the following numbers, which one is third greatest?

(A) $2\sqrt{2} - 1$ (B) $\sqrt{2} + 1$ (C) $1 - \sqrt{2}$

(D) $\sqrt{2} - 1$ (E) $\sqrt{2}$

Since each option involves the $\sqrt{2}$, it is convenient to think of how each quantity compares to the $\sqrt{2}$. Since $\sqrt{2} > 1$, only option C is negative. If A, B, C, D, and E denote the respective quantities, it can be determined by inspection that $B > E > D > C$. Since $A = \sqrt{2} + (\sqrt{2} - 1)$, clearly $A > E$, but $A < B$. Therefore, $B > A > E > D > C$, and the best answer is E.

Alternatively, the value of each option can be estimated by using 1.4 for the $\sqrt{2}$.

188. During the second quarter of 1984, a total of 2,976,000 domestic cars were sold. If this was 24 percent greater than the number sold during the first quarter of 1984, how many were sold during the first quarter?

(A)   714,240
(B)   2,261,760
(C)   2,400,000
(D)   3,690,240
(E)   3,915,790

If q represents the number of cars sold during the first quarter, then 124 percent of q represents the number sold during the second quarter, or $1.24q = 2,976,000$, and $q = 2,400,000$. Thus, the best answer is C.

189. If a positive integer n is divisible by both 5 and 7, the n must also be divisible by which of the following?

I.   12
II. 35
III. 70

(A) None (B) I only (C) II only

(D) I and II (E) II and III

Since 5 and 7 are prime numbers, if n is divisible by both, then n must also be divisible by $5(7) = 35$. Thus, n is of the form $35k$, where k is some integer. Note that if k is an odd integer, n will not be divisible by either 12 or 70. Hence, the best answer is C.

190. An author received $0.80 in royalties for each of the first 100,000 copies of her book sold, and $0.60 in royalties for each additional copy sold. If she received a total of $260,000 in royalties, how many copies of her book were sold?

(A) 130,000
(B) 300,000
(C) 380,000
(D) 400,000
(E) 420,000

If the author sold n copies, then she received $0.80(100,000) or $80,000 for the first 100,000 copies sold, and $0.60 $(n - 100,000)$ for the rest of the copies sold, for a total of $260,000. The equation

$$\$260,000 = \$80,000 + \$0.60\,(n - 100,000)$$

yields $0.6n = 240,000$ and $n = 400,000$. Thus, the best answer is D.

191. Starting from Town S, Fred rode his bicycle 8 miles due east, 3 miles due south, 2 miles due west, and 11 miles due north, finally stopping at Town T. If the entire region is flat, what is the straight-line distance, in miles, between Towns S and T?

(A) 10

(B) $8\sqrt{2}$

(C) $\sqrt{157}$

(D) 14

(E) 24

The map below shows the consecutive paths that Fred rode in his roundabout trip from Town S to Town T.

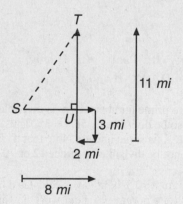

From the map, it can be seen that his path crossed at point U and that $SU = (8 - 2)$ or 6 miles and $TU = (11 - 3)$ or 8 miles. Thus, by the Pythagorean theorem, the straight line distance

(dotted line) is $\sqrt{6^2 + 8^2} = 10$ miles, and the best answer is A.

192. Which of the following describes all values of x for which $1 - x^2 \geq 0$?

(A) $x \geq 1$
(B) $x \leq -1$
(C) $0 \leq x \leq 1$
(D) $x \leq -1$ or $x \geq 1$
(E) $-1 \leq x \leq 1$

An equivalent expression of the inequality is $(1 + x)(1 - x) \geq 0$. The product of the two factors will equal 0 if $x = -1$ or $x = 1$; the product of the two factors will be greater than 0 if both factors are positive or if both factors are negative. In the first case, $1 + x > 0$ and $1 - x > 0$, so that $x > -1$ and $1 > x$, or $-1 < x < 1$. If both factors are negative, then $1 + x < 0$ and $1 - x < 0$, so that $x < -1$ and $1 < x$, which is impossible and, thus, yields no additional values of x. Therefore, taking all cases into consideration, the solution is $-1 \leq x \leq 1$, and the best answer is E.

Alternatively, adding x^2 to both sides of the inequality $1 - x^2 \geq 0$ yields $1 \geq x^2$. To solve this inequality we need to consider cases where $x \geq 0$ and cases where $x < 0$. If $x \geq 0$, then $1 \geq x^2$ whenever $1 \geq x \geq 0$. If $x < 0$, then $1 \geq x^2$ whenever $-1 \leq x < 0$. Thus, $1 \geq x^2$ whenever $-1 \leq x \leq 1$, and the best answer is E.

193. Four hours from now, the population of a colony of bacteria will reach 1.28×10^6. If the population of the colony doubles every 4 hours, what was the population 12 hours ago?

(A) 6.4×10^2
(B) 8.0×10^4
(C) 1.6×10^5
(D) 3.2×10^5
(E) 8.0×10^6

If the population of bacteria doubles every 4 hours, then it must now be half of what it will be in 4 hours or

$\dfrac{1.28 \times 10^6}{2} = 0.64 \times 10^6$. Since 12 hours consists of three

4-hour intervals, the population 12 hours ago was $\left(\dfrac{1}{2}\right)^3$, or $\dfrac{1}{8}$,

of 0.64×10^6, which would be written in scientific notation, not as 0.08×10^6, but as 8.0×10^4. Thus, the best answer is B.

194. At a certain pizzeria, $\frac{1}{8}$ of the pizzas sold in one week were mushroom and $\frac{1}{3}$ of the <u>remaining</u> pizzas sold were pepperoni. If n of the pizzas sold were pepperoni, how many were mushroom?

(A) $\frac{3}{8}n$

(B) $\frac{3}{7}n$

(C) $\frac{7}{16}n$

(D) $\frac{7}{8}n$

(E) $3n$

If t is the total number of pizzas sold, then $\frac{1}{8}t$ of the pizzas sold were mushroom, and $\frac{1}{3}\left(\frac{7}{8}t\right)$ or $\frac{7t}{24}$ of the pizzas sold were pepperoni. The ratio of the number of mushroom pizzas sold to the number of pepperoni pizzas sold was $\frac{3t}{24}$ to $\frac{7t}{24}$, or $\frac{3}{7}$. Thus, if there were n pepperoni pizzas sold, there were $\frac{3}{7}n$ mushroom pizzas sold and the best answer is B.

Alternatively, if $\frac{1}{8}$ of the pizzas sold were mushroom, then $\frac{1}{3}\left(1-\frac{1}{8}\right)$ or $\frac{7}{24}$ of the pizzas were pepperoni. Thus, if n pepperoni pizzas were sold, then a total of $\frac{24}{7}n$ pizzas were sold. Of the $\frac{24}{7}n$ pizzas sold, $\frac{1}{8}\left(\frac{24}{7}\right)n$ were pepperoni, and the best answer is B.

195. If 4 is one solution of the equation $x^2 + 3x + k = 10$, where k is a constant, what is the other solution?

(A) -7 (B) -4 (C) -3 (D) 1 (E) 6

If 4 is one solution of the equation, then $4^2 + 3(4) + k = 10$ and $k = -18$. Thus, the equation to be solved is $x^2 + 3x - 18 = 10$ or $x^2 + 3x - 28 = 0$. Factoring the quadratic yields $(x + 7)(x - 4) = 0$, which has solutions -7 and 4. Therefore, $x = -7$ is the other solution, and the best answer is A.

196. The probability is $\frac{1}{2}$ that a certain coin will turn up heads on any given toss. If the coin is to be tossed three times, what is the probability that on at least one of the tosses the coin will turn up tails?

(A) $\frac{1}{8}$ (B) $\frac{1}{2}$ (C) $\frac{3}{4}$ (D) $\frac{7}{8}$ (E) $\frac{15}{16}$

The probability that on at least one of the tosses the coin will turn up tails is 1 minus the probability that the coin will turn up heads on all three tosses. Since each toss is an independent event, the probability of getting three heads is $\left(\frac{1}{2}\right)^3$, so that the probability of getting at least one tail is $1 - \frac{1}{8} = \frac{7}{8}$. Thus the best answer is D.

197. A caterer ordered 125 ice-cream bars and 125 sundaes. If the total price was $200.00 and the price of each ice-cream bar was $0.60, what was the price of each sundae?

(A) $0.60
(B) $0.80
(C) $1.00
(D) $1.20
(E) $1.60

Let y represent the price of a sundae ordered by the caterer. Since the caterer ordered 125 sundaes and 125 ice-cream bars, and the price of each ice-cream bar was $0.60 and the total price of ice-cream bars and sundaes was $200.00, it follows that $125(0.60) + 125y = 200.00$. Solving this equation yields $y = \$1.00$. Hence, the best answer is C.

198. Lloyd normally works 7.5 hours per day and earns $4.50 per hour. For each hour he works in excess of 7.5 hours on a given day, he is paid 1.5 times his regular rate. If Lloyd works 10.5 hours on a given day, how much does he earn for that day?

(A) $33.75
(B) $47.25
(C) $51.75
(D) $54.00
(E) $70.00

Lloyd's earnings for a 10.5-hour day is calculated by combining his earnings for a normal 7.5-hour work day and his earnings for 3 hours overtime. Since he earns $4.50 per hour regularly and 1.5 times his regular rate for overtime, he earns $7.5(\$4.50) = \$33.75$ for a normal day and $3(1.5)(\$4.50) = \$20.25$ for his overtime. Therefore, his total earnings for the day is $54.00, and the best answer is D.

199. If $x = -3$, what is the value of $-3x^2$?

(A) –27   (B) –18   (C) 18   (D) 27   (E) 81

Since $x = -3$, the value of $-3x^2 = -3(-3)^2 = -27$. Thus, the best answer is A.

200. Of the final grades received by the students in a certain math course, $\frac{1}{5}$ are A's, $\frac{1}{4}$ are B's, $\frac{1}{2}$ are C's, and the remaining 10 grades are D's. What is the number of students in the course?

(A)   80
(B)   110
(C)   160
(D)   200
(E)   400

If there are x students in the course, then $\left(\frac{1}{5} + \frac{1}{4} + \frac{1}{2}\right)x$ or $\left(\frac{19}{20}\right)x$ of the students received grades of A, B, or C, leaving only $\frac{x}{20}$ or 10 students that received a D grade. Thus, $\frac{x}{20} = 10$ and $x = 200$. Hence, the best answer is D.

201. $\dfrac{29^2 + 29}{29} =$

(A) 870   (B) 841   (C) 58   (D) 31   (E) 30

The easiest way to evaluate the expression is to factor 29 out of each term in the numerator. Thus, $\dfrac{29^2 + 29}{29} = \dfrac{29(29+1)}{29} = \dfrac{29(30)}{29} = 30$; so, the best answer is E.

202. Mr. Hernandez, who was a resident of State X for only 8 months last year, had a taxable income of $22,500 for the year. If the state tax rate were 4 percent of the year's taxable income prorated for the proportion of the year during which the taxpayer was a resident, what would be the amount of Mr. Hernandez's State X tax for last year?

(A) $900   (B) $720   (C) $600
(D) $300   (E) $60

Mr. Hernandez's State X tax for last year can be calculated by multiplying the tax rate by his taxable income and then by the fraction of the year that he was a resident. His tax for last year was $(0.04)\ (\$22,500)\left(\dfrac{8}{12}\right) = \$600$. Thus, the best answer is C.

203. If $x = 1 - 3t$ and $y = 2t - 1$, then for what value of t does $x = y$?

(A) $\dfrac{5}{2}$ (B) $\dfrac{3}{2}$ (C) $\dfrac{2}{3}$ (D) $\dfrac{2}{5}$ (E) 0

Since $x = y$, the two expressions for x and y can be set equal to each other. Thus, the equation $1 - 3t = 2t - 1$ yields $t = \dfrac{2}{5}$, and the best answer is D.

204. Which of the following fractions is equal to the decimal 0.0625 ?

(A) $\dfrac{5}{8}$ (B) $\dfrac{3}{8}$ (C) $\dfrac{1}{16}$ (D) $\dfrac{1}{18}$ (E) $\dfrac{3}{80}$

The fraction that is equal to the decimal 0.0625 is $\dfrac{625}{10,000} = \dfrac{1}{16}$. Hence, the best answer is C.

205. In the figure above, if $\dfrac{x}{x+y} = \dfrac{3}{8}$, then $x =$

(A)   60
(B)   67.5
(C)   72
(D)   108
(E)   112.5

If $\dfrac{x}{x+y} = \dfrac{3}{8}$ is multiplied by $8(x + y)$, the result is $8x = 3x + 3y$, or $5x = 3y$. Since the angles of the figure are supplementary, $x + y = 180$. Solving the first equation for y yields $y = \dfrac{5}{3}x$ and substituting into the second equation yields $x + \dfrac{5}{3}x = 180$. Therefore, $x = 67.5$, and the best answer is B.

206. The number of coronary-bypass operations performed in the United States increased from 13,000 in 1970 to 191,000 in 1983. What was the approximate percent increase in the number of coronary-bypass operations from 1970 to 1983 ?

 (A)   90%
 (B)   140%
 (C)   150%
 (D) 1,400%
 (E) 1,600%

The approximate percent increase in the number of coronary-bypass operations from 1970 to 1983 is calculated by dividing the increase in the number of operations by the original number of operations in 1970. Hence, $\dfrac{178,000}{13,000} = 13.7$ or approximately 1,400 percent. Thus, the best answer is D.

207. If positive integers x and y are not both odd, which of the following must be even?

 (A) xy
 (B) $x + y$
 (C) $x - y$
 (D) $x + y - 1$
 (E) $2(x + y) - 1$

Since x and y are not both odd, either one or both of them is even. To determine which answer choice is even, each choice must be checked for both cases as shown in the table below.

	both even	one even and one odd
xy	even	even
$x + y$	even	odd
$x - y$	even	odd
$x + y - 1$	odd	even
$2(x + y) - 1$	odd	odd

Since xy is the only one of the expressions that must be even in both cases, the best answer is A.

208. Two trains, X and Y, started simultaneously from opposite ends of a 100-mile route and traveled toward each other on parallel tracks. Train X, traveling at a constant rate, completed the 100-mile trip in 5 hours; train Y, traveling at a constant rate, completed the 100-mile trip in 3 hours. How many miles had train X traveled when it met train Y ?

 (A) 37.5   (B) 40.0   (C) 60.0
 (D) 62.5   (E) 77.5

Let t be the number of hours the trains had traveled before they met. The rate of the train is determined by dividing the distance by the time. Train X was traveling at $\dfrac{100}{5} = 20$ miles per hour; and train Y was traveling at $\dfrac{100}{3}$ miles per hour. Since the two trains were traveling in opposite directions and $d = rt$, the distance, covered before they met, must add to 100 miles. The equation $20t + \dfrac{100}{3}t = 100$ yields $t = 1.875$ hours. The number of miles train X had traveled before it met train Y was $20t = 20(1.875) = 37.5$ miles. Hence, the best answer is A.

Another way to look at the problem is as follows: the distances that each of the trains traveled in the same amount of time is directly proportional to their relative speeds. The ratio of the speed of train X to that of train Y is $\dfrac{100}{5}$ to $\dfrac{100}{3}$, or 3 to 5. Thus, if the entire trip is divided into eighths, at the time they passed, train X had traveled $\dfrac{3}{8}$ of the distance and train Y had traveled $\dfrac{5}{8}$ of the distance. Hence, $\dfrac{3}{8}(100 \text{ miles}) = 37.5$ and the best answer is A.

209. As x increases from 165 to 166, which of the following must increase?

 I. $2x - 5$

 II. $1 - \dfrac{1}{x}$

 III. $\dfrac{1}{x^2 - x}$

 (A) I only
 (B) III only
 (C) I and II
 (D) I and III
 (E) II and III

With respect to I, as x increases from 165 to 166, expression $2x - 5$ increases since $2x$ increases; therefore, the value of the expression is increasing. With respect to II, as x increases, its reciprocal decreases; therefore, the value of the expression as a whole increases. With respect to III, for integers greater than 1, x^2 increases more rapidly than x increases so that the value of $x^2 - x$ in the denominator increases, causing the reciprocal to decrease. Therefore, I and II increase but III decreases, and the best answer is C.

210. If it is true that $x > -2$ and $x < 7$, which of the following must be true?

(A) $x > 2$
(B) $x > -7$
(C) $x < 2$
(D) $-7 < x < 2$
(E) None of the above

A graph of $x > -2$ and $x < 7$, as shown below, will establish the x values that satisfy the two inequalities ($-2 < x < 7$). $x > 2$ is not true since there are x values on the graph that are not greater than 2. Likewise $x < 2$ is also false, since there are x values on the graph that are not less than 2. $-7 < x < 2$ is also false since it includes values that are not on the graph. Every value on the graph is greater than -7, which implies $x > -7$ is true; thus, the best answer is B.

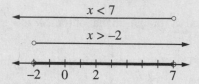

211. A club sold an average (arithmetic mean) of 92 raffle tickets per member. Among the female members, the average number sold was 84, and among the male members, the average number sold was 96. What was the ratio of the number of male members to the number of female members in the club?

(A) 1 : 1
(B) 1 : 2
(C) 1 : 3
(D) 2 : 1
(E) 3 : 1

The average numbers of raffle tickets sold per member, per female member, and per male member were 92, 84, and 96, respectively. If f represents the number of female members and m represents the number of male members, then $84f + 96m = 92(f + m)$, which yields $4m = 8f$; hence,

$\dfrac{m}{f} = \dfrac{8}{4}$. Therefore, the ratio of the number of male members to female members is 2 to 1. Hence, the best answer is D.

212. How many bits of computer memory will be required to store the integer x, where

$x = -\sqrt{810,000}$, if each digit requires 4 bits of memory and the sign of x requires 1 bit?

(A) 25 (B) 24 (C) 17 (D) 13 (E) 12

The expression $-\sqrt{810,000}$ is equivalent to -900, which contains three digits and a negative sign for a total use of $3(4) + 1 = 13$ bits of memory. Therefore, the best answer is D.

213. One week a certain truck rental lot had a total of 20 trucks, all of which were on the lot Monday morning. If 50 percent of the trucks that were rented out during the week were returned to the lot on or before Saturday morning of that week, and if there were at least 12 trucks on the lot that Saturday morning, what is the greatest number of different trucks that could have been rented out during the week?

(A) 18
(B) 16
(C) 12
(D) 8
(E) 4

The difference between the number of trucks on the lot on Monday and the minimum number of trucks on the lot on Saturday is 8 trucks, which is the maximum number of trucks not on the lot Saturday morning. Since 50 percent of the trucks that were rented out during the week were returned to the lot on or before Saturday morning, the greatest number of different trucks that could have been rented out during the week was $2(8) = 16$ or twice the maximum number of trucks not on the lot Saturday morning. Thus, the best answer is B.

214. Ms. Adams sold two properties, X and Y, for $30,000 each. She sold property X for 20 percent more than she paid for it and sold property Y for 20 percent less than she paid for it. If expenses are disregarded, what was her total net gain or loss, if any, on the two properties?

(A) Loss of $1,250
(B) Loss of $2,500
(C) Gain of $1,250
(D) Gain of $2,500
(E) There was neither a net gain nor a net loss.

Let x represent the amount of money Ms. Adams paid for property X and y represent the amount of money Ms. Adams paid for property Y. Since she sold X for 20 percent more than she paid for it, $1.20x = \$30,000$. Since she sold Y for 20 percent less than she paid for it, $0.8y = \$30,000$. Solving the two equations yields $x = \$25,000$ and $y = \$37,500$. It follows that a $5,000 profit was made on property X and a $7,500 loss was realized on property Y. The net outcome was a $2,500 loss; thus, the best answer is B.

215. A rectangular box is 10 inches wide, 10 inches long, and 5 inches high. What is the greatest possible (straight-line) distance, in inches, between any two points on the box?

(A) 15
(B) 20
(C) 25
(D) $10\sqrt{2}$
(E) $10\sqrt{3}$

The greatest possible distance between any two points on the box is the space diagonal (AB) of the rectangular solid as shown below. To compute the length of AB, the Pythagorean theorem must be used twice as follows:

$AB^2 = AC^2 + BC^2$
$AC^2 = 10^2 = 100$
$BC^2 = 5^2 + 10^2 = 125$
$AB^2 = 100 + 125 = 225$
$AB = 15$

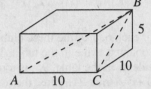

Therefore, the best answer is A.

216. How many positive integers less than 20 are either a multiple of 2, an odd multiple of 9, or the sum of a positive multiple of 2 and a positive multiple of 9 ?

(A) 19 (B) 18 (C) 17 (D) 16 (E) 15

There are 9 multiples of 2 less than 20. The only odd multiple of 9 less than 20 is 9. There are 5 numbers less than 20 that can be written as the sum of a positive multiple of 2 and a positive multiple of 9. They are $9 + 2$, $9 + 4$, $9 + 6$, $9 + 8$, and $9 + 10$. Hence, the total is $9 + 1 + 5 = 15$ and the best answer is E.

217. On 3 sales John has received commissions of $240, $80, and $110, and he has 1 additional sale pending. If John is to receive an average (arithmetic mean) commission of exactly $150 on the 4 sales, then the 4th commission must be

(A) $164
(B) $170
(C) $175
(D) $182
(E) $185

If x is the 4th commission and the average commission is $150, then

$$\frac{240 + 80 + 110 + x}{4} = 150$$
$$430 + x = 600$$
$$x = 170$$

Therefore, the best answer is B.

218. $\sqrt{463}$ is between

(A) 21 and 22
(B) 22 and 23
(C) 23 and 24
(D) 24 and 25
(E) 25 and 26

Since $21^2 = 441$ and $22^2 = 484$, $\sqrt{463}$ is between 21 and 22. The best answer is A.

219. The annual budget of a certain college is to be shown on a circle graph. If the size of each sector of the graph is to be proportional to the amount of the budget it represents, how many degrees of the circle should be used to represent an item that is 15 percent of the budget?

(A) $15°$
(B) $36°$
(C) $54°$
(D) $90°$
(E) $150°$

If the sector is to represent 15 percent of the budget, the measure of its central angle should be 15 percent of $360°$, or $0.15(360°)$, or $54°$. Thus, the best answer is C.

220. A company accountant estimates that airfares next year for business trips of a thousand miles or less will increase by 20 percent and airfares for all other business trips will increase by 10 percent. This year total airfares for business trips of a thousand miles or less were $9,900 and airfares for all other business trips were $13,000. According to the accountant's estimate, if the same business trips will be made next year as this year, how much will be spent for airfares next year?

(A) $22,930
(B) $26,180
(C) $26,330
(D) $26,490
(E) $29,770

Since the airfare for business trips of a thousand miles or less will increase by 20 percent next year, the amount spent will be (1.20) ($9,900), or $11,880. Since the airfares for all other business trips will increase by 10 percent next year, the amount spent will be (1.10) ($13,000), or $14,300. Thus, the total amount spent for airfares next year is estimated to be $11,880 + $14,300 = $26,180. Therefore the best answer is B.

221. What is the value of $2x^2 - 2.4x - 1.7$ for $x = 0.7$?

(A) -0.72
(B) -1.42
(C) -1.98
(D) -2.40
(E) -2.89

For $x = 0.7$, the value of $2x^2 - 2.4x - 1.7$ is
$2(0.7)^2 - 2.4(0.7) - 1.7$, or -2.40. The best answer is D.

222. If $x * y = xy - 2(x + y)$ for all integers x and
y, then $2 * (-3) =$

(A) -16
(B) -11
(C) -4
(D) 4
(E) 16

Since $x * y = xy - 2(x + y)$, therefore $2 * (-3) = 2(-3) - 2(2 + (-3))$,
or -4. The best answer is C.

223. During a two-week period, the price of an ounce of
silver increased by 25 percent by the end of the first
week and then decreased by 20 percent of this new
price by the end of the second week. If the price of
silver was x dollars per ounce at the beginning of
the two-week period, what was the price, in dollars
per ounce, by the end of the period?

(A) $0.8x$
(B) $0.95x$
(C) x
(D) $1.05x$
(E) $1.25x$

At the end of the first week the price of an ounce of silver was
$1.25x$. Therefore, at the end of the second week the price was
20 percent less than $1.25x$, or $(0.80)(1.25)x$, which equals x.
Therefore, the best answer is C.

224. If a cube has a volume of 64, what is its total surface
area?

(A) 16
(B) 24
(C) 48
(D) 64
(E) 96

Since the volume of the cube is 64, $x^3 = 64$, where x is the
length of each edge of the cube. Thus, $x = 4$. The surface area of
each side of the cube is 4^2, or 16, and the cube has 6 sides. Thus,
the total surface area is $(16)(6)$, or 96. The best answer is E.

Club	Number of Students
Chess	40
Drama	30
Math	25

225. The table above shows the number of students in three
clubs at McAuliffe School. Although no student is in all
three clubs, 10 students are in both chess and drama, 5
students are in both chess and math, and
6 students are in both drama and math. How many
different students are in the three clubs?

(A) 68 (B) 69 (C) 74 (D) 79 (E) 84

For each pair of the three clubs, the number of students in both
is counted twice in the table. Therefore, the total number of
students in the table, 95, is too large by an amount equal to
$10 + 5 + 6$, or 21. Thus, the number of different students in the
three clubs is $95 - 21$, or 74. The diagram below shows the
distribution of these 74 students.

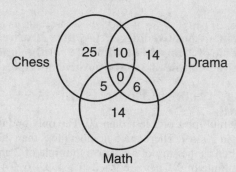

Therefore, the best answer is C.

226. If s, u, and v are positive integers and
$2s = 2u + 2v$, which of the following must
be true?

 I. $s = u$
 II. $u \neq v$
 III. $s > v$

(A) None
(B) I only
(C) II only
(D) III only
(E) II and III

 I. s cannot equal u, because if $s = u$, then $2v = 0$, which is not
 true for any integer v. Thus, statement I is not true.
 II. u can equal v; for example $2^3 = 2^2 + 2^2$. Thus, statement II
 is not true.
 III. Using the same reasoning as in I above $s \neq v$. Since $2u$ must
 be positive, $2s$ must be greater than $2v$. So, s must be
 greater than v. Thus, statement III must be true, and the best
 answer is D.

227. In a nationwide poll, N people were interviewed. If $\frac{1}{4}$ of them answered "yes" to question 1, and of those, $\frac{1}{3}$ answered "yes" to question 2, which of the following expressions represents the number of people interviewed who did <u>not</u> answer "yes" to both questions?

(A) $\frac{N}{7}$

(B) $\frac{6N}{7}$

(C) $\frac{5N}{12}$

(D) $\frac{7N}{12}$

(E) $\frac{11N}{12}$

The number of people who answered "yes" to question 1 was $\frac{N}{4}$. Since $\frac{1}{3}$ of the $\frac{N}{4}$ people answered "yes" to question 2, $\left(\frac{1}{3}\right)\frac{N}{4}$, or $\frac{N}{12}$, people answered "yes" to both questions. Thus the number of people who did <u>not</u> answer "yes" to both questions was $N - \frac{N}{12}$, or $\frac{11N}{12}$. Therefore, the best answer is E.

228. In a certain pond, 50 fish were caught, tagged, and returned to the pond. A few days later, 50 fish were caught again, of which 2 were found to have been tagged. If the percent of tagged fish in the second catch approximates the percent of tagged fish in the pond, what is the approximate number of fish in the pond?

(A) 400
(B) 625
(C) 1,250
(D) 2,500
(E) 10,000

Let N be the number of fish in the pond. Then $\frac{50}{N}$ is the fraction of fish in the pond that were tagged. The fraction of fish in the sample of 50 that were tagged was $\frac{2}{50}$, or $\frac{1}{25}$.

Therefore, $\frac{50}{N} = \frac{1}{25}$, or $N = (50)(25) = 1,250$.
Thus, the best answer is C.

229. The ratio of two quantities is 3 to 4. If each of the quantities is increased by 5, what is the ratio of these two new quantities?

(A) $\frac{3}{4}$

(B) $\frac{8}{9}$

(C) $\frac{18}{19}$

(D) $\frac{23}{24}$

(E) It cannot be determined from the information given.

Let x and y be the two quantities such that $\frac{x}{y} = \frac{3}{4}$.

If $x = 3$ and $y = 4$, then $\frac{x+5}{y+5} = \frac{3+5}{4+5} = \frac{8}{9}$. If $x = 6$ and $y = 8$

(which would still make $\frac{x}{y} = \frac{3}{4}$), then $\frac{x+5}{y+5} = \frac{6+5}{8+5} = \frac{11}{13}$.

Therefore, the ratio of the two new quantities cannot be uniquely determined from the information given. Thus, the best answer is E.

230. In 1986 the book value of a certain car was $\frac{2}{3}$ of the original purchase price, and in 1988 its book value was $\frac{1}{2}$ of the original purchase price. By what percent did the book value of this car decrease from 1986 to 1988 ?

(A) $16\frac{2}{3}\%$

(B) 25%

(C) $33\frac{1}{3}\%$

(D) 50%

(E) 75%

If B is the original purchase price of the car, then the book value of the car in 1986 was $\frac{2B}{3}$ and the book value in 1988 was $\frac{B}{2}$. Therefore, the percent decrease in the book value from 1986 to 1988 was

$$\frac{\frac{2B}{3} - \frac{B}{2}}{\frac{2B}{3}} = \frac{\frac{4B}{6} - \frac{3B}{6}}{\frac{2B}{3}} = \frac{\frac{B}{6}}{\frac{2B}{3}} = \frac{B}{6} \cdot \frac{3}{2B} = \frac{3B}{12B} = \frac{1}{4} = 25\%.$$

Thus, the best answer is B.

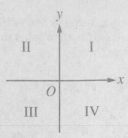

231. In the rectangular coordinate system shown above, which quadrant, if any, contains no point (x, y) that satisfies the inequality $2x - 3y \le -6$?

(A) None
(B) I
(C) II
(D) III
(E) IV

Since $2x - 3y \le -6$, $2x \le 3y - 6$, or $x \le \dfrac{3y - 6}{2}$. Note that if y is negative, x must be negative. Therefore, no point (x, y) that satisfies the inequality can have y negative and x positive. Therefore, no points that satisfy the inequality are in quadrant IV. The best answer is E.

232. A hiker walked for two days. On the second day the hiker walked 2 hours longer and at an average speed 1 mile per hour faster than he walked on the first day. If during the two days he walked a total of 64 miles and spent a total of 18 hours walking, what was his average speed on the first day?

(A) 2 mph
(B) 3 mph
(C) 4 mph
(D) 5 mph
(E) 6 mph

If t is the number of hours the hiker walked on the first day, then $t + 2$ is the number of hours he walked on the second day. Therefore, $t + t + 2 = 18$, or $t = 8$. If s was the hiker's average speed in miles per hour on the first day, then $s + 1$ was his average speed on the second day. So, the total distance hiked in 2 days was $(8)(s) + (10)(s + 1)$. Therefore,

$$8s + 10(s + 1) = 64$$
$$8s + 10s + 10 = 64$$
$$18s = 54$$
$$s = 3$$

Therefore, the best answer is B .

233. If a printer can print 2 pages of text per second, then, at this rate, approximately how many minutes will it take to print 5,000 pages of text?

(A) 4
(B) 25
(C) 42
(D) 250
(E) 417

Since the printer can produce 2 pages per second, it can produce 5,000 pages in $\dfrac{5,000}{2}$, or 2,500 seconds, which is equal to $\dfrac{2,500}{60}$, or approximately 42, minutes. Therefore, the best answer is C.

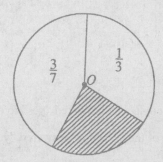

234. In the circular region with center O, shown above, the two unshaded sections comprise $\dfrac{3}{7}$ and $\dfrac{1}{3}$ of the area of the circular region. The shaded section comprises what fractional part of the area of the circular region?

(A) $\dfrac{3}{5}$

(B) $\dfrac{6}{7}$

(C) $\dfrac{2}{21}$

(D) $\dfrac{5}{21}$

(E) $\dfrac{16}{21}$

The two unshaded sections comprise $\dfrac{3}{7} + \dfrac{1}{3} = \dfrac{9}{21} + \dfrac{7}{21} = \dfrac{16}{21}$ of the area of the circular region. Thus, the shaded section comprises $1 - \dfrac{16}{21} = \dfrac{5}{21}$ of the circular region. Therefore, the best answer is D.

235. Envelopes can be purchased for $1.50 per pack of 100, $1.00 per pack of 50, or $0.03 each. What is the greatest number of envelopes that can be purchased for $7.30 ?

   (A) 426
   (B) 430
   (C) 443
   (D) 460
   (E) 486

The cheapest rate is $1.50 per pack of 100, followed by $1.00 per pack of 50, and the most expensive rate is $0.03 per envelope. Therefore, the greatest number of envelopes that can be purchased for $7.30 would be

$$4 \times \$1.50 = \$6.00 \text{ (for 400 envelopes)}$$
$$1 \times \$1.00 = \$1.00 \text{ (for 50 envelopes)}$$
$$10 \times \$0.03 = \underline{\$0.30 \text{ (for 10 envelopes)}}$$
$$\text{Total} = \$7.30 \text{ (for 460 envelopes).}$$

Therefore, the best answer is D.

236. $\sqrt{16+16} =$

   (A) $4\sqrt{2}$

   (B) $8\sqrt{2}$

   (C) $16\sqrt{2}$

   (D) 8

   (E) 16

$\sqrt{16+16} = \sqrt{(16)(2)} = \left(\sqrt{16}\right)\left(\sqrt{2}\right) = 4\sqrt{2}$.
Thus, the best answer is A.

237. An automobile's gasoline mileage varies, depending on the speed of the automobile, between 18.0 and 22.4 miles per gallon, inclusive. What is the maximum distance, in miles, that the automobile could be driven on 15 gallons of gasoline?

   (A) 336
   (B) 320
   (C) 303
   (D) 284
   (E) 270

The maximum distance would occur at the 22.4 miles per gallon rate. Thus, the maximum would be (22.4) (15), or 336 miles. Therefore, the best answer is A.

238. $\dfrac{(0.3)^5}{(0.3)^3} =$

   (A) 0.001
   (B) 0.01
   (C) 0.09
   (D) 0.9
   (E) 1.0

$\dfrac{(0.3)^5}{(0.3)^3} = (0.3)^{5-3} = (0.3)^2 = 0.09$. Therefore, the best answer is C.

239. In a horticultural experiment, 200 seeds were planted in plot I and 300 were planted in plot II. If 57 percent of the seeds in plot I germinated and 42 percent of the seeds in plot II germinated, what percent of the total number of planted seeds germinated?

   (A) 45.5%
   (B) 46.5%
   (C) 48.0%
   (D) 49.5%
   (E) 51.0%

Of the 500 seeds planted, the total number that germinated was 200 (0.57) + 300 (0.42) = 114 + 126 = 240. Thus, the percent of the total planted that germinated was $\dfrac{240}{500} = 0.48$, or 48.0%. Therefore, the best answer is C.

240. The organizers of a fair projected a 25 percent increase in attendance this year over that of last year, but attendance this year actually decreased by 20 percent. What percent of the projected attendance was the actual attendance?

   (A) 45%
   (B) 56%
   (C) 64%
   (D) 75%
   (E) 80%

If A was last year's attendance, then the projected attendance for this year was 25 percent higher than last year, or 1.25A. The actual attendance for this year was 20 percent less than last year, or 0.80A. Thus, the percent of the projected attendance that was the actual attendance is $\dfrac{0.80A}{1.25A} = 0.64 = 64\%$.

Therefore, the best answer is C.

-185-

241. An optometrist charges $150 per pair for soft contact lenses and $85 per pair for hard contact lenses. Last week she sold 5 more pairs of soft lenses than hard lenses. If her total sales for pairs of contact lenses last week were $1,690, what was the total number of pairs of contact lenses that she sold?

(A) 11 (B) 13 (C) 15 (D) 17 (E) 19

If x is the number of hard contact lenses sold last week, then $x + 5$ is the number of soft contact lenses sold. Therefore,

$$x(\$85) + (x + 5)(\$150) = \$1,690$$
$$85x + 150x + 750 = 1,690$$
$$235x = 940$$
$$x = 4$$

So, the total number of hard and soft contact lenses sold was $x + (x + 5) = 4 + 9 = 13$. Therefore, the best answer is B.

242. What is the ratio of $\dfrac{3}{4}$ to the product $4\left(\dfrac{3}{4}\right)$?

(A) $\dfrac{1}{4}$

(B) $\dfrac{1}{3}$

(C) $\dfrac{4}{9}$

(D) $\dfrac{9}{4}$

(E) 4

The ratio of $\dfrac{3}{4}$ to $4\left(\dfrac{3}{4}\right)$ is $\dfrac{\dfrac{3}{4}}{4\left(\dfrac{3}{4}\right)} = \dfrac{1}{4}$. Thus, the best answer is A.

243. The cost to rent a small bus for a trip is x dollars, which is to be shared equally among the people taking the trip. If 10 people take the trip rather than 16, how many more dollars, in terms of x, will it cost per person?

(A) $\dfrac{x}{6}$

(B) $\dfrac{x}{10}$

(C) $\dfrac{x}{16}$

(D) $\dfrac{3x}{40}$

(E) $\dfrac{3x}{80}$

If 16 take the trip, the cost per person would be $\dfrac{x}{16}$ dollars. If 10 take the trip, the cost per person would be $\dfrac{x}{10}$ dollars. Thus, if 10 take the trip, the increase in dollars per person would be $\dfrac{x}{10} - \dfrac{x}{16} = \dfrac{16x - 10x}{160} = \dfrac{6x}{160} = \dfrac{3x}{80}$. Therefore, the best answer is E.

244. If x is an integer and $y = 3x + 2$, which of the following CANNOT be a divisor of y?

(A) 4
(B) 5
(C) 6
(D) 7
(E) 8

Since $3x$ is always divisible by 3, $3x + 2$ cannot be divisible by 3, which means that $3x + 2$ cannot be divisible by 6. Therefore, the answer is C.

245. The size of a television screen is given as the length of the screen's diagonal. If the screens were flat, then the area of a square 21-inch screen would be how many square inches greater than the area of a square 19-inch screen?

(A) 2
(B) 4
(C) 16
(D) 38
(E) 40

If x is the length of a side of a square television screen and d is the length of the diagonal, then by the Pythagorean Theorem,

$$x^2 + x^2 = d^2$$
$$2x^2 = d^2$$
$$x^2 = \dfrac{d^2}{2},$$

which is the area of the screen in square inches.

If $d = 19$, then the area $= \dfrac{19^2}{2} = \dfrac{361}{2} = 180.5$ sq. in.

If $d = 21$, then the area $= \dfrac{21^2}{2} = \dfrac{441}{2} = 220.5$ sq. in.

Thus, the area of the 21-inch screen is greater by $220.5 - 180.5 = 40$ square inches. Therefore, the best answer is E.

246. If the average (arithmetic mean) of x and y is 60 and the average (arithmetic mean) of y and z is 80, what is the value of $z - x$?

(A) 70
(B) 40
(C) 20
(D) 10
(E) It cannot be determined from the information given.

The average of x and $y = \dfrac{x+y}{2} = 60$, so $x + y = 120$. The average of y and $z = \dfrac{y+z}{2} = 80$, so $y + z = 160$. Subtracting $x + y = 120$ from $y + z = 160$, you get

$$y + z - (x + y) = 160 - 120$$
$$y + z - x - y = 40$$
$$z - x = 40$$

Therefore, the best answer is B.

247. If 3 and 8 are the lengths of two sides of a triangular region, which of the following can be the length of the third side?

I. 5
II. 8
III. 11

(A) II only
(B) III only
(C) I and II only
(D) II and III only
(E) I, II, and III

Since 3 and 8 are the lengths of two sides of a triangular region, the length of the third side, x, must be greater than $8 - 3$, or 5, and less than $8 + 3$, or 11. So, $5 < x < 11$. Thus, of the three lengths given, 5, 8, and 11, only 8 can be the length of the third side. Therefore, the best answer is A.

248. One night a certain motel rented $\dfrac{3}{4}$ of its rooms, including $\dfrac{2}{3}$ of its air-conditioned rooms. If $\dfrac{3}{5}$ of its rooms were air-conditioned, what percent of the rooms that were <u>not</u> rented were air-conditioned?

(A) 20%
(B) $33\dfrac{1}{3}$%
(C) 35%
(D) 40%
(E) 80%

The motel rented $\dfrac{3}{4}$ of its rooms, including $\dfrac{2}{3}$ of its air-conditioned rooms. Since $\dfrac{3}{5}$ of its rooms were air-conditioned, $\dfrac{2}{3} \times \dfrac{3}{5}$, or $\dfrac{2}{5}$, of its rooms were rented, air-conditioned rooms. This information is summarized in the table below.

	Rented	Not Rented	
Air-Conditioned	$\dfrac{2}{5}$		$\dfrac{3}{5}$
Not Air-Conditioned			
	$\dfrac{3}{4}$		1

From the table you can see that $\dfrac{3}{5} - \dfrac{2}{5}$, or $\dfrac{1}{5}$, of its rooms were air-conditioned but not rented, and $1 - \dfrac{3}{4}$, or $\dfrac{1}{4}$, of its rooms were not rented. Thus, the percent of air-conditioned rooms among the not-rented rooms was $\dfrac{\frac{1}{5}}{\frac{1}{4}} = \dfrac{4}{5} = 80\%$.

Therefore, the best answer is E.

249. If $3 - x = 2x - 3$, then $4x =$

(A) -24
(B) -8
(C) 0
(D) 8
(E) 24

If $3 - x = 2x - 3$, then adding $x + 3$ to both sides of the equation yields $6 = 3x$. Dividing both sides of the equation by 3 yields $x = 2$. Thus, $4x = 8$ and the answer is D.

250. A certain electronic component is sold in boxes of 54 for $16.20 and in boxes of 27 for $13.20. A customer who needed only 54 components for a project had to buy 2 boxes of 27 because boxes of 54 were unavailable. Approximately how much more did the customer pay for each component due to the unavailability of the larger boxes?

    (A) $0.33
    (B) $0.19
    (C) $0.11
    (D) $0.06
    (E) $0.03

The customer paid $2 \times \$13.20$ or $26.40 for 2 boxes of 27 components. This was $26.40 – $16.20, or $10.20 more than it would have cost to buy one 54-component box. Thus the additional cost per component due to the unavailability of the larger boxes was $\dfrac{\$10.20}{54}$, which is approximately $0.19. This can be seen by noting that $\dfrac{10.20}{50} = 0.204$ which is close to, but slightly greater than, $\dfrac{10.20}{54}$. Thus the answer is B.

251. On a certain street, there is an odd number of houses in a row. The houses in the row are painted alternately white and green, with the first house painted white. If n is the total number of houses in the row, how many of the houses are painted white?

    (A) $\dfrac{n+1}{2}$

    (B) $\dfrac{n-1}{2}$

    (C) $\dfrac{n}{2}+1$

    (D) $\dfrac{n}{2}-1$

    (E) $\dfrac{n}{2}$

Since there are an odd number of houses in the row and they are painted alternately white and green, the number of houses that are white is one more than the number of houses that are green. Denoting the number of houses that are white by w, the number of houses that are green is $w - 1$. Therefore, the total number of houses n is equal to $w + (w - 1)$, so $n = 2w - 1$ and $w = \dfrac{n+1}{2}$. Thus the answer is A.

$$\begin{array}{r} \square\triangle \\ \times\ \triangle\square \\ \hline \end{array}$$

252. The product of the two-digit numbers above is the three-digit number $\square\diamond\square$, where $\square$, $\triangle$, and $\diamond$ are three different nonzero digits. If $\square \times \triangle < 10$, what is the two-digit number $\square\triangle$?

    (A) 11
    (B) 12
    (C) 13
    (D) 21
    (E) 31

It follows, from considering the units column of

$$\begin{array}{r} \square\triangle \\ \times\ \triangle\square \\ \hline \square\ \diamond\ \square \end{array}$$

and the fact that $\square \times \triangle < 10$, that $\square \times \triangle = \square$. So $\triangle = 1$ and $\square \neq 1$.
Writing out the product gives

$$\begin{array}{r} \square\triangle \\ \times\ \triangle\square \\ \hline \square^2\,\square \\ \square\ 1 \\ \hline \square\diamond\square \end{array}$$

Since the circled digits are the same it follows that $\square^2 + 1 < 10$, or $\square^2 < 9$. Thus, since $\square \neq 1$ and $\square^2 < 9$ it follows that $\square = 2$ and $\square\triangle = 21$. Thus the answer is D.

253. As a salesperson, Phyllis can choose one of two methods of annual payment: either an annual salary of $35,000 with no commission or an annual salary of $10,000 plus a 20 percent commission on her total annual sales. What must her total annual sales be to give her the same annual pay with either method?

    (A) $100,000
    (B) $120,000
    (C) $125,000
    (D) $130,000
    (E) $132,000

If s is the amount of sales needed to generate commissions so that $\$35,000 = \$10,000 + 0.2s$, then $0.2s = \$25,000$ and $s = \dfrac{\$25,000}{0.2} = \$125,000$. The best answer is C.

254. A restaurant buys fruit in cans containing $3\frac{1}{2}$ cups of fruit each. If the restaurant uses $\frac{1}{2}$ cup of the fruit in each serving of its fruit compote, what is the least number of cans needed to prepare 60 servings of the compote?

(A) 7
(B) 8
(C) 9
(D) 10
(E) 12

If the restaurant uses $\frac{1}{2}$ cup of fruit per serving, then $\frac{1}{2}(60)$ or 30 cups of fruit are needed for 60 servings. Since there are $3\frac{1}{2}$ cups in one can and 30 cups are needed, $\frac{30}{3\frac{1}{2}}$, or $8\frac{4}{7}$ cans are needed. Because it is not possible to purchase part of a can, 9 cans are needed. Therefore, the best answer is C.

255. If $x > 3{,}000$, then the value of $\frac{x}{2x+1}$ is closest to

(A) $\frac{1}{6}$
(B) $\frac{1}{3}$
(C) $\frac{10}{21}$
(D) $\frac{1}{2}$
(E) $\frac{3}{2}$

If x is greater than 3,000, the value of $\frac{x}{2x+1}$ is very close to the value of $\frac{x}{2x}$, which is equal to $\frac{1}{2}$. The best answer is D.

256. Machine A produces 100 parts twice as fast as machine B does. Machine B produces 100 parts in 40 minutes. If each machine produces parts at a constant rate, how many parts does machine A produce in 6 minutes?

(A) 30
(B) 25
(C) 20
(D) 15
(E) 7.5

If machine A produces the parts twice as fast as machine B does, then machine A requires half as much time as machine B does, or 20 minutes, to produce 100 parts. In 6 minutes, machine A will produce $\frac{100}{20}(6)$ or 30 parts. The best answer is A.

257. If 18 is 15 percent of 30 percent of a certain number, what is the number?

(A) 9
(B) 36
(C) 40
(D) 81
(E) 400

If n represents the number, then $18 = 0.15(0.3n)$ and $n = \frac{18}{0.045} = 400$. The best answer is E.

258. A necklace is made by stringing N individual beads together in the repeating pattern red bead, green bead, white bead, blue bead, and yellow bead. If the necklace design begins with a red bead and ends with a white bead, then N could equal

(A) 16
(B) 32
(C) 41
(D) 54
(E) 68

The pattern of red, green, white, blue, and yellow repeats after every 5th bead. Since the first bead is red (first in the pattern) and the last bead is white (third in the pattern), the number of beads is of the form $5n + 3$, where n is an integer. Of the options, only $68 = 5(13) + 3$ is of this form. Therefore, the best answer is E.

259. If $x = (0.08)^2$, $y = \frac{1}{(0.08)^2}$, and $z = (1 - 0.08)^2 - 1$, which of the following is true?

(A) $x = y = z$
(B) $y < z < x$
(C) $z < x < y$
(D) $y < x$ and $x = z$.
(E) $x < y$ and $x = z$.

It is not necessary to compute the precise values of x, y, and z. It is sufficient to see that x is between 0 and 1, y is greater than 1, and $z = (0.92)^2 - 1$ is less than 0. Therefore, $z < x < y$, and the best answer is C.

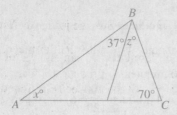

260. In $\triangle ABC$ above, what is x in terms of z ?

(A) $z + 73$
(B) $z - 73$
(C) $70 - z$
(D) $z - 70$
(E) $73 - z$

The sum of the angle measures of $\triangle ABC$ is equal to $x + 37 + z + 70 = 180$. Thus, $x + z = 180 - (37 + 70) = 73$, and $x = 73 - z$. The best answer is E.

261. In 1990 a total of x earthquakes occurred worldwide, some but not all of which occurred in Asia. If m of these earthquakes occurred in Asia, which of the following represents the ratio of the number of earthquakes that occurred in Asia to the number that did <u>not</u> occur in Asia?

(A) $\dfrac{x}{m}$

(B) $\dfrac{m}{x}$

(C) $\dfrac{m}{x - m}$

(D) $\dfrac{x}{x - m}$

(E) $1 - \dfrac{m}{x}$

If there was a total of x earthquakes and m of them occurred in Asia, then $x - m$ of them did not occur in Asia. Therefore, the ratio of the number that occurred in Asia to the number that did not occur in Asia is $\dfrac{m}{x - m}$. The best answer is C.

262. If $\dfrac{x + y}{xy} = 1$, then $y =$

(A) $\dfrac{x}{x - 1}$

(B) $\dfrac{x}{x + 1}$

(C) $\dfrac{x - 1}{x}$

(D) $\dfrac{x + 1}{x}$

(E) x

It follows from the equation that $x + y = xy$; so $x = xy - y$ or $x = y(x - 1)$. Therefore, $y = \dfrac{x}{x - 1}$, and the best answer is A.

263. If $\dfrac{1}{2}$ of the air in a tank is removed with each stroke of a vacuum pump, what fraction of the original amount of air has been removed after 4 strokes?

(A) $\dfrac{15}{16}$

(B) $\dfrac{7}{8}$

(C) $\dfrac{1}{4}$

(D) $\dfrac{1}{8}$

(E) $\dfrac{1}{16}$

With the first stroke of the pump, $\dfrac{1}{2}$ of the air is removed; with the second stroke $\dfrac{1}{2}$ of the remaining $\dfrac{1}{2}$, or $\dfrac{1}{4}$, of the air is removed, leaving $\dfrac{1}{2} - \dfrac{1}{4} = \dfrac{1}{4}$ of the air; with the third stroke $\dfrac{1}{2}$ of $\dfrac{1}{4}$, or $\dfrac{1}{8}$, is removed, leaving $\dfrac{1}{4} - \dfrac{1}{8} = \dfrac{1}{8}$; and with the fourth stroke $\dfrac{1}{2}$ of $\dfrac{1}{8}$, or $\dfrac{1}{16}$, is removed. Therefore, $\dfrac{1}{2} + \dfrac{1}{4} + \dfrac{1}{8} + \dfrac{1}{16} = \dfrac{15}{16}$ of the air has been removed, and the best answer is A.

264. Last year Department Store X had a sales total for December that was 4 times the average (arithmetic mean) of the monthly sales totals for January through November. The sales total for December was what fraction of the sales total for the year?

(A) $\dfrac{1}{4}$

(B) $\dfrac{4}{15}$

(C) $\dfrac{1}{3}$

(D) $\dfrac{4}{11}$

(E) $\dfrac{4}{5}$

If A was the average sales total per month for the first 11 months, the December sales total was $4A$, the sales total for the first 11 months was $11A$, and the sales total for the year was $11A + 4A = 15A$. Thus, the ratio of the sales total for December to the sales total for the year was $\dfrac{4A}{15A} = \dfrac{4}{15}$. The best answer is B.

265. How many integers n are there such that $1 < 5n + 5 < 25$?

    (A) Five
    (B) Four
    (C) Three
    (D) Two
    (E) One

If $1 < 5n + 5 < 25$, then subtracting 5 from each of the three parts of the inequality yields $-4 < 5n < 20$, and dividing by 5 yields $-\dfrac{4}{5} < n < 4$. The four integers that satisfy this inequality are 0, 1, 2, and 3. Therefore, the best answer is B.

266. If the two-digit integers M and N are positive and have the same digits, but in reverse order, which of the following CANNOT be the sum of M and N ?

    (A) 181
    (B) 165
    (C) 121
    (D) 99
    (E) 44

If t and u are the two digits, integer M is 10 times the tens digit plus the units digit, or $10t + u$. Similarly, n is $10u + t$, and the sum of the numbers M and N is $(10t + u) + (10u + t) = 11t + 11u = 11(t + u)$. Because the sum of M and N must be a multiple of 11, you need only find which of the answer choices is *not* a multiple of 11. Since $181 = 11(16) + 5$, 181 is not a multiple of 11, and the best answer is A.

267. Working alone, printers $X, Y,$ and Z can do a certain printing job, consisting of a large number of pages, in 12, 15, and 18 hours, respectively. What is the ratio of the time it takes printer X to do the job, working alone at its rate, to the time it takes printers Y and Z to do the job, working together at their individual rates?

    (A) $\dfrac{4}{11}$

    (B) $\dfrac{1}{2}$

    (C) $\dfrac{15}{22}$

    (D) $\dfrac{22}{15}$

    (E) $\dfrac{11}{4}$

If X requires 12 hours to do the job, then X can do $\dfrac{1}{12}$ of the job per hour. Similarly, Y can do $\dfrac{1}{15}$ of the job per hour and Z can do $\dfrac{1}{18}$ of the job per hour. Together, Y and Z can do $\left(\dfrac{1}{15} + \dfrac{1}{18}\right)$ or $\dfrac{11}{90}$ of the job per hour, which implies that it takes them $\dfrac{90}{11}$ hours to complete the job. Therefore, the ratio of the time required for X to do the job (12 hours) to the time required for Y and Z working together to do the job $\left(\dfrac{90}{11} \text{ hours}\right)$ is $\dfrac{12}{\frac{90}{11}} = \dfrac{12(11)}{90} = \dfrac{22}{15}$. The best answer is D.

268. In 1985 a company sold a brand of shoes to retailers for a fixed price per pair. In 1986 the number of pairs of the shoes that the company sold to retailers decreased by 20 percent, while the price per pair increased by 20 percent. If the company's revenue from the sales of the shoes in 1986 was $3.0 million, what was the approximate revenue from the sale of the shoes in 1985 ?

    (A) $2.4 million
    (B) $2.9 million
    (C) $3.0 million
    (D) $3.1 million
    (E) $3.6 million

Let n be the number of pairs of shoes sold in 1985 and p be the price per pair in 1985. Then in 1986, the number of pairs sold was 20 percent less, or $0.8n$, and the price per pair was 20 percent more, or $1.2p$. The company's revenue in 1986 was $(0.8n)(1.2p) = 0.96np = \$3$ million. Therefore, np, the company's revenue in 1985, was $\dfrac{\$3 \text{ million}}{\$0.96}$ or approximately $3.1 million. The best answer is D.

269. $\dfrac{(3)(0.072)}{0.54} =$

    (A) 0.04
    (B) 0.3
    (C) 0.4
    (D) 0.8
    (E) 4.0

To perform this computation, it is convenient to

multiply $\dfrac{(3)(0.072)}{0.54}$ by $\dfrac{100}{100}$, which gives

$\dfrac{3(7.2)}{54} = \dfrac{21.6}{54} = \dfrac{3.6}{9} = 0.4$. The best answer is C.

270. A car dealer sold x used cars and y new cars during May. If the number of used cars sold was 10 greater than the number of new cars sold, which of the following expresses this relationship?

    (A) $x > 10y$
    (B) $x > y + 10$
    (C) $x > y - 10$
    (D) $x = y + 10$
    (E) $x = y - 10$

According to the problem, if x is 10 greater than y, then $x = y + 10$, and the best answer is D.

271. What is the maximum number of $1\frac{1}{4}$-foot pieces of wire that can be cut from a wire that is 24 feet long?

    (A) 11
    (B) 18
    (C) 19
    (D) 20
    (E) 30

The maximum number is the greatest integer less than or equal to the quotient when 24 feet is divided by $1\frac{1}{4}$ feet. The quotient is 19.2, and the maximum number of $1\frac{1}{4}$-foot pieces is 19. The best answer is C.

272. If each of the two lines ℓ_1 and ℓ_2 is parallel to line ℓ_3, which of the following must be true?

    (A) Lines ℓ_1, ℓ_2, and ℓ_3 lie in the same plane.
    (B) Lines ℓ_1, ℓ_2, and ℓ_3 lie in different planes.
    (C) Line ℓ_1 is parallel to line ℓ_2.
    (D) Line ℓ_1 is the same line as line ℓ_2.
    (E) Line ℓ_1 is the same line as line ℓ_3.

It is a well-known fact that two lines that are parallel to the same line are parallel to each other; thus the best answer is C. To see that the other options are not necessarily true, we

first recall that two lines are parallel if they lie in the same plane and are everywhere equidistant. To show A and B need not be true, consider the figure below;

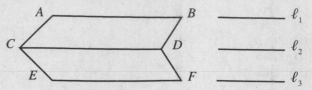

D is not necessarily true because no assumption can be made about whether or not lines ℓ_1 and ℓ_2 are coincident. That E is not necessarily true can be seen from the figures in the discussion of A and B.

$$\dfrac{61.24 \times (0.998)^2}{\sqrt{403}}$$

273. The expression above is approximately equal to

    (A) 1
    (B) 3
    (C) 4
    (D) 5
    (E) 6

Since $\sqrt{403}$ is approximately 20 and $(0.998)^2$ is approximately 1, the value of the expression is approximately $\dfrac{60(1)}{20}$ or 3. The best answer is B.

274. Car X and car Y traveled the same 80-mile route. If car X took 2 hours and car Y traveled at an average speed that was 50 percent faster than the average speed of car X, how many hours did it take car Y to travel the route?

    (A) $\dfrac{2}{3}$

    (B) 1

    (C) $1\dfrac{1}{3}$

    (D) $1\dfrac{3}{5}$

    (E) 3

If car X took 2 hours to drive the 80 miles, then car X drove an average speed of $\dfrac{80}{2}$, or 40 miles per hour, and car Y drove an average speed of $1.5(40) = 60$ miles per hour. Therefore, it took $\dfrac{80}{60}$ or $1\dfrac{1}{3}$ hours for car Y to travel the route. The best answer is C.

275. If the numbers $\dfrac{17}{24}, \dfrac{1}{2}, \dfrac{3}{8}, \dfrac{3}{4},$ and $\dfrac{9}{16}$ were ordered from greatest to least, the middle number of the resulting sequence would be

(A) $\dfrac{17}{24}$

(B) $\dfrac{1}{2}$

(C) $\dfrac{3}{8}$

(D) $\dfrac{3}{4}$

(E) $\dfrac{9}{16}$

The least common denominator of the five fractions is 48.

When the fractions are expressed with denominator 48, they are, in the order given, $\dfrac{34}{48}, \dfrac{24}{48}, \dfrac{18}{48}, \dfrac{36}{48},$ and $\dfrac{27}{48}.$ Once the fractions are expressed with the same denominator, one need only order the numerators from greatest to least. Clearly, the middle number is $\dfrac{27}{48}$ or $\dfrac{9}{16}$, and the best answer is E.

276. If a 10 percent deposit that has been paid toward the purchase of a certain product is $110, how much more remains to be paid?

(A) $880
(B) $990
(C) $1,000
(D) $1,100
(E) $1,210

If 10 percent of the purchase is $110, the 90 percent that remains to be paid is 9($110) = $990. The best answer is B.

277. Kim purchased n items from a catalog for $8 each. Postage and handling charges consisted of $3 for the first item and $1 for each additional item. Which of the following gives the total dollar amount of Kim's purchase, including postage and handling, in terms of n ?

(A) $8n + 2$
(B) $8n + 4$
(C) $9n + 2$
(D) $9n + 3$
(E) $9n + 4$

The purchase price of the n items at $8 each was $8n$ dollars. Postage and handling was $3 for the first item and $1(n-1)$ for the remaining $n-1$ items. The total cost was, therefore, $8n + 3 + 1(n-1) = 9n + 2$ dollars. The best answer is C.

278. $\left(\sqrt{7} + \sqrt{7}\right)^2 =$

(A) 98
(B) 49
(C) 28
(D) 21
(E) 14

$\left(\sqrt{7} + \sqrt{7}\right)^2 = \left(2\sqrt{7}\right)^2 = 4(7) = 28$. The best answer is C.

279. If the average (arithmetic mean) of the four numbers $K,\ 2K + 3,\ 3K - 5,$ and $5K + 1$ is 63, what is the value of K ?

(A) 11

(B) $15\dfrac{3}{4}$

(C) 22

(D) 23

(E) $25\dfrac{3}{10}$

The average of the four numbers is
$$\dfrac{K + (2K + 3) + (3K - 5) + (5K + 1)}{4} = \dfrac{11K - 1}{4} = 63, \text{ or}$$
$11K - 1 = 252;\ 11K = 253$ and $K = 23$. The best answer is D.

280. A rabbit on a controlled diet is fed daily 300 grams of a mixture of two foods, food X and food Y. Food X contains 10 percent protein and food Y contains 15 percent protein. If the rabbit's diet provides exactly 38 grams of protein daily, how many grams of food X are in the mixture?

(A) 100
(B) 140
(C) 150
(D) 160
(E) 200

Let x be the number of grams of food X in the mixture.

Then the number of grams of food Y in the mixture is $300 - x$.

According to the problem, $0.10x + 0.15(300 - x) = 38$ grams; $0.10x - 0.15x = 38 - 45 = -7$. Thus, $x = \dfrac{-7}{-0.05} = 140$ grams.

The best answer is B.

281. A company that ships boxes to a total of 12 distribution centers uses color coding to identify each center. If either a single color or a pair of two different colors is chosen to represent each center and if each center is uniquely represented by that choice of one or two colors, what is the minimum number of colors needed for the coding? (Assume that the order of the colors in a pair does not matter.)

(A) 4
(B) 5
(C) 6
(D) 12
(E) 24

It is sometimes a good idea to look at the answer choices before tackling the problem. For example, if 4 colors were used, 4 centers could be identified with a single color and $_4C_2 = \dfrac{4!}{2!2!} = 6$ centers could be identified with two colors. Thus, only 10 centers could be identified with 4 colors. Similarly, with 5 colors, 5 centers could be identified with a single color and $_5C_2 = \dfrac{5!}{2!3!} = \dfrac{(5)(4)}{2} = 10$ centers could be identified with two colors for a total of 15. Therefore, a minimum of 5 colors is needed, and the best answer is B.

282. If $x + y = a$ and $x - y = b$, then $2xy =$

(A) $\dfrac{a^2 - b^2}{2}$

(B) $\dfrac{b^2 - a^2}{2}$

(C) $\dfrac{a - b}{2}$

(D) $\dfrac{ab}{2}$

(E) $\dfrac{a^2 + b^2}{2}$

$(x + y)^2 = x^2 + 2xy + y^2 = a^2$, and
$(x - y)^2 = x^2 - 2xy + y^2 = b^2$. Subtracting the second equation from the first yields $4xy = a^2 - b^2$ and $2xy = \dfrac{a^2 - b^2}{2}$. The best answer is A.

283. A rectangular circuit board is designed to have width w inches, perimeter p inches, and area k square inches. Which of the following equations must be true?

(A) $w^2 + pw + k = 0$
(B) $w^2 - pw + 2k = 0$
(C) $2w^2 + pw + 2k = 0$
(D) $2w^2 - pw - 2k = 0$
(E) $2w^2 - pw + 2k = 0$

If the perimeter is p and the width is w, the length ℓ can be determined from the formula $2\ell + 2w = p$. Solving this equation for ℓ gives $\ell = \dfrac{p - 2w}{2}$. The area, k, of the rectangle is equal to ℓw. Substituting $\dfrac{p - 2w}{2}$ for ℓ gives $k = \left(\dfrac{p - 2w}{2}\right)w$ or $2k = (p - 2w)w = pw - 2w^2$, which is equivalent to $2w^2 - pw + 2k = 0$. The best answer is E.

284. On a certain road, 10 percent of the motorists exceed the posted speed limit and receive speeding tickets, but 20 percent of the motorists who exceed the posted speed limit do not receive speeding tickets. What percent of the motorists on that road exceed the posted speed limit?

(A) $10\dfrac{1}{2}\%$

(B) $12\dfrac{1}{2}\%$

(C) 15%

(D) 22%

(E) 30%

Let t be the total number of motorists and let e be the number of motorists who exceed the speed limit. Then if 20 percent of the motorists who exceed the speed limit do not receive tickets, 80 percent of those who exceed the speed limit, or $0.8e$, receive tickets. Since $0.1t$ exceed the speed limit and receive tickets, $0.8e = 0.1t$ and the ratio of e to t is 1 to 8, which is equivalent to 12.5 percent. The best answer is B.

285. If p is an even integer and q is an odd integer, which of the following must be an odd integer?

(A) $\dfrac{p}{q}$

(B) pq

(C) $2p + q$

(D) $2(p + q)$

(E) $\dfrac{3p}{q}$

The product of an even integer and any other integer is even, and the sum of an even integer and an odd integer is odd. An examination of the answer choices shows that both B, pq, and D, $2(p + q)$, must be even and that C, $2p + q$, must be an odd integer, since $2p$ is even and it is given that q is odd. With this approach, choices A and E do not have to be examined, but substitution of values for p and q, such as $p = 12$ and $q = 3$, shows that $\dfrac{p}{q}$ and $\dfrac{3p}{q}$ do not have to be odd integers. The best answer is C.

286. A certain college has a student-to-teacher ratio of 11 to 1. The average (arithmetic mean) annual salary for teachers is $26,000. If the college pays a total of $3,380,000 in annual salaries to its teachers, how many students does the college have?

(A) 130
(B) 169
(C) 1,300
(D) 1,430
(E) 1,560

Let s be the number of students and t be the number of teachers. Then $\dfrac{s}{t} = \dfrac{11}{1}$. The number of teachers can be found by dividing total salaries by the average salary per teacher, $\dfrac{\$3,380,000}{\$26,000} = 130$. Substituting this value for t in the equation $\dfrac{s}{t} = \dfrac{11}{1}$ gives $\dfrac{s}{130} = \dfrac{11}{1}$, and $s = 1,430$. The best answer is D.

287. Last year if 97 percent of the revenues of a company came from domestic sources and the remaining revenues, totaling $450,000, came from foreign sources, what was the total of the company's revenues?

(A) $1,350,000
(B) $1,500,000
(C) $4,500,000
(D) $15,000,000
(E) $150,000,000

If 97 percent of the revenues came from domestic sources, then the remaining 3 percent, totaling $450,000, came from foreign sources. If r represents total revenue, then $0.03r = \$450,000$ and $r = \$15,000,000$. The best answer is D.

288. Drum X is $\dfrac{1}{2}$ full of oil and drum Y, which has twice the capacity of drum X, is $\dfrac{2}{3}$ full of oil. If all of the oil in drum X is poured into drum Y, then drum Y will be filled to what fraction of its capacity?

(A) $\dfrac{3}{4}$

(B) $\dfrac{5}{6}$

(C) $\dfrac{11}{12}$

(D) $\dfrac{7}{6}$

(E) $\dfrac{11}{6}$

Let x and y represent the capacities of drums X and Y, respectively. The amount of oil in drum X is $\dfrac{1}{2}x$ and the amount of oil in drum Y is $\dfrac{2}{3}y$. Since the capacity of drum Y is twice the capacity of drum X, it follows that $y = 2x$, or $x = \dfrac{1}{2}y$, and the oil in drum X is $\dfrac{1}{2}x = \dfrac{1}{4}y$. When the oil in drum X is poured into drum Y, Y contains $\dfrac{1}{4}y + \dfrac{2}{3}y = \dfrac{11}{12}y$, which is $\dfrac{11}{12}$ of its capacity. The best answer is C.

289. In a certain population, there are 3 times as many people aged twenty-one or under as there are people over twenty-one. The ratio of those twenty-one or under to the total population is

(A) 1 to 2
(B) 1 to 3
(C) 1 to 4
(D) 2 to 3
(E) 3 to 4

If v represents the number of people over twenty-one, then $3v$ represents the number of people twenty-one or under, and $v + 3v$ represents the total population. Thus, the ratio of those twenty-one or under to the total population is

$\dfrac{3v}{v+3v} = \dfrac{3v}{4v} = \dfrac{3}{4}$, or 3 to 4, and the best answer is E.

290. $\dfrac{2+2\sqrt{6}}{2} =$

(A) $\sqrt{6}$
(B) $2\sqrt{6}$
(C) $1+\sqrt{6}$
(D) $1+2\sqrt{6}$
(E) $2+\sqrt{6}$

$\dfrac{2+2\sqrt{6}}{2} = \dfrac{2(1+\sqrt{6})}{2} = 1+\sqrt{6}$, and the best answer is C.

291. A certain telescope increases the visual range at a particular location from 90 kilometers to 150 kilometers. By what percent is the visual range increased by using the telescope ?

(A) 30%
(B) $33\dfrac{1}{2}$%
(C) 40%
(D) 60%
(E) $66\dfrac{2}{3}$%

The telescope increases the visual range by $150 - 90 = 60$ kilometers. Thus, the increase in visual range is

$\dfrac{60}{90} = \dfrac{2}{3} = 66\dfrac{2}{3}$%. The best answer is E.

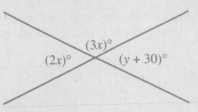

Note: Figure not drawn to scale.

292. In the figure above, the value of y is

(A) 6
(B) 12
(C) 24
(D) 36
(E) 42

Since the indicated angles are formed by the intersection of two lines, the adjacent angles are supplementary (i.e., the sum of their measures is 180°). Thus, $2x + 3x = 180$, or $x = 36$, and $3x + y + 30 = 180$, or $3(36) + y + 30 = 180$, or $y = 42$. The best answer is E.

293. A part-time employee whose hourly wage was increased by 25 percent decided to reduce the number of hours worked per week so that the employee's total weekly income would remain unchanged. By what percent should the number of hours worked be reduced?

(A) 12.5%
(B) 20%
(C) 25%
(D) 50%
(E) 75%

Let h be the original number of hours the employee worked per week and w be the hourly wage, for weekly income of wh. The increased wage is $1.25w$, or $\dfrac{5}{4}w$, and the reduced number of hours can be represented by H, for a weekly income of $\dfrac{5}{4}wH$. If the total weekly income is to be unchanged, then $wh = \dfrac{5}{4}wH$ and $h = \dfrac{5}{4}H$, or $H = \dfrac{4}{5}h$. The reduced hours are $\dfrac{4}{5}$ or 80% of the original hours, which is a reduction of 20%. The best answer is B.

294. If $x > 0$, $\dfrac{x}{50} + \dfrac{x}{25}$ is what percent of x ?

(A) 6%

(B) 25%

(C) $37\dfrac{1}{2}\%$

(D) 60%

(E) 75%

If $x > 0$, $\dfrac{x}{50} + \dfrac{x}{25} = \dfrac{x}{50} + \dfrac{2x}{50} = \dfrac{3x}{50} = \dfrac{6x}{100}$ or 6% of x.
The best answer is A.

295. If the operation $\odot$ is defined for all a and b by

the equation $a \odot b = \dfrac{a^2 b}{3}$, then $2 \odot (3 \odot -1) =$

(A)   4

(B)   2

(C) $-\dfrac{4}{3}$

(D) -2

(E) -4

To find the value of $2 \odot (3 \odot -1)$, the value of $3 \odot -1$

must be found first. By definition, $a \odot b = \dfrac{a^2 b}{3}$; so

$3 \odot -1 = \dfrac{3^2(-1)}{3} = \dfrac{-9}{3} = -3$. Thus, $2 \odot (3 \odot -1) =$

$2 \odot -3 = \dfrac{2^2(-3)}{3} = 4(-1) = -4$, and the best answer is E.

296. A factory that employs 1,000 assembly-line

workers pays each of these workers $5 per hour

for the first 40 hours worked during a week and

$1\dfrac{1}{2}$ times that rate for hours worked in excess

of 40. What was the total payroll for the

assembly-line workers for a week in which 30

percent of them worked 20 hours, 50 percent

worked 40 hours, and the rest worked 50 hours?

(A) $180,000

(B) $185,000

(C) $190,000

(D) $200,000

(E) $205,000

Since there are 1,000 workers, 30 percent, or 300, worked
20 hours each; 50 percent, or 500, worked 40 hours each;
and the remaining 200 worked 50 hours each. The 300
workers earned 300(20)($5) = $30,000, the 500 workers
earned 500(40)($5) = $100,000, and the 200 workers earned
$200[(40)(\$5) + (50 - 40)(1\dfrac{1}{2})(\$5)] = \$55,000$. Thus, the
total payroll was $30,000 + $100,000 + $55,000 = $185,000,
and the best answer is B.

297. If $x \neq 2$, then $\dfrac{3x^2(x-2) - x + 2}{x - 2} =$

(A) $3x^2 - x + 2$

(B) $3x^2 + 1$

(C) $3x^2$

(D) $3x^2 - 1$

(E) $3x^2 - 2$

If $x \neq 2$, then $\dfrac{3x^2(x-2) - x + 2}{x - 2} = \dfrac{3x^2(x-2) - (x - 2)}{x - 2} =$

$\dfrac{(x-2)\left(3x^2 - 1\right)}{x - 2} = 3x^2 - 1$. The best answer is D.

298. In a certain school, 40 more than $\dfrac{1}{3}$ of all the

students are taking a science course and $\dfrac{1}{4}$ of

those taking a science course are taking physics.

If $\dfrac{1}{8}$ of all the students in the school are taking

physics, how many students are in the school?

(A) 240

(B) 300

(C) 480

(D) 720

(E) 960

If s represents the number of students in the school, then

$40 + \dfrac{1}{3}s$ are taking a science course and $\dfrac{1}{4}\left(40 + \dfrac{1}{3}s\right)$

are taking physics. If $\dfrac{1}{8}$ of the students in the school

are taking physics, then $\dfrac{1}{8}s = \dfrac{1}{4}\left(40 + \dfrac{1}{3}s\right)$, or

$s = 2\left(40 + \dfrac{1}{3}s\right) = 80 + \dfrac{2}{3}s$, and $s - \dfrac{2}{3}s = 80$.

Thus, $s = 240$, and the best answer is A.

299. If $d > 0$ and $0 < 1 - \dfrac{c}{d} < 1$, which of the following must be true?

I. $c > 0$

II. $\dfrac{c}{d} < 1$

III. $c^2 + d^2 > 1$

(A) I only
(B) II only
(C) I and II only
(D) II and III only
(E) I, II, and III

If every value of c and d satisfying the inequalities $d > 0$ and $0 < 1 - \dfrac{c}{d} < 1$ also satisfies the inequality in statement I, II, or III, then that statement must be true.

If even one value of c and d satisfying the inequalities $d > 0$ and $0 < 1 - \dfrac{c}{d} < 1$ does not satisfy the inequality in statement I, II, or III, then that statement need not be true.

I. Since $1 - \dfrac{c}{d} < 1$, it follows that $\dfrac{c}{d} > 0$. This together with $d > 0$ implies $c > 0$, and statement I must be true.

II. Since $0 < 1 - \dfrac{c}{d} < 1$, it follows that $-1 < -\dfrac{c}{d} < 0$, which is equivalent to $0 < \dfrac{c}{d} < 1$, and statement II must be true.

III. The inequalities $d > 0$ and $0 < 1 - \dfrac{c}{d} < 1$ give information about the size of $\dfrac{c}{d}$ but do not appear to give information about the size of $c^2 + d^2$; so it is reasonable to try to find positive values of c and d for which $\dfrac{c}{d}$ is less than 1. Choosing $c = \dfrac{1}{4}$ and $d = \dfrac{1}{3}$ yields $c^2 + d^2 = \left(\dfrac{1}{4}\right)^2 + \left(\dfrac{1}{3}\right)^2 = \dfrac{1}{16} + \dfrac{1}{9}$, which is less than 1. Therefore, statement III need not be true.

The best answer is C.

300. The inside dimensions of a rectangular wooden box are 6 inches by 8 inches by 10 inches. A cylindrical cannister is to be placed inside the box so that it stands upright when the closed box rests on one of its six faces. Of all such cannisters that could be used, what is the radius, in inches, of the one that has maximum volume?

(A) 3
(B) 4
(C) 5
(D) 6
(E) 8

The formula for the volume of a right circular cylinder is $v = \pi r^2 h$, where r is the radius and h is the height of the cylinder. The diameter of the circular top of the cannister must equal the length of the shorter dimension of the top of the box, as illustrated in the figure below.

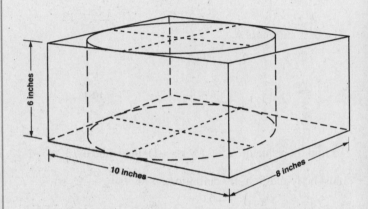

Since the box can rest on any one of its six faces, there are three possibilities to consider. These are summarized in the following table.

Dimensions of the box top	r	h	v
6 by 8	3	10	90π
6 by 10	3	8	72π
8 by 10	4	6	96π

Thus, the radius, in inches, of the cannister having the maximum volume is 4. The best answer is B.

-198-

301. $\dfrac{\dfrac{1}{2}}{\dfrac{1}{4}+\dfrac{1}{6}} =$

(A) $\dfrac{6}{5}$

(B) $\dfrac{5}{6}$

(C) $\dfrac{5}{24}$

(D) $\dfrac{1}{5}$

(E) $\dfrac{1}{12}$

One way to solve the problem is to express all fractions with the common denominator 12, that is, $\dfrac{\dfrac{6}{12}}{\dfrac{3}{12}+\dfrac{2}{12}} = \dfrac{\dfrac{6}{12}}{\dfrac{5}{12}} = \dfrac{6}{5}$.

The best answer is A.

302. Kelly and Chris packed several boxes with books. If Chris packed 60 percent of the total number of boxes, what was the ratio of the number of boxes Kelly packed to the number of boxes Chris packed?

(A) 1 to 6
(B) 1 to 4
(C) 2 to 5
(D) 3 to 5
(E) 2 to 3

If Chris packed 60 percent of the boxes, then Kelly packed 40 percent of the boxes. The ratio of the number of boxes Kelly packed to the number Chris packed is $\dfrac{40\%}{60\%} = \dfrac{2}{3}$.
The best answer is E.

303. A train travels from New York City to Chicago, a distance of approximately 840 miles, at an average rate of 60 miles per hour and arrives in Chicago at 6:00 in the evening, Chicago time. At what hour in the morning, New York City time, did the train depart for Chicago? (Note: Chicago time is one hour earlier than New York City time.)

(A) 4:00
(B) 5:00
(C) 6:00
(D) 7:00
(E) 8:00

Because time is found by dividing distance by rate, the trip took $\dfrac{840}{60} = 14$ hours. The train arrived in Chicago at 6:00 in the evening Chicago time or 7:00 in the evening New York time. New York time 14 hours before 7:00 in the evening is 5:00 in the morning. The best answer is B.

304. Of the following, which is the closest approximation of $\dfrac{50.2 \times 0.49}{199.8}$?

(A) $\dfrac{1}{10}$

(B) $\dfrac{1}{8}$

(C) $\dfrac{1}{4}$

(D) $\dfrac{5}{4}$

(E) $\dfrac{25}{2}$

$\dfrac{50.2 \times 0.49}{199.8}$ is approximately $\dfrac{50 \times 0.5}{200} = \dfrac{25}{200} = \dfrac{1}{8}$.
The best answer is B.

305. Last year Manfred received 26 paychecks. Each of his first 6 paychecks was $750; each of his remaining paychecks was $30 more than each of his first 6 paychecks. To the nearest dollar, what was the average (arithmetic mean) amount of his paychecks for the year?

(A) $752
(B) $755
(C) $765
(D) $773
(E) $775

The total amount in dollars of the 26 paychecks was

$6(750) + (26 - 6)(750 + 30) = 6(750) + 20(780) = 4,500 + 15,600 = 20,100$. Thus, the average paycheck was $\dfrac{\$20,100}{26}$

or approximately $773. The best answer is D.

306. A certain pair of used shoes can be repaired for $12.50 and will last for 1 year. A pair of the same kind of shoes can be purchased new for $28.00 and will last for 2 years. The average cost per year of the new shoes is what percent greater than the cost of repairing the used shoes?

   (A)   3%
   (B)   5%
   (C) 12%
   (D) 15%
   (E) 24%

Having the used shoes repaired will cost $12.50 for 1 year. The new shoes will cost $28.00 and will last for 2 years, which is an average cost of $14.00 for 1 year or $1.50 greater than the cost of repairing the used shoes. Thus, the average cost per year of the new shoes is $\frac{\$1.50}{\$12.50} = 12\%$ greater than the cost of repairing the used shoes. The best answer is C.

307. In a certain brick wall, each row of bricks above the bottom row contains one less brick than the row just below it. If there are 5 rows in all and a total of 75 bricks in the wall, how many bricks does the bottom row contain?

   (A) 14
   (B) 15
   (C) 16
   (D) 17
   (E) 18

If b represents the number of bricks in the bottom row, the numbers of bricks in the next 4 rows are $b-1$, $b-2$, $b-3$, and $b-4$, respectively. The total number of bricks in the 5 rows is $b + (b-1) + (b-2) + (b-3) + (b-4) = 5b - 10 = 75$. Thus, $5b = 85$ and $b = 17$. The best answer is D.

308. If 25 percent of p is equal to 10 percent of q, and $pq \neq 0$, then p is what percent of q ?

   (A)   2.5%
   (B) 15%
   (C) 20%
   (D) 35%
   (E) 40%

If $0.25p = 0.10q$, dividing both sides of the equation by 0.25 gives $p = \frac{0.10q}{0.25} = \frac{10q}{25}$. Thus, p is 40% of q, and the best answer is E.

309. If the length of an edge of cube X is twice the length of an edge of cube Y, what is the ratio of the volume of cube Y to the volume of cube X ?

   (A) $\frac{1}{2}$

   (B) $\frac{1}{4}$

   (C) $\frac{1}{6}$

   (D) $\frac{1}{8}$

   (E) $\frac{1}{27}$

If y represents the length of one edge of cube Y, then the length of one edge of cube X is $2y$. The ratio of the volume of cube Y to the volume of cube X is $\frac{y^3}{(2y)^3} = \frac{y^3}{8y^3} = \frac{1}{8}$. The best answer is D.

310. $(\sqrt{2} + 1)(\sqrt{2} - 1)(\sqrt{3} + 1)(\sqrt{3} - 1) =$

   (A) 2
   (B) 3
   (C) $2\sqrt{6}$
   (D) 5
   (E) 6

From the relationship $(a + b)(a - b) = a^2 - b^2$, $(\sqrt{2} + 1)(\sqrt{2} - 1) = 2 - 1 = 1$ and $(\sqrt{3} + 1)(\sqrt{3} - 1) = 3 - 1 = 2$. Thus, $(\sqrt{2} + 1)(\sqrt{2} - 1)(\sqrt{3} + 1)(\sqrt{3} - 1) = (1)(2) = 2$, and the best answer is A.

311. In a certain calculus class, the ratio of the number of mathematics majors to the number of students who are not mathematics majors is 2 to 5. If 2 more mathematics majors were to enter the class, the ratio would be 1 to 2. How many students are in the class?

(A) 10
(B) 12
(C) 21
(D) 28
(E) 35

Let m be the number of mathematics majors and n be the number of nonmathematics majors in the class. Thus, the ratio of $\frac{m}{n} = \frac{2}{5}$. If the number of mathematics majors is increased by 2, the ratio of $\frac{m+2}{n} = \frac{1}{2}$. From the first equation, $m = \frac{2}{5}n$, and from the second equation, $m+2 = \frac{1}{2}n$, or $m = \frac{1}{2}n - 2$. Thus, $\frac{1}{2}n - 2 = \frac{2}{5}n$ or $\frac{1}{2}n - \frac{2}{5}n = 2$, and $\frac{1}{10}n = 2$. Therefore, $n = 20$ and $m = \frac{2}{5}(20) = 8$, and the total number of students is $m + n = 20 + 8 = 28$.

The best answer is D.

312. Machines A and B always operate independently and at their respective constant rates. When working alone, machine A can fill a production lot in 5 hours, and machine B can fill the same lot in x hours. When the two machines operate simultaneously to fill the production lot, it takes them 2 hours to complete the job. What is the value of x ?

(A) $3\frac{1}{3}$

(B) 3

(C) $2\frac{1}{2}$

(D) $2\frac{1}{3}$

(E) $1\frac{1}{2}$

Since machine A can fill a production lot in 5 hours, machine A can complete $\frac{1}{5}$ of the job in 1 hour. Similarly, machine B can complete $\frac{1}{x}$ of the job in 1 hour, and the two machines operating simultaneously can fill $\frac{1}{2}$ of the job in 1 hour. Therefore, $\frac{1}{5} + \frac{1}{x} = \frac{1}{2}$ and $\frac{1}{x} = \frac{1}{2} - \frac{1}{5} = \frac{3}{10}$ or $x = \frac{10}{3} = 3\frac{1}{3}$. The best answer is A.

313. In the xy-coordinate system, if (a, b) and $(a+3, b+k)$ are two points on the line defined by the equation $x = 3y - 7$, then $k =$

(A) 9

(B) 3

(C) $\frac{7}{3}$

(D) 1

(E) $\frac{1}{3}$

Since the points (a, b) and $(a+3, b+k)$ lie on the line $x = 3y - 7$, their coordinates can be substituted for x and y in the equation for the line. Thus, $a = 3b - 7$ and $a + 3 = 3(b + k) - 7$. Substituting $3b - 7$ for a in the second equation gives $(3b - 7) + 3 = 3b + 3k - 7 = (3b - 7) + 3k$. Thus, $3 = 3k$ and $k = 1$. The best answer is D.

Alternatively, the slope-intercept form of the equation of the line is $y = \frac{1}{3}x + \frac{7}{3}$; so the slope of the line is $\frac{1}{3}$. Since the slope is the $\frac{difference\ of\ y-coordinates}{difference\ of\ x-coordinates}$ of the two points, $\frac{(b+k)-b}{(a+3)-a} = \frac{1}{3}$, or $\frac{k}{3} = \frac{1}{3}$ and $k = 1$.

314. What is the units digit of $(13)^4(17)^2(29)^3$?

(A) 9
(B) 7
(C) 5
(D) 3
(E) 1

The units digit of 13^4 is 1, since $3 \times 3 \times 3 \times 3 = 81$; the units digit of 17^2 is 9, since $7 \times 7 = 49$; and the units digit of 29^3 is 9, since $9 \times 9 \times 9 = 729$. Therefore, the units digit of $(13)^4(17)^2(29)^3$ is 1, since $1 \times 9 \times 9 = 81$, and the best answer is E.

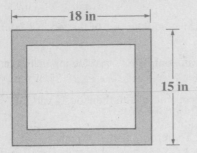

Note: Figure not drawn to scale.

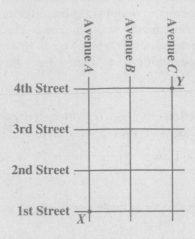

315. The shaded region in the figure above represents a rectangular frame with length 18 inches and width 15 inches. The frame encloses a rectangular picture that has the same area as the frame itself. If the length and width of the picture have the same ratio as the length and width of the frame, what is the length of the picture, in inches?

(A) $9\sqrt{2}$

(B) $\dfrac{3}{2}$

(C) $\dfrac{9}{\sqrt{2}}$

(D) $15\left(1-\dfrac{1}{\sqrt{2}}\right)$

(E) $\dfrac{9}{2}$

Let ℓ and w represent the length and width in inches, respectively, of the picture. Because the length and width of the picture have the same ratio as the length and width of the frame, $\dfrac{\ell}{w}=\dfrac{18}{15}=\dfrac{6}{5}$. The areas, in square inches, of the picture and the frame are ℓw and $(18\times 15)-\ell w=270-\ell w$, respectively. Since the two areas are equal, $\ell w=270-\ell w$ or $\ell w=135$. From the ratio $\dfrac{\ell}{w}=\dfrac{6}{5}$, $w=\dfrac{5}{6}\ell$. Substituting $\dfrac{5}{6}\ell$ for w in the equation $\ell w=135$ yields $\ell(\dfrac{5}{6}\ell)=135$ or $5\ell^2=6(135)$ and $\ell^2=6(27)=(2)(3)(3)(3)(3)=2(9)^2$. Thus, $\sqrt{\ell^2}=\sqrt{2(9)^2}$ and $\ell=9\sqrt{2}$. The best answer is A.

316. Pat will walk from intersection X to intersection Y along a route that is confined to the square grid of four streets and three avenues shown in the map above. How many routes from X to Y can Pat take that have the minimum possible length?

(A) Six
(B) Eight
(C) Ten
(D) Fourteen
(E) Sixteen

In order to walk from intersection X to intersection Y by one of the routes of minimum possible length, Pat must travel upward or rightward between intersections on the map. Thus, the routes of minimum length consist of walking upwards, U , 3 times and rightward, R , twice, for a total of 5 blocks. There are 10 ways in which Pat can walk upward 3 times and rightward twice:

$U\,U\,U\,R\,R$	$U\,R\,R\,U\,U$
$U\,U\,R\,U\,R$	$R\,R\,U\,U\,U$
$U\,U\,R\,R\,U$	$R\,U\,U\,U\,R$
$U\,R\,U\,U\,R$	$R\,U\,U\,R\,U$
$U\,R\,U\,R\,U$	$R\,U\,R\,U\,U$

Thus, there are 10 routes of minimum length, and the best answer is C.

317. A certain fishing boat is chartered by 6 people who are to contribute equally to the total charter cost of $480. If each person contributes equally to a $150 down payment, how much of the charter cost will each person still owe?

(A) $80   (B) $66   (C) $55   (D) $50   (E) $45

Since each person contributed equally to the $150 down payment and the total cost of the chartered boat is $480, each person still owes $\dfrac{\$480-\$150}{6} = \$55$. Thus, the best answer is C.

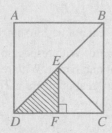

318. In square $ABCD$ above, if $DE = EB$ and $DF = FC$, then the area of the shaded region is what fraction of the area of square region $ABCD$?

(A) $\dfrac{1}{16}$ (B) $\dfrac{1}{8}$ (C) $\dfrac{1}{6}$ (D) $\dfrac{1}{4}$ (E) $\dfrac{1}{3}$

Since $DE = EB$ and $DF = FC$, the area of the shaded region is one-fourth the area of triangular region BCD. Since BD divides square $ABCD$ into two equal triangular regions, the shaded region is $\left(\dfrac{1}{2}\right)\left(\dfrac{1}{4}\right)$, or $\dfrac{1}{8}$, of the area of square region $ABCD$. Hence, the best answer is B.

319. Craig sells major appliances. For each appliance he sells, Craig receives a commission of $50 plus 10 percent of the selling price. During one particular week Craig sold 6 appliances for selling prices totaling $3,620. What was the total of Craig's commissions for that week?

(A) $412   (B) $526   (C) $585
(D) $605   (E) $662

Since Craig receives a commission of $50 on each appliance plus a 10 percent commission on total sales, his commission for that week was $6(\$50) + (0.1)(\$3,620) = \$662$. Thus, the best answer is E.

320. The average (arithmetic mean) of 10, 30, and 50 is 5 more than the average of 20, 40, and

(A) 15   (B) 25   (C) 35   (D) 45   (E) 55

Since the average of 10, 30, and 50 is 30, the average of 20, 40, and some number x is $30 - 5$, or 25. If the average of 20, 40, and x is 25, then the sum of the three numbers is 75, and $x = 15$. The best answer is A.

321. What number when multiplied by $\dfrac{4}{7}$ yields $\dfrac{6}{7}$ as the result?

(A) $\dfrac{2}{7}$ (B) $\dfrac{2}{3}$ (C) $\dfrac{3}{2}$ (D) $\dfrac{24}{7}$ (E) $\dfrac{7}{2}$

If n represents the number, $\dfrac{4}{7}n = \dfrac{6}{7}$, which yields $n = \dfrac{3}{2}$. Thus, the best answer is C.

322. If $y = 4 + (x - 3)^2$, then y is least when $x =$

(A) -4 (B) -3 (C) 0   (D) 3   (E) 4

Since the expression $(x - 3)^2$ must be greater than or equal to zero, y will be least when $(x - 3) = 0$. Therefore, the least value for y occurs when x is 3, and the best answer is D.

323. If 3 pounds of dried apricots that cost x dollars per pound are mixed with 2 pounds of prunes that cost y dollars per pound, what is the cost, in dollars, per pound of the mixture?

(A) $\dfrac{3x + 2y}{5}$

(B) $\dfrac{3x + 2y}{x + y}$

(C) $\dfrac{3x + 2y}{xy}$

(D) $5(3x + 2y)$

(E) $3x + 2y$

The total number of pounds in the mixture is $3 + 2 = 5$ pounds, and the total cost of the mixture is $3x + 2y$ dollars. Therefore, the cost per pound of the mixture is $\dfrac{3x + 2y}{5}$ dollars, and the best answer is A.

324. A cashier mentally reversed the digits of one customer's correct amount of change and thus gave the customer an incorrect amount of change. If the cash register contained 45 cents more than it should have as a result of this error, which of the following could have been the correct amount of change in cents?

(A) 14　(B) 45　(C) 54　(D) 65　(E) 83

Let x represent the units' digit and y represent the tens' digit in the correct amount of change before the digits were reversed. Since the cash register contained 45 cents more than it should have, it follows that $(10x + y) - (10y + x) = 45$. Simplifying yields $9x - 9y = 45$, or $x - y = 5$, which implies that the difference in the two digits is 5. Since 83 is the only number given whose digits have a difference of 5, the best answer is E.

325. Which of the following is NOT equal to the square of an integer?

(A) $\sqrt{\sqrt{1}}$　(B) $\sqrt{4}$　(C) $\dfrac{18}{2}$

(D) $41 - 25$　(E) 36

In choice B, $\sqrt{4} = 2$, which is not the square of an integer. Thus, the best answer is B. It can be verified that the remaining answer choices represent the squares of 1, 3, 4, and 6, respectively.

326. An artist wishes to paint a circular region on a square poster that is 2 feet on a side. If the area of the circular region is to be $\dfrac{1}{2}$ the area of the poster, what must be the radius of the circular region in feet?

(A) $\dfrac{1}{\pi}$　(B) $\sqrt{\dfrac{2}{\pi}}$　(C) 1　(D) $\dfrac{2}{\sqrt{\pi}}$　(E) $\dfrac{\pi}{2}$

The area of the square poster is $2^2 = 4$ square feet. Since the area of the circular region is to be $\dfrac{1}{2}$ the area of the poster, $\pi r^2 = \dfrac{1}{2}(4)$, where r is the radius of the circle. Solving the equation yields $r = \sqrt{\dfrac{2}{\pi}}$. Thus, the best answer is B.

327. Which of the following must be equal to zero for all real numbers x ?

  I.　$-\dfrac{1}{x}$

  II.　$x + (-x)$

  III.　x^0

(A) I only
(B) II only
(C) I and III only
(D) II and III only
(E) I, II, and III

With respect to I, $-\dfrac{1}{x}$ cannot be zero since 1 divided by any number can never be zero. With respect to II, $x + (-x)$ equals zero for all real numbers x. With respect to III, x^0 equals 1 for all nonzero real numbers x. Therefore, the best answer is B.

328. At the rate of m meters per s seconds, how many meters does a cyclist travel in x minutes?

(A) $\dfrac{m}{sx}$　(B) $\dfrac{mx}{s}$　(C) $\dfrac{60m}{sx}$

(D) $\dfrac{60ms}{x}$　(E) $\dfrac{60mx}{s}$

Since the cyclist travels $\dfrac{m}{x}$ meters per second, the cyclist travels $\dfrac{60m}{s}$ meters per minute. Thus, in x minutes the cyclist will travel $\dfrac{60mx}{s}$ meters, and the best answer is E.

	City A	City B	City C	City D	City E	City F
City A						
City B						
City C						
City D						
City E						
City F						

329. In the table above, what is the least number of table entries that are needed to show the mileage between each city and each of the other five cities?

(A) 15　(B) 21　(C) 25　(D) 30　(E) 36

In the table, draw a diagonal from the upper left to the lower right corner. The entries along this diagonal should not be counted since a cell on the diagonal represents the distance from the city to itself. Because the diagonal divides the remaining cells into two equal halves, each of which would contain the same set of distances, count only the cells in one of the halves, $5 + 4 + 3 + 2 + 1 = 15$. Hence, the best answer is A.

330. A certain tax rate is $0.82 per $100.00. What is this rate, expressed as a percent?

(A) 82% (B) 8.2% (C) 0.82%
(D) 0.082% (E) 0.0082%

The tax rate $0.82 per $100.00 can be written as the fraction $\frac{\$0.82}{\$100.00} = 0.82\%$. The best answer is C.

331. Fermat primes are prime numbers that can be written in the form $2^k + 1$, where k is an integer and a power of 2. Which of the following is NOT a Fermat prime?

(A) 3 (B) 5 (C) 17 (D) 31 (E) 257

Since Fermat primes can be written in the form $2^k + 1$, where k is an integer and a power of 2, check each answer choice to find the number that cannot be so expressed.

$3 = 2^1 + 1$, where $k = 1 = 2^0$
$5 = 2^2 + 1$, where $k = 2 = 2^1$
$17 = 2^4 + 1$, where $k = 4 = 2^2$
$31 = 30 + 1$, but 30 cannot be expressed as an integer power of 2
$257 = 2^8 + 1$, where $k = 8 = 2^3$

Thus, the best answer is D.

332. A shipment of 1,500 heads of cabbage, each of which was approximately the same size, was purchased for $600. The day the shipment arrived, $\frac{2}{3}$ of the heads were sold, each at 25 percent above the cost per head. The following day the rest were sold at a price per head equal to 10 percent less than the price each head sold for on the day before. What was the gross profit on this shipment?

(A) $100 (B) $115 (C) $125
(D) $130 (E) $135

The cost of a head of cabbage was $\frac{\$600.00}{1,500} = \$0.40$. Since the selling price of a head of cabbage on the day the shipment arrived was $(1.25)(\$0.40) = \$0.50$, the revenue for

the first day was $\frac{2}{3}(1,500)(\$0.50) = \$500.00$. On the second day the remaining cabbage heads were sold at a selling price of $(0.9)(\$0.50) = \$0.45$ per head, which yields $\frac{1}{3}(1,500)(\$0.45) = \$225.00$ in revenue. The gross profit for the shipment was $\$500.00 + \$225.00 - \$600.00 = \$125.00$. Thus, the best answer is C.

333. If $(t - 8)$ is a factor of $t^2 - kt - 48$, then $k =$

(A) −6 (B) −2 (C) 2 (D) 6 (E) 14

If $(t - 8)$ is a factor of the expression $t^2 - kt - 48$, then the expression can be written as the product $(t - 8)(t + a)$. When multiplying this product, $(-8)(a) = -48$, or $a = 6$. Thus, the product becomes $(t - 8)(t + 6)$, which has the middle term $6t - 8t = -2t$. Therefore, $k = 2$, and the best answer is C.

334. If a is a positive integer, and if the units' digit of a^2 is 9 and the units' digit of $(a + 1)^2$ is 4, what is the units' digit of $(a + 2)^2$?

(A) 1 (B) 3 (C) 5 (D) 7 (E) 9

If 9 is the units' digit of a^2, then either 3 or 7 must be the units' digit of a, since only numbers ending in 3 or 7 would yield a units' digit of 9 when squared. Then $a + 1$ must have a units' digit of either $3 + 1$ or $7 + 1$. But if 4 were the units' digit of $a + 1$, then $(a + 1)^2$ would have units' digit 6 instead of 4 as given. Therefore, the units' digit of $a + 1$ must be 8, which implies that the units' digit of $a + 2$ would have to be $8 + 1 = 9$. Since the units' digit of 9^2 is 1, the units digit of $(a + 2)^2$ must be 1. Thus, the best answer is A.

335. The ratio, by volume, of soap to alcohol to water in a certain solution is 2 : 50 : 100. The solution will be altered so that the ratio of soap to alcohol is doubled while the ratio of soap to water is halved. If the altered solution will contain 100 cubic centimeters of alcohol, how many cubic centimeters of water will it contain?

(A) 50 (B) 200 (C) 400 (D) 625 (E) 800

Originally the ratio of soap to alcohol to water was 2:50:100. When the ratio 2:50 is doubled, the new ratio will be 4:50; when the ratio 2:100 is halved, the new ratio will be 1:100 or 4:400. Thus, the ratio of soap to alcohol to water will be 4:50:400. Since 100 cubic centimeters represents the 50 parts of alcohol in the new solution, 800 cubic centimeters will represent the 400 parts of water in the solution. Thus, the best answer is E.

336. If 75 percent of a class answered the first question on a certain test correctly, 55 percent answered the second question on the test correctly, and 20 percent answered neither of the questions correctly, what percent answered <u>both</u> correctly?

(A) 10% (B) 20% (C) 30%
(D) 50% (E) 65%

For questions of this type, it is convenient to draw a Venn diagram to represent the conditions in the problem. For example:

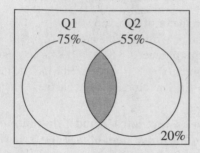

Now it is clear that the two circles represent 80 percent of the students. If x is the percent corresponding to the shaded region (the percent who answered both questions correctly), then $75\% + 55\% - x = 80\%$, and $x = 50\%$. Thus, the best answer is D.

Alternatively, if 75 percent of the class answered the first question correctly and 20 percent of the class answered both questions incorrectly, then 5 percent of the class answered the second question correctly but the first incorrectly. Since 55 percent of the class answered the second question correctly, the percent who answered both questions correctly is $55\% - 5\% = 50\%$.

337. $\dfrac{31}{125} =$

(A) 0.248
(B) 0.252
(C) 0.284
(D) 0.312
(E) 0.320

The fraction $\dfrac{31}{125}$ can be converted to decimal form by dividing 31 by 125, which yields 0.248. Thus, the best answer is A.

Alternatively, since $8(125) = 1,000$, $\dfrac{31}{125} \times \dfrac{8}{8} = \dfrac{248}{1,000} = 0.248$.

338. Members of a social club met to address 280 newsletters. If they addressed $\dfrac{1}{4}$ of the newsletters during the first hour and $\dfrac{2}{5}$ of the remaining newsletters during the second hour, how many newsletters did they address during the second hour?

(A) 28 (B) 42 (C) 63 (D) 84 (E) 112

Three-fourths of 280, or 210, newsletters were not addressed during the first hour. Therefore, $\dfrac{2}{5}(210) = 84$ newsletters were addressed during the second hour, and the best answer is D.

339. If $x^2 = 2y^3$ and $2y = 4$, what is the value of $x^2 + y$?

(A) -14
(B) -2
(C) 3
(D) 6
(E) 18

If $2y = 4$, then $y = 2$ and $x^2 = 2y^3 = 2(2)^3 = 16$. Therefore, $x^2 + y = 16 + 2 = 18$, and the best answer is E.

340. If the cost of 12 eggs varies between \$0.90 and \$1.20, then the cost per egg varies between

(A) \$0.06 and \$0.08
(B) \$0.065 and \$0.085
(C) \$0.07 and \$0.09
(D) \$0.075 and \$0.10
(E) \$0.08 and \$0.105

If the cost of 12 eggs varies between \$0.90 and \$1.20, the cost per egg varies between $\dfrac{\$0.90}{12}$ and $\dfrac{\$1.20}{12}$, or between \$0.075 and \$0.10. Thus, the best answer is D.

341. $(\sqrt{3} + 2)(\sqrt{3} - 2) =$

(A) $\sqrt{3} - 4$ (B) $\sqrt{6} - 4$ (C) -1
(D) 1 (E) 2

$(\sqrt{3} + 2)(\sqrt{3} - 2) = (\sqrt{3})^2 + 2\sqrt{3} - 2\sqrt{3} + 2(-2)$
$$= 3 - 4 = -1$$

Thus, the best answer is C.

342. A glucose solution contains 15 grams of glucose per 100 cubic centimeters of solution. If 45 cubic centimeters of the solution were poured into an empty container, how many grams of glucose would be in the container?

(A) 3.00
(B) 5.00
(C) 5.50
(D) 6.50
(E) 6.75

If x is the number of grams of glucose in the 45 cubic centimeters of solution, then $\frac{x}{45} = \frac{15}{100}$, and $x = 6.75$. Thus, the best answer is E.

343. If Sam were twice as old as he is, he would be 40 years older than Jim. If Jim is 10 years younger than Sam, how old is Sam?

(A) 20
(B) 30
(C) 40
(D) 50
(E) 60

Let S be Sam's current age and let J be Jim's current age. The statement "if Sam were twice as old as he is, he would be 40 years older than Jim" can be represented by the equation $2S = J + 40$, and the statement "Jim is 10 years younger than Sam" can be represented by the equation $S - 10 = J$. Substituting $S - 10$ for J in the equation $2S = J + 40$ yields $2S = S + 30$. Thus, $S = 30$, and the best answer is B.

344. If $\frac{1}{2} + \frac{1}{3} + \frac{1}{4} = \frac{13}{x}$, which of the following must be an integer?

I. $\frac{x}{8}$

II. $\frac{x}{12}$

III. $\frac{x}{24}$

(A) I only
(B) II only
(C) I and III only
(D) II and III only
(E) I, II, and III

The fractions can be added using the least common denominator 12:

$\frac{13}{x} = \frac{1}{2} + \frac{1}{3} + \frac{1}{4} = \frac{6}{12} + \frac{4}{12} + \frac{3}{12} = \frac{13}{12}$, so $x = 12$.

I. $\frac{x}{8} = \frac{12}{8}$, which is not an integer.

II. $\frac{x}{12} = \frac{12}{12} = 1$, which is an integer.

III. $\frac{x}{24} = \frac{12}{24} = \frac{1}{2}$, which is not an integer.

Thus, only II is an integer, and the best answer is B.

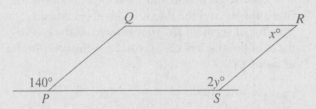

345. In the figure above, if PQRS is a parallelogram, then $y - x =$

(A) 30   (B) 35   (C) 40   (D) 70   (E) 100

Since PQ and SR are parallel, $2y = 140$ and $y = 70$. Since QR and PS are parallel, $x + 2y = 180$; so $x + 2(70) = 180$, or $x = 40$. Thus, $y - x = 30$, and the best answer is A.

346. The temperature in degrees Celsius (C) can be converted to temperature in degrees Fahrenheit (F) by the formula $F = \frac{9}{5}C + 32$. What is the temperature at which $F = C$?

(A) 20°   (B) $\left(\frac{32}{5}\right)°$ (C) 0°
(D) −20°   (E) −40°

Substituting F for C in the equation $F = \frac{9}{5}C + 32$ yields $F = \frac{9}{5}F + 32$. Thus, $-\frac{4}{5}F = 32$, or $F = 32(-\frac{5}{4}) = -40$, and the best answer is E.

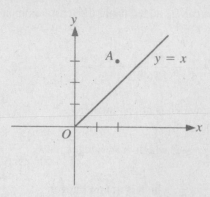

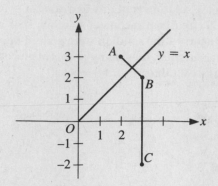

The coordinates of *C* are therefore $(3, -2)$, and the best answer is D.

347. In the rectangular coordinate system above, the line $y = x$ is the perpendicular bisector of segment *AB* (not shown), and the *x*-axis is the perpendicular bisector of segment *BC* (not shown). If the coordinates of point *A* are $(2, 3)$, what are the coordinates of point *C* ?

  (A) $(-3, -2)$
  (B) $(-3, 2)$
  (C) $(2, -3)$
  (D) $(3, -2)$
  (E) $(2, 3)$

Since the line $y = x$ is the perpendicular bisector of *AB*, *B* is the reflection of *A* through this line. In any reflection through the line $y = x$, the *x*-coordinate and *y*-coordinate of a point become interchanged. Thus, the coordinates of *B* are $(3,2)$.

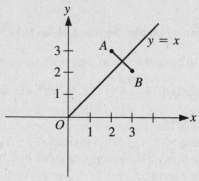

Since the *x*-axis is the perpendicular bisector of *BC*, *C* is the reflection of *B* through the *x*-axis. Thus, the *x*-coordinates of *C* and *B* are the same, and the *y*-coordinate of *C* is the negative of the *y*-coordinate of *B*.

348. If 1 kilometer is approximately 0.6 mile, which of the following best approximates the number of kilometers in 2 miles?

  (A) $\dfrac{10}{3}$ (B) 3 (C) $\dfrac{6}{5}$ (D) $\dfrac{1}{3}$ (E) $\dfrac{3}{10}$

If *x* is the number of kilometers in 2 miles, then $\dfrac{1}{0.6} = \dfrac{x}{2}$. So $x = \dfrac{2}{0.6} = \dfrac{20}{6} = \dfrac{10}{3}$, and the best answer is A.

349. A \$500 investment and a \$1,500 investment have a combined yearly return of 8.5 percent of the total of the two investments. If the \$500 investment has a yearly return of 7 percent, what percent yearly return does the \$1,500 investment have?

  (A) 9%

  (B) 10%

  (C) $10\dfrac{5}{8}$%

  (D) 11%

  (E) 12%

The total of the two investments, or \$2,000, has a yearly return of 8.5 percent, or \$170. The \$500 investment has a yearly return of 7 percent, or \$35. Thus, the \$1,500 investment has a yearly return of \$170 − \$35, or \$135. The \$135 yearly return is $\dfrac{135}{1,500}$, or 9 percent, of \$1,500. The best answer is A.

350. A store currently charges the same price for each towel that it sells. If the current price of each towel were to be increased by $1, 10 fewer of the towels could be bought for $120, excluding sales tax. What is the current price of each towel?

   (A) $1
   (B) $2
   (C) $3
   (D) $4
   (E) $12

Let p be the price per towel and let n be the number of towels that can be sold for $120. Thus, $np = 120$ and $(p + 1)(n - 10) = 120$. Solving the first equation for n yields $n = \dfrac{120}{p}$. Substituting $\dfrac{120}{p}$ for n in the second equation yields $(p + 1)(\dfrac{120}{p} - 10) = 120$, which can be solved as follows:

$$
\begin{aligned}
(p + 1)(120 - 10p) &= 120p \\
10(p + 1)(12 - p) &= 120p \\
(p + 1)(12 - p) &= 12p \\
-p^2 + 11p + 12 &= 12p \\
p^2 + p - 12 &= 0 \\
(p - 3)(p + 4) &= 0 \\
p &= 3 \text{ or } -4
\end{aligned}
$$

Since p is the price per towel, p cannot be -4. Thus, $p = 3$, and the best answer is C.

351. If the sum of n consecutive integers is 0, which of the following must be true?

   I. n is an even number.
   II. n is an odd number.
   III. The average (arithmetic mean) of the n integers is 0.

   (A) I only   (B) II only   (C) III only
   (D) I and III   (E) II and III

Recall that for every integer a, $a + (-a) = 0$. Therefore, by pairing 1 with -1, 2 with -2, and so on, one can see that in order to sum to zero, a list of consecutive integers must contain the same number of positive integers as negative integers, in addition to containing the integer 0. Therefore, the list has an odd number of integers. Thus, I is false and II is true. The average of a list of n numbers is equal to their sum divided by n. Thus, III is true, and the best answer is E.

352. In the formula $V = \dfrac{1}{(2r)^3}$, if r is halved, then V is multiplied by

   (A) 64

   (B) 8

   (C) 1

   (D) $\dfrac{1}{8}$

   (E) $\dfrac{1}{64}$

If $V = \dfrac{1}{(2r)^3} = \dfrac{1}{8r^3}$, then substituting $\dfrac{1}{2}r$ for r yields

$$
\dfrac{1}{8\left(\dfrac{r}{2}\right)^3} = \dfrac{1}{r^3} = 8 \times \dfrac{1}{8r^3} = 8V .
$$

Thus, if r is halved, V is multiplied by 8, and the best answer is B.

353. For any integer n greater than 1, $\lfloor n$ denotes the product of all the integers from 1 to n, inclusive. How many prime numbers are there between $\lfloor 6 + 2$ and $\lfloor 6 + 6$, inclusive?

   (A) None   (B) One   (C) Two
   (D) Three   (E) Four

$\lfloor 6 = (6)(5)(4)(3)(2)(1) = 720$

Thus, the question is asking how many prime numbers are between 722 and 726, inclusive. The numbers 722, 724, and 726 are divisible by 2, and 725 is divisible by 5. The only remaining number is 723, which is divisible by 3. Thus, there are no prime numbers between $\lfloor 6 + 2$ and $\lfloor 6 + 6$, inclusive, and the best answer is A.

354. In how many arrangements can a teacher seat 3 girls and 3 boys in a row of 6 seats if the boys are to have the first, third, and fifth seats?

   (A) 6   (B) 9   (C) 12   (D) 36   (E) 720

Any one of the 3 boys could be seated in the first seat, either of the remaining 2 boys in the third seat, and the remaining boy in the fifth seat. Thus there are $3(2)(1) = 6$ ways the boys could be arranged. There are also 3 girls to be arranged in 3 seats; thus, by the same reasoning, there are 6 ways in which the girls can be arranged. Since for each arrangement of the boys, there are 6 arrangements of the girls, there are $6(6) = 36$ ways in which the 3 boys and the 3 girls can be arranged. Thus, the best answer is D.

355. A circular rim 28 inches in diameter rotates the same number of inches per second as a circular rim 35 inches in diameter. If the smaller rim makes x revolutions per second, how many revolutions per <u>minute</u> does the larger rim make in terms of x ?

   (A) $\dfrac{48\pi}{x}$

   (B) $75x$

   (C) $48x$

   (D) $24x$

   (E) $\dfrac{x}{75}$

One rotation of circular rims of diameters 28 and 35 inches is 28π and 35π inches, respectively. Since the two circular rims rotate the same number of inches per second, the number of rotations per second of the larger rim is $\dfrac{28}{35}$ times the number of rotations of the smaller rim. Thus, if the smaller rim rotates x times per second, the larger rim rotates $\dfrac{28}{35}x$ times per second. Since there are 60 seconds in 1 minute, the larger rim rotates $(60)\dfrac{28}{35}x = 48x$ times per minute, and the best answer is C.

356. The cost C of manufacturing a certain product can be estimated by the formula $C = 0.03rst^2$, where r and s are the amounts, in pounds, of the two major ingredients and t is the production time, in hours. If r is increased by 50 percent, s is increased by 20 percent, and t is decreased by 30 percent, by approximately what percent will the estimated cost of manufacturing the product change?

   (A) 40% increase
   (B) 12% increase
   (C) 4% increase
   (D) 12% decrease
   (E) 24% decrease

If r is increased by 50 percent, s is increased by 20 percent, and t is decreased by 30 percent, then, according to the formula, the new estimated cost of manufacturing the product will be

$$0.03(1.5r)(1.2s)(0.7t)^2 = [0.03(1.5)(1.2)(0.7)^2]rst^2$$
$$= 0.882(0.03rst^2).$$

This is a decrease of approximately 12 percent, and the best answer is D.

357. Reggie purchased a car costing $8,700. As a down payment he used a $2,300 insurance settlement, and an amount from his savings equal to 15 percent of the difference between the cost of the car and the insurance settlement. If he borrowed the rest of the money needed to purchase the car, how much did he borrow?

(A) $6,400
(B) $6,055
(C) $5,440
(D) $5,095
(E) $3,260

The difference between the cost of the car and the insurance settlement was $8,700 – $2,300, or $6,400. Since Reggie used an amount equal to 15 percent of $6,400 as part of the down payment, the rest of the money needed to purchase the car was 85 percent of $6,400, or 0.85 ($6,400), which is $5,440. The best answer is C.

MEMBERSHIP OF ORGANIZATION X, 1988

Honorary Members	78
Fellows	9,209
Members	35,509
Associate Members	27,909
Affiliates	2,372

358. According to the table above, the number of fellows was approximately what percent of the total membership of Organization X ?

(A) 9%
(B) 12%
(C) 18%
(D) 25%
(E) 35%

From the table, the number of fellows is 9,209, and the total membership is the sum of the 5 numbers, which is 75,077. Therefore, the number of fellows is $\frac{9,209}{75,077}$ of the total membership, or approximately 12 percent. The best answer is B.

359. The arithmetic mean and standard deviation of a certain normal distribution are 13.5 and 1.5, respectively. What value is exactly 2 standard deviations less than the mean?

(A) 10.5
(B) 11.0
(C) 11.5
(D) 12.0
(E) 12.5

Since the arithmetic mean is 13.5 and one standard deviation is 1.5, two standard deviations less than the mean is $13.5 – 2(1.5) = 10.5$. The best answer is A.

360. Mark bought a set of 6 flower pots of different sizes at a total cost of $8.25. Each pot cost $0.25 more than the next one below it in size. What was the cost, in dollars, of the largest pot?

(A) $1.75
(B) $1.85
(C) $2.00
(D) $2.15
(E) $2.30

If the largest pot cost x dollars, the next smaller pot cost $x – 0.25$ dollars, the next smaller $x – 0.50$ dollars, and so forth. Thus, the total cost in dollars for the 6 pots was $x + (x – 0.25) + (x – 0.50) + (x – 0.75) + (x – 1.00) + (x – 1.25)$. Therefore, combining terms, $6x – 3.75 = 8.25$, or $x = 2.00$. The best answer is C.

361. When N is divided by T, the quotient is S and the remainder is V. Which of the following expressions is equal to N ?

(A) ST
(B) $S + V$
(C) $ST + V$
(D) $T(S + V)$
(E) $T(S – V)$

The first sentence implies that N equals the product of S and T plus a remainder of V; that is, $N = ST + V$. For example, when 17 is divided by 5, the quotient is 3 and the remainder is 2; so $17 = (3)(5) + 2$. The best answer is C.

38, 69, 22, 73, 31, 47, 13, 82

362. Which of the following numbers is greater than three-fourths of the numbers but less than one-fourth of the numbers in the list above?

(A) 56
(B) 68
(C) 69
(D) 71
(E) 73

The numbers in the list reordered from least to greatest are as follows: 13, 22, 31, 38, 47, 69, 73, 82. Since there are 8 numbers in the list, $\frac{3}{4}(8) = 6$ and $\frac{1}{4}(8) = 2$.

Therefore, any number that is greater than the first 6 numbers on the list must be greater than 69, and any number that is less than the last 2 numbers in the list must be less than 73. Of the answer choices given, the only one that is greater than 69 but less than 73 is 71. The best answer is D.

363. Lucy invested $10,000 in a new mutual fund account exactly three years ago. The value of the account increased by 10 percent during the first year, increased by 5 percent during the second year, and decreased by 10 percent during the third year. What is the value of the account today?

(A) $10,350
(B) $10,395
(C) $10,500
(D) $11,500
(E) $12,705

Since the account increased by 10 percent during the first year, the value of the account at the end of the first year was $10,000 (1.10), or $11,000. The account increased by 5 percent during the second year, so its value at the end of the second year was $11,000 (1.05), or $11,550. The account decreased by 10 percent during the third year, which reduced its value to 90 percent of $11,550 by the end of the third year; or $11,550(0.90) = $10,395. The best answer is B.

364. A certain bakery has 6 employees. It pays annual salaries of $14,000 to each of 2 employees, $16,000 to 1 employee, and $17,000 to each of the remaining 3 employees. The average (arithmetic mean) annual salary of these employees is closest to which of the following?

(A) $15,200
(B) $15,500
(C) $15,800
(D) $16,000
(E) $16,400

The sum of the salaries of the 6 employees is (2)($14,000) + (1)($16,000) + (3)($17,000), which equals $95,000. Therefore, the average salary for the 6 employees is $\frac{\$95,000}{6}$, or $15,833 to the nearest dollar. Of the 5 options given, $15,800 is closest to $15,833. The best answer is C.

365. If x is equal to the sum of the even integers from 40 to 60, inclusive, and y is the number of even integers from 40 to 60, inclusive, what is the value of $x+y$?

(A) 550
(B) 551
(C) 560
(D) 561
(E) 572

There are 21 integers between 40 and 60, inclusive, with 11 of the integers being even. Thus, the value of y is 11. The sum of the 11 even integers from 40 to 60, inclusive, can be obtained by multiplying the average of the integers by 11. Since the integers are consecutive, the average of all the integers is halfway between 40 and 60, or $\frac{40+60}{2} = 50$. Thus, the sum is (11)(50) = 550, which is the value of x. The value of $x + y$ is therefore 550 + 11= 561. The best answer is D.

366. If $\left(7^{\frac{3}{4}}\right)^n = 7$, what is the value of n ?

(A) $\dfrac{1}{3}$

(B) $\dfrac{2}{3}$

(C) $\dfrac{4}{3}$

(D) $\dfrac{5}{3}$

(E) $\dfrac{6}{3}$

Since $\left(7^{\frac{3}{4}}\right)^n = 7^{\frac{3n}{4}} = 7^1$, it follows, by equating

exponents, that $\dfrac{3n}{4} = 1$, or $n = \dfrac{4}{3}$. The best answer is C.

367. Which of the following is equal to the average (arithmetic mean) of $(x + 2)^2$ and $(x - 2)^2$?

(A) x^2
(B) $x^2 + 2$
(C) $x^2 + 4$
(D) $x^2 + 2x$
(E) $x^2 + 4x$

The average of $(x+2)^2$ and $(x-2)^2$ is

$\dfrac{(x+2)^2 + (x-2)^2}{2}$, or

$\dfrac{(x^2 + 4x + 4) + (x^2 - 4x + 4)}{2} = \dfrac{2x^2 + 8}{2} = x^2 + 4$

The best answer is C.

368. If $x^4 + y^4 = 100$ then the greatest possible value of x is between

(A) 0 and 3
(B) 3 and 6
(C) 6 and 9
(D) 9 and 12
(E) 12 and 15

The value of x is greatest when $y = 0$. In that case $x^4 = 100$. Since $3^4 = 81$ and $4^4 = 256$, it follows that the greatest possible value of x is between 3 and 4. The best answer is B.

369. During a car trip, Maria stopped to rest after she traveled $\dfrac{1}{2}$ of the total distance to her destination. She stopped again after she traveled $\dfrac{1}{4}$ of the distance remaining between her first stop and her destination, and then she drove the remaining 120 miles to her destination. What was the total distance, in miles, from Maria's starting point to her destination?

(A) 280
(B) 320
(C) 360
(D) 420
(E) 480

Let D be the total distance, in miles, from starting point to destination. Maria first traveled $\dfrac{D}{2}$ miles, leaving a distance of $\dfrac{D}{2}$ miles to go. She then traveled $\dfrac{1}{4}$ of the remaining distance, which was $\dfrac{1}{4}\left(\dfrac{D}{2}\right)$, or $\dfrac{D}{8}$ miles. So, after the second stop she had traveled a total of $\dfrac{D}{2} + \dfrac{D}{8}$ miles, or $\dfrac{5D}{8}$ miles. She still had $D - \dfrac{5D}{8}$, or $\dfrac{3D}{8}$ miles to go, which is given as 120 miles.

Therefore, $\dfrac{3D}{8} = 120$, or $D = 320$. The best answer is B.

NUMBER OF SOLID-COLORED MARBLES IN THREE JARS

Jar	Number of Red Marbles	Number of Green Marbles	Total Number of Red and Green Marbles
P	x	y	80
Q	y	z	120
R	x	z	160

370. In the table above, what is the number of green marbles in jar R ?

(A) 70
(B) 80
(C) 90
(D) 100
(E) 110

From the table, the total number of red marbles and green marbles in the 3 jars is $2x + 2y + 2z$, which equals $80 + 120 + 160$, or 360. Dividing by 2 gives you $x + y + z = 180$. But the total number of red marbles and green marbles in jar P is $x + y = 80$, so substituting into the previous equation for $x + y$, you get $80 + z = 180$. Therefore z, which is the number of green marbles in jar R, is 100. The best answer is D.

371. The cost of picture frame M is $10.00 less than 3 times the cost of picture frame N. If the cost of frame M is $50.00, what is the cost of frame N ?

(A) $13.33
(B) $16.66
(C) $20.00
(D) $26.66
(E) $40.00

If m is the cost, in dollars, of frame M, and n is the cost, in dollars, of frame N, it follows that $m = 3n - 10$.

Therefore, if $m = 50$, then $50 = 3n - 10$, or $n = \dfrac{60}{3} = 20$.

The best answer is C.

372. If x is to be chosen at random from the set $\{1, 2, 3, 4\}$ and y is to be chosen at random from the set $\{5, 6, 7\}$, what is the probability that xy will be even?

(A) $\dfrac{1}{6}$

(B) $\dfrac{1}{3}$

(C) $\dfrac{1}{2}$

(D) $\dfrac{2}{3}$

(E) $\dfrac{5}{6}$

There are 4 different numbers (x) that can be chosen from $\{1, 2, 3, 4\}$ and 3 different numbers (y) that can be chosen from $\{5, 6, 7\}$. Therefore, the number of different pairs of numbers x and y that can be chosen is 4×3, or 12. Note that if xy is to be even, at least one of x and y must be even. If x is even, then y can be odd or even. Since there are 2 even values of x, there are $2 \times 3 = 6$ possibilities that xy will be even. If x is odd, then y must be even. Since there is 1 even value of y and 2 odd values of x, there are $2 \times 1 = 2$ additional possibilities. Thus, there are $6 + 2 = 8$ possibilities for xy to be even, and the probability that xy will be even is $\dfrac{8}{12} = \dfrac{2}{3}$. The best answer is D.

373. If $S = \{0, 4, 5, 2, 11, 8\}$, how much greater than the median of the numbers in S is the mean of the numbers in S ?

(A) 0.5
(B) 1.0
(C) 1.5
(D) 2.0
(E) 2.5

If the numbers in S are ordered according to size, 0, 2, 4, 5, 8, 11, the median of those numbers, which is the average of the two middle numbers, is $\dfrac{4+5}{2} = 4.5$. The mean of the numbers in S is the sum of all the numbers divided by 6, or $\dfrac{30}{6} = 5$. Therefore, the mean is 0.5 greater than the median. The best answer is A.

374. The value of $\sqrt[3]{-89}$ is

    (A) between –9 and –10
    (B) between –8 and –9
    (C) between –4 and –5
    (D) between –3 and –4
    (E) undefined

The cube root of –89, or $\sqrt[3]{-89}$, is a number x such that $x^3 = -89$. Therefore, x must be negative. Since $(-4)^3 = -64$ and $(-5)^3 = -125$, the cube root of –89 must be a number between –4 and –5. The best answer is C.

Shipment	Number of Defective Chips in the Shipment	Total Number of Chips in the Shipment
S1	2	5,000
S2	5	12,000
S3	6	18,000
S4	4	16,000

375. A computer chip manufacturer expects the ratio of the number of defective chips to the total number of chips in all future shipments to equal the corresponding ratio for shipments $S1$, $S2$, $S3$, and $S4$ combined, as shown in the table above. What is the expected number of defective chips in a shipment of 60,000 chips?

    (A) 14
    (B) 20
    (C) 22
    (D) 24
    (E) 25

According to the table, for the four shipments combined, there are 17 defective chips out of a total of 51,000 chips, which is a ratio of $\frac{17}{51,000} = \frac{1}{3,000}$. Thus, if n is the number of defective chips in a shipment of 60,000 chips, $\frac{1}{3,000} = \frac{n}{60,000}$, or $n = 20$. The best answer is B.

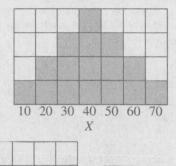

X

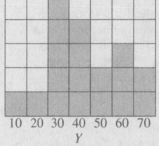

Y

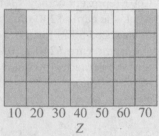

Z

376. If the variables, X, Y, and Z take on only the values 10, 20, 30, 40, 50, 60, or 70 with frequencies indicated by the shaded regions above, for which of the frequency distributions is the mean equal to the median?

    (A) X only
    (B) Y only
    (C) Z only
    (D) X and Y
    (E) X and Z

Note that the frequency distributions for both X and Z are symmetric about 40, which implies that both variables have mean = median = 40. [Note: Although the mean of Y is $42\frac{2}{9}$ and the median is 40, it is not necessary to speculate about or calculate them, since there is no answer choice "X, Y and Z."] The best answer is E.

377. In a certain furniture store, each week Nancy earns a salary of $240 plus 5 percent of the amount of her total sales that exceeds $800 for the week. If Nancy earned a total of $450 one week, what were her total sales that week?

(A) $2,200
(B) $3,450
(C) $4,200
(D) $4,250
(E) $5,000

Let x represent Nancy's total sales for a week. Each week she earns $240 plus 5 percent of her total sales that exceed $800 for the week. Therefore, in a week she would earn $240 + (0.05)(x − $800). It is given that she earned $450 one week, so for that week $240 + (0.05)(x − $800) = $450, or x = $5,000. The best answer is E.

$$A = \{2, 3, 4, 5\}$$
$$B = \{4, 5, 6, 7, 8\}$$

378. Two integers will be randomly selected from the sets above, one integer from set A and one integer from set B. What is the probability that the sum of the two integers will equal 9?

(A) 0.15
(B) 0.20
(C) 0.25
(D) 0.30
(E) 0.33

The number of possible selections from A is 4, and the number of possible selections from B is 5. Therefore, the number of different pairs of numbers, one from A and one from B, is $4 \times 5 = 20$. Of these 20 pairs of numbers, there are 4 possible pairs that sum to 9, namely: 2 and 7, 3 and 6, 4 and 5, and 5 and 4. Therefore, the probability that the sum of the 2 integers selected will equal 9 is $\frac{4}{20} = 0.20$. The best answer is B.

$$p, r, s, t, u$$

379. An arithmetic sequence is a sequence in which each term after the first is equal to the sum of the preceding term and a constant. If the list of numbers shown above is an arithmetic sequence, which of the following must also be an arithmetic sequence?

  I. $2p, 2r, 2s, 2t, 2u$
  II. $p − 3, r − 3, s − 3, t − 3, u − 3$
  III. p^2, r^2, s^2, t^2, u^2

(A) I only
(B) II only
(C) III only
(D) I and II
(E) II and III

It follows from the definition of arithmetic sequence given in the first sentence that there is a constant c such that $r − p = s − r = t − s = u − t = c$. In sequence I, the difference between any two consecutive terms is equal to twice the constant c. For example, $2r − 2p = 2(r − p) = 2c$. Thus, I is an arithmetic sequence. In sequence II, the difference between any two consecutive terms is equal to the same constant c in the original sequence. For example, $r − 3 − (p − 3) = r − p = c$. Thus, II is an arithmetic sequence. In sequence III, the difference between two consecutive terms is *not* constant. For example, if p, q, r, t and u were 1, 2, 3, 4, and 5, then sequence III would be 1, 4, 9, 16 and 25, which is not arithmetic since, for example, $4 − 1 \neq 9 − 4$. The best answer is D.

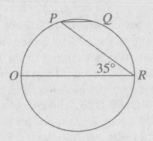

380. In the circle above, PQ is parallel to diameter OR, and OR has length 18. What is the length of minor arc PQ ?

(A) 2π

(B) $\dfrac{9\pi}{4}$

(C) $\dfrac{7\pi}{2}$

(D) $\dfrac{9\pi}{2}$

(E) 3π

Since the measure of inscribed angle PRO is 35°, the measure of minor arc OP is 70°. Since PQ is parallel to OR, the measure of inscribed angle QPR is 35°, and so the measure of minor arc QR is also 70°. Thus, the measure of minor arc PQ is 180° – 70° – 70° = 40°, and the length of minor arc PQ is $\dfrac{40}{360} = \dfrac{1}{9}$ of the length of the circumference of the circle. Since the diameter OR has length 18, the circumference is $\pi d = 18\pi$. Thus the length of minor arc PQ is $\dfrac{1}{9}(18\pi) = 2\pi$. The best answer is A.

381. Dick and Jane each saved $3,000 in 1989. In 1990 Dick saved 8 percent more than in 1989, and together he and Jane saved a total of $5,000. Approximately what percent less did Jane save in 1990 than in 1989 ?

(A) 8%
(B) 25%
(C) 41%
(D) 59%
(E) 70%

In 1990 Dick saved 8 percent more than the $3,000 he saved in 1989, which amounted to (1.08)($3,000), or $3,240. In 1990 he and Jane together saved $5,000. Thus, Jane must have saved only $5,000 – $3,240 = $1,760, which is $1,240 less than she saved in 1990. Therefore, in 1990 Jane saved approximately $\dfrac{\$1,240}{\$3,000} = 41\%$ less than she saved in 1989. The best answer is C.

382. Of the following, which is least?

(A) $\dfrac{1}{0.2}$

(B) $(0.2)^2$

(C) 0.02

(D) $\dfrac{0.2}{2}$

(E) 0.2

The choices can be compared quickly, as follows:

The first choice is $\dfrac{1}{0.2} = 5$, the second choice is $(0.2)^2 = 0.04$, the third choice is 0.02, the fourth choice is $\dfrac{0.2}{2} = 0.1$, and the fifth choice is 0.2. The best answer is C.

383. S represents the sum of the weights of n fish in pounds. Which of the following represents the average (arithmetic mean) of the n weights in ounces? (1 pound = 16 ounces).

(A) $16nS$

(B) $\dfrac{16S}{n}$

(C) $\dfrac{16n}{S}$

(D) $\dfrac{nS}{16}$

(E) $\dfrac{S}{16n}$

The average of the n weights in pounds is represented by $\dfrac{S}{n}$. Since 1 pound = 16 ounces, the average of the n weights in ounces is $16\left(\dfrac{S}{n}\right)$, or $\dfrac{16S}{n}$. The best answer is B.

NET INCOME BY SECTOR, SECOND QUARTER, 1996

Sector	Net Income (in billions)	Percent Change from First Quarter, 1996
Basic Materials	$4.83	−26%
Energy	7.46	+40
Industrial	5.00	−1
Utilities	8.57	+303
Conglomerates	2.07	+10

384. The table above represents the combined net income of all United States companies in each of five sectors for the second quarter of 1996. Which sector had the greatest net income during the first quarter of 1996 ?

(A) Basic Materials
(B) Energy
(C) Industrial
(D) Utilities
(E) Conglomerates

The table shows net income in billions of dollars and the percent change from the first quarter to the second. According to the table, net income in the basic materials sector decreased by 26 percent from the first quarter to the second. If x represents the net income in the first quarter, $(0.74)x = 4.83$, and $x = 6.53$. The energy sector net income increased by 40 percent. If y represents the net income in the first quarter, $(1.40)y = 7.46$, so $y < 6$. The industrial sector changed by only 1 percent to 5.00, so the first quarter value had to be less than 6.53. For utilities, the net income increased about 300 percent, which means that the net income in the first quarter was about $\dfrac{1}{4}$ of 8.57, which is clearly less than 6.53. The conglomerates sector net income the first quarter was less than 2.07, so the basic materials net income was greatest in the first quarter. The best answer is A.

385. For how many integers n is $2^n = n^2$?

(A) None
(B) One
(C) Two
(D) Three
(E) More than three

For all negative values of n, 2^n would be less than 1, and n^2 would be 1 or more. If $n = 0$, $2^n = 1$ and $n^2 = 0$. If $n = 1$, $2^n = 2$ and $n^2 = 1$. If $n = 2$, $2^n = 4$ and $n^2 = 4$. If $n = 3$, $2^n = 8$ and $n^2 = 9$. If $n = 4$, $2^n = 16$ and $n^2 = 16$. And if $n \geq 5$, $2^n > n^2$. So, for only two values of n, namely 2 and 4, is $2^n = n^2$. The best answer is C.

386. The manager of a theater noted that for every 10 admission tickets sold, the theater sells 3 bags of popcorn at $2.25 each, 4 sodas at $1.50 each, and 2 candy bars at $1.00 each. To the nearest cent, what is the average (arithmetic mean) amount of these snack sales per ticket sold?

(A) $1.48
(B) $1.58
(C) $1.60
(D) $1.64
(E) $1.70

For every 10 admission tickets sold, the theater sells $3(\$2.25) = \$6.75$ in popcorn, $4(\$1.50) = \$6.00$ in sodas, and $2(\$1.00), = \$2.00$ in candy bars, for a total of $14.75. Thus, the average amount per ticket sold is $\dfrac{\$14.75}{10}$, or $1.48, to the nearest cent. The best answer is A.

387. If $n = 4p$, where p is a prime number greater than 2, how many different positive <u>even</u> divisors does n have, including n ?

(A) Two
(B) Three
(C) Four
(D) Six
(E) Eight

Since p is a prime greater than 2, p must be odd. Therefore, the possible even divisors of $n = 4p$ are 2, 4, $2p$, and $4p$. The best answer is C.

388. S is a set containing 9 different numbers. T is a set containing 8 different numbers, all of which are members of S. Which of the following statements CANNOT be true?

(A) The mean of S is equal to the mean of T.
(B) The median of S is equal to the median of T.
(C) The range of S is equal to the range of T.
(D) The mean of S is greater than the mean of T.
(E) The range of S is less than the range of T.

To determine which of the statements cannot be true, it may be easiest to consider specific sets of numbers for S and T. For example, suppose S consists of the integers from 1 to 9 and T consists of the same integers except 5. Then the mean and median of S are both 5, and since the median of T is $\frac{4+6}{2} = 5$, the mean and median of T are both 5 as well. Since the range of a set is the difference between the greatest and smallest numbers in the set, S and T also have the same range, $9 - 1 = 8$. Thus, the first three choices can be true. The fourth choice is true if S is the same as above and T is the set of integers from 1 to 8. The mean of S would be 5, as stated earlier, and the mean of T would be 4.5. To see that the fifth choice <u>cannot</u> be true, suppose that x denotes the number in S that is not in T. If x is either the smallest or the greatest number in S, then the range of T would be less than the range of S. However, if x is between the smallest number and greatest number in S, then the range of T would be equal to the range of S. In any case, the range of S cannot be less than the range of T. The best answer is E.

389. In a recent election, James received 0.5 percent of the 2,000 votes cast. To win the election, a candidate needed to receive more than 50 percent of the vote. How many additional votes would James have needed to win the election?

(A) 901
(B) 989
(C) 990
(D) 991
(E) 1,001

James received 0.5 percent of 2,000 votes, which is $(0.005)(2,000) = 10$ votes. To win he needed more than 50 percent of 2,000, so he needed $(0.5)(2,000) + 1 = 1,001$ votes. Therefore, he needed an additional $1,001-10 = 991$ votes. The best answer is D.

390. The regular price per can of a certain brand of soda is $0.40. If the regular price per can is discounted 15 percent when the soda is purchased in 24-can cases, what is the price of 72 cans of this brand of soda purchased in 24-can cases?

(A) $16.32
(B) $18.00
(C) $21.60
(D) $24.48
(E) $28.80

The discounted price of one can of soda is $(0.85)(\$0.40)$, or $0.34. Therefore, the price of 72 cans of soda at the discounted price would be $(72)(\$0.34)$, or $24.48. The best answer is D.

391. If r and s are integers and $rs + r$ is odd, which of the following must be even?

(A) r
(B) s
(C) $r + s$
(D) $rs - r$
(E) $r^2 + s$

Since $rs + r = r(s + 1)$, which is odd, r and $s + 1$ must both be odd. Therefore, r is odd and s is even. Note that the other answer choices $r + s$, $rs - r$, and $r^2 + s$ must all be odd. The best answer is B.

List I: 3, 6, 8, 19
List II: x, 3, 6, 8, 19

392. If the median of the numbers in list I above is equal to the median of the numbers in list II above, what is the value of x ?

(A) 6
(B) 7
(C) 8
(D) 9
(E) 10

In general, to calculate the median of n numbers, first order the numbers from least to greatest. If n is odd, the median is the middle number, while if n is even, the median is the average of the two middle numbers. Thus, the median of the numbers in list I is $\dfrac{6+8}{2}$, or 7. In list II, there are 5 numbers, so the median must be the 3rd number in the list if the numbers are ordered from least to greatest. Since the median must be 7 (the median of list I), x must be 7. The best answer is B.

393. If $d = 2.0453$ and $d*$ is the decimal obtained by rounding d to the nearest hundredth, what is the value of $d* - d$?

(A) −0.0053
(B) −0.0003
(C) 0.0007
(D) 0.0047
(E) 0.0153

d rounded to the nearest hundredth is 2.05. Therefore, $d* = 2.05$, and $d* - d = 2.05 - 2.0453$, or 0.0047. The best answer is D.

394. Right triangle PQR is to be constructed in the xy-plane so that the right angle is at P and PR is parallel to the x-axis. The x- and y-coordinates of P, Q, and R are to be integers that satisfy the inequalities $-4 \le x \le 5$ and $6 \le y \le 16$. How many different triangles with these properties could be constructed?

(A) 110
(B) 1,100
(C) 9,900
(D) 10,000
(E) 12,100

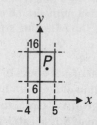

In the xy-plane, point P is located in the rectangular area determined by $-4 \le x \le 5$ and $6 \le y \le 16$ (see above). Since the coordinates of points P, Q, and R are integers, there are 10 possible x values and 11 possible y values, so point P can be any one of $10(11) = 110$ points in the rectangular area. In the horizontal direction (left or right) from each point P there are 9 points that could be point R, and in the vertical direction (up or down) from each point P there are 10 points that could be point Q. Thus, there are $110(9)(10) = 9,900$ sets of 3 points P, Q, and R, each of which determines a right triangle PQR with the right angle at P and PR parallel to the x-axis. The best answer is C.

395. A box contains 100 balls, numbered from 1 to 100. If three balls are selected at random and with replacement from the box, what is the probability that the sum of the three numbers on the balls selected from the box will be odd?

(A) $\frac{1}{4}$

(B) $\frac{3}{8}$

(C) $\frac{1}{2}$

(D) $\frac{5}{8}$

(E) $\frac{3}{4}$

For the sum of the three numbers on the selected balls to be odd, either (1) the numbers must all be odd, or (2) exactly one of the numbers must be odd and the other two numbers must be even. Possibility (2) occurs in three different ways depending on whether the first, second, or third number is odd. Thus, there are four different outcomes in which the sum could be odd. Since the selection is done with replacement, each selection will be made from 50 odd-numbered and 50 even-numbered balls. Therefore, the probability of selecting an odd-numbered ball is

$$\frac{\text{the number of balls with an odd number}}{\text{the total number of balls}} = \frac{50}{100} = \frac{1}{2}.$$

Similarly, the probability of selecting an even-numbered ball is also $\frac{1}{2}$. Since each choice of a ball is independent of another, each of the four outcomes mentioned above has probability $\frac{1}{2} \times \frac{1}{2} \times \frac{1}{2} = \frac{1}{8}$, and so the probability that the sum of the three numbers is odd is $4\left(\frac{1}{8}\right) = \frac{1}{2}$.

The best answer is C.

396. How many different positive integers are factors of 441 ?

(A) 4
(B) 6
(C) 7
(D) 9
(E) 11

$441 = (9)(49) = (3^2)(7^2)$. Therefore, the factors of 441 are 1, 3, 7, 3^2, $(3)(7)$, 7^2, $(3^2)(7)$, $(3)(7^2)$, and 441, or 1, 3, 7, 9, 21, 49, 63, 147, and 441. The best answer is D.

397. Company K's earnings were $12 million last year. If this year's earnings are projected to be 150 percent greater than last year's earnings, what are Company K's projected earnings this year?

(A) $13.5 million
(B) $15 million
(C) $18 million
(D) $27 million
(E) $30 million

If this year's earnings are projected to be 150 percent greater than the $12 million earned last year, then this year's earnings will be 250 percent of $12 million, or (2.5)($12 million) = $30 million. The best answer is E.

2, 4, 6, 8, n, 3, 5, 7, 9

398. In the list above, if n is an integer between 1 and 10, inclusive, then the median must be

(A) either 4 or 5
(B) either 5 or 6
(C) either 6 or 7
(D) n
(E) 5.5

The reordering of the 8 actual numbers in the list from least to greatest is: 2, 3, 4, 5, 6, 7, 8, 9. Since n is an integer, it cannot have a value between the two middle numbers on the list, 5 and 6. Thus, if $n \geq 6$, the median of the 9 numbers would be 6, and if $n \leq 5$, the median of the 9 numbers would be 5. The best answer is B.

399. If $0 < x < 1$, which of the following inequalities must be true?

    I. $x^5 < x^3$
    II. $x^4 + x^5 < x^3 + x^2$
    III. $x^4 - x^5 < x^2 - x^3$

(A) None
(B) I only
(C) II only
(D) I and II only
(E) I, II, and III

If x is between 0 and 1, and if n is a positive integer, then the greater the value of n, the smaller the value of x^n. Thus, in particular, $x^5 < x^4 < x^3 < x^2$. In statement I, x^5 must be less than x^3. Concerning statement II, since x^4 and x^5 are each less than x^3 or x^2, it follows that $x^4 + x^5 < x^3 + x^2$. In statement III, note that $x^4 - x^5 = x^4(1-x)$ and $x^2 - x^3 = x^2(1-x)$. Thus, since $x^4 < x^2$ and $1 - x$ is positive, it follows that $x^4 - x^5 < x^2 - x^3$, and III is also true. The best answer is E.

400. If $(2^x)(2^y) = 8$ and $(9^x)(3^y) = 81$, then $(x, y) =$

(A) $(1, 2)$
(B) $(2, 1)$
(C) $(1, 1)$
(D) $(2, 2)$
(E) $(1, 3)$

Since $(2^x)(2^y) = 8$ can be written as $2^{x+y} = 2^3$, it follows, by equating exponents, that $x + y = 3$. Similarly, $(9^x)(3^y) = 81$ can be written as $3^{2x+y} = 3^4$, so $2x + y = 4$. Therefore, from the first equation $y = 3 - x$, and substituting for y into the second equation gives $2x + 3 - x = 4$, or $x = 1$. Therefore, $y = 2$ and $(x, y) = (1, 2)$. The best answer is A.

401. If $a = 1$ and $\dfrac{a - b}{c} = 1$, which of the following is NOT a possible value of b ?

(A) -2
(B) -1
(C) 0
(D) 1
(E) 2

From $\dfrac{a - b}{c} = 1$, it follows that $a - b \neq 0$, or $a \neq b$. Since it is given that $a = 1$, b cannot be equal to 1. The best answer is D.

402. Which of the following is equal to x^{18} for all positive values of x ?

(A) $x^9 + x^9$
(B) $(x^2)^9$
(C) $(x^9)^9$
(D) $(x^3)^{15}$
(E) $\dfrac{x^4}{x^{22}}$

Note that $x^9 + x^9 = 2x^9$, $\left(x^2\right)^9 = x^{(2)(9)} = x^{18}$, $\left(x^9\right)^9 = x^{81}$, $\left(x^3\right)^{15} = x^{45}$, and $\dfrac{x^4}{x^{22}} = x^{-18}$. The best answer is B.

403. A television manufacturer produces 600 units of a certain model each month at a cost to the manufacturer of $90 per unit and all of the produced units are sold each month. What is the minimum selling price per unit that will ensure that the monthly profit (revenue from sales minus the manufacturer's cost to produce) on the sales of these units will be at least $42,000 ?

(A) $110
(B) $120
(C) $140
(D) $160
(E) $180

If the manufacturer will sell each unit for x dollars, and the cost to manufacture each unit is $90, then the profit per unit is $x - \$90$. To attain a profit of at least $42,000 on the production and sale of 600 units, $600(x - \$90) \geq \$42,000$, or $x \geq \$160$. The best answer is D.

404. A square countertop has a square tile inlay in the center, leaving an untiled strip of uniform width around the tile. If the ratio of the tiled area to the untiled area is 25 to 39, which of the following could be the width, in inches, of the strip?

    I. $1\dfrac{1}{2}$
    II. 3
    III. $4\dfrac{1}{2}$

(A) I only
(B) II only
(C) I and II only
(D) I and III only
(E) I, II, and III

Since the ratio of the tiled area to the untiled area is 25 to 39, the ratio of the total area of the countertop to the tiled area is $\frac{39+25}{25} = \frac{64}{25}$. Therefore, the ratio of the length of a side of the countertop to the length of a side of the tiled area is $\frac{8}{5}$. If x is the length of a side of the countertop and y is the length of a side of the tiled area, this means that $y = \frac{5}{8}x$. If w is the width of the untiled strip, then $w = \frac{x-y}{2}$, which implies that $w = \frac{3}{16}x$. Therefore, for any positive value of w, a countertop with a side of length $\frac{16}{3}w$ inches will have an untiled strip of width w inches, and thus any width is possible for such a countertop. For example, an untiled strip of width 3 inches can be found in a countertop with a side of length $\frac{16}{3}(3) = 16$ inches. Therefore, all of the values I, II, and III could be the width of the strip. The best answer is E.

$$
\begin{array}{r}
4 \,\square\, 7 \\
\triangle\, 2\; 3 \\
+\; 1\; 6\; 2 \\
\hline
1,\; 2\; 2\; 2
\end{array}
$$

405. If $\square$ and $\triangle$ represent single digits in the correctly worked computation above, what is the value of $\square + \triangle$?

(A) 7
(B) 9
(C) 10
(D) 11
(E) 13

Since the sum of the units digits is $7 + 3 + 2 = 12$, the sum of the tens digits must be $1 + \square + 2 + 6 = 12$ because 1 is carried from the sum of the units digits. Thus, $\square = 3$, and 1 is carried to the hundreds column, where the sum of the digits is $1 + 4 + \triangle + 1 = 12$, or $\triangle = 6$. Therefore, $\square + \triangle = 9$. The best answer is B.

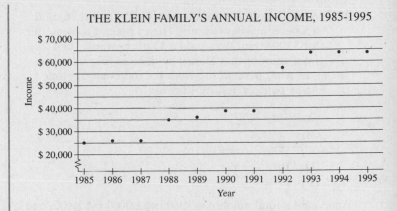

THE KLEIN FAMILY'S ANNUAL INCOME, 1985-1995

406. Which of the following statements can be inferred from the data above?

I. The Klein family's annual income more than doubled from 1985 to 1995.

II. The Klein family's annual income increased by a greater amount from 1985 to 1990 than from 1990 to 1995.

III. The Klein family's average (arithmetic mean) annual income for the period shown was greater than $40,000.

(A) I only
(B) II only
(C) I and III only
(D) II and III only
(E) I, II, and III

The Klein family's income increased from $25,000 in 1985 to over $60,000 in 1995, so it more than doubled, and statement I can be inferred from the data. The family's income increased from $25,000 in 1985 to approximately $38,000 in 1990, an increase of about $13,000. From 1990 to 1995 its income increased by more than $20,000 (from about $38,000 to more than $60,000), so statement II cannot be inferred from the data. The family's average income per year for the 7 years from 1985–1991 appears to be about $35,000, and for the 4 years 1992–1995 it appears to average more than $60,000 per year. Thus, the average annual income for the 11 years is about,

$$
\frac{7\,(\$35,000) + 4\,(\$60,000)}{11} = \frac{\$245,000 + \$240,000}{11} = \frac{\$485,000}{11},
$$

which is greater than $40,000. Therefore, statement III can be inferred from the data. The best answer is C.

407. Anne bought a computer for $2,000 and then paid a 5 percent sales tax, and Henry bought a computer for $1,800 and then paid a 12 percent sales tax. The total amount that Henry paid, including sales tax, was what percent less than the total amount that Anne paid, including sales tax?

(A) 3%
(B) 4%
(C) 7%
(D) 10%
(E) 12%

Anne paid a total amount of $(1.05)(\$2,000) = \$2,100$, and Henry paid a total amount of $(1.12)(1,800) = \$2,016$. Therefore, Henry paid $\$2,100 - \$2,016 = \$84$ less than Anne paid, which was $\dfrac{84}{2,100} = 4$ percent less. The best answer is B.

408. If $\dfrac{x}{y} = \dfrac{2}{3}$, then $\dfrac{x - y}{x} =$

(A) $-\dfrac{1}{2}$

(B) $-\dfrac{1}{3}$

(C) $\dfrac{1}{3}$

(D) $\dfrac{1}{2}$

(E) $\dfrac{5}{2}$

$\dfrac{x}{y} = \dfrac{2}{3}$ and $\dfrac{x - y}{x} = \dfrac{x}{x} - \dfrac{y}{x} = 1 - \dfrac{y}{x}$. Therefore,

$\dfrac{x - y}{x} = 1 - \dfrac{3}{2} = -\dfrac{1}{2}$. The best answer is A.

409. If $4x + 3y = -2$ and $3x + 6 = 0$, what is the value of y ?

(A) $-3\dfrac{1}{3}$

(B) -2

(C) $-\dfrac{2}{3}$

(D) $\dfrac{2}{3}$

(E) 2

Since $3x + 6 = 0$, $x = -2$. Then, substituting -2 into the equation $4x + 3y = -2$ for x, $4(-2) + 3y = -2$, or $y = 2$. The best answer is E.

I. 72, 73, 74, 75, 76
II. 74, 74, 74, 74, 74
III. 62, 74, 74, 74, 89

410. The data sets I, II, and III above are ordered from greatest standard deviation to least standard deviation in which of the following?

(A) I, II, III
(B) I, III, II
(C) II, III, I
(D) III, I, II
(E) III, II, I

In data set II there is no variation, so the standard deviation is 0. Data set I has small deviations from the mean of 74, so the standard deviation is greater in I than in II. Because of the extreme values 62 and 89, the variation in set III is clearly greater than the variation in I. So, the standard deviation in III is greater than the standard deviation in I. The best answer is D.

411. The contents of a certain box consist of 14 apples and 23 oranges. How many oranges must be removed from the box so that 70 percent of the pieces of fruit in the box will be apples?

(A) 3
(B) 6
(C) 14
(D) 17
(E) 20

There are a total of 37 pieces of fruit in the box. If x oranges must be removed, leaving $37 - x$ pieces of fruit, then the 14 apples in the box would constitute 70 percent of $37 - x$. Therefore, $\frac{14}{37 - x} = 0.70$, or $x = 17$. Alternatively, since 14 is 70 percent of 20, the number of oranges must be reduced to 6. Since there are currently 23 oranges in the box, this means that $23 - 6 = 17$ oranges must be removed. The best answer is D.

412. If n is a positive integer and n^2 is divisible by 72, then the largest positive integer that must divide n is

(A)   6
(B) 12
(C) 24
(D) 36
(E) 48

If n^2 is divisible by 72, then $n^2 = 72k$ for some positive integer k. Since n^2 is a perfect square and $72 = 2^3 3^2$, k must be even, so 144 must divide n^2 and 12 must divide n. Now note that if $n = 12$, then $n^2 = 144$ is divisible by 72. Therefore, no integer greater than 12 will necessarily divide all n such that n^2 is divisible by 72. The best answer is B.

413. If -3 is 6 more than x, what is the value of $\frac{x}{3}$?

(A) −9
(B) −6
(C) −3
(D) −1
(E)   1

If -3 is 6 more than x, then $-3 = x + 6$. Therefore, $x = -9$ and $\frac{x}{3} = \frac{-9}{3}$, or -3. The best answer is C.

$$r = 400 \left(\frac{D + S - P}{P} \right)$$

414. If stock is sold three months after it is purchased, the formula above relates P, D, S, and r, where P is the purchase price of the stock, D is the amount of any dividend received, S is the selling price of the stock, and r is the yield of the investment as a percent. If Rose purchased $400 worth of stock, received a dividend of $5, and sold the stock for $420 three months after purchasing it, what was the yield of her investment according to the formula? (Assume that she paid no commissions.)

(A)   1.25%
(B)   5%
(C)   6.25%
(D) 20%
(E) 25%

In this example, D is $5, S is $420, and P is $400. Therefore, according to the formula, the yield r of the investment, as a percent is $400 \left(\frac{5 + 420 - 400}{400} \right)$, or $r = 25$. So, the yield is 25%. The best answer is E.

415. An athlete runs R miles in H hours, then rides a bicycle Q miles in the same number of hours. Which of the following represents the athlete's average speed, in miles per hour, for these two activities combined?

(A) $\dfrac{R - Q}{H}$

(B) $\dfrac{R - Q}{2H}$

(C) $\dfrac{2(R + Q)}{H}$

(D) $\dfrac{2(R + Q)}{2H}$

(E) $\dfrac{R + Q}{2H}$

Average speed in miles per hour is defined as distance in miles divided by time in hours. The athlete travels a total of $R + Q$ miles in $H + H$ hours, so the average speed in miles per hour can be represented by $\frac{R + Q}{2H}$. The best answer is E.

416. If a certain sample of data has a mean of 20.0 and a standard deviation of 3.0, which of the following values is more than 2.5 standard deviations from the mean?

(A) 12.0
(B) 13.5
(C) 17.0
(D) 23.5
(E) 26.5

To be more than 2.5 standard deviations from the mean of a sample of data, a value must be either more than 2.5 standard deviations above the mean or more than 2.5 standard deviations below the mean. So, in this case, to be more than 2.5 standard deviations from the mean of 20, the value must be either greater than $20 + 2.5(3) = 27.5$, or less than $20 - 2.5(3) = 12.5$. The best answer is A.

417. Which of the following is the least positive integer that is divisible by 2, 3, 4, 5, 6, 7, 8, and 9 ?

(A) 15,120
(B) 3,024
(C) 2,520
(D) 1,890
(E) 1,680

The 8 numbers 2, 3, 4, 5, 6, 7, 8, and 9, have only the prime factors 2, 3, 5, and 7. So the least positive integer that is divisible by each of those numbers must have as factors 2^a, 3^b, 5^c and 7^d, where a, b, c, and d are each the maximum number of times that the particular prime occurs as a factor in any of the 8 numbers. The maximum number of times that 2 occurs in any number is 3. (That is, $2^3 = 8$.) The maximum for 3 is 2 (that is, $3^2 = 9$), and the maximum for 5 and 7 are each 1. So, the least positive integer is $2^3 \times 3^2 \times 5^1 \times 7^1$, or 2,520. The best answer is C.

418. Of the 50 researchers in a workgroup, 40 percent will be assigned to team A and the remaining 60 percent to team B. However, 70 percent of the researchers prefer team A and 30 percent prefer team B. What is the least possible number of researchers who will NOT be assigned to the team they prefer?

(A) 15
(B) 17
(C) 20
(D) 25
(E) 30

The number of researchers assigned to team A will be (0.40)(50), or 20. So, 30 will be assigned to team B. The number of researchers who prefer team A is (0.70)(50), or 35, and the rest, 15, prefer team B. Therefore, to minimize the number who will not be assigned to the team they prefer, let the 15 who prefer B be assigned to B. That leaves 35 who prefer A, but only 20 of them can be assigned to A, leaving 15 workers who will not be assigned to the team they prefer. The best answer is A.

419. Last year, a certain public transportation system sold an average (arithmetic mean) of 41,000 tickets per day on weekdays (Monday through Friday) and an average of 18,000 tickets per day on Saturday and Sunday. Which of the following is closest to the total number of tickets sold last year?

(A)   1 million
(B)   1.25 million
(C)   10 million
(D)   12.5 million
(E)   125 million

Last year, on the average, each week the number of tickets sold was 5(41,000) + 2(18,000) or 241,000. Assuming 52 weeks in the year, the total number sold for the year was (52)(241,000), or 12,532,000, which is approximately 12.5 million. For a less detailed calculation, one can note that (52)(241,000) is slightly greater than (50)(240,000) or 12,000,000. The best answer is D.

County	Amount Recycled	Amount Disposed of
A	16,700	142,800
B	8,800	48,000
C	13,000	51,400
D	3,900	20,300
E	3,300	16,200

420. The table above shows the amount of waste material, in tons, recycled by each of five counties in a single year and the amount of waste material, also in tons, that was disposed of in landfills by the five counties in that year. Which county had the lowest ratio of waste material disposed of to waste material recycled in the year reported in the table?

(A) A
(B) B
(C) C
(D) D
(E) E

The county with the lowest ratio of material disposed of to material recycled is the one with the lowest fraction: $\dfrac{\text{Amount Disposed of}}{\text{Amount Recycled}}$. If this fraction were calculated from each county, County C would have the lowest ratio. Without doing the actual calculations, however, a close look at each pair of amounts reveals that the ratio is greater than 4 for Counties A, B, D, and E, but less than 4 for County C. So, the ratio in County C is lowest. The best answer is C.

421. If a number between 0 and $\dfrac{1}{2}$ is selected at random, which of the following will the number most likely be between?

(A) 0 and $\dfrac{3}{20}$

(B) $\dfrac{3}{20}$ and $\dfrac{1}{5}$

(C) $\dfrac{1}{5}$ and $\dfrac{1}{4}$

(D) $\dfrac{1}{4}$ and $\dfrac{3}{10}$

(E) $\dfrac{3}{10}$ and $\dfrac{1}{2}$

Each of the given pairs of numbers defines a segment of the number line between 0 and $\dfrac{1}{2}$, and the length of each segment is found by subtracting the first number from the second. The number selected is most likely to be in the longest of these segments. Therefore, it is most likely that the number selected will be between the given pair of numbers whose difference is greatest. To compare the five differences most easily, one can use 20 as a common denominator when computing each difference. The differences would then be $\dfrac{3}{20}, \dfrac{1}{20}, \dfrac{1}{20}, \dfrac{1}{20}$, and $\dfrac{4}{20}$, respectively. The best answer is E.

District	Number of Votes	Percent of Votes for Candidate P	Percent of Votes for Candidate Q
1	800	60	40
2	1,000	50	50
3	1,500	50	50
4	1,800	40	60
5	1,200	30	70

422. The table above shows the results of a recent school board election in which the candidate with the higher total number of votes from the five districts was declared the winner. Which district had the greatest number of votes for the winner?

(A) 1
(B) 2
(C) 3
(D) 4
(E) 5

A careful look at the table reveals that candidates P and Q were even in districts 2 and 3, and they reversed percents (60 and 40) in districts 1 and 4, although there were many more voters in district 4, in which Q had 60 percent of the vote. Finally, Q clearly won in district 5 with 70 percent of the vote. So, Q was the winner, and Q received 1,800 (0.60), or 1,080 votes in district 4, which was the greatest number of votes for Q in any district. The best answer is D.

423. If m is the average (arithmetic mean) of the first 10 positive multiples of 5 and if M is the median of the first 10 positive multiples of 5, what is the value of $M - m$?

(A) −5
(B)   0
(C)   5
(D) 25
(E) 27.5

The first 10 positive multiples of 5 are 5, 10, 15, . . . , 50. The mean m is the sum of these numbers divided by 10, or $\dfrac{5+10+15+\ldots+50}{10} = \dfrac{5(1+2+3+\ldots+10)}{10} = \dfrac{5(55)}{10} = $ 27.5. The median M of these numbers is the mean of the two middle-valued numbers, 25 and 30. So, $M = \dfrac{25+30}{2}$, or 27.5. Therefore $M - m = 0$. The best answer is B.

424. If n is a positive integer less than 200 and $\dfrac{14n}{60}$ is an integer, then n has how many different positive prime factors?

(A) Two
(B) Three
(C) Five
(D) Six
(E) Eight

Since $\dfrac{14n}{60}$, which equals $\dfrac{7n}{30}$, is an integer, it follows that n is divisible by 30. The possible values of n are therefore 30, 60, 90, 120, 150, and 180. Each of these values has exactly three different positive prime factors: 2, 3, and 5. The best answer is B.

Day	Change in Dollars
Monday	$+1\dfrac{1}{2}$
Tuesday	$-\dfrac{3}{4}$
Wednesday	0
Thursday	$-\dfrac{1}{8}$
Friday	$+2\dfrac{1}{4}$

425. The table above shows the daily change in the price of a certain stock last week. What was the net change in dollars in the price of the stock for the week?

(A) $-4\dfrac{5}{8}$

(B) $-2\dfrac{7}{8}$

(C) $+2\dfrac{7}{8}$

(D) $+3\dfrac{3}{4}$

(E) $+4\dfrac{5}{8}$

The net change in the price of the stock for the week, in dollars, is the sum of all the change values for the week, that is, $1\dfrac{1}{2} + (-\dfrac{3}{4}) + 0 + (-\dfrac{1}{8}) + 2\dfrac{1}{4}$, or $2\dfrac{7}{8}$. The best answer is C.

426. A group of store managers must assemble 280 displays for an upcoming sale. If they assemble 25 percent of the displays during the first hour and 40 percent of the remaining displays during the second hour, how many of the displays will **not** have been assembled by the end of the second hour?

    (A) 70
    (B) 98
    (C) 126
    (D) 168
    (E) 182

During the first hour, (0.25)(280), or 70, displays will be assembled, and during the second hour (0.40)(280 – 70), or 84, will be assembled. Therefore, at the end of the second hour there will be 280 – 70 – 84, or 126, displays that will not have been assembled. The best answer is C.

427. The temperatures in degrees Celsius recorded at 6 in the morning in various parts of a certain country were 10°, 5°, –2°, –1°, –5°, and 15°. What is the median of these temperatures?

    (A) –2°C
    (B) –1°C
    (C) 2°C
    (D) 3°C
    (E) 5°C

There are 6 temperature values, so after the values are listed in increasing order –5°, –2°, –1°, 5°, 10°, 15°, the median of the values is the mean of the 2 middle values.

So, the median is $\dfrac{-1° + 5°}{2} = 2°$. The best answer is C.

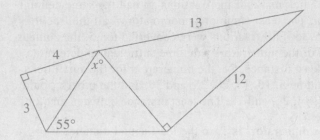

428. In the figure above, what is the value of x ?

    (A) 55
    (B) 60
    (C) 65
    (D) 70
    (E) 75

In the right triangle with sides of lengths 3 and 4, the length of the third side s can be found by using the Pythagorean theorem: $s^2 = 3^2 + 4^2$, so $s = 5$. Similarly, in the other right triangle the same theorem can be used to find the third side: $t^2 + 12^2 = 13^2$, or $t = 5$. Therefore, the

triangle with the angle of $x°$ has two sides of length 5 and the angles opposite these sides must have equal measures. So, in that triangle, $55° + 55° + x° = 180°$, or $x = 70$. The best answer is D.

1	2	3	4	5	6	7
–2	–4	–6	–8	–10	–12	–14
3	6	9	12	15	18	21
–4	–8	–12	–16	–20	–24	–28
5	10	15	20	25	30	35
–6	–12	–18	–24	–30	–36	–42
7	14	21	28	35	42	49

429. What is the sum of the integers in the table above?

    (A) 28
    (B) 112
    (C) 336
    (D) 448
    (E) 784

The sum of the numbers in the first row is: $1 + 2 + 3 + \ldots + 7 = 28$. Note that in each of the other 6 rows, the sum can be expressed as an integer n multiplied by $1 + 2 + 3 + \ldots + 7$, or simply $(n)(28)$. For example, in the 2nd row n would be –2 and the sum would be $(-2)(28)$. For the 7 rows, the values of n are 1, –2, 3, –4, 5, –6, and 7. So, the total sum of all rows is the sum of the 7 values of n multiplied by 28, or $4(28) = 112$. The best answer is B.

430. If $m > 0$ and x is m percent of y, then, in terms of m, y is what percent of x ?

    (A) $100m$

    (B) $\dfrac{1}{100m}$

    (C) $\dfrac{1}{m}$

    (D) $\dfrac{10}{m}$

    (E) $\dfrac{10,000}{m}$

Since x is m percent of y, $\dfrac{x}{y} = \dfrac{m}{100}$, and therefore,

$\dfrac{y}{x} = \dfrac{100}{m}$. To convert the fraction $\dfrac{100}{m}$ to an equivalent

percent, one can multiply by 100 to obtain $\dfrac{10,000}{m}$.

The best answer is E.

$$3, k, 2, 8, m, 3$$

431. The arithmetic mean of the list of numbers above is 4. If k and m are integers and $k \neq m$, what is the median of the list?

(A) 2
(B) 2.5
(C) 3
(D) 3.5
(E) 4

Since the arithmetic mean of the 6 numbers is 4,
$$\frac{3+k+2+8+m+3}{6} = 4,$$ and therefore $k + m = 8$.
The list of the 4 numbers other than k and m, in order of size, is 2, 3, 3, 8. Since k and m are integers such that $k \neq m$ and $k + m = 8$, either $k \leq 3$ and $m \geq 5$ or $m \leq 3$ and $k \geq 5$. Therefore, when the 6 numbers are listed in increasing order, the two middle numbers in the list will both be 3. So the median of the list is 3. The best answer is C.

432. A certain junior class has 1,000 students and a certain senior class has 800 students. Among these students, there are 60 sibling pairs, each consisting of 1 junior and 1 senior. If 1 student is to be selected at random from each class, what is the probability that the 2 students selected will be a sibling pair?

(A) $\dfrac{3}{40,000}$

(B) $\dfrac{1}{3,600}$

(C) $\dfrac{9}{2,000}$

(D) $\dfrac{1}{60}$

(E) $\dfrac{1}{15}$

The probability of selecting a student from the 1,000 juniors who is a member of a sibling pair is $\dfrac{60}{1,000}$.

Then, the probability of selecting the 1 student among the 800 seniors who is the other member of that pair is $\dfrac{1}{800}$. Therefore, the probability that the 2 students selected

will be a sibling pair is $\left(\dfrac{60}{1,000} \right) \left(\dfrac{1}{800} \right) = \dfrac{3}{40,000}$.
The best answer is A.

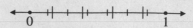

433. On the number line above, the segment from 0 to 1 has been divided into fifths, as indicated by the large tick marks, and also into sevenths, as indicated by the small tick marks. What is the <u>least</u> possible distance between any two of the tick marks?

(A) $\dfrac{1}{70}$

(B) $\dfrac{1}{35}$

(C) $\dfrac{2}{35}$

(D) $\dfrac{1}{12}$

(E) $\dfrac{1}{7}$

The small tick marks are placed at $\dfrac{1}{7}, \dfrac{2}{7}, \dfrac{3}{7}, \dfrac{4}{7}, \dfrac{5}{7},$

and, $\dfrac{6}{7}$ and the large tick marks are at $\dfrac{1}{5}, \dfrac{2}{5}, \dfrac{3}{5},$ and $\dfrac{4}{5}$.
It would be much easier to compare distances between any 2 tick marks if the fractions all had the same denominator. The least common denominator of all the fractions is 35, so if all fractions were converted to 35, the comparison of the numerators would be sufficient to determine the least distance. So, the numerators for the small ticks would be 5, 10, 15, 20, 25, and 30, and the others would be 7, 14, 21, and 28. The least distance between any 2 of these numerators is 1, so the least actual distance is $\dfrac{1}{35}$.

The best answer is B.

434. A certain musical scale has 13 notes, each having a different frequency, measured in cycles per second. In the scale, the notes are ordered by increasing frequency, and the highest frequency is twice the lowest. For each of the 12 lower frequencies, the ratio of a frequency to the next higher frequency is a fixed constant. If the lowest frequency is 440 cycles per second, then the frequency of the 7th note in the scale is how many cycles per second?

(A) $440\sqrt{2}$

(B) $440\sqrt{2^7}$

(C) $440\sqrt{2^{12}}$

(D) $440\sqrt[12]{2^7}$

(E) $440\sqrt[7]{2^{12}}$

If x represents the constant ratio from one frequency to the next, the 2nd frequency, in cycles per second, would be $440x$, the 3rd would be $440x^2$, the 7th would be $440x^6$ and the 13th would be $440x^{12}$. Since the 13th frequency is twice the 1st, $440x^{12}$ must be $(2)(440)$, or 880. Thus, $440x^{12} = 880$, or $x^{12} = 2$. Therefore, since $x^{12} = (x^6)^2 = 2$, $x^6 = \sqrt{2}$, and so the 7th frequency is $440x^6$, $= 440\sqrt{2}$. The best answer is A.

435. If $a = 7$ and $b = -7$, what is the value of $2a - 2b + b^2$?

(A) -49
(B) 21
(C) 49
(D) 63
(E) 77

By substitution, the value of $2a - 2b + b^2 = 2(7) - 2(-7) + (-7)^2 = 14 + 14 + 49$, or 77. The best answer is E.

436. Equal amounts of water were poured into two empty jars of different capacities, which made one jar $\frac{1}{4}$ full and the other jar $\frac{1}{3}$ full. If the water in the jar with the lesser capacity is then poured into the jar with the greater capacity, what fraction of the larger jar will be filled with water?

(A) $\frac{1}{7}$

(B) $\frac{2}{7}$

(C) $\frac{1}{2}$

(D) $\frac{7}{12}$

(E) $\frac{2}{3}$

Since the amounts of water in the two jars were equal, the jar with the greater capacity is $\frac{1}{4}$ full and the jar with the lesser capacity is $\frac{1}{3}$ full. Therefore, when the water in the smaller jar is poured into the larger jar, it will double the amount in the larger jar, which will then be $\frac{1}{2}$ full. The best answer is C.

437. If Mel saved more than \$10 by purchasing a sweater at a 15 percent discount, what is the smallest amount the original price of the sweater could be, to the nearest dollar?

(A) 45
(B) 67
(C) 75
(D) 83
(E) 150

If the original price of the sweater was P dollars, then $(0.15) P$ must be greater than 10, or $(0.15) P > 10$.

Since $P > \frac{10}{0.15}$, $P > 66.67$. The best answer is B.

438. Which of the following CANNOT be the median of the three positive integers x, y, and z ?

(A) x

(B) z

(C) $x + z$

(D) $\dfrac{x+z}{2}$

(E) $\dfrac{x+z}{3}$

If x, y, and z were ordered according to size, any one of them could be the middle one, which is the median. Thus, either of the first two choices is a possible median. Since x, y, and z are all positive, either of the smaller numbers added to the greatest number would be greater than the middle number, and the smallest number added to the middle number would be greater than the middle number. Therefore, $x + z$ cannot be the median. [Note: $\dfrac{x+z}{2}$ could be the median if x, y, and z were 2, 4, and 6, respectively, and $\dfrac{x+z}{3}$ could be the median if x, y, and z were 2, 4, and 10, respectively.] The best answer is C.

439. $\dfrac{(8^2)(3^3)(2^4)}{96^2} =$

(A) 3

(B) 6

(C) 9

(D) 12

(E) 18

$96^2 = (8^2)(12^2) = (8^2)(3^2)(4^2)$ and $4^2 = 2^4$. Thus,

$\dfrac{(8^2)(3^3)(2^4)}{96^2} = \dfrac{(8^2)(3^3)(2^4)}{(8^2)(3^2)(2^4)} = 3$. The best answer is A.

440. What is the 25th digit to the right of the decimal point in the decimal form of $\dfrac{6}{11}$?

(A) 3

(B) 4

(C) 5

(D) 6

(E) 7

In the decimal form of $\dfrac{6}{11}$, the digits 54 repeat indefinitely; that is, $\dfrac{6}{11} = 0.545454\ldots$ Since every odd-numbered digit to the right of the decimal point is 5, the 25th digit must be 5. The best answer is C.

441. Which of the following lists the number of points at which a circle can intersect a triangle?

(A) 2 and 6 only

(B) 2, 4, and 6 only

(C) 1, 2, 3, and 6 only

(D) 1, 2, 3, 4, and 6 only

(E) 1, 2, 3, 4, 5, and 6

A circle can intersect a triangle in 1, 2, 3, 4, 5, or 6 points, as shown:

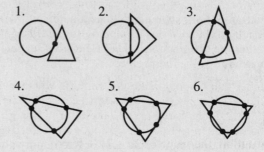

The best answer is E.

5 Data Sufficiency

In these questions, you are to classify each problem according to the five fixed answer choices, rather than find a solution to the problem. Each problem consists of a question and two statements. You are to decide whether the information in each statement alone is sufficient to answer the question or, if neither is, whether the information in the two statements together is sufficient.

The following pages include test-taking strategies, sample questions, and a detailed explanation of every problem. These explanations present possible problem-solving strategies for the examples.

Test-taking Strategies for Data Sufficiency

1. Do not waste valuable time solving a problem; you are only to determine whether sufficient information is given to solve the problem. First consider statement (1) and statement (2) separately and determine whether each alone gives sufficient information to solve the problem. Be sure to disregard the information given in statement (1) when you evaluate the information given in statement (2). If either, or both, of the statements give sufficient information to solve the problem, click on the oval corresponding to the description of which statement(s) give sufficient information to solve the problem. If not, consider the information in both statement (1) and statement (2). Then click on the oval corresponding to the description of whether the statements TOGETHER give sufficient information to solve the problem.

2. Remember that when you are determining whether there is sufficient information to answer a question of the form, "What is the value of y?" the information given must be sufficient to find one and only one value for y. Being able to determine minimum or maximum values or an answer of the form $y = x + 2$ is not sufficient, because such answers constitute a range of values rather than "the value of y."

3. When geometric figures are involved, be very careful not to make unwarranted assumptions based on the figures. Figures are not necessarily drawn to scale; they are generalized figures showing little more than intersecting line segments and the betweenness of points, angles, and regions. So, for example, if a figure described as a rectangle looks like a square you may not conclude that it is, in fact, a square just by looking at the figure.

Beginning

When finished reading directions click on the icon below

This data sufficiency problem consists of a question and two statements, labeled (1) and (2), in which certain data are given. You have to decide whether the data given in the statements are <u>sufficient</u> for answering the question. Using the data given in the statements <u>plus</u> your knowledge of mathematics and everyday facts (such as the number of days in July or the meaning of *counterclockwise*), you must indicate whether

- statement (1) ALONE is sufficient, but statement (2) alone is not sufficient to answer the question asked;
- statement (2) ALONE is sufficient, but statement (1) alone is not sufficient to answer the question asked;
- BOTH statements (1) and (2) TOGETHER are sufficient to answer the question asked; but NEITHER statement ALONE sufficient.
- EACH statement ALONE is sufficient to answer the question asked;
- statements (1) and (2) TOGETHER are NOT sufficient to answer the question asked, and additional data specific to the problem are needed.

<u>Numbers:</u>   All numbers used are real numbers.

<u>Figures:</u>   A figure accompanying a data sufficiency problem will conform to the information given in the question, but will not necessarily

Dismiss

Directions

Test
Quit

Section
Exit

Time

?
Help

Answer
Confirm

➡
Next

More Available

When finished reading directions click on the icon below

Dismiss Directions

conform to the additional information given in statements (1) and (2).

Lines shown as straight can be assumed to be straight and lines that appear jagged can also be assumed to be straight.

You may assume that the positions of points, angles, regions, etc., exist in the order shown and that angle measures are greater than zero.

All figures lie in a plane unless otherwise indicated.

Note: In data sufficiency problems that ask for the value of a quantity the data given in the statements are sufficient only when it is possible to determine exactly one numerical value for the quantity.

Test | Section |  Time
Quit | Exit

? Help | Answer Confirm | ➡ Next

End

When finished reading directions click on the icon below

Dismiss Directions

Example:

In $\triangle PQR$, what is the value of x?

(1) $PQ = PR$

(2) $y = 40$

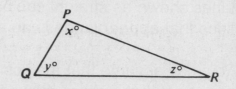

Explanation: According to statement (1), $PQ = PR$; therefore, $\triangle PQR$ is isosceles and $y = z$. Since $x + y + z = 180$, it follows that $x + 2y = 180$. Since statement (1) does not give a value for y, you cannot answer the question using statement (1) alone. According to statement (2), $y = 40$; therefore, $x + z = 140$. Since statement (2) does not give a value for z, you cannot answer the question using statement (2) alone. Using both statements together, since $x + 2y = 180$ and the value of y is given, you can find the value of x. Therefore, BOTH statements (1) and (2) TOGETHER are sufficient to answer the question, but NEITHER statement ALONE is sufficient.

To review these directions for subsequent questions of this type, click on HELP.

Test	Section					?	Answer	→
Quit	Exit	Time				Help	Confirm	Next

DATA SUFFICIENCY SAMPLE QUESTIONS

A   Statement (1) ALONE is sufficient, but statement (2) alone is not sufficient.
B   Statement (2) ALONE is sufficient, but statement (1) alone is not sufficient.
C   BOTH statements TOGETHER are sufficient, but NEITHER statement ALONE is sufficient.
D   EACH statement ALONE is sufficient.
E   Statements (1) and (2) TOGETHER are NOT sufficient.

1. At a certain picnic, each of the guests was served either a single scoop or a double scoop of ice cream. How many of the guests were served a double scoop of ice cream?

   (1) At the picnic, 60 percent of the guests were served a double scoop of ice cream.

   (2) A total of 120 scoops of ice cream were served to all the guests at the picnic.

2. By what percent was the price of a certain candy bar increased?

   (1) The price of the candy bar was increased by 5 cents.

   (2) The price of the candy bar after the increase was 45 cents.

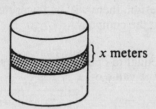
} x meters

3. A circular tub has a band painted around its circumference, as shown above. What is the surface area of this painted band?

   (1) $x = 0.5$

   (2) The height of the tub is 1 meter.

4. Is it true that $a > b$?

   (1) $2a > 2b$

   (2) $a + c > b + c$

5. A thoroughly blended biscuit mix includes only flour and baking powder. What is the ratio of the number of grams of baking powder to the number of grams of flour in the mix?

   (1) Exactly 9.9 grams of flour are contained in 10 grams of the mix.

   (2) Exactly 0.3 gram of baking powder is contained in 30 grams of the mix.

6. If a real estate agent received a commission of 6 percent of the selling price of a certain house, what was the selling price of the house?

   (1) The selling price minus the real estate agent's commission was $84,600.

   (2) The selling price was 250 percent of the original purchase price of $36,000.

7. What is the value of $|x|$?

   (1) $x = -|x|$
   (2) $x^2 = 4$

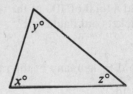

8. What is the value of z in the triangle above?

   (1) $x + y = 139$
   (2) $y + z = 108$

A   Statement (1) ALONE is sufficient, but statement (2) alone is not sufficient.
B   Statement (2) ALONE is sufficient, but statement (1) alone is not sufficient.
C   BOTH statements TOGETHER are sufficient, but NEITHER statement ALONE is sufficient.
D   EACH statement ALONE is sufficient.
E   Statements (1) and (2) TOGETHER are NOT sufficient.

9. A certain bakery sells rye bread in 16-ounce loaves and 24-ounce loaves, and all loaves of the same size sell for the same price per loaf regardless of the number of loaves purchased. What is the price of a 24-ounce loaf of rye bread in this bakery?

   (1) The total price of a 16-ounce loaf and a 24-ounce loaf of this bread is $2.40.

   (2) The total price of two 16-ounce loaves and one 24-ounce loaf of this bread is $3.40.

10. If $\dfrac{\sqrt{x}}{y} = n$, what is the value of x ?

   (1) $yn = 10$

   (2) $y = 40$ and $n = \dfrac{1}{4}$

11. If m and n are consecutive positive integers, is m greater than n ?

   (1) $m - 1$ and $n + 1$ are consecutive positive integers.

   (2) m is an even integer.

12. Paula and Sandy were among those people who sold raffle tickets to raise money for Club X. If Paula and Sandy sold a total of 100 of the tickets, how many of the tickets did Paula sell?

   (1) Sandy sold $\dfrac{2}{3}$ as many of the raffle tickets as Paula did.

   (2) Sandy sold 8 percent of all the raffle tickets sold for Club X.

13. Is the integer n odd?

   (1) n is divisible by 3.
   (2) n is divisible by 5.

3.2 □△6

14. If □ and △ each represent single digits in the decimal above, what digit does □ represent?

   (1) When the decimal is rounded to the nearest tenth, 3.2 is the result.

   (2) When the decimal is rounded to the nearest hundredth, 3.24 is the result.

15. A certain company currently has how many employees?

   (1) If 3 additional employees are hired by the company and all of the present employees remain, there will be at least 20 employees in the company.

   (2) If no additional employees are hired by the company and 3 of the present employees resign, there will be fewer than 15 employees in the company.

16. If x is equal to one of the numbers $\dfrac{1}{4}$, $\dfrac{3}{8}$, or $\dfrac{2}{5}$, what is the value of x ?

   (1) $\dfrac{1}{4} < x < \dfrac{1}{2}$

   (2) $\dfrac{1}{3} < x < \dfrac{3}{5}$

17. If a, b, and c are integers, is $a - b + c$ greater than $a + b - c$?

   (1) b is negative.
   (2) c is positive.

18. If $x + 2y + 1 = y - x$, what is the value of x ?

   (1) $y^2 = 9$
   (2) $y = 3$

A   Statement (1) ALONE is sufficient, but statement (2) alone is not sufficient.
B   Statement (2) ALONE is sufficient, but statement (1) alone is not sufficient.
C   BOTH statements TOGETHER are sufficient, but NEITHER statement ALONE is sufficient.
D   EACH statement ALONE is sufficient.
E   Statements (1) and (2) TOGETHER are NOT sufficient.

19. If n is an integer, then n is divisible by how many positive integers?

   (1) n is the product of two different prime numbers.

   (2) n and 2^3 are each divisible by the same number of positive integers.

20. How many miles long is the route from Houghton to Callahan?

   (1)   It will take 1 hour less time to travel the entire route at an average rate of 55 miles per hour than at an average rate of 50 miles per hour.

   (2)   It will take 11 hours to travel the first half of the route at an average rate of 25 miles per hour.

21. If x and y are positive, what is the value of x?

   (1) $x = 3.927y$
   (2) $y = 2.279$

22. John and David each received a salary increase. Which one received the greater dollar increase?

   (1)   John's salary increased 8 percent.

   (2)   David's salary increased 5 percent.

23. Carlotta can drive from her home to her office by one of two possible routes. If she must also return by one of these routes, what is the distance of the shorter route?

   (1)   When she drives from her home to her office by the shorter route and returns by the longer route, she drives a total of 42 kilometers.

   (2)   When she drives both ways, from her home to her office and back, by the longer route, she drives a total of 46 kilometers.

24. If r and s are positive integers, r is what percent of s?

   (1) $r = \dfrac{3}{4} s$

   (2) $r \div s = \dfrac{75}{100}$

25. A shirt and a pair of gloves cost a total of $41.70. How much does the pair of gloves cost?

   (1)   The shirt costs twice as much as the gloves.

   (2)   The shirt costs $27.80.

26. What is the number of 360-degree rotations that a bicycle wheel made while rolling 100 meters in a straight line without slipping?

   (1)   The diameter of the bicycle wheel, including the tire, was 0.5 meter.

   (2)   The wheel made twenty 360-degree rotations per minute.

27. What is the value of the sum of a list of n odd integers?

   (1) $n = 8$

   (2)   The square of the number of integers on the list is 64.

28. If a certain animated cartoon consists of a total of 17,280 frames on film, how many minutes will it take to run the cartoon?

   (1)   The cartoon runs without interruption at the rate of 24 frames per second.

   (2)   It takes 6 times as long to run the cartoon as it takes to rewind the film, and it takes a total of 14 minutes to do both.

A   Statement (1) ALONE is sufficient, but statement (2) alone is not sufficient.
B   Statement (2) ALONE is sufficient, but statement (1) alone is not sufficient.
C   BOTH statements TOGETHER are sufficient, but NEITHER statement ALONE is sufficient.
D   EACH statement ALONE is sufficient.
E   Statements (1) and (2) TOGETHER are NOT sufficient.

29. What was the average number of miles per gallon of gasoline for a car during a certain trip?

  (1) The total cost of the gasoline used by the car for the 180-mile trip was $12.00.

  (2) The cost of the gasoline used by the car for the trip was $1.20 per gallon.

30. If x and y are positive, is $\frac{x}{y}$ greater than 1 ?

  (1) $xy > 1$

  (2) $x - y > 0$

31. In $\triangle PQR$, if $PQ = x$, $QR = x + 2$, and $PR = y$, which of the three angles of $\triangle PQR$ has the greatest degree measure?

  (1) $y = x + 3$

  (2) $x = 2$

32. Is the prime number p equal to 37 ?

  (1) $p = n^2 + 1$, where n is an integer.

  (2) p^2 is greater than 200.

33. The only contents of a parcel are 25 photographs and 30 negatives. What is the total weight, in ounces, of the parcel's contents?

  (1) The weight of each photograph is 3 times the weight of each negative.

  (2) The total weight of 1 of the photographs and 2 of the negatives is $\frac{1}{3}$ ounce.

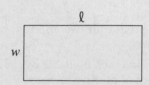

34. If ℓ and w represent the length and width, respectively, of the rectangle above, what is the perimeter?

  (1) $2\ell + w = 40$

  (2) $\ell + w = 25$

35. What is the ratio of x to y ?

  (1) x is 4 more than twice y.

  (2) The ratio of $0.5x$ to $2y$ is 3 to 5.

36. If x, y, and z are three integers, are they consecutive integers?

  (1) $z - x = 2$

  (2) $x < y < z$

37. What is the value of x ?

  (1) $-(x + y) = x - y$

  (2) $x + y = 2$

38. A sum of $200,000 from a certain estate was divided among a spouse and three children. How much of the estate did the youngest child receive?

  (1) The spouse received $\frac{1}{2}$ of the sum from the estate, and the oldest child received $\frac{1}{4}$ of the remainder.

  (2) Each of the two younger children received $12,500 more than the oldest child and $62,500 less than the spouse.

-240-

A   Statement (1) ALONE is sufficient, but statement (2) alone is not sufficient.
B   Statement (2) ALONE is sufficient, but statement (1) alone is not sufficient.
C   BOTH statements TOGETHER are sufficient, but NEITHER statement ALONE is sufficient.
D   EACH statement ALONE is sufficient.
E   Statements (1) and (2) TOGETHER are NOT sufficient.

39. If the Lincoln Library's total expenditure for books, periodicals, and newspapers last year was $35,000, how much of the expenditure was for books?

   (1) The expenditure for newspapers was 40 percent greater than the expenditure for periodicals.

   (2) The total of the expenditure for periodicals and newspapers was 25 percent less than the expenditure for books.

40. The symbol ∇ represents one of the following operations: addition, subtraction, multiplication, or division. What is the value of $3 \nabla 2$?

   (1) $0 \nabla 1 = 1$

   (2) $1 \nabla 0 = 1$

41. The regular price for canned soup was reduced during a sale. How much money could one have saved by purchasing a dozen 7-ounce cans of soup at the reduced price rather than at the regular price?

   (1) The regular price for the 7-ounce cans was 3 for a dollar.

   (2) The reduced price for the 7-ounce cans was 4 for a dollar.

42. If on a fishing trip Jim and Tom each caught some fish, which one caught more fish?

   (1) Jim caught $\frac{2}{3}$ as many fish as Tom.

   (2) After Tom stopped fishing, Jim continued fishing until he had caught 12 fish.

43. If $5x + 3y = 17$, what is the value of x ?

   (1) x is a positive integer.

   (2) $y = 4x$

44. Yesterday Nan parked her car at a certain parking garage that charges more for the first hour than for each additional hour. If Nan's total parking charge at the garage yesterday was $3.75, for how many hours of parking was she charged?

   (1) Parking charges at the garage are $0.75 for the first hour and $0.50 for each additional hour or fraction of an hour.

   (2) If the charge for the first hour had been $1.00, Nan's total parking charge would have been $4.00.

45. If r and s are integers, is $r + s$ divisible by 3 ?

   (1) s is divisible by 3.

   (2) r is divisible by 3.

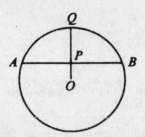

46. What is the radius of the circle above with center O ?

   (1) The ratio of OP to PQ is 1 to 2.

   (2) P is the midpoint of chord AB .

47. A certain 4-liter solution of vinegar and water consists of x liters of vinegar and y liters of water. How many liters of vinegar does the solution contain?

   (1) $\dfrac{x}{4} = \dfrac{3}{8}$

   (2) $\dfrac{y}{4} = \dfrac{5}{8}$

A Statement (1) ALONE is sufficient, but statement (2) alone is not sufficient.
B Statement (2) ALONE is sufficient, but statement (1) alone is not sufficient.
C BOTH statements TOGETHER are sufficient, but NEITHER statement ALONE is sufficient.
D EACH statement ALONE is sufficient.
E Statements (1) and (2) TOGETHER are NOT sufficient.

48. Is $x < 0$?

(1) $-2x > 0$

(2) $x^3 < 0$

49. Of the 230 single-family homes built in City X last year, how many were occupied at the end of the year?

(1) Of all single-family homes in City X, 90 percent were occupied at the end of last year.

(2) A total of 7,200 single-family homes in City X were occupied at the end of last year.

50. Does the product $jkmn$ equal 1 ?

(1) $\dfrac{jk}{mn} = 1$

(2) $j = \dfrac{1}{k}$ and $m = \dfrac{1}{n}$

51. How many of the boys in a group of 100 children have brown hair?

(1) Of the children in the group, 60 percent have brown hair.

(2) Of the children in the group, 40 are boys.

52. Is the perimeter of square S greater than the perimeter of equilateral triangle T ?

(1) The ratio of the length of a side of S to the length of a side of T is $4 : 5$.

(2) The sum of the lengths of a side of S and a side of T is 18.

53. If p and q are positive integers and $pq = 24$, what is the value of p ?

(1) $\dfrac{q}{6}$ is an integer.

(2) $\dfrac{p}{2}$ is an integer.

54. If $x \neq 0$, what is the value of $\left(\dfrac{x^p}{x^q}\right)^4$?

(1) $p = q$

(2) $x = 3$

55. From May 1, 1960, to May 1, 1975, the closing price of a share of stock X doubled. What was the closing price of a share of stock X on May 1, 1960 ?

(1) From May 1, 1975, to May 1, 1984, the closing price of a share of stock X doubled.

(2) From May 1, 1975, to May 1, 1984, the closing price of a share of stock X increased by $4.50.

56. If d is a positive integer, is $\sqrt{d}$ an integer?

(1) d is the square of an integer.

(2) $\sqrt{d}$ is the square of an integer.

57. If Q is an integer between 10 and 100, what is the value of Q ?

(1) One of Q's digits is 3 more than the other, and the sum of its digits is 9.

(2) $Q < 50$

58. If digit h is the hundredths' digit in the decimal $d = 0.2h6$, what is the value of d, rounded to the nearest tenth?

(1) $d < \dfrac{1}{4}$

(2) $h < 5$

59. What is the value of $x^2 - y^2$?

(1) $x - y = y + 2$

(2) $x - y = \dfrac{1}{x + y}$

A   Statement (1) ALONE is sufficient, but statement (2) alone is not sufficient.
B   Statement (2) ALONE is sufficient, but statement (1) alone is not sufficient.
C   BOTH statements TOGETHER are sufficient, but NEITHER statement ALONE is sufficient.
D   EACH statement ALONE is sufficient.
E   Statements (1) and (2) TOGETHER are NOT sufficient.

60. If ∘ represents one of the operations +, −, and ×, is $k \circ (\ell + m) = (k \circ \ell) + (k \circ m)$ for all numbers k, ℓ, and m ?

   (1) $k \circ 1$ is not equal to $1 \circ k$ for some numbers k.

   (2) ∘ represents subtraction.

61. Committee member W wants to schedule a one-hour meeting on Thursday for himself and three other committee members, X, Y, and Z. Is there a one-hour period on Thursday that is open for all four members?

   (1) On Thursday W and X have an open period from 9:00 a.m. to 12:00 noon.

   (2) On Thursday Y has an open period from 10:00 a.m. to 1:00 p.m. and Z has an open period from 8:00 a.m. to 11:00 a.m.

62. If Jack's and Kate's annual salaries in 1985 were each 10 percent higher than their respective annual salaries in 1984, what was Jack's annual salary in 1984 ?

   (1) The sum of Jack's and Kate's annual salaries in 1984 was $50,000.

   (2) The sum of Jack's and Kate's annual salaries in 1985 was $55,000.

63. What is the value of x ?

   (1) $x + 1 = 2 - 3x$

   (2) $\dfrac{1}{2x} = 2$

64. How many newspapers were sold at a certain newsstand today?

   (1) A total of 100 newspapers were sold at the newsstand yesterday, 10 fewer than twice the number sold today.

   (2) The number of newspapers sold at the newsstand yesterday was 45 more than the number sold today.

65. How much did a certain telephone call cost?

   (1) The call lasted 53 minutes.

   (2) The cost for the first 3 minutes was 5 times the cost for each additional minute.

66. A certain expressway has exits J, K, L, and M, in that order. What is the road distance from exit K to exit L ?

   (1) The road distance from exit J to exit L is 21 kilometers.

   (2) The road distance from exit K to exit M is 26 kilometers.

67. Two cars, S and T, each traveled a distance of 50 miles. Did car S use more gasoline than car T ?

   (1) Cars S and T traveled the entire distance at the rates of 55 miles per hour and 50 miles per hour, respectively.

   (2) For the entire distance, car S traveled 20 miles per gallon of gasoline and car T traveled 25 miles per gallon of gasoline.

68. If n is a positive integer, is n odd?

   (1) $3n$ is odd.

   (2) $n + 3$ is even.

69. Does $2m - 3n = 0$?

   (1) $m \neq 0$

   (2) $6m = 9n$

70. If $xy < 3$, is $x < 1$?

   (1) $y > 3$

   (2) $x < 3$

A Statement (1) ALONE is sufficient, but statement (2) alone is not sufficient.
B Statement (2) ALONE is sufficient, but statement (1) alone is not sufficient.
C BOTH statements TOGETHER are sufficient, but NEITHER statement ALONE is sufficient.
D EACH statement ALONE is sufficient.
E Statements (1) and (2) TOGETHER are NOT sufficient.

71. Each of the eggs in a bowl is dyed red, or green, or blue. If one egg is to be removed at random, what is the probability that the egg will be green?

   (1) There are 5 red eggs in the bowl.

   (2) The probability that the egg will be blue is $\frac{1}{3}$.

72. Is the average (arithmetic mean) of x and y greater than 20 ?

   (1) The average (arithmetic mean) of $2x$ and $2y$ is 48.

   (2) $x = 3y$

73. Marcia's bucket can hold a maximum of how many liters of water?

   (1) The bucket currently contains 9 liters of water.

   (2) If 3 liters of water are added to the bucket when it is half full of water, the amount of water in the bucket will increase by $\frac{1}{3}$.

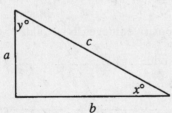

74. In the triangle above, does $a^2 + b^2 = c^2$?

   (1) $x + y = 90$

   (2) $x = y$

75. What is the value of the positive integer n ?

   (1) $n^4 < 25$

   (2) $n \neq n^2$

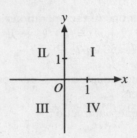

76. If $ab \neq 0$, in what quadrant of the coordinate system above does point (a, b) lie?

   (1) (b, a) lies in quadrant IV.

   (2) $(a, -b)$ lies in quadrant III.

77. From 1984 to 1987, the value of foreign goods consumed annually in the United States increased by what percent?

   (1) In 1984 the value of foreign goods consumed constituted 19.8 percent of the total value of goods consumed in the United States that year.

   (2) In 1987 the value of foreign goods consumed constituted 22.7 percent of the total value of goods consumed in the United States that year.

78. If x, y, and z are positive, is $x = \frac{y}{z^2}$?

   (1) $z = \frac{y}{xz}$

   (2) $z = \sqrt{\frac{y}{x}}$

79. If x and y are positive integers and $x^y = x^{2y-3}$, what is the value of x^y ?

   (1) $x = 2$

   (2) $x^3 = 8$

A Statement (1) ALONE is sufficient, but statement (2) alone is not sufficient.
B Statement (2) ALONE is sufficient, but statement (1) alone is not sufficient.
C BOTH statements TOGETHER are sufficient, but NEITHER statement ALONE is sufficient.
D EACH statement ALONE is sufficient.
E Statements (1) and (2) TOGETHER are NOT sufficient.

80. If k and n are integers, is n divisible by 7 ?

(1) $n - 3 = 2k$
(2) $2k - 4$ is divisible by 7.

81. If x and y are integers and
$y = |x + 3| + |4 - x|$ does y equal 7 ?

(1) $x < 4$
(2) $x > -3$

82. If $1 < d < 2$, is the tenths' digit of the decimal representation of d equal to 9 ?

(1) $d + 0.01 < 2$
(2) $d + 0.05 > 2$

83. The participants in a race consisted of 3 teams with 3 runners on each team. A team was awarded $6 - n$ points if one of its runners finished in nth place, where $1 \le n \le 5$. If all of the runners finished the race and if there were no ties, was each team awarded at least one point?

(1) No team was awarded more than a total of 6 points.

(2) No pair of teammates finished in consecutive places among the top five places.

84. If $x + y + z > 0$, is $z > 1$?

(1) $z > x + y + 1$
(2) $x + y + 1 < 0$

85. How many integers n are there such that $r < n < s$?

(1) $s - r = 5$
(2) r and s are not integers.

86. A total of 9 women and 12 men reside in the 21 apartments that are in a certain apartment building, one person to each apartment. If a poll taker is to select one of the apartments at random, what is the probability that the resident of the apartment selected will be a woman who is a student?

(1) Of the women, 4 are students.
(2) Of the women, 5 are not students.

87. Is x greater than 1.8 ?

(1) $x > 1.7$
(2) $x > 1.9$

88. Hoses X and Y simultaneously fill an empty swimming pool that has a capacity of 50,000 liters. If the flow in each hose is independent of the flow in the other hose, how many hours will it take to fill the pool?

(1) Hose X alone would take 28 hours to fill the pool.

(2) Hose Y alone would take 36 hours to fill the pool.

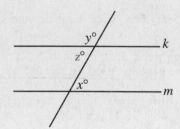

89. In the figure above, if lines k and m are parallel, what is the value of x ?

(1) $y = 120$
(2) $z = 60$

90. If x and y are integers, what is the value of y ?

(1) $xy = 27$
(2) $x = y^2$

A Statement (1) ALONE is sufficient, but statement (2) alone is not sufficient.
B Statement (2) ALONE is sufficient, but statement (1) alone is not sufficient.
C BOTH statements TOGETHER are sufficient, but NEITHER statement ALONE is sufficient.
D EACH statement ALONE is sufficient.
E Statements (1) and (2) TOGETHER are NOT sufficient.

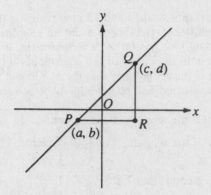

91. In the figure above, segments PR and QR are each parallel to one of the rectangular coordinate axes. Is the ratio of the length of QR to the length of PR equal to 1 ?

    (1) $c = 3$ and $d = 4$.

    (2) $a = -2$ and $b = -1$.

92. In a school election, if each of the 900 voters voted for either Edith or José (but not both), what percent of the female voters in this election voted for José?

    (1) Eighty percent of the female voters voted for Edith.

    (2) Sixty percent of the male voters voted for José.

93. During week W, how much did it cost, per mile, for the gasoline used by car X ?

    (1) During week W, car X used gasoline that cost $1.24 per gallon.

    (2) During week W, car X was driven 270 miles.

94. If r and s are integers, is r divisible by 7 ?

    (1) The product rs is divisible by 7.

    (2) s is not divisible by 7.

95. If $\dfrac{m}{n} = \dfrac{5}{3}$, what is the value of $m + n$?

    (1) $m > 0$

    (2) $2m + n = 26$

96. If P and Q are each circular regions, what is the radius of the larger of these regions?

    (1) The area of P plus the area of Q is equal to 90π.

    (2) The larger circular region has a radius that is 3 times the radius of the smaller circular region.

97. Is z less than 0 ?

    (1) $xy > 0$ and $yz < 0$.

    (2) $x > 0$

98. If the total price of n equally priced shares of a certain stock was $12,000, what was the price per share of the stock?

    (1) If the price per share of the stock had been $1 more, the total price of the n shares would have been $300 more.

    (2) If the price per share of the stock had been $2 less, the total price of the n shares would have been 5 percent less.

99. What is the ratio of $x : y : z$?

    (1) $z = 1$ and $xy = 32$.

    (2) $\dfrac{x}{y} = 2$ and $\dfrac{z}{y} = \dfrac{1}{4}$.

100. What is Ricky's age now?

    (1) Ricky is now twice as old as he was exactly 8 years ago.

    (2) Ricky's sister Teresa is now 3 times as old as Ricky was exactly 8 years ago.

101. Is $xy > 5$?

    (1) $1 \le x \le 3$ and $2 \le y \le 4$.

    (2) $x + y = 5$

102. In year X, 8.7 percent of the men in the labor force were unemployed in June compared with 8.4 percent in May. If the number of men in the labor force was the same for both months, how many men were unemployed in June of that year?

    (1) In May of year X, the number of unemployed men in the labor force was 3.36 million.

    (2) In year X, 120,000 more men in the labor force were unemployed in June than in May.

103. If the average (arithmetic mean) of 4 numbers is 50, how many of the numbers are greater than 50 ?

    (1) None of the four numbers is equal to 50.

    (2) Two of the numbers are equal to 25.

104. On Monday morning a certain machine ran continuously at a uniform rate to fill a production order. At what time did it completely fill the order that morning?

    (1) The machine began filling the order at 9:30 a.m.

    (2) The machine had filled $\frac{1}{2}$ of the order by

    10:30 a.m. and $\frac{5}{6}$ of the order by 11:10 a.m.

105. If $n + k = m$, what is the value of k ?

    (1) $n = 10$
    (2) $m + 10 = n$

106. Town T has 20,000 residents, 60 percent of whom are female. What percent of the residents were born in Town T ?

    (1) The number of female residents who were born in Town T is twice the number of male residents who were <u>not</u> born in Town T.

    (2) The number of female residents who were <u>not</u> born in Town T is twice the number of female residents who were born in Town T.

107. Can the positive integer n be written as the sum of two different positive prime numbers?

    (1) n is greater than 3.
    (2) n is odd.

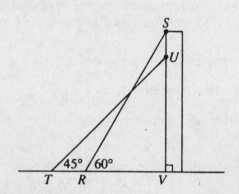

108. In the figure above, segments RS and TU represent two positions of the same ladder leaning against the side SV of a wall. The length of TV is how much greater than the length of RV ?

    (1) The length of TU is 10 meters.
    (2) The length of RV is 5 meters.

109. If both x and y are nonzero numbers, what is the value of $\frac{y}{x}$?

    (1) $x = 6$
    (2) $y^2 = x^2$

110. If $x = 0.rstu$, where r, s, t, and u each represent a nonzero digit of x, what is the value of x ?

    (1) $r = 3s = 2t = 6u$
    (2) The product of r and u is equal to the product of s and t.

A   Statement (1) ALONE is sufficient, but statement (2) alone is not sufficient.
B   Statement (2) ALONE is sufficient, but statement (1) alone is not sufficient.
C   BOTH statements TOGETHER are sufficient, but NEITHER statement ALONE is sufficient.
D   EACH statement ALONE is sufficient.
E   Statements (1) and (2) TOGETHER are NOT sufficient.

111. What were the gross revenues from ticket sales for a certain film during the second week in which it was shown?

(1) Gross revenues during the second week were $1.5 million less than during the first week.

(2) Gross revenues during the third week were $2.0 million less than during the first week.

112. What number is 15 percent of x ?

(1) 18 is 6 percent of x.

(2) $\frac{2}{3}$ of x is 200.

113. How many books does Ricardo have?

(1) If Ricardo had 15 fewer books, he would have only half as many as he actually has.

(2) Ricardo has twice as many fiction books as nonfiction books.

114. What was the amount of money donated to a certain charity?

(1) Of the amount donated, 40 percent came from corporate donations.

(2) Of the amount donated, $1.5 million came from noncorporate donations.

115. Is x a negative number?

(1) $9x > 10x$

(2) $x + 3$ is positive.

116. John took a test that had 60 questions numbered from 1 to 60. How many of the questions did he answer correctly?

(1) The number of questions he answered correctly in the first half of the test was 7 more than the number he answered correctly in the second half of the test.

(2) He answered $\frac{5}{6}$ of the odd-numbered

questions correctly and $\frac{4}{5}$ of the

even-numbered questions correctly.

117. The perimeter of a rectangular garden is 360 feet. What is the length of the garden?

(1) The length of the garden is twice the width.

(2) The difference between the length and width of the garden is 60 feet.

118. If $2^x(5^n) = t$, what is the value of t ?

(1) $x = n + 3$

(2) $2^x = 32$

119. In $\triangle XYZ$, what is the length of YZ ?

(1) The length of XY is 3.

(2) The length of XZ is 5.

120. If Jill's average (arithmetic mean) score for three games of bowling was 168, what was her lowest score?

(1) Jill's highest score was 204.

(2) The sum of Jill's two highest scores was 364.

121. An empty rectangular swimming pool has uniform depth. How long will it take to fill the pool with water?

(1) Water will be pumped in at the rate of 240 gallons per hour (1 cubic foot = 7.5 gallons).

(2) The pool is 60 feet long and 25 feet wide.

122. In Jefferson School, 300 students study French or Spanish or both. If 100 of these students do not study French, how many of these students study both French and Spanish?

(1) Of the 300 students, 60 do not study Spanish.

(2) A total of 240 of the students study Spanish.

123. Is the value of n closer to 50 than to 75 ?

    (1) $75 - n > n - 50$
    (2) $n > 60$

124. In the equation $x^2 + bx + 12 = 0$, x is a variable and b is a constant. What is the value of b ?

    (1) $x - 3$ is a factor of $x^2 + bx + 12$.
    (2) 4 is a root of the equation $x^2 + bx + 12 = 0$.

125. If Juan had a doctor's appointment on a certain day, was the appointment on a Wednesday?

    (1) Exactly 60 hours before the appointment, it was Monday.
    (2) The appointment was between 1:00 p.m. and 9:00 p.m.

126. What is the value of $b + c$?

    (1) $ab + cd + ac + bd = 6$
    (2) $a + d = 4$

127. If m is an integer, is m odd ?

    (1) $\dfrac{m}{2}$ is not an even integer.
    (2) $m - 3$ is an even integer.

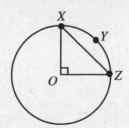

128. What is the circumference of the circle above with center O ?

    (1) The perimeter of $\triangle OXZ$ is $20 + 10\sqrt{2}$.
    (2) The length of arc XYZ is 5π.

129. At the beginning of last month, a stationery store had in stock 250 writing pads, which had cost the store $0.75 each. During the same month, the store made only one purchase of writing pads. What was the total amount spent by the store on the writing pads it had in stock at the end of last month?

    (1) Last month the store purchased 150 writing pads for $0.80 each.
    (2) Last month the total revenue from the sale of writing pads was $180.

130. If y is an integer, is y^3 divisible by 9 ?

    (1) y is divisible by 4.
    (2) y is divisible by 6.

131. What was the ratio of the number of cars to the number of trucks produced by Company X last year?

    (1) Last year, if the number of cars produced by Company X had been 8 percent greater, the number of cars produced would have been 150 percent of the number of trucks produced by Company X.
    (2) Last year Company X produced 565,000 cars and 406,800 trucks.

132. How long did it take Betty to drive nonstop on a trip from her home to Denver, Colorado?

    (1) If Betty's average speed for the trip had been $1\dfrac{1}{2}$ times as fast, the trip would have taken 2 hours.

    (2) Betty's average speed for the trip was 50 miles per hour.

A Statement (1) ALONE is sufficient, but statement (2) alone is not sufficient.
B Statement (2) ALONE is sufficient, but statement (1) alone is not sufficient.
C BOTH statements TOGETHER are sufficient, but NEITHER statement ALONE is sufficient.
D EACH statement ALONE is sufficient.
E Statements (1) and (2) TOGETHER are NOT sufficient.

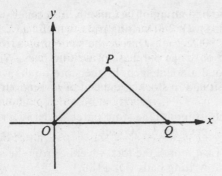

133. In the rectangular coordinate system above, if $OP < PQ$, is the area of region OPQ greater than 48 ?

   (1) The coordinates of point P are $(6, 8)$.

   (2) The coordinates of point Q are $(13, 0)$.

$$S = \frac{\dfrac{2}{n}}{\dfrac{1}{x} + \dfrac{2}{3x}}$$

134. In the expression above, if $xn \neq 0$, what is the value of S ?

   (1) $x = 2n$

   (2) $n = \dfrac{1}{2}$

135. If S is the infinite sequence
   $S_1 = 9, S_2 = 99, S_3 = 999, \ldots, S_k = 10^k - 1, \ldots,$
   is every term in S divisible by the prime number p ?

   (1) p is greater than 2.

   (2) At least one term in sequence S is divisible by p.

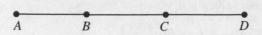

136. In the figure above, is $CD > BC$?

   (1) $AD = 20$

   (2) $AB = CD$

137. How many more men than women are in the room?

   (1) There is a total of 20 women and men in the room.

   (2) The number of men in the room equals the square of the number of women in the room.

138. If n is an integer, is $\dfrac{100 - n}{n}$ an integer?

   (1) $n > 4$

   (2) $n^2 = 25$

139. Last Friday a certain shop sold $\dfrac{3}{4}$ of the sweaters in its inventory. Each sweater sold for $20. What was the total revenue last Friday from the sale of these sweaters?

   (1) When the shop opened last Friday, there were 160 sweaters in its inventory.

   (2) All but 40 sweaters in the shop's inventory were sold last Friday.

140. A jar contains 30 marbles, of which 20 are red and 10 are blue. If 9 of the marbles are removed, how many of the marbles left in the jar are red?

   (1) Of the marbles removed, the ratio of the number of red ones to the number of blue ones is 2 : 1.

   (2) Of the first 6 marbles removed, 4 are red.

A   Statement (1) ALONE is sufficient, but statement (2) alone is not sufficient.
B   Statement (2) ALONE is sufficient, but statement (1) alone is not sufficient.
C   BOTH statements TOGETHER are sufficient, but NEITHER statement ALONE is sufficient.
D   EACH statement ALONE is sufficient.
E   Statements (1) and (2) TOGETHER are NOT sufficient.

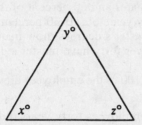

141. Is the triangle above equilateral?

   (1) $x = y$
   (2) $z = 60$

142. If $w + z = 28$, what is the value of wz ?

   (1) w and z are positive integers.
   (2) w and z are consecutive odd integers.

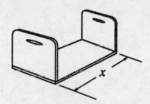

143. Will the first 10 volumes of a 20-volume encyclopedia fit upright in the bookrack shown above?

   (1) $x = 50$ centimeters
   (2) Twelve of the volumes have an average (arithmetic mean) thickness of 5 centimeters.

144. Is $ax = 3 - bx$?

   (1) $x(a + b) = 3$
   (2) $a = b = 1.5$ and $x = 1$.

145. What is the value of the integer x ?

   (1) x is a prime number.
   (2) $31 \le x \le 37$

146. While on a straight road, car X and car Y are traveling at different constant rates. If car X is now 1 mile ahead of car Y, how many minutes from now will car X be 2 miles ahead of car Y ?

   (1) Car X is traveling at 50 miles per hour and car Y is traveling at 40 miles per hour.
   (2) 3 minutes ago car X was $\dfrac{1}{2}$ mile ahead of car Y.

147. In what year was Ellen born?

   (1) Ellen's brother Pete, who is $1\dfrac{1}{2}$ years older than Ellen, was born in 1956.
   (2) In 1975 Ellen turned 18 years old.

148. Is 2^x greater than 100 ?

   (1) $2^{\sqrt{x}} = 8$
   (2) $\dfrac{1}{2^x} < 0.01$

149. What is the number of female employees in Company X?

   (1) If Company X were to hire 14 more people and all of these people were females, the ratio of the number of male employees to the number of female employees would then be 16 to 9.
   (2) Company X has 105 more male employees than female employees.

150. Is the integer x divisible by 36 ?

   (1) x is divisible by 12.
   (2) x is divisible by 9.

A   Statement (1) ALONE is sufficient, but statement (2) alone is not sufficient.
B   Statement (2) ALONE is sufficient, but statement (1) alone is not sufficient.
C   BOTH statements TOGETHER are sufficient, but NEITHER statement ALONE is sufficient.
D   EACH statement ALONE is sufficient.
E   Statements (1) and (2) TOGETHER are NOT sufficient.

151. What is the average (arithmetic mean) of j and k ?

   (1) The average (arithmetic mean) of $j + 2$ and $k + 4$ is 11.

   (2) The average (arithmetic mean) of j, k, and 14 is 10.

152. What is the value of $a - b$?

   (1) $a = b + 4$

   (2) $(a - b)^2 = 16$

153. Is $rst = 1$?

   (1) $rs = 1$

   (2) $st = 1$

154. In a certain office, 50 percent of the employees are college graduates and 60 percent of the employees are over forty years old. If 30 percent of those over forty have master's degrees, how many of the employees over forty have master's degrees?

   (1) Exactly 100 of the employees are college graduates.

   (2) Of the employees forty years old or less, 25 percent have master's degrees.

155. Is $xy < 6$?

   (1) $x < 3$ and $y < 2$.

   (2) $\frac{1}{2} < x < \frac{2}{3}$ and $y^2 < 64$.

A Statement (1) ALONE is sufficient, but statement (2) alone is not sufficient.
B Statement (2) ALONE is sufficient, but statement (1) alone is not sufficient.
C BOTH statements TOGETHER are sufficient, but NEITHER statement ALONE is sufficient.
D EACH statement ALONE is sufficient.
E Statements (1) and (2) TOGETHER are NOT sufficient.

156. The regular price per eight-ounce can of brand X soup is \$0.37, regardless of the number of cans purchased. What amount will be saved on the purchase of 3 eight-ounce cans of brand X soup if the regular price is reduced?

(1) At the reduced price, 3 eight-ounce cans of brand X soup will cost \$0.99.
(2) The amount that will be saved on each eight-ounce can of brand X soup purchased at the reduced price is \$0.04.

157. Does Joe weigh more than Tim?

(1) Tim's weight is 80 percent of Joe's weight.
(2) Joe's weight is 125 percent of Tim's weight.

158. Is p^2 an odd integer?

(1) p is an odd integer.

(2) $\sqrt{p}$ is an odd integer.

159. What is the value of xy ?

(1) $x + y = 10$
(2) $x - y = 6$

160. Elena receives a salary plus a commission that is equal to a fixed percentage of her sales revenue. What was the total of Elena's salary and commission last month?

(1) Elena's monthly salary is \$1,000.
(2) Elena's commission is 5 percent of her sales revenue.

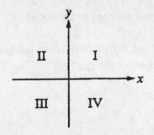

161. Point (x, y) lies in which quadrant of the rectangular coordinate system shown above?

(1) $x + y < 0$
(2) $x = 4$ and $y = -7$.

162. What is the average (arithmetic mean) of x, y, and z ?

(1) $x + y = 5$
(2) $y + z = 7$

163. Chan and Mieko drove separate cars along the entire length of a certain route. If Chan made the trip in 15 minutes, how many minutes did it take Mieko to make the same trip?

(1) Mieko's average speed for the trip was $\frac{3}{4}$ of Chan's average speed.

(2) The route is 14 miles long.

164. If $xy \neq 0$, is $\frac{x}{y} < 0$?

(1) $x = -y$
(2) $-x = -(-y)$

165. What is the value of the two-digit integer x ?

(1) The sum of the two digits is 3.
(2) x is divisible by 3.

166. Is the number x between 0.2 and 0.7 ?

(1) $560x < 280$
(2) $700x > 280$

167. Is x an integer?

(1) $\frac{x}{2}$ is an integer.

(2) $2x$ is an integer.

168. A swim club that sold only individual and family memberships charged \$300 for an individual membership. If the club's total revenue from memberships was \$480,000, what was the charge for a family membership?

(1) The revenue from individual memberships was $\frac{1}{4}$ of the total revenue from memberships.
(2) The club sold 1.5 times as many family memberships as individual memberships.

A   Statement (1) ALONE is sufficient, but statement (2) alone is not sufficient.
B   Statement (2) ALONE is sufficient, but statement (1) alone is not sufficient.
C   BOTH statements TOGETHER are sufficient, but NEITHER statement ALONE is sufficient.
D   EACH statement ALONE is sufficient.
E   Statements (1) and (2) TOGETHER are NOT sufficient.

169. If x, y, and z are positive numbers, is $x > y > z$?

(1) $xz > yz$
(2) $yx > yz$

170. Can the positive integer p be expressed as the product of two integers, each of which is greater than 1 ?

(1) $31 < p < 37$
(2) p is odd.

171. Currently there are 50 picture books on each shelf in the children's section of a library. If these books were to be placed on smaller shelves with 30 picture books on each shelf, how many of the smaller shelves would be needed to hold all of these books?

(1) The number of smaller shelves needed is 6 more than the current number of shelves.
(2) Currently there are 9 shelves in the children's section.

172. Is $y = 6$?

(1) $y^2 = 36$
(2) $y^2 - 7y + 6 = 0$

173. The figure above represents the floor plan of an art gallery that has a lobby and 18 rooms. If Lisa goes from the lobby into room A at the same time that Paul goes from the lobby into room R, and each goes through all of the rooms in succession, entering by one door and exiting by the other, which room will they be in at the same time?

(1) Lisa spends $2x$ minutes in each room and Paul spends $3x$ minutes in each room.
(2) Lisa spends 10 minutes less time in each room than Paul does.

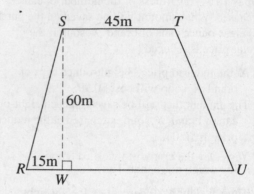

174. Quadrilateral $RSTU$ shown above is a site plan for a parking lot in which side RU is parallel to side ST and RU is longer than ST. What is the area of the parking lot?

(1) $RU = 80$ meters
(2) $TU = 20\sqrt{10}$ meters

175. If $xy = -6$, what is the value of $xy(x + y)$?

(1) $x - y = 5$
(2) $xy^2 = 18$

176. If the list price of a new car was $12,300, what was the cost of the car to the dealer?

(1) The cost to the dealer was equal to 80 percent of the list price.
(2) The car was sold for $11,070, which was 12.5 percent more than the cost to the dealer.

177. If p, q, x, y, and z are different positive integers, which of the five integers is the median?

(1) $p + x < q$
(2) $y < z$

A Statement (1) ALONE is sufficient, but statement (2) alone is not sufficient.
B Statement (2) ALONE is sufficient, but statement (1) alone is not sufficient.
C BOTH statements TOGETHER are sufficient, but NEITHER statement ALONE is sufficient.
D EACH statement ALONE is sufficient.
E Statements (1) and (2) TOGETHER are NOT sufficient.

178. A certain employee is paid \$6 per hour for an 8-hour workday. If the employee is paid $1\frac{1}{2}$ times this rate for time worked in excess of 8 hours during a single day, how many hours did the employee work today?

   (1) The employee was paid \$18 more for hours worked today than for hours worked yesterday.
   (2) Yesterday the employee worked 8 hours.

179. If n is a member of the set
   $$\{33, 36, 38, 39, 41, 42\},$$
   what is the value of n ?

   (1) n is even.
   (2) n is a multiple of 3.

180. What is the value of x ?

   (1) $2x + 1 = 0$
   (2) $(x + 1)^2 = x^2$

$A \qquad B \qquad C \qquad D$

181. In the figure above, what is the length of AD ?

   (1) $AC = 6$
   (2) $BD = 6$

182. A retailer purchased a television set for x percent less than its list price, and then sold it for y percent less than its list price. What was the list price of the television set?

   (1) $x = 15$
   (2) $x - y = 5$

183. Is x^2 greater than x ?

   (1) x^2 is greater than 1.
   (2) x is greater than -1.

184. What is the value of $\dfrac{r}{2} + \dfrac{s}{2}$?

   (1) $\dfrac{r+s}{2} = 5$
   (2) $r + s = 10$

185. If x, y, and z are numbers, is $z = 18$?

   (1) The average (arithmetic mean) of x, y, and z is 6.
   (2) $x = -y$

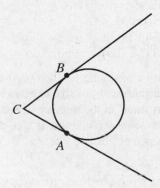

186. The circular base of an above-ground swimming pool lies in a level yard and just touches two straight sides of a fence at points A and B, as shown in the figure above. Point C is on the ground where the two sides of the fence meet. How far from the center of the pool's base is point A ?

   (1) The base has area 250 square feet.
   (2) The center of the base is 20 feet from point C.

187. In 1979 Mr. Jackson bought a total of n shares of stock X and Mrs. Jackson bought a total of 300 shares of stock X. If the couple held all of their respective shares throughout 1980, and Mr. Jackson's 1980 dividends on his n shares totaled \$150, what was the total amount of Mrs. Jackson's 1980 dividends on her 300 shares?

   (1) In 1980 the annual dividend on each share of stock X was \$0.75.
   (2) In 1979 Mr. Jackson bought a total of 200 shares of stock X.

A Statement (1) ALONE is sufficient, but statement (2) alone is not sufficient.
B Statement (2) ALONE is sufficient, but statement (1) alone is not sufficient.
C BOTH statements TOGETHER are sufficient, but NEITHER statement ALONE is sufficient.
D EACH statement ALONE is sufficient.
E Statements (1) and (2) TOGETHER are NOT sufficient.

188. If Sara's age is exactly twice Bill's age, what is Sara's age?

   (1) Four years ago, Sara's age was exactly 3 times Bill's age.
   (2) Eight years from now, Sara's age will be exactly 1.5 times Bill's age.

189. What is the value of $\dfrac{x}{yz}$?

   (1) $x = \dfrac{y}{2}$ and $z = \dfrac{2x}{5}$.

   (2) $\dfrac{x}{z} = \dfrac{5}{2}$ and $\dfrac{1}{y} = \dfrac{1}{10}$.

190. An infinite sequence of positive integers is called an "alpha sequence" if the number of even integers in the sequence is finite. If S is an infinite sequence of positive integers, is S an alpha sequence?

   (1) The first ten integers in S are even.
   (2) An infinite number of integers in S are odd.

191. If $xy > 0$, does $(x - 1)(y - 1) = 1$?

   (1) $x + y = xy$
   (2) $x = y$

192. After winning 50 percent of the first 20 games it played, Team A won all of the remaining games it played. What was the total number of games that Team A won?

   (1) Team A played 25 games altogether.
   (2) Team A won 60 percent of all the games it played.

$$\begin{array}{r}\square \\ + \triangle \\ \hline \bigstar \end{array}$$

193. In the addition problem above, each of the symbols $\square$, $\triangle$, and $\bigstar$ represents a positive digit. If $\square < \triangle$, what is the value of $\triangle$?

   (1) $\bigstar = 4$
   (2) $\square = 1$

CANCELATION FEES

Days Prior to Departure	Percent of Package Price
46 or more	10%
45-31	35%
30-16	50%
15-5	65%
4 or fewer	100%

194. The table above shows the cancelation fee schedule that a travel agency uses to determine the fee charged to a tourist who cancels a trip prior to departure. If a tourist canceled a trip with a package price of $1,700 and a departure date of September 4, on what day was the trip canceled?

   (1) The cancelation fee was $595.
   (2) If the trip had been canceled one day later, the cancelation fee would have been $255 more.

195. Is 5^k less than 1,000 ?

   (1) $5^{k+1} > 3,000$
   (2) $5^{k-1} = 5^k - 500$

196. If Hans purchased a pair of skis and a ski jacket, what was the cost of the skis?

   (A) The ratio of the cost of the skis to the cost of the jacket was 5 to 1.
   (2) The total cost of the skis and the jacket was $360.

197. Is $x < y$?

   (1) $z < y$
   (2) $z < x$

A Statement (1) ALONE is sufficient, but statement (2) alone is not sufficient.
B Statement (2) ALONE is sufficient, but statement (1) alone is not sufficient.
C BOTH statements TOGETHER are sufficient, but NEITHER statement ALONE is sufficient.
D EACH statement ALONE is sufficient.
E Statements (1) and (2) TOGETHER are NOT sufficient.

198. If a certain city is losing 12 percent of its daily water supply each day because of water-main breaks, what is the dollar cost to the city per day for this loss?

(1) The city's daily water supply is 350 million gallons.
(2) The cost to the city for each 12,000 gallons of water lost is $2.

199. Machine X runs at a constant rate and produces a lot consisting of 100 cans in 2 hours. How much less time would it take to produce the lot of cans if both machines X and Y were run simultaneously?

(1) Both machines X and Y produce the same number of cans per hour.
(2) It takes machine X twice as long to produce the lot of cans as it takes machines X and Y running simultaneously to produce the lot.

200. If x and y are positive, what is the value of x ?

(1) 200 percent of x equals 400 percent of y.
(2) xy is the square of a positive integer.

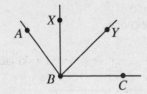

201. In the figure above, what is the measure of $\angle ABC$?

(1) BX bisects $\angle ABY$ and BY bisects $\angle XBC$.
(2) The measure of $\angle ABX$ is 40°.

202. If $-10 < k < 10$, is $k > 0$?

(1) $\dfrac{1}{k} > 0$
(2) $k^2 > 0$

	R	S	T	U
R	0	y	x	62
S	y	0	56	75
T	x	56	0	69
U	62	75	69	0

203. The table above shows the distance, in kilometers, by the most direct route, between any two of the four cities, $R, S, T,$ and U. For example, the distance between City R and City U is 62 kilometers. What is the value of x ?

(1) By the most direct route, the distance between S and T is twice the distance between S and R.
(2) By the most direct route, the distance between T and U is 1.5 times the distance between R and T.

204. Buckets X and Y contained only water and bucket Y was $\dfrac{1}{2}$ full. If all of the water in bucket X was then poured into bucket Y, what fraction of the capacity of Y was then filled with water?

(1) Before the water from X was poured, X was $\dfrac{1}{3}$ full.
(2) X and Y have the same capacity.

205. If n is an integer, is $n + 2$ a prime number?

(1) n is a prime number
(2) $n + 1$ is not a prime number.

206. Is x between 0 and 1 ?

(1) x^2 is less than x.
(2) x^3 is positive.

207. Did Sally pay less than x dollars, including sales tax, for her bicycle?

(1) The price Sally paid for the bicycle was $(0.9)x$ dollars, excluding the 10 percent sales tax.
(2) The price Sally paid for the bicycle was $170, excluding sales tax.

A Statement (1) ALONE is sufficient, but statement (2) alone is not sufficient.
B Statement (2) ALONE is sufficient, but statement (1) alone is not sufficient.
C BOTH statements TOGETHER are sufficient, but NEITHER statement ALONE is sufficient.
D EACH statement ALONE is sufficient.
E Statements (1) and (2) TOGETHER are NOT sufficient.

208. Is the positive square root of x an integer?

(1) $x = n^4$ and n is an integer.
(2) $x = 16$

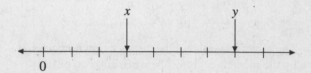

209. If the successive tick marks shown on the number line above are equally spaced and if x and y are the numbers designating the end points of intervals as shown, what is the value of y ?

(1) $x = \dfrac{1}{2}$

(2) $y - x = \dfrac{2}{3}$

210. In a certain senior citizens' club, are more than $\dfrac{1}{4}$ of the members over 75 years of age?

(1) Exactly 60 percent of the female members are over 60 years of age, and, of these, $\dfrac{1}{3}$ are over 75 years of age.

(2) Exactly 10 male members are over 75 years of age.

211. If $t \neq 0$, is r greater than zero?

(1) $rt = 12$
(2) $r + t = 7$

212. If x is an integer, is y an integer?

(1) The average (arithmetic mean) of x, y, and $y - 2$ is x.
(2) The average (arithmetic mean) of x and y is not an integer.

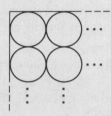

213. The inside of a rectangular carton is 48 centimeters long, 32 centimeters wide, and 15 centimeters high. The carton is filled to capacity with k identical cylindrical cans of fruit that stand upright in rows and columns, as indicated in the figure above. If the cans are 15 centimeters high, what is the value of k ?

(1) Each of the cans has a radius of 4 centimeters.
(2) 6 of the cans fit exactly along the length of the carton.

214. If $R = \dfrac{8x}{3y}$ and $y \neq 0$, what is the value of R ?

(1) $x = \dfrac{2}{3}$
(2) $x = 2y$

215. Is the positive integer n a multiple of 24 ?

(1) n is a multiple of 4.
(2) n is a multiple of 6.

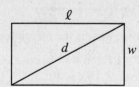

216. What is the area of the rectangular region above?

(1) $\ell + w = 6$
(2) $d^2 = 20$

217. If Aaron, Lee, and Tony have a total of $36, how much money does Tony have?

    (1) Tony has twice as much money as Lee and $\frac{1}{3}$ as much as Aaron.
    (2) The sum of the amounts of money that Tony and Lee have is half the amount that Aaron has.

218. If n is a positive integer, is the value of $b - a$ at least twice the value of $3^n - 2^n$?

    (1) $a = 2^{n+1}$ and $b = 3^{n+1}$
    (2) $n = 3$

219. The price per share of stock X increased by 10 percent over the same time period that the price per share of stock Y decreased by 10 percent. The reduced price per share of stock Y was what percent of the original price per share of stock X ?

    (1) The increased price per share of stock X was equal to the original price per share of stock Y.
    (2) The increase in the price per share of stock X was $\frac{10}{11}$ the decrease in the price per share of stock Y.

220. Any decimal that has only a finite number of non-zero digits is a terminating decimal. For example, 24, 0.82, and 5.096 are three terminating decimals.

    If r and s are positive integers and the ratio $\frac{r}{s}$ is expressed as a decimal, is $\frac{r}{s}$ a terminating decimal?
    (1) $90 < r < 100$
    (2) $s = 4$

221. What is the value of integer n ?

    (1) $n(n+1) = 6$
    (2) $2^{2n} = 16$

222. If x is a positive integer, is $\sqrt{x}$ an integer?

    (1) $\sqrt{4x}$ is an integer.
    (2) $\sqrt{3x}$ is not an integer.

223. Are at least 10 percent of the people in Country X who are 65 years old or older employed?

    (1) In Country X, 11.3 percent of the population is 65 years old or older.

    (2) In Country X, of the population 65 years old or older, 20 percent of the men and 10 percent of the women are employed.

224. If x is a positive number less than 10, is z greater than the average (arithmetic mean) of x and 10 ?

    (1) On the number line, z is closer to 10 than it is to x.
    (2) $z = 5x$

225. If y is greater than 110 percent of x, is y greater than 75 ?

    (1) $x > 75$
    (2) $y - x = 10$

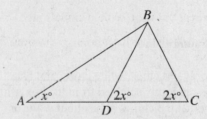

226. In triangle ABC above, what is the length of side BC ?

    (1) Line segment AD has length 6.
    (2) $x = 36$

A Statement (1) ALONE is sufficient, but statement (2) alone is not sufficient.
B Statement (2) ALONE is sufficient, but statement (1) alone is not sufficient.
C BOTH statements TOGETHER are sufficient, but NEITHER statement ALONE is sufficient.
D EACH statement ALONE is sufficient.
E Statements (1) and (2) TOGETHER are NOT sufficient.

227. If the two floors in a certain building are 9 feet apart, how many steps are there in a set of stairs that extends from the first floor to the second floor of the building?

   (1) Each step is $\frac{3}{4}$ foot high.

   (2) Each step is 1 foot wide.

228. A bookstore that sells used books sells each of its paperback books for a certain price and each of its hardcover books for a certain price. If Joe, Maria, and Paul bought books in this store, how much did Maria pay for 1 paperback book and 1 hardcover book?

   (1) Joe bought 2 paperback books and 3 hardcover books for $12.50.

   (2) Paul bought 4 paperback books and 6 hardcover books for $25.00.

229. If S is a set of four numbers w, x, y, and z, is the range of the numbers in S greater than 2 ?

   (1) $w - z > 2$
   (2) z is the least number in S.

230. A box contains only red chips, white chips, and blue chips. If a chip is randomly selected from the box, what is the probability that the chip will be either white or blue?

   (1) The probability that the chip will be blue is $\frac{1}{5}$.

   (2) The probability that the chip will be red is $\frac{1}{3}$.

231. Of the 4,800 voters who voted for or against Resolution K, 1,800 were Democrats and 3,000 were Republicans. What was the total number of female voters who voted for Resolution K ?

   (1) $\frac{3}{4}$ of the Democrats and $\frac{2}{3}$ of the Republicans voted for Resolution K.

   (2) $\frac{1}{3}$ of the Democrats who voted for Resolution K and $\frac{1}{2}$ of the Republicans who voted for Resolution K were females.

232. If n is a positive integer, is $n^3 - n$ divisible by 4 ?

   (1) $n = 2k + 1$, where k is an integer.
   (2) $n^2 + n$ is divisible by 6.

233. If $x \neq -y$, is $\dfrac{x-y}{x+y} > 1$?

   (1) $x > 0$
   (2) $y < 0$

234. If x is a positive integer and w is a negative integer, what is the value of xw ?

   (1) $x^w = \dfrac{1}{2}$

   (2) $w = -1$

235. A certain group of car dealerships agreed to donate x dollars to a Red Cross chapter for each car sold during a 30-day period. What was the total amount that was expected to be donated?

   (1) A total of 500 cars were expected to be sold.
   (2) 60 more cars were sold than expected, so that the total amount actually donated was $28,000.

A Statement (1) ALONE is sufficient, but statement (2) alone is not sufficient.
B Statement (2) ALONE is sufficient, but statement (1) alone is not sufficient.
C BOTH statements TOGETHER are sufficient, but NEITHER statement ALONE is sufficient.
D EACH statement ALONE is sufficient.
E Statements (1) and (2) TOGETHER are NOT sufficient.

236. Is $|x| = y - z$?

(1) $x + y = z$
(2) $x < 0$

237. If x is an integer, is $9^x + 9^{-x} = b$?

(1) $3^x + 3^{-x} = \sqrt{b+2}$
(2) $x > 0$

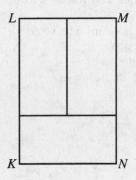

238. In the figure above, what is the ratio $\dfrac{KN}{MN}$?

(1) The perimeter of rectangle $KLMN$ is 30 meters.
(2) The three small rectangles have the same dimensions.

239. If n is an integer between 2 and 100 and if n is also the square of an integer, what is the value of n ?

(1) n is even.
(2) The cube root of n is an integer.

240. If x and y are positive integers such that $x = 8y + 12$, what is the greatest common divisor of x and y ?

(1) $x = 12u$, where u is an integer.
(2) $y = 12z$, where z is an integer.

241. If r and s are positive integers, is $\dfrac{r}{s}$ an integer?

(1) Every factor of s is also a factor of r.
(2) Every prime factor of s is also a prime factor of r.

242. On Jane's credit card account, the average daily balance for a 30-day billing cycle is the average (arithmetic mean) of the daily balances at the end of each of the 30 days. At the beginning of a certain 30-day billing cycle, Jane's credit card account had a balance of $600. Jane made a payment of $300 on the account during the billing cycle. If no other amounts were added to or subtracted from the account during the billing cycle, what was the average daily balance on Jane's account for the billing cycle?

(1) Jane's payment was credited on the 21st day of the billing cycle.
(2) The average daily balance through the 25th day of the billing cycle was $540.

243. If the integer n is greater than 1, is n equal to 2 ?

(1) n has exactly two positive factors.
(2) The difference of any two distinct positive factors of n is odd.

244. Is $x > y$?

(1) $x = y + 2$

(2) $\dfrac{x}{2} = y - 1$

245. Is $\dfrac{1}{a-b} < b - a$?

(1) $a < b$
(2) $1 < |a-b|$

A Statement (1) ALONE is sufficient, but statement (2) alone is not sufficient.
B Statement (2) ALONE is sufficient, but statement (1) alone is not sufficient.
C BOTH statements TOGETHER are sufficient, but NEITHER statement ALONE is sufficient.
D EACH statement ALONE is sufficient.
E Statements (1) and (2) TOGETHER are NOT sufficient.

246. If $rs \neq 0$, is $\dfrac{1}{r} + \dfrac{1}{s} = 4$?

(1) $r + s = 4rs$
(2) $r = s$

247. If m and n are positive integers, is $\sqrt{n-m}$ an integer?

(1) $n > m + 15$
(2) $n = m(m + 1)$

248. Is $\dfrac{1}{p} > \dfrac{r}{r^2 + 2}$?

(1) $p = r$
(2) $r > 0$

249. What is the value of $5x^2 + 4x - 1$?

(1) $x(x + 2) = 0$
(2) $x = 0$

250. What is the value of $a^4 - b^4$?

(1) $a^2 - b^2 = 16$
(2) $a + b = 8$

251. What is the average (arithmetic mean) of a, b, and c?

(1) $a + 2b + 3c = 10$
(2) $3a + 2b + c = 14$

252. Are positive integers p and q both greater than n?

(1) $p - q$ is greater than n.
(2) $q > p$

253. In the rectangular coordinate system, are the points (r, s) and (u, v) equidistant from the origin?

(1) $r + s = 1$
(2) $u = 1 - r$ and $v = 1 - s$.

254. Is $\dfrac{x}{m}(m^2 + n^2 + k^2) = xm + yn + zk$?

(1) $\dfrac{z}{k} = \dfrac{x}{m}$

(2) $\dfrac{x}{m} = \dfrac{y}{n}$

255. If x is to be selected at random from set T, what is the probability that $\dfrac{1}{4}x - 5 \leq 0$?

(1) T is a set of 8 integers.
(2) T is contained in the set of integers from 1 to 25, inclusive.

256. If $m > 0$ and $n > 0$, is $\dfrac{m + x}{n + x} > \dfrac{m}{n}$?

(1) $m < n$
(2) $x > 0$

257. Does the integer k have a factor p such that $1 < p < k$?

(1) $k > 4!$
(2) $13! + 2 \leq k \leq 13! + 13$

258. What is the value of xy?

(1) $y = x + 1$
(2) $y = x^2 + 1$

259. If v and w are different integers, does $v = 0$?

(1) $vw = v^2$
(2) $w = 2$

260. Is $\sqrt{(x-5)^2} = 5 - x$?

(1) $-x|x| > 0$
(2) $5 - x > 0$

A   Statement (1) ALONE is sufficient, but statement (2) alone is not sufficient.
B   Statement (2) ALONE is sufficient, but statement (1) alone is not sufficient.
C   BOTH statements TOGETHER are sufficient, but NEITHER statement ALONE is sufficient.
D   EACH statement ALONE is sufficient.
E   Statements (1) and (2) TOGETHER are NOT sufficient.

261. What is the number of members of Club X who are at least 35 years of age?

(1) Exactly $\frac{3}{4}$ of the members of Club X are under 35 years of age.
(2) The 64 women in Club X constitute 40 percent of the club's membership.

262. If $z^n = 1$, what is the value of z ?

(1) n is a nonzero integer.
(2) $z > 0$

263. Is $m \neq n$?

(1) $m + n < 0$
(2) $mn < 0$

264. Is $2x - 3y < x^2$?

(1) $2x - 3y = -2$
(2) $x > 2$ and $y > 0$.

265. If $\frac{x}{2} = \frac{3}{y}$, is x less than y ?

(1) $y \geq 3$
(2) $y \leq 4$

266. Marta bought several pencils. If each pencil was either a 23-cent pencil or a 21-cent pencil, how many 23-cent pencils did Marta buy?

(1) Marta bought a total of 6 pencils.
(2) The total value of the pencils Marta bought was 130 cents.

267. For a certain set of n numbers, where $n > 1$, is the average (arithmetic mean) equal to the median?

(1) If the n numbers in the set are listed in increasing order, then the difference between any pair of successive numbers in the set is 2.
(2) The range of the n numbers in the set is $2(n-1)$.

268. Henry purchased 3 items during a sale. He received a 20 percent discount off the regular price of the most expensive item and a 10 percent discount off the regular price of each of the other 2 items. Was the total amount of the 3 discounts greater than 15 percent of the sum of the regular prices of the 3 items?

(1) The regular price of the most expensive item was $50, and the regular price of the next most expensive item was $20.
(2) The regular price of the least expensive item was $15.

269. Whenever Martin has a restaurant bill with an amount between $10 and $99, he calculates the dollar amount of the tip as 2 times the tens digit of the amount of his bill. If the amount of Martin's most recent restaurant bill was between $10 and $99, was the tip calculated by Martin on this bill greater than 15 percent of the amount of the bill?

(1) The amount of the bill was between $15 and $50.
(2) The tip calculated by Martin was $8.

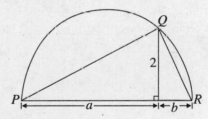

270. If arc PQR above is a semicircle, what is the length of diameter PR ?

(1) $a = 4$
(2) $b = 1$

271. If r and s are nonzero integers, is $\frac{r}{s}$ an integer?

(1) $r - 1 = (s + 1)(s - 1)$
(2) $r - s = 20$

A   Statement (1) ALONE is sufficient, but statement (2) alone is not sufficient.
B   Statement (2) ALONE is sufficient, but statement (1) alone is not sufficient.
C   BOTH statements TOGETHER are sufficient, but NEITHER statement ALONE is sufficient.
D   EACH statement ALONE is sufficient.
E   Statements (1) and (2) TOGETHER are NOT sufficient.

272. In the fraction $\frac{x}{y}$, where x and y are positive

   integers, what is the value of y ?

   (1) The least common denominator

      of $\frac{x}{y}$ and $\frac{1}{3}$ is 6.

   (2) $x = 1$

273. If x and y are nonzero integers, is $x^y < y^x$?

   (1) $x = y^2$
   (2) $y > 2$

274. If n is an integer, is $\frac{n}{7}$ an integer?

   (1) $\frac{3n}{7}$ is an integer.

   (2) $\frac{5n}{7}$ is an integer.

Explanatory Material:
Data Sufficiency

The following discussion of data sufficiency is intended to familiarize you with the most efficient and effective approaches to the kinds of problems common to data sufficiency. The problems on the sample questions in this chapter are generally representative of the kinds of questions you will encounter in this section of the GMAT. Remember that it is the problem-solving strategy that is important, not the specific details of a particular question.

1. At a certain picnic, each of the guests was served either a single scoop or a double scoop of ice cream. How many of the guests were served a double scoop of ice cream?

    (1) At the picnic, 60 percent of the guests were served a double scoop of ice cream.

    (2) A total of 120 scoops of ice cream were served to all the guests at the picnic.

Statement (1) alone is not sufficient because the total number of guests is unknown. Thus, the answer must be B, C, or E. Statement (2) alone is not sufficient since there is no information indicating how the 120 scoops were divided into single-scoop and double-scoop servings. Thus, the answer must be C or E. From (1) the ratio of the number of guests who were served a single scoop to the number of guests who were served a double scoop can be determined and can be used with (2) to determine the number of guests who were served a double scoop. Thus, the best answer is C. (It may be helpful to set up equations to determine whether there is sufficient information given in (1) and (2) for answering the question, but it is not actually necessary to solve the equations.)

2. By what percent was the price of a certain candy bar increased?

    (1) The price of the candy bar was increased by 5 cents.
    (2) The price of the candy bar after the increase was 45 cents.

In (1), only the increase in price is given, and both the original and final prices are unknown. Thus, the percent increase cannot be determined from (1) alone, and the answer must be B, C, or E. In (2), only the final price is given, so the percent increase cannot be determined from (2) alone, and the answer must be C or E. From (1) and (2) together, the amount of the increase is known and the price before the increase can be computed. Therefore, the percent increase can be determined, and the best answer is C.

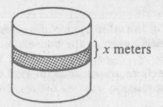
} x meters

3. A circular tub has a band painted around its circumference, as shown above. What is the surface area of this painted band?

    (1) $x = 0.5$
    (2) The height of the tub is 1 meter.

The surface area of the band is the product of the circumference of the band and the width of the band. In (1) the width of the band is given, but the circumference is unknown, so the surface area cannot be determined. Therefore, (1) alone is not sufficient, and the answer must be B, C, or E. In (2) the height of the tub is given, which has no relation to the circumference or the width of the band. Thus, (2) is not sufficient, with or without (1), so the best answer is E.

4. Is it true that $a > b$?

    (1) $2a > 2b$
    (2) $a + c > b + c$

In (1), when both sides of $2a > 2b$ are divided by 2, the result is $a > b$. Thus, (1) alone is sufficient, and the answer must be A or D. In (2), when c is subtracted from both sides of $a + c > b + c$, the result is $a > b$. Thus, (2) alone is also sufficient, and the best answer is D.

5. A thoroughly blended biscuit mix includes only flour and baking powder. What is the ratio of the number of grams of baking powder to the number of grams of flour in the mix?

    (1) Exactly 9.9 grams of flour is contained in 10 grams of the mix.

    (2) Exactly 0.3 gram of baking powder is contained in 30 grams of the mix.

In any amount of the mix, once both ingredient amounts are known, their ratio can be determined. (This ratio must be the same in any amount of the mix since the mix is thoroughly blended.) Each of statements (1) and (2) alone gives the amount of one ingredient in some amount of the mix, so the amount of the other ingredient can be determined. Thus, each of (1) and (2) alone is sufficient, and the best answer is D.

6. If a real estate agent received a commission of 6 percent of the selling price of a certain house, what was the selling price of the house?

   (1) The selling price minus the real estate agent's commission was $84,600.

   (2) The selling price was 250 percent of the original purchase price of $36,000.

From (1) it follows that $84,600 is 94% (100% − 6%) of the selling price, and thus the selling price, $\frac{\$84,600}{0.94}$, can be determined. Therefore, (1) alone is sufficient, and the answer must be A or D. From (2) it follows that the selling price is 2.5($36,000). Thus, (2) alone is also sufficient, and the best answer is D.

7. What is the value of $|x|$?

   (1) $x = -|x|$

   (2) $x^2 = 4$

From (1) all that can be determined is that x is negative (or 0) since $|x|$, the absolute value of x, is always positive (or 0). Thus, (1) alone is not sufficient, and the answer must be B, C, or E. From (2) it can be determined that $x = \pm 2$; in either case $|x| = 2$. Since (2) alone is sufficient to determine the value of $|x|$, the best answer is B.

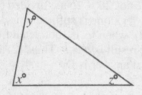

8. What is the value of z in the triangle above?

   (1) $x + y = 139$

   (2) $y + z = 108$

Note that, as in any triangle, $x + y + z = 180$. Using (1), the value 139 can be substituted for $x + y$ in $x + y + z = 180$ to obtain the value of z. Thus, (1) alone is sufficient, and the answer must be A or D. When the equation in (2) is combined with $x + y + z = 180$, all that can be deduced is the value of x. Thus, (2) alone is not sufficient, and the best answer is A.

9. A certain bakery sells rye bread in 16-ounce loaves and 24-ounce loaves, and all loaves of the same size sell for the same price per loaf regardless of the number of loaves purchased. What is the price of a 24-ounce loaf of rye bread in this bakery?

   (1) The total price of a 16-ounce loaf and a 24-ounce loaf of this bread is $2.40.

   (2) The total price of two 16-ounce loaves and one 24-ounce loaf of this bread is $3.40.

Let s and t be the prices of a 16-ounce loaf and a 24-ounce loaf, respectively. According to (1), $s + t = \$2.40$. Since t cannot be determined without knowing s, statement (1) alone is not sufficient, and the answer must be B, C, or E. Similarly, according to (2), $2s + t = \$3.40$, so t cannot be determined. Therefore, (2) alone is not sufficient, and the answer must be C or E. Using both equations from (1) and (2), $t = \$2.40 - s = \$3.40 - 2s$, from which s, and thus t, can be determined. The best answer is therefore C.

10. If $\frac{\sqrt{x}}{y} = n$, what is the value of x ?

   (1) $yn = 10$

   (2) $y = 40$ and $n = \frac{1}{4}$

Note that $\frac{\sqrt{x}}{y} = n$ is equivalent to $\sqrt{x} = yn$ (if $y \neq 0$). From this information and (1), $\sqrt{x} = yn = 10$, and x can be determined. Therefore, the answer must be A or D. From (2), $yn = (40)\left(\frac{1}{4}\right) = 10$, as in (1). Therefore, (2) alone is also sufficient and the best answer is D.

11. If m and n are consecutive positive integers, is m greater than n ?

   (1) $m - 1$ and $n + 1$ are consecutive positive integers.

   (2) m is an even integer.

Note that for two consecutive integers the larger must be 1 more than the smaller. That (1) alone is sufficient can probably be seen most easily by considering particular values for m and n. For example, if $m = 4$, then $n = 3$ or 5 since m and n are consecutive. Then $m - 1 = 3$ and $n + 1 = 4$ or 6. Since $m - 1$ and $n + 1$ are consecutive, $n = 3$ and $m > n$. More generally, since m and n are consecutive, either $m = n + 1$ or $n = m + 1$. But, if $n = m + 1$, then $n + 1 = m + 2$, which is 3 more than $m - 1$, contradicting the fact that $m - 1$ and $n + 1$ are consecutive integers. Thus, $m = n + 1$, or $m > n$, and the answer must be A or D. Because the fact given in (2) that m is even is irrelevant, the best answer is A.

12. **Paula and Sandy were among those people who sold raffle tickets to raise money for Club X. If Paula and Sandy sold a total of 100 of the tickets, how many of the tickets did Paula sell?**

   (1) Sandy sold $\frac{2}{3}$ as many of the raffle tickets as Paula did.

   (2) Sandy sold 8 percent of all the raffle tickets sold for Club X.

If Paula sold p tickets and Sandy sold s tickets, then $p + s = 100$. According to (1), $s = \frac{2}{3}p$. The value of p can be determined by solving both equations simultaneously. Therefore, the answer must be A or D. From (2) the number of raffle tickets that Sandy (and thus Paula) sold cannot be determined since the total number of raffle tickets sold is unknown. Thus, (2) alone is not sufficient, and the best answer is A.

13. **Is the integer n odd?**

   (1) n is divisible by 3.

   (2) n is divisible by 5.

In statement (1), n is divisible by 3, but n may be even or odd as the examples $n = 6$ and $n = 9$ show. Similarly, in statement (2), n is divisible by 5, but it may be even or odd as the examples $n = 10$ and $n = 15$ show. Since neither statement alone is sufficient, the answer must be C or E. From (1) and (2) together, n must be divisible by 15, and the examples $n = 30$ and $n = 45$ show that n may be even or odd. Thus, the best answer is E.

3.2 □△6

14. **If □ and △ each represent single digits in the decimal above, what digit does □ represent?**

   (1) When the decimal is rounded to the nearest tenth, 3.2 is the result.

   (2) When the decimal is rounded to the nearest hundredth, 3.24 is the result.

From (1) the decimal must have been rounded down since the tenths digit is 2 in both 3.2 □△6 and 3.2. Hence, □ represents 0, 1, 2, 3, or 4. Since it cannot be determined from (1) alone what digit □ represents, the answer must be B, C, or E. From (2), □ can represent 3 or 4, depending upon the value of △. For, example, both 3.2376 and 3.2416, when rounded to the nearest hundredth, are 3.24. Since (2) alone is not sufficient, the answer must be C or E, and since the numbers 3.2376 and 3.2416 also satisfy (1) and (2) together, the best answer is E.

15. **A certain company currently has how many employees?**

   (1) If 3 additional employees are hired by the company and all of the present employees remain, there will be at least 20 employees in the company.

   (2) If no additional employees are hired by the company and 3 of the present employees resign, there will be fewer than 15 employees in the company.

Let n be the current number of employees. According to (1), $n + 3 \geq 20$, or $n \geq 17$, which gives a range of possible values of n. Thus, (1) alone is not sufficient, and the answer must be B, C, or E. According to (2), $n - 3 < 15$, or $n < 18$, which also gives a range for n. Thus, (2) alone is not sufficient, and the answer must be C or E. From (1) and (2) together, the value of n can be determined to be 17. Therefore, the best answer is C.

16. **If x is equal to one of the numbers $\frac{1}{4}$, $\frac{3}{8}$, or $\frac{2}{5}$, what is the value of x?**

   (1) $\frac{1}{4} < x < \frac{1}{2}$

   (2) $\frac{1}{3} < x < \frac{3}{5}$

In decimal form, $\frac{1}{4} = 0.25$, $\frac{3}{8} = 0.375$, and $\frac{2}{5} = 0.4$, and statement (1) can be written as $0.25 < x < 0.5$, so that both $\frac{3}{8}$ and $\frac{2}{5}$ are possible values of x. Thus, (1) alone is not sufficient, and the answer must be B, C, or E. Statement (2) can be written as $0.333\ldots < x < 0.6$, so that both $\frac{3}{8}$ and $\frac{2}{5}$ are possible values of x. Thus, (2) alone is not sufficient, and the answer must be C or E. When both (1) and (2) are considered, it follows that $0.333\ldots < x < 0.5$, so that, again, $\frac{3}{8}$ and $\frac{2}{5}$ are both possible values of x. Therefore, the best answer is E.

17. **If a, b, and c are integers, is $a - b + c$ greater than $a + b - c$?**

   (1) b is negative.

   (2) c is positive.

The inequality, $a - b + c > a + b - c$, is equivalent to $-b + c > b - c$, which is equivalent to $2c > 2b$, or $c > b$. Thus, the simpler inequality, $c > b$, may be considered. In (1), $b < 0$ is not sufficient to determine whether $c > b$ since no information is given about c. Hence, the answer must be B, C, or E. Similarly, in (2), $c > 0$ is not sufficient since no information is given about b, and so the answer must be C or E. Using (1) and (2) together, $b < 0 < c$, so that $c > b$, or equivalently, $a - b + c > a + b - c$. Thus, the best answer is C.

18. If $x + 2y + 1 = y - x$, what is the value of x ?

   (1) $y^2 = 9$
   (2) $y = 3$

The equation $x + 2y + 1 = y - x$ is equivalent to $2x = -y - 1$, or $x = -\dfrac{1}{2}(y + 1)$. Thus, the value of x can be determined if and only if the value of y is known. From (1) it follows that $y = 3$ or $y = -3$, so that x has two possible values as well. Thus, (1) alone is not sufficient, and the answer must be B, C, or E. In (2) the value of y is given; therefore, the value of x can be determined. Thus, (2) alone is sufficient, and the best answer is B.

19. If n is an integer, then n is divisible by how many positive integers?

   (1) n is the product of two different prime numbers.

   (2) n and 2^3 are each divisible by the same number of positive integers.

According to (1), $n = pq$, where both p and q are prime numbers and $p \neq q$. Thus, n is divisible by the positive integers 1, p, q, pq, and no others. Statement (1) alone is therefore sufficient to determine the number of positive divisors of n, and the answer must be A or D. Since $2^3 = 8$ and the number of positive divisors of 8 can be determined, statement (2) alone is also sufficient, and the best answer is D.

20. How many miles long is the route from Houghton to Callahan?

   (1) It will take 1 hour less time to travel the entire route at an average rate of 55 miles per hour than at an average rate of 50 miles per hour.

   (2) It will take 11 hours to travel the first half of the route at an average rate of 25 miles per hour.

Using the standard formula rate × time = distance, or $rt = d$, it can be determined from (1) that $d = 50t$ and $d = 55(t - 1)$, where t is the time it takes to travel the entire route at an average rate of 50 miles per hour. These equations can be solved simultaneously for t, and then d can be determined. Therefore, (1) alone is sufficient, and the answer must be A or D. Statement (2) can be expressed as $\dfrac{d}{2} = 25(11)$, which can be solved for d. Thus, statement (2) alone is also sufficient, and the best answer is D.

21. If x and y are positive, what is the value of x ?

   (1) $x = 3.927y$
   (2) $y = 2.279$

Statement (1) indicates that the value of x is 3.927 times the value of y, and statement (2) gives the value of y. Therefore, (1) and (2) together are sufficient to determine the value of x, but neither statement alone is sufficient, and so the best answer is C.

22. John and David each received a salary increase. Which one received the greater dollar increase?

   (1) John's salary increased 8 percent.
   (2) David's salary increased 5 percent.

In (1) there is no information about David's salary and in (2) there is no information about John's salary; thus, neither statement alone is sufficient, and the answer must be C or E. Since (1) and (2) together give only the percentage increases in salary, it cannot be determined which person received the greater dollar increase. For example, if John's salary was the larger salary, then his salary increase would evidently be the greater amount; however, if David's salary was more than $\dfrac{8}{5}$ times John's salary, then David's salary increase would be the greater amount. Therefore, (1) and (2) together are not sufficient, and the best answer is E.

23. Carlotta can drive from her home to her office by one of two possible routes. If she must also return by one of these routes, what is the distance of the shorter route?

   (1) When she drives from her home to her office by the shorter route and returns by the longer route, she drives a total of 42 kilometers.

   (2) When she drives both ways, from her home to her office and back, by the longer route, she drives a total of 46 kilometers.

Statement (1) alone is not sufficient because only the sum of the distances of the two routes is given and there are infinitely many pairs of numbers with a given sum. Thus, the answer must be B, C, or E. From (2) the distance of the longer route can be found, but there is no information about the distance of the shorter route. Statement (2) alone is therefore not sufficient, so the answer must be C or E. From (1) and (2) together, the distance of the shorter route can be determined $(42 - \dfrac{46}{2})$, and the best answer is C.

24. If r and s are positive integers, r is what percent of s ?

   (1) $r = \dfrac{3}{4}s$

   (2) $r \div s = \dfrac{75}{100}$

To determine r as a percent of s it suffices to know the ratio of r to s, since any ratio can be converted to an equivalent ratio with denominator 100. Since (1) and (2) both give the ratio of r to s, each alone is sufficient, and the best answer is D.

25. A shirt and a pair of gloves cost a total of $41.70. How much does the pair of gloves cost?

   (1) The shirt costs twice as much as the gloves.
   (2) The shirt costs $27.80.

From (1) it can be determined that the total cost of the shirt and gloves is three times the cost of the gloves alone; in other words, the gloves cost one third as much as the shirt and gloves together. Thus, (1) alone is sufficient, and the answer must be A or D. Since the cost of the gloves is the difference between the total cost, $41.70, and the cost of the shirt, statement (2) alone is also sufficient. The best answer is therefore D.

26. What is the number of 360-degree rotations that a bicycle wheel made while rolling 100 meters in a straight line without slipping?

   (1) The diameter of the bicycle wheel, including the tire, was 0.5 meter.
   (2) The wheel made twenty 360-degree rotations per minute.

For each 360-degree rotation, the wheel has traveled a distance equal to its circumference. Thus, the number of 360-degree rotations is equal to the number of times the circumference of the wheel can be laid out along the straight-line path that is 100 meters long; so it suffices to know the size of the wheel. From (1) the circumference of the wheel can be determined. Thus, (1) alone is sufficient, and the answer must be A or D. Statement (2) gives the speed at which the wheel is traveling; however, the size of the wheel cannot be determined, and (2) alone is not sufficient. Therefore, the best answer is A.

27. What is the value of the sum of a list of n odd integers?

   (1) $n = 8$
   (2) The square of the number of integers on the list is 64.

Statements (1) and (2) give only the number of integers in the list. Since additional information is needed to determine the sum of the integers (for example, their average), the best answer is E.

28. If a certain animated cartoon consists of a total of 17,280 frames on film, how many minutes will it take to run the cartoon?

   (1) The cartoon runs without interruption at the rate of 24 frames per second.
   (2) It takes 6 times as long to run the cartoon as it takes to rewind the film, and it takes a total of 14 minutes to do both.

From (1) it can be determined that it takes $\frac{17,280}{24 \times 60}$ minutes to run the cartoon. Thus, (1) alone is sufficient, and the answer must be A or D. From (2) it can be determined that the time it takes to run the cartoon is $\frac{6}{7}$ of the 14 minutes it takes both to run the cartoon and to rewind the film, and so (2) alone is also sufficient. The best answer is therefore D.

29. What was the average number of miles per gallon of gasoline for a car during a certain trip?

   (1) The total cost of the gasoline used by the car for the 180-mile trip was $12.00.
   (2) The cost of the gasoline used by the car for the trip was $1.20 per gallon.

Statement (1) gives the number of miles the car traveled; however, the number of gallons of gasoline used cannot be determined, since only the total cost of the gasoline used is given. Thus, (1) alone is not sufficient, and the answer must be B, C, or E. Statement (2) alone is obviously not sufficient, but it gives the additional information needed in (1) to determine the number of gallons of gasoline used. Once the number of miles traveled and the number of gallons used are known, the average number of miles per gallon can be determined. Therefore, (1) and (2) together are sufficient, and the best answer is C.

30. If x and y are positive, is $\frac{x}{y}$ greater than 1 ?

   (1) $xy > 1$
   (2) $x - y > 0$

Since $y > 0$, it follows that $\frac{x}{y} > 1$ if and only if $x > y$. Thus, to answer the question it suffices to determine whether $x > y$. In (1) there are innumerable pairs of different numbers x and y whose product xy is greater than 1, and the larger number in each such pair can be either x or y. Thus, (1) alone is not sufficient, and the answer must be B, C, or E. In (2), $x - y > 0$ is equivalent to $x > y$, so (2) alone is sufficient. The best answer is B.

31. In $\triangle PQR$, if $PQ = x$, $QR = x + 2$, and $PR = y$, which of the three angles of $\triangle PQR$ has the greatest degree measure?

   (1) $y = x + 3$
   (2) $x = 2$

In any triangle, the largest angle is opposite the longest side. To determine the longest side it suffices to determine whether $y > x + 2$. Since $x + 3 > x + 2$, it follows from (1) that $y > x + 2$. Statement (1) alone is therefore sufficient, and the answer must be A or D. From (2) it follows that $PQ = 2$ and $QR = 4$. Thus, y can be any value between 2 and 6; it follows that $y > x$, but it cannot be concluded that $y > x + 2$. Statement (2) alone is therefore not sufficient, so the best answer is A.

32. Is the prime number p equal to 37 ?

    (1) $p = n^2 + 1$, where n is an integer.
    (2) p^2 is greater than 200.

In (1) the expression $n^2 + 1$ can represent a prime number less than 37, equal to 37, or greater than 37, depending on the value of n. For example, if $n = 4$, then $4^2 + 1 = 17$; if $n = 6$, then $6^2 + 1 = 37$; if $n = 10$, then $10^2 + 1 = 101$; and 17, 37, and 101 are all prime numbers. Thus, (1) alone is not sufficient, and the answer must be B, C, or E. Since $14^2 = 196$ and $15^2 = 225$, it follows from (2) that $p > 14$, so that p might or might not equal 37. Thus, (2) alone is not sufficient, and the answer must be C or E. The values of p for $n = 4$ and for $n = 6$ given above show that (1) and (2) together are not sufficient, and the best answer is E.

33. The only contents of a parcel are 25 photographs and 30 negatives. What is the total weight, in ounces, of the parcel's contents?

    (1) The weight of each photograph is 3 times the weight of each negative.
    (2) The total weight of 1 of the photographs and 2 of the negatives is $\frac{1}{3}$ ounce.

Let p and n denote the weight, in ounces, of a photograph and a negative, respectively. Then the total weight of the parcel's contents can be written as $25p + 30n$. The information in (1) can be written as $p = 3n$. By substituting $3n$ for p in the expression $25p + 30n$, it can be seen that the resulting expression depends on n. Thus, (1) alone is not sufficient, and the answer must be B, C, or E. The information in (2) can be written as $p + 2n = \frac{1}{3}$ and is, similarly, not sufficient. Thus, the answer must be C or E. The two linear equations summarizing the information in (1) and (2) can be solved simultaneously for p and n, so that statements (1) and (2) together are sufficient. The best answer is therefore C.

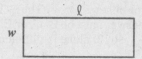

34. If ℓ and w represent the length and width, respectively, of the rectangle above, what is the perimeter?

    (1) $2\ell + w = 40$
    (2) $\ell + w = 25$

The formula for the perimeter of a rectangle is $P = 2\ell + 2w = 2(\ell + w)$, where ℓ and w represent the length and width, respectively. The perimeter can therefore be determined once $\ell + w$ is known. The value of $\ell + w$ cannot be determined from (1), since $2\ell + w = 40$ is equivalent to $\ell + w = 40 - \ell$, which depends on ℓ. Thus, (1) alone is not sufficient, and the answer must be B, C, or E. However, (2) alone is sufficient because $\ell + w$ is known, and the best answer is B.

35. What is the ratio of x to y ?

    (1) x is 4 more than twice y.
    (2) The ratio of $0.5x$ to $2y$ is 3 to 5.

Statement (1) can be expressed as $x = 2y + 4$, which is not sufficient since $\frac{x}{y} = 2 + \frac{4}{y}$, showing that $\frac{x}{y}$ depends on y. Thus, the answer must be B, C, or E. Statement (2) can be expressed as $\frac{0.5x}{2y} = \frac{3}{5}$; so $\frac{x}{y} = \frac{3}{5} \div \frac{0.5}{2}$. Therefore, (2) alone is sufficient, and the best answer is B.

36. If x, y, and z are three integers, are they consecutive integers?

    (1) $z - x = 2$
    (2) $x < y < z$

From (1) it follows that there is exactly one integer between x and z, but there is no information about y. Thus, (1) alone is not sufficient, and the answer must be B, C, or E. Statement (2) alone is not sufficient because there could be other integers between x and z besides y, so the answer must be C or E. From (1) and (2) together, it follows that y is the unique integer between x and z; that is, $y = x + 1$ and $z = y + 1$, and the integers are consecutive. The best answer is therefore C.

37. What is the value of x ?

    (1) $-(x + y) = x - y$
    (2) $x + y = 2$

In (1) the equation $-(x + y) = x - y$ can be written as $-x - y = x - y$, which reduces to $-x = x$. The expression $-x$ denotes the additive inverse of x. Because 0 is the only number that is equal to its additive inverse, it follows that $x = 0$, and (1) alone is sufficient. Alternatively, $-x = x$ can be written as $2x = 0$ so that $x = 0$. Thus, the answer must be A or D. In (2) the value of x depends on the value of y, so (2) alone is not sufficient. The best answer is therefore A.

38. A sum of $200,000 from a certain estate was divided among a spouse and three children. How much of the estate did the youngest child receive?

(1) The spouse received $\frac{1}{2}$ of the sum from the estate, and the oldest child received $\frac{1}{4}$ of the remainder.

(2) Each of the two younger children received $12,500 more than the oldest child and $62,500 less than the spouse.

From (1) the combined amount of the estate that the two younger children received can be determined, but not the individual amount received by either of them. Thus, (1) alone is not sufficient, and the answer must be B, C, or E. In (2) the amount of the estate received by the oldest child and by the spouse can each be expressed in terms of the amount, x, received by each of the two younger children. An equation expressing the sum of $200,000 in terms of x can then be set up and solved for x. It follows that (2) alone is sufficient, so the best answer is B.

39. If the Lincoln Library's total expenditure for books, periodicals, and newspapers last year was $35,000, how much of the expenditure was for books?

(1) The expenditure for newspapers was 40 percent greater than the expenditure for periodicals.

(2) The total of the expenditure for periodicals and newspapers was 25 percent less than the expenditure for books.

Let b, p, and n denote the expenditure, in dollars, for books, periodicals, and newspapers, respectively. Then $b + p + n = 35,000$. In (1) it follows that $n = 1.4p$, so $b + 2.4p = 35,000$. Since the value of b cannot be determined, (1) alone is not sufficient, and the answer must be B, C, or E. In (2) it follows that $p + n = 0.75b$. Then $0.75b$ can be substituted for $p + n$ in the equation $b + p + n = 35,000$, resulting in an equation involving b alone. Since the value of b can be determined by solving this equation, (2) alone is sufficient, and the best answer is B.

40. The symbol ∇ represents one of the following operations: addition, subtraction, multiplication, or division. What is the value of $3 \nabla 2$?

(1) $0 \nabla 1 = 1$
(2) $1 \nabla 0 = 1$

Since $0 + 1 = 1$, $0 - 1 = -1$, $0 \times 1 = 0$, and $0 \div 1 = 0$, it follows from (1) that ∇ represents addition, so the value of $3 \nabla 2$ can be determined. Thus, (1) alone is sufficient, and the answer must be A or D. Since $1 + 0 = 1$, $1 - 0 = 1$, $1 \times 0 = 0$, and $1 \div 0$ is undefined, it follows from (2) that ∇ could represent either addition or subtraction, so $3 \nabla 2$ could equal 5 or 1. Thus, (2) alone is not sufficient, and the best answer is A.

41. The regular price for canned soup was reduced during a sale. How much money could one have saved by purchasing a dozen 7-ounce cans of soup at the reduced price rather than at the regular price?

(1) The regular price for the 7-ounce cans was 3 for a dollar.

(2) The reduced price for the 7-ounce cans was 4 for a dollar.

The saving is the difference between the regular price of a dozen cans and their reduced price. Since (1) gives no information about the reduced price, (1) alone is not sufficient to determine the saving, and the answer must be B, C, or E. Statement (2) alone gives no information about the regular price. Therefore, (2) alone is not sufficient, and the answer must be C or E. From (1) and (2) together, both prices can be computed, and the saving can be determined. Therefore, the best answer is C.

42. If on a fishing trip Jim and Tom each caught some fish, which one caught more fish?

(1) Jim caught $\frac{2}{3}$ as many fish as Tom.

(2) After Tom stopped fishing, Jim continued fishing until he had caught 12 fish.

Statement (1) indicates that Jim caught fewer fish than Tom. Therefore, (1) alone is sufficient to answer the question, and the answer must be A or D. Statement (2) gives no information about the number of fish Tom caught. Therefore, (2) alone is not sufficient, and the best answer is A.

43. If $5x + 3y = 17$, what is the value of x ?

(1) x is a positive integer.
(2) $y = 4x$

Statement (1) alone is not sufficient because it gives no information about the value of y. Thus, the answer must be B, C, or E. From (2) it follows that $5x + 3(4x) = 17$, which can be solved for x. Therefore, the best answer is B.

44. Yesterday Nan parked her car at a certain parking garage that charges more for the first hour than for each additional hour. If Nan's total parking charge at the garage yesterday was $3.75, for how many hours of parking was she charged?

  (1) Parking charges at the garage are $0.75 for the first hour and $0.50 for each additional hour or fraction of an hour.

  (2) If the charge for the first hour had been $1.00, Nan's total parking charge would have been $4.00.

Statement (1) gives the charge for the first hour and for subsequent hours. From this information, together with the total charge that is given, the number of hours after the first hour can be computed. Thus, the answer must be A or D. From statement (2) the charge for the first hour can be determined; however, there is no information about charges after the first hour. Therefore, (2) alone is not sufficient, and the best answer is A.

45. If r and s are integers, is $r + s$ divisible by 3 ?

  (1) s is divisible by 3.
  (2) r is divisible by 3.

One approach to answering this question is to choose values for r and s. In statement (1), for example, let $s = 6$, which is divisible by 3. Then, $r + s$ is divisible by 3 if $r = 9$ but not if $r = 10$, and similarly for statement (2). In more general terms, $r + s$ is divisible by 3 if both r and s are divisible by 3. If either r or s is not divisible by 3, then $r + s$ might or might not be divisible by 3. Since neither (1) alone nor (2) alone gives information about both r and s, neither statement alone is sufficient, and the answer must be C or E. Statements (1) and (2) together state that both r and s are divisible by 3, however, so the best answer is C.

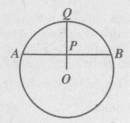

46. What is the radius of the circle above with center O ?

  (1) The ratio of OP to PQ is 1 to 2.
  (2) P is the midpoint of chord AB.

From statement (1) it can be concluded only that the radius is 3 times the length of OP. Since there are many possible lengths of OP and PQ that would have a ratio of 1 to 2, statement (1) alone is not sufficient, and the answer must be B, C, or E. Similarly, knowing that P is the midpoint of chord AB is of no help in determining the radius, so (2) alone is not sufficient. Therefore, the answer must be C or E. Statements (1) and (2) together do not give the length of any line segment shown in the circle, so they are not sufficient to determine the radius. Thus, the best answer is E.

47. A certain 4-liter solution of vinegar and water consists of x liters of vinegar and y liters of water. How many liters of vinegar does the solution contain?

  (1) $\dfrac{x}{4} = \dfrac{3}{8}$

  (2) $\dfrac{y}{4} = \dfrac{5}{8}$

Statement (1) can be solved for x, so (1) alone is sufficient. Therefore, the answer must be A or D. Statement (2) can be solved for y. Since $x + y = 4$, substituting the value of y in the equation will give the value of x. Thus, statement (2) alone is also sufficient, and the best answer is D.

48. Is $x < 0$?

  (1) $-2x > 0$
  (2) $x^3 < 0$

A negative number times a positive number is negative, whereas a negative number times a negative number is positive. Thus, from statement (1) it can be determined that x must be negative, since -2 times x is positive. Therefore, (1) alone is sufficient, and the answer must be A or D. Statement (2) alone is also sufficient, since the cube of a positive number is positive and the cube of a negative number is negative. Therefore, each statement alone is sufficient, and the best answer is D.

49. Of the 230 single-family homes built in City X last year, how many were occupied at the end of the year?

  (1) Of all single-family homes in City X, 90 percent were occupied at the end of last year.

  (2) A total of 7,200 single-family homes in City X were occupied at the end of last year.

Statement (1) does not give the percentage of homes built last year that were occupied. Any number of the 230 homes could be included in the 90 percent of the total. Therefore, the answer must be B, C, or E. Similarly, any number of the 230 homes could be included in the total, and (2) alone is not sufficient. Therefore, the answer must be C or E. From (1) and (2) together, only the total number of single-family homes can be determined. Thus, the best answer is E.

50. Does the product $jkmn$ equal 1 ?

  (1) $\dfrac{jk}{mn} = 1$

  (2) $j = \dfrac{1}{k}$ and $m = \dfrac{1}{n}$

From statement (1) it can be determined only that $jk = mn$. Since this information is not sufficient, the answer must be B, C, or E. From (2) alone, it can be determined that $jk = 1$ and $mn = 1$, so $jkmn = 1$. Thus, (2) alone is sufficient, and the best answer is B.

51. How many of the boys in a group of 100 children have brown hair?

(1) Of the children in the group, 60 percent have brown hair.

(2) Of the children in the group, 40 are boys.

From statement (1), only the total number of children who have brown hair can be determined, so (1) alone is not sufficient. Therefore, the answer must be B, C, or E. Clearly (2) alone is not sufficient because nothing is said about brown hair. Therefore, the answer must be C or E. From statements (1) and (2) together, only the total number of children who have brown hair and the number of boys in the group are known. Thus, (1) and (2) together are not sufficient, and the best answer is E.

52. Is the perimeter of square S greater than the perimeter of equilateral triangle T ?

(1) The ratio of the length of a side of S to the length of a side of T is $4:5$.

(2) The sum of the lengths of a side of S and a side of T is 18.

In considering (1), let the length of each side of S be $4x$ and the length of each side of T be $5x$, which is consistent with the ratio given. Thus, the perimeter of S is $4(4x)$ and the perimeter of T is $3(5x)$, and statement (1) alone is sufficient. Thus, the answer must be A or D. Statement (2) alone is not sufficient because there are many pairs of numbers whose sum is 18, and for some of these pairs the perimeter of S is less than that of T, while for other pairs it is greater. The best answer is A.

53. If p and q are positive integers and $pq = 24$, what is the value of p ?

(1) $\dfrac{q}{6}$ is an integer.

(2) $\dfrac{p}{2}$ is an integer.

There are four pairs of positive integers whose product is 24 : 1 and 24, 2 and 12, 3 and 8, and 4 and 6. From statement (1) the possible values of q are 24, 12, and 6, and there is a value of p corresponding to each of these three values. Thus, statement (1) alone is not sufficient, and the answer must be B, C, or E. From (2), the possible values of p are 2, 4, 6, 8, 12, and 24. Thus, (2) alone is not sufficient, and the answer must be C or E. From (1) and (2) together, it can be determined only that q can be either 12 or 6, so p can be either 2 or 4. Thus, (1) and (2) together are not sufficient, and the best answer is E.

54. If $x \neq 0$, what is the value of $\left(\dfrac{x^p}{x^q}\right)^4$?

(1) $p = q$

(2) $x = 3$

From statement (1) it follows, by substitution, that $\dfrac{x^p}{x^q} = 1$, and thus (1) alone is sufficient to determine the value of $\left(\dfrac{x^p}{x^q}\right)^4$.

Therefore, the answer must be A or D. Statement (2) alone is not sufficient because it gives no information about the values of p and q. Thus, the best answer is A.

55. From May 1, 1960, to May 1, 1975, the closing price of a share of stock X doubled. What was the closing price of a share of stock X on May 1, 1960 ?

(1) From May 1, 1975, to May 1, 1984, the closing price of a share of stock X doubled.

(2) From May 1, 1975, to May 1, 1984, the closing price of a share of stock X increased by $4.50.

Neither statement (1) alone nor statement (2) alone gives any information about the price from 1960 to 1975. Thus, the answer must be C or E. From statements (1) and (2) together, the closing price of a share of the stock on May 1, 1975, can be determined ($4.50) and the closing price on May 1, 1960, can be determined (half of $4.50). Therefore, (1) and (2) together are sufficient, and the best answer is C.

56. If d is a positive integer, is $\sqrt{d}$ an integer?

(1) d is the square of an integer.

(2) $\sqrt{d}$ is the square of an integer.

Statement (1) can be expressed as $d = x^2$, where x is a nonzero integer. Then $\sqrt{d} = \sqrt{x^2}$ equals x or $-x$, depending on whether x is positive or negative, respectively. In either case, $\sqrt{d}$ is an integer. For example, $\sqrt{10^2} = 10$ and $\sqrt{(-4)^2} = \sqrt{16} = 4 = -(-4)$. Therefore, (1) alone is sufficient, and the answer must be A or D. In (2) the square of an integer must also be an integer. Thus, (2) alone is also sufficient, and the best answer is D.

57. If Q is an integer between 10 and 100, what is the value of Q ?

    (1)   One of Q's digits is 3 more than the other, and the sum of its digits is 9.

    (2) $Q < 50$

If x and y are the digits of Q, statement (1) can be expressed as $x = y + 3$ and $x + y = 9$, which can be solved for x and y. It is also possible to see that only the numbers 36 and 63 satisfy (1) without actually setting up equations, but the order of the digits is not known regardless of the method used. Thus, (1) alone is not sufficient, and the answer must be B, C, or E. Clearly, (2) alone is not sufficient because it only narrows the range of possible values of Q. Therefore, the answer must be C or E. When the two possible values of Q are considered and it is noted that only one of the values is less than 50, it can be seen that (1) and (2) together are sufficient to determine the value of Q, and the best answer is C.

58. If digit h is the hundredths' digit in the decimal $d = 0.2h6$, what is the value of d, rounded to the nearest tenth?

    (1) $d < \dfrac{1}{4}$

    (2) $h < 5$

The value of d, rounded to the nearest tenth, is 0.3 for $h \geq 5$ and 0.2 for $h < 5$. Statement (1) can be written $d < 0.250$, so $h < 5$. Thus, (1) alone is sufficient, and the answer must be A or D. Statement (2) gives the information that $h < 5$ directly, so (2) alone is also sufficient. The best answer is D.

59. What is the value of $x^2 - y^2$?

    (1) $x - y = y + 2$

    (2) $x - y = \dfrac{1}{x + y}$

From statement (1) it can be determined only that $x = 2y + 2$ and that $x^2 - y^2 = (2y + 2)^2 - y^2$, which depends on the value of y. Thus, (1) alone is not sufficient to determine the value of $x^2 - y^2$, and the answer must be B, C, or E. Statement (2) can be rewritten $(x - y)(x + y) = 1$, or $x^2 - y^2 = 1$. Therefore, (2) alone is sufficient, and the best answer is B.

60. If ∘ represents one of the operations $+$, $-$, and $\times$, is $k \circ (\ell + m) = (k \circ \ell) + (k \circ m)$ for all numbers k, ℓ, and m ?

    (1) $k \circ 1$ is not equal to $1 \circ k$ for some numbers k.

    (2)   ∘ represents subtraction.

Since $k \circ 1 = 1 \circ k$ for both $+$ and $\times$ (i.e., $k + 1 = 1 + k$ and $k \times 1 = 1 \times k$ for all values of k), according to statement (1), ∘ must represent subtraction. Thus, it can be determined whether $k - (\ell + m) = (k - \ell) + (k - m)$ holds for all k, ℓ, and m. Note, however, that it is not actually necessary to answer this question, only to see that the answer can be determined. Thus, (1) alone is sufficient, and the answer must be A or D. Because statement (2) gives the information directly that ∘ represents subtraction, (2) alone is also sufficient, and the best answer is D.

61. Committee member W wants to schedule a one-hour meeting on Thursday for himself and three other committee members, X, Y, and Z. Is there a one-hour period on Thursday that is open for all four members?

    (1)   On Thursday W and X have an open period from 9:00 a.m. to 12:00 noon.

    (2)   On Thursday Y has an open period from 10:00 a.m. to 1:00 p.m. and Z has an open period from 8:00 a.m. to 11:00 a.m.

Statement (1) alone is not sufficient, since it gives no information about Y and Z. Thus, the answer must be B, C, or E. Similarly, statement (2) alone is not sufficient, since it gives no information about W and X. Therefore, the answer must be C or E. From statements (1) and (2) together, it can be determined that all four committee members have an open one-hour period from 10:00 a.m. to 11:00 a.m. Thus, the best answer is C.

62. If Jack's and Kate's annual salaries in 1985 were each 10 percent higher than their respective annual salaries in 1984, what was Jack's annual salary in 1984 ?

    (1)   The sum of Jack's and Kate's annual salaries in 1984 was $50,000.

    (2)   The sum of Jack's and Kate's annual salaries in 1985 was $55,000.

Statement (1) alone is not sufficient because it gives only the total salaries for Jack and Kate. Thus, the answer must be B, C, or E. From statement (2) alone, it can be determined only that the sum of Jack's and Kate's salaries in 1984 was $55,000 \div 1.1 = $50,000$, which was given directly in (1). Since statements (1) and (2) give the same information, taken together they still do not provide enough information to determine Jack's salary in 1984. Thus, the best answer is E.

63. What is the value of x ?

    (1) $x + 1 = 2 - 3x$

    (2) $\dfrac{1}{2x} = 2$

Each equation, taken separately, can be solved for a unique value of x. Therefore, the best answer is D.

64. How many newspapers were sold at a certain newsstand today?

   (1) A total of 100 newspapers were sold at the newsstand yesterday, 10 fewer than twice the number sold today.

   (2) The number of newspapers sold at the newsstand yesterday was 45 more than the number sold today.

Let t be the number of newspapers sold today. Then statement (1) can be translated as $100 = 2t - 10$, which can be solved for t. Therefore, the answer must be A or D. From statement (2) alone, it can be determined only that the number of newspapers sold yesterday was $t + 45$. Since the number sold yesterday is not known, t cannot be determined and the best answer is A.

65. How much did a certain telephone call cost?

   (1) The call lasted 53 minutes.

   (2) The cost for the first 3 minutes was 5 times the cost for each additional minute.

The cost of the call depends on the duration of the call and the telephone rates. Since statement (1) gives only the duration, it is not sufficient. Therefore, the answer must be B, C, or E. Since statement (2) gives relative rather than actual rates, statement (2) alone is not sufficient, and the answer must be C or E. If c is the cost for the first 3 minutes, then statements (1) and (2) taken together imply that the cost of the call is $c + \frac{c}{5}(50)$. Since the value of c cannot be determined, the best answer is E.

66. A certain expressway has exits $J, K, L,$ and M, in that order. What is the road distance from exit K to exit L?

   (1) The road distance from exit J to exit L is 21 kilometers.

   (2) The road distance from exit K to exit M is 26 kilometers.

Let JK, KL, and LM be the distances between adjacent exits. From statement (1), it can be determined only that $KL = 21 - JK$. Therefore, the answer must be B, C, or E. Similarly, from statement (2), it can be determined only that $KL = 26 - LM$, and the answer must be C or E. Statements (1) and (2) taken together do not provide any of the distances $JK, LM,$ or $JM,$ any of which would give the needed information to find KL. Thus, the best answer is E.

67. Two cars, S and T, each traveled a distance of 50 miles. Did car S use more gasoline than car T?

   (1) Cars S and T traveled the entire distance at the rates of 55 miles per hour and 50 miles per hour, respectively.

   (2) For the entire distance, car S traveled 20 miles per gallon of gasoline and car T traveled 25 miles per gallon of gasoline.

From statement (1), it can be determined only that T traveled more slowly and thus took more time to make the trip than S. Therefore, the answer must be B, C, or E. From statement (2), it can be determined that S traveled fewer miles per gallon and thus used more gasoline to travel the same distance than T. The best answer is B.

68. If n is a positive integer, is n odd?

   (1) $3n$ is odd.

   (2) $n + 3$ is even.

Statement (1) implies that n is odd, for if n were even, any multiple of n would be even. Therefore, the answer must be A or D. Statement (2) also implies that n is odd, since 3 less than any even number is an odd number. Since either (1) or (2), taken separately, is sufficient to answer the question, the best answer is D.

69. Does $2m - 3n = 0$?

   (1) $m \neq 0$
   (2) $6m = 9n$

The question is equivalent to the question, "Does $2m = 3n$?" Statement (1) alone is not sufficient since it does not give any information about the relationship between m and n. Therefore, the answer must be B, C, or E. Statement (2) is equivalent to $2m = 3n$, so it is sufficient to answer the question. The best answer is B.

70. If $xy < 3$, is $x < 1$?

   (1) $y > 3$
   (2) $x < 3$

Statement (1) and the information that $xy < 3$ are sufficient to determine that $x < 1$. For if it were true that $x \geq 1$ and $y > 3$, then $xy > 3$, which is not the case. Therefore, the answer must be A or D. Statement (2) alone does not give sufficient information. For example, if $y = 1$, then x can be any number less than 3, so it is possible that $x \leq 1$ or $x > 1$. The best answer is A.

71. Each of the eggs in a bowl is dyed red, or green, or blue. If one egg is to be removed at random, what is the probability that the egg will be green?

   (1) There are 5 red eggs in the bowl.

   (2) The probability that the egg will be blue is $\frac{1}{3}$.

To determine the probability that the egg removed is green, one must know the number of green eggs and the total number of eggs, or know what proportion of the eggs are green. None of this information is provided by either statement. Therefore, the answer must be C or E. From statements (1) and (2) together, it can be determined only that the probability is less than $\frac{2}{3}$. The best answer is E.

72. Is the average (arithmetic mean) of x and y greater than 20 ?

    (1)   The average (arithmetic mean) of $2x$ and $2y$ is 48.

    (2) $x = 3y$

According to statement (1), $\dfrac{2x+2y}{2} = 48$ and so $\dfrac{x+y}{2} = 24$, which is greater than 20. Therefore, the answer must be either A or D. Statement (2) alone implies that the average of x and y equals $\dfrac{x+y}{2} = \dfrac{3y+y}{2} = 2y$. Since the value of y is not known, it cannot be determined whether $2y > 20$. The best answer is A.

73. Marcia's bucket can hold a maximum of how many liters of water?

    (1)   The bucket currently contains 9 liters of water.

    (2)   If 3 liters of water are added to the bucket when it is half full of water, the amount of water in the bucket will increase by $\dfrac{1}{3}$.

Statement (1) is not sufficient since it implies only that the bucket will hold at least 9 liters. Therefore, the answer must be B, C, or E. With respect to statement (2), if c is the capacity of Marcia's bucket and the addition of 3 liters of water increases the volume of the water from $\dfrac{1}{2}c$ to $\dfrac{4}{3}\left(\dfrac{1}{2}c\right)$, then $\dfrac{4}{3}\left(\dfrac{1}{2}c\right) - \dfrac{1}{2}c = 3$, which can be solved for c. The best answer is B.

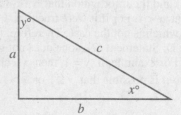

74. In the triangle above, does $a^2 + b^2 = c^2$?

    (1) $x + y = 90$

    (2) $x = y$

The Pythagorean theorem states that $a^2 + b^2 = c^2$ for any right triangle with legs of lengths a and b and hypotenuse of length c. Statement (1) implies that the triangle is a right triangle since the degree measure of the unmarked angle is $180 - (x + y) = 90$. Therefore, $a^2 + b^2 = c^2$ and the answer must be A or D. Statement (2) alone is not sufficient, since $x = y$ does not provide enough information to determine that the largest angle measures 90 degrees. The best answer is A.

75. What is the value of the positive integer n ?

    (1) $n^4 < 25$

    (2) $n \neq n^2$

Statement (1) alone is not sufficient, for if $n^4 < 25$, then $n = 1$ or $n = 2$, since $1^4 = 1$ and $2^4 = 16$, and $n \geq 3$ implies $n^4 \geq 81$. Therefore, the answer must be B, C, or E. Statement (2) implies only that n is not equal to 1. Statements (1) and (2) together are sufficient, since eliminating $n = 1$ leaves $n = 2$. The best answer is C.

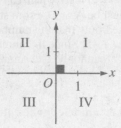

76. If $ab \neq 0$, in what quadrant of the coordinate system above does point (a, b) lie?

    (1) (b, a) lies in quadrant IV.

    (2) $(a, -b)$ lies in quadrant III.

With respect to statement (1), if (b, a) lies in quadrant IV, then $b > 0$ and $a < 0$, which implies that (a, b) lies in quadrant II. Therefore, the answer must be A or D. With respect to statement (2), if $(a, -b)$ lies in quadrant III, then $a < 0$, $-b < 0$, and $b > 0$. Again, $a < 0$ and $b > 0$ imply that (a, b) lies in quadrant II. The best answer is D.

77. From 1984 to 1987, the value of foreign goods consumed annually in the United States increased by what percent?

    (1)   In 1984 the value of foreign goods consumed constituted 19.8 percent of the total value of goods consumed in the United States that year.

    (2)   In 1987 the value of foreign goods consumed constituted 22.7 percent of the total value of goods consumed in the United States that year.

To compute the percent increase, the values of foreign goods consumed in both 1984 and 1987 must be known. Each statement gives only the value of foreign goods as a percentage of the total value of goods consumed in one of the years. Thus, the answer must be C or E. Since statements (1) and (2) together do not provide the values of goods consumed in 1984 and 1987, either total or foreign, they do not give sufficient information to answer the question. Thus, the best answer is E.

78. If x, y, and z are positive, is $x = \dfrac{y}{z^2}$?

(1) $z = \dfrac{y}{xz}$

(2) $z = \sqrt{\dfrac{y}{x}}$

With respect to statement (1), since x, y, and z are positive, both sides of the equation can be multiplied by $\dfrac{x}{z}$ to produce the identical equation $x = \dfrac{y}{z^2}$. Thus, the answer must be A or D. Statement (2) is also an equivalent equation, which can be seen by squaring both sides of the equation and then solving for x. Since each statement gives sufficient information, the best answer is D.

79. If x and y are positive integers and $xy = x^2y^{-3}$, what is the value of xy ?

(1) $x = 2$
(2) $x^3 = 8$

If $x^y = x^{2y-3}$, then $y = 2y - 3$, or $y = 3$. To determine x^y, or x^3, one only needs the value of x. Statement (1) gives the value of x, and the value of x can be found from statement (2). Thus, the best answer is D.

80. If k and n are integers, is n divisible by 7 ?

(1) $n - 3 = 2k$
(2) $2k - 4$ is divisible by 7.

Statement (1) alone is not sufficient since it implies only that $n = 2k + 3$, which could be any odd number. Therefore, the answer must be B, C, or E. Statement (2) alone is not sufficient since it does not give any information about n. Therefore, the answer must be C or E. Statement (2) does imply that $2k - 4 = 7x$, where x is an integer. Also note that $2k + 3$, from (1), can be expressed as $(2k - 4) + 7$. Thus, combining the information in (1) and (2), $n = 2k + 3 = (2k - 4) + 7$, which is divisible by 7 since it is the sum of two terms, each of which is divisible by 7. The best answer is C.

81. If x and y are integers and $y = |x + 3| + |4 - x|$, does y equal 7 ?

(1) $x < 4$
(2) $x > -3$

Statement (1) alone is not sufficient since $y > 7$ if $x < -3$ and $y = 7$ if $-3 \leq x < 4$. This can be found by trying a few values of x. Therefore, the answer must be B, C, or E. Statement (2) alone is also not sufficient since $y > 7$ if $x > 4$. The answer must be C or E. Taken together, statements (1) and (2) determine values of x for which $y = 7$. The best answer is C.

82. If $1 < d < 2$, is the tenths' digit of the decimal representation of d equal to 9 ?

(1) $d + 0.01 < 2$
(2) $d + 0.05 > 2$

Statement (1) indicates that $d < 1.99$, which means that the tenths' digit could be any of the ten digits. Therefore, the answer must be B, C, or E. Statement (2) indicates that $d > 1.95$. Since it is given that $d < 2$, the tenths' digit of d must be 9. The best answer is B.

83. The participants in a race consisted of 3 teams with 3 runners on each team. A team was awarded $6 - n$ points if one of its runners finished in nth place, where $1 \leq n \leq 5$. If all the runners finished the race and if there were no ties, was each team awarded at least one point?

(1) No team was awarded more than a total of 6 points.
(2) No pair of teammates finished in consecutive places among the top five places.

The problem indicates that 5 points were awarded for first place, 4 points for second place, 3 points for third place, 2 points for fourth place, and 1 point for fifth place, for a total of 15 points. Statement (1) indicates that no team was awarded more than 6 points. Suppose that two teams got the maximum of 6 points each, accounting for a total of 12 of the 15 points. Clearly, the third team would have gotten the other 3 points. Therefore, the answer must be A or D. Statement (2) is not conclusive. If no pair of teammates finished in consecutive order, then no team was awarded consecutive numbers of points. From this information alone, one team could have received $(5 + 3 + 1)$ points and a second team $(2 + 4)$ points, leaving no points for the third team; alternatively, one team could have received $(5 + 2)$ points, a second team $(3 + 1)$ points, leaving 4 points for the third team, etc. The best answer is A.

84. If $x + y + z > 0$, is $z > 1$?

(1) $z > x + y + 1$
(2) $x + y + 1 < 0$

Statement (1) alone is not sufficient. Note that $x + y + z > 0$ implies $x + y > -z$ so that, using (1), $z > x + y + 1 > -z + 1$, and $z > -z + 1$ implies $z > 0.5$. For example, let $z = 0.7$ and $x + y = -0.6$; then $x + y + z > 0$ and $z > x + y + 1$, but $z < 1$. Therefore, the answer must be B, C, or E. Statement (2) alone indicates that $x + y < -1$. If $(x + y) + z > 0$, then $z > 1$. Therefore, statement (2) alone is sufficient and the best answer is B.

85. How many integers n are there such that $r < n < s$?

(1) $s - r = 5$

(2) r and s are not integers.

From statement (1), it can be concluded that the number of integers is 4 if r and s are integers (e.g., 7 and 12) and the number of integers is 5 if r and s are not integers (e.g., 6.5 and 11.5). Therefore, the answer must be B, C, or E. Statement (2) alone is not sufficient since it gives no information about how far apart r and s are. From statements (1) and (2) together it follows that there are 5 integers between r and s. The best answer is C.

86. A total of 9 women and 12 men reside in the 21 apartments that are in a certain apartment building, one person to each apartment. If a poll taker is to select one of the apartments at random, what is the probability that the resident of the apartment selected will be a woman who is a student?

(1) Of the women, 4 are students.

(2) Of the women, 5 are not students.

The probability that the person selected will be a woman who is a student is equal to:

$$\frac{\text{the number of women students}}{\text{the total number of people in the apartments}}.$$

Statement (1) says the number of women students is 4, and since the total number of people in the apartments is known to be 21, statement (1) alone is sufficient. Thus, the answer must be A or D. Statement (2) is also sufficient, since if 5 women are not students and there are 9 women altogether, then $9 - 5 = 4$ women must be students. Since each of the statements alone is sufficient, the best answer is D.

87. Is x greater than 1.8 ?

(1) $x > 1.7$

(2) $x > 1.9$

Statement (1) alone is not sufficient to determine whether $x > 1.8$, because x could be a number between 1.7 and 1.8. Thus, the answer must be B, C, or E. Statement (2), together with the fact that $1.9 > 1.8$, implies that $x > 1.8$. Thus, (2) alone is sufficient. The best answer is B.

88. Hoses X and Y simultaneously fill an empty swimming pool that has a capacity of 50,000 liters. If the flow in each hose is independent of the flow in the other hose, how many hours will it take to fill the pool?

(1) Hose X alone would take 28 hours to fill the pool.

(2) Hose Y alone would take 36 hours to fill the pool.

Clearly neither statement (1) nor (2) alone is sufficient, since information about the filling rate for both hoses is needed. Thus, the answer must be C or E. Since hose X fills the pool in 28 hours, hose X fills $\frac{1}{28}$ of the pool in 1 hour. Since hose Y fills the pool in 36 hours, hose Y fills $\frac{1}{36}$ of the pool in 1 hour. Therefore, together they fill $\frac{1}{28} + \frac{1}{36} = \frac{4}{63}$ of the pool in 1 hour, so the time it will take them to fill the pool can be found by solving for t in $\frac{4}{63}(t) = 1$. Note that it is not actually necessary to do any of the computations. Since the two statements together are sufficient, the best answer is C.

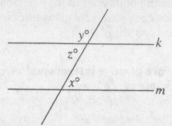

89. In the figure above, if lines k and m are parallel, what is the value of x ?

(1) $y = 120$

(2) $z = 60$

Because y and z are the degree measures of supplementary angles, statement (1) alone implies that $z = 180 - 120 = 60$. Since z and x are the degree measures of alternate interior angles, it follows that $z = x = 60$. Hence, statement (1) alone is sufficient and the answer must be A or D. Statement (2) implies that $x = 60$ also, since z and x must be equal, as stated above. Therefore, each statement alone is sufficient, and the best answer is D.

90. If x and y are integers, what is the value of y ?

(1) $xy = 27$

(2) $x = y^2$

Statement (1) alone is not sufficient to determine the value of y, since different pairs of integers could have the product 27, i.e., $(-3)(-9)$ or $(1)(27)$. Thus, the answer must be B, C, or E. Clearly statement (2), which states that $x = y^2$, does not determine the value of y, since x could have many different values. Hence, the answer must be C or E. From (2), if y^2 is substituted for x in statement (1), the result, $y^3 = 27$, implies that $y = 3$. Thus, both (1) and (2) together are sufficient to determine the value of y. The best answer is C.

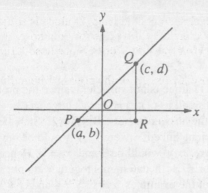

91. In the figure above, segments PR and QR are each parallel to one of the rectangular coordinate axes. Is the ratio of the length of QR to the length of PR equal to 1 ?

(1) $c = 3$ and $d = 4$.

(2) $a = -2$ and $b = -1$.

Note that the ratio of QR to PR is the slope of the line. Since two points are necessary to determine a line, and thus its slope, (1) and (2) together are sufficient, but neither alone is sufficient. Therefore, the best answer is C.

92. In a school election, if each of the 900 voters voted for either Edith or José (but not both), what percent of the female voters in this election voted for José?

(1) Eighty percent of the female voters voted for Edith.

(2) Sixty percent of the male voters voted for José.

Statement (1) is sufficient, since if 80 percent of the female voters voted for Edith, then $100\% - 80\% = 20\%$ of the female voters voted for José. Thus, the answer must be A or D. Statement (2) alone is not sufficient to answer the question, since it gives no information about female voters. Therefore, the best answer is A.

93. During week W, how much did it cost, per mile, for the gasoline used by car X ?

(1) During week W, car X used gasoline that cost $1.24 per gallon.

(2) During week W, car X was driven 270 miles.

Statement (1) is not sufficient, because it does not specify how many gallons of gasoline were bought or how many miles were driven. Thus, the answer must be B, C, or E. Statement (2) is also not sufficient since it does not specify how much money was spent on gasoline. Thus, the answer must be C or E. Since it is not known either how many gallons of gasoline were bought or the total amount spent on gasoline for the week, the two statements together are not sufficient to answer the question. The best answer is E.

94. If r and s are integers, is r divisible by 7 ?

(1) The product rs is divisible by 7.

(2) s is not divisible by 7.

If a product rs is divisible by the prime number 7, then either r is divisible by 7 or s is divisible by 7. Hence, statement (1) alone implies that either r or s is divisible by 7, but it is not sufficient to determine that r is divisible by 7. Therefore, the answer must be B, C, or E. Statement (2) alone is clearly not sufficient, since no information is given about r. Hence, the answer must be C or E. The two statements together are sufficient: If rs is divisible by 7 and s is not divisible by 7, then r is divisible by 7. Thus, the best answer is C.

95. If $\dfrac{m}{n} = \dfrac{5}{3}$, what is the value of $m + n$?

(1) $m > 0$

(2) $2m + n = 26$

Statement (1) alone is not sufficient since m and n could be any positive numbers in the ratio 5 : 3, e.g., 10 and 6 or 5 and 3. Thus, the answer must be B, C, or E. However, statement (2) alone is sufficient, since the equation in the question together with statement (2) form two equations in two unknowns, which can be solved. The values of n, m, and $n + m$ can then be determined. Therefore, the best answer is B.

96. If P and Q are each circular regions, what is the radius of the larger of these regions?

(1) The area of P plus the area of Q is equal to 90π.

(2) The larger circular region has a radius that is 3 times the radius of the smaller circular region.

Let r represent the radius of the smaller circular region, and let R represent the radius of the larger circular region. Then statement (1) implies that $\pi r^2 + \pi R^2 = 90\pi$, which is not enough to determine R. Therefore, the answer must be B, C, or E. Statement (2) implies that $R = 3r$, which by itself is clearly not enough to determine R. Hence, the answer is either C or E. If $R/3$ is substituted for r in $\pi r^2 + \pi R^2 = 90\pi$, the result is a single equation in R, which does determine R. Thus, the two statements together are sufficient, and the best answer is C.

97. Is z less than 0 ?

(1) $xy > 0$ and $yz < 0$.

(2) $x > 0$

Statement (1) is not sufficient to answer the question since both of the sets of values $x = 1$, $y = 1$, $z = -1$ and $x = -1$, $y = -1$, $z = 1$ are consistent with statement (1). Hence, the answer must be B, C, or E. Statement (2) alone is clearly not sufficient since it gives no information about z. Therefore, the answer must be C or E. The two statements together are sufficient. Since $xy > 0$ and $x > 0$, y must be positive; since $yz < 0$ and $y > 0$, z must be negative. Thus, the best answer is C.

98. If the total price of n equally priced shares of a certain stock was $12,000, what was the price per share of the stock?

   (1) If the price per share of the stock had been $1 more, the total price of the n shares would have been $300 more.

   (2) If the price per share of the stock had been $2 less, the total price of the n shares would have been 5 percent less.

Since the price per share of the stock is $\dfrac{\$12,000}{n}$, it suffices to determine the value of n. Statement (1) says that if the price of each of the n shares of the stock had been $1 more, the total increase would have been $300, or $n(\$1) = \$300$. It follows that $n = 300$, and statement (1) alone is sufficient. Thus, the answer must be A or D. Similarly, statement (2) says that if the price of each of the n shares had been reduced by $2, the total reduction in price would have been $0.05(\$12,000)$, or $2n = 0.05(\$12,000)$. Since the value of n can be determined from this equation, statement (2) alone is also sufficient, and the best answer is D.

99. What is the ratio of $x : y : z$?

   (1) $z = 1$ and $xy = 32$

   (2) $\dfrac{x}{y} = 2$ and $\dfrac{z}{y} = \dfrac{1}{4}$

Statement (1) alone is clearly not sufficient to answer the question. For example, if $x = 4$ and $y = 8$, the ratio is $4 : 8 : 1$, but if $x = 16$ and $y = 2$, then the ratio is $16 : 2 : 1$. Thus, the answer must be B, C, or E. Statement (2) alone is sufficient, since multiplying the two equations by y yields $x = 2y$ and $z = \dfrac{1}{4}y$. Therefore, the ratio is $2y : y : \dfrac{1}{4}y = 2 : 1 : \dfrac{1}{4}$. The best answer is B.

100. What is Ricky's age now?

   (1) Ricky is now twice as old as he was exactly 8 years ago.

   (2) Ricky's sister Teresa is now 3 times as old as Ricky was exactly 8 years ago.

Let r stand for Ricky's age now. Statement (1) implies that $r = 2(r - 8)$, so $r = 16$. Hence, statement (1) alone is sufficient, and the answer must be A or D. Letting t represent Teresa's age now, statement (2) implies that $t = 3(r - 8)$, which is not enough to determine Ricky's age. Thus, the best answer is A.

101. Is $xy > 5$?

   (1) $1 \le x \le 3$ and $2 \le y \le 4$.

   (2) $x + y = 5$

Statement (1) alone is not sufficient, since the product xy could be as small as $(1)(2) = 2$ or as large as $(3)(4) = 12$. Therefore, the answer must be B, C, or E. Statement (2) alone is not sufficient since if x were 1, y would be 4 and $xy = 4$; but if x were 2, y would be 3 and $xy = 6$. Hence, the answer must be C or E. Both statements together are not sufficient since both of the examples $x = 1$, $y = 4$ and $x = 2$, $y = 3$ are consistent with both statements. Therefore, the best answer is E.

102. In year X, 8.7 percent of the men in the labor force were unemployed in June compared with 8.4 percent in May. If the number of men in the labor force was the same for both months, how many men were unemployed in June of that year?

   (1) In May of year X, the number of unemployed men in the labor force was 3.36 million.

   (2) In year X, 120,000 more men in the labor force were unemployed in June than in May.

Since 8.7 percent of the men in the labor force were unemployed in June, the number of unemployed men could be calculated if the total number of men in the labor force were known. Let t represent the total number of men in the labor force. Statement (1) implies that $(8.4\%)t = 3,360,000$, from which the value of t can be determined. Therefore, statement (1) alone is sufficient, and the answer must be A or D. Statement (2) implies that $(8.7\% - 8.4\%)t = 120,000$. Since this can be solved for t, statement (2) alone is also sufficient to answer the question. The best answer is D.

103. If the average (arithmetic mean) of 4 numbers is 50, how many of the numbers are greater than 50?

   (1) None of the four numbers is equal to 50.

   (2) Two of the numbers are equal to 25.

If the four numbers were 25, 25, 26, and 124, their average would be 50 and they would satisfy both statement (1) and statement (2). But if the four numbers were 25, 25, 75, and 75, their average would also be 50 and they would also satisfy both statement (1) and statement (2). Since in the first case only one number is greater than 50 and in the second case two of the numbers are greater than 50, both statements together are not sufficient to answer the question. Thus, the best answer is E.

104. On Monday morning a certain machine ran continuously at a uniform rate to fill a production order. At what time did it completely fill the order that morning?

(1) The machine began filling the order at 9:30 a.m.

(2) The machine had filled $\frac{1}{2}$ of the order by 10:30 a.m. and $\frac{5}{6}$ of the order by 11:10 a.m.

Statement (1) is clearly not sufficient, since it merely states what time the machine began filling the order. Hence, the answer must be B, C, or E. From statement (2) it can be concluded that $\frac{5}{6} - \frac{1}{2} = \frac{1}{3}$ of the order was filled in 40 minutes; so the entire order was completely filled in $3 \times 40 = 120$ minutes, or 2 hours. Since half of the order was filled by 10:30 a.m., the entire order was filled by 11:30 a.m. Thus, statement (2) alone is sufficient, and the best answer is B.

105. If $n + k = m$, what is the value of k?

(1) $n = 10$
(2) $m + 10 = n$

It is given that $n + k = m$, so $k = m - n$. Thus, it suffices to determine the value of $m - n$. Clearly statement (1) alone is not sufficient because no information involving m is given. Thus, the answer must be B, C, or E. Statement (2) can be expressed as $m - n = -10$; so $k = -10$. Statement (2) alone is therefore sufficient, and the best answer is B.

106. A Town T has 20,000 residents, 60 percent of whom are female. What percent of the residents were born in Town T?

(1) The number of female residents who were born in Town T is twice the number of male residents who were <u>not</u> born in Town T.

(2) The number of female residents who were <u>not</u> born in Town T is twice the number of female residents who were born in Town T.

Statement (1) is not sufficient since the total number of male and female residents born in Town T cannot be determined; so the answer must be B, C, or E. From statement (2) alone, one third of the female residents were born in Town T, but no information is given about the male residents born in town; so (2) is not sufficient to answer the question. Thus, the answer must be C or E. From (1) and (2) together the entries in the table below can be determined. First calculate the number of female and male residents: 60% of 20,000 = 12,000 female residents, and 20,000 – 12,000 = 8,000 male residents. Statement (2) implies that one third of the 12,000 female residents, or 4,000, were born in town. Then statement (1) implies that the number of male residents who were not born in town is half the number of females born in town, or 2,000. Hence, the number of males born in town is 8,000 – 2,000 = 6,000. So, out of 20,000 residents, 4,000 + 6,000 = 10,000 were born in town, or 50% of the residents. Thus, the best answer is C.

	Female	Male	Total
Born in Town T	4,000	6,000	10,000
Not Born in Town T	8,000	2,000	10,000
Total	12,000	8,000	20,000

107. Can the positive integer n be written as the sum of two different positive prime numbers?

(1) n is greater than 3.
(2) n is odd.

The prime numbers are 2, 3, 5, 7, 11, 13, 17, 19, etc., that is, integers $p > 1$ whose only positive factors are 1 and p. Statement (1) is not sufficient to answer the question since $n = 4$ cannot be written as the sum of two different primes, but $n = 5$ can ($5 = 2 + 3$). Note that $4 = 1 + 3 = 2 + 2$, but neither of these sums satisfies both requirements of the question. Hence, the answer must be B, C, or E. Statement (2) is not sufficient since some odd integers can be written as the sum of two different primes (e.g., 5), whereas others cannot (e.g., 11). Note that if 11 were the sum of two primes, one of them would have to be even, since the sum of two odd integers is even. But the only even prime is 2, and $11 - 2 = 9$, which is not a prime. This reasoning shows that the only odd integers n greater than 3 that can be expressed as the sum of two different prime numbers are those for which $n - 2$ is an odd prime. Thus, (2) alone is not sufficient, nor are (1) and (2) together, and the best answer is E.

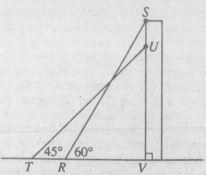

108. In the figure above, segments *RS* and *TU* represent two positions of the same ladder leaning against the side *SV* of a wall. The length of *TV* is how much greater than the length of *RV* ?

(1) The length of *TU* is 10 meters.

(2) The length of *RV* is 5 meters.

Since the triangle *TUV* is a 45°– 45°– 90° triangle, the lengths of the sides are in the ratio $1 : 1 : \sqrt{2}$; so the length of any one side determines the length of the other two sides. Similarly, the triangle *RSV* is a 30°– 60° – 90° triangle with the lengths of the sides in the ratio $1 : \sqrt{3} : 2$; so the length of any one side determines the length of the other two sides. Also, the length of the hypotenuse is the same in both triangles, because it is the length of the ladder. Hence, the length of any one side of either triangle determines the lengths of all sides of both triangles. Each statement alone is sufficient since each statement gives a side of one of the triangles. Therefore, the best answer is D.

109. If both *x* and *y* are nonzero numbers, what is the value of $\dfrac{y}{x}$?

(1) $x = 6$

(2) $y^2 = x^2$

Statement (1) alone is not sufficient, since it states only the value of *x*. Thus, the answer must be B, C, or E. Statement (2) alone is not sufficient because $\dfrac{x}{y}$ could be 1 or –1, but it cannot be determined which of the two values $\dfrac{x}{y}$ equals. Thus, the answer must be C or E. The two statements together are not sufficient since *y* could be either 6 or – 6, which implies $\dfrac{x}{y}$ could be either 1 or –1. The best answer is E.

110. If $x = 0. rstu$, where *r, s, t,* and *u* each represent a nonzero digit of *x*, what is the value of *x* ?

(1) $r = 3s = 2t = 6u$

(2) The product of *r* and *u* is equal to the product of *s* and *t*.

If the values of *r, s, t,* and *u* were known, the value of *x* could be found. Statement (1) alone is sufficient to find these values. Since $r = 6u$ and *r* and *u* must be nonzero digits,

u = 1 and *r* = 6. If *u* were any larger, *r* could not be a digit (i.e., 0, 1, 2, 3, 4, 5, 6, 7, 8, or 9). Since *u* = 1 and $2t = 6u$, *t* = 3. Since $3s = 6u$, *s* = 2, so *x* = 0.6231, and statement (1) is sufficient to answer the question. Thus, the answer must be A or D. Statement (2) alone is not sufficient since, for example, any digits with *r* = *s* and *u* = *t* would satisfy statement (2). Therefore, the best answer is A.

111. What were the gross revenues from ticket sales for a certain film during the second week in which it was shown?

(1) Gross revenues during the second week were $1.5 million less than during the first week.

(2) Gross revenues during the third week were $2.0 million less than during the first week.

Statement (1) alone is not sufficient, since the amount of gross revenues during the first week is not given; so the answer must be B, C, or E. Statement (2) alone is also not sufficient, since it gives no information about gross revenues during the second week. Thus, the answer must be C or E. Statements (1) and (2) together are still not sufficient, since additional information is needed, such as the amount of gross revenues during either the first or the third week. Therefore, the best answer is E.

112. What number is 15 percent of *x* ?

(1) 18 is 6 percent of *x*.

(2) $\dfrac{2}{3}$ of *x* is 200.

The question can be answered if the value of *x* is known. According to statement (1), $18 = 0.06x$, which can be solved for *x*. Thus, (1) alone is sufficient, and the answer must be A or D. Statement (2) alone is also sufficient, since it states that $\dfrac{2}{3}x = 200$, which can be solved for *x*. Therefore, the best answer is D.

113. How many books does Ricardo have?

(1) If Ricardo had 15 fewer books, he would have only half as many as he actually has.

(2) Ricardo has twice as many fiction books as nonfiction books.

From statement (1) it can be concluded that 15 books represent half the total number of books that Ricardo has. Alternatively, if *n* represents the number of books that Ricardo has, then it follows from (1) that $n - 15 = \dfrac{1}{2}n$, which can be solved for *n*.

Thus (1) alone is sufficient, and the answer must be A or D. Statement (2) alone is not sufficient, since it gives only the ratio of the number of fiction to the number of nonfiction books. Thus, the best answer is A.

114. What was the amount of money donated to a certain charity?

   (1) Of the amount donated, 40 percent came from corporate donations.

   (2) Of the amount donated, $1.5 million came from noncorporate donations.

The amount of money donated was the total of corporate and noncorporate donations. Statement (1) alone is not sufficient, since it gives only the portion that represented corporate donations. Thus, the answer must be B, C, or E. Similarly, statement (2) alone is not sufficient, since it gives only the dollar amount that represented noncorporate donations. Thus, the answer must be C or E. If the dollar amount donated was x, then (1) and (2) together can be expressed as $0.40x + \$1,500,000 = x$, which can be solved for x. Thus, the best answer is C.

115. Is x a negative number?

   (1) $9x > 10x$

   (2) $x + 3$ is positive.

Statement (1) alone is sufficient to conclude that x is a negative number, since $9x$ cannot be greater than $10x$ if x is zero or positive. Thus, the answer must be A or D. Statement (2) alone is not sufficient, since $x + 3$ is positive for values of $x > -3$, which include -2 and -1, for example, but also all positive values of x. The best answer is therefore A.

116. John took a test that had 60 questions numbered from 1 to 60. How many of the questions did he answer correctly?

   (1) The number of questions he answered correctly in the first half of the test was 7 more than the number he answered correctly in the second half of the test.

   (2) He answered $\frac{5}{6}$ of the odd-numbered questions correctly and $\frac{4}{5}$ of the even-numbered questions correctly.

Statement (1) is not sufficient because it states that $f = 7 + s$, where f is the number of questions answered correctly in the first half of the test and s is the number answered correctly in the second half. Since the equation cannot be solved for $f + s$, the total number of questions answered correctly, the answer must be B, C, or E. From statement (2) alone it can be determined that the number of questions answered correctly was $\frac{5}{6}(30) + \frac{4}{5}(30)$. Thus, the best answer is B.

117. The perimeter of a rectangular garden is 360 feet. What is the length of the garden?

   (1) The length of the garden is twice the width.

   (2) The difference between the length and width of the garden is 60 feet.

If ℓ and w denote the length and width of the garden, respectively, then it is given that the perimeter is $2(\ell + w) = 360$, or $\ell + w = 180$. Statement (1) says that $\ell = 2w$; so ℓ can be determined by substituting $\frac{\ell}{2}$ for w in the equation $\ell + w = 180$ and solving the resulting equation. Thus, (1) alone is sufficient, and the answer must be A or D. Statement (2) says that $\ell - w = 60$; so ℓ can be determined by solving the two equations $\ell - w = 60$ and $\ell + w = 180$ simultaneously. Thus, (2) alone is also sufficient, and the best answer is D.

118. If $2x(5n) = t$, what is the value of t?

   (1) $x = n + 3$

   (2) $2x = 32$

To determine the value of t, the values of x and n must both be known. Statement (1) alone is not sufficient because it merely relates the values of x and n, and statement (2) alone is not sufficient because it yields only the value of x. Thus, the answer must be C or E. Since the value of x determined from equation (2) can be used in equation (1) to determine the value of n, statements (1) and (2) together are sufficient, and the best answer is C.

119. In $\triangle XYZ$, what is the length of YZ?

   (1) The length of XY is 3.

   (2) The length of XZ is 5.

Given the length of one side of a triangle, it can be concluded that the sum of the lengths of the other two sides is greater than that given length; but the length of either of the other two sides can be any positive number. Thus, neither statement (1) alone nor statement (2) alone is sufficient, and the answer must be C or E. From (1) and (2) together, by using the triangle inequality mentioned above, only a range of values for YZ can be determined. If the length of YZ is k, then $3 + 5 > k$ and $3 + k > 5$, or $2 < k < 8$. Alternatively, note that the length of YZ depends on the size of the angle having sides XY and XZ. The best answer is E.

120. If Jill's average (arithmetic mean) score for three games of bowling was 168, what was her lowest score?

    (1)   Jill's highest score was 204.

    (2)   The sum of Jill's two highest scores was 364.

Jill's average score was the sum of her scores divided by 3, or $168 = \dfrac{\ell + m + h}{3}$, where ℓ, m, and h are her lowest, middle, and highest scores, respectively. Statement (1) alone is not sufficient, since substituting $h = 204$ in the equation yields only the value of $\ell + m$. Thus, the answer must be B, C, or E. Statement (2) alone is sufficient, since substituting $m + h = 364$ yields $168 = \dfrac{\ell + 364}{3}$, which can be solved for ℓ. Therefore, the best answer is B.

121. An empty rectangular swimming pool has uniform depth. How long will it take to fill the pool with water?

    (1)   Water will be pumped in at the rate of 240 gallons per hour (1 cubic foot = 7.5 gallons).

    (2)   The pool is 60 feet long and 25 feet wide.

To determine how long it will take to fill the pool, it suffices to know the capacity of the pool and the filling rate, that is, the rate at which the water will be pumped into the pool. Statement (1) gives the filling rate, but gives no information about the size of the pool; statement (2) gives incomplete information about the size of the pool and no information about the filling rate. Thus, neither statement alone is sufficient, and the answer must be C or E. Statements (1) and (2) together are still not sufficient, since the depth of the pool is not specified, and so the capacity of the pool cannot be determined. Thus, the best answer is E.

122. In Jefferson School, 300 students study French or Spanish or both. If 100 of these students do not study French, how many of these students study both French and Spanish?

    (1)   Of the 300 students, 60 do not study Spanish.

    (2)   A total of 240 of the students study Spanish.

One way to solve a problem of this kind is to represent the data by a Venn diagram. Thus, if x is the number of students who study both French and Spanish, y is the number who do not study Spanish (i.e., study only French), and 100 do not study French, then the information can be represented by the Venn diagram below, where $300 = x + y + 100$:

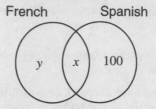

Statement (1) alone is sufficient, since it gives the number of students who do not study Spanish, i.e., gives the value of y in the equation $300 = x + y + 100$, from which the value of x can be determined. Thus, the answer must be A or D. Statement (2) alone is also sufficient, since $240 = x + 100$, from which the value of x can again be determined. The best answer is therefore D.

123. Is the value of n closer to 50 than to 75 ?

    (1) $75 - n > n - 50$

    (2) $n > 60$

The value of n is equidistant between 50 and 75 provided that n is the midpoint between 75 and 50, i.e., $n = \dfrac{50 + 75}{2} = 62.5$. Alternatively, n is equidistant between 50 and 75 provided that $75 - n = n - 50$, as indicated on the number line below.

$$n - 50 \;=\; 75 - n$$

$$\underset{\substack{\;\\ 50 \qquad\quad n \qquad\quad 75}}{n \,\vdash\!\!-\!\!-\!\!-\!\!\dashv\!\!-\!\!-\!\!-\!\!\dashv}$$

It follows that the value of n is closer to 50 than to 75 provided that $75 - n > n - 50$, which is statement (1). Thus, (1) alone is sufficient, and the answer must be A or D. Statement (2) alone is not sufficient, since for values of n between 60 and 62.5, n is closer to 50; whereas, for values of n greater than 62.5, n is closer to 75. Thus, the best answer is A.

124. In the equation $x^2 + bx + 12 = 0$, x is a variable and b is a constant. What is the value of b ?

    (1) $x - 3$ is a factor of $x^2 + bx + 12$.

    (2)   4 is a root of the equation $x^2 + bx + 12 = 0$.

Statement (1) implies that the other factor of $x^2 + bx + 12$ is $x - 4$, since $\dfrac{12}{-3} = -4$. This gives $(x - 3)(x - 4) = x^2 - 7x + 12 = x^2 + bx + 12$, which determines the value of b. Thus, the answer must be A or D. Statement (2) implies that $4^2 + 4b + 12 = 0$, from which the value of b can again be determined. Therefore, the best answer is D.

-284-

125. **If Juan had a doctor's appointment on a certain day, was the appointment on a Wednesday?**

    (1)   **Exactly 60 hours before the appointment, it was Monday.**

    (2)   **The appointment was between 1:00 p.m. and 9:00 p.m.**

Statement (1) alone is not sufficient, since it is not known at what time on Monday it was 60 hours before the appointment. For example, if it was 9:00 Monday morning, 60 hours later would be 9:00 Wednesday evening; but if it was 9:00 Monday evening, 60 hours later would be 9:00 Thursday morning. Thus, the answer must be B, C, or E. Statement (2) alone is clearly not sufficient since no information is given about the day of the appointment, and the answer must be C or E. From (1) and (2) together it can be concluded that the appointment was on a Wednesday: 60 hours before any time in the afternoon is a time in the morning two days earlier; so 60 hours before the appointment it was Monday morning, and the appointment was Wednesday afternoon. Thus, (1) and (2) together are sufficient, and the best answer is C.

126. **What is the value of $b + c$?**

    (1) $ab + cd + ac + bd = 6$

    (2) $a + d = 4$

Statement (1) can be reordered $(ab + bd) + (ac + cd)$ and factored to give $b(a + d) + c(a + d) = (a + d)(b + c)$, which equals 6; but the value of $b + c$ cannot be determined unless the value of $a + d$ is known. Thus, (1) alone is not sufficient, and the answer must be B, C, or E. Statement (2) alone is clearly not sufficient because it gives no information about b and c, but it does give the needed information in (1). Thus, (1) and (2) together are sufficient, and the best answer is C.

127. **If m is an integer, is m odd?**

    (1) $\dfrac{m}{2}$ is <u>not</u> an even integer.

    (2) $m - 3$ is an even integer.

Statement (1) alone is not sufficient since m could be the odd integer 3 or the even integer 10 and satisfy the condition in (1). Thus, the answer must be B, C, or E. Statement (2) alone is sufficient, since an odd integer minus an odd integer is even (e.g., $9 - 3 = 6$); whereas, an even integer minus an odd integer is odd (e.g., $8 - 3 = 5$). Thus, the best answer is B.

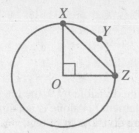

128. **What is the circumference of the circle above with center O ?**

    (1)   **The perimeter of $\triangle OXZ$ is $20 + 10\sqrt{2}$.**

    (2)   **The length of arc XYZ is 5π.**

The circumference of the circle can be found if the radius r is known. $\triangle OXZ$ is a right triangle with $OX = OZ = r$ and perimeter $2r + XZ$. From the Pythagorean theorem,

$$XZ = \sqrt{r^2 + r^2} = \sqrt{2r^2} = r\sqrt{2} \; ;$$ the perimeter is then $2r + r\sqrt{2}$. According to statement (1), the perimeter of $\triangle OXZ$ is

$20 + 10\sqrt{2}$. Thus, $2r + r\sqrt{2} = 20 + 10\sqrt{2} = 2(10) + 10\sqrt{2}$, and (1) alone is sufficient. The answer must be A or D. Statement (2) alone is sufficient, since the length of arc XYZ is

$\dfrac{1}{4}$ of the circumference. Therefore, the best answer is D.

129. **At the beginning of last month, a stationery store had in stock 250 writing pads, which had cost the store $0.75 each. During the same month, the store made only one purchase of writing pads. What was the total amount spent by the store on the writing pads it had in stock at the end of last month?**

    (1)   **Last month the store purchased 150 writing pads for $0.80 each.**

    (2)   **Last month the total revenue from the sale of writing pads was $180.**

It is known that the pads in stock at the beginning of the month cost the store $250 \times \$0.75$, but the cost of the additional pads purchased is not known. In addition, the number of pads sold and their cost is not known. Since statement (1) gives no information about the number and cost of the pads sold, it is not sufficient, and the answer must be B, C, or E. Statement (2) alone is not sufficient since it does not provide any of the information needed. Thus, the answer must be C or E. Statements (1) and (2) together still do not provide sufficient information, since the number of pads sold and their cost cannot be determined. The best answer is E.

130. If y is an integer, is y^3 divisible by 9 ?

(1) y is divisible by 4.

(2) y is divisible by 6.

In order for y^3 to be divisible by 9, the integer y must be divisible by 3. Statement (1) alone is not sufficient because not all multiples of 4 are divisible by 3 (e.g., $y = 12$ is, but $y = 16$ is not); however, statement (2) alone is sufficient, since any number divisible by 6 is also divisible by 3. Thus, the best answer is B.

131. What was the ratio of the number of cars to the number of trucks produced by Company X last year?

(1) Last year, if the number of cars produced by Company X had been 8 percent greater, the number of cars produced would have been 150 percent of the number of trucks produced by Company X.

(2) Last year Company X produced 565,000 cars and 406,800 trucks.

Let c equal the number of cars and t the number of trucks produced by Company X last year. Statement (1) can be expressed as $1.08c = 1.5t$, so that the ratio $\dfrac{c}{t}$ equals $\dfrac{1.5}{1.08}$. Thus, (1) alone is sufficient, and the answer must be A or D. In statement (2), the values of c and t are given; so the ratio $\dfrac{c}{t}$ can be determined. Thus, (2) alone is also sufficient, and the best answer is D.

132. How long did it take Betty to drive nonstop on a trip from her home to Denver, Colorado?

(1) If Betty's average speed for the trip had been $1\dfrac{1}{2}$ times as fast, the trip would have taken 2 hours.

(2) Betty's average speed for the trip was 50 miles per hour.

Given that $rt = d$ where r is the rate in miles per hour, t is the time in hours, and d is the distance in miles, the distance Betty drove was rt. According to the information in statement (1), if Betty drove $\dfrac{3}{2}$ times as fast, then it took her $\dfrac{2}{3}$ as much time, since $\left(\dfrac{3}{2}r\right)\left(\dfrac{2}{3}t\right) = rt$. Thus, $\dfrac{2t}{3} = 2$ or $t = 3$; so (1) alone is sufficient, and the answer must be A or D. Statement (2) can be expressed as $50t = d$, but the time cannot be determined without knowing the distance. Thus, (2) alone is not sufficient, and the best answer is A.

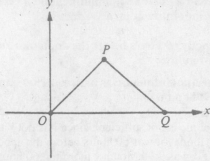

133. In the rectangular coordinate system above, if $OP < PQ$, is the area of region OPQ greater than 48 ?

(1) The coordinates of point P are (6, 8).

(2) The coordinates of point Q are (13, 0).

The area of a triangle with base b and altitude h is $\dfrac{hb}{2}$. From statement (1), $h = 8$, which is the y-coordinate of P, but the x-coordinate gives the length of only part of the base, as can be seen in the figure below.

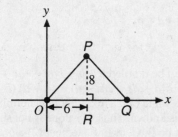

From the Pythagorean theorem $OP = 10$, and since $OP < PQ$ it follows that $PQ > 10$, and so $RQ > 6$. Thus, base $OQ > 12$ and the area of $\triangle OPQ$ is greater than $\dfrac{(8)(12)}{2} = 48$. Therefore, (1) alone is sufficient, and the answer must be A or D. From statement (2) it can be concluded that the length of OQ is 13, the x-coordinate of Q; however, there is no information given about the altitude. Therefore, (2) alone is not sufficient, and the best answer is A.

$$S = \frac{\dfrac{2}{n}}{\dfrac{1}{x} + \dfrac{2}{3x}}$$

134. In the expression above, if $xn \neq 0$, what is the value of S ?

    (1) $x = 2n$

    (2) $n = \dfrac{1}{2}$

It may be helpful first to simplify the given equation:

$$S = \frac{\dfrac{2}{n}}{\dfrac{1}{x} + \dfrac{2}{3x}} = \frac{\dfrac{2}{n}}{\dfrac{3}{3x} + \dfrac{2}{3x}} = \frac{\dfrac{2}{n}}{\dfrac{5}{3x}} = \frac{2}{n}\left(\frac{3x}{5}\right) = \frac{6x}{5n}$$

Substituting $x = 2n$ from statement (1) gives $S = \dfrac{6(2n)}{5n} = \dfrac{12}{5}$.
Thus, (1) alone is sufficient, and the answer must be A or D.

Statement (2) alone is not sufficient, since substituting $n = \dfrac{1}{2}$

gives $S = \dfrac{6x}{5\left(\dfrac{1}{2}\right)}$, and the value of S cannot be determined

unless the value of x is known. The best answer is A.

135. If S is the infinite sequence
$S_1 = 9$, $S_2 = 99$, $S_3 = 999, \ldots, S_k = 10^k - 1, \ldots,$
is every term in S divisible by the prime number p ?

    (1) p is greater than 2.

    (2) At least one term in sequence S is divisible by p.

For a problem of this kind it may be helpful to examine various prime numbers subject to the constraints imposed by statements (1) and (2). Regarding statement (1), p could be any of the prime numbers 3, 5, 7, 11, etc. Since each of the numbers 9, 99, 999, etc., is divisible by 3, whereas none of them is divisible by 5, it follows that (1) alone is not sufficient. Thus, the answer must be B, C, or E. Regarding statement (2), if the second term, 99, is examined it can be seen that it is divisible by both 3 and 11; the first term, 9, is divisible by only 3. Thus, (2) alone is not sufficient, and the answer must be C or E. Since the prime numbers considered in (2), namely, 3 and 11, satisfy statement (1), it follows that (1) and (2) together are not sufficient, and the best answer is E.

136. In the figure above, is $CD > BC$?

    (1) $AD = 20$

    (2) $AB = CD$

Statement (1) gives the total length of the segment shown, which has no bearing on the relative sizes of CD and BC. Statement (2) says that AB and CD are equal, which also has no bearing on the relative sizes of BC and CD. Thus the answer must be C or E. Considering statements (1) and (2) together, if lengths AB and CD were each a little larger than pictured, e.g.,

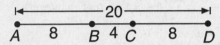

then $BC < CD$. But if lengths AB and CD were a little smaller than pictured, e.g., then $BC > CD$. Therefore, both statements together are not sufficient to answer the question, and the answer is E.

137. How many more men than women are in the room?

    (1) There is a total of 20 women and men in the room.

    (2) The number of men in the room equals the square of the number of women in the room.

If w is the number of women in the room and m is the number of men in the room, then the question is: what is the value of $m - w$? Statement (1) says that $w + m = 20$, which is not sufficient to answer the question, and the answer must be B, C, or E. Statement (2) says that $m = w^2$, which has several solutions: e.g., $m = 4$, $w = 2$, or $m = 9$, $w = 3$. These cases would give different answers to the value of $m - w$. So, statement (2) is not sufficient to answer the question. However, if both statements are used, then

$$w + m = 20 = w + w^2$$

Therefore,
$$w^2 + w - 20 = 0$$
$$(w + 5)(w - 4) = 0$$
$$w = -5 \text{ or } 4$$

Thus, the two statements together yield a single positive solution, $w = 4$, which means that $m = 16$ and $m - w = 12$. Therefore, both statements together are sufficient to answer the question, and the answer is C.

138. If n is an integer, is $\dfrac{100-n}{n}$ an integer?

    (1) $n > 4$

    (2) $n^2 = 25$

Statement (1) states that $n > 4$, which means that n could be 5 or 6 (among many other possibilities).

If $n = 5$, $\dfrac{100-n}{n} = \dfrac{100-5}{5} = 19$ (an integer)

If $n = 6$, $\dfrac{100-n}{n} = \dfrac{100-6}{6} = 15.6$ (not an integer)

So statement (1) is not sufficient, and the answer must be B, C, or E. Statement (2) says $n^2 = 25$, or $n = 5$ or -5

If $n = 5$, $\dfrac{100-n}{n}$ is an integer (see above).

If $n = -5$, $\dfrac{100-n}{n} = \dfrac{100-(-5)}{n} = \dfrac{105}{-5} = -21$ (an integer).

Therefore, statement (2) alone is sufficient, and the answer is B.

139. Last Friday a certain shop sold $\dfrac{3}{4}$ of the sweaters in its inventory. Each sweater sold for $20. What was the total revenue last Friday from the sale of these sweaters?

    (1) When the shop opened last Friday, there were 160 sweaters in its inventory.

    (2) All but 40 sweaters in the shop's inventory were sold last Friday.

Statement (1) says there are 160 sweaters in the inventory.

Thus, the total revenue would be $\dfrac{3}{4}(160)$, the number sold, times $20, or $2,400. So, statement (1) is sufficient to answer the question and the answer must be A or D. Statement (2) alone is also sufficient to answer the question because the number not sold, 40 sweaters, must equal $\dfrac{1}{4}$ of the inventory.

Thus, the inventory must be 4×40, or 160 sweaters, which is what statement (1) says. Therefore, each statement alone is sufficient to answer the question, and the answer is D.

140. A jar contains 30 marbles, of which 20 are red and 10 are blue. If 9 of the marbles are removed, how many of the marbles left in the jar are red?

    (1) Of the marbles removed, the ratio of the number of red ones to the number of blue ones is 2 : 1.

    (2) Of the first 6 marbles removed, 4 are red.

From statement (1) we know that of the 9 marbles removed, the ratio of red to blue was 2 to 1; thus 6 red and 3 blue marbles were removed. Since there were originally 20 red marbles in the jar, the number of red marbles remaining in the jar is $20 - 6$, or 14. Therefore, statement (1) alone is sufficient to answer the question, and the answer must be A or D. Statement (2) is not sufficient alone to answer the question because knowing that 4 of the first 6 marbles removed were red does not tell us how many of the other 3 marbles removed were red. Therefore, statement (1) alone is sufficient but statement (2) alone is not sufficient, and the answer is A.

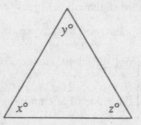

141. Is the triangle above equilateral?

    (1) $x = y$

    (2) $z = 60$

For the triangle to be equilateral, it must be true that $x = y = z = 60$. Statement (1) says that x and y are equal, but not necessarily equal to 60. Therefore, statement (1) alone is not sufficient to answer the question, and the answer must be B, C, or E. Statement (2) says that $z = 60$, which means that $x + y$ must be 120. However, x and y are not necessarily 60 and 60. Thus statement (2) alone is not sufficient. But, both statements (1) and (2) together are sufficient since $x = y$ and $z = 60$ is sufficient to show that $x = y = z = 60$, and the answer is C.

142. If $w + z = 28$, what is the value of wz ?

    (1) w and z are positive integers.

    (2) w and z are consecutive odd integers.

Statement (1) says that w and z are both positive, which is not sufficient to answer the question because, for example, if $w = 20$ and $z = 8$, then $wz = 160$, and if $w = 10$ and $z = 18$, then $wz = 180$, and the answer must be B, C, or E. Statement (2) says that w and z are consecutive odd integers. You can look at some consecutive odd integers that are less than 28, e.g.,

          . . . 11, 13, 15, 17, 19, 21, 23 . . .

and note that the only two consecutive integers that add to 28 are 13 and 15, which means that wz must be (13)(15), or 195. Or, more formally, the consecutive odd integers w and z could be represented by $2n + 1$ and $2n + 3$, where n is any integer. Therefore,

$$w + z = (2n + 1) + (2n + 3) = 28$$

$$4n + 4 = 28$$
$$4n = 24$$
$$n = 6$$

Thus, $w = 2(6) + 1 = 13$, and $z = 2(6) + 3 = 15$. So, statement (2) alone is sufficient but statement (1) alone is not sufficient, and the answer is B.

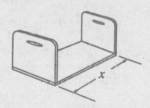

143. Will the first 10 volumes of a 20-volume encyclopedia fit upright in the bookrack shown above?

    (1) $x = 50$ centimeters

    (2) Twelve of the volumes have an average (arithmetic mean) thickness of 5 centimeters.

Statement (1) establishes the length of the bookrack but does not give any information about the thickness of the volumes, so it is not sufficient to answer the question, and the answer is B, C, or E. Statement (2) establishes the average thickness of 12 of the volumes, but does not give any information about the average thickness of the first ten volumes. So statement (2) is not sufficient to answer the question. By the same reasoning used in the discussion of statement (2), statements (1) and (2) together are not sufficient to answer the question, and the answer is E.

144. Is $ax = 3 - bx$?

    (1) $x(a + b) = 3$

    (2) $a = b = 1.5$ and $x = 1$.

From statement (1)
$$x(a + b) = 3$$
$$ax + bx = 3$$
$$ax = 3 - bx$$

Thus statement (1) alone is sufficient, and the answer is A or D. From statement (2), substituting the values into $ax = 3 - bx$, you can see that $1.5(1) = 3 - (1.5)(1)$ is true. Therefore, statement (2) alone is sufficient. Therefore, each statement alone is sufficient, and the answer is D.

145. What is the value of the integer x ?

    (1) x is a prime number.

    (2) $31 \leq x \leq 37$

Statement (1) allows integer x to be any prime, so the statement is not sufficient to determine the value of x, and the answer is B, C, or E. Statement (2) allows integer x to be 31, 32, 33, 34, 35, 36, or 37, two of which, 31 and 37, are prime numbers. Thus, neither statement (2) alone nor statements (1) and (2) together are sufficient to determine a single numerical value of x, and the answer is E.

146. While on a straight road, car X and car Y are traveling at different constant rates. If car X is now 1 mile ahead of car Y, how many minutes from now will car X be 2 miles ahead of car Y ?

    (1) Car X is traveling at 50 miles per hour and car Y is traveling at 40 miles per hour.

    (2) 3 minutes ago car X was $\frac{1}{2}$ mile ahead of car Y.

The question is how long will it take car X to get 1 mile farther ahead of car Y than it is now. Statement (1) tells you that at their constant rates, car X would increase its distance from car Y by 10 miles every hour or, equivalently, 1 mile every 6 minutes. Thus, statement (1) alone is sufficient to answer the question, and the answer is A or D. Statement (2) tells you that car X increases its distance from car Y by 0.5 mile every 3 minutes, which is equivalent to 1 mile every 6 minutes. Therefore, each statement alone is sufficient to answer the question, and the answer is D.

147. In what year was Ellen born?

    (1)   Ellen's brother Pete, who is $1\frac{1}{2}$ years older than Ellen, was born in 1956.

    (2)   In 1975 Ellen turned 18 years old.

Statement (1) tells you that Pete was born sometime in 1956. If he was born in the latter half of 1956, then Ellen, who is $1\frac{1}{2}$ years younger than Pete, was born in 1958. If Pete was born in the first half of 1956, then Ellen was born in 1957. Thus statement (1) alone is not sufficient to determine in what year Ellen was born, and the answer is B, C, or E. Statement (2) tells you that Ellen had her 18th birthday sometime during 1975. Thus, Ellen had to have been born 18 years earlier sometime during 1957. Therefore, statement (2) alone is sufficient but statement (1) alone is not sufficient, and the answer is B.

148. Is 2^x greater than 100 ?

    (1) $2^{\sqrt{x}} = 8$

    (2) $\dfrac{1}{2^x} < 0.01$

From statement (1), $2^{\sqrt{x}} = 8 = 2^3$. Thus, $\sqrt{x} = 3$, which implies that $x = 9$. Since 2^9 is greater than 100, statement (1) alone is sufficient to answer the question, and the answer is A or D. From statement (2), $\dfrac{1}{2^x} < 0.01$ implies that $2^x > \dfrac{1}{0.01}$, or $2^x > 100$, which is sufficient to answer the question. Therefore, each statement alone is sufficient to answer the question, and the answer is D.

149. What is the number of female employees in Company X ?

    (1)   If Company X were to hire 14 more people and all of these people were females, the ratio of the number of male employees to the number of female employees would then be 16 to 9.

    (2)   Company X has 105 more male employees than female employees.

If you let the number of female employees in Company X be f and the number of male employees be m, then according to statement (1), if 14 females are hired, the ratio of males to females can be expressed as $\dfrac{m}{f+14}$, which equals $\dfrac{16}{9}$. Since the equation $\dfrac{m}{f+14} = \dfrac{16}{9}$ has two unknowns, it is not sufficient to determine the value of f, and the answer is B, C, or E. Statement (2) tells you that $m = f + 105$. Again, this equation involves two unknowns and is not sufficient alone to determine the value of f. However, if the two equations are used together, f can be determined. Substituting $f + 105$ for m in the first equation yields

$$\frac{f+105}{f+14} = \frac{16}{9}$$

$$16f + 224 = 9f + 945$$

$$7f = 721$$

$$f = 103$$

Thus, both statements together are sufficient, and the answer is C.

150. Is the integer x divisible by 36 ?

    (1) x is divisible by 12.

    (2) x is divisible by 9.

When x is expressed as a product of prime numbers, this product contains at least two 2's and two 3's (since $36 = 2 \times 2 \times 3 \times 3$). By similar reasoning statement (1) implies that the prime factorization of x contains at least two 2's and at least one 3, and statement (2) implies that the prime factorization of x contains at least two 3's and may or may not contain 2's. So neither statement alone is sufficient, and the answer is C or E. However, both statements together imply that the prime factorization of x contains at least two 2's and two 3's, so x is divisible by 36. Thus, both statements together are sufficient, and the answer is C.

151. What is the average (arithmetic mean) of j and k ?

    (1)   The average (arithmetic mean) of $j + 2$ and $k + 4$ is 11.

    (2)   The average (arithmetic mean) of $j, k,$ and 14 is 10.

From statement (1) the average of $j + 2$ and $k + 4$ is 11. Thus,

$$\frac{(j+2)+(k+4)}{2} = 11$$

$$\frac{j+k+6}{2} = 11$$

$$\frac{j+k}{2} + \frac{6}{2} = 11$$

$$\frac{j+k}{2} = 8$$

So, statement (1) alone is sufficient to determine the average of j and $k,$ and the answer is A or D. Statement (2) says that the mean of $j, k,$ and 14 is 10, or

$$\frac{j+k+14}{3} = 10$$

$$j + k + 14 = 30$$

$$j + k = 16$$

$$\frac{j+k}{2} = \frac{16}{2} = 8$$

So, statement (2) alone is also sufficient to determine the average of j and $k.$ Therefore, each statement alone is sufficient, and the answer is D.

152. What is the value of $a - b$?

    (1) $a = b + 4$
    (2) $(a - b)^2 = 16$

From statement (1), $a = b + 4,$ or $a - b = 4.$ Thus statement (1) alone is sufficient to find a single numerical value of $a - b,$ and the answer is A or D. In statement (2) you can conclude that since $(a - b)^2 = 16,$ either $a - b = 4$ or $a - b = -4.$ Thus, statement (2) alone is not sufficient to determine a single numerical value of $a - b.$ Therefore, statement (1) alone is sufficient, and the answer is A.

153. Is $rst = 1$?

    (1) $rs = 1$
    (2) $st = 1$

Statement (1) establishes that $rs = 1,$ but since you do not know the value of $t,$ you do not know if $rst = 1.$ Thus, statement (1) alone is not sufficient to answer the question,

and the answer is B, C, or E. Similarly, statement (2) alone is also not sufficient because you do not know the value of $r.$ Both statements together are still not sufficient to determine whether or not $rst = 1.$ For example, if $r = s = t = 1,$ then

$rs = 1,$ $st = 1,$ and $rst = 1.$ However, if $r = t = 5,$ and $s = \dfrac{1}{5},$

then $rs = 1,$ $st = 1,$ but $rst = 5.$ Therefore, both statements together are not sufficient, and the answer is E.

154. In a certain office, 50 percent of the employees are college graduates and 60 percent of the employees are over forty years old. If 30 percent of those over forty have master's degrees, how many of the employees over forty have master's degrees?

    (1)   Exactly 100 of the employees are college graduates.

    (2)   Of the employees forty years old or less, 25 percent have master's degrees.

It is given that 50 percent of the employees are college graduates, and statement (1) says that exactly 100 of the employees are college graduates. Thus, the total number of employees in the company is 200. It is also given that 60 percent of the employees are over forty years old, which would be (0.60)(200), or 120 employees. Since 30 percent of those over forty have master's degrees (also given), (0.30)(120), or 36, employees are over forty and have master's degrees. Thus statement (1) alone is sufficient to answer the question, and the answer is A or D. Statement (2) says that of the employees forty years old or less, 25 percent have master's degrees. But since there is no information in statement (2) regarding how many employees fall into any of the categories, you cannot determine how many employees over forty have master's degrees. Thus, statement (1) alone is sufficient but statement (2) alone is not sufficient, and the answer is A.

155. Is $xy < 6$?

    (1) $x < 3$ and $y < 2.$

    (2) $\dfrac{1}{2} < x < \dfrac{2}{3}$ and $y^2 < 64.$

If x and y were restricted to nonnegative values, statement (1) would be sufficient to determine that $xy < 6.$ However, if x and y were both negative and sufficiently large, xy would not be less than 6. For example, if $x = y = -3,$ then xy would be $(-3)^2,$ or 9, which is greater than 6. Thus, statement (1) alone is not sufficient to answer the question, and the answer is B, C, or E. Statement (2) restricts x to the interval $\dfrac{1}{2} < x < \dfrac{2}{3}$ and y to the interval $-8 < y < 8.$ Thus, the largest value possible for xy would be less than $\left(\dfrac{2}{3}\right)(8),$ or $5\dfrac{1}{3},$ which is less than 6.

Thus, statement (2) alone is sufficient but statement (1) alone is not sufficient, and the answer is B.

156. The regular price per eight-ounce can of brand X soup is $0.37, regardless of the number of cans purchased. What amount will be saved on the purchase of 3 eight-ounce cans of brand X soup if the regular price is reduced?

   (1) At the reduced price, 3 eight-ounce cans of brand X soup will cost $0.99.
   (2) The amount that will be saved on each eight-ounce can of brand X soup purchased at the reduced price is $0.04.

From statement (1) it can be determined that the saving on 3 cans of the soup will be 3($0.37) – $0.99 = $0.12. Thus, (1) alone is sufficient, and the answer must be A or D. From statement (2), the saving is 3($0.04) = $0.12. Since each statement alone is sufficient, the best answer is D.

157. Does Joe weigh more than Tim?

   (1) Tim's weight is 80 percent of Joe's weight.
   (2) Joe's weight is 125 percent of Tim's weight.

Statement (1) indicates that Tim's weight is 80 percent of Joe's weight, so Joe weighs more than Tim. Thus, (1) alone is sufficient, and the answer must be A or D. According to statement (2), Joe's weight is more than 100 percent of Tim's weight, so Joe weighs more than Tim. The best answer is therefore D.

158. Is p^2 an odd integer?

   (1) p is an odd integer.
   (2) $\sqrt{p}$ is an odd integer.

Statement (1) indicates that p is an odd integer, which implies that any positive integer power of p will be an odd integer since the product of two or more odd integers is odd. Statement (2) indicates $\sqrt{p}$ is an odd integer. Since $p^2 = (\sqrt{p})^4$, p^2 is a product of odd integers, which, as stated in the discussion of (1), must be odd. Because each statement alone gives sufficient information to answer the question, the best answer is D.

159. What is the value of xy ?

   (1) $x + y = 10$
   (2) $x - y = 6$

From statement (1), $x = 10 - y$ and from statement (2), $x = 6 + y$. Neither statement alone gives sufficient information, so the answer must be C or E. The two statements can be solved simultaneously for x and y, so xy can be found. The best answer is C.

160. Elena receives a salary plus a commission that is equal to a fixed percentage of her sales revenue. What was the total of Elena's salary and commission last month?

   (1) Elena's monthly salary is $1,000.
   (2) Elena's commission is 5 percent of her sales revenue.

From the information in the question and statement (1), it is known that Elena's salary is $1,000 and that her commission is equal to a fixed percentage of her sales revenue, but there is no information about the percentage or sales revenue. Thus, (1) alone is not sufficient, and the answer must be B, C, or E. Statement (2) gives the percent but nothing about the sales revenue or her salary. Therefore, (2) alone is not sufficient, and the answer must be C or E. Both statements are still insufficient because they provide no information about her sales revenue. The best answer is E.

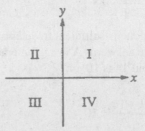

161. Point (x, y) lies in which quadrant of the rectangular coordinate system shown above?

   (1) $x + y < 0$
   (2) $x = 4$ and $y = -7$.

From statement (1) alone, it is not possible to determine whether x, y, or both x and y are negative; therefore, the answer must be B, C, or E. From statement (2) alone, it can be determined that the point $(4, -7)$ lies in quadrant IV. The best answer is B.

162. What is the average (arithmetic mean) of x, y, and z ?

   (1) $x + y = 5$
   (2) $y + z = 7$

The average of x, y, and z equals $\dfrac{x + y + z}{3}$. Statement (1) gives no information about z, and statement (2) gives no information about x. Therefore, neither statement alone is sufficient, and the answer must be C or E. From the two statements taken together, $x + 2y + z = 12$, but the value of $x + y + z$ cannot be determined. The best answer is E.

163. Chan and Mieko drove separate cars along the entire length of a certain route. If Chan made the trip in 15 minutes, how many minutes did it take Mieko to make the same trip?

(1) Mieko's average speed for the trip was $\frac{3}{4}$ of Chan's average speed.
(2) The route is 14 miles long.

For a fixed distance, the average speed is inversely related to the amount of time required to make the trip. Therefore, from the information given in the question and statement (1), since Mieko's average speed was $\frac{3}{4}$ of Chan's, her time was $\frac{4}{3}$ as long or $\frac{4}{3}(15)$ minutes. Thus, the answer is A or D. Because statement (2) gives no information about Mieko's average speed, it is not sufficient. The best answer is A.

164. If $xy \neq 0$, is $\frac{x}{y} < 0$?

(1) $x = -y$
(2) $-x = -(-y)$

Dividing both sides of the equation given in (1) by y yields $\frac{x}{y} = -1$; thus $\frac{x}{y} < 0$, so the correct answer must be A or D. From statement (2), if each side of the equation is divided by -1, the result will be the same as statement (1), so either statement alone is sufficient to answer the question and the best answer is D.

165. What is the value of the two-digit integer x ?

(1) The sum of the two digits is 3.
(2) x is divisible by 3.

From statement (1), the two-digit integer must be either 12, 21, or 30. Because a single numerical value of x cannot be determined from (1), the answer must be B, C, or E. Statement (2) alone is not sufficient because there are many two-digit integers divisible by 3, for example, 15, 24, and 27. Since all three numbers from (1) are divisible by 3, statements (1) and (2) together do not provide sufficient information, and the best answer is E.

166. Is the number x between 0.2 and 0.7 ?

(1) $560x < 280$
(2) $700x > 280$

From statement (1) it can be determined that $x < 0.5$. Since it cannot be determined whether x is greater than 0.2, the best answer must be B, C, or E. From statement (2) it can be determined that x is greater than 0.4, but it cannot be determined whether x is less than 0.7, and the answer must be C or E. Both statements taken together imply that $0.4 < x < 0.5$, which implies that x is between 0.2 and 0.7. The best answer is C.

167. Is x an integer?

(1) $\frac{x}{2}$ is an integer.
(2) $2x$ is an integer.

Statement (1) implies that x is an even integer. Therefore, the answer must be either A or D. From statement (2), x could be an integer; but x could also be an odd number divided by 2, such as $\frac{1}{2}$ or $-\frac{1}{2}$, neither of which is an integer. Therefore, (2) alone is not sufficient, and the best answer is A.

168. A swim club that sold only individual and family memberships charged $300 for an individual membership. If the club's total revenue from memberships was $480,000, what was the charge for a family membership?

(1) The revenue from individual memberships was $\frac{1}{4}$ of the total revenue from memberships.
(2) The club sold 1.5 times as many family memberships as individual memberships.

Let n be the number of individual memberships at $300 each and m be the number of family memberships at x dollars each. Then the total revenue is $300n + mx = \$480,000$. Statement (1) yields the equation $\$300n = \frac{1}{4}(\$480,000)$, which can be solved for n, so $n = 40$. Substituting 40 for n in the equation $\$300n + mx = \$480,000$ and solving for mx yields $mx = \frac{3}{4}(\$480,000)$, but since there is no information about m or x, statement (1) is not sufficient. Statement (2) gives only the information that $m = 1.5n$, so $\$300n + 1.5n(x) = \$480,000$, which cannot be solved for x. Statement (1) yields $n = 400$, and statement (2) taken with (1) yields $\$300(400) + 1.5(400)(x) = \$480,000$, which can be solved for x. The best answer is C.

169. If x, y, and z are positive numbers, is $x > y > z$?

    (1) $xz > yz$
    (2) $yx > yz$

Dividing each side of the inequality in (1) by z yields $x > y$, but there is no information relating z to either x or y. Therefore, the answer must be B, C, or E. Similarly, (2) yields only $x > z$, and the answer must be C or E. From both statements it can be determined that x is greater than both y and z. Because it cannot be determined whether y or z is least, the correct ordering of the three numbers cannot be determined, so the best answer is E.

170. Can the positive integer p be expressed as the product of two integers, each of which is greater than 1 ?

    (1) $31 < p < 37$
    (2) p is odd.

From statement (1), p can be any of the integers 32, 33, 34, 35, or 36. Because each of these integers can be expressed as the product of two integers, each of which is greater than 1, the question can be answered even though the specific value of p is not known. Thus, the answer must be A or D. Statement (2) is not sufficient since some odd numbers are prime and so cannot be expressed as a product of two integers, each of which is greater than 1; other odd numbers are composite and so can be expressed as a product of two integers, each of which is greater than 1. The best answer is A.

171. Currently there are 50 picture books on each shelf in the children's section of a library. If these books were to be placed on smaller shelves with 30 picture books on each shelf, how many of the smaller shelves would be needed to hold all of these books?

    (1) The number of smaller shelves needed is 6 more than the current number of shelves.
    (2) Currently there are 9 shelves in the children's section.

The missing information in this problem is the total number of books to be distributed, 30 to a shelf, which will give the total number of smaller shelves. If s is the current number of shelves, there are $50s$ books, and statement (1) says that $30(s + 6) = 50s$, or $s = 9$. Therefore, there are $9(50)$ or 450 books to be distributed on 30 shelves. Thus, the answer must be A or D. Statement (2) also implies that there is a total of $9(50) = 450$ books. Therefore, the best answer is D.

172. Is $y = 6$?

    (1) $y^2 = 36$
    (2) $y^2 - 7y + 6 = 0$

From statement (1) it cannot be determined whether $y = 6$ or $y = -6$. Thus, the answer must be B, C, or E.

Factoring the equation in (2) yields $(y - 6)(y - 1) = 0$, which implies that $y = 1$ or $y = 6$. Since a single numerical value of y cannot be determined from either equation alone, the answer must be C or E. From both equations taken together, it can be determined that $y = 6$. The best answer is C.

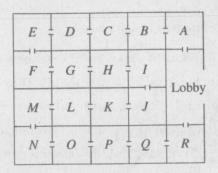

173. The figure above represents the floor plan of an art gallery that has a lobby and 18 rooms. If Lisa goes from the lobby into room A at the same time that Paul goes from the lobby into room R, and each goes through all of the rooms in succession, entering by one door and exiting by the other, which room will they be in at the same time?

    (1) Lisa spends $2x$ minutes in each room and Paul spends $3x$ minutes in each room.
    (2) Lisa spends 10 minutes less time in each room than Paul does.

From statement (1), if Lisa spends $\frac{2}{3}$ as much time in each room as Paul does, then Lisa will go through $\frac{3}{2}$ as many rooms as Paul does, or if r is the number of rooms Paul goes through, then $r + \frac{3r}{2} = 18$, and $r = 7.2$ and $\frac{3r}{2} = 10.5$. Thus, they will meet in room K, and the answer must be A or D. Since statement (2) does not relate Lisa's time with Paul's time in a way that is useful, the best answer is A.

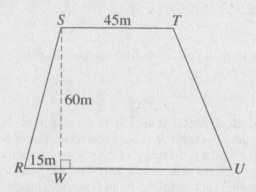

174. Quadrilateral *RSTU* shown above is a site plan for a parking lot in which side *RU* is parallel to side *ST* and *RU* is longer than *ST*. What is the area of the parking lot?

(1) $RU = 80$ meters

(2) $TU = 20\sqrt{10}$ meters

The area of a quadrilateral region that has parallel sides of lengths a and b and altitude h is $\frac{1}{2}(a + b)h$. Statement (1) gives the length of the base of the quadrilateral lot. Thus, the area of the lot, in square meters, is $\frac{(45 + 80)}{2}(60)$, and the answer must be A or D. If you do not know the formula, drawing the altitude from *T*, as shown in the figure below, can be helpful.

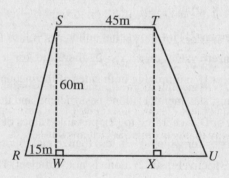

It can be seen that, in meters, $RU = 15 + 45 + XU$, and from (1), $80 = 15 + 45 + XU$, so $XU = 20$. The area of *RSTU* is the sum of the areas of the two triangles and the rectangle. From (2), using the Pythagorean theorem gives $60^2 + XU^2 = TU^2 = (20\sqrt{10})^2$, or $XU = 20$ meters. Then the length of *RU*, in square meters, is $15 + 45 + 20 = 80$, and since this is the information given in (1), it can similarly be used to find the area of *RSTU*. Therefore, the best answer is D.

175. If $xy = -6$, what is the value of $xy(x + y)$?

(1) $x - y = 5$

(2) $xy^2 = 18$

The question can be simplified to "What is the value of $-6(x + y)$?" From (1), $x = y + 5$, so substituting $y + 5$ for x in the equation $xy = -6$ yields $(y + 5)y = -6$, or $y^2 + 5y + 6 = 0$. Factoring the equation gives $(y + 2)(y + 3) = 0$, and $y = -2$ or $y = -3$. Since the value of y is not known, neither the value of x nor the value of $x + y$ can be determined. Thus, (1) alone is not sufficient. From statement (2), it follows that $xy^2 = (xy)y = 18$. Substituting -6 for xy in this equation yields $-6y = 18$ or $y = -3$. Since $y = -3$ and $xy = -6$, it follows that $x = 2$. Therefore, statement (2) alone is sufficient to determine the value of $x + y$ and of $-6(x + y)$. The best answer is B.

176. If the list price of a new car was \$12,300, what was the cost of the car to the dealer?

(1) The cost to the dealer was equal to 80 percent of the list price.

(2) The car was sold for \$11,070, which was 12.5 percent more than the cost to the dealer.

If C represents the cost to the dealer, then statement (1) can be written as $C = 0.80(\$12,300)$, which can be solved for C. Thus, statement (1) alone is sufficient, and the answer must be A or D. From (2) it follows that $\$11,070 = C + 0.125C$, which can be solved for C. Thus, (2) alone is also sufficient, and the best answer is D.

177. If p, q, x, y, and z are different positive integers, which of the five integers is the median?

(1) $p + x < q$

(2) $y < z$

Since there are five different integers, there are two integers greater and two integers less than the median, which is the middle number. Statement (1) gives no information about the order of y and z with respect to the other three numbers. Thus, (1) alone is not sufficient, and the answer must be B, C, or E. Similarly, statement (2) does not relate y and z to the other three integers and is also not sufficient, so the answer must be C or E. Because the two statements taken together do not relate $p, x,$ and q to y and z, it is impossible to tell which is the median. Thus, the two statements together are not sufficient, and the best answer is E.

178. A certain employee is paid \$6 per hour for an 8-hour workday. If the employee is paid $1\frac{1}{2}$ times this rate for time worked in excess of 8 hours during a single day, how many hours did the employee work today?

    (1) The employee was paid \$18 more for hours worked today than for hours worked yesterday.
    (2) Yesterday the employee worked 8 hours.

The employee is paid \$6 per hour for 8 hours and $1\frac{1}{2}$ times this rate, or \$9 per hour, for time worked in excess of 8 hours. Statement (1) gives information only about the additional amount paid for hours worked today compared with hours worked yesterday. The \$18 could have been for 3 hours at \$6, for 2 hours at \$9, or for a combination of base and overtime hours. Thus, without information about the number of hours the employee worked yesterday, (1) alone is not sufficient, and the answer must be B, C, or E. Statement (2) gives only the number of hours the employee worked yesterday. Thus, (2) alone is not sufficient, and the answer must be C or E. From (1) and (2) together, it can be determined that the employee was paid for $8 + 2$, or 10 hours today. The best answer is C.

179. If n is a member of the set
$$\{33, 36, 38, 39, 41, 42\},$$
what is the value of n?

    (1) n is even.
    (2) n is a multiple of 3.

Statement (1) alone implies that n is 36, or 38, or 42, and (2) alone implies that n is 33, 36, 39, or 42; so neither statement alone is sufficient. Thus, the answer must be C or E. From (1) and (2) together, it can be determined that n is either 36 or 42. Therefore, the best answer is E.

180. What is the value of x?

    (1) $2x + 1 = 0$
    (2) $(x + 1)^2 = x^2$

Since $2x + 1 = 0$ can be solved for x, (1) alone is sufficient. Statement (2) can be expanded to $x^2 + 2x + 1 = x^2$, from which it follows that $2x + 1 = 0$, which was given in (1). Thus, each statement alone is sufficient, and the best answer is D.

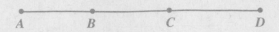

181. In the figure above, what is the length of AD?

    (1) $AC = 6$
    (2) $BD = 6$

Since the length of AD is the sum of the lengths of AC and CD, but the length of CD is not known, (1) alone is not sufficient. Similarly, the length of AD is the sum of the lengths of AB and BD, but the length of AB is not known, and (2) alone is not sufficient. From (1) and (2) together, $AC + BD = 12$, but the two line segments overlap. Since BC, the length of the overlap, is not known, the best answer is E.

182. A retailer purchased a television set for x percent less than its list price, and then sold it for y percent less than its list price. What was the list price of the television set?

    (1) $x = 15$
    (2) $x - y = 5$

Statements (1) and (2) provide information only about the values of x and y. Since no dollar values are given, knowing the percent decreases from the list price is insufficient to determine the list price. The statements alone or together are not sufficient, and the best answer is E.

183. Is x^2 greater than x?

    (1) x^2 is greater than 1.
    (2) x is greater than -1.

From statement (1) it follows that either $x < -1$ or $x > 1$. For all nonzero values of x, $x^2 > 0$; therefore, for $x < -1$, $x^2 > x$. If $x > 1$, multiplying both sides of the inequality gives $x^2 > x$. Thus, statement (1) alone is sufficient, and the answer must be A or D. According to (2), possible values of x are $\frac{1}{2}$, or 0, or 2, for which x^2 is less than, equal to, or greater than x, respectively; so (2) alone is not sufficient. The best answer is A.

184. What is the value of $\frac{r}{2} + \frac{s}{2}$?

    (1) $\frac{r + s}{2} = 5$
    (2) $r + s = 10$

The sum $\frac{r}{2} + \frac{s}{2} = \frac{r + s}{2}$. Thus, since the value of $r + s$ can be found from (1) and is given in (2), each statement alone is sufficient, and the best answer is D.

185. If x, y, and z are numbers, is $z = 18$?

    (1) The average (arithmetic mean) of x, y, and z is 6.
    (2) $x = -y$

From (1) it is known that $\frac{x+y+z}{3} = 6$, or $x + y + z = 18$, but nothing is known about the value of $x + y$. Therefore, (1) alone is not sufficient, and the answer must be B, C, or E. Statement (2) alone is not sufficient because it implies that $x + y = 0$ but gives no information about the values of $x, y,$ and z. Thus, the answer must be C or E. Statements (1) and (2) together are sufficient since 0 can be substituted for $x + y$ in the equation $x + y + z = 18$ to yield $z = 18$. The best answer is C.

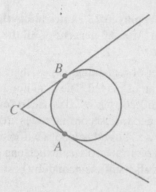

186. The circular base of an above-ground swimming pool lies in a level yard and just touches two straight sides of a fence at points A and B, as shown in the figure above. Point C is on the ground where the two sides of the fence meet. How far from the center of the pool's base is point A ?

    (1) The base has area 250 square feet.
    (2) The center of the base is 20 feet from point C.

Let Q be the center of the pool's base and r be the distance from Q to A, as shown in the figure below.

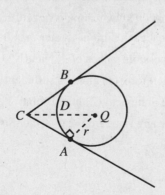

Since A is a point on the circular base, QA is a radius of the base. Thus, (1) can be written Area $= \pi r^2 = 250$ square feet, which can be solved for r. Thus, (1) alone is sufficient, and the answer must be A or D. Since CA is tangent to the base, QAC is a right triangle. From (2), $QC = 20$, but there is not enough information to determine the length of QA. Therefore, (2) alone is not sufficient, and the best answer is A.

187. In 1979 Mr. Jackson bought a total of n shares of stock X and Mrs. Jackson bought a total of 300 shares of stock X. If the couple held all of their respective shares throughout 1980, and Mr. Jackson's 1980 dividends on his n shares totaled \$150, what was the total amount of Mrs. Jackson's 1980 dividends on her 300 shares?

    (1) In 1980 the annual dividend on each share of stock X was \$0.75.
    (2) In 1979 Mr. Jackson bought a total of 200 shares of stock X.

Statement (1) alone is sufficient because the total amount of Mrs. Jackson's 1980 dividends on her 300 shares was 300 times the annual dividend per share, which is given in (1). Thus, the answer must be A or D. It is given that Mr. Jackson's 1980 dividends totaled \$150, and (2) gives the number of shares of stock Mr. Jackson bought. Thus, the dividend per share was $\frac{\$150}{200} = \$0.75$, which is the information given in (1), and it follows that (2) alone is also sufficient. The best answer is D.

188. If Sara's age is exactly twice Bill's age, what is Sara's age?

    (1) Four years ago, Sara's age was exactly 3 times Bill's age.
    (2) Eight years from now, Sara's age will be exactly 1.5 times Bill's age.

If s and b represent Sara's and Bill's ages in years, respectively, then $s = 2b$, or $b = \frac{s}{2}$. Statement (1) can then be written algebraically as $s - 4 = 3(b - 4)$. Substituting $\frac{s}{2}$ for b in this equation gives $s - 4 = 3(\frac{s}{2} - 4)$, which can be solved for s. Similarly, (2) can be written algebraically as $s + 8 = 1.5(b + 8)$ or $s + 8 = 1.5(\frac{s}{2} + 8)$, which can be solved for s. Thus, both (1) alone and (2) alone are sufficient, and the best answer is D.

189. What is the value of $\dfrac{x}{yz}$?

(1) $x = \dfrac{y}{2}$ and $z = \dfrac{2x}{5}$.

(2) $\dfrac{x}{z} = \dfrac{5}{2}$ and $\dfrac{1}{y} = \dfrac{1}{10}$.

From statement (1), z can be expressed in terms of y by

substituting $\dfrac{y}{2}$ for x in $z = \dfrac{2x}{5}$, which gives

$z = \dfrac{2\left(\dfrac{y}{2}\right)}{5} = \dfrac{y}{5}$. The value of $\dfrac{x}{yz}$ in terms of y is then

$\dfrac{\dfrac{y}{2}}{y\left(\dfrac{y}{5}\right)} = \dfrac{y}{2}\left(\dfrac{5}{y^2}\right) = \dfrac{5}{2y}$. Since no information about the value

of y is given, (1) alone is not sufficient, and the answer must

be B, C, or E. Statement (2) alone is sufficient because

$\dfrac{x}{yz} = \left(\dfrac{1}{y}\right)\left(\dfrac{x}{z}\right)$ or $\left(\dfrac{1}{10}\right)\left(\dfrac{5}{2}\right)$. The best answer is B.

190. An infinite sequence of positive integers is called an "alpha sequence" if the number of even integers in the sequence is finite. If S is an infinite sequence of positive integers, is S an alpha sequence?

(1) The first ten integers in S are even.
(2) An infinite number of integers in S are odd.

Statement (1) alone is not sufficient because it gives no information about the integers in S other than the first ten; in addition to the first ten integers in S there may be any number of other even integers. Statement (2) is irrelevant because it gives information about the number of odd integers but no information about the number of even integers in S. S could have an infinite number of even integers as in the case of the set of all positive integers, or S could have a finite number of even integers. Thus, statement (2) alone is not sufficient, and since together the two statements do not give enough information about even integers, it follows that (1) and (2) together are not sufficient. The best answer is E.

191. If $xy > 0$, does $(x-1)(y-1) = 1$?

(1) $x + y = xy$
(2) $x = y$

The product $(x-1)(y-1)$ is equivalent to $xy - y - x + 1$. From statement (1), $x+y$ can be substituted for xy, which gives $x+y-y-x+1 = 1$. Thus, $(x-1)(y-1) = 1$, and (1) alone is sufficient. From statement (2), substituting y for x in $(x-1)(y-1)$ gives $(y-1)(y-1)$. Since the value of y is not given, statement (2) alone is not sufficient, and the best answer is A.

192. After winning 50 percent of the first 20 games it played, Team A won all of the remaining games it played. What was the total number of games that Team A won?

(1) Team A played 25 games altogether.
(2) Team A won 60 percent of all the games it played.

If r is the number of remaining games, then $20 + r$ is the total number of games played. The total number of games the team won was $0.50(20) + r$ or $10 + r$. To solve the problem, the value of r is needed. According to (1), $20 + r = 25$, which can be solved for r. Thus, (1) alone is sufficient. Statement (2) implies that $0.60(20 + r) = 10 + r$, which can be solved for r. Thus, (2) alone is also sufficient, and the best answer is D.

193. In the addition problem above, each of the symbols $\square$, $\triangle$, and $\star$ represents a positive digit. If $\square < \triangle$, what is the value of $\triangle$?

(1) $\star = 4$
(2) $\square = 1$

Since each of the three symbols represents a positive digit, $\square + \triangle < 10$. Statement (1) says that $\star = 4$, so $\square + \triangle = 4$, and it is given that each digit is greater than 0 and $\square < \triangle$. Thus, the only possible values of $\square$ and $\triangle$ are 1 and 3, respectively. Therefore, (1) alone is sufficient and the answer must be A or D. Statement (2) implies that $1 + \triangle = \star$, and $\triangle$ can have any value from 2 to 8, inclusive. The best answer is A.

CANCELATION FEES

Days Prior to Departure	Percent of Package Price
46 or more	10%
45-31	35%
30-16	50%
15-5	65%
4 or fewer	100%

194. The table above shows the cancelation fee schedule that a travel agency uses to determine the fee charged to a tourist who cancels a trip prior to departure. If a tourist canceled a trip with a package price of $1,700 and a departure date of September 4, on what day was the trip canceled?

(1) The cancelation fee was $595.
(2) If the trip had been canceled one day later, the cancelation fee would have been $255 more.

The cancelation fee given in (1) is $\frac{\$595}{\$1,700} = 35\%$ of the package price, which is the percent charged for cancelation 45-31 days prior to the departure date of September 4. Thus, (1) alone is not sufficient, and the answer must be B, C, or E. Statement (2) implies that the increase in the cancelation fee for canceling one day later would have been $\frac{\$255}{\$1,700} = 15\%$ of the package price; so the cancelation could have occurred either 31 days or 16 days prior to the departure date of September 4. Therefore, (2) alone is not sufficient, and the answer must be C or E, but (1) and (2) together imply that the trip was canceled 31 days prior to September 4. The best answer is C.

195. Is 5^k less than 1,000 ?

(1) $5^{k+1} > 3,000$
(2) $5^{k-1} = 5^k - 500$

Since $5^{k+1} = 5^k(5)$, or $5^k = 5\frac{5^{k+1}}{5}$, it follows from statement (1) that $\frac{5^{k+1}}{5} > \frac{3,000}{5}$, or $5^k > 600$. Thus, (1) alone is not sufficient. From statement (2), $5^k - 5^{k-1} = 500$, or $5^k - 5^k(5^{-1}) = 5^k - 5^k(\frac{1}{5}) = 500$. Factoring out 5^k gives $5^k(1 - \frac{1}{5}) = 500$, or $5^k = 500(\frac{5}{4}) = 625$, which is less than 1,000. Therefore, (2) alone is sufficient, and the best answer is B.

196. If Hans purchased a pair of skis and a ski jacket, what was the cost of the skis?

(1) The ratio of the cost of the skis to the cost of the jacket was 5 to 1.
(2) The total cost of the skis and the jacket was $360.

Statement (1) alone is not sufficient because only the relative cost of the skis and jacket is given; there is no information about dollar costs. Thus, the answer must be B, C, or E. Statement (2) alone is not sufficient since it does not give information about the relative cost of the jacket and the skis. Hence, the answer must be C or E. From (1) and (2) together, if x is the cost of the jacket, then $5x$ is the cost of the skis and $5x + x = 360$. Because this equation can be solved for x, the best answer is C.

197. Is $x < y$?

(1) $z < y$
(2) $z < x$

Since statement (1) gives no information about x and statement (2) gives no information about y, neither statement alone is sufficient, and the answer must be C or E. From (1) and (2) together, it can be determined only that z is less than either x or y. Since x can be greater than, equal to, or less than y, the best answer is E.

198. If a certain city is losing 12 percent of its daily water supply each day because of water-main breaks, what is the dollar cost to the city per day for this loss?

(1) The city's daily water supply is 350 million gallons.
(2) The cost to the city for each 12,000 gallons of water lost is $2.

In order to solve this problem, the cost of the water and the number of gallons in the daily water supply must be known. Statement (1) gives the daily water supply, which is not sufficient by itself, and statement (2) gives the cost of water, which also is not sufficient by itself. Thus, the answer must be C or E. From both statements together, it can be concluded that the dollar cost for the water lost is $\frac{0.12(350,000,000) \times \$2}{12,000}$. The best answer is C.

199. Machine X runs at a constant rate and produces a lot consisting of 100 cans in 2 hours. How much less time would it take to produce the lot of cans if both machines X and Y were run simultaneously?

    (1) Both machines X and Y produce the same number of cans per hour.

    (2) It takes machine X twice as long to produce the lot of cans as it takes machines X and Y running simultaneously to produce the lot.

Since the problem states that the job is to produce 100 cans and machine X can do it in 2 hours, the only information needed to answer the question is either the rate for machine Y or the time for X and Y together. Statement (1) says that the rate for Y is the same as that for X, which is given; so the answer must be A or D. From statement (2) alone, it can be determined that X and Y together take 1 hour, since the rate for X is twice that for X and Y running simultaneously. Thus each statement alone is sufficient, and the best answer is D.

200. If x and y are positive, what is the value of x ?

    (1) 200 percent of x equals 400 percent of y.
    (2) xy is the square of a positive integer.

From statement (1) alone, it can only be determined that $x = 2y$. Since this equation has an infinite number of solutions, the answer must be B, C, or E. From statement (2) alone, it can only be determined that $xy = k^2$, where k is a positive integer. This equation has an infinite number of solutions. If (1) and (2) are taken together, the two equations in three unknowns cannot be solved for a unique value of x. The best answer is E.

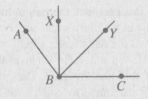

201. In the figure above, what is the measure of $\angle ABC$?

    (1) BX bisects $\angle ABY$ and BY bisects $\angle XBC$.
    (2) The measure of $\angle ABX$ is 40°.

From statement (1) alone it can be determined that $\angle ABX$, $\angle XBY$, and $\angle YBC$ are equal in measure, but the measure of $\angle ABC$ cannot be determined. Therefore, the answer must be B, C, or E. Statement (2) alone is also not sufficient since it gives no information about the measure of $\angle XBC$. Therefore, the answer must be C or E. From (1) and (2) together, it can be determined that the measure of $\angle ABX =$ the measure of $\angle XBY =$ the measure of $\angle YBC = 40°$, so $\angle ABC$ measures $3(40) = 120$ degrees. Thus, the best answer is C.

202. If $-10 < k < 10$, is $k > 0$?

    (1) $\dfrac{1}{k} > 0$
    (2) $k^2 > 0$

Statement (1) alone is sufficient since k must be a positive number if its reciprocal $\dfrac{1}{k}$ is positive; so the answer must be A or D. Statement (2) alone is not sufficient since it permits k to be either positive or negative. The best answer is A.

	R	S	T	U
R	0	y	x	62
S	y	0	56	75
T	x	56	0	69
U	62	75	69	0

203. The table above shows the distance, in kilometers, by the most direct route, between any two of the four cities, R, S, T, and U. For example, the distance between City R and City U is 62 kilometers. What is the value of x ?

    (1) By the most direct route, the distance between S and T is twice the distance between S and R.
    (2) By the most direct route, the distance between T and U is 1.5 times the distance between R and T.

The value of x is the distance between City R and City T; the value of y is the distance between City R and City S. From statement (1) alone, it can be determined only that $56 = 2y$. Since no information is given about x, the answer must be B, C, or E. Statement (2) alone yields the equation $1.5x = 69$, which can be solved for x. Hence, the best answer is B.

204. Buckets X and Y contained only water and bucket Y was $\dfrac{1}{2}$ full. If all of the water in bucket X was then poured into bucket Y, what fraction of the capacity of Y was then filled with water?

    (1) Before the water from X was poured, X was $\dfrac{1}{3}$ full.
    (2) X and Y have the same capacity.

Statement (1) alone is not sufficient since it gives no information about the relative capacities of the two buckets. Thus, the answer must be B, C, or E. Statement (2) alone is not sufficient since it gives no information about the amount of water in bucket X. Thus, the answer must be C or E. If (1) and (2) are considered together, it can be determined that bucket Y is filled to $\left(\dfrac{1}{2}+\dfrac{1}{3}\right)$ of its capacity. Therefore, the best answer is C.

205. If n is an integer, is $n + 2$ a prime number?

    (1) n is a prime number.
    (2) $n + 1$ is <u>not</u> a prime number.

For problems such as this, trying out two or three values of n can be very helpful. In statement (1), consider the prime numbers 2, 3, or 7, for example. Statement (1) alone is not sufficient since for these values $n + 2 = 4, 5,$ or 9, respectively, and only 5 is prime. Thus, the answer must be B, C, or E. Similarly, for statement (2), if $n = 3$ or 7, then $n + 1 = 4$ or 8, and $n + 2 = 5$ or 9. Thus, the answer must be C or E. Since neither of the statements gives any definitive information about $n + 2$, the two statements taken together are still not sufficient to determine whether $n + 2$ is a prime number, and the best answer is E.

206. Is x between 0 and 1?

    (1) x^2 is less than x.
    (2) x^3 is positive.

Since x^2 is always nonnegative, it follows from statement (1) that x must be positive. For $x = 0$ or 1, $x^2 = x$; for $x > 1$, $x^2 > x$. Therefore, x must be between 0 and 1. Thus, statement (1) alone is sufficient, and the answer must be A or D. Statement (2) alone is not sufficient since x can be any positive number. Thus, the best answer is A.

207. Did Sally pay less than x dollars, including sales tax, for her bicycle?

    (1) The price Sally paid for the bicycle was $(0.9)x$ dollars, excluding the 10 percent sales tax.
    (2) The price Sally paid for the bicycle was $170, excluding sales tax.

Statement (1) alone is sufficient since the price, including sales tax, was $(0.9)x + (0.1)(0.9)x = 0.99x$, which is less than x. Thus, the answer must be A or D. Statement (2) alone is not sufficient since there is no information given relating the $170 Sally paid and the value of x. Thus, the best answer is A.

208. Is the positive square root of x an integer?

    (1) $x = n^4$ and n is an integer.
    (2) $x = 16$

Statement (1) alone is sufficient since the positive square root of x is n^2, which must be an integer since n is an integer. Thus, the answer must be A or D. Statement (2) alone is also sufficient since the positive square root of 16 is the integer 4. The best answer is D.

209. If the successive tick marks shown on the number line above are equally spaced and if x and y are the numbers designating the end points of intervals as shown, what is the value of y?

    (1) $x = \dfrac{1}{2}$

    (2) $y - x = \dfrac{2}{3}$

From statement (1) it can be established that each subdivision of the line represents $\dfrac{1}{3}\left(\dfrac{1}{2}\right) = \dfrac{1}{6}$, so the value of y is $\dfrac{7}{6}$. Thus, (1) alone is sufficient, and the answer must be A or D. From statement (2) alone, the four equal subdivisions represent a total distance of $\dfrac{2}{3}$ which implies that each subdivision of the number line has length $\dfrac{1}{4}\left(\dfrac{2}{3}\right) = \dfrac{1}{6}$. Therefore, the best answer is D.

210. In a certain senior citizens' club, are more than $\dfrac{1}{4}$ of the members over 75 years of age?

    (1) Exactly 60 percent of the female members are over 60 years of age, and, of these, $\dfrac{1}{3}$ are over 75 years of age.

    (2) Exactly 10 male members are over 75 years of age.

From statement (1) it can be determined only that $\dfrac{1}{3}\left(\dfrac{3}{5}\right) = \dfrac{1}{5}$ of the female members are over 75. Thus, (1) alone is not sufficient, and the answer must be B, C, or E. Statement (2) gives only the number of male members over 75. Thus, (2) alone is not sufficient, and the answer must be C or E. Both statements together are still insufficient since they provide no information about the number of female members and the total number of members. The best answer is E.

211. If $t \neq 0$, is r greater than zero?

    (1) $rt = 12$
    (2) $r + t = 7$

Statement (1) alone is not sufficient since r and t could be either both positive or both negative. Statement (2) alone is not sufficient since both r and t can be positive or t can be positive and r negative (e.g., $r = 3$ and $t = 4$, or $r = -3$ and $t = 10$). If (1) and (2) are considered together, the system of equations can be solved to show that r must be either 3 or 4. Thus, the best answer is C.

212. If x is an integer, is y an integer?

   (1) The average (arithmetic mean) of x, y, and $y - 2$ is x.
   (2) The average (arithmetic mean) of x and y is <u>not</u> an integer.

From statement (1), $\dfrac{x + y + (y - 2)}{3} = x$ simplifies to $y = x + 1$. Since x is an integer, x and y are consecutive integers. Thus, (1) alone is sufficient, and the answer must be A or D. From statement (2) alone, y might be an integer (e.g., $x = 5$ and $y = 6$) or y might not be an integer (e.g., $x = 5$ and $y = 6.2$). In both examples the average is <u>not</u> an integer. Therefore, (2) alone is not sufficient, and the best answer is A.

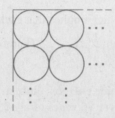

213. The inside of a rectangular carton is 48 centimeters long, 32 centimeters wide, and 15 centimeters high. The carton is filled to capacity with k identical cylindrical cans of fruit that stand upright in rows and columns, as indicated in the figure above. If the cans are 15 centimeters high, what is the value of k ?

   (1) Each of the cans has a radius of 4 centimeters.
   (2) 6 of the cans fit exactly along the length of the carton.

Statement (1) alone establishes that the diameter of each can is 8 centimeters. Along the length of the carton 6 cans ($48 \div 8$) can be placed; along the width of the carton 4 cans ($32 \div 8$) can be placed. Hence, $k = 24$, and (1) alone is sufficient. Thus, the answer must be A or D. Statement (2) also implies that the diameter of each can is 8 centimeters since 6 cans fit along the length of the carton ($48 \div 6$). Thus, (2) alone is also sufficient, and the best answer is D.

214. If $R = \dfrac{8x}{3y}$ and $y \neq 0$, what is the value of R ?

   (1) $x = \dfrac{2}{3}$
   (2) $x = 2y$

Statement (1) alone is not sufficient to determine the value of R since the value of y is not known. Thus, the answer

must be B, C, or E. Statement (2) alone is sufficient since $R = \dfrac{8x}{3y} = \dfrac{8(2y)}{3y} = \dfrac{16}{3}$. The best answer is B.

215. Is the positive integer n a multiple of 24 ?

   (1) n is a multiple of 4.
   (2) n is a multiple of 6.

Statement (1) alone is not sufficient because it says only that n is a multiple of 4 (e.g., n could be 8 or 24), and statement 2 alone is not sufficient because it says only that n is a multiple of 6 (e.g., n could be 12 or 48). Since both statements together imply only that n is a multiple of the least common multiple of 4 and 6, namely, 12, the best answer is E.

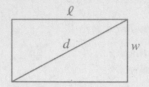

216. What is the area of the rectangular region above?

   (1) $\ell + w = 6$
   (2) $d^2 = 20$

The area of the rectangular region is ℓw. Statement (1) alone is not sufficient since the dimensions ℓ and w cannot be determined. Thus, the answer must be B, C, or E. Statement (2) alone is not sufficient because the length of the diagonal will not uniquely determine the length and width of the rectangle. Thus, the answer must be C or E. The Pythagorean theorem together with both (1) and (2) yield the equations $\ell^2 + w^2 = d^2 = 20$ and $(\ell + w)^2 = \ell^2 + 2\ell w + w^2 = 36$. Combining these equations gives $\ell w = 8$. Hence, the best answer is C.

217. If Aaron, Lee, and Tony have a total of \$36, how much money does Tony have?

   (1) Tony has twice as much money as Lee and $\dfrac{1}{3}$ as much as Aaron.
   (2) The sum of the amounts of money that Tony and Lee have is half the amount that Aaron has.

From statement (1) alone it can be determined that if Lee has x dollars, then Tony has $2x$ dollars, Aaron has $6x$ dollars, and together they have $9x = 36$ dollars. Thus, the amount that Tony has can be determined, and the answer must be A or D. From statement (2), if the sum of the amounts that Tony and Lee have is y dollars, then Aaron has $2y$ dollars, and y can be determined. However, the individual amounts for Tony and Lee cannot be determined. Thus, (2) alone is not sufficient, and the best answer is A.

218. If n is a positive integer, is the value of $b - a$ at least twice the value of $3^n - 2^n$?

    (1) $a = 2^{n+1}$ and $b = 3^{n+1}$
    (2) $n = 3$

From statement (1) alone it can be determined that $b - a$ is more than twice $3^n - 2^n$, since

$$b - a = 3^{n+1} - 2^{n+1} = 3(3^n) - 2(2^n), \text{ and}$$
$$3(3^n) - 2(2^n) > 2(3^n) - 2(2^n), \text{ or } 2(3^n - 2^n).$$

Therefore, the answer must be either A or D. Since statement (2) alone gives no information about $b - a$, it is not sufficient. Thus, the best answer is A.

219. The price per share of stock X increased by 10 percent over the same time period that the price per share of stock Y decreased by 10 percent. The reduced price per share of stock Y was what percent of the original price per share of stock X?

    (1) The increased price per share of stock X was equal to the original price per share of stock Y.
    (2) The increase in the price per share of stock X was $\dfrac{10}{11}$ the decrease in the price per share of stock Y.

The amount that stock X increased per share can be represented by $0.1x$, where x represents the original price per share of stock X. The amount that stock Y decreased per share can be represented by $0.1y$, where y represents the original price per share of stock Y. The reduced price per share of stock Y as a percent of the original price per share of stock X can be determined if a relationship between x and y is known. Statement (1) establishes that $1.1x = y$, and statement (2) establishes that $0.1x = \dfrac{10}{11}(0.1y)$. Since each statement alone is sufficient, the best answer is D.

220. Any decimal that has only a finite number of nonzero digits is a terminating decimal. For example, 24, 0.82, and 5.096 are three terminating decimals. If r and s are positive integers and the ratio $\dfrac{r}{s}$ is expressed as a decimal, is $\dfrac{r}{s}$ a terminating decimal?

    (1) $90 < r < 100$
    (2) $s = 4$

Statement (1) alone is not sufficient to determine that $\dfrac{r}{s}$ is a terminating decimal since there is no information about the value of s. For example, $\dfrac{92}{5} = 18.4$ terminates, but $\dfrac{92}{3} = 30.666\ldots$ does not terminate. Therefore, the answer must be B, C, or E. Statement (2) alone is sufficient since division by the number 4 must terminate: the remainder when dividing by 4 must be 0, 1, 2, or 3, so the quotient must end with .0, .25, .5, or .75, respectively. Thus, the best answer is B.

221. What is the value of integer n?

    (1) $n(n+1) = 6$
    (2) $2^{2n} = 16$

From statement (1), $n^2 + n - 6 = 0$, or $(n + 3)(n - 2) = 0$. Therefore, n could be -3 or 2, so (1) alone is not sufficient. From statement (2), $2^{2n} = 16 = 2^4$, so $2n = 4$ and $n = 2$. Thus, statement (2) ALONE is sufficient, but statement (1) alone is not sufficient to answer the question. The best answer is B.

222. If x is a positive integer, is $\sqrt{x}$ an integer?

    (1) $\sqrt{4x}$ is an integer.
    (2) $\sqrt{3x}$ is not an integer.

From statement (1), since $\sqrt{4x}$ is an integer, it follows that $4x$ must be the square of an integer, and so x must be the square of an integer. Therefore $\sqrt{x}$ must be an integer. Thus, statement (1) alone is sufficient. From statement (2), if x is the square of an integer, say 4, then $\sqrt{3x}$ is not an integer and $\sqrt{x}$ is an integer. However, if x is not the square of an integer, say 2, then $\sqrt{3x}$ is still not an integer, and $\sqrt{x}$ is also not an integer. Therefore statement (2) alone is not sufficient. Thus, statement (1) ALONE is sufficient, but statement (2) alone is not sufficient to answer the question. The best answer is A.

223. Are at least 10 percent of the people in Country X who are 65 years old or older employed?

    (1) In Country X, 11.3 percent of the population is 65 years old or older.

    (2) In Country X, of the population 65 years old or older, 20 percent of the men and 10 percent of the women are employed.

Statement (1) says that a certain percent of the population is 65 years old or older, but states nothing about what percent of them are employed. So, (1) alone is not sufficient. Statement (2) says that 20 percent of the men and 10 percent of the women who are 65 years old or older are employed, which means that at least 10 percent of the people in that age group are employed. Thus, statement (2) ALONE is sufficient, but statement (1) alone is not sufficient to answer the question. The best answer is B.

224. If x is a positive number less than 10, is z greater than the average (arithmetic mean) of x and 10 ?

    (1) On the number line, z is closer to 10 than it is to x.
    (2) $z = 5x$

From statement (1), z is closer (on the number line) to 10 than it is to x. The average of x and 10 must be the number halfway between x and 10 on the number line. Thus, if z is closer to 10 than it is to x, then z must be greater than the average of x and 10. Therefore (1) alone is sufficient. Statement (2) alone is not sufficient because, for example, if $x = 1$, then $z = 5$. However, the average of x and 10 is $\frac{1+10}{2} = 5.5$, which is greater than z. Whereas, if $x = 1.6$, then $z = 8$, and the average of 1.6 and 10 is $\frac{1.6+10}{2} = 5.8$, which is less than z. Thus, statement (1) ALONE is sufficient, but statement (2) alone is not sufficient to answer the question. The best answer is A.

225. If y is greater than 110 percent of x, is y greater than 75 ?

    (1) $x > 75$
    (2) $y - x = 10$

In statement (1), $x > 75$. Since y is greater than 110 percent of x, and since 110 percent of 75 is greater than 75, statement (1) alone is sufficient. In statement (2), $y - x = 10$; however, more information would be needed about the value of x. For example, if $x = 20$, then $y = 30$, which is less than 75; however, if $x = 80$, then $y = 90$, which is greater than 75. In both cases y would be greater than 110 percent of x. Thus, statement (1) ALONE is sufficient, but statement (2) alone is not sufficient to answer the question. The best answer is A.

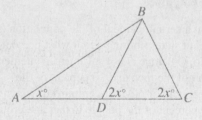

226. In triangle ABC above, what is the length of side BC ?

    (1) Line segment AD has length 6.
    (2) $x = 36$

Before considering statements (1) and (2), note that angle BDC is an exterior angle of triangle ADB. Thus, if angle ABD has measure $y°$, then $x + y = 2x$, or $y = x$. (The degree measure of an exterior angle of a triangle is equal to the sum of the remote interior angles.) Thus $AD = DB$ (the 2 sides are opposite angles with equal measure), and for the same reason $DB = BC$. Therefore $AD = BC$. Statement (1) says that $AD = 6$,

so BC must equal 6. Thus, statement (1) alone is sufficient. Since statement (2) gives no information about the length of any line segments, the length of side BC cannot be determined from (2) alone. Thus, statement (1) ALONE is sufficient, but statement (2) alone is not sufficient to answer the question. The best answer is A.

227. If the two floors in a certain building are 9 feet apart, how many steps are there in a set of stairs that extends from the first floor to the second floor of the building?

    (1) Each step is $\frac{3}{4}$ foot high.
    (2) Each step is 1 foot wide.

Statement (1) says that each step in the set of stairs is $\frac{3}{4}$ foot high. Since the set of stairs rises 9 feet from the first floor to the second, the number of steps must be $9 \div \frac{3}{4}$, or 12. Thus, statement (1) alone is sufficient. Statement (2) alone is not sufficient because it provides no information regarding the height of the steps. Thus, statement (1) ALONE is sufficient, but statement (2) alone is not sufficient to answer the question. The best answer is A.

228. A bookstore that sells used books sells each of its paperback books for a certain price and each of its hardcover books for a certain price. If Joe, Maria, and Paul bought books in this store, how much did Maria pay for 1 paperback book and 1 hardcover book?

    (1) Joe bought 2 paperback books and 3 hardcover books for $12.50.

    (2) Paul bought 4 paperback books and 6 hardcover books for $25.00.

If p is the price for each paperback book and h is the price for each hardcover book, statement (1) says that $2p + 3h = \$12.50$. Without more information, this equation alone is not sufficient to determine the cost of 1 paperback and 1 hardcover. Statement (2) says that $4p + 6h = \$25.00$. If you divide both sides of this equation by 2, you get exactly the same equation as in (1). Therefore, statements (1) and (2) TOGETHER are NOT sufficient to answer the question. The best answer is E.

229. If S is a set of four numbers w, x, y, and z, is the range of the numbers in S greater than 2 ?

(1) $w - z > 2$
(2) z is the least number in S.

The range of the numbers w, x, y, and z is equal to the greatest of those numbers minus the least of the numbers. Statement (1) reveals that the difference between two of the numbers is greater than 2, which means that the range of the four numbers must also be greater than 2. Thus, statement (1) alone is sufficient. Statement (2) alone is not sufficient because it says only that z is the least number without giving any information regarding the other numbers. Thus, statement (1) ALONE is sufficient, but statement (2) alone is not sufficient to answer the question. The best answer is A.

230. A box contains only red chips, white chips, and blue chips. If a chip is randomly selected from the box, what is the probability that the chip will be either white or blue?

(1) The probability that the chip will be blue is $\frac{1}{5}$.

(2) The probability that the chip will be red is $\frac{1}{3}$.

From statement (1), only the probability that the chip will be white or red can be determined. Therefore, statement (1) alone is not sufficient. From statement (2), the probability that the chip will be red is $\frac{1}{3}$. Note that the probability that the chip will be either white or blue is the same as the probability that it will <u>not</u> be red, which is $1 - \frac{1}{3} = \frac{2}{3}$. Thus, statement (2) ALONE is sufficient, but statement (1) alone is not sufficient to answer the question. The best answer is B.

231. Of the 4,800 voters who voted for or against Resolution K, 1,800 were Democrats and 3,000 were Republicans. What was the total number of female voters who voted for Resolution K ?

(1) $\frac{3}{4}$ of the Democrats and $\frac{2}{3}$ of the Republicans voted for Resolution K.

(2) $\frac{1}{3}$ of the Democrats who voted for Resolution K and $\frac{1}{2}$ of the Republicans who voted for Resolution K were females.

Statement (1) does not mention female voters at all, so (1) alone is not sufficient. Statement (2) does not tell how many Democrats or Republicans voted for Resolution K, so knowing what fraction of each of those unknowns were females is not sufficient. From statements (1) and (2) together, it can be concluded that $\frac{1}{3} \left(\frac{3}{4} \right) = \frac{1}{4}$ of the Democrats and $\frac{1}{2} \left(\frac{2}{3} \right) = \frac{1}{3}$ of the Republicans voted for K and were females. Since the number of Democrats and Republicans who voted is given, statements (1) and (2) are sufficient to determine the total number of females who voted for K. Thus, BOTH statements TOGETHER are sufficient to answer the question. The best answer is C.

232. If n is a positive integer, is $n^3 - n$ divisible by 4 ?

(1) $n = 2k + 1$, where k is an integer.
(2) $n^2 + n$ is divisible by 6.

Since n is a positive integer and $n^3 - n = n(n^2 - 1) = n(n - 1)(n + 1)$, it follows that $n^3 - n$ is the product of the three consecutive integers $n - 1$, n, and $n + 1$. From statement (1), $n = 2k + 1$, which must be an odd integer. Therefore, the consecutive integers, $n - 1$, n, and $n + 1$ are even, odd, and even, respectively, and since two of the three numbers are divisible by 2, the product of the three numbers must be divisible by 4. Thus, statement (1) alone is sufficient. From statement (2), $n^2 + n = n(n + 1)$, which represents the product of two consecutive integers. The fact that $n(n + 1)$ is divisible by 6 does not guarantee that $n(n - 1)(n + 1)$ is divisible by 4. For example, $(6)(7) = 42$ is divisible by 6, but $(5)(6)(7)$ is not divisible by 4. However $(5)(6)$ is divisible by 6 and $(4)(5)(6)$ is divisible by 4. Therefore, statement (2) alone is not sufficient. Thus statement (1) ALONE is sufficient, but statement (2) alone is not sufficient to answer the question. The best answer is A.

233. If $x \neq -y$, is $\dfrac{x-y}{x+y} > 1$?

    (1) $x > 0$
    (2) $y < 0$

From statement (1), $x > 0$. If $x = 4$ and $y = -3$ then $\dfrac{x-y}{x+y} =$ 7, which is greater than 1. However, if $x = 4$ and $y = 0$, then $\dfrac{x-y}{x+y} = 1$, which is not greater than 1. Therefore, statement (1) alone is not sufficient. From statement (2), $y < 0$. If $x = 4$ and $y = -3$, then as above, $\dfrac{x-y}{x+y}$ would be greater than 1.

However, if $x = 0$ and $y = -3$, then $\dfrac{x-y}{x+y} = -1$, which is not greater than 1. Thus, statement (2) alone is not sufficient. Even statements (1) and (2) together, $x > 0$ and $y < 0$, are not sufficient. As before, if $x = 4$ and $y = -3$, then $\dfrac{x-y}{x+y}$ is greater than 1, but if $x = 2$ and $y = -3$ (also satisfying both statements), then $\dfrac{x-y}{x+y} = -5$, which is not greater than 1.

Therefore, statements (1) and (2) TOGETHER are NOT sufficient to answer the question. The best answer is E.

234. If x is a positive integer and w is a negative integer, what is the value of xw ?

    (1) $x^w = \dfrac{1}{2}$
    (2) $w = -1$

In statement (1), since x is a positive integer and w is a negative integer, the only values for which $x^w = \dfrac{1}{2}$ are $x = 2$ and $w = -1$, that is, $2^{-1} = \dfrac{1}{2}$. Therefore, $xw = (2)(-1) = -2$, and statement (1) alone is sufficient. Statement (2) does not mention x, so xw cannot be evaluated, and (2) alone is not sufficient. Thus, statement (1) ALONE is sufficient, but statement (2) alone is not sufficient to answer the question. The best answer is A.

235. A certain group of car dealerships agreed to donate x dollars to a Red Cross chapter for each car sold during a 30-day period. What was the total amount that was expected to be donated?

    (1) A total of 500 cars were expected to be sold.
    (2) 60 more cars were sold than expected, so that the total amount actually donated was $28,000.

From statement (1), 500 cars were expected to be sold, so $500x$ represents the total amount of the expected donation. However, x is unknown, so (1) alone is not sufficient. From statement (2), the total amount expected to be donated would be $28,000 minus $60x$. Again, x is unknown, so (2) alone is not sufficient. If the information in (1) and in (2) are used together, then $500x = \$28,000 - 60x$, from which the value of x can be determined and thus also the total amount expected to be donated. Thus, BOTH statements TOGETHER are sufficient to answer the question. The best answer is C.

236. Is $|x| = y - z$?

    (1) $x + y = z$
    (2) $x < 0$

From statement (1), $x + y = z$, or equivalently, $x = z - y$. If x is positive, then $|x| = x$, and so $|x| = z - y$. If x is negative, then $|x| = -x$, and so $|x| = -(z - y) = y - z$. Thus $|x|$ could equal $y - z$ or $z - y$ depending on whether x is negative or positive. Therefore, (1) alone is not sufficient. Statement (2) says that x is negative, but does not mention y or z, so (2) alone is not sufficient. If (2), which states that x is negative, is taken together with (1), then, as explained above, $|x|$ would equal $y - z$. Thus, BOTH statements TOGETHER are sufficient to answer the question. The best answer is C.

237. If x is an integer, is $9^x + 9^{-x} = b$?

    (1) $3^x + 3^{-x} = \sqrt{b+2}$
    (2) $x > 0$

From statement (1), $3^x + 3^{-x} = \sqrt{b+2}$. Squaring both sides gives $(3^x + 3^{-x})^2 = b + 2$. But, $(3^x + 3^{-x})^2 = 3^{2x} + 2(3^x 3^{-x}) + 3^{-2x}$, or $9^x + 2 + 9^{-x}$. Therefore, $9^x + 2 + 9^{-x} = b + 2$, or $9^x + 9^{-x} = b$, and so (1) alone is sufficient. Statement (2) gives no information about the relationship between x and b, so (2) alone is not sufficient. Thus, statement (1) ALONE is sufficient, but statement (2) alone is not sufficient to answer the question. The best answer is A.

238. In the figure above, what is the ratio $\dfrac{KN}{MN}$?

  (1) The perimeter of rectangle KLMN is 30 meters.
  (2) The three small rectangles have the same dimensions.

In statement (1), it is given that *KLMN* is a rectangle and that it has a perimeter of 30 meters, so $2(KN) + 2(MN) = 30$, but there is no information about the relative sizes of *KN* and *MN*. Thus, (1) alone is not sufficient. Since statement (2) says that the three small rectangles have the same dimensions, their shorter dimensions are equal to $\dfrac{1}{2}KN$, and their longer dimensions are equal to *KN*. Therefore, $MN = KN + \dfrac{1}{2}KN = \dfrac{3}{2}KN$, and the ratio $\dfrac{KN}{MN}$ is $\dfrac{KN}{\dfrac{3}{2}KN}$, or $\dfrac{2}{3}$. Thus, statement (2) ALONE is sufficient, but statement (1) alone is not sufficient to answer the question. The best answer is B.

239. If *n* is an integer between 2 and 100 and if *n* is also the square of an integer, what is the value of *n*?

  (1) *n* is even.
  (2) The cube root of *n* is an integer.

Statement (1) says that *n* is even, but there are several possible even values of *n* that are squares of integers and are between 2 and 100; namely, 4, 16, 36, and 64. Thus, statement (1) is not sufficient. Statement (2) says that the cube root of *n* is an integer, which means that *n* must not only be the square of an integer but also the cube of an integer. There is only one such value of *n* between 2 and 100, which is 64. Thus, statement (2) ALONE is sufficient, but statement (1) alone is not sufficient to answer the question. The best answer is B.

240. If *x* and *y* are positive integers such that $x = 8y + 12$, what is the greatest common divisor of *x* and *y*?

  (1) $x = 12u$, where *u* is an integer.
  (2) $y = 12z$, where *z* is an integer.

Statement (1) implies that *x* is a multiple of 12. If $x = 36$, then $y = \dfrac{36 - 12}{8} = 3$ and the greatest common divisor of *x* and *y* is 3. However, if $x = 60$, then $y = 6$ and the greatest common divisor of *x* and *y* is 6. Therefore, statement (1) alone is not sufficient. Statement (2) implies that *y* is a multiple of 12 or that 12 is a divisor of *y*. Since $x = 8y + 12$, it follows that 12 is a divisor of *x*, and thus 12 is a common divisor of *x* and *y*. Since $12 = x - 8y$, any common divisor of *x* and *y* must be a divisor of 12. Therefore no integer greater than 12 is a common divisor of *x* and *y*, and 12 is the greatest common divisor of *x* and *y*. Thus, statement (2) ALONE is sufficient, but statement (1) alone is not sufficient to answer the question. The best answer is B.

241. If *r* and *s* are positive integers, is $\dfrac{r}{s}$ an integer?

  (1) Every factor of *s* is also a factor of *r*.
  (2) Every prime factor of *s* is also a prime factor of *r*.

From statement (1), every factor of *s* is also a factor of *r*. Since *s* is a factor of itself, *s* is a factor of *r*, and therefore $\dfrac{r}{s}$ must be an integer. Thus, (1) alone is sufficient. From statement (2), every prime factor of *s* is also a prime factor of *r*. For example, if $r = 18$ and $s = 6$, then 6 has the prime factors 2 and 3, each of which is a factor of 18, and $\dfrac{r}{s} = \dfrac{18}{6}$ is an integer. However, if $r = 18$ and $s = 8$, then *r* has prime factors 2 and 3, and *s* has prime factor 2. Therefore, every prime factor of *s* is a prime factor of *r*, but $\dfrac{r}{s} = \dfrac{18}{8}$ is not an integer. Thus, statement (1) ALONE is sufficient, but statement (2) alone is not sufficient to answer the question. The best answer is A.

242. On Jane's credit card account, the average daily balance for a 30-day billing cycle is the average (arithmetic mean) of the daily balances at the end of each of the 30 days. At the beginning of a certain 30-day billing cycle, Jane's credit card account had a balance of $600. Jane made a payment of $300 on the account during the billing cycle. If no other amounts were added to or subtracted from the account during the billing cycle, what was the average daily balance on Jane's account for the billing cycle?

  (1) Jane's payment was credited on the 21st day of the billing cycle.
  (2) The average daily balance through the 25th day of the billing cycle was $540.

From statement (1), if the payment was made on the 21st day, Jane's balance was $600 for 20 days and $300 for 10 days. Therefore, her average daily balance, which equals

$$\frac{20(\$600)+10(\$300)}{30},$$ can be determined. So (1) alone is

sufficient. From statement (2), if x represents the number of days for which the daily balance stayed $600, then the value of x can be determined by solving the equation

$$\frac{x(\$600)+(25-x)(\$300)}{25} = \$540,$$ where the left side is the

average daily balance for the first 25 days. The value of the average daily balance for the 30 days, which equals

$$\frac{x(\$600)+(30-x)(\$300)}{30},$$ can then be determined. Thus,

EACH statement ALONE is sufficient to answer the question. The best answer is D.

243. If the integer n is greater than 1, is n equal to 2 ?

  (1) n has exactly two positive factors.
  (2) The difference of any two distinct positive factors of n is odd.

Statement (1) says that n has exactly 2 positive factors, which is true for all prime numbers, since each prime number p has only the factors p and 1. So (1) alone is not sufficient. Regarding statement (2), note that if $n > 2$ and n is odd, then 1 and n are factors of n whose difference is even. Also, if $n > 2$ and n is even, then 2 and n are factors of n whose difference is even. Thus, no integer greater than 2 satisfies statement (2), but 2 itself does since 1 and 2 are the only positive factors of 2. Thus, statement (2) ALONE is sufficient, but statement (1) alone is not sufficient to answer the question. The best answer is B.

244. Is $x > y$?

  (1) $x = y + 2$
  (2) $\frac{x}{2} = y - 1$

Statement (1) shows that x is 2 greater than y, so statement (1) alone is sufficient. The equation in statement (2) is equivalent to $x = 2y - 2$. Thus, $x > y$ if and only if $2y - 2 > y$, or $y > 2$, which cannot be determined. Thus, statement (1) ALONE is sufficient, but statement (2) alone is not sufficient to answer the question. The best answer is A.

245. Is $\frac{1}{a-b} < b - a$?

  (1) $a < b$
  (2) $1 < |a-b|$

In statement (1), $a < b$, so $\frac{1}{a-b}$ is negative and $b - a$ is

positive. Therefore, $\frac{1}{a-b} < b - a$, and (1) alone is sufficient. Statement (2) says that the absolute value of $a - b$ is greater than 1, so $a - b$ could be either positive or negative, which makes $b - a$ negative if $a - b$ is positive, and vice versa.

For example, if $a = 7$ and $b = 4$, then $\frac{1}{3} > -3$, but if $a = 4$

and $b = 7$, then $-\frac{1}{3} < 3$. Therefore, (2) alone is not sufficient.

Thus, statement (1) ALONE is sufficient, but statement (2) alone is not sufficient to answer the question. The best answer is A.

246. If $rs \neq 0$, is $\frac{1}{r} + \frac{1}{s} = 4$?

  (1) $r + s = 4rs$
  (2) $r = s$

In statement (1), if both sides of the equation were divided by

rs, the result would be $\frac{r}{rs} + \frac{s}{rs} = \frac{4rs}{rs}$, or $\frac{1}{s} + \frac{1}{r} = 4$. Therefore,

statement (1) alone is sufficient. In statement (2), if $r = s = \frac{1}{2}$,

then $\frac{1}{r} + \frac{1}{s} = 4$, but if $r = s = 1$, then $\frac{1}{r} + \frac{1}{s} = 2$. Therefore,

statement (2) alone is not sufficient. Thus, statement (1) ALONE is sufficient, but statement (2) alone is not sufficient to answer the question. The best answer is A.

247. If m and n are positive integers, is $\sqrt{n-m}$ an integer?

    (1) $n > m + 15$
    (2) $n = m(m + 1)$

From statement (1) it follows that $n - m > 15$. If $n - m = 16$, then $\sqrt{n-m} = 4$, an integer; however, if $n - m = 17$, then $\sqrt{n-m} = \sqrt{17}$, which is not an integer. Thus, statement (1) alone is not sufficient. From statement (2), $n = m(m + 1) = m^2 + m$, so $n - m = m^2$. Therefore, $\sqrt{n-m} = \sqrt{m^2} = m$, an integer. Thus, statement (2) ALONE is sufficient, but statement (1) alone is not sufficient to answer the question. The best answer is B.

248. Is $\dfrac{1}{p} > \dfrac{r}{r^2 + 2}$?

    (1) $p = r$
    (2) $r > 0$

In statement (1), $p = r$, so it must be determined whether $\dfrac{1}{r} > \dfrac{r}{r^2 + 2}$. If $r > 0$, then multiplying both sides by r gives $1 > \dfrac{r^2}{r^2 + 2}$, which is always true because r^2 must be less than $r^2 + 2$. But, if $r < 0$, then multiplying both sides by r changes the inequality sign and gives $1 < \dfrac{r^2}{r^2 + 2}$, which by the same reasoning is not true. Thus, statement (1) alone is not sufficient. Statement (2) says that $r > 0$, but does not mention p, so (2) alone is not sufficient to determine whether $\dfrac{1}{p} > \dfrac{r}{r^2 + 2}$. However, if both (1) and (2) are considered together, as discussed above, $r > 0$ and $p = r$ would be sufficient. Thus, BOTH statements TOGETHER are sufficient to answer the question. The best answer is C.

249. What is the value of $5x^2 + 4x - 1$?

    (1) $x(x + 2) = 0$
    (2) $x = 0$

In statement (1), since $x(x + 2) = 0$, either $x = 0$ or $x = -2$, and each of these two values of x yields a different value for $5x^2 + 4x - 1$. Therefore, statement (1) alone is not sufficient to determine the value of the expression. Since statement (2) says that $x = 0$, the value of the expression can be determined. Thus, statement (2) ALONE is sufficient, but statement (1) alone is not sufficient to answer the question. The best answer is B.

250. What is the value of $a^4 - b^4$?

    (1) $a^2 - b^2 = 16$
    (2) $a + b = 8$

The expression $a^4 - b^4$ can be factored as $(a^2 + b^2)(a^2 - b^2) = (a^2 + b^2)(a + b)(a - b)$. Statement (1) gives the value of $a^2 - b^2$, which is $(a + b)(a - b)$, but without the value of $a^2 + b^2$, statement (1) alone is not sufficient. Statement (2) gives the value of $a + b$, but without values for $a^2 + b^2$ and $a - b$, statement (2) alone is not sufficient. From statements (1) and (2) together, $a^2 - b^2 = 16$ and $a + b = 8$. Since $a^2 - b^2 = (a + b)(a - b)$, it follows that $a - b = 2$. Thus, the two equations $a - b = 2$ and $a + b = 8$ can be solved for a and b, and the value of $a^4 - b^4$ can be determined. Thus, BOTH statements TOGETHER are sufficient to answer the question. The best answer is C.

251. What is the average (arithmetic mean) of a, b, and c?

    (1) $a + 2b + 3c = 10$
    (2) $3a + 2b + c = 14$

The average of a, b, and c is $\dfrac{a+b+c}{3}$. Statement (1) says that $a + 2b + 3c = 10$, but there is not enough information to determine the value of $a + b + c$. Thus, statement (1) alone is not sufficient. Similarly, the equation in statement (2) also fails to give enough information, so statement (2) alone is not sufficient. If the equations in statements (1) and (2) are added together, term by term, the result is $4a + 4b + 4c = 24$, which means that $a + b + c = 6$. The average is therefore $\dfrac{6}{3} = 2$.

Thus, BOTH statements TOGETHER are sufficient to answer the question. The best answer is C.

252. Are positive integers p and q both greater than n?

    (1) $p - q$ is greater than n.
    (2) $q > p$

Statement (1) says $p - q > n$, or $p > n + q$. Since q is positive, p must be greater than n, but there is not enough information to determine whether q is greater than n. Thus, (1) alone is not sufficient. Statement (2) does not mention n at all, so (2) alone is not sufficient. Since statement (1) establishes that $p > n$, and statement (2) says that $q > p$, the two statements together are sufficient to show that p and q are both greater than n. Thus, BOTH statements TOGETHER are sufficient to answer the question. The best answer is C.

253. In the rectangular coordinate system, are the points (r, s) and (u, v) equidistant from the origin?

    (1) $r + s = 1$
    (2) $u = 1 - r$ and $v = 1 - s$.

The distance from (r, s) to $(0, 0)$ is $\sqrt{(r-0)^2 + (s-0)^2}$, or $\sqrt{r^2 + s^2}$. Similarly, the distance from (u, v) to $(0, 0)$ is $\sqrt{u^2 + v^2}$. Therefore, if $r^2 + s^2 = u^2 + v^2$, the two points would be equidistant from the origin. Statement (1) says nothing about coordinates u and v, so (1) alone is not sufficient. From statement (2), $u^2 = (1 - r)^2 = 1 - 2r + r^2$ and $v^2 = (1 - s)^2 = 1 - 2s + s^2$, and $u^2 + v^2 = 1 - 2r + r^2 + 1 - 2s + s^2 = 2 - 2(r + s) + r^2 + s^2$, but there is no information about the value of $r + s$. Thus, (2) alone is not sufficient. From statements (1) and (2) together, since $r + s = 1$, it follows by substitution that $u^2 + v^2 = 2 - 2(1) + r^2 + s^2$, or $u^2 + v^2 = r^2 + s^2$. Thus, BOTH statements TOGETHER are sufficient to answer the question. The best answer is C.

254. Is $\dfrac{x}{m}(m^2 + n^2 + k^2) = xm + yn + zk$?

    (1) $\dfrac{z}{k} = \dfrac{x}{m}$

    (2) $\dfrac{x}{m} = \dfrac{y}{n}$

The equation $\dfrac{x}{m}(m^2 + n^2 + k^2) = xm + yn + zk$ is equivalent to $xm^2 + xn^2 + xk^2 = m^2x + myn + mzk$, which is equivalent to $xn^2 + xk^2 = myn + mzk$. Statement (1) implies that $xk = mz$, or $xk^2 = mzk$; but it is not sufficient to determine whether $xn^2 + xk^2 = myn + mzk$, since it cannot be concluded that $xn^2 = myn$. Statement (2) implies that $xn = my$, or $xn^2 = myn$; but it cannot be concluded that $xn^2 + xk^2 = myn + mzk$ unless it were known that $xk^2 = mzk$. Thus, statement (2) alone is not sufficient. Combining the information in (1) and (2) gives $xn^2 + xk^2 = myn + mzk$. Thus, BOTH statements TOGETHER are sufficient to answer the question. The best answer is C.

255. If x is to be selected at random from set T, what is the probability that $\dfrac{1}{4}x - 5 \le 0$?

    (1) T is a set of 8 integers.
    (2) T is contained in the set of integers from 1 to 25, inclusive.

The inequality $\dfrac{1}{4}x - 5 \le 0$ is equivalent to $x \le 20$, so the question could be stated: "what is the probability that $x \le 20$?" Statement (1) says that there are 8 integers in T. Without knowing what integers are in T, the probability cannot be determined. Thus (1) alone is not sufficient. Statement (2) says that T is a subset of the integers from 1 to 25, inclusive, but the particular integers that are in T are not given. Thus (2) alone is not sufficient. Even both statements together are not sufficient because the number of integers in T that are less than or equal to 20 is still unknown. Therefore, statements (1) and (2) TOGETHER are NOT sufficient to answer the question. The best answer is E.

256. If $m > 0$ and $n > 0$, is $\dfrac{m + x}{n + x} > \dfrac{m}{n}$?

    (1) $m < n$
    (2) $x > 0$

Note that $\dfrac{m + x}{n + x} > \dfrac{m}{n}$ implies that $\dfrac{m + x}{n + x} - \dfrac{m}{n} = \dfrac{(n - m)x}{(n + x)n} > 0$. From statement (1), it follows that $0 < m < n$. Thus, $n - m > 0$; but it cannot be determined whether $\dfrac{(n - m)x}{(n + x)n}$ is positive unless it were known whether $(n - m)x$ and $(n + x)n$ are both positive or both negative. Thus, statement (1) alone is not sufficient. From statement (2), it follows that $(n + x)n > 0$, but it cannot be determined whether $(n - m)x$ is positive, so statement (2) alone is not sufficient. From (1) and (2) together it can be concluded that $(n - m)x > 0$ and $(n + x)n > 0$, and so $\dfrac{(n - m)x}{(n + x)n} > 0$. Thus, BOTH statements TOGETHER are sufficient to answer the question. The best answer is C.

257. Does the integer k have a factor p such that $1 < p < k$?

(1) $k > 4!$
(2) $13! + 2 \leq k \leq 13! + 13$

Note that, if n is any integer greater than 1, then $n!$, read "n factorial," is defined as the product of all the integers from 1 to n. Also k will have a factor p between 1 and k if and only if k is not a prime number. In statement (1), $k > 24$, since $4! = (1)(2)(3)(4) = 24$. However, k may or may not be a prime number. For example if $k = 27$, then the factor p could be 3 or 9; but if $k = 29$, then k does not have any factors between 1 and 29, that is, 29 is a prime number. Thus, statement (1) alone is not sufficient. In statement (2), k could be any of the twelve integers $13! + 2$, $13! + 3$, $13! + 4$, ..., $13! + 13$ where $13!$ is the product of the integers from 1 to 13. Note that 2 is a factor of $13! + 2$, since it is a factor of $13!$ and 2. Also 3 is a factor of $13! + 3$, since 3 is a factor of $13!$ and 3. Similarly, 4 is a factor of $13! + 4$, 5 is a factor of $13! + 5$, and so on for all the values of k. Thus, for each number k from $13! + 2$ to $13! + 13$, there is a factor p such that $1 < p < k$. Thus, statement (2) ALONE is sufficient, but statement (1) alone is not sufficient to answer the question. The best answer is B.

258. What is the value of xy?

(1) $y = x + 1$
(2) $y = x^2 + 1$

From statement (1), $y = x + 1$, but the value of xy cannot be determined. Thus, (1) alone is not sufficient. From statement (2), $y = x^2 + 1$, but again there is not sufficient information to determine the value of xy. Thus, (2) alone is not sufficient. The two statements together imply that $x + 1 = x^2 + 1$, or $x = x^2$. Therefore, $x = 1$ or 0. If x equals 1, then $y = 2$, and $xy = 2$. But if $x = 0$, then $y = 1$, and $xy = 0$. So, the value of xy cannot be determined. Thus, statements (1) and (2) TOGETHER are not sufficient to answer the question. The best answer is E.

259. If v and w are different integers, does $v = 0$?

(1) $vw = v^2$
(2) $w = 2$

In statement (1), if v were not zero, then the equation $vw = v^2$ would be equivalent to $w = v$, which is not possible because it is given that w and v are different integers. Therefore, v must be 0, and (1) alone is sufficient. In statement (2), $w = 2$, so v could be 0, but v could also be any other integer except 2. So, (2) alone is not sufficient. Thus, statement (1) ALONE is sufficient, but statement (2) alone is not sufficient to answer the question. The best answer is A.

260. Is $\sqrt{(x-5)^2} = 5 - x$?

(1) $-x|x| > 0$
(2) $5 - x > 0$

Note that $\sqrt{y^2} = |y|$ for every y. Since $\sqrt{(x-5)^2} = |x-5|$, the given equation $\sqrt{(x-5)^2} = 5 - x$ is equivalent to $|x-5| = 5 - x$, which is true if and only if $5 - x \geq 0$, or $x \leq 5$, because the absolute value must be nonnegative. In statement (1), $|x| > 0$ and, since the product of $-x$ and $|x|$ is positive, $-x > 0$. Thus, $x < 0$, so $x < 5$ and statement (1) alone is sufficient. In statement (2), since $5 - x > 0$, it follows that $x < 5$, and thus statement (2) alone is sufficient. Thus, EACH statement ALONE is sufficient to answer the question. The best answer is D.

261. What is the number of members of Club X who are at least 35 years of age?

(1) Exactly $\frac{3}{4}$ of the members of Club X are under 35 years of age.
(2) The 64 women in Club X constitute 40 percent of the club's membership.

Statement (1) says that $\frac{3}{4}$ of the members are less than 35 years old, which means that $\frac{1}{4}$ of the members are at least 35 years old, but without any information about the number of members, (1) alone is not sufficient. In statement (2), let $m = $ total membership. Since 64 women constitute 40 percent of the membership, $(0.4)(m) = 64$, or $m = 160$. However, there is no mention of age, so (2) alone is not sufficient. From statements (1) and (2) together, $\frac{1}{4}$ of the total membership of 160 are at least 35 years old, so $\frac{1}{4}(160) = 40$. Thus, BOTH statements TOGETHER are sufficient to answer the question. The best answer is C.

262. If $z^n = 1$, what is the value of z?

(1) n is a nonzero integer.
(2) $z > 0$

From statement (1), n is a nonzero integer. If n were odd, then it would follow from $z^n = 1$ that $z = 1$; however, if n were even, then z could be 1 or -1. Therefore, statement (1) alone is not sufficient. From statement (2), z is positive, but if n were 0, any positive value of z would satisfy $z^n = 1$. Thus, statement (2) alone is not sufficient. Statements (1) and (2) together are sufficient because statement (1) limits z to 1 or -1 and statement (2) eliminates -1. Thus, BOTH statements TOGETHER are sufficient to answer the question. The best answer is C.

263. Is $m \neq n$?

    (1) $m + n < 0$
    (2) $mn < 0$

In statement (1), $m + n < 0$, so it is possible that $m = n$, for example, $m = -2, n = -2$, and it is possible that $m \neq n$, for example, $m = -2, n = -3$. So (1) alone is not sufficient. In statement (2), since mn is negative, one of the 2 numbers must be negative and the other positive, which means that $m \neq n$. Thus, statement (2) ALONE is sufficient, but statement (1) alone is not sufficient to answer the question. The best answer is B.

264. Is $2x - 3y < x^2$?

    (1) $2x - 3y = -2$
    (2) $x > 2$ and $y > 0$.

Whatever is the value of x, the value of x^2 must be at least 0. So, in statement (1), since $2x - 3y = -2$, and $-2 < x^2$, it follows that $2x - 3y < x^2$. So, statement (1) alone is sufficient. In statement (2), $x > 2$, so $x^2 > 2x$, and since $y > 0$, $-3y$ is negative. Therefore, $2x - 3y$ must be less than x^2. Thus, EACH statement ALONE is sufficient to answer the question. The best answer is D.

265. If $\dfrac{x}{2} = \dfrac{3}{y}$, is x less than y ?

    (1) $y \geq 3$
    (2) $y \leq 4$

The equation $\dfrac{x}{2} = \dfrac{3}{y}$ can be written $x = \dfrac{6}{y}$. So, using statement (1) alone, $y \geq 3$, which makes $x \leq 2$, or $x < y$. Therefore, (1) alone is sufficient. Using statement (2) alone, $y \leq 4$, so x could be less than y, or not. For example, if $y = 2$, then $x = 3$, but if $y = 3$, then $x = 2$. Thus, statement (1) ALONE is sufficient, but statement (2) alone is not sufficient to answer the question. The best answer is A.

266. Marta bought several pencils. If each pencil was either a 23-cent pencil or a 21-cent pencil, how many 23-cent pencils did Marta buy?

    (1) Marta bought a total of 6 pencils.
    (2) The total value of the pencils Marta bought was 130 cents.

From statement (1), Marta bought 6 pencils, but the number of 23-cent pencils cannot be determined. Thus, (1) alone is not sufficient. From statement (2), the total value of the pencils is 130 cents, so if x is the number of 23-cent pencils and y is the number of 21-cent pencils, then $23x + 21y = 130$. The possible values of x are 0, 1, 2, 3, 4, and 5, but the only value of x that allows y to be an integer is $x = 2$; that is $x = 2$ and $y = 4$. Thus, statement (2) ALONE is sufficient, but statement (1) alone is not sufficient to answer the question. The best answer is B.

267. For a certain set of n numbers, where $n > 1$, is the average (arithmetic mean) equal to the median?

    (1) If the n numbers in the set are listed in increasing order, then the difference between any pair of successive numbers in the set is 2.
    (2) The range of the n numbers in the set is $2(n - 1)$.

From statement (1), the numbers can be written as $x, x + 2, x + 4$, etc. If n is odd then the median is the middle number, which will also be the average. For example, if $n = 5$, the numbers are $x, x + 2, x + 4, x + 6, x + 8$. The average is the sum divided by 5 or $\dfrac{5x + 20}{5} = x + 4$, which is the middle number or median. If n is even, the median is the average of the two middle numbers, which will also be the average of all the numbers. For example, if $n = 6$, then, adding $x + 10$ to the five numbers above, the average is $\dfrac{6x + 30}{6} = x + 5$, when equals $\dfrac{(x + 4) + (x + 6)}{2}$, or the median. Thus, statement (1) alone is sufficient. In statement (2) the range is the difference between the least and greatest numbers; however, it does not give information about the rest of the numbers affecting the average and the median. For example, if $n = 3$, then the range of the three numbers is 4. However, the numbers could be 2, 4, 6, for which the average is equal to the median, or the numbers could be 2, 3, 6, for which the average is greater than the median. Thus statement (1) ALONE is sufficient, but statement (2) alone is not sufficient to answer the question. The best answer is A.

268. Henry purchased 3 items during a sale. He received a 20 percent discount off the regular price of the most expensive item and a 10 percent discount off the regular price of each of the other 2 items. Was the total amount of the 3 discounts greater than 15 percent of the sum of the regular prices of the 3 items?

    (1) The regular price of the most expensive item was $50, and the regular price of the next most expensive item was $20.

    (2) The regular price of the least expensive item was $15.

From statement (1), Henry received a 20 percent discount off the $50 item, so the discount was $10. Also, he received a 10 percent discount off the $20 item, so that discount was $2. He also received a 10 percent discount off the least expensive item, so if x is the price of the least expensive item, then the question is equivalent to asking whether x satisfies the inequality $\frac{12 + (0.1)x}{70 + x} > \frac{15}{100}$, which can be shown to be equivalent to the inequality $x < 30$ using algebra. Since statement (1) implies that $x < 20$, x does satisfy these inequalities, and statement (1) alone is sufficient. Statement (2) alone is not sufficient since it reveals only the price of the third item. Thus, statement (1) ALONE is sufficient, but statement (2) alone is not sufficient to answer the question. The best answer is A.

269. Whenever Martin has a restaurant bill with an amount between $10 and $99, he calculates the dollar amount of the tip as 2 times the tens digit of the amount of his bill. If the amount of Martin's most recent restaurant bill was between $10 and $99, was the tip calculated by Martin on this bill greater than 15 percent of the amount of the bill?

    (1) The amount of the bill was between $15 and $50.

    (2) The tip calculated by Martin was $8.

From Statement (1), the amount of the bill was between $15 and $50, which means that, say, for a bill of $20, the tip would have been $4, which is $\frac{4}{20}$, or 20%; however, for a bill of $19, the tip would be $2, which is $\frac{2}{19} < 15\%$. So, (1) alone is not sufficient. From statement (2) the tip was calculated at $8, which means that the bill was at most $49.99, and the tip was at least $\frac{8}{49.99}$, or 16%, of the bill. Thus, statement (2) ALONE is sufficient, but statement (1) alone is not sufficient to answer the question. The best answer is B.

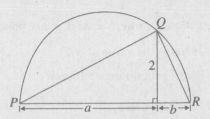

270. If arc PQR above is a semicircle, what is the length of diameter PR ?

    (1) $a = 4$
    (2) $b = 1$

Since angle PQR is inscribed in a semicircle, it is a right angle, and $\triangle PQR$ is a right triangle. $\triangle PQR$ is divided into two right triangles by the vertical line from Q to side PR. Let $x = PQ$ and $y = QR$. The larger right triangle has hypotenuse x, so $x^2 = 4 + a^2$, and the smaller right triangle has hypotenuse y, so $y^2 = 4 + b^2$. From $\triangle PQR$, $(a + b)^2 = x^2 + y^2$, so by substitution, $(a + b)^2 = (4 + a^2) + (4 + b^2)$. Therefore, $a^2 + 2ab + b^2 = 8 + a^2 + b^2$, or $ab = 4$. From statement (1), $a = 4$, so b must be 1, and diameter PR is 5. Thus, (1) alone is sufficient. From statement (2), $b = 1$, so a must be 4, and (2) alone is sufficient. Thus, EACH statement ALONE is sufficient to answer the question. The best answer is D.

271. If r and s are nonzero integers, is $\frac{r}{s}$ an integer?

    (1) $r - 1 = (s + 1)(s - 1)$
    (2) $r - s = 20$

From statement (1), $r - 1 = (s + 1)(s - 1) = s^2 - 1$, so $r = s^2$. Therefore, $\frac{r}{s} = \frac{s^2}{s} = s$, which is an integer. Thus, statement (1) alone is sufficient. In statement (2), if $r = 40$ and $s = 20$, then $r - s = 20$ and $\frac{r}{s}$ is an integer; but, if $r = 39$ and $s = 19$, then $r - s = 20$ and $\frac{r}{s}$ is <u>not</u> an integer. Thus, statement (1) ALONE is sufficient, but statement (2) alone is not sufficient to answer the question. The best answer is A.

272. In the fraction $\dfrac{x}{y}$, where x and y are positive integers, what is the value of y ?

    (1) The least common denominator

       of $\dfrac{x}{y}$ and $\dfrac{1}{3}$ is 6.

    (2) $x = 1$

In statement (1), the least common denominator of the fractions $\dfrac{x}{y}$ and $\dfrac{1}{3}$ is 6, which would be the case if $\dfrac{x}{y}$ were $\dfrac{x}{2}$ or $\dfrac{x}{6}$, so (1) alone is not sufficient. In statement (2), $x = 1$, but y could be any positive integer. Thus, (2) alone is not sufficient. If the two statements are taken together, $\dfrac{x}{y} = \dfrac{1}{2}$ or $\dfrac{1}{6}$, and y is either 2 or 6. Therefore, statements (1) and (2) TOGETHER are not sufficient to answer the question. The best answer is E.

273. If x and y are nonzero integers, is $x^y < y^x$?

    (1) $x = y^2$
    (2) $y > 2$

In statement (1), $x = y^2$, so by substitution $x^y = (y^2)^y = y^{2y}$, and $y^x = y^{y^2}$. Comparing x^y to y^x can then be done by comparing y^{2y} to y^{y^2}, or simply comparing $2y$ to y^2. If $y = 2$, then $2y = 4$ and $y^2 = 4$, and so $x^y = y^x$. If $y = 3$, then $2y = 6$ and $y^2 = 9$, and so $x^y < y^x$. Thus, (1) alone is not sufficient. In statement (2), $y > 2$, but no information about x is given, so statement (2) alone is not sufficient. If both statements are taken together, then from (1) you are comparing $2y$ to y^2, and from (2) $y > 2$, so $2y$ will always be less than y^2. Therefore, $x^y < y^x$. Thus, BOTH statements TOGETHER are sufficient to answer the question. The best answer is C.

274. If n is an integer, is $\dfrac{n}{7}$ an integer?

    (1) $\dfrac{3n}{7}$ is an integer.

    (2) $\dfrac{5n}{7}$ is an integer.

In statement (1), if $\dfrac{3n}{7} = \dfrac{3}{7}n$ is an integer, then n must be divisible by 7, and so $\dfrac{n}{7}$ must be an integer. Thus, (1) alone is sufficient. In statement (2), $\dfrac{5n}{7}$ is an integer, and the same reasoning used above can also be applied here to show that $\dfrac{n}{7}$ must be an integer. Therefore, (2) alone is sufficient. Thus, EACH statement ALONE is sufficient to answer the question. The best answer is D.

6 Reading Comprehension

There are six kinds of reading comprehension questions, each of which tests a different reading skill. The following pages include descriptions of the various question types, test-taking strategies, sample questions, and detailed explanations for all the questions. The explanations further illustrate the ways in which reading comprehension questions evaluate basic reading skills.

Reading comprehension questions include:

1. Questions that ask about the main idea of a passage

Each reading comprehension passage in the GMAT is a unified whole—that is, the individual sentences and paragraphs support and develop one main idea or central point. Sometimes you will be told the central point in the passage itself, and sometimes it will be necessary for you to determine the central point from the overall organization or development of the passage. You may be asked in this kind of question to recognize a correct restatement, or paraphrase, of the main idea of a passage; to identify the author's primary purpose, or objective, in writing the passage; or to assign a title that summarizes briefly and pointedly the main idea developed in the passage.

2. Questions that ask about the supporting ideas presented in a passage

These questions measure your ability to comprehend the supporting ideas in a passage and to differentiate those supporting ideas from the main idea. The questions also measure your ability to differentiate ideas that are *explicitly stated* in a passage from ideas that are *implied* by the author but are not explicitly stated. You may be asked about facts cited in a passage, or about the specific content of arguments presented by the author in support of his or her views, or about descriptive details used to support or elaborate on the main idea. Whereas questions about the main idea ask you to determine the meaning of a passage *as a whole*, questions about supporting ideas ask you to determine the meanings of individual sentences and paragraphs that *contribute* to the meaning of the passage as a whole. One way to think about these questions is to see them as questions asking for the main point of *one small part* of the passage.

3. Questions that ask for inferences based on information presented in a passage

These questions ask about ideas that are not explicitly stated in a passage but are *strongly implied* by the author. Unlike questions about supporting details, which ask about information that is directly stated in a passage, inference questions ask about ideas or meanings that must be inferred from information that is directly stated. Authors can make their points in indirect ways, suggesting ideas without actually stating them. These questions measure your ability to infer an author's intended meaning in parts of a passage where the meaning is only suggested. The questions do not ask about meanings or implications that are remote from the passage but about meanings that are developed indirectly or implications specifically suggested by the author. To answer these questions, you may have to carry statements made by the author one step beyond their literal meanings, or recognize the *opposite* of a statement made by the author, or identify the intended meaning of a word used figuratively in a passage. If a passage explicitly states an effect, for example, you may be asked to infer its cause. If the author compares two phenomena, you may be asked to infer the basis for the comparison. You may be asked to infer the characteristics of an old policy from an explicit description of a new one. When you read a passage, therefore, you should concentrate not only on the explicit meaning of the author's words, but also on the more subtle meaning implied by those words.

4. **Questions that ask how information given in a passage can be applied to a context outside the passage itself**
These questions measure your ability to discern the relationships between situations or ideas presented by the author and other situations or ideas that might parallel those in the passage. In this kind of question, you may be asked to identify a hypothetical situation that is comparable to a situation presented in the passage, or to select an example that is similar to an example provided in the passage, or to apply ideas given in the passage to a situation not mentioned by the author, or to recognize ideas that the author would probably agree or disagree with on the basis of statements made in the passage. Unlike inference questions, these questions use ideas or situations *not* taken from the passage. Ideas and situations given in a question are *like* those given in the passage, and they parallel ideas and situations given in the passage. Therefore, to answer the question, you must do more than recall what you read. You must recognize the essential attributes of ideas and situations presented in the passage when they appear in different words and in an entirely new context.

5. **Questions that ask about the logical structure of a passage**
These questions ask you to analyze and evaluate the organization and the logic of a passage. They may ask how a passage is constructed: for instance, does it define, does it compare or contrast, does it present a new idea, does it refute an idea? They may also ask how the author persuades readers to accept his or her assertions, or about the reason behind the author's use of any particular supporting detail. You may also be asked to identify assumptions that the author is making, to assess the strengths and weaknesses of the author's arguments, or to recognize appropriate counter-arguments. These questions measure your ability not only to comprehend a passage but to evaluate it critically. However, it is important for you to realize that these questions do not rely on any kind of formal logic, nor do they require that you be familiar with specific terms of logic or argumentation. You can answer these questions using only the information in the passage and careful reasoning.

6. **Questions that ask about the style and tone of a passage**
These questions ask about the language of a passage and about the ideas in a passage that may be expressed through its language. You may be asked to deduce the author's attitude toward an idea, a fact, or a situation from the words that he or she uses to describe it. You may also be asked to select a word that accurately describes the tone of a passage—for instance, "critical," "questioning," "objective," or "enthusiastic." To answer this type of question, you will have to consider the language of the passage as a whole: it takes more than one pointed critical word to make the tone of an entire passage "critical." Sometimes, these questions ask what audience the passage was probably intended for or what type of publication it probably appeared in. Style and tone questions may apply to one small part of the passage or to the passage as a whole. To answer them, you must ask yourself what meanings are contained in the words of a passage beyond their literal meanings. Were such words selected because of their emotional content, or because a particular audience would expect to hear them? Remember, these questions measure your ability to discern meaning expressed by the author through his or her choice of words.

Test-taking Strategies for Reading Comprehension

1. You should not expect to be completely familiar with any of the material presented in reading comprehension passages. You may find some passages easier to understand than others, but all passages are designed to present a challenge. If you have some familiarity with the material being presented in a passage, do not let this knowledge influence your choice of answers to the questions. Answer all questions on the basis of what is *stated or implied* in the passage itself.

2. Since the questions require specific and detailed understanding of the material in a passage, analyze each passage carefully the first time you read it. However, there are other ways of approaching reading comprehension passages: some test takers prefer to skim the passages the first time through or even to read the first question before reading the passage. You should choose the method most suitable for you.

3. Focus on key words and phrases, and make every effort to avoid losing the sense of what is being discussed. Keep the following in mind:

    * Note how each fact relates to an idea or an argument.
    * Note where the passage moves from one idea to the next.
    * Separate main ideas from supporting ideas.
    * Determine what conclusions are reached and why.

4. Read the questions carefully, making certain that you understand what is being asked. An answer choice may be incorrect, even though it accurately restates information given in the passage, if it does not answer the question. If you need to, refer back to the passage for clarification.

5. Read all the choices carefully. Never assume that you have selected the best answer without first reading all the choices.

6. Select the choice that best answers the question in terms of the information given in the passage. Do not rely on outside knowledge of the material for answering the questions.

7. Remember that understanding, not speed, is the critical factor in reading comprehension.

READING COMPREHENSION DIRECTIONS

When finished reading directions click on the icon below

Dismiss Directions

The questions in this group are based on the content of a passage. After reading the passage, choose the best answer to each question. Answer all questions following the passage on the basis of what is <u>stated</u> or <u>implied</u> in the passage.

To review these directions for subsequent questions of this type, click on HELP.

| Test | Section | | | | ? | Answer | → |
| Quit | Exit | Time | | | Help | Confirm | Next |

READING COMPREHENSION SAMPLE QUESTIONS

Caffeine, the stimulant in coffee, has been called "the most widely used psychoactive substance on Earth." Snyder, Daly, and Bruns have recently proposed that
Line caffeine affects behavior by countering the activity in
(5) the human brain of a naturally occurring chemical called adenosine. Adenosine normally depresses neuron firing in many areas of the brain. It apparently does this by inhibiting the release of neurotransmitters, chemicals that carry nerve impulses from one neuron to the next.
(10) Like many other agents that affect neuron firing, adenosine must first bind to specific receptors on neuronal membranes. There are at least two classes of these receptors, which have been designated A_1 and A_2. Snyder et al propose that caffeine, which is struc-
(15) turally similar to adenosine, is able to bind to both types of receptors, which prevents adenosine from attaching there and allows the neurons to fire more readily than they otherwise would.

For many years, caffeine's effects have been attri-
(20) buted to its inhibition of the production of phosphodi-esterase, an enzyme that breaks down the chemical called cyclic AMP. A number of neurotransmitters exert their effects by first increasing cyclic AMP concentra-tions in target neurons. Therefore, prolonged periods at
(25) the elevated concentrations, as might be brought about by a phosphodiesterase inhibitor, could lead to a greater amount of neuron firing and, consequently, to behav-ioral stimulation. But Snyder et al point out that the caffeine concentrations needed to inhibit the production
(30) of phosphodiesterase in the brain are much higher than those that produce stimulation. Moreover, other com-pounds that block phosphodiesterase's activity are not stimulants.

To buttress their case that caffeine acts instead by pre-
(35) venting adenosine binding, Snyder et al compared the stimulatory effects of a series of caffeine derivatives with their ability to dislodge adenosine from its receptors in the brains of mice. "In general," they reported, "the ability of the compounds to compete at the receptors
(40) correlates with their ability to stimulate locomotion in the mouse; i.e., the higher their capacity to bind at the receptors, the higher their ability to stimulate locomo-tion." Theophylline, a close structural relative of caffeine and the major stimulant in tea, was one of the most
(45) effective compounds in both regards.

There were some apparent exceptions to the general correlation observed between adenosine-receptor binding and stimulation. One of these was a compound called 3-isobutyl-l-methylxanthine (IBMX), which bound very

(50) well but actually depressed mouse locomotion. Snyder et al suggest that this is not a major stumbling block to their hypothesis. The problem is that the compound has mixed effects in the brain, a not unusual occurrence with psychoactive drugs. Even caffeine, which is generally
(55) known only for its stimulatory effects, displays this property, depressing mouse locomotion at very low concentrations and stimulating it at higher ones.

1. The primary purpose of the passage is to

   (A) discuss a plan for investigation of a phe-nomenon that is not yet fully understood
   (B) present two explanations of a phenomenon and reconcile the differences between them
   (C) summarize two theories and suggest a third theory that overcomes the problems encoun-tered in the first two
   (D) describe an alternative hypothesis and provide evidence and arguments that support it
   (E) challenge the validity of a theory by exposing the inconsistencies and contradictions in it

2. According to Snyder et al, caffeine differs from adenosine in that caffeine

   (A) stimulates behavior in the mouse and in humans, whereas adenosine stimulates behavior in humans only
   (B) has mixed effects in the brain, whereas adenosine has only a stimulatory effect
   (C) increases cyclic AMP concentrations in target neurons, whereas adenosine decreases such concentrations
   (D) permits release of neurotransmitters when it is bound to adenosine receptors, whereas adenosine inhibits such release
   (E) inhibits both neuron firing and the production of phosphodiesterase when there is a suffi-cient concentration in the brain, whereas adenosine inhibits only neuron firing

3. In response to experimental results concerning IBMX, Snyder et al contended that it is not uncommon for psychoactive drugs to have

   (A) mixed effects in the brain
   (B) inhibitory effects on enzymes in the brain
   (C) close structural relationships with caffeine
   (D) depressive effects on mouse locomotion
   (E) the ability to dislodge caffeine from receptors in the brain

4. According to Snyder et al, all of the following compounds can bind to specific receptors in the brain EXCEPT

   (A) IBMX
   (B) caffeine
   (C) adenosine
   (D) theophylline
   (E) phosphodiesterase

5. Snyder et al suggest that caffeine's ability to bind to A_1 and A_2 receptors can be at least partially attributed to which of the following?

   (A) The chemical relationship between caffeine and phosphodiesterase
   (B) The structural relationship between caffeine and adenosine
   (C) The structural similarity between caffeine and neurotransmitters
   (D) The ability of caffeine to stimulate behavior
   (E) The natural occurrence of caffeine and adenosine in the brain

6. The author quotes Snyder et al in lines 38-43 most probably in order to

   (A) reveal some of the assumptions underlying their theory
   (B) summarize a major finding of their experiments
   (C) point out that their experiments were limited to the mouse
   (D) indicate that their experiments resulted only in general correlations
   (E) refute the objections made by supporters of the older theory

Archaeology as a profession faces two major problems. First, it is the poorest of the poor. Only paltry sums are available for excavating and even less is available for publishing the results and preserving the sites once excavated. Yet archaeologists deal with priceless objects every day. Second, there is the problem of illegal excavation, resulting in museum-quality pieces being sold to the highest bidder.

I would like to make an outrageous suggestion that would at one stroke provide funds for archaeology and reduce the amount of illegal digging. I would propose that scientific archaeological expeditions and governmental authorities sell excavated artifacts on the open market. Such sales would provide substantial funds for the excavation and preservation of archaeological sites and the publication of results. At the same time, they would break the illegal excavator's grip on the market, thereby decreasing the inducement to engage in illegal activities

You might object that professionals excavate to acquire knowledge, not money. Moreover, ancient artifacts are part of our global cultural heritage, which should be available for all to appreciate, not sold to the highest bidder. I agree. Sell nothing that has unique artistic merit or scientific value. But, you might reply, everything that comes out of the ground has scientific value. Here we part company. Theoretically, you may be correct in claiming that every artifact has potential scientific value. Practically, you are wrong.

I refer to the thousands of pottery vessels and ancient lamps that are essentially duplicates of one another. In one small excavation in Cyprus, archaeologists recently uncovered 2,000 virtually indistinguishable small jugs in a single courtyard. Even precious royal seal impressions known as *l'melekh* handles have been found in abundance—more than 4,000 examples so far.

The basements of museums are simply not large enough to store the artifacts that are likely to be discovered in the future. There is not enough money even to catalogue the finds; as a result, they cannot be found again and become as inaccessible as if they had never been discovered. Indeed, with the help of a computer, sold artifacts could be more accessible than are the pieces stored in bulging museum basements. Prior to sale, each could be photographed and the list of the purchasers could be maintained on the computer. A purchaser could even be required to agree to return the piece if it should become needed for scientific purposes.

It would be unrealistic to suggest that illegal digging would stop if artifacts were sold on the open market. But the demand for the clandestine product would be substantially reduced. Who would want an unmarked pot when another was available whose provenance was known, and that was dated stratigraphically by the professional archaeologist who excavated it?

7. The primary purpose of the passage is to propose

(A) an alternative to museum display of artifacts
(B) a way to curb illegal digging while benefiting the archaeological profession
(C) a way to distinguish artifacts with scientific value from those that have no such value
(D) the governmental regulation of archaeological sites
(E) a new system for cataloguing duplicate artifacts

8. The author implies that all of the following statements about duplicate artifacts are true EXCEPT:

(A) A market for such artifacts already exists.
(B) Such artifacts seldom have scientific value.
(C) There is likely to be a continuing supply of such artifacts.
(D) Museums are well supplied with examples of such artifacts.
(E) Such artifacts frequently exceed in quality those already catalogued in museum collections.

9. Which of the following is mentioned in the passage as a disadvantage of storing artifacts in museum basements?

(A) Museum officials rarely allow scholars access to such artifacts.
(B) Space that could be better used for display is taken up for storage.
(C) Artifacts discovered in one excavation often become separated from each other.
(D) Such artifacts are often damaged by variations in temperature and humidity.
(E) Such artifacts often remain uncatalogued and thus cannot be located once they are put in storage.

10. The author mentions the excavation in Cyprus (lines 31-34) to emphasize which of the following points?

(A) Ancient lamps and pottery vessels are less valuable, although more rare, than royal seal impressions.
(B) Artifacts that are very similar to each other present cataloguing difficulties to archaeologists.
(C) Artifacts that are not uniquely valuable, and therefore could be sold, are available in large quantities.
(D) Cyprus is the most important location for unearthing large quantities of salable artifacts.
(E) Illegal sales of duplicate artifacts are widespread, particularly on the island of Cyprus.

11. The author's argument concerning the effect of the official sale of duplicate artifacts on illegal excavation is based on which of the following assumptions?

(A) Prospective purchasers would prefer to buy authenticated artifacts.
(B) The price of illegally excavated artifacts would rise.
(C) Computers could be used to trace sold artifacts.
(D) Illegal excavators would be forced to sell only duplicate artifacts.
(E) Money gained from selling authenticated artifacts could be used to investigate and prosecute illegal excavators.

12. The author anticipates which of the following initial objections to the adoption of his proposal?

(A) Museum officials will become unwilling to store artifacts.
(B) An oversupply of salable artifacts will result and the demand for them will fall.
(C) Artifacts that would have been displayed in public places will be sold to private collectors.
(D) Illegal excavators will have an even larger supply of artifacts for resale.
(E) Counterfeiting of artifacts will become more commonplace.

(This passage is excerpted from material published in 1980.)

Federal efforts to aid minority businesses began in the 1960's when the Small Business Administration (SBA) began making federally guaranteed loans and govern-
Line ment-sponsored management and technical assistance
(5) available to minority business enterprises. While this program enabled many minority entrepreneurs to form new businesses, the results were disappointing, since managerial inexperience, unfavorable locations, and capital shortages led to high failure rates. Even 15
(10) years after the program was implemented, minority business receipts were not quite two percent of the national economy's total receipts.

Recently federal policymakers have adopted an approach intended to accelerate development of the
(15) minority business sector by moving away from directly aiding small minority enterprises and toward supporting larger, growth-oriented minority firms through intermediary companies. In this approach, large corporations participate in the development of successful and stable
(20) minority businesses by making use of government-sponsored venture capital. The capital is used by a participating company to establish a Minority Enterprise Small Business Investment Company or MESBIC. The MESBIC then provides capital and guidance to minority
(25) businesses that have potential to become future suppliers or customers of the sponsoring company.

MESBIC's are the result of the belief that providing established firms with easier access to relevant management techniques and more job-specific experience, as
(30) well as substantial amounts of capital, gives those firms a greater opportunity to develop sound business foundations than does simply making general management experience and small amounts of capital available. Further, since potential markets for the minority busi-
(35) nesses already exist through the sponsoring companies, the minority businesses face considerably less risk in terms of location and market fluctuation. Following early financial and operating problems, sponsoring corporations began to capitalize MESBIC's far above
(40) the legal minimum of $500,000 in order to generate sufficient income and to sustain the quality of management needed. MESBIC's are now emerging as increasingly important financing sources for minority enterprises.

(45) Ironically, MESBIC staffs, which usually consist of Hispanic and Black professionals, tend to approach investments in minority firms more pragmatically than do many MESBIC directors, who are usually senior managers from sponsoring corporations. The latter
(50) often still think mainly in terms of the "social responsibility approach" and thus seem to prefer deals that are riskier and less attractive than normal investment criteria would warrant. Such differences in viewpoint have produced uneasiness among many minority staff members,

(55) who feel that minority entrepreneurs and businesses should be judged by established business considerations. These staff members believe their point of view is closer to the original philosophy of MESBIC's and they are concerned that, unless a more prudent course is fol-
(60) lowed, MESBIC directors may revert to policies likely to re-create the disappointing results of the original SBA approach.

13. Which of the following best states the central idea of the passage?

(A) The use of MESBIC's for aiding minority entrepreneurs seems to have greater potential for success than does the original SBA approach.
(B) There is a crucial difference in point of view between the staff and directors of some MESBIC's.
(C) After initial problems with management and marketing, minority businesses have begun to expand at a steady rate.
(D) Minority entrepreneurs wishing to form new businesses now have several equally successful federal programs on which to rely.
(E) For the first time since 1960, large corporations are making significant contributions to the development of minority businesses.

14. According to the passage, the MESBIC approach differs from the SBA approach in that MESBIC's

(A) seek federal contracts to provide markets for minority businesses
(B) encourage minority businesses to provide markets for other minority businesses
(C) attempt to maintain a specified rate of growth in the minority business sector
(D) rely on the participation of large corporations to finance minority businesses
(E) select minority businesses on the basis of their location

15. Which of the following does the author cite to support the conclusion that the results of the SBA program were disappointing?

(A) The small number of new minority enterprises formed as a result of the program
(B) The small number of minority enterprises that took advantage of the management and technical assistance offered under the program
(C) The small percentage of the nation's business receipts earned by minority enterprises following the program's implementation
(D) The small percentage of recipient minority enterprises that were able to repay federally guaranteed loans made under the program
(E) The small number of minority enterprises that chose to participate in the program

-324-

16. Which of the following statements about the SBA program can be inferred from the passage?

(A) The maximum term for loans made to recipient businesses was 15 years.
(B) Business loans were considered to be more useful to recipient businesses than was management and technical assistance.
(C) The anticipated failure rate for recipient businesses was significantly lower than the rate that actually resulted.
(D) Recipient businesses were encouraged to relocate to areas more favorable for business development.
(E) The capitalization needs of recipient businesses were assessed and then provided for adequately.

17. The author refers to the "financial and operating problems" (line 38) encountered by MESBIC's primarily in order to

(A) broaden the scope of the discussion to include the legal considerations of funding MESBIC's through sponsoring companies
(B) call attention to the fact that MESBIC's must receive adequate funding in order to function effectively
(C) show that sponsoring companies were willing to invest only $500,000 of government-sponsored venture capital in the original MESBIC's
(D) compare SBA and MESBIC limits on minimum funding
(E) refute suggestions that MESBIC's have been only marginally successful

18. The author's primary objective in the passage is to

(A) disprove the view that federal efforts to aid minority businesses have been ineffective
(B) explain how federal efforts to aid minority businesses have changed since the 1960's
(C) establish a direct link between the federal efforts to aid minority businesses made before the 1960's and those made in the 1980's
(D) analyze the basis for the belief that job-specific experience is more useful to minority businesses than is general management experience
(E) argue that the "social responsibility approach" to aiding minority businesses is superior to any other approach

The majority of successful senior managers do not closely follow the classical rational model of first clarifying goals, assessing the problem, formulating options, estimating likelihoods of success, making a decision, and only then taking action to implement the decision. Rather, in their day-by-day tactical maneuvers, these senior executives rely on what is vaguely termed "intuition" to manage a network of interrelated problems that require them to deal with ambiguity, inconsistency, novelty, and surprise; and to integrate action into the process of thinking.

Generations of writers on management have recognized that some practicing managers rely heavily on intuition. In general, however, such writers display a poor grasp of what intuition is. Some see it as the opposite of rationality; others view it as an excuse for capriciousness.

Isenberg's recent research on the cognitive processes of senior managers reveals that managers' intuition is neither of these. Rather, senior managers use intuition in at least five distinct ways. First, they intuitively sense when a problem exists. Second, managers rely on intuition to perform well-learned behavior patterns rapidly. This intuition is not arbitrary or irrational, but is based on years of painstaking practice and hands-on experience that build skills. A third function of intuition is to synthesize isolated bits of data and practice into an integrated picture, often in an "Aha!" experience. Fourth, some managers use intuition as a check on the results of more rational analysis. Most senior executives are familiar with the formal decision analysis models and tools, and those who use such systematic methods for reaching decisions are occasionally leery of solutions suggested by these methods which run counter to their sense of the correct course of action. Finally, managers can use intuition to bypass in-depth analysis and move rapidly to engender a plausible solution. Used in this way, intuition is an almost instantaneous cognitive process in which a manager recognizes familiar patterns.

One of the implications of the intuitive style of executive management is that "thinking" is inseparable from acting. Since managers often "know" what is right before they can analyze and explain it, they frequently act first and explain later. Analysis is inextricably tied to action in thinking/acting cycles, in which managers develop thoughts about their companies and organizations not by analyzing a problematic situation and then acting, but by acting and analyzing in close concert.

Given the great uncertainty of many of the management issues that they face, senior managers often instigate a course of action simply to learn more about an issue. They then use the results of the action to develop a more complete understanding of the issue. One implication of thinking/acting cycles is that action is often part of defining the problem, not just of implementing the solution.

19. According to the passage, senior managers use intuition in all of the following ways EXCEPT to

(A) speed up the creation of a solution to a problem
(B) identify a problem
(C) bring together disparate facts
(D) stipulate clear goals
(E) evaluate possible solutions to a problem

20. The passage suggests which of the following about the "writers on management" mentioned in line 12 ?

(A) They have criticized managers for not following the classical rational model of decision analysis.
(B) They have not based their analyses on a sufficiently large sample of actual managers.
(C) They have relied in drawing their conclusions on what managers say rather than on what managers do.
(D) They have misunderstood how managers use intuition in making business decisions.
(E) They have not acknowledged the role of intuition in managerial practice.

21. Which of the following best exemplifies "an 'Aha!' experience" (line 28) as it is presented in the passage?

   (A) A manager risks taking an action whose outcome is unpredictable to discover whether the action changes the problem at hand.
   (B) A manager performs well-learned and familiar behavior patterns in creative and uncharacteristic ways to solve a problem.
   (C) A manager suddenly connects seemingly unrelated facts and experiences to create a pattern relevant to the problem at hand.
   (D) A manager rapidly identifies the methodology used to compile data yielded by systematic analysis.
   (E) A manager swiftly decides which of several sets of tactics to implement in order to deal with the contingencies suggested by a problem.

22. According to the passage, the classical model of decision analysis includes all of the following EXCEPT

   (A) evaluation of a problem
   (B) creation of possible solutions to a problem
   (C) establishment of clear goals to be reached by the decision
   (D) action undertaken in order to discover more information about a problem
   (E) comparison of the probable effects of different solutions to a problem

23. It can be inferred from the passage that which of the following would most probably be one major difference in behavior between Manager X, who uses intuition to reach decisions, and Manager Y, who uses only formal decision analysis?

   (A) Manager X analyzes first and then acts; Manager Y does not.
   (B) Manager X checks possible solutions to a problem by systematic analysis; Manager Y does not.
   (C) Manager X takes action in order to arrive at the solution to a problem; Manager Y does not.
   (D) Manager Y draws on years of hands-on experience in creating a solution to a problem; Manager X does not.
   (E) Manager Y depends on day-to-day tactical maneuvering; Manager X does not.

24. The passage provides support for which of the following statements?

   (A) Managers who rely on intuition are more successful than those who rely on formal decision analysis.
   (B) Managers cannot justify their intuitive decisions.
   (C) Managers' intuition works contrary to their rational and analytical skills.
   (D) Logical analysis of a problem increases the number of possible solutions.
   (E) Intuition enables managers to employ their practical experience more efficiently.

Nearly a century ago, biologists found that if they separated an invertebrate animal embryo into two parts at an early stage of its life, it would survive and develop as two normal embryos. This led them to believe that the cells in the early embryo are undetermined in the sense that each cell has the potential to develop in a variety of different ways. Later biologists found that the situation was not so simple. It matters in which plane the embryo is cut. If it is cut in a plane different from the one used by the early investigators, it will not form two whole embryos.

A debate arose over what exactly was happening. Which embryo cells are determined, just when do they become irreversibly committed to their fates, and what are the "morphogenetic determinants" that tell a cell what to become? But the debate could not be resolved because no one was able to ask the crucial questions in a form in which they could be pursued productively. Recent discoveries in molecular biology, however, have opened up prospects for a resolution of the debate. Now investigators think they know at least some of the molecules that act as morphogenetic determinants in early development. They have been able to show that, in a sense, cell determination begins even before an egg is fertilized.

Studying sea urchins, biologist Paul Gross found that an unfertilized egg contains substances that function as morphogenetic determinants. They are located in the cytoplasm of the egg cell, i.e., in that part of the cell's protoplasm that lies outside of the nucleus. In the unfertilized egg, the substances are inactive and are not distributed homogeneously. When the egg is fertilized, the substances become active and, presumably, govern the behavior of the genes they interact with. Since the substances are unevenly distributed in the egg, when the fertilized egg divides, the resulting cells are different from the start and so can be qualitatively different in their own gene activity.

The substances that Gross studied are maternal messenger RNA's—products of certain of the maternal genes. He and other biologists studying a wide variety of organisms have found that these particular RNA's direct, in large part, the synthesis of histones, a class of proteins that bind to DNA. Once synthesized, the histones move into the cell nucleus, where sections of DNA wrap around them to form a structure that resembles beads, or knots, on a string. The beads are DNA segments wrapped around the histones; the string is the intervening DNA. And it is the structure of these beaded DNA strings that guides the fate of the cells in which they are located.

25. It can be inferred from the passage that the morphogenetic determinants present in the early embryo are

(A) located in the nucleus of the embryo cells
(B) evenly distributed unless the embryo is not developing normally
(C) inactive until the embryo cells become irreversibly committed to their final function
(D) identical to those that were already present in the unfertilized egg
(E) present in larger quantities than is necessary for the development of a single individual

26. The main topic of the passage is

(A) the early development of embryos of lower marine organisms
(B) the main contribution of modern embryology to molecular biology
(C) the role of molecular biology in disproving older theories of embryonic development
(D) cell determination as an issue in the study of embryonic development
(E) scientific dogma as a factor in the recent debate over the value of molecular biology

27. According to the passage, when biologists believed that the cells in the early embryo were undetermined, they made which of the following mistakes?

(A) They did not attempt to replicate the original experiment of separating an embryo into two parts.
(B) They did not realize that there was a connection between the issue of cell determination and the outcome of the separation experiment.
(C) They assumed that the results of experiments on embryos did not depend on the particular animal species used for such experiments.
(D) They assumed that it was crucial to perform the separation experiment at an early stage in the embryo's life.
(E) They assumed that different ways of separating an embryo into two parts would be equivalent as far as the fate of the two parts was concerned.

28. It can be inferred from the passage that the initial production of histones after an egg is fertilized takes place

(A) in the cytoplasm
(B) in the maternal genes
(C) throughout the protoplasm
(D) in the beaded portions of the DNA strings
(E) in certain sections of the cell nucleus

29. It can be inferred from the passage that which of the following is dependent on the fertilization of an egg?

(A) Copying of maternal genes to produce maternal messenger RNA's
(B) Synthesis of proteins called histones
(C) Division of a cell into its nucleus and the cytoplasm
(D) Determination of the egg cell's potential for division
(E) Generation of all of a cell's morphogenetic determinants

30. According to the passage, the morphogenetic determinants present in the unfertilized egg cell are which of the following?

(A) Proteins bound to the nucleus
(B) Histones
(C) Maternal messenger RNA's
(D) Cytoplasm
(E) Nonbeaded intervening DNA

In the two decades between 1910 and 1930, over ten percent of the Black population of the United States left the South, where the preponderance of the Black
Line population had been located, and migrated to northern
(5) states, with the largest number moving, it is claimed, between 1916 and 1918. It has been frequently assumed, but not proved, that the majority of the migrants in what has come to be called the Great Migration came from rural areas and were motivated by two concurrent
(10) factors: the collapse of the cotton industry following the boll weevil infestation, which began in 1898, and increased demand in the North for labor following the cessation of European immigration caused by the outbreak of the First World War in 1914. This assump-
(15) tion has led to the conclusion that the migrants' subsequent lack of economic mobility in the North is tied to rural background, a background that implies unfamiliarity with urban living and a lack of industrial skills.

But the question of who actually left the South has
(20) never been rigorously investigated. Although numerous investigations document an exodus from rural southern areas to southern cities prior to the Great Migration, no one has considered whether the same migrants then moved on to northern cities. In 1910 over 600,000
(25) Black workers, or ten percent of the Black work force, reported themselves to be engaged in "manufacturing and mechanical pursuits," the federal census category roughly encompassing the entire industrial sector. The Great Migration could easily have been made up entirely
(30) of this group and their families. It is perhaps surprising to argue that an employed population could be enticed to move, but an explanation lies in the labor conditions then prevalent in the South.

About thirty-five percent of the urban Black popu-
(35) lation in the South was engaged in skilled trades. Some were from the old artisan class of slavery—blacksmiths, masons, carpenters—which had had a monopoly of certain trades, but they were gradually being pushed out by competition, mechanization, and obsolescence.
(40) The remaining sixty-five percent, more recently urbanized, worked in newly developed industries—tobacco, lumber, coal and iron manufacture, and railroads. Wages in the South, however, were low, and Black workers were aware, through labor recruiters and the
(45) Black press, that they could earn more even as unskilled workers in the North than they could as artisans in the South. After the boll weevil infestation, urban Black workers faced competition from the continuing influx of both Black and White rural workers, who were driven
(50) to undercut the wages formerly paid for industrial jobs. Thus, a move north would be seen as advantageous to a group that was already urbanized and steadily employed, and the easy conclusion tying their subsequent economic problems in the North to their rural background comes into question.

31. The author indicates explicitly that which of the following records has been a source of information in her investigation?

(A) United States Immigration Service reports from 1914 to 1930
(B) Payrolls of southern manufacturing firms between 1910 and 1930
(C) The volume of cotton exports between 1898 and 1910
(D) The federal census of 1910
(E) Advertisements of labor recruiters appearing in southern newspapers after 1910

32. In the passage, the author anticipates which of the following as a possible objection to her argument?

(A) It is uncertain how many people actually migrated during the Great Migration.
(B) The eventual economic status of the Great Migration migrants has not been adequately traced.
(C) It is not likely that people with steady jobs would have reason to move to another area of the country.
(D) It is not true that the term "manufacturing and mechanical pursuits" actually encompasses the entire industrial sector.
(E) Of the Black workers living in southern cities, only those in a small number of trades were threatened by obsolescence.

33. According to the passage, which of the following is true of wages in southern cities in 1910?

(A) They were being pushed lower as a result of increased competition.
(B) They had begun to rise so that southern industry could attract rural workers.
(C) They had increased for skilled workers but decreased for unskilled workers.
(D) They had increased in large southern cities but decreased in small southern cities.
(E) They had increased in newly developed industries but decreased in the older trades.

34. The author cites each of the following as possible influences in a Black worker's decision to migrate north in the Great Migration EXCEPT

    (A) wage levels in northern cities
    (B) labor recruiters
    (C) competition from rural workers
    (D) voting rights in northern states
    (E) the Black press

35. It can be inferred from the passage that the "easy conclusion" mentioned in line 53 is based on which of the following assumptions?

    (A) People who migrate from rural areas to large cities usually do so for economic reasons.
    (B) Most people who leave rural areas to take jobs in cities return to rural areas as soon as it is financially possible for them to do so.
    (C) People with rural backgrounds are less likely to succeed economically in cities than are those with urban backgrounds.
    (D) Most people who were once skilled workers are not willing to work as unskilled workers.
    (E) People who migrate from their birthplaces to other regions of a country seldom undertake a second migration.

36. The primary purpose of the passage is to

    (A) support an alternative to an accepted methodology
    (B) present evidence that resolves a contradiction
    (C) introduce a recently discovered source of information
    (D) challenge a widely accepted explanation
    (E) argue that a discarded theory deserves new attention

In 1896 a Georgia couple suing for damages in the accidental death of their two year old was told that since the child had made no real economic contribution to the family, there was no liability for damages. In contrast, less than a century later, in 1979, the parents of a three year old sued in New York for accidental-death damages and won an award of $750,000.

The transformation in social values implicit in juxtaposing these two incidents is the subject of Viviana Zelizer's excellent book, *Pricing the Priceless Child*. During the nineteenth century, she argues, the concept of the "useful" child who contributed to the family economy gave way gradually to the present-day notion of the "useless" child who, though producing no income for, and indeed extremely costly to, its parents, is yet considered emotionally "priceless." Well established among segments of the middle and upper classes by the mid-1800's, this new view of childhood spread throughout society in the late-nineteenth and early-twentieth centuries as reformers introduced child-labor regulations and compulsory education laws predicated in part on the assumption that a child's emotional value made child labor taboo.

For Zelizer the origins of this transformation were many and complex. The gradual erosion of children's productive value in a maturing industrial economy, the decline in birth and death rates, especially in child mortality, and the development of the companionate family (a family in which members were united by explicit bonds of love rather than duty) were all factors critical in changing the assessment of children's worth. Yet "expulsion of children from the 'cash nexus,' . . . although clearly shaped by profound changes in the economic, occupational, and family structures," Zelizer maintains, "was also part of a cultural process of 'sacralization' of children's lives." Protecting children from the crass business world became enormously important for late-nineteenth-century middle-class Americans, she suggests; this sacralization was a way of resisting what they perceived as the relentless corruption of human values by the marketplace.

In stressing the cultural determinants of a child's worth, Zelizer takes issue with practitioners of the new "sociological economics," who have analyzed such traditionally sociological topics as crime, marriage, education, and health solely in terms of their economic determinants. Allowing only a small role for cultural forces in the form of individual "preferences," these sociologists tend to view all human behavior as directed primarily by the principle of maximizing economic gain. Zelizer is highly critical of this approach, and emphasizes instead the opposite phenomenon: the power of social values to transform price. As children became more valuable in emotional terms, she argues, their "exchange" or "surrender" value on the market, that is, the conversion of their intangible worth into cash terms, became much greater.

37. It can be inferred from the passage that accidental-death damage awards in America during the nineteenth century tended to be based principally on the

(A) earnings of the person at time of death
(B) wealth of the party causing the death
(C) degree of culpability of the party causing the death
(D) amount of money that had been spent on the person killed
(E) amount of suffering endured by the family of the person killed

38. It can be inferred from the passage that in the early 1800's children were generally regarded by their families as individuals who

(A) needed enormous amounts of security and affection
(B) required constant supervision while working
(C) were important to the economic well-being of a family
(D) were unsuited to spending long hours in school
(E) were financial burdens assumed for the good of society

39. Which of the following alternative explanations of the change in the cash value of children would be most likely to be put forward by sociological economists as they are described in the passage?

(A) The cash value of children rose during the nineteenth century because parents began to increase their emotional investment in the upbringing of their children.

(B) The cash value of children rose during the nineteenth century because their expected earnings over the course of a lifetime increased greatly.

(C) The cash value of children rose during the nineteenth century because the spread of humanitarian ideals resulted in a wholesale reappraisal of the worth of an individual.

(D) The cash value of children rose during the nineteenth century because compulsory education laws reduced the supply, and thus raised the costs, of available child labor.

(E) The cash value of children rose during the nineteenth century because of changes in the way negligence law assessed damages in accidental-death cases.

40. The primary purpose of the passage is to

(A) review the literature in a new academic subfield

(B) present the central thesis of a recent book

(C) contrast two approaches to analyzing historical change

(D) refute a traditional explanation of a social phenomenon

(E) encourage further work on a neglected historical topic

41. It can be inferred from the passage that which of the following statements was true of American families over the course of the nineteenth century?

(A) The average size of families grew considerably.

(B) The percentage of families involved in industrial work declined dramatically.

(C) Family members became more emotionally bonded to one another.

(D) Family members spent an increasing amount of time working with each other.

(E) Family members became more economically dependent on each other.

42. Zelizer refers to all of the following as important influences in changing the assessment of children's worth EXCEPT changes in

(A) the mortality rate

(B) the nature of industry

(C) the nature of the family

(D) attitudes toward reform movements

(E) attitudes toward the marketplace

Prior to 1975, union efforts to organize public-sector clerical workers, most of whom are women, were somewhat limited. The factors favoring unionization drives

Line seem to have been either the presence of large numbers
(5) of workers, as in New York City, to make it worth the effort, or the concentration of small numbers in one or two locations, such as a hospital, to make it relatively easy. Receptivity to unionization on the workers' part was also a consideration, but when there were large
(10) numbers involved or the clerical workers were the only unorganized group in a jurisdiction, the multioccupational unions would often try to organize them regardless of the workers' initial receptivity. The strategic reasoning was based, first, on the concern that politi-
(15) cians and administrators might play off unionized against nonunionized workers, and, second, on the conviction that a fully unionized public work force meant power, both at the bargaining table and in the legislature. In localities where clerical workers were few
(20) in number, were scattered in several workplaces, and expressed no interest in being organized, unions more often than not ignored them in the pre-1975 period.

But since the mid-1970's, a different strategy has emerged. In 1977, 34 percent of government clerical
(25) workers were represented by a labor organization, compared with 46 percent of government professionals, 44 percent of government blue-collar workers, and 41 percent of government service workers. Since then, however, the biggest increases in public-sector unioniza-
(30) tion have been among clerical workers. Between 1977 and 1980, the number of unionized government workers in blue-collar and service occupations increased only about 1.5 percent, while in the white-collar occupations the increase was 20 percent and among clerical workers
(35) in particular the increase was 22 percent.

What accounts for this upsurge in unionization among clerical workers? First, more women have entered the work force in the past few years, and more of them plan to remain working until retirement age. Conse-
(40) quently, they are probably more concerned than their predecessors were about job security and economic benefits. Also, the women's movement has succeeded in legitimizing the economic and political activism of women on their own behalf, thereby producing a more positive atti-
(45) tude toward unions. The absence of any comparable increase in unionization among private-sector clerical workers, however, identifies the primary catalyst—the structural change in the multioccupational public-sector unions themselves. Over the past twenty years, the occu-
(50) pational distribution in these unions has been steadily shifting from predominantly blue-collar to predominantly white-collar. Because there are far more women in white-collar jobs, an increase in the proportion of female members has accompanied the occupational shift
(55) and has altered union policy-making in favor of organizing women and addressing women's issues.

43. According to the passage, the public-sector workers who were most likely to belong to unions in 1977 were

(A) professionals
(B) managers
(C) clerical workers
(D) service workers
(E) blue-collar workers

44. The author cites union efforts to achieve a fully unionized work force (lines 13-19) in order to account for why

(A) politicians might try to oppose public-sector union organizing
(B) public-sector unions have recently focused on organizing women
(C) early organizing efforts often focused on areas where there were large numbers of workers
(D) union efforts with regard to public-sector clerical workers increased dramatically after 1975
(E) unions sometimes tried to organize workers regardless of the workers' initial interest in unionization

45. The author's claim that, since the mid-1970's, a new strategy has emerged in the unionization of public-sector clerical workers (line 23) would be strengthened if the author

(A) described more fully the attitudes of clerical workers toward labor unions
(B) compared the organizing strategies employed by private-sector unions with those of public-sector unions
(C) explained why politicians and administrators sometimes oppose unionization of clerical workers
(D) indicated that the number of unionized public-sector clerical workers was increasing even before the mid-1970's
(E) showed that the factors that favored unionization drives among these workers prior to 1975 have decreased in importance

46. According to the passage, in the period prior to 1975, each of the following considerations helped determine whether a union would attempt to organize a certain group of clerical workers EXCEPT

(A) the number of clerical workers in that group
(B) the number of women among the clerical workers in that group
(C) whether the clerical workers in that area were concentrated in one workplace or scattered over several workplaces
(D) the degree to which the clerical workers in that group were interested in unionization
(E) whether all the other workers in the same jurisdiction as that group of clerical workers were unionized

47. The author states that which of the following is a consequence of the women's movement of recent years?

(A) An increase in the number of women entering the work force
(B) A structural change in multioccupational public-sector unions
(C) A more positive attitude on the part of women toward unions
(D) An increase in the proportion of clerical workers that are women
(E) An increase in the number of women in administrative positions

48. The main concern of the passage is to

(A) advocate particular strategies for future efforts to organize certain workers into labor unions
(B) explain differences in the unionized proportions of various groups of public-sector workers
(C) evaluate the effectiveness of certain kinds of labor unions that represent public-sector workers
(D) analyze and explain an increase in unionization among a certain category of workers
(E) describe and distinguish strategies appropriate to organizing different categories of workers

Milankovitch proposed in the early twentieth century that the ice ages were caused by variations in the Earth's orbit around the Sun. For sometime this theory was considered untestable, largely because there was no suffi-
Line
(5) ciently precise chronology of the ice ages with which the orbital variations could be matched.

To establish such a chronology it is necessary to determine the relative amounts of land ice that existed at various times in the Earth's past. A recent discovery
(10) makes such a determination possible: relative land-ice volume for a given period can be deduced from the ratio of two oxygen isotopes, 16 and 18, found in ocean sediments. Almost all the oxygen in water is oxygen 16, but a few molecules out of every thousand incorporate the
(15) heavier isotope 18. When an ice age begins, the continental ice sheets grow, steadily reducing the amount of water evaporated from the ocean that will eventually return to it. Because heavier isotopes tend to be left behind when water evaporates from the ocean surfaces,
(20) the remaining ocean water becomes progressively enriched in oxygen 18. The degree of enrichment can be determined by analyzing ocean sediments of the period, because these sediments are composed of calcium carbonate shells of marine organisms, shells that were
(25) constructed with oxygen atoms drawn from the surrounding ocean. The higher the ratio of oxygen 18 to oxygen 16 in a sedimentary specimen, the more land ice there was when the sediment was laid down.

As an indicator of shifts in the Earth's climate, the
(30) isotope record has two advantages. First, it is a global record: there is remarkably little variation in isotope ratios in sedimentary specimens taken from different continental locations. Second, it is a more continuous record than that taken from rocks on land. Because of
(35) these advantages, sedimentary evidence can be dated with sufficient accuracy by radiometric methods to establish a precise chronology of the ice ages. The dated isotope record shows that the fluctuations in global ice volume over the past several hundred thousand years
(40) have a pattern: an ice age occurs roughly once every 100,000 years. These data have established a strong connection between variations in the Earth's orbit and the periodicity of the ice ages.

However, it is important to note that other factors,
(45) such as volcanic particulates or variations in the amount of sunlight received by the Earth, could potentially have affected the climate. The advantage of the Milankovitch theory is that it is testable; changes in the Earth's orbit can be calculated and dated by applying Newton's laws
(50) of gravity to progressively earlier configurations of the bodies in the solar system. Yet the lack of information about other possible factors affecting global climate does not make them unimportant.

49. In the passage, the author is primarily interested in

(A) suggesting an alternative to an outdated research method
(B) introducing a new research method that calls an accepted theory into question
(C) emphasizing the instability of data gathered from the application of a new scientific method
(D) presenting a theory and describing a new method to test that theory
(E) initiating a debate about a widely accepted theory

50. The author of the passage would be most likely to agree with which of the following statements about the Milankovitch theory?

(A) It is the only possible explanation for the ice ages.
(B) It is too limited to provide a plausible explanation for the ice ages, despite recent research findings.
(C) It cannot be tested and confirmed until further research on volcanic activity is done.
(D) It is one plausible explanation, though not the only one, for the ice ages.
(E) It is not a plausible explanation for the ice ages, although it has opened up promising possibilities for future research.

51. It can be inferred from the passage that the isotope record taken from ocean sediments would be less useful to researchers if which of the following were true?

(A) It indicated that lighter isotopes of oxygen predominated at certain times.
(B) It had far more gaps in its sequence than the record taken from rocks on land.
(C) It indicated that climate shifts did not occur every 100,000 years.
(D) It indicated that the ratios of oxygen 16 and oxygen 18 in ocean water were not consistent with those found in fresh water.
(E) It stretched back for only a million years.

52. According to the passage, which of the following is true of the ratios of oxygen isotopes in ocean sediments?

   (A) They indicate that sediments found during an ice age contain more calcium carbonate than sediments formed at other times.
   (B) They are less reliable than the evidence from rocks on land in determining the volume of land ice.
   (C) They can be used to deduce the relative volume of land ice that was present when the sediment was laid down.
   (D) They are more unpredictable during an ice age than in other climatic conditions.
   (E) They can be used to determine atmospheric conditions at various times in the past.

53. It can be inferred from the passage that precipitation formed from evaporated ocean water has

   (A) the same isotopic ratio as ocean water
   (B) less oxygen 18 than does ocean water
   (C) less oxygen 18 than has the ice contained in continental ice sheets
   (D) a different isotopic composition than has precipitation formed from water on land
   (E) more oxygen 16 than has precipitation formed from fresh water

54. It can be inferred from the passage that calcium carbonate shells

   (A) are not as susceptible to deterioration as rocks
   (B) are less common in sediments formed during an ice age
   (C) are found only in areas that were once covered by land ice
   (D) contain radioactive material that can be used to determine a sediment's isotopic composition
   (E) reflect the isotopic composition of the water at the time the shells were formed

Many United States companies have, unfortunately, made the search for legal protection from import competition into a major line of work. Since 1980 the United States International Trade Commission (ITC) has received about 280 complaints alleging damage from imports that benefit from subsidies by foreign governments. Another 340 charge that foreign companies "dumped" their products in the United States at "less than fair value." Even when no unfair practices are alleged, the simple claim that an industry has been injured by imports is sufficient grounds to seek relief.

Contrary to the general impression, this quest for import relief has hurt more companies than it has helped. As corporations begin to function globally, they develop an intricate web of marketing, production, and research relationships. The complexity of these relationships makes it unlikely that a system of import relief laws will meet the strategic needs of all the units under the same parent company.

Internationalization increases the danger that foreign companies will use import relief laws against the very companies the laws were designed to protect. Suppose a United States-owned company establishes an overseas plant to manufacture a product while its competitor makes the same product in the United States. If the competitor can prove injury from the imports—and that the United States company received a subsidy from a foreign government to build its plant abroad—the United States company's products will be uncompetitive in the United States, since they would be subject to duties.

Perhaps the most brazen case occurred when the ITC investigated allegations that Canadian companies were injuring the United States salt industry by dumping rock salt, used to de-ice roads. The bizarre aspect of the complaint was that a foreign conglomerate with United States operations was crying for help against a United States company with foreign operations. The "United States" company claiming injury was a subsidiary of a Dutch conglomerate, while the "Canadian" companies included a subsidiary of a Chicago firm that was the second-largest domestic producer of rock salt.

Line
(5)

(10)

(15)

(20)

(25)

(30)

(35)

(40)

55. The passage is chiefly concerned with

(A) arguing against the increased internationalization of United States corporations
(B) warning that the application of laws affecting trade frequently has unintended consequences
(C) demonstrating that foreign-based firms receive more subsidies from their governments than United States firms receive from the United States government
(D) advocating the use of trade restrictions for "dumped" products but not for other imports
(E) recommending a uniform method for handling claims of unfair trade practices

56. It can be inferred from the passage that the minimal basis for a complaint to the International Trade Commission is which of the following?

(A) A foreign competitor has received a subsidy from a foreign government.
(B) A foreign competitor has substantially increased the volume of products shipped to the United States.
(C) A foreign competitor is selling products in the United States at less than fair market value.
(D) The company requesting import relief has been injured by the sale of imports in the United States.
(E) The company requesting import relief has been barred from exporting products to the country of its foreign competitor.

57. The last paragraph performs which of the following functions in the passage?

(A) It summarizes the discussion thus far and suggests additional areas for research.
(B) It presents a recommendation based on the evidence presented earlier.
(C) It discusses an exceptional case in which the results expected by the author of the passage were not obtained.
(D) It introduces an additional area of concern not mentioned earlier.
(E) It cites a specific case that illustrates a problem presented more generally in the previous paragraph.

58. The passage warns of which of the following dangers?

(A) Companies in the United States may receive no protection from imports unless they actively seek protection from import competition.
(B) Companies that seek legal protection from import competition may incur legal costs that far exceed any possible gain.
(C) Companies that are United States-owned but operate internationally may not be eligible for protection from import competition under the laws of the countries in which their plants operate.
(D) Companies that are not United States-owned may seek legal protection from import competition under United States import relief laws.
(E) Companies in the United States that import raw materials may have to pay duties on those materials.

59. The passage suggests that which of the following is most likely to be true of United States trade laws?

(A) They will eliminate the practice of "dumping" products in the United States.
(B) They will enable manufacturers in the United States to compete more profitably outside the United States.
(C) They will affect United States trade with Canada more negatively than trade with other nations.
(D) Those that help one unit within a parent company will not necessarily help other units in the company.
(E) Those that are applied to international companies will accomplish their intended result.

60. It can be inferred from the passage that the author believes which of the following about the complaint mentioned in the last paragraph?

(A) The ITC acted unfairly toward the complainant in its investigation.
(B) The complaint violated the intent of import relief laws.
(C) The response of the ITC to the complaint provided suitable relief from unfair trade practices to the complainant.
(D) The ITC did not have access to appropriate information concerning the case.
(E) Each of the companies involved in the complaint acted in its own best interest.

At the end of the nineteenth century, a rising interest in Native American customs and an increasing desire to understand Native American culture prompted ethnologists to begin recording the life stories of Native Americans. Ethnologists had a distinct reason for wanting to hear the stories: they were after linguistic or anthropological data that would supplement their own field observations, and they believed that the personal stories, even of a single individual, could increase their understanding of the cultures that they had been observing from without. In addition many ethnologists at the turn of the century believed that Native American manners and customs were rapidly disappearing, and that it was important to preserve for posterity as much information as could be adequately recorded before the cultures disappeared forever.

There were, however, arguments against this method as a way of acquiring accurate and complete information. Franz Boas, for example, described autobiographies as being "of limited value, and useful chiefly for the study of the perversion of truth by memory," while Paul Radin contended that investigators rarely spent enough time with the tribes they were observing, and inevitably derived results too tinged by the investigator's own emotional tone to be reliable.

Even more importantly, as these life stories moved from the traditional oral mode to recorded written form, much was inevitably lost. Editors often decided what elements were significant to the field research on a given tribe. Native Americans recognized that the essence of their lives could not be communicated in English and that events that they thought significant were often deemed unimportant by their interviewers. Indeed, the very act of telling their stories could force Native American narrators to distort their cultures, as taboos had to be broken to speak the names of dead relatives crucial to their family stories.

Despite all of this, autobiography remains a useful tool for ethnological research: such personal reminiscences and impressions, incomplete as they may be, are likely to throw more light on the working of the mind and emotions than any amount of speculation from an ethnologist or ethnological theorist from another culture.

61. Which of the following best describes the organization of the passage?

(A) The historical backgrounds of two currently used research methods are chronicled.
(B) The validity of the data collected by using two different research methods is compared.
(C) The usefulness of a research method is questioned and then a new method is proposed.
(D) The use of a research method is described and the limitations of the results obtained are discussed.
(E) A research method is evaluated and the changes necessary for its adaptation to other subject areas are discussed.

62. Which of the following is most similar to the actions of nineteenth-century ethnologists in their editing of the life stories of Native Americans?

(A) A witness in a jury trial invokes the Fifth Amendment in order to avoid relating personally incriminating evidence.
(B) A stockbroker refuses to divulge the source of her information on the possible future increase in a stock's value.
(C) A sports announcer describes the action in a team sport with which he is unfamiliar.
(D) A chef purposely excludes the special ingredient from the recipe of his prizewinning dessert.
(E) A politician fails to mention in a campaign speech the similarities in the positions held by her opponent for political office and by herself.

63. According to the passage, collecting life stories can be a useful methodology because

(A) life stories provide deeper insights into a culture than the hypothesizing of academics who are not members of that culture
(B) life stories can be collected easily and they are not subject to invalid interpretations
(C) ethnologists have a limited number of research methods from which to choose
(D) life stories make it easy to distinguish between the important and unimportant features of a culture
(E) the collection of life stories does not require a culturally knowledgeable investigator

64. Information in the passage suggests that which of the following may be a possible way to eliminate bias in the editing of life stories?

(A) Basing all inferences made about the culture on an ethnological theory
(B) Eliminating all of the emotion-laden information reported by the informant
(C) Translating the informant's words into the researcher's language
(D) Reducing the number of questions and carefully specifying the content of the questions that the investigator can ask the informant
(E) Reporting all of the information that the informant provides regardless of the investigator's personal opinion about its intrinsic value

65. The primary purpose of the passage as a whole is to

(A) question an explanation
(B) correct a misconception
(C) critique a methodology
(D) discredit an idea
(E) clarify an ambiguity

66. It can be inferred from the passage that a characteristic of the ethnological research on Native Americans conducted during the nineteenth century was the use of which of the following?

(A) Investigators familiar with the culture under study
(B) A language other than the informant's for recording life stories
(C) Life stories as the ethnologist's primary source of information
(D) Complete transcriptions of informants' descriptions of tribal beliefs
(E) Stringent guidelines for the preservation of cultural data

All of the cells in a particular plant start out with the same complement of genes. How then can these cells differentiate and form structures as different as roots, stems, leaves, and fruits? The answer is that only a small subset of the genes in a particular kind of cell are expressed, or turned on, at a given time. This is accomplished by a complex system of chemical messengers that in plants include hormones and other regulatory molecules. Five major hormones have been identified: auxin, abscisic acid, cytokinin, ethylene, and gibberellin. Studies of plants have now identified a new class of regulatory molecules called oligosaccharins.

Unlike the oligosaccharins, the five well-known plant hormones are pleiotropic rather than specific; that is, each has more than one effect on the growth and development of plants. The five have so many simultaneous effects that they are not very useful in artificially controlling the growth of crops. Auxin, for instance, stimulates the rate of cell elongation, causes shoots to grow up and roots to grow down, and inhibits the growth of lateral shoots. Auxin also causes the plant to develop a vascular system, to form lateral roots, and to produce ethylene.

The pleiotropy of the five well-studied plant hormones is somewhat analogous to that of certain hormones in animals. For example, hormones from the hypothalamus in the brain stimulate the anterior lobe of the pituitary gland to synthesize and release many different hormones, one of which stimulates the release of hormones from the adrenal cortex. These hormones have specific effects on target organs all over the body. One hormone stimulates the thyroid gland, for example, another the ovarian follicle cells, and so forth. In other words, there is a hierarchy of hormones.

Such a hierarchy may also exist in plants. Oligosaccharins are fragments of the cell wall released by enzymes: different enzymes release different oligosaccharins. There are indications that pleiotropic plant hormones may actually function by activating the enzymes that release these other, more specific chemical messengers from the cell wall.

67. According to the passage, the five well-known plant hormones are not useful in controlling the growth of crops because

(A) it is not known exactly what functions the hormones perform
(B) each hormone has various effects on plants
(C) none of the hormones can function without the others
(D) each hormone has different effects on different kinds of plants
(E) each hormone works on only a small subset of a cell's genes at any particular time

68. The passage suggests that the place of hypothalamic hormones in the hormonal hierarchies of animals is similar to the place of which of the following in plants?

(A) Plant cell walls
(B) The complement of genes in each plant cell
(C) A subset of a plant cell's gene complement
(D) The five major hormones
(E) The oligosaccharins

69. The passage suggests that which of the following is a function likely to be performed by an oligosaccharin?

(A) To stimulate a particular plant cell to become part of a plant's root system
(B) To stimulate the walls of a particular cell to produce other oligosaccharins
(C) To activate enzymes that release specific chemical messengers from plant cell walls
(D) To duplicate the gene complement in a particular plant cell
(E) To produce multiple effects on a particular subsystem of plant cells

70. The author mentions specific effects that auxin has on plant development in order to illustrate the

   (A) point that some of the effects of plant hormones can be harmful
   (B) way in which hormones are produced by plants
   (C) hierarchical nature of the functioning of plant hormones
   (D) differences among the best-known plant hormones
   (E) concept of pleiotropy as it is exhibited by plant hormones

71. According to the passage, which of the following best describes a function performed by oligo-saccharins?

   (A) Regulating the daily functioning of a plant's cells
   (B) Interacting with one another to produce different chemicals
   (C) Releasing specific chemical messengers from a plant's cell walls
   (D) Producing the hormones that cause plant cells to differentiate to perform different functions
   (E) Influencing the development of a plant's cells by controlling the expression of the cells' genes

72. The passage suggests that, unlike the pleiotropic hormones, oligosaccharins could be used effectively to

   (A) trace the passage of chemicals through the walls of cells
   (B) pinpoint functions of other plant hormones
   (C) artificially control specific aspects of the development of crops
   (D) alter the complement of genes in the cells of plants
   (E) alter the effects of the five major hormones on plant development

Two recent publications offer different assessments of the career of the famous British nurse Florence Nightingale. A book by Anne Summers seeks to debunk the idealizations and present a reality at odds with Nightingale's heroic reputation. According to Summers, Nightingale's importance during the Crimean War has been exaggerated: not until near the war's end did she become supervisor of the female nurses. Additionally, Summers writes that the contribution of the nurses to the relief of the wounded was at best marginal. The prevailing problems of military medicine were caused by army organizational practices, and the addition of a few nurses to the medical staff could be no more than symbolic. Nightingale's place in the national pantheon, Summers asserts, is largely due to the propagandistic efforts of contemporary newspaper reporters.

By contrast, the editors of a new volume of Nightingale's letters view Nightingale as a person who significantly influenced not only her own age but also subsequent generations. They highlight her ongoing efforts to reform sanitary conditions after the war. For example, when she learned that peacetime living conditions in British barracks were so horrible that the death rate of enlisted men far exceeded that of neighboring civilian populations, she succeeded in persuading the government to establish a Royal Commission on the Health of the Army. She used sums raised through public contributions to found a nurses' training hospital in London. Even in administrative matters, the editors assert, her practical intelligence was formidable: as recently as 1947 the British Army's medical services were still using the cost-accounting system she had devised in the 1860's.

I believe that the evidence of her letters supports continued respect for Nightingale's brilliance and creativity. When counseling a village schoolmaster to encourage children to use their faculties of observation, she sounds like a modern educator. Her insistence on classifying the problems of the needy in order to devise appropriate treatments is similar to the approach of modern social workers. In sum, although Nightingale may not have achieved all of her goals during the Crimean War, her breadth of vision and ability to realize ambitious projects have earned her an eminent place among the ranks of social pioneers.

73. The passage is primarily concerned with evaluating

(A) the importance of Florence Nightingale's innovations in the field of nursing
(B) contrasting approaches to the writing of historical biography
(C) contradictory accounts of Florence Nightingale's historical significance
(D) the quality of health care in nineteenth-century England
(E) the effect of the Crimean War on developments in the field of health care

74. According to the passage, the editors of Nightingale's letters credit her with contributing to which of the following?

(A) Improvement of the survival rate for soldiers in British Army hospitals during the Crimean War
(B) The development of a nurses' training curriculum that was far in advance of its day
(C) The increase in the number of women doctors practicing in British Army hospitals
(D) Establishment of the first facility for training nurses at a major British university
(E) The creation of an organization for monitoring the peacetime living conditions of British soldiers

75. The passage suggests which of the following about Nightingale's relationship with the British public of her day?

(A) She was highly respected, her projects receiving popular and governmental support.
(B) She encountered resistance both from the army establishment and the general public.
(C) She was supported by the working classes and opposed by the wealthier classes.
(D) She was supported by the military establishment but had to fight the governmental bureaucracy.
(E) After initially being received with enthusiasm, she was quickly forgotten.

76. The passage suggests which of the following about sanitary conditions in Britain after the Crimean War?

(A) While not ideal, they were superior to those in other parts of the world.
(B) Compared with conditions before the war, they had deteriorated.
(C) They were more advanced in rural areas than in the urban centers.
(D) They were worse in military camps than in the neighboring civilian populations.
(E) They were uniformly crude and unsatisfactory throughout England.

77. With which of the following statements regarding the differing interpretations of Nightingale's importance would the author most likely agree?

(A) Summers misunderstood both the importance of Nightingale's achievements during the Crimean War and her subsequent influence on British policy.
(B) The editors of Nightingale's letters made some valid points about her practical achievements, but they still exaggerated her influence on subsequent generations.
(C) Although Summers' account of Nightingale's role in the Crimean War may be accurate, she ignored evidence of Nightingale's subsequent achievement that suggests that her reputation as an eminent social reformer is well deserved.
(D) The editors of Nightingale's letters mistakenly propagated the outdated idealization of Nightingale that only impedes attempts to arrive at a balanced assessment of her true role.
(E) The evidence of Nightingale's letters supports Summers' conclusions both about Nightingale's activities and about her influence.

78. Which of the following is an assumption underlying the author's assessment of Nightingale's creativity?

(A) Educational philosophy in Nightingale's day did not normally emphasize developing children's ability to observe.
(B) Nightingale was the first to notice the poor living conditions in British military barracks in peacetime.
(C) No educator before Nightingale had thought to enlist the help of village schoolmasters in introducing new teaching techniques.
(D) Until Nightingale began her work, there was no concept of organized help for the needy in nineteenth-century Britain.
(E) The British Army's medical services had no cost-accounting system until Nightingale devised one in the 1860's.

79. In the last paragraph, the author is primarily concerned with

(A) summarizing the arguments about Nightingale presented in the first two paragraphs
(B) refuting the view of Nightingale's career presented in the preceding paragraph
(C) analyzing the weaknesses of the evidence presented elsewhere in the passage
(D) citing evidence to support a view of Nightingale's career
(E) correcting a factual error occurring in one of the works under review

A meteor stream is composed of dust particles that have been ejected from a parent comet at a variety of velocities. These particles follow the same orbit as the parent comet, but due to their differing velocities they slowly gain on or fall behind the disintegrating comet until a shroud of dust surrounds the entire cometary orbit. Astronomers have hypothesized that a meteor stream should broaden with time as the dust particles' individual orbits are perturbed by planetary gravitational fields. A recent computer-modeling experiment tested this hypothesis by tracking the influence of planetary gravitation over a projected 5,000-year period on the positions of a group of hypothetical dust particles. In the model, the particles were randomly distributed throughout a computer simulation of the orbit of an actual meteor stream, the Geminid. The researcher found, as expected, that the computer-model stream broadened with time. Conventional theories, however, predicted that the distribution of particles would be increasingly dense toward the center of a meteor stream. Surprisingly, the computer-model meteor stream gradually came to resemble a thick-walled, hollow pipe.

Whenever the Earth passes through a meteor stream, a meteor shower occurs. Moving at a little over 1,500,000 miles per day around its orbit, the Earth would take, on average, just over a day to cross the hollow, computer-model Geminid stream if the stream were 5,000 years old. Two brief periods of peak meteor activity during the shower would be observed, one as the Earth entered the thick-walled "pipe" and one as it exited. There is no reason why the Earth should always pass through the stream's exact center, so the time interval between the two bursts of activity would vary from one year to the next.

Has the predicted twin-peaked activity been observed for the actual yearly Geminid meteor shower? The Geminid data between 1970 and 1979 show just such a bifurcation, a secondary burst of meteor activity being clearly visible at an average of 19 hours (1,200,000 miles) after the first burst. The time intervals between the bursts suggest the actual Geminid stream is about 3,000 years old.

80. The primary focus of the passage is on which of the following?

(A) Comparing two scientific theories and contrasting the predictions that each would make concerning a natural phenomenon
(B) Describing a new theoretical model and noting that it explains the nature of observations made of a particular natural phenomenon
(C) Evaluating the results of a particular scientific experiment and suggesting further areas for research
(D) Explaining how two different natural phenomena are related and demonstrating a way to measure them
(E) Analyzing recent data derived from observations of an actual phenomenon and constructing a model to explain the data

81. According to the passage, which of the following is an accurate statement concerning meteor streams?

(A) Meteor streams and comets start out with similar orbits, but only those of meteor streams are perturbed by planetary gravitation.
(B) Meteor streams grow as dust particles are attracted by the gravitational fields of comets.
(C) Meteor streams are composed of dust particles derived from comets.
(D) Comets may be composed of several kinds of materials, while meteor streams consist only of large dust particles.
(E) Once formed, meteor streams hasten the further disintegration of comets.

82. The author states that the research described in the first paragraph was undertaken in order to

(A) determine the age of an actual meteor stream
(B) identify the various structural features of meteor streams
(C) explore the nature of a particularly interesting meteor stream
(D) test the hypothesis that meteor streams become broader as they age
(E) show that a computer model could help in explaining actual astronomical data

83. It can be inferred from the passage that which of the following would most probably be observed during the Earth's passage through a meteor stream if the conventional theories mentioned in line 18 were correct?

(A) Meteor activity would gradually increase to a single, intense peak, and then gradually decline.
(B) Meteor activity would be steady throughout the period of the meteor shower.
(C) Meteor activity would rise to a peak at the beginning and at the end of the meteor shower.
(D) Random bursts of very high meteor activity would be interspersed with periods of very little activity.
(E) In years in which the Earth passed through only the outer areas of a meteor stream, meteor activity would be absent.

84. According to the passage, why do the dust particles in a meteor stream eventually surround a comet's original orbit?

(A) They are ejected by the comet at differing velocities.
(B) Their orbits are uncontrolled by planetary gravitational fields.
(C) They become part of the meteor stream at different times.
(D) Their velocity slows over time.
(E) Their ejection velocity is slower than that of the comet.

85. The passage suggests that which of the following is a prediction concerning meteor streams that can be derived from both the conventional theories mentioned in line 18 and the new computer-derived theory?

(A) Dust particles in a meteor stream will usually be distributed evenly throughout any cross section of the stream.
(B) The orbits of most meteor streams should cross the orbit of the Earth at some point and give rise to a meteor shower.
(C) Over time the distribution of dust in a meteor stream will usually become denser at the outside edges of the stream than at the center.
(D) Meteor showers caused by older meteor streams should be, on average, longer in duration than those caused by very young meteor streams.
(E) The individual dust particles in older meteor streams should be, on average, smaller than those that compose younger meteor streams.

86. It can be inferred from the last paragraph of the passage that which of the following must be true of the Earth as it orbits the Sun?

(A) Most meteor streams it encounters are more than 2,000 years old.
(B) When passing through a meteor stream, it usually passes near to the stream's center.
(C) It crosses the Geminid meteor stream once every year.
(D) It usually takes over a day to cross the actual Geminid meteor stream.
(E) It accounts for most of the gravitational perturbation affecting the Geminid meteor stream.

87. Which of the following is an assumption underlying the last sentence of the passage?

(A) In each of the years between 1970 and 1979, the Earth took exactly 19 hours to cross the Geminid meteor stream.
(B) The comet associated with the Geminid meteor stream has totally disintegrated.
(C) The Geminid meteor stream should continue to exist for at least 5,000 years.
(D) The Geminid meteor stream has not broadened as rapidly as the conventional theories would have predicted.
(E) The computer-model Geminid meteor stream provides an accurate representation of the development of the actual Geminid stream.

Most large corporations in the United States were once run by individual capitalists who owned enough stock to dominate the board of directors and dictate company policy. Because putting such large amounts of
(5) stock on the market would only depress its value, they could not sell out for a quick profit and instead had to concentrate on improving the long-term productivity of their companies. Today, with few exceptions, the stock of large United States corporations is held by large insti-
(10) tutions—pension funds, for example—and because these institutions are prohibited by antitrust laws from owning a majority of a company's stock and from actively influencing a company's decision-making, they can enhance their wealth only by buying and selling
(15) stock in anticipation of fluctuations in its value. A minority shareholder is necessarily a short-term trader. As a result, United States productivity is unlikely to improve unless shareholders and the managers of the companies in which they invest are encouraged to
(20) enhance long-term productivity (and hence long-term profitability), rather than simply to maximize short-term profits.

Since the return of the old-style capitalist is unlikely, today's short-term traders must be remade into tomor-
(25) row's long-term capitalistic investors. The legal limits that now prevent financial institutions from acquiring a dominant shareholding position in a corporation should be removed, and such institutions encouraged to take a more active role in the operations of the companies in
(30) which they invest. In addition, any institution that holds 20 percent or more of a company's stock should be forced to give the public one day's notice of the intent to sell those shares. Unless the announced sale could be explained to the public on grounds other than antici-
(35) pated future losses, the value of the stock would plummet and, like the old-time capitalists, major investors could cut their losses only by helping to restore their companies' productivity. Such measures would force financial institutions to become capitalists whose success
(40) depends not on trading shares at the propitious moment, but on increasing the productivity of the companies in which they invest.

88. In the passage, the author is primarily concerned with doing which of the following?

(A) Comparing two different approaches to a problem
(B) Describing a problem and proposing a solution
(C) Defending an established method
(D) Presenting data and drawing conclusions from the data
(E) Comparing two different analyses of a current situation

89. It can be inferred from the passage that which of the following is true of majority shareholders in a corporation?

(A) They make the corporation's operational management decisions.
(B) They are not allowed to own more than 50 percent of the corporation's stock.
(C) They cannot make quick profits by selling off large amounts of their stock in the corporation.
(D) They are more interested in profits than in productivity.
(E) They cannot sell any of their stock in the corporation without giving the public advance notice.

90. According to the passage, the purpose of the requirement suggested in lines 30-33 would be which of the following?

(A) To encourage institutional stockholders to sell stock that they believe will decrease in value
(B) To discourage institutional stockholders from intervening in the operation of a company whose stock they own
(C) To discourage short-term profit-taking by institutional stockholders
(D) To encourage a company's employees to take an active role in the ownership of stock in the company
(E) To encourage investors to diversify their stock holdings

91. The author suggests that which of the following is a true statement about people who typify the "old-style capitalist" referred to in line 23 ?

(A) They now rely on outdated management techniques.
(B) They seldom engaged in short-term trading of the stock they owned.
(C) They did not influence the investment policies of the corporations in which they invested.
(D) They now play a very small role in the stock market as a result of antitrust legislation.
(E) They were primarily concerned with maximizing the short-term profitability of the corporations in which they owned stock.

92. It can be inferred that the author makes which of the following assumptions about the businesses once controlled by individual capitalists?

(A) These businesses were less profitable than are businesses today.
(B) Improving long-term productivity led to increased profits.
(C) Each business had only a few stockholders.
(D) There was no short-term trading in the stock of these businesses.
(E) Institutions owned no stock in these companies.

93. The author suggests that the role of large institutions as stockholders differs from that of the "old-style capitalist" in part because large institutions

(A) invest in the stock of so many companies that they cannot focus attention on the affairs of any single corporation
(B) are prohibited by law from owning a majority of a corporation's stock
(C) are influenced by brokers who advise against long-term ownership of stocks
(D) are able to put large amounts of stock on the market without depressing the stock's value
(E) are attracted to the stocks of corporations that demonstrate long-term gains in productivity

94. The primary function of the second paragraph of the passage is to

(A) identify problems
(B) warn of consequences
(C) explain effects
(D) evaluate solutions
(E) recommend actions

Traditionally, the first firm to commercialize a new technology has benefited from the unique opportunity to shape product definitions, forcing followers to adapt to a standard or invest in an unproven alternative. Today, however, the largest payoffs may go to companies that lead in developing integrated approaches for successful mass production and distribution.

Producers of the Beta format for videocassette recorders (VCR's), for example, were first to develop the VCR commercially in 1975, but producers of the rival VHS (Video Home System) format proved to be more successful at forming strategic alliances with other producers and distributors to manufacture and market their VCR format. Seeking to maintain exclusive control over VCR distribution, Beta producers were reluctant to form such alliances and eventually lost ground to VHS in the competition for the global VCR market.

Despite Beta's substantial technological head start and the fact that VHS was neither technically better nor cheaper than Beta, developers of VHS quickly turned a slight early lead in sales into a dominant position. Strategic alignments with producers of prerecorded tapes reinforced the VHS advantage. The perception among consumers that prerecorded tapes were more available in VHS format further expanded VHS's share of the market. By the end of the 1980's, Beta was no longer in production.

95. The passage is primarily concerned with which of the following?

(A) Evaluating two competing technologies
(B) Tracing the impact of a new technology by narrating a sequence of events
(C) Reinterpreting an event from contemporary business history
(D) Illustrating a business strategy by means of a case history
(E) Proposing an innovative approach to business planning

96. According to the passage, today's successful firms, unlike successful firms in the past, may earn the greatest profits by

(A) investing in research to produce cheaper versions of existing technology
(B) being the first to market a competing technology
(C) adapting rapidly to a technological standard previously set by a competing firm
(D) establishing technological leadership in order to shape product definitions in advance of competing firms
(E) emphasizing the development of methods for the mass production and distribution of a new technology

97. According to the passage, consumers began to develop a preference for VCR's in the VHS format because they believed which of the following?

(A) VCR's in the VHS format were technically better than competing-format VCR's.
(B) VCR's in the VHS format were less expensive than competing-format VCR's.
(C) VHS was the first standard format for VCR's.
(D) VHS prerecorded videotapes were more available than Beta-format tapes.
(E) VCR's in the Beta format would soon cease to be produced.

98. The author implies that one way that VHS producers won control over the VCR market was by

(A) carefully restricting access to VCR technology
(B) giving up a slight early lead in VCR sales in order to improve long-term prospects
(C) retaining a strict monopoly on the production of prerecorded videotapes
(D) sharing control of the marketing of VHS-format VCR's
(E) sacrificing technological superiority over Beta-format VCR's in order to remain competitive in price

99. The alignment of producers of VHS-format VCR's with producers of prerecorded videotapes is most similar to which of the following?

(A) The alignment of an automobile manufacturer with another automobile manufacturer to adopt a standard design for automobile engines
(B) The alignment of an automobile manufacturer with an automotive glass company whereby the manufacturer agrees to purchase automobile windshields only from that one glass company
(C) The alignment of an automobile manufacturer with a petroleum company to ensure the widespread availability of the fuel required by a new type of engine developed by the manufacturer
(D) The alignment of an automobile manufacturer with its dealers to adopt a plan to improve automobile design
(E) The alignment of an automobile dealer with an automobile rental chain to adopt a strategy for an advertising campaign to promote a new type of automobile

100. Which of the following best describes the relation of the first paragraph to the passage as a whole?

(A) It makes a general observation to be exemplified.
(B) It outlines a process to be analyzed.
(C) It poses a question to be answered.
(D) It advances an argument to be disputed.
(E) It introduces conflicting arguments to be reconciled.

Australian researchers have discovered electroreceptors (sensory organs designed to respond to electrical fields) clustered at the tip of the spiny anteater's snout. The
Line researchers made this discovery by exposing small areas of
(5) the snout to extremely weak electrical fields and recording the transmission of resulting nervous activity to the brain. While it is true that tactile receptors, another kind of sensory organ on the anteater's snout, can also respond to electrical stimuli, such receptors do so only in response to
(10) electrical field strengths about 1,000 times greater than those known to excite electroreceptors.

Having discovered the electroreceptors, researchers are now investigating how anteaters utilize such a sophisticated sensory system. In one behavioral experiment, researchers
(15) successfully trained an anteater to distinguish between two troughs of water, one with a weak electrical field and the other with none. Such evidence is consistent with researchers' hypothesis that anteaters use electroreceptors to detect electrical signals given off by prey; however,
(20) researchers as yet have been unable to detect electrical signals emanating from termite mounds, where the favorite food of anteaters live. Still, researchers have observed anteaters breaking into a nest of ants at an oblique angle and quickly locating nesting chambers. This ability to quickly
(25) locate unseen prey suggests, according to the researchers, that the anteaters were using their electroreceptors to locate the nesting chambers.

101. According to the passage, which of the following is a characteristic that distinguishes electroreceptors from tactile receptors?

(A) The manner in which electroreceptors respond to electrical stimuli
(B) The tendency of electroreceptors to be found in clusters
(C) The unusual locations in which electroreceptors are found in most species
(D) The amount of electrical stimulation required to excite electroreceptors
(E) The amount of nervous activity transmitted to the brain by electroreceptors when they are excited

102. Which of the following can be inferred about the experiment described in the first paragraph?

(A) Researchers had difficulty verifying the existence of electroreceptors in the anteater because electroreceptors respond to such a narrow range of electrical field strengths.
(B) Researchers found that the level of nervous activity in the anteater's brain increased dramatically as the strength of the electrical stimulus was increased.
(C) Researchers found that some areas of the anteater's snout were not sensitive to a weak electrical stimulus.
(D) Researchers found that the anteater's tactile receptors were more easily excited by a strong electrical stimulus than were the electroreceptors.
(E) Researchers tested small areas of the anteater's snout in order to ensure that only electroreceptors were responding to the stimulus.

103. The author of the passage most probably discusses the function of tactile receptors (lines 7-11) in order to

(A) eliminate an alternative explanation of anteaters' response to electrical stimuli
(B) highlight a type of sensory organ that has a function identical to that of electroreceptors
(C) point out a serious complication in the research on electroreceptors in anteaters
(D) suggest that tactile receptors assist electroreceptors in the detection of electrical signals
(E) introduce a factor that was not addressed in the research on electroreceptors in anteaters

104. Which of the following can be inferred about anteaters from the behavioral experiment mentioned in the second paragraph?

(A) They are unable to distinguish between stimuli detected by their electroreceptors and stimuli detected by their tactile receptors.
(B) They are unable to distinguish between the electrical signals emanating from termite mounds and those emanating from ant nests.
(C) They can be trained to recognize consistently the presence of a particular stimulus.
(D) They react more readily to strong than to weak stimuli.
(E) They are more efficient at detecting stimuli in a controlled environment than in a natural environment.

105. The passage suggests that the researchers mentioned in the second paragraph who observed anteaters break into a nest of ants would most likely agree with which of the following statements?

(A) The event they observed provides conclusive evidence that anteaters use their electroreceptors to locate unseen prey.
(B) The event they observed was atypical and may not reflect the usual hunting practices of anteaters.
(C) It is likely that the anteaters located the ants' nesting chambers without the assistance of electroreceptors.
(D) Anteaters possess a very simple sensory system for use in locating prey.
(E) The speed with which the anteaters located their prey is greater than what might be expected on the basis of chance alone.

106. Which of the following, if true, would most strengthen the hypothesis mentioned in lines 17-19 ?

(A) Researchers are able to train anteaters to break into an underground chamber that is emitting a strong electrical signal.
(B) Researchers are able to detect a weak electrical signal emanating from the nesting chamber of an ant colony.
(C) Anteaters are observed taking increasingly longer amounts of time to locate the nesting chambers of ants.
(D) Anteaters are observed using various angles to break into nests of ants.
(E) Anteaters are observed using the same angle used with nests of ants to break into the nests of other types of prey.

When A. Philip Randolph assumed the leadership of the
Brotherhood of Sleeping Car Porters, he began a ten-year
battle to win recognition from the Pullman Company, the
largest private employer of Black people in the United
States and the company that controlled the railroad
industry's sleeping car and parlor service. In 1935 the
Brotherhood became the first Black union recognized by a
major corporation. Randolph's efforts in the battle helped
transform the attitude of Black workers toward unions and
toward themselves as an identifiable group; eventually,
Randolph helped to weaken organized labor's antagonism
toward Black workers.

In the Pullman contest Randolph faced formidable
obstacles. The first was Black workers' understandable
skepticism toward unions, which had historically barred
Black workers from membership. An additional obstacle
was the union that Pullman itself had formed, which
weakened support among Black workers for an independent
entity.

The Brotherhood possessed a number of advantages,
however, including Randolph's own tactical abilities. In
1928 he took the bold step of threatening a strike against
Pullman. Such a threat, on a national scale, under Black
leadership, helped replace the stereotype of the Black
worker as servant with the image of the Black worker as
wage earner. In addition, the porters' very isolation aided
the Brotherhood. Porters were scattered throughout the
country, sleeping in dormitories in Black communities;
their segregated life protected the union's internal
communications from interception. That the porters were a
homogeneous group working for a single employer with a
single labor policy, thus sharing the same grievances from
city to city, also strengthened the Brotherhood and encouraged racial identity and solidarity as well. But it was only
in the early 1930's that federal legislation prohibiting a
company from maintaining its own unions with company
money eventually allowed the Brotherhood to become
recognized as the porters' representative.

Not content with this triumph, Randolph brought the
Brotherhood into the American Federation of Labor, where
it became the equal of the Federation's 105 other unions.
He reasoned that as a member union, the Brotherhood
would be in a better position to exert pressure on member
unions that practiced race restrictions. Such restrictions
were eventually found unconstitutional in 1944.

Line (5), (10), (15), (20), (25), (30), (35), (40)

107. According to the passage, by 1935 the skepticism of
Black workers toward unions was

(A) unchanged except among Black employees of
railroad-related industries
(B) reinforced by the actions of the Pullman
Company's union
(C) mitigated by the efforts of Randolph
(D) weakened by the opening up of many unions to
Black workers
(E) largely alleviated because of the policies of the
American Federation of Labor

108. In using the word "understandable" (line 14), the
author most clearly conveys

(A) sympathy with attempts by the Brotherhood
between 1925 and 1935 to establish an
independent union
(B) concern that the obstacles faced by Randolph
between 1925 and 1935 were indeed formidable
(C) ambivalence about the significance of unions to
most Black workers in the 1920's
(D) appreciation of the attitude of many Black workers
in the 1920's toward unions
(E) regret at the historical attitude of unions toward
Black workers

109. The passage suggests which of the following about the
response of porters to the Pullman Company's own
union?

(A) Few porters ever joined this union.
(B) Some porters supported this union before 1935.
(C) Porters, more than other Pullman employees,
enthusiastically supported this union.
(D) The porters' response was most positive after
1935.
(E) The porters' response was unaffected by the
general skepticism of Black workers concerning
unions.

110. The passage suggests that if the grievances of porters in one part of the United States had been different from those of porters in another part of the country, which of the following would have been the case?

(A) It would have been more difficult for the Pullman Company to have had a single labor policy.
(B) It would have been more difficult for the Brotherhood to control its channels of communication.
(C) It would have been more difficult for the Brotherhood to build its membership.
(D) It would have been easier for the Pullman Company's union to attract membership.
(E) It would have been easier for the Brotherhood to threaten strikes.

111. The passage suggests that in the 1920's a company in the United States was able to

(A) use its own funds to set up a union
(B) require its employees to join the company's own union
(C) develop a single labor policy for all its employees with little employee dissent
(D) pressure its employees to contribute money to maintain the company's own union
(E) use its resources to prevent the passage of federal legislation that would have facilitated the formation of independent unions

112. The passage supplies information concerning which of the following matters related to Randolph?

(A) The steps he took to initiate the founding of the Brotherhood
(B) His motivation for bringing the Brotherhood into the American Federation of Labor
(C) The influence he had on the passage of legislation overturning race restrictions in 1944
(D) The influence he had on the passage of legislation to bar companies from financing their own unions
(E) The success he and the Brotherhood had in influencing the policies of the other unions in the American Federation of Labor

Seeking a competitive advantage, some professional service firms (for example, firms providing advertising, accounting, or health care services) have considered offering unconditional guarantees of satisfaction. Such guarantees specify what clients can expect and what the firm will do if it fails to fulfill these expectations. Particularly with first-time clients, an unconditional guarantee can be an effective marketing tool if the client is very cautious, the firm's fees are high, the negative consequences of bad service are grave, or business is difficult to obtain through referrals and word-of-mouth.

However, an unconditional guarantee can sometimes hinder marketing efforts. With its implication that failure is possible, the guarantee may, paradoxically, cause clients to doubt the service firm's ability to deliver the promised level of service. It may conflict with a firm's desire to appear sophisticated, or may even suggest that a firm is begging for business. In legal and health care services, it may mislead clients by suggesting that lawsuits or medical procedures will have guaranteed outcomes. Indeed, professional service firms with outstanding reputations and performance to match have little to gain from offering unconditional guarantees. And any firm that implements an unconditional guarantee without undertaking a commensurate commitment to quality of service is merely employing a potentially costly marketing gimmick.

Line (5)

(10)

(15)

(20)

(25)

113. The primary function of the passage as a whole is to

(A) account for the popularity of a practice
(B) evaluate the utility of a practice
(C) demonstrate how to institute a practice
(D) weigh the ethics of using a strategy
(E) explain the reasons for pursuing a strategy

114. All of the following are mentioned in the passage as circumstances in which professional service firms can benefit from offering an unconditional guarantee EXCEPT:

(A) The firm is having difficulty retaining its clients of long standing.
(B) The firm is having difficulty getting business through client recommendations.
(C) The firm charges substantial fees for its services.
(D) The adverse effects of poor performance by the firm are significant for the client.
(E) The client is reluctant to incur risk.

115. Which of the following is cited in the passage as a goal of some professional service firms in offering unconditional guarantees of satisfaction?

(A) A limit on the firm's liability
(B) Successful competition against other firms
(C) Ability to justify fee increases
(D) Attainment of an outstanding reputation in a field
(E) Improvement in the quality of the firm's service

116. The passage's description of the issue raised by unconditional guarantees for health care or legal services most clearly implies that which of the following is true?

(A) The legal and medical professions have standards of practice that would be violated by attempts to fulfill such unconditional guarantees.
(B) The result of a lawsuit or medical procedure cannot necessarily be determined in advance by the professionals handling a client's case.
(C) The dignity of the legal and medical professions is undermined by any attempts at marketing of professional services, including unconditional guarantees.
(D) Clients whose lawsuits or medical procedures have unsatisfactory outcomes cannot be adequately compensated by financial settlements alone.
(E) Predicting the monetary cost of legal or health care services is more difficult than predicting the monetary cost of other types of professional services.

117. Which of the following hypothetical situations best exemplifies the potential problem noted in the second sentence of the second paragraph (lines 14-17) ?

(A) A physician's unconditional guarantee of satisfaction encourages patients to sue for malpractice if they are unhappy with the treatment they receive.

(B) A lawyer's unconditional guarantee of satisfaction makes clients suspect that the lawyer needs to find new clients quickly to increase the firm's income.

(C) A business consultant's unconditional guarantee of satisfaction is undermined when the consultant fails to provide all of the services that are promised.

(D) An architect's unconditional guarantee of satisfaction makes clients wonder how often the architect's buildings fail to please clients.

(E) An accountant's unconditional guarantee of satisfaction leads clients to believe that tax returns prepared by the accountant are certain to be accurate.

118. The passage most clearly implies which of the following about the professional service firms mentioned in line 22 ?

(A) They are unlikely to have offered unconditional guarantees of satisfaction in the past.

(B) They are usually profitable enough to be able to compensate clients according to the terms of an unconditional guarantee.

(C) They usually practice in fields in which the outcomes are predictable.

(D) Their fees are usually more affordable than those charged by other professional service firms.

(E) Their clients are usually already satisfied with the quality of service that is delivered.

Although genetic mutations in bacteria and viruses can lead to epidemics, some epidemics are caused by bacteria and viruses that have undergone no significant *Line* genetic change. In analyzing the latter, scientists have
(5) discovered the importance of social and ecological factors to epidemics. Poliomyelitis, for example, emerged as an epidemic in the United States in the twentieth century; by then, modern sanitation was able to delay exposure to polio until adolescence or adulthood, at
(10) which time polio infection produced paralysis. Previously, infection had occurred during infancy, when it typically provided lifelong immunity without paralysis. Thus, the hygiene that helped prevent typhoid epidemics indirectly fostered a paralytic polio epidemic. Another
(15) example is Lyme disease, which is caused by bacteria that are transmitted by deer ticks. It occurred only sporadically during the late nineteenth century but has recently become prevalent in parts of the United States, largely due to an increase in the deer population that
(20) occurred simultaneously with the growth of the suburbs and increased outdoor recreational activities in the deer's habitat. Similarly, an outbreak of dengue hemorrhagic fever became an epidemic in Asia in the 1950's because of ecological changes that caused *Aedes aegypti*,
(25) the mosquito that transmits the dengue virus, to proliferate. The stage is now set in the United States for a dengue epidemic because of the inadvertent introduction and wide dissemination of another mosquito, *Aedes albopictus*.

119. The passage suggests that a lack of modern sanitation would make which of the following most likely to occur?

(A) An outbreak of Lyme disease
(B) An outbreak of dengue hemorrhagic fever
(C) An epidemic of typhoid
(D) An epidemic of paralytic polio among infants
(E) An epidemic of paralytic polio among adolescents and adults

120. According to the passage, the outbreak of dengue hemorrhagic fever in the 1950's occurred for which of the following reasons?

(A) The mosquito *Aedes aegypti* was newly introduced into Asia.
(B) The mosquito *Aedes aegypti* became more numerous.
(C) The mosquito *Aedes albopictus* became infected with the dengue virus.
(D) Individuals who would normally acquire immunity to the dengue virus as infants were not infected until later in life.
(E) More people began to visit and inhabit areas in which mosquitos live and breed.

121. It can be inferred from the passage that Lyme disease has become prevalent in parts of the United States because of which of the following?

(A) The inadvertent introduction of Lyme disease bacteria to the United States
(B) The inability of modern sanitation methods to eradicate Lyme disease bacteria
(C) A genetic mutation in Lyme disease bacteria that makes them more virulent
(D) The spread of Lyme disease bacteria from infected humans to noninfected humans
(E) An increase in the number of humans who encounter deer ticks

122. Which of the following can most reasonably be concluded about the mosquito *Aedes albopictus* on the basis of information given in the passage?

(A) It is native to the United States.
(B) It can proliferate only in Asia.
(C) It transmits the dengue virus.
(D) It caused an epidemic of dengue hemorrhagic fever in the 1950's.
(E) It replaced *Aedes aegypti* in Asia when ecological changes altered *Aedes aegypti's* habitat.

123. Which of the following best describes the organization of the passage?

(A) A paradox is stated, discussed, and left unresolved.
(B) Two opposing explanations are presented, argued, and reconciled.
(C) A theory is proposed and is then followed by descriptions of three experiments that support the theory.
(D) A generalization is stated and is then followed by three instances that support the generalization.
(E) An argument is described and is then followed by three counterexamples that refute the argument.

124. Which of the following, if true, would most strengthen the author's assertion about the cause of the Lyme disease outbreak in the United States?

(A) The deer population was smaller in the late nineteenth century than in the mid-twentieth century.
(B) Interest in outdoor recreation began to grow in the late nineteenth century.
(C) In recent years the suburbs have stopped growing.
(D) Outdoor recreation enthusiasts routinely take measures to protect themselves against Lyme disease.
(E) Scientists have not yet developed a vaccine that can prevent Lyme disease.

Two modes of argumentation have been used on behalf of women's emancipation in Western societies. Arguments in what could be called the "relational" feminist tradition maintain the doctrine of "equality in difference," or equity as distinct from equality. They posit that biological distinctions between the sexes result in a necessary sexual division of labor in the family and throughout society and that women's procreative labor is currently undervalued by society, to the disadvantage of women. By contrast, the individualist feminist tradition emphasizes individual human rights and celebrates women's quest for personal autonomy, while downplaying the importance of gender roles and minimizing discussion of childbearing and its attendant responsibilities.

Before the late nineteenth century, these views coexisted within the feminist movement, often within the writings of the same individual. Between 1890 and 1920, however, relational feminism, which had been the dominant strain in feminist thought, and which still predominates among European and non-Western feminists, lost ground in England and the United States. Because the concept of individual rights was already well established in the Anglo-Saxon legal and political tradition, individualist feminism came to predominate in English-speaking countries. At the same time, the goals of the two approaches began to seem increasingly irreconcilable. Individualist feminists began to advocate a totally gender-blind system with equal rights for all. Relational feminists, while agreeing that equal educational and economic opportunities outside the home should be available for all women, continued to emphasize women's special contributions to society as homemakers and mothers; they demanded special treatment for women, including protective legislation for women workers, state-sponsored maternity benefits, and paid compensation for housework.

Relational arguments have a major pitfall: because they underline women's physiological and psychological distinctiveness, they are often appropriated by political adversaries and used to endorse male privilege. But the individualist approach, by attacking gender roles, denying the significance of physiological difference, and condemning existing familial institutions as hopelessly patriarchal, has often simply treated as irrelevant the family roles important to many women. If the individualist framework, with its claim for women's autonomy, could be harmonized with the family-oriented concerns of relational feminists, a more fruitful model for contemporary feminist politics could emerge.

125. The author of the passage alludes to the well-established nature of the concept of individual rights in the Anglo-Saxon legal and political tradition in order to

(A) illustrate the influence of individualist feminist thought on more general intellectual trends in English history
(B) argue that feminism was already a part of the larger Anglo-Saxon intellectual tradition, even though this has often gone unnoticed by critics of women's emancipation
(C) explain the decline in individualist thinking among feminists in non-English-speaking countries
(D) help account for an increasing shift toward individualist feminism among feminists in English-speaking countries
(E) account for the philosophical differences between individualist and relational feminists in English-speaking countries

126. The passage suggests that the author of the passage believes which of the following?

(A) The predominance of individualist feminism in English-speaking countries is a historical phenomenon, the causes of which have not yet been investigated.
(B) The individualist and relational feminist views are irreconcilable, given their theoretical differences concerning the foundations of society.
(C) A consensus concerning the direction of future feminist politics will probably soon emerge, given the awareness among feminists of the need for cooperation among women.
(D) Political adversaries of feminism often misuse arguments predicated on differences between the sexes to argue that the existing social system should be maintained.
(E) Relational feminism provides the best theoretical framework for contemporary feminist politics, but individualist feminism could contribute much toward refining and strengthening modern feminist thought.

127. It can be inferred from the passage that the individualist feminist tradition denies the validity of which of the following causal statements?

(A) A division of labor in a social group can result in increased efficiency with regard to the performance of group tasks.
(B) A division of labor in a social group causes inequities in the distribution of opportunities and benefits among group members.
(C) A division of labor on the basis of gender in a social group is necessitated by the existence of sex-linked biological differences between male and female members of the group.
(D) Culturally determined distinctions based on gender in a social group foster the existence of differing attitudes and opinions among group members.
(E) Educational programs aimed at reducing inequalities based on gender among members of a social group can result in a sense of greater well-being for all members of the group.

128. According to the passage, relational feminists and individualist feminists agree that

(A) individual human rights take precedence over most other social claims
(B) the gender-based division of labor in society should be eliminated
(C) laws guaranteeing equal treatment for all citizens regardless of gender should be passed
(D) a greater degree of social awareness concerning the importance of motherhood would be beneficial to society
(E) the same educational and economic opportunities should be available to both sexes

129. According to the author, which of the following was true of feminist thought in Western societies before 1890 ?

(A) Individualist feminist arguments were not found in the thought or writing of non-English-speaking feminists.
(B) Individualist feminism was a strain in feminist thought, but another strain, relational feminism, predominated.
(C) Relational and individualist approaches were equally prevalent in feminist thought and writing.
(D) The predominant view among feminists held that the welfare of women was ultimately less important than the welfare of children.
(E) The predominant view among feminists held that the sexes should receive equal treatment under the law.

130. The author implies that which of the following was true of most feminist thinkers in England and the United States after 1920 ?

(A) They were less concerned with politics than with intellectual issues.
(B) They began to reach a broader audience and their programs began to be adopted by mainstream political parties.
(C) They called repeatedly for international cooperation among women's groups to achieve their goals.
(D) They moderated their initial criticism of the economic systems that characterized their societies.
(E) They did not attempt to unite the two different feminist approaches in their thought.

The new school of political history that emerged in the 1960's and 1970's sought to go beyond the traditional focus of political historians on leaders and government institutions by examining directly the political practices of ordinary citizens. Like the old approach, however, this new approach excluded women. The very techniques these historians used to uncover mass political behavior in the nineteenth-century United States—quantitative analyses of election returns, for example—were useless in analyzing the political activities of women, who were denied the vote until 1920.

By redefining "political activity," historian Paula Baker has developed a political history that includes women. She concludes that among ordinary citizens, political activism by women in the nineteenth century prefigured trends in twentieth-century politics. Defining "politics" as "any action taken to affect the course of behavior of government or of the community," Baker concludes that, while voting and holding office were restricted to men, women in the nineteenth century organized themselves into societies committed to social issues such as temperance and poverty. In other words, Baker contends, women activists were early practitioners of nonpartisan, issue-oriented politics and thus were more interested in enlisting lawmakers, regardless of their party affiliation, on behalf of certain issues than in ensuring that one party or another won an election. In the twentieth century, more men drew closer to women's ideas about politics and took up modes of issue-oriented politics that Baker sees women as having pioneered.

131. The primary purpose of the passage is to

(A) enumerate reasons why both traditional scholarly methods and newer scholarly methods have limitations
(B) identify a shortcoming in a scholarly approach and describe an alternative approach
(C) provide empirical data to support a long-held scholarly assumption
(D) compare two scholarly publications on the basis of their authors' backgrounds
(E) attempt to provide a partial answer to a long-standing scholarly dilemma

132. The passage suggests which of the following concerning the techniques used by the new political historians described in the first paragraph of the passage?

(A) They involved the extensive use of the biographies of political party leaders and political theoreticians.
(B) They were conceived by political historians who were reacting against the political climates of the 1960's and 1970's.
(C) They were of more use in analyzing the positions of United States political parties in the nineteenth century than in analyzing the positions of those in the twentieth century.
(D) They were of more use in analyzing the political behavior of nineteenth-century voters than in analyzing the political activities of those who could not vote during that period.
(E) They were devised as a means of tracing the influence of nineteenth-century political trends on twentieth-century political trends.

133. It can be inferred that the author of the passage quotes Baker directly in the second paragraph primarily in order to

(A) clarify a position before providing an alternative to that position
(B) differentiate between a novel definition and traditional definitions
(C) provide an example of a point agreed on by different generations of scholars
(D) provide an example of the prose style of an important historian
(E) amplify a definition given in the first paragraph

134. According to the passage, Paula Baker and the new political historians of the 1960's and 1970's shared which of the following?

(A) A commitment to interest-group politics
(B) A disregard for political theory and ideology
(C) An interest in the ways in which nineteenth-century politics prefigured contemporary politics
(D) A reliance on such quantitative techniques as the analysis of election returns
(E) An emphasis on the political involvement of ordinary citizens

135. Which of the following best describes the structure of the first paragraph of the passage?

(A) Two scholarly approaches are compared, and a shortcoming common to both is identified.
(B) Two rival schools of thought are contrasted, and a third is alluded to.
(C) An outmoded scholarly approach is described, and a corrective approach is called for.
(D) An argument is outlined, and counterarguments are mentioned.
(E) A historical era is described in terms of its political trends.

136. The information in the passage suggests that a pre-1960's political historian would have been most likely to undertake which of the following studies?

(A) An analysis of voting trends among women voters of the 1920's
(B) A study of male voters' gradual ideological shift from party politics to issue-oriented politics
(C) A biography of an influential nineteenth-century minister of foreign affairs
(D) An analysis of narratives written by previously unrecognized women activists
(E) A study of voting trends among naturalized immigrant laborers in a nineteenth-century logging camp

New observations about the age of some globular clusters in our Milky Way galaxy have cast doubt on a long-held theory about how the galaxy was formed. The Milky Way contains about 125 globular clusters (compact groups of anywhere from several tens of thousands to perhaps a million stars) distributed in a roughly spherical halo around the galactic nucleus. The stars in these clusters are believed to have been born during the formation of the galaxy, and so may be considered relics of the original galactic nebula, holding vital clues to the way the formation took place.

The conventional theory of the formation of the galaxy contends that roughly 12 to 13 billion years ago the Milky Way formed over a relatively short time (about 200 million years) when a spherical cloud of gas collapsed under the pressure of its own gravity into a disc surrounded by a halo. Such a rapid formation of the galaxy would mean that all stars in the halo should be very nearly the same age.

However, the astronomer Michael Bolte has found considerable variation in the ages of globular clusters. One of the clusters studied by Bolte is 2 billion years older than most other clusters in the galaxy, while another is 2 billion years younger. A colleague of Bolte contends that the cluster called Palomar 12 is 5 billion years younger than most other globular clusters.

To explain the age differences among the globular clusters, astronomers are taking a second look at "renegade" theories. One such newly fashionable theory, first put forward by Richard Larson in the early 1970's, argues that the halo of the Milky Way formed over a period of a billion or more years as hundreds of small gas clouds drifted about, collided, lost orbital energy, and finally collapsed into a centrally condensed elliptical system. Larson's conception of a "lumpy and turbulent" protogalaxy is complemented by computer modeling done in the 1970's by mathematician Alan Toomre, which suggests that closely interacting spiral galaxies could lose enough orbital energy to merge into a single galaxy.

137. The passage is primarily concerned with discussing

(A) the importance of determining the age of globular clusters in assessing when the Milky Way galaxy was formed
(B) recent changes in the procedures used by astronomers to study the formation of the Milky Way galaxy
(C) current disputes among astronomers regarding the size and form of the Milky Way galaxy
(D) the effect of new discoveries regarding globular clusters on theories about the formation of the Milky Way galaxy
(E) the origin, nature, and significance of groups of stars known as globular clusters

138. According to the passage, one way in which Larson's theory and the conventional theory of the formation of the Milky Way galaxy differ is in their assessment of the

(A) amount of time it took to form the galaxy
(B) size of the galaxy immediately after its formation
(C) particular gases involved in the formation of the galaxy
(D) importance of the age of globular clusters in determining how the galaxy was formed
(E) shape of the halo that formed around the galaxy

139. Which of the following, if true, would be most useful in supporting the conclusions drawn from recent observations about globular clusters?

(A) There is firm evidence that the absolute age of the Milky Way galaxy is between 10 and 17 billion years.

(B) A survey reveals that a galaxy close to the Milky Way galaxy contains globular clusters of ages close to the age of Palomar 12.

(C) A mathematical model proves that small gas clouds move in regular patterns.

(D) Space probes indicate that the stars in the Milky Way galaxy are composed of several different types of gas.

(E) A study of over 1,500 individual stars in the halo of the Milky Way galaxy indicates wide discrepancies in their ages.

140. If Bolte and his colleague are both correct, it can be inferred that the globular cluster Palomar 12 is approximately

(A) 5 billion years younger than any other cluster in the galaxy

(B) the same age as most other clusters in the galaxy

(C) 7 billion years younger than another cluster in the galaxy

(D) 12 billion years younger than most other clusters in the galaxy

(E) 2 billion years younger than most other clusters in the galaxy

141. The passage suggests that Toomre's work complements Larson's theory because it

(A) specifies more precisely the time frame proposed by Larson

(B) subtly alters Larson's theory to make it more plausible

(C) supplements Larson's hypothesis with direct astronomical observations

(D) provides theoretical support for the ideas suggested by Larson

(E) expands Larson's theory to make it more widely applicable

142. Which of the following most accurately states a finding of Bolte's research, as described in the passage?

(A) The globular clusters in the Milky Way galaxy are 2 billion years older than predicted by the conventional theory.

(B) The ages of at least some globular clusters in the Milky Way galaxy differ by at least 4 billion years.

(C) One of the globular clusters in the Milky Way galaxy is 5 billion years younger than most others.

(D) The globular clusters in the Milky Way galaxy are significantly older than the individual stars in the halo.

(E) Most globular clusters in the Milky Way galaxy are between 11 and 15 billion years old.

143. The author of the passage puts the word "renegade" (line 29) in quotation marks most probably in order to

(A) emphasize the lack of support for the theories in question

(B) contrast the controversial quality of the theories in question with the respectable character of their formulators

(C) generate skepticism about the theories in question

(D) ridicule the scientists who once doubted the theories in question

(E) indicate that the theories in question are no longer as unconventional as they once seemed

During the 1960's and 1970's, the primary economic development strategy of local governments in the United States was to attract manufacturing industries. Unfortu-
Line nately, this strategy was usually implemented at another
(5) community's expense: many manufacturing facilities were lured away from their moorings elsewhere through tax incentives and slick promotional efforts. Through the transfer of jobs and related revenues that resulted from this practice, one town's triumph could become another
(10) town's tragedy.

In the 1980's the strategy shifted from this zero-sum game to one called "high-technology development," in which local governments competed to attract newly formed high-technology manufacturing firms. Although
(15) this approach was preferable to victimizing other geo-graphical areas by taking their jobs, it also had its shortcomings: high-tech manufacturing firms employ only a specially trained fraction of the manufacturing workforce, and there simply are not enough high-tech
(20) firms to satisfy all geographic areas.

Recently, local governments have increasingly come to recognize the advantages of yet a third strategy: the promotion of homegrown small businesses. Small indig-enous businesses are created by a nearly ubiquitous
(25) resource, local entrepreneurs. With roots in their com-munities, these individuals are less likely to be enticed away by incentives offered by another community. Indig-enous industry and talent are kept at home, creating an environment that both provides jobs and fosters further entrepreneurship.

144. The primary purpose of the passage is to

(A) advocate more effective strategies for encour-aging the development of high-technology enterprises in the United States
(B) contrast the incentives for economic develop-ment offered by local governments with those offered by the private sector
(C) acknowledge and counter adverse criticism of programs being used to stimulate local economic development
(D) define and explore promotional efforts used by local governments to attract new industry
(E) review and evaluate strategies and programs that have been used to stimulate economic development

145. The passage suggests which of the following about the majority of United States manufacturing indus-tries before the high-technology development era of the 1980's?

(A) They lost many of their most innovative per-sonnel to small entrepreneurial enterprises.
(B) They experienced a major decline in profits during the 1960's and 1970's.
(C) They could provide real economic benefits to the areas in which they were located.
(D) They employed workers who had no specialized skills.
(E) They actively interfered with local entre-preneurial ventures.

146. The tone of the passage suggests that the author is most optimistic about the economic development potential of which of the following groups?

(A) Local governments
(B) High-technology promoters
(C) Local entrepreneurs
(D) Manufacturing-industry managers
(E) Economic development strategists

147. The passage does NOT state which of the following about local entrepreneurs?

(A) They are found nearly everywhere.
(B) They encourage further entrepreneurship.
(C) They attract out-of-town investors.
(D) They employ local workers.
(E) They are established in their communities.

148. The author of the passage mentions which of the following as an advantage of high-technology development?

(A) It encourages the modernization of existing manufacturing facilities.
(B) It promotes healthy competition between rival industries.
(C) It encourages the growth of related industries.
(D) It takes full advantage of the existing workforce.
(E) It does not advantage one local workforce at the expense of another.

In an attempt to improve the overall performance of clerical workers, many companies have introduced computerized performance monitoring and control systems (CPMCS) that record and report a worker's computer-driven activities. However, at least one study has shown that such monitoring may not be having the desired effect. In the study, researchers asked monitored clerical workers and their supervisors how assessments of productivity affected supervisors' ratings of workers' performance. In contrast to unmonitored workers doing the same work, who without exception identified the most important element in their jobs as customer service, the monitored workers and their supervisors all responded that productivity was the critical factor in assigning ratings. This finding suggested that there should have been a strong correlation between a monitored worker's productivity and the overall rating the worker received. However, measures of the relationship between overall rating and individual elements of performance clearly supported the conclusion that supervisors gave considerable weight to criteria such as attendance, accuracy, and indications of customer satisfaction.

It is possible that productivity may be a "hygiene factor"; that is, if it is too low, it will hurt the overall rating. But the evidence suggests that beyond the point at which productivity becomes "good enough," higher productivity per se is unlikely to improve a rating.

149. According to the passage, before the final results of the study were known, which of the following seemed likely?

(A) That workers with the highest productivity would also be the most accurate

(B) That workers who initially achieved high productivity ratings would continue to do so consistently

(C) That the highest performance ratings would be achieved by workers with the highest productivity

(D) That the most productive workers would be those whose supervisors claimed to value productivity

(E) That supervisors who claimed to value productivity would place equal value on customer satisfaction

150. It can be inferred that the author of the passage discusses "unmonitored workers" (line 10) primarily in order to

(A) compare the ratings of these workers with the ratings of monitored workers

(B) provide an example of a case in which monitoring might be effective

(C) provide evidence of an inappropriate use of CPMCS

(D) emphasize the effect that CPMCS may have on workers' perceptions of their jobs

(E) illustrate the effect that CPMCS may have on workers' ratings

151. Which of the following, if true, would most clearly have supported the conclusion referred to in lines 19-21 ?

(A) Ratings of productivity correlated highly with ratings of both accuracy and attendance.
(B) Electronic monitoring greatly increased productivity.
(C) Most supervisors based overall ratings of performance on measures of productivity alone.
(D) Overall ratings of performance correlated more highly with measures of productivity than the researchers expected.
(E) Overall ratings of performance correlated more highly with measures of accuracy than with measures of productivity.

152. According to the passage, a "hygiene factor" (lines 22-23) is an aspect of a worker's performance that

(A) has no effect on the rating of a worker's performance
(B) is so basic to performance that it is assumed to be adequate for all workers
(C) is given less importance than it deserves in rating a worker's performance
(D) is not likely to affect a worker's rating unless it is judged to be inadequate
(E) is important primarily because of the effect it has on a worker's rating

153. The primary purpose of the passage is to

(A) explain the need for the introduction of an innovative strategy
(B) discuss a study of the use of a particular method
(C) recommend a course of action
(D) resolve a difference of opinion
(E) suggest an alternative approach

Schools expect textbooks to be a valuable source of information for students. My research suggests, however, that textbooks that address the place of Native Americans
Line within the history of the United States distort history to suit
(5) a particular cultural value system. In some textbooks, for example, settlers are pictured as more humane, complex, skillful, and wise than Native Americans. In essence, textbooks stereotype and deprecate the numerous Native American cultures while reinforcing the attitude that the
(10) European conquest of the New World denotes the superiority of European cultures. Although textbooks evaluate Native American architecture, political systems, and home-making, I contend that they do it from an ethnocentric, European perspective without recognizing that other per-
(15) spectives are possible.

One argument against my contention asserts that, by nature, textbooks are culturally biased and that I am simply underestimating children's ability to see through these biases. Some researchers even claim that by the time
(20) students are in high school, they know they cannot take textbooks literally. Yet substantial evidence exists to the contrary. Two researchers, for example, have conducted studies that suggest that children's attitudes about particular cultures are strongly influenced by the textbooks used in
(25) schools. Given this, an ongoing, careful review of how school textbooks depict Native Americans is certainly warranted.

154. Which of the following would most logically be the topic of the paragraph immediately following the passage?

(A) Specific ways to evaluate the biases of United States history textbooks
(B) The centrality of the teacher's role in United States history courses
(C) Nontraditional methods of teaching United States history
(D) The contributions of European immigrants to the development of the United States
(E) Ways in which parents influence children's political attitudes

155. The primary purpose of the passage is to

(A) describe in detail one research study regarding the impact of history textbooks on children's attitudes and beliefs about certain cultures
(B) describe revisions that should be made to United States history textbooks
(C) discuss the difficulty of presenting an accurate history of the United States
(D) argue that textbooks used in schools stereotype Native Americans and influence children's attitudes
(E) summarize ways in which some textbooks give distorted pictures of the political systems developed by various Native American groups

156. The author mentions two researchers' studies (lines 22-25) most likely in order to

(A) suggest that children's political attitudes are formed primarily through textbooks
(B) counter the claim that children are able to see through stereotypes in textbooks
(C) suggest that younger children tend to interpret the messages in textbooks more literally than do older children
(D) demonstrate that textbooks carry political messages meant to influence their readers
(E) prove that textbooks are not biased in terms of their political presentations

157. The author's attitude toward the content of the history textbooks discussed in the passage is best described as one of

(A) indifference
(B) hesitance
(C) neutrality
(D) amusement
(E) disapproval

158. It can be inferred from the passage that the researchers mentioned in line 19 would be most likely to agree with which of the following statements?

(A) Students form attitudes about cultures other than their own primarily inside the school environment.
(B) For the most part, seniors in high school know that textbooks can be biased.
(C) Textbooks play a crucial role in shaping the attitudes and beliefs of students.
(D) Elementary school students are as likely to recognize biases in textbooks as are high school students.
(E) Students are less likely to give credence to history textbooks than to mathematics textbooks.

159. The author implies that which of the following will occur if textbooks are not carefully reviewed?

(A) Children will remain ignorant of the European settlers' conquest of the New World.
(B) Children will lose their ability to recognize biases in textbooks.
(C) Children will form negative stereotypes of Native Americans.
(D) Children will develop an understanding of ethnocentrism.
(E) Children will stop taking textbooks seriously.

Until recently, scientists did not know of a close vertebrate analogue to the extreme form of altruism observed in
eusocial insects like ants and bees, whereby individuals
Line cooperate, sometimes even sacrificing their own oppor-
(5) "unities to survive and reproduce, for the good of others.
However, such a vertebrate society may exist among underground colonies of the highly social rodent *Heterocephalus
glaber,* the naked mole rat.

A naked mole rat colony, like a beehive, wasp's nest, or
(10) termite mound, is ruled by its queen, or reproducing
female. Other adult female mole rats neither ovulate nor
breed. The queen is the largest member of the colony, and
she maintains her breeding status through a mixture of
behavioral and, presumably, chemical control. Queens have
(15) been long-lived in captivity, and when they die or are
removed from a colony one sees violent fighting for breeding status among the larger remaining females, leading to a
takeover by a new queen.

Eusocial insect societies have rigid caste systems, each
(20) insect's role being defined by its behavior, body shape, and
physiology. In naked mole rat societies, on the other hand,
differences in behavior are related primarily to reproductive
status (reproduction being limited to the queen and a few
males), body size, and perhaps age. Smaller nonbreeding
(25) members, both male and female, seem to participate primarily in gathering food, transporting nest material, and
tunneling. Larger nonbreeders are active in defending the
colony and perhaps in removing dirt from the tunnels.
Jarvis' work has suggested that differences in growth rates
(30) may influence the length of time that an individual performs
a task, regardless of its age.

Cooperative breeding has evolved many times in vertebrates, but unlike naked mole rats, most cooperatively
breeding vertebrates (except the wild dog, *Lycaon pictus*)
(35) are dominated by a pair of breeders rather than by a single
breeding female. The division of labor within social groups
is less pronounced among other vertebrates than among
naked mole rats, colony size is much smaller, and mating
by subordinate females may not be totally suppressed,
(40) whereas in naked mole rat colonies subordinate females are
not sexually active, and many never breed.

160. Which of the following most accurately states the main
idea of the passage?

(A) Naked mole rat colonies are the only known
examples of cooperatively breeding vertebrate
societies.
(B) Naked mole rat colonies exhibit social organization based on a rigid caste system.
(C) Behavior in naked mole rat colonies may well be
a close vertebrate analogue to behavior in
eusocial insect societies.
(D) The mating habits of naked mole rats differ from
those of any other vertebrate species.
(E) The basis for the division of labor among naked
mole rats is the same as that among eusocial
insects.

161. The passage suggests that Jarvis' work has called into
question which of the following explanatory variables
for naked mole rat behavior?

(A) Size
(B) Age
(C) Reproductive status
(D) Rate of growth
(E) Previously exhibited behavior

162. It can be inferred from the passage that the performance of tasks in naked mole rat colonies differs from
task performance in eusocial insect societies in which
of the following ways?

(A) In naked mole rat colonies, all tasks are performed
cooperatively.
(B) In naked mole rat colonies, the performance of
tasks is less rigidly determined by body shape.
(C) In naked mole rat colonies, breeding is limited to
the largest animals.
(D) In eusocial insect societies, reproduction is limited
to a single female.
(E) In eusocial insect societies, the distribution of
tasks is based on body size.

163. According to the passage, which of the following is a supposition rather than a fact concerning the queen in a naked mole rat colony?

(A) She is the largest member of the colony.
(B) She exerts chemical control over the colony.
(C) She mates with more than one male.
(D) She attains her status through aggression.
(E) She is the only breeding female.

164. The passage supports which of the following inferences about breeding among *Lycaon pictus* ?

(A) The largest female in the social group does not maintain reproductive status by means of behavioral control.
(B) An individual's ability to breed is related primarily to its rate of growth.
(C) Breeding is the only task performed by the breeding female.
(D) Breeding in the social group is not cooperative.
(E) Breeding is not dominated by a single pair of dogs.

165. According to the passage, naked mole rat colonies may differ from all other known vertebrate groups in which of the following ways?

(A) Naked mole rats exhibit an extreme form of altruism.
(B) Naked mole rats are cooperative breeders.
(C) Among naked mole rats, many males are permitted to breed with a single dominant female.
(D) Among naked mole rats, different tasks are performed at different times in an individual's life.
(E) Among naked mole rats, fighting results in the selection of a breeding female.

166. One function of the third paragraph of the passage is to

(A) state a conclusion about facts presented in an earlier paragraph
(B) introduce information that is contradicted by information in the fourth paragraph
(C) qualify the extent to which two previously mentioned groups might be similar
(D) show the chain of reasoning that led to the conclusions of a specific study
(E) demonstrate that, of three explanatory factors offered, two may be of equal significance

Joseph Glatthaar's *Forged in Battle* is not the first excellent study of Black soldiers and their White officers in the
Civil War, but it uses more soldiers' letters and diaries—
Line including rare material from Black soldiers—and concen-
(5) trates more intensely on Black-White relations in Black
regiments than do any of its predecessors. Glatthaar's title
expresses his theses: loyalty, friendship, and respect among
White officers and Black soldiers were fostered by the
mutual dangers they faced in combat.
(10) Glatthaar accurately describes the government's discriminatory treatment of Black soldiers in pay, promotion, medical care, and job assignments, appropriately emphasizing
the campaign by Black soldiers and their officers to get the
opportunity to fight. That chance remained limited through-
(15) out the war by army policies that kept most Black units
serving in rear-echelon assignments and working in labor
battalions. Thus, while their combat death rate was only
one-third that of White units, their mortality rate from
disease, a major killer in this war, was twice as great.
(20) Despite these obstacles, the courage and effectiveness of
several Black units in combat won increasing respect from
initially skeptical or hostile White soldiers. As one White
officer put it, "they have fought their way into the respect
of all the army."
(25) In trying to demonstrate the magnitude of this attitudinal change, however, Glatthaar seems to exaggerate the
prewar racism of the White men who became officers in
Black regiments. "Prior to the war," he writes of these
men, "virtually all of them held powerful racial prejudices."
(30) While perhaps true of those officers who joined Black
units for promotion or other self-serving motives, this statement misrepresents the attitudes of the many abolitionists
who became officers in Black regiments. Having spent
years fighting against the race prejudice endemic in Ameri-
(35) can society, they participated eagerly in this military experiment, which they hoped would help African Americans
achieve freedom and postwar civil equality. By current standards of racial egalitarianism, these men's paternalism
toward African Americans was racist. But to call their feel-
(40) ings "powerful racial prejudices" is to indulge in generational chauvinism—to judge past eras by present standards.

167. The passage as a whole can best be characterized as
which of the following?

(A) An evaluation of a scholarly study
(B) A description of an attitudinal change
(C) A discussion of an analytical defect
(D) An analysis of the causes of a phenomenon
(E) An argument in favor of revising a view

168. According to the author, which of the following is true
of Glatthaar's *Forged in Battle* compared with previous
studies on the same topic?

(A) It is more reliable and presents a more complete
picture of the historical events on which it
concentrates than do previous studies.
(B) It uses more of a particular kind of source material and focuses more closely on a particular
aspect of the topic than do previous studies.
(C) It contains some unsupported generalizations, but
it rightly emphasizes a theme ignored by most
previous studies.
(D) It surpasses previous studies on the same topic in
that it accurately describes conditions often
neglected by those studies.
(E) It makes skillful use of supporting evidence to
illustrate a subtle trend that previous studies
have failed to detect.

169. The author implies that the title of Glatthaar's book
refers specifically to which of the following?

(A) The sense of pride and accomplishment that Black
soldiers increasingly felt as a result of their
Civil War experiences
(B) The civil equality that African Americans
achieved after the Civil War, partly as a result of
their use of organizational skills honed by
combat
(C) The changes in the discriminatory army policies that
were made as a direct result of the performance
of Black combat units during the Civil War
(D) The improved interracial relations that were
formed by the races' facing of common
dangers and their waging of a common fight
during the Civil War
(E) The standards of racial egalitarianism that came to
be adopted as a result of the White Civil War
veterans' repudiation of their previous racism

170. The passage mentions which of the following as an
important theme that receives special emphasis in
Glatthaar's book?

(A) The attitudes of abolitionist officers in Black units
(B) The struggle of Black units to get combat assign-
ments
(C) The consequences of the poor medical care
received by Black soldiers
(D) The motives of officers serving in Black units
(E) The discrimination that Black soldiers faced when
trying for promotions.

171. The passage suggests that which of the following was true of Black units' disease mortality rates in the Civil War?

(A) They were almost as high as the combat mortality rates of White units.
(B) They resulted in part from the relative inexperience of these units when in combat.
(C) They were especially high because of the nature of these units' usual duty assignments.
(D) They resulted in extremely high overall casualty rates in Black combat units.
(E) They exacerbated the morale problems that were caused by the army's discriminatory policies.

172. The author of the passage quotes the White officer in lines 23-24 primarily in order to provide evidence to support the contention that

(A) virtually all White officers initially had hostile attitudes toward Black soldiers
(B) Black soldiers were often forced to defend themselves from physical attacks initiated by soldiers from White units
(C) the combat performance of Black units changed the attitudes of White soldiers toward Black soldiers
(D) White units paid especially careful attention to the performance of Black units in battle
(E) respect in the army as a whole was accorded only to those units, whether Black or White, that performed well in battle

173. Which of the following best describes the kind of error attributed to Glatthaar in lines 25-28 ?

(A) Insisting on an unwarranted distinction between two groups of individuals in order to render an argument concerning them internally consistent
(B) Supporting an argument in favor of a given interpretation of a situation with evidence that is not particularly relevant to the situation
(C) Presenting a distorted view of the motives of certain individuals in order to provide grounds for a negative evaluation of their actions
(D) Describing the conditions prevailing before a given event in such a way that the contrast with those prevailing after the event appears more striking than it actually is
(E) Asserting that a given event is caused by another event merely because the other event occurred before the given event occurred

174. Which of the following actions can best be described as indulging in "generational chauvinism" (lines 40-41) as that practice is defined in the passage?

(A) Condemning a present-day monarch merely because many monarchs have been tyrannical in the past
(B) Clinging to the formal standards of politeness common in one's youth to such a degree that any relaxation of those standards is intolerable
(C) Questioning the accuracy of a report written by an employee merely because of the employee's gender
(D) Deriding the superstitions accepted as "science" in past eras without acknowledging the prevalence of irrational beliefs today
(E) Labeling a nineteenth-century politician as "corrupt" for engaging in once-acceptable practices considered intolerable today

It was once assumed that all living things could be divided into two fundamental and exhaustive categories. Multicellular plants and animals, as well as many unicellu-
Line lar organisms, are eukaryotic—their large, complex cells
(5) have a well-formed nucleus and many organelles. On the other hand, the true bacteria are prokaryotic cells, which are simple and lack a nucleus. The distinction between eukaryotes and bacteria, initially defined in terms of subcellular structures visible with a microscope, was ulti-
(10) mately carried to the molecular level. Here prokaryotic and eukaryotic cells have many features in common. For instance, they translate genetic information in proteins according to the same type of genetic coding. But even where the molecular processes are the same, the details in
(15) the two forms are different and characteristic of the respec- tive forms. For example, the amino acid sequences of vari- ous enzymes tend to be typically prokaryotic or eukaryotic. The differences between the groups and the similarities within each group made it seem certain to most biologists
(20) that the tree of life had only two stems. Moreover, argu- ments pointing out the extent of both structural and func- tional differences between eukaryotes and true bacteria convinced many biologists that the precursors of the eukaryotes must have diverged from the common ancestor
(25) before the bacteria arose.

Although much of this picture has been sustained by more recent research, it seems fundamentally wrong in one respect. Among the bacteria, there are organisms that are significantly different both from the cells of eukaryotes and
(30) from the true bacteria, and it now appears that there are three stems in the tree of life. New techniques for deter- mining the molecular sequence of the RNA of organisms have produced evolutionary information about the degree to which organisms are related, the time since they diverged
(35) from a common ancestor, and the reconstruction of ances- stral versions of genes. These techniques have strongly suggested that although the true bacteria indeed form a large coherent group, certain other bacteria, the archaebac- teria, which are also prokaryotes and which resemble true
(40) bacteria, represent a distinct evolutionary branch that far antedates the common ancestor of all true bacteria.

175. The passage is primarily concerned with

(A) detailing the evidence that has led most biologists to replace the trichotomous picture of living organisms with a dichotomous one
(B) outlining the factors that have contributed to the current hypothesis concerning the number of basic categories of living organisms
(C) evaluating experiments that have resulted in proof that the prokaryotes are more ancient than had been expected
(D) summarizing the differences in structure and func- tion found among true bacteria, archaebacteria, and eukaryotes
(E) formulating a hypothesis about the mechanisms of evolution that resulted in the ancestors of the prokaryotes

176. According to the passage, investigations of eukaryotic and prokaryotic cells at the molecular level supported the conclusions that

(A) most eukaryotic organisms are unicellular
(B) complex cells have well-formed nuclei
(C) prokaryotes and eukaryotes form two fundamental categories
(D) subcellular structures are visible with a micro- scope
(E) prokaryotic and eukaryotic cells have similar enzymes

177. According to the passage, which of the following state- ments about the two-category hypothesis is likely to be true?

(A) It is promising because it explains the presence of true bacteria-like organisms such as organelles in eukaryotic cells.
(B) It is promising because it explains why eukaryotic cells, unlike prokaryotic cells, tend to form multicellular organisms.
(C) It is flawed because it fails to account for the great variety among eukaryotic organisms.
(D) It is flawed because it fails to account for the similarity between prokaryotes and eukaryotes.
(E) It is flawed because it fails to recognize an impor- tant distinction among prokaryotes.

178. It can be inferred from the passage that which of the following have recently been compared in order to clarify the fundamental classifications of living things?

(A) The genetic coding in true bacteria and that in other prokaryotes
(B) The organelle structures of archaebacteria, true bacteria, and eukaryotes
(C) The cellular structures of multicellular organisms and unicellular organisms
(D) The molecular sequences in eukaryotic RNA, true bacterial RNA, and archaebacterial RNA
(E) The amino acid sequences in enzymes of various eukaryotic species and those of enzymes in archaebacterial species.

179. If the "new techniques" mentioned in line 31 were applied in studies of biological classifications other than bacteria, which of the following is most likely?

(A) Some of those classifications will have to be reevaluated.
(B) Many species of bacteria will be reclassified.
(C) It will be determined that there are four main categories of living things rather than three.
(D) It will be found that true bacteria are much older than eukaryotes.
(E) It will be found that there is a common ancestor of the eukaryotes, archaebacteria, and true bacteria.

180. According to the passage, researchers working under the two-category hypothesis were correct in thinking that

(A) prokaryotes form a coherent group
(B) the common ancestor of all living things had complex properties
(C) eukaryotes are fundamentally different from true bacteria
(D) true bacteria are just as complex as eukaryotes
(E) ancestral versions of eukaryotic genes functioned differently from their modern counterparts

181. All of the following statements are supported by the passage EXCEPT:

(A) True bacteria form a distinct evolutionary group.
(B) Archaebacteria are prokaryotes that resemble true bacteria.
(C) True bacteria and eukaryotes employ similar types of genetic coding.
(D) True bacteria and eukaryotes are distinguishable at the subcellular level.
(E) Amino acid sequences of enzymes are uniform for eukaryotic and prokaryotic organisms.

182. The author's attitude toward the view that living things are divided into three categories is best described as one of

(A) tentative acceptance
(B) mild skepticism
(C) limited denial
(D) studious criticism
(E) wholehearted endorsement

Excess inventory, a massive problem for many businesses, has several causes, some of which are unavoidable. Overstocks may accumulate through production overruns or
Line errors. Certain styles and colors prove unpopular. With
(5) some products—computers and software, toys, and books—last year's models are difficult to move even at huge discounts. Occasionally the competition introduces a better product. But in many cases the public's buying tastes simply change, leaving a manufacturer or distributor with
(10) thousands (or millions) of items that the fickle public no longer wants.

One common way to dispose of this merchandise is to sell it to a liquidator, who buys as cheaply as possible and then resells the merchandise through catalogs, discount
(15) stores, and other outlets. However, liquidators may pay less for the merchandise than it cost to make it. Another way to dispose of excess inventory is to dump it. The corporation takes a straight cost write-off on its taxes and hauls the merchandise to a landfill. Although it is hard to believe,
(20) there is a sort of convoluted logic to this approach. It is perfectly legal, requires little time or preparation on the company's part, and solves the problem quickly. The drawback is the remote possibility of getting caught by the news media. Dumping perfectly useful products can turn into a
(25) public relations nightmare. Children living in poverty are freezing and XYZ Company has just sent 500 new snowsuits to the local dump. Parents of young children are barely getting by and QRS Company dumps 1,000 cases of disposable diapers because they have slight imperfections.
(30) The managers of these companies are not deliberately wasteful; they are simply unaware of all their alternatives. In 1976 the Internal Revenue Service provided a tangible incentive for businesses to contribute their products to charity. The new tax law allowed corporations to deduct the
(35) cost of the product donated plus half the difference between cost and fair market selling price, with the proviso that deductions cannot exceed twice cost. Thus, the federal government sanctions—indeed, encourages—an above-cost federal tax deductions for companies that donate inventory to charity.

183. The author mentions each of the following as a cause of excess inventory EXCEPT

(A) production of too much merchandise
(B) inaccurate forecasting of buyers' preferences
(C) unrealistic pricing policies
(D) products' rapid obsolescence
(E) availability of a better product

184. The passage suggests that which of the following is a kind of product that a liquidator who sells to discount stores would be unlikely to wish to acquire?

(A) Furniture
(B) Computers
(C) Kitchen equipment
(D) Baby-care products
(E) Children's clothing

185. The passage provides information that supports which of the following statements?

(A) Excess inventory results most often from insufficient market analysis by the manufacturer.
(B) Products with slight manufacturing defects may contribute to excess inventory.
(C) Few manufacturers have taken advantage of the changes in the federal tax laws.
(D) Manufacturers who dump their excess inventory are often caught and exposed by the news media.
(E) Most products available in discount stores have come from manufacturers' excess-inventory stock.

186. The author cites the examples in lines 25-29 most probably in order to illustrate

(A) the fiscal irresponsibility of dumping as a policy for dealing with excess inventory
(B) the waste-management problems that dumping new products creates
(C) the advantages to the manufacturers of dumping as a policy
(D) alternatives to dumping explored by different companies
(E) how the news media could portray dumping to the detriment of the manufacturer's reputation

187. By asserting that manufacturers "are simply unaware" (line 31), the author suggests which of the following?

(A) Manufacturers might donate excess inventory to charity rather than dump it if they knew about the provision in the federal tax code.
(B) The federal government has failed to provide sufficient encouragement to manufacturers to make use of advantageous tax policies.
(C) Manufacturers who choose to dump excess inventory are not aware of the possible effects on their reputation of media coverage of such dumping.
(D) The manufacturers of products disposed of by dumping are unaware of the needs of those people who would find the products useful.
(E) The manufacturers who dump their excess inventory are not familiar with the employment of liquidators to dispose of overstock.

188. The information in the passage suggests that which of the following, if true, would make donating excess inventory to charity less attractive to manufacturers than dumping?

(A) The costs of getting the inventory to the charitable destination are greater than the above-cost tax deduction.
(B) The news media give manufacturers' charitable contributions the same amount of coverage that they give dumping.
(C) No straight-cost tax benefit can be claimed for items that are dumped.
(D) The fair-market value of an item in excess inventory is 1.5 times its cost.
(E) Items end up as excess inventory because of a change in the public's preferences.

189. Information in the passage suggests that one reason manufacturers might take advantage of the tax provision mentioned in the last paragraph is that

(A) there are many kinds of products that cannot be legally dumped in a landfill
(B) liquidators often refuse to handle products with slight imperfections
(C) the law allows a deduction in excess of the cost of manufacturing the product
(D) media coverage of contributions of excess-inventory products to charity is widespread and favorable
(E) no tax deduction is available for products dumped or sold to a liquidator

Historians of women's labor in the United States at first largely disregarded the story of female service workers — women earning wages in occupations such as salesclerk, domestic servant, and office secretary. These historians
(5) focused instead on factory work, primarily because it seemed so different from traditional, unpaid "women's work" in the home, and because the underlying economic forces of industrialism were presumed to be gender-blind and hence emancipatory in effect. Unfortunately, emanci-
(10) pation has been less profound than expected, for not even industrial wage labor has escaped continued sex segregation in the workplace.

To explain this unfinished revolution in the status of women, historians have recently begun to emphasize the
(15) way a prevailing definition of femininity often determines the kinds of work allocated to women, even when such allocation is inappropriate to new conditions. For instance, early textile-mill entrepreneurs, in justifying women's employment in wage labor, made much of the assumption
(20) that women were by nature skillful at detailed tasks and patient in carrying out repetitive chores; the mill owners thus imported into the new industrial order hoary stereo-types associated with the homemaking activities they presumed to have been the purview of women. Because
(25) women accepted the more unattractive new industrial tasks more readily than did men, such jobs came to be regarded as female jobs. And employers, who assumed that women's "real" aspirations were for marriage and family life, declined to pay women wages commensurate with those of
(30) men. Thus many lower-skilled, lower-paid, less secure jobs came to be perceived as "female."

More remarkable than the original has been the persistence of such sex segregation in twentieth-century industry. Once an occupation came to be perceived as "female," employers
(35) showed surprisingly little interest in changing that perception, even when higher profits beckoned. And despite the urgent need of the United States during the Second World War to mobilize its human resources fully, job segregation by sex characterized even the most important
(40) war industries. Moreover, once the war ended, employers quickly returned to men most of the "male" jobs that women had been permitted to master.

190. According to the passage, job segregation by sex in the United States was

(A) greatly diminished by labor mobilization during the Second World War
(B) perpetuated by those textile-mill owners who argued in favor of women's employment in wage labor
(C) one means by which women achieved greater job security
(D) reluctantly challenged by employers except when the economic advantages were obvious
(E) a constant source of labor unrest in the young textile industry

191. According to the passage, historians of women's labor focused on factory work as a more promising area of research than service-sector work because factory work

(A) involved the payment of higher wages
(B) required skill in detailed tasks
(C) was assumed to be less characterized by sex segregation
(D) was more readily accepted by women than by men
(E) fitted the economic dynamic of industrialism better

192. It can be inferred from the passage that early historians of women's labor in the United States paid little attention to women's employment in the service sector of the economy because

(A) the extreme variety of these occupations made it very difficult to assemble meaningful statistics about them
(B) fewer women found employment in the service sector than in factory work
(C) the wages paid to workers in the service sector were much lower than those paid in the industrial sector
(D) women's employment in the service sector tended to be much more short term than in factory work
(E) employment in the service sector seemed to have much in common with the unpaid work associated with homemaking

193. The passage supports which of the following statements about the early mill owners mentioned in the
second paragraph?

(A) They hoped that by creating relatively unattractive
"female" jobs they would discourage women
from losing interest in marriage and family life.
(B) They sought to increase the size of the available
labor force as a means to keep men's wages low.
(C) They argued that women were inherently suited to
do well in particular kinds of factory work.
(D) They though that factory work bettered the
condition of women by emancipating them from
dependence on income earned by men.
(E) They felt guilty about disturbing the traditional
division of labor in the family.

194. It can be inferred from the passage that the "unfinished
revolution" the author mentions in line 13 refers to the

(A) entry of women into the industrial labor market
(B) recognition that work done by women as
homemakers should be compensated at rates
comparable to those prevailing in the service
sector of the economy
(C) development of a new definition of femininity
unrelated to the economic forces of industrialism
(D) introduction of equal pay for equal work in all
professions
(E) emancipation of women wage earners from
gender-determined job allocation

195. The passage supports which of the following
statements about hiring policies in the United States?

(A) After a crisis many formerly "male" jobs are
reclassified as "female" jobs.
(B) Industrial employers generally prefer to hire
women with previous experience as
homemakers.
(C) Post-Second World War hiring policies caused
women to lose many of their wartime gains in
employment opportunity.
(D) Even war industries during the Second World War
were reluctant to hire women for factory work.
(E) The service sector of the economy has proved
more nearly gender-blind in its hiring policies
than has the manufacturing sector.

196. Which of the following words best expresses the
opinion of the author of the passage concerning the
notion that women are more skillful than men in
carrying out detailed tasks?

(A) "patient" (line 21)
(B) "repetitive" (line 21)
(C) "hoary" (line 22)
(D) "homemaking" (line 23)
(E) "purview" (line 24)

197. Which of the following best describes the relationship
of the final paragraph to the passage as a whole?

(A) The central idea is reinforced by the citation of
evidence drawn from twentieth-century history.
(B) The central idea is restated in such a way as to
form a transition to a new topic for discussion.
(C) The central idea is restated and juxtaposed with
evidence that might appear to contradict it.
(D) A partial exception to the generalizations of the
central idea is dismissed as unimportant.
(E) Recent history is cited to suggest that the central
idea's validity is gradually diminishing.

According to a recent theory, Archean-age gold-quartz vein systems were formed over two billion years ago from magmatic fluids that originated from molten granitelike bodies deep beneath the surface of the Earth. This theory is
(5) contrary to the widely held view that the systems were deposited from metamorphic fluids, that is, from fluids that formed during the dehydration of wet sedimentary rocks.

The recently developed theory has considerable practical importance. Most of the gold deposits discovered during
(10) the original gold rushes were exposed at the Earth's surface and were found because they had shed trails of alluvial gold that were easily traced by simple prospecting methods. Although these same methods still lead to an occasional discovery, most deposits not yet discovered have gone
(15) undetected because they are buried and have no surface expression.

The challenge in exploration is therefore to unravel the subsurface geology of an area and pinpoint the position of buried minerals. Methods widely used today include
(20) analysis of aerial images that yield a broad geological overview; geophysical techniques that provide data on the magnetic, electrical, and mineralogical properties of the rocks being investigated; and sensitive chemical tests that are able to detect the subtle chemical halos that often
(25) envelop mineralization. However, none of these high-technology methods are of any value if the sites to which they are applied have never mineralized, and to maximize the chances of discovery the explorer must therefore pay particular attention to selecting the ground formations most
(30) likely to be mineralized. Such ground selection relies to varying degrees on conceptual models, which take into account theoretical studies of relevant factors.

These models are constructed primarily from empirical observations of known mineral deposits and from theories
(35) of ore-forming processes. The explorer uses the models to identify those geological features that are critical to the formation of the mineralization being modeled, and then tries to select areas for exploration that exhibit as many of the critical features as possible.

198. The author is primarily concerned with

(A) advocating a return to an older methodology
(B) explaining the importance of a recent theory
(C) enumerating differences between two widely used methods
(D) describing events leading to a discovery
(E) challenging the assumptions on which a theory is based

199. According to the passage, the widely held view of Archean-age gold-quartz vein systems is that such systems

(A) were formed from metamorphic fluids
(B) originated in molten granitelike bodies
(C) were formed from alluvial deposits
(D) generally have surface expression
(E) are not discoverable through chemical tests

200. The passage implies that which of the following steps would be the first performed by explorers who wish to maximize their chances of discovering gold?

(A) Surveying several sites known to have been formed more than two billion years ago
(B) Limiting exploration to sites known to have been formed from metamorphic fluid
(C) Using an appropriate conceptual model to select a site for further exploration
(D) Using geophysical methods to analyze rocks over a broad area
(E) Limiting exploration to sites where alluvial gold has previously been found

201. Which of the following statements about discoveries of gold deposits is supported by information in the passage?

(A) The number of gold discoveries made annually has increased between the time of the original gold rushes and the present.
(B) New discoveries of gold deposits are likely to be the result of exploration techniques designed to locate buried mineralization.
(C) It is unlikely that newly discovered gold deposits will ever yield as much as did those deposits discovered during the original gold rushes.
(D) Modern explorers are divided on the question of the utility of simple prospecting methods as a source of new discoveries of gold deposits.
(E) Models based on the theory that gold originated from magmatic fluids have already led to new discoveries of gold deposits.

202. It can be inferred from the passage that which of the following is easiest to detect?

(A) A gold-quartz vein system originating in magmatic fluids
(B) A gold-quartz vein system originating in metamorphic fluids
(C) A gold deposit that is mixed with granite
(D) A gold deposit that has shed alluvial gold
(E) A gold deposit that exhibits chemical halos

203. The theory mentioned in line 1 relates to the conceptual models discussed in the passage in which of the following ways?

(A) It may furnish a valid account of ore-forming processes, and, hence, can support conceptual models that have great practical significance.
(B) It suggests that certain geological formations, long believed to be mineralized, are in fact mineralized, thus confirming current conceptual models.
(C) It suggests that there may not be enough similarity across Archean-age gold-quartz vein systems to warrant the formation of conceptual models.
(D) It corrects existing theories about the chemical halos of gold deposits, and thus provides a basis for correcting current conceptual models.
(E) It suggests that simple prospecting methods still have a higher success rate in the discovery of gold deposits than do more modern methods.

204. According to the passage, methods of exploring for gold that are widely used today are based on which of the following facts?

(A) Most of the Earth's remaining gold deposits are still molten.
(B) Most of the Earth's remaining gold deposits are exposed at the surface.
(C) Most of the Earth's remaining gold deposits are buried and have no surface expression.
(D) Only one type of gold deposit warrants exploration, since the other types of gold deposits are found in regions difficult to reach.
(E) Only one type of gold deposit warrants exploration, since the other types of gold deposits are unlikely to yield concentrated quantities of gold.

205. It can be inferred from the passage that the efficiency of model-based gold exploration depends on which of the following?

I. The closeness of the match between the geological features identified by the model as critical and the actual geological features of a given area
II. The degree to which the model chosen relies on empirical observation of known mineral deposits rather than on theories of ore-forming processes
III. The degree to which the model chosen is based on an accurate description of the events leading to mineralization

(A) I only
(B) II only
(C) I and II only
(D) I and III only
(E) I, II, and III

While there is no blueprint for transforming a largely government-controlled economy into a free one, the experience of the United Kingdom since 1979 clearly
Line shows one approach that works: privatization, in which
(5) state-owned industries are sold to private companies. By 1979, the total borrowings and losses of state-owned industries were running at about £3 billion a year. By selling many of these industries, the government has decreased these borrowings and losses, gained over £34
(10) billion from the sales, and now receives tax revenues from the newly privatized companies. Along with a dramatically improved overall economy, the government has been able to repay 12.5 percent of the net national debt over a two-year period.
(15) In fact, privatization has not only rescued individual industries and a whole economy headed for disaster, but has also raised the level of performance in every area. At British Airways and British Gas, for example, productivity per employee has risen by 20 percent. At Associated
(20) British Ports, labor disruptions common in the 1970's and early 1980's have now virtually disappeared. At British Telecom, there is no longer a waiting list—as there always was before privatization—to have a telephone installed.
Part of this improved productivity has come about
(25) because the employees of privatized industries were given the opportunity to buy shares in their own companies. They responded enthusiastically to the offer of shares: at British Aerospace, 89 percent of the eligible work force bought shares; at Associated British Ports, 90 percent; and at
(30) British Telecom, 92 percent. When people have a personal stake in something, they think about it, care about it, work to make it prosper. At the National Freight Consortium, the new employee-owners grew so concerned about their company's profits that during wage negotiations they
(35) actually pressed their union to lower its wage demands.
Some economists have suggested that giving away free shares would provide a needed acceleration of the privatization process. Yet they miss Thomas Paine's point that "what we obtain too cheap we esteem too lightly." In
(40) order for the far-ranging benefits of individual ownership to be achieved by owners, companies, and countries, employees and other individuals must make their own decisions to buy, and they must commit some of their own resources to the choice.

206. According to the passage, all of the following were benefits of privatizing state-owned industries in the United Kingdom EXCEPT:

(A) Privatized industries paid taxes to the government.
(B) The government gained revenue from selling state-owned industries.
(C) The government repaid some of its national debt.
(D) Profits from industries that were still state-owned increased.
(E) Total borrowings and losses of state-owned industries decreased.

207. According to the passage, which of the following resulted in increased productivity in companies that have been privatized?

(A) A large number of employees chose to purchase shares in their companies.
(B) Free shares were widely distributed to individual shareholders.
(C) The government ceased to regulate major industries.
(D) Unions conducted wage negotiations for employees.
(E) Employee-owners agreed to have their wages lowered.

208. It can be inferred from the passage that the author considers labor disruptions to be

(A) an inevitable problem in a weak national economy
(B) a positive sign of employee concern about a company
(C) a predictor of employee reactions to a company's offer to sell shares to them
(D) a phenomenon found more often in state-owned industries than in private companies
(E) a deterrence to high performance levels in an industry

209. The passage supports which of the following statements about employees buying shares in their own companies?

(A) At three different companies, approximately nine out of ten of the workers were eligible to buy shares in their companies.

(B) Approximately 90 percent of the eligible workers at three different companies chose to buy shares in their companies.

(C) The opportunity to buy shares was discouraged by at least some labor unions.

(D) Companies that demonstrated the highest productivity were the first to allow their employees the opportunity to buy shares.

(E) Eligibility to buy shares was contingent on employees' agreeing to increased work loads

210. Which of the following statements is most consistent with the principle described in lines 30-32 ?

(A) A democratic government that decides it is inappropriate to own a particular industry has in no way abdicated its responsibilities as guardian of the public interest.

(B) The ideal way for a government to protect employee interests is to force companies to maintain their share of a competitive market without government subsidies.

(C) The failure to harness the power of self-interest is an important reason that state-owned industries perform poorly.

(D) Governments that want to implement privatization programs must try to eliminate all resistance to the free-market system.

(E) The individual shareholder will reap only a minute share of the gains from whatever sacrifices he or she makes to achieve these gains.

211. Which of the following can be inferred from the passage about the privatization process in the United Kingdom?

(A) It depends to a potentially dangerous degree on individual ownership of shares.

(B) It conforms in its most general outlines to Thomas Paine's prescription for business ownership.

(C) It was originally conceived to include some giving away of free shares.

(D) It has been successful, even through privatization has failed in other countries.

(E) It is taking place more slowly than some economists suggest is necessary.

212. The quotation in line 39 is most probably used to

(A) counter a position that the author of the passage believes is incorrect

(B) state a solution to a problem described in the previous sentence

(C) show how opponents of the viewpoint of the author of the passage have supported their arguments

(D) point out a paradox contained in a controversial viewpoint

(E) present a historical maxim to challenge the principle introduced in the third paragraph

Coral reefs are one of the most fragile, biologically complex, and diverse marine ecosystems on Earth. This ecosystem is one of the fascinating paradoxes of the bio-
Line
(5) sphere: how do clear, and thus nutrient-poor, waters support such prolific and productive communities? Part of the answer lies within the tissues of the corals themselves. Symbiotic cells of algae known as zooxanthellae carry out photosynthesis using the metabolic wastes of the corals, thereby producing food for themselves, for their coral
(10) hosts, and even for other members of the reef community. This symbiotic process allows organisms in the reef community to use sparse nutrient resources efficiently.

Unfortunately for coral reefs, however, a variety of human activities are causing worldwide degradation of
(15) shallow marine habitats by adding nutrients to the water. Agriculture, slash-and-burn land clearing, sewage disposal, and manufacturing that creates waste by-products all increase nutrient loads in these waters. Typical symptoms of reef decline are destabilized herbivore populations and
(20) an increasing abundance of algae and filter-feeding animals. Declines in reef communities are consistent with observations that nutrient input is increasing in direct proportion to growing human populations, thereby threatening reef communities sensitive to subtle changes in nutrient input to their waters.

213. The passage is primarily concerned with

(A) describing the effects of human activities on algae in coral reefs
(B) explaining how human activities are posing a threat to coral reef communities
(C) discussing the process by which coral reefs deteriorate in nutrient-poor waters
(D) explaining how coral reefs produce food for themselves
(E) describing the abundance of algae and filter-feeding animals in coral reef areas

214. The passage suggests which of the following about coral reef communities?

(A) Coral reef communities may actually be more likely to thrive in waters that are relatively low in nutrients.
(B) The nutrients on which coral reef communities thrive are only found in shallow waters.
(C) Human population growth has led to changing ocean temperatures, which threatens coral reef communities.
(D) The growth of coral reef communities tends to destabilize underwater herbivore populations.
(E) Coral reef communities are more complex and diverse than most ecosystems located on dry land.

215. The author refers to "filter-feeding animals" (line 20) in order to

(A) provide an example of a characteristic sign of reef deterioration
(B) explain how reef communities acquire sustenance for survival
(C) identify a factor that helps herbivore populations thrive
(D) indicate a cause of decreasing nutrient input in waters that reefs inhabit
(E) identify members of coral reef communities that rely on coral reefs for nutrients

216. According to the passage, which of the following is a factor that is threatening the survival of coral reef communities?

(A) The waters they inhabit contain few nutrient resources.
(B) A decline in nutrient input is disrupting their symbiotic relationship with zooxanthellae.
(C) The degraded waters of their marine habitats have reduced their ability to carry out photosynthesis.
(D) They are too biologically complex to survive in habitats with minimal nutrient input.
(E) Waste by-products result in an increase in nutrient input to reef communities.

217. It can be inferred from the passage that the author describes coral reef communities as paradoxical most likely for which of the following reasons?

(A) They are thriving even though human activities have depleted the nutrients in their environment.
(B) They are able to survive in spite of an over-abundance of algae inhabiting their waters.
(C) They are able to survive in an environment with limited food resources.
(D) Their metabolic wastes contribute to the degradation of the waters that they inhabit.
(E) They are declining even when the water surrounding them remains clear.

Two divergent definitions have dominated sociologists' discussions of the nature of ethnicity. The first emphasizes the primordial and unchanging character of ethnicity. In
Line
(5) this view, people have an essential need for belonging that is satisfied by membership in groups based on shared ancestry and culture. A different conception of ethnicity de-emphasizes the cultural component and defines ethnic groups as interest groups. In this view, ethnicity serves as a way of mobilizing a certain population behind issues
(10) relating to its economic position. While both of these definitions are useful, neither fully captures the dynamic and changing aspects of ethnicity in the United States. Rather, ethnicity is more satisfactorily conceived of as a process in which preexisting communal bonds and common
(15) cultural attributes are adapted for instrumental purposes according to changing real-life situations.

One example of this process is the rise of participation by Native American people in the broader United States political system since the Civil Rights movement of the
(20) 1960's. Besides leading Native Americans to participate more actively in politics (the number of Native American legislative officeholders more than doubled), this movement also evoked increased interest in tribal history and traditional culture. Cultural and instrumental components of
(25) ethnicity are not mutually exclusive, but rather reinforce one another.

The Civil Rights movement also brought changes in the uses to which ethnicity was put by Mexican American people. In the 1960's, Mexican Americans formed
(30) community-based political groups that emphasized ancestral heritage as a way of mobilizing constituents. Such emerging issues as immigration and voting rights gave Mexican American advocacy groups the means by which to promote ethnic solidarity. Like European ethnic groups in the
(35) nineteenth-century United States, late-twentieth-century Mexican American leaders combined ethnic with contemporary civic symbols. In 1968 Henry Cisneros, later mayor of San Antonio, Texas, cited Mexican leader Benito Juárez as a model for Mexican Americans in their fight for con-
(40) temporary civil rights. And every year, Mexican Americans celebrate *Cinco de Mayo* as fervently as many Irish American people embrace St. Patrick's Day (both are major holidays in the countries of origin), with both holidays having been reinvented in the context of the United States
(45) and linked to ideals, symbols, and heroes of the United States.

218. Which of the following best states the main idea of the passage?

(A) In their definitions of the nature of ethnicity, sociologists have underestimated the power of the primordial human need to belong.

(B) Ethnicity is best defined as a dynamic process that combines cultural components with shared political and economic interests.

(C) In the United States in the twentieth century, ethnic groups have begun to organize in order to further their political and economic interests.

(D) Ethnicity in the United States has been significantly changed by the Civil Rights movement.

(E) The two definitions of ethnicity that have dominated sociologists' discussions are incompatible and should be replaced by an entirely new approach.

219. Which of the following statements about the first two definitions of ethnicity discussed in the first paragraph is supported by the passage?

(A) One is supported primarily by sociologists, and the other is favored by members of ethnic groups.

(B) One emphasizes the political aspects of ethnicity, and the other focuses on the economic aspects.

(C) One is the result of analysis of United States populations, and the other is the result of analysis of European populations.

(D) One focuses more on the ancestral components of ethnicity than does the other.

(E) One focuses more on immigrant groups than does the other.

220. The author of the passage refers to Native American people in the second paragraph in order to provide an example of

(A) the ability of membership in groups based on shared ancestry and culture to satisfy an essential human need
(B) how ethnic feelings have both motivated and been strengthened by political activity
(C) how the Civil Rights movement can help promote solidarity among United States ethnic groups
(D) how participation in the political system has helped to improve a group's economic situation
(E) the benefits gained from renewed study of ethnic history and culture

221. The passage supports which of the following statements about the Mexican American community?

(A) In the 1960's the Mexican American community began to incorporate the customs of another ethnic group in the United States into the observation of its own ethnic holidays.
(B) In the 1960's Mexican American community groups promoted ethnic solidarity primarily in order to effect economic change.
(C) In the 1960's leaders of the Mexican American community concentrated their efforts on promoting a renaissance of ethnic history and culture.
(D) In the 1960's members of the Mexican American community were becoming increasingly concerned about the issue of voting rights.
(E) In the 1960's the Mexican American community had greater success in mobilizing constituents than did other ethnic groups in the United States.

222. Which of the following types of ethnic cultural expression is discussed in the passage?

(A) The retelling of traditional narratives
(B) The wearing of traditional clothing
(C) The playing of traditional music
(D) The celebration of traditional holidays
(E) The preparation of traditional cuisine

223. Information in the passage supports which of the following statements about many European ethnic groups in the nineteenth-century United States?

(A) They emphasized economic interests as a way of mobilizing constituents behind certain issues.
(B) They conceived of their own ethnicity as being primordial in nature.
(C) They created cultural traditions that fused United States symbols with those of their countries of origin.
(D) They de-emphasized the cultural components of their communities in favor of political interests.
(E) They organized formal community groups designed to promote a renaissance of ethnic history and culture.

224. The passage suggests that in 1968 Henry Cisneros most likely believed that

(A) many Mexican Americans would respond positively to the example of Benito Juárez
(B) many Mexican Americans were insufficiently educated in Mexican history
(C) the fight for civil rights in the United States had many strong parallels in both Mexican and Irish history
(D) the quickest way of organizing community-based groups was to emulate the tactics of Benito Juárez
(E) Mexican Americans should emulate the strategies of Native American political leaders

The fact that superior service can generate a competitive advantage for a company does not mean that every attempt at improving service will create such an advantage. Invest-
Line
(5) ments in service, like those in production and distribution, must be balanced against other types of investments on the basis of direct, tangible benefits such as cost reduction and increased revenues. If a company is already effectively on a par with its competitors because it provides service that avoids a damaging reputation and keeps customers from
(10) leaving at an unacceptable rate, then investment in higher service levels may be wasted, since service is a deciding factor for customers only in extreme situations.

This truth was not apparent to managers of one regional bank, which failed to improve its competitive position
(15) despite its investment in reducing the time a customer had to wait for a teller. The bank managers did not recognize the level of customer inertia in the consumer banking industry that arises from the inconvenience of switching banks. Nor did they analyze their service improvement to
(20) determine whether it would attract new customers by producing a new standard of service that would excite customers or by proving difficult for competitors to copy. The only merit of the improvement was that it could easily be described to customers.

225. The primary purpose of the passage is to

(A) contrast possible outcomes of a type of business investment
(B) suggest more careful evaluation of a type of business investment
(C) illustrate various ways in which a type of business investment could fail to enhance revenues
(D) trace the general problems of a company to a certain type of business investment
(E) criticize the way in which managers tend to analyze the costs and benefits of business investments

226. According to the passage, investments in service are comparable to investments in production and distribution in terms of the

(A) tangibility of the benefits that they tend to confer
(B) increased revenues that they ultimately produce
(C) basis on which they need to be weighed
(D) insufficient analysis that managers devote to them
(E) degree of competitive advantage that they are likely to provide

227. The passage suggests which of the following about service provided by the regional bank prior to its investment in enhancing that service?

(A) It enabled the bank to retain customers at an acceptable rate.
(B) It threatened to weaken the bank's competitive position with respect to other regional banks.
(C) It had already been improved after having caused damage to the bank's reputation in the past.
(D) It was slightly superior to that of the bank's regional competitors.
(E) It needed to be improved to attain parity with the service provided by competing banks.

228. The passage suggests that bank managers failed to consider whether or not the service improvement mentioned in line 19

(A) was too complicated to be easily described to prospective customers
(B) made a measurable change in the experiences of customers in the bank's offices
(C) could be sustained if the number of customers increased significantly
(D) was an innovation that competing banks could have imitated
(E) was adequate to bring the bank's general level of service to a level that was comparable with that of its competitors

229. The discussion of the regional bank (lines 13-24) serves which of the following functions within the passage as a whole?

(A) It describes an exceptional case in which investment in service actually failed to produce a competitive advantage.

(B) It illustrates the pitfalls of choosing to invest in service at a time when investment is needed more urgently in another area.

(C) It demonstrates the kind of analysis that managers apply when they choose one kind of service investment over another.

(D) It supports the argument that investments in certain aspects of service are more advantageous than investments in other aspects of service.

(E) It provides an example of the point about investment in service made in the first paragraph.

230. The author uses the word "only" in line 23 most likely in order to

(A) highlight the oddity of the service improvement

(B) emphasize the relatively low value of the investment in service improvement

(C) distinguish the primary attribute of the service improvement from secondary attributes

(D) single out a certain merit of the service improvement from other merits

(E) point out the limited duration of the actual service improvement

A recent study has provided clues to predator-prey dynamics in the late Pleistocene era. Researchers compared the number of tooth fractures in present-day carnivores with tooth fractures in carnivores that lived
Line
(5) 36,000 to 10,000 years ago and that were preserved in the Rancho La Brea tar pits in Los Angeles. The breakage frequencies in the extinct species were strikingly higher than those in the present-day species.

In considering possible explanations for this finding,
(10) the researchers dismissed demographic bias because older individuals were not overrepresented in the fossil samples. They rejected preservational bias because a total absence of breakage in two extinct species demonstrated that the fractures were not the result of
(15) abrasion within the pits. They ruled out local bias because breakage data obtained from other Pleistocene sites were similar to the La Brea data. The explanation they consider most plausible is behavioral differences between extinct and present-day carnivores—in par-
(20) ticular, more contact between the teeth of predators and the bones of prey due to more thorough consumption of carcasses by the extinct species. Such thorough carcass consumption implies to the researchers either that prey availability was low, at least seasonally, or that there
(25) was intense competition over kills and a high rate of carcass theft due to relatively high predator densities.

231. The primary purpose of the passage is to

(A) present several explanations for a well-known fact
(B) suggest alternative methods for resolving a debate
(C) argue in favor of a controversial theory
(D) question the methodology used in a study
(E) discuss the implications of a research finding

232. The passage suggests that, compared with Pleistocene carnivores in other areas, Pleistocene carnivores in the La Brea area

(A) included the same species, in approximately the same proportions
(B) had a similar frequency of tooth fractures
(C) populated the La Brea area more densely
(D) consumed their prey more thoroughly
(E) found it harder to obtain sufficient prey

233. According to the passage, the researchers believe that the high frequency of tooth breakage in carnivores found at La Brea was caused primarily by

(A) the aging process in individual carnivores
(B) contact between the fossils in the pits
(C) poor preservation of the fossils after they were removed from the pits
(D) the impact of carnivores' teeth against the bones of their prey
(E) the impact of carnivores' teeth against the bones of other carnivores during fights over kills

234. The researchers' conclusion concerning the absence of demographic bias would be most seriously undermined if it were found that

   (A) the older an individual carnivore is, the more likely it is to have a large number of tooth fractures
   (B) the average age at death of a present-day carnivore is greater than was the average age at death of a Pleistocene carnivore
   (C) in Pleistocene carnivore species, older individuals consumed carcasses as thoroughly as did younger individuals
   (D) the methods used to determine animals' ages in fossil samples tend to misidentify many older individuals as younger individuals
   (E) data concerning the ages of fossil samples cannot provide reliable information about behavioral differences between extinct carnivores and present-day carnivores

235. The passage suggests that if the researchers had not found that two extinct carnivore species were free of tooth breakage, the researchers would have concluded that

   (A) the difference in breakage frequencies could have been the result of damage to the fossil remains in the La Brea pits
   (B) the fossils in other Pleistocene sites could have higher breakage frequencies than do the fossils in the La Brea pits
   (C) Pleistocene carnivore species probably behaved very similarly to one another with respect to consumption of carcasses
   (D) all Pleistocene carnivore species differed behaviorally from present-day carnivore species
   (E) predator densities during the Pleistocene era were extremely high

During the nineteenth century, occupational information about women that was provided by the United States census—a population count conducted
Line each decade—became more detailed and precise in
(5) response to social changes. Through 1840, simple enumeration by household mirrored a home-based agricultural economy and hierarchical social order: the head of the household (presumed male or absent) was specified by name, whereas other household members
(10) were only indicated by the total number of persons counted in various categories, including occupational categories. Like farms, most enterprises were family-run, so that the census measured economic activity as an attribute of the entire household, rather than of indi-
(15) viduals.

The 1850 census, partly responding to antislavery and women's rights movements, initiated the collection of specific information about each individual in a household. Not until 1870 was occupational information
(20) analyzed by gender: the census superintendent reported 1.8 million women employed outside the home in "gainful and reputable occupations." In addition, he arbitrarily attributed to each family one woman "keeping house." Overlap between the two groups was not
(25) calculated until 1890, when the rapid entry of women into the paid labor force and social issues arising from industrialization were causing women's advocates and women statisticians to press for more thorough and accurate accounting of women's occupations and wages.

236. The primary purpose of the passage is to

(A) explain and critique the methods used by early statisticians
(B) compare and contrast a historical situation with a current-day one
(C) describe and explain a historical change
(D) discuss historical opposition to an established institution
(E) trace the origin of a contemporary controversy

237. Each of the following aspects of nineteenth-century United States censuses is mentioned in the passage EXCEPT the

(A) year in which data on occupations began to be analyzed by gender
(B) year in which specific information began to be collected on individuals in addition to the head of the household
(C) year in which overlap between women employed outside the home and women keeping house was first calculated
(D) way in which the 1890 census measured women's income levels and educational backgrounds
(E) way in which household members were counted in the 1840 census

238. It can be inferred from the passage that the 1840 United States census provided a count of which of the following?

(A) Women who worked exclusively in the home
(B) People engaged in nonfarming occupations
(C) People engaged in social movements
(D) Women engaged in family-run enterprises
(E) Men engaged in agriculture

239. The author uses the adjective "simple" in line 5 most probably to emphasize that the

(A) collection of census information became progressively more difficult throughout the nineteenth century
(B) technology for tabulating census information was rudimentary during the first half of the nineteenth century
(C) home-based agricultural economy of the early nineteenth century was easier to analyze than the later industrial economy
(D) economic role of women was better defined in the early nineteenth century than in the late nineteenth century
(E) information collected by early-nineteenth-century censuses was limited in its amount of detail

240. The passage suggests which of the following about the "women's advocates and women statisticians" mentioned in lines 27-28 ?

(A) They wanted to call attention to the lack of pay for women who worked in the home.
(B) They believed that previous census information was inadequate and did not reflect certain economic changes in the United States.
(C) They had begun to press for changes in census-taking methods as part of their participation in the antislavery movement.
(D) They thought that census statistics about women would be more accurate if more women were employed as census officials.
(E) They had conducted independent studies that disputed the official statistics provided by previous United States censuses.

The modern multinational corporation is described as having originated when the owner-managers of nineteenth-century British firms carrying on international
Line trade were replaced by teams of salaried managers
(5) organized into hierarchies. Increases in the volume of transactions in such firms are commonly believed to have necessitated this structural change. Nineteenth-century inventions like the steamship and the telegraph, by facilitating coordination of managerial activities, are
(10) described as key factors. Sixteenth- and seventeenth-century chartered trading companies, despite the international scope of their activities, are usually considered irrelevant to this discussion: the volume of their transactions is assumed to have been too low and the
(15) communications and transport of their day too primitive to make comparisons with modern multinationals interesting.

In reality, however, early trading companies successfully purchased and outfitted ships, built and
(20) operated offices and warehouses, manufactured trade goods for use abroad, maintained trading posts and production facilities overseas, procured goods for import, and sold those goods both at home and in other countries. The large volume of transactions associated
(25) with these activities seems to have necessitated hierarchical management structures well before the advent of modern communications and transportation. For example, in the Hudson's Bay Company, each far-flung trading outpost was managed by a salaried
(30) agent, who carried out the trade with the Native Americans, managed day-to-day operations, and oversaw the post's workers and servants. One chief agent, answerable to the Court of Directors in London through the correspondence committee, was appointed with
(35) control over all of the agents on the bay.

The early trading companies did differ strikingly from modern multinationals in many respects. They depended heavily on the national governments of their home countries and thus characteristically acted abroad to
(40) promote national interests. Their top managers were typically owners with a substantial minority share, whereas senior managers' holdings in modern multinationals are usually insignificant. They operated in a preindustrial world, grafting a system of capitalist
(45) international trade onto a premodern system of artisan and peasant production. Despite these differences, however, early trading companies organized effectively in remarkably modern ways and merit further study as analogues of more modern structures.

241. The author's main point is that

(A) modern multinationals originated in the sixteenth and seventeenth centuries with the establishment of chartered trading companies

(B) the success of early chartered trading companies, like that of modern multinationals, depended primarily on their ability to carry out complex operations

(C) early chartered trading companies should be more seriously considered by scholars studying the origins of modern multinationals

(D) scholars are quite mistaken concerning the origins of modern multinationals

(E) the management structures of early chartered trading companies are fundamentally the same as those of modern multinationals

242. According to the passage, early chartered trading companies are usually described as

(A) irrelevant to a discussion of the origins of the modern multinational corporation

(B) interesting but ultimately too unusual to be good subjects for economic study

(C) analogues of nineteenth-century British trading firms

(D) rudimentary and very early forms of the modern multinational corporation

(E) important national institutions because they existed to further the political aims of the governments of their home countries

243. It can be inferred from the passage that the author would characterize the activities engaged in by early chartered trading companies as being

(A) complex enough in scope to require a substantial amount of planning and coordination on the part of management
(B) too simple to be considered similar to those of a modern multinational corporation
(C) as intricate as those carried out by the largest multinational corporations today
(D) often unprofitable due to slow communications and unreliable means of transportation
(E) hampered by the political demands imposed on them by the governments of their home countries

244. The author lists the various activities of early chartered trading companies in order to

(A) analyze the various ways in which these activities contributed to changes in management structure in such companies
(B) demonstrate that the volume of business transactions of such companies exceeded that of earlier firms
(C) refute the view that the volume of business undertaken by such companies was relatively low
(D) emphasize the international scope of these companies' operations
(E) support the argument that such firms coordinated such activities by using available means of communication and transport

245. With which of the following generalizations regarding management structures would the author of the passage most probably agree?

(A) Hierarchical management structures are the most efficient management structures possible in a modern context.
(B) Firms that routinely have a high volume of business transactions find it necessary to adopt hierarchical management structures.
(C) Hierarchical management structures cannot be successfully implemented without modern communications and transportation.
(D) Modern multinational firms with a relatively small volume of business transactions usually do not have hierarchically organized management structures.
(E) Companies that adopt hierarchical management structures usually do so in order to facilitate expansion into foreign trade.

246. The passage suggests that modern multinationals differ from early chartered trading companies in that

(A) the top managers of modern multinationals own stock in their own companies rather than simply receiving a salary
(B) modern multinationals depend on a system of capitalist international trade rather than on less modern trading systems
(C) modern multinationals have operations in a number of different foreign countries rather than merely in one or two
(D) the operations of modern multinationals are highly profitable despite the more stringent environmental and safety regulations of modern governments
(E) the overseas operations of modern multinationals are not governed by the national interests of their home countries

247. The author mentions the artisan and peasant production systems of early chartered trading companies as an example of

(A) an area of operations of these companies that was unhampered by rudimentary systems of communications and transport
(B) a similarity that allows fruitful comparison of these companies with modern multinationals
(C) a positive achievement of these companies in the face of various difficulties
(D) a system that could not have emerged in the absence of management hierarchies
(E) a characteristic that distinguishes these companies from modern multinationals

248. The passage suggests that one of the reasons that early chartered trading companies deserve comparison with early modern multinationals is

(A) the degree to which they both depended on new technology
(B) the similar nature of their management structures
(C) similarities in their top managements' degree of ownership in the company
(D) their common dependence on political stability abroad in order to carry on foreign operations
(E) their common tendency to revolutionize systems of production

In an unfinished but highly suggestive series of essays, the late Sarah Eisenstein has focused attention on the evolution of working women's values from the turn of the century to the First World War. Eisenstein argues
(5) that turn-of-the-century women neither wholly accepted nor rejected what she calls the dominant "ideology of domesticity," but rather took this and other available ideologies—feminism, socialism, trade unionism—and modified or adapted them in light of their own experi-
(10) ences and needs. In thus maintaining that wage-work helped to produce a new "consciousness" among women, Eisenstein to some extent challenges the recent, controversial proposal by Leslie Tentler that for women the work experience only served to reinforce the attrac-
(15) tiveness of the dominant ideology. According to Tentler, the degrading conditions under which many female wage earners worked made them view the family as a source of power and esteem available nowhere else in their social world. In contrast, Eisenstein's study insists that
(20) wage-work had other implications for women's identities and consciousness. Most importantly, her work aims to demonstrate that wage-work enabled women to become aware of themselves as a distinct social group capable of defining their collective circumstance. Eisenstein insists
(25) that as a group working-class women were not able to come to collective consciousness of their situation until they began entering the labor force, because domestic work tended to isolate them from one another.

Unfortunately, Eisenstein's unfinished study does not
(30) develop these ideas in sufficient depth or detail, offering tantalizing hints rather than an exhaustive analysis. Whatever Eisenstein's overall plan may have been, in its current form her study suffers from the limited nature of the sources she depended on. She uses the speeches and
(35) writings of reformers and labor organizers, who she acknowledges were far from representative, as the voice of the typical woman worker. And there is less than adequate attention given to the differing values of immi- grant groups that made up a significant proportion of
(40) the population under investigation. While raising impor- tant questions, Eisenstein's essays do not provide defini- tive answers, and it remains for others to take up the challenges they offer.

249. The primary purpose of the passage is to

(A) criticize a scholar's assumptions and methodology
(B) evaluate an approach to women's history
(C) compare two sociological theories
(D) correct a misconception about feminist theory
(E) defend an unpopular ideology

250. It can be inferred from the passage that, in Eisen- stein's view, working women at the turn of the century had which of the following attitudes toward the dominant ideology of their time?

(A) They resented the dominant ideology as degrad- ing.
(B) They preferred the dominant ideology to other available ideologies.
(C) They began to view the dominant ideology more favorably as a result of their experi- ences in the labor force.
(D) They accepted some but not all aspects of the dominant ideology.
(E) They believed that the dominant ideology isolated them from one another.

251. Which of the following best describes the organization of the first paragraph of the passage?

(A) A chronological account of a historical development is presented, and then future developments are predicted.
(B) A term is defined according to several different schools of thought, and then a new definition is formulated.
(C) A theory is presented, an alternative viewpoint is introduced, and then the reasoning behind the initial theory is summarized.
(D) A tentative proposal is made, reasons for and against it are weighed, and then a modified version of the proposal is offered.
(E) A controversy is described, its historical implications are assessed, and then a compromise is suggested.

252. Which of the following would the author of the passage be most likely to approve as a continuation of Eisenstein's study?

(A) An oral history of prominent women labor organizers
(B) An analysis of letters and diaries written by typical female wage earners at the turn of the century
(C) An assessment of what different social and political groups defined as the dominant ideology in the early twentieth century
(D) A theoretical study of how socialism and feminism influenced one another at the turn of the century
(E) A documentary account of labor's role in the introduction of women into the labor force

Neotropical coastal mangrove forests are usually "zonal," with certain mangrove species found predominantly in the seaward portion of the habitat and other

Line
(5) mangrove species on the more landward portions of the coast. The earliest research on mangrove forests produced descriptions of species distribution from shore to land, without exploring the causes of the distributions.

The idea that zonation is caused by plant succession
(10) was first expressed by J. H. Davis in a study of Florida mangrove forests. According to Davis' scheme, the shoreline is being extended in a seaward direction because of the "land-building" role of mangroves, which, by trapping sediments over time, extend the
(15) shore. As a habitat gradually becomes more inland as the shore extends, the "land-building" species are replaced. This continuous process of accretion and succession would be interrupted only by hurricanes or storm flushings.

(20) Recently the universal application of Davis' succession paradigm has been challenged. It appears that in areas where weak currents and weak tidal energies allow the accumulation of sediments, mangroves will follow land formation and accelerate the rate of soil accretion;
(25) succession will proceed according to Davis' scheme. But on stable coastlines, the distribution of mangrove species results in other patterns of zonation; "land building" does not occur.

To find a principle that explains the various distribu-
(30) tion patterns, several researchers have looked to salinity and its effects on mangroves. While mangroves can develop in fresh water, they can also thrive in salinities as high as 2.5 times that of seawater. However, those mangrove species found in freshwater habitats do well
(35) only in the absence of competition, thus suggesting that salinity tolerance is a critical factor in competitive success among mangrove species. Research suggests that mangroves will normally dominate highly saline regions, although not because they require salt. Rather, they are
(40) metabolically efficient (and hence grow well) in portions of an environment whose high salinity excludes plants adapted to lower salinities. Tides create different degrees of salinity along a coastline. The characteristic mangrove species of each zone should exhibit a higher metabolic
(45) efficiency at that salinity than will any potential invader, including other species of mangrove.

253. The primary purpose of the passage is to

(A) refute the idea that the zonation exhibited in mangrove forests is caused by adaptation to salinity
(B) describe the pattern of zonation typically found in Florida mangrove forests
(C) argue that Davis' succession paradigm cannot be successfully applied to Florida mangrove forests
(D) discuss hypotheses that attempt to explain the zonation of coastal mangrove forests
(E) establish that plants that do well in saline forest environments require salt to achieve maximum metabolic efficiency

254. According to the passage, the earliest research on mangrove forests produced which of the following?

(A) Data that implied random patterns of mangrove species distribution
(B) Descriptions of species distributions suggesting zonation
(C) Descriptions of the development of mangrove forests over time
(D) Reclassification of species formerly thought to be identical
(E) Data that confirmed the "land-building" role of mangroves

255. It can be inferred from the passage that Davis'
paradigm does NOT apply to which of the following?

(A) The shoreline of Florida mangrove forests first
studied by Davis
(B) A shoreline in an area with weak currents
(C) A shoreline in an area with weak tidal energy
(D) A shoreline extended by "land-building" species
of mangroves
(E) A shoreline in which few sediments can accu-
mulate

256. Information in the passage indicates that the author
would most probably regard which of the following
statements as INCORRECT?

(A) Coastal mangrove forests are usually zonal.
(B) Hurricanes interrupt the process of accretion
and succession that extends existing
shorelines.
(C) Species of plants that thrive in a saline habitat
require salt to flourish.
(D) Plants with the highest metabolic efficiency in a
given habitat tend to exclude other plants
from that habitat.
(E) Shorelines in areas with weak currents and tides
are more likcly to be extended through the
process of accumulation of sediment than are
shorelines with strong currents and tides.

Modern manufacturers, who need reliable sources of materials and technologically advanced components to operate profitably, face an increasingly difficult choice between owning the producers of these items (a practice known as backward integration) and buying from independent producers. Manufacturers who integrate may reap short-term rewards, but they often restrict their future capacity for innovative product development.

Backward integration removes the need for some purchasing and marketing functions, centralizes overhead, and permits manufacturers to eliminate duplicated efforts in research and development. Where components are commodities (ferrous metals or petroleum, for example), backward integration almost certainly boosts profits. Nevertheless, because product innovation means adopting the most technologically advanced and cost-effective ways of making components, backward integration may entail a serious risk for a technologically active company—for example, a producer of sophisticated consumer electronics.

A company that decides to make rather than buy important parts can lock itself into an outdated technology. Independent suppliers may be unwilling to share innovations with assemblers with whom they are competing. Moreover, when an assembler sets out to master the technology of producing advanced components, the resulting demands on its resources may compromise its ability to assemble these components successfully into end products. Long-term contracts with suppliers can achieve many of the same cost benefits as backward integration without compromising a company's ability to innovate.

However, moving away from backward integration is not a complete solution either. Developing innovative technologies requires independent suppliers of components to invest huge sums in research and development. The resulting low profit margins on the sale of components threaten the long-term financial stability of these firms. Because the ability of end-product assemblers to respond to market opportunities depends heavily on suppliers of components, assemblers are often forced to integrate by purchasing the suppliers of components just to keep their suppliers in business.

257. According to the passage, all of the following are benefits associated with backward integration EXCEPT

(A) improvement in the management of overhead expenses
(B) enhancement of profit margins on sales of components
(C) simplification of purchasing and marketing operations
(D) reliability of a source of necessary components
(E) elimination of unnecessary research efforts

258. According to the passage, when an assembler buys a firm that makes some important component of the end product that the assembler produces, independent suppliers of the same component may

(A) withhold technological innovations from the assembler
(B) experience improved profit margins on sales of their products
(C) lower their prices to protect themselves from competition
(D) suffer financial difficulties and go out of business
(E) stop developing new versions of the component

259. Which of the following best describes the way the last paragraph functions in the context of the passage?

(A) The last in a series of arguments supporting the central argument of the passage is presented.
(B) A viewpoint is presented which qualifies one presented earlier in the passage.
(C) Evidence is presented in support of the argument developed in the preceding paragraph.
(D) Questions arising from the earlier discussion are identified as points of departure for further study of the topic.
(E) A specific example is presented to illustrate the main elements of the argument presented in the earlier paragraphs.

260. According to the passage, which of the following relationships between profits and investments in research and development holds true for producers of technologically advanced components?

(A) Modest investments are required and the profit margins on component sales are low.
(B) Modest investments are required but the profit margins on component sales are quite high.
(C) Despite the huge investments that are required, the profit margins on component sales are high.
(D) Because huge investments are required, the profit margins on component sales are low.
(E) Long-term contractual relationships with purchasers of components ensure a high ratio of profits to investment costs.

Homeostasis, an animal's maintenance of certain internal variables within an acceptable range, particularly in extreme physical environments, has long interested biologists. The desert rat and the camel in the
Line
(5) most water-deprived environments, and marine vertebrates in an all-water environment, encounter the same regulatory problem: maintaining adequate internal fluid balance.

For desert rats and camels, the problem is conser-
(10) vation of water in an environment where standing water is nonexistent, temperature is high, and humidity is low. Despite these handicaps, desert rats are able to maintain the osmotic pressure of their blood, as well as their total body-water content, at approximately the same
(15) levels as other rats. One countermeasure is behavioral: these rats stay in burrows during the hot part of the day, thus avoiding loss of fluid through panting or sweating, which are regulatory mechanisms for maintaining internal body temperature by evaporative cooling.
(20) Also, desert rats' kidneys can excrete a urine having twice as high a salt content as sea water.

Camels, on the other hand, rely more on simple endurance. They cannot store water, and their reliance on an entirely unexceptional kidney results in a rate
(25) of water loss through renal function significantly higher than that of desert rats. As a result, camels must tolerate losses in body water of up to thirty percent of their body weight. Nevertheless, camels do rely on a special mechanism to keep water loss within a tolerable range:
(30) by sweating and panting only when their body temperature exceeds that which would kill a human, they conserve internal water.

Marine vertebrates experience difficulty with their water balance because though there is no shortage of
(35) seawater to drink, they must drink a lot of it to maintain their internal fluid balance. But the excess salts from the seawater must be discharged somehow, and the kidneys of most marine vertebrates are unable to excrete a urine in which the salts are more concentrated than in
(40) seawater. Most of these animals have special salt-secreting organs outside the kidney that enable them to eliminate excess salt.

261. Which of the following most accurately states the purpose of the passage?

(A) To compare two different approaches to the study of homeostasis
(B) To summarize the findings of several studies regarding organisms' maintenance of internal variables in extreme environments
(C) To argue for a particular hypothesis regarding various organisms' conservation of water in desert environments
(D) To cite examples of how homeostasis is achieved by various organisms
(E) To defend a new theory regarding the maintenance of adequate fluid balance

262. According to the passage, the camel maintains internal fluid balance in which of the following ways?

I. By behavioral avoidance of exposure to conditions that lead to fluid loss
II. By an ability to tolerate high body temperatures
III. By reliance on stored internal fluid supplies

(A) I only
(B) II only
(C) I and II only
(D) II and III only
(E) I, II, and III

263. It can be inferred from the passage that some mechanisms that regulate internal body temperature, like sweating and panting, can lead to which of the following?

(A) A rise in the external body temperature
(B) A drop in the body's internal fluid level
(C) A decrease in the osmotic pressure of the blood
(D) A decrease in the amount of renal water loss
(E) A decrease in the urine's salt content

264. It can be inferred from the passage that the author characterizes the camel's kidney as "entirely unexceptional" (line 24) primarily to emphasize that it

(A) functions much as the kidney of a rat functions
(B) does not aid the camel in coping with the exceptional water loss resulting from the extreme conditions of its environment
(C) does not enable the camel to excrete as much salt as do the kidneys of marine vertebrates
(D) is similar in structure to the kidneys of most mammals living in water-deprived environments
(E) requires the help of other organs in eliminating excess salt

In the seventeenth-century Florentine textile industry, women were employed primarily in low-paying, low-skill jobs. To explain this segregation of labor by gender, economists have relied on the useful theory of human capital. According to this theory, investment in human capital—the acquisition of difficult job-related skills—generally benefits individuals by making them eligible to engage in well-paid occupations. Women's role as child bearers, however, results in interruptions in their participation in the job market (as compared with men's) and thus reduces their opportunities to acquire training for highly skilled work. In addition, the human capital theory explains why there was a high concentration of women workers in certain low-skill jobs, such as weaving, but not in others, such as combing or carding, by positing that because of their primary responsibility in child rearing women took occupations that could be carried out in the home.

There were, however, differences in pay scales that cannot be explained by the human capital theory. For example, male construction workers were paid significantly higher wages than female taffeta weavers. The wage difference between these two low-skill occupations stems from the segregation of labor by gender: because a limited number of occupations were open to women, there was a large supply of workers in their fields, and this "overcrowding" resulted in women receiving lower wages and men receiving higher wages.

265. The passage suggests that combing and carding differ from weaving in that combing and carding are

(A) low-skill jobs performed primarily by women employees
(B) low-skill jobs that were not performed in the home
(C) low-skill jobs performed by both male and female employees
(D) high-skill jobs performed outside the home
(E) high-skill jobs performed by both male and female employees

266. Which of the following, if true, would most weaken the explanation provided by the human capital theory for women's concentration in certain occupations in seventeenth-century Florence?

(A) Women were unlikely to work outside the home even in occupations whose hours were flexible enough to allow women to accommodate domestic tasks as well as paid labor.

(B) Parents were less likely to teach occupational skills to their daughters than they were to their sons.

(C) Women's participation in the Florentine paid labor force grew steadily throughout the sixteenth and seventeenth centuries.

(D) The vast majority of female weavers in the Florentine wool industry had children.

(E) Few women worked as weavers in the Florentine silk industry, which was devoted to making cloths that required a high degree of skill to produce.

267. The author of the passage would be most likely to describe the explanation provided by the human capital theory for the high concentration of women in certain occupations in the seventeenth-century Florentine textile industry as

(A) well founded though incomplete
(B) difficult to articulate
(C) plausible but poorly substantiated
(D) seriously flawed
(E) contrary to recent research

Maps made by non-Native Americans to depict Native American land tenure, resources, and population distributions appeared almost as early as Europeans'

Line
(5)
first encounters with Native Americans and took many forms: missionaries' field sketches, explorers' drawings, and surveyors' maps, as well as maps rendered in connection with treaties involving land transfers. Most existing maps of Native American lands are reconstructions that are based largely on archaeology, oral reports,

(10)
and evidence gathered from observers' accounts in letters, diaries, and official reports; accordingly, the accuracy of these maps is especially dependent on the mapmakers' own interpretive abilities.

Many existing maps also reflect the 150-year role of

(15)
the Bureau of Indian Affairs (BIA) in administering tribal lands. Though these maps incorporate some information gleaned directly from Native Americans, rarely has Native American cartography contributed to this official record, which has been compiled, surveyed, and

(20)
authenticated by non-Native Americans. Thus our current cartographic record relating to Native American tribes and their migrations and cultural features, as well as territoriality and contemporary trust lands, reflects the origins of the data, the mixed purposes for which

(25)
the maps have been prepared, and changes both in United States government policy and in non-Native Americans' attitudes toward an understanding of Native Americans.

268. Which of the following best describes the content of the passage?

(A) A chronology of the development of different methods for mapping Native American lands

(B) A discussion of how the mapmaking techniques of Native Americans differed from those of Europeans

(C) An argument concerning the present-day uses to which historical maps of Native American lands are put

(D) An argument concerning the nature of information contained in maps of Native American lands

(E) A proposal for improving the accuracy of maps of Native American lands

269. The passage mentions each of the following as a factor affecting current maps of Native American lands EXCEPT

(A) United States government policy

(B) non-Native Americans' perspectives on Native Americans

(C) origins of the information utilized to produce the maps

(D) changes in the ways that tribal lands are used

(E) the reasons for producing the maps

270. The passage suggests which of the following about most existing maps of Native American lands?

(A) They do not record the migrations of Native American tribes.
(B) They have been preserved primarily because of their connection with treaties involving land transfers.
(C) They tend to reflect archaeological evidence that has become outdated.
(D) They tend to be less accurate when they are based on oral reports than when they are based on written documents.
(E) They are not based primarily on the mapmakers' firsthand observations of Native American lands.

271. All of the following are examples of the type of evidence used in creating "Most existing maps"(lines 7-8) EXCEPT

(A) a nineteenth-century government report on population distributions of a particular tribe
(B) taped conversations with people who lived on Native American tribal lands in the early twentieth century
(C) aerial photographs of geological features of lands inhabited by Native Americans
(D) findings from a recently excavated site once inhabited by a certain Native American people
(E) a journal kept by a non-Native American explorer who traveled in Native American territory in the early nineteenth century

(This passage was written in 1984.)

It is now possible to hear a recording of Caruso's singing that is far superior to any made during his lifetime. A decades-old wax-cylinder recording of this *Line* great operatic tenor has been digitized, and the digi-
(5) tized signal has been processed by computer to remove the extraneous sound, or "noise," introduced by the now "ancient" wax-cylinder recording process.

Although this digital technique needs improvement, it represents a new and superior way of recording and
(10) processing sound which overcomes many of the limitations of analog recording. In analog recording systems, the original sound is represented as a continuous waveform created by variations in the sound's amplitude over time. When analog playback systems reproduce
(15) this waveform, however, they invariably introduce distortions. First, the waveform produced during playback differs somewhat from the original waveform. Second, the medium that stores the analog recording creates noise during playback which gets added to the
(20) recorded sounds.

Digital recordings, by contrast, reduce the original sound to a series of discrete numbers that represent the sound's waveform. Because the digital playback system "reads" only numbers, any noise and distortion
(25) that may accumulate during storage and manipulation of the digitized signal will have little effect: as long as the numbers remain recognizable, the original waveform will be reconstructed with little loss in quality. However, because the waveform is continuous, while
(30) its digital representation is composed of discrete numbers, it is impossible for digital systems to avoid some distortion. One kind of distortion, called "sampling error," occurs if the sound is sampled (i.e., its amplitude is measured) too infrequently, so that the
(35) amplitude changes more than one quantum (the smallest change in amplitude measured by the digital system) between samplings. In effect, the sound is changing too quickly for the system to record it accurately. A second form of distortion is "quantizing error," which
(40) arises when the amplitude being measured is not a whole number of quanta, forcing the digital recorder to round off. Over the long term, these errors are random, and the noise produced (a background buzzing) is similar to analog noise except that it only occurs when recorded sounds are being reproduced.

272. Which of the following best describes the relationship of the first paragraph to the passage as a whole?

(A) The first paragraph introduces a general thesis that is elaborated on in detail elsewhere in the passage.
(B) The first paragraph presents a concrete instance of a problem that is discussed elsewhere in the passage.
(C) The first paragraph describes a traditional process that is contrasted unfavorably with a newer process described elsewhere in the passage.
(D) The first paragraph presents a dramatic example of the potential of a process that is described elsewhere in the passage.
(E) The first paragraph describes a historic incident that served as the catalyst for developments described elsewhere in the passage.

273. According to the passage, one of the ways in which analog recording systems differ from digital recording systems is that analog systems

(A) can be used to reduce background noise in old recordings
(B) record the original sound as a continuous waveform
(C) distort the original sound somewhat
(D) can avoid introducing extraneous and nonmusical sounds
(E) can reconstruct the original waveform with little loss in quality

274. Which of the following statements about the numbers by which sound is represented in a digital system can be inferred from the passage?

(A) They describe the time interval between successive sounds in a passage of music.
(B) They model large changes in the amplitude of the initial sound with relatively poor precision.
(C) They are slightly altered each time they are read by the playback apparatus.
(D) They are not readily altered by distortion and noise accumulated as the digital signal is stored and manipulated.
(E) They are stored in the recording medium in small groups that can be read simultaneously by the playback apparatus.

275. Which of the following can be inferred from the passage about the digital approach to the processing of sound?

(A) It was developed in competition with wax-cylinder recording technology.
(B) It has resulted in the first distortion-free playback system.
(C) It has been extensively applied to nonmusical sounds.
(D) It cannot yet process music originally recorded on analog equipment.
(E) It is not yet capable of reprocessing old recordings in a completely distortion-free manner.

The function of capital markets is to facilitate an exchange of funds among all participants, and yet in practice we find that certain participants are not on a par
Line with others. Members of society have varying degrees
(5) of market strength in terms of information they bring to a transaction, as well as of purchasing power and creditworthiness, as defined by lenders.

For example, within minority communities, capital markets do not properly fulfill their functions; they do
(10) not provide access to the aggregate flow of funds in the United States. The financial system does not generate the credit or investment vehicles needed for underwriting economic development in minority areas. The problem underlying this dysfunction is found in a rationing
(15) mechanism affecting both the available alternatives for investment and the amount of financial resources. This creates a distributive mechanism penalizing members of minority groups because of their socioeconomic differences from others. The existing system expresses defi-
(20) nite socially based investment preferences that result from the previous allocation of income and that influence the allocation of resources for the present and future. The system tends to increase the inequality of income distribution. And, in the United States economy, a greater
(25) inequality of income distribution leads to a greater concentration of capital in certain types of investments.

Most traditional financial-market analysis studies ignore financial markets' deficiencies in allocation because of analysts' inherent preferences for the simple
(30) model of perfect competition. Conventional financial analysis pays limited attention to issues of market structure and dynamics, relative costs of information, and problems of income distribution. Market participants are viewed as acting as entirely independent and homo-
(35) geneous individuals with perfect foresight about capital-market behavior. Also, it is assumed that each individual in the community at large has the same access to the market and the same opportunity to transact and to express the preference appropriate to his or her indi-
(40) vidual interest. Moreover, it is assumed that transaction costs for various types of financial instruments (stocks, bonds, etc.) are equally known and equally divided among all community members.

276. The main point made by the passage is that

(A) financial markets provide for an optimum allocation of resources among all competing participants by balancing supply and demand

(B) the allocation of financial resources takes place among separate individual participants, each of whom has access to the market

(C) the existence of certain factors adversely affecting members of minority groups shows that financial markets do not function as conventional theory says they function

(D) investments in minority communities can be made by the use of various alternative financial instruments, such as stocks and bonds

(E) since transaction costs for stocks, bonds, and other financial instruments are not equally apportioned among all minority-group members, the financial market is subject to criticism

277. The passage states that traditional studies of the financial market overlook imbalances in the allocation of financial resources because

(A) an optimum allocation of resources is the final result of competition among participants

(B) those performing the studies choose an oversimplified description of the influences on competition

(C) such imbalances do not appear in the statistics usually compiled to measure the market's behavior

(D) the analysts who study the market are unwilling to accept criticism of their methods as biased

(E) socioeconomic differences form the basis of a rationing mechanism that puts minority groups at a disadvantage

278. The author's main point is argued by

(A) giving examples that support a conventional generalization
(B) showing that the view opposite to the author's is self-contradictory
(C) criticizing the presuppositions of a proposed plan
(D) showing that omissions in a theoretical description make it inapplicable in certain cases
(E) demonstrating that an alternative hypothesis more closely fits the data

279. A difference in which of the following would be an example of inequality in transaction costs as alluded to in lines 40-43 ?

(A) Maximum amounts of loans extended by a bank to businesses in different areas
(B) Fees charged to large and small investors for purchasing stocks
(C) Prices of similar goods offered in large and small stores in an area
(D) Stipends paid to different attorneys for preparing legal suits for damages
(E) Exchange rates in dollars for currencies of different countries

280. Which of the following can be inferred about minority communities on the basis of the passage?

(A) They provide a significant portion of the funds that become available for investment in the financial market.
(B) They are penalized by the tax system, which increases the inequality of the distribution of income between investors and wage earners.
(C) They do not receive the share of the amount of funds available for investment that would be expected according to traditional financial-market analysis.
(D) They are not granted governmental subsidies to assist in underwriting the cost of economic development.
(E) They provide the same access to alternative sources of credit to finance businesses as do majority communities.

281. According to the passage, a questionable assumption of the conventional theory about the operation of financial markets is that

(A) creditworthiness as determined by lenders is a factor determining market access
(B) market structure and market dynamics depend on income distribution
(C) a scarcity of alternative sources of funds would result from taking socioeconomic factors into consideration
(D) those who engage in financial-market transactions are perfectly well informed about the market
(E) inequalities in income distribution are increased by the functioning of the financial market

282. According to the passage, analysts have conventionally tended to view those who participate in financial markets as

(A) judging investment preferences in terms of the good of society as a whole
(B) influencing the allocation of funds through prior ownership of certain kinds of assets
(C) varying in market power with respect to one another
(D) basing judgments about future events mainly on chance
(E) having equal opportunities to engage in transactions

(The following is based on material written in 1996.)

The Montreal Protocol on Substances that Deplete
the Ozone Layer, signed in 1987 by more than 150
nations, has attained its short-term goals: it has decreased
Line the rate of increase in amounts of most ozone-deplet-
(5) ing chemicals reaching the atmosphere and has even
reduced the atmospheric levels of some of them. The
projection that the ozone layer will substantially recover
from ozone depletion by 2050 is based on the assumption that the protocol's regulations will be strictly fol-
(10) lowed. Yet there is considerable evidence of violations,
particularly in the form of the release of ozone-depleting
chlorofluorocarbons (CFC's), which are commonly
used in the refrigeration, heating, and air conditioning
industries. These violations reflect industry attitudes;
(15) for example, in the United States, 48 percent of
respondents in a recent survey of subscribers to *Air
Conditioning, Heating, and Refrigeration News*, an
industry trade journal, said that they did not believe that
CFC's damage the ozone layer. Moreover, some in the
(20) industry apparently do not want to pay for CFC
substitutes, which can run five times the cost of CFC's.
Consequently, a black market in imported illicit CFC's
has grown. Estimates of the contraband CFC trade
range from 10,000 to 22,000 tons a year, with most of
(25) the CFC's originating in India and China, whose agreements under the Protocol still allow them to produce
CFC's. In fact, the United States Customs Service
reports that CFC-12 is a contraband problem second
only to illicit drugs.

283. According to the passage, which of the following best describes most ozone-depleting
chemicals in 1996 as compared to those
in 1987 ?

(A) The levels of such chemicals in the
atmosphere had decreased.
(B) The number of such chemicals that
reached the atmosphere had
declined.
(C) The amounts of such chemicals
released had increased but the
amounts that reached the atmosphere
had decreased.
(D) The rate of increase in amounts of such
chemicals reaching the atmosphere
had decreased.
(E) The rate at which such chemicals were
being reduced in the atmosphere had
slowed.

284. The author of the passage compares the smuggling of CFC's to the illicit drug trade most likely for which of the following reasons?

(A) To qualify a previous claim
(B) To emphasize the extent of a problem
(C) To provide an explanation for an earlier assertion
(D) To suggest that the illicit CFC trade, like the illicit drug trade, will continue to increase
(E) To suggest that the consequences of a relatively little-known problem are as serious as those of a well-known one

285. The passage suggests which of the following about the illicit trade in CFC's ?

(A) It would cease if manufacturers in India and China stopped producing CFC's.
(B) Most people who participate in such trade do not believe that CFC's deplete the ozone layer.
(C) It will probably surpass illicit drugs as the largest contraband problem faced by the United States Customs Service.
(D) It is fostered by people who do not want to pay the price of CFC substitutes.
(E) It has grown primarily because of the expansion of the refrigeration, heating, and air-conditioning industries in foreign countries.

Explanatory Material: Reading Comprehension

The following discussion of reading comprehension is intended to familiarize you with the most efficient and effective approaches to the kinds of problems common to reading comprehension. The particular questions in this chapter are generally representative of the kinds of reading comprehension questions you will encounter on the GMAT®. Remember that it is the problem-solving strategy that is important, not the specific details of a particular question.

Questions 1-6 refer to the passage on page 320.

1. The primary purpose of the passage is to

   (A) discuss a plan for investigation of a phenomenon that is not yet fully understood
   (B) present two explanations of a phenomenon and reconcile the differences between them
   (C) summarize two theories and suggest a third theory that overcomes the problems encountered in the first two
   (D) describe an alternative hypothesis and provide evidence and arguments that support it
   (E) challenge the validity of a theory by exposing the inconsistencies and contradictions in it

The best answer is D. This question requires you to identify the primary concern of the passage as a whole. The first paragraph presents a recent hypothesis about how caffeine affects behavior. The second paragraph describes an earlier and widely accepted hypothesis about how caffeine affects behavior, and then presents evidence that is not consistent with that hypothesis. The third and fourth paragraphs return to the newer hypothesis introduced in the first paragraph and provide "evidence and arguments" that support this alternative hypothesis.

2. According to Snyder et al, caffeine differs from adenosine in that caffeine

   (A) stimulates behavior in the mouse and in humans, whereas adenosine stimulates behavior in humans only
   (B) has mixed effects in the brain, whereas adenosine has only a stimulatory effect
   (C) increases cyclic AMP concentrations in target neurons, whereas adenosine decreases such concentrations
   (D) permits release of neurotransmitters when it is bound to adenosine receptors, whereas adenosine inhibits such release
   (E) inhibits both neuron firing and the production of phosphodiesterase when there is a sufficient concentration in the brain, whereas adenosine inhibits only neuron firing

The best answer is D. Lines 6-12 state that adenosine "depresses neuron firing" by binding to specific receptors on neuronal membranes, which in turn inhibits the release of neurotransmitters. Lines 14-18 describe Snyder et al's hypothesis about caffeine. They propose that caffeine binds to specific receptors on neuronal membranes, which prevents adenosine from binding to those receptors and "allows the neurons to fire more readily than they otherwise would." Therefore, according to Snyder et al, caffeine differs from adenosine in that caffeine permits neurotransmitter release when it is bound to adenosine receptors, whereas adenosine inhibits neurotransmitter release.

3. In response to experimental results concerning IBMX, Snyder et al contended that it is not uncommon for psychoactive drugs to have

   (A) mixed effects in the brain
   (B) inhibitory effects on enzymes in the brain
   (C) close structural relationships with caffeine
   (D) depressive effects on mouse locomotion
   (E) the ability to dislodge caffeine from receptors in the brain

The best answer is A. The effects of IBMX are discussed in the last paragraph of the passage. IBMX apparently binds to adenosine-specific receptors on neuronal membranes, but, in contrast to the other caffeine derivatives that Snyder et al experimented with, IBMX depresses rather than stimulates mouse locomotion. Snyder et al respond to this experimental result by stating that IBMX has "mixed effects in the brain, a not unusual occurrence with psychoactive drugs" (lines 53-54).

4. According to Snyder et al, all of the following compounds can bind to specific receptors in the brain EXCEPT

(A) IBMX
(B) caffeine
(C) adenosine
(D) theophylline
(E) phosphodiesterase

The best answer is E. This question asks you to identify which compound, according to Snyder et al, does NOT bind to specific receptors in the brain. The last paragraph describes IBMX (A) as a compound that binds to specific receptors in the brain. Lines 14-18 describe Snyder et al's proposal that caffeine (B) can bind to specific receptors in the brain. Lines 6-12 state that adenosine (C) inhibits neuron firing by binding to specific receptors in the brain. Lines 43-45 mention theophylline (D) as an example of a caffeine derivative that binds to specific receptors in the brain. Phosphodiesterase (E), identified as an "enzyme that breaks down the chemical called cyclic AMP" (lines 21-22), is the only compound that is not identified as one that binds to specific receptors in the brain.

5. Snyder et al suggest that caffeine's ability to bind to A_1 and A_2 receptors can be at least partially attributed to which of the following?

(A) The chemical relationship between caffeine and phosphodiesterase
(B) The structural relationship between caffeine and adenosine
(C) The structural similarity between caffeine and neurotransmitters
(D) The ability of caffeine to stimulate behavior
(E) The natural occurrence of caffeine and adenosine in the brain

The best answer is B. This question asks you to identify information that is suggested rather than directly stated in the passage. To answer it, first look for the location in the passage of the information specified in the question. The A_1 and A_2 receptors are mentioned in lines 12-14. Lines 14-18 go on to describe Snyder et al's hypothesis about the effects of caffeine on behavior. They propose that caffeine, "which is structurally similar to adenosine," is able to bind to A_1 and A_2 receptors in the brain, the same receptors that adenosine normally binds to. Thus, the passage suggests that the structural relationship between caffeine and adenosine may be partially responsible for caffeine's ability to bind to A_1 and A_2 receptors.

6. The author quotes Snyder et al in lines 38-43 most probably in order to

(A) reveal some of the assumptions underlying their theory
(B) summarize a major finding of their experiments
(C) point out that their experiments were limited to the mouse
(D) indicate that their experiments resulted only in general correlations
(E) refute the objections made by supporters of the older theory

The best answer is B. This question asks you to identify the function of a quotation in the third paragraph of the passage. The third paragraph provides evidence for Snyder et al's hypothesis by discussing experiments they conducted on mice. The quotation in lines 38-43 "summarizes" the findings of these experiments. Snyder et al found that a number of caffeine derivatives are able to bind to specific receptors in the brains of mice just as adenosine does, and that the derivatives that are most successful at stimulating locomotion are also the most successful in competing with adenosine in binding at the receptors. This finding is "major" in that it supports their hypothesis that the stimulative effects of caffeine are a result of its ability to compete with adenosine.

Questions 7-12 refer to the passage on page 322.

7. The primary purpose of the passage is to propose

(A) an alternative to museum display of artifacts
(B) a way to curb illegal digging while benefiting the archaeological profession
(C) a way to distinguish artifacts with scientific value from those that have no such value
(D) the governmental regulation of archaeological sites
(E) a new system for cataloguing duplicate artifacts

The best answer is B. The first paragraph identifies two major problems faced by the archaeological profession: inadequate funding and illegal digging. Lines 9-11 indicate that the author is going to suggest how to remedy both problems, thereby benefiting the archaeological profession. The author proceeds to propose allowing the sale of excavated artifacts (lines 11-14) and to explain how this would solve both problems (lines 14-19). The author then supports the proposal by countering possible objections to it, and in the last paragraph explains how the proposal would curb illegal digging (lines 51-55). Thus, the way information is organized in the passage indicates that the author's purpose is to suggest that allowing the sale of excavated artifacts would provide funds for the archaeological profession and curb illegal digging.

8. The author implies that all of the following statements about duplicate artifacts are true EXCEPT

(A) A market for such artifacts already exists.
(B) Such artifacts seldom have scientific value.
(C) There is likely to be a continuing supply of such artifacts.
(D) Museums are well supplied with examples of such artifacts.
(E) Such artifacts frequently exceed in quality those already catalogued in museum collections.

The best answer is E. The question requires you to identify the answer choice that CANNOT be inferred from the passage. Choice A asserts that potential purchasers for duplicate artifacts exist; this is implied in lines 51-55, which suggest that purchasers would prefer legally acquired duplicate artifacts, thereby reducing demand for clandestine products. Choice B is implied in lines 25-31, which deny the practical scientific value of duplicate artifacts. Choice C is implied in lines 37-39, which express doubt about storing all the artifacts that "are likely to be discovered in the future." Choice D is implied by the reference to "pieces stored in bulging museum basements" (line 44). Nothing in the passage implies that duplicate artifacts exceed museum objects in quality (choice E).

9. Which of the following is mentioned in the passage as a disadvantage of storing artifacts in museum basements?

(A) Museum officials rarely allow scholars access to such artifacts.
(B) Space that could be better used for display is taken up for storage.
(C) Artifacts discovered in one excavation often become separated from each other.
(D) Such artifacts are often damaged by variations in temperature and humidity.
(E) Such artifacts often remain uncatalogued and thus cannot be located once they are put in storage.

The best answer is E. The disadvantages of storing artifacts in museum basements are discussed in the fifth paragraph. Lines 39-42 state that "There is not enough money . . . to catalogue the finds" and declare that as a result stored objects cannot be located. The fact that such objects become "inaccessible" (line 41) is clearly connected to the problems in cataloguing, not to museum policy toward scholars, as choice A states. No mention is made of the situations discussed in choices B, C, and D.

10. The author mentions the excavation in Cyprus (lines 31-34) to emphasize which of the following points?

(A) Ancient lamps and pottery vessels are less valuable, although more rare, than royal seal impressions.
(B) Artifacts that are very similar to each other present cataloguing difficulties to archaeologists.
(C) Artifacts that are not uniquely valuable, and therefore could be sold, are available in large quantities.
(D) Cyprus is the most important location for unearthing large quantities of salable artifacts.
(E) Illegal sales of duplicate artifacts are widespread, particularly on the island of Cyprus.

The best answer is C. In lines 27-29, the author refutes the assertion that every object excavated has potential scientific value and therefore should not be sold. In lines 30-31, the author defines those objects that do not have scientific value: "the thousands of pottery vessels . . . that are essentially duplicates of one another." The Cyprus excavation appears in the next sentence as an example of one location in which such duplicate artifacts have been found in large quantities. The reference to "2,000 virtually indistinguishable small jugs" highlights the profusion and uniformity of the Cyprus finds. Thus, the excavation is mentioned in order to emphasize the ready availability of objects that lack unique value and therefore could be sold.

11. The author's argument concerning the effect of the official sale of duplicate artifacts on illegal excavation is based on which of the following assumptions?

(A) Prospective purchasers would prefer to buy authenticated artifacts.
(B) The price of illegally excavated artifacts would rise.
(C) Computers could be used to trace sold artifacts.
(D) Illegal excavators would be forced to sell only duplicate artifacts.
(E) Money gained from selling authenticated artifacts could be used to investigate and prosecute illegal excavators.

The best answer is A. The author's argument concerning the effect of the official sale of duplicate artifacts on illegal excavation appears in lines 51-52, in which the author predicts that such official sale would reduce demand for "the clandestine product." The rhetorical question that follows (lines 52-55) indicates that the author finds it unlikely that any purchaser would prefer objects of unknown provenance to objects of known origin, or, to rephrase, the author assumes that most people would prefer to purchase objects of authenticated provenance, as choice A states. The author's argument concerning the effect of such sales on illegal excavation does not assume any of the other answer choices.

12. The author anticipates which of the following initial objections to the adoption of his proposal?

(A) Museum officials will become unwilling to store artifacts.
(B) An oversupply of salable artifacts will result and the demand for them will fall.
(C) Artifacts that would have been displayed in public places will be sold to private collectors.
(D) Illegal excavators will have an even larger supply of artifacts for resale.
(E) Counterfeiting of artifacts will become more commonplace.

The best answer is C. The author begins the third paragraph by saying "You might object . . ." in order to anticipate possible objections to the adoption of his proposal. In the next sentence the author asserts that "ancient artifacts . . . should be available for all to appreciate, not sold to the highest bidder" (lines 21-24), acknowledging an opponent's fear that individuals might be allowed to purchase objects that ought to be displayed in public institutions. This objection is paraphrased in choice C. Choice A alludes to a situation that shows the benefits, not the drawbacks, of the author's proposal; B, D, and E describe situations that are not discussed in the passage.

Questions 13-18 refer to the passage on page 324.

13. Which of the following best states the central idea of the passage?

(A) The use of MESBIC's for aiding minority entrepreneurs seems to have greater potential for success than does the original SBA approach.
(B) There is a crucial difference in point of view between the staff and directors of some MESBIC's.
(C) After initial problems with management and marketing, minority businesses have begun to expand at a steady rate.
(D) Minority entrepreneurs wishing to form new businesses now have several equally successful federal programs on which to rely.
(E) For the first time since 1960, large corporations are making significant contributions to the development of minority businesses.

The best answer is A. The passage begins by indicating that the results of the SBA approach to aiding minority entrepreneurs "were disappointing" (line 7). Lines 42-44 state that "MESBIC's are now emerging as increasingly important financing sources for minority enterprises." Much of the passage is devoted to supporting the author's view that MESBIC's have the greater potential for success, and the last sentence in the passage confirms this view. Choice B accurately restates a point made by the author, that differences exist between staff and directors of MESBIC's, but the point is not central to the author's discussion. The statements in C, D, and E are not supported by information in the passage.

14. According to the passage, the MESBIC approach differs from the SBA approach in that MESBIC's

(A) seek federal contracts to provide markets for minority businesses
(B) encourage minority businesses to provide markets for other minority businesses
(C) attempt to maintain a specified rate of growth in the minority business sector
(D) rely on the participation of large corporations to finance minority businesses
(E) select minority businesses on the basis of their location

The best answer is D. In the second paragraph, the author describes the MESBIC approach as one in which "large corporations participate in the development of successful and stable minority businesses by making use of government-sponsored venture capital" (lines 18-21). There is no indication in the passage that the SBA approach relies on the participation of large corporations. Although any of the other answer choices might actually be true of MESBIC's, there is no information in the passage that confirms that these statements are correct.

15. Which of the following does the author cite to support the conclusion that the results of the SBA program were disappointing?

(A) The small number of new minority enterprises formed as a result of the program
(B) The small number of minority enterprises that took advantage of the management and technical assistance offered under the program
(C) The small percentage of the nation's business receipts earned by minority enterprises following the program's implementation
(D) The small percentage of recipient minority enterprises that were able to repay federally guaranteed loans made under the program
(E) The small number of minority enterprises that chose to participate in the program

The best answer is C. The author concludes that the results of the SBA approach "were disappointing" (line 7) and then supports the conclusion by citing the fact that "Even 15 years after the program was implemented, minority business receipts were not quite two percent of the national economy's total receipts" (lines 9-12). The statements in A, B, D, and E are not supported by the information in the passage.

16. Which of the following statements about the SBA program can be inferred from the passage?

(A) The maximum term for loans made to recipient businesses was 15 years.
(B) Business loans were considered to be more useful to recipient businesses than was management and technical assistance.
(C) The anticipated failure rate for recipient businesses was significantly lower than the rate that actually resulted.
(D) Recipient businesses were encouraged to relocate to areas more favorable for business development.
(E) The capitalization needs of recipient businesses were assessed and then provided for adequately.

The best answer is C. This question asks you to draw an inference about the SBA program. Although the passage does not actually state that the failure rate for SBA recipient businesses was higher than anticipated, in the first paragraph the author does state that the results of the SBA program were disappointing, in part because of the high failure rate among SBA-sponsored businesses. From this it can be inferred that the anticipated failure rate was lower than the actual rate. There is no information in the passage to suggest that A, B, D, and E could be true.

17. The author refers to the "financial and operating problems" (line 38) encountered by MESBIC's primarily in order to

(A) broaden the scope of the discussion to include the legal considerations of funding MESBIC's through sponsoring companies
(B) call attention to the fact that MESBIC's must receive adequate funding in order to function effectively
(C) show that sponsoring companies were willing to invest only $500,000 of government-sponsored venture capital in the original MESBIC's
(D) compare SBA and MESBIC limits on minimum funding
(E) refute suggestions that MESBIC's have been only marginally successful

The best answer is B. The reference in line 38 to "financial and operating problems" appears in the context of a discussion of why corporations came to capitalize MESBIC's "far above the legal minimum of $500,000." The problems are cited to illustrate the reasons that MESBIC's need more than the minimum funding required by law, and thus call attention to this need. The reference is not primarily concerned with legal considerations as suggested in A, or with a comparison with SBA funding limits as suggested in D. The $500,000 mentioned in the passage is the *minimum* level of funding required, not a maximum as suggested in C. There is no suggestion in the passage that MESBIC's have been only marginally successful; thus, choice E is not correct.

18. The author's primary objective in the passage is to

(A) disprove the view that federal efforts to aid minority businesses have been ineffective
(B) explain how federal efforts to aid minority businesses have changed since the 1960's
(C) establish a direct link between the federal efforts to aid minority businesses made before the 1960's and those made in the 1980's
(D) analyze the basis for the belief that job-specific experience is more useful to minority businesses than is general management experience
(E) argue that the "social responsibility approach" to aiding minority businesses is superior to any other approach

The best answer is B. The passage describes efforts undertaken in the 1960's to aid minority businesses and then describes MESBIC's, a newer approach to such efforts. Choice A is not correct because, although the author does suggest that MESBIC's have been effective in aiding minority businesses, there is no indication in the passage that the author's purpose is to disprove the view that federal efforts have been ineffective. Because the passage does not discuss efforts undertaken during the 1980's to aid minority businesses, C cannot be correct. The passage neither attempts to analyze the basis for the belief mentioned in D nor argues that the "social responsibility approach" is the most effective. Therefore, neither D nor E can be correct.

Questions 19-24 refer to the passage on page 326.

19. According to the passage, senior managers use intuition in all of the following ways EXCEPT to

(A) speed up the creation of a solution to a problem
(B) identify a problem
(C) bring together disparate facts
(D) stipulate clear goals
(E) evaluate possible solutions to a problem

The best answer is D. The question requires you to recognize which of the choices is NOT mentioned in the passage as a way in which senior managers use intuition. Choice A, speeding up the creation of a solution, is mentioned in lines 36-37, which describe intuition as enabling managers to "move rapidly to engender a plausible solution." B appears in lines 21-22: "they intuitively sense when a problem exists." C is a restatement of the sentence in lines 26-28. E may be gathered from lines 29-30, which state that intuition is used "as a check on the results of more rational analysis"; those results are identified in the next sentence as "solutions." The passage does not mention stipulating goals (choice D).

20. The passage suggests which of the following about the "writers on management" mentioned in line 12 ?

(A) They have criticized managers for not following the classical rational model of decision analysis.
(B) They have not based their analyses on a sufficiently large sample of actual managers.
(C) They have relied in drawing their conclusions on what managers say rather than on what managers do.
(D) They have misunderstood how managers use intuition in making business decisions.
(E) They have not acknowledged the role of intuition in managerial practice.

The best answer is D. The author asserts that the writers in question "display a poor grasp of what intuition is" (lines 14-15). The next paragraph presents a view that, according to the author of the passage, characterizes intuition more accurately than the writers on management do. Isenberg's research is specifically described as showing the ways in which managers use intuition (lines 20-21). Therefore, what Isenberg correctly comprehends, and the writers in question misunderstand, is how managers use intuition, as D states.

21. Which of the following best exemplifies "an 'Aha!' experience" (line 28) as it is presented in the passage?

(A) A manager risks taking an action whose outcome is unpredictable to discover whether the action changes the problem at hand.
(B) A manager performs well-learned and familiar behavior patterns in creative and uncharacteristic ways to solve a problem.
(C) A manager suddenly connects seemingly unrelated facts and experiences to create a pattern relevant to the problem at hand.
(D) A manager rapidly identifies the methodology used to compile data yielded by systematic analysis.
(E) A manager swiftly decides which of several sets of tactics to implement in order to deal with the contingencies suggested by a problem.

The best answer is C. An "Aha! experience" is said in lines 26-28 to result from the synthesizing of "isolated bits of data and practice into an integrated picture." C is the best example of this kind of process. The connecting of seemingly unrelated facts and experiences mentioned in the answer choice is equivalent to synthesizing "isolated bits of data and practice," and the pattern referred to is comparable to an "integrated picture."

22. According to the passage, the classical model of decision analysis includes all of the following EXCEPT

(A) evaluation of a problem
(B) creation of possible solutions to a problem
(C) establishment of clear goals to be reached by the decision
(D) action undertaken in order to discover more information about a problem
(E) comparison of the probable effects of different solutions to a problem

The best answer is D. The question requires you to recognize which of the choices is NOT mentioned in the passage as a component of the classical model of decision analysis. Four of the answer choices are mentioned in the first sentence of the passage, which describes the classical model of analysis: "clarifying goals" (C), "assessing the problem" (A), "formulating options" (B), and "estimating likelihoods of success" (E). Only D, "action undertaken in order to discover more information about a problem," does not appear in the passage.

23. It can be inferred from the passage that which of the following would most probably be one major difference in behavior between Manager X, who uses intuition to reach decisions, and Manager Y, who uses only formal decision analysis?

(A) Manager X analyzes first and then acts; Manager Y does not.
(B) Manager X checks possible solutions to a problem by systematic analysis; Manager Y does not.
(C) Manager X takes action in order to arrive at the solution to a problem; Manager Y does not.
(D) Manager Y draws on years of hands-on experience in creating a solution to a problem; Manager X does not.
(E) Manager Y depends on day-to-day tactical maneuvering; Manager X does not.

The best answer is C. The question requires you to compare behavior based on intuition with behavior based on formal decision analysis. Choice C specifies that the manager who uses intuition incorporates action into the decision-making process, but the manager who uses formal analysis does not. This distinction is made in several places in the passage. Lines 4-5 emphasize that decision-making and action-taking are separate steps in formal decision analysis: "making a decision, and only then taking action." On the other hand, those who use intuition "integrate action into the process of thinking" (lines 10-11). Again, the author mentions that in the intuitive style of management, " 'thinking' is inseparable from acting" (lines 41-42), and "action is often part of defining the problem" (lines 54-55).

24. The passage provides support for which of the following statements?

   (A) Managers who rely on intuition are more successful than those who rely on formal decision analysis.
   (B) Managers cannot justify their intuitive decisions.
   (C) Managers' intuition works contrary to their rational and analytical skills.
   (D) Logical analysis of a problem increases the number of possible solutions.
   (E) Intuition enables managers to employ their practical experience more efficiently.

The best answer is E. The question requires you to identify a statement that can be inferred from information in the passage but is not explicitly stated. The author asserts that intuitive managers can "move rapidly to engender a plausible solution" (lines 36-37) and that their intuition is based on "experience that builds skills" (lines 25-26). This implies that the combination of skill and rapidity enables managers to employ their practical experience more efficiently, as E states. Choice A cannot be inferred from the passage, which states only that a majority of successful managers are intuitive (lines 1-11), not that their degree of success is greater. B and C are directly contradicted by the passage, and the passage provides no support for D.

Questions 25-30 refer to the passage on page 328.

25. It can be inferred from the passage that the morphogenetic determinants present in the early embryo are

   (A) located in the nucleus of the embryo cells
   (B) evenly distributed unless the embryo is not developing normally
   (C) inactive until the embryo cells become irreversibly committed to their final function
   (D) identical to those that were already present in the unfertilized egg
   (E) present in larger quantities than is necessary for the development of a single individual

The best answer is E. The second and third paragraphs of the passage indicate that morphogenetic determinants are substances in the embryo that are activated after the egg has been fertilized and that "tell a cell what to become" (lines 15-16). If, as the author asserts in the first paragraph, biologists have succeeded in dividing an embryo into two parts, each of which survives and develops into a normal embryo, it can be concluded that the quantity of morphogenetic determinants in the early embryo is greater than that required for the development of a single individual. Choices A, B, and C are directly contradicted by information in the passage, and D makes an assertion that cannot be inferred from the passage.

26. The main topic of the passage is

   (A) the early development of embryos of lower marine organisms
   (B) the main contribution of modern embryology to molecular biology
   (C) the role of molecular biology in disproving older theories of embryonic development
   (D) cell determination as an issue in the study of embryonic development
   (E) scientific dogma as a factor in the recent debate over the value of molecular biology

The best answer is D. In identifying the main topic of the passage, you must consider the passage as a whole. In the first paragraph, the author provides a historical context for the debate described in the second paragraph, concerning when and how the determination of embryo cells takes place. The third and fourth paragraphs provide a specific example of the "Recent discoveries in molecular biology" (line 19) that may lead to the resolution of that debate. C is incorrect because although the passage does indicate that biologists revised their initial belief that early embryo cells are undetermined, this revision is seen as having taken place prior to the "Recent discoveries in molecular biology." Choices A, B, and E do not accurately reflect the content of the passage.

27. According to the passage, when biologists believed that the cells in the early embryo were undetermined, they made which of the following mistakes?

   (A) They did not attempt to replicate the original experiment of separating an embryo into two parts.
   (B) They did not realize that there was a connection between the issue of cell determination and the outcome of the separation experiment.
   (C) They assumed that the results of experiments on embryos did not depend on the particular animal species used for such experiments.
   (D) They assumed that it was crucial to perform the separation experiment at an early stage in the embryo's life.
   (E) They assumed that different ways of separating an embryo into two parts would be equivalent as far as the fate of the two parts was concerned.

The best answer is E. According to the author, early investigators arrived at the conclusion that the cells of the embryo are undetermined because they "found that if they separated an invertebrate animal embryo into two parts at an early stage of its life, it would survive and develop as two normal embryos" (lines 1-4). However, later biologists discovered that when an embryo was cut in planes different from the one used by the early investigators, it did not form two whole embryos. Because the earlier biologists apparently arrived at their conclusion without attempting to cut an embryo in different planes, it would appear that they assumed, erroneously, that different ways of separating the embryos would not affect the fate of the two embryo parts.

28. It can be inferred from the passage that the initial production of histones after an egg is fertilized takes place

(A) in the cytoplasm
(B) in the maternal genes
(C) throughout the protoplasm
(D) in the beaded portions of the DNA strings
(E) in certain sections of the cell nucleus

The best answer is A. In the third paragraph, the author asserts that substances that function as morphogenetic determinants are located in the cytoplasm of the cell and become active after the cell is fertilized. In the fourth paragraph we learn that these substances are "maternal messenger RNA's" and that they "direct, in large part, the synthesis of histones," which, after being synthesized, "move into the cell nucleus" (lines 39-45). Thus, it can be inferred that after the egg is fertilized, the initial production of histones occurs in the cytoplasm.

29. It can be inferred from the passage that which of the following is dependent on the fertilization of an egg?

(A) Copying of maternal genes to produce maternal messenger RNA's
(B) Synthesis of proteins called histones
(C) Division of a cell into its nucleus and the cytoplasm
(D) Determination of the egg cell's potential for division
(E) Generation of all of a cell's morphogenetic determinants

The best answer is B. Lines 30-34 indicate that substances that function as morphogenetic determinants are inactive in the unfertilized egg and that when the egg is fertilized, they "become active and, presumably, govern the behavior of the genes they interact with." In the fourth paragraph, we learn that these substances exert their control over the fate of the cell by directing "the synthesis of histones." Because these histones cannot be synthesized until the substances that function as morphogenetic determinants become active, and because these substances do not become active until the egg is fertilized, it can be inferred that the synthesis of the histones is dependent on the fertilization of the egg.

30. According to the passage, the morphogenetic determinants present in the unfertilized egg cell are which of the following?

(A) Proteins bound to the nucleus
(B) Histones
(C) Maternal messenger RNA's
(D) Cytoplasm
(E) Nonbeaded intervening DNA

The best answer is C. Lines 26-28 inform us that in his study of sea urchins, Gross "found that an unfertilized egg contains substances that function as morphogenetic determinants." Lines 39-40 assert that the "substances that Gross studied are maternal messenger RNA's," and in lines 41-42 we learn that these maternal messenger RNA's can be found in "a wide variety of organisms." B is incorrect. Although after becoming active these messenger RNA's are said to direct the synthesis of histones, the synthesis of the histones is said to occur after, not before, the egg has been fertilized.

Questions 31-36 refer to the passage on page 330.

31. The author indicates explicitly that which of the following records has been a source of information in her investigation?

(A) United States Immigration Service reports from 1914 to 1930
(B) Payrolls of southern manufacturing firms between 1910 and 1930
(C) The volume of cotton exports between 1898 and 1910
(D) The federal census of 1910
(E) Advertisements of labor recruiters appearing in southern newspapers after 1910

The best answer is D. In lines 24-28, the author states that ten percent of the Black workers in the South were employed in "manufacturing and mechanical pursuits" and then identifies "manufacturing and mechanical pursuits" as the general federal census category for industrial occupations in 1910. Thus, she indicates that she used the federal census as a source of information. Although the author discusses information that may have been included in the records mentioned in A, B, C, and E, she does not "explicitly" identify any of those records as sources used in her investigation.

32. In the passage, the author anticipates which of the following as a possible objection to her argument?

(A) It is uncertain how many people actually migrated during the Great Migration.
(B) The eventual economic status of the Great Migration migrants has not been adequately traced.
(C) It is not likely that people with steady jobs would have reason to move to another area of the country.
(D) It is not true that the term "manufacturing and mechanical pursuits" actually encompasses the entire industrial sector.
(E) Of the Black workers living in southern cities, only those in a small number of trades were threatened by obsolescence.

The best answer is C. To answer this question, you must first identify the author's argument. The author argues that it is possible that Black migrants to the North were living and working in urban areas of the South rather than in rural areas, as researchers had previously assumed. In lines 30-33, the author states that it may be "surprising" that an employed population would relocate. Thus, the author anticipates an objection to her argument on the grounds that Black urban workers in the South would have been unlikely to leave an economically secure existence. She meets that objection by stating that "an explanation lies in the labor conditions then prevalent in the South" (lines 32-33), and discusses the low wages that may have motivated Black workers to migrate north for higher pay.

33. According to the passage, which of the following is true of wages in southern cities in 1910?

(A) They were being pushed lower as a result of increased competition.
(B) They had begun to rise so that southern industry could attract rural workers.
(C) They had increased for skilled workers but decreased for unskilled workers.
(D) They had increased in large southern cities but decreased in small southern cities.
(E) They had increased in newly developed industries but decreased in the older trades.

The best answer is A. The author discusses wages in southern cities in the third paragraph. Lines 47-50 state that an increase in the number of rural workers who migrated to southern cities after the collapse of the cotton industry led to increased competition for jobs and resulted in wages being pushed lower. There is no indication in the passage that B, C, D, or E was true.

34. The author cites each of the following as possible influences in a Black worker's decision to migrate north in the Great Migration EXCEPT

(A) wage levels in northern cities
(B) labor recruiters
(C) competition from rural workers
(D) voting rights in northern states
(E) the Black press

The best answer is D. This question asks you to identify the possible influences that motivated Black workers in their decision to migrate north, and then to recognize which of the choices is NOT mentioned as an influence on Black workers. Choices A, B, C, and E are all discussed in the third paragraph. Lines 48-50 state that "competition from . . . rural workers" (C) resulted in even lower wages in the South. Lines 43-47 state that Black workers were aware through "labor recruiters" (B) and the "Black press" (E) that "wage levels in northern cities" (A) were higher than they were in the South. D—"voting rights in northern states"—is the only option not mentioned in the passage as an influence that may have motivated southern Black workers to move north.

35. It can be inferred from the passage that the "easy conclusion" mentioned in line 53 is based on which of the following assumptions?

(A) People who migrate from rural areas to large cities usually do so for economic reasons.
(B) Most people who leave rural areas to take jobs in cities return to rural areas as soon as it is financially possible for them to do so.
(C) People with rural backgrounds are less likely to succeed economically in cities than are those with urban backgrounds.
(D) Most people who were once skilled workers are not willing to work as unskilled workers.
(E) People who migrate from their birthplaces to other regions of a country seldom undertake a second migration.

The best answer is C. To answer this question, you must first identify the "easy conclusion" mentioned in line 53, which ties Black migrants' "subsequent economic problems in the North to their rural background." This linkage of rural background to economic difficulty after migration to the North is first mentioned in lines 14-18. Here, the author points out that researchers have assumed that Black migrants encountered economic difficulties in northern cities because they were from rural rather than urban backgrounds, and that rural backgrounds imply "unfamiliarity with urban living and a lack of industrial skills." Choice C provides an assumption about the relationship between rural backgrounds and economic difficulty that underlies this conclusion. It states that people with rural backgrounds are more likely to have economic difficulty in urban areas than are people with urban backgrounds. A, B, D, and E can be eliminated because they do not deal with the connection between economic difficulties and rural backgrounds.

36. The primary purpose of the passage is to

   (A) support an alternative to an accepted methodology
   (B) present evidence that resolves a contradiction
   (C) introduce a recently discovered source of information
   (D) challenge a widely accepted explanation
   (E) argue that a discarded theory deserves new attention

The best answer is D. The first paragraph describes a common assumption about the Great Migration, that the majority of migrants came from rural areas. It also restates the conclusion that is based on this assumption, that the subsequent economic difficulties of Black migrants in the North were a result of their unfamiliarity with urban life. In the second paragraph, the author states that the "question of who actually left the South" (line 19) has never been adequately researched. She goes on to argue that Black migrants may actually have been from urban areas rather than rural areas, and thus that their subsequent economic problems in northern cities were not caused by their rural background. In making this argument, the author is challenging the "widely accepted explanation" presented in the first paragraph.

Questions 37-42 refer to the passage on page 332.

37. It can be inferred from the passage that accidental-death damage awards in America during the nineteenth century tended to be based principally on the

   (A) earnings of the person at time of death
   (B) wealth of the party causing the death
   (C) degree of culpability of the party causing the death
   (D) amount of money that had been spent on the person killed
   (E) amount of suffering endured by the family of the person killed

The best answer is A. In the first paragraph, the author cites an accidental-death case from nineteenth-century America in which the absence of economic contribution on the part of a deceased child was ruled sufficient grounds to deny the awarding of damages to the child's parents. The author goes on to discuss how this case typified attitudes that persisted even into the twentieth century. It can be inferred from this that in nineteenth-century America the chief consideration in determining damages in an accidental-death case was the deceased person's earnings. There is no evidence in the passage to suggest that the factors cited in B, C, D, and E were of primary concern in determining accidental-death damages in nineteenth-century America.

38. It can be inferred from the passage that in the early 1800's children were generally regarded by their families as individuals who

   (A) needed enormous amounts of security and affection
   (B) required constant supervision while working
   (C) were important to the economic well-being of a family
   (D) were unsuited to spending long hours in school
   (E) were financial burdens assumed for the good of society

The best answer is C. In the second paragraph, the author describes how during the nineteenth century the concept of the "'useful' child who contributed to the family economy" (lines 12-13) gradually gave way to the present-day notion of the economically "useless" but emotionally "priceless" child; this new view of childhood was "Well established among segments of the middle and upper classes by the mid-1800's" and "spread throughout society in the late-nineteenth and early-twentieth centuries" (lines 16-20). Thus in the early 1800's, prior to the shift in the valuation of children, families valued the role children had to play in the family's economic well-being. Choices A and E describe attitudes more in accord with the present-day view of childhood, and B and D address issues that are not raised in the passage.

39. Which of the following alternative explanations of the change in the cash value of children would be most likely to be put forward by sociological economists as they are described in the passage?

   (A) The cash value of children rose during the nineteenth century because parents began to increase their emotional investment in the upbringing of their children.
   (B) The cash value of children rose during the nineteenth century because their expected earnings over the course of a lifetime increased greatly.
   (C) The cash value of children rose during the nineteenth century because the spread of humanitarian ideals resulted in a wholesale reappraisal of the worth of an individual.
   (D) The cash value of children rose during the nineteenth century because compulsory education laws reduced the supply, and thus raised the costs, of available child labor.
   (E) The cash value of children rose during the nineteenth century because of changes in the way negligence law assessed damages in accidental-death cases.

The best answer is B. According to the author, practitioners of the new "sociological economics" explain sociological phenomena "solely in terms of their economic determinants" and "tend to view all human behavior as directed primarily by the principle of maximizing economic gain" (lines 46-50).

Choice B provides just such an economic explanation for the nineteenth-century rise in the cash value of children. Choice A paraphrases Zelizer's own explanation, which is at odds with that of the sociological economists, and C uses social values and emotional factors to explain an even broader revaluation of individual worth. D uses an economic argument to explain the change, but here the economic factors at work are the result of a change in social values. E provides a legal explanation for the change.

40. **The primary purpose of the passage is to**

   (A) review the literature in a new academic subfield
   (B) present the central thesis of a recent book
   (C) contrast two approaches to analyzing historical change
   (D) refute a traditional explanation of a social phenomenon
   (E) encourage further work on a neglected historical topic

The best answer is B. In the first paragraph, the author contrasts two incidents that are said to exemplify the transformation in social values that forms the subject of Zelizer's book. The second and third paragraphs consist of a brief history of that transformation, as Zelizer presents it, and an account of the factors she considers important in bringing it about. In the last paragraph, the author explains how Zelizer's thesis differs from that of sociological economists. Thus, the passage serves primarily to present the central thesis of Zelizer's book. Choice C is incorrect because although the passage does contrast two approaches, this contrast takes place only in the final paragraph. The other answer choices misrepresent either the author's approach or the subject matter of the passage.

41. **It can be inferred from the passage that which of the following statements was true of American families over the course of the nineteenth century?**

   (A) The average size of families grew considerably.
   (B) The percentage of families involved in industrial work declined dramatically.
   (C) Family members became more emotionally bonded to one another.
   (D) Family members spent an increasing amount of time working with each other.
   (E) Family members became more economically dependent on each other.

The best answer is C. In the third paragraph, the author cites Zelizer's contention that the new view of childhood that developed in nineteenth-century America was due in part to "the development of the companionate family (a family in which members were united by explicit bonds of love rather than duty)" (lines 28-30). From this it can be inferred that the emotional bonds between family members became increasingly important during this period. There is no information in the passage to support the other answer choices.

42. **Zelizer refers to all of the following as important influences in changing the assessment of children's worth EXCEPT changes in**

   (A) the mortality rate
   (B) the nature of industry
   (C) the nature of the family
   (D) attitudes toward reform movements
   (E) attitudes toward the marketplace

The best answer is D. Choices A, B, and C are mentioned in lines 25-31 as factors Zelizer regards as "critical in changing the assessment of children's worth"; E is mentioned in lines 36-41, which describe how the "sacralization" of children's lives represented "a way of resisting what they [middle-class Americans] perceived as the relentless corruption of human values by the marketplace." Although reform movements are mentioned in lines 20-23, the passage does not discuss attitudes or changes in attitudes toward those movements. D is therefore *not* among the influences Zelizer is said to regard as important in changing the assessment of children's worth.

Questions 43-48 refer to the passage on page 334.

43. **According to the passage, the public-sector workers who were most likely to belong to unions in 1977 were**

   (A) professionals
   (B) managers
   (C) clerical workers
   (D) service workers
   (E) blue-collar workers

The best answer is A. In the second paragraph, the author gives the percentages of workers who were unionized in different categories of the public sector in 1977. Forty-six percent of government professionals were unionized; this is greater than the percentage for any of the other categories of unionized workers from among the listed categories of public-sector workers. Therefore, professionals were more likely to belong to unions than were other public-sector workers.

44. The author cites union efforts to achieve a fully unionized work force (lines 13-19) in order to account for
why

(A) politicians might try to oppose public-sector union
organizing
(B) public-sector unions have recently focused on
organizing women
(C) early organizing efforts often focused on areas
where there were large numbers of workers
(D) union efforts with regard to public-sector clerical
workers increased dramatically after 1975
(E) unions sometimes tried to organize workers
regardless of the workers' initial interest in
organizing

The best answer is E. In lines 13-19, the author describes the
reasoning behind the multioccupational unions' attempt to
achieve a fully unionized workplace. This reasoning is provided to explain why "the multioccupational unions would
often try to organize them [clerical workers] regardless of the
workers' initial receptivity" (lines 11-13). Choice A helps to
explain, but is not explained by, the attempt to achieve a fully
unionized work force. An explanation for C is given in lines
3-6; B and D are explained in the second and third paragraphs
of the passage.

45. The author's claim that, since the mid-1970's, a new
strategy has emerged in the unionization of public-
sector clerical workers (lines 23-24) would be strengthened if the author

(A) described more fully the attitudes of clerical
workers toward labor unions
(B) compared the organizing strategies employed by
private-sector unions with those of public-sector
unions
(C) explained why politicians and administrators
sometimes oppose unionization of clerical
workers
(D) indicated that the number of unionized public-
sector clerical workers was increasing even
before the mid-1970's
(E) showed that the factors that favored unionization
drives among these workers prior to 1975 have
decreased in importance

The best answer is E. The question asks what would
strengthen the author's claim that a new strategy for unionization has emerged since the mid-1970's. Lines 23-24 cite
the appearance of the new strategy. The paragraphs that follow
describe the changed circumstances that provided a context
for such new strategies, and lines 52-56 explain precisely
how these changed circumstances created a reason for new
unionizing strategies. The author's claim would be strengthened if it could be shown not only that there are such new
circumstances, but that the old circumstances discussed in
the first paragraph have become less important, further nec-
essitating the adoption of a new strategy in place of an old
strategy suitable to those older circumstances.

46. According to the passage, in the period prior to 1975,
each of the following considerations helped determine
whether a union would attempt to organize a certain
group of clerical workers EXCEPT

(A) the number of clerical workers in that group
(B) the number of women among the clerical workers
in that group
(C) whether the clerical workers in that area were
concentrated in one workplace or scattered
over several workplaces
(D) the degree to which the clerical workers in that
group were interested in unionization
(E) whether all the other workers in the same
jurisdiction as that group of clerical workers
were unionized

The best answer is B. In the first paragraph, the author
describes the considerations relevant to a union's attempt to
organize a certain group of clerical workers prior to 1975.
Choices A, C, D, and E are all cited as important considerations. In line 2, the author notes the fact that most of these
clerical workers were women, but does not suggest that this
was an important consideration for unionizers.

47. The author states that which of the following is a
consequence of the women's movement of recent
years?

(A) An increase in the number of women entering the
work force
(B) A structural change in multioccupational public-
sector unions
(C) A more positive attitude on the part of women
toward unions
(D) An increase in the proportion of clerical workers
that are women
(E) An increase in the number of women in administrative positions

The best answer is C. According to the author, "the women's
movement has succeeded in legitimizing the economic and
political activism of women on their own behalf," and this in
turn has produced in women "a more positive attitude toward
unions" (lines 42-45). Although A, B, D, and E describe developments mentioned in the passage, none of these are said to
have been a consequence of the women's movement.

48. The main concern of the passage is to

(A) advocate particular strategies for future efforts to organize certain workers into labor unions
(B) explain differences in the unionized proportions of various groups of public-sector workers
(C) evaluate the effectiveness of certain kinds of labor unions that represent public-sector workers
(D) analyze and explain an increase in unionization among a certain category of workers
(E) describe and distinguish strategies appropriate to organizing different categories of workers

The best answer is D. In the first paragraph of the passage, the author asserts that efforts to unionize public-sector clerical workers prior to 1975 were limited and then goes on to describe these limited efforts. In the second paragraph, the author asserts that a new strategy developed after 1975 and cites an increase in union membership among public-sector clerical workers. The author begins the last paragraph by asking what can explain this increase in union membership, and then proceeds to provide an explanation. Thus, the passage is primarily concerned with analyzing and explaining the increase in unionization among public-sector clerical workers.

Questions 49-54 refer to the passage on page 336.

49. In the passage, the author is primarily interested in

(A) suggesting an alternative to an outdated research method
(B) introducing a new research method that calls an accepted theory into question
(C) emphasizing the instability of data gathered from the application of a new scientific method
(D) presenting a theory and describing a new method to test that theory
(E) initiating a debate about a widely accepted theory

The best answer is D. In the first paragraph, the author describes Milankovitch's theory and explains why the theory previously had been considered untestable. In the second and third paragraphs, the author describes a scientific breakthrough that has made it possible to test and provide support for Milankovitch's theory. Although the author also mentions other factors that potentially could have affected the Earth's climate, the passage as a whole is concerned primarily with Milankovitch's theory and the scientific method that has been used to test that theory. Choices A, C, and E do not accurately reflect the content of the passage, and, although the passage does describe a new research method as B suggests, this method supports rather than casts doubt on Milankovitch's theory.

50. The author of the passage would be most likely to agree with which of the following statements about the Milankovitch theory?

(A) It is the only possible explanation for the ice ages.
(B) It is too limited to provide a plausible explanation for the ice ages, despite recent research findings.
(C) It cannot be tested and confirmed until further research on volcanic activity is done.
(D) It is one plausible explanation, though not the only one, for the ice ages.
(E) It is not a plausible explanation for the ice ages, although it has opened up promising possibilities for future research.

The best answer is D. In lines 7-13, the author states that a recent discovery has made it possible to establish a precise chronology of the Earth's ice ages. Scientists have used this discovery to test the basic premise of Milankovitch's theory —that the ice ages were caused by variations in the Earth's orbit around the Sun. The author notes in lines 41-43 that the data have established a "strong connection" between orbital variation and ice ages, which confirms the plausibility of Milankovitch's theory. However, one can infer from the last paragraph that the author believes factors other than variations in the Earth's orbit could provide plausible explanations for global climate change.

51. It can be inferred from the passage that the isotope record taken from ocean sediments would be less useful to researchers if which of the following were true?

(A) It indicated that lighter isotopes of oxygen predominated at certain times.
(B) It had far more gaps in its sequence than the record taken from rocks on land.
(C) It indicated that climate shifts did not occur every 100,000 years.
(D) It indicated that the ratios of oxygen 16 and oxygen 18 in ocean water were not consistent with those found in fresh water.
(E) It stretched back for only a million years.

The best answer is B. The author states that one advantage of obtaining an isotopic record from ocean sediment is that the ocean's isotopic record is "a more continuous record than that taken from rocks on land" (lines 33-34). Because a continuous record can indicate more precisely when shifts in the Earth's climate have occurred, the ocean's isotopic record would be less useful if it had more gaps in it than the record taken from rocks. Choice A describes a circumstance that is in fact true, since oxygen 16 is the lighter isotope and, according to the passage, "Almost all the oxygen in water is oxygen 16" (line 13); but this fact clearly has not compromised the usefulness of the ocean's isotopic record as an indicator of climatic shifts. Likewise, E would not diminish its usefulness, since isotopic records showing "fluctuations in global ice volume over the past several hundred thousand years" have been sufficient to determine a meaningful pattern (lines 37-41). If C were shown to be true, Milankovitch's theory would be weakened, but this would not diminish the value of the isotopic record. If D were true, researchers would need to accommodate the inconsistency described in evaluating the isotopic record, but, again, this would not compromise the usefulness of the record itself.

52. According to the passage, which of the following is true of the ratios of oxygen isotopes in ocean sediments?

(A) They indicate that sediments found during an ice age contain more calcium carbonate than sediments formed at other times.
(B) They are less reliable than the evidence from rocks on land in determining the volume of land ice.
(C) They can be used to deduce the relative volume of land ice that was present when the sediment was laid down.
(D) They are more unpredictable during an ice age than in other climatic conditions.
(E) They can be used to determine atmospheric conditions at various times in the past.

The best answer is C. Lines 10-13 state that the relative volume of land ice can be deduced from the ratio of oxygen 18 to oxygen 16 in ocean sediments. Choices A, D, and E are incorrect because there is no information in the passage to support these statements. B is incorrect because it contradicts lines 33-34, in which the author states that ocean sediment provides "a more continuous record than that taken from rocks on land."

53. It can be inferred from the passage that precipitation formed from evaporated ocean water has

(A) the same isotopic ratio as ocean water
(B) less oxygen 18 than does ocean water
(C) less oxygen 18 than has the ice contained in continental ice sheets
(D) a different isotopic composition than has precipitation formed from water on land
(E) more oxygen 16 than has precipitation formed from fresh water

The best answer is B. Lines 18-21 state that when water evaporates from the ocean surface, oxygen 18, a heavier isotope than oxygen 16, tends to be left behind in the remaining ocean water. Thus, one can infer that evaporated ocean water would contain less oxygen 18 than would the remaining ocean water. Choice A is incorrect because it contradicts information stated in lines 15-21. C is incorrect because the passage suggests that the water evaporated from the ocean contributes to the growth of continental ice sheets, which should therefore have an isotopic composition similar to that of the precipitation formed from evaporated ocean water. Choices D and E describe information that cannot be inferred from the passage.

54. It can be inferred from the passage that calcium carbonate shells

(A) are not as susceptible to deterioration as rocks
(B) are less common in sediments formed during an ice age
(C) are found only in areas that were once covered by land ice
(D) contain radioactive material that can be used to determine a sediment's isotopic composition
(E) reflect the isotopic composition of the water at the time the shells were formed

The best answer is E. Lines 23-26 of the passage state that the calcium carbonate shells of marine organisms are constructed with "oxygen atoms drawn from the surrounding ocean." This water contains varying proportions of oxygen 16 and oxygen 18 and, according to the passage, "becomes progressively enriched in oxygen 18" with the onset of an ice age (lines 15-21). The author states that "The degree of enrichment can be determined by analyzing ocean sediments . . . composed of calcium carbonate shells of marine organisms" (lines 21-24). Thus, it can be inferred that the shells of marine organisms would reflect the isotopic composition of the surrounding ocean water at the time when the shells were formed.

55. The passage is chiefly concerned with

   (A) arguing against the increased internationalization of United States corporations
   (B) warning that the application of laws affecting trade frequently has unintended consequences
   (C) demonstrating that foreign-based firms receive more subsidies from their governments than United States firms receive from the United States government
   (D) advocating the use of trade restrictions for "dumped" products but not for other imports
   (E) recommending a uniform method for handling claims of unfair trade practices

The best answer is B. In the first sentence of the passage, the author characterizes the preoccupation of many United States companies with the search for legal protection from import competition as unfortunate. Then, in lines 12-14, the author explains that the "quest for import relief has hurt more companies than it has helped." The third paragraph discusses one situation in which United States companies might experience such injury—when import relief laws are used against foreign subsidiaries of United States companies—and the last paragraph provides a specific example of this situation. Thus, it can be inferred that the author's primary concern is to warn about possible unintended negative consequences of applying trade laws.

56. It can be inferred from the passage that the minimal basis for a complaint to the International Trade Commission is which of the following?

   (A) A foreign competitor has received a subsidy from a foreign government.
   (B) A foreign competitor has substantially increased the volume of products shipped to the United States.
   (C) A foreign competitor is selling products in the United States at less than fair market value.
   (D) The company requesting import relief has been injured by the sale of imports in the United States.
   (E) The company requesting import relief has been barred from exporting products to the country of its foreign competitor.

The best answer is D. Bases for complaints to the International Trade Commission are discussed in the first paragraph. In lines 3-9 the author mentions the two specific kinds of complaints referred to in choices A and C (about imports benefiting from subsidies provided by foreign governments and about "dumping"), but goes on to conclude the paragraph with the comment that "the simple claim that an industry has been injured by imports is sufficient grounds to seek relief." That a "simple claim" is "sufficient grounds to seek relief" suggests that the minimal basis for a complaint to the ITC is injury from the sale of imports in the United States, as stated in choice D. The situations in choices B and E are not discussed in the passage.

57. The last paragraph performs which of the following functions in the passage?

   (A) It summarizes the discussion thus far and suggests additional areas for research.
   (B) It presents a recommendation based on the evidence presented earlier.
   (C) It discusses an exceptional case in which the results expected by the author of the passage were not obtained.
   (D) It introduces an additional area of concern not mentioned earlier.
   (E) It cites a specific case that illustrates a problem presented more generally in the previous paragraph.

The best answer is E. The last paragraph discusses a specific case in which a United States subsidiary of a Dutch conglomerate accused a Canadian branch of a United States company of "dumping" rock salt in the United States market. This incident is cited as "the most brazen case" (line 32) of the problem stated in lines 20-22 of the previous paragraph: the use of import relief laws by foreign companies against U.S. companies. No recommendations, discussion of unexpected results, or additional areas of research or concern are mentioned in the paragraph. Thus, choices A, B, C, and D are not correct.

58. The passage warns of which of the following dangers?

   (A) Companies in the United States may receive no protection from imports unless they actively seek protection from import competition.
   (B) Companies that seek legal protection from import competition may incur legal costs that far exceed any possible gain.
   (C) Companies that are United States-owned but operate internationally may not be eligible for protection from import competition under the laws of the countries in which their plants operate.
   (D) Companies that are not United States-owned may seek legal protection from import competition under United States import relief laws.
   (E) Companies in the United States that import raw materials may have to pay duties on those materials.

The best answer is D. The "danger" of import relief laws is stated in lines 20-22: "that foreign companies will use import relief laws against the very companies the laws were designed to protect." Import relief laws are the legal protection referred to in choice D. The passage does not mention the situations described in choices A, B, C, and E.

59. The passage suggests that which of the following is most likely to be true of United States trade laws?

(A) They will eliminate the practice of "dumping" products in the United States.
(B) They will enable manufacturers in the United States to compete more profitably outside the United States.
(C) They will affect United States trade with Canada more negatively than trade with other nations.
(D) Those that help one unit within a parent company will not necessarily help other units in the company.
(E) Those that are applied to international companies will accomplish their intended result.

The best answer is D. In lines 16-19 the author warns that it is "unlikely that a system of import relief laws will meet the strategic needs of all the units under the same parent company." Thus, it can be inferred that the United States trade laws dealing with import relief will not necessarily help all units of a company, as stated in choice D. There is no indication in the passage that United States trade laws are expected to eliminate dumping, as is stated in choice A. Choice E is directly contradicted by the sentence in lines 20-22. There is no discussion in the passage of the situations mentioned in choices B and C.

60. It can be inferred from the passage that the author believes which of the following about the complaint mentioned in the last paragraph?

(A) The ITC acted unfairly toward the complainant in its investigation.
(B) The complaint violated the intent of import relief laws.
(C) The response of the ITC to the complaint provided suitable relief from unfair trade practices to the complainant.
(D) The ITC did not have access to appropriate information concerning the case.
(E) Each of the companies involved in the complaint acted in its own best interest.

The best answer is B. In lines 35-38 the author states that "The bizarre aspect of the complaint was that a foreign conglomerate. . .was crying for help against a United States company. . . ." It can be inferred from lines 20-22 that import relief laws were designed to protect United States companies from foreign competition. Thus, the lodging of a complaint by a foreign conglomerate against a United States company violated the intent of the laws.

Questions 61-66 refer to the passage on page 340.

61. Which of the following best describes the organization of the passage?

(A) The historical backgrounds of two currently used research methods are chronicled.
(B) The validity of the data collected by using two different research methods is compared.
(C) The usefulness of a research method is questioned and then a new method is proposed.
(D) The use of a research method is described and the limitations of the results obtained are discussed.
(E) A research method is evaluated and the changes necessary for its adaptation to other subject areas are discussed.

The best answer is D. The first paragraph of the passage identifies a research method (recording life stories) and explains the method's uses. The second and third paragraphs explain limitations of the method's results. The final paragraph explains why the research method is useful despite its limitations. Choices A, B, and C are incorrect because only one research method is discussed, not two. Choice E can be eliminated because the passage does not discuss changing the method or adapting it to any other subject area.

62. Which of the following is most similar to the actions of nineteenth-century ethnologists in their editing of the life stories of Native Americans?

(A) A witness in a jury trial invokes the Fifth Amendment in order to avoid relating personally incriminating evidence.
(B) A stockbroker refuses to divulge the source of her information on the possible future increase in a stock's value.
(C) A sports announcer describes the action in a team sport with which he is unfamiliar.
(D) A chef purposely excludes the special ingredient from the recipe of his prizewinning dessert.
(E) A politician fails to mention in a campaign speech the similarities in the positions held by her opponent for political office and by herself.

The best answer is C. Lines 22-23 suggest that ethnologists "rarely spent enough time with the tribes they were observing." Ethnologists who did not spend enough time with tribes they were observing were unlikely to be sufficiently familiar with the culture and customs of those tribes. Such ethnologists nevertheless attempted to describe the lives of tribal members. This attempt can be seen as analogous to the announcer's attempt to describe the actions in a team sport with which he is unfamiliar. Choices A, B, and D can be eliminated because the passage does not suggest that ethnologists deliberately withheld information. Choice E is incorrect because the passage does not mention any common ideas or positions held by both the ethnologists and the Native Americans.

63. According to the passage, collecting life stories can be a useful methodology because

(A) life stories provide deeper insights into a culture than the hypothesizing of academics who are not members of that culture
(B) life stories can be collected easily and they are not subject to invalid interpretations
(C) ethnologists have a limited number of research methods from which to choose
(D) life stories make it easy to distinguish between the important and unimportant features of a culture
(E) the collection of life stories does not require a culturally knowledgeable investigator

The best answer is A, which paraphrases the passage's assertion that life stories "are likely to throw more light on the working of the mind and emotions than any amount of speculation from an ethnologist or ethnological theorist from another culture" (lines 40-44). Choice B is incorrect because the passage does not assess the difficulty of collecting life stories, and because the second paragraph discusses ways in which life stories became distorted. Choice C is incorrect because the passage does not specify how many research methods are available to ethnologists. Choice D can be eliminated because the third paragraph mentions distortion arising from ethnologists' failure to recognize significant events in life stories. Choice E is incorrect because the second paragraph suggests that life stories would be more useful if collected by culturally knowledgeable investigators.

64. Information in the passage suggests that which of the following may be a possible way to eliminate bias in the editing of life stories?

(A) Basing all inferences made about the culture on an ethnological theory
(B) Eliminating all of the emotion-laden information reported by the informant
(C) Translating the informant's words into the researcher's language
(D) Reducing the number of questions and carefully specifying the content of the questions that the investigator can ask the informant
(E) Reporting all of the information that the informant provides regardless of the investigator's personal opinion about its intrinsic value

The best answer is E. In the third paragraph, the passage asserts that editors made their own decisions about which elements of the Native Americans' life stories were important. It can therefore be inferred from the passage that reporting all of an informant's information would help eliminate bias, because editing had involved subjective judgments about the intrinsic value of the information. Choices A, C, and D can be eliminated because the passage does not attribute bias to failures in adhering to ethnological theory, to translations into the researchers' language, or to problems in the numbers and content of questions posed. Choice B is not supported because the second paragraph criticizes the emotion of the reporter, not that of the informant, for introducing bias.

65. The primary purpose of the passage as a whole is to

(A) question an explanation
(B) correct a misconception
(C) critique a methodology
(D) discredit an idea
(E) clarify an ambiguity

The best answer is C. The passage describes a methodology, explains the methodology's intended uses, criticizes the methodology's accurateness and comprehensiveness, and reaffirms the methodology's usefulness despite its limitations. Thus, the primary purpose of the passage is to evaluate or critique a methodology.

66. It can be inferred from the passage that a characteristic of the ethnological research on Native Americans conducted during the nineteenth century was the use of which of the following?

(A) Investigators familiar with the culture under study
(B) A language other than the informant's for recording life stories
(C) Life stories as the ethnologist's primary source of information
(D) Complete transcriptions of informants' descriptions of tribal beliefs
(E) Stringent guidelines for the preservation of cultural data

The best answer is B. Lines 30-32 state that "Native Americans recognized that the essence of their lives could not be communicated in English," that is, in the language of the ethnologists recording the life stories. Since this statement supports the idea that "much was inevitably lost," it can be inferred that the informants used a language other than that used to record their life stories. Choice A is incorrect because, in the second paragraph, the investigators are criticized for lacking familiarity with the cultures they studied. Choice C is incorrect because ethnologists recorded life stories to "supplement their own field observations" (lines 7-8). Choice D is incorrect because the passage indicates that life stories were edited; choice E is incorrect because the passage provides no information about guidelines used by the researchers.

Questions 67-72 refer to the passage on page 342.

67. According to the passage, the five well-known plant hormones are not useful in controlling the growth of crops because

   (A) it is not known exactly what functions the hormones perform
   (B) each hormone has various effects on plants
   (C) none of the hormones can function without the others
   (D) each hormone has different effects on different kinds of plants
   (E) each hormone works on only a small subset of a cell's genes at any particular time

The best answer is B. The passage states that each of the five well-known plant hormones "has more than one effect on the growth and development of plants" (lines 15-16) and that, for this reason, "they are not very useful in artificially controlling the growth of crops" (lines 17-18). Choice A is not correct because lines 18-23 describe some of the functions performed by the hormone auxin. Choice E is consistent with information presented in the passage, but by emphasizing the specific effect hormones have at the cellular level rather than the multiplicity of effects they have on the entire plant, E fails to provide the reason stated in the passage that the five hormones are not useful in controlling the growth of crops. Neither C nor D is suggested by anything in the passage.

68. The passage suggests that the place of hypothalamic hormones in the hormonal hierarchies of animals is similar to the place of which of the following in plants?

   (A) Plant cell walls
   (B) The complement of genes in each plant cell
   (C) A subset of a plant cell's gene complement
   (D) The five major hormones
   (E) The oligosaccharins

The best answer is D. According to the passage, "The pleiotropy of the five well-studied plant hormones is somewhat analogous to that of certain hormones in animals" (lines 24-26). The example given involves certain hypothalamic hormones that "stimulate the anterior lobe of the pituitary gland to synthesize and release many different hormones, one of which stimulates the release of hormones from the adrenal cortex" (lines 27-30). These hormones in turn "have specific effects on target organs all over the body" (line 31). This "hierarchy of hormones," as the author calls it, "may also exist in plants" (line 35), where the five pleiotropic hormones may "function by activating the enzymes that release . . . more specific chemical messengers" (lines 39-41). Thus, hypothalamic hormones in animals and the five major hormones in plants occupy a similar place in the respective organisms' hormonal hierarchy.

69. The passage suggests that which of the following is a function likely to be performed by an oligosaccharin?

   (A) To stimulate a particular plant cell to become part of a plant's root system
   (B) To stimulate the walls of a particular cell to produce other oligosaccharins
   (C) To activate enzymes that release specific chemical messengers from plant cell walls
   (D) To duplicate the gene complement in a particular plant cell
   (E) To produce multiple effects on a particular subsystem of plant cells

The best answer is A. The last paragraph characterizes oligosaccharins as "specific chemical messengers" (lines 40-41). The passage indicates that these chemical messengers are "specific" in that, unlike the pleiotropic hormones, they are likely to have particular effects on particular plant cells. Choice A is correct because it is the only answer choice that describes an effect on a specific aspect of plant growth and development: stimulating a particular plant cell to become part of a plant's root system. Choices B and C are incorrect because the last paragraph indicates that enzymes activate the release of oligosaccharins. Choice D is incorrect because, although oligosaccharins do affect the activity of the gene complement of a particular cell, they do not duplicate that complement. Choice E is incorrect because the second paragraph indicates that an oligosaccharin has a specific effect rather than multiple effects on plant cells.

70. The author mentions specific effects that auxin has on plant development in order to illustrate the

   (A) point that some of the effects of plant hormones can be harmful
   (B) way in which hormones are produced by plants
   (C) hierarchical nature of the functioning of plant hormones
   (D) differences among the best-known plant hormones
   (E) concept of pleiotropy as it is exhibited by plant hormones

The best answer is E. The second paragraph states that the five major plant hormones, including auxin, are pleiotropic and indicates that each pleiotropic hormone has "more than one effect on the growth and development of plants" (lines 15-16). The effects of auxin are then listed in detail to provide an example of the different effects a pleiotropic hormone can have on a plant. Thus, the specific effects of auxin are mentioned to illustrate the concept of pleiotropy as it is exhibited by plant hormones. Choice C can be eliminated because the specific effects that auxin has on plant development are not discussed in the context of the hierarchy of hormones. Choices A, B, and D are incorrect because they cite topics that are not discussed in the passage.

71. According to the passage, which of the following best describes a function performed by oligosaccharins?

(A) Regulating the daily functioning of a plant's cells
(B) Interacting with one another to produce different chemicals
(C) Releasing specific chemical messengers from a plant's cell walls
(D) Producing the hormones that cause plant cells to differentiate to perform different functions
(E) Influencing the development of a plant's cells by controlling the expression of the cells' genes

The best answer is E. The first paragraph states that plant cells "differentiate and form structures" (line 3) when a "complex system of chemical messengers" (line 7) activates a "small subset of the genes in a particular kind of cell" (lines 5-6). In lines 38-41, the author elaborates on the hormonal system in plants by indicating that the pleiotropic plant hormones activate enzymes, which in turn release oligosaccharins—the "more specific chemical messengers" (lines 40-41). The second paragraph indicates these specific chemical messengers have specific effects on plant development. Thus, the passage indicates that it is the oligosaccharins that directly influence the development of a plant cell by controlling the expression of a plant cell's genes. Choices C and D are incorrect because the oligosaccharins are themselves specific chemical messengers and are not said to produce any hormones. The passage provides no information to support A or B.

72. The passage suggests that, unlike the pleiotropic hormones, oligosaccharins could be used effectively to

(A) trace the passage of chemicals through the walls of cells
(B) pinpoint functions of other plant hormones
(C) artificially control specific aspects of the development of crops
(D) alter the complement of genes in the cells of plants
(E) alter the effects of the five major hormones on plant development

The best answer is C. Lines 16-18 state that because each pleiotropic hormone has so many different effects on a plant, pleiotropic hormones "are not very useful in artificially controlling the growth of crops" (lines 17-18). In contrast, the passage indicates that oligosaccharins have specific effects on the growth and development of plants. Thus, in comparison to the pleiotropic hormones, oligosaccharins could potentially be effective in artificially controlling specific aspects of crop development. Choices A, B, D, and E can be eliminated because they describe functions that are not attributed in the passage either to the pleiotropic hormones or to oligosaccharins.

Questions 73-79 refer to the passage on page 344.

73. The passage is primarily concerned with evaluating

(A) the importance of Florence Nightingale's innovations in the field of nursing
(B) contrasting approaches to the writing of historical biography
(C) contradictory accounts of Florence Nightingale's historical significance
(D) the quality of health care in nineteenth-century England
(E) the effect of the Crimean War on developments in the field of health care

This question asks you to identify the primary concern of the passage.

The best answer is C. According to the first paragraph, the passage is about two different assessments of Florence Nightingale's career. The first paragraph summarizes one of these assessments; the second paragraph presents a contrasting account of Nightingale's career that contradicts the central point of the first account.

Choice A is incorrect. Although the passage discusses various aspects of Florence Nightingale's involvement in the field of nursing, it does not mention any innovations that she introduced to that field. Choice B is not correct because the passage does not discuss approaches to the writing of historical biography. Choice D is also incorrect. Although the passage refers to the specific problems of military medicine during the Crimean War (lines 10-11) and to the poor living conditions of British soldiers after the war (lines 22-23), the passage does not discuss the broader, more general issue of the quality of health care in nineteenth-century England. And choice E is not the answer because the passage does not mention the effects of the Crimean War on developments in health care.

74. According to the passage, the editors of Nightingale's letters credit her with contributing to which of the following?

(A) Improvement of the survival rate for soldiers in British Army hospitals during the Crimean War
(B) The development of a nurses' training curriculum that was far in advance of its day
(C) The increase in the number of women doctors practicing in British Army hospitals
(D) Establishment of the first facility for training nurses at a major British university
(E) The creation of an organization for monitoring the peacetime living conditions of British soldiers

This question asks you to identify a contribution that the editors of Nightingale's letters attribute to her.

The best answer is E. In the second paragraph, several of Nightingale's post-war accomplishments that are highlighted by the editors of her letters are mentioned. In lines 22-27, her contribution to the creation of an organization for monitoring the peacetime living conditions of British soldiers is mentioned as one of these.

Choice A is not correct. In lines 22-25 the editors of Nightingale's letters cite the relatively high death rate of British soldiers after the Crimean War, but they do not mention their survival rate during the war. Choice B is incorrect, because the passage does not provide any information about the curriculum of the nurses' training hospital that Nightingale founded. Choice C is also not the correct answer. The passage does not mention women doctors, only women nurses. And choice D is incorrect because there is no indication in the passage that the nurses' training hospital that Nightingale founded was at a university or that it was the first of its kind.

75. **The passage suggests which of the following about Nightingale's relationship with the British public of her day?**

    (A) **She was highly respected, her projects receiving popular and governmental support.**
    (B) **She encountered resistance both from the army establishment and the general public.**
    (C) **She was supported by the working classes and opposed by the wealthier classes.**
    (D) **She was supported by the military establishment but had to fight the governmental bureaucracy.**
    (E) **After initially being received with enthusiasm, she was quickly forgotten.**

To answer this question, you must use information contained in the passage to infer something about Nightingale's relationship with the British public of her day.

The best answer is A. Line 5 refers to Nightingale's "heroic reputation"; line 14 refers to "Nightingale's place in the national pantheon"; and lines 25-28 discuss her persuasiveness with the British government and her fund-raising successes. From this information it can be inferred that Nightingale was highly respected, as evidenced by both popular and governmental support for her projects.

Choices B, C, and D are incorrect for the same reason: each one refers to an element of social or governmental opposition or resistance to Nightingale's ideas, none of which is mentioned or suggested by the passage. Choice E is also incorrect. The information in the passage contradicts the notion that Nightingale was "quickly forgotten." To the contrary, the passage discusses the "famous British nurse Florence Nightingale" (lines 2-3), her "heroic reputation" (line 5), and her "place in the national pantheon" (line 14), as well as her "eminent place among the ranks of social pioneers" (lines 43-44).

76. **The passage suggests which of the following about sanitary conditions in Britain after the Crimean War?**

    (A) **While not ideal, they were superior to those in other parts of the world.**
    (B) **Compared with conditions before the war, they had deteriorated.**
    (C) **They were more advanced in rural areas than in the urban centers.**
    (D) **They were worse in military camps than in the neighboring civilian populations.**
    (E) **They were uniformly crude and unsatisfactory throughout England.**

This question asks you to draw a conclusion about sanitary conditions in Britain after the Crimean War that is suggested, rather than stated expressly, in the passage.

The best answer is D. In the second paragraph Nightingale's efforts to reform sanitary conditions in Britain are illustrated by her response to the death rate among enlisted men in British barracks, which is described as unusually high relative to that of neighboring civilian populations. From this it can be inferred that sanitary conditions in the barracks were worse than in these civilian populations.

Choices A, B, and C are incorrect: in each, a comparison is made between sanitary conditions in post-war Britain and sanitary conditions elsewhere or at other times. However, because the passage provides no basis on which to make any of these comparisons, all three of these choices are incorrect. The passage does not mention sanitary conditions "in other parts of the world," as in Choice A; "before the war," as in choice B; or in "rural areas" as compared with "urban centers," as in choice C. Choice E is also incorrect, because the passage provides no information about the general state of sanitary conditions "throughout England."

77. **With which of the following statements regarding the differing interpretations of Nightingale's importance would the author most likely agree?**

    (A) **Summers misunderstood both the importance of Nightingale's achievements during the Crimean War and her subsequent influence on British policy.**
    (B) **The editors of Nightingale's letters made some valid points about her practical achievements, but they still exaggerated her influence on subsequent generations.**
    (C) **Although Summers' account of Nightingale's role in the Crimean War may be accurate, she ignored evidence of Nightingale's subsequent achievement that suggests that her reputation as an eminent social reformer is well deserved.**
    (D) **The editors of Nightingale's letters mistakenly propagated the outdated idealization of Nightingale that only impedes attempts to arrive at a balanced assessment of her true role.**
    (E) **The evidence of Nightingale's letters supports Summers' conclusions both about Nightingale's activities and about her influence.**

This question asks you to select a statement about the two contrasting accounts of Nightingale's importance with which the author of the passage would be most likely to agree.

The best answer is C. In the last paragraph, the author concedes that "Nightingale may not have achieved all of her goals during the Crimean War." This is consistent with Summers' view that Nightingale's importance during the war has been exaggerated (lines 5-7), but the author of the passage nonetheless describes Nightingale as a great social pioneer because of her vision and achievements. These achievements, which the second paragraph states occurred primarily after the Crimean War, apparently did not influence Summers' interpretation of

Nightingale's importance. Given the author's favorable assessment of Nightingale's reputation, it is likely that the author would agree that Summers' interpretation ignores this important evidence.

Choice A is not the correct answer. Although, in lines 40-42, the author concedes that Summers may be correct in her assessment of Nightingale's wartime achievements, nothing is said in the passage about Summers' discussion, if any, of Nightingale's postwar influence or activities. Choice B is also incorrect. In lines 33-35, the author cites the editors' collection of Nightingale's letters as evidence of Nightingale's "brilliance and creativity." Therefore, it is unlikely that the author would agree that the editors only made valid points about Nightingale's "practical" achievements. In addition, in light of the author's statement that Nightingale has earned "an eminent place among the ranks of social pioneers" (lines 43-44), there is no reason to think the author would agree that the editors exaggerated Nightingale's influence on later generations.

Choice D is not the correct answer. In the last paragraph of the passage, the author refers to Nightingale's letters as evidence of her "brilliance and creativity" (lines 33-35), and as the basis for a conclusion that Nightingale has earned "an eminent place among the ranks of social pioneers" (lines 43-44). It is therefore highly unlikely that the author believes that the editors of these letters have "mistakenly propagated" outdated notions or impeded a balanced assessment of Nightingale's role. Choice E is also incorrect. In the last paragraph of the passage, the author states that "the evidence of Nightingale's letters supports continued respect for Nightingale's brilliance and creativity." Summers, on the other hand, seeks in her book to "debunk" Nightingale's "heroic reputation" (lines 3-5). Rather than supporting Summers' conclusions about Nightingale, the evidence of Nightingale's letters contradicts them.

78. Which of the following is an assumption underlying the author's assessment of Nightingale's creativity?

   (A) Educational philosophy in Nightingale's day did not normally emphasize developing children's ability to observe.
   (B) Nightingale was the first to notice the poor living conditions in British military barracks in peacetime.
   (C) No educator before Nightingale had thought to enlist the help of village schoolmasters in introducing new teaching techniques.
   (D) Until Nightingale began her work, there was no concept of organized help for the needy in nineteenth-century Britain.
   (E) The British Army's medical services had no cost-accounting system until Nightingale devised one in the 1860's.

This question asks you to identify something the author has assumed in assessing Nightingale's creativity. The author's assessment of Nightingale's creativity is discussed in the last paragraph of the passage.

The best answer is A. In the last paragraph of the passage, the author presents two examples of Nightingale's "brilliance and creativity." In the first of these, the author compares Nightingale to "a modern educator" for counseling a village schoolmaster to encourage children's powers of observation. The fact that the author believes that this is evidence of Nightingale's creativity suggests that it was unusual at that time to emphasize developing children's ability to observe.

Choice B is not the correct answer. Nightingale's efforts to improve conditions in British military barracks are not cited as evidence of her creativity, nor is it suggested that Nightingale was the "first" to notice the poor living conditions in British barracks. Choice C is also incorrect. The passage describes Nightingale's counseling a village schoolmaster, not enlisting schoolmasters' help (lines 35-36); moreover, nothing in the passage suggests that educators had failed to enlist such help prior to the incident the author describes. Choice D is incorrect: although the author cites Nightingale's contributions to the care of the needy (lines 37-40), the passage does not suggest that no organized help for the needy existed before Nightingale began her work. And choice E is incorrect, because although Nightingale's cost-accounting system is presented in the passage as having made a lasting contribution to the British Army's medical services, the passage never suggests that before Nightingale the Army lacked a cost-accounting system.

79. In the last paragraph, the author is primarily concerned with

   (A) summarizing the arguments about Nightingale presented in the first two paragraphs
   (B) refuting the view of Nightingale's career presented in the preceding paragraph
   (C) analyzing the weaknesses of the evidence presented elsewhere in the passage
   (D) citing evidence to support a view of Nightingale's career
   (E) correcting a factual error occurring in one of the works under review

This question asks you to identify the author's primary concern in the last paragraph of the passage.

The best answer is D. In the last paragraph, the author cites examples of Nightingale's achievements to support the author's conclusion that Nightingale is worthy of respect and has earned "an eminent place among the ranks of social pioneers" (lines 43-44).

Choice A is incorrect. The third paragraph does not summarize the arguments presented in the first two paragraphs. Choice B is also not the correct answer: in the third paragraph, the author expresses essential agreement with the positive view of Nightingale's career described in the second paragraph. Choice C is incorrect because in the last paragraph the author does not analyze the weaknesses of any evidence cited elsewhere in the passage. And choice E is not the correct answer because the author does not correct any factual errors in the two works under review.

Questions 80-87 refer to the passage on page 346.

80. The primary focus of the passage is on which of the following?

(A) Comparing two scientific theories and contrasting the predictions that each would make concerning a natural phenomenon
(B) Describing a new theoretical model and noting that it explains the nature of observations made of a particular natural phenomenon
(C) Evaluating the results of a particular scientific experiment and suggesting further areas for research
(D) Explaining how two different natural phenomena are related and demonstrating a way to measure them
(E) Analyzing recent data derived from observations of an actual phenomenon and constructing a model to explain the data

This question asks you to identify the primary focus of the passage.

The best answer is B. The author describes the new theoretical model in the first paragraph; in the final paragraph the author states that the data obtained from actual observations, which are discussed in the second and third paragraphs, is consistent with the new theoretical model.

Choice A is not correct; the computer model confirmed the astronomers' hypothesis that meteor streams broaden with time, and although the model yielded an unexpected result, the passage does not contrast the predictions yielded by competing theories. Choices C and D are not correct because the passage makes no reference to further areas for research, and only a single phenomenon is described in the passage. And choice E is not correct because it reverses the order of events. The model yielded a prediction that was subsequently confirmed by observational data; the model was not constructed to explain the data.

81. According to the passage, which of the following is an accurate statement concerning meteor streams?

(A) Meteor streams and comets start out with similar orbits, but only those of meteor streams are perturbed by planetary gravitation.
(B) Meteor streams grow as dust particles are attracted by the gravitational fields of comets.
(C) Meteor streams are composed of dust particles derived from comets.
(D) Comets may be composed of several kinds of materials, while meteor streams consist only of large dust particles.
(E) Once formed, meteor streams hasten the further disintegration of comets.

This question asks you to identify an accurate statement about meteor streams. Choice C, the best answer, restates information about the composition of meteor streams from the first sentence of the passage.

Choice A is not correct. The passage discusses the influence of planetary gravitation on meteor streams but says nothing about its influence on the orbits of comets. According to the passage, it is planetary gravitation, not the gravitational fields of comets, that causes meteor streams to increase in size, so choice B is not correct. And choices D and E are not correct because the passage says nothing about the composition of comets or the role that meteor streams play in their further disintegration.

82. The author states that the research described in the first paragraph was undertaken in order to

(A) determine the age of an actual meteor stream
(B) identify the various structural features of meteor streams
(C) explore the nature of a particularly interesting meteor stream
(D) test the hypothesis that meteor streams become broader as they age
(E) show that a computer model could help in explaining actual astronomical data

This question asks what the author says about the purpose of the research described in the first paragraph.

The best answer is D. According to the author, the purpose of the computer-modeling experiment was to test the hypothesis that meteor streams broaden with time.

Choice A is not correct; although the observational data described in the last paragraph allowed scientists to estimate the age of the Geminid stream, this data was analyzed to confirm a surprising prediction made by the computer model. This analysis was not part of the original experiment.

Choice B is also incorrect. Although the experiment yielded a surprising prediction about a particular feature of meteor streams, the purpose of the experiment was to determine whether meteor streams broaden with time, not to identify the various structural features of meteor streams.

Choice C is not correct because the experiment was undertaken to test a general hypothesis about meteor streams. It was not undertaken to explore the nature of any particular meteor stream, and the passage never suggests that the actual meteor stream used in the computer model was "particularly interesting."

Choice E is not correct. Although the computer model did confirm the astronomers' hypothesis, the purpose of the experiment was not to show that such models are useful.

83. It can be inferred from the passage that which of the following would most probably be observed during the Earth's passage through a meteor stream if the conventional theories mentioned in line 18 were correct?

(A) Meteor activity would gradually increase to a single, intense peak, and then gradually decline.
(B) Meteor activity would be steady throughout the period of the meteor shower.
(C) Meteor activity would rise to a peak at the beginning and at the end of the meteor shower.
(D) Random bursts of very high meteor activity would be interspersed with periods of very little activity.
(E) In years in which the Earth passed through only the outer areas of a meteor stream, meteor activity would be absent.

This question asks you to make an inference about what would most probably be observed during the Earth's passage through a meteor stream if the conventional theories mentioned in the passage were correct. According to lines 18-20, the conventional theories predicted that the meteor stream would be most dense at the center. The computer model, on the other hand, predicted that a meteor stream would come to resemble a thick-walled, hollow pipe (lines 21-22). The passage states that, if the computer model were correct, two peak periods of meteor activity would be observed as the Earth passed through the walls of the "pipe" (lines 28-31). According to lines 36-38, observational data confirmed the prediction of the computer model. If, on the other hand, the conventional theories were correct, it can be inferred that a bifurcation of meteor activity would not be observed; instead, it can be inferred that scientists would expect to observe a single peak of meteor activity as the Earth passed through the dense center of the stream. Choice A identifies this single peak of activity as the most likely observation if the conventional theories were correct.

Choices B and D are not correct because they describe meteor activity that is either steady or erratic, neither of which is consistent with the conventional theories. Choice C describes meteor activity more in line with the bifurcation predicted by the computer model, rather than the single peak of activity that the conventional theories would suggest. Choice E is incorrect because the passage says that meteor showers occur whenever the Earth passes through a meteor stream; it cannot be inferred that either theory would predict otherwise.

84. According to the passage, why do the dust particles in a meteor stream eventually surround a comet's original orbit?

(A) They are ejected by the comet at differing velocities.
(B) Their orbits are uncontrolled by planetary gravitational fields.
(C) They become part of the meteor stream at different times.
(D) Their velocity slows over time.
(E) Their ejection velocity is slower than that of the comet.

This question asks for the reason given in the passage for a characteristic feature of meteor streams. According to lines 1-7, the dust particles in a meteor stream eventually surround a comet's original orbit because of the different velocities at which they are ejected, as stated in choice A, the best answer.

Choice B is directly contradicted by information in the passage (lines 8-10). The other answer choices are incorrect because the passage does not say that the dust particles become part of the meteor stream at different times, or that their velocity slows over time, or that their ejection velocity is slower than that of the comet.

85. The passage suggests that which of the following is a prediction concerning meteor streams that can be derived from both the conventional theories mentioned in line 18 and the new computer-derived theory?

(A) Dust particles in a meteor stream will usually be distributed evenly throughout any cross section of the stream.
(B) The orbits of most meteor streams should cross the orbit of the Earth at some point and give rise to a meteor shower.
(C) Over time the distribution of dust in a meteor stream will usually become denser at the outside edges of the stream than at the center.
(D) Meteor showers caused by older meteor streams should be, on average, longer in duration than those caused by very young meteor streams.
(E) The individual dust particles in older meteor streams should be, on average, smaller than those that compose younger meteor streams.

This question asks you to identify a prediction that can be derived from both the conventional theories about meteor streams and the new computer-derived model. You must base your answer on information that is suggested by, but not expressly stated in, the passage.

According to lines 7-8 of the passage, the conventional theories hypothesized that meteor streams should broaden with time, and the computer simulation confirmed this hypothesis. The passage also suggests that the time it takes for the Earth to cross a meteor stream (and, by implication, the duration of the resulting meteor shower) is directly related to the breadth of the stream (lines 23-28). From these pieces of information, which are supported by both the conventional theories and the new computer-derived theory, it can be inferred that on average the meteor showers caused by older (and therefore broader) meteor streams would be longer in duration than those caused by very young (and therefore narrower) meteor streams, as stated in D, the best answer.

Choice A is incorrect because it contradicts the predictions of both the conventional theories (that the particles will be most dense at the center of the stream) and the computer model (that the stream will resemble a thick-walled, hollow pipe). Choice C is also incorrect because it is inconsistent with the conventional theories that suggested the distribution of dust in a meteor stream is denser at the center. And choices B and E are incorrect because the theories discussed in the passage do not suggest anything about the likelihood that the Earth's orbit will cross that of any particular meteor stream, nor do they suggest anything about the size of the dust particles that compose meteor streams.

86. It can be inferred from the last paragraph of the passage that which of the following must be true of the Earth as it orbits the Sun?

(A) Most meteor streams it encounters are more than 2,000 years old.
(B) When passing through a meteor stream, it usually passes near to the stream's center.
(C) It crosses the Geminid meteor stream once every year.
(D) It usually takes over a day to cross the actual Geminid meteor stream.
(E) It accounts for most of the gravitational perturbation affecting the Geminid meteor stream.

This question asks you to draw an inference from information in the last paragraph of the passage.

The best answer is C. According to the passage, the Geminid meteor shower occurs yearly; because meteor showers occur whenever the Earth passes through a meteor stream, one can infer that the Earth crosses the Geminid stream once every year.

Choice A is incorrect because the passage provides no information from which to generalize about the age of meteor streams. Choice B, which is directly contradicted by lines 31-32, is also incorrect. Choice D is incorrect. In lines 25-28, the passage says that the Earth would take just over a day to cross the stream if the stream were 5,000 years old. However, in lines 38-42 the passage states that in fact an average of only 19 hours elapsed between the time that the Earth entered the stream until the time that it exited, leading researchers to conclude that the stream is only about 3,000 years old. Choice E is incorrect because the passage says only that planetary gravitational fields perturb the orbits of dust particles in a meteor stream; it does not say that the effect of the Earth's gravitation is greater than that of other planets.

87. Which of the following is an assumption underlying the last sentence of the passage?

(A) In each of the years between 1970 and 1979, the Earth took exactly 19 hours to cross the Geminid meteor stream.
(B) The comet associated with the Geminid meteor stream has totally disintegrated.
(C) The Geminid meteor stream should continue to exist for at least 5,000 years.
(D) The Geminid meteor stream has not broadened as rapidly as the conventional theories would have predicted.
(E) The computer-model Geminid meteor stream provides an accurate representation of the development of the actual Geminid stream.

This question asks you to identify an assumption underlying the last sentence of the passage. In this sentence, the author of the passage draws a conclusion about the age of the Geminid stream. This conclusion is based on two pieces of information. The first is the length of time the Earth would take to cross the computer-model Geminid stream if the stream were 5,000 years old (lines 24-28). The second is the actual elapsed time between the two peaks of meteor activity predicted by the computer model (lines 36-40). In concluding from this information that the Geminid stream is actually only 3,000 years old, the author is assuming the accuracy of the computer model, as stated in E, the best answer.

Choice A is incorrect because the passage says that the time the Earth takes to cross the stream would vary from year to year (lines 32-34) and that 19 hours was the average time, not the exact time, observed from 1970 to 1979 (lines 36-40). Choices B and C are incorrect because the passage does not suggest anything about the current state of the comet associated with the Geminid stream or about the expected longevity of the stream. Choice D is incorrect because the computer model is said to confirm the broadening predicted by the conventional theories; the fact that the model projected the positions of the particles in the stream over a 5,000-year period does not suggest that researchers expected the stream to be older (and therefore broader) than it turned out to be.

Questions 88-94 refer to the passage on page 348.

88. In the passage, the author is primarily concerned with doing which of the following?

(A) Comparing two different approaches to a problem
(B) Describing a problem and proposing a solution
(C) Defending an established method
(D) Presenting data and drawing conclusions from the data
(E) Comparing two different analyses of a current situation

This question asks you to determine the main task that the passage is designed to accomplish.

The best answer is B. The passage identifies a problem (shareholders' and managers' failure to enhance companies' long-term productivity) in the first paragraph, most pointedly in the last sentence of that paragraph. In the second paragraph, the author recommends certain actions as a means of solving that problem.

Choice A is not correct. The author of the passage identifies a problem in the first paragraph, but the author does not compare two different approaches to that problem. Rather, in the second paragraph, the author proposes a single, unified approach to solving the problem. Choice C is incorrect. The author does not defend an established method in the passage. Instead, the author criticizes the current method of institutional shareholding in the United States and recommends a different method in the second paragraph. Choice D is also incorrect. The author describes a situation in the first paragraph but does not provide data or draw any conclusions from data. Choice E is not the correct answer. The author does not compare alternative analyses of the current situation discussed in the passage.

89. It can be inferred from the passage that which of the following is true of majority shareholders in a corporation?

(A) They make the corporation's operational management decisions.
(B) They are not allowed to own more than 50 percent of the corporation's stock.
(C) They cannot make quick profits by selling off large amounts of their stock in the corporation.
(D) They are more interested in profits than in productivity.
(E) They cannot sell any of their stock in the corporation without giving the public advance notice.

This question asks you to decide what the passage implies, rather than states directly, about majority shareholders in a corporation.

The best answer is C. According to lines 4-8 of the passage, those individual capitalists who were once majority shareholders in a corporation would not be able to make a quick profit by selling a large amount of stock because such a sale would depress the stock's value. It can be inferred from the passage that this would be true of any majority shareholders.

Choice A is not the correct answer. The passage suggests, in lines 11-13, that majority shareholders can actively influence a company's decision-making, but it does not suggest that this influence is equal to the absolute authority suggested by the language of this answer choice. The passage also does not discuss the "operational management decisions" of corporations. Choice B is not correct. The passage does not specify what percentage of a corporation's stock any one shareholder is allowed to own. Choice D is not the correct answer. The author does not imply that majority shareholders are more interested in profits than in productivity. In fact, the author argues the opposite, stating that majority shareholders such as the old-style capitalists concentrated more on long-term productivity than on quick profits. Choice E is also incorrect. In lines 30-33, the author proposes that shareholders of more than 20 percent of a company's stock should be required to give advance public notice before a stock sale, but the passage does not suggest that majority shareholders are currently required to do so.

90. According to the passage, the purpose of the requirement suggested in lines 30-33 would be which of the following?

(A) To encourage institutional stockholders to sell stock that they believe will decrease in value
(B) To discourage institutional stockholders from intervening in the operation of a company whose stock they own
(C) To discourage short-term profit-taking by institutional stockholders
(D) To encourage a company's employees to take an active role in the ownership of stock in the company
(E) To encourage investors to diversify their stock holdings

This question asks you to identify the stated purpose of the author's suggestion in lines 30-33, namely, that any institution holding 20 percent or more of a corporation's stock be required to give the public one day's notice of the intent to sell that stock.

The best answer is C. The purpose of the requirement that institutions holding 20 percent or more of a company's stock be required to give advance public notice of the sale of that stock is stated in lines 38-42: to prevent institutions from "trading shares at the propitious moment" and to encourage them to concentrate on increasing a company's productivity.

Choice A is incorrect. The suggested requirement that an institution give advance notice of its intent to sell a significant amount of stock tends to discourage institutional stockholders from selling stock they believe will decrease in value, since, according to the passage, such an announcement would cause the stock's value to plummet (lines 33-36). Choice B is also incorrect. In lines 28-30, the author argues that institutional stockholders should be "encouraged to take a more active role in the operations of the companies in which they invest." The advance notice requirement discussed in lines 30-33 is proposed by the author as a means of fostering, not discouraging, institutional stockholders' participation in the operation of the companies they invest in. Choice D is not the correct answer. The passage does not discuss ownership of company stock by that company's employees. Choice E is also incorrect. The passage states only that institutions should be allowed to acquire "a dominant shareholding position in a corporation," but it does not discuss whether investors should diversify their stock holdings by investing in different companies.

91. The author suggests that which of the following is a true statement about people who typify the "old-style capitalist" referred to in line 23 ?

(A) They now rely on outdated management techniques.
(B) They seldom engaged in short-term trading of the stock they owned.
(C) They did not influence the investment policies of the corporations in which they invested.
(D) They now play a very small role in the stock market as a result of antitrust legislation.
(E) They were primarily concerned with maximizing the short-term profitability of the corporations in which they owned stock.

To answer this question, you must use information contained in the passage to infer something about the "old-style capitalist" referred to in line 23.

The best answer is B. According to lines 1-7 of the passage, the individual capitalists of the past, referred to later in the passage as "old-style" capitalists (line 23), could not "sell out for a quick profit" because to do so would depress the value of their stocks. From this statement it can be inferred that someone who typifies the "old-style capitalist" would be unlikely to engage in short-term stock trading.

Choice A is incorrect. A comparison between the old-style capitalists and their modern counterparts is made in lines 36-38, but the passage does not express an opinion about whether or not the management techniques used by these capitalists are outdated.

Choice C is not the correct answer. The passage does not discuss the investment policies of the corporations in which financial institutions invest. Choice D is also incorrect. According to the passage (lines 1-2; line 23), the old-style capitalists were individual investors, not large institutions. While the passage states that large institutions are affected by anti-trust legislation (lines 8-12), it says nothing about whether this legislation affects individual investors. In addition, the passage does not mention anything about how great a role individual investors now play in the stock market. Choice E is also incorrect. The passage states that the old-style capitalists focused on long-term productivity (lines 5-8), and hence not on short-term profitability.

92. It can be inferred that the author makes which of the following assumptions about the businesses once controlled by individual capitalists?

(A) These businesses were less profitable than are businesses today.
(B) Improving long-term productivity led to increased profits.
(C) Each business had only a few stockholders.
(D) There was no short-term trading in the stock of these businesses.
(E) Institutions owned no stock in these companies.

This question asks you to infer, from information stated in the passage, what the author assumes about the companies once controlled by individual capitalists.

The best answer is B. In lines 5-8, the author asserts that individual capitalists "had to concentrate on improving the long-term productivity of their companies. "Then, in lines 20-21, the author identifies improved long-term profitability as a consequence of improved long-term productivity. From this it can be inferred that the author assumes that if the businesses controlled by individual capitalists had improved long-term productivity, they would also have become more profitable.

Choice A is not correct. The author does not make any direct comparison between the profitability of past and present corporations. Choice C is not the correct answer. The first sentence of the passage states that most large corporations were once dominated by individual capitalists who owned large portions of the companies' stock, but the passage does not specify whether many or few people owned the remainder of each company's stock. Choice D is incorrect. In lines 4-6, the passage states that the individual capitalists who once dominated large corporations "could not sell out for a quick profit," but the passage does not indicate whether or not the other shareholders of these corporations were involved in short-term trading of their stock. Choice E is not correct. The passage does not suggest that institutions owned no stock in most large corporations, only that individual capitalists owned enough stock to dominate these corporations.

93. The author suggests that the role of large institutions as stockholders differs from that of the "old-style capitalist" in part because large institutions

(A) invest in the stock of so many companies that they cannot focus attention on the affairs of any single corporation
(B) are prohibited by law from owning a majority of a corporation's stock
(C) are influenced by brokers who advise against long-term ownership of stocks
(D) are able to put large amounts of stock on the market without depressing the stock's value
(E) are attracted to the stocks of corporations that demonstrate long-term gains in productivity

This question asks you to infer, from information stated in the passage, a way in which the role of large institutions as stockholders differs from that of the "old-style capitalist."

The best answer is B. According to the passage, the old-style capitalists were able to play a dominant role in the corporations in which they held stock because they owned enough stock to do so (lines 1-4). The passage also states that large institutions are legally barred from owning a majority of a company's stock (lines 8-12). From this it can be inferred that large institutions, because their ability to own stock is limited, do not play as dominant a role in the corporations of which they are stockholders as did the old-style capitalists.

Choice A is not correct. The passage does not indicate whether large institutions invest in many companies, few companies, or even just a single company. Choice C is not the correct answer. The passage does not mention brokers or any other parties who might influence the investment choices made by large institutions. Choice D is incorrect. In lines 33-36 of the passage, the author notes that an institution's sale of a large amount of stock would, in fact, decrease the stock's value. Choice E is not the correct answer. The passage does not suggest any reasons why large institutions are attracted to the stock of any particular corporations.

94. The primary function of the second paragraph of the passage is to

(A) identify problems
(B) warn of consequences
(C) explain effects
(D) evaluate solutions
(E) recommend actions

This question asks you to determine the main purpose served by the second paragraph of the passage in the context of the passage as a whole.

The best answer is E. The second paragraph is devoted to the author's recommendations of certain actions, namely, the adoption of new regulations concerning the holding and selling of stock by institutional investors.

Choice A is not the correct answer. The author of the passage identifies a problem—short-term trading done by institutional shareholders—but does so in the first paragraph, not in the second. Choice B is incorrect. In the second paragraph, the author recommends new regulations regarding shareholding by institutions. Although in lines 38-42 the author mentions some consequences of the suggested regulations, the author clearly views these consequences as desirable. Choice C is not correct. The second paragraph contains suggestions about new ways to regulate shareholding by institutions. Although the author asserts that certain effects would result from the proposed regulations, these effects are not explained. Choice D is not correct. The second paragraph proposes measures to solve the problem presented in the first paragraph, but it simply describes, rather than evaluates, these proposed solutions.

Questions 95-100 refer to the passage on page 350.

95. The passage is primarily concerned with which of the following?

(A) Evaluating two competing technologies
(B) Tracing the impact of a new technology by narrating a sequence of events
(C) Reinterpreting an event from contemporary business history
(D) Illustrating a business strategy by means of a case history
(E) Proposing an innovative approach to business planning

The best answer is D. In the first paragraph, the author outlines a business strategy, "developing integrated approaches for successful mass production and distribution." The rest of the passage discusses the rivalry between Beta and VHS producers for control of the global VCR market, an illustration of the use of this strategy by VHS producers. The author briefly evaluates the two competing technologies and traces the impact of each on the market, but neither of these is the passage's primary concern, so A and B are incorrect. Choices C and E are incorrect because no events are reinterpreted in the passage and no new approaches to business planning are proposed.

96. According to the passage, today's successful firms, unlike successful firms in the past, may earn the greatest profits by

(A) investing in research to produce cheaper versions of existing technology
(B) being the first to market a competing technology
(C) adapting rapidly to a technological standard previously set by a competing firm
(D) establishing technological leadership in order to shape product definitions in advance of competing firms
(E) emphasizing the development of methods for the mass production and distribution of a new technology

The best answer is E. Lines 4-8 of the passage set up a contrast with "traditional" ways to benefit from marketing a product by stating that marketplace success based on leadership in "mass production and distribution" is characteristic of today's companies, not those of the past. Choices B and D are incorrect because they describe ways in which companies have achieved success in the past. Choices A and C are incorrect: they present ways of earning profits that are not discussed in the passage.

97. According to the passage, consumers began to develop a preference for VCR's in the VHS format because they believed which of the following?

(A) VCR's in the VHS format were technically better than competing-format VCR's.
(B) VCR's in the VHS format were less expensive than competing-format VCR's.
(C) VHS was the first standard format for VCR's.
(D) VHS prerecorded videotapes were more available than Beta-format tapes.
(E) VCR's in the Beta format would soon cease to be produced.

The best answer is D. Lines 23-25 of the passage state that the "perception among consumers that prerecorded tapes were more available in VHS format further expanded VHS's share of the market." None of the information given in the passage suggests that consumers thought the VHS-format was technically better (A) or less expensive than Beta (B). Nor does the passage indicate that consumers believed that VHS-format VCR's were the first on the market (C) or that VHS-format VCR's would eventually drive Beta VCR's out of production entirely (E).

98. The author implies that one way that VHS producers won control over the VCR market was by

   (A) carefully restricting access to VCR technology
   (B) giving up a slight early lead in VCR sales in order to improve long-term prospects
   (C) retaining a strict monopoly on the production of prerecorded videotapes
   (D) sharing control of the marketing of VHS-format VCR's
   (E) sacrificing technological superiority over Beta-format VCR's in order to remain competitive in price

The best answer is D. VHS producers formed "strategic alliances with other producers and distributors" (lines 10-13) that helped manufacture and market their product, whereas Beta manufacturers "were reluctant to form such alliances and eventually lost ground" (lines 15-16). Choice A is incorrect because it describes the strategy used by Beta producers. Choice B is incorrect because, although VHS producers held an early lead in sales, they did not give up their advantage. Choice C is also incorrect: the passage states that VHS manufacturers took advantage of "[s]trategic alignments with producers of prerecorded tapes" (lines 21-22), but no mention is made of a strict VHS monopoly on such tapes. Choice E is incorrect because the passage does not suggest that VHS producers sacrificed technological superiority over Beta-format VCR's.

99. The alignment of producers of VHS-format VCR's with producers of prerecorded videotapes is most similar to which of the following?

   (A) The alignment of an automobile manufacturer with another automobile manufacturer to adopt a standard design for automobile engines
   (B) The alignment of an automobile manufacturer with an automotive glass company whereby the manufacturer agrees to purchase automobile windshields only from that one glass company
   (C) The alignment of an automobile manufacturer with a petroleum company to ensure the widespread availability of the fuel required by a new type of engine developed by the manufacturer
   (D) The alignment of an automobile manufacturer with its dealers to adopt a plan to improve automobile design
   (E) The alignment of an automobile dealer with an automobile rental chain to adopt a strategy for an advertising campaign to promote a new type of automobile

The best answer is C. The alliances formed by VHS producers with videotape manufacturers created partnerships between companies whose products were mutually interdependent. Choice C, an alignment with the producer of a complementary product that is necessary for the original product to function correctly, offers the closest analogy. An alignment between manufacturers of competing products (A) is not analogous, nor is an alignment with a parts manufacturer (B). Choices D and E describe alignments with companies that distribute and market the product and are similar to some of the strategic alliances formed by VHS producers, but not to their alignment with videotape producers.

100. Which of the following best describes the relation of the first paragraph to the passage as a whole?

   (A) It makes a general observation to be exemplified.
   (B) It outlines a process to be analyzed.
   (C) It poses a question to be answered.
   (D) It advances an argument to be disputed.
   (E) It introduces conflicting arguments to be reconciled.

The best answer is A. In the first paragraph, the author presents a general observation about contemporary business; the rest of the passage narrates a specific series of recent events concerning two companies in particular. The story of these companies serves as an example that illustrates the observation being made in the first paragraph of the passage. Choices B, C, and E can be eliminated because the author does not describe a process, pose any questions, or introduce conflicting arguments. Although the passage does advance an argument, the author does not anticipate that the conclusions being drawn will be disputed, so choice D is also incorrect.

Questions 101-106 refer to the passage on page 352.

101. According to the passage, which of the following is a characteristic that distinguishes electroreceptors from tactile receptors?

   (A) The manner in which electroreceptors respond to electrical stimuli
   (B) The tendency of electroreceptors to be found in clusters
   (C) The unusual locations in which electroreceptors are found in most species
   (D) The amount of electrical stimulation required to excite electroreceptors
   (E) The amount of nervous activity transmitted to the brain by electroreceptors when they are excited

The best answer is D. According to the passage, the electroreceptors in the snouts of spiny anteaters respond to extremely weak electrical fields. In lines 7-11, the author of the passage contrasts these electroreceptors with tactile receptors, stating that it takes field strengths "about 1,000 times greater than those known to excite electroreceptors" to excite the tactile receptors on an anteater's snout. The passage does not contrast the two types of receptors with regard to the characteristics mentioned in choices A, B, C, and E.

102. Which of the following can be inferred about the experiment described in the first paragraph?

(A) Researchers had difficulty verifying the existence of electroreceptors in the anteater because electroreceptors respond to such a narrow range of electrical field strengths.
(B) Researchers found that the level of nervous activity in the anteater's brain increased dramatically as the strength of the electrical stimulus was increased.
(C) Researchers found that some areas of the anteater's snout were not sensitive to a weak electrical stimulus.
(D) Researchers found that the anteater's tactile receptors were more easily excited by a strong electrical stimulus than were the electroreceptors.
(E) Researchers tested small areas of the anteater's snout in order to ensure that only electroreceptors were responding to the stimulus.

The best answer is C. In the experiment described in the first passage, researchers described the electroreceptors in the anteater's snout as "clustered" at the tip. Thus, it can be inferred that nervous activity was not recorded across the entire snout, but only in certain areas. Therefore, some areas of the snout, including those containing the tactile receptors, were not stimulated by the weak fields used in the experiment, as choice C suggests. There is no information in the description of the experiment provided in the passage to suggest A, B, D, or E.

103. The author of the passage most probably discusses the function of tactile receptors (lines 7-11) in order to

(A) eliminate an alternative explanation of anteaters' response to electrical stimuli
(B) highlight a type of sensory organ that has a function identical to that of electroreceptors
(C) point out a serious complication in the research on electroreceptors in anteaters
(D) suggest that tactile receptors assist electroreceptors in the detection of electrical signals
(E) introduce a factor that was not addressed in the research on electroreceptors in anteaters

The best answer is A. Because tactile receptors also respond to electrical stimulation, the researchers' conclusion that electroreceptors exist is valid only if it can be demonstrated that the nervous activity recorded in the anteater's brain did not originate in the tactile receptors. There is no indication in the passage that tactile receptors function like electroreceptors (B) or that tactile receptors assist electroreceptors (D). There is no information in the passage to suggest that the presence of tactile receptors complicated research on electroreceptors, so C is not correct. Choice E is not correct because the information in lines 7-11 is presented in addition to information about the experiment and not as a criticism or to point out an omission.

104. Which of the following can be inferred about anteaters from the behavioral experiment mentioned in the second paragraph?

(A) They are unable to distinguish between stimuli detected by their electroreceptors and stimuli detected by their tactile receptors.
(B) They are unable to distinguish between the electrical signals emanating from termite mounds and those emanating from ant nests.
(C) They can be trained to recognize consistently the presence of a particular stimulus.
(D) They react more readily to strong than to weak stimuli.
(E) They are more efficient at detecting stimuli in a controlled environment than in a natural environment.

The best answer is C. Lines 14-17 state that anteaters were "successfully trained" by researchers "to distinguish between two troughs of water," only one of which had an electrical field. Choices A, B, D, and E can be eliminated because they present hypotheses about anteater behavior that were not tested in the experiment and are not discussed in the passage.

105. The passage suggests that the researchers mentioned in the second paragraph who observed anteaters break into a nest of ants would most likely agree with which of the following statements?

(A) The event they observed provides conclusive evidence that anteaters use their electroreceptors to locate unseen prey.
(B) The event they observed was atypical and may not reflect the usual hunting practices of anteaters.
(C) It is likely that the anteaters located the ants' nesting chambers without the assistance of electroreceptors.
(D) Anteaters possess a very simple sensory system for use in locating prey.
(E) The speed with which the anteaters located their prey is greater than what might be expected on the basis of chance alone.

The best answer is E. The last sentence in the passage implies that the researchers believed that the anteaters' locating of their unseen prey was too prompt and too deliberate to be accidental. Choice A is incorrect: researchers were unable to confirm that the anteaters' favorite prey, termites, emitted electrical signals, and the observation of anteaters locating ants' nesting chambers "suggests" (line 25), rather than proves conclusively, that anteaters use their electroreceptors to find prey. Choice B is incorrect because there is no indication in the passage that researchers believed that the anteaters' behavior was atypical. Choice C is incorrect because, according to lines 24-27, the researchers believed that the anteaters "were using their electroreceptors to locate the nesting chambers." Choice D is contradicted by the passage: in line 13, the anteater's sensory system is described as "sophisticated."

106. Which of the following, if true, would most strengthen the hypothesis mentioned in lines 17-19 ?

    (A) Researchers are able to train anteaters to break into an underground chamber that is emitting a strong electrical signal.
    (B) Researchers are able to detect a weak electrical signal emanating from the nesting chamber of an ant colony.
    (C) Anteaters are observed taking increasingly longer amounts of time to locate the nesting chambers of ants.
    (D) Anteaters are observed using various angles to break into nests of ants.
    (E) Anteaters are observed using the same angle used with nests of ants to break into the nests of other types of prey.

The best answer is B. The researchers' hypothesis is "that anteaters use electroreceptors to detect electrical signals given off by prey." Evidence that electrical signals emanate from the nesting chamber of an ant colony—on which anteaters are known to prey—would strengthen the hypothesis. Choice C may actually weaken the hypothesis: the passage implies that the rapidity with which anteaters were able to locate ants' nesting chambers suggested to researchers that anteaters were using electroreceptors to locate prey. Choices A, D, and E provide evidence that does not strengthen the hypothesis.

Questions 107-112 refer to the passage on page 354.

107. According to the passage, by 1935 the skepticism of Black workers toward unions was

    (A) unchanged except among Black employees of railroad-related industries
    (B) reinforced by the actions of the Pullman Company's union
    (C) mitigated by the efforts of Randolph
    (D) weakened by the opening up of many unions to Black workers
    (E) largely alleviated because of the policies of the American Federation of Labor

The best answer is C. According to lines 8-10 of the passage, Randolph's efforts to obtain recognition for the Brotherhood of Sleeping Car Porters, a goal achieved in 1935, "helped transform the attitude of Black workers toward unions." Lines 14-15 state that prior to 1935 that attitude was one of skepticism. Therefore, the passage indicates that the workers' skepticism was diminished as a result of Randolph's work. Choice A is incorrect because the passage does not indicate that the attitudes among Black workers in other industries toward unions remained unchanged by 1935. Choice B is incorrect because the passage does not state that the actions of the Pullman Company's union made Black workers more skeptical of unions by 1935. No information is given in the passage to support either D or E.

108. In using the word "understandable" (line 14), the author most clearly conveys

    (A) sympathy with attempts by the Brotherhood between 1925 and 1935 to establish an independent union
    (B) concern that the obstacles faced by Randolph between 1925 and 1935 were indeed formidable
    (C) ambivalence about the significance of unions to most Black workers in the 1920's
    (D) appreciation of the attitude of many Black workers in the 1920's toward unions
    (E) regret at the historical attitude of unions toward Black workers

The best answer is D. In lines 14-16, the author of the passage describes the skepticism of Black workers toward unions, "which had historically barred Black workers from membership," as "understandable," thus conveying an appreciation that the attitude of Black workers had a legitimate basis. Choices A and B can be eliminated because they concern Randolph and the Brotherhood rather than the attitude of the workers mentioned in line 14. Choice C is incorrect because the author expresses no ambivalence about the significance of unions to Black workers. Choice E is incorrect because the word "understandable" is used in the passage to describe the attitude of the Black workers rather than the historical attitude of unions toward Black workers.

109. The passage suggests which of the following about the response of porters to the Pullman Company's own union?

    (A) Few porters ever joined this union.
    (B) Some porters supported this union before 1935.
    (C) Porters, more than other Pullman employees, enthusiastically supported this union.
    (D) The porters' response was most positive after 1935.
    (E) The porters' response was unaffected by the general skepticism of Black workers concerning unions.

The best answer is B. Lines 16-19 of the passage state that the existence of a Pullman-owned union "weakened support among Black workers for an independent entity" such as Randolph's Brotherhood of Sleeping Car Porters. Thus, the passage suggests that some porters did support the Pullman Company union. Lines 16-19 directly contradict A, which implies virtually no support of the Pullman company union. Choice C is incorrect because the passage does not suggest anything about Pullman employees other than porters. Choice D is incorrect: in fact, the passage suggests that the porters' attitude was less positive after Randolph's union achieved recognition in 1935. Choice E is incorrect because the passage nowhere suggests that the general skepticism of Black workers had no effect on their response to the Pullman Company's union.

110. The passage suggests that if the grievances of porters in one part of the United States had been different from those of porters in another part of the country, which of the following would have been the case?

(A) It would have been more difficult for the Pullman Company to have had a single labor policy.
(B) It would have been more difficult for the Brotherhood to control its channels of communication.
(C) It would have been more difficult for the Brotherhood to build its membership.
(D) It would have been easier for the Pullman Company's union to attract membership.
(E) It would have been easier for the Brotherhood to threaten strikes.

The best answer is C. The passage indicates that it was an advantage to Randolph in building the Brotherhood's membership that Black workers shared "the same grievances from city to city" (lines 32-33), suggesting that it would have been more difficult to build the membership of the Brotherhood if Black workers in different parts of the country had had different grievances. There is no information in the passage to support A, B, D, and E.

111. The passage suggests that in the 1920's a company in the United States was able to

(A) use its own funds to set up a union
(B) require its employees to join the company's own union
(C) develop a single labor policy for all its employees with little employee dissent
(D) pressure its employees to contribute money to maintain the company's own union
(E) use its resources to prevent the passage of federal legislation that would have facilitated the formation of independent unions

The best answer is A. Lines 34-38 indicate that in the early 1930's it became illegal for a company to maintain its own union with company funds. Thus, the passage suggests that prior to the 1930's a company was permitted to fund its own union. Choices B, C, D, and E describe practices that are not implied in the passage.

112. The passage supplies information concerning which of the following matters related to Randolph?

(A) The steps he took to initiate the founding of the Brotherhood
(B) His motivation for bringing the Brotherhood into the American Federation of Labor
(C) The influence he had on the passage of legislation overturning race restrictions in 1944
(D) The influence he had on the passage of legislation to bar companies from financing their own unions
(E) The success he and the Brotherhood had in influencing the policies of the other unions in the American Federation of Labor

The best answer is B. Lines 42-44 state Randolph's reason for bringing the Brotherhood into the American Federation of Labor: "as a member union, the Brotherhood would be in a better position to exert pressure on member unions that practiced race restrictions." No information is given in the passage to support choices A, C, D, and E.

Questions 113-118 refer to the passage on page 356.

113. The primary function of the passage as a whole is to

(A) account for the popularity of a practice
(B) evaluate the utility of a practice
(C) demonstrate how to institute a practice
(D) weigh the ethics of using a strategy
(E) explain the reasons for pursuing a strategy

The best answer is B. The passage describes a marketing strategy practiced by some professional service firms, outlines the arguments in favor of its use, and then describes the drawbacks associated with the strategy. Choice A is incorrect because the popularity of the practice is not discussed in the passage. Choice C is incorrect because the passage does not include a demonstration of how to institute unconditional guarantees. Choice D is incorrect because ethical issues are not addressed by the author. In the first paragraph, the author does give reasons for why firms pursue the strategy, but that is not the purpose of the passage as a whole, so E is also incorrect.

114. All of the following are mentioned in the passage as circumstances in which professional service firms can benefit from offering an unconditional guarantee EXCEPT:

(A) The firm is having difficulty retaining its clients of long standing.
(B) The firm is having difficulty getting business through client recommendations.
(C) The firm charges substantial fees for its services.
(D) The adverse effects of poor performance by the firm are significant for the client.
(E) The client is reluctant to incur risk.

The best answer is A. In lines 7-8, the passage explicitly states that offering unconditional guarantees works best with first-time clients, but no mention is made of the relative success of this practice with clients of long standing. The circumstances referred to in B, C, D, and E are mentioned in lines 8-12 of the passage.

115. Which of the following is cited in the passage as a goal of some professional service firms in offering unconditional guarantees of satisfaction?

   (A) A limit on the firm's liability
   (B) Successful competition against other firms
   (C) Ability to justify fee increases
   (D) Attainment of an outstanding reputation in a field
   (E) Improvement in the quality of the firm's service

The best answer is B. In lines 1-4, the author states that firms offering unconditional guarantees are "seeking a competitive advantage." Choices A, C, and E can be eliminated because no mention is made in the passage of liability limits, justification for fee increases, or improvement of service as objectives in offering unconditional guarantees. Choice D is incorrect because the passage does not associate the offering of unconditional guarantees with the attainment of an outstanding reputation.

116. The passage's description of the issue raised by unconditional guarantees for health care or legal services most clearly implies that which of the following is true?

   (A) The legal and medical professions have standards of practice that would be violated by attempts to fulfill such unconditional guarantees.
   (B) The result of a lawsuit or medical procedure cannot necessarily be determined in advance by the professionals handling a client's case.
   (C) The dignity of the legal and medical professions is undermined by any attempts at marketing of professional services, including unconditional guarantees.
   (D) Clients whose lawsuits or medical procedures have unsatisfactory outcomes cannot be adequately compensated by financial settlements alone.
   (E) Predicting the monetary cost of legal or health care services is more difficult than predicting the monetary cost of other types of professional services.

The best answer is B. The passage states that a guarantee "may mislead clients by suggesting that lawsuits or medical procedures will have guaranteed outcomes" (lines 20-22). This implies that legal and medical outcomes cannot be predicted with absolute certainty. Although the statements in A, C, D, and E could be true, none of these statements is implied by the description in lines 20-22 of the passage.

117. Which of the following hypothetical situations best exemplifies the potential problem noted in the second sentence of the second paragraph (lines 14-17) ?

   (A) A physician's unconditional guarantee of satisfaction encourages patients to sue for malpractice if they are unhappy with the treatment they receive.
   (B) A lawyer's unconditional guarantee of satisfaction makes clients suspect that the lawyer needs to find new clients quickly to increase the firm's income.
   (C) A business consultant's unconditional guarantee of satisfaction is undermined when the consultant fails to provide all of the services that are promised.
   (D) An architect's unconditional guarantee of satisfaction makes clients wonder how often the architect's buildings fail to please clients.
   (E) An accountant's unconditional guarantee of satisfaction leads clients to believe that tax returns prepared by the accountant are certain to be accurate.

The best answer is D. Lines 14-17 state that an unconditional guarantee "may, paradoxically, cause clients to doubt the service firm's ability to deliver the promised level of service." In D, an architect's unconditional guarantee leads prospective clients to wonder whether previous clients have been satisfied with that architect's work, a situation that exemplifies the paradox described in the passage. Choice A describes a problem that would occur after a service has been rendered. Similarly, in C, a guaranteed service has actually been judged unsatisfactory. Choice B exemplifies the situation described in lines 18-19 of the passage: guarantees may suggest that a firm is "begging for business." Choice E is incorrect because it presents a situation that is the reverse of the potential problem mentioned in the passage.

118. The passage most clearly implies which of the following about the professional service firms mentioned in line 22 ?

(A) They are unlikely to have offered unconditional guarantees of satisfaction in the past.
(B) They are usually profitable enough to be able to compensate clients according to the terms of an unconditional guarantee.
(C) They usually practice in fields in which the outcomes are predictable.
(D) Their fees are usually more affordable than those charged by other professional service firms.
(E) Their clients are usually already satisfied with the quality of service that is delivered.

The best answer is E. The passage states in lines 22-24 that "professional service firms with outstanding reputations and performance to match have little to gain from offering unconditional guarantees." If a firm has an outstanding reputation based on a high level of performance, it is likely that its clients are satisfied with the quality of service that is delivered. Choice A is not implied: the passage indicates that the author believes that firms with outstanding reputations have little to gain from offering unconditional guarantees, but the passage implies nothing about whether such firms either currently offer guarantees or have offered them in the past. The passage does not provide information concerning the profitability (B) or the fees charged by highly reputed firms (D). In addition, it does not suggest that such firms practice in fields in which outcomes are predictable (C).

Questions 119-124 refer to the passage on page 358.

119. The passage suggests that a lack of modern sanitation would make which of the following most likely to occur?

(A) An outbreak of Lyme disease
(B) An outbreak of dengue hemorrhagic fever
(C) An epidemic of typhoid
(D) An epidemic of paralytic polio among infants
(E) An epidemic of paralytic polio among adolescents and adults

The best answer is C. Line 13 states that modern hygiene practices prevented the spread of typhoid, suggesting that if modern sanitation were discontinued, the likelihood of a typhoid epidemic would increase. Choices A and B can be eliminated because the passage ties Lyme disease and dengue hemorrhagic fever to animal carriers rather than to lack of hygiene. Choice D is incorrect because, according to lines 10-12, polio in infants does not typically cause paralysis. Choice E is incorrect because if modern sanitation is not practiced, polio immunity is acquired during infancy.

120. According to the passage, the outbreak of dengue hemorrhagic fever in the 1950's occurred for which of the following reasons?

(A) The mosquito *Aedes aegypti* was newly introduced into Asia.
(B) The mosquito *Aedes aegypti* became more numerous.
(C) The mosquito *Aedes albopictus* became infected with the dengue virus.
(D) Individuals who would normally acquire immunity to the dengue virus as infants were not infected until later in life.
(E) More people began to visit and inhabit areas in which mosquitos live and breed.

The best answer is B. Lines 22-26 of the passage state that the dengue hemorrhagic fever outbreak occurred when *Aedes aegypti* began to proliferate as a result of ecological changes. Choice A is incorrect because the passage implies that the mosquito was already present in Asia in the 1950's. Choice C can be eliminated because the 1950's epidemic is attributed by the author to *Aedes aegypti*, not *Aedes albopictus*. Choices D and E suggest possibilities mentioned in the passage as causes for epidemics of other diseases but not of dengue hemorrhagic fever.

121. It can be inferred from the passage that Lyme disease has become prevalent in parts of the United States because of which of the following?

(A) The inadvertent introduction of Lyme disease bacteria to the United States
(B) The inability of modern sanitation methods to eradicate Lyme disease bacteria
(C) A genetic mutation in Lyme disease bacteria that makes them more virulent
(D) The spread of Lyme disease bacteria from infected humans to noninfected humans
(E) An increase in the number of humans who encounter deer ticks

The best answer is E. The passage mentions two reasons for the rise in the prevalence of Lyme disease: an increase in the number of deer and thus of the number of the deer ticks that carry the bacteria, and the proliferation of human activity in the deer's habitat, suggesting that contact between humans and deer ticks has increased significantly since the late nineteenth century. No mention is made of the transmission of Lyme disease bacteria to the United States, or of any genetic mutations in the bacteria, so A and C can be eliminated. Choice B is incorrect because the passage does not suggest that any attempt was made to eradicate Lyme disease through better sanitation. Choice D is incorrect because the passage describes only deer ticks as a source of the Lyme disease bacterium, not infected humans.

122. Which of the following can most reasonably be concluded about the mosquito *Aedes albopictus* on the basis of information given in the passage?

(A) It is native to the United States.
(B) It can proliferate only in Asia.
(C) It transmits the dengue virus.
(D) It caused an epidemic of dengue hemorrhagic fever in the 1950's.
(E) It replaced *Aedes aegypti* in Asia when ecological changes altered *Aedes aegypti's* habitat.

The best answer is C. Lines 26-29 state that the presence of *Aedes albopictus* creates the risk of a dengue epidemic, thus implying strongly that the mosquito is a carrier of the disease. Choices A and B are directly contradicted by the passage, which states that the mosquito was introduced into the United States inadvertently and that it has proliferated widely there. The passage attributes the dengue epidemic of the 1950's to *Aedes aegypti,* not *Aedes albopictus,* making choice D incorrect. Choice E is incorrect because the passage does not discuss the ecological relationship between the two mosquitoes.

123. Which of the following best describes the organization of the passage?

(A) A paradox is stated, discussed, and left unresolved.
(B) Two opposing explanations are presented, argued, and reconciled.
(C) A theory is proposed and is then followed by descriptions of three experiments that support the theory.
(D) A generalization is stated and is then followed by three instances that support the generalization.
(E) An argument is described and is then followed by three counterexamples that refute the argument.

The best answer is D. The passage begins with a general statement that epidemics can occur without genetic changes in the bacteria and viruses that cause them, and then presents three instances of epidemics that did not have their origins in genetic changes. Choices C and E are incorrect because the passage does not describe experiments or provide counter-examples to refute an argument. Choices A and B do not accurately describe the organization of the passage.

124. Which of the following, if true, would most strengthen the author's assertion about the cause of the Lyme disease outbreak in the United States?

(A) The deer population was smaller in the late nineteenth century than in the mid-twentieth century.
(B) Interest in outdoor recreation began to grow in the late nineteenth century.
(C) In recent years the suburbs have stopped growing.
(D) Outdoor recreation enthusiasts routinely take measures to protect themselves against Lyme disease.
(E) Scientists have not yet developed a vaccine that can prevent Lyme disease.

The best answer is A. The author asserts that the recent high incidence of Lyme disease can be attributed to an increase in the deer population. The author's assertion would be supported if it were to be shown that the deer population was lower in the late nineteenth century, when the incidence of Lyme disease was sporadic. Choice B is incorrect because it does not provide information clearly supporting the author's assertion that Lyme disease increased as a result of an increase of the deer population and an increase in outdoor recreational activities in the deer's habitat. Choice C, if true, could actually weaken the author's argument that the outbreak of Lyme disease is related to the growth of the suburbs. Choices D and E are incorrect because they are not relevant to what the author claims has caused the recent outbreak of Lyme disease.

Questions 125-130 refer to the passage on page 360.

125. The author of the passage alludes to the well-established nature of the concept of individual rights in the Anglo-Saxon legal and political tradition in order to

   (A) illustrate the influence of individualist feminist thought on more general intellectual trends in English history

   (B) argue that feminism was already a part of the larger Anglo-Saxon intellectual tradition, even though this has often gone unnoticed by critics of women's emancipation

   (C) explain the decline in individualist thinking among feminists in non-English-speaking countries

   (D) help account for an increasing shift toward individualist feminism among feminists in English-speaking countries

   (E) account for the philosophical differences between individualist and relational feminists in English-speaking countries

The best answer is D. In lines 18-26, the author states that relational feminism "lost ground" in England and the United States while individualist feminism came to predominate, as a result of the well-established concept of individual rights. Choice A is incorrect: lines 22-26 of the passage suggest that individualist feminism was influenced by broader trends in English legal and political tradition. Choice B can be eliminated: the passage does not suggest that feminism was part of the Anglo-Saxon tradition. Choice C is incorrect: individualist feminism is described in lines 18-26 of the passage as growing, not declining. Choice E is incorrect because, although individualist and relational feminists did have philosophical differences, the author does not mention the Anglo-Saxon legal and political tradition in order to account for these differences.

126. The passage suggests that the author of the passage believes which of the following?

   (A) The predominance of individualist feminism in English-speaking countries is a historical phenomenon, the causes of which have not yet been investigated.

   (B) The individualist and relational feminist views are irreconcilable, given their theoretical differences concerning the foundations of society.

   (C) A consensus concerning the direction of future feminist politics will probably soon emerge, given the awareness among feminists of the need for cooperation among women.

   (D) Political adversaries of feminism often misuse arguments predicated on differences between the sexes to argue that the existing social system should be maintained.

   (E) Relational feminism provides the best theoretical framework for contemporary feminist politics, but individualist feminism could contribute much toward refining and strengthening modern feminist thought.

The best answer is D. In lines 38-41 of the passage, the author contends that a significant liability of relational arguments is that "because they underline women's physiological and psychological distinctiveness, they are often appropriated by political adversaries and used to endorse male privilege." Therefore, D states an idea with which the author would likely concur. Choice A is contradicted by the passage: the author attributes the predominance of individualist feminism in English-speaking countries to Anglo-Saxon legal and political tradition. Choice B is incorrect: the passage does not suggest that the author believes that individualist and relational feminism have views concerning the foundations of society that prevent their eventual reconciliation. There is no indication in the passage that the author would be likely to agree with the statements given in C and E.

127. It can be inferred from the passage that the individualist feminist tradition denies the validity of which of the following causal statements?

   (A) A division of labor in a social group can result in increased efficiency with regard to the performance of group tasks.

   (B) A division of labor in a social group causes inequities in the distribution of opportunities and benefits among group members.

   (C) A division of labor on the basis of gender in a social group is necessitated by the existence of sex-linked biological differences between male and female members of the group.

   (D) Culturally determined distinctions based on gender in a social group foster the existence of differing attitudes and opinions among group members.

   (E) Educational programs aimed at reducing inequalities based on gender among members of a social group can result in a sense of greater well-being for all members of the group.

The best answer is C. In lines 5-8, the author states that relational feminists "posit that biological distinctions between the sexes result in a necessary sexual division of labor." In lines 10-15, when describing the individualist feminist philosophy, the author begins with the phrase "by contrast," thus implying that the position taken by relational feminists on a necessary gender-based division of labor is not accepted in the individualist feminist tradition. In line 13, the author further states that individualist feminists downplay the importance of gender roles. Nothing in the passage suggests that individualist feminists would disagree with the statements in A, B, D, and E.

128. According to the passage, relational feminists and individualist feminists agree that

(A) individual human rights take precedence over most other social claims
(B) the gender-based division of labor in society should be eliminated
(C) laws guaranteeing equal treatment for all citizens regardless of gender should be passed
(D) a greater degree of social awareness concerning the importance of motherhood would be beneficial to society
(E) the same educational and economic opportunities should be available to both sexes

The best answer is E. Lines 28-29 indicate that individualist feminists advocate equal rights for all. Lines 30-32 go on to state that relational feminists agree that "equal educational and economic opportunities outside the home should be available for all women." Choices A and B are incorrect because the passage suggests that they are beliefs held only by individualist feminists. Choice C represents a belief with which relational feminists disagree, and D represents a belief with which only relational feminists would agree.

129. According to the author, which of the following was true of feminist thought in Western societies before 1890 ?

(A) Individualist feminist arguments were not found in the thought or writing of non-English-speaking feminists.
(B) Individualist feminism was a strain in feminist thought, but another strain, relational feminism, predominated.
(C) Relational and individualist approaches were equally prevalent in feminist thought and writing.
(D) The predominant view among feminists held that the welfare of women was ultimately less important than the welfare of children.
(E) The predominant view among feminists held that the sexes should receive equal treatment under the law.

The best answer is B. In lines 16-20, the passage states that prior to the late nineteenth century, relational feminism and individualist feminism "coexisted within the feminist movement" but that relational feminism was the "dominant strain." Choices A and C are contradicted by lines 16-20. There is no information in the passage to support the statements presented in D and E.

130. The author implies that which of the following was true of most feminist thinkers in England and the United States after 1920 ?

(A) They were less concerned with politics than with intellectual issues.
(B) They began to reach a broader audience and their programs began to be adopted by mainstream political parties.
(C) They called repeatedly for international cooperation among women's groups to achieve their goals.
(D) They moderated their initial criticism of the economic systems that characterized their societies.
(E) They did not attempt to unite the two different feminist approaches in their thought.

The best answer is E. In lines 22-28, the passage states that, between 1890 and 1920, individualist feminism became predominant among feminists in England and the United States, and that the "goals of the two approaches began to seem increasingly irreconcilable." The discussion that follows suggests that the two schools of thought continued to remain separate and that no attempt was being made to unite them. In lines 46-50, the author concludes by suggesting a way that relational and individualist feminism could be harmonized. Choices A, B, C, and D are not suggested by information presented in the passage.

Questions 131-136 refer to the passage on page 362.

131. The primary purpose of the passage is to

(A) enumerate reasons why both traditional scholarly methods and newer scholarly methods have limitations
(B) identify a shortcoming in a scholarly approach and describe an alternative approach
(C) provide empirical data to support a long-held scholarly assumption
(D) compare two scholarly publications on the basis of their authors' backgrounds
(E) attempt to provide a partial answer to a long-standing scholarly dilemma

The best answer is B. The first paragraph states that reliance on techniques that overlooked the political activities of women was a shortcoming shared by traditional political historians and the new school of political history that emerged in the 1960's and 1970's. The second paragraph describes an alternative approach that overcomes this shortcoming. Choice A can be eliminated because the passage discusses only one reason why both traditional and some new approaches were limited. Because the passage does not discuss a long-held assumption, authors' backgrounds, or a long-standing scholarly dilemma, C, D, and E can be eliminated.

132. The passage suggests which of the following concerning the techniques used by the new political historians described in the first paragraph of the passage?

(A) They involved the extensive use of the biographies of political party leaders and political theoreticians.
(B) They were conceived by political historians who were reacting against the political climates of the 1960's and 1970's.
(C) They were of more use in analyzing the positions of United States political parties in the nineteenth century than in analyzing the positions of those in the twentieth century.
(D) They were of more use in analyzing the political behavior of nineteenth-century voters than in analyzing the political activities of those who could not vote during that period.
(E) They were devised as a means of tracing the influence of nineteenth-century political trends on twentieth-century political trends.

The best answer is D. Lines 6-11 provide an example of the techniques used by the new political historians—quantitative analyses of election returns—and state that these techniques were unsuited for analyzing the political activities of women, who could not vote in the nineteenth century. This suggests that, in general, the techniques used by these historians were of more use in analyzing the political behavior of nineteenth-century voters than in analyzing the political activities of those who could not vote during that period. Choice A can be eliminated because the first sentence of the passage states that the new historians sought to go beyond a focus on leaders. There is no information in the passage to support B, C, or E.

133. It can be inferred that the author of the passage quotes Baker directly in the second paragraph primarily in order to

(A) clarify a position before providing an alternative to that position
(B) differentiate between a novel definition and traditional definitions
(C) provide an example of a point agreed on by different generations of scholars
(D) provide an example of the prose style of an important historian
(E) amplify a definition given in the first paragraph

The best answer is B. The first paragraph suggests that political activity had been defined in terms of voting, party politics, and office holding, whereas the second paragraph indicates that Baker broadened the definition to include any action influencing government or community issues. Thus, the author's direct quotation serves to display the difference between Baker's definition and more traditional definitions. Because no alternative view is discussed after the discussion of Baker's, A can be eliminated. Choice C is incorrect because, as the passage indicates, the definition offered by Baker is not one on which different generations of scholars agree. Choice D can be eliminated because the author displays no interest in Baker's prose style. Choice E is incorrect because no definition like Baker's is discussed in the first paragraph.

134. According to the passage, Paula Baker and the new political historians of the 1960's and 1970's shared which of the following?

(A) A commitment to interest-group politics
(B) A disregard for political theory and ideology
(C) An interest in the ways in which nineteenth-century politics prefigured contemporary politics
(D) A reliance on such quantitative techniques as the analysis of election returns
(E) An emphasis on the political involvement of ordinary citizens

The best answer is E. The first sentence of the passage states that the new historians of the 1960's and 1970's examined the political practices of ordinary citizens, and the second paragraph recounts how Baker extended this examination to include the political activities of ordinary women. Choice A is incorrect because the passage implies that the new historians failed to examine interest groups. The passage does not provide information to support B. Choice C can be eliminated because only Baker is described as displaying an interest in a way in which nineteenth-century politics prefigured contemporary politics. Because the second paragraph emphasizes that Baker did not rely primarily on quantitative techniques such as the analysis of election returns, D is incorrect.

135. Which of the following best describes the structure of the first paragraph of the passage?

(A) Two scholarly approaches are compared, and a shortcoming common to both is identified.
(B) Two rival schools of thought are contrasted, and a third is alluded to.
(C) An outmoded scholarly approach is described, and a corrective approach is called for.
(D) An argument is outlined, and counterarguments are mentioned.
(E) A historical era is described in terms of its political trends.

The best answer is A. The first sentence of the paragraph compares the traditional approach of political historians with the approach of the school that emerged in the 1960's and 1970's, and the remainder of the paragraph identifies a shortcoming shared by both approaches, namely, a reliance on techniques unsuited for examining the political activities of women. Since no third group of historians and no corrective approach are discussed in the first paragraph, B and C are incorrect. Choices D and E do not describe the structure of the first paragraph.

136. The information in the passage suggests that a pre-1960's political historian would have been most likely to undertake which of the following studies?

(A) An analysis of voting trends among women voters of the 1920's
(B) A study of male voters' gradual ideological shift from party politics to issue-oriented politics
(C) A biography of an influential nineteenth-century minister of foreign affairs
(D) An analysis of narratives written by previously unrecognized women activists
(E) A study of voting trends among naturalized immigrant laborers in a nineteenth-century logging camp

The best answer is C. The first sentence of the passage implies that prior to the 1960's, political historians tended to focus on leaders and institutions. A biography of an influential nineteenth-century minister of foreign affairs thus would have been a typical project for a political historian prior to the 1960's. Choices A and E are incorrect because the first sentence implies that traditional historians tended not to focus on ordinary citizens. Choices B and D are incorrect for the additional reason that, as the first paragraph makes clear, traditional historians employed techniques that were unsuited for the study of the sorts of activities described in these choices.

Questions 137-143 refer to the passage on page 364.

137. The passage is primarily concerned with discussing

(A) the importance of determining the age of globular clusters in assessing when the Milky Way galaxy was formed
(B) recent changes in the procedures used by astronomers to study the formation of the Milky Way galaxy
(C) current disputes among astronomers regarding the size and form of the Milky Way galaxy
(D) the effect of new discoveries regarding globular clusters on theories about the formation of the Milky Way galaxy
(E) the origin, nature, and significance of groups of stars known as globular clusters

The best answer is D. The first sentence of the passage states: "New observations about the age of some globular clusters in our Milky Way galaxy have cast doubt on a long-held theory about how the galaxy was formed." The second paragraph describes this long-held theory, and the third paragraph describes the new findings. The final paragraph discusses the effect of these new findings on theorizing about the formation of the galaxy. Choices A and E are incorrect—although globular clusters are discussed in the passage, they are not the primary focus. Choices B and C refer to topics not discussed in the passage.

138. According to the passage, one way in which Larson's theory and the conventional theory of the formation of the Milky Way galaxy differ is in their assessment of the

(A) amount of time it took to form the galaxy
(B) size of the galaxy immediately after its formation
(C) particular gases involved in the formation of the galaxy
(D) importance of the age of globular clusters in determining how the galaxy was formed
(E) shape of the halo that formed around the galaxy

The best answer is A. Lines 12-15 indicate that, according to the conventional theory, the galaxy "formed over a relatively short time (about 200 million years)." Lines 29-32 state that, according to Larson's theory, the halo of the galaxy "formed over a period of a billion or more years." Choice D is incorrect because it can be inferred from the passage that these theories are both based on the assumption that the age of globular clusters is important in determining how the galaxy was formed. Since the passage does not indicate any position taken by the conventional theory on the original shape of the halo, E can be eliminated. The passage does not provide any information about the factors mentioned in B and C.

139. Which of the following, if true, would be most useful in supporting the conclusions drawn from recent observations about globular clusters?

(A) There is firm evidence that the absolute age of the Milky Way galaxy is between 10 and 17 billion years.
(B) A survey reveals that a galaxy close to the Milky Way galaxy contains globular clusters of ages close to the age of Palomar 12.
(C) A mathematical model proves that small gas clouds move in regular patterns.
(D) Space probes indicate that the stars in the Milky Way galaxy are composed of several different types of gas.
(E) A study of over 1,500 individual stars in the halo of the Milky Way galaxy indicates wide discrepancies in their ages.

The best answer is E. The recent observations have to do with the age of globular clusters in the Milky Way galaxy. One conclusion that has been drawn from these observations is that the galaxy may have formed over a long period of time (lines 27-32). The discovery that stars in the halo of the galaxy vary greatly in age would support this conclusion and weaken the conventional theory, which suggests that "all stars in the halo should be very nearly the same age" (lines 18-19). The information contained in the other choices is of little or no relevance to any conclusions drawn from the recent observations.

140. If Bolte and his colleague are both correct, it can be inferred that the globular cluster Palomar 12 is approximately

(A) 5 billion years younger than any other cluster in the galaxy
(B) the same age as most other clusters in the galaxy
(C) 7 billion years younger than another cluster in the galaxy
(D) 12 billion years younger than most other clusters in the galaxy
(E) 2 billion years younger than most other clusters in the galaxy

The best answer is C. Bolte claims that one cluster is 2 billion years older than most other clusters in the galaxy (lines 22-23). The colleague claims that Palomar 12 is 5 billion years younger than most other clusters (lines 24-26). If both claims are correct, Palomar 12 is 7 billion years younger than another cluster in the galaxy. The statement made in A is not implied by the two claims made by Bolte and his colleague, whereas the statements made in B, D, and E are false if the two claims are correct.

141. The passage suggests that Toomre's work complements Larson's theory because it

(A) specifies more precisely the time frame proposed by Larson
(B) subtly alters Larson's theory to make it more plausible
(C) supplements Larson's hypothesis with direct astronomical observations
(D) provides theoretical support for the ideas suggested by Larson
(E) expands Larson's theory to make it more widely applicable

The best answer is D. Larson's theory holds that numerous gas clouds "drifted about, collided, lost orbital energy, and finally collapsed into a centrally condensed elliptical system" (lines 33-35). Toomre's computer modeling apparently indicates a way in which this process could have occurred. The computer modeling thus provides theoretical support for Larson's theory. Nothing in the passage suggests that Toomre's computer modeling does any of the things mentioned in the other choices.

142. Which of the following most accurately states a finding of Bolte's research, as described in the passage?

(A) The globular clusters in the Milky Way galaxy are 2 billion years older than predicted by the conventional theory.
(B) The ages of at least some globular clusters in the Milky Way galaxy differ by at least 4 billion years.
(C) One of the globular clusters in the Milky Way galaxy is 5 billion years younger than most others.
(D) The globular clusters in the Milky Way galaxy are significantly older than the individual stars in the halo.
(E) Most globular clusters in the Milky Way galaxy are between 11 and 15 billion years old.

The best answer is B. Bolte found that one cluster "is 2 billion years older than most other clusters in the galaxy, while another is 2 billion years younger" (lines 22-24). Thus, he found that at least these two clusters differ in age by at least 4 billion years. Choice C is incorrect, because the passage states that it was a colleague of Bolte's who claimed that a cluster is 5 billion years younger than most. The passage does not indicate any finding by Bolte that corresponds to the statements in the other choices.

143. The author of the passage puts the word "renegade" (line 29) in quotation marks most probably in order to

(A) emphasize the lack of support for the theories in question
(B) contrast the controversial quality of the theories in question with the respectable character of their formulators
(C) generate skepticism about the theories in question
(D) ridicule the scientists who once doubted the theories in question
(E) indicate that the theories in question are no longer as unconventional as they once seemed

The best answer is E. To describe a theory as "renegade" is to suggest that it is unconventional. However, the author puts the word "renegade" in quotation marks (line 29) when using it to describe theories that, the author says, are "newly fashionable" (line 29). The use of quotation marks with this word in this way serves to indicate that the theories in question are no longer as unconventional as they once seemed. There is nothing in the passage to suggest that any of the other choices describe goals of the author.

Questions 144-148 refer to the passage on page 366.

144. The primary purpose of the passage is to

(A) advocate more effective strategies for encouraging the development of high-technology enterprises in the United States
(B) contrast the incentives for economic development offered by local governments with those offered by the private sector
(C) acknowledge and counter adverse criticism of programs being used to stimulate local economic development
(D) define and explore promotional efforts used by local governments to attract new industry
(E) review and evaluate strategies and programs that have been used to stimulate economic development

The best answer is E. Each paragraph of the passage describes a strategy or program used by local governments in an attempt to stimulate economic development in their locales. In each case, an evaluation is made of the strategy or program that is discussed. Choices A and D are incorrect because only parts of the passage are concerned with specific strategies focusing on high-technology enterprises or attracting new industry. Since no incentives offered by the private sector are discussed, B can be eliminated. Choice C is incorrect because no attempt is made in the passage to counter the criticisms that are raised against the strategies discussed in the first two paragraphs.

145. The passage suggests which of the following about the majority of United States manufacturing industries before the high-technology development era of the 1980's?

(A) They lost many of their most innovative personnel to small entrepreneurial enterprises.
(B) They experienced a major decline in profits during the 1960's and 1970's.
(C) They could provide real economic benefits to the areas in which they were located.
(D) They employed workers who had no specialized skills.
(E) They actively interfered with local entrepreneurial ventures.

The best answer is C. The final sentence of the first paragraph suggests that, during the 1960's and 1970's, a town that attracted a manufacturer thereby achieved a "triumph" (line 9), whereas a town losing one of these industries suffered a "tragedy" (line 10). It is thus suggested that the majority of these industries prior to the 1980's could provide real economic benefits to the areas in which they were located. Choice D can be eliminated, because although the last sentence of the second paragraph suggests that manufacturing industries prior to the 1980's did not limit their employment to a specially trained fraction of manufacturing workers, it does not suggest that the majority of these industries employed workers who had no specialized skills. Nothing in the passage suggests any of the statements made in A, B, and E.

146. The tone of the passage suggests that the author is most optimistic about the economic development potential of which of the following groups?

(A) Local governments
(B) High-technology promoters
(C) Local entrepreneurs
(D) Manufacturing-industry managers
(E) Economic development strategists

The best answer is C. The first two paragraphs describe shortcomings of the strategies of attracting manufacturing industries and high-technology industries, and the third paragraph describes the advantages, and mentions no disadvantages, of promoting small businesses run by local entrepreneurs. Thus, the author appears to be most optimistic about the economic development potential of local entrepreneurs. The passage's tone does not indicate that the author is more optimistic about groups mentioned in A, B, D, and E than about local entrepreneurs.

147. The passage does NOT state which of the following about local entrepreneurs?

(A) They are found nearly everywhere.
(B) They encourage further entrepreneurship.
(C) They attract out-of-town investors.
(D) They employ local workers.
(E) They are established in their communities.

The best answer is C. The third paragraph discusses local entrepreneurs, and nowhere is it said that they attract out-of-town investors. However, it is said that they are "nearly ubiquitous" (line 24), that their local businesses both foster "further entrepreneurship" (lines 29-30) and create an environment that "provides jobs" (lines 28-29), and that they have "roots in their communities" (lines 25-26), thus ruling out A, B, D, and E, respectively.

148. The author of the passage mentions which of the following as an advantage of high-technology development?

(A) It encourages the modernization of existing manufacturing facilities.
(B) It promotes healthy competition between rival industries.
(C) It encourages the growth of related industries.
(D) It takes full advantage of the existing workforce.
(E) It does not advantage one local workforce at the expense of another.

The best choice is E. The first paragraph mentions that a shortcoming of the strategy of attracting manufacturing industries was that jobs moved from one town to another. The second paragraph states that the strategy of high-technology development was "preferable to victimizing other geographical areas by taking their jobs" (lines 15-16). Nothing in the passage suggests that high-technology development has any of the advantages mentioned in choices A, B, and C. Lines 16-20 imply that high-technology development does not have the advantage mentioned in choice D.

Questions 149-153 refer to the passage on page 368.

149. According to the passage, before the final results of the study were known, which of the following seemed likely?

  (A) That workers with the highest productivity would also be the most accurate
  (B) That workers who initially achieved high productivity ratings would continue to do so consistently
  (C) That the highest performance ratings would be achieved by workers with the highest productivity
  (D) That the most productive workers would be those whose supervisors claimed to value productivity
  (E) That supervisors who claimed to value productivity would place equal value on customer satisfaction

The best answer is C. Lines 15-17 indicate that before the study's results were known it seemed likely that there would be a "strong correlation between a monitored worker's productivity and the overall rating the worker received." Thus, the passage indicates that it was expected that workers with high productivity would receive high ratings. Choices A and B are incorrect because the passage does not state that highly productive workers were predicted either to be exceptionally accurate or to continue at a high rate of productivity and receive consistently high ratings. Choices D and E are incorrect because the passage does not suggest that certain workers were predicted to be more productive than others or that supervisors' relative weighting of productivity and customer service was predicted beforehand.

150. It can be inferred that the author of the passage discusses "unmonitored workers" (line 10) primarily in order to

  (A) compare the ratings of these workers with the ratings of monitored workers
  (B) provide an example of a case in which monitoring might be effective
  (C) provide evidence of an inappropriate use of CPMCS
  (D) emphasize the effect that CPMCS may have on workers' perceptions of their jobs
  (E) illustrate the effect that CPMCS may have on workers' ratings

The best answer is D. In lines 9-14, the passage states that monitored workers whose productivity was being tracked through CPMCS all reported that productivity was the most important factor in assigning ratings, whereas unmonitored workers who were doing the same work reported that customer service was the most important element in their jobs. The author mentions this difference in perception between monitored workers and unmonitored workers to illustrate the effect that CPMCS can have on the way employees think about their jobs. Choices A and E are incorrect because the passage provides no information concerning unmonitored workers' ratings. Choices B and C are incorrect because the author does not discuss the suitability or effectiveness of CPMCS in relation to unmonitored workers.

151. Which of the following, if true, would most clearly have supported the conclusion referred to in lines 19-21 ?

  (A) Ratings of productivity correlated highly with ratings of both accuracy and attendance.
  (B) Electronic monitoring greatly increased productivity.
  (C) Most supervisors based overall ratings of performance on measures of productivity alone.
  (D) Overall ratings of performance correlated more highly with measures of productivity than the researchers expected.
  (E) Overall ratings of performance correlated more highly with measures of accuracy than with measures of productivity.

The best answer is E. According to lines 17-21, it was concluded that supervisors gave considerable weight to factors other than worker productivity, such as "attendance, accuracy, and indications of customer satisfaction." If this were true, one would expect that one of these other elements would correlate with the supervisor's rating of a worker as highly as or more highly than would productivity. The evidence indicated in E— a higher correlation between accuracy and overall ratings than between productivity and overall ratings—would therefore support the conclusion that supervisors gave considerable weight to criteria other than productivity. Choices A and B can be eliminated because they are not directly relevant to the conclusion that supervisors' ratings suggested that they valued aspects of performance other than productivity. Choices C and D can be eliminated because they help refute the conclusion that employee ratings were not based on productivity alone.

152. According to the passage, a "hygiene factor" (lines 22-23) is an aspect of a worker's performance that

  (A) has no effect on the rating of a worker's performance
  (B) is so basic to performance that it is assumed to be adequate for all workers
  (C) is given less importance than it deserves in rating a worker's performance
  (D) is not likely to affect a worker's rating unless it is judged to be inadequate
  (E) is important primarily because of the effect it has on a worker's rating

The best answer is D. Lines 23-26 define a hygiene factor as a factor that can harm a performance rating if it is too low but is unlikely to raise a performance rating if it is higher than is adequate. Choices A and B can be eliminated because the passage suggests both that hygiene factors are measured and that they do have some effect on employee performance ratings. No information in the passage is provided to support C and E.

153. The primary purpose of the passage is to

(A) explain the need for the introduction of an innovative strategy
(B) discuss a study of the use of a particular method
(C) recommend a course of action
(D) resolve a difference of opinion
(E) suggest an alternative approach

The best answer is B. The passage begins by identifying a method that is used to track employees' productivity and then goes on to discuss a study of this method. Choices A and C are incorrect because the passage does not advocate or explain the need for anything; it simply reports the results of a study on a particular method. Choice D can be eliminated because the passage records objective data concerning CPMCS, not contrasting opinions of them. Choice E is incorrect because the passage does not suggest an alternative approach to CPMCS.

Questions 154-159 refer to the passage on page 370.

154. Which of the following would most logically be the topic of the paragraph immediately following the passage?

(A) Specific ways to evaluate the biases of United States history textbooks
(B) The centrality of the teacher's role in United States history courses
(C) Nontraditional methods of teaching United States history
(D) The contributions of European immigrants to the development of the United States
(E) Ways in which parents influence children's political attitudes

The best answer is A. The passage ends by recommending an "ongoing, careful review of how school textbooks depict Native Americans" (lines 25-26). Of the five choices, A presents the most logical topic to follow the author's recommendation for a careful review of biases against Native Americans in United States textbooks. Choices B, C, and E can be eliminated because the passage focuses on textbooks and how they affect students, not on teaching methods, teachers, or parents' effects on students. Choice D can be eliminated because after suggesting that European immigrants' contributions have been overemphasized in United States textbooks at the expense of Native Americans' achievements, the passage is unlikely to go on to discuss European immigrants' contributions.

155. The primary purpose of the passage is to

(A) describe in detail one research study regarding the impact of history textbooks on children's attitudes and beliefs about certain cultures
(B) describe revisions that should be made to United States history textbooks
(C) discuss the difficulty of presenting an accurate history of the United States
(D) argue that textbooks used in schools stereotype Native Americans and influence children's attitudes
(E) summarize ways in which some textbooks give distorted pictures of the political systems developed by various Native American groups

The best answer is D. In the first paragraph, the author argues that United States textbooks stereotype Native American cultures. In the second paragraph, the author cites evidence that students' attitudes are affected by material they encounter in textbooks. Choice A can be eliminated because the passage mentions the work of different researchers on children's attitudes about particular cultures. Choice B can be eliminated because although the author may believe that revisions should be made to United States history textbooks, those revisions are not described in the passage. Choice C can be eliminated because it cites a topic much broader than that discussed in the passage. Choice E can be eliminated because the passage is concerned with distorted depictions of Native Americans in general, not just of their political systems.

156. The author mentions two researchers' studies (lines 22-25) most likely in order to

(A) suggest that children's political attitudes are formed primarily through textbooks
(B) counter the claim that children are able to see through stereotypes in textbooks
(C) suggest that younger children tend to interpret the messages in textbooks more literally than do older children
(D) demonstrate that textbooks carry political messages meant to influence their readers
(E) prove that textbooks are not biased in terms of their political presentations

The best answer is B. The author begins the second paragraph by describing the argument that children are able to see through the cultural biases of textbooks. The author then counters this argument by mentioning two researchers whose work suggests that "children's attitudes about particular cultures are strongly influenced by the textbooks used in schools" (lines 23-25). Choices A and E can be eliminated because the studies mentioned in the passage do not support these assertions. Choices C and D can be eliminated because the researchers' work is not described as addressing age effects or speculating about the intentions of textbook authors.

157. The author's attitude toward the content of the history textbooks discussed in the passage is best described as one of

(A) indifference
(B) hesitance
(C) neutrality
(D) amusement
(E) disapproval

The best answer is E. In the first paragraph, the author suggests that the way in which Native Americans are treated in United States history textbooks is objectionable: "textbooks stereotype and deprecate the numerous Native American cultures" (lines 8-9). The author then goes on to indicate that children's attitudes toward Native American cultures are affected by the material the children encounter in textbooks and ends by recommending an "ongoing, careful review of how school textbooks depict Native Americans" (lines 25-26), which indicates that the author is dissatisfied with the content of the textbooks as they currently stand. None of the other choices correctly describes the author's attitude toward the textbooks discussed in the passage.

158. It can be inferred from the passage that the researchers mentioned in line 19 would be most likely to agree with which of the following statements?

(A) Students form attitudes about cultures other than their own primarily inside the school environment.
(B) For the most part, seniors in high school know that textbooks can be biased.
(C) Textbooks play a crucial role in shaping the attitudes and beliefs of students.
(D) Elementary school students are as likely to recognize biases in textbooks as are high school students.
(E) Students are less likely to give credence to history textbooks than to mathematics textbooks.

The best answer is B. The author begins the second paragraph by noting the view that children can see through cultural biases in textbooks and then, as an example of this view, describes the claim of the researchers mentioned in line 19, that high school students "know they cannot take textbooks literally" (lines 20-21). This suggests that the researchers would be likely to agree that high school seniors know that textbooks can be biased. Choice A cannot be inferred, because there is no suggestion of a comparison, by the researchers, of the school environment with other environments. Choice C can be eliminated because it contradicts the view of the researchers. Choices D and E cannot be inferred: the passage does not report the researchers' views on elementary school students or mathematics textbooks.

159. The author implies that which of the following will occur if textbooks are not carefully reviewed?

(A) Children will remain ignorant of the European settlers' conquest of the New World.
(B) Children will lose their ability to recognize biases in textbooks.
(C) Children will form negative stereotypes of Native Americans.
(D) Children will develop an understanding of ethnocentrism.
(E) Children will stop taking textbooks seriously.

The best answer is C. In the first paragraph, the author argues that textbooks on United States history contain negative stereotypes of Native Americans. In the second paragraph, the author cites and concurs with research indicating that students' attitudes are affected by the material they encounter in textbooks. Thus, the author implies that if textbooks are not reviewed in order to identify and eliminate the stereotypes, students will be likely to develop negative biases regarding Native Americans. Choice A can be eliminated because the author indicates that United States textbooks do mention the European conquest of the New World. Choices B, D, and E can be eliminated because there is no indication in the passage that the author believes these represent likely outcomes of failure to review textbooks.

Questions 160-166 refer to the passage on page 372.

160. Which of the following most accurately states the main idea of the passage?

(A) Naked mole rat colonies are the only known examples of cooperatively breeding vertebrate societies.
(B) Naked mole rat colonies exhibit social organization based on a rigid caste system.
(C) Behavior in naked mole rat colonies may well be a close vertebrate analogue to behavior in eusocial insect societies.
(D) The mating habits of naked mole rats differ from those of any other vertebrate species.
(E) The basis for the division of labor among naked mole rats is the same as that among eusocial insects.

The best answer is C. The first paragraph of the passage introduces the idea that the naked mole rat colony is similar to certain insect colonies. The rest of the passage provides comparisons of naked mole rat behavior with the behavior of eusocial insects (paragraphs 2 and 3) and contrasts naked mole rat behavior with that of other vertebrates (paragraph 4). None of the other choices states a main idea included in the passage. Choices A and D are not correct according to lines 32-33. Choices B and E are also incorrect: in lines 19-27, naked mole rat social systems are contrasted with rigid caste systems like those of eusocial insects.

161. The passage suggests that Jarvis' work has called into question which of the following explanatory variables for naked mole rat behavior?

(A) Size
(B) Age
(C) Reproductive status
(D) Rate of growth
(E) Previously exhibited behavior

The best answer is B. All that the passage reveals about Jarvis' work is that it suggested that "differences in growth rates may influence the length of time that an individual performs a task, regardless of its age" (lines 29-31). Thus, in Jarvis' view, age may not be a crucial variable in explaining what naked mole rats do.

162. It can be inferred from the passage that the performance of tasks in naked mole rat colonies differs from task performance in eusocial insect societies in which of the following ways?

(A) In naked mole rat colonies, all tasks are performed cooperatively.
(B) In naked mole rat colonies, the performance of tasks is less rigidly determined by body shape.
(C) In naked mole rat colonies, breeding is limited to the largest animals.
(D) In eusocial insect societies, reproduction is limited to a single female.
(E) In eusocial insect societies, the distribution of tasks is based on body size.

The best answer is B. According to lines 19-24, in eusocial insect societies, role is defined by "behavior, body shape, and physiology." For naked mole rats, in contrast, "reproductive status . . . , body size, and perhaps age" influence behavior; no mention is made of body shape. The passage does not indicate whether all tasks are performed cooperatively in eusocial societies, so A is incorrect. Choice C is incorrect: the passage contains no information about the relative size of breeders in insect societies. Choice D is incorrect because reproduction is limited to a single female in both insect and naked mole rat societies. Choice E is not correct: body size is not mentioned as affecting the distribution of tasks in eusocial insect societies.

163. According to the passage, which of the following is a supposition rather than a fact concerning the queen in a naked mole rat colony?

(A) She is the largest member of the colony.
(B) She exerts chemical control over the colony.
(C) She mates with more than one male.
(D) She attains her status through aggression.
(E) She is the only breeding female.

The best answer is B. The word "presumably" in line 14 of the passage indicates that it is not certain that the queen in a naked mole rat colony exerts chemical control over the colony. The passage states that the queen is the largest member of the colony (choice A). There is no indication of doubt concerning

either the number of males the queen mates with (C) or her status as the only breeding female (E). The queen's attainment of her status through aggression is indicated by the statement that when a queen dies other females fight violently for breeding status (D).

164. The passage supports which of the following inferences about breeding among *Lycaon pictus* ?

(A) The largest female in the social group does not maintain reproductive status by means of behavioral control.
(B) An individual's ability to breed is related primarily to its rate of growth.
(C) Breeding is the only task performed by the breeding female.
(D) Breeding in the social group is not cooperative.
(E) Breeding is not dominated by a single pair of dogs.

The best answer is E. According to lines 33-36 in the passage, most cooperatively breeding vertebrates are dominated by a pair of breeders, but the wild dog, *Lycoon pictus,* is an exception to this statement, and therefore breeding among these dogs is *not* dominated by a single pair. The passage provides no information to support the inferences in choices A, B, C, and D.

165. According to the passage, naked mole rat colonies may differ from all other known vertebrate groups in which of the following ways?

(A) Naked mole rats exhibit an extreme form of altruism.
(B) Naked mole rats are cooperative breeders.
(C) Among naked mole rats, many males are permitted to breed with a single dominant female.
(D) Among naked mole rats, different tasks are performed at different times in an individual's life.
(E) Among naked mole rats, fighting results in the selection of a breeding female.

The best answer is A. The passage indicates that scientists once knew of no vertebrate group exhibiting extreme altruism like that of eusocial insects but the naked mole rat does exhibit such altruism. Choice B is incorrect: lines 32-36 indicate that other vertebrate groups breed cooperatively. Choice C is also incorrect: the passage does not indicate that naked mole rats are the only vertebrates having a single breeding female. The passage indicates that a naked mole rat may perform different tasks during its lifetime but does not discuss this for other vertebrates, so D cannot be correct. Choice E is not correct: although the passage indicates that fighting results in the selection of the queen, no information is given about the selection of breeding females in other vertebrate groups.

166. One function of the third paragraph of the passage is to

(A) state a conclusion about facts presented in an earlier paragraph
(B) introduce information that is contradicted by information in the fourth paragraph
(C) qualify the extent to which two previously mentioned groups might be similar
(D) show the chain of reasoning that led to the conclusions of a specific study
(E) demonstrate that, of three explanatory factors offered, two may be of equal significance

The best answer is C. The third paragraph provides information contrasting naked mole rat societies with eusocial insect societies, whereas earlier in the passage, similarities between the two kinds of societies have been emphasized. Choice A is not correct: the author of the passage presents factual information rather than drawing a conclusion in the third paragraph. Because the fourth paragraph presents information about breeding among other vertebrate groups, it does not contradict information in the third paragraph, so B is not correct. Choice D is incorrect because the mention of Jarvis' work serves to provide new information, rather than being the culmination of another discussion. Choice E is incorrect because no explanatory factors are discussed in the third paragraph.

Questions 167-174 refer to the passage on page 374.

167. The passage as a whole can best be characterized as which of the following?

(A) An evaluation of a scholarly study
(B) A description of an attitudinal change
(C) A discussion of an analytical defect
(D) An analysis of the causes of a phenomenon
(E) An argument in favor of revising a view

The best answer is A. This question requires you to identify the option that best describes the passage as a whole. In the first paragraph, the author of the passage compares Glatthaar's scholarly study with other "excellent" studies of its kind, noting that Glatthaar's makes more extensive use of certain types of material. The second paragraph summarizes several points of the study, noting that one point is presented "accurately" and another "appropriately." Paragraph three assesses Glatthaar's ability to "demonstrate the magnitude" of a change, asserting that he exaggerates a particular element. Thus, the passage as a whole is concerned with offering an overall "evaluation of a scholarly study"; it does not present a sustained discussion of any of the matters described by the other options.

168. According to the author, which of the following is true of Glatthaar's *Forged in Battle* compared with previous studies on the same topic?

(A) It is more reliable and presents a more complete picture of the historical events on which it concentrates than do previous studies.
(B) It uses more of a particular kind of source material and focuses more closely on a particular aspect of the topic than do previous studies.
(C) It contains some unsupported generalizations, but it rightly emphasizes a theme ignored by most previous studies.
(D) It surpasses previous studies on the same topic in that it accurately describes conditions often neglected by those studies.
(E) It makes skillful use of supporting evidence to illustrate a subtle trend that previous studies have failed to detect.

The best answer is B. Lines 3-6 state that *Forged in Battle* "uses more soldiers' letters and diaries" and "concentrates more intensely on Black-White relations in Black regiments than do any of its predecessors." Thus, the author of the passage asserts, as B states, that *Forged in Battle* "uses more of a particular kind of source material and relies more closely on a particular aspect of the topic than do previous studies." Nowhere does the passage compare the reliability of Glatthaar's work to that of earlier studies, as A and D assert. Similarly, C and E can be eliminated because the passage does not assert that previous studies neglected any particular subject, only that Glatthaar's work "concentrates more intensely on Black-White relations than do . . . its predecessors."

169. The author implies that the title of Glatthaar's book refers specifically to which of the following?

(A) The sense of pride and accomplishment that Black soldiers increasingly felt as a result of their Civil War experiences

(B) The civil equality that African Americans achieved after the Civil War, partly as a result of their use of organizational skills honed by combat

(C) The changes in discriminatory army policies that were made as a direct result of the performance of Black combat units during the Civil War

(D) The improved interracial relations that were formed by the races' facing of common dangers and their waging of a common fight during the Civil War

(E) The standards of racial egalitarianism that came to be adopted as a result of White Civil War veterans' repudiation of their previous racism

The best answer is D. In lines 6-9, the author of the passage asserts that the title of Glatthaar's work, *Forged in Battle*, "expresses his [Glatthaar's] thesis: loyalty, friendship, and respect among White officers and Black soldiers were fostered by the mutual dangers they faced in combat." That the combat dangers "fostered" such attributes suggests that they acted to improve the relations among the Black and White soldiers; thus the passage implies, as D states, that the title *Forged in Battle* refers specifically to the idea that interracial relations between Black and White soldiers fighting in the Civil War were improved by their shared experience of combat dangers. The other options describe factors that the author of the passage in no way relates to the book's title.

170. The passage mentions which of the following as an important theme that receives special emphasis in Glatthaar's book?

(A) The attitudes of abolitionist officers in Black units
(B) The struggle of Black units to get combat assignments
(C) The consequences of the poor medical care received by Black soldiers
(D) The motives of officers serving in Black units
(E) The discrimination that Black soldiers faced when trying for promotions

The best answer is B. In the second paragraph, the author of the passage describes Glatthaar's work as "appropriately emphasizing the campaign by Black soldiers and their officers to get the opportunity to fight." Thus, the "struggle of Black units to get combat assignments" (choice B) is identified as rightfully emphasized by Glatthaar—that is, as being important and receiving emphasis. None of the other options describe such themes: (choice A) is mentioned only by the author of the passage; C and E are wrong because medical care and discrimination are mentioned merely as realities that Glatthaar "accurately describes"; and D because, although the passage mentions the motives of White officers in Black units, Glatthaar is nowhere described as giving special emphasis to the motives of all officers in such units.

171. The passage suggests that which of the following was true of Black units' disease mortality rates in the Civil War?

(A) They were almost as high as the combat mortality rates of White units.
(B) They resulted in part from the relative inexperience of these units when in combat.
(C) They were especially high because of the nature of these units' usual duty assignments.
(D) They resulted in extremely high overall casualty rates in Black combat units.
(E) They exacerbated the morale problems that were caused by the army's discriminatory policies.

The best answer is C. In lines 15-19, the passage describes "army policies that kept most Black units serving in rear-echelon assignments and working in labor battalions." The passage continues: "Thus . . . their mortality rate from disease . . . was twice as great." The use of the word "thus" here suggests that some aspect of these conditions was the cause of the high mortality rates, as C states. Nothing can be inferred from the passage about the absolute relationship between disease mortality rates of Black units and combat mortality rates of White units (choice A), or about the relative severity of overall casualty rates in Black combat units (choice D). Nor does the passage mention or suggest the role of either the inexperience (choice B) or the morale (choice E) of Black units.

172. The author of the passage quotes the White officer in lines 23-24 primarily in order to provide evidence to support the contention that

(A) virtually all White officers initially had hostile attitudes toward Black soldiers
(B) Black soldiers were often forced to defend themselves from physical attacks initiated by soldiers from White units
(C) the combat performance of Black units changed the attitudes of White soldiers toward Black soldiers
(D) White units paid especially careful attention to the performance of Black units in battle
(E) respect in the army as a whole was accorded only to those units, whether Black or White, that performed well in battle

The best answer is C. Lines 20-22 assert that the combat performance of Black units "won increasing respect from initially skeptical or hostile White soldiers." To support the assertion that the performance of the Black units changed White soldiers' attitudes toward them, the author of the passage then quotes a comment made by one of those White officers about the Black units: "they fought their way into the respect of all the army" (lines 22-24). The passage makes no assertions about whether "virtually all White officers" were hostile (choice A); or about whether White units either physically attacked Black units (choice B) or paid particular attention to the performance of Black units (choice D). Nor does it address the relationship "in the army as a whole" between a unit's performance and the respect accorded it (choice E).

173. Which of the following best describes the kind of error attributed to Glatthaar in lines 25-28 ?

(A) Insisting on an unwarranted distinction between two groups of individuals in order to render an argument concerning them internally consistent
(B) Supporting an argument in favor of a given interpretation of a situation with evidence that is not particularly relevant to the situation
(C) Presenting a distorted view of the motives of certain individuals in order to provide grounds for a negative evaluation of their actions
(D) Describing the conditions prevailing before a given event in such a way that the contrast with those prevailing after the event appears more striking than it actually is
(E) Asserting that a given event is caused by another event merely because the other event occurred before the given event occurred

The best answer is D. To answer this question, you must determine what "kind of error" the author of the passage directly attributes to Glatthaar in lines 25-28. These lines assert that "in trying to demonstrate the magnitude of this attitudinal change"— the change in White soldiers' attitudes toward Black units— "Glatthaar seems to exaggerate the prewar racism of the White men who became officers in Black regiments." The error attributed to Glatthaar is one of exaggerating conditions before the Civil War so as to overstate the contrast between prewar and postwar conditions. Glatthaar is not specifically faulted in lines 25-28 for presenting either "an unwarranted distinction between two groups" (choice A); or irrelevant evidence (choice B); or for distorting motives in order to evaluate actions negatively (choice C); or for misattributing causality (choice E).

174. Which of the following actions can best be described as indulging in "generational chauvinism" (lines 40-41) as that practice is defined in the passage?

(A) Condemning a present-day monarch merely because many monarchs have been tyrannical in the past
(B) Clinging to the formal standards of politeness common in one's youth to such a degree that any relaxation of those standards is intolerable
(C) Questioning the accuracy of a report written by an employee merely because of the employee's gender
(D) Deriding the superstitions accepted as "science" in past eras without acknowledging the prevalence of irrational beliefs today
(E) Labeling a nineteenth-century politician as "corrupt" for engaging in once-acceptable practices considered intolerable today

The best answer is E. This question requires you to identify a hypothetical situation that exemplifies the concept of "generational chauvinism" as it is defined in the passage. This term is defined in lines 37-41, where the author of the passage criticizes the use of "current standards of racial egalitarianism" to judge the motives of abolitionist White officers serving in Black regiments: "to call their feelings 'powerful racial prejudices' is to indulge in generational chauvinism— to judge past eras by present standards." The last phrase serves to define "generational chauvinism," a concept exemplified by the situation described in choice E, in which the "once-acceptable practices" of a nineteenth-century politician are labeled as "corrupt." None of the other options exemplify this "generational chauvinism" as it is defined in the passage.

Questions 175-182 refer to the passage on page 376.

175. The passage is primarily concerned with

   (A) detailing the evidence that has led most biologists to replace the trichotomous picture of living organisms with a dichotomous one
   (B) outlining the factors that have contributed to the current hypothesis concerning the number of basic categories of living organisms
   (C) evaluating experiments that have resulted in proof that the prokaryotes are more ancient than had been expected
   (D) summarizing the differences in structure and function found among true bacteria, archaebacteria, and eukaryotes
   (E) formulating a hypothesis about the mechanisms of evolution that resulted in the ancestors of the prokaryotes

The best answer is B. The first paragraph reviews inquiries leading to the hypothesis that two categories of organism exist; the second explains how "more recent research" (line 27) supports a three-category hypothesis. Thus, the passage is primarily concerned with outlining factors contributing to the current hypothesis about the number of such categories. Choice A is wrong because the passage describes the replacement of a dichotomous with a trichotomous model, not the reverse. C is wrong because the passage mentions no experimental proof that the prokaryotes were older than expected; D is wrong because the passage only briefly discusses the structure and function of eukaryotes and prokaryotes, never mentioning those of archaebacteria. E is wrong because the passage mentions no particular "mechanisms of evolution" that created the ancestors of the prokaryotes.

176. According to the passage, investigations of eukaryotic and prokaryotic cells at the molecular level supported the conclusion that

   (A) most eukaryotic organisms are unicellular
   (B) complex cells have well-formed nuclei
   (C) prokaryotes and eukaryotes form two fundamental categories
   (D) subcellular structures are visible with a microscope
   (E) prokaryotic and eukaryotic cells have similar enzymes

The best answer is C. In lines 10-20, the passage states that, although molecular investigation revealed some similarities between prokaryotic and eukaryotic cells, "the differences between the groups and the similarities within each group made it seem certain to most biologists that the tree of life had only two stems" (lines 18-20)—that is, "two fundamental categories," as C asserts. The passage does not address what proportion of eukaryotic organisms are unicellular (choice A) or whether all complex cells have well-formed nuclei (choice B). That "subcellular structures are visible with a microscope" (choice D) is described as established "initially"—that is, before the research was "ultimately carried to the molecular level" (lines 7-10). According to the passage, molecular investigation supports the idea that "sequences of . . . enzymes tend to be typically prokaryotic or eukaryotic"—not that those enzymes are similar (lines 16-17), as E claims.

177. According to the passage, which of the following statements about the two-category hypothesis is likely to be true?

   (A) It is promising because it explains the presence of true bacteria-like organisms such as organelles in eukaryotic cells.
   (B) It is promising because it explains why eukaryotic cells, unlike prokaryotic cells, tend to form multicellular organisms.
   (C) It is flawed because it fails to account for the great variety among eukaryotic organisms.
   (D) It is flawed because it fails to account for the similarity between prokaryotes and eukaryotes.
   (E) It is flawed because it fails to recognize an important distinction among prokaryotes.

The best answer is E. According to the passage, the two-category hypothesis, which assumed "that all living things could be divided into two . . . categories," (lines 1-2) now "seems fundamentally wrong" (line 27) because it does not account for evidence that two kinds of prokaryotic organisms exist: true bacteria and "a distinct evolutionary branch," archaebacteria (line 40). Thus, the hypothesis is said to ignore an important distinction among prokaryotes, as E states. Choice A is wrong because the passage does not even mention bacteria-like organisms existing within eukaryotic cells. B contradicts the passage, which states that "many unicellular organisms . . . are eukaryotic." C and D are wrong because each identifies as a flaw the failure to "account for" conditions that the passage indicates the hypothesis accounted for.

178. It can be inferred from the passage that which of the following have recently been compared in order to clarify the fundamental classifications of living things?

(A) The genetic coding in true bacteria and that in other prokaryotes
(B) The organelle structures of archaebacteria, true bacteria, and eukaryotes
(C) The cellular structures of multicellular organisms and unicellular organisms
(D) The molecular sequences in eukaryotic RNA, true bacterial RNA, and archaebacterial RNA
(E) The amino acid sequences in enzymes of various eukaryotic species and those of enzymes in archaebacterial species

This question requires you to identify information implied rather than stated in the passage. D, the best answer, can be inferred from lines 30-31, which state that it "now appears that there are three stems in the tree of life"—that is, three categories of organism—because "new techniques for determining the molecular sequence of the RNA of organisms have produced evolutionary information . . . ." From this it can be inferred, as D states, that researchers compared the molecular sequences in the RNA of each kind of organism postulated by the new view—eukaryotic, bacterial, and archaebacterial. The other choices cannot be inferred from the passage; each describes types of features discussed in the context of earlier, not later, research.

179. If the "new techniques" mentioned in line 31 were applied in studies of biological classifications other than bacteria, which of the following is most likely?

(A) Some of those classifications will have to be reevaluated.
(B) Many species of bacteria will be reclassified.
(C) It will be determined that there are four main categories of living things rather than three.
(D) It will be found that true bacteria are much older than eukaryotes.
(E) It will be found that there is a common ancestor of the eukaryotes, archaebacteria, and true bacteria.

The best answer is A. This question requires you to select the answer that, based on information presented in the passage, describes the most likely result of applying the "new techniques" (line 31) to biological classifications other than bacteria. Lines 31-36 state that these techniques "produced . . . information about the degree to which organisms are related." Specifically, the techniques "strongly suggested" that the prokaryote category includes two distinct kinds of organisms (lines 36-37). This information, which suggests a reevaluation of the prokaryote classification, provides support for the statement that "classifications other than bacteria" are also likely to require reevaluation if the same techniques are used to study them, as A states.

180. According to the passage, researchers working under the two-category hypothesis were correct in thinking that

(A) prokaryotes form a coherent group
(B) the common ancestor of all living things had complex properties
(C) eukaryotes are fundamentally different from true bacteria
(D) true bacteria are just as complex as eukaryotes
(E) ancestral versions of eukaryotic genes functioned differently from their modern counterparts

The best answer is C. Lines 26-28 indicate that C is an aspect of the two-category hypothesis that "has been sustained by more recent research." Thus, the passage supports the assumption, made by proponents of the two-category hypothesis, that "eukaryotes are fundamentally different from true bacteria" (choice C). The passage contradicts the idea that prokaryotes "form a coherent group" (choice A) because it states that there is "one respect" (lines 27-28) in which new evidence contradicts the hypothesis: in addition to the eukaryotes and the "true bacteria," which are prokaryotes, there exists another distinct "evolutionary branch" within the prokaryotes: the archaebacteria (38-41). The two-category hypothesis, as presented in the passage, proposes neither B nor E and asserts the opposite of D.

181. All of the following statements are supported by the passage EXCEPT:

(A) True bacteria form a distinct evolutionary group.
(B) Archaebacteria are prokaryotes that resemble true bacteria.
(C) True bacteria and eukaryotes employ similar types of genetic coding.
(D) True bacteria and eukaryotes are distinguishable at the subcellular level.
(E) Amino acid sequences of enzymes are uniform for eukaryotic and prokaryotic organisms.

The best answer is E, the only choice NOT supported by the passage. Lines 37-38 support the idea that "true bacteria indeed form a large coherent group" of the kind postulated by the two-category hypothesis—that is, that they are a "distinct evolutionary group" (choice A). Lines 38-40 assert that "archaebacteria . . . are prokaryotes and . . . resemble true bacteria," as B states. Lines 10-13 support C: "prokaryotic and eukaryotic cells . . . translate genetic information . . . according to the same type of genetic coding." D is supported by lines 7-10 in the passage, which state that "the distinction between eukaryotes and bacteria" was "initially defined in terms of subcellular structures visible with a microscope." E, however, is contradicted by lines 25-27: "the amino acid sequences of various enzymes tend to be typically prokaryotic or eukaryotic."

182. The author's attitude toward the view that living things are divided into three categories is best described as one of

(A) tentative acceptance
(B) mild skepticism
(C) limited denial
(D) studious criticism
(E) wholehearted endorsement

The best answer is A, which aptly describes the author's attitude toward the hypothesis that there are three categories of living things. In lines 30-31 the author states that "it now appears that there are three stems in the tree of life" because new techniques "have strongly suggested" the accuracy of the three-category view (lines 31-41). That the author accepts the three-category hypothesis is suggested by this mention of "strong" support. That this acceptance is "cautious" is conveyed by the use of the terms "seems" (line 27), "appears," and "suggested." Such caution rules out the "wholehearted endorsement" described by E; nor does the author express "denial" of (choice C), "criticism" about (choice D), or "skepticism" about (choice B) the three-category hypothesis.

Questions 183-189 refer to the passage on page 378.

183. The author mentions each of the following as a cause of excess inventory EXCEPT

(A) production of too much merchandise
(B) inaccurate forecasting of buyers' preferences
(C) unrealistic pricing policies
(D) products' rapid obsolescence
(E) availability of a better product

The best answer is C. The question requires you to recognize which of the choices is NOT mentioned in the passage as a cause of excess inventory. Choice A, "production of too much merchandise," is listed as a cause in lines 2-3, where the passage states that "overstocks may accumulate through production overruns." In line 4, the assertion that "certain styles and colors prove unpopular" identifies "inaccurate forecasting of buyers' preferences" (choice B), as a cause. D, "products' rapid obsolescence," appears in lines 4-7, which indicate that "with some products . . . last year's models are difficult to move." E, "availability of a better product," is listed as a cause in lines 7-8: "Occasionally the competition introduces a better product." C, "unrealistic pricing policies," is not mentioned in the passage.

184. The passage suggests that which of the following is a kind of product that a liquidator who sells to discount stores would be unlikely to wish to acquire?

(A) Furniture
(B) Computers
(C) Kitchen equipment
(D) Baby-care products
(E) Children's clothing

The best answer is B. This question requires you to identify a kind of product that information in the passage suggests a liquidator selling to discount stores is UNLIKELY to want to buy. About computers, lines 4-7 state that "last year's models are difficult to move even at a huge discount." A liquidator buying excess inventory for resale to discount stores would therefore probably avoid buying computers because demand for them would be low; thus, the passage suggests choice B. The passage does not mention choice A or choice C. Choices D and E, baby-care products and children's clothing, are mentioned as examples of products that, if dumped, might cause public relations problems; there is no information in the passage about the attractiveness of these products to liquidators.

185. The passage provides information that supports which of the following statements?

(A) Excess inventory results most often from insufficient market analysis by the manufacturer.
(B) Products with slight manufacturing defects may contribute to excess inventory.
(C) Few manufacturers have taken advantage of the changes in the federal tax laws.
(D) Manufacturers who dump their excess inventory are often caught and exposed by the news media.
(E) Most products available in discount stores have come from manufacturers' excess-inventory stock.

The best answer is B. "Products with slight manufacturing defects may contribute to excess inventory," is supported by lines 2-3, which assert that "production . . . errors" can contribute to excess inventory. Lines 27-29, which describe a scenario illustrating the exposure of excess-inventory dumping, also support B: "QRS Company dumps . . . diapers because they have slight imperfections." The passage does not mention "market analysis" (choice A), nor does it include information about the relative proportion either of "manufacturers that have taken advantage of tax laws" (choice C) or of products in discount stores that come from excess-inventory stock (choice E). Far from being supported, D groundlessly asserts that the "remote possibility" described in lines 23-24 occurs "often."

186. The author cites the examples in lines 25-29 most probably in order to illustrate

(A) the fiscal irresponsibility of dumping as a policy for dealing with excess inventory
(B) the waste-management problems that dumping new products creates
(C) the advantages to the manufacturer of dumping as a policy
(D) alternatives to dumping explored by different companies
(E) how the news media could portray dumping to the detriment of the manufacturer's reputation

The best answer is E. Lines 25-29 immediately follow the author's description of how manufacturers choosing excess-inventory dumping may be "caught by the news media," in which case "dumping perfectly useful products can turn into a public relations nightmare" (lines 22-25). Both scenarios described in lines 25-29 illustrate the kind of statement that, if made by the news media, would "portray dumping to the detriment of the manufacturer's reputation," as E states. Each emphasizes the reputation-damaging perception that a manufacturer has dumped useful, much-needed goods. Neither scenario illustrates A-D. Neither "fiscal responsibility" (choice A) nor "waste-management" (choice B) is mentioned in the passage. Choices C and D are mentioned elsewhere in the passage but are not organizationally or logically connected with lines 25-29.

187. By asserting that manufacturers "are simply unaware" (line 31), the author suggests which of the following?

(A) Manufacturers might donate excess inventory to charity rather than dump it if they knew about the provision in the federal tax code.
(B) The federal government has failed to provide sufficient encouragement to manufacturers to make use of advantageous tax policies.
(C) Manufacturers who choose to dump excess inventory are not aware of the possible effects on their reputation of media coverage of such dumping.
(D) The manufacturers of products disposed of by dumping are unaware of the needs of those people who would find the products useful.
(E) The manufacturers who dump their excess inventory are not familiar with the employment of liquidators to dispose of overstock.

The best answer is A. Lines 30-31 state: "The managers of these companies are not deliberately wasteful; they are simply unaware of all their alternatives." The single such "alternative" identified is one encouraged by "an above-cost federal tax deduction for companies that donate inventory to charity." By stating that the manufacturers "are simply unaware" of this more cost-saving alternative, the author suggests that, if aware of the provision, they might choose inventory-donation over inventory-dumping. Nowhere does the author suggest that the

government "failed to provide sufficient encouragement" for donation (choice B), or that the manufacturers were unaware in the ways described by C, D, or E.

188. The information in the passage suggests that which of the following, if true, would make donating excess inventory to charity less attractive to manufacturers than dumping?

(A) The costs of getting the inventory to the charitable destination are greater than the above-cost tax deduction.
(B) The news media give manufacturers' charitable contributions the same amount of coverage that they give dumping.
(C) No straight-cost tax benefit can be claimed for items that are dumped.
(D) The fair-market value of an item in excess inventory is 1.5 times its cost.
(E) Items end up as excess inventory because of a change in the public's preferences.

The best answer is A. Lines 34-36 indicate that a manufacturer can save money by donating excess inventory to charity. However, if the cost of transporting inventory to a charitable destination is greater than that savings, as A indicates, the attractiveness of donating excess inventory would be lessened. Because inventory dumping involves "straight cost write-off" (line 18) and "requires little time or preparation" (line 21), dumping might seem more attractive than a donation that does not save the manufacturer money. Choices B, C, and D are consistent with the author's suggestion that inventory donation is more attractive; D is irrelevant to the comparison.

189. Information in the passage suggests that one reason manufacturers might take advantage of the tax provision mentioned in the last paragraph is that

(A) there are many kinds of products that cannot be legally dumped in a landfill
(B) liquidators often refuse to handle products with slight imperfections
(C) the law allows a deduction in excess of the cost of manufacturing the product
(D) media coverage of contributions of excess-inventory products to charity is widespread and favorable
(E) no tax deduction is available for products dumped or sold to a liquidator

The best answer is C. Lines 34-39 describe the 1976 tax provision as a financial "incentive" (line 34) that the manufacturers would take advantage of if they were not "unaware of all their alternatives" for disposing of excess inventory (line 31). This provision allows "an above-cost federal tax deduction for companies that donate inventory to charity"—specifically, deduction of up to "twice cost" for donated goods (lines 34-39). This information suggests that one reason manufacturers might take advantage of the provision is that, as C states, it allows "a deduction in excess of the cost of manufacturing the product." Choices A, B, and D each describe factors that are neither mentioned nor suggested by the passage; E contradicts lines 17-18, which state that inventory-dumping entails "a straight cost write-off on . . . taxes."

Questions 190-197 refer to the passage on page 380.

190. According to the passage, job segregation by sex in the United States was

(A) greatly diminished by labor mobilization during the Second World War
(B) perpetuated by those textile-mill owners who argued in favor of women's employment in wage labor
(C) one means by which women achieved greater job security
(D) reluctantly challenged by employers except when the economic advantages were obvious
(E) a constant source of labor unrest in the young textile industry

The best answer is B. Lines 13-17 state that sex segregation persisted in the workplace because "a prevailing definition of femininity" dictated the kinds of tasks women performed. The passage then provides an example of this phenomenon by citing early textile-mill entrepreneurs who, "in justifying women's employment in wage labor, made much of the assumption that women were by nature skillful at detailed tasks and patient in carrying out repetitive chores" (lines 18-21). Thus, job segregation by sex in the United States was perpetuated by those textile-mill owners. A is incorrect because lines 36-40 state job segregation by sex was not diminished during World War II. Choice C is wrong because lines 30-31 state that many "female" jobs were "less secure." Choices D and E are not supported by the passage.

191. According to the passage, historians of women's labor focused on factory work as a more promising area of research than service-sector work because factory work

(A) involved the payment of higher wages
(B) required skill in detailed tasks
(C) was assumed to be less characterized by sex segregation
(D) was more readily accepted by women than by men
(E) fitted the economic dynamic of industrialism better

The best answer is C. Lines 4-9 state that historians of women's labor focused on factory work rather than service-sector work because the "underlying economic forces of industrialism were presumed to be gender-blind and hence emancipatory in effect." Thus, the passage indicates that these historians assumed that sex segregation was less prevalent in factory work than in service-sector work. Choices A, B, D, and E can be eliminated because the passage does not state that historians focused on factory work because it involved higher wages, required skill in detailed tasks, was accepted more readily by women, or fitted the economic dynamic of industrialism better.

192. It can be inferred from the passage that early historians of women's labor in the United States paid little attention to women's employment in the service sector of the economy because

(A) the extreme variety of these occupations made it very difficult to assemble meaningful statistics about them
(B) fewer women found employment in the service sector than in factory work
(C) the wages paid to workers in the service sector were much lower than those paid in the industrial sector
(D) women's employment in the service sector tended to be much more short-term than in factory work
(E) employment in the service sector seemed to have much in common with the unpaid work associated with homemaking

The best answer is E. In lines 4-7 the author states that historians of women's labor in the United States focused on factory work rather than the service sector because factory work "seemed so different from traditional, unpaid 'women's work' in the home." By indicating that historians preferred to study women's work in factories rather than women's work in the service sector because factory work seemed less like women's work at home, the passage suggests that historians believed that women's work in the service sector was similar to women's work at home. Choice A is incorrect because the passage does not discuss statistics. Choices B, C, and D can be eliminated because the passage does not compare women factory workers and women service workers.

193. The passage supports which of the following statements about the early mill owners mentioned in the second paragraph?

(A) They hoped that by creating relatively unattractive "female" jobs they would discourage women from losing interest in marriage and family life.
(B) They sought to increase the size of the available labor force as a means to keep men's wages low.
(C) They argued that women were inherently suited to do well in particular kinds of factory work.
(D) They thought that factory work bettered the condition of women by emancipating them from dependence on income earned by men.
(E) They felt guilty about disturbing the traditional division of labor in the family.

The best answer is C. In lines 19-21, the author states that early textile-mill owners "made much of the assumption that women were by nature skillful at detailed tasks and patient in carrying out repetitive chores." Choice A is incorrect because the passage states that the early mill owners were interested in "justifying women's employment in wage labor" (lines 18-19). Choices B and D can be eliminated because the passage does not state that the mill owners were interested in keeping men's wages low or in bettering the condition of women. Choice E can be eliminated because the passage does not discuss mill owners' attitudes toward the traditional division of labor in the family.

194. It can be inferred from the passage that the "unfinished revolution" the author mentions in line 13 refers to the

(A) entry of women into the industrial labor market
(B) recognition that work done by women as homemakers should be compensated at rates comparable to those prevailing in the service sector of the economy
(C) development of a new definition of femininity unrelated to the economic forces of industrialism
(D) introduction of equal pay for equal work in all professions
(E) emancipation of women wage earners from gender-determined job allocation

The best answer is E. In the last sentence of the first paragraph, the author states that emancipation for women in factory work was "less profound than expected, for not even industrial wage labor has escaped continued sex segregation in the workplace." The author goes on in the first sentence of the second paragraph to discuss "this unfinished revolution in the status of women"; the phrase "this unfinished revolution" refers back to the last sentence of the first paragraph, where the author has just mentioned the persistence of sex segregation in the industrialized work force. Choice A is incorrect because the first paragraph indicates that women have entered the industrial labor market. Choice C is wrong because the passage does not refer to any new definition of femininity unrelated to industrialism. Choices B and D are incorrect because the first paragraph discusses women's work in terms of sex segregation and not in terms of equal pay for men and women in various professions.

195. The passage supports which of the following statements about hiring policies in the United States?

(A) After a crisis many formerly "male" jobs are reclassified as "female" jobs.
(B) Industrial employers generally prefer to hire women with previous experience as homemakers.
(C) Post-Second World War hiring policies caused women to lose many of their wartime gains in employment opportunity.
(D) Even war industries during the Second World War were reluctant to hire women for factory work.
(E) The service sector of the economy has proved more nearly gender-blind in its hiring policies than has the manufacturing sector.

The best answer is C. The last sentence of the passage states that after World War II "employers quickly returned to men most of the 'male' jobs that women had been permitted to master." Choice A is incorrect because the passage states that in the case of World War II many jobs occupied by women were returned to men. Choice D is incorrect because the last paragraph of the passage indicates that war industries did hire

women, although those women were subject to job segregation by sex. The passage does not provide any information to support B or E.

196. Which of the following words best expresses the opinion of the author of the passage concerning the notion that women are more skillful than men in carrying out detailed tasks?

(A) "patient" (line 21)
(B) "repetitive" (line 21)
(C) "hoary" (line 22)
(D) "homemaking" (line 23)
(E) "purview" (line 24)

The best answer is C. The author of the passage uses the word "hoary" in line 22 to characterize the kinds of stereotypes about women that mill owners imported into the new industrial order. Through this word, the author expresses a negative opinion about stereotypes propagating the notion that women are more skillful than men in carrying out certain tasks. Choices A and B can be eliminated because the author uses them to paraphrase the assumptions of the mill owners about the kinds of work women excelled at; the mill owners subscribed to the very stereotypes that the author describes as "hoary." Choices D and E are incorrect because the words "homemaking" and "purview" do not convey attitudes.

197. Which of the following best describes the relationship of the final paragraph to the passage as a whole?

(A) The central idea is reinforced by the citation of evidence drawn from twentieth-century history.
(B) The central idea is restated in such a way as to form a transition to a new topic for discussion.
(C) The central idea is restated and juxtaposed with evidence that might appear to contradict it.
(D) A partial exception to the generalizations of the central idea is dismissed as unimportant.
(E) Recent history is cited to suggest that the central idea's validity is gradually diminishing.

The best answer is A. To answer this question you must identify the central idea of the passage so as to determine the relationship of the content of the last paragraph to that idea. The central idea is introduced in lines 10-12 of the first paragraph: "not even industrial wage labor has escaped continued sex segregation in the workplace." The second paragraph goes on to discuss the origins of sex segregation in the industrialized workforce. The author begins the last paragraph by mentioning the persistence of sex segregation and goes on to describe such segregation in industry during and after the Second World War. Choice B is incorrect because the last paragraph focuses on the topic under discussion and does not introduce any new and different topic. Choices C, D, and E can be eliminated because the last paragraph cites evidence to support the central idea rather than to challenge it.

198. The author is primarily concerned with

(A) advocating a return to an older methodology
(B) explaining the importance of a recent theory
(C) enumerating differences between two widely used methods
(D) describing events leading to a discovery
(E) challenging the assumptions on which a theory is based

The best answer is B. In the first paragraph the author describes a recent theory concerning the formation of Archean-age gold-quartz vein systems, and in the second paragraph this theory is said to have "considerable practical importance" (lines 8-9). The remaining paragraphs explain why such theories of ore-forming processes are important for explorers seeking to locate gold deposits. The older method of prospecting for gold is mentioned, but rather than advocating this method (choice A), the author explains why prospecting is no longer viable. The author neither discusses differences between widely used methods (choice C) nor describes the events leading to a discovery (choice D). Although another, widely held view concerning ore-forming processes is mentioned, the author does not challenge the assumptions on which this view is based (choice E).

199. According to the passage, the widely held view of Archea-age gold-quartz vein systems is that such systems

(A) were formed from metamorphic fluids
(B) originated in molten granitelike bodies
(C) were formed from alluvial deposits
(D) generally have surface expression
(E) are not discoverable through chemical tests

The best answer is A. In lines 5-6 the author mentions "the widely held view that the [Archean-age gold-quartz vein] systems were deposited from metamorphic fluids." This view is said to be contrary to the recent theory that these systems originated in molten granitelike bodies, so choice B is not correct. Alluvial deposits are mentioned in the passage as having aided simple prospecting methods, but such deposits are not said to have formed the Archean-age gold-quartz vein systems (choice C). According to the author, "most deposits not yet discovered have gone undetected because they are buried and have no surface expression" (lines 14-16), so choice D is not correct. And choice E is incorrect because the author says that chemical tests can aid the discovery of gold deposits if they are conducted in areas where mineralization is likely to have taken place (lines 23-27).

200. The passage implies that which of the following steps would be the first performed by explorers who wish to maximize their chances of discovering gold?

(A) Surveying several sites known to have been formed more than two billion years ago
(B) Limiting exploration to sites known to have been formed from metamorphic fluid
(C) Using an appropriate conceptual model to select a site for further exploration
(D) Using geophysical methods to analyze rocks over a broad area
(E) Limiting exploration to sites where alluvial gold has previously been found

The best answer is C. According to the author, "to maximize the chances of discovery the explorer must . . . pay particular attention to selecting the ground formations most likely to be mineralized" (lines 27-30); the explorer begins by using conceptual models "to identify those geological features that are critical to the formation of the mineralization being modeled, and then tries to select areas for exploration" (lines 35-38). According to the author, geophysical methods are of no value if they are applied to sites that have never mineralized (lines 25-27), so choice D is not correct, and there is no indication in the passage that age of formation would narrow the explorer's choices, so choice A is not correct. Choice B is not correct because the new theory, which is said to have "considerable practical importance" (lines 8-9) for the discovery of gold, is contrary to the view that gold deposits were deposited from metamorphic fluids. And the passage says that simple prospecting methods that trace alluvial gold only occasionally lead to new discoveries, so choice E is incorrect.

201. Which of the following statements about discoveries of gold deposits is supported by information in the passage?

(A) The number of gold discoveries made annually has increased between the time of the original gold rushes and the present.

(B) New discoveries of gold deposits are likely to be the result of exploration techniques designed to locate buried mineralization.

(C) It is unlikely that newly discovered gold deposits will ever yield as much as did those deposits discovered during the original gold rushes.

(D) Modern explorers are divided on the question of the utility of simple prospecting methods as a source of new discoveries of gold deposits.

(E) Models based on the theory that gold originated from magmatic fluids have already led to new discoveries of gold deposits.

The best answer is B. According to the passage, "most [gold] deposits not yet discovered have gone undetected because they are buried and have no surface expression" (lines 14-16); as a result, an explorer uses conceptual models "to identify those geological features that are critical to the formation of the mineralization being modeled, and then tries to select areas for exploration" (lines 35-38). The passage provides no information about the number of gold discoveries or the yield of gold deposits past or present, so choices A and C are not correct. The author does not suggest that there is any disagreement concerning the utility of simple prospecting methods, which the author says only occasionally lead to new discoveries, so choice D is incorrect. And although the author indicates that the theory that gold originated from magmatic fluids has considerable practical importance, there is no information in the passage indicating that models based on this theory have already led to new discoveries of gold deposits, so choice E is incorrect.

202. It can be inferred from the passage that which of the following is easiest to detect?

(A) A gold-quartz vein system originating in magmatic fluids

(B) A gold-quartz vein system originating in metamorphic fluids

(C) A gold deposit that is mixed with granite

(D) A gold deposit that has shed alluvial gold

(E) A gold deposit that exhibits chemical halos

The best answer is D. According to the passage, "Most of the gold deposits discovered during the original gold rushes were exposed at the Earth's surface and were found because they had shed trails of alluvial gold that were easily traced by simple prospecting methods" (lines 9-12). By contrast, "most deposits not yet discovered have gone undetected because they are buried and have no surface expression" (lines 14-16), and the passage gives no indication that gold-quartz vein systems and gold deposits like those described in choices A, B, C, and E would have the kind of surface expression that would make them easy to detect.

203. The theory mentioned in line 1 relates to the conceptual models discussed in the passage in which of the following ways?

(A) It may furnish a valid account of ore-forming processes, and, hence, can support conceptual models that have great practical significance.

(B) It suggests that certain geological formations, long believed to be mineralized, are in fact mineralized, thus confirming current conceptual models.

(C) It suggests that there may not be enough similarity across Archean-age gold-quartz vein systems to warrant the formulation of conceptual models.

(D) It corrects existing theories about the chemical halos of gold deposits, and thus provides a basis for correcting current conceptual models.

(E) It suggests that simple prospecting methods still have a higher success rate in the discovery of gold deposits than do more modern methods.

The best answer is A. The passage says that the theory has "considerable practical importance" (lines 8-9), and the bulk of the passage is devoted to explaining that importance for the discovery of new gold deposits: since most remaining gold deposits are buried and have no surface expression, the passage says, conceptual models derived from theories of ore-forming processes are used to identify sites where mineralization is likely to have taken place. The theory is not said to confirm or correct current models (choices B and D), nor does it suggest that simple prospecting methods have any current value (choice E). And choice C is incorrect because it contradicts what the passage suggests about the importance of the theory for the formulation of conceptual models.

204. According to the passage, methods of exploring for gold that are widely used today are based on which of the following facts?

(A) Most of the Earth's remaining gold deposits are still molten.

(B) Most of the Earth's remaining gold deposits are exposed at the surface.

(C) Most of the Earth's remaining gold deposits are buried and have no surface expression.

(D) Only one type of gold deposit warrants exploration, since the other types of gold deposits are found in regions difficult to reach.

(E) Only one type of gold deposit warrants exploration, since the other types of gold deposits are unlikely to yield concentrated quantities of gold.

The best answer is C. According to the passage, "most deposits not yet discovered have gone undetected because they are buried and have no surface expression" (lines 14-16), and "The challenge in exploration is therefore to unravel the subsurface geology of an area and pinpoint the position of buried minerals" (lines 17-19). The "Methods widely used today" (line 19) are based on these facts, which directly contradict choice B.

Choices A, D, and E are incorrect because there is no information in the passage to support these statements about methods of exploring for gold.

205. It can be inferred from the passage that the efficiency of model-based gold exploration depends on which of the following?

    I. The closeness of the match between the geological features identified by the model as critical and the actual geological features of a given area

   II. The degree to which the model chosen relies on empirical observation of known mineral deposits rather than on theories of ore-forming processes

  III. The degree to which the model chosen is based on an accurate description of the events leading to mineralization

    (A) I only
    (B) II only
    (C) I and II only
    (D) I and III only
    (E) I, II, and III

The best answer is D. According to the passage, after constructing conceptual models based on observations of known mineral deposits and theories of ore-forming processes, "The explorer uses the models to identify those geological features that are critical to the formation of the mineralization being modeled, and then tries to select areas for exploration that exhibit as many of the critical features as possible" (lines 35-39). It can be inferred from this that the efficiency of the resulting exploration will depend on how closely the features of the selected area match the features identified by the model as critical (Statement I) and on how accurately the process of mineralization has been modeled (Statement III). According to the passage, both empirical observations of known mineral deposits and theories of ore-forming processes are important in constructing the models, so Statement II cannot be part of the correct answer.

Questions 206-212 refer to the passage on page 384.

206. According to the passage, all of the following were benefits of privatizing state-owned industries in the United Kingdom EXCEPT:

    (A) Privatized industries paid taxes to the government.
    (B) The government gained revenue from selling state-owned industries.
    (C) The government repaid some of its national debt.
    (D) Profits from industries that were still state-owned increased.
    (E) Total borrowings and losses of state-owned industries decreased.

The best answer is D. The passage does not mention how industries that were still state-owned fared in terms of profits. Choice A is not the answer because lines 10-11 state that the government "now receives tax revenues from the newly privatized companies." Choice B is not the answer because lines 9-10

state that the government gained billions of pounds from selling state-owned industries. Choice C is not the answer because lines 12-14 state that "the government has been able to repay 12.5 percent of the net national debt over a two-year period." Choice E is not the answer because lines 8-9 state that the government has decreased borrowings and losses of the state-owned industries mentioned in lines 6-7.

207. According to the passage, which of the following resulted in increased productivity in companies that have been privatized?

    (A) A large number of employees chose to purchase shares in their companies.
    (B) Free shares were widely distributed to individual shareholders.
    (C) The government ceased to regulate major industries.
    (D) Unions conducted wage negotiations for employees.
    (E) Employee-owners agreed to have their wages lowered.

The best answer is A. In lines 24-26, the author attributes improved productivity partly to the opportunity given to employees of privatized industries to purchase shares in their own companies. The next sentence gives examples of how employees "responded enthusiastically to the offer of shares," thereby implying that many employees bought shares in the privatized companies. Choice B is incorrect because, although the passage mentions that some economists suggested giving away free shares, the passage does not indicate that any shares were given away. Choice C is incorrect because the subject of regulation is not addressed, and choices D and E are incorrect because the passage does not discuss the relationship between wages and productivity.

208. It can be inferred from the passage that the author considers labor disruptions to be

    (A) an inevitable problem in a weak national economy
    (B) a positive sign of employee concern about a company
    (C) a predictor of employee reactions to a company's offer to sell shares to them
    (D) a phenomenon found more often in state-owned industries than in private companies
    (E) a deterrence to high performance levels in an industry

The best answer is E. In lines 15-17, the author states that privatization has "raised the level of performance" in industry. As an example, the author mentions in lines 19-21 that at one company, "labor disruptions common in the 1970's and early 1980's have now virtually disappeared." Thus, the author is implying that an absence of labor disruptions raises the level of performance, and the converse—that labor disruptions adversely affect performance levels. Choices A, B, and C are incorrect because the passage makes no generalization about

-471-

labor disruptions in a weak national economy, nor does it connect labor disruptions with employee concern or employee shareholding. Choice D is incorrect because the passage makes no generalization about the frequency of labor disruptions throughout either state-owned or private companies.

209. The passage supports which of the following statements about employees buying shares in their own companies?

(A) At three different companies, approximately nine out of ten of the workers were eligible to buy shares in their companies.
(B) Approximately 90 percent of the eligible workers at three different companies chose to buy shares in their companies.
(C) The opportunity to buy shares was discouraged by at least some labor unions.
(D) Companies that demonstrated the highest productivity were the first to allow their employees the opportunity to buy shares.
(E) Eligibility to buy shares was contingent on employees' agreeing to increased work loads.

The best answer is B. In lines 27-30, the passage cites the percentage of eligible workers (rather than the percentage of total workers) who bought shares at three different companies; these percentages were respectively 89 percent, 90 percent, and 92 percent—that is, approximately 90 percent in each case. Choice A is incorrect because the passage does not state what portion of the workforce at each company was actually eligible to buy shares. Choice C is incorrect because the passage does not state labor unions' position on employee shareholding. Choices D and E are incorrect because the passage does not mention any contingency on which employees' opportunity to buy shares was based.

210. Which of the following statements is most consistent with the principle described in lines 30-32 ?

(A) A democratic government that decides it is inappropriate to own a particular industry has in no way abdicated its responsibilities as guardian of the public interest.
(B) The ideal way for a government to protect employee interests is to force companies to maintain their share of a competitive market without government subsidies.
(C) The failure to harness the power of self-interest is an important reason that state-owned industries perform poorly.
(D) Governments that want to implement privatization programs must try to eliminate all resistance to the free-market system.
(E) The individual shareholder will reap only a minute share of the gains from whatever sacrifices he or she makes to achieve these gains.

The best answer is C. Lines 30-32 assert that people who have a personal stake in an endeavor will "work to make it prosper." In other words, self-interest is an incentive to make people perform better. Choice C makes the same assumption and uses that assumption in the context of state-owned industries to assert that the converse is also true: that when workers lack a personal stake in the fate of their industry, their performance will be poor. Thus, state-owned industries, in which employees receive no additional benefit from increased profits, perform poorly because the industries have failed to use employees' self-interest as motivation for those employees to perform well.

211. Which of the following can be inferred from the passage about the privatization process in the United Kingdom?

(A) It depends to a potentially dangerous degree on individual ownership of shares.
(B) It conforms in its most general outlines to Thomas Paine's prescription for business ownership.
(C) It was originally conceived to include some giving away of free shares.
(D) It has been successful, even though privatization has failed in other countries.
(E) It is taking place more slowly than some economists suggest is necessary.

The best answer is E. In lines 36-38, the author notes that some economists have suggested a way to "provide a needed acceleration of the privatization process." That the acceleration is considered to be "needed" suggests that these economists see the privatization process as occurring more slowly than it should be occurring. Choice A is incorrect because the passage does not attribute any danger to individual ownership of shares. Choice B is incorrect because the sale of shares to employees was optional rather than a part of the actual privatization process. Choice C is incorrect because the passage presents no evidence that this idea was part of the original conception. Choice D is incorrect because the passage does not mention how privatization has fared elsewhere.

212. The quotation in line 39 is most probably used to

(A) counter a position that the author of the passage believes is incorrect
(B) state a solution to a problem described in the previous sentence
(C) show how opponents of the viewpoint of the author of the passage have supported their arguments
(D) point out a paradox contained in a controversial viewpoint
(E) present a historical maxim to challenge the principle introduced in the third paragraph

The best answer is A. Paine's saying asserts that people do not hold in high esteem something that comes to them too easily; in this case, the author of the passage is applying the maxim to workers in privatized industries. The author of the passage states that Paine's point is missed by those economists who believe that giving away, rather than selling, company shares to the employees of a privatized company would spur the privatization process. Thus, the author of the passage believes that the position taken by these economists is incorrect, and that the opposing position as represented by Paine's maxim is correct—that workers will value the shares more if the shares have a cost.

Questions 213-217 refer to the passage on page 386.

213. The passage is primarily concerned with

(A) describing the effects of human activities on algae in coral reefs
(B) explaining how human activities are posing a threat to coral reef communities
(C) discussing the process by which coral reefs deteriorate in nutrient-poor waters
(D) explaining how coral reefs produce food for themselves
(E) describing the abundance of algae and filter-feeding animals in coral reef areas

This question asks you to identify the primary concern of the passage. The best answer is B. The first paragraph describes how coral reefs survive in nutrient-poor waters. The second paragraph states that human activities are adding nutrients to shallow marine habitats, thus threatening the survival of coral reef communities. Choices A and E can be eliminated because an increase in algae and filter-feeding animals is mentioned in the context of the passage's larger concern with the negative effects of human activities on coral reefs. Choice C is incorrect because the first paragraph of the passage explains how coral reefs survive in nutrient-poor waters; the deterioration of coral reef communities has occurred as a result of the increase in nutrients in their habitats. Choice D can be eliminated because the first paragraph states that symbiotic cells of algae known as zooxanethellae produce food for coral reef communities.

214. The passage suggests which of the following about coral reef communities?

(A) Coral reef communities may actually be more likely to thrive in waters that are relatively low in nutrients.
(B) The nutrients on which coral reef communities thrive are only found in shallow waters.
(C) Human population growth has led to changing ocean temperatures, which threatens coral reef communities.
(D) The growth of coral reef communities tends to destabilize underwater herbivore populations.
(E) Coral reef communities are more complex and diverse than most ecosystems located on dry land.

This question asks you to identify what the passage suggests about coral reef communities. The best answer is A. The first paragraph of the passage describes how coral reef communities have survived in nutrient-poor waters. Lines 21-22 go on to state that recent "Declines in reef communities are consistent with observations that nutrient input is increasing" in habitats occupied by coral reefs. Thus, the passage suggests that coral reef communities are more likely to survive in nutrient-poor waters. Both B and C can be eliminated because the passage does not state that human population growth has led to changing ocean temperatures, nor does it state that the nutrients on which coral reef communities thrive are found only in shallow waters. Choice D is incorrect because the passage states that destabilized herbivore populations are a symptom of the decline of coral reef communities rather than a result of the growth of coral reef communities. Choice E can also be eliminated because the first sentence of the passage states that coral reefs "are one of the most fragile, biologically complex, and diverse marine ecosystems on Earth"; it does not, however, discuss the complexity of coral reefs communities in the context of ecosystems on dry land.

215. The author refers to "filter-feeding animals" (line 20) in order to

(A) provide an example of a characteristic sign of reef deterioration
(B) explain how reef communities acquire sustenance for survival
(C) identify a factor that helps herbivore populations thrive
(D) indicate a cause of decreasing nutrient input in waters that reefs inhabit
(E) identify members of coral reef communities that rely on coral reefs for nutrients.

This question asks you to identify the purpose of the author's reference to filter-feeding animals. The best answer is A. In the second paragraph, the author asserts that human activities are adding nutrients to coral reef habitats, thus causing reef decline. In lines 18-20, the author identifies "an increasing abundance of . . . filter-feeding animals" as a typical symptom of this decline. Choice B can be eliminated because the way in which reef communities acquire sustenance for survival is described in the first paragraph of the passage, prior to the author's reference to filter-feeding animals. Choice C is not the correct answer because filter-feeding animals are not identified as a factor that helps herbivore populations survive; in fact, destabilized herbivore populations and an increase in filter-feeding animals are signs of coral reef decline. Choice D can be eliminated because the passage indicates that an increase in filter-feeding animals is a symptom of coral reef decline that is brought about by an increase in nutrient input in coral reef habitats, not a decrease in nutrient input. Choice E can be eliminated also because the passage does not mention filter-feeding animals in order to identify coral reef community members that rely on coral reefs for sustenance.

216. According to the passage, which of the following is a factor that is threatening the survival of coral reef communities?

(A) The waters they inhabit contain few nutrient resources.
(B) A decline in nutrient input is disrupting their symbiotic relationship with zooxanthellae.
(C) The degraded waters of their marine habitats have reduced their ability to carry out photosynthesis.
(D) They are too biologically complex to survive in habitats with minimal nutrient input.
(E) Waste by-products result in an increase in nutrient input to reef communities.

This question asks you to identify a factor, mentioned in the passage, that is threatening the survival of coral reef communities. The best answer is E. In lines 16-18, the author indicates that waste by-products created by manufacturing increase the nutrient input in coral reef habitats. In lines 21-25, the author states that the increase in nutrient input is threatening the coral reef communities. Choice A can be eliminated because the first paragraph of the passage indicates that coral reef communities have thrived in nutrient-poor waters. Choice B can be eliminated because the second paragraph of the passage indicates that there has been an increase in the nutrient input in their habitats, not a decline. Choice C is not the correct answer. Although the passage does indicate that the waters of coral reefs' marine habitats have become degraded, the passage does not state that this degradation reduces the ability of coral reef communities to carry out photosynthesis. Choice D is incorrect because the passage does indicate that coral reef communities are complex, but it also states that they have been able to thrive in nutrient-poor waters.

217. It can be inferred from the passage that the author describes coral reef communities as paradoxical most likely for which of the following reasons?

(A) They are thriving even though human activities have depleted the nutrients in their environment.
(B) They are able to survive in spite of an over-abundance of algae inhabiting their waters.
(C) They are able to survive in an environment with limited food resources.
(D) Their metabolic wastes contribute to the degradation of the waters that they inhabit.
(E) They are declining even when the water surrounding them remains clear.

To answer this question, you must use information contained in the passage to draw an inference about why the author labels coral reef communities as paradoxical. The best answer is C. In line 3, the author calls coral reefs "one of the fascinating paradoxes of the biosphere." The author goes on to explain the nature of this paradox: the "prolific and productive" coral reef communities survive in nutrient-poor waters. Choice A contradicts information presented in the passage. The second paragraph indicates that human activities have increased, not decreased, the nutrients in coral reef communities' waters, and that this increase has threatened the survival of such communities. Choice B does not present a reason why the author describes coral reef communities as paradoxical. In addition, lines 18-20 of the passage indicate that an abundance of algae is a symptom of reef decline, not reef survival. Choice D does not describe a paradox, and it misrepresents information presented in the passage. Lines 7-10 indicate that the metabolic wastes of coral reefs are used by zooxanthellae to carry out photosynthesis, thereby sustaining themselves and the coral reefs. Choice E contradicts information presented in the passage. Lines 2-5 indicate that coral reef communities thrive in "clear, and thus nutrient-poor, waters." However, they have begun to decline because of an addition of nutrients in their waters, thus suggesting that the water surrounding them is no longer as clear.

Questions 218-224 refer to the passage on page 388.

218. Which of the following best states the main idea of the passage?

(A) In their definitions of the nature of ethnicity, sociologists have underestimated the power of the primordial human need to belong.
(B) Ethnicity is best defined as a dynamic process that combines cultural components with shared political and economic interests.
(C) In the United States in the twentieth century, ethnic groups have begun to organize in order to further their political and economic interests.
(D) Ethnicity in the United States has been significantly changed by the Civil Rights movement.
(E) The two definitions of ethnicity that have dominated sociologists' discussions are incompatible and should be replaced by an entirely new approach.

This question asks you to identify the statement that best expresses the main idea of the passage. The best answer is B. The passage defines ethnicity and provides examples to illustrate how ethnicity is a "process" that combines cultural concerns with the "shared political and economic interests" mentioned in choice B. Choice A can be eliminated because the "primordial" character of ethnicity is mentioned only as a feature of the first definition of ethnicity mentioned in the passage. Choices C and D can be eliminated because ethnic groups' efforts to further their political and economic interests and changes brought about by the Civil Rights movement are merely used by the author as evidence supporting the main idea. Choice E is not correct because although the passage suggests a new conception of ethnicity, there is no indication that the other definitions discussed are incompatible with each other.

219. Which of the following statements about the first two definitions of ethnicity discussed in the first paragraph is supported by the passage?

    (A) One is supported primarily by sociologists, and the other is favored by members of ethnic groups.

    (B) One emphasizes the political aspects of ethnicity, and the other focuses on the economic aspects.

    (C) One is the result of analysis of United States populations, and the other is the result of analysis of European populations.

    (D) One focuses more on the ancestral components of ethnicity than does the other.

    (E) One focuses more on immigrant groups than does the other.

Since the question simply asks which of the given statements is supported by the passage, you must read each of the choices in order to answer. Reading the first two definitions of ethnicity will be helpful in answering this question. The best answer is D because only the first definition mentions ancestry as a component of ethnicity. The two definitions are contrasted in the passage as well as in choices A, B, and C, but there is no information in the passage to suggest that the definitions are different in any of the specific ways mentioned in these choices. Choice E can be eliminated because neither definition mentions or focuses on immigrant groups.

220. The author of the passage refers to Native American people in the second paragraph in order to provide an example of

    (A) the ability of membership in groups based on shared ancestry and culture to satisfy an essential human need

    (B) how ethnic feelings have both motivated and been strengthened by political activity

    (C) how the Civil Rights movement can help promote solidarity among United States ethnic groups

    (D) how participation in the political system has helped to improve a group's economic situation

    (E) the benefits gained from renewed study of ethnic history and culture

This question asks you to determine why the author uses the actions of Native American people as an example. To answer it, you must decide what the phrase "this process" in line 17 means. The best answer is B because the "process" of ethnicity mentioned in line 17 is described generally in the first paragraph. The reference to Native American people provides a specific example, in terms of political activity, of that process. Specifically, in lines 20-24, the author states that Native Americans' political activities, which were inspired by the Civil Rights movement, have in turn increased interest in Native American history and culture. Choice A can be eliminated because the discussion of Native American people is not concerned with the concept of essential human need, which is mentioned in the first paragraph in the first definition of ethnicity. Choice C can be eliminated because the Civil Rights

movement is mentioned in the second paragraph because of its encouragement of Native American participation in politics, rather than its promoting of solidarity among groups. Both D and E are incorrect because no mention is made of improvement in Native Americans' economic situation or of the benefits gained from studying ethnic history and culture.

221. The passage supports which of the following statements about the Mexican American community?

    (A) In the 1960's the Mexican American community began to incorporate the customs of another ethnic group in the United States into the observation of its own ethnic holidays.

    (B) In the 1960's Mexican American community groups promoted ethnic solidarity primarily in order to effect economic change.

    (C) In the 1960's leaders of the Mexican American community concentrated their efforts on promoting a renaissance of ethnic history and culture.

    (D) In the 1960's members of the Mexican American community were becoming increasingly concerned about the issue of voting rights.

    (E) In the 1960's the Mexican American community had greater success in mobilizing constituents than did other ethnic groups in the United States.

Since the question asks which statement is supported by the passage, you must read the information about the Mexican American community in order to answer. The best answer is D because voting rights is characterized as an emerging issue —an issue of increasing concern. Choice A can be eliminated because Cinco de Mayo and other ethnic holidays are not characterized as having been combined. Choice B can be eliminated because no mention is made of economic change as a motivation for ethnic solidarity. Choice C is incorrect because the passage suggests that ethnic history and culture were not ends in themselves but were used to promote political ends. Choice E is incorrect also because the Mexican American community is not characterized as more successful than other ethnic groups.

222. Which of the following types of ethnic cultural expression is discussed in the passage?

    (A) The retelling of traditional narratives

    (B) The wearing of traditional clothing

    (C) The playing of traditional music

    (D) The celebration of traditional holidays

    (E) The preparation of traditional cuisine

This question simply requires that you select the type of ethnic cultural expression that is mentioned in the passage. The best answer is D. The celebration of Cinco de Mayo and St. Patrick's Day, which are both traditional ethnic holidays, is mentioned in the passage. Choices A, B, C, and E are not correct: these types of ethnic cultural expressions are not mentioned anywhere in the passage.

223. Information in the passage supports which of the following statements about many European ethnic groups in the nineteenth-century United States?

(A) They emphasized economic interests as a way of mobilizing constituents behind certain issues.
(B) They conceived of their own ethnicity as being primordial in nature.
(C) They created cultural traditions that fused United States symbols with those of their countries of origin.
(D) They de-emphasized the cultural components of their communities in favor of political interests.
(E) They organized formal community groups designed to promote a renaissance of ethnic history and culture.

Reference to the "many European ethnic groups in the nine-teenth-century United States" is found in the last paragraph of the passage. The best answer is C. "United States symbols" in choice C paraphrases "civic symbols" in the passage, and "those [symbols] of their countries of origin" in C paraphrases "ethnic . . . symbols." Although the statements in choices A, B, D, and E are not necessarily incorrect, there is no information in the passage that clearly supports any of them.

224. The passage suggests that in 1968 Henry Cisneros most likely believed that

(A) many Mexican Americans would respond posi-tively to the example of Benito Juárez
(B) many Mexican Americans were insufficiently educated in Mexican history
(C) the fight for civil rights in the United States had many strong parallels in both Mexican and Irish history
(D) the quickest way of organizing community-based groups was to emulate the tactics of Benito Juárez
(E) Mexican Americans should emulate the strategies of Native American political leaders

This question asks you to use the information in the passage to draw a conclusion about Henry Cisneros, a Mexican American leader who is discussed in the passage. According to the pas-sage, Cisneros cited Juárez as a model for Mexican Americans. Choice A, the best answer, is another way of saying that Cis-neros believed that his constituents would respond positively to Juárez' example. Choice B can be eliminated because although Cisneros believed a particular historical figure to be important to Mexican Americans, there is no indication that he thought of Mexican Americans as insufficiently educated in Mexican history. Choice C is incorrect because the author men-tions only a parallel between a holiday celebrated by Mexican Americans and a holiday celebrated by Irish Americans. Choice D can be eliminated because the passage states only that Juárez would provide a model for Mexican Americans; it does not refer to his tactics. Choice E can be eliminated because there is no indication in the passage that Cisneros recommended that Mexican Americans emulate strategies used by other groups.

Questions 225-230 refer to the passage on page 390.

225. The primary purpose of the passage is to

(A) contrast possible outcomes of a type of business investment
(B) suggest more careful evaluation of a type of busi-ness investment
(C) illustrate various ways in which a type of business investment could fail to enhance revenues
(D) trace the general problems of a company to a cer-tain type of business investment
(E) criticize the way in which managers tend to analyze the costs and benefits of business investments

This question asks you to identify the primary purpose of the passage as a whole. The best answer is B. The first two sen-tences of the passage point out that attempts to create superior service do not always result in a competitive advantage for a company and that investments in service need to be weighed against other possible methods for improving a company's competitiveness. These statements suggest that more careful evaluation is needed when service improvements are being contemplated for the purpose of increasing competitiveness. Choice A is incorrect because the passage does not contrast possible outcomes of investment in service. The only outcome of such investment that is discussed in the passage is that of lack of improvement in competitive advantage. Choice C can be eliminated because although the passage illustrates a case in which investments in service did not result in increased com-petitiveness, it does not illustrate various ways in which such investments fail to enhance revenues. Choice D is incorrect because the passage is not primarily about the regional bank referred to in the second paragraph and its problems. Rather, the bank is discussed as an example of the larger issue about which the passage is concerned. Choice E can be eliminated because the passage does not explain or criticize *how* man-agers actually analyze the costs and benefits of business invest-ments: it indicates only that managers' analysis is inadequate.

226. According to the passage, investments in service are comparable to investments in production and distribu-tion in terms of the

(A) tangibility of the benefits that they tend to confer
(B) increased revenues that they ultimately produce
(C) basis on which they need to be weighed
(D) insufficient analysis that managers devote to them
(E) degree of competitive advantage that they are likely to provide

This question asks you to identify a similarity between invest-ments in service and investments in production and distribu-tion that is explicitly noted by the author in the passage. The best answer is C. In lines 3-7, the author observes that invest-ments in service are comparable to investments in production and distribution in that both types of investments need to be evaluated on the same basis; specifically the author states that both "must be balanced against other types of investments on the basis of direct, tangible benefits such as cost reduction and increased revenues." Choice A is not correct: lines 3-7 suggest that the author believes that both investments in service and investments in production and distribution may be worthwhile if they result in tangible benefits, but the author neither states nor suggests that the tangibility of investments in service is comparable to the tangibility of investments in production and distribution. Choice B can be eliminated because there is no indication in the passage that when, in fact, investments in service do raise revenues, these revenues are comparable to the revenues raised by investments in production and distribution. Choice D is incorrect because although the passage does suggest that managers' analysis of investments in service is insufficient, there is no indication in the passage that managers' analysis of investments in production and distribution is also insufficient. Choice E can be eliminated because there is no discussion in the passage of the extent to which either investments in service or investments in production and distribution are likely to enhance competitive advantage.

227. **The passage suggests which of the following about service provided by the regional bank prior to its investment in enhancing that service?**

   (A) **It enabled the bank to retain customers at an acceptable rate.**

   (B) **It threatened to weaken the bank's competitive position with respect to other regional banks.**

   (C) **It had already been improved after having caused damage to the bank's reputation in the past.**

   (D) **It was slightly superior to that of the bank's regional competitors.**

   (E) **It needed to be improved to attain parity with the service provided by competing banks.**

This question asks you to draw a conclusion about the service provided by the regional bank discussed in lines 13-24, prior to this bank's investments in service. The best answer is A. The words "This truth" in line 13 refer to the information presented in the previous sentence (lines 7-12). By putting together the information in this sentence and the information in the first sentence of the following paragraph, one can infer that even before this regional bank had instituted its service improvements, it was "already effectively on a par with its competitors because it provide[d] service that avoid[ed] a damaging reputation and ke[pt] customers from leaving at an unacceptable rate, ..." (lines 8-10). Choice B can be eliminated because there is no indication in the passage that the bank's competitive position was threatened by its service. On the contrary, the passage suggests that the bank's service was equal to that of its competitors. Choice C can be eliminated because there is no suggestion in the passage that the bank's reputation had been damaged in the past by its service; indeed, the passage suggests that the bank had avoided a damaging reputation (lines 7-9). Choices D and E are incorrect in that they contradict the passage's implication that the bank was "on a par with its competitors" (lines 7-8) by suggesting that the bank's service was either superior to (choice D) or inferior to (choice E) that of its competitors.

228. **The passage suggests that bank managers failed to consider whether or not the service improvement mentioned in line 19**

   (A) **was too complicated to be easily described to prospective customers**

   (B) **made a measurable change in the experiences of customers in the bank's offices**

   (C) **could be sustained if the number of customers increased significantly**

   (D) **was an innovation that competing banks could have imitated**

   (E) **was adequate to bring the bank's general level of service to a level that was comparable with that of its competitors**

This question asks you to infer, from information in the passage, what managers of the regional bank failed to consider concerning the service improvement mentioned in line 19. The best answer is D. Lines 19-22 state that the bank managers did not "analyze" whether their investments in service "would attract new customers by . . . proving difficult for competitors to copy." From this statement it can be inferred that the bank managers failed to consider whether or not the service improvement could be imitated by competing banks. Choices A, B, and C each raise an issue that could conceivably have been overlooked by the managers of the regional bank. However, the passage provides no indication or suggestion that, in fact, the managers failed to consider any of these issues. Choice E mistakenly presumes that prior to the service improvement referred to in line 19, the service of the regional bank was inferior to that of competitors, whereas lines 7-16 suggest the bank's service was on a par with that of its competitors.

229. **The discussion of the regional bank (lines 13-24) serves which of the following functions within the passage as a whole?**

   (A) **It describes an exceptional case in which investment in service actually failed to produce a competitive advantage.**

   (B) **It illustrates the pitfalls of choosing to invest in service at a time when investment is needed more urgently in another area.**

   (C) **It demonstrates the kind of analysis that managers apply when they choose one kind of service investment over another.**

   (D) **It supports the argument that investments in certain aspects of service are more advantageous than investments in other aspects of service.**

   (E) **It provides an example of the point about investment in service made in the first paragraph.**

This question asks you to select the choice that best describes how the second paragraph (lines 13-24) logically relates to the rest of the passage. The best answer is E because the author's purpose in the passage is to suggest that investments in service do not necessarily translate into a competitive advantage. The second paragraph logically relates to this purpose by presenting an example of a company that did not improve its competitive advantage by investments in service, even though it did improve service. Choice A can be eliminated: while it is true that the bank's investment in service failed to produce a competitive advantage, there is no indication that the bank was unusual in this respect. Choice B is incorrect because although the passage suggests that the regional bank's investments in service were unwise in that they failed to improve the bank's competitiveness, the second paragraph does not illustrate problems, or pitfalls, arising from the bank's decision to invest in service rather than in other aspects of its business. Choices C and D are incorrect because the passage does not discuss the kind of analysis managers use in deciding which services to invest in (choice C), or the relative advantages of investing in different aspects of service (choice D).

230. The author uses the word "only" in line 23 most likely in order to

(A) highlight the oddity of the service improvement
(B) emphasize the relatively low value of the investment in service improvement
(C) distinguish the primary attribute of the service improvement from secondary attributes
(D) single out a certain merit of the service improvement from other merits
(E) point out the limited duration of the actual service improvement

This question requires you to identify the author's most likely rhetorical purpose in using the word "only" in line 23 of the passage. The best answer is B. The word "only" in line 23 appears in a sentence that identifies the sole benefit of the bank's investment in service. In this context, the word "only" highlights the low return on the bank's investments in service: whereas the bank's managers clearly had hoped to gain a competitive edge, in fact they gained only a single, seemingly insignificant benefit as a result of their investments in service, that is, the ease with which the improvement in service could be described to the bank's customers. Choice A can be eliminated because there is no suggestion in the passage that it is odd either for service to improve as a result of investments in service or for businesses to invest in service improvements. Choice C is not correct because the passage does not discuss any particular attributes of the improvement. Choice D can be eliminated because the passage mentions only one incidental merit of the service improvement: ease of explanation (lines 22-24). It cannot, therefore, be accurately described as singling out a certain merit from other merits. Choice E is incorrect because the passage does not discuss the duration of the single benefit described.

Questions 231-235 refer to the passage on page 392.

231. The primary purpose of the passage is to

(A) present several explanations for a well-known fact
(B) suggest alternative methods for resolving a debate
(C) argue in favor of a controversial theory
(D) question the methodology used in a study
(E) discuss the implications of a research finding

This question asks you to identify the primary purpose of the passage. Choice E is the best answer. The first paragraph of the passage mentions evidence discovered at the Rancho La Brea tar pits and suggests that this evidence provides information about predator-prey dynamics in the late Pleistocene era. After dismissing possible alternative explanations, the second paragraph describes what is considered to be the most likely explanation for the findings. Choice A is incorrect because the passage discusses several explanations for the findings but only in order to eliminate them as rivals of the explanation that credits behavioral differences. In addition, there is no indication of how well known the evidence regarding tooth fractures is. Choice B is incorrect because no alternative methods for resolving a debate are mentioned. Choice C is incorrect because there is no suggestion in the passage that the preferred explanation for the tooth fractures is controversial. Choice D is incorrect: there is nothing in the passage to suggest that the evidence discussed in the passage or the way in which it is analyzed is questionable.

232. The passage suggests that, compared with Pleistocene carnivores in other areas, Pleistocene carnivores in the La Brea area

(A) included the same species, in approximately the same proportions
(B) had a similar frequency of tooth fractures
(C) populated the La Brea area more densely
(D) consumed their prey more thoroughly
(E) found it harder to obtain sufficient prey

This question asks you to recognize what is implied in the passage's comparison of data obtained from La Brea with data obtained from other Pleistocene sites. The best answer is B. The passage says ". . . breakage data obtained from other Pleistocene sites were similar to the La Brea data" (lines 16-17). Since there is no suggestion in the passage that this data is misleading, the implication is that the frequencies of tooth fractures ("breakage data") in the two groups were similar. Choice A is incorrect because this issue is not addressed in the passage. There is no discussion of differences between or similarities in species found in the two areas. Choices C, D, and E can be eliminated because the passage does not suggest that carnivore populations at La Brea differed from carnivore populations at other Pleistocene sites.

233. According to the passage, the researchers believe that the high frequency of tooth breakage in carnivores found at La Brea was caused primarily by

(A) the aging process in individual carnivores
(B) contact between the fossils in the pits
(C) poor preservation of the fossils after they were removed from the pits
(D) the impact of carnivores' teeth against the bones of their prey
(E) the impact of carnivores' teeth against the bones of other carnivores during fights over kills

This question asks you what the researchers believe was primarily responsible for the high frequency of tooth breakage in carnivores found at La Brea. Choice D is the best answer. According to the passage, the explanation for the high frequency of breakage that is considered most plausible by researchers is "more contact between the teeth of the predators and the bones of the prey" (lines 20-21). Choice A is an example of demographic bias. Choice B is an example of preservational bias. Lines 9-15 of the passage indicate that researchers reject these explanations. Choice C is incorrect because preservation of fossils after removal from the pits is not discussed in the passage. Choice E is incorrect: although the passage mentions competition over kills, there is no mention of carnivores' teeth impacting the bones of other carnivores during fights.

234. The researchers' conclusion concerning the absence of demographic bias would be most seriously undermined if it were found that

(A) the older an individual carnivore is, the more likely it is to have a large number of tooth fractures
(B) the average age at death of a present-day carnivore is greater than was the average age at death of a Pleistocene carnivore
(C) in Pleistocene carnivore species, older individuals consumed carcasses as thoroughly as did younger individuals
(D) the methods used to determine animals' ages in fossil samples tend to misidentify many older individuals as younger individuals
(E) data concerning the ages of fossil samples cannot provide reliable information about behavioral differences between extinct carnivores and present-day carnivores

This question asks you to identify a statement that would undermine the researchers' conclusion regarding demographic bias. The researchers concluded that demographic bias was not a factor because older individuals were not disproportionately represented among the fossils. The implication of this conclusion is that older individuals might be expected to have a higher rate of tooth breakage. The best answer is D. The researchers' conclusions with regard to the demographic bias are dependent upon reliable information about the age of the individuals in the fossil samples. If there were a demographic

bias—in this case, a preponderance of older individuals—in the fossil samples, the misidentification of older individuals as younger ones would have concealed the bias from researchers. Choice A is not correct. The researchers' conclusions imply that older individuals might be expected to have a higher rate of tooth breakage. Findings that confirmed this would not undermine the researchers' conclusion that the samples were representative. The information in choices B, C, and E is irrelevant to the issue of whether older individuals were disproportionately represented among the fossil samples.

235. The passage suggests that if the researchers had <u>not</u> found that two extinct carnivore species were free of tooth breakage, the researchers would have concluded that

(A) the difference in breakage frequencies could have been the result of damage to the fossil remains in the La Brea pits
(B) the fossils in other Pleistocene sites could have higher breakage frequencies than do the fossils in the La Brea pits
(C) Pleistocene carnivore species probably behaved very similarly to one another with respect to consumption of carcasses
(D) all Pleistocene carnivore species differed behaviorally from present-day carnivore species
(E) predator densities during the Pleistocene era were extremely high

This question asks you to identify a conclusion that the researchers might have reached if they had not found the two extinct carnivore species that were free of tooth breakage. The best answer is A. The researchers used the evidence of extinct carnivore species that were free of tooth breakage to eliminate preservational bias, that is, to eliminate the possibility that fractures were caused by abrasion in the pits. If every extinct species found had shown tooth breakage, the possibility that fractures were caused by abrasion within the pits could not have been eliminated, and the researchers would have concluded that the damage could have occurred in the La Brea pits. Choice B is incorrect because there is nothing in the passage to suggest the relevance of these two species to predicting breakage frequency at other sites. Choice C can be eliminated because the passage suggests that if every extinct species found in the La Brea pits showed tooth breakage, researchers would have considered that preservational bias, not similarity of consumption behavior in Pleistocene carnivore species, was responsible for the finding. Choice D can be eliminated because the passage suggests that if every extinct species found in the La Brea pits showed tooth breakage, researchers would have concluded that the fractures could have been caused by preservational bias rather than by behavior in Pleistocene carnivore species that differed from behavior in present-day species. Choice E is incorrect: if every extinct species found in the La Brea pits showed tooth breakage, the breakage could have been attributable to preservational bias rather than to high predator densities during the Pleistocene era.

Questions 236-240 refer to the passage on page 394.

236. The primary purpose of the passage is to

(A) explain and critique the methods used by early statisticians
(B) compare and contrast a historical situation with a current-day one
(C) describe and explain a historical change
(D) discuss historical opposition to an established institution
(E) trace the origin of a contemporary controversy

This question asks you to identify what the passage is mainly concerned with doing. The best answer is choice C. Lines 1-5 state that the United States census' occupational information about women became more detailed and precise during the nineteenth century. The rest of the passage discusses how and why this change occurred. Choice A is incorrect because it is overly broad. The passage does not describe methods used by early statisticians. Rather, it concerns the more narrow topic of information about women provided by the United States census during the nineteenth century. Choice B is incorrect. Although the passage does deal with a historical topic—namely, the United States censuses during the nineteenth century—it does not describe the current-day United States census. Choice D is incorrect: although the passage describes a series of changes made to the United States census during the nineteenth century, there is no mention in the passage of opposition to the census. Choice E is incorrect because the passage is concerned with certain historical changes in the census, not with a contemporary controversy.

237. Each of the following aspects of nineteenth-century United States censuses is mentioned in the passage EXCEPT the

(A) year in which data on occupations began to be analyzed by gender
(B) year in which specific information began to be collected on individuals in addition to the head of the household
(C) year in which overlap between women employed outside the home and women keeping house was first calculated
(D) way in which the 1890 census measured women's income levels and educational backgrounds
(E) way in which household members were counted in the 1840 census

This question asks you to identify which of several pieces of information about nineteenth-century United States censuses is NOT presented in the passage. The best answer is D. Lines 24-29 of the passage, which describe the 1890 United States census, suggest that this census gathered information about women's occupations and wages. There is, however, no indication of how (or whether) the census measured women's overall income levels, and the passage does not mention women's educational backgrounds in connection with the census. Choice A is incorrect: lines 19-20 of the passage indicate that 1870 was the year in which occupational information was first analyzed by gender. Choice B is incorrect: lines 16-19 of the passage state that 1850 was the year in which information about individuals was first collected. Choice C is incorrect: lines 19-29 of the passage indicate that 1890 was the year in which overlap between women who were employed outside the home and women who kept house was first determined. Choice E is incorrect: lines 5-15 of the passage state that in the 1840 United States census, the head of household was specified by name while other household members were indicated by occupational and other categories.

238. It can be inferred from the passage that the 1840 United States census provided a count of which of the following?

(A) Women who worked exclusively in the home
(B) People engaged in nonfarming occupations
(C) People engaged in social movements
(D) Women engaged in family-run enterprises
(E) Men engaged in agriculture

This question asks you to draw a conclusion about the 1840 United States census that is suggested by, rather than explicitly stated in, the passage. Choice B is the best answer. Lines 5-15 indicate that in the 1840 United States census, individuals were classified by occupational categories. It can be inferred from this information that the 1840 census provided a count of persons in occupations other than farming. Choice A is incorrect: lines 19-29 suggest that the number of women who worked exclusively in the home could not have been determined from United States census data before 1890, since the 1890 census was the first in which overlap between women who worked outside the home and women who worked in the home was determined. Choice C is incorrect: although lines 16-19 state that changes to the 1850 census were made partly in response to the antislavery and women's rights movements, there is no indication in the passage that any nineteenth-century census collected information about persons' participation in social movements. Choices D and E are incorrect. Lines 19-20 indicate that the 1870 United States census was the first in which occupational information was analyzed by gender. From this information it is possible to infer that no United States census prior to 1870 could have provided a count either of women engaged in family-run enterprises or of men engaged in agriculture.

239. The author uses the adjective "simple" in line 5 most probably to emphasize that the

(A) collection of census information became progressively more difficult throughout the nineteenth century
(B) technology for tabulating census information was rudimentary during the first half of the nineteenth century
(C) home-based agricultural economy of the early nineteenth century was easier to analyze than the later industrial economy
(D) economic role of women was better defined in the early nineteenth century than in the late nineteenth century
(E) information collected by early-nineteenth-century censuses was limited in its amount of detail

This question asks you to identify the idea that the author emphasizes by using the word "simple" in line 5 of the passage. Choice E is the best answer. The word "simple" appears in a sentence that describes the United States census from the beginning of the nineteenth century through 1840. This sentence appears immediately after a statement indicating that during the nineteenth century, the United States census became more detailed and precise. In this context, the word "simple" in line 5 emphasizes the idea that occupational information in United States censuses of the early nineteenth century was limited in its amount of detail. Choices A, B, C, and D are incorrect for the same reason: none represents a claim which the passage makes. The passage does not discuss the difficulty of collecting census data, the technology for tabulating census information, or the relative ease with which various nineteenth-century economies could be analyzed. The passage also does not discuss the degree to which women's economic role was well defined in the early nineteenth century as compared with the late part of the century.

240. The passage suggests which of the following about the "women's advocates and women statisticians" mentioned in lines 27-28 ?

(A) They wanted to call attention to the lack of pay for women who worked in the home.
(B) They believed that previous census information was inadequate and did not reflect certain economic changes in the United States.
(C) They had begun to press for changes in census-taking methods as part of their participation in the antislavery movement.
(D) They thought that census statistics about women would be more accurate if more women were employed as census officials.
(E) They had conducted independent studies that disputed the official statistics provided by previous United States censuses.

This question asks you to choose which of several statements about the "women's advocates and women statisticians" mentioned in lines 27-28 can best be inferred from information presented in the passage. Choice B is the best answer. Lines 25-29 of the passage state that "the rapid entry of women into the paid labor force and social issues arising from industrialization" had caused "women's advocates and women statisticians" to press for "more thorough and accurate accounting of women's occupations and wages" in the 1890 census. Their pressing for fuller information implies that the women's advocates and women statisticians believed earlier United States censuses had not provided adequate information about women's occupations and wages. The fact that recent economic changes such as women's increased participation in the paid labor force are described as causing the request for a fuller census accounting implies that these changes were among the things which the advocates believed were not reflected in census information previously. Both A and C attribute the desire of women's advocates and women statisticians for more thorough and accurate census information to an explanation other than the one given in lines 24-29 of the passage. The passage does not indicate that these advocates and statisticians were participants in the antislavery movement or that they wanted to call attention to the lack of pay for women who worked at home. Choice D is incorrect because it cannot be determined from the information presented in the passage whether these advocates and statisticians thought that census statistics about women would be more accurate if more women were employed as census officials. Choice E is incorrect because it cannot be determined from the information presented in the passage whether these advocates and statisticians personally conducted independent studies relating to census statistics.

Questions 241-248 refer to the passage on page 396.

241. The author's main point is that

(A) modern multinationals originated in the sixteenth and seventeenth centuries with the establishment of chartered trading companies
(B) the success of early chartered trading companies, like that of modern multinationals, depended primarily on their ability to carry out complex operations
(C) early chartered trading companies should be more seriously considered by scholars studying the origins of modern multinationals
(D) scholars are quite mistaken concerning the origins of modern multinationals
(E) the management structures of early chartered trading companies are fundamentally the same as those of modern multinationals

This question asks you to identify the author's main point in the passage. The best answer is C. In the first paragraph, the author states that early chartered trading companies are usually not considered to be precursors of the modern multinational corporation. In the second paragraph, however, the author goes on to discuss similarities between early chartered trading companies and the modern multinational corporation. At the end of the passage the author asserts that early chartered trading companies "merit further study as analogues of more modern structures." Choice A is incorrect: although the passage indicates similarities between early chartered trading companies and the modern multinational corporation, it does not assert that these trading companies originated the modern multinational corporation. Choice B is incorrect because the passage focuses on the similarities between early chartered trading companies and the modern multinational, not on the factors that determined their success. Choice D is incorrect because the author does not suggest that scholars are mistaken that the modern multinational corporation originated with nineteenth-century British firms; instead, the author suggests that certain similarities between early chartered trading companies and the modern multinational merit further attention. Choice E can be eliminated because the author does not assert that the management structures of early chartered trading companies were fundamentally the same as those of modern multinationals.

242. According to the passage, early chartered trading companies are usually described as

(A) irrelevant to a discussion of the origins of the modern multinational corporation
(B) interesting but ultimately too unusual to be good subjects for economic study
(C) analogues of nineteenth-century British trading firms
(D) rudimentary and very early forms of the modern multinational corporation
(E) important national institutions because they existed to further the political aims of the governments of their home countries

This question asks you to identify a typical characterization of early chartered trading companies that is mentioned in the passage. The best answer is A. Lines 10-13 of the passage state that early chartered trading companies are not usually considered relevant to the discussion of the origin of the modern multinational corporation. Choices B and E are incorrect because the passage does not indicate that early chartered trading companies are considered unusual nor does it indicate that their importance is considered to stem from their furthering of political aims. Choices C and D are incorrect because the first paragraph of the passage indicates that nineteenth-century British trading firms, but not early chartered trading companies, are described as having originated the modern multinational.

243. It can be inferred from the passage that the author would characterize the activities engaged in by early chartered trading companies as being

(A) complex enough in scope to require a substantial amount of planning and coordination on the part of management
(B) too simple to be considered similar to those of a modern multinational corporation
(C) as intricate as those carried out by the largest multinational corporations today
(D) often unprofitable due to slow communications and unreliable means of transportation
(E) hampered by the political demands imposed on them by the governments of their home countries

This question asks you to draw an inference about how the author of the passage would describe the activities engaged in by early chartered trading companies. The best answer is A. The first sentence of the second paragraph of the passage outlines the activities of early chartered trading companies. The author then goes on to say that the "large volume of transactions associated with these activities seems to have necessitated hierarchical management structures." The last two sentences of the second paragraph provide an example of the activity required to manage the work of early chartered trading companies. Thus it can be inferred from the passage that the author would agree that the activities of early chartered trading companies were complex enough to require a high level of planning on the part of management. Both B and C misrepresent the author's description of the activities engaged in by early chartered trading companies. The author suggests that the activities are fairly complex and in some ways similar to those of a modern multinational corporation, but does not indicate how the activities compare in complexity with those carried out by the largest multinational corporations today. Choice D is incorrect: lines 18-24 of the passage indicate that early chartered trading companies were successful. Choice E is incorrect: although the author of the passage indicates that early chartered trading companies depended heavily on their national governments, the author does not suggest that such companies were hampered by their governments' political demands.

244. The author lists the various activities of early chartered trading companies in order to

   (A) analyze the various ways in which these activities contributed to changes in management structure in such companies
   (B) demonstrate that the volume of business transactions of such companies exceeded that of earlier firms
   (C) refute the view that the volume of business undertaken by such companies was relatively low
   (D) emphasize the international scope of these companies' operations
   (E) support the argument that such firms coordinated such activities by using available means of communication and transport

This question asks you to identify the function served by the author's listing the various activities of early chartered trading companies. The best answer is C. In the last sentence of the first paragraph of the passage, the author states that the volume of early chartered trading companies' transactions is usually assumed to have been low. The author then contradicts this view in the second paragraph by listing many different kinds of trade-related activities undertaken by trading companies that indicate a significant volume of business. Thus the author's list serves to refute the belief that the volume of early chartered trading companies' transactions was relatively low. Choice A is incorrect because the passage indicates that the nature of the various transactions engaged in by early chartered trading companies required a complex management structure, but the author's

listing of activities does not indicate ways in which the management structure changed. Choices B, D, and E can be eliminated: the list of examples of the various activities engaged in by early chartered trading companies does not follow a statement about the international scope of these companies or a comparison with the activities of earlier firms, and it is not offered in support of an argument about how chartered trading companies used available means of communication and transport.

245. With which of the following generalizations regarding management structures would the author of the passage most probably agree?

   (A) Hierarchical management structures are the most efficient management structures possible in a modern context.
   (B) Firms that routinely have a high volume of business transactions find it necessary to adopt hierarchical management structures.
   (C) Hierarchical management structures cannot be successfully implemented without modern communications and transportation.
   (D) Modern multinational firms with a relatively small volume of business transactions usually do not have hierarchically organized management structures.
   (E) Companies that adopt hierarchical management structures usually do so in order to facilitate expansion into foreign trade.

This question asks you to use information in the passage to choose which of several generalizations about management structures the author of the passage would be most likely to agree with. The best answer is B. In the first sentence of the second paragraph of the passage, the author lists activities that early chartered trading companies engaged in. In lines 24-27, the author goes on to state that the high volume of transactions associated with these activities apparently "necesitated hierarchical management structures." This suggests that the author accepts the idea that hierarchical management structures are necessary for dealing with a large volume of transactions. Choices A and E make assertions about hierarchical management structures for which there is no support in the passage: the author does not suggest that hierarchical management structures are the most efficient ones possible in a modern context or that such structures are adopted to facilitate expansion into foreign trade. Choice C is incorrect because it is an assertion that the author would be likely to disagree with. Lines 24-27 of the passage indicate that early chartered trading companies did implement hierarchical management structures "before the advent of modern communications and transportation." Choice D is incorrect because the author does not indicate that hierarchical management structures are found only in firms that have a large number of transactions.

246. The passage suggests that modern multinationals differ from early chartered trading companies in that

(A) the top managers of modern multinationals own stock in their own companies rather than simply receiving a salary
(B) modern multinationals depend on a system of capitalist international trade rather than on less modern trading systems
(C) modern multinationals have operations in a number of different foreign countries rather than merely in one or two
(D) the operations of modern multinationals are highly profitable despite the more stringent environmental and safety regulations of modern governments
(E) the overseas operations of modern multinationals are not governed by the national interests of their home countries

This question asks you to identify a difference between modern multinationals and early chartered trading companies that is mentioned in the passage. The best answer is E. Lines 36-40 of the passage state that a difference between modern multinationals and early chartered trading companies is that early chartered trading companies were governed by the interests of their home countries. Choice A is incorrect: lines 40-43 of the passage indicate that top managers in early chartered trading companies owned a substantial amount of stock in their own companies, whereas stock holdings by senior managers of modern multinationals typically are insignificant. Choice B is incorrect: lines 43-46 of the passage indicate that early chartered trading companies did depend on a system of capitalist international trade. Choice C is incorrect because the passage does not indicate that early chartered trading companies had operations in only one or two foreign countries. Choice D is incorrect because the passage does not suggest that the operations of early chartered trading companies were not profitable.

247. The author mentions the artisan and peasant production systems of early chartered trading companies as an example of

(A) an area of operations of these companies that was unhampered by rudimentary systems of communications and transport
(B) a similarity that allows fruitful comparison of these companies with modern multinationals
(C) a positive achievement of these companies in the face of various difficulties
(D) a system that could not have emerged in the absence of management hierarchies
(E) a characteristic that distinguishes these companies from modern multinationals

This question requires you to recognize how the author uses the reference to artisan and peasant production systems in the passage. The correct answer is E. The third paragraph of the passage describes differences between early trading companies

and modern multinationals. The author mentions the artisan and peasant production systems of early trading companies as an example of one of those differences. Choices A, C, and D are incorrect because the author does not suggest that artisan and peasant production systems were unhampered by rudimentary systems of communications and transport, nor does the author indicate that such systems were a positive achievement or that they were dependent on management hierarchies. Choice B can be eliminated because the author mentions artisan and peasant production systems in the context of a discussion of the differences, not the similarities, between early trading companies and modern multinationals.

248. The passage suggests that one of the reasons that early chartered trading companies deserve comparison with early modern multinationals is

(A) the degree to which they both depended on new technology
(B) the similar nature of their management structures
(C) similarities in their top managements' degree of ownership in the company
(D) their common dependence on political stability abroad in order to carry on foreign operations
(E) their common tendency to revolutionize systems of production

This question asks you to draw an inference from information presented in the passage about why early chartered trading companies deserve comparison with modern multinationals. The correct answer is B. Lines 1-5 of the passage indicate that modern multinationals originated when "teams of salaried managers organized into hierarchies" replaced owner-managers of nineteenth-century British firms, suggesting that hierarchical management structures are a typical feature of modern multinationals. In lines 24-27, the passage indicates that early chartered trading companies had hierarchical management structures also. The passage implies that similarity of organization is one of the reasons why early chartered trading companies "merit further study as analogues of more modern structures" (lines 48-49). Choices A, D, and E can be eliminated because the passage does not indicate the degree of dependence on technology or discuss the tendency to revolutionize production systems of either early trading companies or modern multinationals, nor does it suggest that either kind of company relied on political stability. Choice C is incorrect. Lines 40-43 of the passage indicate that top managers in early trading companies owned a substantial minority share of their companies, whereas senior managers in modern multinationals own little if any of their companies.

Questions 249-252 refer to the passage on page 398.

249. The primary purpose of the passage is to

(A) criticize a scholar's assumptions and
   methodology
(B) evaluate an approach to women's history
(C) compare two sociological theories
(D) correct a misconception about feminist theory
(E) defend an unpopular ideology

This question asks you to identify the primary purpose of the passage as a whole. Choice B is the best answer. The passage gives an overview of Eisenstein's approach to women's history and then offers an evaluation of that approach. Choice A is not correct: while the passage mentions certain criticisms of Eisenstein's work, it is not her underlying assumptions that are being challenged. Furthermore, the criticisms do not constitute the primary concern of the passage. Choice C is not correct: while two theories are mentioned, a passage whose primary purpose were to compare those two theories would have to discuss the second theory in greater detail. Choices D and E are incorrect because the passage does not suggest that there have been misconceptions about feminist theory, and no particular ideology is being defended.

250. It can be inferred from the passage that, in Eisenstein's view, working women at the turn of the century had which of the following attitudes toward the dominant ideology of their time?

(A) They resented the dominant ideology as degrading.
(B) They preferred the dominant ideology to other available ideologies.
(C) They began to view the dominant ideology more favorably as a result of their experiences in the labor force.
(D) They accepted some but not all aspects of the dominant ideology.
(E) They believed that the dominant ideology isolated them from one another.

This question requires you to make an inference, based on Eisenstein's arguments, regarding her view of the attitudes of the women she studied. The best answer is D. The first paragraph of the passage notes Eisenstein's argument that women neither wholly accepted nor rejected the dominant ideology of the time, and that they modified this and other ideologies to suit their needs. Choice A is incorrect. The dominant ideology is one among several ideologies that Eisenstein argues were adapted and modified by working women; the passage does not suggest that Eisenstein believed that working women resented that ideology or considered it degrading. Choice B is incorrect because Eisenstein's argument is that women took aspects of several available ideologies and modified them; there is no suggestion that any one ideology was preferred over others. Choice C can be eliminated because according to the passage, it is Tentler, not Eisenstein, who argues that working conditions increased the attractiveness of the dominant ideology. Choice E is not correct. Eisenstein argues that domestic work tended to isolate women from one another; there is no indication in the passage that the women themselves believed the dominant ideology was responsible for this.

251. Which of the following best describes the organization of the first paragraph of the passage?

(A) A chronological account of a historical development is presented, and then future developments are predicted.
(B) A term is defined according to several different schools of thought, and then a new definition is formulated.
(C) A theory is presented, an alternative viewpoint is introduced, and then the reasoning behind the initial theory is summarized.
(D) A tentative proposal is made, reasons for and against it are weighed, and then a modified version of the proposal is offered.
(E) A controversy is described, its historical implications are assessed, and then a compromise is suggested.

This question asks you to identify the structure of the first paragraph of the passage. The best answer is C. The first paragraph presents Eisenstein's theory, then makes note of Tentler's opposing views, then continues with further explication of Eisenstein's argument. Choice A can be eliminated because the paragraph discusses a certain historical development, the evolution of working women's values, but it does not make predictions about future developments. Choice B is not correct because the paragraph is not concerned with contrasting definitions of any term. Choices D and E are not correct because the paragraph does not discuss a tentative proposal that requires evaluation or a controversy that calls for resolution.

252. Which of the following would the author of the passage be most likely to approve as a continuation of Eisenstein's study?

   (A) An oral history of prominent women labor organizers

   (B) An analysis of letters and diaries written by typical female wage earners at the turn of the century

   (C) An assessment of what different social and political groups defined as the dominant ideology in the early twentieth century

   (D) A theoretical study of how socialism and feminism influenced one another at the turn of the century

   (E) A documentary account of labor's role in the introduction of women into the labor force

To answer this question you must decide which answer would best provide the sort of information that the author feels is lacking in Eisenstein's study. The author's critique of Eisenstein's argument is found primarily in the second paragraph. Choice B is the best answer because the author points out that Eisenstein's study is flawed in that it relies on sources that are not representative of the average female worker. An analysis of writings by typical female wage earners would help to rectify this problem. Choice A is not correct. Eisenstein's study already focuses on labor organizers; it is unlikely that the author feels that even more attention to this group is necessary. Choice C is not correct because the passage does not suggest that there were disagreements among social and political groups as to the definition of the dominant ideology. Choices D and E are incorrect because Eisenstein's study is not concerned with the interaction between socialism and feminism, nor with labor's particular role in the introduction of women into the workforce.

Questions 253-256 refer to the passage on page 400.

253. The primary purpose of the passage is to

   (A) refute the idea that the zonation exhibited in mangrove forests is caused by adaptation to salinity

   (B) describe the pattern of zonation typically found in Florida mangrove forests

   (C) argue that Davis' succession paradigm cannot be successfully applied to Florida mangrove forests

   (D) discuss hypotheses that attempt to explain the zonation of coastal mangrove forests

   (E) establish that plants that do well in saline forest environments require salt to achieve maximum metabolic efficiency

This question asks you to identify the primary purpose of the passage as a whole. The best answer is D. The passage discusses two hypotheses concerning zonation of mangrove forests. Choice A can be eliminated because the passage presents as a viable hypothesis the idea that mangrove zonation may be caused by adaptation to salinity. Choice B is incorrect because

the passage is concerned with the causes of zonation patterns, not simply with a description of those patterns. Both C and E contradict information that is presented in the passage.

254. According to the passage, the earliest research on mangrove forests produced which of the following?

   (A) Data that implied random patterns of mangrove species distribution

   (B) Descriptions of species distributions suggesting zonation

   (C) Descriptions of the development of mangrove forests over time

   (D) Reclassification of species formerly thought to be identical

   (E) Data that confirmed the "land-building" role of mangroves

This question asks you to identify information provided in the passage about early research on mangrove forests. That research is discussed in the first paragraph. Choice B is the best answer. Early research on mangrove forests is characterized as having produced descriptions of species distribution from shore to land. Such a distribution is described in the first sentence of the passage as "zonal." Choice A is not correct. Early research described mangrove distribution from shore to land. This implies a regular pattern of distribution, not a random one. Choices C and D are not correct because there is no indication in the passage that early studies of mangrove forests were concerned with the plants' chronological development or with the reclassification of species. Choice E is incorrect because the passage does not say that the research in question did anything except describe species distribution.

255. It can be inferred from the passage that Davis' paradigm does NOT apply to which of the following?

   (A) The shoreline of Florida mangrove forests first studied by Davis

   (B) A shoreline in an area with weak currents

   (C) A shoreline in an area with weak tidal energy

   (D) A shoreline extended by "land-building" species of mangroves

   (E) A shoreline in which few sediments can accumulate

Here you are asked to make an inference based on information that is stated in the passage. Note that the best answer will refer to a situation where Davis' paradigm does NOT apply. Choice E is the best answer. Davis' succession paradigm states that mangroves trap sediments over time, thus extending the shore. A shoreline where few sediments could accumulate would be unable to develop according to such a scheme. Choice A is not correct. Davis first expressed his theory of "land-building" in his study of Florida mangrove forests. Thus his paradigm presumably applies to the shoreline of those forests. Choices B and C are incorrect because the passage states that areas with weak currents and weak tidal energies are areas where land formation will progress according to Davis' paradigm. Choice D is not correct because Davis' paradigm describes the "land-building" process of mangroves, so a shoreline that had been extended by that process would fall within the paradigm.

256. Information in the passage indicates that the author would most probably regard which of the following statements as INCORRECT?

(A) Coastal mangrove forests are usually zonal.
(B) Hurricanes interrupt the process of accretion and succession that extends existing shorelines.
(C) Species of plants that thrive in a saline habitat require salt to flourish.
(D) Plants with the highest metabolic efficiency in a given habitat tend to exclude other plants from that habitat.
(E) Shorelines in areas with weak currents and tides are more likely to be extended through the process of accumulation of sediment than are shorelines with strong currents and tides.

Here you are asked to make an inference about the likely view of the author of the passage. Note that the best answer must be a statement that the author would most likely judge to be INCORRECT. Choice C is best. The author points out that while mangroves normally thrive in highly saline regions, this is not because they require salt. That assertion contradicts the claim made in this answer, so the author would likely regard the claim made in this answer as incorrect. Choice A is incorrect because it paraphrases an assertion the author makes in the first sentence of the passage. Choice B is incorrect because it paraphrases an assertion the author makes in the last sentence of the second paragraph. Choice D is incorrect because the passage does not provide sufficient information to determine whether the author would agree with this statement. Choice E is not correct. The author notes that areas with weak currents and tides are likely to be extended through land formation. Thus the author would consider the assertion made here to be correct, not incorrect.

Questions 257-260 refer to the passage on page 402.

257. According to the passage, all of the following are benefits associated with backward integration EXCEPT

(A) improvement in the management of overhead expenses
(B) enhancement of profit margins on sales of components
(C) simplification of purchasing and marketing operations
(D) reliability of a source of necessary components
(E) elimination of unnecessary research efforts

This question asks you to identify which one of the five answer choices is NOT mentioned in the passage as a benefit associated with backward integration. The best answer is B. The passage does not indicate how backward integration affects the profit margins on sales of components by independent suppliers. Choices A, C, and E are mentioned in the passage as a benefit of backward integration. Choice D is incorrect because the passage indicates that backward integration is a way of having a reliable source of necessary components.

258. According to the passage, when an assembler buys a firm that makes some important component of the end product that the assembler produces, independent suppliers of the same component may

(A) withhold technological innovations from the assembler
(B) experience improved profit margins on sales of their products
(C) lower their prices to protect themselves from competition
(D) suffer financial difficulties and go out of business
(E) stop developing new versions of the component

This question asks you to identify information presented in the passage about independent suppliers of product components. Choice A is the best answer. The passage asserts that independent suppliers making the same components as assemblers may not share technological innovations with assemblers. Choices B, C, D, and E can be eliminated because there is no indication in the passage that independent suppliers making the same components as assemblers experience improved profit margins, lower their prices, suffer financial difficulties, or stop developing new versions of the component.

259. Which of the following best describes the way the last paragraph functions in the context of the passage?

(A) The last in a series of arguments supporting the central argument of the passage is presented.
(B) A viewpoint is presented which qualifies one presented earlier in the passage.
(C) Evidence is presented in support of the argument developed in the preceding paragraph.
(D) Questions arising from the earlier discussion are identified as points of departure for further study of the topic.
(E) A specific example is presented to illustrate the main elements of the argument presented in the earlier paragraphs.

This question asks you to choose the statement that best describes the function of the last paragraph of the passage. The best answer is B. At the end of the third paragraph, the author indicates that assemblers benefit from contracting with, rather than owning, independent suppliers. In the last paragraph, however, the author indicates that contracting with independent suppliers can itself present problems. Thus the last paragraph qualifies the viewpoint presented at the end of the third paragraph. Choice A is not the correct answer because the passage makes several points about backward integration, but does not present a central argument about this topic. Choice C is not the correct answer because the final paragraph qualifies rather than supports an argument made in the third paragraph about contracting with independent suppliers. Choices D and E are incorrect because the final paragraph does not identify questions or present a specific example.

260. According to the passage, which of the following relationships between profits and investments in research and development holds true for producers of technologically advanced components?

(A) Modest investments are required and the profit margins on component sales are low.
(B) Modest investments are required but the profit margins on component sales are quite high.
(C) Despite the huge investments that are required, the profit margins on component sales are high.
(D) Because huge investments are required, the profit margins on component sales are low.
(E) Long-term contractual relationships with purchasers of components ensure a high ratio of profits to investment costs.

This question asks you to identify information presented in the passage about the relationship between profits and investments for producers of technologically advanced components. The best answer is D. The passage indicates that the high investments required to develop technologically advanced components can lead to low profit margins for producers of such components. Choice A is incorrect because the passage indicates that large, not modest, investments in research and development are required. Choices B and C are incorrect because the passage indicates that profit margins for producers of technologically

advanced components are low, not high as these answer choices assert. Choice E is incorrect: although the author claims that long-term contracts with suppliers are beneficial to assemblers, the passage does not indicate that long-term contracts with purchasers lead to high profits for producers of technologically advanced components.

Questions 261-264 refer to the passage on page 404.

261. Which of the following most accurately states the purpose of the passage?

(A) To compare two different approaches to the study of homeostasis
(B) To summarize the findings of several studies regarding organisms' maintenance of internal variables in extreme environments
(C) To argue for a particular hypothesis regarding various organisms' conservation of water in desert environments
(D) To cite examples of how homeostasis is achieved by various organisms
(E) To defend a new theory regarding the maintenance of adequate fluid balance

This question asks you to identify the primary concern of the passage. The best answer is D. The passage focuses primarily on a discussion of how various animals achieve homeostasis. Choice A is not correct: while the passage does discuss the regulatory mechanisms employed by animals in two very different environments, it does not compare two different approaches to the study of those mechanisms. Choice B is not correct because no particular studies are cited in the passage. Choices C and E can be eliminated because the passage is concerned with a straightforward description of certain regulatory processes in various animals. It does not argue in favor of any particular hypothesis, nor does it defend any new theory concerning homeostasis.

262. According to the passage, the camel maintains internal fluid balance in which of the following ways?

I. By behavioral avoidance of exposure to conditions that lead to fluid loss
II. By an ability to tolerate high body temperatures
III. By reliance on stored internal fluid supplies

(A) I only
(B) II only
(C) I and II only
(D) II and III only
(E) I, II, and III

In order to answer this question you must first determine which of the numbered statements correctly describes a way in which the camel maintains internal fluid balance. The correct answer will be the answer choice that lists *only* the numeral or numerals that represent statements supported by information in the passage. Choice B is the best answer because the passage states that camels conserve internal water by sweating and panting only upon reaching high body temperatures. Choices A, C, D, and E are incorrect. Statement I describes a behavior attributed to desert rats, not camels, so no answer choice that includes I can be correct. Statement III contradicts information provided in the passage about camels, namely that they cannot store water (line 23); thus no answer choice that includes III can be correct.

263. It can be inferred from the passage that some mechanisms that regulate internal body temperature, like sweating and panting, can lead to which of the following?

(A) A rise in the external body temperature
(B) A drop in the body's internal fluid level
(C) A decrease in the osmotic pressure of the blood
(D) A decrease in the amount of renal water loss
(E) A decrease in the urine's salt content

To answer this question, you must use information contained in the passage to draw an inference about the effects of certain regulatory mechanisms in animals. Choice B is the best answer. The passage states that camels conserve internal water by sweating and panting *only* when they reach very high body temperatures. Since camels conserve internal water by *not* panting and sweating, it can be inferred that sweating and panting decrease the body's internal fluid level. Choice A can be eliminated because the passage suggests that a rise in body temperature can result in panting and sweating, not vice versa. Choices C and D can be eliminated because there is no information in the passage to suggest that internal body temperature regulation methods result in a decrease in osmotic pressure of the blood or in the amount of water lost through the kidneys. Choice E is incorrect because the passage mentions the salt content of desert rats' urine, but does not suggest that the salt content decreases in response to body temperature regulation mechanisms.

264. It can be inferred from the passage that the author characterizes the camel's kidney as "entirely unexceptional" (lines 23-24) primarily to emphasize that it

(A) functions much as the kidney of a rat functions
(B) does not aid the camel in coping with the exceptional water loss resulting from the extreme conditions of its environment
(C) does not enable the camel to excrete as much salt as do the kidneys of marine vertebrates
(D) is similar in structure to the kidneys of most mammals living in water-deprived environments
(E) requires the help of other organs in eliminating excess salt

This question asks you to identify an attribute of the camel's kidney that the description "entirely unexceptional" emphasizes in the passage. The best answer is choice B. The preceding paragraph concludes with a statement about how desert rats' unusual kidney function aids their homeostasis; by calling the camel's kidney, in contrast, "entirely unexceptional," the author emphasizes the fact that camels, who also inhabit the desert, cannot similarly rely on specialized kidney function to aid in homeostasis. Choice A can be eliminated because the author has just pointed out that desert rats' kidney function is unusual, so calling the camel's kidney "entirely unexceptional" suggests that the two animals' kidneys in fact function differently. Choice C is not correct because there is no suggestion that the author is attempting to compare the functioning of camels' kidneys with the functioning of marine vertebrates' kidneys. Choice D is incorrect because the passage does not provide sufficient information to infer what kidney structure is typical of mammals who inhabit water-deprived environments. Choice E is incorrect because it is marine vertebrates, not camels, whom the author describes as having special organs that help in eliminating excess salt.

Questions 265-267 refer to the passage on page 406.

265. The passage suggests that combing and carding differ from weaving in that combing and carding are

(A) low-skill jobs performed primarily by women employees
(B) low-skill jobs that were not performed in the home
(C) low-skill jobs performed by both male and female employees
(D) high-skill jobs performed outside the home
(E) high-skill jobs performed by both male and female employees

This question asks you draw an inference about something that *differentiates* weaving from combing and carding. The best answer is B. First, the phrase "there was a high concentration of women workers in certain low-skill jobs, such as weaving, but not in others, such as combing and carding" indicates that all three jobs in question were low-skill jobs. Second, the passage states that women tended to take occupations that could be carried out in the home; the fact that there was a high concentration of female weavers, but not of female combers and carders, thus suggests that weaving was performed in the home, but combing and carding were not. Choice A is not correct because the passage suggests that relatively small numbers of women did combing and carding; furthermore, even if combing and carding had been performed mainly by women, this fact would not distinguish those occupations from weaving. Choice C is incorrect because the passage mentions relative *levels of concentration* of women in the occupations of weaving, combing, and carding, suggesting that all three jobs were performed to some extent by men as well. Thus, combing and carding would not differ from weaving in this regard. Choices D and E can be eliminated. The phrase "there was a high concentration of women workers in certain low-skill jobs, such as weaving, but not in others, such as combing and carding" indicates that all three jobs in question were low-skill jobs. Thus any choice that characterizes combing and carding as high-skill jobs is incorrect.

266. Which of the following, if true, would most weaken the explanation provided by the human capital theory for women's concentration in certain occupations in seventeenth-century Florence?

(A) Women were unlikely to work outside the home even in occupations whose hours were flexible enough to allow women to accommodate domestic tasks as well as paid labor.
(B) Parents were less likely to teach occupational skills to their daughters than they were to their sons.
(C) Women's participation in the Florentine paid labor force grew steadily throughout the sixteenth and seventeenth centuries.
(D) The vast majority of female weavers in the Florentine wool industry had children.
(E) Few women worked as weavers in the Florentine silk industry, which was devoted to making cloths that required a high degree of skill to produce.

This question asks you to consider the effect that certain additional information would have on the strength of an explanation provided in the passage. The correct answer choice will be the one that would, if true, most *weaken* the explanation. Choice A is the best answer. The human capital theory explanation posits that women were more likely to take jobs that could be done at home because that allowed the women also to attend to domestic child-rearing duties. If women had been unlikely to work outside the home even in jobs with hours flexible enough to accommodate domestic work as well, then the need to attend to domestic tasks would not appear to be a sufficient explanation for the high concentrations of women who opted to work at home. Choice B is incorrect because a differential teaching of occupational skills by parents to their children according to gender does not weaken the human capital theory explanation. Choice C is incorrect: since women who worked at home and women who worked outside the home were all part of the paid labor force, a growth in the female paid labor force would not necessarily weaken the human capital theory explanation. Choice D is not correct because the explanation asserts that women tended to choose weaving as an occupation because it allowed them to stay home and attend to child rearing. If the vast majority of female weavers had children this would support the explanation, not weaken it. Choice E is incorrect. If the Florentine silk industry was a high-skilled sector of the weaving industry, the human capital theory explanation would lead you to expect few women to be employed in that sector. Thus choice E, rather than weakening the explanation, accords with it.

267. The author of the passage would be most likely to describe the explanation provided by the human capital theory for the high concentration of women in certain occupations in the seventeenth-century Florentine textile industry as

(A) well founded though incomplete
(B) difficult to articulate
(C) plausible but poorly substantiated
(D) seriously flawed
(E) contrary to recent research

This question asks you to make a judgment about the author's attitude toward the human capital explanation for women's distribution among certain types of jobs in the seventeenth-century Florentine textile industry. The best answer is A. The author presents the human-capital theory as one that explains the disparate concentrations of female workers in certain jobs, but also notes that the theory fails to account for differences in pay scales. The author also specifically characterizes the human capital theory as "useful" (line 3). Thus the theory is presented as valid, yet insufficient to account for all aspects of labor segregation by gender. Choice B is incorrect because there is no indication that the author finds the explanation provided by human capital theory difficult to express. Choices C and D are incorrect because the author characterizes the human capital theory as "useful" (line 3) and presents it as a theory that can explain a relatively complex feature of women's labor history —namely, the varied concentration of women in certain occupations in seventeenth-century Florence. Thus it is unlikely that the author considers the explanation itself to be poorly substantiated, and certainly the author does not consider it seriously flawed. Choice E is not correct because the author does not discuss recent research in the passage.

Questions 268-271 refer to the passage on page 408.

268. Which of the following best describes the content of the passage?

(A) A chronology of the development of different methods for mapping Native American lands
(B) A discussion of how the mapmaking techniques of Native Americans differed from those of Europeans
(C) An argument concerning the present-day uses to which historical maps of Native American lands are put
(D) An argument concerning the nature of information contained in maps of Native American lands
(E) A proposal for improving the accuracy of maps of Native American lands

This question asks you to identify the answer that most clearly describes the content of the passage as a whole. Choice D is the best answer. The passage is mainly concerned with arguing that the information contained in maps of Native American lands reflects certain important aspects of the maps' original production. While certain mapping techniques are mentioned in the passage, the passage is not concerned with tracing the development of those techniques as indicated in choice A. Choice B can be eliminated because the passage focuses on non-Native Americans' mapping techniques and is not concerned with comparing those techniques with Native Americans' techniques. Choice C is not correct because the argument in the passage concerns the origins of the information in certain historical maps, not any specific present-day uses of those maps. Choice E is incorrect because the passage does not offer any proposal to amend the accuracy of the maps being discussed.

269. **The passage mentions each of the following as a factor affecting current maps of Native American lands EXCEPT**

(A) **United States government policy**
(B) **non-Native Americans' perspectives on Native Americans**
(C) **origins of the information utilized to produce the maps**
(D) **changes in the ways that tribal lands are used**
(E) **the reasons for producing the maps**

To answer this question correctly you must locate certain pieces of information that are presented explicitly in the passage. Note that the correct answer will be the only answer choice that describes information that is *not* provided in the passage. The best answer is D. While it is possible that changes in tribal land usage could be reflected in historical maps of Native American lands, the passage does not specifically mention this as a factor affecting the maps in question. Choices A, B, C, and E are incorrect. Each of these describes a factor mentioned in the final sentence of the passage.

270. **The passage suggests which of the following about most existing maps of Native American lands?**

(A) **They do not record the migrations of Native American tribes.**
(B) **They have been preserved primarily because of their connection with treaties involving land transfers.**
(C) **They tend to reflect archaeological evidence that has become outdated.**
(D) **They tend to be less accurate when they are based on oral reports than when they are based on written documents.**
(E) **They are not based primarily on the mapmakers' firsthand observations of Native American lands.**

This question requires you to use the information provided in the passage to draw an inference about existing Native American land maps. Choice E is the best answer. The passage points

out that most existing maps are based on second-hand information and that their accuracy is largely dependent on the mapmakers' ability to interpret that information. Thus it can be inferred that most of these maps are not based on firsthand observations by the mapmakers. Choice A is not correct because the passage mentions the "current cartographic record relating to Native American tribes and their migrations," indicating that migrations are at least in part recorded on existing maps. Choice B is not correct: while the passage mentions that some maps were produced in connection with treaties involving land transfers, there is no indication in the passage that this connection was the primary impetus for preservation of the maps. Choice C is incorrect because the passage mentions that some maps are based on archaeological findings, but does not provide information that would support a claim that the archaeological evidence reflected in the maps has become outdated. While the statement in choice D could be true, the passage does not provide information to support such an inference.

271. **All of the following are examples of the type of evidence used in creating "Most existing maps"(lines 7-8) EXCEPT**

(A) **a nineteenth-century government report on population distributions of a particular tribe**
(B) **taped conversations with people who lived on Native American tribal lands in the early twentieth century**
(C) **aerial photographs of geological features of lands inhabited by Native Americans**
(D) **findings from a recently excavated site once inhabited by a certain Native American people**
(E) **a journal kept by a non-Native American explorer who traveled in Native American territory in the early nineteenth century**

To answer this question correctly you must consider the types of evidence that are listed in the passage and determine whether or not each answer choice would represent one of those types of evidence. Note that the correct answer will be the only choice that describes a type of evidence that does *not* represent one of the types mentioned in the passage. The best answer is C because aerial photographs of geological features do not provide an example of a type of evidence mentioned in the passage. Evidence in choice A is an example of an "official report" (lines 10-11). Evidence in choice B is an example of an "oral report" (line 9). Evidence in choice D is an example of "archaeology" (line 9). Evidence in choice E is an example of a "diary" (line 10).

Questions 272-275 refer to the passage on page 410.

272. Which of the following best describes the relationship of the first paragraph to the passage as a whole?

(A) The first paragraph introduces a general thesis that is elaborated on in detail elsewhere in the passage.

(B) The first paragraph presents a concrete instance of a problem that is discussed elsewhere in the passage.

(C) The first paragraph describes a traditional process that is contrasted unfavorably with a newer process described elsewhere in the passage.

(D) The first paragraph presents a dramatic example of the potential of a process that is described elsewhere in the passage.

(E) The first paragraph describes a historic incident that served as the catalyst for developments described elsewhere in the passage.

This question asks you to select the choice that best describes how the first paragraph (lines 1-7) relates to the rest of the passage. The best answer is choice D. The first paragraph presents an example of what may be accomplished with a modern digital recording and processing technique. The remainder of the passage goes into detail about the technique itself. Choice A is not correct in that the first paragraph presents a particular instance of digitization, not a general thesis. Choice B can be eliminated: while the first paragraph does present a concrete example, it is an example of a successful use of digitization, not an example of a problem. Choice C is incorrect because the first paragraph is primarily concerned with presenting an example of a new process, not with describing an old process. Choice E also can be eliminated because the first paragraph mentions a historic recording, not a historic incident, and it does not describe a catalyst for developments discussed elsewhere in the passage.

273. According to the passage, one of the ways in which analog recording systems differ from digital recording systems is that analog systems

(A) can be used to reduce background noise in old recordings

(B) record the original sound as a continuous waveform

(C) distort the original sound somewhat

(D) can avoid introducing extraneous and nonmusical sounds

(E) can reconstruct the original waveform with little loss in quality

This question asks you to identify something mentioned specifically in the passage that is a feature of analog recording systems that is not shared by digital recording systems.

Choice B is the best answer. The passage states in lines 10-13 that analog recording systems represent the original sound as a continuous waveform, while in lines 21-23 it notes that digital recordings reduce the original sound to a series of discrete numbers. Neither A, D, or E are features of analog systems, according to the passage. Choice C is not correct: while the passage does say that analog recording systems distort the original sound, the passage also notes that "it is impossible for digital systems to avoid some distortion" (lines 31-32). Thus some amount of sound distortion is involved in *both* analog and digital recording processes.

274. Which of the following statements about the numbers by which sound is represented in a digital system can be inferred from the passage?

(A) They describe the time interval between successive sounds in a passage of music.

(B) They model large changes in the amplitude of the initial sound with relatively poor precision.

(C) They are slightly altered each time they are read by the playback apparatus.

(D) They are not readily altered by distortion and noise accumulated as the digital signal is stored and manipulated.

(E) They are stored in the recording medium in small groups that can be read simultaneously by the playback apparatus.

To answer this question, you must use information contained in the passage to draw an inference about the numbers by which sound is represented in digital recording systems. The best answer is D because the passage states that storage and manipulation have little effect on the sound quality of digital recordings. Since the sounds of a digital recording are represented by numbers, it may thus be inferred that the numbers themselves are not easily altered by storage and manipulation. Choice A is not correct: since the passage makes no mention of time intervals between successive sounds, one cannot infer that the numbers describe such intervals. Choice B can be eliminated because in its description of sampling error, the passage suggests that small changes in amplitude are sometimes recorded inaccurately in digital systems. However, the passage does not indicate that digital systems have difficulty modeling large changes in amplitude. Choices C and E are incorrect because there is no indication in the passage that the numbers representing sounds in a digital recording are altered in any way during playback, nor that the numbers are stored and read in groups.

275. Which of the following can be inferred from the passage about the digital approach to the processing of sound?

(A) It was developed in competition with wax-cylinder recording technology.

(B) It has resulted in the first distortion-free playback system.

(C) It has been extensively applied to nonmusical sounds.

(D) It cannot yet process music originally recorded on analog equipment.

(E) It is not yet capable of reprocessing old recordings in a completely distortion-free manner.

To answer this question, you must use information contained in the passage to draw an inference about the digital approach to sound processing. Choice E is the best answer. The passage notes that it is impossible for digital systems to avoid some distortion, so it may be inferred that it is not possible to digitally reprocess old recordings without at least some measure of distortion. Choice A is not correct because the wax-cylinder process is characterized as "ancient" (line 7), while digital recording is called "new and superior" (line 9). The wax-cylinder recording mentioned in line 3 is described as "decades-old." The suggestion thus is that the two processes were developed at different times, not that they were developed in competition with each other. Both choices B and D contradict information presented in the passage: it is stated that it is impossible for digital recordings to avoid distortion completely (lines 29-32), and an example is provided in the first paragraph of an analog recording being digitally reprocessed. While the statement in choice C could be true without contradicting any information provided in the passage, the passage does not furnish enough information to justify such an inference.

Questions 276-282 refer to the passage on page 412.

276. The main point made by the passage is that

(A) financial markets provide for an optimum allocation of resources among all competing participants by balancing supply and demand

(B) the allocation of financial resources takes place among separate individual participants, each of whom has access to the market

(C) the existence of certain factors adversely affecting members of minority groups shows that financial markets do not function as conventional theory says they function

(D) investments in minority communities can be made by the use of various alternative financial instruments, such as stocks and bonds

(E) since transaction costs for stocks, bonds, and other financial instruments are not equally apportioned among all minority-group members, the financial market is subject to criticism

This question asks you to identify the main point that is conveyed by the passage. C is the best answer. The overarching message of the passage is that certain factors affecting minority communities are essentially ignored in conventional financial-market analyses. Choice A is not correct because the passage does not discuss issues of supply and demand. Both B and D present a general claim about issues mentioned in the passage, but neither statement expresses the main point of the passage. Choice E can be eliminated because while the passage does criticize certain aspects of the financial market, it is chiefly concerned with differences between minority and non-minority communities, not with any differences among minority-group members.

277. The passage states that traditional studies of the financial market overlook imbalances in the allocation of financial resources because

  (A) an optimum allocation of resources is the final result of competition among participants
  (B) those performing the studies choose an oversimplified description of the influences on competition
  (C) such imbalances do not appear in the statistics usually compiled to measure the market's behavior
  (D) the analysts who study the market are unwilling to accept criticism of their methods as biased
  (E) socioeconomic differences form the basis of a rationing mechanism that puts minority groups at a disadvantage

This question asks you to identify an explicit claim made in the passage about traditional financial-market studies. The best answer is B because the passage states that most studies are affected by analysts' preference for simplicity in their models. Choice A is incorrect because the passage does not suggest that competition eventually results in an optimum allocation of resources. While the statements in C and D could be true, they do not express claims presented in the passage. Choice E can be eliminated: although the passage does make a similar point about rationing mechanisms, it does not do so in explanation of alleged flaws in financial-market analyses.

278. The author's main point is argued by

  (A) giving examples that support a conventional generalization
  (B) showing that the view opposite to the author's is self-contradictory
  (C) criticizing the presuppositions of a proposed plan
  (D) showing that omissions in a theoretical description make it inapplicable in certain cases
  (E) demonstrating that an alternative hypothesis more closely fits the data

This question asks you to identify the answer that best captures the author's approach to the main argument presented in the passage. Choice D is the best answer. In constructing an argument about flaws in conventional market-analysis models, the author focuses on various factors that are typically ignored —that is, omitted—in those models. Choice A can be eliminated because the author is arguing against a conventional viewpoint, not in favor of one. Choice B is incorrect because the author characterizes the opposing point of view as flawed in certain respects, but does not claim that the view is self-contradictory. Choices C and E are incorrect because there is no proposed plan discussed in the passage, nor is an alternative hypothesis offered.

279. A difference in which of the following would be an example of inequality in transaction costs as alluded to in lines 40-43 ?

  (A) Maximum amounts of loans extended by a bank to businesses in different areas
  (B) Fees charged to large and small investors for purchasing stocks
  (C) Prices of similar goods offered in large and small stores in an area
  (D) Stipends paid to different attorneys for preparing legal suits for damages
  (E) Exchange rates in dollars for currencies of different countries

To answer this question correctly you must choose the answer that most clearly offers an example of the phenomenon alluded to in lines 40-43. Note that the question asks you to consider what it would mean if there were *differences in* what is described in the answer choices. The best answer is B. A fee to purchase stock is a transaction cost, and stock is mentioned in the passage as an example of a type of financial instrument. Differences in fees charged to buy stock would thus be an example of inequality in transaction costs for financial instruments. Choices A, C, and E are not correct because amounts of loans, prices of goods, and exchange rates would not be considered transaction costs for financial instruments. Choice D is incorrect: while a stipend paid for a service might be considered a type of transaction cost, this choice does not describe a transaction cost involving the purchase or sale of financial instruments.

280. Which of the following can be inferred about minority communities on the basis of the passage?

  (A) They provide a significant portion of the funds that become available for investment in the financial market.
  (B) They are penalized by the tax system, which increases the inequality of the distribution of income between investors and wage earners.
  (C) They do not receive the share of the amount of funds available for investment that would be expected according to traditional financial-market analysis.
  (D) They are not granted governmental subsidies to assist in underwriting the cost of economic development.
  (E) They provide the same access to alternative sources of credit to finance businesses as do majority communities

This question asks you to use information provided in the passage in order to draw an inference about minority communities. Choice C is the best answer. According to the passage, traditional financial-market analysis assumes equal access to the market for all participants; according to the author, however, minority communities do *not* have equal access to the market. Thus it may be inferred that while traditional analysis assumes

-494-

that all communities will receive their share of available funds, in reality those funds are disproportionately allocated to majority communities. Choices A and B are incorrect because the passage does not discuss either the origins of funds available for investment or any tax penalties that may be incurred by certain investors. While this statement in D could be true, there is not enough information provided in the passage to support such an inference. Choice E is incorrect because the passage does not assert or suggest that equal access to any sources of credit is provided in minority communities.

281. According to the passage, a questionable assumption of the conventional theory about the operation of financial markets is that

(A) creditworthiness as determined by lenders is a factor determining market access
(B) market structure and market dynamics depend on income distribution
(C) a scarcity of alternative sources of funds would result from taking socioeconomic factors into consideration
(D) those who engage in financial-market transactions are perfectly well informed about the market
(E) inequalities in income distribution are increased by the functioning of the financial market

This question asks you to identify a claim about conventional financial-market theory that is made explicitly in the passage. The best answer is choice D. The author points out this assumption within the context of criticizing the conventional theory about financial markets. Choice A is not correct because creditworthiness is mentioned in the first paragraph of the passage, but not in the context of assumptions made in conventional theory. Choices B and E can be eliminated: with regard to the consideration of income distribution, the passage states only that conventional analysis tends to pay little attention to the topic. Choice C is incorrect because the passage does not mention any assumption on the part of conventional theory with regard to the consequences of considering socioeconomic factors.

282. According to the passage, analysts have conventionally tended to view those who participate in financial markets as

(A) judging investment preferences in terms of the good of society as a whole
(B) influencing the allocation of funds through prior ownership of certain kinds of assets
(C) varying in market power with respect to one another
(D) basing judgments about future events mainly on chance
(E) having equal opportunities to engage in transactions

This question asks you to identify a claim made in the passage about the conventional viewpoint of financial market analysts. The best answer is E. The passage states that conventional financial analysis has assumed that all market participants have the same access to the market and the same opportunity to make transactions in the market. Choice A is incorrect because the passage does not suggest that analysts have traditionally assumed any attention to societal good on the part of market participants. Choice B can be eliminated because the effect of prior allocation of funds is mentioned in the second paragraph (lines 8-14), prior to any discussion of traditional financial-market analysis. Both C and D contradict a claim made in the passage about conventional financial-market analysis. First, conventional analysis is said to assume that all participants have equal access, not varying market power. Second, conventional analysis is said to assume that market participants act with perfect foresight about capital-market behavior, not that they rely on chance.

Questions 283-285 refer to the passage on page 414.

283. According to the passage, which of the following best describes most ozone-depleting chemicals in 1996 as compared to those in 1987 ?

(A) The levels of such chemicals in the atmosphere had decreased.
(B) The number of such chemicals that reached the atmosphere had declined.
(C) The amounts of such chemicals released had increased but the amounts that reached the atmosphere had decreased.
(D) The rate of increase in amounts of such chemicals reaching the atmosphere had decreased.
(E) The rate at which such chemicals were being reduced in the atmosphere had slowed.

This question asks you to identify a claim that is made in the passage about ozone-depleting chemicals. The best answer is D. The passage, written in 1996, states that the rate of increase in amounts of most ozone-depleting chemicals reaching the atmosphere had been reduced since 1987. Choice A can be eliminated because the passage states that the atmospheric levels of *some* ozone-depleting chemicals had been reduced, not that the levels of most had been reduced. Choice B is incorrect because the actual number of different chemicals reaching the atmosphere is not provided in the passage, nor is it claimed that the number had declined. Choice C is not correct because the passage does not claim that there was an increase in the amounts of ozone-depleting chemicals released between 1987 and 1996. Choice E is incorrect because there is no indication in the passage that the rate of reduction of atmospheric chemicals had slowed between 1987 and 1996.

284. The author of the passage compares the smuggling of CFC's to the illicit drug trade most likely for which of the following reasons?

(A) To qualify a previous claim
(B) To emphasize the extent of a problem
(C) To provide an explanation for an earlier assertion
(D) To suggest that the illicit CFC trade, like the illicit drug trade, will continue to increase
(E) To suggest that the consequences of a relatively little-known problem are as serious as those of a well-known one

This question asks you to identify the purpose of the author's comparison of CFC smuggling and the illicit drug trade. The best answer is B. The author notes that the smuggling of CFC's is, in the view of the United States Customs Service, a problem "second only" to the illicit drug trade. This provides a point of reference that emphasizes the extent of the CFC smuggling problem. Choice A is not correct. To qualify a claim is to weaken or soften it. The author's comparison of CFC smuggling to the illicit drug trade in fact underscores the previous claim, which has to do with the amount of contraband CFC's traded each year on the black market. Choice C is not correct because the comparison of CFC smuggling to the illicit drug trade does not provide an explanation for an assertion made in the passage. Choices D and E are not correct because the comparison of CFC smuggling to the illicit drug trade illustrates the extent of the CFC smuggling problem, but does not suggest further similarities between the two phenomena, such as the likelihood of their increase. The author also does not express any opinion as to the relative seriousness of the two problems' consequences.

285. The passage suggests which of the following about the illicit trade in CFC's ?

(A) It would cease if manufacturers in India and China stopped producing CFC's.
(B) Most people who participate in such trade do not believe that CFC's deplete the ozone layer.
(C) It will probably surpass illicit drugs as the largest contraband problem faced by the United States Customs Service.
(D) It is fostered by people who do not want to pay the price of CFC substitutes.
(E) It has grown primarily because of the expansion of the refrigeration, heating, and air-conditioning industries in foreign countries.

This question asks what the passage implies about the illicit trade in CFC's. The best answer is D. The passage states that some industry members appear not to want to pay the price of CFC substitutes, and that consequently a black market in cheaper CFC's has emerged. This implies that the black market is fostered at least in part by those industry members who are unwilling to pay the higher price of CFC substitutes. Choice A can be eliminated because the passage states only that most contraband CFC's originate in India and China. This does not imply that the illicit trade in CFC's could not continue without manufacturers in those countries. Choice B is not correct because the passage does not provide information about the beliefs of participants in the illicit CFC trade. Choice C is incorrect because the passage states only that the United States Customs Service considers the illicit CFC trade to be a problem second only to the illicit drug trade; there is no suggestion in the passage that the illicit CFC trade is expected to develop into a larger problem than the illicit drug trade. Choice E is incorrect because the passage attributes the growth of the illicit trade in CFC's to the high cost of CFC substitutes, not to an expansion of refrigeration, heating, and air-conditioning industries in foreign countries.

7 Critical Reasoning

In these questions you are to analyze the situation on which each question is based, and then select the answer choice that is the most appropriate response to the question. No specialized knowledge of any particular field is required for answering the questions, and no knowledge of the terminology and conventions of formal logic is presupposed. The sample critical reasoning questions that begin on page 499 provide good illustrations of the variety of topics that may be covered, of the kinds of questions that may be asked, and of the level of analysis that will generally be required.

Test-taking Strategies for Critical Reasoning

1. The set of statements on which a question is based should be read very carefully, with close attention to such matters as (1) what is put forward as factual information, (2) what is not said but necessarily follows from what is said, (3) what is claimed to follow from facts that have been put forward, and (4) how well substantiated are any claims to the effect that a particular conclusion follows from the facts that have been put forward. In reading arguments, it is important to attend to the soundness of the reasoning employed; it is not necessary to make a judgment of the actual truth of anything that is put forward as factual information.

2. If a question is based on an argument, be careful to identify clearly which part of the argument is its conclusion. The conclusion does not necessarily come at the end of the text of the argument; it may come somewhere in the middle, or it may even come at the beginning. Be alert to clues in the text that one of the statements made is not simply asserted but is said to follow logically from another statement or other statements in the text.

3. It is important to determine exactly what the question is asking; in fact, you might find it helpful to read the question first, before reading the material on which it is based. For example, an argument may appear to have an obvious flaw, and you may expect to be asked to detect that flaw; but the question may actually ask you to recognize the one among the answer choices that does NOT describe a weakness of the argument.

4. Read all the answer choices carefully. You should not assume that a given answer is the best answer without first reading all the choices.

CRITICAL REASONING DIRECTIONS

When finished reading directions click on the icon below

Dismiss Directions

For this question, select the best of the answer choices given.

To review these directions for subsequent questions of this type, click on HELP.

Test
Quit

Section
Exit

Time

?
Help

Answer
Confirm

Next

CRITICAL REASONING SAMPLE QUESTIONS

1. Which of the following best completes the passage below?

   In a survey of job applicants, two-fifths admitted to being at least a little dishonest. However, the survey may underestimate the proportion of job applicants who are dishonest, because _____.

   (A) some dishonest people taking the survey might have claimed on the survey to be honest
   (B) some generally honest people taking the survey might have claimed on the survey to be dishonest
   (C) some people who claimed on the survey to be at least a little dishonest may be very dishonest
   (D) some people who claimed on the survey to be dishonest may have been answering honestly
   (E) some people who are not job applicants are probably at least a little dishonest

Questions 2-3 are based on the following.

   The average life expectancy for the United States population as a whole is 73.9 years, but children born in Hawaii will live an average of 77 years, and those born in Louisiana, 71.7 years. If a newlywed couple from Louisiana were to begin their family in Hawaii, therefore, their children would be expected to live longer than would be the case if the family remained in Louisiana.

2. Which of the following, if true, would most seriously weaken the conclusion drawn in the passage?

   (A) Insurance company statisticians do not believe that moving to Hawaii will significantly lengthen the average Louisianian's life.
   (B) The governor of Louisiana has falsely alleged that statistics for his state are inaccurate.
   (C) The longevity ascribed to Hawaii's current population is attributable mostly to genetically determined factors.
   (D) Thirty percent of all Louisianians can expect to live longer than 77 years.
   (E) Most of the Hawaiian Islands have levels of air pollution well below the national average for the United States.

3. Which of the following statements, if true, would most significantly strengthen the conclusion drawn in the passage?

   (A) As population density increases in Hawaii, life expectancy figures for that state are likely to be revised downward.
   (B) Environmental factors tending to favor longevity are abundant in Hawaii and less numerous in Louisiana.
   (C) Twenty-five percent of all Louisianians who move to Hawaii live longer than 77 years.
   (D) Over the last decade, average life expectancy has risen at a higher rate for Louisianians than for Hawaiians.
   (E) Studies show that the average life expectancy for Hawaiians who move permanently to Louisiana is roughly equal to that of Hawaiians who remain in Hawaii.

4. Insurance Company X is considering issuing a new policy to cover services required by elderly people who suffer from diseases that afflict the elderly. Premiums for the policy must be low enough to attract customers. Therefore, Company X is concerned that the income from the policies would not be sufficient to pay for the claims that would be made.

   Which of the following strategies would be most likely to minimize Company X's losses on the policies?

   (A) Attracting middle-aged customers unlikely to submit claims for benefits for many years
   (B) Insuring only those individuals who did not suffer any serious diseases as children
   (C) Including a greater number of services in the policy than are included in other policies of lower cost
   (D) Insuring only those individuals who were rejected by other companies for similar policies
   (E) Insuring only those individuals who are wealthy enough to pay for the medical services

5. A program instituted in a particular state allows parents to prepay their children's future college tuition at current rates. The program then pays the tuition annually for the child at any of the state's public colleges in which the child enrolls. Parents should participate in the program as a means of decreasing the cost for their children's college education.

Which of the following, if true, is the most appropriate reason for parents not to participate in the program?

(A) The parents are unsure about which public college in the state the child will attend.
(B) The amount of money accumulated by putting the prepayment funds in an interest-bearing account today will be greater than the total cost of tuition for any of the public colleges when the child enrolls.
(C) The annual cost of tuition at the state's public colleges is expected to increase at a faster rate than the annual increase in the cost of living.
(D) Some of the state's public colleges are contemplating large increases in tuition next year.
(E) The prepayment plan would not cover the cost of room and board at any of the state's public colleges.

6. Company Alpha buys free-travel coupons from people who are awarded the coupons by Bravo Airlines for flying frequently on Bravo airplanes. The coupons are sold to people who pay less for the coupons than they would pay by purchasing tickets from Bravo. This marketing of coupons results in lost revenue for Bravo.

To discourage the buying and selling of free-travel coupons, it would be best for Bravo Airlines to restrict the

(A) number of coupons that a person can be awarded in a particular year
(B) use of the coupons to those who were awarded the coupons and members of their immediate families
(C) days that the coupons can be used to Monday through Friday
(D) amount of time that the coupons can be used after they are issued
(E) number of routes on which travelers can use the coupons

7. The ice on the front windshield of the car had formed when moisture condensed during the night. The ice melted quickly after the car was warmed up the next morning because the defrosting vent, which blows only on the front windshield, was turned on full force.

Which of the following, if true, most seriously jeopardizes the validity of the explanation for the speed with which the ice melted?

(A) The side windows had no ice condensation on them.
(B) Even though no attempt was made to defrost the back window, the ice there melted at the same rate as did the ice on the front windshield.
(C) The speed at which ice on a window melts increases as the temperature of the air blown on the window increases.
(D) The warm air from the defrosting vent for the front windshield cools rapidly as it dissipates throughout the rest of the car.
(E) The defrosting vent operates efficiently even when the heater, which blows warm air toward the feet or faces of the driver and passengers, is on.

8. To prevent some conflicts of interest, Congress could prohibit high-level government officials from accepting positions as lobbyists for three years after such officials leave government service. One such official concluded, however, that such a prohibition would be unfortunate because it would prevent high-level government officials from earning a livelihood for three years.

The official's conclusion logically depends on which of the following assumptions?

(A) Laws should not restrict the behavior of former government officials.
(B) Lobbyists are typically people who have previously been high-level government officials.
(C) Low-level government officials do not often become lobbyists when they leave government service.
(D) High-level government officials who leave government service are capable of earning a livelihood only as lobbyists.
(E) High-level government officials who leave government service are currently permitted to act as lobbyists for only three years.

9. A conservation group in the United States is trying to change the long-standing image of bats as frightening creatures. The group contends that bats are feared and persecuted solely because they are shy animals that are active only at night.

Which of the following, if true, would cast the most serious doubt on the accuracy of the group's contention?

(A) Bats are steadily losing natural roosting places such as caves and hollow trees and are thus turning to more developed areas for roosting.
(B) Bats are the chief consumers of nocturnal insects and thus can help make their hunting territory more pleasant for humans.
(C) Bats are regarded as frightening creatures not only in the United States but also in Europe, Africa, and South America.
(D) Raccoons and owls are shy and active only at night; yet they are not generally feared and persecuted.
(E) People know more about the behavior of other greatly feared animal species, such as lions, alligators, and snakes, than they do about the behavior of bats.

10. Meteorite explosions in the Earth's atmosphere as large as the one that destroyed forests in Siberia, with approximately the force of a twelve-megaton nuclear blast, occur about once a century.

The response of highly automated systems controlled by complex computer programs to unexpected circumstances is unpredictable.

Which of the following conclusions can most properly be drawn, if the statements above are true, about a highly automated nuclear-missile defense system controlled by a complex computer program?

(A) Within a century after its construction, the system would react inappropriately and might accidentally start a nuclear war.
(B) The system would be destroyed if an explosion of a large meteorite occurred in the Earth's atmosphere.
(C) It would be impossible for the system to distinguish the explosion of a large meteorite from the explosion of a nuclear weapon.
(D) Whether the system would respond inappropriately to the explosion of a large meteorite would depend on the location of the blast.
(E) It is not certain what the system's response to the explosion of a large meteorite would be, if its designers did not plan for such a contingency.

Questions 11-12 are based on the following.

The fewer restrictions there are on the advertising of legal services, the more lawyers there are who advertise their services, and the lawyers who advertise a specific service usually charge less for that service than lawyers who do not advertise. Therefore, if the state removes any of its current restrictions, such as the one against advertisements that do not specify fee arrangements, overall consumer legal costs will be lower than if the state retains its current restrictions.

11. If the statements above are true, which of the following must be true?

(A) Some lawyers who now advertise will charge more for specific services if they do not have to specify fee arrangements in the advertisements.
(B) More consumers will use legal services if there are fewer restrictions on the advertising of legal services.
(C) If the restriction against advertisements that do not specify fee arrangements is removed, more lawyers will advertise their services.
(D) If more lawyers advertise lower prices for specific services, some lawyers who do not advertise will also charge less than they currently charge for those services.
(E) If the only restrictions on the advertising of legal services were those that apply to every type of advertising, most lawyers would advertise their services.

12. Which of the following, if true, would most seriously weaken the argument concerning overall consumer legal costs?

(A) The state has recently removed some other restrictions that had limited the advertising of legal services.
(B) The state is unlikely to remove all of the restrictions that apply solely to the advertising of legal services.
(C) Lawyers who do not advertise generally provide legal services of the same quality as those provided by lawyers who do advertise.
(D) Most lawyers who now specify fee arrangements in their advertisements would continue to do so even if the specification were not required.
(E) Most lawyers who advertise specific services do not lower their fees for those services when they begin to advertise.

13. Defense Department analysts worry that the ability of the United States to wage a prolonged war would be seriously endangered if the machine-tool manufacturing base shrinks further. Before the Defense Department publicly connected this security issue with the import quota issue, however, the machine-tool industry raised the national security issue in its petition for import quotas.

Which of the following, if true, contributes most to an explanation of the machine-tool industry's raising the issue above regarding national security?

(A) When the aircraft industries retooled, they provided a large amount of work for tool builders.

(B) The Defense Department is only marginally concerned with the effects of foreign competition on the machine-tool industry.

(C) The machine-tool industry encountered difficulty in obtaining governmental protection against imports on grounds other than defense.

(D) A few weapons important for defense consist of parts that do not require extensive machining.

(E) Several federal government programs have been designed which will enable domestic machine-tool manufacturing firms to compete successfully with foreign toolmakers.

14. Opponents of laws that require automobile drivers and passengers to wear seat belts argue that in a free society people have the right to take risks as long as the people do not harm others as a result of taking the risks. As a result, they conclude that it should be each person's decision whether or not to wear a seat belt.

Which of the following, if true, most seriously weakens the conclusion drawn above?

(A) Many new cars are built with seat belts that automatically fasten when someone sits in the front seat.

(B) Automobile insurance rates for all automobile owners are higher because of the need to pay for the increased injuries or deaths of people not wearing seat belts.

(C) Passengers in airplanes are required to wear seat belts during takeoffs and landings.

(D) The rate of automobile fatalities in states that do not have mandatory seat-belt laws is greater than the rate of fatalities in states that do have such laws.

(E) In automobile accidents, a greater number of passengers who do not wear seat belts are injured than are passengers who do wear seat belts.

15. The cost of producing radios in Country Q is ten percent less than the cost of producing radios in Country Y. Even after transportation fees and tariff charges are added, it is still cheaper for a company to import radios from Country Q to Country Y than to produce radios in Country Y.

The statements above, if true, best support which of the following assertions?

(A) Labor costs in Country Q are ten percent below those in Country Y.

(B) Importing radios from Country Q to Country Y will eliminate ten percent of the manufacturing jobs in Country Y.

(C) The tariff on a radio imported from Country Q to Country Y is less than ten percent of the cost of manufacturing the radio in Country Y.

(D) The fee for transporting a radio from Country Q to Country Y is more than ten percent of the cost of manufacturing the radio in Country Q.

(E) It takes ten percent less time to manufacture a radio in Country Q than it does in Country Y.

16. During the Second World War, about 375,000 civilians died in the United States and about 408,000 members of the United States armed forces died overseas. On the basis of those figures, it can be concluded that it was not much more dangerous to be overseas in the armed forces during the Second World War than it was to stay at home as a civilian.

Which of the following would reveal most clearly the absurdity of the conclusion drawn above?

(A) Counting deaths among members of the armed forces who served in the United States in addition to deaths among members of the armed forces serving overseas

(B) Expressing the difference between the numbers of deaths among civilians and members of the armed forces as a percentage of the total number of deaths

(C) Separating deaths caused by accidents during service in the armed forces from deaths caused by combat injuries

(D) Comparing death rates per thousand members of each group rather than comparing total numbers of deaths

(E) Comparing deaths caused by accidents in the United States to deaths caused by combat in the armed forces

17. Toughened hiring standards have not been the primary cause of the present staffing shortage in public schools. The shortage of teachers is primarily caused by the fact that in recent years teachers have not experienced any improvements in working conditions and their salaries have not kept pace with salaries in other professions.

Which of the following, if true, would most support the claims above?

(A) Many teachers already in the profession would not have been hired under the new hiring standards.
(B) Today more teachers are entering the profession with a higher educational level than in the past.
(C) Some teachers have cited higher standards for hiring as a reason for the current staffing shortage.
(D) Many teachers have cited low pay and lack of professional freedom as reasons for their leaving the profession.
(E) Many prospective teachers have cited the new hiring standards as a reason for not entering the profession.

18. A proposed ordinance requires the installation in new homes of sprinklers automatically triggered by the presence of a fire. However, a home builder argued that because more than 90 percent of residential fires are extinguished by a household member, residential sprinklers would only marginally decrease property damage caused by residential fires.

Which of the following, if true, would most seriously weaken the home builder's argument?

(A) Most individuals have no formal training in how to extinguish fires.
(B) Since new homes are only a tiny percentage of available housing in the city, the new ordinance would be extremely narrow in scope.
(C) The installation of smoke detectors in new residences costs significantly less than the installation of sprinklers.
(D) In the city where the ordinance was proposed, the average time required by the fire department to respond to a fire was less than the national average.
(E) The largest proportion of property damage that results from residential fires is caused by fires that start when no household member is present.

19. Even though most universities retain the royalties from faculty members' inventions, the faculty members retain the royalties from books and articles they write. Therefore, faculty members should retain the royalties from the educational computer software they develop.

The conclusion above would be more reasonably drawn if which of the following were inserted into the argument as an additional premise?

(A) Royalties from inventions are higher than royalties from educational software programs.
(B) Faculty members are more likely to produce educational software programs than inventions.
(C) Inventions bring more prestige to universities than do books and articles.
(D) In the experience of most universities, educational software programs are more marketable than are books and articles.
(E) In terms of the criteria used to award royalties, educational software programs are more nearly comparable to books and articles than to inventions.

20. Increases in the level of high-density lipoprotein (HDL) in the human bloodstream lower bloodstream-cholesterol levels by increasing the body's capacity to rid itself of excess cholesterol. Levels of HDL in the bloodstream of some individuals are significantly increased by a program of regular exercise and weight reduction.

Which of the following can be correctly inferred from the statements above?

(A) Individuals who are underweight do not run any risk of developing high levels of cholesterol in the bloodstream.
(B) Individuals who do not exercise regularly have a high risk of developing high levels of cholesterol in the bloodstream late in life.
(C) Exercise and weight reduction are the most effective methods of lowering bloodstream cholesterol levels in humans.
(D) A program of regular exercise and weight reduction lowers cholesterol levels in the bloodstream of some individuals.
(E) Only regular exercise is necessary to decrease cholesterol levels in the bloodstream of individuals of average weight.

21. When limitations were in effect on nuclear-arms testing, people tended to save more of their money, but when nuclear-arms testing increased, people tended to spend more of their money. The perceived threat of nuclear catastrophe, therefore, decreases the willingness of people to postpone consumption for the sake of saving money.

The argument above assumes that

(A) the perceived threat of nuclear catastrophe has increased over the years
(B) most people supported the development of nuclear arms
(C) people's perception of the threat of nuclear catastrophe depends on the amount of nuclear-arms testing being done
(D) the people who saved the most money when nuclear-arms testing was limited were the ones who supported such limitations
(E) there are more consumer goods available when nuclear-arms testing increases

22. Which of the following best completes the passage below?

People buy prestige when they buy a premium product. They want to be associated with something special. Mass-marketing techniques and price-reduction strategies should not be used because _____.

(A) affluent purchasers currently represent a shrinking portion of the population of all purchasers
(B) continued sales depend directly on the maintenance of an aura of exclusivity
(C) purchasers of premium products are concerned with the quality as well as with the price of the products
(D) expansion of the market niche to include a broader spectrum of consumers will increase profits
(E) manufacturing a premium brand is not necessarily more costly than manufacturing a standard brand of the same product

23. A cost-effective solution to the problem of airport congestion is to provide high-speed ground transportation between major cities lying 200 to 500 miles apart. The successful implementation of this plan would cost far less than expanding existing airports and would also reduce the number of airplanes clogging both airports and airways.

Which of the following, if true, could proponents of the plan above most appropriately cite as a piece of evidence for the soundness of their plan?

(A) An effective high-speed ground-transportation system would require major repairs to many highways and mass-transit improvements.
(B) One-half of all departing flights in the nation's busiest airport head for a destination in a major city 225 miles away.
(C) The majority of travelers departing from rural airports are flying to destinations in cities over 600 miles away.
(D) Many new airports are being built in areas that are presently served by high-speed ground-transportation systems.
(E) A large proportion of air travelers are vacationers who are taking long-distance flights.

Questions 24-25 are based on the following.

If there is an oil-supply disruption resulting in higher international oil prices, domestic oil prices in open-market countries such as the United States will rise as well, whether such countries import all or none of their oil.

24. If the statement above concerning oil-supply disruptions is true, which of the following policies in an open-market nation is most likely to reduce the long-term economic impact on that nation of sharp and unexpected increases in international oil prices?

(A) Maintaining the quantity of oil imported at constant yearly levels
(B) Increasing the number of oil tankers in its fleet
(C) Suspending diplomatic relations with major oil-producing nations
(D) Decreasing oil consumption through conservation
(E) Decreasing domestic production of oil

25. Which of the following conclusions is best supported by the statement above?

(A) Domestic producers of oil in open-market countries are excluded from the international oil market when there is a disruption in the international oil supply.
(B) International oil-supply disruptions have little, if any, effect on the price of domestic oil as long as an open-market country has domestic supplies capable of meeting domestic demand.
(C) The oil market in an open-market country is actually part of the international oil market, even if most of that country's domestic oil is usually sold to consumers within its borders.
(D) Open-market countries that export little or none of their oil can maintain stable domestic oil prices even when international oil prices rise sharply.
(E) If international oil prices rise, domestic distributors of oil in open-market countries will begin to import more oil than they export.

26. The average normal infant born in the United States weighs between twelve and fourteen pounds at the age of three months. Therefore, if a three-month-old child weighs only ten pounds, its weight gain has been below the United States average.

Which of the following indicates a flaw in the reasoning above?

(A) Weight is only one measure of normal infant development.
(B) Some three-month-old children weigh as much as seventeen pounds.
(C) It is possible for a normal child to weigh ten pounds at birth.
(D) The phrase "below average" does not necessarily mean insufficient.
(E) Average weight gain is not the same as average weight.

27. Red blood cells in which the malarial-fever parasite resides are eliminated from a person's body after 120 days. Because the parasite cannot travel to a new generation of red blood cells, any fever that develops in a person more than 120 days after that person has moved to a malaria-free region is not due to the malarial parasite.

Which of the following, if true, most seriously weakens the conclusion above?

(A) The fever caused by the malarial parasite may resemble the fever caused by flu viruses.
(B) The anopheles mosquito, which is the principal insect carrier of the malarial parasite, has been eradicated in many parts of the world.
(C) Many malarial symptoms other than the fever, which can be suppressed with antimalarial medication, can reappear within 120 days after the medication is discontinued.
(D) In some cases, the parasite that causes malarial fever travels to cells of the spleen, which are less frequently eliminated from a person's body than are red blood cells.
(E) In any region infested with malaria-carrying mosquitoes, there are individuals who appear to be immune to malaria.

28. Fact 1: Television advertising is becoming less effective: the proportion of brand names promoted on television that viewers of the advertising can recall is slowly decreasing.

Fact 2: Television viewers recall commercials aired first or last in a cluster of consecutive commercials far better than they recall commercials aired somewhere in the middle.

Fact 2 would be most likely to contribute to an explanation of fact 1 if which of the following were also true?

(A) The average television viewer currently recalls fewer than half the brand names promoted in commercials he or she saw.
(B) The total time allotted to the average cluster of consecutive television commercials is decreasing.
(C) The average number of hours per day that people spend watching television is decreasing.
(D) The average number of clusters of consecutive commercials per hour of television is increasing.
(E) The average number of television commercials in a cluster of consecutive commercials is increasing.

29. The number of people diagnosed as having a certain intestinal disease has dropped significantly in a rural county this year, as compared to last year. Health officials attribute this decrease entirely to improved sanitary conditions at water-treatment plants, which made for cleaner water this year and thus reduced the incidence of the disease.

Which of the following, if true, would most seriously weaken the health officials' explanation for the lower incidence of the disease?

(A) Many new water-treatment plants have been built in the last five years in the rural county.
(B) Bottled spring water has not been consumed in significantly different quantities by people diagnosed as having the intestinal disease, as compared to people who did not contract the disease.
(C) Because of a new diagnostic technique, many people who until this year would have been diagnosed as having the intestinal disease are now correctly diagnosed as suffering from intestinal ulcers.
(D) Because of medical advances this year, far fewer people who contract the intestinal disease will develop severe cases of the disease.
(E) The water in the rural county was brought up to the sanitary standards of the water in neighboring counties ten years ago.

30. The price the government pays for standard weapons purchased from military contractors is determined by a pricing method called "historical costing." Historical costing allows contractors to protect their profits by adding a percentage increase, based on the current rate of inflation, to the previous year's contractual price.

Which of the following statements, if true, is the best basis for a criticism of historical costing as an economically sound pricing method for military contracts?

(A) The government might continue to pay for past inefficient use of funds.
(B) The rate of inflation has varied considerably over the past twenty years.
(C) The contractual price will be greatly affected by the cost of materials used for the products.
(D) Many taxpayers question the amount of money the government spends on military contracts.
(E) The pricing method based on historical costing might not encourage the development of innovative weapons.

31. Some who favor putting governmental enterprises into private hands suggest that conservation objectives would in general be better served if private environmental groups were put in charge of operating and financing the national park system, which is now run by the government.

Which of the following, assuming that it is a realistic possibility, argues most strongly against the suggestion above?

(A) Those seeking to abolish all restrictions on exploiting the natural resources of the parks might join the private environmental groups as members and eventually take over their leadership.
(B) Private environmental groups might not always agree on the best ways to achieve conservation objectives.
(C) If they wished to extend the park system, the private environmental groups might have to seek contributions from major donors and the general public.
(D) There might be competition among private environmental groups for control of certain park areas.
(E) Some endangered species, such as the California condor, might die out despite the best efforts of the private environmental groups, even if those groups are not hampered by insufficient resources.

32. A recent spate of launching and operating mishaps with television satellites led to a corresponding surge in claims against companies underwriting satellite insurance. As a result, insurance premiums shot up, making satellites more expensive to launch and operate. This, in turn, has added to the pressure to squeeze more performance out of currently operating satellites.

Which of the following, if true, taken together with the information above, best supports the conclusion that the cost of television satellites will continue to increase?

(A) Since the risk to insurers of satellites is spread over relatively few units, insurance premiums are necessarily very high.
(B) When satellites reach orbit and then fail, the causes of failure are generally impossible to pinpoint with confidence.
(C) The greater the performance demands placed on satellites, the more frequently those satellites break down.
(D) Most satellites are produced in such small numbers that no economies of scale can be realized.
(E) Since many satellites are built by unwieldy international consortia, inefficiencies are inevitable.

33. Rural households have more purchasing power than do urban or suburban households at the same income level, since some of the income urban and suburban households use for food and shelter can be used by rural households for other needs.

Which of the following inferences is best supported by the statement made above?

(A) The average rural household includes more people than does the average urban or suburban household.
(B) Rural households have lower food and housing costs than do either urban or suburban households.
(C) Suburban households generally have more purchasing power than do either rural or urban households.
(D) The median income of urban and suburban households is generally higher than that of rural households.
(E) All three types of households spend more of their income on food and housing than on all other purchases combined.

34. In 1985 state border colleges in Texas lost the enrollment of more than half, on average, of the Mexican nationals they had previously served each year. Teaching faculties have alleged that this extreme drop resulted from a rise in tuition for international and out-of-state students from $40 to $120 per credit hour.

Which of the following, if feasible, offers the best prospects for alleviating the problem of the drop in enrollment of Mexican nationals as the teaching faculties assessed it?

(A) Providing grants-in-aid to Mexican nationals to study in Mexican universities
(B) Allowing Mexican nationals to study in Texas border colleges and to pay in-state tuition rates, which are the same as the previous international rate
(C) Reemphasizing the goals and mission of the Texas state border colleges as serving both in-state students and Mexican nationals
(D) Increasing the financial resources of Texas colleges by raising the tuition for in-state students attending state institutions
(E) Offering career counseling for those Mexican nationals who graduate from state border colleges and intend to return to Mexico

35. Affirmative action is good business. So asserted the National Association of Manufacturers while urging retention of an executive order requiring some federal contractors to set numerical goals for hiring minorities and women. "Diversity in work force participation has produced new ideas in management, product development, and marketing," the association claimed.

The association's argument as it is presented in the passage above would be most strengthened if which of the following were true?

(A) The percentage of minority and women workers in business has increased more slowly than many minority and women's groups would prefer.
(B) Those businesses with the highest percentages of minority and women workers are those that have been the most innovative and profitable.
(C) Disposable income has been rising as fast among minorities and women as among the population as a whole.
(D) The biggest growth in sales in the manufacturing sector has come in industries that market the most innovative products.
(E) Recent improvements in management practices have allowed many manufacturers to experience enormous gains in worker productivity.

Questions 36-37 refer to the following.

If the airspace around centrally located airports were restricted to commercial airliners and only those private planes equipped with radar, most of the private-plane traffic would be forced to use outlying airfields. Such a reduction in the amount of private-plane traffic would reduce the risk of midair collision around the centrally located airports.

36. The conclusion drawn in the first sentence depends on which of the following assumptions?

(A) Outlying airfields would be as convenient as centrally located airports for most pilots of private planes.
(B) Most outlying airfields are not equipped to handle commercial-airline traffic.
(C) Most private planes that use centrally located airports are not equipped with radar.
(D) Commercial airliners are at greater risk of becoming involved in midair collisions than are private planes.
(E) A reduction in the risk of midair collision would eventually lead to increases in commercial-airline traffic.

37. Which of the following, if true, would most strengthen the conclusion drawn in the second sentence?

   (A) Commercial airliners are already required by law to be equipped with extremely sophisticated radar systems.
   (B) Centrally located airports are experiencing overcrowded airspace primarily because of sharp increases in commercial-airline traffic.
   (C) Many pilots of private planes would rather buy radar equipment than be excluded from centrally located airports.
   (D) The number of midair collisions that occur near centrally located airports has decreased in recent years.
   (E) Private planes not equipped with radar systems cause a disproportionately large number of midair collisions around centrally located airports.

38. Which of the following best completes the passage below?

   Established companies concentrate on defending what they already have. Consequently, they tend not to be innovative themselves and tend to underestimate the effects of the innovations of others. The clearest example of this defensive strategy is the fact that _____.

   (A) ballpoint pens and soft-tip markers have eliminated the traditional market for fountain pens, clearing the way for the marketing of fountain pens as luxury or prestige items
   (B) a highly successful automobile was introduced by the same company that had earlier introduced a model that had been a dismal failure
   (C) a once-successful manufacturer of slide rules reacted to the introduction of electronic calculators by trying to make better slide rules
   (D) one of the first models of modern accounting machines, designed for use in the banking industry, was purchased by a public library as well as by banks
   (E) the inventor of a commonly used anesthetic did not intend the product to be used by dentists, who currently account for almost the entire market for that drug

39. Most archaeologists have held that people first reached the Americas less than 20,000 years ago by crossing a land bridge into North America. But recent discoveries of human shelters in South America dating from 32,000 years ago have led researchers to speculate that people arrived in South America first, after voyaging across the Pacific, and then spread northward.

   Which of the following, if it were discovered, would be pertinent evidence against the speculation above?

   (A) A rock shelter near Pittsburgh, Pennsylvania, contains evidence of use by human beings 19,000 years ago.
   (B) Some North American sites of human habitation predate any sites found in South America.
   (C) The climate is warmer at the 32,000-year-old South American site than at the oldest known North American site.
   (D) The site in South America that was occupied 32,000 years ago was continuously occupied until 6,000 years ago.
   (E) The last Ice Age, between 11,500 and 20,000 years ago, considerably lowered worldwide sea levels.

40. In Asia, where palm trees are non-native, the trees' flowers have traditionally been pollinated by hand, which has kept palm fruit productivity unnaturally low. When weevils known to be efficient pollinators of palm flowers were introduced into Asia in 1980, palm fruit productivity increased—by up to 50 percent in some areas—but then decreased sharply in 1984.

   Which of the following statements, if true, would best explain the 1984 decrease in productivity?

   (A) Prices for palm fruit fell between 1980 and 1984 following the rise in production and a concurrent fall in demand.
   (B) Imported trees are often more productive than native trees because the imported ones have left behind their pests and diseases in their native lands.
   (C) Rapid increases in productivity tend to deplete trees of nutrients needed for the development of the fruit-producing female flowers.
   (D) The weevil population in Asia remained at approximately the same level between 1980 and 1984.
   (E) Prior to 1980 another species of insect pollinated the Asian palm trees, but not as efficiently as the species of weevil that was introduced in 1980.

41. Since the mayor's publicity campaign for Greenville's bus service began six months ago, morning automobile traffic into the midtown area of the city has decreased seven percent. During the same period, there has been an equivalent rise in the number of persons riding buses into the midtown area. Obviously, the mayor's publicity campaign has convinced many people to leave their cars at home and ride the bus to work.

Which of the following, if true, casts the most serious doubt on the conclusion drawn above?

(A) Fares for all bus routes in Greenville have risen an average of five percent during the past six months.
(B) The mayor of Greenville rides the bus to City Hall in the city's midtown area.
(C) Road reconstruction has greatly reduced the number of lanes available to commuters in major streets leading to the midtown area during the past six months.
(D) The number of buses entering the midtown area of Greenville during the morning hours is exactly the same now as it was one year ago.
(E) Surveys show that longtime bus riders are no more satisfied with the Greenville bus service than they were before the mayor's publicity campaign began.

42. In the aftermath of a worldwide stock-market crash, Country T claimed that the severity of the stock-market crash it experienced resulted from the accelerated process of denationalization many of its industries underwent shortly before the crash.

Which of the following, if it could be carried out, would be most useful in an evaluation of Country T's assessment of the causes of the severity of its stock-market crash?

(A) Calculating the average loss experienced by individual traders in Country T during the crash
(B) Using economic theory to predict the most likely date of the next crash in Country T
(C) Comparing the total number of shares sold during the worst days of the crash in Country T to the total number of shares sold in Country T just prior to the crash
(D) Comparing the severity of the crash in Country T to the severity of the crash in countries otherwise economically similar to Country T that have not experienced recent denationalization
(E) Comparing the long-term effects of the crash on the purchasing power of the currency of Country T to the immediate, more severe short-term effects of the crash on the purchasing power of the currency of Country T

43. With the emergence of biotechnology companies, it was feared that they would impose silence about proprietary results on their in-house researchers and their academic consultants. This constraint, in turn, would slow the development of biological science and engineering.

Which of the following, if true, would tend to weaken most seriously the prediction of scientific secrecy described above?

(A) Biotechnological research funded by industry has reached some conclusions that are of major scientific importance.
(B) When the results of scientific research are kept secret, independent researchers are unable to build on those results.
(C) Since the research priorities of biotechnology companies are not the same as those of academic institutions, the financial support of research by such companies distorts the research agenda.
(D) To enhance the companies' standing in the scientific community, the biotechnology companies encourage employees to publish their results, especially results that are important.
(E) Biotechnology companies devote some of their research resources to problems that are of fundamental scientific importance and that are not expected to produce immediate practical applications.

44. Some people have questioned the judge's objectivity in cases of sex discrimination against women. But the record shows that in sixty percent of such cases, the judge has decided in favor of the women. This record demonstrates that the judge has not discriminated against women in cases of sex discrimination against women.

The argument above is flawed in that it ignores the possibility that

(A) a large number of the judge's cases arose out of allegations of sex discrimination against women
(B) many judges find it difficult to be objective in cases of sex discrimination against women
(C) the judge is biased against women defendants or plaintiffs in cases that do not involve sex discrimination
(D) the majority of the cases of sex discrimination against women that have reached the judge's court have been appealed from a lower court
(E) the evidence shows that the women should have won in more than 60 percent of the judge's cases involving sex discrimination against women

45. The tobacco industry is still profitable and projections are that it will remain so. In the United States this year, the total amount of tobacco sold by tobacco-farmers has increased, even though the number of adults who smoke has decreased.

Each of the following, if true, could explain the simultaneous increase in tobacco sales and decrease in the number of adults who smoke EXCEPT:

(A) During this year, the number of women who have begun to smoke is greater than the number of men who have quit smoking.
(B) The number of teen-age children who have begun to smoke this year is greater than the number of adults who have quit smoking during the same period.
(C) During this year, the number of nonsmokers who have begun to use chewing tobacco or snuff is greater than the number of people who have quit smoking.
(D) The people who have continued to smoke consume more tobacco per person than they did in the past.
(E) More of the cigarettes made in the United States this year were exported to other countries than was the case last year.

46. Kale has more nutritional value than spinach. But since collard greens have more nutritional value than lettuce, it follows that kale has more nutritional value than lettuce.

Any of the following, if introduced into the argument as an additional premise, makes the argument above logically correct EXCEPT:

(A) Collard greens have more nutritional value than kale.
(B) Spinach has more nutritional value than lettuce.
(C) Spinach has more nutritional value than collard greens.
(D) Spinach and collard greens have the same nutritional value.
(E) Kale and collard greens have the same nutritional value.

47. On the basis of a decrease in the college-age population, many colleges now anticipate increasingly smaller freshman classes each year. Surprised by a 40 percent increase in qualified applicants over the previous year, however, administrators at Nice College now plan to hire more faculty for courses taken by all freshmen.

Which of the following statements about Nice College's current qualified applicants, if true, would strongly suggest that the administrators' plan is flawed?

(A) A substantially higher percentage than usual plan to study for advanced degrees after graduation from college.
(B) According to their applications, their level of participation in extracurricular activities and varsity sports is unusually high.
(C) According to their applications, none of them lives in a foreign country.
(D) A substantially lower percentage than usual rate Nice College as their first choice among the colleges to which they are applying.
(E) A substantially lower percentage than usual list mathematics as their intended major.

48. A researcher discovered that people who have low levels of immune-system activity tend to score much lower on tests of mental health than do people with normal or high immune-system activity. The researcher concluded from this experiment that the immune system protects against mental illness as well as against physical disease.

The researcher's conclusion depends on which of the following assumptions?

(A) High immune-system activity protects against mental illness better than normal immune-system activity does.
(B) Mental illness is similar to physical disease in its effects on body systems.
(C) People with high immune-system activity cannot develop mental illness.
(D) Mental illness does not cause people's immune-system activity to decrease.
(E) Psychological treatment of mental illness is not as effective as is medical treatment.

49. A milepost on the towpath read "21" on the side facing the hiker as she approached it and "23" on its back. She reasoned that the next milepost forward on the path would indicate that she was halfway between one end of the path and the other. However, the milepost one mile further on read "20" facing her and "24" behind.

Which of the following, if true, would explain the discrepancy described above?

(A) The numbers on the next milepost had been reversed.

(B) The numbers on the mileposts indicate kilometers, not miles.

(C) The facing numbers indicate miles to the end of the path, not miles from the beginning.

(D) A milepost was missing between the two the hiker encountered.

(E) The mileposts had originally been put in place for the use of mountain bikers, not for hikers.

50. Airline: Newly developed collision-avoidance systems, although not fully tested to discover potential malfunctions, must be installed immediately in passenger planes. Their mechanical warnings enable pilots to avoid crashes.

Pilots: Pilots will not fly in planes with collision-avoidance systems that are not fully tested. Malfunctioning systems could mislead pilots, causing crashes.

The pilots' objection is most strengthened if which of the following is true?

(A) It is always possible for mechanical devices to malfunction.

(B) Jet engines, although not fully tested when first put into use, have achieved exemplary performance and safety records.

(C) Although collision-avoidance systems will enable pilots to avoid some crashes, the likely malfunctions of the not-fully-tested systems will cause even more crashes.

(D) Many airline collisions are caused in part by the exhaustion of overworked pilots.

(E) Collision-avoidance systems, at this stage of development, appear to have worked better in passenger planes than in cargo planes during experimental flights made over a six-month period.

51. Guitar strings often go "dead"—become less responsive and bright in tone—after a few weeks of intense use. A researcher whose son is a classical guitarist hypothesized that dirt and oil, rather than changes in the material properties of the string, were responsible.

Which of the following investigations is most likely to yield significant information that would help to evaluate the researcher's hypothesis?

(A) Determining if a metal alloy is used to make the strings used by classical guitarists

(B) Determining whether classical guitarists make their strings go dead faster than do folk guitarists

(C) Determining whether identical lengths of string, of the same gauge, go dead at different rates when strung on various brands of guitars

(D) Determining whether a dead string and a new string produce different qualities of sound

(E) Determining whether smearing various substances on new guitar strings causes them to go dead

52. Most consumers do not get much use out of the sports equipment they purchase. For example, seventeen percent of the adults in the United States own jogging shoes, but only 45 percent of the owners jog more than once a year, and only 17 percent jog more than once a week.

Which of the following, if true, casts most doubt on the claim that most consumers get little use out of the sports equipment they purchase?

(A) Joggers are most susceptible to sports injuries during the first six months in which they jog.

(B) Joggers often exaggerate the frequency with which they jog in surveys designed to elicit such information.

(C) Many consumers purchase jogging shoes for use in activities other than jogging.

(D) Consumers who take up jogging often purchase an athletic shoe that can be used in other sports.

(E) Joggers who jog more than once a week are often active participants in other sports as well.

53. Two decades after the Emerald River Dam was built, none of the eight fish species native to the Emerald River was still reproducing adequately in the river below the dam. Since the dam reduced the annual range of water temperature in the river below the dam from 50 degrees to 6 degrees, scientists have hypothesized that sharply rising water temperatures must be involved in signaling the native species to begin the reproductive cycle.

Which of the following statements, if true, would most strengthen the scientists' hypothesis?

(A) The native fish species were still able to reproduce only in side streams of the river below the dam where the annual temperature range remains approximately 50 degrees.

(B) Before the dam was built, the Emerald River annually overflowed its banks, creating backwaters that were critical breeding areas for the native species of fish.

(C) The lowest recorded temperature of the Emerald River before the dam was built was 34 degrees, whereas the lowest recorded temperature of the river after the dam was built has been 43 degrees.

(D) Nonnative species of fish, introduced into the Emerald River after the dam was built, have begun competing with the declining native fish species for food and space.

(E) Five of the fish species native to the Emerald River are not native to any other river in North America.

54. It is true that it is against international law to sell plutonium to countries that do not yet have nuclear weapons. But if United States companies do not do so, companies in other countries will.

Which of the following is most like the argument above in its logical structure?

(A) It is true that it is against the police department's policy to negotiate with kidnappers. But if the police want to prevent loss of life, they must negotiate in some cases.

(B) It is true that it is illegal to refuse to register for military service. But there is a long tradition in the United States of conscientious objection to serving in the armed forces.

(C) It is true that it is illegal for a government official to participate in a transaction in which there is an apparent conflict of interest. But if the facts are examined carefully, it will clearly be seen that there was no actual conflict of interest in the defendant's case.

(D) It is true that it is against the law to burglarize people's homes. But someone else certainly would have burglarized that house if the defendant had not done so first.

(E) It is true that company policy forbids supervisors to fire employees without two written warnings. But there have been many supervisors who have disobeyed this policy.

55. In recent years many cabinetmakers have been winning acclaim as artists. But since furniture must be useful, cabinetmakers must exercise their craft with an eye to the practical utility of their product. For this reason, cabinetmaking is not art.

Which of the following is an assumption that supports drawing the conclusion above from the reason given for that conclusion?

(A) Some furniture is made to be placed in museums, where it will not be used by anyone.

(B) Some cabinetmakers are more concerned than others with the practical utility of the products they produce.

(C) Cabinetmakers should be more concerned with the practical utility of their products than they currently are.

(D) An object is not an art object if its maker pays attention to the object's practical utility.

(E) Artists are not concerned with the monetary value of their products.

56. Although custom prosthetic bone replacements produced through a new computer-aided design process will cost more than twice as much as ordinary replacements, custom replacements should still be cost-effective. Not only will surgery and recovery time be reduced, but custom replacements should last longer, thereby reducing the need for further hospital stays.

Which of the following must be studied in order to evaluate the argument presented above?

(A) The amount of time a patient spends in surgery *versus* the amount of time spent recovering from surgery

(B) The amount by which the cost of producing custom replacements has declined with the introduction of the new technique for producing them

(C) The degree to which the use of custom replacements is likely to reduce the need for repeat surgery when compared with the use of ordinary replacements

(D) The degree to which custom replacements produced with the new technique are more carefully manufactured than are ordinary replacements

(E) The amount by which custom replacements produced with the new technique will drop in cost as the production procedures become standardized and applicable on a larger scale

57. Extinction is a process that can depend on a variety of ecological, geographical, and physiological variables. These variables affect different species of organisms in different ways, and should, therefore, yield a random pattern of extinctions. However, the fossil record shows that extinction occurs in a surprisingly definite pattern, with many species vanishing at the same time.

Which of the following, if true, forms the best basis for at least a partial explanation of the patterned extinctions revealed by the fossil record?

(A) Major episodes of extinction can result from widespread environmental disturbances that affect numerous different species.

(B) Certain extinction episodes selectively affect organisms with particular sets of characteristics unique to their species.

(C) Some species become extinct because of accumulated gradual changes in their local environments.

(D) In geologically recent times, for which there is no fossil record, human intervention has changed the pattern of extinctions.

(E) Species that are widely dispersed are the least likely to become extinct.

58. Neither a rising standard of living nor balanced trade, by itself, establishes a country's ability to compete in the international marketplace. Both are required simultaneously since standards of living can rise because of growing trade deficits and trade can be balanced by means of a decline in a country's standard of living.

If the facts stated in the passage above are true, a proper test of a country's ability to be competitive is its ability to

(A) balance its trade while its standard of living rises

(B) balance its trade while its standard of living falls

(C) increase trade deficits while its standard of living rises

(D) decrease trade deficits while its standard of living falls

(E) keep its standard of living constant while trade deficits rise

59. Certain messenger molecules fight damage to the lungs from noxious air by telling the muscle cells encircling the lungs' airways to contract. This partially seals off the lungs. An asthma attack occurs when the messenger molecules are activated unnecessarily, in response to harmless things like pollen or household dust.

Which of the following, if true, points to the most serious flaw of a plan to develop a medication that would prevent asthma attacks by blocking receipt of any messages sent by the messenger molecules referred to above?

(A) Researchers do not yet know how the body produces the messenger molecules that trigger asthma attacks.

(B) Researchers do not yet know what makes one person's messenger molecules more easily activated than another's.

(C) Such a medication would not become available for several years, because of long lead times in both development and manufacture.

(D) Such a medication would be unable to distinguish between messages triggered by pollen and household dust and messages triggered by noxious air.

(E) Such a medication would be a preventative only and would be unable to alleviate an asthma attack once it had started.

60. Since the routine use of antibiotics can give rise to resistant bacteria capable of surviving antibiotic environments, the presence of resistant bacteria in people could be due to the human use of prescription antibiotics. Some scientists, however, believe that most resistant bacteria in people derive from human consumption of bacterially infected meat.

Which of the following statements, if true, would most significantly strengthen the hypothesis of the scientists?

(A) Antibiotics are routinely included in livestock feed so that livestock producers can increase the rate of growth of their animals.
(B) Most people who develop food poisoning from bacterially infected meat are treated with prescription antibiotics.
(C) The incidence of resistant bacteria in people has tended to be much higher in urban areas than in rural areas where meat is of comparable quality.
(D) People who have never taken prescription antibiotics are those least likely to develop resistant bacteria.
(E) Livestock producers claim that resistant bacteria in animals cannot be transmitted to people through infected meat.

61. The recent decline in the value of the dollar was triggered by a prediction of slower economic growth in the coming year. But that prediction would not have adversely affected the dollar had it not been for the government's huge budget deficit, which must therefore be decreased to prevent future currency declines.

Which of the following, if true, would most seriously weaken the conclusion about how to prevent future currency declines?

(A) The government has made little attempt to reduce the budget deficit.
(B) The budget deficit has not caused a slowdown in economic growth.
(C) The value of the dollar declined several times in the year prior to the recent prediction of slower economic growth.
(D) Before there was a large budget deficit, predictions of slower economic growth frequently caused declines in the dollar's value.
(E) When there is a large budget deficit, other events in addition to predictions of slower economic growth sometimes trigger declines in currency value.

62. Which of the following best completes the passage below?

At a recent conference on environmental threats to the North Sea, most participating countries favored uniform controls on the quality of effluents, whether or not specific environmental damage could be attributed to a particular source of effluent. What must, of course, be shown, in order to avoid excessively restrictive controls, is that _____.

(A) any uniform controls that are adopted are likely to be implemented without delay
(B) any substance to be made subject to controls can actually cause environmental damage
(C) the countries favoring uniform controls are those generating the largest quantities of effluents
(D) all of any given pollutant that is to be controlled actually reaches the North Sea at present
(E) environmental damage already inflicted on the North Sea is reversible

63. Traditionally, decision making by managers that is reasoned step-by-step has been considered preferable to intuitive decision making. However, a recent study found that top managers used intuition significantly more than did most middle- or lower-level managers. This confirms the alternative view that intuition is actually more effective than careful, methodical reasoning.

The conclusion above is based on which of the following assumptions?

(A) Methodical, step-by-step reasoning is inappropriate for making many real-life management decisions.
(B) Top managers have the ability to use either intuitive reasoning or methodical, step-by-step reasoning in making decisions.
(C) The decisions made by middle- and lower-level managers can be made as easily by using methodical reasoning as by using intuitive reasoning.
(D) Top managers use intuitive reasoning in making the majority of their decisions.
(E) Top managers are more effective at decision making than middle- or lower-level managers.

64. The imposition of quotas limiting imported steel will not help the big American steel mills. In fact, the quotas will help "mini-mills" flourish in the United States. Those small domestic mills will take more business from the big American steel mills than would have been taken by the foreign steel mills in the absence of quotas.

Which of the following, if true, would cast the most serious doubt on the claim made in the last sentence above?

(A) Quality rather than price is a major factor in determining the type of steel to be used for a particular application.
(B) Foreign steel mills have long produced grades of steel comparable in quality to the steel produced by the big American mills.
(C) American quotas on imported goods have often induced other countries to impose similar quotas on American goods.
(D) Domestic "mini-mills" consistently produce better grades of steel than do the big American mills.
(E) Domestic "mini-mills" produce low-volume, specialized types of steels that are not produced by the big American steel mills.

65. Correctly measuring the productivity of service workers is complex. Consider, for example, postal workers: they are often said to be more productive if more letters are delivered per postal worker. But is this really true? What if more letters are lost or delayed per worker at the same time that more are delivered?

The objection implied above to the productivity measure described is based on doubts about the truth of which of the following statements?

(A) Postal workers are representative of service workers in general.
(B) The delivery of letters is the primary activity of the postal service.
(C) Productivity should be ascribed to categories of workers, not to individuals.
(D) The quality of services rendered can appropriately be ignored in computing productivity.
(E) The number of letters delivered is relevant to measuring the productivity of postal workers.

66. Male bowerbirds construct elaborately decorated nests, or bowers. Basing their judgment on the fact that different local populations of bowerbirds of the same species build bowers that exhibit different building and decorative styles, researchers have concluded that the bowerbirds' building styles are a culturally acquired, rather than a genetically transmitted, trait.

Which of the following, if true, would most strengthen the conclusion drawn by the researchers?

(A) There are more common characteristics than there are differences among the bower-building styles of the local bowerbird population that has been studied most extensively.
(B) Young male bowerbirds are inept at bower-building and apparently spend years watching their elders before becoming accomplished in the local bower style.
(C) The bowers of one species of bowerbird lack the towers and ornamentation characteristic of the bowers of most other species of bowerbird.
(D) Bowerbirds are found only in New Guinea and Australia, where local populations of the birds apparently seldom have contact with one another.
(E) It is well known that the song dialects of some songbirds are learned rather than transmitted genetically.

67. A greater number of newspapers are sold in Town S than in Town T. Therefore, the citizens of Town S are better informed about major world events than are the citizens of Town T.

Each of the following, if true, weakens the conclusion above EXCEPT:

(A) Town S has a larger population than Town T.
(B) Most citizens of Town T work in Town S and buy their newspapers there.
(C) The average citizen of Town S spends less time reading newspapers than does the average citizen of Town T.
(D) A weekly newspaper restricted to the coverage of local events is published in Town S.
(E) The average newsstand price of newspapers sold in Town S is lower than the average price of newspapers sold in Town T.

68. A drug that is highly effective in treating many types of infection can, at present, be obtained only from the bark of the ibora, a tree that is quite rare in the wild. It takes the bark of 5,000 trees to make one kilogram of the drug. It follows, therefore, that continued production of the drug must inevitably lead to the ibora's extinction.

Which of the following, if true, most seriously weakens the argument above?

(A) The drug made from ibora bark is dispensed to doctors from a central authority.
(B) The drug made from ibora bark is expensive to produce.
(C) The leaves of the ibora are used in a number of medical products.
(D) The ibora can be propagated from cuttings and grown under cultivation.
(E) The ibora generally grows in largely inaccessible places.

69. High levels of fertilizer and pesticides, needed when farmers try to produce high yields of the same crop year after year, pollute water supplies. Experts therefore urge farmers to diversify their crops and to rotate their plantings yearly.

To receive governmental price-support benefits for a crop, farmers must have produced that same crop for the past several years.

The statements above, if true, best support which of the following conclusions?

(A) The rules for governmental support of farm prices work against efforts to reduce water pollution.
(B) The only solution to the problem of water pollution from fertilizers and pesticides is to take farmland out of production.
(C) Farmers can continue to make a profit by rotating diverse crops, thus reducing costs for chemicals, but not by planting the same crop each year.
(D) New farming techniques will be developed to make it possible for farmers to reduce the application of fertilizers and pesticides.
(E) Governmental price supports for farm products are set at levels that are not high enough to allow farmers to get out of debt.

70. Shelby Industries manufactures and sells the same gauges as Jones Industries. Employee wages account for forty percent of the cost of manufacturing gauges at both Shelby Industries and Jones Industries. Shelby Industries is seeking a competitive advantage over Jones Industries. Therefore, to promote this end, Shelby Industries should lower employee wages.

Which of the following, if true, would most weaken the argument above?

(A) Because they make a small number of precision instruments, gauge manufacturers cannot receive volume discounts on raw materials.
(B) Lowering wages would reduce the quality of employee work, and this reduced quality would lead to lowered sales.
(C) Jones Industries has taken away twenty percent of Shelby Industries' business over the last year.
(D) Shelby Industries pays its employees, on average, ten percent more than does Jones Industries.
(E) Many people who work for manufacturing plants live in areas in which the manufacturing plant they work for is the only industry.

71. Some communities in Florida are populated almost exclusively by retired people and contain few, if any, families with small children. Yet these communities are home to thriving businesses specializing in the rental of furniture for infants and small children.

Which of the following, if true, best reconciles the seeming discrepancy described above?

(A) The businesses specializing in the rental of children's furniture buy their furniture from distributors outside of Florida.
(B) The few children who do reside in these communities all know each other and often make overnight visits to one another's houses.
(C) Many residents of these communities who move frequently prefer renting their furniture to buying it outright.
(D) Many residents of these communities must provide for the needs of visiting grandchildren several weeks a year.
(E) Children's furniture available for rental is of the same quality as that available for sale in the stores.

72. Large national budget deficits do not cause large trade deficits. If they did, countries with the largest budget deficits would also have the largest trade deficits. In fact, when deficit figures are adjusted so that different countries are reliably comparable to each other, there is no such correlation.

If the statements above are all true, which of the following can properly be inferred on the basis of them?

(A) Countries with large national budget deficits tend to restrict foreign trade.
(B) Reliable comparisons of the deficit figures of one country with those of another are impossible.
(C) Reducing a country's national budget deficit will not necessarily result in a lowering of any trade deficit that country may have.
(D) When countries are ordered from largest to smallest in terms of population, the smallest countries generally have the smallest budget and trade deficits.
(E) Countries with the largest trade deficits never have similarly large national budget deficits.

73. "Fast cycle time" is a strategy of designing a manufacturing organization to eliminate bottlenecks and delays in production. Not only does it speed up production, but it also assures quality. The reason is that the bottlenecks and delays cannot be eliminated unless all work is done right the first time.

The claim about quality made above rests on a questionable presupposition that

(A) any flaw in work on a product would cause a bottleneck or delay and so would be prevented from occurring on a "fast cycle" production line
(B) the strategy of "fast cycle time" would require fundamental rethinking of product design
(C) the primary goal of the organization is to produce a product of unexcelled quality, rather than to generate profits for stockholders
(D) "fast cycle time" could be achieved by shaving time off each of the component processes in a production cycle
(E) "fast cycle time" is a concept in business strategy that has not yet been put into practice in a factory

74. Many breakfast cereals are fortified with vitamin supplements. Some of these cereals provide 100 percent of the recommended daily requirement of vitamins. Nevertheless, a well-balanced breakfast, including a variety of foods, is a better source of those vitamins than are such fortified breakfast cereals alone.

Which of the following, if true, would most strongly support the position above?

(A) In many foods, the natural combination of vitamins with other nutrients makes those vitamins more usable by the body than are vitamins added in vitamin supplements.
(B) People who regularly eat cereals fortified with vitamin supplements sometimes neglect to eat the foods in which the vitamins occur naturally.
(C) Foods often must be fortified with vitamin supplements because naturally occurring vitamins are removed during processing.
(D) Unprocessed cereals are naturally high in several of the vitamins that are usually added to fortified breakfast cereals.
(E) Cereals containing vitamin supplements are no harder to digest than similar cereals without added vitamins.

75. Which of the following best completes the passage below?

The more worried investors are about losing their money, the more they will demand a high potential return on their investment; great risks must be offset by the chance of great rewards. This principle is the fundamental one in determining interest rates, and it is illustrated by the fact that _____.

(A) successful investors are distinguished by an ability to make very risky investments without worrying about their money
(B) lenders receive higher interest rates on unsecured loans than on loans backed by collateral
(C) in times of high inflation, the interest paid to depositors by banks can actually be below the rate of inflation
(D) at any one time, a commercial bank will have a single rate of interest that it will expect all of its individual borrowers to pay
(E) the potential return on investment in a new company is typically lower than the potential return on investment in a well-established company

76. A famous singer recently won a lawsuit against an advertising firm for using another singer in a commercial to evoke the famous singer's well-known rendition of a certain song. As a result of the lawsuit, advertising firms will stop using imitators in commercials. Therefore, advertising costs will rise, since famous singers' services cost more than those of their imitators.

The conclusion above is based on which of the following assumptions?

(A) Most people are unable to distinguish a famous singer's rendition of a song from a good imitator's rendition of the same song.
(B) Commercials using famous singers are usually more effective than commercials using imitators of famous singers.
(C) The original versions of some well-known songs are unavailable for use in commercials.
(D) Advertising firms will continue to use imitators to mimic the physical mannerisms of famous singers.
(E) The advertising industry will use well-known renditions of songs in commercials.

77. A certain mayor has proposed a fee of five dollars per day on private vehicles entering the city, claiming that the fee will alleviate the city's traffic congestion. The mayor reasons that, since the fee will exceed the cost of round-trip bus fare from many nearby points, many people will switch from using their cars to using the bus.

Which of the following statements, if true, provides the best evidence that the mayor's reasoning is flawed?

(A) Projected increases in the price of gasoline will increase the cost of taking a private vehicle into the city.
(B) The cost of parking fees already makes it considerably more expensive for most people to take a private vehicle into the city than to take a bus.
(C) Most of the people currently riding the bus do not own private vehicles.
(D) Many commuters opposing the mayor's plan have indicated that they would rather endure traffic congestion than pay a five-dollar-per-day fee.
(E) During the average workday, private vehicles owned and operated by people living within the city account for 20 percent of the city's traffic congestion.

78. A group of children of various ages was read stories in which people caused harm, some of those people doing so intentionally, and some accidentally. When asked about appropriate punishments for those who had caused harm, the younger children, unlike the older ones, assigned punishments that did not vary according to whether the harm was done intentionally or accidentally. Younger children, then, do not regard people's intentions as relevant to punishment.

Which of the following, if true, would most seriously weaken the conclusion above?

(A) In interpreting these stories, the listeners had to draw on a relatively mature sense of human psychology in order to tell whether harm was produced intentionally or accidentally.
(B) In these stories, the severity of the harm produced was clearly stated.
(C) Younger children are as likely to produce harm unintentionally as are older children.
(D) The older children assigned punishment in a way that closely resembled the way adults had assigned punishment in a similar experiment.
(E) The younger children assigned punishments that varied according to the severity of the harm done by the agents in the stories.

79. When hypnotized subjects are told that they are deaf and are then asked whether they can hear the hypnotist, they reply, "No." Some theorists try to explain this result by arguing that the selves of hypnotized subjects are dissociated into separate parts, and that the part that is deaf is dissociated from the part that replies.

Which of the following challenges indicates the most serious weakness in the attempted explanation described above?

(A) Why does the part that replies not answer, "Yes"?
(B) Why are the observed facts in need of any special explanation?
(C) Why do the subjects appear to accept the hypnotist's suggestion that they are deaf?
(D) Why do hypnotized subjects all respond the same way in the situation described?
(E) Why are the separate parts of the self the same for all subjects?

Questions 80-81 are based on the following.

The program to control the entry of illegal drugs into the country was a failure in 1987. If the program had been successful, the wholesale price of most illegal drugs would not have dropped substantially in 1987.

80. The argument in the passage depends on which of the following assumptions?

   (A) The supply of illegal drugs dropped substantially in 1987.
   (B) The price paid for most illegal drugs by the average consumer did not drop substantially in 1987.
   (C) Domestic production of illegal drugs increased at a higher rate than did the entry of such drugs into the country.
   (D) The wholesale price of a few illegal drugs increased substantially in 1987.
   (E) A drop in demand for most illegal drugs in 1987 was not the sole cause of the drop in their wholesale price.

81. The argument in the passage would be most seriously weakened if it were true that

   (A) in 1987 smugglers of illegal drugs, as a group, had significantly more funds at their disposal than did the country's customs agents
   (B) domestic production of illegal drugs increased substantially in 1987
   (C) the author's statements were made in order to embarrass the officials responsible for the drug-control program
   (D) in 1987 illegal drugs entered the country by a different set of routes than they did in 1986
   (E) the country's citizens spent substantially more money on illegal drugs in 1987 than they did in 1986

82. Excavation of the ancient city of Kourion on the island of Cyprus revealed a pattern of debris and collapsed buildings typical of towns devastated by earthquakes. Archaeologists have hypothesized that the destruction was due to a major earthquake known to have occurred near the island in A.D. 365.

Which of the following, if true, most strongly supports the archaeologists' hypothesis?

   (A) Bronze ceremonial drinking vessels that are often found in graves dating from years preceding and following A.D. 365 were also found in several graves near Kourion.
   (B) No coins minted after A.D. 365 were found in Kourion, but coins minted before that year were found in abundance.
   (C) Most modern histories of Cyprus mention that an earthquake occurred near the island in A.D. 365.
   (D) Several small statues carved in styles current in Cyprus in the century between A.D. 300 and 400 were found in Kourion.
   (E) Stone inscriptions in a form of the Greek alphabet that was definitely used in Cyprus after A.D. 365 were found in Kourion.

83. Sales of telephones have increased dramatically over the last year. In order to take advantage of this increase, Mammoth Industries plans to expand production of its own model of telephone, while continuing its already very extensive advertising of this product.

Which of the following, if true, provides most support for the view that Mammoth Industries cannot increase its sales of telephones by adopting the plan outlined above?

   (A) Although it sells all of the telephones that it produces, Mammoth Industries' share of all telephone sales has declined over the last year.
   (B) Mammoth Industries' average inventory of telephones awaiting shipment to retailers has declined slightly over the last year.
   (C) Advertising has made the brand name of Mammoth Industries' telephones widely known, but few consumers know that Mammoth Industries owns this brand.
   (D) Mammoth Industries' telephone is one of three brands of telephone that have together accounted for the bulk of the last year's increase in sales.
   (E) Despite a slight decline in the retail price, sales of Mammoth Industries' telephones have fallen in the last year.

84. Many institutions of higher education suffer declining enrollments during periods of economic slowdown. At two-year community colleges, however, enrollment figures boom during these periods when many people have less money and there is more competition for jobs.

Each of the following, if true, helps to explain the enrollment increases in two-year community colleges described above EXCEPT:

(A) During periods of economic slowdown, two-year community colleges are more likely than four-year colleges to prepare their students for the jobs that are still available.
(B) During periods of economic prosperity, graduates of two-year community colleges often continue their studies at four-year colleges.
(C) Tuition at most two-year community colleges is a fraction of that at four-year colleges.
(D) Two-year community colleges devote more resources than do other colleges to attracting those students especially affected by economic slowdowns.
(E) Students at two-year community colleges, but not those at most four-year colleges, can control the cost of their studies by choosing the number of courses they take each term.

Questions 85-86 are based on the following.

Hardin argued that grazing land held in common (that is, open to any user) would always be used less carefully than private grazing land. Each rancher would be tempted to overuse common land because the benefits would accrue to the individual, while the costs of reduced land quality that results from overuse would be spread among all users. But a study comparing 217 million acres of common grazing land with 433 million acres of private grazing land showed that the common land was in better condition.

85. The answer to which of the following questions would be most useful in evaluating the significance, in relation to Hardin's claim, of the study described above?

(A) Did any of the ranchers whose land was studied use both common and private land?
(B) Did the ranchers whose land was studied tend to prefer using common land over using private land for grazing?
(C) Was the private land that was studied of comparable quality to the common land before either was used for grazing?
(D) Were the users of the common land that was studied at least as prosperous as the users of the private land?
(E) Were there any owners of herds who used only common land, and no private land, for grazing?

86. Which of the following, if true and known by the ranchers, would best help explain the results of the study?

(A) With private grazing land, both the costs and the benefits of overuse fall to the individual user.
(B) The cost in reduced land quality that is attributable to any individual user is less easily measured with common land than it is with private land.
(C) An individual who overuses common grazing land might be able to achieve higher returns than other users can, with the result that he or she would obtain a competitive advantage.
(D) If one user of common land overuses it even slightly, the other users are likely to do so even more, with the consequence that the costs to each user outweigh the benefits.
(E) There are more acres of grazing land held privately than there are held in common.

87. In tests for pironoma, a serious disease, a false positive result indicates that people have pironoma when, in fact, they do not; a false negative result indicates that people do not have pironoma when, in fact, they do. To detect pironoma most accurately, physicians should use the laboratory test that has the lowest proportion of false positive results.

Which of the following, if true, gives the most support to the recommendation above?

(A) The accepted treatment for pironoma does not have damaging side effects.
(B) The laboratory test that has the lowest proportion of false positive results causes the same minor side effects as do the other laboratory tests used to detect pironoma.
(C) In treating pironoma patients, it is essential to begin treatment as early as possible, since even a week of delay can result in loss of life.
(D) The proportion of inconclusive test results is equal for all laboratory tests used to detect pironoma.
(E) All laboratory tests to detect pironoma have the same proportion of false negative results.

Questions 88-89 are based on the following.

In many corporations, employees are being replaced by automated equipment in order to save money. However, many workers who lose their jobs to automation will need government assistance to survive, and the same corporations that are laying people off will eventually pay for that assistance through increased taxes and unemployment insurance payments.

88. The author is arguing that

   (A) higher taxes and unemployment insurance payments will discourage corporations from automating
   (B) replacing people through automation to reduce production costs will result in increases of other costs to corporations
   (C) many workers who lose their jobs to automation will have to be retrained for new jobs
   (D) corporations that are laying people off will eventually rehire many of them
   (E) corporations will not save money by automating because people will be needed to run the new machines

89. Which of the following, if true, most strengthens the author's argument?

   (A) Many workers who have already lost their jobs to automation have been unable to find new jobs.
   (B) Many corporations that have failed to automate have seen their profits decline.
   (C) Taxes and unemployment insurance are paid also by corporations that are not automating.
   (D) Most of the new jobs created by automation pay less than the jobs eliminated by automation did.
   (E) The initial investment in machinery for automation is often greater than the short-term savings in labor costs.

90. The sustained massive use of pesticides in farming has two effects that are especially pernicious. First, it often kills off the pests' natural enemies in the area. Second, it often unintentionally gives rise to insecticide-resistant pests, since those insects that survive a particular insecticide will be the ones most resistant to it, and they are the ones left to breed.

From the passage above, it can be properly inferred that the effectiveness of the sustained massive use of pesticides can be extended by doing which of the following, assuming that each is a realistic possibility?

   (A) Using only chemically stable insecticides
   (B) Periodically switching the type of insecticide used
   (C) Gradually increasing the quantities of pesticides used
   (D) Leaving a few fields fallow every year
   (E) Breeding higher-yielding varieties of crop plants

91. When a polygraph test is judged inconclusive, this is no reflection on the examinee. Rather, such a judgment means that the test has failed to show whether the examinee was truthful or untruthful. Nevertheless, employers will sometimes refuse to hire a job applicant because of an inconclusive polygraph test result.

Which of the following conclusions can most properly be drawn from the information above?

   (A) Most examinees with inconclusive polygraph test results are in fact untruthful.
   (B) Polygraph tests should not be used by employers in the consideration of job applicants.
   (C) An inconclusive polygraph test result is sometimes unfairly held against the examinee.
   (D) A polygraph test indicating that an examinee is untruthful can sometimes be mistaken.
   (E) Some employers have refused to consider the results of polygraph tests when evaluating job applicants.

92. According to the new office smoking regulations, only employees who have enclosed offices may smoke at their desks. Virtually all employees with enclosed offices are at the professional level, and virtually all secretarial employees lack enclosed offices. Therefore, secretaries who smoke should be offered enclosed offices.

Which of the following is an assumption that enables the conclusion above to be properly drawn?

(A) Employees at the professional level who do not smoke should keep their enclosed offices.
(B) Employees with enclosed offices should not smoke at their desks, even though the new regulations permit them to do so.
(C) Employees at the secretarial level should be allowed to smoke at their desks, even if they do not have enclosed offices.
(D) The smoking regulations should allow all employees who smoke an equal opportunity to do so, regardless of an employee's job level.
(E) The smoking regulations should provide equal protection from any hazards associated with smoking to all employees who do not smoke.

93. Dental researchers recently discovered that toothbrushes can become contaminated with bacteria that cause pneumonia and strep throat. They found that contamination usually occurs after toothbrushes have been used for four weeks. For that reason, people should replace their toothbrushes at least once a month.

Which of the following, if true, would most weaken the conclusion above?

(A) The dental researchers could not discover why toothbrush contamination usually occurred only after toothbrushes had been used for four weeks.
(B) The dental researchers failed to investigate contamination of toothbrushes by viruses, yeasts, and other pathogenic microorganisms.
(C) The dental researchers found that among people who used toothbrushes contaminated with bacteria that cause pneumonia and strep throat, the incidence of these diseases was no higher than among people who used uncontaminated toothbrushes.
(D) The dental researchers found that people who rinsed their toothbrushes thoroughly in hot water after each use were as likely to have contaminated toothbrushes as were people who only rinsed their toothbrushes hurriedly in cold water after each use.
(E) The dental researchers found that, after six weeks of use, greater length of use of a toothbrush did not correlate with a higher number of bacteria being present.

Questions 94-95 are based on the following.

To protect certain fledgling industries, the government of country Z banned imports of the types of products those industries were starting to make. As a direct result, the cost of those products to the buyers, several export-dependent industries in Z, went up, sharply limiting the ability of those industries to compete effectively in their export markets.

94. Which of the following can be most properly inferred from the passage about the products whose importation was banned?

(A) Those products had been cheaper to import than they were to make within country Z's fledgling industries.
(B) Those products were ones that country Z was hoping to export in its turn, once the fledgling industries matured.
(C) Those products used to be imported from just those countries to which country Z's exports went.
(D) Those products had become more and more expensive to import, which resulted in a foreign trade deficit just before the ban.
(E) Those products used to be imported in very small quantities, but they were essential to country Z's economy.

95. Which of the following conclusions about country Z's adversely affected export-dependent industries is best supported by the passage?

(A) Profit margins in those industries were not high enough to absorb the rise in costs mentioned above.
(B) Those industries had to contend with the fact that other countries banned imports from country Z.
(C) Those industries succeeded in expanding the domestic market for their products.
(D) Steps to offset rising materials costs by decreasing labor costs were taken in those industries.
(E) Those industries started to move into export markets that they had previously judged unprofitable.

96. The difficulty with the proposed high-speed train line is that a used plane can be bought for one-third the price of the train line, and the plane, which is just as fast, can fly anywhere. The train would be a fixed linear system, and we live in a world that is spreading out in all directions and in which consumers choose the free-wheel systems (cars, buses, aircraft), which do not have fixed routes. Thus a sufficient market for the train will not exist.

Which of the following, if true, most severely weakens the argument presented above?

(A) Cars, buses, and planes require the efforts of drivers and pilots to guide them, whereas the train will be guided mechanically.
(B) Cars and buses are not nearly as fast as the high-speed train will be.
(C) Planes are not a free-wheel system because they can fly only between airports, which are less convenient for consumers than the high-speed train's stations would be.
(D) The high-speed train line cannot use currently underutilized train stations in large cities.
(E) For long trips, most people prefer to fly rather than to take ground-level transportation.

97. Leaders of a miners' union on strike against Coalco are contemplating additional measures to pressure the company to accept the union's contract proposal. The union leaders are considering as their principal new tactic a consumer boycott against Gasco gas stations, which are owned by Energy Incorporated, the same corporation that owns Coalco.

The answer to which of the following questions is LEAST directly relevant to the union leaders' consideration of whether attempting a boycott of Gasco will lead to acceptance of their contract proposal?

(A) Would revenue losses by Gasco seriously affect Energy Incorporated?
(B) Can current Gasco customers easily obtain gasoline elsewhere?
(C) Have other miners' unions won contracts similar to the one proposed by this union?
(D) Have other unions that have employed a similar tactic achieved their goals with it?
(E) Do other corporations that own coal companies also own gas stations?

Questions 98-99 are based on the following.

Transnational cooperation among corporations is experiencing a modest renaissance among United States firms, even though projects undertaken by two or more corporations under a collaborative agreement are less profitable than projects undertaken by a single corporation. The advantage of transnational cooperation is that such joint international projects may allow United States firms to win foreign contracts that they would not otherwise be able to win.

98. Which of the following statements by a United States corporate officer best fits the situation of United States firms as described in the passage above?

(A) "We would rather make only a share of the profit and also risk only a share of a possible loss than run the full risk of a loss."
(B) "We would rather make a share of a relatively modest profit than end up making none of a potentially much bigger profit."
(C) "We would rather cooperate and build good will than poison the business climate by all-out competition."
(D) "We would rather have foreign corporations join us in American projects than join them in projects in their home countries."
(E) "We would rather win a contract with a truly competitive bid of our own than get involved in less profitable collaborative agreements."

99. Which of the following is information provided by the passage above?

(A) Transnational cooperation involves projects too big for a single corporation to handle.
(B) Transnational cooperation results in a pooling of resources leading to high-quality performance.
(C) Transnational cooperation has in the past been both more common and less common than it is now among United States firms.
(D) Joint projects between United States and foreign corporations are not profitable enough to be worth undertaking.
(E) Joint projects between United States and foreign corporations benefit only those who commission the projects.

100. A compelling optical illusion called the illusion of velocity and size makes objects appear to be moving more slowly the larger the objects are. Therefore, a motorist's estimate of the time available for crossing a highway with a small car approaching is bound to be lower than it would be with a large truck approaching.

The conclusion above would be more properly drawn if it were made clear that the

(A) truck's speed is assumed to be lower than the car's
(B) truck's speed is assumed to be the same as the car's
(C) truck's speed is assumed to be higher than the car's
(D) motorist's estimate of time available is assumed to be more accurate with cars approaching than with trucks approaching
(E) motorist's estimate of time available is assumed to be more accurate with trucks approaching than with cars approaching

101. Biological functions of many plants and animals vary in cycles that are repeated every 24 hours. It is tempting to suppose that alteration in the intensity of incident light is the stimulus that controls these daily biological rhythms. But there is much evidence to contradict this hypothesis.

Which of the following, if known, is evidence that contradicts the hypothesis stated in lines 2-5 above?

(A) Human body temperature varies throughout the day, with the maximum occurring in the late afternoon and the minimum in the morning.
(B) While some animals, such as the robin, are more active during the day, others, such as mice, show greater activity at night.
(C) When people move from one time zone to another, their daily biological rhythms adjust in a matter of days to the periods of sunlight and darkness in the new zone.
(D) Certain single-cell plants display daily biological rhythms even when the part of the cell containing the nucleus is removed.
(E) Even when exposed to constant light intensity around the clock, some algae display rates of photosynthesis that are much greater during daylight hours than at night.

102. Although migraine headaches are believed to be caused by food allergies, putting patients on diets that eliminate those foods to which the patients have been demonstrated to have allergic migraine reactions frequently does not stop headaches. Obviously, some other cause of migraine headaches besides food allergies must exist.

Which of the following, if true, would most weaken the conclusion above?

(A) Many common foods elicit an allergic response only after several days, making it very difficult to observe links between specific foods patients eat and headaches they develop.
(B) Food allergies affect many people who never develop the symptom of migraine headaches.
(C) Many patients report that the foods that cause them migraine headaches are among the foods that they most enjoy eating.
(D) Very few patients have allergic migraine reactions as children and then live migraine-free adult lives once they have eliminated from their diets foods to which they have been demonstrated to be allergic.
(E) Very rarely do food allergies cause patients to suffer a symptom more severe than that of migraine headaches.

103. The technological conservatism of bicycle manufacturers is a reflection of the kinds of demand they are trying to meet. The only cyclists seriously interested in innovation and willing to pay for it are bicycle racers. Therefore, innovation in bicycle technology is limited by what authorities will accept as standard for purposes of competition in bicycle races.

Which of the following is an assumption made in drawing the conclusion above?

(A) The market for cheap, traditional bicycles cannot expand unless the market for high-performance competition bicycles expands.
(B) High-performance bicycles are likely to be improved more as a result of technological innovations developed in small workshops than as a result of technological innovations developed in major manufacturing concerns.
(C) Bicycle racers do not generate a strong demand for innovations that fall outside what is officially recognized as standard for purposes of competition.
(D) The technological conservatism of bicycle manufacturers results primarily from their desire to manufacture a product that can be sold without being altered to suit different national markets.
(E) The authorities who set standards for high-performance bicycle racing do not keep informed about innovative bicycle design.

104. Spending on research and development by United States businesses for 1984 showed an increase of about 8 percent over the 1983 level. This increase actually continued a downward trend evident since 1981—when outlays for research and development increased 16.4 percent over 1980 spending. Clearly, the 25 percent tax credit enacted by Congress in 1981, which was intended to promote spending on research and development, did little or nothing to stimulate such spending.

The conclusion of the argument above cannot be true unless which of the following is true?

(A) Business spending on research and development is usually directly proportional to business profits.
(B) Business spending for research and development in 1985 could not increase by more than 8.3%.
(C) Had the 1981 tax credit been set higher than 25%, business spending for research and development after 1981 would have increased more than it did.
(D) In the absence of the 25% tax credit, business spending for research and development after 1981 would not have been substantially lower than it was.
(E) Tax credits marked for specific investments are rarely effective in inducing businesses to make those investments.

105. Treatment for hypertension forestalls certain medical expenses by preventing strokes and heart disease. Yet any money so saved amounts to only one-fourth of the expenditures required to treat the hypertensive population. Therefore, there is no economic justification for preventive treatment for hypertension.

Which of the following, if true, is most damaging to the conclusion above?

(A) The many fatal strokes and heart attacks resulting from untreated hypertension cause insignificant medical expenditures but large economic losses of other sorts.
(B) The cost, per patient, of preventive treatment for hypertension would remain constant even if such treatment were instituted on a large scale.
(C) In matters of health care, economic considerations should ideally not be dominant.
(D) Effective prevention presupposes early diagnosis, and programs to ensure early diagnosis are costly.
(E) The net savings in medical resources achieved by some preventive health measures are smaller than the net losses attributable to certain other measures of this kind.

106. Property taxes are typically set at a flat rate per $1,000 of officially assessed value. Reassessments should be frequent in order to remove distortions that arise when property values change at differential rates. In practice, however, reassessments typically occur when they benefit the government— that is, when their effect is to increase total tax revenue.

If the statements above are true, which of the following describes a situation in which a reassessment should occur but is unlikely to do so?

(A) Property values have risen sharply and uniformly.
(B) Property values have all risen—some very sharply, some less so.
(C) Property values have for the most part risen sharply; yet some have dropped slightly.
(D) Property values have for the most part dropped significantly; yet some have risen slightly.
(E) Property values have dropped significantly and uniformly.

107. The number of patents granted to inventors by the United States Patent Office dropped from 56,000 in 1971 to 45,000 in 1978. Spending on research and development, which peaked at 3 percent of the gross national product (GNP) in 1964, was only 2.2 percent of the GNP in 1978. During this period, when the United States percentage was steadily decreasing, West Germany and Japan increased the percentage of their GNP's spent on research and development to 3.2 percent and 1.6 percent, respectively.

Which of the following conclusions is best supported by the information above?

(A) There is a direct relationship between the size of a nation's GNP and the number of inventions it produces.
(B) Japan and West Germany spent more money on research and development in 1978 than did the United States.
(C) The amount of money a nation spends on research and development is directly related to the number of inventions patented in that nation.
(D) Between 1964 and 1978 the United States consistently spent a larger percentage of its GNP on research and development than did Japan.
(E) Both West Germany and Japan will soon surpass the United States in the number of patents granted to inventors.

108. When three Everett-owned Lightning-built airplanes crashed in the same month, the Everett company ordered three new Lightning-built airplanes as replacements. This decision surprised many in the airline industry because, ordinarily when a product is involved in accidents, users become reluctant to buy that product.

Which of the following, if true, provides the best indication that the Everett company's decision was logically well supported?

(A) Although during the previous year only one Lightning-built airplane crashed, competing manufacturers had a perfect safety record.
(B) The Lightning-built airplanes crashed due to pilot error, but because of the excellent quality of the planes there were many survivors.
(C) The Federal Aviation Association issued new guidelines for airlines in order to standardize safety requirements governing preflight inspections.
(D) Consumer advocates pressured two major airlines into purchasing safer airplanes so that the public would be safer while flying.
(E) Many Lightning Airplane Company employees had to be replaced because they found jobs with the competition.

109. Recently a court ruled that current law allows companies to reject a job applicant if working in the job would entail a 90 percent chance that the applicant would suffer a heart attack. The presiding judge justified the ruling, saying that it protected both employees and employers.

The use of this court ruling as part of the law could not be effective in regulating employment practices if which of the following were true?

(A) The best interests of employers often conflict with the interests of employees.
(B) No legally accepted methods exist for calculating the risk of a job applicant's having a heart attack as a result of being employed in any particular occupation.
(C) Some jobs might involve health risks other than the risk of heart attack.
(D) Employees who have a 90 percent chance of suffering a heart attack may be unaware that their risk is so great.
(E) The number of people applying for jobs at a company might decline if the company, by screening applicants for risk of heart attack, seemed to suggest that the job entailed high risk of heart attack.

110. Robot satellites relay important communications and identify weather patterns. Because the satellites can be repaired only in orbit, astronauts are needed to repair them. Without repairs, the satellites would eventually malfunction. Therefore, space flights carrying astronauts must continue.

Which of the following, if true, would most seriously weaken the argument above?

(A) Satellites falling from orbit because of malfunctions burn up in the atmosphere.
(B) Although satellites are indispensable in the identification of weather patterns, weather forecasters also make some use of computer projections to identify weather patterns.
(C) The government, responding to public pressure, has decided to cut the budget for space flights and put more money into social welfare programs.
(D) Repair of satellites requires heavy equipment, which adds to the amount of fuel needed to lift a spaceship carrying astronauts into orbit.
(E) Technical obsolescence of robot satellites makes repairing them more costly and less practical than sending new, improved satellites into orbit.

111. Advocates of a large-scale space-defense research project conclude that it will represent a net benefit to civilian business. They say that since government-sponsored research will have civilian applications, civilian businesses will reap the rewards of government-developed technology.

Each of the following, if true, raises a consideration arguing against the conclusion above, EXCEPT:

(A) The development of cost-efficient manufacturing techniques is of the highest priority for civilian business and would be neglected if resources go to military projects, which do not emphasize cost efficiency.
(B) Scientific and engineering talent needed by civilian business will be absorbed by the large-scale project.
(C) Many civilian businesses will receive subcontracts to provide materials and products needed by the research project.
(D) If government research money is devoted to the space project, it will not be available for specifically targeted needs of civilian business, where it could be more efficiently used.
(E) The increase in taxes or government debt needed to finance the project will severely reduce the vitality of the civilian economy.

112. In an attempt to promote the widespread use of paper rather than plastic, and thus reduce nonbiodegradable waste, the council of a small town plans to ban the sale of disposable plastic goods for which substitutes made of paper exist. The council argues that since most paper is entirely biodegradable, paper goods are environmentally preferable.

Which of the following, if true, indicates that the plan to ban the sale of disposable plastic goods is ill suited to the town council's environmental goals?

(A) Although biodegradable plastic goods are now available, members of the town council believe biodegradable paper goods to be safer for the environment.
(B) The paper factory at which most of the townspeople are employed plans to increase production of biodegradable paper goods.
(C) After other towns enacted similar bans on the sale of plastic goods, the environmental benefits were not discernible for several years.
(D) Since most townspeople prefer plastic goods to paper goods in many instances, they are likely to purchase them in neighboring towns where plastic goods are available for sale.
(E) Products other than those derived from wood pulp are often used in the manufacture of paper goods that are entirely biodegradable.

113. Since the deregulation of airlines, delays at the nation's increasingly busy airports have increased by 25 percent. To combat this problem, more of the takeoff and landing slots at the busiest airports must be allocated to commercial airlines.

Which of the following, if true, casts the most doubt on the effectiveness of the solution proposed above?

(A) The major causes of delays at the nation's busiest airports are bad weather and overtaxed air traffic control equipment.
(B) Since airline deregulation began, the number of airplanes in operation has increased by 25 percent.
(C) Over 60 percent of the takeoff and landing slots at the nation's busiest airports are reserved for commercial airlines.
(D) After a small midwestern airport doubled its allocation of takeoff and landing slots, the number of delays that were reported decreased by 50 percent.
(E) Since deregulation the average length of delay at the nation's busiest airports has doubled.

114. The more frequently employees take time to exercise during working hours each week, the fewer sick days they take. Even employees who exercise only once a week during working hours take less sick time than those who do not exercise. Therefore, if companies started fitness programs, the absentee rate in those companies would decrease significantly.

Which of the following, if true, most seriously weakens the argument above?

(A) Employees who exercise during working hours occasionally fall asleep for short periods of time after they exercise.
(B) Employees who are frequently absent are the least likely to cooperate with or to join a corporate fitness program.
(C) Employees who exercise only once a week in their company's fitness program usually also exercise after work.
(D) Employees who exercise in their company's fitness program use their working time no more productively than those who do not exercise.
(E) Employees who exercise during working hours take slightly longer lunch breaks than employees who do not exercise.

115. Many people argue that tobacco advertising plays a crucial role in causing teen-agers to start or continue smoking. In Norway, however, where there has been a ban on tobacco advertising since 1975, smoking is at least as prevalent among teen-agers as it is in countries that do not ban such advertising.

Which of the following statements draws the most reliable conclusion from the information above?

(A) Tobacco advertising cannot be the only factor that affects the prevalence of smoking among teen-agers.
(B) Advertising does not play a role in causing teen-agers to start or continue smoking.
(C) Banning tobacco advertising does not reduce the consumption of tobacco.
(D) More teen-agers smoke if they are not exposed to tobacco advertising than if they are.
(E) Most teen-agers who smoked in 1975 did not stop when the ban on tobacco advertising was implemented.

116. Laws requiring the use of headlights during daylight hours can prevent automobile collisions. However, since daylight visibility is worse in countries farther from the equator, any such laws would obviously be more effective in preventing collisions in those countries. In fact, the only countries that actually have such laws are farther from the equator than is the continental United States.

Which of the following conclusions could be most properly drawn from the information given above?

(A) Drivers in the continental United States who used their headlights during the day would be just as likely to become involved in a collision as would drivers who did not use their headlights.

(B) In many countries that are farther from the equator than is the continental United States poor daylight visibility is the single most important factor in automobile collisions.

(C) The proportion of automobile collisions that occur in the daytime is greater in the continental United States than in the countries that have daytime headlight laws.

(D) Fewer automobile collisions probably occur each year in countries that have daytime headlight laws than occur within the continental United States.

(E) Daytime headlight laws would probably do less to prevent automobile collisions in the continental United States than they do in the countries that have the laws.

117. A company's two divisions performed with remarkable consistency over the past three years: in each of those years, the pharmaceuticals division has accounted for roughly 20 percent of dollar sales and 40 percent of profits, and the chemicals division for the balance.

Which of the following can properly be inferred regarding the past three years from the statement above?

(A) Total dollar sales for each of the company's divisions have remained roughly constant.

(B) The pharmaceuticals division has faced stiffer competition in its markets than has the chemicals division.

(C) The chemicals division has realized lower profits per dollar of sales than has the pharmaceuticals division.

(D) The product mix offered by each of the company's divisions has remained unchanged.

(E) Highly profitable products accounted for a higher percentage of the chemicals division's sales than of those of the pharmaceuticals division.

118. According to a review of 61 studies of patients suffering from severely debilitating depression, a large majority of the patients reported that missing a night's sleep immediately lifted their depression. Yet sleep-deprivation is not used to treat depression even though the conventional treatments, which use drugs and electric shocks, often have serious side effects.

Which of the following, if true, best explains the fact that sleep-deprivation is not used as a treatment for depression?

(A) For a small percentage of depressed patients, missing a night's sleep induces a temporary sense of euphoria.

(B) Keeping depressed patients awake is more difficult than keeping awake people who are not depressed.

(C) Prolonged loss of sleep can lead to temporary impairment of judgment comparable to that induced by consuming several ounces of alcohol.

(D) The dramatic shifts in mood connected with sleep and wakefulness have not been traced to particular changes in brain chemistry.

(E) Depression returns in full force as soon as the patient sleeps for even a few minutes.

Questions 119-120 are based on the following.

According to the Tristate Transportation Authority, making certain improvements to the main commuter rail line would increase ridership dramatically. The authority plans to finance these improvements over the course of five years by raising automobile tolls on the two highway bridges along the route the rail line serves. Although the proposed improvements are indeed needed, the authority's plan for securing the necessary funds should be rejected because it would unfairly force drivers to absorb the entire cost of something from which they receive no benefit.

119. Which of the following, if true, would cast the most doubt on the effectiveness of the authority's plan to finance the proposed improvements by increasing bridge tolls?

(A) Before the authority increases tolls on any of the area bridges, it is required by law to hold public hearings at which objections to the proposed increase can be raised.

(B) Whenever bridge tolls are increased, the authority must pay a private contractor to adjust the automated toll-collecting machines.

(C) Between the time a proposed toll increase is announced and the time the increase is actually put into effect, many commuters buy more tokens than usual to postpone the effects of the increase.

(D) When tolls were last increased on the two bridges in question, almost 20 percent of the regular commuter traffic switched to a slightly longer alternative route that has since been improved.

(E) The chairman of the authority is a member of the Tristate Automobile Club that has registered strong opposition to the proposed toll increase.

120. Which of the following, if true, would provide the authority with the strongest counter to the objection that its plan is unfair?

(A) Even with the proposed toll increase, the average bridge toll in the tristate region would remain less than the tolls charged in neighboring states.

(B) Any attempt to finance the improvements by raising rail fares would result in a decrease in ridership and so would be self-defeating.

(C) Automobile commuters benefit from well-maintained bridges, and in the tristate region bridge maintenance is funded out of general income tax revenues to which both automobile and rail commuters contribute.

(D) The roads along the route served by the rail line are highly congested and drivers benefit when commuters are diverted from congested roadways to mass transit.

(E) The only alternative way of funding the proposed improvements now being considered is through a regional income tax surcharge, which would affect automobile commuters and rail commuters alike.

121. Manufacturers sometimes discount the price of a product to retailers for a promotion period when the product is advertised to consumers. Such promotions often result in a dramatic increase in amount of product sold by the manufacturers to retailers. Nevertheless, the manufacturers could often make more profit by not holding the promotions.

Which of the following, if true, most strongly supports the claim above about the manufacturers' profit?

(A) The amount of discount generally offered by manufacturers to retailers is carefully calculated to represent the minimum needed to draw consumers' attention to the product.
(B) For many consumer products the period of advertising discounted prices to consumers is about a week, not sufficiently long for consumers to become used to the sale price.
(C) For products that are not newly introduced, the purpose of such promotions is to keep the products in the minds of consumers and to attract consumers who are currently using competing products.
(D) During such a promotion retailers tend to accumulate in their warehouses inventory bought at discount; they then sell much of it later at their regular price.
(E) If a manufacturer fails to offer such promotions but its competitor offers them, that competitor will tend to attract consumers away from the manufacturer's product.

122. When people evade income taxes by not declaring taxable income, a vicious cycle results. Tax evasion forces lawmakers to raise income tax rates, which causes the tax burden on nonevading taxpayers to become heavier. This, in turn, encourages even more taxpayers to evade income taxes by hiding taxable income.

The vicious cycle described above could not result unless which of the following were true?

(A) An increase in tax rates tends to function as an incentive for taxpayers to try to increase their pretax incomes.
(B) Some methods for detecting tax evaders, and thus recovering some tax revenue lost through evasion, bring in more than they cost, but their success rate varies from year to year.
(C) When lawmakers establish income tax rates in order to generate a certain level of revenue, they do not allow adequately for revenue that will be lost through evasion.
(D) No one who routinely hides some taxable income can be induced by a lowering of tax rates to stop hiding such income unless fines for evaders are raised at the same time.
(E) Taxpayers do not differ from each other with respect to the rate of taxation that will cause them to evade taxes.

123. Advertisement: Today's customers expect high quality. Every advance in the quality of manufactured products raises customer expectations. The company that is satisfied with the current quality of its products will soon find that its customers are not. At MegaCorp, meeting or exceeding customer expectations is our goal.

Which of the following must be true on the basis of the statements in the advertisement above?

(A) MegaCorp's competitors will succeed in attracting customers only if those competitors adopt MegaCorp's goal as their own.
(B) A company that does not correctly anticipate the expectations of its customers is certain to fail in advancing the quality of its products.
(C) MegaCorp's goal is possible to meet only if continuing advances in product quality are possible.
(D) If a company becomes satisfied with the quality of its products, then the quality of its products is sure to decline.
(E) MegaCorp's customers are currently satisfied with the quality of its products.

124. The local board of education found that, because the current physics curriculum has little direct relevance to today's world, physics classes attracted few high school students. So to attract students to physics classes, the board proposed a curriculum that emphasizes principles of physics involved in producing and analyzing visual images.

Which of the following, if true, provides the strongest reason to expect that the proposed curriculum will be successful in attracting students?

(A) Several of the fundamental principles of physics are involved in producing and analyzing visual images.
(B) Knowledge of physics is becoming increasingly important in understanding the technology used in today's world.
(C) Equipment that a large producer of photographic equipment has donated to the high school could be used in the proposed curriculum.
(D) The number of students interested in physics today is much lower than the number of students interested in physics 50 years ago.
(E) In today's world the production and analysis of visual images is of major importance in communications, business, and recreation.

125. Unlike the wholesale price of raw wool, the wholesale price of raw cotton has fallen considerably in the last year. Thus, although the retail price of cotton clothing at retail clothing stores has not yet fallen, it will inevitably fall.

Which of the following, if true, most seriously weakens the argument above?

(A) The cost of processing raw cotton for cloth has increased during the last year.
(B) The wholesale price of raw wool is typically higher than that of the same volume of raw cotton.
(C) The operating costs of the average retail clothing store have remained constant during the last year.
(D) Changes in retail prices always lag behind changes in wholesale prices.
(E) The cost of harvesting raw cotton has increased in the last year.

126. Many companies now have employee assistance programs that enable employees, free of charge, to improve their physical fitness, reduce stress, and learn ways to stop smoking. These programs increase worker productivity, reduce absenteeism, and lessen insurance costs for employee health care. Therefore, these programs benefit the company as well as the employee.

Which of the following, if true, most significantly strengthens the conclusion above?

(A) Physical fitness programs are often the most popular services offered to employees.
(B) Studies have shown that training in stress management is not effective for many people.
(C) Regular exercise reduces people's risk of heart disease and provides them with increased energy.
(D) Physical injuries sometimes result from entering a strenuous physical fitness program too quickly.
(E) Employee assistance programs require companies to hire people to supervise the various programs offered.

127. Small-business groups are lobbying to defeat proposed federal legislation that would substantially raise the federal minimum wage. This opposition is surprising since the legislation they oppose would, for the first time, exempt all small businesses from paying any minimum wage.

Which of the following, if true, would best explain the opposition of small-business groups to the proposed legislation?

(A) Under the current federal minimum-wage law, most small businesses are required to pay no less than the minimum wage to their employees.
(B) In order to attract workers, small companies must match the wages offered by their larger competitors, and these competitors would not be exempt under the proposed laws.
(C) The exact number of companies that are currently required to pay no less than the minimum wage but that would be exempt under the proposed laws is unknown.
(D) Some states have set their own minimum wages— in some cases, quite a bit above the level of the minimum wage mandated by current federal law—for certain key industries.
(E) Service companies make up the majority of small businesses and they generally employ more employees per dollar of revenues than do retail or manufacturing businesses.

128. Reviewer: The book *Art's Decline* argues that European painters today lack skills that were common among European painters of preceding centuries. In this the book must be right, since its analysis of 100 paintings, 50 old and 50 contemporary, demonstrates convincingly that none of the contemporary paintings are executed as skillfully as the older paintings.

Which of the following points to the most serious logical flaw in the reviewer's argument?

(A) The paintings chosen by the book's author for analysis could be those that most support the book's thesis.

(B) There could be criteria other than the technical skill of the artist by which to evaluate a painting.

(C) The title of the book could cause readers to accept the book's thesis even before they read the analysis of the paintings that supports it.

(D) The particular methods currently used by European painters could require less artistic skill than do methods used by painters in other parts of the world.

(E) A reader who was not familiar with the language of art criticism might not be convinced by the book's analysis of the 100 paintings.

129. The pharmaceutical industry argues that because new drugs will not be developed unless heavy development costs can be recouped in later sales, the current 20 years of protection provided by patents should be extended in the case of newly developed drugs. However, in other industries new-product development continues despite high development costs, a fact that indicates that the extension is unnecessary.

Which of the following, if true, most strongly supports the pharmaceutical industry's argument against the challenge made above?

(A) No industries other than the pharmaceutical industry have asked for an extension of the 20-year limit on patent protection.

(B) Clinical trials of new drugs, which occur after the patent is granted and before the new drug can be marketed, often now take as long as 10 years to complete.

(C) There are several industries in which the ratio of research and development costs to revenues is higher than it is in the pharmaceutical industry.

(D) An existing patent for a drug does not legally prevent pharmaceutical companies from bringing to market alternative drugs, provided they are sufficiently dissimilar to the patented drug.

(E) Much recent industrial innovation has occurred in products—for example, in the computer and electronics industries—for which patent protection is often very ineffective.

Questions 130-131 are based on the following.

Bank depositors in the United States are all financially protected against bank failure because the government insures all individuals' bank deposits. An economist argues that this insurance is partly responsible for the high rate of bank failures, since it removes from depositors any financial incentive to find out whether the bank that holds their money is secure against failure. If depositors were more selective, then banks would need to be secure in order to compete for depositors' money.

130. The economist's argument makes which of the following assumptions?

(A) Bank failures are caused when big borrowers default on loan repayments.

(B) A significant proportion of depositors maintain accounts at several different banks.

(C) The more a depositor has to deposit, the more careful he or she tends to be in selecting a bank.

(D) The difference in the interest rates paid to depositors by different banks is not a significant factor in bank failures.

(E) Potential depositors are able to determine which banks are secure against failure.

131. Which of the following, if true, most seriously weakens the economist's argument?

(A) Before the government started to insure depositors against bank failure, there was a lower rate of bank failure than there is now.

(B) When the government did not insure deposits, frequent bank failures occurred as a result of depositors' fears of losing money in bank failures.

(C) Surveys show that a significant proportion of depositors are aware that their deposits are insured by the government.

(D) There is an upper limit on the amount of an individual's deposit that the government will insure, but very few individuals' deposits exceed this limit.

(E) The security of a bank against failure depends on the percentage of its assets that are loaned out and also on how much risk its loans involve.

132. Passengers must exit airplanes swiftly after accidents, since gases released following accidents are toxic to humans and often explode soon after being released. In order to prevent passenger deaths from gas inhalation, safety officials recommend that passengers be provided with smoke hoods that prevent inhalation of the gases.

Which of the following, if true, constitutes the strongest reason not to require implementation of the safety officials' recommendation?

(A) Test evacuations showed that putting on the smoke hoods added considerably to the overall time it took passengers to leave the cabin.
(B) Some airlines are unwilling to buy the smoke hoods because they consider them to be prohibitively expensive.
(C) Although the smoke hoods protect passengers from the toxic gases, they can do nothing to prevent the gases from igniting.
(D) Some experienced flyers fail to pay attention to the safety instructions given on every commercial flight before takeoff.
(E) In many airplane accidents, passengers who were able to reach emergency exits were overcome by toxic gases before they could exit the airplane.

133. In 1960, 10 percent of every dollar paid in automobile insurance premiums went to pay costs arising from injuries incurred in car accidents. In 1990, 50 percent of every dollar paid in automobile insurance premiums went toward such costs, despite the fact that cars were much safer in 1990 than in 1960.

Which of the following, if true, best explains the discrepancy outlined above?

(A) There were fewer accidents in 1990 than in 1960.
(B) On average, people drove more slowly in 1990 than in 1960.
(C) Cars grew increasingly more expensive to repair over the period in question.
(D) The price of insurance increased more rapidly than the rate of inflation between 1960 and 1990.
(E) Health-care costs rose sharply between 1960 and 1990.

134. Caterpillars of all species produce an identical hormone called "juvenile hormone" that maintains feeding behavior. Only when a caterpillar has grown to the right size for pupation to take place does a special enzyme halt the production of juvenile hormone. This enzyme can be synthesized and will, on being ingested by immature caterpillars, kill them by stopping them from feeding.

Which of the following, if true, most strongly supports the view that it would not be advisable to try to eradicate agricultural pests that go through a caterpillar stage by spraying croplands with the enzyme mentioned above?

(A) Most species of caterpillar are subject to some natural predation.
(B) Many agricultural pests do not go through a caterpillar stage.
(C) Many agriculturally beneficial insects go through a caterpillar stage.
(D) Since caterpillars of different species emerge at different times, several sprayings would be necessary.
(E) Although the enzyme has been synthesized in the laboratory, no large-scale production facilities exist as yet.

135. Although aspirin has been proven to eliminate moderate fever associated with some illnesses, many doctors no longer routinely recommend its use for this purpose. A moderate fever stimulates the activity of the body's disease-fighting white blood cells and also inhibits the growth of many strains of disease-causing bacteria.

If the statements above are true, which of the following conclusions is most strongly supported by them?

(A) Aspirin, an effective painkiller, alleviates the pain and discomfort of many illnesses.
(B) Aspirin can prolong a patient's illness by eliminating moderate fever helpful in fighting some diseases.
(C) Aspirin inhibits the growth of white blood cells, which are necessary for fighting some illnesses.
(D) The more white blood cells a patient's body produces, the less severe the patient's illness will be.
(E) The focus of modern medicine is on inhibiting the growth of disease-causing bacteria within the body.

136. Because postage rates are rising, *Home Decorator* magazine plans to maximize its profits by reducing by one-half the number of issues it publishes each year. The quality of articles, the number of articles published per year, and the subscription price will not change. Market research shows that neither subscribers nor advertisers will be lost if the magazine's plan is instituted.

Which of the following, if true, provides the strongest evidence that the magazine's profits are likely to decline if the plan is instituted?

(A) With the new postage rates, a typical issue under the proposed plan would cost about one-third more to mail than a typical current issue would.

(B) The majority of the magazine's subscribers are less concerned about a possible reduction in the quantity of the magazine's articles than about a possible loss of the current high quality of its articles.

(C) Many of the magazine's long-time subscribers would continue their subscriptions even if the subscription price were increased.

(D) Most of the advertisers that purchase advertising space in the magazine will continue to spend the same amount on advertising per issue as they have in the past.

(E) Production costs for the magazine are expected to remain stable.

137. A study of marital relationships in which one partner's sleeping and waking cycles differ from those of the other partner reveals that such couples share fewer activities with each other and have more violent arguments than do couples in a relationship in which both partners follow the same sleeping and waking patterns. Thus, mismatched sleeping and waking cycles can seriously jeopardize a marriage.

Which of the following, if true, most seriously weakens the argument above?

(A) Married couples in which both spouses follow the same sleeping and waking patterns also occasionally have arguments that can jeopardize the couple's marriage.

(B) The sleeping and waking cycles of individuals tend to vary from season to season.

(C) The individuals who have sleeping and waking cycles that differ significantly from those of their spouses tend to argue little with colleagues at work.

(D) People in unhappy marriages have been found to express hostility by adopting a different sleeping and waking cycle from that of their spouses.

(E) According to a recent study, most people's sleeping and waking cycles can be controlled and modified easily.

Questions 138-139 are based on the following.

Roland: The alarming fact is that 90 percent of the people in this country now report that they know someone who is unemployed.

Sharon: But a normal, moderate level of unemployment is 5 percent, with 1 out of 20 workers unemployed. So at any given time if a person knows approximately 50 workers, 1 or more will very likely be unemployed.

138. Sharon's argument is structured to lead to which of the following as a conclusion?

(A) The fact that 90 percent of the people know someone who is unemployed is not an indication that unemployment is abnormally high.

(B) The current level of unemployment is not moderate.

(C) If at least 5 percent of workers are unemployed, the result of questioning a representative group of people cannot be the percentage Roland cites.

(D) It is unlikely that the people whose statements Roland cites are giving accurate reports.

(E) If an unemployment figure is given as a certain percent, the actual percentage of those without jobs is even higher.

139. Sharon's argument relies on the assumption that

(A) normal levels of unemployment are rarely exceeded

(B) unemployment is not normally concentrated in geographically isolated segments of the population

(C) the number of people who each know someone who is unemployed is always higher than 90 percent of the population

(D) Roland is not consciously distorting the statistics he presents

(E) knowledge that a personal acquaintance is unemployed generates more fear of losing one's job than does knowledge of unemployment statistics

140. A report on acid rain concluded, "Most forests in Canada are not being damaged by acid rain." Critics of the report insist the conclusion be changed to, "Most forests in Canada do not show visible symptoms of damage by acid rain, such as abnormal loss of leaves, slower rates of growth, or higher mortality."

Which of the following, if true, provides the best logical justification for the critics' insistence that the report's conclusion be changed?

(A) Some forests in Canada are being damaged by acid rain.
(B) Acid rain could be causing damage for which symptoms have not yet become visible.
(C) The report does not compare acid rain damage to Canadian forests with acid rain damage to forests in other countries.
(D) All forests in Canada have received acid rain during the past fifteen years.
(E) The severity of damage by acid rain differs from forest to forest.

141. In the past most airline companies minimized aircraft weight to minimize fuel costs. The safest airline seats were heavy, and airlines equipped their planes with few of these seats. This year the seat that has sold best to airlines has been the safest one—a clear indication that airlines are assigning a higher priority to safe seating than to minimizing fuel costs.

Which of the following, if true, most seriously weakens the argument above?

(A) Last year's best-selling airline seat was not the safest airline seat on the market.
(B) No airline company has announced that it would be making safe seating a higher priority this year.
(C) The price of fuel was higher this year than it had been in most of the years when the safest airline seats sold poorly.
(D) Because of increases in the cost of materials, all airline seats were more expensive to manufacture this year than in any previous year.
(E) Because of technological innovations, the safest airline seat on the market this year weighed less than most other airline seats on the market.

142. A computer equipped with signature-recognition software, which restricts access to a computer to those people whose signatures are on file, identifies a person's signature by analyzing not only the form of the signature but also such characteristics as pen pressure and signing speed. Even the most adept forgers cannot duplicate all of the characteristics the program analyzes.

Which of the following can be logically concluded from the passage above?

(A) The time it takes to record and analyze a signature makes the software impractical for everyday use.
(B) Computers equipped with the software will soon be installed in most banks.
(C) Nobody can gain access to a computer equipped with the software solely by virtue of skill at forging signatures.
(D) Signature-recognition software has taken many years to develop and perfect.
(E) In many cases even authorized users are denied legitimate access to computers equipped with the software.

143. Division manager: I want to replace the Microton computers in my division with Vitech computers.

General manager: Why?

Division manager: It costs 28 percent less to train new staff on the Vitech.

General manager: But that is not a good enough reason. We can simply hire only people who already know how to use the Microton computer.

Which of the following, if true, most seriously undermines the general manager's objection to the replacement of Microton computers with Vitechs?

(A) Currently all employees in the company are required to attend workshops on how to use Microton computers in new applications.
(B) Once employees learn how to use a computer, they tend to change employers more readily than before.
(C) Experienced users of Microton computers command much higher salaries than do prospective employees who have no experience in the use of computers.
(D) The average productivity of employees in the general manager's company is below the average productivity of the employees of its competitors.
(E) The high costs of replacement parts make Vitech computers more expensive to maintain than Microton computers.

144. An airplane engine manufacturer developed a new engine model with safety features lacking in the earlier model, which was still being manufactured. During the first year that both were sold, the earlier model far outsold the new model; the manufacturer thus concluded that safety was not the customers' primary consideration.

Which of the following, if true, would most seriously weaken the manufacturer's conclusion?

(A) Both private plane owners and commercial airlines buy engines from this airplane engine manufacturer.
(B) Many customers consider earlier engine models better safety risks than new engine models, since more is usually known about the safety of the earlier models.
(C) Many customers of this airplane engine manufacturer also bought airplane engines from manufacturers who did not provide additional safety features in their newer models.
(D) The newer engine model can be used in all planes in which the earlier engine model can be used.
(E) There was no significant difference in price between the newer engine model and the earlier engine model.

145. Between 1975 and 1985, nursing-home occupancy rates averaged 87 percent of capacity, while admission rates remained constant, at an average of 95 admissions per 1,000 beds per year. Between 1985 and 1988, however, occupancy rates rose to an average of 92 percent of capacity, while admission rates declined to 81 per 1,000 beds per year.

If the statements above are true, which of the following conclusions can be most properly drawn?

(A) The average length of time nursing-home residents stayed in nursing homes increased between 1985 and 1988.
(B) The proportion of older people living in nursing homes was greater in 1988 than in 1975.
(C) Nursing home admission rates tend to decline whenever occupancy rates rise.
(D) Nursing homes built prior to 1985 generally had fewer beds than did nursing homes built between 1985 and 1988.
(E) The more beds a nursing home has, the higher its occupancy rate is likely to be.

146. Firms adopting "profit-related-pay" (PRP) contracts pay wages at levels that vary with the firm's profits. In the metalworking industry last year, firms with PRP contracts in place showed productivity per worker on average 13 percent higher than that of their competitors who used more traditional contracts.

If, on the basis of the evidence above, it is argued that PRP contracts increase worker productivity, which of the following, if true, would most seriously weaken that argument?

(A) Results similar to those cited for the metalworking industry have been found in other industries where PRP contracts are used.
(B) Under PRP contracts costs other than labor costs, such as plant, machinery, and energy, make up an increased proportion of the total cost of each unit of output.
(C) Because introducing PRP contracts greatly changes individual workers' relationships to the firm, negotiating the introduction of PRP contracts is complex and time-consuming.
(D) Many firms in the metalworking industry have modernized production equipment in the last five years, and most of these introduced PRP contracts at the same time.
(E) In firms in the metalworking industry where PRP contracts are in place, the average take-home pay is 15 percent higher than it is in those firms where workers have more traditional contracts.

147. Crops can be traded on the futures market before they are harvested. If a poor corn harvest is predicted, prices of corn futures rise; if a bountiful corn harvest is predicted, prices of corn futures fall. This morning meteorologists are predicting much-needed rain for the corn-growing region starting tomorrow. Therefore, since adequate moisture is essential for the current crop's survival, prices of corn futures will fall sharply today.

Which of the following, if true, most weakens the argument above?

(A) Corn that does not receive adequate moisture during its critical pollination stage will not produce a bountiful harvest.
(B) Futures prices for corn have been fluctuating more dramatically this season than last season.
(C) The rain that meteorologists predicted for tomorrow is expected to extend well beyond the corn-growing region.
(D) Agriculture experts announced today that a disease that has devastated some of the corn crop will spread widely before the end of the growing season.
(E) Most people who trade in corn futures rarely take physical possession of the corn they trade.

148. A discount retailer of basic household necessities employs thousands of people and pays most of them at the minimum wage rate. Yet following a federally mandated increase of the minimum wage rate that increased the retailer's operating costs considerably, the retailer's profits increased markedly.

Which of the following, if true, most helps to resolve the apparent paradox?

(A) Over half of the retailer's operating costs consist of payroll expenditures; yet only a small percentage of those expenditures go to pay management salaries.
(B) The retailer's customer base is made up primarily of people who earn, or who depend on the earnings of others who earn, the minimum wage.
(C) The retailer's operating costs, other than wages, increased substantially after the increase in the minimum wage rate went into effect.
(D) When the increase in the minimum wage rate went into effect, the retailer also raised the wage rate for employees who had been earning just above minimum wage.
(E) The majority of the retailer's employees work as cashiers, and most cashiers are paid the minimum wage.

149. The cotton farms of Country Q became so productive that the market could not absorb all that they produced. Consequently, cotton prices fell. The government tried to boost cotton prices by offering farmers who took 25 percent of their cotton acreage out of production direct support payments up to a specified maximum per farm.

The government's program, if successful, will not be a net burden on the budget. Which of the following, if true, is the best basis for an explanation of how this could be so?

(A) Depressed cotton prices meant operating losses for cotton farms, and the government lost revenue from taxes on farm profits.
(B) Cotton production in several countries other than Q declined slightly the year that the support-payment program went into effect in Q.
(C) The first year that the support-payment program was in effect, cotton acreage in Q was 5 percent below its level in the base year for the program.
(D) The specified maximum per farm meant that for very large cotton farms the support payments were less per acre for those acres that were withdrawn from production than they were for smaller farms.
(E) Farmers who wished to qualify for support payments could not use the cotton acreage that was withdrawn from production to grow any other crop.

150. United States hospitals have traditionally relied primarily on revenues from paying patients to offset losses from unreimbursed care. Almost all paying patients now rely on governmental or private health insurance to pay hospital bills. Recently, insurers have been strictly limiting what they pay hospitals for the care of insured patients to amounts at or below actual costs.

Which of the following conclusions is best supported by the information above?

(A) Although the advance of technology has made expensive medical procedures available to the wealthy, such procedures are out of the reach of low-income patients.

(B) If hospitals do not find ways of raising additional income for unreimbursed care, they must either deny some of that care or suffer losses if they give it.

(C) Some patients have incomes too high for eligibility for governmental health insurance but are unable to afford private insurance for hospital care.

(D) If the hospitals reduce their costs in providing care, insurance companies will maintain the current level of reimbursement, thereby providing more funds for unreimbursed care.

(E) Even though philanthropic donations have traditionally provided some support for the hospitals, such donations are at present declining.

151. Generally scientists enter their field with the goal of doing important new research and accept as their colleagues those with similar motivation. Therefore, when any scientist wins renown as an expounder of science to general audiences, most other scientists conclude that this popularizer should no longer be regarded as a true colleague.

The explanation offered above for the low esteem in which scientific popularizers are held by research scientists assumes that

(A) serious scientific research is not a solitary activity, but relies on active cooperation among a group of collegues

(B) research scientists tend not to regard as colleagues those scientists whose renown they envy

(C) a scientist can become a famous popularizer without having completed any important research

(D) research scientists believe that those who are well known as popularizers of science are not motivated to do important new research

(E) no important new research can be accessible to or accurately assessed by those who are not themselves scientists

152. Mouth cancer is a danger for people who rarely brush their teeth. In order to achieve early detection of mouth cancer in these individuals, a town's public health officials sent a pamphlet to all town residents, describing how to perform weekly self-examinations of the mouth for lumps.

Which of the following, if true, is the best criticism of the pamphlet as a method of achieving the public health officials' goal?

(A) Many dental diseases produce symptoms that cannot be detected in a weekly self-examination.

(B) Once mouth cancer has been detected, the effectiveness of treatment can vary from person to person.

(C) The pamphlet was sent to all town residents, including those individuals who brush their teeth regularly.

(D) Mouth cancer is much more common in adults than in children.

(E) People who rarely brush their teeth are unlikely to perform a weekly examination of their mouth.

153. Technological improvements and reduced equipment costs have made converting solar energy directly into electricity far more cost-efficient in the last decade. However, the threshold of economic viability for solar power (that is, the price per barrel to which oil would have to rise in order for new solar power plants to be more economical than new oil-fired power plants) is unchanged at thirty-five dollars.

Which of the following, if true, does most to help explain why the increased cost-efficiency of solar power has not decreased its threshold of economic viability?

(A) The cost of oil has fallen dramatically.

(B) The reduction in the cost of solar-power equipment has occurred despite increased raw material costs for that equipment.

(C) Technological changes have increased the efficiency of oil-fired power plants.

(D) Most electricity is generated by coal-fired or nuclear, rather than oil-fired, power plants.

(E) When the price of oil increases, reserves of oil not previously worth exploiting become economically viable.

154. Start-up companies financed by venture capitalists have a much lower failure rate than companies financed by other means. Source of financing, therefore, must be a more important causative factor in the success of a start-up company than are such factors as the personal characteristics of the entrepreneur, the quality of strategic planning, or the management structure of the company.

Which of the following, if true, most seriously weakens the argument above?

(A) Venture capitalists tend to be more responsive than other sources of financing to changes in a start-up company's financial needs.

(B) The strategic planning of a start-up company is a less important factor in the long-term success of the company than are the personal characteristics of the entrepreneur.

(C) More than half of all new companies fail within five years.

(D) The management structures of start-up companies are generally less formal than the management structures of ongoing businesses.

(E) Venture capitalists base their decisions to fund start-up companies on such factors as the characteristics of the entrepreneur and quality of strategic planning of the company.

155. The proportion of women among students enrolled in higher education programs has increased over the past decades. This is partly shown by the fact that in 1959, only 11 percent of the women between twenty and twenty-one were enrolled in college, while in 1981, 30 percent of the women between twenty and twenty-one were enrolled in college.

To evaluate the argument above, it would be most useful to compare 1959 and 1981 with regard to which of the following characteristics?

(A) The percentage of women between twenty and twenty-one who were not enrolled in college

(B) The percentage of women between twenty and twenty-five who graduated from college

(C) The percentage of women who, after attending college, entered highly paid professions

(D) The percentage of men between twenty and twenty-one who were enrolled in college

(E) The percentage of men who graduated from high school

Questions 156-157 are based on the following.

Companies O and P each have the same number of employees who work the same number of hours per week. According to records maintained by each company, the employees of Company O had fewer job-related accidents last year than did the employees of Company P. Therefore, employees of Company O are less likely to have job-related accidents than are employees of Company P.

156. Which of the following, if true, would most strengthen the conclusion above?

(A) Company P manufactures products that are more hazardous for workers to produce than does Company O.

(B) Company P holds more safety inspections than does Company O.

(C) Company P maintains a more modern infirmary than does Company O.

(D) Company O paid more for new job-related medical claims than did Company P.

(E) Company P provides more types of health-care benefits than does Company O.

157. Which of the following, if true, would most weaken the conclusion above?

(A) The employees of Company P lost more time at work due to job-related accidents than did the employees of Company O.

(B) Company P considered more types of accidents to be job-related than did Company O.

(C) The employees of Company P were sick more often than were the employees of Company O.

(D) Several employees of Company O each had more than one job-related accident.

(E) The majority of job-related accidents at Company O involved a single machine.

158. In comparison to the standard typewriter keyboard, the EFCO keyboard, which places the most-used keys nearest the typist's strongest fingers, allows faster typing and results in less fatigue. Therefore, replacement of standard keyboards with the EFCO keyboard will result in an immediate reduction of typing costs.

Which of the following, if true, would most weaken the conclusion drawn above?

(A) People who use both standard and EFCO keyboards report greater difficulty in the transition from the EFCO keyboard to the standard keyboard than in the transition from the standard keyboard to the EFCO keyboard.

(B) EFCO keyboards are no more expensive to manufacture than are standard keyboards and require less frequent repair than do standard keyboards.

(C) The number of businesses and government agencies that use EFCO keyboards is increasing each year.

(D) The more training and experience an employee has had with the standard keyboard, the more costly it is to train that employee to use the EFCO keyboard.

(E) Novice typists can learn to use the EFCO keyboard in about the same amount of time it takes them to learn to use the standard keyboard.

Questions 159-160 are based on the following.

Half of the subjects in an experiment—the experimental group—consumed large quantities of a popular artificial sweetener. Afterward, this group showed lower cognitive abilities than did the other half of the subjects—the control group—who did not consume the sweetener. The detrimental effects were attributed to an amino acid that is one of the sweetener's principal constituents.

159. Which of the following, if true, would best support the conclusion that some ingredient of the sweetener was responsible for the experimental results?

(A) Most consumers of the sweetener do not consume as much of it as the experimental group members did.

(B) The amino acid referred to in the conclusion is a component of all proteins, some of which must be consumed for adequate nutrition.

(C) The quantity of the sweetener consumed by individuals in the experimental group is considered safe by federal food regulators.

(D) The two groups of subjects were evenly matched with regard to cognitive abilities prior to the experiment.

(E) A second experiment in which subjects consumed large quantities of the sweetener lacked a control group of subjects who were not given the sweetener.

160. Which of the following, if true, would best help explain how the sweetener might produce the observed effect?

(A) The government's analysis of the artificial sweetener determined that it was sold in relatively pure form.

(B) A high level of the amino acid in the blood inhibits the synthesis of a substance required for normal brain functioning.

(C) Because the sweetener is used primarily as a food additive, adverse reactions to it are rarely noticed by consumers.

(D) The amino acid that is a constituent of the sweetener is also sold separately as a dietary supplement.

(E) Subjects in the experiment did not know whether they were consuming the sweetener or a second, harmless substance.

161. Adult female rats who have never before encountered rat pups will start to show maternal behaviors after being confined with a pup for about seven days. This period can be considerably shortened by disabling the female's sense of smell or by removing the scent-producing glands of the pup.

Which of the following hypotheses best explains the contrast described above?

(A) The sense of smell in adult female rats is more acute than that in rat pups.
(B) The amount of scent produced by rat pups increases when they are in the presence of a female rat that did not bear them.
(C) Female rats that have given birth are more affected by olfactory cues than are female rats that have never given birth.
(D) A female rat that has given birth shows maternal behavior toward rat pups that she did not bear more quickly than does a female rat that has never given birth.
(E) The development of a female rat's maternal interest in a rat pup that she did not bear is inhibited by the odor of the pup.

162. The interview is an essential part of a successful hiring program because, with it, job applicants who have personalities that are unsuited to the requirements of the job will be eliminated from consideration.

The argument above logically depends on which of the following assumptions?

(A) A hiring program will be successful if it includes interviews.
(B) The interview is a more important part of a successful hiring program than is the development of a job description.
(C) Interviewers can accurately identify applicants whose personalities are unsuited to the requirements of the job.
(D) The only purpose of an interview is to evaluate whether job applicants' personalities are suited to the requirements of the job.
(E) The fit of job applicants' personalities to the requirements of the job was once the most important factor in making hiring decisions.

163. An overly centralized economy, not the changes in the climate, is responsible for the poor agricultural production in Country X since its new government came to power. Neighboring Country Y has experienced the same climatic conditions, but while agricultural production has been falling in Country X, it has been rising in Country Y.

Which of the following, if true, would most weaken the argument above?

(A) Industrial production also is declining in Country X.
(B) Whereas Country Y is landlocked, Country X has a major seaport.
(C) Both Country X and Country Y have been experiencing drought conditions.
(D) The crops that have always been grown in Country X are different from those that have always been grown in Country Y.
(E) Country X's new government instituted a centralized economy with the intention of ensuring an equitable distribution of goods.

164. Useful protein drugs, such as insulin, must still be administered by the cumbersome procedure of injection under the skin. If proteins are taken orally, they are digested and cannot reach their target cells. Certain nonprotein drugs, however, contain chemical bonds that are not broken down by the digestive system. They can, thus, be taken orally.

The statements above most strongly support a claim that a research procedure that successfully accomplishes which of the following would be beneficial to users of protein drugs?

(A) Coating insulin with compounds that are broken down by target cells, but whose chemical bonds are resistant to digestion
(B) Converting into protein compounds, by procedures that work in the laboratory, the nonprotein drugs that resist digestion
(C) Removing permanently from the digestive system any substances that digest proteins
(D) Determining, in a systematic way, what enzymes and bacteria are present in the normal digestive system and whether they tend to be broken down within the body
(E) Determining the amount of time each nonprotein drug takes to reach its target cells

165. Country Y uses its scarce foreign-exchange reserves to buy scrap iron for recycling into steel. Although the steel thus produced earns more foreign exchange than it costs, that policy is foolish. Country Y's own territory has vast deposits of iron ore, which can be mined with minimal expenditure of foreign exchange.

Which of the following, if true, provides the strongest support for Country Y's policy of buying scrap iron abroad?

(A) The price of scrap iron on international markets rose significantly in 1987.
(B) Country Y's foreign-exchange reserves dropped significantly in 1987.
(C) There is virtually no difference in quality between steel produced from scrap iron and that produced from iron ore.
(D) Scrap iron is now used in the production of roughly half the steel used in the world today, and experts predict that scrap iron will be used even more extensively in the future.
(E) Furnaces that process scrap iron can be built and operated in Country Y with substantially less foreign exchange than can furnaces that process iron ore.

166. Last year the rate of inflation was 1.2 percent, but for the current year it has been 4 percent. We can conclude that inflation is on an upward trend and the rate will be still higher next year.

Which of the following, if true, most seriously weakens the conclusion above?

(A) The inflation figures were computed on the basis of a representative sample of economic data rather than all of the available data.
(B) Last year a dip in oil prices brought inflation temporarily below its recent stable annual level of 4 percent.
(C) Increases in the pay of some workers are tied to the level of inflation, and at an inflation rate of 4 percent or above, these pay raises constitute a force causing further inflation.
(D) The 1.2 percent rate of inflation last year represented a ten-year low.
(E) Government intervention cannot affect the rate of inflation to any significant degree.

167. Because no employee wants to be associated with bad news in the eyes of a superior, information about serious problems at lower levels is progressively softened and distorted as it goes up each step in the management hierarchy. The chief executive is, therefore, less well informed about problems at lower levels than are his or her subordinates at those levels.

The conclusion drawn above is based on the assumption that

(A) problems should be solved at the level in the management hierarchy at which they occur
(B) employees should be rewarded for accurately reporting problems to their superiors
(C) problem-solving ability is more important at higher levels than it is at lower levels of the management hierarchy
(D) chief executives obtain information about problems at lower levels from no source other than their subordinates
(E) some employees are more concerned about truth than about the way they are perceived by their superiors

168. In the United States in 1986, the average rate of violent crime in states with strict gun-control laws was 645 crimes per 100,000 persons—about 50 percent higher than the average rate in the eleven states where strict gun-control laws had never been passed. Thus one way to reduce violent crime is to repeal strict gun control laws.

Which of the following, if true, would most weaken the argument above?

(A) The annual rate of violent crime in states with strict gun-control laws has decreased since the passage of those laws.
(B) In states with strict gun-control laws, few individuals are prosecuted for violating such laws.
(C) In states without strict gun-control laws, many individuals have had no formal training in the use of firearms.
(D) The annual rate of nonviolent crime is lower in states with strict gun-control laws than in states without such laws.
(E) Less than half of the individuals who reside in states without strict gun-control laws own a gun.

169. Corporate officers and directors commonly buy and sell, for their own portfolios, stock in their own corporations. Generally, when the ratio of such inside sales to inside purchases falls below 2 to 1 for a given stock, a rise in stock prices is imminent. In recent days, while the price of MEGA Corporation stock has been falling, the corporation's officers and directors have bought up to nine times as much of it as they have sold.

The facts above best support which of the following predictions?

(A) The imbalance between inside purchases and inside sales of MEGA stock will grow even further.
(B) Inside purchases of MEGA stock are about to cease abruptly.
(C) The price of MEGA stock will soon begin to go up.
(D) The price of MEGA stock will continue to drop, but less rapidly.
(E) The majority of MEGA stock will soon be owned by MEGA's own officers and directors.

170. The proposal to hire ten new police officers in Middletown is quite foolish. There is sufficient funding to pay the salaries of the new officers, but not the salaries of additional court and prison employees to process the increased caseload of arrests and convictions that new officers usually generate.

Which of the following, if true, will most seriously weaken the conclusion drawn above?

(A) Studies have shown that an increase in a city's police force does not necessarily reduce crime.
(B) When one major city increased its police force by 19 percent last year, there were 40 percent more arrests and 13 percent more convictions.
(C) If funding for the new police officers' salaries is approved, support for other city services will have to be reduced during the next fiscal year.
(D) In most United States cities, not all arrests result in convictions, and not all convictions result in prison terms.
(E) Middletown's ratio of police officers to citizens has reached a level at which an increase in the number of officers will have a deterrent effect on crime.

171. A recent report determined that although only 3 percent of drivers on Maryland highways equipped their vehicles with radar detectors, 33 percent of all vehicles ticketed for exceeding the speed limit were equipped with them. Clearly, drivers who equip their vehicles with radar detectors are more likely to exceed the speed limit regularly than are drivers who do not.

The conclusion drawn above depends on which of the following assumptions?

(A) Drivers who equip their vehicles with radar detectors are less likely to be ticketed for exceeding the speed limit than are drivers who do not.
(B) Drivers who are ticketed for exceeding the speed limit are more likely to exceed the speed limit regularly than are drivers who are not ticketed.
(C) The number of vehicles that were ticketed for exceeding the speed limit was greater than the number of vehicles that were equipped with radar detectors.
(D) Many of the vehicles that were ticketed for exceeding the speed limit were ticketed more than once in the time period covered by the report.
(E) Drivers on Maryland highways exceeded the speed limit more often than did drivers on other state highways not covered in the report.

172. There is a great deal of geographical variation in the frequency of many surgical procedures—up to tenfold variation per hundred thousand between different areas in the numbers of hysterectomies, prostatectomies, and tonsillectomies.

To support a conclusion that much of the variation is due to unnecessary surgical procedures, it would be most important to establish which of the following?

(A) A local board of review at each hospital examines the records of every operation to determine whether the surgical procedure was necessary.

(B) The variation is unrelated to factors (other than the surgical procedures themselves) that influence the incidence of diseases for which surgery might be considered.

(C) There are several categories of surgical procedure (other than hysterectomies, prostatectomies, and tonsillectomies) that are often performed unnecessarily.

(D) For certain surgical procedures, it is difficult to determine after the operation whether the procedures were necessary or whether alternative treatment would have succeeded.

(E) With respect to how often they are performed unnecessarily, hysterectomies, prostatectomies, and tonsillectomies are representative of surgical procedures in general.

173. Researchers have found that when very overweight people, who tend to have relatively low metabolic rates, lose weight primarily through dieting, their metabolisms generally remain unchanged. They will thus burn significantly fewer calories at the new weight than do people whose weight is normally at that level. Such newly thin persons will, therefore, ultimately regain weight until their body size again matches their metabolic rate.

The conclusion of the argument above depends on which of the following assumptions?

(A) Relatively few very overweight people who have dieted down to a new weight tend to continue to consume substantially fewer calories than do people whose normal weight is at that level.

(B) The metabolisms of people who are usually not overweight are much more able to vary than the metabolisms of people who have been very overweight.

(C) The amount of calories that a person usually burns in a day is determined more by the amount that is consumed that day than by the current weight of the individual.

(D) Researchers have not yet determined whether the metabolic rates of formerly very overweight individuals can be accelerated by means of chemical agents.

(E) Because of the constancy of their metabolic rates, people who are at their usual weight normally have as much difficulty gaining weight as they do losing it.

174. In 1987 sinusitis was the most common chronic medical condition in the United States, followed by arthritis and high blood pressure, in that order.

The incidence rates for both arthritis and high blood pressure increase with age, but the incidence rate for sinusitis is the same for people of all ages.

The average age of the United States population will increase between 1987 and 2000.

Which of the following conclusions can be most properly drawn about chronic medical conditions in the United States from the information given above?

(A) Sinusitis will be more common than either arthritis or high blood pressure in 2000.
(B) Arthritis will be the most common chronic medical condition in 2000.
(C) The average age of people suffering from sinusitis will increase between 1987 and 2000.
(D) Fewer people will suffer from sinusitis in 2000 than suffered from it in 1987.
(E) A majority of the population will suffer from at least one of the medical conditions mentioned above by the year 2000.

175. Parasitic wasps lay their eggs directly into the eggs of various host insects in exactly the right numbers for any suitable size of host egg. If they laid too many eggs in a host egg, the developing wasp larvae would compete with each other to the death for nutrients and space. If too few eggs were laid, portions of the host egg would decay, killing the wasp larvae.

Which of the following conclusions can properly be drawn from the information above?

(A) The size of the smallest host egg that a wasp could theoretically parasitize can be determined from the wasp's egg-laying behavior.
(B) Host insects lack any effective defenses against the form of predation practiced by parasitic wasps.
(C) Parasitic wasps learn from experience how many eggs to lay into the eggs of different host species.
(D) Failure to lay enough eggs would lead to the death of the developing wasp larvae more quickly than would laying too many eggs.
(E) Parasitic wasps use visual clues to calculate the size of a host egg.

176. Northern Air has dozens of flights daily into and out of Belleville Airport, which is highly congested. Northern Air depends for its success on economy and quick turnaround and consequently is planning to replace its large planes with Skybuses, whose novel aerodynamic design is extremely fuel efficient. The Skybus' fuel efficiency results in both lower fuel costs and reduced time spent refueling.

Which of the following, if true, could present the most serious disadvantage for Northern Air in replacing their large planes with Skybuses?

(A) The Skybus would enable Northern Air to schedule direct flights to destinations that currently require stops for refueling.
(B) Aviation fuel is projected to decline in price over the next several years.
(C) The fuel efficiency of the Skybus would enable Northern Air to eliminate refueling at some of its destinations, but several mechanics would lose their jobs.
(D) None of Northern Air's competitors that use Belleville Airport are considering buying Skybuses.
(E) The aerodynamic design of the Skybus causes turbulence behind it when taking off that forces other planes on the runway to delay their takeoffs.

177. Products sold under a brand name used to command premium prices because, in general, they were superior to nonbrand rival products. Technical expertise in product development has become so widespread, however, that special quality advantages are very hard to obtain these days and even harder to maintain. As a consequence, brand-name products generally neither offer higher quality nor sell at higher prices. Paradoxically, brand names are a bigger marketing advantage than ever.

Which of the following, if true, most helps to resolve the paradox outlined above?

(A) Brand names are taken by consumers as a guarantee of getting a product as good as the best rival products.

(B) Consumers recognize that the quality of products sold under invariant brand names can drift over time.

(C) In many acquisitions of one corporation by another, the acquiring corporation is interested more in acquiring the right to use certain brand names than in acquiring existing production facilities.

(D) In the days when special quality advantages were easier to obtain than they are now, it was also easier to get new brand names established.

(E) The advertising of a company's brand-name products is at times transferred to a new advertising agency, especially when sales are declining.

178. In countries in which new life-sustaining drugs cannot be patented, such drugs are sold at widely affordable prices; those same drugs, where patented, command premium prices because the patents shield patent-holding manufacturers from competitors. These facts show that future access to new life-sustaining drugs can be improved if the practice of granting patents on newly developed life-sustaining drugs were to be abolished everywhere.

Which of the following, if true, most seriously weakens the argument?

(A) In countries in which life-sustaining drugs cannot be patented, their manufacture is nevertheless a profitable enterprise.

(B) Countries that do not currently grant patents on life-sustaining drugs are, for the most part, countries with large populations.

(C) In some countries specific processes for the manufacture of pharmaceutical drugs can be patented even in cases in which the drugs themselves cannot be patented.

(D) Pharmaceutical companies can afford the research that goes into the development of new drugs only if patents allow them to earn high profits.

(E) Countries that grant patents on life-sustaining drugs almost always ban their importation from countries that do not grant such patents.

179. A museum has been offered an undocumented statue, supposedly Greek and from the sixth century B.C. Possibly the statue is genuine but undocumented because it was recently unearthed or because it has been privately owned. However, an ancient surface usually has uneven weathering, whereas the surface of this statue has the uniform quality characteristically produced by a chemical bath used by forgers to imitate a weathered surface. Therefore, the statue is probably a forgery.

Which of the following, if true, most seriously weakens the argument?

(A) Museums can accept a recently unearthed statue only with valid export documentation from its country of origin.
(B) The subject's pose and other aspects of the subject's treatment exhibit all the most common features of Greek statues of the sixth century B.C.
(C) The chemical bath that forgers use was at one time used by dealers and collectors to remove the splotchy surface appearance of genuinely ancient sculptures.
(D) Museum officials believe that forgers have no technique that can convincingly simulate the patchy weathering characteristic of the surfaces of ancient sculptures.
(E) An allegedly Roman sculpture with a uniform surface similar to that of the statue being offered to the museum was recently shown to be a forgery.

180. In the arid land along the Colorado River, use of the river's water supply is strictly controlled: farms along the river each have a limited allocation that they are allowed to use for irrigation. But the trees that grow in narrow strips along the river's banks also use its water. Clearly, therefore, if farmers were to remove those trees, more water would be available for crop irrigation.

Which of the following, if true, most seriously weakens the argument?

(A) The trees along the river's banks shelter it from the sun and wind, thereby greatly reducing the amount of water lost through evaporation.
(B) Owners of farms along the river will probably not undertake the expense of cutting down trees along the banks unless they are granted a greater allocation of water in return.
(C) Many of the tree species currently found along the river's banks are specifically adapted to growing in places where tree roots remain constantly wet.
(D) The strip of land where trees grow along the river's banks would not be suitable for growing crops if the trees were removed.
(E) The distribution of water allocations for irrigation is intended to prevent farms farther upstream from using water needed by farms farther downstream.

181. Consumer health advocate: Your candy company adds caffeine to your chocolate candy bars so that each one delivers a specified amount of caffeine. Since caffeine is highly addictive, this indicates that you intend to keep your customers addicted.

Candy manufacturer: Our manufacturing process results in there being less caffeine in each chocolate candy bar than in the unprocessed cacao beans from which the chocolate is made.

The candy manufacturer's response is flawed as a refutation of the consumer health advocate's argument because it

(A) fails to address the issue of whether the level of caffeine in the candy bars sold by the manufacturer is enough to keep people addicted
(B) assumes without warrant that all unprocessed cacao beans contain a uniform amount of caffeine
(C) does not specify exactly how caffeine is lost in the manufacturing process
(D) treats the consumer health advocate's argument as though it were about each candy bar rather than about the manufacturer's candy in general
(E) merely contradicts the consumer health advocate's conclusion without giving any reason to believe that the advocate's reasoning is unsound

182. The earliest Mayan pottery found at Colha, in Belize, is about 3,000 years old. Recently, however, 4,500-year-old stone agricultural implements were unearthed at Colha. These implements resemble Mayan stone implements of a much later period, also found at Colha. Moreover, the implements' designs are strikingly different from the designs of stone implements produced by other cultures known to have inhabited the area in prehistoric times. Therefore, there were surely Mayan settlements in Colha 4,500 years ago.

Which of the following, if true, most seriously weakens the argument?

(A) Ceramic ware is not known to have been used by the Maya to make agricultural implements.
(B) Carbon dating of corn pollen in Colha indicates that agriculture began there around 4,500 years ago.
(C) Archaeological evidence indicates that some of the oldest stone implements found at Colha were used to cut away vegetation after controlled burning of trees to open areas of swampland for cultivation.
(D) Successor cultures at a given site often adopt the style of agricultural implements used by earlier inhabitants of the same site.
(E) Many religious and social institutions of the Mayan people who inhabited Colha 3,000 years ago relied on a highly developed system of agricultural symbols.

183. Editorial:

Regulations recently imposed by the government of Risemia call for unprecedented reductions in the amounts of pollutants manufacturers are allowed to discharge into the environment. It will take costly new pollution control equipment requiring expensive maintenance to comply with these regulations. Resultant price increases for Risemian manufactured goods will lead to the loss of some export markets. Clearly, therefore, annual exports of Risemian manufactured goods will in the future occur at diminished levels.

Which of the following, if true, most seriously weakens the argument in the editorial?

(A) The need to comply with the new regulations will stimulate the development within Risemia of new pollution control equipment for which a strong worldwide demand is likely to emerge.

(B) The proposed regulations include a schedule of fines for noncompliance that escalate steeply in cases of repeated noncompliance.

(C) Savings from utilizing the chemicals captured by the pollution control equipment will remain far below the cost of maintaining the equipment.

(D) By international standards, the levels of pollutants currently emitted by some of Risemia's manufacturing plants are not considered excessive.

(E) The stockholders of most of Risemia's manufacturing corporations exert substantial pressure on the corporations to comply with environmental laws.

184. Codex Berinensis, a Florentine copy of an ancient Roman medical treatise, is undated but contains clues to when it was produced. Its first eighty pages are by a single copyist, but the remaining twenty pages are by three different copyists, which indicates some significant disruption. Since a letter in handwriting identified as that of the fourth copyist mentions a plague that killed many people in Florence in 1148, Codex Berinensis was probably produced in that year.

Which of the following, if true, most strongly supports the hypothesis that Codex Berinensis was produced in 1148 ?

(A) Other than Codex Berinensis, there are no known samples of the handwriting of the first three copyists.

(B) According to the account by the fourth copyist, the plague went on for ten months.

(C) A scribe would be able to copy a page of text the size and style of Codex Berinensis in a day.

(D) There was only one outbreak of plague in Florence in the 1100's.

(E) The number of pages of Codex Berinensis produced by a single scribe becomes smaller with each successive change of copyist.

185. Near Chicago a newly built hydroponic spinach "factory," a completely controlled environment for growing spinach, produces on 1 acre of floor space what it takes 100 acres of fields to produce. Expenses, especially for electricity, are high, however, and the spinach produced costs about four times as much as washed California field spinach, the spinach commonly sold throughout the United States.

Which of the following, if true, best supports a projection that the spinach-growing facility near Chicago will be profitable?

(A) Once the operators of the facility are experienced, they will be able to cut operating expenses by about 25 percent.

(B) There is virtually no scope for any further reduction in the cost per pound for California field spinach.

(C) Unlike washed field spinach, the hydroponically grown spinach is untainted by any pesticides or herbicides and thus will sell at exceptionally high prices to such customers as health food restaurants.

(D) Since spinach is a crop that ships relatively well, the market for the hydroponically grown spinach is no more limited to the Chicago area than the market for California field spinach is to California.

(E) A second hydroponic facility is being built in Canada, taking advantage of inexpensive electricity and high vegetable prices.

186. Offshore oil-drilling operations entail an unavoidable risk of an oil spill, but importing oil on tankers presently entails an even greater such risk per barrel of oil. Therefore, if we are to reduce the risk of an oil spill without curtailing our use of oil, we must invest more in offshore operations and import less oil on tankers.

Which of the following, if true, most seriously weakens the argument above?

(A) Tankers can easily be redesigned so that their use entails less risk of an oil spill.
(B) Oil spills caused by tankers have generally been more serious than those caused by offshore operations.
(C) The impact of offshore operations on the environment can be controlled by careful management.
(D) Offshore operations usually damage the ocean floor, but tankers rarely cause such damage.
(E) Importing oil on tankers is currently less expensive than drilling for it offshore.

187. Automobile Dealer's Advertisement:

The Highway Traffic Safety Institute reports that the PZ 1000 has the fewest injuries per accident of any car in its class. This shows that the PZ 1000 is one of the safest cars available today.

Which of the following, if true, most seriously weakens the argument in the advertisement?

(A) The Highway Traffic Safety Institute report listed many cars in other classes that had more injuries per accident than did the PZ 1000.
(B) In recent years many more PZ 1000's have been sold than have any other kind of car in its class.
(C) Cars in the class to which the PZ 1000 belongs are more likely to be involved in accidents than are other types of cars.
(D) The difference between the number of injuries per accident for the PZ 1000 and that for other cars in its class is quite pronounced.
(E) The Highway Traffic Safety Institute issues reports only once a year.

188. When demand for a factory's products is high, more money is spent at the factory for safety precautions and machinery maintenance than when demand is low. Thus the average number of on-the-job accidents per employee each month should be lower during periods when demand is high than when demand is low and less money is available for safety precautions and machinery maintenance.

Which of the following, if true about a factory when demand for its products is high, casts the most serious doubt on the conclusion drawn above?

(A) Its employees ask for higher wages than they do at other times.
(B) Its management hires new workers but lacks the time to train them properly.
(C) Its employees are less likely to lose their jobs than they are at other times.
(D) Its management sponsors a monthly safety award for each division in the factory.
(E) Its old machinery is replaced with modern, automated models.

189. Studies have shown that elderly people who practice a religion are much more likely to die immediately after an important religious holiday period than immediately before one. Researchers have concluded that the will to live can prolong life, at least for short periods of time.

Which of the following, if true, would most strengthen the researchers' conclusion?

(A) Elderly people who practice a religion are less likely to die immediately before or during an important religious holiday than at any other time of the year.
(B) Elderly people who practice a religion appear to experience less anxiety at the prospect of dying than do other people.
(C) Some elderly people who do practice a religion live much longer than most elderly people who do not.
(D) Most elderly people who participate in religious holidays have different reasons for participating than young people do.
(E) Many religions have important holidays in the spring and fall, seasons with the lowest death rates for elderly people.

190. Manufacturers of mechanical pencils make most of their profit on pencil leads rather than on the pencils themselves. The Write Company, which cannot sell its leads as cheaply as other manufacturers can, plans to alter the design of its mechanical pencil so that it will accept only a newly designed Write Company lead, which will be sold at the same price as the Write Company's current lead.

Which of the following, if true, most strongly supports the Write Company's projection that its plan will lead to an increase in its sales of pencil leads?

(A) First-time buyers of mechanical pencils tend to buy the least expensive mechanical pencils available.
(B) Annual sales of mechanical pencils are expected to triple over the next five years.
(C) A Write Company executive is studying ways to reduce the cost of manufacturing pencil leads.
(D) A rival manufacturer recently announced similar plans to introduce a mechanical pencil that would accept only the leads produced by that manufacturer.
(E) In extensive test marketing, mechanical-pencil users found the new Write Company pencil markedly superior to other mechanical pencils they had used.

191. To evaluate a plan to save money on office-space expenditures by having its employees work at home, XYZ Company asked volunteers from its staff to try the arrangement for six months. During this period, the productivity of these employees was as high as or higher than before.

Which of the following, if true, would argue most strongly against deciding, on the basis of the trial results, to implement the company's plan?

(A) The employees who agreed to participate in the test of the plan were among the company's most self-motivated and independent workers.
(B) The savings that would accrue from reduced office-space expenditures alone would be sufficient to justify the arrangement for the company, apart from any productivity increases.
(C) Other companies that have achieved successful results from work-at-home plans have work forces that are substantially larger than that of XYZ.
(D) The volunteers who worked at home were able to communicate with other employees as necessary for performing the work.
(E) Minor changes in the way office work is organized at XYZ would yield increases in employee productivity similar to those achieved in the trial.

192. Mourdet Winery: Danville Winery's new wine was introduced to compete with our most popular wine, which is sold in a distinctive tall, black bottle. Danville uses a similar bottle. Thus, it is likely that many customers intending to buy our wine will mistakenly buy theirs instead.

Danville Winery: Not so. The two bottles can be readily distinguished: the label on ours, but not on theirs, is gold colored.

Which of the following, if true, most undermines Danville Winery's response?

(A) Gold is the background color on the label of many of the wines produced by Danville Winery.
(B) When the bottles are viewed side by side, Danville Winery's bottle is perceptibly taller than Mourdet Winery's.
(C) Danville Winery, unlike Mourdet Winery, displays its wine's label prominently in advertisements.
(D) It is common for occasional purchasers to buy a bottle of wine on the basis of a general impression of the most obvious feature of the bottle.
(E) Many popular wines are sold in bottles of a standard design.

193. Editorial:

The mayor plans to deactivate the city's fire alarm boxes, because most calls received from them are false alarms. The mayor claims that the alarm boxes are no longer necessary, since most people now have access to either public or private telephones. But the city's commercial district, where there is the greatest risk of fire, has few residents and few public telephones, so some alarm boxes are still necessary.

Which of the following, if true, most seriously weakens the editorial's argument?

(A) Maintaining the fire alarm boxes costs the city more than five million dollars annually.
(B) Commercial buildings have automatic fire alarm systems that are linked directly to the fire department.
(C) The fire department gets less information from an alarm box than it does from a telephone call.
(D) The city's fire department is located much closer to the residential areas than to the commercial district.
(E) On average, almost 25 percent of the public telephones in the city are out of order.

194. A major impediment to wide acceptance of electric vehicles even on the part of people who use their cars almost exclusively for commuting is the inability to use electric vehicles for occasional extended trips. In an attempt to make purchasing electric vehicles more attractive to commuters, one electric vehicle producer is planning to offer customers three days free rental of a conventional car for every 1,000 miles that they drive their electric vehicle.

Which of the following, if true, most threatens the plan's prospects for success?

(A) Many electric vehicles that are used for commercial purposes are not needed for extended trips.

(B) Because a majority of commuters drive at least 100 miles a week, the cost to the producer of making good the offer would add considerably to the already high price of electric vehicles.

(C) The relatively long time it takes to recharge the battery of an electric vehicle can easily be fitted into the regular patterns of car use characteristic of commuters.

(D) Although electric vehicles are essentially emission-free in actual use, generating the electricity necessary for charging an electric vehicle's battery can burden the environment.

(E) Some family vehicles are used primarily not for commuting but for making short local trips, such as to do errands.

195. A proposed change to federal income tax laws would eliminate deductions from taxable income for donations a taxpayer has made to charitable and educational institutions. If this change were adopted, wealthy individuals would no longer be permitted such deductions. Therefore, many charitable and educational institutions would have to reduce services, and some would have to close their doors.

The argument above assumes which of the following?

(A) Without the incentives offered by federal income tax laws, at least some wealthy individuals would not donate as much money to charitable and educational institutions as they otherwise would have.

(B) Money contributed by individuals who make their donations because of provisions in the federal tax laws provides the only source of funding for many charitable and educational institutions.

(C) The primary reason for not adopting the proposed change in the federal income tax laws cited above is to protect wealthy individuals from having to pay higher taxes.

(D) Wealthy individuals who donate money to charitable and educational institutions are the only individuals who donate money to such institutions.

(E) Income tax laws should be changed to make donations to charitable and educational institutions the only permissible deductions from taxable income.

196. An unusually severe winter occurred in Europe after the continent was blanketed by a blue haze resulting from the eruption of the Laki Volcano in the European republic of Iceland in the summer of 1984. Thus, it is evident that major eruptions cause the atmosphere to become cooler than it would be otherwise.

Which of the following statements, if true, most seriously weakens the argument above?

(A) The cooling effect triggered by volcanic eruptions in 1985 was counteracted by an unusual warming of Pacific waters.

(B) There is a strong statistical link between volcanic eruptions and the severity of the rainy season in India.

(C) A few months after El Chichón's large eruption in April 1982, air temperatures throughout the region remained higher than expected, given the long-term weather trends.

(D) The climatic effects of major volcanic eruptions can temporarily mask the general warming trend resulting from an excess of carbon dioxide in the atmosphere.

(E) Three months after an early springtime eruption in South America during the late 19th century, sea surface temperatures near the coast began to fall.

197. To persuade consumers to buy its personal computers for home use, SuperComp has enlisted computer dealers in shopping centers to sell its product and launched a major advertising campaign that has already increased public awareness of the SuperComp brand. Despite the fact that these dealers achieved dramatically increased sales of computers last month, however, analysts doubt that the marketing plan is bringing SuperComp the desired success.

Which of the following, if true, best supports the claim that the analysts' doubt is well founded?

(A) In market surveys, few respondents who had been exposed to SuperComp's advertising campaign said they thought there was no point in owning a home computer.

(B) People who own a home computer often buy a second such computer, but only rarely do people buy a third computer.

(C) SuperComp's dealers also sell other brands of computers that are very similar to SuperComp's but less expensive and that afford the dealers a significantly higher markup.

(D) The dealers who were chosen to sell SuperComp's computers were selected in part because their stores are located in shopping centers that attract relatively wealthy shoppers.

(E) Computer-industry analysts believed before the SuperComp campaign began that most consumers who already owned home computers were not yet ready to replace them.

198. A factory was trying out a new process for producing one of its products, with the goal of reducing production costs. A trial production run using the new process showed a 15 percent reduction in costs compared with past performance using the standard process. The production managers therefore concluded that the new process did produce a cost savings.

Which of the following, if true, casts most doubt on the production managers' conclusion?

(A) In the cost reduction project that eventually led to the trial of the new process, production managers had initially been seeking cost reductions of 50 percent.

(B) Analysis of the trial of the new process showed that the cost reduction during the trial was entirely attributable to a reduction in the number of finished products rejected by quality control.

(C) While the trial was being conducted, production costs at the factory for a similar product, produced without benefit of the new process, also showed a 15 percent reduction.

(D) Although some of the factory's managers have been arguing that the product is outdated and ought to be redesigned, the use of the new production process does not involve any changes in the finished product.

(E) Since the new process differs from the standard process only in the way in which the stages of production are organized and ordered, the cost of the materials used in the product is the same in both processes.

199. Vitacorp, a manufacturer, wishes to make its information booth at an industry convention more productive in terms of boosting sales. The booth offers information introducing the company's new products and services. To achieve the desired result, Vitacorp's marketing department will attempt to attract more people to the booth. The marketing director's first measure was to instruct each salesperson to call his or her five best customers and personally invite them to visit the booth.

Which of the following, if true, most strongly supports the prediction that the marketing director's first measure will contribute to meeting the goal of boosting sales?

(A) Vitacorp's salespeople routinely inform each important customer about new products and services as soon as the decision to launch them has been made.

(B) Many of Vitacorp's competitors have made plans for making their own information booths more productive in increasing sales.

(C) An information booth that is well attended tends to attract visitors who would not otherwise have attended the booth.

(D) Most of Vitacorp's best customers also have business dealings with Vitacorp's competitors.

(E) Vitacorp has fewer new products and services available this year than it had in previous years.

200. Outsourcing is the practice of obtaining from an independent supplier a product or service that a company has previously provided for itself. Since a company's chief objective is to realize the highest possible year-end profits, any product or service that can be obtained from an independent supplier for less than it would cost the company to provide the product or service on its own should be outsourced.

Which of the following, if true, most seriously weakens the argument?

(A) If a company decides to use independent suppliers for a product, it can generally exploit the vigorous competition arising among several firms that are interested in supplying that product.

(B) Successful outsourcing requires a company to provide its suppliers with information about its products and plans that can fall into the hands of its competitors and give them a business advantage.

(C) Certain tasks, such as processing a company's payroll, are commonly outsourced, whereas others, such as handling the company's core business, are not.

(D) For a company to provide a product or service for itself as efficiently as an independent supplier can provide it, the managers involved need to be as expert in the area of that product or service as the people in charge of that product or service at an independent supplier are.

(E) When a company decides to use an independent supplier for a product or service, the independent supplier sometimes hires members of the company's staff who formerly made the product or provided the service that the independent supplier now supplies.

201. State spokesperson: Many businesspeople who have not been to our state believe that we have an inadequate road system. Those people are mistaken, as is obvious from the fact that in each of the past six years, our state has spent more money per mile on road improvements than any other state.

Which of the following, if true, most seriously undermines the reasoning in the spokesperson's argument?

(A) In the spokesperson's state, spending on road improvements has been increasing more slowly over the past six years than it has in several other states.

(B) Adequacy of a state's road system is generally less important to a businessperson considering doing business there than is the availability of qualified employees.

(C) Over the past six years, numerous businesses have left the spokesperson's state, but about as many businesses have moved into the state.

(D) In general, the number of miles of road in a state's road system depends on both the area and the population of the state.

(E) Only states with seriously inadequate road systems need to spend large amounts of money on road improvements.

202. Gortland has long been narrowly self-sufficient in both grain and meat. However, as per capita income in Gortland has risen toward the world average, per capita consumption of meat has also risen toward the world average, and it takes several pounds of grain to produce one pound of meat. Therefore, since per capita income continues to rise, whereas domestic grain production will not increase, Gortland will soon have to import either grain or meat or both.

Which of the following is an assumption on which the argument depends?

(A) The total acreage devoted to grain production in Gortland will not decrease substantially.

(B) The population of Gortland has remained relatively constant during the country's years of growing prosperity.

(C) The per capita consumption of meat in Gortland is roughly the same across all income levels.

(D) In Gortland, neither meat nor grain is subject to government price controls.

(E) People in Gortland who increase their consumption of meat will not radically decrease their consumption of grain.

203. Journalist: In physics journals, the number of articles reporting the results of experiments involving particle accelerators was lower last year than it had been in previous years. Several of the particle accelerators at major research institutions were out of service the year before last for repairs, so it is likely that the low number of articles was due to the decline in availability of particle accelerators.

Which of the following, if true, most seriously undermines the journalist's argument?

(A) Every article based on experiments with particle accelerators that was submitted for publication last year actually was published.
(B) The average time scientists must wait for access to a particle accelerator has declined over the last several years.
(C) The number of physics journals was the same last year as in previous years.
(D) Particle accelerators can be used for more than one group of experiments in any given year.
(E) Recent changes in the editorial policies of several physics journals have decreased the likelihood that articles concerning particle-accelerator research will be accepted for publication.

204. An eyeglass manufacturer tried to boost sales for the summer quarter by offering its distributors a special discount if their orders for that quarter exceeded those for last year's summer quarter by at least 20 percent. Many distributors qualified for this discount. Even with much merchandise discounted, sales increased enough to produce a healthy gain in net profits. The manufacturer plans to repeat this success by offering the same sort of discount for the fall quarter.

Which of the following, if true, most clearly points to a flaw in the manufacturer's plan to repeat the successful performance of the summer quarter?

(A) In general, a distributor's orders for the summer quarter are no higher than those for the spring quarter.
(B) Along with offering special discounts to qualifying distributors, the manufacturer increased newspaper and radio advertising in those distributors' sales areas.
(C) The distributors most likely to qualify for the manufacturer's special discount are those whose orders were unusually low a year earlier.
(D) The distributors who qualified for the manufacturer's special discount were free to decide how much of that discount to pass on to their own customers.
(E) The distributors' ordering more goods in the summer quarter left them overstocked for the fall quarter.

205. Consumer advocate: It is generally true, at least in this state, that lawyers who advertise a specific service charge less for that service than lawyers who do not advertise. It is also true that **each time restrictions on the advertising of legal services have been eliminated, the number of lawyers advertising their services has increased and legal costs to consumers have declined in consequence.** However, eliminating the state requirement that legal advertisements must specify fees for specific services would almost certainly increase rather than further reduce consumers' legal costs. Lawyers would no longer have an incentive to lower their fees when they begin advertising and **if no longer required to specify fee arrangements, many lawyers who now advertise would increase their fees.**

In the consumer advocate's argument, the two portions in **boldface** play which of the following roles?

(A) The first is a generalization that the consumer advocate accepts as true; the second is presented as a consequence that follows from the truth of that generalization.

(B) The first is a pattern of cause and effect that the consumer advocate argues will be repeated in the case at issue; the second acknowledges a circumstance in which that pattern would not hold.

(C) The first is a pattern of cause and effect that the consumer advocate predicts will not hold in the case at issue; the second offers a consideration in support of that prediction.

(D) The first is evidence that the consumer advocate offers in support of a certain prediction; the second is that prediction.

(E) The first acknowledges a consideration that weighs against the main position that the consumer advocate defends; the second is that position.

Explanatory Material: Critical Reasoning

The following discussion is intended to illustrate the variety of ways critical reasoning questions may be approached, and to give you an indication of the degree of precision and depth of reasoning that solving these problems will typically require. The particular questions in this chapter are generally representative of the kinds of questions you will encounter in the GMAT®. Remember that the subject matter of a particular question is less important than the reasoning task you are asked to perform.

1. Which of the following best completes the passage below?

   In a survey of job applicants, two-fifths admitted to being at least a little dishonest. However, the survey may underestimate the proportion of job applicants who are dishonest, because _____.

   (A) some dishonest people taking the survey might have claimed on the survey to be honest
   (B) some generally honest people taking the survey might have claimed on the survey to be dishonest
   (C) some people who claimed on the survey to be at least a little dishonest may be very dishonest
   (D) some people who claimed on the survey to be dishonest may have been answering honestly
   (E) some people who are not job applicants are probably at least a little dishonest

If applicants who are in fact dishonest claimed to be honest, the survey results would show a smaller proportion of dishonest applicants than actually exists. Therefore, A is the best answer.

Choice B is inappropriate because generally honest applicants who claimed to be dishonest could contribute to the overestimation, but not to the underestimation, of dishonest applicants. Choice D is inappropriate because applicants who admitted their dishonesty would not contribute to an underestimation of the proportion of dishonest applicants. Choices C and E are inappropriate because the argument is concerned neither with degrees of dishonesty nor with the honesty of nonapplicants.

Questions 2-3 are based on the following.

The average life expectancy for the United States population as a whole is 73.9 years, but children born in Hawaii will live an average of 77 years, and those born in Louisiana, 71.7 years. If a newlywed couple from Louisiana were to begin their family in Hawaii, therefore, their children would be expected to live longer than would be the case if the family remained in Louisiana.

2. Which of the following, if true, would most seriously weaken the conclusion drawn in the passage?

   (A) Insurance company statisticians do not believe that moving to Hawaii will significantly lengthen the average Louisianian's life.
   (B) The governor of Louisiana has falsely alleged that statistics for his state are inaccurate.
   (C) The longevity ascribed to Hawaii's current population is attributable mostly to genetically determined factors.
   (D) Thirty percent of all Louisianians can expect to live longer than 77 years.
   (E) Most of the Hawaiian Islands have levels of air pollution well below the national average for the United States.

Choice C suggests that a significant proportion of Hawaii's population is genetically predisposed to be long-lived. Since Louisianians are not necessarily so predisposed, and since the Louisianians' children will acquire their genetic characteristics from their parents, not from their birthplace, choice C presents a reason to doubt that Hawaiian-born children of native Louisianians will have an increased life expectancy. Therefore, C is the best answer.

Because the conclusion concerns people born in Hawaii, not the average Louisianian, A does not weaken the conclusion. Because the governor's allegation is false (choice B), it cannot affect the conclusion. Choice D fails to weaken the conclusion because it is consistent with the information given and the conclusion about life expectancy. By suggesting that Hawaii's environment is in one respect particularly healthy, E supports the conclusion.

3. Which of the following statements, if true would most significantly strengthen the conclusion drawn in the passage?

    (A) As population density increases in Hawaii, life expectancy figures for that state are likely to be revised downward.

    (B) Environmental factors tending to favor longevity are abundant in Hawaii and less numerous in Louisiana.

    (C) Twenty-five percent of all Louisianians who move to Hawaii live longer than 77 years.

    (D) Over the last decade, average life expectancy has risen at a higher rate for Louisianians than for Hawaiians.

    (E) Studies show that the average life expectancy for Hawaiians who move permanently to Louisiana is roughly equal to that of Hawaiians who remain in Hawaii.

If B is true, the greater abundance of longevity-promoting environmental factors it mentions is probably at least partly responsible for the higher life expectancy in Hawaii. Children born in Hawaii benefit from these factors from birth, and thus Louisianians who have children in Hawaii increase their children's chances of living longer. Therefore, B is the best answer.

    If life expectancy in Hawaii is likely to be falling, as A says, the argument is weakened rather than strengthened. Choices C and E, in the absence of other relevant information, have no bearing on the conclusion; thus, C and E are inappropriate. Choice D is irrelevant, because the information it mentions about rates would already have been incorporated into the statistics cited in the passage.

4. Insurance Company X is considering issuing a new policy to cover services required by elderly people who suffer from diseases that afflict the elderly. Premiums for the policy must be low enough to attract customers. Therefore, Company X is concerned that the income from the policies would not be sufficient to pay for the claims that would be made.

Which of the following strategies would be most likely to minimize Company X's losses on the policies?

    (A) Attracting middle-aged customers unlikely to submit claims for benefits for many years

    (B) Insuring only those individuals who did not suffer any serious diseases as children

    (C) Including a greater number of services in the policy than are included in other policies of lower cost

    (D) Insuring only those individuals who were rejected by other companies for similar policies

    (E) Insuring only those individuals who are wealthy enough to pay for the medical services

Insurance companies can improve the ratio of revenues to claims paid, thus minimizing losses, if they insure as many people belonging to low-risk groups as they can. Because the strategy described in A adds a low-risk group to the pool of policyholders, A is the best answer.

    Choice B is irrelevant, since no link is established between childhood diseases and diseases affecting the elderly. Choice C is inappropriate, since increasing the number of services covered is unlikely to minimize losses. Choice D is inappropriate, since it would increase the likelihood that claims against the policy will be made. Because policyholders will file claims against the policy for services covered rather than pay for the cost of the services themselves, E is irrelevant.

5. A program instituted in a particular state allows parents to prepay their children's future college tuition at current rates. The program then pays the tuition annually for the child at any of the state's public colleges in which the child enrolls. Parents should participate in the program as a means of decreasing the cost for their children's college education.

Which of the following, if true, is the most appropriate reason for parents not to participate in the program?

    (A) The parents are unsure about which public college in the state the child will attend.

    (B) The amount of money accumulated by putting the prepayment funds in an interest-bearing account today will be greater than the total cost of tuition for any of the public colleges when the child enrolls.

    (C) The annual cost of tuition at the state's public colleges is expected to increase at a faster rate than the annual increase in the cost of living.

    (D) Some of the state's public colleges are contemplating large increases in tuition next year.

    (E) The prepayment plan would not cover the cost of room and board at any of the state's public colleges.

The passage recommends that parents participate in a tuition prepayment program as a means of decreasing the cost of their children's future college education. If B were true, placing the funds in an interest-bearing account would be more cost-effective than participating in the prepayment program. Therefore B would be a reason for *not* participating and is the best answer.

    Neither A nor E is clearly relevant to deciding whether to participate. Since the program applies to whatever public college the child might choose to attend, contingency A is covered by the plan. Regardless of whether the parents participate, the expenses E mentions would not be included in the cost of tuition. Choices C and D, by stating that tuition will increase, provide support for participating in the program.

6. Company Alpha buys free-travel coupons from people who are awarded the coupons by Bravo Airlines for flying frequently on Bravo airplanes. The coupons are sold to people who pay less for the coupons than they would pay by purchasing tickets from Bravo. This marketing of coupons results in lost revenue for Bravo.

To discourage the buying and selling of free-travel coupons, it would be best for Bravo Airlines to restrict the

(A) number of coupons that a person can be awarded in a particular year
(B) use of the coupons to those who were awarded the coupons and members of their immediate families
(C) days that the coupons can be used to Monday through Friday
(D) amount of time that the coupons can be used after they are issued
(E) number of routes on which travelers can use the coupons

Restricting use of the coupons to the immediate families of those awarded them, as B suggests, would make the coupons valueless for anyone else, so that marketing the coupons would no longer be possible. The coupons, however, would still allow the people to whom Bravo gives them to enjoy free travel. Thus, awarding coupons would remain a strong incentive to frequent travel on Bravo. Therefore, B is the best answer.

Choice A, conversely, would do nothing to reduce the resale value of the coupons. Choices C, D, and E all not only fail to prevent Alpha's coupon sales from competing with Bravo's own ticket sales, but also potentially reduce the usefulness of the coupons to the people to whom they are awarded.

7. The ice on the front windshield of the car had formed when moisture condensed during the night. The ice melted quickly after the car was warmed up the next morning because the defrosting vent, which blows only on the front windshield, was turned on full force.

Which of the following, if true, most seriously jeopardizes the validity of the explanation for the speed with which the ice melted?

(A) The side windows had no ice condensation on them.
(B) Even though no attempt was made to defrost the back window, the ice there melted at the same rate as did the ice on the front windshield.
(C) The speed at which ice on a window melts increases as the temperature of the air blown on the window increases.
(D) The warm air from the defrosting vent for the front windshield cools rapidly as it dissipates throughout the rest of the car.
(E) The defrosting vent operates efficiently even when the heater, which blows warm air toward the feet or faces of the driver and passengers, is on.

The speed with which the ice on the windshield melted is attributed to the air blowing full force from the defrosting vent onto the front windshield. This explanation is undermined if, as B states, no attempt was made to defrost the back window and the ice on the back window melted as quickly as did the ice on the windshield. Therefore, B is the best answer.

In the absence of other information, the lack of ice condensation on the side windows that is mentioned in A is irrelevant to the validity of the explanation. Choice C might support the explanation, since the air from the defrosting vent was warm. Neither D nor E gives a reason to doubt that air from the vent caused the ice's melting, and thus neither jeopardizes the explanation's validity.

8. To prevent some conflicts of interest, Congress could prohibit high-level government officials from accepting positions as lobbyists for three years after such officials leave government service. One such official concluded, however, that such a prohibition would be unfortunate because it would prevent high-level government officials from earning a livelihood for three years.

The official's conclusion logically depends on which of the following assumptions?

(A) Laws should not restrict the behavior of former government officials.
(B) Lobbyists are typically people who have previously been high-level government officials.
(C) Low-level government officials do not often become lobbyists when they leave government service.
(D) High-level government officials who leave government service are capable of earning a livelihood only as lobbyists.
(E) High-level government officials who leave government service are currently permitted to act as lobbyists for only three years.

The official argues that prohibiting high-level government officials from accepting positions as lobbyists for three years would prevent the officials from earning a livelihood for that period. This reasoning tacitly excludes the possibility of such officials earning a living through work other than lobbying. Therefore, D, which expresses this tacit assumption, is the best answer.

The official's argument does not depend on assumption A, B, C, or E, since the argument would not be invalidated if some restrictions on the behavior of government officials were desirable (A), or if lobbyists were not typically former high-level government officials (B), or if former low-level government officials did often become lobbyists (C), or if former high-level government officials could act as lobbyists indefinitely (E).

9. A conservation group in the United States is trying to change the long-standing image of bats as frightening creatures. The group contends that bats are feared and persecuted solely because they are shy animals that are active only at night.

Which of the following, if true, would cast the most serious doubt on the accuracy of the group's contention?

(A) Bats are steadily losing natural roosting places such as caves and hollow trees and are thus turning to more developed areas for roosting.
(B) Bats are the chief consumers of nocturnal insects and thus can help make their hunting territory more pleasant for humans.
(C) Bats are regarded as frightening creatures not only in the United States but also in Europe, Africa, and South America.
(D) Raccoons and owls are shy and active only at night; yet they are not generally feared and persecuted.
(E) People know more about the behavior of other greatly feared animal species, such as lions, alligators, and snakes, than they do about the behavior of bats.

The group's contention suggests that animals that are shy and active at night are feared and persecuted for that reason. Choice D establishes that raccoons and owls are shy and active at night, but that they are neither feared nor persecuted. Therefore, D is the best answer.

Although an increasing prevalence of bats might explain the importance of addressing people's fear of bats, A does not address the original causes of that fear. Choices B and E, while relevant to the rationality of people's fear of bats, do not affect the assessment of the accuracy of the group's contention. That bats are feared outside the United States, as C states, does not conflict with the group's explanation for fear of bats in the United States.

10. Meteorite explosions in the Earth's atmosphere as large as the one that destroyed forests in Siberia, with approximately the force of a twelve-megaton nuclear blast, occur about once a century.

The response of highly automated systems controlled by complex computer programs to unexpected circumstances is unpredictable.

Which of the following conclusions can most properly be drawn, if the statements above are true, about a highly automated nuclear-missile defense system controlled by a complex computer program?

(A) Within a century after its construction, the system would react inappropriately and might accidentally start a nuclear war.
(B) The system would be destroyed if an explosion of a large meteorite occurred in the Earth's atmosphere.
(C) It would be impossible for the system to distinguish the explosion of a large meteorite from the explosion of a nuclear weapon.
(D) Whether the system would respond inappropriately to the explosion of a large meteorite would depend on the location of the blast.
(E) It is not certain what the system's response to the explosion of a large meteorite would be, if its designers did not plan for such a contingency.

If the defense system designers did not plan for the contingency of large meteorite explosions, such explosions would, from the system's perspective, be unexpected. The system's response to such explosions is consequently unpredictable. Choice E expresses this inference and is thus the best answer.

Choices A and C cannot be inferred since it is consistent with the stated information that no meteorite explosion will occur within a century and that an appropriately designed nuclear defense system might be able to distinguish nuclear from meteorite explosions. Choices B and D cannot be inferred since there is no information to suggest either that meteorite explosions in the atmosphere would destroy the system or that the location of blasts would determine the appropriateness of the defense system's response.

Questions 11-12 are based on the following.

The fewer restrictions there are on the advertising of legal services, the more lawyers there are who advertise their services, and the lawyers who advertise a specific service usually charge less for that service than lawyers who do not advertise. Therefore, if the state removes any of its current restrictions, such as the one against advertisements that do not specify fee arrangements, overall consumer legal costs will be lower than if the state retains its current restrictions.

11. If the statements above are true, which of the following must be true?

(A) Some lawyers who now advertise will charge more for specific services if they do not have to specify fee arrangements in the advertisements.
(B) More consumers will use legal services if there are fewer restrictions on the advertising of legal services.
(C) If the restriction against advertisements that do not specify fee arrangements is removed, more lawyers will advertise their services.
(D) If more lawyers advertise lower prices for specific services, some lawyers who do not advertise will also charge less than they currently charge for those services.
(E) If the only restrictions on the advertising of legal services were those that apply to every type of advertising, most lawyers would advertise their services.

The supposition in C involves reducing by one the number of restrictions on the advertising of legal services. Any such reduction will, if the stated correlation exists, be accompanied by an increase in the number of lawyers advertising their services, as C predicts. Therefore, C is the best answer.

Choices A, B, D, and E do not follow from the stated information since it is still possible that no lawyers would raise their fees (contrary to A); there would be no increase in the number of consumers using legal services (contrary to B); none of the lawyers who do not advertise would decide to lower their prices (contrary to D); and few lawyers would advertise their legal services (contrary to E).

12. Which of the following, if true, would most seriously weaken the argument concerning overall consumer legal costs?

   (A) The state has recently removed some other restrictions that had limited the advertising of legal services.
   (B) The state is unlikely to remove all of the restrictions that apply solely to the advertising of legal services.
   (C) Lawyers who do not advertise generally provide legal services of the same quality as those provided by lawyers who do advertise.
   (D) Most lawyers who now specify fee arrangements in their advertisements would continue to do so even if the specification were not required.
   (E) Most lawyers who advertise specific services do not lower their fees for those services when they begin to advertise.

If E is true, the lawyers who begin advertising when the restriction is removed might all be among those who do not lower their fees on beginning to advertise, in which case no decrease in consumer legal costs will occur. Therefore, E weakens the argument and is the best answer.

   Since A does not relate the recent removal of restrictions to changes in consumer legal costs, A alone does not weaken the argument. Since the argument is unconcerned with whatever restrictions remain in effect but focuses only on those that will be removed, B does not weaken the argument. Choices C and D are irrelevant to an evaluation of the argument, which is concerned with cost considerations, not with the quality of legal services or the content of lawyers' advertisements.

13. Defense Department analysts worry that the ability of the United States to wage a prolonged war would be seriously endangered if the machine-tool manufacturing base shrinks further. Before the Defense Department publicly connected this security issue with the import quota issue, however, the machine-tool industry raised the national security issue in its petition for import quotas.

   Which of the following, if true, contributes most to an explanation of the machine-tool industry's raising the issue above regarding national security?

   (A) When the aircraft industries retooled, they provided a large amount of work for tool builders.
   (B) The Defense Department is only marginally concerned with the effects of foreign competition on the machine-tool industry.
   (C) The machine-tool industry encountered difficulty in obtaining governmental protection against imports on grounds other than defense.
   (D) A few weapons important for defense consist of parts that do not require extensive machining.
   (E) Several federal government programs have been designed which will enable domestic machine-tool manufacturing firms to compete successfully with foreign toolmakers.

Since the size of the machine-tool manufacturing base presumably has implications in areas beyond national security, one might find it surprising that the industry raised the security issue in its petition. Choice C, the best answer, explains that the industry turned to this issue because others tended to be ineffective in efforts to obtain governmental protection.

   Choices A and B, on the other hand, merely explain why the industry might *not* raise the security issue. Choice A suggests that the industry might have raised the issue of jobs instead. Choice B suggests that the part of the government concerned with security is not concerned enough with the industry's import problem to take action. Neither D nor E is relevant to the industry's choice of strategy for securing import quotas.

14. Opponents of laws that require automobile drivers and passengers to wear seat belts argue that in a free society people have the right to take risks as long as the people do not harm others as a result of taking the risks. As a result, they conclude that it should be each person's decision whether or not to wear a seat belt.

Which of the following, if true, most seriously weakens the conclusion drawn above?

(A) Many new cars are built with seat belts that automatically fasten when someone sits in the front seat.
(B) Automobile insurance rates for all automobile owners are higher because of the need to pay for the increased injuries or deaths of people not wearing seat belts.
(C) Passengers in airplanes are required to wear seat belts during takeoffs and landings.
(D) The rate of automobile fatalities in states that do not have mandatory seat-belt laws is greater than the rate of fatalities in states that do have such laws.
(E) In automobile accidents, a greater number of passengers who do not wear seat belts are injured than are passengers who do wear seat belts.

The principle that people are entitled to risk injury provided they do not thereby harm others fails to justify the individual's right to decide not to wear seat belts if it can be shown, as B shows, that that decision does harm others. Therefore, B is the best answer.

The argument implicitly concedes that individuals take risks by not wearing seat belts; therefore, D and E, which simply confirm this concession, do not weaken the conclusion. Choice C cites a requirement analogous to the one at issue, but its existence alone does not bear on the legitimacy of the one at issue. Choice A suggests that the law may be irrelevant in some cases, but it does not address the issue of the law's legitimacy.

15. The cost of producing radios in Country Q is ten percent less than the cost of producing radios in Country Y. Even after transportation fees and tariff charges are added, it is still cheaper for a company to import radios from Country Q to Country Y than to produce radios in Country Y.

The statements above, if true, best support which of the following assertions?

(A) Labor costs in Country Q are ten percent below those in Country Y.
(B) Importing radios from Country Q to Country Y will eliminate ten percent of the manufacturing jobs in Country Y.
(C) The tariff on a radio imported from Country Q to Country Y is less than ten percent of the cost of manufacturing the radio in Country Y.
(D) The fee for transporting a radio from Country Q to Country Y is more than ten percent of the cost of manufacturing the radio in Country Q.
(E) It takes ten percent less time to manufacture a radio in Country Q than it does in Country Y.

If the tariff on importing radios from Country Q to Country Y were as high as ten percent or more of the cost of producing radios in Y, then, contrary to what the passage says, the cost of importing radios from Q to Y would be equal to or more than the cost of producing radios in Y. Thus, the tariff cannot be that high, and C is the best answer.

Choices A and E give possible partial explanations for the cost difference, but neither is supported by the passage because the cost advantage in Q might be attributable to other factors. Choices B and D are both consistent with the information in the passage, but the passage provides no evidence to support them.

16. During the Second World War, about 375,000 civilians died in the United States and about 408,000 members of the United States armed forces died overseas. On the basis of those figures, it can be concluded that it was not much more dangerous to be overseas in the armed forces during the Second World War than it was to stay at home as a civilian.

Which of the following would reveal most clearly the absurdity of the conclusion drawn above?

(A) Counting deaths among members of the armed forces who served in the United States in addition to deaths among members of the armed forces serving overseas
(B) Expressing the difference between the numbers of deaths among civilians and members of the armed forces as a percentage of the total number of deaths
(C) Separating deaths caused by accidents during service in the armed forces from deaths caused by combat injuries
(D) Comparing death rates per thousand members of each group rather than comparing total numbers of deaths
(E) Comparing deaths caused by accidents in the United States to deaths caused by combat in the armed forces

Concluding from the similar numbers of deaths in two groups that the relative danger of death was similar for both groups is absurd if, as here, one group was far smaller. Choice D exposes this absurdity by pointing out the need to compare death rates of the two groups, which would reveal the higher death rate for the smaller group. Therefore, D is the best answer.

Since the conclusion acknowledges the difference between the number of civilian and armed forces deaths, expressing this difference as a percentage, as suggested by B, is beside the point. Choice A is inappropriate because it simply adds a third group to the two being compared. Because cause of death is not at issue, C and E are irrelevant.

17. Toughened hiring standards have not been the primary cause of the present staffing shortage in public schools. The shortage of teachers is primarily caused by the fact that in recent years teachers have not experienced any improvements in working conditions and their salaries have not kept pace with salaries in other professions.

Which of the following, if true, would most support the claims above?

(A) Many teachers already in the profession would not have been hired under the new hiring standards.
(B) Today more teachers are entering the profession with a higher educational level than in the past.
(C) Some teachers have cited higher standards for hiring as a reason for the current staffing shortage.
(D) Many teachers have cited low pay and lack of professional freedom as reasons for their leaving the profession.
(E) Many prospective teachers have cited the new hiring standards as a reason for not entering the profession.

The passage rejects one explanation of the shortage of teachers—that it results from toughened hiring standards—and advances an alternative—that it results from deficiencies in pay and working conditions. Choice D provides corroborative evidence for the latter explanation by suggesting that, for many former teachers, poor pay and working conditions were reasons for their quitting the profession. Therefore, D is the best answer.

Choices A, C, and E provide evidence that tends to implicate new hiring standards in the staffing shortage, and thus support the explanation that the passage rejects. Choice B describes what may be a result of the new hiring standards, but it provides no evidence favoring one explanation of the staffing shortage over the other.

18. A proposed ordinance requires the installation in new homes of sprinklers automatically triggered by the presence of a fire. However, a home builder argued that because more than 90 percent of residential fires are extinguished by a household member, residential sprinklers would only marginally decrease property damage caused by residential fires.

Which of the following, if true, would most seriously weaken the home builder's argument?

(A) Most individuals have no formal training in how to extinguish fires.

(B) Since new homes are only a tiny percentage of available housing in the city, the new ordinance would be extremely narrow in scope.

(C) The installation of smoke detectors in new residences costs significantly less than the installation of sprinklers.

(D) In the city where the ordinance was proposed, the average time required by the fire department to respond to a fire was less than the national average.

(E) The largest proportion of property damage that results from residential fires is caused by fires that start when no household member is present.

The home builder reasons from evidence about most residential fires to a conclusion about the effectiveness of sprinklers in preventing property damage. But this reasoning is faulty because of the possibility that most of the property damage results from the minority of fires excluded from the builder's evidence. This possibility is realized if E is true. Thus, E is the best answer.

Because the builder's argument concerns neither the cost of installing sprinklers nor a comparison with fire department performance in other locations, choices C and D are irrelevant. The evidence the home builder cites suggests that formal training (choice A) is not needed in order to extinguish fires. Choice B supports the builder's view that requiring sprinklers would have a limited effect.

19. Even though most universities retain the royalties from faculty members' inventions, the faculty members retain the royalties from books and articles they write. Therefore, faculty members should retain the royalties from the educational computer software they develop.

The conclusion above would be more reasonably drawn if which of the following were inserted into the argument as an additional premise?

(A) Royalties from inventions are higher than royalties from educational software programs.

(B) Faculty members are more likely to produce educational software programs than inventions.

(C) Inventions bring more prestige to universities than do books and articles.

(D) In the experience of most universities, educational software programs are more marketable than are books and articles.

(E) In terms of the criteria used to award royalties, educational software programs are more nearly comparable to books and articles than to inventions.

The passage concludes that, where royalty retention of faculty members' works is concerned, software should be treated as books and articles are, not as inventions are. The conclusion requires an additional premise establishing that software is, in relevant respects, more comparable to books and articles than to inventions. Choice E provides this kind of premise and is therefore the best answer.

Choices A, B, C, and D, conversely, each describe some difference between software and inventions (choices A and B), or between inventions and books and articles (choice C), or between software and books and articles (choice D), but none establishes the required relationship among inventions, software, and books and articles.

20. Increases in the level of high-density lipoprotein (HDL) in the human bloodstream lower bloodstream-cholesterol levels by increasing the body's capacity to rid itself of excess cholesterol. Levels of HDL in the bloodstream of some individuals are significantly increased by a program of regular exercise and weight reduction.

Which of the following can be correctly inferred from the statements above?

(A) Individuals who are underweight do not run any risk of developing high levels of cholesterol in the bloodstream.

(B) Individuals who do not exercise regularly have a high risk of developing high levels of cholesterol in the bloodstream late in life.

(C) Exercise and weight reduction are the most effective methods of lowering bloodstream cholesterol levels in humans.

(D) A program of regular exercise and weight reduction lowers cholesterol levels in the bloodstream of some individuals.

(E) Only regular exercise is necessary to decrease cholesterol levels in the bloodstream of individuals of average weight.

If increased HDL levels cause reduced cholesterol levels and if a certain program increases HDL levels in some individuals, it follows that some individuals who undertake that program achieve reduced cholesterol levels. Choice D is thus correctly inferable and the best answer.

Choice A cannot be correctly inferred because the statements do not establish any connection between being underweight and levels of cholesterol. Neither B nor E is inferable, since there is no indication that exercise alone is either necessary or sufficient to increase HDL levels or to decrease cholesterol levels. Choice C is inappropriate because other methods of cholesterol reduction are not addressed.

21. When limitations were in effect on nuclear-arms testing, people tended to save more of their money, but when nuclear-arms testing increased, people tended to spend more of their money. The perceived threat of nuclear catastrophe, therefore, decreases the willingness of people to postpone consumption for the sake of saving money.

The argument above assumes that

(A) the perceived threat of nuclear catastrophe has increased over the years

(B) most people supported the development of nuclear arms

(C) people's perception of the threat of nuclear catastrophe depends on the amount of nuclear-arms testing being done

(D) the people who saved the most money when nuclear-arms testing was limited were the ones who supported such limitations

(E) there are more consumer goods available when nuclear-arms testing increases

On the basis of an observed correlation between arms testing and people's tendency to save money, the argument concludes that there is a causal connection between a perception of threat and the tendency not to save. That connection cannot be made unless C, linking the perception of threat to the amount of testing being done, is assumed to be true. Therefore, C is the best answer.

The conclusion does not depend on there having been an increase in the perceived threat over time or on how many people supported the development of nuclear arms. Hence, neither A nor B is assumed. Furthermore, the argument does not deal with those who supported arms limitations or with the availability of consumer goods. Thus, D and E are not assumed.

22. Which of the following best completes the passage below?

People buy prestige when they buy a premium product. They want to be associated with something special. Mass-marketing techniques and price-reduction strategies should not be used because _____.

(A) affluent purchasers currently represent a shrinking portion of the population of all purchasers

(B) continued sales depend directly on the maintenance of an aura of exclusivity

(C) purchasers of premium products are concerned with the quality as well as with the price of the products

(D) expansion of the market niche to include a broader spectrum of consumers will increase profits

(E) manufacturing a premium brand is not necessarily more costly than manufacturing a standard brand of the same product

The incomplete passage calls for an explanation of why price-reduction and mass-marketing methods should not be used for premium products. Choice B, which states that sales of these products require that they appear special, provides such an explanation. Therefore, B is the best answer.

No other choice offers an appropriate explanation. Choice C suggests that purchasers of premium products find reduced prices attractive, and it has not been established that the methods affect quality or perception of quality. The diminishing proportion of affluent buyers cited in A argues for using price reductions to attract buyers of lesser means, while D argues for, rather than against, using mass marketing. Choice E is inappropriate, since there is no indication that manufacturing costs are relevant.

23. A cost-effective solution to the problem of airport congestion is to provide high-speed ground transportation between major cities lying 200 to 500 miles apart. The successful implementation of this plan would cost far less than expanding existing airports and would also reduce the number of airplanes clogging both airports and airways.

Which of the following, if true, could proponents of the plan above most appropriately cite as a piece of evidence for the soundness of their plan?

(A) An effective high-speed ground-transportation system would require major repairs to many highways and mass-transit improvements.
(B) One-half of all departing flights in the nation's busiest airport head for a destination in a major city 225 miles away.
(C) The majority of travelers departing from rural airports are flying to destinations in cities over 600 miles away.
(D) Many new airports are being built in areas that are presently served by high-speed ground-transportation systems.
(E) A large proportion of air travelers are vacationers who are taking long-distance flights.

The plan proposes that high-speed ground transportation would be a less expensive solution to airport congestion than would airport expansion. Choice B indicates that between the cities to be served by the plan there is substantial air travel to which ground transportation would represent an alternative. Therefore, B is the best answer.

No other choice could be cited appropriately. Choices A and D both provide some evidence against the plan, A by emphasizing the likely costs of providing high-speed ground transportation, and D by indicating that such an alternative is not by itself a solution to airport congestion. Choices C and E say that there are many travelers for whom the proposed system would actually provide no alternative.

Questions 24-25 are based on the following.

If there is an oil-supply disruption resulting in higher international oil prices, domestic oil prices in open-market countries such as the United States will rise as well, whether such countries import all or none of their oil.

24. If the statement above concerning oil-supply disruptions is true, which of the following policies in an open-market nation is most likely to reduce the long-term economic impact on that nation of sharp and unexpected increases in international oil prices?

(A) Maintaining the quantity of oil imported at constant yearly levels
(B) Increasing the number of oil tankers in its fleet
(C) Suspending diplomatic relations with major oil-producing nations
(D) Decreasing oil consumption through conservation
(E) Decreasing domestic production of oil

If the statement about oil-supply disruption is true, domestic oil prices in an open-market country will rise when an oil-supply disruption causes increased international oil prices. A reduction in the amount of oil an open-market country consumes could reduce the economic impact of these increases. Choice D gives a way to reduce oil consumption and is thus the best answer.

None of the other choices is appropriate. Choices A and E describe policies that could actually increase the long-term impact of increases in international oil prices. No relationship is established between the economic impact and either the number of oil tankers (choice B) or diplomatic relations (choice C).

25. Which of the following conclusions is best supported by the statement above?

(A) Domestic producers of oil in open-market countries are excluded from the international oil market when there is a disruption in the international oil supply.
(B) International oil-supply disruptions have little, if any, effect on the price of domestic oil as long as an open-market country has domestic supplies capable of meeting domestic demand.
(C) The oil market in an open-market country is actually part of the international oil market, even if most of that country's domestic oil is usually sold to consumers within its borders.
(D) Open-market countries that export little or none of their oil can maintain stable domestic oil prices even when international oil prices rise sharply.
(E) If international oil prices rise, domestic distributors of oil in open-market countries will begin to import more oil than they export.

If the oil market in an open-market country were independent, fluctuations in international oil prices would not affect domestic oil prices. However, if the statement about oil-supply disruption is true, it is evidence that domestic oil prices are dependent on the international market and hence that the domestic oil market is a part of the international oil market. Therefore, C is the best answer.

Choices B and D are not supported, since each contradicts the claim that an international oil-supply disruption will lead to rising oil prices in an open-market nation. Neither are A and E supported, since the statement provides information only about the effect of disruption on oil prices, not domestic producers or distributors.

26. The average normal infant born in the United States weighs between twelve and fourteen pounds at the age of three months. Therefore, if a three-month-old child weighs only ten pounds, its weight gain has been below the United States average.

Which of the following indicates a flaw in the reasoning above?

(A) Weight is only one measure of normal infant development.
(B) Some three-month-old children weigh as much as seventeen pounds.
(C It is possible for a normal child to weigh ten pounds at birth.
(D) The phrase "below average" does not necessarily mean insufficient.
(E) Average weight gain is not the same as average weight.

The evidence on which the conclusion is based concerns only average weight, but the conclusion concerns average weight gain. Because there is not necessarily a connection between an absolute measurement—such as weight—and a rate of increase—such as weight gain—this argument is flawed. The relevant reasoning error is described in E, which is the best answer.

Neither A nor D identifies a reasoning error in the passage, since the passage makes no claim that weight is the only relevant measure of infant development in general (choice A), and no claim about sufficiency (choice D). Both B and C are consistent with the claims in the passage, and neither identifies a flaw in the argument.

27. Red blood cells in which the malarial-fever parasite resides are eliminated from a person's body after 120 days. Because the parasite cannot travel to a new generation of red blood cells, any fever that develops in a person more than 120 days after that person has moved to a malaria-free region is not due to the malarial parasite.

Which of the following, if true, most seriously weakens the conclusion above?

(A) The fever caused by the malarial parasite may resemble the fever caused by flu viruses.
(B) The anopheles mosquito, which is the principal insect carrier of the malarial parasite, has been eradicated in many parts of the world.
(C) Many malarial symptoms other than the fever, which can be suppressed with antimalarial medication, can reappear within 120 days after the medication is discontinued.
(D) In some cases, the parasite that causes malarial fever travels to cells of the spleen, which are less frequently eliminated from a person's body than are red blood cells.
(E) In any region infested with malaria-carrying mosquitoes, there are individuals who appear to be immune to malaria.

The passage concludes that, because the malarial parasite cannot reside in red blood cells for more than 120 days, the malarial parasite cannot cause fever more than 120 days after infection. However, according to D, there is a site in the body where the parasite could reside for more than 120 days after infection. Therefore, D weakens the conclusion and is the best answer.

The resemblance between malarial-fever symptoms and those of other diseases (choice A), the existence of other malarial symptoms (choice C), and the possibility of immunity to malaria (choice E) are irrelevant to the issue of the conditions under which malarial fever can occur. Choice B provides confirmation for the existence of malaria-free regions but does not otherwise bear on the conclusion.

28. Fact 1: Television advertising is becoming less effective: the proportion of brand names promoted on television that viewers of the advertising can recall is slowly decreasing.

Fact 2: Television viewers recall commercials aired first or last in a cluster of consecutive commercials far better than they recall commercials aired somewhere in the middle.

Fact 2 would be most likely to contribute to an explanation of fact 1 if which of the following were also true?

(A) The average television viewer currently recalls fewer than half the brand names promoted in commercials he or she saw.
(B) The total time allotted to the average cluster of consecutive television commercials is decreasing.
(C) The average number of hours per day that people spend watching television is decreasing.
(D) The average number of clusters of consecutive commercials per hour of television is increasing.
(E) The average number of television commercials in a cluster of consecutive commercials is increasing.

Because E indicates that the number of commercials in a cluster is increasing, E entails that proportionally more commercials are aired in intermediate positions. Hence, E helps fact 2 explain fact 1 by showing that increasingly more commercials are aired in positions in which viewers find them difficult to recall. E is the best answer.

Choice A testifies to the ineffectiveness of television advertising but does not help fact 2 explain fact 1. Choice B indicates that fact 2 contradicts rather than explains fact 1, since it suggests that the number of commercials per cluster is decreasing. Choices C and D help to explain fact 1—C by describing a change in viewing habits and D by describing a change in programming—but neither relates fact 2 to fact 1.

29. The number of people diagnosed as having a certain intestinal disease has dropped significantly in a rural county this year, as compared to last year. Health officials attribute this decrease entirely to improved sanitary conditions at water-treatment plants, which made for cleaner water this year and thus reduced the incidence of the disease.

Which of the following, if true, would most seriously weaken the health officials' explanation for the lower incidence of the disease?

(A) Many new water-treatment plants have been built in the last five years in the rural county.
(B) Bottled spring water has not been consumed in significantly different quantities by people diagnosed as having the intestinal disease, as compared to people who did not contract the disease.
(C) Because of a new diagnostic technique, many people who until this year would have been diagnosed as having the intestinal disease are now correctly diagnosed as suffering from intestinal ulcers.
(D) Because of medical advances this year, far fewer people who contract the intestinal disease will develop severe cases of the disease.
(E) The water in the rural county was brought up to the sanitary standards of the water in neighboring counties ten years ago.

The health officials' explanation assumes that the decrease in the number of people diagnosed with the disease accurately reflects a diminution in cases of the disease. By pointing out that this assumption is false, C undermines the officials' explanation and thus is the best answer.

Since A supports the view that sanitary conditions have been improving, it tends to support the officials' explanation. So does B, which eliminates a factor that might have differentiated between those contracting and those not contracting the disease and thus rules out an alternative explanation. The reduction of the severity of the diagnosed cases (choice D) does not bear on the officials' explanation. Since the standards in neighboring counties might themselves have been inadequate, E does not weaken the officials' explanation.

30. The price the government pays for standard weapons purchased from military contractors is determined by a pricing method called "historical costing." Historical costing allows contractors to protect their profits by adding a percentage increase, based on the current rate of inflation, to the previous year's contractual price.

Which of the following statements, if true, is the best basis for a criticism of historical costing as an economically sound pricing method for military contracts?

(A) The government might continue to pay for past inefficient use of funds.
(B) The rate of inflation has varied considerably over the past twenty years.
(C) The contractual price will be greatly affected by the cost of materials used for the products.
(D) Many taxpayers question the amount of money the government spends on military contracts.
(E) The pricing method based on historical costing might not encourage the development of innovative weapons.

If the original contractual price for the weapons purchased incorporated an inefficient use of funds, then, since historical costing merely adds to the original price, it preserves these inefficiencies. An economically sound pricing method should at least allow the possibility of reductions in price as such inefficiencies are removed. Hence, A is the best answer.

Because historical costing responds to inflation, both B and C are consistent with the economic soundness of historical costing—B because it refers to the rate of inflation and C because it refers to costs that are reflected in inflation. Choice D offers no grounds for questioning the economic soundness of historical costing in particular. Historical costing applies to standard weapons only, not to the innovative weapons that are mentioned in E.

31. Some who favor putting governmental enterprises into private hands suggest that conservation objectives would in general be better served if private environmental groups were put in charge of operating and financing the national park system, which is now run by the government.

Which of the following, assuming that it is a realistic possibility, argues most strongly against the suggestion above?

(A) Those seeking to abolish all restrictions on exploiting the natural resources of the parks might join the private environmental groups as members and eventually take over their leadership.

(B) Private environmental groups might not always agree on the best ways to achieve conservation objectives.

(C) If they wished to extend the park system, the private environmental groups might have to seek contributions from major donors and the general public.

(D) There might be competition among private environmental groups for control of certain park areas.

(E) Some endangered species, such as the California condor, might die out despite the best efforts of the private environmental groups, even if those groups are not hampered by insufficient resources.

If those seeking to abolish restrictions on exploiting the natural resources of the parks assumed the leadership of a group that was placed in charge of operating the park system, conservation objectives would not be better served. Choice A suggests that such a scenario might result from the proposed policy and is thus the best answer.

Choices C, D, and E list problems that might confront private environmental groups in charge of parks, but they do not give reason to believe that such groups would not be better able to pursue conservation objectives than is the current administration of the park system. Choice B indicates the potential for disagreement among various private environmental groups, but it does not suggest that disagreements could not be resolved.

32. A recent spate of launching and operating mishaps with television satellites led to a corresponding surge in claims against companies underwriting satellite insurance. As a result, insurance premiums shot up, making satellites more expensive to launch and operate. This, in turn, had added to the pressure to squeeze more performance out of currently operating satellites.

Which of the following, if true, taken together with the information above, best supports the conclusion that the cost of television satellites will continue to increase?

(A) Since the risk to insurers of satellites is spread over relatively few units, insurance premiums are necessarily very high.

(B) When satellites reach orbit and then fail, the causes of failure are generally impossible to pinpoint with confidence.

(C) The greater the performance demands placed on satellites, the more frequently those satellites break down.

(D) Most satellites are produced in such small numbers that no economies of scale can be realized.

(E) Since many satellites are built by unwieldy international consortia, inefficiencies are inevitable.

According to the passage, satellite mishaps caused a surge in insurance claims, which, in turn, caused increased insurance premiums. Higher premiums made the satellites more costly, resulting in increased performance demands. If C is true, the greater demands on performance will lead to further increases in costs by increasing the number of mishaps, and thus pushing insurance premiums still higher. Thus, C is the best answer.

Choices A, D, and E all describe factors relevant to costs, but there is no reason to think that the situation described in the passage will cause the costs resulting from these factors to increase. Similarly, the impossibility of pinpointing the causes of failure, mentioned in B, is consistent with the cost of satellites remaining stable.

33. Rural households have more purchasing power than do urban or suburban households at the same income level, since some of the income urban and suburban households use for food and shelter can be used by rural households for other needs.

Which of the following inferences is best supported by the statement made above?

(A) The average rural household includes more people than does the average urban or suburban household.

(B) Rural households have lower food and housing costs than do either urban or suburban households.

(C) Suburban households generally have more purchasing power than do either rural or urban households.

(D) The median income of urban and suburban households is generally higher than that of rural households.

(E) All three types of households spend more of their income on housing than on all other purchases combined.

If the greater purchasing power of rural households results from their having more money left over after meeting basic expenses, it follows, as B says, that those expenses are lower for those households than they are for suburban or urban households at the same income level. Consequently, B is the best answer.

Choice A is not a supported inference, since there is no information to suggest that larger households are not more likely to have either more purchasing power or lower food and shelter expenses. Choices C and D are not supported, since the passage compares only households that share the same income level. Because the relative amounts spent on different types of expenditures are not specified for any of the categories of households, E is not supported.

34. In 1985 state border colleges in Texas lost the enrollment of more than half, on average, of the Mexican nationals they had previously served each year. Teaching faculties have alleged that this extreme drop resulted from a rise in tuition for international and out-of-state students from $40 to $120 per credit hour.

Which of the following, if feasible, offers the best prospects for alleviating the problem of the drop in enrollment of Mexican nationals as the teaching faculties assessed it?

(A) Providing grants-in-aid to Mexican nationals to study in Mexican universities

(B) Allowing Mexican nationals to study in Texas border colleges and to pay in-state tuition rates, which are the same as the previous international rate

(C) Reemphasizing the goals and mission of the Texas state border colleges as serving both in-state students and Mexican nationals

(D) Increasing the financial resources of Texas colleges by raising the tuition for in-state students attending state institutions

(E) Offering career counseling for those Mexican nationals who graduate from state border colleges and intend to return to Mexico

The teaching faculties attribute the drop in enrollment of Mexican nationals to an increase in tuition costs. If the faculties are correct, reducing these costs should halt the drop in enrollment. Choice B offers a plan for reducing these costs and so is the best answer.

Neither C nor D nor E offers a plan that would reduce the costs taken to be responsible for the drop in enrollment. Nor does A offer such a plan: because the problem to be addressed is a drop in enrollment of Mexican nationals at Texas border colleges, providing financial incentive for Mexican nationals to study at Mexican universities, as A suggests, would offer no prospect of alleviating the problem.

35. Affirmative action is good business. So asserted the National Association of Manufacturers while urging retention of an executive order requiring some federal contractors to set numerical goals for hiring minorities and women. "Diversity in work force participation has produced new ideas in management, product development, and marketing," the association claimed.

The association's argument as it is presented in the passage above would be most strengthened if which of the following were true?

(A) The percentage of minority and women workers in business has increased more slowly than many minority and women's groups would prefer.

(B) Those businesses with the highest percentages of minority and women workers are those that have been the most innovative and profitable.

(C) Disposable income has been rising as fast among minorities and women as among the population as a whole.

(D) The biggest growth in sales in the manufacturing sector has come in industries that market the most innovative products.

(E) Recent improvements in management practices have allowed many manufacturers to experience enormous gains in worker productivity.

If, as B says, businesses with the highest percentages of minorities and women have been the most profitable, there is reason to believe that, because it increases the level of participation of women and minorities in the work force, affirmative action is good business. Thus, B is the best answer.

Choice A suggests that minority and women's groups have reason to support affirmative action, but it does not indicate that affirmative action is good business. Because there is no indication that the improvement in disposable income noted in C is due to affirmative action, C does not strengthen the argument given for affirmative action. Choice D addresses growth in sales and E addresses improvements in management; neither, however, asserts that these benefits are due to affirmative action.

Questions 36-37 refer to the following.

If the airspace around centrally located airports were restricted to commercial airliners and only those private planes equipped with radar, most of the private-plane traffic would be forced to use outlying airfields. Such a reduction in the amount of private-plane traffic would reduce the risk of midair collision around the centrally located airports.

36. The conclusion drawn in the first sentence depends on which of the following assumptions?

(A) Outlying airfields would be as convenient as centrally located airports for most pilots of private planes.

(B) Most outlying airfields are not equipped to handle commercial-airline traffic.

(C) Most private planes that use centrally located airports are not equipped with radar.

(D) Commercial airliners are at greater risk of becoming involved in midair collisions than are private planes.

(E) A reduction in the risk of midair collision would eventually lead to increases in commercial-airline traffic.

The first sentence concludes that prohibiting private planes that are not radar-equipped from centrally located airports would force most private planes away from those airports. This conclusion cannot be true unless it is true that, as choice C says, most private planes that use these airports are not radar-equipped. Therefore the first sentence's conclusion assumes choice C, which is thus the best answer.

The conclusion need not assume that outlying airfields are convenient for private planes (choice A), since the restrictions would give planes that are not radar equipped no choice. The conclusion concerns only how the radar requirement would affect the volume of private plane traffic, so choice B, which deals with commercial planes, and choices D and E, which deal with risk of midair collision, need not be assumed.

37. Which of the following, if true, would most strengthen the conclusion drawn in the second sentence?

   (A) Commercial airliners are already required by law to be equipped with extremely sophisticated radar systems.
   (B) Centrally located airports are experiencing overcrowded airspace primarily because of sharp increases in commercial-airline traffic.
   (C) Many pilots of private planes would rather buy radar equipment than be excluded from centrally located airports.
   (D) The number of midair collisions that occur near centrally located airports has decreased in recent years.
   (E) Private planes not equipped with radar systems cause a disproportionately large number of midair collisions around centrally located airports.

The second sentence concludes that the reduction described in the first sentence would reduce the risk of midair collisions around centrally located airports. According to E, such a reduction would remove precisely the kind of plane that causes a disproportionate number of midair collisions. Thus E is the best answer.

   Choices B and C concern the question of whether or not the proposed restrictions would reduce plane traffic, but not the question of whether any resulting reductions would reduce the risk of midair collisions. Because A does not address the question of whether reducing private-plane traffic would reduce the risk of midair collisions, A is inappropriate. That the number of midair collisions has recently decreased is irrelevant to whether the proposed reduction would further reduce collisions, so D is inappropriate.

38. Which of the following best completes the passage below?

   Established companies concentrate on defending what they already have. Consequently, they tend not to be innovative themselves and tend to underestimate the effects of the innovations of others. The clearest example of this defensive strategy is the fact that _____.

   (A) ballpoint pens and soft-tip markers have eliminated the traditional market for fountain pens, clearing the way for the marketing of fountain pens as luxury or prestige items
   (B) a highly successful automobile was introduced by the same company that had earlier introduced a model that had been a dismal failure
   (C) a once-successful manufacturer of slide rules reacted to the introduction of electronic calculators by trying to make better slide rules
   (D) one of the first models of modern accounting machines, designed for use in the banking industry, was purchased by a public library as well as by banks
   (E) the inventor of a commonly used anesthetic did not intend the product to be used by dentists, who currently account for almost the entire market for that drug

Choice C is a clear example of a defensive, noninnovative strategy that underestimates the effects of others' innovations: the slide-rule manufacturer acted as though any advantages offered by the newer and fundamentally different technology of a competing product, the electronic calculator, could be matched by improving the older, more familiar product. Choice C is thus the best answer.

   The other choices are not examples of the defensive strategy the author cites. Choices D and E are cases of new products finding unintended users, not of responses to innovations of others; nor does B describe such a response. Choice A presents a case in which innovative products displaced an older product from its traditional market but in so doing made possible a new marketing strategy for the older product.

39. Most archaeologist have held that people first reached the Americas less than 20,000 years ago by crossing a land bridge into North America. But recent discoveries of human shelters in South America dating from 32,000 years ago have led researchers to speculate that people arrived in South America first, after voyaging across the Pacific, and then spread northward.

Which of the following, if it were discovered, would be pertinent evidence against the speculation above?

(A) A rock shelter near Pittsburgh, Pennsylvania, contains evidence of use by human beings 19,000 years ago.
(B) Some North American sites of human habitation predate any sites found in South America.
(C) The climate is warmer at the 32,000-year-old South American site than at the oldest known North American site.
(D) The site in South America that was occupied 32,000 years ago was continuously occupied until 6,000 years ago.
(E) The last Ice Age, between 11,500 and 20,000 years ago, considerably lowered worldwide sea levels.

The reasoning behind the researchers' speculation that people first arrived in South America is that there is no evidence of North American sites that predate the human shelters discovered in South America. If it were discovered that, as B states, some North American sites predate those in South America, the reasoning behind the speculation would no longer hold. Thus, B is the best answer.

The facts related in A and E both involve time periods occurring after those discussed in the passage, and so create no conflict with the speculation. Although C and D describe discoveries about the South American site, neither the relative climates mentioned in C nor the duration of occupation mentioned in D provides evidence against the speculation.

40. In Asia, where palm trees are non-native, the trees' flowers have traditionally been pollinated by hand, which has kept palm fruit productivity unnaturally low. When weevils known to be efficient pollinators of palm flowers were introduced into Asia in 1980, palm fruit productivity increased—by up to 50 percent in some areas—but then decreased sharply in 1984.

Which of the following statements, if true, would best explain the 1984 decrease in productivity?

(A) Prices for palm fruit fell between 1980 and 1984 following the rise in production and a concurrent fall in demand.
(B) Imported trees are often more productive than native trees because the imported ones have left behind their pests and diseases in their native lands.
(C) Rapid increases in productivity tend to deplete trees of nutrients needed for the development of the fruit-producing female flowers.
(D) The weevil population in Asia remained at approximately the same level between 1980 and 1984.
(E) Prior to 1980 another species of insect pollinated the Asian palm trees, but not as efficiently as the species of weevil that was introduced in 1980.

If C is true, the rapid increase in productivity among Asian palm trees after 1980 probably depleted nutrients needed for the development of fruit-producing flowers. Thus C explains why the palms' productivity could subsequently decline and is the best answer.

Choice A relates a drop in the price of palm fruit to a rise in production and a fall in demand, but it does not explain the subsequent drop in the trees' productivity. Choice B gives no reason for the decrease in productivity of the trees introduced to Asia. Nor does D, since the stability of the weevil population described in D would support stability of palm fruit productivity between 1980 and 1984 rather than a decrease. Because E describes the pollination of the trees prior to 1980, it cannot explain a change occurring in 1984.

41. Since the mayor's publicity campaign for Greenville's bus service began six months ago, morning automobile traffic into the midtown area of the city has decreased seven percent. During the same period, there has been an equivalent rise in the number of persons riding buses into the midtown area. Obviously, the mayor's publicity campaign has convinced many people to leave their cars at home and ride the bus to work.

Which of the following, if true, casts the most serious doubt on the conclusion drawn above?

(A) Fares for all bus routes in Greenville have risen an average of five percent during the past six months.
(B) The mayor of Greenville rides the bus to City Hall in the city's midtown area.
(C) Road reconstruction has greatly reduced the number of lanes available to commuters in major streets leading to the midtown area during the past six months.
(D) The number of buses entering the midtown area of Greenville during the morning hours is exactly the same now as it was one year ago.
(E) Surveys show that longtime bus riders are no more satisfied with the Greenville bus service than they were before the mayor's publicity campaign began.

The passage concludes that the mayor's publicity campaign has persuaded people to ride the bus to work instead of driving, and it cites as evidence the decreased morning automobile traffic and increased bus ridership into the midtown area. But the road reconstruction described in C provides an alternative explanation for this evidence, so C is the best answer.

Choice A eliminates decreased fares as a possible explanation for the increased ridership, so it supports rather than casts doubt on the conclusion. Similarly, D and E each eliminate a possible explanation: the unchanged number of buses cited in D, and longtime bus riders' attitudes cited in E suggest that the increased ridership is not explained by improved service. The fact that the mayor rides the bus, cited in B, may contribute to the effectiveness of the publicity campaign, but it is irrelevant to assessing whether the campaign caused the increased ridership.

42. In the aftermath of a worldwide stock-market crash, Country T claimed that the severity of the stock-market crash it experienced resulted from the accelerated process of denationalization many of its industries underwent shortly before the crash.

Which of the following, if it could be carried out, would be most useful in an evaluation of Country T's assessment of the causes of the severity of its stock-market crash?

(A) Calculating the average loss experienced by individual traders in Country T during the crash
(B) Using economic theory to predict the most likely date of the next crash in Country T
(C) Comparing the total number of shares sold during the worst days of the crash in Country T to the total number of shares sold in Country T just prior to the crash
(D) Comparing the severity of the crash in Country T to the severity of the crash in countries otherwise economically similar to Country T that have not experienced recent denationalization
(E) Comparing the long-term effects of the crash on the purchasing power of the currency of Country T to the immediate, more severe short-term effects of the crash on the purchasing power of the currency of Country T

The comparison suggested in D would be useful in evaluating Country T's assessment of the causes of the severity of its stock-market crash. If the severity of the crash is at least as great in the countries that are, except for recent nationalization, economically similar to Country T, Country T's assessment is undermined. If the severity of the crash is not as great in these countries as in Country T, however, the assessment is supported. Thus, D is the best answer.

Choices A, C, and E are not good answers because each concerns only determining the severity of the crash in Country T, not assessing a hypothesis about the causes of the crash. Nor is the date of Country T's next crash relevant to assessing such a hypothesis; thus, B is inappropriate.

43. With the emergence of biotechnology companies, it was feared that they would impose silence about proprietary results on their in-house researchers and their academic consultants. This constraint, in turn, would slow the development of biological science and engineering.

Which of the following, if true, would tend to weaken most seriously the prediction of scientific secrecy described above?

(A) Biotechnological research funded by industry has reached some conclusions that are of major scientific importance.
(B) When the results of scientific research are kept secret, independent researchers are unable to build on those results.
(C) Since the research priorities of biotechnology companies are not the same as those of academic institutions, the financial support of research by such companies distorts the research agenda.
(D) To enhance the companies' standing in the scientific community, the biotechnology companies encourage employees to publish their results, especially results that are important.
(E) Biotechnology companies devote some of their research resources to problems that are of fundamental scientific importance and that are not expected to produce immediate practical applications.

Choice D weakens the prediction of secrecy by establishing that biotechnology companies have a strong motive to encourage their researchers to publicize results. Therefore, D is the best answer.

Neither A nor B nor E provides any reason to expect that the prediction will be or will not be fulfilled. Choices A and B support the argument that developments in biological science and engineering would be slowed if the prediction of secrecy were fulfilled. Choice E, which says that biotechnology companies devote some resources to fundamental problems without immediate practical benefits, is merely consistent with that argument and so does not weaken the prediction. The distortion of the research agenda asserted in C is not relevant to the question of scientific secrecy.

44. Some people have questioned the judge's objectivity in cases of sex discrimination against women. But the record shows that in sixty percent of such cases, the judge has decided in favor of the women. This record demonstrates that the judge has not discriminated against women in cases of sex discrimination against women.

The argument above is flawed in that it ignores the possibility that

(A) a large number of the judge's cases arose out of allegations of sex discrimination against women
(B) many judges find it difficult to be objective in cases of sex discrimination against women
(C) the judge is biased against women defendants or plaintiffs in cases that do not involve sex discrimination
(D) the majority of the cases of sex discrimination against women that have reached the judge's court have been appealed from a lower court
(E) the evidence shows that the women should have won in more than 60 percent of the judge's cases involving sex discrimination against women

The flaw in the argument is that it assumes erroneously that a majority of decisions favorable to women in sex discrimination cases demonstrates absence of discriminatory behavior against women on the part of the judge who made those decisions. Choice E exposes this flaw by pointing out that the judge may well have failed to decide in favor of women in cases where evidence shows that the women should have won. Therefore, E is the best answer.

Choices B and C introduce considerations with no bearing on the reasoning of the argument. Because the argument concerns a particular judge, B is inappropriate; because it concerns cases of a particular type, C is inappropriate. Choices A and D also have no bearing, because the origin of these cases is not at issue in the argument.

45. The tobacco industry is still profitable and projections are that it will remain so. In the United States this year, the total amount of tobacco sold by tobacco-farmers has increased, even though the number of adults who smoke has decreased.

Each of the following, if true, could explain the simultaneous increase in tobacco sales and decrease in the number of adults who smoke EXCEPT:

(A) During this year, the number of women who have begun to smoke is greater than the number of men who have quit smoking.
(B) The number of teen-age children who have begun to smoke this year is greater than the number of adults who have quit smoking during the same period.
(C) During this year, the number of nonsmokers who have begun to use chewing tobacco or snuff is greater than the number of people who have quit smoking.
(D) The people who have continued to smoke consume more tobacco per person than they did in the past.
(E) More of the cigarettes made in the United States this year were exported to other countries than was the case last year.

If the number of men beginning to smoke and the number of women quitting smoking during the year are equal, choice A would result in an increase, not a decrease, in the number of adults who smoke. Hence, A does *not* explain the facts cited and is the best answer.

Given the decrease in the number of adults who smoke, the increase in tobacco sales could be explained by a proportionally greater increase in the nonadults who smoke or the nonsmokers who use tobacco. An increase in total tobacco use by smokers or in the sales of United States tobacco abroad would also explain the facts cited. Thus, because B, C, D, and E could explain the facts cited, none of them can be the best answer.

46. Kale has more nutritional value than spinach. But since collard greens have more nutritional value than lettuce, it follows that kale has more nutritional value than lettuce.

Any of the following, if introduced into the argument as an additional premise, makes the argument above logically correct EXCEPT:

(A) Collard greens have more nutritional value than kale.
(B) Spinach has more nutritional value than lettuce.
(C) Spinach has more nutritional value than collard greens.
(D) Spinach and collard greens have the same nutritional value.
(E) Kale and collard greens have the same nutritional value.

The question asks for an additional premise that does *not* make the argument logically correct. Adding choice A to the information given in the passage leaves open the possibility that, in order of nutritional value, the vegetables rank: collard greens, lettuce, kale, spinach. Because this order is contrary to the conclusion of the argument, A leaves open the possibility that the conclusion of the argument is false; A is thus the best answer.

By contrast, any of choices B, C, D, and E, when added to the information that the nutritional value of kale is greater than that of spinach and that the nutritional value of collard greens is greater than that of lettuce, makes the conclusion—that kale has more nutritional value than lettuce—follow logically.

47. On the basis of a decrease in the college-age population, many colleges now anticipate increasingly smaller freshman classes each year. Surprised by a 40 percent increase in qualified applicants over the previous year, however, administrators at Nice College now plan to hire more faculty for courses taken by all freshmen.

Which of the following statements about Nice College's current qualified applicants, if true, would strongly suggest that the administrators' plan is flawed?

(A) A substantially higher percentage than usual plan to study for advanced degrees after graduation from college.
(B) According to their applications, their level of participation in extracurricular activities and varsity sports is unusually high.
(C) According to their applications, none of them lives in a foreign country.
(D) A substantially lower percentage than usual rate Nice College as their first choice among the colleges to which they are applying.
(E) A substantially lower percentage than usual list mathematics as their intended major.

If, as D states, a substantial percentage of the qualified applicants do not rate Nice College as their first choice, then, provided many of these applicants are accepted at and enroll in the colleges that are their first choices, the increase in applications to Nice College might not result in any increase in the size of its freshman class. So D is the best answer.

Nothing can be determined from A, B, C, or E about the size of the freshman class, so none of these choices is relevant to the question of whether Nice College should hire more faculty to teach courses taken by all freshmen. Thus, these choices are inappropriate.

48. A researcher discovered that people who have low levels of immune-system activity tend to score much lower on tests of mental health than do people with normal or high immune-system activity. The researcher concluded from this experiment that the immune system protects against mental illness as well as against physical disease.

The researcher's conclusion depends on which of the following assumptions?

(A) High immune-system activity protects against mental illness better than normal immune-system activity does.
(B) Mental illness is similar to physical disease in its effects on body systems.
(C) People with high immune-system activity cannot develop mental illness.
(D) Mental illness does not cause people's immune-system activity to decrease.
(E) Psychological treatment of mental illness is not as effective as is medical treatment.

The researcher concludes from the association of low immune-system activity with low mental-health scores that, in effect, immune system activity can inhibit mental illness. If, contrary to D, mental illness can depress immune-system activity, the association mentioned does not support the researcher's conclusion. So D must be assumed.

Normal immune-system activity could protect against mental illness without high immune-system activity offering increased protection, contrary to what A states, or prevention, contrary to what C states, so neither A nor C is assumed. The conclusion does not depend on there being a similarity between mental and physical illness, so B is not assumed; nor does it depend on there being a difference in treatments, so E is not assumed.

49. A milepost on the towpath read "21" on the side facing the hiker as she approached it and "23" on its back. She reasoned that the next milepost forward on the path would indicate that she was halfway between one end of the path and the other. However, the milepost one mile further on read "20" facing her and "24" behind.

Which of the following, if true, would explain the discrepancy described above?

(A) The numbers on the next milepost had been reversed.
(B) The numbers on the mileposts indicate kilometers, not miles.
(C) The facing numbers indicate miles to the end of the path, not miles from the beginning.
(D) A milepost was missing between the two the hiker encountered.
(E) The mileposts had originally been put in place for the use of mountain bikers, not for hikers.

The hiker's reasoning assumes that the number that faced her indicated distance from the path's beginning. The numbers on the second milepost show that this assumption was erroneous. They are, however, the numbers that would be expected if the facing number indicated the distance to the path's end with the number on the back indicating the distance from the beginning. Thus choice C explains the discrepancy and is the best answer.

The next milepost being reversed (choice A) cannot be the explanation, because if the hiker's reasoning were accurate both numbers on the milepost would be 22. The units (choice B) would not affect whether the number became smaller or larger. Nor would a missing milepost (choice D) affect the direction of change. The mode of transportation (choice E) is irrelevant to distance.

50. Airline: Newly developed collision-avoidance systems, although not fully tested to discover potential malfunctions, must be installed immediately in passenger planes. Their mechanical warnings enable pilots to avoid crashes.

Pilots: Pilots will not fly in planes with collision avoidance systems that are not fully tested. Malfunctioning systems could mislead pilots, causing crashes.

The pilots' objection is most strengthened if which of the following is true?

(A) It is always possible for mechanical devices to malfunction.
(B) Jet engines, although not fully tested when first put into use, have achieved exemplary performance and safety records.
(C) Although collision-avoidance systems will enable pilots to avoid some crashes, the likely malfunctions of the not-fully-tested systems will cause even more crashes.
(D) Many airline collisions are caused in part by the exhaustion of overworked pilots.
(E) Collision-avoidance systems, at this stage of development, appear to have worked better in passenger planes than in cargo planes during experimental flights made over a six-month period.

Choice C states that what the pilots think could happen is likely to happen. Thus, C is the best answer.

Choice A is inappropriate because it says nothing about the malfunctions that most concern the pilots—those that might mislead. Nor does A distinguish tested from not-fully-tested systems. Choice B is inappropriate. The only outcome of using insufficiently tested equipment that might strengthen the pilots' objection is an unfavorable one, but B reports on a favorable outcome. Choice D is inappropriate because it mentions a problem that needs to be addressed whether or not the collision-avoidance systems are installed immediately. Choice E is inappropriate because it provides no evidence that any malfunctions were of a sort to mislead pilots and cause crashes.

51. Guitar strings often go "dead"—become less responsive and bright in tone—after a few weeks of intense use. A researcher whose son is a classical guitarist hypothesized that dirt and oil, rather than changes in the material properties of the string, were responsible.

Which of the following investigations is most likely to yield significant information that would help to evaluate the researcher's hypothesis?

(A) Determining if a metal alloy is used to make the strings used by classical guitarists
(B) Determining whether classical guitarists make their strings go dead faster than do folk guitarists
(C) Determining whether identical lengths of string, of the same gauge, go dead at different rates when strung on various brands of guitars
(D) Determining whether a dead string and a new string produce different qualities of sound
(E) Determining whether smearing various substances on new guitar strings causes them to go dead

The hypothesis has two parts: first, that intense use does not bring material changes that cause the string to go dead and, second, that dirt and oil do cause the phenomenon. The experiment suggested in choice E directly tests this hypothesis by contaminating strings that are known to have their original material properties. Thus, E is the best answer.

Because factors associated with style of play (choice B) and brand of guitar (choice C) might affect how the strings become contaminated, no result of the investigations in B and C will allow clear evaluation of the hypothesis. Information about the strings' material (choice A) will need considerable supplementation before its bearing on the hypothesis is clear. The passage already gives the information promised by investigation D.

52. Most consumers do not get much use out of the sports equipment they purchase. For example, seventeen percent of the adults in the United States own jogging shoes, but only 45 percent of the owners jog more than once a year, and only 17 percent jog more than once a week.

Which of the following, if true, casts most doubt on the claim that most consumers get little use out of the sports equipment they purchase?

(A) Joggers are most susceptible to sports injuries during the first six months in which they jog.
(B) Joggers often exaggerate the frequency with which they jog in surveys designed to elicit such information.
(C) Many consumers purchase jogging shoes for use in activities other than jogging.
(D) Consumers who take up jogging often purchase an athletic shoe that can be used in other sports.
(E) Joggers who jog more than once a week are often active participants in other sports as well.

The claim that most consumers do not get much use out of the sports equipment they purchase is supported by the infrequency with which jogging shoes are used for jogging. This reasoning overlooks the possibility that jogging shoes are used for other purposes; thus, choice C is the best answer.

Because injured joggers are less likely to use their jogging shoes, choice A is inappropriate. If B is true, joggers use their jogging shoes even less than the study cited states. So choice B is inappropriate. Because the consumers and joggers mentioned in D and E respectively are most likely to be among those who frequently use sports equipment and whose existence the argument concedes, D and E are inappropriate.

53. Two decades after the Emerald River Dam was built, none of the eight fish species native to the Emerald River was still reproducing adequately in the river below the dam. Since the dam reduced the annual range of water temperature in the river below the dam from 50 degrees to 6 degrees, scientists have hypothesized that sharply rising water temperatures must be involved in signaling the native species to begin the reproductive cycle.

Which of the following statements, if true, would most strengthen the scientists' hypothesis?

(A) The native fish species were still able to reproduce only in side streams of the river below the dam where the annual temperature range remains approximately 50 degrees.
(B) Before the dam was built, the Emerald River annually overflowed its banks, creating backwaters that were critical breeding areas for the native species of fish.
(C) The lowest recorded temperature of the Emerald River before the dam was built was 34 degrees, whereas the lowest recorded temperature of the river after the dam was built has been 43 degrees.
(D) Nonnative species of fish, introduced into the Emerald River after the dam was built, have begun competing with the declining native fish species for food and space.
(E) Five of the fish species native to the Emerald River are not native to any other river in North America.

For the hypothesis to be tenable it is important that the fish in streams in the Emerald River area that retain a wide temperature difference have not lost their ability to reproduce. Choice A asserts that these fish could still reproduce and is thus the best answer.

Choice B undermines the hypothesis by suggesting a completely different hypothesis; choice C tends to support the claim that the temperature variation has lessened but does not show that this is the right explanation; since D relates a development after the native species began to decline, it does not bear on the hypothesis, which concerns the decline's original cause; and choice E emphasizes the seriousness of the problem but sheds no light on what causes it.

54. It is true that it is against international law to sell plutonium to countries that do not yet have nuclear weapons. But if United States companies do not do so, companies in other countries will.

Which of the following is most like the argument above in its logical structure?

(A) It is true that it is against the police department's policy to negotiate with kidnappers. But if the police want to prevent loss of life, they must negotiate in some cases.

(B) It is true that it is illegal to refuse to register for military service. But there is a long tradition in the United States of conscientious objection to serving in the armed forces.

(C) It is true that it is illegal for a government official to participate in a transaction in which there is an apparent conflict of interest. But if the facts are examined carefully, it will clearly be seen that there was no actual conflict of interest in the defendant's case.

(D) It is true that it is against the law to burglarize people's homes. But someone else certainly would have burglarized that house if the defendant had not done so first.

(E) It is true that company policy forbids supervisors to fire employees without two written warnings. But there have been many supervisors who have disobeyed this policy.

The argument in the passage acknowledges that a certain action contravenes a law, but it presents an excuse for the action by presupposing that someone will inevitably break this law. Only choice D shares all these features, and is thus the best answer.

In choice A, an excuse is presented for contravening a stated policy. However, unlike in the passage and choice D, there is no presupposition that the policy will inevitably be contravened. Similarly, choices B and E report that illegal activities have occurred, without presupposing that they inevitably will. Choice C describes a case as being one to which the law that is stated is inapplicable.

55. In recent years, many cabinetmakers have been winning acclaim as artists. But since furniture must be useful, cabinetmakers must exercise their craft with an eye to the practical utility of their product. For this reason, cabinetmaking is not art.

Which of the following is an assumption that supports drawing the conclusion above from the reason given for that conclusion?

(A) Some furniture is made to be placed in museums, where it will not be used by anyone.

(B) Some cabinetmakers are more concerned than others with the practical utility of the products they produce.

(C) Cabinetmakers should be more concerned with the practical utility of their products than they currently are.

(D) An object is not an art object if its maker pays attention to the object's practical utility.

(E) Artists are not concerned with the monetary value of their products.

The argument concludes that cabinetmaking is not an art because cabinetmakers must consider the practical utility of their products. If it is true that an object is not a work of art if its maker pays attention to the object's practical utility, as choice D says, the conclusion is supported. Thus, choice D is the best answer.

The argument is concerned with whether or not the cabinetmakers must take the practical utility of their products into consideration, not with either their monetary value (choice E) or what actually happens to them (choice A). The argument is not concerned with the precise degree to which individual cabinetmakers take the practical utility of cabinets into consideration. Thus, neither B nor C is appropriate.

56. Although custom prosthetic bone replacements produced through a new computer-aided design process will cost more than twice as much as ordinary replacements, custom replacements should still be cost-effective. Not only will surgery and recovery time be reduced, but custom replacements should last longer, thereby reducing the need for further hospital stays.

Which of the following must be studied in order to evaluate the argument presented above?

(A) The amount of time a patient spends in surgery *versus* the amount of time spent recovering from surgery

(B) The amount by which the cost of producing custom replacements has declined with the introduction of the new technique for producing them

(C) The degree to which the use of custom replacements is likely to reduce the need for repeat surgery when compared with the use of ordinary replacements

(D) The degree to which custom replacements produced with the new technique are more carefully manufactured than are ordinary replacements

(E) The amount by which custom replacements produced with the new technique will drop in cost as the production procedures become standardized and applicable on a larger scale

Although costly to produce, custom bone replacements are tentatively projected to be cost-effective because of other savings. To evaluate the argument it must be determined whether these savings will compensate for the increased cost. Thus, study of the expected reduction in the need for further hospital stays is needed, and choice C is the best answer.

The argument requires no study of the ratio between surgery and recovery time, so choice A is inappropriate. Past and future changes in cost are irrelevant to evaluating an argument that is based on the currently projected cost, so choices B and E are inappropriate. Finally, since studying the care with which the custom replacements are made does not itself provide information about costs, choice D is also incorrect.

57. Extinction is a process that can depend on a variety of ecological, geographical, and physiological variables. These variables affect different species of organisms in different ways, and should, therefore, yield a random pattern of extinctions. However, the fossil record shows that extinction occurs in a surprisingly definite pattern, with many species vanishing at the same time.

Which of the following, if true, forms the best basis for at least a partial explanation of the patterned extinctions revealed by the fossil record?

(A) Major episodes of extinction can result from widespread environmental disturbances that affect numerous different species.

(B) Certain extinction episodes selectively affect organisms with particular sets of characteristics unique to their species.

(C) Some species become extinct because of accumulated gradual changes in their local environments.

(D) In geologically recent times, for which there is no fossil record, human intervention has changed the pattern of extinctions.

(E) Species that are widely dispersed are the least likely to become extinct.

Choice A, the best answer, asserts that some environmental disturbances can be so widespread as to cause the extinction of numerous species. This fact helps to explain why the fossil record frequently shows many species becoming extinct at the same time, despite the variety of factors that can cause a species to become extinct.

None of the other choices explains how numerous extinctions could have occurred simultaneously in the past. Choice B explains why sometimes only a very limited range of species becomes extinct. Choice C explains how some individual species become extinct. Choice D explains why the modern period is unlike the period of the fossil record, and choice E states which species are least likely to become extinct.

58. Neither a rising standard of living nor balanced trade, by itself, establishes a country's ability to compete in the international marketplace. Both are required simultaneously since standards of living can rise because of growing trade deficits and trade can be balanced by means of a decline in a country's standard of living.

If the facts stated in the passage above are true, a proper test of a country's ability to be competitive is its ability to

(A) balance its trade while its standard of living rises
(B) balance its trade while its standard of living falls
(C) increase trade deficits while its standard of living rises
(D) decrease trade deficits while its standard of living falls
(E) keep its standard of living constant while trade deficits rise

The passage states that a country capable of competing in the international marketplace must balance trade while its standard of living rises. In view of this information, a proper test of a country's ability to compete in the international marketplace will establish that both of these conditions are met simultaneously. Since neither choice B, nor choice C, nor choice D, nor choice E describes tests that incorporate both of these criteria, these answers are inappropriate. Choice A, which describes a test that does, is the best answer.

59. Certain messenger molecules fight damage to the lungs from noxious air by telling the muscle cells encircling the lungs' airways to contract. This partially seals off the lungs. An asthma attack occurs when the messenger molecules are activated unnecessarily, in response to harmless things like pollen or household dust.

Which of the following, if true, points to the most serious flaw of a plan to develop a medication that would prevent asthma attacks by blocking receipt of any messages sent by the messenger molecules referred to above?

(A) Researchers do not yet know how the body produces the messenger molecules that trigger asthma attacks.
(B) Researchers do not yet know what makes one person's messenger molecules more easily activated than another's.
(C) Such a medication would not become available for several years, because of long lead times in both development and manufacture.
(D) Such a medication would be unable to distinguish between messages triggered by pollen and household dust and messages triggered by noxious air.
(E) Such a medication would be a preventative only and would be unable to alleviate an asthma attack once it had started.

The medication to be developed is intended to prevent asthma attacks by suppressing the natural action of certain molecules in the lungs. Choice D asserts that this suppression would occur not only when the molecules' action is superfluous, but also when it is necessary. This would be a serious flaw in the medication, so D is the best answer.

Choices A and B refer to a lack of knowledge about how the messenger molecules are produced or activated, but not about how they act in the lungs. Choice C describes how long the development might take, but does not rule out the possibility of success. Choice E asserts merely that the medication would be unable to do something it was not intended to do.

60. Since the routine use of antibiotics can give rise to resistant bacteria capable of surviving antibiotic environments, the presence of resistant bacteria in people could be due to the human use of prescription antibiotics. Some scientists, however, believe that most resistant bacteria in people derive from human consumption of bacterially infected meat.

Which of the following statements, if true, would most significantly strengthen the hypothesis of the scientists?

(A) Antibiotics are routinely included in livestock feed so that livestock producers can increase the rate of growth of their animals.
(B) Most people who develop food poisoning from bacterially infected meat are treated with prescription antibiotics.
(C) The incidence of resistant bacteria in people has tended to be much higher in urban areas than in rural areas where meat is of comparable quality.
(D) People who have never taken prescription antibiotics are those least likely to develop resistant bacteria.
(E) Livestock producers claim that resistant bacteria in animals cannot be transmitted to people through infected meat.

If livestock are routinely fed antibiotics, as choice A states, meat from livestock is likely to contain the resistant bacteria, since any routine of antibiotics can result in resistant bacteria. Thus, choice A is the best answer.

How cases of food poisoning are treated (choice B) fails to indicate whether the infecting bacteria are resistant bacteria. Choice C suggests that meat consumption is not the primary culprit for the high incidence of resistant bacteria. Choice D tends to support the competing hypothesis that prescription antibiotics are responsible. Choice E asserts that livestock farmers claim that the hypothesis is false, but it provides no basis for evaluating the truth of this claim.

61. The recent decline in the value of the dollar was triggered by a prediction of slower economic growth in the coming year. But that prediction would not have adversely affected the dollar had it not been for the government's huge budget deficit, which must therefore be decreased to prevent future currency declines.

Which of the following, if true, would most seriously weaken the conclusion about how to prevent future currency declines?

(A) The government has made little attempt to reduce the budget deficit.
(B) The budget deficit has not caused a slowdown in economic growth.
(C) The value of the dollar declined several times in the year prior to the recent prediction of slower economic growth.
(D) Before there was a large budget deficit, predictions of slower economic growth frequently caused declines in the dollar's value.
(E) When there is a large budget deficit, other events in addition to predictions of slower economic growth sometimes trigger declines in currency value.

The argument assumes that a particular prediction can cause a currency decline only if accompanied by a large budget deficit. Since choice D states that this prediction can cause a currency decline without a large budget deficit, choice D is the best answer.

That a method is not fully implemented does not imply that the method is ineffective. Thus, choice A is inappropriate. Since no slowdown in economic growth is asserted, what might cause such a slowdown is irrelevant. Thus, choice B is inappropriate. Since C supports the claim that a budget deficit is the underlying cause of the currency decline, C is inappropriate. Choice E is inappropriate because it supports the claim that a decrease in the budget deficit is necessary.

62. Which of the following best completes the passage below?

At a recent conference on environmental threats to the North Sea, most participating countries favored uniform controls on the quality of effluents, whether or not specific environmental damage could be attributed to a particular source of effluent. What must, of course, be shown, in order to avoid excessively restrictive controls, is that _____.

(A) any uniform controls that are adopted are likely to be implemented without delay
(B) any substance to be made subject to controls can actually cause environmental damage
(C) the countries favoring uniform controls are those generating the largest quantities of effluents
(D) all of any given pollutant that is to be controlled actually reaches the North Sea at present
(E) environmental damage already inflicted on the North Sea is reversible

If a substance that causes no environmental damage were subject to controls, those controls would be more restrictive than necessary. Choice B is therefore the best answer.

Ensuring prompt implementation of controls, as choice A claims, is not a necessary part of avoiding excessively restrictive controls. Although it would probably help to avoid excessive restrictions if some of the countries producing the most effluents favored uniform controls, it is not necessary that all such countries do, as choice C claims. Not all of any given pollutant need reach the North Sea, as choice D claims, since at most some needs to. Since the controls can be excessively restrictive even if the damage already inflicted is reversible, choice E is incorrect.

63. Traditionally, decision making by managers that is reasoned step-by-step has been considered preferable to intuitive decision making. However, a recent study found that top managers used intuition significantly more than did most middle- or lower-level managers. This confirms the alternative view that intuition is actually more effective than careful, methodical reasoning.

The conclusion above is based on which of the following assumptions?

(A) Methodical, step-by-step reasoning is inappropriate for making many real-life management decisions.
(B) Top managers have the ability to use either intuitive reasoning or methodical, step-by-step reasoning in making decisions.
(C) The decisions made by middle- and lower-level managers can be made as easily by using methodical reasoning as by using intuitive reasoning.
(D) Top managers use intuitive reasoning in making the majority of their decisions.
(E) Top managers are more effective at decision making than middle- or lower-level managers.

If top managers are not the more effective decision makers, then the fact that they use intuition more often than lower-level managers does not support the conclusion that intuition is more effective. Because the argument must assume E, choice E is the best answer.

To the extent that less effective methods are inappropriate, the passage does not assume A, but argues for it. Since the argument leaves open the possibility of situations in which top managers are unable to use one of the methods, choice B is inappropriate. Since the ease with which a method is implemented is not at issue, choice C is inappropriate. The argument is consistent with managers at all levels using intuition in the minority of decisions made. Thus, choice D is inappropriate.

64. The imposition of quotas limiting imported steel will not help the big American steel mills. In fact, the quotas will help "mini-mills" flourish in the United States. Those small domestic mills will take more business from the big American steel mills than would have been taken by the foreign steel mills in the absence of quotas.

Which of the following, if true, would cast the most serious doubt on the claim made in the last sentence above?

(A) Quality rather than price is a major factor in determining the type of steel to be used for a particular application.
(B) Foreign steel mills have long produced grades of steel comparable in quality to the steel produced by the big American mills.
(C) American quotas on imported goods have often induced other countries to impose similar quotas on American goods.
(D) Domestic "mini-mills" consistently produce better grades of steel than do the big American mills.
(E) Domestic "mini-mills" produce low-volume, specialized types of steels that are not produced by the big American steel mills.

If, as choice E asserts, large and small mills produce different types of steels, increasing sales by small mills need not lead to decreasing sales by large ones. Thus, choice E casts a serious doubt on the claim and is the best answer.

Choice A does not present enough information about the relative quality of steel from foreign and domestic mills to cast any doubt on the claim. Similarly, choice B does not provide enough information about small American mills, nor does choice C provide enough information about the likely consequences of quotas imposed by foreign countries to cast doubt on the claim. Choice D tends to support the claim, since better steel should sell better than poorer steel.

65. Correctly measuring the productivity of service workers is complex. Consider, for example, postal workers: they are often said to be more productive if more letters are delivered per postal worker. But is this really true? What if more letters are lost or delayed per worker at the same time that more are delivered?

The objection implied above to the productivity measure described is based on doubts about the truth of which of the following statements?

(A) Postal workers are representative of service workers in general.
(B) The delivery of letters is the primary activity of the postal service.
(C) Productivity should be ascribed to categories of workers, not to individuals.
(D) The quality of services rendered can appropriately be ignored in computing productivity.
(E) The number of letters delivered is relevant to measuring the productivity of postal workers.

The critique of the proposed purely quantitative measure of productivity raises the issue of quality of service, which implies that quality of service is a potentially relevant consideration. Thus, choice D is the best answer.

The objection assumes that postal workers are a suitable illustrative example of service workers in general; thus, choice A is inappropriate. By deriving the proposed productivity measure from the delivery of letters, the argument treats letter delivery as the primary activity of postal workers; thus, choice B is inappropriate. Because the passage explicitly ascribes productivity to entire categories of workers, choice C is inappropriate. Choice E is inappropriate, since the objector does not question the relevance of the number of letters delivered but implies that something else might also be relevant.

66. Male bowerbirds construct elaborately decorated nests, or bowers. Basing their judgment on the fact that different local populations of bowerbirds of the same species build bowers that exhibit different building and decorative styles, researchers have concluded that the bowerbirds' building styles are a culturally acquired, rather than a genetically transmitted, trait.

Which of the following, if true, would most strengthen the conclusion drawn by the researchers?

(A) There are more common characteristics than there are differences among the bower-building styles of the local bowerbird population that has been studied most extensively.
(B) Young male bowerbirds are inept at bower-building and apparently spend years watching their elders before becoming accomplished in the local bower style.
(C) The bowers of one species of bowerbird lack the towers and ornamentation characteristic of the bowers of most other species of bowerbird.
(D) Bowerbirds are found only in New Guinea and Australia, where local populations of the birds apparently seldom have contact with one another.
(E) It is well known that the song dialects of some songbirds are learned rather than transmitted genetically.

The information in choice B says that young bowerbirds progress slowly toward mastery of a bower-building style, which suggests that the skill is one they must learn, rather than one whose transmission is wholly genetic. Choice B also suggests a means of cultural transmission, namely, observation of older birds' techniques. Thus, B supports the conclusion and is the best answer.

That differences within building styles are outnumbered by similarities (choice A) and that local populations have little contact (choice D) are both equally consistent with building-style differences being culturally acquired or genetically transmitted. Nor are differences among species of bowerbird (choice C) the issue. Finally, choice E confirms the possibility of birds learning skills, but it is not evidence that bower-building styles are learned.

67. A greater number of newspapers are sold in Town S than in Town T. Therefore, the citizens of Town S are better informed about major world events than are the citizens of Town T.

Each of the following, if true, weakens the conclusion above EXCEPT:

(A) Town S has a larger population than Town T.
(B) Most citizens of Town T work in Town S and buy their newspapers there.
(C) The average citizen of Town S spends less time reading newspapers than does the average citizen of Town T.
(D) A weekly newspaper restricted to the coverage of local events is published in Town S.
(E) The average newsstand price of newspapers sold in Town S is lower than the average price of newspapers sold in Town T.

The conclusion is based on comparing newspaper sales in Town S and Town T. Four answer choices indicate why greater newspaper sales in S need not imply that citizens of S are better informed about world events. Choice B suggests that many newspapers sold in S inform citizens of T, not S. Choices A and C both show how greater newspaper sales can occur without the average citizen having greater familiarity with the news. Finally, choice D suggests that much newspaper reading in S is not a source of information about world events.

The price differential noted in E might help to explain the difference in sales, but it does not undermine the conclusion based on that difference. Therefore, E is the best answer.

68. A drug that is highly effective in treating many types of infection can, at present, be obtained only from the bark of the ibora, a tree that is quite rare in the wild. It takes the bark of 5,000 trees to make one kilogram of the drug. It follows, therefore, that continued production of the drug must inevitably lead to the ibora's extinction.

Which of the following, if true, most seriously weakens the argument above?

(A) The drug made from ibora bark is dispensed to doctors from a central authority.
(B) The drug made from ibora bark is expensive to produce.
(C) The leaves of the ibora are used in a number of medical products.
(D) The ibora can be propagated from cuttings and grown under cultivation.
(E) The ibora generally grows in largely inaccessible places.

If the ibora can be successfully cultivated, it is possible to continue production of the drug without threatening the ibora with extinction. Therefore, choice D is the best answer.

If production continues, the method for distributing the drug after it has been produced (choice A) is not likely, on its own, to have consequences for the continued existence of the ibora. Nor is the price of the drug (choice B). If the leaves of the ibora also have a use (choice C), the threat of extinction is strengthened rather than weakened. Finally, if the ibora is largely inaccessible (choice E), this bears on the question of whether production of the drug could continue, not on what would happen if it did continue.

69. High levels of fertilizer and pesticides, needed when farmers try to produce high yields of the same crop year after year, pollute water supplies. Experts therefore urge farmers to diversify their crops and to rotate their plantings yearly.

To receive governmental price-support benefits for a crop, farmers must have produced that same crop for the past several years.

The statements above, if true, best support which of the following conclusions?

(A) The rules for governmental support of farm prices work against efforts to reduce water pollution.
(B) The only solution to the problem of water pollution from fertilizers and pesticides is to take farmland out of production.
(C) Farmers can continue to make a profit by rotating diverse crops, thus reducing costs for chemicals, but not by planting the same crop each year.
(D) New farming techniques will be developed to make it possible for farmers to reduce the application of fertilizers and pesticides.
(E) Governmental price supports for farm products are set at levels that are not high enough to allow farmers to get out of debt.

Farmers benefit from governmental price supports only when they produce the same crops from year to year. Farmers who wish to receive the benefit of these price supports will be unlikely to reduce water pollution because they will not follow the experts' advice regarding diversification and rotation. Thus, A is the best answer.

Since the experts' advice is evidently their favored solution, the notion that the sole solution is something else (choice B) is not supported. The statements mention neither farmers' costs and revenues nor developments in farming techniques, and thus support no conclusions about prospects for profits (choice C) or future farming techniques (choice D). Because no information is given about either the amount of price support or farmers' debt, choice E is not supported.

70. Shelby Industries manufactures and sells the same gauges as Jones Industries. Employee wages account for forty percent of the cost of manufacturing gauges at both Shelby Industries and Jones Industries. Shelby Industries is seeking a competitive advantage over Jones Industries. Therefore, to promote this end, Shelby Industries should lower employee wages.

Which of the following, if true, would most weaken the argument above?

(A) Because they make a small number of precision instruments, gauge manufacturers cannot receive volume discounts on raw materials.
(B) Lowering wages would reduce the quality of employee work, and this reduced quality would lead to lowered sales.
(C) Jones Industries has taken away twenty percent of Shelby Industries' business over the last year.
(D) Shelby Industries pays its employees, on average, ten percent more than does Jones Industries.
(E) Many people who work for manufacturing plants live in areas in which the manufacturing plant they work for is the only industry.

According to choice B, the effect of lowering wages is to reduce quality sufficiently to reduce sales. This is a good reason to doubt that wage cuts would give Shelby Industries any competitive advantage, so choice B is the best answer.

Some of the other choices provide good reasons for, rather than against, lowering wages. Choice A implies that reducing the cost of raw materials is not possible, choice D indicates that Shelby Industries' wages are relatively high, and choice E suggests that Shelby Industries would not lose many workers if it did reduce wages. Choice C gives a reason for Shelby Industries to be concerned about its competitive position but no reason to think wage cuts would not improve that position.

71. Some communities in Florida are populated almost exclusively by retired people and contain few, if any, families with small children. Yet these communities are home to thriving businesses specializing in the rental of furniture for infants and small children.

Which of the following, if true, best reconciles the seeming discrepancy described above?

(A) The businesses specializing in the rental of children's furniture buy their furniture from distributors outside of Florida.
(B) The few children who do reside in these communities all know each other and often make overnight visits to one another's houses.
(C) Many residents of these communities who move frequently prefer renting their furniture to buying it outright.
(D) Many residents of these communities must provide for the needs of visiting grandchildren several weeks a year.
(E) Children's furniture available for rental is of the same quality as that available for sale in the stores.

If many residents of these communities host visiting grandchildren several weeks a year, as D states, that in itself might generate sufficient demand for rented children's furniture to support thriving businesses. Thus, D helps reconcile the apparent discrepancy and is the best answer.

The few households mentioned in choice B are unlikely to generate sufficient demand for rental businesses to thrive. Similarly, choices A and E, though they provide information concerning the furniture that is rented in these communities, do not address the prior issue of why there should be such demand for children's furniture. Choice C helps explain why these communities have an unusually high demand for rental furniture, but not why such a demand would extend to children's furniture.

72. Large national budget deficits do not cause large trade deficits. If they did, countries with the largest budget deficits would also have the largest trade deficits. In fact, when deficit figures are adjusted so that different countries are reliably comparable to each other, there is no such correlation.

If the statements above are all true, which of the following can properly be inferred on the basis of them?

(A) Countries with large national budget deficits tend to restrict foreign trade.
(B) Reliable comparisons of the deficit figures of one country with those of another are impossible.
(C) Reducing a country's national budget deficit will not necessarily result in a lowering of any trade deficit that country may have.
(D) When countries are ordered from largest to smallest in terms of population, the smallest countries generally have the smallest budget and trade deficits.
(E) Countries with the largest trade deficits never have similarly large national budget deficits.

The passage asserts that large budget deficits do not cause large trade deficits. If this is so, it is possible that a country with large budget and trade deficits could reduce its budget deficit and yet retain a large trade deficit. Thus, choice C is the best answer.

None of the other choices can be inferred. The passage says nothing about how countries respond to large budget deficits (choice A). The passage states that comparing deficit figures for different countries can be reliable (contrary to choice B). Correlation between deficit size and population size (choice D) is not at issue in the passage. Finally, it is consistent with the passage that countries with the largest trade deficits sometimes have similarly large budget deficits (choice E).

73. "Fast cycle time" is a strategy of designing a manufacturing organization to eliminate bottlenecks and delays in production. Not only does it speed up production, but it also assures quality. The reason is that the bottlenecks and delays cannot be eliminated unless all work is done right the first time.

The claim about quality made above rests on a questionable presupposition that

(A) any flaw in work on a product would cause a bottleneck or delay and so would be prevented from occurring on a "fast cycle" production line
(B) the strategy of "fast cycle time" would require fundamental rethinking of product design
(C) the primary goal of the organization is to produce a product of unexcelled quality, rather than to generate profits for stockholders
(D) "fast cycle time" could be achieved by shaving time off each of the component processes in a production cycle
(E) "fast cycle time" is a concept in business strategy that has not yet been put into practice in a factory

The argument presupposes that, if bottlenecks and delays are eliminated, production work must have been accomplished flawlessly. This presupposition is questionable, since there might well be flaws that do not impede the manufacturing process. The best answer is thus choice A.

None of the other choices is presupposed. The argument is consistent with redesigning the manufacturing process and not the product (choice B). The primary goal might be profits, and quality merely a means to that end (choice C). The argument does not rely on the feasibility of any one method of implementing "fast cycle time" (choice D). Finally, the concept of "fast cycle time" could already have been implemented operationally (choice E).

74. Many breakfast cereals are fortified with vitamin supplements. Some of these cereals provide 100 percent of the recommended daily requirement of vitamins. Nevertheless, a well-balanced breakfast, including a variety of foods, is a better source of those vitamins than are such fortified breakfast cereals alone.

Which of the following, if true, would most strongly support the position above?

(A) In many foods, the natural combination of vitamins with other nutrients makes those vitamins more usable by the body than are vitamins added in vitamin supplements.
(B) People who regularly eat cereals fortified with vitamin supplements sometimes neglect to eat the foods in which the vitamins occur naturally.
(C) Foods often must be fortified with vitamin supplements because naturally occurring vitamins are removed during processing.
(D) Unprocessed cereals are naturally high in several of the vitamins that are usually added to fortified breakfast cereals.
(E) Cereals containing vitamin supplements are no harder to digest than similar cereals without added vitamins.

By pointing out that, when occurring in natural combination with other nutrients, vitamins are more usable by the body than are those same vitamins when added as a supplement, choice A provides reason to believe that a well-balanced breakfast is a better source of vitamins than is a fortified breakfast cereal. A is the best answer.

Choice B does not support the position taken, although the position taken, if correct, is relevant to the people mentioned. Choice E describes a similarity between fortified cereals and other cereals. Choice C provides a reason for adding supplements to processed cereals, and choice D gives information about unprocessed cereals, but neither adds support for the alleged advantage of a well-balanced breakfast over a fortified cereal.

75. Which of the following best completes the passage below?

The more worried investors are about losing their money, the more they will demand a high potential return on their investment; great risks must be offset by the chance of great rewards. This principle is the fundamental one in determining interest rates, and it is illustrated by the fact that _____.

(A) successful investors are distinguished by an ability to make very risky investments without worrying about their money
(B) lenders receive higher interest rates on unsecured loans than on loans backed by collateral
(C) in times of high inflation, the interest paid to depositors by banks can actually be below the rate of inflation
(D) at any one time, a commercial bank will have a single rate of interest that it will expect all of its individual borrowers to pay
(E) the potential return on investment in a new company is typically lower than the potential return on investment in a well-established company

Since an unsecured loan is more risky, from the lender's point of view, than a loan backed by collateral, the fact that lenders receive higher interest rates for unsecured loans is an illustration of the principle outlined in the passage. Thus, choice B is the best answer.

None of the other choices gives a clear instance in which increased risk is compensated by the potential for increased return. Choice A does not concern return on investment at all. Choice C is an instance of low return unrelated to risk. In choice D, contrary to the principle, the rate of return remains constant despite possible variations in risk, and choice E also runs counter to the principle if investments in well-established companies entail less risk.

76. A famous singer recently won a lawsuit against an advertising firm for using another singer in a commercial to evoke the famous singer's well-known rendition of a certain song. As a result of the lawsuit, advertising firms will stop using imitators in commercials. Therefore, advertising costs will rise, since famous singers' services cost more than those of their imitators.

The conclusion above is based on which of the following assumptions?

(A) Most people are unable to distinguish a famous singer's rendition of a song from a good imitator's rendition of the same song.
(B) Commercials using famous singers are usually more effective than commercials using imitators of famous singers.
(C) The original versions of some well-known songs are unavailable for use in commercials.
(D) Advertising firms will continue to use imitators to mimic the physical mannerisms of famous singers.
(E) The advertising industry will use well-known renditions of songs in commercials.

If choice E were not assumed, the costs of the services of the famous singers of well-known renditions of songs would not be said to affect advertising costs. Since advertising costs are, however, projected to rise because of the relatively high cost of famous singers' services, choice E is assumed and is the best answer.

Choice A is irrelevant to the argument, since famous singers' services cost more than imitators' anyway. The argument addresses commercials' cost, not their effectiveness, so choice B is not assumed. The argument assumes that some well-known renditions of songs are available, but does not require that any versions be unavailable (choice C). Since the argument states that advertising firms will stop using imitators, choice D is not assumed.

77. A certain mayor has proposed a fee of five dollars per day on private vehicles entering the city, claiming that the fee will alleviate the city's traffic congestion. The mayor reasons that, since the fee will exceed the cost of round-trip bus fare from many nearby points, many people will switch from using their cars to using the bus.

Which of the following statements, if true, provides the best evidence that the mayor's reasoning is flawed?

(A) Projected increases in the price of gasoline will increase the cost of taking a private vehicle into the city.
(B) The cost of parking fees already makes it considerably more expensive for most people to take a private vehicle into the city than to take a bus.
(C) Most of the people currently riding the bus do not own private vehicles.
(D) Many commuters opposing the mayor's plan have indicated that they would rather endure traffic congestion than pay a five-dollar-per-day fee.
(E) During the average workday, private vehicles owned and operated by people living within the city account for 20 percent of the city's traffic congestion.

The mayor's reasoning rests on assuming that, if it costs more to travel to the city by car than by bus, people will choose to travel by bus rather than by car. Choice B provides evidence that this assumption is false, and is therefore the best answer.

Choice A does not undermine the mayor's view that the five-dollar fee will provide an incentive to switch to buses. Choice C makes it unlikely that the bus system will lose current riders if new riders are attracted. Choice D is inappropriate since many drivers not switching to buses is entirely consistent with many people making the switch. Choice E supports the mayor's proposal by indicating that vehicles entering the city produce most of the city's congestion.

78. A group of children of various ages was read stories in which people caused harm, some of those people doing so intentionally, and some accidentally. When asked about appropriate punishments for those who had caused harm, the younger children, unlike the older ones, assigned punishments that did not vary according to whether the harm was done intentionally or accidentally. Younger children, then, do not regard people's intentions as relevant to punishment.

Which of the following, if true, would most seriously weaken the conclusion above?

(A) In interpreting these stories, the listeners had to draw on a relatively mature sense of human psychology in order to tell whether harm was produced intentionally or accidentally.

(B) In these stories, the severity of the harm produced was clearly stated.

(C) Younger children are as likely to produce harm unintentionally as are older children.

(D) The older children assigned punishment in a way that closely resembled the way adults had assigned punishment in a similar experiment.

(E) The younger children assigned punishments that varied according to the severity of the harm done by the agents in the stories.

Choice A, the best answer, indicates that younger children might be unable to tell whether the harm in the stories was produced intentionally. Thus, even if younger children do regard people's intentions as relevant, they might be unable to apply this criterion here. Therefore, A undermines the conclusion's support.

Choices B and E support the conclusion by suggesting that another factor—severity of harm—either possibly (choice B) or actually (choice E) motivated variations in the punishments assigned by younger children. Neither choice C nor choice D affects the conclusion. The conclusion concerns what children recognize about others' behavior, not children's own behavior (choice C). The similarity between older children's and adult's assignments (choice D) leaves open the question of why younger children's assignments differed.

79. When hypnotized subjects are told that they are deaf and are then asked whether they can hear the hypnotist, they reply, "No." Some theorists try to explain this result by arguing that the selves of hypnotized subjects are dissociated into separate parts, and that the part that is deaf is dissociated from the part that replies.

Which of the following challenges indicates the most serious weakness in the attempted explanation described above?

(A) Why does the part that replies not answer, "Yes"?

(B) Why are the observed facts in need of any special explanation?

(C) Why do the subjects appear to accept the hypnotist's suggestion that they are deaf?

(D) Why do hypnotized subjects all respond the same way in the situation described?

(E) Why are the separate parts of the self the same for all subjects?

Since the question elicits a reply, the question was presumably heard, but presumably not by the part that is deaf. The explanation's obvious weakness, therefore, is that it fails to indicate why the part that replies would reply as if it were the part that is deaf. Choice A points to this failure and is the best answer.

Choice B does not challenge the explanation itself, but the need for an explanation in the first place. Choices C and D raise pertinent questions concerning the facts described, but do not address the proffered explanation of those facts. Choice E points to a question to which the attempted explanation gives rise, but does not challenge the adequacy of the explanation.

Questions 80-81 are based on the following.

The program to control the entry of illegal drugs into the country was a failure in 1987. If the program had been successful, the wholesale price of most illegal drugs would not have dropped substantially in 1987.

80. The argument in the passage depends on which of the following assumptions?

(A) The supply of illegal drugs dropped substantially in 1987.

(B) The price paid for most illegal drugs by the average consumer did not drop substantially in 1987.

(C) Domestic production of illegal drugs increased at a higher rate than did the entry of such drugs into the country.

(D) The wholesale price of a few illegal drugs increased substantially in 1987.

(E) A drop in demand for most illegal drugs in 1987 was not the sole cause of the drop in their wholesale price.

The only choice that must be true in order to conclude legitimately from the drop in the wholesale price of illegal drugs that the program was a failure is choice E, the best answer. If the drop in price was caused by a drop in demand, there is no reason to suspect that there has been any increase in supply caused by drugs entering the country.

The other choices can be false without affecting the argument. The supply of illegal drugs need not have dropped (choice A), and the retail price could have dropped (choice B). The entry of illegal drugs could have risen at a higher rate than domestic production (choice C), and no illegal drug need have undergone a substantial price rise (choice D).

81. The argument in the passage would be most seriously weakened if it were true that

   (A) in 1987 smugglers of illegal drugs, as a group, had significantly more funds at their disposal than did the country's customs agents
   (B) domestic production of illegal drugs increased substantially in 1987
   (C) the author's statements were made in order to embarrass the officials responsible for the drug-control program
   (D) in 1987 illegal drugs entered the country by a different set of routes than they did in 1986
   (E) the country's citizens spent substantially more money on illegal drugs in 1987 than they did in 1986

If domestic production of illegal drugs increased substantially, the overall supply could have increased (and the price fallen) without more illegal drugs entering the country, and without any failure of the program. Thus, choice B is the best answer.

None of the other choices weakens the argument. The smugglers' having more money (choice A) suggests that they would have resources to evade controls. The author's intention (choice C) is irrelevant to whether the reasoning the statements express is cogent. A change of routes (choice D) would have increased the chance of the program failing, and an increase in the amount of money spent (choice E) also provides evidence that the program did fail, given the low price levels.

82. Excavation of the ancient city of Kourion on the island of Cyprus revealed a pattern of debris and collapsed buildings typical of towns devastated by earthquakes. Archaeologists have hypothesized that the destruction was due to a major earthquake known to have occurred near the island in A.D. 365.

Which of the following, if true, most strongly supports the archaeologists' hypothesis?

   (A) Bronze ceremonial drinking vessels that are often found in graves dating from years preceding and following A.D. 365 were also found in several graves near Kourion.
   (B) No coins minted after A.D. 365 were found in Kourion, but coins minted before that year were found in abundance.
   (C) Most modern histories of Cyprus mention that an earthquake occurred near the island in A.D. 365.
   (D) Several small statues carved in styles current in Cyprus in the century between A.D. 300 and 400 were found in Kourion.
   (E) Stone inscriptions in a form of the Greek alphabet that was definitely used in Cyprus after A.D. 365 were found in Kourion.

The archaeologists hypothesized that Kourion was devastated by an earthquake known to have occurred in A.D. 365. Since choice B provides evidence that A.D. 365 was the date when life in Kourion was disrupted, B supports the hypothesis that it was the A.D. 365 earthquake that devastated Kourion. Thus, B is the best answer.

By contrast, choices A, D, and E all give information about artifacts found in or used in Kourion, but they do not specifically point to A.D. 365 as the date of the devastation. Thus, A, D, and E are inappropriate. Since choice C supports something already established, namely, that an earthquake occurred in A.D. 365, C is inappropriate.

83. Sales of telephones have increased dramatically over the last year. In order to take advantage of this increase, Mammoth Industries plans to expand production of its own model of telephone, while continuing its already very extensive advertising of this product.

Which of the following, if true, provides most support for the view that Mammoth Industries *cannot* increase its sales of telephones by adopting the plan outlined above?

(A) Although it sells all of the telephones that it produces, Mammoth Industries' share of all telephone sales has declined over the last year.

(B) Mammoth Industries' average inventory of telephones awaiting shipment to retailers has declined slightly over the last year.

(C) Advertising has made the brand name of Mammoth Industries' telephones widely known, but few consumers know that Mammoth Industries owns this brand.

(D) Mammoth Industries' telephone is one of three brands of telephone that have together accounted for the bulk of the last year's increase in sales.

(E) Despite a slight decline in the retail price, sales of Mammoth Industries' telephones have fallen in the last year.

Choice E indicates that Mammoth's telephones already fail to participate in the industry trend of higher sales despite heavy advertising. Producing more of the same model would thus be unlikely to generate increased sales for Mammoth, so E is the best answer.

If Mammoth has sold all the telephones it produced, it might increase sales by producing more, even if it has lost market share, as choice A states. Choice D indicates that Mammoth's sales are increasing, and similarly for B if the decrease in inventory results from retailers taking delivery of more telephones. So long as consumers recognize the brand name of Mammoth's telephones, as choice C states, it probably does not matter whether they associate it with Mammoth.

84. Many institutions of higher education suffer declining enrollments during periods of economic slowdown. At two-year community colleges, however, enrollment figures boom during these periods when many people have less money and there is more competition for jobs.

Each of the following, if true, helps to explain the enrollment increases in two-year community colleges described above EXCEPT:

(A) During periods of economic slowdown, two-year community colleges are more likely than four-year colleges to prepare their students for the jobs that are still available.

(B) During periods of economic prosperity, graduates of two-year community colleges often continue their studies at four-year colleges.

(C) Tuition at most two-year community colleges is a fraction of that at four-year colleges.

(D) Two-year community colleges devote more resources than do other colleges to attracting those students especially affected by economic slowdowns.

(E) Students at two-year community colleges, but not those at most four-year colleges, can control the cost of their studies by choosing the number of courses they take each term.

Four of the choices give reasons why, in an economic slowdown, many people would choose a two-year college. Choice A indicates that a two-year college education gives one a better chance of finding a job when economic conditions are poor. Choices C and E indicate why people with less money might prefer two-year colleges. Finally, choice D suggests that more is being done to attract people whose lives are affected by the slowdown to two-year than to four-year colleges.

Choice B, the best answer, might explain the decreased enrollment at four-year colleges during the slowdown, but because it deals with graduates of two-year colleges it cannot explain why enrollment at these colleges might increase.

Hardin argued that grazing land held in common (that is, open to any user) would always be used less carefully than private grazing land. Each rancher would be tempted to overuse common land because the benefits would accrue to the individual, while the costs of reduced land quality that results from overuse would be spread among all users. But a study comparing 217 million acres of common grazing land with 433 million acres of private grazing land showed that the common land was in better condition.

85. The answer to which of the following questions would be most useful in evaluating the significance, in relation to Hardin's claim, of the study described above?

   (A) Did any of the ranchers whose land was studied use both common and private land?
   (B) Did the ranchers whose land was studied tend to prefer using common land over using private land for grazing?
   (C) Was the private land that was studied of comparable quality to the common land before either was used for grazing?
   (D) Were the users of the common land that was studied at least as prosperous as the users of the private land?
   (E) Were there any owners of herds who used only common land, and no private land, for grazing?

Hardin's claim is that common grazing land deteriorates more quickly than private grazing land because of overuse. The study indicates that common grazing land is currently in better shape, but this would not undermine Hardin's claim if common grazing land was in far better shape before grazing began. Thus, choice C is the best answer.

   Choices A and E are inappropriate since the study can undermine Hardin's claim whether or not some ranchers use both sorts of land, or use only common land. Similarly, the study can undermine Hardin's claim whether or not ranchers prefer to use common land, as B says. Finally, D is inappropriate since the force of the study is not diminished if users of common land are more or less prosperous.

86. Which of the following, if true and known by the ranchers, would best help explain the results of the study?

   (A) With private grazing land, both the costs and the benefits of overuse fall to the individual user.
   (B) The cost in reduced land quality that is attributable to any individual user is less easily measured with common land than it is with private land.
   (C) An individual who overuses common grazing land might be able to achieve higher returns than other users can, with the result that he or she would obtain a competitive advantage.
   (D) If one user of common land overuses it even slightly, the other users are likely to do so even more, with the consequence that the costs to each user outweigh the benefits.
   (E) There are more acres of grazing land held privately than there are held in common.

The study indicates that common lands are in better shape than private lands. The best answer, D, indicates that, contrary to Hardin's claim, it is in each rancher's self-interest not to overuse common land, which would explain why common lands are in relatively good shape.

   Choices A and C can only explain why private land is in better shape than common land, not the reverse. Neither the fact that it is more difficult to attribute deterioration of common land to any particular user (choice B) nor the fact that the relative amounts of common and private land differ (choice E) gives a reason for farmers not to graze their herds on common land as much as possible.

87. In tests for pironoma, a serious disease, a false positive result indicates that people have pironoma when, in fact, they do not; a false negative result indicates that people do not have pironoma when, in fact, they do. To detect pironoma most accurately, physicians should use the laboratory test that has the lowest proportion of false positive results.

Which of the following, if true, gives the most support to the recommendation above?

(A) The accepted treatment for pironoma does not have damaging side effects.
(B) The laboratory test that has the lowest proportion of false positive results causes the same minor side effects as do the other laboratory tests used to detect pironoma.
(C) In treating pironoma patients, it is essential to begin treatment as early as possible, since even a week of delay can result in loss of life.
(D) The proportion of inconclusive test results is equal for all laboratory tests used to detect pironoma.
(E) All laboratory tests to detect pironoma have the same proportion of false negative results.

The most accurate test for pironoma would be the one with the fewest false results. If all tests have the same proportion of false negatives, then the most accurate is the one that has the lowest proportion of false positives. Thus, E supports the recommendation and is the best answer.

Choices A and C deal with the treatment for pironoma and are irrelevant to the accuracy of tests for pironoma. Choice B deals with the side effects of tests for pironoma, and does not address their accuracy. That the proportion of inconclusive test results is equal for all tests (choice D) leaves open the question of which test is more accurate, since it does not indicate which test has fewest false results.

Questions 88-89 are based on the following.

In many corporations, employees are being replaced by automated equipment in order to save money. However, many workers who lose their jobs to automation will need government assistance to survive, and the same corporations that are laying people off will eventually pay for that assistance through increased taxes and unemployment insurance payments.

88. The author is arguing that

(A) higher taxes and unemployment insurance payments will discourage corporations from automating
(B) replacing people through automation to reduce production costs will result in increases of other costs to corporations
(C) many workers who lose their jobs to automation will have to be retrained for new jobs
(D) corporations that are laying people off will eventually rehire many of them
(E) corporations will not save money by automating because people will be needed to run the new machines

The author argues that replacing employees with automated equipment might lend to less savings for corporations than anticipated, since laying off workers will lead to other costs. Choice B states the author's main points and thus is the best answer.

The author argues that corporations that automate might incur unexpected costs, but the author does not argue that these costs will discourage corporations from automating (choice A). The author does not address the issues of retraining (choice C) and rehiring (choice D). Although the author argues that some unanticipated costs might offset savings resulting from automation, the cost of running the new machines (choice E) is clearly not one of these unanticipated costs.

89. **Which of the following, if true, most strengthens the author's argument?**

    (A) Many workers who have already lost their jobs to automation have been unable to find new jobs.

    (B) Many corporations that have failed to automate have seen their profits decline.

    (C) Taxes and unemployment insurance are paid also by corporations that are not automating.

    (D) Most of the new jobs created by automation pay less than the jobs eliminated by automation did.

    (E) The initial investment in machinery for automation is often greater than the short-term savings in labor costs.

The threat envisioned by the author to the economic survival of workers displaced by automation will be serious only if they cannot find new jobs. Choice A, the best answer, says that there are already many such workers unable to find new jobs, and so strengthens the author's argument.

Since the causes for declining profits for corporations that fail to automate are not analyzed in the passage, B is inappropriate. By saying that costs associated with unemployment are not carried solely by corporations that automate, choice C weakens the argument. Since the author tacitly grants that, initially, automation will cut costs, the detail given in D provides us added support. Choice E is inappropriate because it concerns short-term rather than long-term results of automation.

90. **The sustained massive use of pesticides in farming has two effects that are especially pernicious. First, it often kills off the pests' natural enemies in the area. Second, it often unintentionally gives rise to insecticide-resistant pests, since those insects that survive a particular insecticide will be the ones most resistant to it, and they are the ones left to breed.**

From the passage above, it can be properly inferred that the effectiveness of the sustained massive use of pesticides can be extended by doing which of the following, assuming that each is a realistic possibility?

    (A) Using only chemically stable insecticides

    (B) Periodically switching the type of insecticide used

    (C) Gradually increasing the quantities of pesticides used

    (D) Leaving a few fields fallow every year

    (E) Breeding higher-yielding varieties of crop plants

Choice B gives a way of counteracting a serious drawback of the sustained massive use of pesticides. By periodically changing the pesticide used, pests resistant to one pesticide might be killed by the next pesticide, and those resistant to that pesticide might be killed by another, and so on. Therefore, B is the best answer.

Choice A is inappropriate, since the effects of stable pesticides would simply be more persistent. Gradually increasing pesticide amounts (choice C) will likely have no effect on pests already resistant to massive amounts. Leaving a few fields fallow (choice D) is not relevant to the effectiveness of sustained use of pesticides. Breeding higher-yielding crops (choice E) might temporarily increase yields, but not because of anything to do with pesticides.

91. **When a polygraph test is judged inconclusive, this is no reflection on the examinee. Rather, such a judgment means that the test has failed to show whether the examinee was truthful or untruthful. Nevertheless, employers will sometimes refuse to hire a job applicant because of an inconclusive polygraph test result.**

Which of the following conclusions can most properly be drawn from the information above?

    (A) Most examinees with inconclusive polygraph test results are in fact untruthful.

    (B) Polygraph tests should not be used by employers in the consideration of job applicants.

    (C) An inconclusive polygraph test result is sometimes unfairly held against the examinee.

    (D) A polygraph test indicating that an examinee is untruthful can sometimes be mistaken.

    (E) Some employers have refused to consider the results of polygraph tests when evaluating job applicants.

The passage indicates that an inconclusive polygraph test tells nothing about the person who has taken the test, and yet employers sometimes refuse to hire someone whose results from such a test are inconclusive. Treating lack of information as if it were unfavorable evidence about a person can reasonably be considered unfair. Therefore, C is the best answer.

Choice A is not supported, since the passage says that an inconclusive polygraph test is no reflection on the examinee. Neither B nor D is supported, since the information given includes nothing either implicit or explicit about polygraph tests that yield conclusive results. Since the passage is consistent with both E and its denial, E is not supported.

92. According to the new office smoking regulations, only employees who have enclosed offices may smoke at their desks. Virtually all employees with enclosed offices are at the professional level, and virtually all secretarial employees lack enclosed offices. Therefore, secretaries who smoke should be offered enclosed offices.

Which of the following is an assumption that enables the conclusion above to be properly drawn?

(A) Employees at the professional level who do not smoke should keep their enclosed offices.
(B) Employees with enclosed offices should not smoke at their desks, even though the new regulations permit them to do so.
(C) Employees at the secretarial level should be allowed to smoke at their desks, even if they do not have enclosed offices.
(D) The smoking regulations should allow all employees who smoke an equal opportunity to do so, regardless of an employee's job level.
(E) The smoking regulations should provide equal protection from any hazards associated with smoking to all employees who do not smoke.

The regulations allow some employees—those with enclosed offices—but not others the opportunity to smoke at their desks. If it is assumed that the regulations should allow all employees equal opportunity to smoke, those who are currently denied this opportunity should be given it, and so secretaries who smoke should be offered enclosed offices. Therefore, choice D is the best answer.

None of the other choices enables the conclusion to be properly drawn. Choice A tends to conflict with the conclusion, unless some enclosed offices are vacant. Choice B supports no conclusion about how secretaries should be treated, and choice C undermines the conclusion. Finally, nonsmokers already have equal protection from hazards, so choice E cannot be used to justify making any changes.

93. Dental researchers recently discovered that toothbrushes can become contaminated with bacteria that cause pneumonia and strep throat. They found that contamination usually occurs after toothbrushes have been used for four weeks. For that reason, people should replace their toothbrushes at least once a month.

Which of the following, if true, would most weaken the conclusion above?

(A) The dental researchers could not discover why toothbrush contamination usually occurred only after toothbrushes had been used for four weeks.
(B) The dental researchers failed to investigate contamination of toothbrushes by viruses, yeasts, and other pathogenic microorganisms.
(C) The dental researchers found that among people who used toothbrushes contaminated with bacteria that cause pneumonia and strep throat, the incidence of these diseases was no higher than among people who used uncontaminated toothbrushes.
(D) The dental researchers found that people who rinsed their toothbrushes thoroughly in hot water after each use were as likely to have contaminated toothbrushes as were people who only rinsed their toothbrushes hurriedly in cold water after each use.
(E) The dental researchers found that, after six weeks of use, greater length of use of a toothbrush did not correlate with a higher number of bacteria being present.

According to choice C, using a contaminated toothbrush does not increase the incidence of infection, so the recommendation to replace a toothbrush before it becomes contaminated is greatly undermined. Choice C is therefore the best answer.

Since the recommendation is based on the discovery that bacterial contamination occurs after about four weeks, the researchers' inability to discover why contamination takes that long to appear does not weaken the recommendation (choice A), nor does their failure to investigate other forms of contamination (choice B), nor does the discovery that contamination does not worsen after six weeks (choice E). According to choice D, even thorough washing cannot prevent contamination, so replacing the toothbrush appears more essential, rather than less so.

Questions 94-95 are based on the following.

To protect certain fledgling industries, the government of country Z banned imports of the types of products those industries were starting to make. As a direct result, the cost of those products to the buyers, several export-dependent industries in Z, went up, sharply limiting the ability of those industries to compete effectively in their export markets.

94. Which of the following can be most properly inferred from the passage about the products whose importation was banned?

(A) Those products had been cheaper to import than they were to make within country Z's fledgling industries.
(B) Those products were ones that country Z was hoping to export in its turn, once the fledgling industries matured.
(C) Those products used to be imported from just those countries to which country Z's exports went.
(D) Those products had become more and more expensive to import, which resulted in a foreign trade deficit just before the ban.
(E) Those products used to be imported in very small quantities, but they were essential to country Z's economy.

In Z, when the government banned imports of certain products the cost of those products rose, so the products must have been cheaper to import than they were to make in Z. Therefore choice A is the best answer.

None of the other choices can be inferred. Country Z need have had no plan to export those products later (choice B), nor need the products have come previously from those countries to which country Z exported goods (choice C). The products need not have become more expensive before the ban (choice D), and they could have been imported in relatively large quantities (choice E).

95. Which of the following conclusions about country Z's adversely affected export-dependent industries is best supported by the passage?

(A) Profit margins in those industries were not high enough to absorb the rise in costs mentioned above.
(B) Those industries had to contend with the fact that other countries banned imports from country Z.
(C) Those industries succeeded in expanding the domestic market for their products.
(D) Steps to offset rising materials costs by decreasing labor costs were taken in those industries.
(E) Those industries started to move into export markets that they had previously judged unprofitable.

When the cost of the products rose, the competitive ability of those export-dependent industries that bought them was sharply limited. This fact strongly supports the claim that those industries did not have sufficiently high profit margins to enable them to absorb the price increase, so choice A is the best answer.

Given the limitation on their competitive ability, it is unlikely that those industries would be able either to expand their domestic markets (choice C) or to enter into new export markets (choice E). The other choices relate situations that would be possible but that are not strongly supported: other countries could have continued to permit imports from Z (choice B), and the industries may have been unable to decrease labor costs (choice D).

96. The difficulty with the proposed high-speed train line is that a used plane can be bought for one-third the price of the train line, and the plane, which is just as fast, can fly anywhere. The train would be a fixed linear system, and we live in a world that is spreading out in all directions and in which consumers choose the free-wheel systems (cars, buses, aircraft), which do not have fixed routes. Thus a sufficient market for the train will not exist.

Which of the following, if true, most severely weakens the argument presented above?

(A) Cars, buses, and planes require the efforts of drivers and pilots to guide them, whereas the train will be guided mechanically.
(B) Cars and buses are not nearly as fast as the high-speed train will be.
(C) Planes are not a free-wheel system because they can fly only between airports, which are less convenient for consumers than the high-speed train's stations would be.
(D) The high-speed train line cannot use currently underutilized train stations in large cities.
(E) For long trips, most people prefer to fly rather than to take ground-level transportation.

The author argues that planes, since they are a free-wheel system, will be preferred to the high-speed train. Choice C weakens the argument by pointing out that planes are not a free-wheel system and are less convenient than the high-speed train would be. Thus C is the best answer.

The special feature of the high-speed train described in A is not one that clearly affects consumer choice one way or the other way. Since it is planes that would compete effectively with the proposed trains, the fact that cars and buses might not do so is irrelevant. Nonavailability of certain stations (choice D) and the consumer preferences described in choice E tend to make the proposed train less, not more, attractive and so both choices strengthen the argument.

97. Leaders of a miners' union on strike against Coalco are contemplating additional measures to pressure the company to accept the union's contract proposal. The union leaders are considering as their principal new tactic a consumer boycott against Gasco gas stations, which are owned by Energy Incorporated, the same corporation that owns Coalco.

The answer to which of the following questions is LEAST directly relevant to the union leaders' consideration of whether attempting a boycott of Gasco will lead to acceptance of their contract proposal?

(A) Would revenue losses by Gasco seriously affect Energy Incorporated?
(B) Can current Gasco customers easily obtain gasoline elsewhere?
(C) Have other miners' unions won contracts similar to the one proposed by this union?
(D) Have other unions that have employed a similar tactic achieved their goals with it?
(E) Do other corporations that own coal companies also own gas stations?

Whether corporations, other than Energy Incorporated, that own coal companies also own gas stations is not directly relevant to whether attempting a boycott of Gasco gas stations will coerce Coalco to accept the contract proposal. Thus choice E is the best answer.

Each of the other four questions is relevant to evaluating the chances the union strategy has of succeeding. Choice A bears on whether the strategy would apply sufficient economic pressure on Energy Incorporated. Choice B is relevant to whether consumers can respond to the call for a boycott. Choice C is relevant to whether the union's contract proposal is a reasonable one. Choice D is relevant because a successful precedent would favorably reflect on the union's chances of success.

Questions 98-99 are based on the following.

Transnational cooperation among corporations is experiencing a modest renaissance among United States firms, even though projects undertaken by two or more corporations under a collaborative agreement are less profitable than projects undertaken by a single corporation. The advantage of transnational cooperation is that such joint international projects may allow United States firms to win foreign contracts that they would not otherwise be able to win.

98. Which of the following statements by a United States corporate officer best fits the situation of United States firms as described in the passage above?

(A) "We would rather make only a share of the profit and also risk only a share of a possible loss than run the full risk of a loss."
(B) "We would rather make a share of a relatively modest profit than end up making none of a potentially much bigger profit."
(C) "We would rather cooperate and build good will than poison the business climate by all-out competition."
(D) "We would rather have foreign corporations join us in American projects than join them in projects in their home countries."
(E) "We would rather win a contract with a truly competitive bid of our own than get involved in less profitable collaborative agreements."

According to the passage, for certain foreign contracts United States firms can either cooperate and hope to earn a modest profit, or not cooperate, not win the contract, and earn no part of a larger profit. This is how choice B describes the situation, so choice B is the best answer.

In order to earn a profit, United States firms must cooperate, so the alternatives described in several of the choices are not in practice open to them: the alternatives of a modest risk versus a full risk (choice A), cooperation versus competition (choice C), and winning on their own versus collaborating (choice E). Since they do not have the same need to cooperate with foreign corporations to win American contracts, choice D does not fit either.

99. Which of the following is information provided by the passage above?

   (A) Transnational cooperation involves projects too big for a single corporation to handle.

   (B) Transnational cooperation results in a pooling of resources leading to high-quality performance.

   (C) Transnational cooperation has in the past been both more common and less common than it is now among United States firms.

   (D) Joint projects between United States and foreign corporations are not profitable enough to be worth undertaking.

   (E) Joint projects between United States and foreign corporations benefit only those who commission the projects.

To say that transnational cooperation is experiencing a modest renaissance means that it used to be relatively common, became less so, and is now becoming more common again. Therefore choice C is the best answer, since it follows from that statement.

None of the other choices presents information provided by the passage. The passage says nothing about the size of the projects (choice A), nor about the quality of work in cases of transnational cooperation (choice B). Since the passage strongly suggests transnational cooperation can be profitable for the firms concerned, it thereby tends to contradict both the claims that joint projects are not profitable (choice D) and that they only benefit those who commission the projects (choice E).

100. A compelling optical illusion called the illusion of velocity and size makes objects appear to be moving more slowly the larger the objects are. Therefore, a motorist's estimate of the time available for crossing a highway with a small car approaching is bound to be lower than it would be with a large truck approaching.

The conclusion above would be more properly drawn if it were made clear that the

   (A) truck's speed is assumed to be lower than the car's

   (B) truck's speed is assumed to be the same as the car's

   (C) truck's speed is assumed to be higher than the car's

   (D) motorist's estimate of time available is assumed to be more accurate with cars approaching than with trucks approaching

   (E) motorist's estimate of time available is assumed to be more accurate with trucks approaching than with cars approaching

If the truck's speed is assumed to be the same as the car's, then since the truck is larger, the optical illusion will make it appear that there is more time to cross the highway with the truck approaching than with the car approaching. Thus, choice B helps in establishing the conclusion and is the best answer.

If the truck's speed is lower than the car's (choice A), the conclusion does not depend on the illusion. If the truck's speed is higher than the car's (choice C), the speed of the truck might counteract the illusion's effect. Since the illusion works as stated regardless of what vehicle the estimate happens to be accurate for, neither choice D nor choice E assists in drawing the conclusion.

101. Biological functions of many plants and animals vary in cycles that are repeated every 24 hours. It is tempting to suppose that alteration in the intensity of incident light is the stimulus that controls these daily biological rhythms. But there is much evidence to contradict this hypothesis.

Which of the following, if known, is evidence that contradicts the hypothesis stated in lines 2-5 above?

   (A) Human body temperature varies throughout the day, with the maximum occurring in the late afternoon and the minimum in the morning.

   (B) While some animals, such as the robin, are more active during the day, others, such as mice, show greater activity at night.

   (C) When people move from one time zone to another, their daily biological rhythms adjust in a matter of days to the periods of sunlight and darkness in the new zone.

   (D) Certain single-cell plants display daily biological rhythms even when the part of the cell containing the nucleus is removed.

   (E) Even when exposed to constant light intensity around the clock, some algae display rates of photosynthesis that are much greater during daylight hours than at night.

Algae whose rate of photosynthesis varies on a 24-hour basis even when they are under constant light constitute evidence against the hypothesis that it is alterations in light that control biological cycles. Therefore choice E is the best answer.

Choices A and B describe biological cycles, but provide no evidence about what controls them. Choice C says that cycles can become adapted to new patterns of light, weakly supporting the hypothesis that alterations in light control cycles. Finally, choice D provides evidence against a different hypothesis, namely, that it is the cell nucleus of single-cell plants that controls their biological cycles.

102. Although migraine headaches are believed to be caused by food allergies, putting patients on diets that eliminate those foods to which the patients have been demonstrated to have allergic migraine reactions frequently does not stop headaches. Obviously, some other cause of migraine headaches besides food allergies must exist.

Which of the following, if true, would most weaken the conclusion above?

(A) Many common foods elicit an allergic response only after several days, making it very difficult to observe links between specific foods patients eat and headaches they develop.
(B) Food allergies affect many people who never develop the symptom of migraine headaches.
(C) Many patients report that the foods that cause them migraine headaches are among the foods that they most enjoy eating.
(D) Very few patients have allergic migraine reactions as children and then live migraine-free adult lives once they have eliminated from their diets foods to which they have been demonstrated to be allergic.
(E) Very rarely do food allergies cause patients to suffer a symptom more severe than that of migraine headaches.

If it is difficult to determine which foods cause migraines, then some foods that cause allergic reactions might not have been demonstrated to do so. Hence, if choice A is true, eliminating foods that have been demonstrated to cause migraines might not eliminate migraines, even if food allergies are the only cause of migraines. Choice A is the best answer.

Neither the fact that some food allergies do not result in migraines (choice B), nor the fact that few allergies result in symptoms more severe than migraines (choice E), explains why restricting one's diet does not stop migraines. Choice C suggests that migraine sufferers do not naturally avoid the foods at issue. Choice D reiterates the information that eliminating certain foods does not usually solve the problem.

103. The technological conservatism of bicycle manufacturers is a reflection of the kinds of demand they are trying to meet. The only cyclists seriously interested in innovation and willing to pay for it are bicycle racers. Therefore, innovation in bicycle technology is limited by what authorities will accept as standard for purposes of competition in bicycle races.

Which of the following is an assumption made in drawing the conclusion above?

(A) The market for cheap, traditional bicycles cannot expand unless the market for high-performance competition bicycles expands.
(B) High-performance bicycles are likely to be improved more as a result of technological innovations developed in small workshops than as a result of technological innovations developed in major manufacturing concerns.
(C) Bicycle racers do not generate a strong demand for innovations that fall outside what is officially recognized as standard for purposes of competition.
(D) The technological conservatism of bicycle manufacturers results primarily from their desire to manufacture a product that can be sold without being altered to suit different national markets.
(E) The authorities who set standards for high-performance bicycle racing do not keep informed about innovative bicycle design.

If racers, the only cyclists interested in innovation, created a strong demand for innovations for purposes other than official competition, then the conclusion would not follow. Therefore choice C—which asserts that racers generate no such demand—is assumed and is the best answer.

Since the argument is stated generally in terms of where demand for innovation lies and how manufacturers respond to demand, no assumption is made about the structure of the market for bicycles themselves (choice A) nor about which manufacturers are most likely to produce innovations (choice B). Choice D presents another pressure toward technological conservatism, but this pressure is not required by the argument. Finally, the authorities may keep a close eye on innovation (choice E) without the argument being affected.

104. Spending on research and development by United States businesses for 1984 showed an increase of about 8 percent over the 1983 level. This increase actually continued a downward trend evident since 1981—when outlays for research and development increased 16.4 percent over 1980 spending. Clearly, the 25 percent tax credit enacted by Congress in 1981, which was intended to promote spending on research and development, did little or nothing to stimulate such spending.

The conclusion of the argument above cannot be true unless which of the following is true?

(A) Business spending on research and development is usually directly proportional to business profits.
(B) Business spending for research and development in 1985 could not increase by more than 8.3 percent.
(C) Had the 1981 tax credit been set higher than 25 percent, business spending for research and development after 1981 would have increased more than it did.
(D) In the absence of the 25 percent tax credit, business spending for research and development after 1981 would not have been substantially lower than it was.
(E) Tax credits marked for specific investments are rarely effective in inducing businesses to make those investments.

The conclusion that the tax credit did nothing to stimulate spending on research and development would not be true if, without the credit, such spending would have been even lower than it actually was. Thus choice D must be true for the conclusion to be true and is the best answer.

Since a tax credit generally improves business profits, if the conclusion is true choice A is unlikely to be true. If the tax credit was ineffective, some other factors must determine the level of spending, and could lead to much higher levels of spending in 1985 (against choice B), and could render a higher level of tax credit ineffective (against choice C), but it could be that credits are generally effective (against choice E).

105. Treatment for hypertension forestalls certain medical expenses by preventing strokes and heart disease. Yet any money so saved amounts to only one-fourth of the expenditures required to treat the hypertensive population. Therefore, there is no economic justification for preventive treatment for hypertension.

Which of the following, if true, is most damaging to the conclusion above?

(A) The many fatal strokes and heart attacks resulting from untreated hypertension cause insignificant medical expenditures but large economic losses of other sorts.
(B) The cost, per patient, of preventive treatment for hypertension would remain constant even if such treatment were instituted on a large scale.
(C) In matters of health care, economic considerations should ideally not be dominant.
(D) Effective prevention presupposes early diagnosis, and programs to ensure early diagnosis are costly.
(E) The net savings in medical resources achieved by some preventive health measures are smaller than the net losses attributable to certain other measures of this kind.

If the results of untreated hypertension cause large economic losses, as choice A claims, then the treatment of hypertension may well be economically justifiable. Therefore choice A is most damaging to the conclusion and is the best answer.

Choices B and D tend to support the conclusion; choice B says that making preventive treatment widespread would not introduce economies of scale, and choice D identifies one aspect of prevention that is both costly and essential. Choice C undermines a different conclusion—that society should not support treatment for hypertension—but does not damage the conclusion actually drawn. The fact that different preventive health measures have different economic consequences (choice D) gives no specific information about treatment for hypertension, and so cannot affect the conclusion drawn.

106. Property taxes are typically set at a flat rate per $1,000 of officially assessed value. Reassessments should be frequent in order to remove distortions that arise when property values change at differential rates. In practice, however, reassessments typically occur when they benefit the government—that is, when their effect is to increase total tax revenue.

If the statements above are true, which of the following describes a situation in which a reassessment should occur but is unlikely to do so?

(A) Property values have risen sharply and uniformly.
(B) Property values have all risen—some very sharply, some less so.
(C) Property values have for the most part risen sharply; yet some have dropped slightly.
(D) Property values have for the most part dropped significantly; yet some have risen slightly.
(E) Property values have dropped significantly and uniformly.

If most property values have dropped significantly, but some have risen slightly, a reassessment should occur (since values have changed at different rates) but is unlikely (since it will not benefit the government). Thus choice D describes the required situation and is the best answer.

According to the passage, choices A and E describe situations in which there is no need for a reassessment, since change has occurred uniformly. Similarly, choices B and C both describe situations in which a reassessment should occur, and is likely to, since the government will benefit.

107. The number of patents granted to inventors by the United States Patent Office dropped from 56,000 in 1971 to 45,000 in 1978. Spending on research and development, which peaked at 3 percent of the gross national product (GNP) in 1964, was only 2.2 percent of the GNP in 1978. During this period, when the United States percentage was steadily decreasing, West Germany and Japan increased the percentage of their GNP's spent on research and development to 3.2 percent and 1.6 percent, respectively.

Which of the following conclusions is best supported by the information above?

(A) There is a direct relationship between the size of a nation's GNP and the number of inventions it produces.
(B) Japan and West Germany spent more money on research and development in 1978 than did the United States.
(C) The amount of money a nation spends on research and development is directly related to the number of inventions patented in that nation.
(D) Between 1964 and 1978 the United States consistently spent a larger percentage of its GNP on research and development than did Japan.
(E) Both West Germany and Japan will soon surpass the United States in the number of patents granted to inventors.

From 1964 to 1978, spending on research and development never fell below 2.2 percent of the GNP in the United States and never rose above 1.6 percent in Japan. Therefore choice D follows from the information given and is the best answer.

Since no information is provided about the size of the GNP of any of the countries mentioned, neither choice A nor choice B is supported. The amount of information given about numbers of patents granted is insufficient to establish any general relation between spending and numbers of patents, so choice C is unsupported; and given that there is no information about the number of inventions patented in Japan and West Germany, choice E is not supported either.

108. When three Everett-owned Lightning-built airplanes crashed in the same month, the Everett company ordered three new Lightning-built airplanes as replacements. This decision surprised many in the airline industry because, ordinarily when a product is involved in accidents, users become reluctant to buy that product.

Which of the following, if true, provides the best indication that the Everett company's decision was logically well supported?

(A) Although during the previous year only one Lightning-built airplane crashed, competing manufacturers had a perfect safety record.

(B) The Lightning-built airplanes crashed due to pilot error, but because of the excellent quality of the planes there were many survivors.

(C) The Federal Aviation Association issued new guidelines for airlines in order to standardize safety requirements governing preflight inspections.

(D) Consumer advocates pressured two major airlines into purchasing safer airplanes so that the public would be safer while flying.

(E) Many Lightning Airplane Company employees had to be replaced because they found jobs with the competition.

Everett's decision is most logically well supported if the crashes were not due to deficiencies in the planes, particularly if there is evidence that the airplanes provide significant protection to occupants in the event of a crash. Thus choice B is the best answer.

Choices A and E are incorrect because each suggests that the decision might be ill founded. Competing manufacturers' models might actually be safer (choice A), and Lightning might have lost its most able employees—those able to get new jobs (choice E). Choice C is incorrect because it provides no reason for preferring Lightning-built airplanes to other makes of airplane. Choice D is incorrect because, though it underscores the advisability of buying safe airplanes, it offers no evidence that the airplanes that Everett bought were safe.

109. Recently a court ruled that current law allows companies to reject a job applicant if working in the job would entail a 90 percent chance that the applicant would suffer a heart attack. The presiding judge justified the ruling, saying that it protected both employees and employers.

The use of this court ruling as part of the law could not be effective in regulating employment practices if which of the following were true?

(A) The best interests of employers often conflict with the interests of employees.

(B) No legally accepted methods exist for calculating the risk of a job applicant's having a heart attack as a result of being employed in any particular occupation.

(C) Some jobs might involve health risks other than the risk of heart attack.

(D) Employees who have a 90 percent chance of suffering a heart attack may be unaware that their risk is so great.

(E) The number of people applying for jobs at a company might decline if the company, by screening applicants for risk of heart attack, seemed to suggest that the job entailed high risk of heart attack.

The ruling would be ineffective in regulating employment practices if it could never be used to justify rejecting some application. According to choice B the ruling cannot be applied in a legally acceptable way. Thus choice B is the best answer.

None of the other choices casts doubt on the effectiveness of the ruling. Choice A suggests that the judge's justification for the ruling would be unavailable in many situations but not that the ruling itself would be ineffective. Choice C raises the possibility that there might be further rulings of a similar nature in the future. Choice D concerns employees, not job applicants; its concern is thus outside the scope of the ruling. Choice E describes one indirect effect on the job market that might stem from the ruling.

110. Robot satellites relay important communications and identify weather patterns. Because the satellites can be repaired only in orbit, astronauts are needed to repair them. Without repairs, the satellites would eventually malfunction. Therefore, space flights carrying astronauts must continue.

Which of the following, if true, would most seriously weaken the argument above?

(A) Satellites falling from orbit because of malfunctions burn up in the atmosphere.
(B) Although satellites are indispensable in the identification of weather patterns, weather forecasters also make some use of computer projections to identify weather patterns.
(C) The government, responding to public pressure, has decided to cut the budget for space flights and put more money into social welfare programs.
(D) Repair of satellites requires heavy equipment, which adds to the amount of fuel needed to lift a spaceship carrying astronauts into orbit.
(E) Technical obsolescence of robot satellites makes repairing them more costly and less practical than sending new, improved satellites into orbit.

The argument presented in support of manned spaceflights rests on the notion that astronauts are needed to repair satellites. If sending up a new, improved satellite is less costly and more practical than repairing an old one, however, as choice E states, the argument is weakened. Choice E is therefore the best answer.

None of the other choices gives any reason to think that manned spaceflights are not a necessity, so none of them is correct. Choice A describes one consequence of not repairing satellites, while choice B refers to another tool that weather forecasters use in addition to satellites. Choice C describes the circumstances in which defending manned spaceflight has become an issue, and choice D states a practical, but not insuperable, difficulty faced by flights intended for repair projects.

111. Advocates of a large-scale space-defense research project conclude that it will represent a net benefit to civilian business. They say that since government-sponsored research will have civilian applications, civilian businesses will reap the rewards of government-developed technology.

Each of the following, if true, raises a consideration arguing against the conclusion above, EXCEPT:

(A) The development of cost-efficient manufacturing techniques is of the highest priority for civilian business and would be neglected if resources go to military projects, which do not emphasize cost efficiency.
(B) Scientific and engineering talent needed by civilian business will be absorbed by the large-scale project.
(C) Many civilian businesses will receive subcontracts to provide materials and products needed by the research project.
(D) If government research money is devoted to the space project, it will not be available for specifically targeted needs of civilian business, where it could be more efficiently used.
(E) The increase in taxes or government debt needed to finance the project will severely reduce the vitality of the civilian economy.

Choice C describes a benefit to civilian business of the research project, and therefore provides support to the conclusion that the project will represent a net benefit to civilian business, rather than arguing against that conclusion. Choice C is therefore the best answer.

Each of the other choices presents a disadvantage of the project for civilian business that might outweigh the stated benefit, so none is correct. Cost efficiency, vital to civilian business, would be neglected (choice A); technical talent needed by civilian business would be unavailable (choice B); the government funding could be used more efficiently if directed specifically to the needs of civilian business (choice D); and the burden of financing the project would hamper civilian business (choice E).

112. In an attempt to promote the widespread use of paper rather than plastic, and thus reduce nonbiodegradable waste, the council of a small town plans to ban the sale of disposable plastic goods for which substitutes made of paper exist. The council argues that since most paper is entirely biodegradable, paper goods are environmentally preferable.

Which of the following, if true, indicates that the plan to ban the sale of disposable plastic goods is ill suited to the town council's environmental goals?

(A) Although biodegradable plastic goods are now available, members of the town council believe biodegradable paper goods to be safer for the environment.

(B) The paper factory at which most of the townspeople are employed plans to increase production of biodegradable paper goods.

(C) After other towns enacted similar bans on the sale of plastic goods, the environmental benefits were not discernible for several years.

(D) Since most townspeople prefer plastic goods to paper goods in many instances, they are likely to purchase them in neighboring towns where plastic goods are available for sale.

(E) Products other than those derived from wood pulp are often used in the manufacture of paper goods that are entirely biodegradable.

If choice D is true, townspeople are likely to circumvent the local ban by purchasing disposable plastic goods in neighboring towns. The ban is thus likely to be largely ineffectual. Choice D is therefore the best answer.

None of choices A, B, C, or E indicates that the ban is ill chosen as a means of reaching the town council's environmental goals. Choice A indicates that the town council's basic criterion is avoidance of harm to the environment, not merely biodegradability. Choice B does nothing to call the ban into question, whether or not the factory sells biodegradable paper goods locally. Choice C suggests that environmental benefits would ensue, albeit not immediately. Choice E merely provides background details about paper that is completely biodegradable.

113. Since the deregulation of airlines, delays at the nation's increasingly busy airports have increased by 25 percent. To combat this problem, more of the takeoff and landing slots at the busiest airports must be allocated to commercial airlines.

Which of the following, if true, casts the most doubt on the effectiveness of the solution proposed above?

(A) The major causes of delays at the nation's busiest airports are bad weather and overtaxed air traffic control equipment.

(B) Since airline deregulation began, the number of airplanes in operation has increased by 25 percent.

(C) Over 60 percent of the takeoff and landing slots at the nation's busiest airports are reserved for commercial airlines.

(D) After a small midwestern airport doubled its allocation of takeoff and landing slots, the number of delays that were reported decreased by 50 percent.

(E) Since deregulation the average length of delay at the nation's busiest airports has doubled.

The passage presents a problem—delays at airports—and proposes a solution—allocating more slots to commercial airlines. Choice A states, however, that the major causes of the delays lie elsewhere, thereby casting doubt on the effectiveness of the proposed solution, and is thus the best answer.

None of the other choices gives any reason to think that allocating slots will not be an effective solution. Choice B describes another part of the problem, but says nothing about who uses the additional airplanes. Choice C implies that at least some slots are available to be allocated to commercial airlines. Choice D gives one example where allocation was in fact successful, and choice E gives additional information about the scope of the problem.

114. The more frequently employees take time to exercise during working hours each week, the fewer sick days they take. Even employees who exercise only once a week during working hours take less sick time than those who do not exercise. Therefore, if companies started fitness programs, the absentee rate in those companies would decrease significantly.

Which of the following, if true, most seriously weakens the argument above?

(A) Employees who exercise during working hours occasionally fall asleep for short periods of time after they exercise.
(B) Employees who are frequently absent are the least likely to cooperate with or to join a corporate fitness program.
(C) Employees who exercise only once a week in their company's fitness program usually also exercise after work.
(D) Employees who exercise in their company's fitness program use their working time no more productively than those who do not exercise.
(E) Employees who exercise during working hours take slightly longer lunch breaks than employees who do not exercise.

Even supposing that increasing the frequency of exercise leads to less sick time being taken, starting a company-supported fitness program might not produce significantly lowered absentee rates if employees who are frequently absent would not cooperate with such a program. Choice B says that such cooperation is unlikely and is the best answer.

Choices A and E suggest that exercise during working hours has undesirable consequences, and choice D indicates that such exercise fails to produce an added benefit, but none of these bears on sick time taken. Choice C concerns exercise done after work by employees participating in a fitness program, but provides no indication of the effect, if any, of that exercise on sick time taken.

115. Many people argue that tobacco advertising plays a crucial role in causing teen-agers to start or continue smoking. In Norway, however, where there has been a ban on tobacco advertising since 1975, smoking is at least as prevalent among teen-agers as it is in countries that do not ban such advertising.

Which of the following statements draws the most reliable conclusion from the information above?

(A) Tobacco advertising cannot be the only factor that affects the prevalence of smoking among teen-agers.
(B) Advertising does not play a role in causing teen-agers to start or continue smoking.
(C) Banning tobacco advertising does not reduce the consumption of tobacco.
(D) More teen-agers smoke if they are not exposed to tobacco advertising than if they are.
(E) Most teen-agers who smoked in 1975 did not stop when the ban on tobacco advertising was implemented.

If tobacco advertising were the only factor that affected teenage smoking, there would be a difference in the prevalence of smoking between countries that ban such advertising and those that do not. According to the passage, there is no difference, so tobacco advertising cannot be the only factor. Therefore, choice A is the best answer.

Since no information is given about what effect, if any, the Norwegian ban on tobacco advertising had on teenage smoking in Norway, none of choices B through E can be concluded, since each makes some claim about the effects of tobacco advertising, or of banning such advertising, on teenage smoking or on tobacco consumption.

116. Laws requiring the use of headlights during daylight hours can prevent automobile collisions. However, since daylight visibility is worse in countries farther from the equator, any such laws would obviously be more effective in preventing collisions in those countries. In fact, the only countries that actually have such laws are farther from the equator than is the continental United States.

Which of the following conclusions could be most properly drawn from the information given above?

(A) Drivers in the continental United States who used their headlights during the day would be just as likely to become involved in a collision as would drivers who did not use their headlights.

(B) In many countries that are farther from the equator than is the continental United States poor daylight visibility is the single most important factor in automobile collisions.

(C) The proportion of automobile collisions that occur in the daytime is greater in the continental United States than in the countries that have daytime headlight laws.

(D) Fewer automobile collisions probably occur each year in countries that have daytime headlight laws than occur within the continental United States.

(E) Daytime headlight laws would probably do less to prevent automobile collisions in the continental United States than they do in the countries that have the laws.

Since the laws are more effective in countries farther from the equator than the United States, the laws would probably do less to prevent collisions in the United States than they do in the countries that now have such laws—countries that are all farther from the equator than the United States. So choice E is the best answer.

The passage does not indicate that the use of headlights during the day is totally ineffective, so choice A is incorrect. No information is given about the importance of daylight visibility relative to other causes of collisions, so choice B is incorrect. The passage contains no quantitative information for comparing the United States to countries that have the laws, so neither C nor D is correct.

117. A company's two divisions performed with remarkable consistency over the past three years: in each of those years, the pharmaceuticals division has accounted for roughly 20 percent of dollar sales and 40 percent of profits, and the chemicals division for the balance.

Which of the following can properly be inferred regarding the past three years from the statement above?

(A) Total dollar sales for each of the company's divisions have remained roughly constant.

(B) The pharmaceuticals division has faced stiffer competition in its markets than has the chemicals division.

(C) The chemicals division has realized lower profits per dollar of sales than has the pharmaceuticals division.

(D) The product mix offered by each of the company's divisions has remained unchanged.

(E) Highly profitable products accounted for a higher percentage of the chemicals division's sales than of those of the pharmaceuticals division.

The pharmaceuticals division made 40 percent of the profits on only 20 percent of the sales, while the chemicals division, making up the balance, made 60 percent of the profits on 80 percent of the sales. Thus, the chemicals division made a lower profit per dollar of sale than the pharmaceuticals division, as choice C asserts. Choice C is the best answer.

The passage provides no information about total dollar sales, so choice A is incorrect, nor about the severity of competition, so choice B is incorrect. Similarly, no information is provided about the mix of products offered, nor about the breakdown between highly profitable and not highly profitable products in either division, so neither choice D nor choice E is correct.

118. According to a review of 61 studies of patients suffering from severely debilitating depression, a large majority of the patients reported that missing a night's sleep immediately lifted their depression. Yet sleep-deprivation is not used to treat depression even though the conventional treatments, which use drugs and electric shocks, often have serious side effects.

Which of the following, if true, best explains the fact that sleep-deprivation is not used as a treatment for depression?

(A) For a small percentage of depressed patients, missing a night's sleep induces a temporary sense of euphoria.

(B) Keeping depressed patients awake is more difficult than keeping awake people who are not depressed.

(C) Prolonged loss of sleep can lead to temporary impairment of judgment comparable to that induced by consuming several ounces of alcohol.

(D) The dramatic shifts in mood connected with sleep and wakefulness have not been traced to particular changes in brain chemistry.

(E) Depression returns in full force as soon as the patient sleeps for even a few minutes.

The more severely sleep-deprived a patient would be, the more likely it would be that the patient would, whenever possible, catch at least a few minutes of sleep, and according to choice E, depression would then return in full force. This could explain why sleep-deprivation is not used to treat depression, so choice E is the best answer.

If sleep-deprivation could be used as an effective treatment for severely debilitating depression, the benefit derived would be so great that the occasional extra benefit of euphoria (choice A), the need for expending some extra effort (choice B), the occasional drawback of impaired judgment (choice C), and the lack of thorough scientific understanding (choice D) would each be a comparatively insignificant consideration.

Questions 119-120 are based on the following.

According to the Tristate Transportation Authority, making certain improvements to the main commuter rail line would increase ridership dramatically. The authority plans to finance these improvements over the course of five years by raising automobile tolls on the two highway bridges along the route the rail line serves. Although the proposed improvements are indeed needed, the authority's plan for securing the necessary funds should be rejected because it would unfairly force drivers to absorb the entire cost of something from which they receive no benefit.

119. Which of the following, if true, would cast the most doubt on the effectiveness of the authority's plan to finance the proposed improvements by increasing bridge tolls?

(A) Before the authority increases tolls on any of the area bridges, it is required by law to hold public hearings at which objections to the proposed increase can be raised.

(B) Whenever bridge tolls are increased, the authority must pay a private contractor to adjust the automated toll-collecting machines.

(C) Between the time a proposed toll increase is announced and the time the increase is actually put into effect, many commuters buy more tokens than usual to postpone the effects of the increase.

(D) When tolls were last increased on the two bridges in question, almost 20 percent of the regular commuter traffic switched to a slightly longer alternative route that has since been improved.

(E) The chairman of the authority is a member of the Tristate Automobile Club that has registered strong opposition to the proposed toll increase.

Increasing bridge tolls might not increase revenues if such increases prompt a significant percentage of regular bridge users to switch to alternative routes. Choice D says that a previous increase prompted such switches. Choice D, by establishing a strong precedent for commuters' responding to higher tolls by avoiding them altogether, raises doubts about the plan's effectiveness and is thus the best answer.

Choices A and E suggest that the plan might face opposition but not that it will be defeated nor that the anticipated revenue will not be generated. Therefore neither A nor E is correct. Weighed against five years' projected revenues, the considerations raised in choices B and C would not have a significant impact. Thus neither B nor C is correct.

120. Which of the following, if true, would provide the authority with the strongest counter to the objection that its plan is unfair?

(A) Even with the proposed toll increase, the average bridge toll in the tristate region would remain less than the tolls charged in neighboring states.

(B) Any attempt to finance the improvements by raising rail fares would result in a decrease in ridership and so would be self-defeating.

(C) Automobile commuters benefit from well-maintained bridges, and in the tristate region bridge maintenance is funded out of general income tax revenues to which both automobile and rail commuters contribute.

(D) The roads along the route served by the rail line are highly congested and drivers benefit when commuters are diverted from congested roadways to mass transit.

(E) The only alternative way of funding the proposed improvements now being considered is through a regional income tax surcharge, which would affect automobile commuters and rail commuters alike.

The plan is called unfair because it forces drivers to pay for something from which they receive no benefit. Choice D, however, claims that drivers would receive a benefit: a decrease in traffic congestion on the roads along the rail line. Choice D thereby strongly counters the charge of unfairness and is thus the best answer.

The charge of unfairness is not countered by indicating that the amounts involved are relatively low (choice A), or that a seemingly fair funding alternative is unworkable (choice B). Income tax funding as described in choices C and E might be viewed as less unfair than the proposed funding from bridge tolls, but it gives no reason for regarding the bridge tolls as anything but unfair.

121. Manufacturers sometimes discount the price of a product to retailers for a promotion period when the product is advertised to consumers. Such promotions often result in a dramatic increase in amount of product sold by the manufacturers to retailers. Nevertheless, the manufacturers could often make more profit by not holding the promotions.

Which of the following, if true, most strongly supports the claim above about the manufacturers' profit?

(A) The amount of discount generally offered by manufacturers to retailers is carefully calculated to represent the minimum needed to draw consumers' attention to the product.

(B) For many consumer products the period of advertising discounted prices to consumers is about a week, not sufficiently long for consumers to become used to the sale price.

(C) For products that are not newly introduced, the purpose of such promotions is to keep the products in the minds of consumers and to attract consumers who are currently using competing products.

(D) During such a promotion retailers tend to accumulate in their warehouses inventory bought at discount; they then sell much of it later at their regular price.

(E) If a manufacturer fails to offer such promotions but its competitor offers them, that competitor will tend to attract consumers away from the manufacturer's product.

Choice D indicates that during promotions retailers buy much greater quantities of products at discounted prices than they in turn sell to consumers during those promotions. There is, then, much merchandise that retailers sell at their regular price on which the manufacturers, however, do not realize normal profits. Since this loss of normal profits might outweigh the benefits of attracting new consumers during the promotion period, the manufacturers might be better off not holding the promotions. Choice D is, therefore, the best answer.

Attracting consumers' attention (choice A), noninterference with sales at regular, nonpromotional prices (choice B), and attracting and holding customers (choices C and E) are all features of promotions compatible with manufacturers making high profits, so none of these choices is correct.

122. When people evade income taxes by not declaring taxable income, a vicious cycle results. Tax evasion forces lawmakers to raise income tax rates, which causes the tax burden on nonevading taxpayers to become heavier. This, in turn, encourages even more taxpayers to evade income taxes by hiding taxable income.

The vicious cycle described above could not result unless which of the following were true?

(A) An increase in tax rates tends to function as an incentive for taxpayers to try to increase their pretax incomes.

(B) Some methods for detecting tax evaders, and thus recovering some tax revenue lost through evasion, bring in more than they cost, but their success rate varies from year to year.

(C) When lawmakers establish income tax rates in order to generate a certain level of revenue, they do not allow adequately for revenue that will be lost through evasion.

(D) No one who routinely hides some taxable income can be induced by a lowering of tax rates to stop hiding such income unless fines for evaders are raised at the same time.

(E) Taxpayers do not differ from each other with respect to the rate of taxation that will cause them to evade taxes.

For tax evasion to force a raise in income tax rates it must be true that tax evasion causes actual tax revenues to fall short of revenue needs. This is the situation that choice C describes; choice C is therefore the best answer.

None of the other choices states a requirement for the vicious cycle to result. Increases in pretax incomes (choice A) would tend to work against perpetuation of the cycle. Success at catching tax evaders (choice B) should likewise have an inhibiting effect. Choice D describes how problems in breaking existing habits of tax evasion might be overcome. Choice E essentially denies that raising the tax rate in response to some tax evasion could cause additional taxpayers to evade taxes.

123. Advertisement: Today's customers expect high quality. Every advance in the quality of manufactured products raises customer expectations. The company that is satisfied with the current quality of its products will soon find that its customers are not. At MegaCorp, meeting or exceeding customer expectations is our goal.

Which of the following must be true on the basis of the statements in the advertisement above?

(A) MegaCorp's competitors will succeed in attracting customers only if those competitors adopt MegaCorp's goal as their own.

(B) A company that does not correctly anticipate the expectations of its customers is certain to fail in advancing the quality of its products.

(C) MegaCorp's goal is possible to meet only if continuing advances in product quality are possible.

(D) If a company becomes satisfied with the quality of its products, then the quality of its products is sure to decline.

(E) MegaCorp's customers are currently satisfied with the quality of its products.

MegaCorp wishes to at least meet customer expectations. Since these expectations will always tend to move beyond whatever level of quality MegaCorp happens to have attained, MegaCorp will, as choice C indicates, be able to meet its goal only if continuing improvements in the quality of its products are possible. Choice C is thus the best answer.

Choice A is incorrect since success in attracting customers depends only on actual product quality, not on a company's goals regarding quality. Since quality improvements can themselves shape customer expectations, choice B is incorrect. Since nothing has been said to indicate a difficulty with maintaining a given level of product quality, choice D is incorrect. Since having a goal does not imply meeting it, choice E is incorrect.

124. The local board of education found that, because the current physics curriculum has little direct relevance to today's world, physics classes attracted few high school students. So to attract students to physics classes, the board proposed a curriculum that emphasizes principles of physics involved in producing and analyzing visual images.

Which of the following, if true, provides the strongest reason to expect that the proposed curriculum will be successful in attracting students?

(A) Several of the fundamental principles of physics are involved in producing and analyzing visual images.
(B) Knowledge of physics is becoming increasingly important in understanding the technology used in today's world.
(C) Equipment that a large producer of photographic equipment has donated to the high school could be used in the proposed curriculum.
(D) The number of students interested in physics today is much lower than the number of students interested in physics 50 years ago.
(E) In today's world the production and analysis of visual images is of major importance in communications, business, and recreation.

For the proposed curriculum change to attract students to physics classes, producing and analyzing visual images must have direct relevance to today's world. Choice E provides evidence that this is so, and thus is the best answer.

Choices A and C mention things relevant to the new curriculum: that it would indeed teach physics and that equipment facilitating its implementation is available. Choice B underscores how desirable it would be for the new curriculum to succeed, and choice D establishes that there is past precedent that more students can be attracted to physics. Not one of choices A, B, C, or D, however, indicates why the new curriculum would be thought to be attractive to students, so none of them is correct.

125. Unlike the wholesale price of raw wool, the wholesale price of raw cotton has fallen considerably in the last year. Thus, although the retail price of cotton clothing at retail clothing stores has not yet fallen, it will inevitably fall.

Which of the following, if true, most seriously weakens the argument above?

(A) The cost of processing raw cotton for cloth has increased during the last year.
(B) The wholesale price of raw wool is typically higher than that of the same volume of raw cotton.
(C) The operating costs of the average retail clothing store have remained constant during the last year.
(D) Changes in retail prices always lag behind changes in wholesale prices.
(E) The cost of harvesting raw cotton has increased in the last year.

The argument concludes that declining wholesale prices for raw cotton, will produce declining retail prices for cotton products. Choice A weakens the argument by pointing to higher processing costs for raw cotton, which could offset lower wholesale prices. A is therefore the best answer.

Choice B is incorrect because the argument focuses on price changes, not on relative price levels. Choice C is incorrect because it in effect denies that lower wholesale prices for cotton have been offset by rising operating costs. Choice D is incorrect because it is entirely consistent with the prediction made. Choice E is incorrect because the rising cost of harvesting raw cotton, though possibly affecting wholesale prices, cannot affect the relationship between wholesale and retail prices.

126. Many companies now have employee assistance programs that enable employees, free of charge, to improve their physical fitness, reduce stress, and learn ways to stop smoking. These programs increase worker productivity, reduce absenteeism, and lessen insurance costs for employee health care. Therefore, these programs benefit the company as well as the employee.

Which of the following, if true, most significantly strengthens the conclusion above?

(A) Physical fitness programs are often the most popular services offered to employees.
(B) Studies have shown that training in stress management is not effective for many people.
(C) Regular exercise reduces people's risk of heart disease and provides them with increased energy.
(D) Physical injuries sometimes result from entering a strenuous physical fitness program too quickly.
(E) Employee assistance programs require companies to hire people to supervise the various programs offered.

The conclusion is that the programs benefit both companies and employees. For companies, reducing employees' risk of heart disease is likely to reduce insurance costs, and increasing employee energy is likely to increase worker productivity. For employees, the benefits of having a reduced risk of heart disease and of having increased energy are self-evident. Choice C is the best answer.

Knowing which programs are popular does not bear on what benefits the programs confer, so choice A is incorrect. B and D indicate ways in which the programs can fail to provide the intended results, so neither of these is the correct answer. Having to hire additional personnel does not benefit a company, so choice E is not correct.

127. Small-business groups are lobbying to defeat proposed federal legislation that would substantially raise the federal minimum wage. This opposition is surprising since the legislation they oppose would, for the first time, exempt all small businesses from paying any minimum wage.

Which of the following, if true, would best explain the opposition of small-business groups to the proposed legislation?

(A) Under the current federal minimum-wage law, most small businesses are required to pay no less than the minimum wage to their employees.
(B) In order to attract workers, small companies must match the wages offered by their larger competitors, and these competitors would not be exempt under the proposed laws.
(C) The exact number of companies that are currently required to pay no less than the minimum wage but that would be exempt under the proposed laws is unknown.
(D) Some states have set their own minimum wages— in some cases, quite a bit above the level of the minimum wage mandated by current federal law—for certain key industries.
(E) Service companies make up the majority of small businesses and they generally employ more employees per dollar of revenues than do retail or manufacturing businesses.

The opposition of small-business groups despite an exemption apparently favoring them would be less surprising if, in fact, the exemption did not favor them. Choice B is thus the best answer because it explains that small businesses would have to match the higher wages that larger businesses are required to pay.

Choice A confirms that the new exemption constitutes a significant change but does not explain small-business opposition to that change, so choice A is incorrect. Choice C is incorrect because the exact numbers represented by the small-business groups are surely irrelevant. Choice D suggests that in some states the proposed legislation would make no difference, and choice E suggests that most small businesses should value the exemption. Neither choice explains small-business opposition.

128. Reviewer: The book *Art's Decline* argues that European painters today lack skills that were common among European painters of preceding centuries. In this the book must be right, since its analysis of 100 paintings, 50 old and 50 contemporary, demonstrates convincingly that none of the contemporary paintings are executed as skillfully as the older paintings.

Which of the following points to the most serious logical flaw in the reviewer's argument?

(A) The paintings chosen by the book's author for analysis could be those that most support the book's thesis.
(B) There could be criteria other than the technical skill of the artist by which to evaluate a painting.
(C) The title of the book could cause readers to accept the book's thesis even before they read the analysis of the paintings that supports it.
(D) The particular methods currently used by European painters could require less artistic skill than do methods used by painters in other parts of the world.
(E) A reader who was not familiar with the language of art criticism might not be convinced by the book's analysis of the 100 paintings.

Because the number of old and contemporary paintings vastly exceeds the 50 of each type analyzed by *Art's Decline*, the reviewer's argument will be logically flawed if those 100 paintings do not constitute a reasonably representative sample. Choice A says that the sample might be grossly biased, so A is the best answer.

Choices B and D are both incorrect because a sharply defined focus is not a flaw in an argument; the reviewer makes clear that only artistic skill and only European painters are being considered. The reviewer's argument that the book supports its central thesis well is not weakened just because there may be readers less methodical and less competent than the reviewer. Therefore, neither C nor E is correct.

129. The pharmaceutical industry argues that because new drugs will not be developed unless heavy development costs can be recouped in later sales, the current 20 years of protection provided by patents should be extended in the case of newly developed drugs. However, in other industries new-product development continues despite high development costs, a fact that indicates that the extension is unnecessary.

Which of the following, if true, most strongly supports the pharmaceutical industry's argument against the challenge made above?

(A) No industries other than the pharmaceutical industry have asked for an extension of the 20-year limit on patent protection.

(B) Clinical trials of new drugs, which occur after the patent is granted and before the new drug can be marketed, often now take as long as 10 years to complete.

(C) There are several industries in which the ratio of research and development costs to revenues is higher than it is in the pharmaceutical industry.

(D) An existing patent for a drug does not legally prevent pharmaceutical companies from bringing to market alternative drugs, provided they are sufficiently dissimilar to the patented drug.

(E) Much recent industrial innovation has occurred in products—for example, in the computer and electronics industries—for which patent protection is often very ineffective.

The pharmaceutical industry's argument is best supported by an explanation of why the patent period sufficient for other industries to recoup their development costs is insufficient for the pharmaceutical industry. Choice B is the best answer because it provides an explanation: required clinical trials prevent new drugs from being sold for much of the time they receive patent protection.

Choice A is incorrect: the fact that the pharmaceutical industry's request is unique does nothing to justify that request. Choices C and E, if true, could undermine the pharmaceutical industry's argument, so they are incorrect. Choice D indicates that alternative drugs might render patent protection worthless, but that is clearly no reason to extend the protection.

Questions 130-131 are based on the following.

Bank depositors in the United States are all financially protected against bank failure because the government insures all individuals' bank deposits. An economist argues that this insurance is partly responsible for the high rate of bank failures, since it removes from depositors any financial incentive to find out whether the bank that holds their money is secure against failure. If depositors were more selective, then banks would need to be secure in order to compete for depositors' money.

130. The economist's argument makes which of the following assumptions?

(A) Bank failures are caused when big borrowers default on loan repayments.

(B) A significant proportion of depositors maintain accounts at several different banks.

(C) The more a depositor has to deposit, the more careful he or she tends to be in selecting a bank.

(D) The difference in the interest rates paid to depositors by different banks is not a significant factor in bank failures.

(E) Potential depositors are able to determine which banks are secure against failure.

Giving potential depositors a financial incentive to select only secure banks will not lead to increased bank security unless the potential depositors can distinguish banks that actually are secure from those that are not. Choice E is a statement of this prerequisite and is thus the best answer.

The argument is about choosing or avoiding banks likely to fail, regardless of how the failure comes about, so neither choice A nor choice D is specifically assumed. The argument is consistent with each depositor's money being held by a single bank, so B is not assumed. The argument neither asserts nor assumes that depositors currently exercise care in selecting the banks where they deposit their money. Therefore choice C, in particular, is not assumed.

131. Which of the following, if true, most seriously weakens the economist's argument?

(A) Before the government started to insure depositors against bank failure, there was a lower rate of bank failure than there is now.

(B) When the government did not insure deposits, frequent bank failures occurred as a result of depositors' fears of losing money in bank failures.

(C) Surveys show that a significant proportion of depositors are aware that their deposits are insured by the government.

(D) There is an upper limit on the amount of an individual's deposit that the government will insure, but very few individuals' deposits exceed this limit.

(E) The security of a bank against failure depends on the percentage of its assets that are loaned out and also on how much risk its loans involve.

The argument that deposit insurance, because of its impact on depositors' choice of banks, is partially responsible for the high rate of bank failures would be weakened if deposit insurance also prevented certain bank failures. Choice B suggests that deposit insurance does prevent certain bank failures, and is thus the best answer.

Choice A weakly supports the view that insuring deposits contributes to bank failures. Choice C supports the economist's position that depositors take the safety of deposits into account. Choice D supports the argument's relevance by indicating that virtually all depositors can afford to be nonselective. It follows that none of these three choices is correct. Choice E is incorrect because it fails to establish any connection between deposit insurance and the factors controlling bank failures.

132. Passengers must exit airplanes swiftly after accidents, since gases released following accidents are toxic to humans and often explode soon after being released. In order to prevent passenger deaths from gas inhalation, safety officials recommend that passengers be provided with smoke hoods that prevent inhalation of the gases.

Which of the following, if true, constitutes the strongest reason <u>not</u> to require implementation of the safety officials' recommendation?

(A) Test evacuations showed that putting on the smoke hoods added considerably to the overall time it took passengers to leave the cabin.

(B) Some airlines are unwilling to buy the smoke hoods because they consider them to be prohibitively expensive.

(C) Although the smoke hoods protect passengers from the toxic gases, they can do nothing to prevent the gases from igniting.

(D) Some experienced flyers fail to pay attention to the safety instructions given on every commercial flight before takeoff.

(E) In many airplane accidents, passengers who were able to reach emergency exits were overcome by toxic gases before they could exit the airplane.

A strong reason for rejecting the recommendation would be that the hoods endanger passengers. Passengers delayed in exiting the plane are more exposed to the risk of a gas explosion. Choice A says that the hoods would delay passengers and is thus the best answer.

If some airlines are unwilling to buy the hoods, it might be necessary to require them to, so B is incorrect. That the hoods protect from only one major risk is no reason in itself for rejection, so C is not correct. That some passengers ignore safety instructions is also no reason for rejection, so D is incorrect. Choice E is not a good answer; it supports the recommendation by indicating that the hoods might enable more passengers to exit a plane.

133. In 1960, 10 percent of every dollar paid in automobile insurance premiums went to pay costs arising from injuries incurred in car accidents. In 1990, 50 percent of every dollar paid in automobile insurance premiums went toward such costs, despite the fact that cars were much safer in 1990 than in 1960.

Which of the following, if true, best explains the discrepancy outlined above?

(A) There were fewer accidents in 1990 than in 1960.

(B) On average, people drove more slowly in 1990 than in 1960.

(C) Cars grew increasingly more expensive to repair over the period in question.

(D) The price of insurance increased more rapidly than the rate of inflation between 1960 and 1990.

(E) Health-care costs rose sharply between 1960 and 1990.

If cars were safer in 1990 than in 1960, car accidents should have resulted in fewer and in less severe injuries. Yet coverage of injuries took up a greater share of insurance premiums. One possible explanation is that the treatment cost per injury rose sharply. Choice E supports this explanation and is thus the best answer.

Choices A and B both suggest that the number of injuries decreased. Since such a decrease would not explain why injuries take up a greater share of insurance premiums, both of these choices are incorrect. Choice C is incorrect because it suggests, falsely, that costs not related to injuries rose disproportionately. Choice D is incorrect because it does not deal with shifts in the cost components that insurance premiums cover.

134. Caterpillars of all species produce an identical hormone called "juvenile hormone" that maintains feeding behavior. Only when a caterpillar has grown to the right size for pupation to take place does a special enzyme halt the production of juvenile hormone. This enzyme can be synthesized and will, on being ingested by immature caterpillars, kill them by stopping them from feeding.

Which of the following, if true, most strongly supports the view that it would <u>not</u> be advisable to try to eradicate agricultural pests that go through a caterpillar stage by spraying croplands with the enzyme mentioned above?

(A) Most species of caterpillar are subject to some natural predation.

(B) Many agricultural pests do not go through a caterpillar stage.

(C) Many agriculturally beneficial insects go through a caterpillar stage.

(D) Since caterpillars of different species emerge at different times, several sprayings would be necessary.

(E) Although the enzyme has been synthesized in the laboratory, no large-scale production facilities exist as yet.

Since the enzyme kills caterpillars of all species, spraying croplands might not be advisable if caterpillars of beneficial insect species would also be killed. According to choice C, there are many such beneficial species. Choice C thus supports the view that spraying would be inadvisable and is the best answer.

Choice A is incorrect because spraying, if effective, would make natural predation irrelevant. Choice B is incorrect because the existence of pests that the spraying is not intended to control does not make the spraying inadvisable. Choices D and E each raise a point concerning details of how and when spraying programs might be implemented, without challenging the advisability of such programs. Both choices are therefore incorrect.

135. Although aspirin has been proven to eliminate moderate fever associated with some illnesses, many doctors no longer routinely recommend its use for this purpose. A moderate fever stimulates the activity of the body's disease-fighting white blood cells and also inhibits the growth of many strains of disease-causing bacteria.

If the statements above are true, which of the following conclusions is most strongly supported by them?

(A) Aspirin, an effective painkiller, alleviates the pain and discomfort of many illnesses.

(B) Aspirin can prolong a patient's illness by eliminating moderate fever helpful in fighting some diseases.

(C) Aspirin inhibits the growth of white blood cells, which are necessary for fighting some illnesses.

(D) The more white blood cells a patient's body produces, the less severe the patient's illness will be.

(E) The focus of modern medicine is on inhibiting the growth of disease-causing bacteria within the body.

By stimulating disease-fighting white blood cells and inhibiting the growth of disease-causing bacteria, moderate fever can aid the body in fighting infection. However, aspirin can eliminate moderate fever. Thus, as choice B states, aspirin can prolong a patient's illness by eliminating moderate fever and thereby also eliminating its disease-fighting effects. B is the best answer.

Choice A is not the correct answer because no mention is made of aspirin's role as a painkiller. The passage also says nothing about aspirin's effect on the growth or production of white blood cells, mentioning only its effect on their activity, so neither C nor D is correct. Because the statements given could be true regardless of the focus of modern medicine, E is also incorrect.

136. Because postage rates are rising, *Home Decorator* magazine plans to maximize its profits by reducing by one-half the number of issues it publishes each year. The quality of articles, the number of articles published per year, and the subscription price will not change. Market research shows that neither subscribers nor advertisers will be lost if the magazine's plan is instituted.

Which of the following, if true, provides the strongest evidence that the magazine's profits are likely to decline if the plan is instituted?

(A) With the new postage rates, a typical issue under the proposed plan would cost about one-third more to mail than a typical current issue would.

(B) The majority of the magazine's subscribers are less concerned about a possible reduction in the quantity of the magazine's articles than about a possible loss of the current high quality of its articles.

(C) Many of the magazine's long-time subscribers would continue their subscriptions even if the subscription price were increased.

(D) Most of the advertisers that purchase advertising space in the magazine will continue to spend the same amount on advertising per issue as they have in the past.

(E) Production costs for the magazine are expected to remain stable.

Home Decorator magazine's profits would be likely to decline if, as a result of instituting the plan, revenues were to decrease substantially. Choice D indicates that the plan would produce substantially lower revenues because most advertisers will pay the magazine the same amount per issue, but there will be only half as many issues. Therefore, D is the best answer.

Choice A notes that mailing costs per issue will rise by one-third, but since there will be fewer issues, total annual mailing costs will fall. Therefore, A is incorrect. Choices B and C are incorrect because neither describes concerns that subscribers have about the plan under consideration. Choice E is incorrect because stable production costs would not lead to lower profits.

137. A study of marital relationships in which one partner's sleeping and waking cycles differ from those of the other partner reveals that such couples share fewer activities with each other and have more violent arguments than do couples in a relationship in which both partners follow the same sleeping and waking patterns. Thus, mismatched sleeping and waking cycles can seriously jeopardize a marriage.

Which of the following, if true, most seriously weakens the argument above?

(A) Married couples in which both spouses follow the same sleeping and waking patterns also occasionally have arguments that can jeopardize the couple's marriage.

(B) The sleeping and waking cycles of individuals tend to vary from season to season.

(C) The individuals who have sleeping and waking cycles that differ significantly from those of their spouses tend to argue little with colleagues at work.

(D) People in unhappy marriages have been found to express hostility by adopting a different sleeping and waking cycle from that of their spouses.

(E) According to a recent study, most people's sleeping and waking cycles can be controlled and modified easily.

The argument assumes that mismatched sleeping and waking cycles precede marital problems. Choice D weakens the argument by indicating that this assumption is false, and D is the best answer.

The argument does not depend on there being only one cause of marital problems, so choice A is incorrect. That sleeping and waking cycles can change seasonally or might not affect interactions with colleagues does not address the issue of how mismatched cycles between spouses affect their marriage, so B and C are incorrect. Choice E suggests that there is a way to test the conclusion—by bringing a couple's sleeping and waking cycles into alignment—but this by itself does not weaken the argument, so E is incorrect.

Roland: The alarming fact is that 90 percent of the people in this country now report that they know someone who is unemployed.

Sharon: But a normal, moderate level of unemployment is 5 percent, with 1 out of 20 workers unemployed. So at any given time if a person knows approximately 50 workers, 1 or more will very likely be unemployed.

138. Sharon's argument is structured to lead to which of the following as a conclusion?

    (A) The fact that 90 percent of the people know someone who is unemployed is not an indication that unemployment is abnormally high.
    (B) The current level of unemployment is not moderate.
    (C) If at least 5 percent of workers are unemployed, the result of questioning a representative group of people cannot be the percentage Roland cites.
    (D) It is unlikely that the people whose statements Roland cites are giving accurate reports.
    (E) If an unemployment figure is given as a certain percent, the actual percentage of those without jobs is even higher.

Sharon's argument is essentially that, even if the facts are as Roland presents them, they are not in and of themselves a cause for alarm. Even circumstances reassuringly normal and unremarkable—a normal, moderate unemployment rate and having 50 or more workers among one's acquaintances—imply the sort of fact Roland cites. Thus, that fact does not indicate that things are not normal (for example, that unemployment is alarmingly high). Choice A, therefore, is the best answer.

Sharon's argument focuses exclusively on whether Roland's alarm is logically warranted, given the fact he cites. Sharon herself takes no position whatsoever on what the actual facts concerning unemployment statistics and concerning people's self-reports are. Because choices B, C, D, and E are assertions about such matters, each is incorrect.

139. Sharon's argument relies on the assumption that

    (A) normal levels of unemployment are rarely exceeded
    (B) unemployment is not normally concentrated in geographically isolated segments of the population
    (C) the number of people who each know someone who is unemployed is always higher than 90 percent of the population
    (D) Roland is not consciously distorting the statistics he presents
    (E) knowledge that a personal acquaintance is unemployed generates more fear of losing one's job than does knowledge of unemployment statistics

Sharon's argument assumes that people are generally similar in how likely they are to have among their acquaintances people who are unemployed. Since heavy concentrations of unemployment in geographically isolated segments of the population would produce great differences in this respect, Sharon's argument assumes few, if any, such concentrations. Choice B is therefore the best answer.

If normal levels of unemployment were exceeded relatively frequently, and if Roland's figure of 90 percent were an exaggeration, Sharon's argument would be unaffected, so choices A and D are incorrect. At exceptionally low levels of unemployment, Sharon's argument suggests that choice C is likely to be false, so C is not assumed. The fear of losing one's job is not part of Sharon's argument, so choice E is incorrect.

140. A report on acid rain concluded, "Most forests in Canada are not being damaged by acid rain." Critics of the report insist the conclusion be changed to, "Most forests in Canada do not show visible symptoms of damage by acid rain, such as abnormal loss of leaves, slower rates of growth, or higher mortality."

Which of the following, if true, provides the best logical justification for the critics' insistence that the report's conclusion be changed?

    (A) Some forests in Canada are being damaged by acid rain.
    (B) Acid rain could be causing damage for which symptoms have not yet become visible.
    (C) The report does not compare acid rain damage to Canadian forests with acid rain damage to forests in other countries.
    (D) All forests in Canada have received acid rain during the past fifteen years.
    (E) The severity of damage by acid rain differs from forest to forest.

If, as choice B says, acid rain damage could be occurring without there yet being any visible symptoms, the absence of visible symptoms would not justify the conclusion that no damage was occurring. Thus, choice B is the best answer since it justifies the critics' insistence that the conclusion be changed.

Because the authors of the report evidently resist the change being demanded, any claim on which they and their critics are likely to be in agreement cannot provide justification for the change. Choices A, C, D, and E are all claims both parties can agree on, so none of them is correct.

141. In the past most airline companies minimized aircraft weight to minimize fuel costs. The safest airline seats were heavy, and airlines equipped their planes with few of these seats. This year the seat that has sold best to airlines has been the safest one—a clear indication that airlines are assigning a higher priority to safe seating than to minimizing fuel costs.

Which of the following, if true, most seriously weakens the argument above?

(A) Last year's best-selling airline seat was not the safest airline seat on the market.
(B) No airline company has announced that it would be making safe seating a higher priority this year.
(C) The price of fuel was higher this year than it had been in most of the years when the safest airline seats sold poorly.
(D) Because of increases in the cost of materials, all airline seats were more expensive to manufacture this year than in any previous year.
(E) Because of technological innovations, the safest airline seat on the market this year weighed less than most other airline seats on the market.

If the safest airline seats are now among the lightest, as choice E says, then buying them could be part of a strategy of minimizing fuel costs, rather than indicating a shift away from that goal. Choice E, therefore, is the best answer.

Choice A merely confirms that seat safety has improved, and thus does not weaken the argument. Many policy shifts take place without being publicly announced, so choice B does not weaken the argument. Choice C indicates that minimizing fuel costs remains a priority, but it is neutral on whether safety has become more important, so C is incorrect. Choice D does not distinguish between safe and unsafe seats, and is thus also incorrect.

142. A computer equipped with signature-recognition software, which restricts access to a computer to those people whose signatures are on file, identifies a person's signature by analyzing not only the form of the signature but also such characteristics as pen pressure and signing speed. Even the most adept forgers cannot duplicate all of the characteristics the program analyzes.

Which of the following can be logically concluded from the passage above?

(A) The time it takes to record and analyze a signature makes the software impractical for everyday use.
(B) Computers equipped with the software will soon be installed in most banks.
(C) Nobody can gain access to a computer equipped with the software solely by virtue of skill at forging signatures.
(D) Signature-recognition software has taken many years to develop and perfect.
(E) In many cases even authorized users are denied legitimate access to computers equipped with the software.

The passage asserts that skill at forging signatures is not by itself sufficient to match all of the characteristics that the software analyzes to identify signatures. Because the software gives access only after identifying a signature, access cannot be achieved by someone employing forging skill alone. Choice C is thus the best answer.

The passage gives no information about how fast the software operates or about how long the software was under development, so neither A nor D can be concluded. Choice B is incorrect since the software might have features not mentioned in the passage that make it unattractive to banks. The passages give no reason to think that errors of the sort that choice E describes, even if made, would be numerous.

143. **Division manager:** I want to replace the Microton computers in my division with Vitech computers.

General manager: Why?

Division manager: It costs 28 percent less to train new staff on the Vitech.

General manager: But that is not a good enough reason. We can simply hire only people who already know how to use the Microton computer.

Which of the following, if true, most seriously undermines the general manager's objection to the replacement of Microton computers with Vitechs?

(A) Currently all employees in the company are required to attend workshops on how to use Microton computers in new applications.

(B) Once employees learn how to use a computer, they tend to change employers more readily than before.

(C) Experienced users of Microton computers command much higher salaries than do prospective employees who have no experience in the use of computers.

(D) The average productivity of employees in the general manager's company is below the average productivity of the employees of its competitors.

(E) The high costs of replacement parts make Vitech computers more expensive to maintain than Microton computers.

The general manager's objection is based on avoiding training costs altogether. But if, as choice C says, hiring experienced users of Microton computers is significantly more costly than hiring otherwise qualified people who would have to be trained to use Vitech computers, the force of the objection is weakened. Choice C, therefore, is the best answer.

Choices A, B, and D are all incorrect; none of them provides information relevant to an evaluation of Microton computers as compared with Vitech computers. Choice E argues independently against replacing Microton computers with Vitechs and thus is also incorrect.

144. An airplane engine manufacturer developed a new engine model with safety features lacking in the earlier model, which was still being manufactured. During the first year that both were sold, the earlier model far outsold the new model; the manufacturer thus concluded that safety was not the customers' primary consideration.

Which of the following, if true, would most seriously weaken the manufacturer's conclusion?

(A) Both private plane owners and commercial airlines buy engines from this airplane engine manufacturer.

(B) Many customers consider earlier engine models better safety risks than new engine models, since more is usually known about the safety of the earlier models.

(C) Many customers of this airplane engine manufacturer also bought airplane engines from manufacturers who did not provide additional safety features in their newer models.

(D) The newer engine model can be used in all planes in which the earlier engine model can be used.

(E) There was no significant difference in price between the newer engine model and the earlier engine model.

The manufacturer's conclusion would be weakened if it could be argued that, in the opinion of customers, safety considerations favor the earlier model. Choice B supports such an argument and is the best answer.

The groups mentioned in choice A would both be expected to consider safety important, so their failing to buy the new model would be striking, without casting doubt on the conclusion; thus, choice A is incorrect. Choice C might support the conclusion, because customers bought other engine models that might not include the newer safety features. Choices D and E suggest that usability and price, respectively, were not the customers' primary consideration in favoring the earlier model, but neither choice weakens the conclusion that safety was not their primary consideration.

145. Between 1975 and 1985, nursing-home occupancy rates averaged 87 percent of capacity, while admission rates remained constant, at an average of 95 admissions per 1,000 beds per year. Between 1985 and 1988, however, occupancy rates rose to an average of 92 percent of capacity, while admission rates declined to 81 per 1,000 beds per year.

If the statements above are true, which of the following conclusions can be most properly drawn?

(A) The average length of time nursing-home residents stayed in nursing homes increased between 1985 and 1988.
(B) The proportion of older people living in nursing homes was greater in 1988 than in 1975.
(C) Nursing home admission rates tend to decline whenever occupancy rates rise.
(D) Nursing homes built prior to 1985 generally had fewer beds than did nursing homes built between 1985 and 1988.
(E) The more beds a nursing home has, the higher its occupancy rate is likely to be.

Between 1985 and 1988, nursing home occupancy rates rose although admission rates declined. Choice A receives support from these facts since it would be a basis for an adequate account of how they arose. Because it is the only choice that receives support, A is therefore the best answer.

Without information about the total population of older people, nothing can be concluded about percentages in nursing homes; thus, choice B is incorrect. Since there is nothing to indicate whether the development that took place between 1985 and 1988 was an unusual development or a common one, choice C receives no support. No information about numbers of beds is provided, so neither choice D nor choice E is correct.

146. Firms adopting "profit-related-pay" (PRP) contracts pay wages at levels that vary with the firm's profits. In the metalworking industry last year, firms with PRP contracts in place showed productivity per worker on average 13 percent higher than that of their competitors who used more traditional contracts.

If, on the basis of the evidence above, it is argued that PRP contracts increase worker productivity, which of the following, if true, would most seriously weaken that argument?

(A) Results similar to those cited for the metalworking industry have been found in other industries where PRP contracts are used.
(B) Under PRP contracts costs other than labor costs, such as plant, machinery, and energy, make up an increased proportion of the total cost of each unit of output.
(C) Because introducing PRP contracts greatly changes individual workers' relationships to the firm, negotiating the introduction of PRP contracts is complex and time-consuming.
(D) Many firms in the metalworking industry have modernized production equipment in the last five years, and most of these introduced PRP contracts at the same time.
(E) In firms in the metalworking industry where PRP contracts are in place, the average take-home pay is 15 percent higher than it is in those firms where workers have more traditional contracts.

According to choice D, many firms with PRP contracts also have modernized equipment. Since the cause of their improved productivity might be the modernized equipment, not the PRP contracts, this weakens the argument, so D is the best answer.

Choice A does not weaken the argument: it is merely more evidence of the sort already being used. Choice B is incorrect because it is a natural consequence of increased worker productivity if other costs remain stable. Choice C is incorrect because it explains why introducing PRP contracts is difficult, but says nothing about the results of doing so. Choice E is incorrect because it is not implausible that workers' pay should roughly correspond to their productivity.

147. Crops can be traded on the futures market before they are harvested. If a poor corn harvest is predicted, prices of corn futures rise; if a bountiful corn harvest is predicted, prices of corn futures fall. This morning meteorologists are predicting much-needed rain for the corn-growing region starting tomorrow. Therefore, since adequate moisture is essential for the current crop's survival, prices of corn futures will fall sharply today.

Which of the following, if true, most weakens the argument above?

(A) Corn that does not receive adequate moisture during its critical pollination stage will not produce a bountiful harvest.

(B) Futures prices for corn have been fluctuating more dramatically this season than last season.

(C) The rain that meteorologists predicted for tomorrow is expected to extend well beyond the corn-growing region.

(D) Agriculture experts announced today that a disease that has devastated some of the corn crop will spread widely before the end of the growing season.

(E) Most people who trade in corn futures rarely take physical possession of the corn they trade.

The argument, in predicting a drop in the price of corn futures, relies on news suggesting a good-sized corn crop. This prediction is undermined if there is, at the same time, news suggesting a small crop. Choice D presents such news and is therefore the best answer.

Choice A provides background information describing a stage at which rains are essential, and choice C makes rain over the entire corn-growing area seem more certain. Both are fully compatible with the argument and do nothing to weaken it. Past price changes (choice B) and details of who handles harvested corn (choice E) cannot affect the eventual size of this year's corn crop, so neither is relevant to the argument.

148. A discount retailer of basic household necessities employs thousands of people and pays most of them at the minimum wage rate. Yet following a federally mandated increase of the minimum wage rate that increased the retailer's operating costs considerably, the retailer's profits increased markedly.

Which of the following, if true, most helps to resolve the apparent paradox?

(A) Over half of the retailer's operating costs consist of payroll expenditures; yet only a small percentage of those expenditures go to pay management salaries.

(B) The retailer's customer base is made up primarily of people who earn, or who depend on the earnings of others who earn, the minimum wage.

(C) The retailer's operating costs, other than wages, increased substantially after the increase in the minimum wage rate went into effect.

(D) When the increase in the minimum wage rate went into effect, the retailer also raised the wage rate for employees who had been earning just above minimum wage.

(E) The majority of the retailer's employees work as cashiers, and most cashiers are paid the minimum wage.

The question to be resolved is why the mandated wage increase, which increased operating costs, was accompanied by an increase in profits. By showing how the wage increase might have led to an increase in the retailer's sales, choice B helps resolve this question, and thus is the best answer.

Choices A and E are incorrect, since they suggest that the wages that rose as a result of the mandated increase constituted a significant proportion of the retailer's expenditures, which if anything adds to the seeming paradox. Choices C and D also contribute to the paradox, since they indicate that along with increases in the minimum wage there were increases in the retailer's operating costs; so choices C and D are also incorrect.

149. The cotton farms of Country Q became so productive that the market could not absorb all that they produced. Consequently, cotton prices fell. The government tried to boost cotton prices by offering farmers who took 25 percent of their cotton acreage out of production direct support payments up to a specified maximum per farm.

The government's program, if successful, will not be a net burden on the budget. Which of the following, if true, is the best basis for an explanation of how this could be so?

(A) Depressed cotton prices meant operating losses for cotton farms, and the government lost revenue from taxes on farm profits.

(B) Cotton production in several countries other than Q declined slightly the year that the support-payment program went into effect in Q.

(C) The first year that the support-payment program was in effect, cotton acreage in Q was 5 percent below its level in the base year for the program.

(D) The specified maximum per farm meant that for very large cotton farms the support payments were less per acre for those acres that were withdrawn from production than they were for smaller farms.

(E) Farmers who wished to qualify for support payments could not use the cotton acreage that was withdrawn from production to grow any other crop.

If the government's program of support payments to cotton farmers succeeded in raising revenue for the government that would, in the absence of the program, not be raised, this could explain why the program will not be a net burden on the budget. Choice A suggests that the program would raise revenue: by raising the price of cotton, the direct support payments will boost cotton farmers' profits and thereby increase the tax revenues the government receives from cotton farmers. Therefore, A is the best answer.

None of the other choices provides a source of revenue to the government or suggests that savings would be realized in a governmental expense category, so choices B, C, D, and E are all incorrect.

150. United States hospitals have traditionally relied primarily on revenues from paying patients to offset losses from unreimbursed care. Almost all paying patients now rely on governmental or private health insurance to pay hospital bills. Recently, insurers have been strictly limiting what they pay hospitals for the care of insured patients to amounts at or below actual costs.

Which of the following conclusions is best supported by the information above?

(A) Although the advance of technology has made expensive medical procedures available to the wealthy, such procedures are out of the reach of low-income patients.

(B) If hospitals do not find ways of raising additional income for unreimbursed care, they must either deny some of that care or suffer losses if they give it.

(C) Some patients have incomes too high for eligibility for governmental health insurance but are unable to afford private insurance for hospital care.

(D) If the hospitals reduce their costs in providing care, insurance companies will maintain the current level of reimbursement, thereby providing more funds for unreimbursed care.

(E) Even though philanthropic donations have traditionally provided some support for the hospitals, such donations are at present declining.

The passage explains that the primary way hospitals have covered the cost of unreimbursed care in the past is no longer available to them. It follows that they have three options: finding a new way to cover that cost, reducing it by giving less unreimbursed care, or suffering a loss. This is essentially what choice B concludes, so B is the best answer.

The passage touches neither on kinds of medical procedures administered in hospitals (choice A) nor on revenue other than that received from patients or their insurers (choice E), so neither choice is correct. The passage gives no hint of who the paying patients are who do not rely on insurance, so choice C is unsupported. Concerning choice D, the passage actually suggests that it is false.

151. Generally scientists enter their field with the goal of doing important new research and accept as their colleagues those with similar motivation. Therefore, when any scientist wins renown as an expounder of science to general audiences, most other scientists conclude that this popularizer should no longer be regarded as a true colleague.

The explanation offered above for the low esteem in which scientific popularizers are held by research scientists assumes that

(A) serious scientific research is not a solitary activity, but relies on active cooperation among a group of collegues

(B) research scientists tend not to regard as colleagues those scientists whose renown they envy

(C) a scientist can become a famous popularizer without having completed any important research

(D) research scientists believe that those who are well known as popularizers of science are not motivated to do important new research

(E) no important new research can be accessible to or accurately assessed by those who are not themselves scientists

The passage indicates that research scientists accept as colleagues only scientists with motivation to do important new research. This fact explains the tendency of scientists to reject scientists who are renowned popularizers of science only if research scientists believe popularizers lack such motivation; choice D is the best answer.

Since the passage is concerned only with whether certain scientists have the goal of doing important new research, not with how research is done, or with who understands new research, choices A and E are both incorrect. Choice B is incorrect because it suggests an alternative explanation of rejection of popularizers. Since the explanation offered remains unaffected even if unsuccessful research scientists cannot become famous popularizers, choice C is incorrect.

152. Mouth cancer is a danger for people who rarely brush their teeth. In order to achieve early detection of mouth cancer in these individuals, a town's public health officials sent a pamphlet to all town residents, describing how to perform weekly self-examinations of the mouth for lumps.

Which of the following, if true, is the best criticism of the pamphlet as a method of achieving the public health officials' goal?

(A) Many dental diseases produce symptoms that cannot be detected in a weekly self-examination.

(B) Once mouth cancer has been detected, the effectiveness of treatment can vary from person to person.

(C) The pamphlet was sent to all town residents, including those individuals who brush their teeth regularly.

(D) Mouth cancer is much more common in adults than in children.

(E) People who rarely brush their teeth are unlikely to perform a weekly examination of their mouth.

If choice E is true, the very people said to be at risk for mouth cancer are unlikely to be led by the content of the pamphlet to an early detection of this cancer. Choice E thus questions the pamphlet's utility and is the best answer.

Choice A is incorrect because it does not specifically cast doubt on self-examination as a means of detecting mouth cancer. Choice B is concerned with the situation following detection, but not with detection itself, so it is incorrect. Choice C is incorrect: although it suggests a certain inefficiency in handling the pamphlets, it does not suggest that the pamphlets will not achieve their purpose. Choice D supports the general appropriateness of sending written instructions, and is thus incorrect.

153. Technological improvements and reduced equipment costs have made converting solar energy directly into electricity far more cost-efficient in the last decade. However, the threshold of economic viability for solar power (that is, the price per barrel to which oil would have to rise in order for new solar power plants to be more economical than new oil-fired power plants) is unchanged at thirty-five dollars.

Which of the following, if true, does most to help explain why the increased cost-efficiency of solar power has not decreased its threshold of economic viability?

(A) The cost of oil has fallen dramatically.
(B) The reduction in the cost of solar-power equipment has occurred despite increased raw material costs for that equipment.
(C) Technological changes have increased the efficiency of oil-fired power plants.
(D) Most electricity is generated by coal-fired or nuclear, rather than oil-fired, power plants.
(E) When the price of oil increases, reserves of oil not previously worth exploiting become economically viable.

If gains in cost-efficiency of solar power have not improved its economical viability relative to oil-derived power, the explanation must be that oil-derived power itself has become more cost-efficient. Choice C points to this explanation and is thus the best answer.

Actual oil prices control how far, given the viability threshold, solar power is from economic viability but do not figure in the determination of the threshold, so choices A and E are incorrect. Choice B provides background on data that give rise to the puzzle but leaves the puzzle unresolved, so it is incorrect. Because the viability threshold for solar power is defined in relation to generating electricity from oil, choice D is irrelevant to determining the threshold and thus incorrect.

154. Start-up companies financed by venture capitalists have a much lower failure rate than companies financed by other means. Source of financing, therefore, must be a more important causative factor in the success of a start-up company than are such factors as the personal characteristics of the entrepreneur, the quality of strategic planning, or the management structure of the company.

Which of the following, if true, most seriously weakens the argument above?

(A) Venture capitalists tend to be more responsive than other sources of financing to changes in a start-up company's financial needs.
(B) The strategic planning of a start-up company is a less important factor in the long-term success of the company than are the personal characteristics of the entrepreneur.
(C) More than half of all new companies fail within five years.
(D) The management structures of start-up companies are generally less formal than the management structures of ongoing businesses.
(E) Venture capitalists base their decisions to fund start-up companies on such factors as the characteristics of the entrepreneur and quality of strategic planning of the company.

Given choice E, it is possible that companies with those combinations of factors that are most likely to lead to success are the very companies that venture capitalists select for financing. This weakens the argument that the financing itself must be more important for success than those factors. Thus, E is the best answer.

Choice A is incorrect because, rather than weakening the argument, it provides an explanation for how funding by venture capitalists could aid the success of a company. None of choices B, C, and D weakens because each of them makes a statement about start-up companies in general, without regard to their source of financing.

155. The proportion of women among students enrolled in higher education programs has increased over the past decades. This is partly shown by the fact that in 1959, only 11 percent of the women between twenty and twenty-one were enrolled in college, while in 1981, 30 percent of the women between twenty and twenty-one were enrolled in college.

To evaluate the argument above, it would be most useful to compare 1959 and 1981 with regard to which of the following characteristics?

(A) The percentage of women between twenty and twenty-one who were not enrolled in college
(B) The percentage of women between twenty and twenty-five who graduated from college
(C) The percentage of women who, after attending college, entered highly paid professions
(D) The percentage of men between twenty and twenty-one who were enrolled in college
(E) The percentage of men who graduated from high school

The argument presents a substantial increase in the proportion of women between twenty and twenty-one who were enrolled in college as evidence that there was an increase in the proportion of higher education students who were women. This evidence would lack force if a similar increase in college enrollment had occurred among men. Choice D is therefore the best answer.

Since percentages of men graduating from high school do not indicate the percentages enrolling in college that year, choice E is incorrect. Choices A, B, and C are incorrect because the information they refer to, being about women only, does not facilitate a comparison of women's enrollment to men's enrollment in higher education programs.

Questions 156-157 are based on the following.

Companies O and P each have the same number of employees who work the same number of hours per week. According to records maintained by each company, the employees of Company O had fewer job-related accidents last year than did the employees of Company P. Therefore, employees of Company O are less likely to have job-related accidents than are employees of Company P.

156. Which of the following, if true, would most strengthen the conclusion above?

(A) Company P manufactures products that are more hazardous for workers to produce than does Company O.
(B) Company P holds more safety inspections than does Company O.
(C) Company P maintains a more modern infirmary than does Company O.
(D) Company O paid more for new job-related medical claims than did Company P.
(E) Company P provides more types of health-care benefits than does Company O.

The passage's statistical data support the conclusion, but give information about one year only and identify no factor that would cause a higher accident rate at Company P. By describing such a factor, choice A, the best answer, suggests that these data can support a generalization like the conclusion.

Company P's greater number of safety inspections (choice B) may simply indicate greater attention to workers' safety. The infirmary (choice C) and health benefits (choice E) perhaps indicate that Company P makes better provisions for accident victims, but do not mean that accidents are more frequent there. That Company O paid more in job-related medical claims (choice D) says something about the consequences of accidents at the two companies, but not about causes of accidents.

157. Which of the following, if true, would most weaken the conclusion above?

(A) The employees of Company P lost more time at work due to job-related accidents than did the employees of Company O.
(B) Company P considered more types of accidents to be job-related than did Company O.
(C) The employees of Company P were sick more often than were the employees of Company O.
(D) Several employees of Company O each had more than one job-related accident.
(E) The majority of job-related accidents at Company O involved a single machine.

The data used to support the conclusion come from the companies' own records. Since, however, choice B indicates that, as compared with Company O, Company P tends to overstate the number of job-related accidents, choice B weakens the conclusion drawn and is the best answer. Choice A does not weaken the conclusion, but is simply a consequence that would be expected given the data. The relevance of employees' sicknesses (choice C) cannot be assessed without information about the links, if any, between sickness and job-related accidents. Choices D and E both give reasons for predicting a smaller likelihood that any arbitrary employee of Company O will have a job-related accident, and thus support the conclusion.

158. In comparison to the standard typewriter keyboard, the EFCO keyboard, which places the most-used keys nearest the typist's strongest fingers, allows faster typing and results in less fatigue. Therefore, replacement of standard keyboards with the EFCO keyboard will result in an immediate reduction of typing costs.

Which of the following, if true, would most weaken the conclusion drawn above?

(A) People who use both standard and EFCO keyboards report greater difficulty in the transition from the EFCO keyboard to the standard keyboard than in the transition from the standard keyboard to the EFCO keyboard.

(B) EFCO keyboards are no more expensive to manufacture than are standard keyboards and require less frequent repair than do standard keyboards.

(C) The number of businesses and government agencies that use EFCO keyboards is increasing each year.

(D) The more training and experience an employee has had with the standard keyboard, the more costly it is to train that employee to use the EFCO keyboard.

(E) Novice typists can learn to use the EFCO keyboard in about the same amount of time it takes them to learn to use the standard keyboard.

Choice D, the best answer, undermines the conclusion by pointing to a serious short-term cost of replacing standard keyboards with EFCO keyboards. The employees who are probably the most productive currently, those with the most training and experience, will cause the greatest retraining costs, according to choice D.

Choice A, by contrast, suggests that the transition to the EFCO keyboard is comparatively easy, at least for typists already experienced with both types of keyboards. Choices B and E both eliminate possible sources of increased expense associated with the EFCO keyboard, namely equipment expenses (choice B) and training of new typists (choice E). Choice C, which suggests that some offices have found the switch advantageous, is consistent with there being an immediate reduction of typing costs.

Questions 159-160 are based on the following.

Half of the subjects in an experiment—the experimental group—consumed large quantities of a popular artificial sweetener. Afterward, this group showed lower cognitive abilities than did the other half of the subjects—the control group—who did not consume the sweetener. The detrimental effects were attributed to an amino acid that is one of the sweetener's principal constituents.

159. Which of the following, if true, would best support the conclusion that some ingredient of the sweetener was responsible for the experimental results?

(A) Most consumers of the sweetener do not consume as much of it as the experimental group members did.

(B) The amino acid referred to in the conclusion is a component of all proteins, some of which must be consumed for adequate nutrition.

(C) The quantity of the sweetener consumed by individuals in the experimental group is considered safe by federal food regulators.

(D) The two groups of subjects were evenly matched with regard to cognitive abilities prior to the experiment.

(E) A second experiment in which subjects consumed large quantities of the sweetener lacked a control group of subjects who were not given the sweetener.

If, as choice D indicates, the two groups were evenly matched with regard to cognitive abilities prior to the experiment, the conclusion that some ingredient of the sweetener was detrimental to cognitive functioning is strongly supported. Thus, D is the best answer.

Neither choice A nor choice C provides additional reason to believe that some ingredient in the sweetener was responsible for the experimental results, because neither is relevant to interpreting the experimental results. Choice B indicates that, outside of the experiment, both groups consume the amino acid. If relatively small quantities are involved, the conclusion is unaffected; otherwise it is weakened. Choice E claims that a second experiment lacked a control group; yet this failing has no bearing on the experiment at issue.

160. Which of the following, if true, would best help explain how the sweetener might produce the observed effect?

(A) The government's analysis of the artificial sweetener determined that it was sold in relatively pure form.
(B) A high level of the amino acid in the blood inhibits the synthesis of a substance required for normal brain functioning.
(C) Because the sweetener is used primarily as a food additive, adverse reactions to it are rarely noticed by consumers.
(D) The amino acid that is a constituent of the sweetener is also sold separately as a dietary supplement.
(E) Subjects in the experiment did not know whether they were consuming the sweetener or a second, harmless substance.

Choice B entails that a principal constituent of the sweetener can impede normal brain functioning if high levels of it occur in the blood. Since diminished brain functioning would account for a decline in cognitive abilities, choice B helps explain the results and is the best answer.

Choice A suggests that the effect was not due to an impurity in the sweetener, and choice D suggests that further testing could be done using the amino acid alone, but neither helps explain how the sweetener might produce the effect. Neither does choice C: what it helps explain is how the sweetener could be thought harmless even if the sweetener is responsible for diminished cognitive functioning. Choice E gives a reason to trust the experimental results, but it does not explain them.

161. Adult female rats who have never before encountered rat pups will start to show maternal behaviors after being confined with a pup for about seven days. This period can be considerably shortened by disabling the female's sense of smell or by removing the scent-producing glands of the pup.

Which of the following hypotheses best explains the contrast described above?

(A) The sense of smell in adult female rats is more acute than that in rat pups.
(B) The amount of scent produced by rat pups increases when they are in the presence of a female rat that did not bear them.
(C) Female rats that have given birth are more affected by olfactory cues than are female rats that have never given birth.
(D) A female rat that has given birth shows maternal behavior toward rat pups that she did not bear more quickly than does a female rat that has never given birth.
(E) The development of a female rat's maternal interest in a rat pup that she did not bear is inhibited by the odor of the pup.

The contrast to be explained is that female rats develop maternal behaviors toward pups that are not their own faster when they cannot smell the pups than when they can. If the odor of a strange pup inhibits the development of maternal interest, the contrast is explained, so E is the best answer.

The other choices can only explain different contrasts. Choice A explains contrasts between pups and adult females. Choice B explains contrasts between pups that are in different circumstances. Choices C and D explain contrasts between two different groups of females, those that have given birth and those that have not.

162. The interview is an essential part of a successful hiring program because, with it, job applicants who have personalities that are unsuited to the requirements of the job will be eliminated from consideration.

The argument above logically depends on which of the following assumptions?

(A) A hiring program will be successful if it includes interviews.
(B) The interview is a more important part of a successful hiring program than is the development of a job description.
(C) Interviewers can accurately identify applicants whose personalities are unsuited to the requirements of the job.
(D) The only purpose of an interview is to evaluate whether job applicants' personalities are suited to the requirements of the job.
(E) The fit of job applicants' personalities to the requirements of the job was once the most important factor in making hiring decisions.

If interviewers cannot accurately identify unsuitable applicants, then interviews cannot play the role that is claimed to make them an essential part of a successful hiring program. Thus the argument depends on choice C being true, making C the best answer.

Although the argument claims that the interview is an essential part of a successful hiring program, the interview need not ensure success (contrary to choice A), nor need it be more important than another part (contrary to choice B). The interview can also have other purposes, such as checking on technical qualifications, so D is not depended upon. Nothing is implied about how past hiring decisions were made, so there is no dependence on choice E either.

163. An overly centralized economy, not the changes in the climate, is responsible for the poor agricultural production in Country X since its new government came to power. Neighboring Country Y has experienced the same climatic conditions, but while agricultural production has been falling in Country X, it has been rising in Country Y.

Which of the following, if true, would most weaken the argument above?

(A) Industrial production also is declining in Country X.
(B) Whereas Country Y is landlocked, Country X has a major seaport.
(C) Both Country X and Country Y have been experiencing drought conditions.
(D) The crops that have always been grown in Country X are different from those that have always been grown in Country Y.
(E) Country X's new government instituted a centralized economy with the intention of ensuring an equitable distribution of goods.

The argument assumes that agricultural production in Countries X and Y would be affected in the same way by given climatic changes. By pointing out that the crops grown in the two countries differ, choice D undermines this assumption and is the best answer.

   The dissimilarity between Country X and Country Y that choice B describes is unlikely to explain why their trends in agricultural production have diverged. The information in choice A cannot be evaluated without more information about industries in Country X, whereas choice C merely supplies a detail about climate, which has already been explicitly considered in the argument. Choice E explains why Country X's government chose a centralized economy, but it does not address the effects of that choice.

164. Useful protein drugs, such as insulin, must still be administered by the cumbersome procedure of injection under the skin. If proteins are taken orally, they are digested and cannot reach their target cells. Certain nonprotein drugs, however, contain chemical bonds that are not broken down by the digestive system. They can, thus, be taken orally.

The statements above most strongly support a claim that a research procedure that successfully accomplishes which of the following would be beneficial to users of protein drugs?

(A) Coating insulin with compounds that are broken down by target cells, but whose chemical bonds are resistant to digestion
(B) Converting into protein compounds, by procedures that work in the laboratory, the nonprotein drugs that resist digestion
(C) Removing permanently from the digestive system any substances that digest proteins
(D) Determining, in a systematic way, what enzymes and bacteria are present in the normal digestive system and whether they tend to be broken down within the body
(E) Determining the amount of time each nonprotein drug takes to reach its target cells

Coating insulin as described in choice A, the best answer, would benefit protein-drug users by removing the obstacle identified in the passage that prevents protein drugs, such as insulin, from being taken orally. The insulin would become available to the target cells, since these cells would break down the coating.

   Converting nonprotein drugs into protein compounds (choice B) would necessitate administration by injection, benefiting neither their users nor users of protein drugs. If removing substances that digest proteins (choice C) enabled protein drugs to be taken orally, it would be at the expense of normal digestive function. The breakdown of normally occurring bacteria and enzymes (choice D) and the activity of nonprotein drugs (choice E) are irrelevant to the problems associated with protein drugs.

165. Country Y uses its scarce foreign-exchange reserves to buy scrap iron for recycling into steel. Although the steel thus produced earns more foreign exchange than it costs, that policy is foolish. Country Y's own territory has vast deposits of iron ore, which can be mined with minimal expenditure of foreign exchange.

Which of the following, if true, provides the strongest support for Country Y's policy of buying scrap iron abroad?

(A) The price of scrap iron on international markets rose significantly in 1987.
(B) Country Y's foreign-exchange reserves dropped significantly in 1987.
(C) There is virtually no difference in quality between steel produced from scrap iron and that produced from iron ore.
(D) Scrap iron is now used in the production of roughly half the steel used in the world today, and experts predict that scrap iron will be used even more extensively in the future.
(E) Furnaces that process scrap iron can be built and operated in Country Y with substantially less foreign exchange than can furnaces that process iron ore.

Choice E, the best answer, furnishes two pieces of information that together support the policy. First, furnaces that process scrap iron may be unable to process iron ore. Second, obtaining and operating furnaces that can process iron ore would require substantially more foreign exchange, thus possibly offsetting any advantage from processing domestic iron ore.

The possibility of increases in scrap iron's price (choice A) speaks against the policy. The vulnerability of Country Y's foreign-exchange reserves (choice B) emphasizes the need to conserve foreign exchange, but does not indicate which mode of steel production best accomplishes this. Choice C is neutral between the modes of production. Choice D would support the policy only with assumptions about the reasons for the experts' prediction.

166. Last year the rate of inflation was 1.2 percent, but for the current year it has been 4 percent. We can conclude that inflation is on an upward trend and the rate will be still higher next year.

Which of the following, if true, most seriously weakens the conclusion above?

(A) The inflation figures were computed on the basis of a representative sample of economic data rather than all of the available data.
(B) Last year a dip in oil prices brought inflation temporarily below its recent stable annual level of 4 percent.
(C) Increases in the pay of some workers are tied to the level of inflation, and at an inflation rate of 4 percent or above, these pay raises constitute a force causing further inflation.
(D) The 1.2 percent rate of inflation last year represented a ten-year low.
(E) Government intervention cannot affect the rate of inflation to any significant degree.

According to choice B, last year's inflation figure was an anomaly, and inflation has returned to its recent stable level. There is thus less reason to conclude that inflation will rise any further, making B the best answer.

So long as the sample on which the figures are based is representative, there is no reason to doubt that they are essentially accurate, so choice A does not affect the argument. Choice C supports the conclusion by suggesting that there are forces in place to push inflation higher, and choice E supports it indirectly by suggesting that the government is powerless to prevent further increases. Finally, choice D by itself has no clearly defined consequences one way or the other with respect to the conclusion.

167. Because no employee wants to be associated with bad news in the eyes of a superior, information about serious problems at lower levels is progressively softened and distorted as it goes up each step in the management hierarchy. The chief executive is, therefore, less well informed about problems at lower levels than are his or her subordinates at those levels.

The conclusion drawn above is based on the assumption that

(A) problems should be solved at the level in the management hierarchy at which they occur
(B) employees should be rewarded for accurately reporting problems to their superiors
(C) problem-solving ability is more important at higher levels than it is at lower levels of the management hierarchy
(D) chief executives obtain information about problems at lower levels from no source other than their subordinates
(E) some employees are more concerned about truth than about the way they are perceived by their superiors

Unless chief executives rely solely on their subordinates for information about problems at lower levels, the progressive softening and distorting of information described in the passage need not bar the chief executive from obtaining accurate information. Thus, the conclusion that the chief executive is comparatively poorly informed about such problems is based on assuming choice D, which is therefore the best answer.

None of the other choices is assumed. Choices A and B are recommendations that the facts in the passage might support. The issue of where problem-solving ability is best deployed (choice C) may be affected by the conclusion's truth or falsity, but need not be decided in order to draw the conclusion. Choice E, if true, would tend to counteract the phenomenon the passage describes.

168. In the United States in 1986, the average rate of violent crime in states with strict gun-control laws was 645 crimes per 100,000 persons—about 50 percent higher than the average rate in the eleven states where strict gun-control laws had never been passed. Thus one way to reduce violent crime is to repeal strict gun control laws.

Which of the following, if true, would most weaken the argument above?

(A) The annual rate of violent crime in states with strict gun-control laws has decreased since the passage of those laws.
(B) In states with strict gun-control laws, few individuals are prosecuted for violating such laws.
(C) In states without strict gun-control laws, many individuals have had no formal training in the use of firearms.
(D) The annual rate of nonviolent crime is lower in states with strict gun-control laws than in states without such laws.
(E) Less than half of the individuals who reside in states without strict gun-control laws own a gun.

The argument assumes that it is because of their strict gun-control laws that states with such laws have a high rate of violent crime. If that were so, passage of these laws should be associated with increased violent crime. Choice A, the best answer, indicates that the opposite is true and so weakens the argument.

No other choice undermines the argument. The infrequency of prosecutions under strict gun-control laws (choice B) does not indicate that these laws have no effect on violent crime. For choices C and E to be relevant more information is needed, such as comparative data about states with strict gun-control laws. Similarly, without more information the relevance of the nonviolent crime rate (choice D) cannot be assessed.

169. Corporate officers and directors commonly buy and sell, for their own portfolios, stock in their own corporations. Generally, when the ratio of such inside sales to inside purchases falls below 2 to 1 for a given stock, a rise in stock prices is imminent. In recent days, while the price of MEGA Corporation stock has been falling, the corporation's officers and directors have bought up to nine times as much of it as they have sold.

The facts above best support which of the following predictions?

(A) The imbalance between inside purchases and inside sales of MEGA stock will grow even further.
(B) Inside purchases of MEGA stock are about to cease abruptly.
(C) The price of MEGA stock will soon begin to go up.
(D) The price of MEGA stock will continue to drop, but less rapidly.
(E) The majority of MEGA stock will soon be owned by MEGA's own officers and directors.

Since MEGA's officers and directors have bought almost nine times as much of MEGA's stock as they have sold, the ratio of inside sales to inside purchases is roughly 1 to 9, well below 2 to 1. Hence, by the generalization stated in the passage, a rise in MEGA's stock price is imminent and choice C is the best answer.

Since the prediction in choice D runs counter to the stated generalization, choice D is not supported. The passage does not suggest there will be an increase in the imbalance between such purchases and sales. Thus, choice A is not supported. Similarly, the passage suggests neither that inside purchases are about to cease nor that the majority of MEGA stocks will soon be owned by MEGA officers and directors. Thus, neither choice B nor choice E is supported.

170. The proposal to hire ten new police officers in Middletown is quite foolish. There is sufficient funding to pay the salaries of the new officers, but not the salaries of additional court and prison employees to process the increased caseload of arrests and convictions that new officers usually generate.

Which of the following, if true, will most seriously weaken the conclusion drawn above?

(A) Studies have shown that an increase in a city's police force does not necessarily reduce crime.
(B) When one major city increased its police force by 19 percent last year, there were 40 percent more arrests and 13 percent more convictions.
(C) If funding for the new police officers' salaries is approved, support for other city services will have to be reduced during the next fiscal year.
(D) In most United States cities, not all arrests result in convictions, and not all convictions result in prison terms.
(E) Middletown's ratio of police officers to citizens has reached a level at which an increase in the number of officers will have a deterrent effect on crime.

The passage says that hiring new officers usually brings new court expenses, but according to choice E hiring new officers in Middletown will lead to a reduction in crime and thus, perhaps, a reduction in court and prison expenses. Therefore, choice E weakens the conclusion drawn and is the best answer.

Three of the other choices tend to support claims made in the passage; choice A suggests that arrests will increase, choice B says that in one city arrests did increase, and choice C confirms the scarcity of funds. Choice D is irrelevant; it merely states the obvious about rates of arrest, conviction, and imprisonment.

171. A recent report determined that although only 3 percent of drivers on Maryland highways equipped their vehicles with radar detectors, 33 percent of all vehicles ticketed for exceeding the speed limit were equipped with them. Clearly, drivers who equip their vehicles with radar detectors are more likely to exceed the speed limit regularly than are drivers who do not.

The conclusion drawn above depends on which of the following assumptions?

(A) Drivers who equip their vehicles with radar detectors are less likely to be ticketed for exceeding the speed limit than are drivers who do not.

(B) Drivers who are ticketed for exceeding the speed limit are more likely to exceed the speed limit regularly than are drivers who are not ticketed.

(C) The number of vehicles that were ticketed for exceeding the speed limit was greater than the number of vehicles that were equipped with radar detectors.

(D) Many of the vehicles that were ticketed for exceeding the speed limit were ticketed more than once in the time period covered by the report.

(E) Drivers on Maryland highways exceeded the speed limit more often than did drivers on other state highways not covered in the report.

The conclusion concerns regularly exceeding the speed limit, but the data derive from isolated occasions when drivers exceed the speed limit and are ticketed. The conclusion thus assumes that these instances provide evidence of regular behavior—that drivers ticketed for exceeding the speed limit are likely to be drivers who regularly exceed it. Choice B states this assumption and is the best answer.

Choices A, C, and D provide additional data that might be relevant to the conclusion, but if choice B is assumed, the additional data are unnecessary for drawing the conclusion. The difference that choice E describes between Maryland and other states would simply suggest that the report's findings cannot be extrapolated to other states. It does not help in drawing the conclusion.

172. There is a great deal of geographical variation in the frequency of many surgical procedures—up to tenfold variation per hundred thousand people between different areas in the numbers of hysterectomies, prostatectomies, and tonsillectomies.

To support a conclusion that much of the variation is due to unnecessary surgical procedures, it would be most important to establish which of the following?

(A) A local board of review at each hospital examines the records of every operation to determine whether the surgical procedure was necessary.

(B) The variation is unrelated to factors (other than the surgical procedures themselves) that influence the incidence of diseases for which surgery might be considered.

(C) There are several categories of surgical procedure (other than hysterectomies, prostatectomies, and tonsillectomies) that are often performed unnecessarily.

(D) For certain surgical procedures, it is difficult to determine after the operation whether the procedures were necessary or whether alternative treatment would have succeeded.

(E) With respect to how often they are performed unnecessarily, hysterectomies, prostatectomies, and tonsillectomies are representative of surgical procedures in general.

To establish that much of the variation is due to unnecessary surgical procedures, it is necessary to eliminate the possibility that the geographical variation reflects variation in the incidence of diseases treated with these procedures. Choice B, if established, would eliminate this possibility and is thus the best answer.

Review boards (choice A) would provide some control against unnecessary procedures, so choice A would, if anything, tell against the suggested conclusion. Neither choice C nor choice E bears on the conclusion, since neither the conclusion nor the cited geographical variation involves procedures other than the three specified. Even if these procedures are of the kind choice D describes, the difficulty of determining an individual operation's necessity would merely increase the difficulty of verifying the suggested conclusion.

173. Researchers have found that when very overweight people, who tend to have relatively low metabolic rates, lose weight primarily through dieting, their metabolisms generally remain unchanged. They will thus burn significantly fewer calories at the new weight than do people whose weight is normally at that level. Such newly thin persons will, therefore, ultimately regain weight until their body size again matches their metabolic rate.

The conclusion of the argument above depends on which of the following assumptions?

(A) Relatively few very overweight people who have dieted down to a new weight tend to continue to consume substantially fewer calories than do people whose normal weight is at that level.
(B) The metabolisms of people who are usually not overweight are much more able to vary than the metabolisms of people who have been very overweight.
(C) The amount of calories that a person usually burns in a day is determined more by the amount that is consumed that day than by the current weight of the individual.
(D) Researchers have not yet determined whether the metabolic rates of formerly very overweight individuals can be accelerated by means of chemical agents.
(E) Because of the constancy of their metabolic rates, people who are at their usual weight normally have as much difficulty gaining weight as they do losing it.

If, compared with people who have not been overweight, newly thin people burned fewer calories but also generally consumed fewer calories, one could not reliably conclude that the newly thin people would regain weight. Therefore, the conclusion assumes that the newly thin do not generally consume fewer calories, making choice A the best answer.

The conclusion does not rely on differences in the variability of the metabolism (choice B), just on differences in the rate of metabolism, nor does it rely on the relative significance of different factors in determining how many calories a person burns in a day (choice C). Neither does the conclusion assume anything about whether accelerators for the metabolism have been discovered (choice D), or about why some people have difficulty gaining weight (choice E).

174. In 1987 sinusitis was the most common chronic medical condition in the United States, followed by arthritis and high blood pressure, in that order.

The incidence rates for both arthritis and high blood pressure increase with age, but the incidence rate for sinusitis is the same for people of all ages.

The average age of the United States population will increase between 1987 and 2000.

Which of the following conclusions can be most properly drawn about chronic medical conditions in the United States from the information given above?

(A) Sinusitis will be more common than either arthritis or high blood pressure in 2000.
(B) Arthritis will be the most common chronic medical condition in 2000.
(C) The average age of people suffering from sinusitis will increase between 1987 and 2000.
(D) Fewer people will suffer from sinusitis in 2000 than suffered from it in 1987.
(E) A majority of the population will suffer from at least one of the medical conditions mentioned above by the year 2000.

Given that the incidence rate for sinusitis is the same for people of all ages, and that the average age of the population will increase, it follows that the average age of people suffering from sinusitis will increase. Therefore, C is the best answer.

Although it follows that sinusitis will become less common relative to arthritis and high blood pressure, nothing can be concluded about the exact ranking of the three diseases, so choices A and B are ruled out. Just because sinusitis will become relatively less common, one cannot conclude that it will become absolutely less common (choice D). Lacking information about levels of incidence of the diseases, one cannot conclude what proportion of the population has at least one of them (choice E).

175. Parasitic wasps lay their eggs directly into the eggs of various host insects in exactly the right numbers for any suitable size of host egg. If they laid too many eggs in a host egg, the developing wasp larvae would compete with each other to the death for nutrients and space. If too few eggs were laid, portions of the host egg would decay, killing the wasp larvae.

Which of the following conclusions can properly be drawn from the information above?

(A) The size of the smallest host egg that a wasp could theoretically parasitize can be determined from the wasp's egg-laying behavior.
(B) Host insects lack any effective defenses against the form of predation practiced by parasitic wasps.
(C) Parasitic wasps learn from experience how many eggs to lay into the eggs of different host species.
(D) Failure to lay enough eggs would lead to the death of the developing wasp larvae more quickly than would laying too many eggs.
(E) Parasitic wasps use visual clues to calculate the size of a host egg.

Comparing two host eggs in which parasitic wasps have laid different numbers of eggs, it is theoretically possible to determine what size of host egg would be required for a single wasp egg. This would be the smallest egg the wasp could parasitize, so A is the best answer.

None of the other choices follows from the information given. Host insects could conceal their eggs from the wasps (choice B), and the wasps could have inborn abilities to lay appropriate numbers of eggs (choice C). Laying too many eggs could lead to the death of the larvae faster than laying too few (choice D), and the wasps could use tactile clues to calculate the size of a host egg (choice E).

176. Northern Air has dozens of flights daily into and out of Belleville Airport, which is highly congested. Northern Air depends for its success on economy and quick turnaround and consequently is planning to replace its large planes with Skybuses, whose novel aerodynamic design is extremely fuel efficient. The Skybus' fuel efficiency results in both lower fuel costs and reduced time spent refueling.

Which of the following, if true, could present the most serious disadvantage for Northern Air in replacing their large planes with Skybuses?

(A) The Skybus would enable Northern Air to schedule direct flights to destinations that currently require stops for refueling.
(B) Aviation fuel is projected to decline in price over the next several years.
(C) The fuel efficiency of the Skybus would enable Northern Air to eliminate refueling at some of its destinations, but several mechanics would lose their jobs.
(D) None of Northern Air's competitors that use Belleville Airport are considering buying Skybuses.
(E) The aerodynamic design of the Skybus causes turbulence behind it when taking off that forces other planes on the runway to delay their takeoffs.

The passage presents some facts about Northern Air's business—in particular that its success depends on quick turnaround and economy. The airline plans to promote these goals by purchasing Skybuses, which will reduce fuel costs and time spent refueling. The question asks you to identify a disadvantage for the airline in this plan.

Choice E is the best answer because from the passage we know that Belleville Airport is highly congested and that Northern Air has many flights out of this airport daily. Therefore, the delay that Skybus takeoffs cause for other planes will impact Northern Air's flights, reducing the airline's ability to achieve rapid turnaround.

Choices A and C are incorrect since the ability to have more destinations served by direct flights (choice A) and to eliminate refueling at some destinations (choice C) are both potential advantages of Northern Air's plan. Choice B is incorrect for the reason that although a decline in the price of aviation fuel would reduce the cost savings from introducing the Skybus, a reduction in fuel costs would still be an advantage, although a smaller one. Choice D is incorrect. The simple fact that Northern Air's competitors are not considering buying Skybuses does not itself present either an advantage or a disadvantage for Northern Air, although the reasons the competitors might have could include both advantages and disadvantages.

177. Products sold under a brand name used to command premium prices because, in general, they were superior to nonbrand rival products. Technical expertise in product development has become so widespread, however, that special quality advantages are very hard to obtain these days and even harder to maintain. As a consequence, brand-name products generally neither offer higher quality nor sell at higher prices. Paradoxically, brand names are a bigger marketing advantage than ever.

Which of the following, if true, most helps to resolve the paradox outlined above?

(A) Brand names are taken by consumers as a guarantee of getting a product as good as the best rival products.
(B) Consumers recognize that the quality of products sold under invariant brand names can drift over time.
(C) In many acquisitions of one corporation by another, the acquiring corporation is interested more in acquiring the right to use certain brand names than in acquiring existing production facilities.
(D) In the days when special quality advantages were easier to obtain than they are now, it was also easier to get new brand names established.
(E) The advertising of a company's brand-name products is at times transferred to a new advertising agency, especially when sales are declining.

The passage explains that brand-name products can generally no longer be sold for higher prices than nonbrand rival products, since many nonbrand products now equal brand-name products in quality. Yet despite this parity, brand-name products have a larger marketing advantage than before over nonbrand products.

The question asks for a fact that would resolve this paradox. That is, the best answer will explain how it can be advantageous to be marketing a product with a recognized brand name even when that product can be priced no higher than rival nonbrand products.

Choice A is the best answer because a product that consumers believe not to be bettered in quality by any equally priced competing product will tend to sell better than products whose quality consumers are less sure about.

Choices B and E are incorrect since both choices point to difficulties that brand-name products sometimes have in the marketplace but without identifying any compensating advantage that they enjoy. Choice C is incorrect as this choice attests to the fact that corporations believe brand names to be valuable but does not explain why that should be so. Answer choice D works in the wrong direction: it is the information in the passage—that quality advantages cannot be obtained or maintained yet brand names confer marketing advantages—that might explain the difficulty of establishing new brand names.

178. In countries in which new life-sustaining drugs cannot be patented, such drugs are sold at widely affordable prices; those same drugs, where patented, command premium prices because the patents shield patent-holding manufacturers from competitors. These facts show that future access to new life-sustaining drugs can be improved if the practice of granting patents on newly developed life-sustaining drugs were to be abolished everywhere.

Which of the following, if true, most seriously weakens the argument?

(A) In countries in which life-sustaining drugs cannot be patented, their manufacture is nevertheless a profitable enterprise.
(B) Countries that do not currently grant patents on life-sustaining drugs are, for the most part, countries with large populations.
(C) In some countries specific processes for the manufacture of pharmaceutical drugs can be patented even in cases in which the drugs themselves cannot be patented.
(D) Pharmaceutical companies can afford the research that goes into the development of new drugs only if patents allow them to earn high profits.
(E) Countries that grant patents on life-sustaining drugs almost always ban their importation from countries that do not grant such patents.

The passage argues that access to life-sustaining drugs would be improved if patents on them were abolished, based on information about the lower cost of such drugs in countries where there are no patents. You are asked to identify the answer choice that most weakens the argument.

If without patents pharmaceutical companies could not afford to develop new drugs, then abolishing patents would mean that people would have reduced access to new life-sustaining drugs, thereby weakening the argument presented. Therefore, choice D is the correct answer.

Choices A and B both present advantages available in countries without patents on the drugs—manufacturing the drugs can be profitable (choice A) and there is a large potential market (choice B). Neither presents a drawback to abolishing the patents. Choice C is incorrect since the possibility of patenting manufacturing processes introduces some limitation to the benefits of abolishing patents on the drugs, but does not mean that there would be no benefits. Choice E presents a further way in which patents are linked to restrictions on the availability of new life-sustaining drugs, and therefore it supports rather than weakens the argument in favor of abolishing patents.

179. A museum has been offered an undocumented statue, supposedly Greek and from the sixth century B.C. Possibly the statue is genuine but undocumented because it was recently unearthed or because it has been privately owned. However, an ancient surface usually has uneven weathering, whereas the surface of this statue has the uniform quality characteristically produced by a chemical bath used by forgers to imitate a weathered surface. Therefore, the statue is probably a forgery.

Which of the following, if true, most seriously weakens the argument?

(A) Museums can accept a recently unearthed statue only with valid export documentation from its country of origin.
(B) The subject's pose and other aspects of the subject's treatment exhibit all the most common features of Greek statues of the sixth century B.C.
(C) The chemical bath that forgers use was at one time used by dealers and collectors to remove the splotchy surface appearance of genuinely ancient sculptures.
(D) Museum officials believe that forgers have no technique that can convincingly simulate the patchy weathering characteristic of the surfaces of ancient sculptures.
(E) An allegedly Roman sculpture with a uniform surface similar to that of the statue being offered to the museum was recently shown to be a forgery.

The passage presents an argument that a particular statue is a forgery because its surface appears to have been given a chemical treatment that forgers typically use. You are then asked to identify the answer choice that weakens the argument.

If the treatment often used by forgers was also used by others on genuine antiquities, the argument that the statue is a forgery is weakened. Therefore choice C is the best answer. Choice A is not correct because information about whether the museum can accept the statue is not relevant to the question of whether the statue is a forgery, which is the focus of the argument. Since both genuine antiquities and forgeries would share the most common features, choice B does not cast any doubt on the argument that the statue is a forgery. Choice D indicates that a statue that showed uneven weathering would not be a forgery. Since the statue in question does not have uneven weathering, this choice leaves the argument unaffected, and is therefore incorrect. Choice E reinforces the possibility that the statue is a forgery, so does not weaken the argument.

180. In the arid land along the Colorado River, use of the river's water supply is strictly controlled: farms along the river each have a limited allocation that they are allowed to use for irrigation. But the trees that grow in narrow strips along the river's banks also use its water. Clearly, therefore, if farmers were to remove those trees, more water would be available for crop irrigation.

Which of the following, if true, most seriously weakens the argument?

(A) The trees along the river's banks shelter it from the sun and wind, thereby greatly reducing the amount of water lost through evaporation.
(B) Owners of farms along the river will probably not undertake the expense of cutting down trees along the banks unless they are granted a greater allocation of water in return.
(C) Many of the tree species currently found along the river's banks are specifically adapted to growing in places where tree roots remain constantly wet.
(D) The strip of land where trees grow along the river's banks would not be suitable for growing crops if the trees were removed.
(E) The distribution of water allocations for irrigation is intended to prevent farms farther upstream from using water needed by farms farther downstream.

The passage argues that cutting down the trees along the banks of the Colorado River would make more water available for crop irrigation, given that the trees use water. You are asked to identify the choice that most weakens this argument.

If trees also help conserve water, the argument that cutting them down would make more water available for irrigation is weakened, so choice A is the best answer. Choice B is incorrect because it focuses on the farmers' motivations for cutting the trees down, not on what effects cutting them down would have on the availability of water. The additional information presented in choice C about the trees involved is irrelevant to the question whether removing them would make more water available for irrigation. Although choice D presents a drawback to removing the trees, the drawback does not weaken the argument that removing them would make more water available. Choice E is incorrect because it provides background information that does not address the relationship between the trees and the water that is central to the argument.

181. **Consumer health advocate:** Your candy company adds caffeine to your chocolate candy bars so that each one delivers a specified amount of caffeine. Since caffeine is highly addictive, this indicates that you intend to keep your customers addicted.

Candy manufacturer: Our manufacturing process results in there being less caffeine in each chocolate candy bar than in the unprocessed cacao beans from which the chocolate is made.

The candy manufacturer's response is flawed as a refutation of the consumer health advocate's argument because it

(A) fails to address the issue of whether the level of caffeine in the candy bars sold by the manufacturer is enough to keep people addicted

(B) assumes without warrant that all unprocessed cacao beans contain a uniform amount of caffeine

(C) does not specify exactly how caffeine is lost in the manufacturing process

(D) treats the consumer health advocate's argument as though it were about each candy bar rather than about the manufacturer's candy in general

(E) merely contradicts the consumer health advocate's conclusion without giving any reason to believe that the advocate's reasoning is unsound

In the dialogue, the candy manufacturer tries to rebut the claim that caffeine is added to chocolate candy bars in order to keep consumers addicted. The rebuttal is that the caffeine added is restoring to the product caffeine that was lost during manufacture. The question asks you to identify why this rebuttal is inadequate.

Choice A is the best answer. The candy manufacturer's rebuttal amounts to an admission that the candy bars could be manufactured to contain less caffeine than they do. Therefore, the crucial issue for assessing the health advocate's account of the reason for adding the caffeine is whether the amount of caffeine added is enough to make the candy addictive.

Although choices B and D both describe possible flaws in a response, neither of them is a correct description of the response the manufacturer actually gives. With respect to choice C, although the manufacturer does not specify how the caffeine is lost, the mechanism of manufacture is not relevant to the issue that the health advocate raises. With respect to choice E, the manufacturer does not give any reason for thinking the advocate's reason is unsound. But contrary to what this choice says, the manufacturer does not actually contradict the health advocate's conclusion.

182. The earliest Mayan pottery found at Colha, in Belize, is about 3,000 years old. Recently, however, 4,500-year-old stone agricultural implements were unearthed at Colha. These implements resemble Mayan stone implements of a much later period, also found at Colha. Moreover, the implements' designs are strikingly different from the designs of stone implements produced by other cultures known to have inhabited the area in prehistoric times. Therefore, there were surely Mayan settlements in Colha 4,500 years ago.

Which of the following, if true, most seriously weakens the argument?

(A) Ceramic ware is not known to have been used by the Maya to make agricultural implements.

(B) Carbon dating of corn pollen in Colha indicates that agriculture began there around 4,500 years ago.

(C) Archaeological evidence indicates that some of the oldest stone implements found at Colha were used to cut away vegetation after controlled burning of trees to open areas of swampland for cultivation.

(D) Successor cultures at a given site often adopt the style of agricultural implements used by earlier inhabitants of the same site.

(E) Many religious and social institutions of the Mayan people who inhabited Colha 3,000 years ago relied on a highly developed system of agricultural symbols.

The passage argues that the Maya inhabited Colha 4,500 years ago from the fact that 4,500-year-old stone implements from Colha are like much later stone implements that are known to be Mayan. You are asked to identify the choice that weakens the argument.

Choice D suggests a different explanation for the similarity of the implements: the Maya copied the design from an earlier culture. Choice D therefore weakens the argument that the Maya inhabited Colha 4,500 years ago and is thus the best answer.

Since the argument in choice A is based on the similarity of stone implements of different ages, the lack of ceramic agricultural implements leaves the argument unaffected. Choices B and C provide no information about who was practicing agriculture in Colha 4,500 years ago, so they fail to weaken the argument. In choice E the fact that by 3,000 years ago Mayan culture was deeply rooted in agriculture indicates a history that goes back before that date and does nothing to weaken the argument.

183. Editorial:

Regulations recently imposed by the government of Risemia call for unprecedented reductions in the amounts of pollutants manufacturers are allowed to discharge into the environment. It will take costly new pollution control equipment requiring expensive maintenance to comply with these regulations. Resultant price increases for Risemian manufactured goods will lead to the loss of some export markets. Clearly, therefore, annual exports of Risemian manufactured goods will in the future occur at diminished levels.

Which of the following, if true, most seriously weakens the argument in the editorial?

(A) The need to comply with the new regulations will stimulate the development within Risemia of new pollution control equipment for which a strong worldwide demand is likely to emerge.
(B) The proposed regulations include a schedule of fines for noncompliance that escalate steeply in cases of repeated noncompliance.
(C) Savings from utilizing the chemicals captured by the pollution control equipment will remain far below the cost of maintaining the equipment.
(D) By international standards, the levels of pollutants currently emitted by some of Risemia's manufacturing plants are not considered excessive.
(E) The stockholders of most of Risemia's manufacturing corporations exert substantial pressure on the corporations to comply with environmental laws.

The passage argues that because new pollution control equipment will reduce the competitiveness of some goods manufactured in Risemia, annual exports will be at a lower level in the future. You are asked to identify something that weakens this argument.

Choice A is the best answer, since if the new pollution control equipment itself becomes a product that Risemian manufacturers can export, the loss of certain other export markets will not necessarily lead to a reduction in exports. Therefore this fact weakens the argument.

Choices B and C both emphasize that Risemian manufacturers will have additional costs whether they comply with the regulations or not, so they increase the likelihood that the manufacturers will be less competitive on world markets. Thus these choices strengthen rather than weaken the argument. Choice D is incorrect; the passage states that the pollution control equipment will be expensive, so even if the level of pollution to be controlled is not excessive, exports will still be more expensive. Choice E strengthens the argument rather than weakens it, since it asserts that the stockholders will encourage Risemian manufacturers to comply with the regulations despite the economic disadvantages of doing so.

184. Codex Berinensis, a Florentine copy of an ancient Roman medical treatise, is undated but contains clues to when it was produced. Its first eighty pages are by a single copyist, but the remaining twenty pages are by three different copyists, which indicates some significant disruption. Since a letter in handwriting identified as that of the fourth copyist mentions a plague that killed many people in Florence in 1148, Codex Berinensis was probably produced in that year.

Which of the following, if true, most strongly supports the hypothesis that Codex Berinensis was produced in 1148 ?

(A) Other than Codex Berinensis, there are no known samples of the handwriting of the first three copyists.
(B) According to the account by the fourth copyist, the plague went on for ten months.
(C) A scribe would be able to copy a page of text the size and style of Codex Berinensis in a day.
(D) There was only one outbreak of plague in Florence in the 1100's.
(E) The number of pages of Codex Berinensis produced by a single scribe becomes smaller with each successive change of copyist.

The passage points out that the changes in copyists indicates that something prevented the first three copyists from completing the work. The passage then identifies this disruptive factor as the plague of 1148, thus dating the production of the Codex. The question asks you to identify information that would support this dating.

Choice D is the best answer because if there had been other outbreaks of plague in the relevant period, one of these, instead of the plague of 1148, might have disrupted the manuscript's production. This information therefore supports the hypothesis.

Choice A is incorrect since other documents with handwriting by any of the first three copyists might help in establishing a date for the Codex, but the absence of this evidence provides no additional support for the 1148 dating. Choices B, C, and D are incorrect for the reason that information about the duration of the plague, the length of time it took to produce the Codex, and the length of time each scribe worked on the Codex cannot, without considerable further data, provide evidence for or against the 1148 dating.

185. Near Chicago a newly built hydroponic spinach "factory," a completely controlled environment for growing spinach, produces on 1 acre of floor space what it takes 100 acres of fields to produce. Expenses, especially for electricity, are high, however, and the spinach produced costs about four times as much as washed California field spinach, the spinach commonly sold throughout the United States.

Which of the following, if true, best supports a projection that the spinach-growing facility near Chicago will be profitable?

(A) Once the operators of the facility are experienced, they will be able to cut operating expenses by about 25 percent.

(B) There is virtually no scope for any further reduction in the cost per pound for California field spinach.

(C) Unlike washed field spinach, the hydroponically grown spinach is untainted by any pesticides or herbicides and thus will sell at exceptionally high prices to such customers as health food restaurants.

(D) Since spinach is a crop that ships relatively well, the market for the hydroponically grown spinach is no more limited to the Chicago area than the market for California field spinach is to California.

(E) A second hydroponic facility is being built in Canada, taking advantage of inexpensive electricity and high vegetable prices.

This item presents a scenario in which hydroponically grown spinach is four times as expensive as California field spinach. You are asked to identify an option that shows how, despite this disadvantage, the hydroponic spinach-growing facility can be profitable.

Choice C presents an advantage to the hydroponically grown spinach—it can be sold to certain customers who are prepared to pay very high prices for it. This supports the projection that the facility will be profitable, and is thus the best answer.

Choices A and B present the likelihood of changes in the cost of the two kinds of spinach, but neither choice suggests that the current large price differential can be overcome, so neither supports the projection. Choice D presents one advantage shared by the two kinds of spinach, but it does nothing to diminish the cost disadvantage of hydroponic spinach. Choice E gives some reason to think that another hydroponic facility can be profitable but gives no reason to think that the facility under discussion can be so.

186. Offshore oil-drilling operations entail an unavoidable risk of an oil spill, but importing oil on tankers presently entails an even greater such risk per barrel of oil. Therefore, if we are to reduce the risk of an oil spill without curtailing our use of oil, we must invest more in offshore operations and import less oil on tankers.

Which of the following, if true, most seriously weakens the argument above?

(A) Tankers can easily be redesigned so that their use entails less risk of an oil spill.

(B) Oil spills caused by tankers have generally been more serious than those caused by offshore operations.

(C) The impact of offshore operations on the environment can be controlled by careful management.

(D) Offshore operations usually damage the ocean floor, but tankers rarely cause such damage.

(E) Importing oil on tankers is currently less expensive than drilling for it offshore.

The passage presents an argument for increasing offshore oil-drilling operations and decreasing oil imports on tankers, relying on information about the risk of oil spills. You are then asked to identify something that weakens this argument.

According to choice A, tankers can be easily redesigned to reduce the risk of oil spills; if so, increasing offshore drilling operations may not be the only way to reduce the risk of one. Therefore, choice A weakens the argument and is the best answer.

Choices B and C present further evidence against the use of tankers and for offshore operations, so neither of them weakens the argument, and neither is correct. Choice D raises a concern about offshore operations, but it is not a concern related to the risk of oil spills, and hence does not weaken the argument. Choice E presents a factor in favor of importing oil on tankers, but because this factor is not related to the risk of an oil spill, it does not weaken the argument.

187. Automobile Dealer's Advertisement:

The Highway Traffic Safety Institute reports that the PZ 1000 has the fewest injuries per accident of any car in its class. This shows that the PZ 1000 is one of the safest cars available today.

Which of the following, if true, most seriously weakens the argument in the advertisement?

(A) The Highway Traffic Safety Institute report listed many cars in other classes that had more injuries per accident than did the PZ 1000.
(B) In recent years many more PZ 1000's have been sold than have any other kind of car in its class.
(C) Cars in the class to which the PZ 1000 belongs are more likely to be involved in accidents than are other types of cars.
(D) The difference between the number of injuries per accident for the PZ 1000 and that for other cars in its class is quite pronounced.
(E) The Highway Traffic Safety Institute issues reports only once a year.

The advertisement argues that the PZ 1000 is one of the safest cars available, on the basis of the fact that, within its class, the PZ 1000 has the fewest injuries per accident. You are asked to find something that challenges this argument.

According to choice C, the class of cars to which the PZ 1000 belongs is more dangerous than average in a certain respect, so having the lowest injury rate per accident within that class does not count as strong evidence that the PZ 1000 is a highly safe car overall. Therefore this choice weakens the argument, and is the best answer.

Choice A tends to confirm that the PZ 1000 has a low rate of injuries per accident and so supports the argument, rather than weakening it. Since the argument is about injury rates rather than overall numbers, whether the PZ 1000 has sold well or poorly (choice B) has no bearing on the argument.

Choice D emphasizes the difference between the PZ 1000 and other cars in the same class but makes no comparison with cars in general, so it neither supports nor weakens the argument. The frequency with which the safety reports are issued (choice E) has no bearing on the argument presented.

188. When demand for a factory's products is high, more money is spent at the factory for safety precautions and machinery maintenance than when demand is low. Thus the average number of on-the-job accidents per employee each month should be lower during periods when demand is high than when demand is low and less money is available for safety precautions and machinery maintenance.

Which of the following, if true about a factory when demand for its products is high, casts the most serious doubt on the conclusion drawn above?

(A) Its employees ask for higher wages than they do at other times.
(B) Its management hires new workers but lacks the time to train them properly.
(C) Its employees are less likely to lose their jobs than they are at other times.
(D) Its management sponsors a monthly safety award for each division in the factory.
(E) Its old machinery is replaced with modern, automated models.

The passage concludes that in a factory the average number of on-the-job accidents per employee is likely to decline when demand for the factory's products is high, on the grounds that more money gets spent on safety measures when demand is high than at other times. You are asked to identify a fact that casts doubt on this conclusion.

Choice B is the best answer. Factory workers who are newly hired and not properly trained are more likely to have on-the-job accidents than are trained and experienced factory workers, so the presence of such workers could very well counteract the benefits of spending more on safety.

That employees ask for higher wages has no direct bearing on how likely they are to have on-the-job accidents, so choice A is not a correct answer. There is no straightforward connection between factory employees' job security and their likelihood of suffering an on-the-job accident, so choice C is not correct. Choice D suggests that at least part of the money spent on safety precautions is spent to reward safe work practices, and so tends to support rather than cast doubt on the conclusion. Since modern, automated machinery is likely to be safer to operate than machinery it replaces, choice E casts no doubt on the conclusion.

189. Studies have shown that elderly people who practice a religion are much more likely to die immediately after an important religious holiday period than immediately before one. Researchers have concluded that the will to live can prolong life, at least for short periods of time.

Which of the following, if true, would most strengthen the researchers' conclusion?

(A) Elderly people who practice a religion are less likely to die immediately before or during an important religious holiday than at any other time of the year.

(B) Elderly people who practice a religion appear to experience less anxiety at the prospect of dying than do other people.

(C) Some elderly people who do practice a religion live much longer than most elderly people who do not.

(D) Most elderly people who participate in religious holidays have different reasons for participating than young people do.

(E) Many religions have important holidays in the spring and fall, seasons with the lowest death rates for elderly people.

According to the passage, the death rate among elderly people who practice a religion is higher after an important religious holiday than before. From this fact researchers have concluded that people can prolong their lives by willpower, presumably thinking that such people can hold off death long enough to enable them to experience the holiday. You are asked to find a fact that supports the researchers' conclusion.

Choice A is the correct answer. The fact that before and during an important religious holiday the death rate is lower than usual is crucial additional information that helps to support the idea that for the duration of the holiday people succeed in holding off death, and hence it helps to support the researchers' conclusion.

Choice B is incorrect since this information applies to all times of the year, not just to holiday times, and so provides no support for the conclusion. Choice C is irrelevant because the researchers' conclusion is about what can affect the precise time of a person's death, not how long people live overall. Choice D is incorrect; the fact that there is some difference in motivation gives no particular reason to think that the motivation can have the effect that the researchers claim. The researchers' conclusion is based on a striking pattern of death rates over the range of a few days. Therefore, the general seasonal information provided by choice E lends no support to their conclusion.

190. Manufacturers of mechanical pencils make most of their profit on pencil leads rather than on the pencils themselves. The Write Company, which cannot sell its leads as cheaply as other manufacturers can, plans to alter the design of its mechanical pencil so that it will accept only a newly designed Write Company lead, which will be sold at the same price as the Write Company's current lead.

Which of the following, if true, most strongly supports the Write Company's projection that its plan will lead to an increase in its sales of pencil leads?

(A) First-time buyers of mechanical pencils tend to buy the least expensive mechanical pencils available.

(B) Annual sales of mechanical pencils are expected to triple over the next five years.

(C) A Write Company executive is studying ways to reduce the cost of manufacturing pencil leads.

(D) A rival manufacturer recently announced similar plans to introduce a mechanical pencil that would accept only the leads produced by that manufacturer.

(E) In extensive test marketing, mechanical-pencil users found the new Write Company pencil markedly superior to other mechanical pencils they had used.

The passage presents difficulties the Write Company has in selling pencil leads and making a profit, and then presents a plan the company has: to produce a pencil that will accept only a special lead of the company's own. You are asked to find something that supports the company's projection that its sales of pencil leads will increase as a result.

Choice E is the best answer since the evident superiority of the redesigned pencil gives consumers an incentive to buy it. Once consumers have bought the pencil, sales of the special leads for it will follow, so the company's sales of lead are likely to increase.

Choice A provides no support for the company's projection, since there is no indication that the company's redesigned pencil will be very inexpensive. Choice B implies that sales of pencil leads will increase in general, but gives no indication that the Write Company's sales will increase, and in particular it gives no indication that the particular plan that the company has adopted will cause its sales to increase.

The plan as described is to sell the special leads at the same price as current leads, so even if the study described in choice C proves successful, the most that could be achieved would be an increase in profits, not in sales. With respect to choice D, the fact that another manufacturer is considering the same strategy does not help answer the question at issue here—whether this will be a successful strategy for the Write Company—and thus gives no support to the company's projection.

191. To evaluate a plan to save money on office-space expenditures by having its employees work at home, XYZ Company asked volunteers from its staff to try the arrangement for six months. During this period, the productivity of these employees was as high as or higher than before.

Which of the following, if true, would argue most strongly against deciding, on the basis of the trial results, to implement the company's plan?

(A) The employees who agreed to participate in the test of the plan were among the company's most self-motivated and independent workers.

(B) The savings that would accrue from reduced office-space expenditures alone would be sufficient to justify the arrangement for the company, apart from any productivity increases.

(C) Other companies that have achieved successful results from work-at-home plans have work forces that are substantially larger than that of XYZ.

(D) The volunteers who worked at home were able to communicate with other employees as necessary for performing the work.

(E) Minor changes in the way office work is organized at XYZ would yield increases in employee productivity similar to those achieved in the trial.

According to the passage a limited trial of a plan had favorable results. The question asks you to identify information that indicates that those favorable results would not be reproduced if the plan were put into effect.

Choice A is the best answer, since if it is true, then the employees who took part in the trial were the ones likely to do best working at home. So the trial's results cannot be taken as representative of what would happen if the plan was extended to other employees.

Although choices B, C, and D provide information that might be relevant to assessing the likely success of the plan, if implemented, none of them specifically casts doubt on the validity of the trial results; thus they are incorrect choices. Choice E is incorrect; since reduced office-space expenditures, rather than productivity increases, would be the goal of implementing the plan, the fact that alternative measures might achieve equal productivity gains is not directly relevant.

192. Mourdet Winery: Danville Winery's new wine was introduced to compete with our most popular wine, which is sold in a distinctive tall, black bottle. Danville uses a similar bottle. Thus, it is likely that many customers intending to buy our wine will mistakenly buy theirs instead.

Danville Winery: Not so. The two bottles can be readily distinguished: the label on ours, but not on theirs, is gold colored.

Which of the following, if true, most undermines Danville Winery's response?

(A) Gold is the background color on the label of many of the wines produced by Danville Winery.

(B) When the bottles are viewed side by side, Danville Winery's bottle is perceptibly taller than Mourdet Winery's.

(C) Danville Winery, unlike Mourdet Winery, displays its wine's label prominently in advertisements.

(D) It is common for occasional purchasers to buy a bottle of wine on the basis of a general impression of the most obvious feature of the bottle.

(E) Many popular wines are sold in bottles of a standard design.

Mourdet Winery claims that it will lose customers because Danville Winery has imitated its distinctive bottle. Danville denies this claim, and points out that the two bottles can be told apart by the difference in their labels. You are asked to find something that undermines this response.

Choice D is the best answer. According to this choice, at least some of Mourdet's occasional customers are likely to overlook the difference in labels and buy Danville's wine instead of theirs, so Danville's response to Mourdet's complaint is undermined.

Choice A supports, rather than undermines, Danville's response; the gold color is a common feature of Danville's bottles, so a bottle bearing a gold label is more likely to be recognized as a Danville wine. Choice B provides another respect in which the bottles are different, and does not undermine Danville's response.

If the Danville label is emphasized in advertising, it is more likely rather than less that the difference in labels will help prevent customers from buying the wrong wine, so choice C supports rather than undermines Danville's response. The fact that some popular wines can be distinguished from Mourdet's by their bottle shape (choice E) says nothing about whether the difference in labels is enough to prevent consumers from buying Danville's wine instead of Mourdet's.

193. Editorial:

The mayor plans to deactivate the city's fire alarm boxes, because most calls received from them are false alarms. The mayor claims that the alarm boxes are no longer necessary, since most people now have access to either public or private telephones. But the city's commercial district, where there is the greatest risk of fire, has few residents and few public telephones, so some alarm boxes are still necessary.

Which of the following, if true, most seriously weakens the editorial's argument?

(A) Maintaining the fire alarm boxes costs the city more than five million dollars annually.
(B) Commercial buildings have automatic fire alarm systems that are linked directly to the fire department.
(C) The fire department gets less information from an alarm box than it does from a telephone call.
(D) The city's fire department is located much closer to the residential areas than to the commercial district.
(E) On average, almost 25 percent of the public telephones in the city are out of order.

The editorial argues that fire alarm boxes remain necessary in the commercial district, because the specific alternatives to the alarm boxes to which the mayor refers—public and private phones—are not common there. The question asks you to identify a weakness in the editorial's argument in favor of keeping alarm boxes in the commercial district.

Choice B is the best answer. If commercial businesses use a different alternative—alarm systems connected to the fire department—then the editorial's conclusion is not well supported.

Neither choice A nor choice C gives any reason to think that the alarm boxes are not necessary, although both choices provide grounds for deactivating the boxes if they are no longer necessary. Choice D emphasizes the need to make sure that fires in the commercial district are reported quickly and does not weaken the editorial's argument. If public telephones are often out of order (choice E), there is more, rather than less, reason to think that the alarm boxes are necessary.

194. A major impediment to wide acceptance of electric vehicles even on the part of people who use their cars almost exclusively for commuting is the inability to use electric vehicles for occasional extended trips. In an attempt to make purchasing electric vehicles more attractive to commuters, one electric vehicle producer is planning to offer customers three days free rental of a conventional car for every 1,000 miles that they drive their electric vehicle.

Which of the following, if true, most threatens the plan's prospects for success?

(A) Many electric vehicles that are used for commercial purposes are not needed for extended trips.
(B) Because a majority of commuters drive at least 100 miles a week, the cost to the producer of making good the offer would add considerably to the already high price of electric vehicles.
(C) The relatively long time it takes to recharge the battery of an electric vehicle can easily be fitted into the regular patterns of car use characteristic of commuters.
(D) Although electric vehicles are essentially emission-free in actual use, generating the electricity necessary for charging an electric vehicle's battery can burden the environment.
(E) Some family vehicles are used primarily not for commuting but for making short local trips, such as to do errands.

The producer wants to make buying an electric vehicle more attractive to commuters and aims to do so by removing one obstacle: commuters who bought an electric vehicle would not be able to use it for long trips. The question asks you to identify something that might prevent the plan from succeeding.

Choice B is the best answer because if the plan would add considerably to the price of an electric vehicle, then it in effect replaces one obstacle to buying an electric vehicle with another. Choices A and E are incorrect because the producer's plan is focused on commuters, so the way some electric vehicles are used for commercial purposes (A) or for running errands (E) is of no relevance to the plan. Choice C poses no threat to the plan. Choice D presents both an advantage and a disadvantage of using an electric vehicle, but even the disadvantage does not threaten the plan's prospects of making electric vehicles more attractive to commuters than they currently are.

195. A proposed change to federal income tax laws would eliminate deductions from taxable income for donations a taxpayer has made to charitable and educational institutions. If this change were adopted, wealthy individuals would no longer be permitted such deductions. Therefore, many charitable and educational institutions would have to reduce services, and some would have to close their doors.

The argument above assumes which of the following?

(A) Without the incentives offered by federal income tax laws, at least some wealthy individuals would not donate as much money to charitable and educational institutions as they otherwise would have.

(B) Money contributed by individuals who make their donations because of provisions in the federal tax laws provides the only source of funding for many charitable and educational institutions.

(C) The primary reason for not adopting the proposed change in the federal income tax laws cited above is to protect wealthy individuals from having to pay higher taxes.

(D) Wealthy individuals who donate money to charitable and educational institutions are the only individuals who donate money to such institutions.

(E) Income tax laws should be changed to make donations to charitable and educational institutions the only permissible deductions from taxable income.

The passage argues that charitable and educational institutions, part of whose income comes from donations, would be negatively affected if wealthy individuals could not count such donations as deductions from their income. The question asks you to identify an assumption of the argument — that is, something that has to be true in order for the evidence presented to establish the conclusion.

Choice A is the best answer, since if this statement is false, all wealthy individuals would, even without the incentive provided by federal tax laws, donate as much money as they do now. In that case, the evidence used in the argument provides no support for the conclusion.

Choice B is not assumed: the argument need only assume that many institutions depend heavily, but not necessarily exclusively, on donations from such individuals. Choice C is incorrect given that the argument is concerned only with the consequences of the proposed change and makes no assumption about any reasons for making or not making the change. Choice D is not assumed: as far as the argument is concerned, there can be many other individuals who donate money to the institutions. Choice E is incorrect since the argument, being about the consequences of the particular proposed change, does not make any assumption about what alternative changes to the tax laws ought to be made.

196. An unusually severe winter occurred in Europe after the continent was blanketed by a blue haze resulting from the eruption of the Laki Volcano in the European republic of Iceland in the summer of 1984. Thus, it is evident that major eruptions cause the atmosphere to become cooler than it would be otherwise.

Which of the following statements, if true, most seriously weakens the argument above?

(A) The cooling effect triggered by volcanic eruptions in 1985 was counteracted by an unusual warming of Pacific waters.

(B) There is a strong statistical link between volcanic eruptions and the severity of the rainy season in India.

(C) A few months after El Chichón's large eruption in April 1982, air temperatures throughout the region remained higher than expected, given the long-term weather trends.

(D) The climatic effects of major volcanic eruptions can temporarily mask the general warming trend resulting from an excess of carbon dioxide in the atmosphere.

(E) Three months after an early springtime eruption in South America during the late 19th century, sea surface temperatures near the coast began to fall.

The passage makes a general claim — that major eruptions cause the atmosphere to cool down — on the basis of a single episode in which an eruption was followed by an unusually severe winter. You are asked to identify a fact that weakens the argument.

Choice C is the best answer. It describes an occasion when an eruption was followed by temperatures that were warmer than usual, not colder, and thus counterbalances the evidence offered in the passage.

Choice A announces that certain eruptions did have a cooling effect, so although an independent warming effect counteracted the effect, the argument is supported, not weakened. Choice B supports the claim that there is some connection between eruptions and the climate, but it provides no evidence one way or the other about whether eruptions specifically produce cooling. Choices D and E both present further evidence suggesting that eruptions can have a cooling effect: in choice D, the cooling interacts with an independent warming trend, and in choice E an eruption is followed by a cooling of sea temperatures.

197. To persuade consumers to buy its personal computers for home use, SuperComp has enlisted computer dealers in shopping centers to sell its product and launched a major advertising campaign that has already increased public awareness of the SuperComp brand. Despite the fact that these dealers achieved dramatically increased sales of computers last month, however, analysts doubt that the marketing plan is bringing SuperComp the desired success.

Which of the following, if true, best supports the claim that the analysts' doubt is well founded?

(A) In market surveys, few respondents who had been exposed to SuperComp's advertising campaign said they thought there was no point in owning a home computer.
(B) People who own a home computer often buy a second such computer, but only rarely do people buy a third computer.
(C) SuperComp's dealers also sell other brands of computers that are very similar to SuperComp's but less expensive and that afford the dealers a significantly higher markup.
(D) The dealers who were chosen to sell SuperComp's computers were selected in part because their stores are located in shopping centers that attract relatively wealthy shoppers.
(E) Computer-industry analysts believed before the SuperComp campaign began that most consumers who already owned home computers were not yet ready to replace them.

The passage states that the stores through which SuperComp is selling its computers are experiencing dramatically increased sales. Analysts doubt, however, that SuperComp's plan for selling its computers for home use is really working. The question asks you to identify a fact that justifies the analysts' doubt.

Choice C is the best answer. If consumers who are drawn to a SuperComp dealer find less expensive alternatives that the dealer has a strong incentive to sell to them, the analysts' doubt is justified, since it is likely that the increase in the dealer's sales is due not to sales of SuperComp's computers, but rather to sales of these other brands.

Choice A is incorrect; it suggests that there is a market for home computers, so does nothing to justify the analysts' doubts. Choice B is incorrect because it provides information about the consumers' buying inclinations, but does not provide justification for the analysts' doubts, given that the dealers were actually selling more computers than usual. Choice D is incorrect since it suggests that SuperComp chose well-located dealers, and does nothing to justify the analysts' doubts. Finally, the beliefs mentioned in choice E, which were formed before the campaign, cannot justify the analysts' doubts in the face of the evidence about increased sales.

198. A factory was trying out a new process for producing one of its products, with the goal of reducing production costs. A trial production run using the new process showed a 15 percent reduction in costs compared with past performance using the standard process. The production managers therefore concluded that the new process did produce a cost savings.

Which of the following, if true, casts most doubt on the production managers' conclusion?

(A) In the cost reduction project that eventually led to the trial of the new process, production managers had initially been seeking cost reductions of 50 percent.
(B) Analysis of the trial of the new process showed that the cost reduction during the trial was entirely attributable to a reduction in the number of finished products rejected by quality control.
(C) While the trial was being conducted, production costs at the factory for a similar product, produced without benefit of the new process, also showed a 15 percent reduction.
(D) Although some of the factory's managers have been arguing that the product is outdated and ought to be redesigned, the use of the new production process does not involve any changes in the finished product.
(E) Since the new process differs from the standard process only in the way in which the stages of production are organized and ordered, the cost of the materials used in the product is the same in both processes.

The managers concluded that the new process produced a cost savings on the basis of a trial run of the process in which costs were 15 percent lower than they had been previously. You are asked to identify something that casts doubt on their conclusion.

Choice C is the best answer. If production costs at the factory fell for a similar product that was produced without using the new process, it is more doubtful that the observed production cost reductions achieved during the trial run were actually produced by the new process.

Choice A is incorrect; the fact that the managers had hoped for cost reductions of fifty percent does not cast any doubt on their conclusion that the new process had produced at least some savings. Choice B is incorrect since finding the source of the cost savings in the trial shows that the savings were no mere accident and so reinforces the managers' conclusion. Choices D and E are incorrect since by emphasizing that certain aspects of the product—its design and raw materials—were the same in the standard process and the new process, these two answer choices support, rather than cast doubt on, the conclusion that the process itself produced the savings.

199. Vitacorp, a manufacturer, wishes to make its information booth at an industry convention more productive in terms of boosting sales. The booth offers information introducing the company's new products and services. To achieve the desired result, Vitacorp's marketing department will attempt to attract more people to the booth. The marketing director's first measure was to instruct each salesperson to call his or her five best customers and personally invite them to visit the booth.

Which of the following, if true, most strongly supports the prediction that the marketing director's first measure will contribute to meeting the goal of boosting sales?

(A) Vitacorp's salespeople routinely inform each important customer about new products and services as soon as the decision to launch them has been made.

(B) Many of Vitacorp's competitors have made plans for making their own information booths more productive in increasing sales.

(C) An information booth that is well attended tends to attract visitors who would not otherwise have attended the booth.

(D) Most of Vitacorp's best customers also have business dealings with Vitacorp's competitors.

(E) Vitacorp has fewer new products and services available this year than it had in previous years.

The passage introduces a goal: to get the information booth at the industry convention to be more effective at boosting sales. It also introduces a plan for achieving that goal: to increase attendance at the booth by having the salesforce invite its best customers to visit the booth. The question asks you to identify a reason for thinking that inviting the customers will help Vitacorp to achieve its goal.

Choice C is the best answer, since it explains how having Vitacorp's best customers attend the booth might encourage new customers to attend. Hence there would be a chance to boost sales even if the invited visitors, who are already good customers of Vitacorp, do not increase their purchases as a result of their visits.

According to choice A, the customers who will be especially invited to attend the booth will not as a result be any better informed about Vitacorp's products, so it gives no reason for thinking that sales to these customers will be stimulated. Choice B is incorrect because successful information booths belonging to Vitacorp's competitors might cut into Vitacorp's sales. Choice D presents a difficulty for the plan— Vitacorp's best customers also use its competitors—and provides no way of overcoming this difficulty. Choice E strongly suggests that the booth will be less effective at boosting sales than normal.

200. Outsourcing is the practice of obtaining from an independent supplier a product or service that a company has previously provided for itself. Since a company's chief objective is to realize the highest possible year-end profits, any product or service that can be obtained from an independent supplier for less than it would cost the company to provide the product or service on its own should be outsourced.

Which of the following, if true, most seriously weakens the argument?

(A) If a company decides to use independent suppliers for a product, it can generally exploit the vigorous competition arising among several firms that are interested in supplying that product.

(B) Successful outsourcing requires a company to provide its suppliers with information about its products and plans that can fall into the hands of its competitors and give them a business advantage.

(C) Certain tasks, such as processing a company's payroll, are commonly outsourced, whereas others, such as handling the company's core business, are not.

(D) For a company to provide a product or service for itself as efficiently as an independent supplier can provide it, the managers involved need to be as expert in the area of that product or service as the people in charge of that product or service at an independent supplier are.

(E) When a company decides to use an independent supplier for a product or service, the independent supplier sometimes hires members of the company's staff who formerly made the product or provided the service that the independent supplier now supplies.

The passage argues that a company should obtain a needed product or service from an outside supplier whenever a comparison between the price the outside supplier asks and the cost of a company's making that product or service for itself shows the outside supplier's price to be lower. The reason given is that doing so will lower the company's cost and so contribute to its profits.

The question asks you to identify the answer choice that weakens this argument. The correct answer, therefore, will give a reason why using an outside supplier might not help the company's profitability even though the price the outside supplier asks is low.

Choice B is the best answer since the possible leakage of sensitive information to the company's competitors is a hidden cost of relying on outside suppliers and gives a reason why outsourcing might not, ultimately, enhance profitability even if it offers an immediate reduction in costs.

Choices A and D are incorrect because they present benefits of outsourcing, not drawbacks—choice A refers to competition between independent suppliers, and choice D refers to the experienced management ability available. Information about which tasks are in fact commonly outsourced (choice C) does not affect the argument, which is about what tasks should be outsourced. Choice E points out a common consequence of outsourcing, but presents no disadvantage of this consequence to the company.

201.   State spokesperson: Many businesspeople who have not been to our state believe that we have an inadequate road system. Those people are mistaken, as is obvious from the fact that in each of the past six years, our state has spent more money per mile on road improvements than any other state.

Which of the following, if true, most seriously undermines the reasoning in the spokesperson's argument?

(A)   In the spokesperson's state, spending on road improvements has been increasing more slowly over the past six years than it has in several other states.

(B)   Adequacy of a state's road system is generally less important to a businessperson considering doing business there than is the availability of qualified employees.

(C)   Over the past six years, numerous businesses have left the spokesperson's state, but about as many businesses have moved into the state.

(D)   In general, the number of miles of road in a state's road system depends on both the area and the population of the state.

(E)   Only states with seriously inadequate road systems need to spend large amounts of money on road improvements.

The spokesperson argues that the state's road system is not inadequate, since the amount the state spends on road improvement is more, per mile of road, than any other state spends. The question asks you to find the answer choice that most seriously undermines this reasoning. This will be the choice that shows how a large amount of spending on road improvement need not indicate that the road system is good.

Choice E is the best answer. It points out that spending an unusually large amount on road improvements tends to indicate that the roads being improved must be in unusually poor condition.

Choice A is incorrect since it gives no reason for thinking that spending a large amount of money on road improvements is a poor indicator of the quality of the road system. Choices B and C are incorrect. Although the spokesperson's argument is addressed to businesspeople, it is solely about whether the state's road system is adequate. The importance of the road system in attracting business to the state is therefore not relevant to this argument (choice B). The number of businesses relocating into or out of the state is also therefore not relevant to the argument (choice C). Choice D is incorrect since the relevance of the statistic that the spokesperson uses about spending per mile of road is not affected by the information provided here about road systems and state size.

202.   Gortland has long been narrowly self-sufficient in both grain and meat. However, as per capita income in Gortland has risen toward the world average, per capita consumption of meat has also risen toward the world average, and it takes several pounds of grain to produce one pound of meat. Therefore, since per capita income continues to rise, whereas domestic grain production will not increase, Gortland will soon have to import either grain or meat or both.

Which of the following is an assumption on which the argument depends?

(A)   The total acreage devoted to grain production in Gortland will not decrease substantially.

(B)   The population of Gortland has remained relatively constant during the country's years of growing prosperity.

(C)   The per capita consumption of meat in Gortland is roughly the same across all income levels.

(D)   In Gortland, neither meat nor grain is subject to government price controls.

(E)   People in Gortland who increase their consumption of meat will not radically decrease their consumption of grain.

The argument in the passage concludes that, although Gortland currently produces enough grain and meat for its own needs, it will soon not do so. This conclusion is based on the continuing increase in per capita consumption of meat as per capita income increases, and the fact that several pounds of grain must be used to produce each pound of meat.

The question asks you to identify an assumption on which the argument depends. An assumption is something that must be true in order for the argument's conclusion to be established by the evidence the argument gives.

Choice E is the best answer. If the people who increase their consumption of meat at the same time radically reduce their consumption of grain, the evidence given in the argument cannot establish its conclusion. So for the conclusion to be established this possibility must be ruled out, which is what this answer choice does.

Choice A is incorrect. The argument does not assume that grain production in Gortland will decline, only that demand for grain will increase. Choice B is not assumed, since the argument would be unaffected even if the population had been increasing. Choice C is not assumed; no particular assumption about the distribution of meat consumption across income levels is required, although it is required that meat consumption overall will continue to increase. Choice D is incorrect. While it is assumed, for example, that the government will not freeze meat consumption at current levels, it is not assumed that the government has no role in the pricing of meat and grain.

203. Journalist: In physics journals, the number of articles reporting the results of experiments involving particle accelerators was lower last year than it had been in previous years. Several of the particle accelerators at major research institutions were out of service the year before last for repairs, so it is likely that the low number of articles was due to the decline in availability of particle accelerators.

Which of the following, if true, most seriously undermines the journalist's argument?

(A) Every article based on experiments with particle accelerators that was submitted for publication last year actually was published.

(B) The average time scientists must wait for access to a particle accelerator has declined over the last several years.

(C) The number of physics journals was the same last year as in previous years.

(D) Particle accelerators can be used for more than one group of experiments in any given year.

(E) Recent changes in the editorial policies of several physics journals have decreased the likelihood that articles concerning particle-accelerator research will be accepted for publication.

The journalist's argument offers an explanation for the decline in published articles reporting the results of experiments involving particle accelerators. The explanation given is that fewer than usual particle accelerators were available for physicists' experiments the year before last, and thus that the decline reflects a reduction in the number of experiments with results to report.

The question asks for the answer choice that undermines the journalist's argument. The argument can be undermined either by indications that the explanation offered by the journalist cannot explain the decline or by evidence that strongly supports an alternative explanation to the one the journalist offers.

Choice E is the best answer. This choice strongly supports an alternative explanation for the decline: that it was brought about by changes in editorial policy. This possibility undermines the journalist's argument.

Choice A is incorrect because it implies that there was indeed a decline in the number of articles submitted and so supports the journalist's explanation. Choice B is incorrect since the fact that scientists have to wait for access implies that the accelerators continue to be fully used, thereby lending support to the idea that it is the reduced number of accelerators that led to a reduced number of articles. Since a decline in the number of physics journals would be one alternative explanation for the decline in the number of articles published, and choice C rules out that alternative explanation, it somewhat supports the explanation the journalist offers. Choice D does not weaken the journalist's argument: even if accelerators can be used for several experiments, a reduction in the number of accelerators is likely to lead to a reduction in the number of experiments, and hence of articles.

204. An eyeglass manufacturer tried to boost sales for the summer quarter by offering its distributors a special discount if their orders for that quarter exceeded those for last year's summer quarter by at least 20 percent. Many distributors qualified for this discount. Even with much merchandise discounted, sales increased enough to produce a healthy gain in net profits. The manufacturer plans to repeat this success by offering the same sort of discount for the fall quarter.

Which of the following, if true, most clearly points to a flaw in the manufacturer's plan to repeat the successful performance of the summer quarter?

(A) In general, a distributor's orders for the summer quarter are no higher than those for the spring quarter.

(B) Along with offering special discounts to qualifying distributors, the manufacturer increased newspaper and radio advertising in those distributors' sales areas.

(C) The distributors most likely to qualify for the manufacturer's special discount are those whose orders were unusually low a year earlier.

(D) The distributors who qualified for the manufacturer's special discount were free to decide how much of that discount to pass on to their own customers.

(E) The distributors' ordering more goods in the summer quarter left them overstocked for the fall quarter.

Based on the success of the discount offer over the summer, the manufacturer plans to extend the same offer for the fall quarter. The question asks you to find the answer choice that identifies a flaw in this plan, that is, a reason for thinking that, even though the plan was successful in the summer quarter, it will not succeed in the fall.

Choice E is the best answer since it indicates that the increase in sales during the summer quarter has reduced the number of potential sales during the fall quarter. That makes it unlikely that the discount plan can continue to boost sales in the same way.

Choice A is incorrect because the discount program is based on a comparison between a distributor's sales in a quarter and the sales in the same quarter the previous year, rather than in the previous quarter. Since advertising helps the distributors sell to their retail customers, choice B provides no reason for thinking the plan will not succeed in the fall. Choice C is incorrect: although part of the success of the discount incentives in the summer may have come from distributors' recovering to more normal sales, that does not provide a reason for thinking that the same increase in sales cannot occur in the fall quarter. Choice D is also incorrect: distributors' flexibility in deciding how to take advantage of the discounts give no reason for thinking that the discounts will fail to increase fall sales

205. Consumer advocate: It is generally true, at least in this state, that lawyers who advertise a specific service charge less for that service than lawyers who do not advertise. It is also true that **each time restrictions on the advertising of legal services have been eliminated, the number of lawyers advertising their services has increased and legal costs to consumers have declined in consequence.** However, eliminating the state requirement that legal advertisements must specify fees for specific services would almost certainly increase rather than further reduce consumers' legal costs. Lawyers would no longer have an incentive to lower their fees when they begin advertising and **if no longer required to specify fee arrangements, many lawyers who now advertise would increase their fees.**

In the consumer advocate's argument, the two portions in **boldface** play which of the following roles?

(A) The first is a generalization that the consumer advocate accepts as true; the second is presented as a consequence that follows from the truth of that generalization.

(B) The first is a pattern of cause and effect that the consumer advocate argues will be repeated in the case at issue; the second acknowledges a circumstance in which that pattern would not hold.

(C) The first is a pattern of cause and effect that the consumer advocate predicts will not hold in the case at issue; the second offers a consideration in support of that prediction.

(D) The first is evidence that the consumer advocate offers in support of a certain prediction; the second is that prediction.

(E) The first acknowledges a consideration that weighs against the main position that the consumer advocate defends; the second is that position.

In the passage, the consumer advocate argues for a certain position:

> . . . eliminating the state requirement that legal advertisements must specify fees for specific services would almost certainly increase rather than further reduce consumers' legal costs.

What follows the statement is preceded by two concessions that, the advocate admits, tend to point in the opposite direction; what follows the statement of the position are the reasons the advocate has for holding that position. To answer the question, you must find the choice that correctly describes the roles played by **both** of the portions that are in boldface.

Choice C is the correct answer. The first boldface portion does present a pattern of cause and effect, and the advocate's prediction is that this time the pattern will be different. In addition, the second boldface portion is one of the considerations that the advocate uses in support of that prediction.

While the description of the first boldface portion given in choice A is correct, that of the second is not: the generalization in fact tends to run counter to the prediction made in the second boldface portion. Therefore this choice is incorrect.

Choice B is incorrect, since although the first boldface portion presents a pattern of cause and effect, the advocate's prediction is that in this case that pattern will not hold. Thus the role of the first boldface portion is incorrectly described. Choice D is incorrect: the advocate does not use the first boldface portion in support of any prediction and instead concedes that it runs counter to the advocate's own prediction.

While the role of the first boldface portion is correctly described in choice E, that of the second is not, since the position the advocate is defending is not the second boldface portion, but rather the position identified above. Thus this choice is incorrect.

8 Sentence Correction

Sample sentence correction questions begin on page 653; following the questions are explanations for all the questions. The explanations address types of grammatical and syntactical problems you are likely to encounter in the sentence correction questions of the GMAT®.

Study Suggestions

1. One way to gain familiarity with the basic conventions of standard written English is to read material that reflects standard usage. Suitable material will usually be found in good magazines and nonfiction books, editorials in outstanding newspapers, and the collections of essays used by many college and university writing courses.

2. A general review of basic rules of grammar and practice with writing exercises are also ways of studying for the sentence correction questions. If you have papers that have been carefully evaluated for grammatical errors, it may be helpful to review the comments and corrections.

Test-taking Strategies for Sentence Correction

1. Read the entire sentence carefully. Try to understand the specific idea or relationship that the sentence should express.

2. Since the part of the sentence that *may* be incorrect is underlined, concentrate on evaluating the underlined part for errors and possible corrections before reading the answer choices.

3. Read each answer choice carefully. The first answer choice always repeats the underlined portion of the original sentence. Choose this answer if you think that the sentence is best as it stands, but only after examining all of the other choices.

4. Try to determine how well each choice corrects whatever you consider wrong with the original sentence.

5. Make sure that you evaluate the sentence and the choices in terms of general clarity, grammatical and idiomatic usage, economy and precision of language, and appropriateness of diction.

6. Read the whole sentence, substituting the choice that you prefer for the underlined part. A choice may be wrong because it does not fit grammatically or structurally with the rest of the sentence. Remember that some sentences will require no corrections. The answer to such a sentence should be the first answer choice.

SENTENCE CORRECTION SAMPLE QUESTIONS

When finished reading directions click on the icon below

Dismiss Directions

The question presents a sentence, part of which or all of which is underlined. Beneath the sentence you will find five ways of phrasing the underlined part. The first of these repeats the original; the other four are different. If you think the original is best, choose the first answer; otherwise choose one of the others.

This question tests correctness and effectiveness of expression. In choosing your answer, follow the requirements of standard written English; that is, pay attention to grammar, choice of words, and sentence construction. Choose the answer that produces the most effective sentence; this answer should be clear and exact, without awkwardness, ambiguity, redundancy, or grammatical error.

To review these directions for subsequent questions of this type, click on HELP.

Test
Quit

Section
Exit

Time

?
Help

Answer
Confirm

Next

SENTENCE CORRECTION SAMPLE QUESTIONS

1. The Wallerstein study indicates that even after a decade young men and women still experience some of the effects of a divorce <u>occurring when a child</u>.

   (A) occurring when a child
   (B) occurring when children
   (C) that occurred when a child
   (D) that occurred when they were children
   (E) that has occurred as each was a child

2. Since 1981, when the farm depression began, the number of acres overseen by professional farm-management companies <u>have grown from 48 million to nearly 59 million, an area that is about Colorado's size</u>.

   (A) have grown from 48 million to nearly 59 million, an area that is about Colorado's size
   (B) have grown from 48 million to nearly 59 million, about the size of Colorado
   (C) has grown from 48 million to nearly 59 million, an area about the size of Colorado
   (D) has grown from 48 million up to nearly 59 million, an area about the size of Colorado's
   (E) has grown from 48 million up to nearly 59 million, about Colorado's size

3. Some bat caves, like honeybee hives, have residents that take on different duties such as defending the entrance, <u>acting as sentinels and to sound</u> a warning at the approach of danger, and scouting outside the cave for new food and roosting sites.

   (A) acting as sentinels and to sound
   (B) acting as sentinels and sounding
   (C) to act as sentinels and sound
   (D) to act as sentinels and to sound
   (E) to act as a sentinel sounding

4. The only way for growers to salvage frozen citrus is <u>to process them quickly into juice concentrate before they rot when warmer weather returns</u>.

   (A) to process them quickly into juice concentrate before they rot when warmer weather returns
   (B) if they are quickly processed into juice concentrate before warmer weather returns to rot them
   (C) for them to be processed quickly into juice concentrate before the fruit rots when warmer weather returns
   (D) if the fruit is quickly processed into juice concentrate before they rot when warmer weather returns
   (E) to have it quickly processed into juice concentrate before warmer weather returns and rots the fruit

5. Carbon-14 dating reveals that the megalithic monuments in Brittany are nearly 2,000 years <u>as old as any of their supposed</u> Mediterranean predecessors.

   (A) as old as any of their supposed
   (B) older than any of their supposed
   (C) as old as their supposed
   (D) older than any of their supposedly
   (E) as old as their supposedly

6. In virtually all types of tissue in every animal species, dioxin induces the production of enzymes that are the organism's <u>trying to metabolize, or render harmless, the chemical that is irritating it</u>.

   (A) trying to metabolize, or render harmless, the chemical that is irritating it
   (B) trying that it metabolize, or render harmless, the chemical irritant
   (C) attempt to try to metabolize, or render harmless, such a chemical irritant
   (D) attempt to try and metabolize, or render harmless, the chemical irritating it
   (E) attempt to metabolize, or render harmless, the chemical irritant

7. Dr. Hakuta's research among Hispanic children in the United States indicates that the more the children use both Spanish and English, <u>their intellectual advantage is greater in skills underlying reading ability and nonverbal logic</u>.

(A) their intellectual advantage is greater in skills underlying reading ability and nonverbal logic
(B) their intellectual advantage is the greater in skills underlaying reading ability and nonverbal logic
(C) the greater their intellectual advantage in skills underlying reading ability and nonverbal logic
(D) in skills that underlay reading ability and nonverbal logic, their intellectual advantage is the greater
(E) in skills underlying reading ability and nonverbal logic, the greater intellectual advantage is theirs

8. Lacking information about energy use, people tend to overestimate the amount of energy used by <u>equipment, such as lights, that are visible and must be turned on and off and underestimate that</u> used by unobtrusive equipment, such as water heaters.

(A) equipment, such as lights, that are visible and must be turned on and off and underestimate that
(B) equipment, such as lights, that are visible and must be turned on and off and underestimate it when
(C) equipment, such as lights, that is visible and must be turned on and off and underestimate it when
(D) visible equipment, such as lights, that must be turned on and off and underestimate that
(E) visible equipment, such as lights, that must be turned on and off and underestimate it when

9. Astronomers at the Palomar Observatory have discovered a distant supernova explosion, one <u>that they believe is</u> a type previously unknown to science.

(A) that they believe is
(B) that they believe it to be
(C) they believe that it is of
(D) they believe that is
(E) they believe to be of

10. <u>However much United States voters may agree that</u> there is waste in government and that the government as a whole spends beyond its means, it is difficult to find broad support for a movement toward a minimal state.

(A) However much United States voters may agree that
(B) Despite the agreement among United States voters to the fact
(C) Although United States voters agree
(D) Even though United States voters may agree
(E) There is agreement among United States voters that

11. <u>Based on accounts of various ancient writers,</u> scholars have painted a sketchy picture of the activities of an all-female cult that, perhaps as early as the sixth century B.C., worshipped a goddess known in Latin as Bona Dea, "the good goddess."

(A) Based on accounts of various ancient writers
(B) Basing it on various ancient writers' accounts
(C) With accounts of various ancient writers used for a basis
(D) By the accounts of various ancient writers they used
(E) Using accounts of various ancient writers

12. <u>Formulas for cash flow and the ratio of debt to equity do not apply to new small businesses in the same way as they do to established big businesses, because they are growing and are seldom in equilibrium.</u>

(A) Formulas for cash flow and the ratio of debt to equity do not apply to new small businesses in the same way as they do to established big businesses, because they are growing and are seldom in equilibrium.
(B) Because they are growing and are seldom in equilibrium, formulas for cash flow and the ratio of debt to equity do not apply to new small businesses in the same way as they do to established big businesses.
(C) Because they are growing and are seldom in equilibrium, new small businesses are not subject to the same applicability of formulas for cash flow and the ratio of debt to equity as established big businesses.
(D) Because new small businesses are growing and are seldom in equilibrium, formulas for cash flow and the ratio of debt to equity do not apply to them in the same way as to established big businesses.
(E) New small businesses are not subject to the applicability of formulas for cash flow and the ratio of debt to equity in the same way as established big businesses, because they are growing and are seldom in equilibrium.

13. State officials report that soaring <u>rates of liability insurance have risen to force</u> cutbacks in the operations of everything from local governments and school districts to day-care centers and recreational facilities.

(A) rates of liability insurance have risen to force
(B) rates of liability insurance are a force for
(C) rates for liability insurance are forcing
(D) rises in liability insurance rates are forcing
(E) liability insurance rates have risen to force

14. Paleontologists believe that fragments of a primate jawbone unearthed in Burma and estimated <u>at 40 to 44 million years old provide evidence of</u> a crucial step along the evolutionary path that led to human beings.

(A) at 40 to 44 million years old provide evidence of
(B) as being 40 to 44 million years old provides evidence of
(C) that it is 40 to 44 million years old provides evidence of what was
(D) to be 40 to 44 million years old provide evidence of
(E) as 40 to 44 million years old provides evidence of what was

15. In his research paper, Dr. Frosh, medical director of the Payne Whitney Clinic, distinguishes <u>mood swings, which may be violent without their being grounded in mental disease, from genuine manic-depressive psychosis</u>.

(A) mood swings, which may be violent without their being grounded in mental disease, from genuine manic-depressive psychosis
(B) mood swings, perhaps violent without being grounded in mental disease, and genuine manic-depressive psychosis
(C) between mood swings, which may be violent without being grounded in mental disease, and genuine manic-depressive psychosis
(D) between mood swings, perhaps violent without being grounded in mental disease, from genuine manic-depressive psychosis
(E) genuine manic-depressive psychosis and mood swings, which may be violent without being grounded in mental disease

16. Unlike a typical automobile loan, which requires a fifteen- to twenty-percent down payment, <u>the lease-loan buyer is not required to make</u> an initial deposit on the new vehicle.

(A) the lease-loan buyer is not required to make
(B) with lease-loan buying there is no requirement of
(C) lease-loan buyers are not required to make
(D) for the lease-loan buyer there is no requirement of
(E) a lease-loan does not require the buyer to make

17. Native American burial sites dating back 5,000 years indicate that the residents of Maine at that time <u>were part of a widespread culture of Algonquian-speaking people</u>.

(A) were part of a widespread culture of Algonquian-speaking people
(B) had been part of a widespread culture of people who were Algonquian-speaking
(C) were people who were part of a widespread culture that was Algonquian-speaking
(D) had been people who were part of a widespread culture that was Algonquian-speaking
(E) were a people which had been part of a widespread, Algonquian-speaking culture

18. <u>Each of Hemingway's wives — Hadley Richardson, Pauline Pfeiffer, Martha Gelhorn, and Mary Welsh — were strong and interesting women,</u> very different from the often pallid women who populate his novels.

(A) Each of Hemingway's wives — Hadley Richardson, Pauline Pfeiffer, Martha Gelhorn, and Mary Welsh — were strong and interesting women,
(B) Hadley Richardson, Pauline Pfeiffer, Martha Gelhorn, and Mary Welsh — each of them Hemingway's wives — were strong and interesting women,
(C) Hemingway's wives — Hadley Richardson, Pauline Pfeiffer, Martha Gelhorn, and Mary Welsh — were all strong and interesting women,
(D) Strong and interesting women — Hadley Richardson, Pauline Pfeiffer, Martha Gelhorn, and Mary Welsh — each a wife of Hemingway, was
(E) Strong and interesting women — Hadley Richardson, Pauline Pfeiffer, Martha Gelhorn, and Mary Welsh — every one of Hemingway's wives were

19. In addition to having more protein than wheat does, <u>the protein in rice is higher quality than that in</u> wheat, with more of the amino acids essential to the human diet.

    (A) the protein in rice is higher quality than that in
    (B) rice has protein of higher quality than that in
    (C) the protein in rice is higher in quality than it is in
    (D) rice protein is higher in quality than it is in
    (E) rice has a protein higher in quality than

20. An array of tax incentives has led to a boom in the construction of new office buildings; <u>so abundant has capital been for commercial real estate that</u> investors regularly scour the country for areas in which to build.

    (A) so abundant has capital been for commercial real estate that
    (B) capital has been so abundant for commercial real estate, so that
    (C) the abundance of capital for commercial real estate has been such,
    (D) such has the abundance of capital been for commercial real estate that
    (E) such has been an abundance of capital for commercial real estate,

21. Defense attorneys have occasionally argued that their clients' misconduct stemmed from a reaction to something ingested, but <u>in attributing criminal or delinquent behavior to some food allergy</u>, the perpetrators are in effect told that they are not responsible for their actions.

    (A) in attributing criminal or delinquent behavior to some food allergy
    (B) if criminal or delinquent behavior is attributed to an allergy to some food
    (C) in attributing behavior that is criminal or delinquent to an allergy to some food
    (D) if some food allergy is attributed as the cause of criminal or delinquent behavior
    (E) in attributing a food allergy as the cause of criminal or delinquent behavior

22. The voluminous personal papers of Thomas Alva Edison reveal that his inventions typically <u>sprang to life not in a flash of inspiration but evolved slowly</u> from previous works.

    (A) sprang to life not in a flash of inspiration but evolved slowly
    (B) sprang to life not in a flash of inspiration but were slowly evolved
    (C) did not spring to life in a flash of inspiration but evolved slowly
    (D) did not spring to life in a flash of inspiration but had slowly evolved
    (E) did not spring to life in a flash of inspiration but they were slowly evolved

23. A Labor Department study states that the <u>numbers of women employed outside the home grew by more than a thirty-five percent increase</u> in the past decade and accounted for more than sixty-two percent of the total growth in the civilian work force.

    (A) numbers of women employed outside the home grew by more than a thirty-five percent increase
    (B) numbers of women employed outside the home grew more than thirty-five percent
    (C) numbers of women employed outside the home were raised by more than thirty-five percent
    (D) number of women employed outside the home increased by more than thirty-five percent
    (E) number of women employed outside the home was raised by more than a thirty-five percent increase

24. The first decision for most tenants living in a building undergoing <u>being converted to cooperative ownership is if to sign</u> a no-buy pledge with the other tenants.

    (A) being converted to cooperative ownership is if to sign
    (B) being converted to cooperative ownership is whether they should be signing
    (C) being converted to cooperative ownership is whether or not they sign
    (D) conversion to cooperative ownership is if to sign
    (E) conversion to cooperative ownership is whether to sign

25. The end of the eighteenth century saw the emergence of prize-stock breeding, with individual bulls and cows receiving awards, fetching unprecedented prices, and <u>excited</u> enormous interest whenever they were put on show.

(A) excited
(B) it excited
(C) exciting
(D) would excite
(E) it had excited

26. Of all the possible disasters that threaten American agriculture, the possibility of an adverse change in climate <u>is maybe the more difficult for analysis</u>.

(A) is maybe the more difficult for analysis
(B) is probably the most difficult to analyze
(C) is maybe the most difficult for analysis
(D) is probably the more difficult to analyze
(E) is, it may be, the analysis that is most difficult

27. <u>Published in Harlem, the owner and editor of the Messenger were two young journalists, Chandler Owen and A. Philip Randolph, who would later make his reputation as a labor leader.</u>

(A) Published in Harlem, the owner and editor of the *Messenger* were two young journalists, Chandler Owen and A. Philip Randolph, who would later make his reputation as a labor leader.
(B) Published in Harlem, two young journalists, Chandler Owen and A. Philip Randolph, who would later make his reputation as a labor leader, were the owner and editor of the *Messenger*.
(C) Published in Harlem, the *Messenger* was owned and edited by two young journalists, A. Philip Randolph, who would later make his reputation as a labor leader, and Chandler Owen.
(D) The *Messenger* was owned and edited by two young journalists, Chandler Owen and A. Philip Randolph, who would later make his reputation as a labor leader, and published in Harlem.
(E) The owner and editor being two young journalists, Chandler Owen and A. Philip Randolph, who would later make his reputation as a labor leader, the *Messenger* was published in Harlem.

28. The rise in the Commerce Department's index of leading economic indicators <u>suggest that the economy should continue its expansion into the coming months, but that</u> the mixed performance of the index's individual components indicates that economic growth will proceed at a more moderate pace than in the first quarter of this year.

(A) suggest that the economy should continue its expansion into the coming months, but that
(B) suggest that the economy is to continue expansion in the coming months, but
(C) suggests that the economy will continue its expanding in the coming months, but that
(D) suggests that the economy is continuing to expand into the coming months, but that
(E) suggests that the economy will continue to expand in the coming months, but

29. In three centuries — from 1050 to 1350 — several million tons of stone were quarried in France <u>for the building of eighty cathedrals, five hundred large churches, and some</u> tens of thousands of parish churches.

(A) for the building of eighty cathedrals, five hundred large churches, and some
(B) in order that they might build eighty cathedrals, five hundred large churches, and some
(C) so as they might build eighty cathedrals, five hundred large churches, and some
(D) so that there could be built eighty cathedrals, five hundred large churches, and
(E) such that they could build eighty cathedrals, five hundred large churches, and

30. <u>What was as remarkable as the development of the compact disc</u> has been the use of the new technology to revitalize, in better sound than was ever before possible, some of the classic recorded performances of the pre-LP era.

(A) What was as remarkable as the development of the compact disc
(B) The thing that was as remarkable as developing the compact disc
(C) No less remarkable than the development of the compact disc
(D) Developing the compact disc has been none the less remarkable than
(E) Development of the compact disc has been no less remarkable as

31. Unlike computer skills or other technical skills, there is a disinclination on the part of many people to recognize the degree to which their analytical skills are weak.

 (A) Unlike computer skills or other technical skills, there is a disinclination on the part of many people to recognize the degree to which their analytical skills are weak.
 (B) Unlike computer skills or other technical skills, which they admit they lack, many people are disinclined to recognize that their analytical skills are weak.
 (C) Unlike computer skills or other technical skills, analytical skills bring out a disinclination in many people to recognize that they are weak to a degree.
 (D) Many people, willing to admit that they lack computer skills or other technical skills, are disinclined to recognize that their analytical skills are weak.
 (E) Many people have a disinclination to recognize the weakness of their analytical skills while willing to admit their lack of computer skills or other technical skills.

32. Some buildings that were destroyed and heavily damaged in the earthquake last year were constructed in violation of the city's building code.

 (A) Some buildings that were destroyed and heavily damaged in the earthquake last year were
 (B) Some buildings that were destroyed or heavily damaged in the earthquake last year had been
 (C) Some buildings that the earthquake destroyed and heavily damaged last year have been
 (D) Last year the earthquake destroyed or heavily damaged some buildings that have been
 (E) Last year some of the buildings that were destroyed or heavily damaged in the earthquake had been

33. From the earliest days of the tribe, kinship determined the way in which the Ojibwa society organized its labor, provided access to its resources, and defined rights and obligations involved in the distribution and consumption of those resources.

 (A) and defined rights and obligations involved in the distribution and consumption of those resources
 (B) defining rights and obligations involved in their distribution and consumption
 (C) and defined rights and obligations as they were involved in its distribution and consumption
 (D) whose rights and obligations were defined in their distribution and consumption
 (E) the distribution and consumption of them defined by rights and obligations

34. A report by the American Academy for the Advancement of Science has concluded that much of the currently uncontrolled dioxins to which North Americans are exposed comes from the incineration of wastes.

 (A) much of the currently uncontrolled dioxins to which North Americans are exposed comes
 (B) much of the currently uncontrolled dioxins that North Americans are exposed to come
 (C) much of the dioxins that are currently uncontrolled and that North Americans are exposed to comes
 (D) many of the dioxins that are currently uncontrolled and North Americans are exposed to come
 (E) many of the currently uncontrolled dioxins to which North Americans are exposed come

35. In June of 1987, *The Bridge of Trinquetaille,* Vincent van Gogh's view of an iron bridge over the Rhone sold for $20.2 million and it was the second highest price ever paid for a painting at auction.

 (A) Rhone sold for $20.2 million and it was
 (B) Rhone, which sold for $20.2 million, was
 (C) Rhone, was sold for $20.2 million,
 (D) Rhone was sold for $20.2 million, being
 (E) Rhone, sold for $20.2 million, and was

36. *Bufo marinus* toads, fierce predators that will eat frogs, lizards, and even small birds, are native to South America but were introduced into Florida during the 1930's in an attempt to control pests in the state's vast sugarcane fields.

 (A) are native to South America but were introduced into Florida during the 1930's in an attempt to control
 (B) are native in South America but were introduced into Florida during the 1930's as attempts to control
 (C) are natives of South America but were introduced into Florida during the 1930's in an attempt at controlling
 (D) had been native to South America but were introduced to Florida during the 1930's as an attempt at controlling
 (E) had been natives of South America but were introduced to Florida during the 1930's as attempts at controlling

37. While some academicians believe that business ethics should be integrated into every business course, others say that students will take ethics seriously only if it would be taught as a separately required course.

(A) only if it would be taught as a separately required course
(B) only if it is taught as a separate, required course
(C) if it is taught only as a course required separately
(D) if it was taught only as a separate and required course
(E) if it would only be taught as a required course, separately

38. Scientists have observed large concentrations of heavy-metal deposits in the upper twenty centimeters of Baltic Sea sediments, which are consistent with the growth of industrial activity there.

(A) Baltic Sea sediments, which are consistent with the growth of industrial activity there
(B) Baltic Sea sediments, where the growth of industrial activity is consistent with these findings
(C) Baltic Sea sediments, findings consistent with its growth of industrial activity
(D) sediments from the Baltic Sea, findings consistent with the growth of industrial activity in the area
(E) sediments from the Baltic Sea, consistent with the growth of industrial activity there

39. For members of the seventeenth-century Ashanti nation in Africa, animal-hide shields with wooden frames were essential items of military equipment, a method to protect warriors against enemy arrows and spears.

(A) a method to protect
(B) as a method protecting
(C) protecting
(D) as a protection of
(E) to protect

40. In metalwork one advantage of adhesive-bonding over spot-welding is that the contact, and hence the bonding, is effected continuously over a broad surface instead of a series of regularly spaced points with no bonding in between.

(A) instead of
(B) as opposed to
(C) in contrast with
(D) rather than at
(E) as against being at

41. Under a provision of the Constitution that was never applied, Congress has been required to call a convention for considering possible amendments to the document when formally asked to do it by the legislatures of two-thirds of the states.

(A) was never applied, Congress has been required to call a convention for considering possible amendments to the document when formally asked to do it
(B) was never applied, there has been a requirement that Congress call a convention for consideration of possible amendments to the document when asked to do it formally
(C) was never applied, whereby Congress is required to call a convention for considering possible amendments to the document when asked to do it formally
(D) has never been applied, whereby Congress is required to call a convention to consider possible amendments to the document when formally asked to do so
(E) has never been applied, Congress is required to call a convention to consider possible amendments to the document when formally asked to do so

42. The current administration, being worried over some foreign trade barriers being removed and our exports failing to increase as a result of deep cuts in the value of the dollar, has formed a group to study ways to sharpen our competitiveness.

(A) being worried over some foreign trade barriers being removed and our exports failing
(B) worrying over some foreign trade barriers being removed, also over the failure of our exports
(C) worried about the removal of some foreign trade barriers and the failure of our exports
(D) in that they were worried about the removal of some foreign trade barriers and also about the failure of our exports
(E) because of its worry concerning the removal of some foreign trade barriers, also concerning the failure of our exports

43. In the minds of many people living in England, before Australia was Australia, it was the antipodes, the opposite pole to civilization, an obscure and unimaginable place that was considered the end of the world.

(A) before Australia was Australia, it was the antipodes
(B) before there was Australia, it was the antipodes
(C) it was the antipodes that was Australia
(D) Australia was what was the antipodes
(E) Australia was what had been known as the antipodes

44. Using a Doppler ultrasound device, fetal heartbeats can be detected by the twelfth week of pregnancy.

(A) Using a Doppler ultrasound device, fetal heartbeats can be detected by the twelfth week of pregnancy.
(B) Fetal heartbeats can be detected by the twelfth week of pregnancy, using a Doppler ultrasound device.
(C) Detecting fetal heartbeats by the twelfth week of pregnancy, a physician can use a Doppler ultrasound device.
(D) By the twelfth week of pregnancy, fetal heartbeats can be detected using a Doppler ultrasound device by a physician.
(E) Using a Doppler ultrasound device, a physician can detect fetal heartbeats by the twelfth week of pregnancy.

45. Delighted by the reported earnings for the first quarter of the fiscal year, it was decided by the company manager to give her staff a raise.

(A) it was decided by the company manager to give her staff a raise
(B) the decision of the company manager was to give her staff a raise
(C) the company manager decided to give her staff a raise
(D) the staff was given a raise by the company manager
(E) a raise was given to the staff by the company manager

46. A study commissioned by the Department of Agriculture showed that if calves exercise and associated with other calves, they will require less medication and gain weight quicker than do those raised in confinement.

(A) associated with other calves, they will require less medication and gain weight quicker than do
(B) associated with other calves, they require less medication and gain weight quicker than
(C) associate with other calves, they required less medication and will gain weight quicker than do
(D) associate with other calves, they have required less medication and will gain weight more quickly than do
(E) associate with other calves, they require less medication and gain weight more quickly than

47. Displays of the aurora borealis, or "northern lights," can heat the atmosphere over the arctic enough to affect the trajectories of ballistic missiles, induce electric currents that can cause blackouts in some areas and corrosion in north-south pipelines.

(A) to affect the trajectories of ballistic missiles, induce
(B) that the trajectories of ballistic missiles are affected, induce
(C) that it affects the trajectories of ballistic missiles, induces
(D) that the trajectories of ballistic missiles are affected and induces
(E) to affect the trajectories of ballistic missiles and induce

48. The golden crab of the Gulf of Mexico has not been fished commercially in great numbers, primarily on account of living at great depths — 2,500 to 3,000 feet down.

(A) on account of living
(B) on account of their living
(C) because it lives
(D) because of living
(E) because they live

49. The cameras of the Voyager II spacecraft detected six small, previously unseen moons circling Uranus, which doubles to twelve the number of satellites now known as orbiting the distant planet.

(A) which doubles to twelve the number of satellites now known as orbiting
(B) doubling to twelve the number of satellites now known to orbit
(C) which doubles to twelve the number of satellites now known in orbit around
(D) doubling to twelve the number of satellites now known as orbiting
(E) which doubles to twelve the number of satellites now known that orbit

50. As a baby emerges from the darkness of the womb with a rudimentary sense of vision, it would be rated about 20/500, or legally blind if it were an adult with such vision.

(A) As a baby emerges from the darkness of the womb with a rudimentary sense of vision, it would be rated about 20/500, or legally blind if it were an adult with such vision.
(B) A baby emerges from the darkness of the womb with a rudimentary sense of vision that would be rated about 20/500, or legally blind as an adult.
(C) As a baby emerges from the darkness of the womb, its rudimentary sense of vision would be rated about 20/500; qualifying it to be legally blind if an adult.
(D) A baby emerges from the darkness of the womb with a rudimentary sense of vision that would be rated about 20/500; an adult with such vision would be deemed legally blind.
(E) As a baby emerges from the darkness of the womb, its rudimentary sense of vision, which would be deemed legally blind for an adult, would be rated about 20/500.

51. While Jackie Robinson was a Brooklyn Dodger, his courage in the face of physical threats and verbal attacks was not unlike that of Rosa Parks, who refused to move to the back of a bus in Montgomery, Alabama.

(A) not unlike that of Rosa Parks, who refused
(B) not unlike Rosa Parks, who refused
(C) like Rosa Parks and her refusal
(D) like that of Rosa Parks for refusing
(E) as that of Rosa Parks, who refused

52. The rising of costs of data-processing operations at many financial institutions has created a growing opportunity for independent companies to provide these services more efficiently and at lower cost.

(A) The rising of costs
(B) Rising costs
(C) The rising cost
(D) Because the rising cost
(E) Because of rising costs

53. There is no consensus on what role, if any, is played by acid rain in slowing the growth or damaging forests in the eastern United States.

(A) slowing the growth or damaging
(B) the damage or the slowing of the growth of
(C) the damage to or the slowness of the growth of
(D) damaged or slowed growth of
(E) damaging or slowing the growth of

54. Galileo was convinced that natural phenomena, as manifestations of the laws of physics, would appear the same to someone on the deck of a ship moving smoothly and uniformly through the water as a person standing on land.

(A) water as a
(B) water as to a
(C) water; just as it would to a
(D) water, as it would to the
(E) water; just as to the

55. A recent study has found that within the past few years, many doctors had elected early retirement rather than face the threats of lawsuits and the rising costs of malpractice insurance.

(A) had elected early retirement rather than face
(B) had elected early retirement instead of facing
(C) have elected retiring early instead of facing
(D) have elected to retire early rather than facing
(E) have elected to retire early rather than face

56. Architects and stonemasons, huge palace and temple clusters were built by the Maya without benefit of the wheel or animal transport.

(A) huge palace and temple clusters were built by the Maya without benefit of the wheel or animal transport
(B) without the benefits of animal transport or the wheel, huge palace and temple clusters were built by the Maya
(C) the Maya built huge palace and temple clusters without the benefit of animal transport or the wheel
(D) there were built, without the benefit of the wheel or animal transport, huge palace and temple clusters by the Maya
(E) were the Maya who, without the benefit of the wheel or animal transport, built huge palace and temple clusters

57. In astronomy the term "red shift" denotes the extent to which light from a distant galaxy has been shifted toward the red, or long-wave, end of the light spectrum by the rapid motion of the galaxy away from the Earth.

(A) to which light from a distant galaxy has been shifted
(B) to which light from a distant galaxy has shifted
(C) that light from a distant galaxy has been shifted
(D) of light from a distant galaxy shifting
(E) of the shift of light from a distant galaxy

58. William H. Johnson's artistic debt to Scandinavia is evident in paintings that range from sensitive portraits of citizens in his wife's Danish home, Kerteminde, and awe-inspiring views of fjords and mountain peaks in the western and northern regions of Norway.

(A) and
(B) to
(C) and to
(D) with
(E) in addition to

59. In 1978 only half the women granted child support by a court received the amount awarded; at least as much as a million and more others had not any support agreements whatsoever.

(A) at least as much as a million and more others had not any
(B) at least as much as more than a million others had no
(C) more than a million others had not any
(D) more than a million others had no
(E) there was at least a million or more others without any

60. According to a recent poll, owning and living in a freestanding house on its own land is still a goal of a majority of young adults, like that of earlier generations.

(A) like that of earlier generations
(B) as that for earlier generations
(C) just as earlier generations did
(D) as have earlier generations
(E) as it was of earlier generations

61. The Gorton-Dodd bill requires that a bank disclose to their customers how long they will delay access to funds from deposited checks.

(A) that a bank disclose to their customers how long they will delay access to funds from deposited checks
(B) a bank to disclose to their customers how long they will delay access to funds from a deposited check
(C) that a bank disclose to its customers how long it will delay access to funds from deposited checks
(D) a bank that it should disclose to its customers how long it will delay access to funds from a deposited check
(E) that banks disclose to customers how long access to funds from their deposited check is to be delayed

62. Geologists believe that the warning signs for a major earthquake may include sudden fluctuations in local seismic activity, tilting and other deformations of the Earth's crust, changing the measured strain across a fault zone, and varying the electrical properties of underground rocks.

(A) changing the measured strain across a fault zone, and varying
(B) changing measurements of the strain across a fault zone, and varying
(C) changing the strain as measured across a fault zone, and variations of
(D) changes in the measured strain across a fault zone, and variations in
(E) changes in measurements of the strain across a fault zone, and variations among

63. Health officials estimate that 35 million Africans are in danger of contracting trypanosomiasis, or "African sleeping sickness," a parasitic disease spread by the bites of tsetse flies.

(A) are in danger of contracting
(B) are in danger to contract
(C) have a danger of contracting
(D) are endangered by contraction
(E) have a danger that they will contract

64. Unlike a funded pension system, in which contributions are invested to pay future beneficiaries, <u>a pay-as-you-go approach is the foundation of Social Security</u>.

(A) a pay-as-you-go approach is the foundation of Social Security
(B) the foundation of Social Security is a pay-as-you-go approach
(C) the approach of Social Security is pay-as-you-go
(D) Social Security's approach is pay-as-you-go
(E) Social Security is founded on a pay-as-you-go approach

65. Critics of the trend toward privately operated prisons consider corrections facilities <u>to be an integral part of the criminal justice system and question if</u> profits should be made from incarceration.

(A) to be an integral part of the criminal justice system and question if
(B) as an integral part of the criminal justice system and they question if
(C) as being an integral part of the criminal justice system and question whether
(D) an integral part of the criminal justice system and question whether
(E) are an integral part of the criminal justice system, and they question whether

66. The Federal Reserve Board's <u>reduction of interest rates on loans to financial institutions is both an acknowledgement of past economic trends and an effort</u> to influence their future direction.

(A) reduction of interest rates on loans to financial institutions is both an acknowledgement of past economic trends and an effort
(B) reduction of interest rates on loans to financial institutions is an acknowledgement both of past economic trends as well as an effort
(C) reduction of interest rates on loans to financial institutions both acknowledge past economic trends and attempt
(D) reducing interest rates on loans to financial institutions is an acknowledgement both of past economic trends and an effort
(E) reducing interest rates on loans to financial institutions both acknowledge past economic trends as well as attempt

67. Congress is debating a bill requiring certain employers <u>provide workers with unpaid leave so as to</u> care for sick or newborn children.

(A) provide workers with unpaid leave so as to
(B) to provide workers with unpaid leave so as to
(C) provide workers with unpaid leave in order that they
(D) to provide workers with unpaid leave so that they can
(E) provide workers with unpaid leave and

68. Often visible as smog, <u>ozone is formed in the atmosphere from</u> hydrocarbons and nitrogen oxides, two major pollutants emitted by automobiles, react with sunlight.

(A) ozone is formed in the atmosphere from
(B) ozone is formed in the atmosphere when
(C) ozone is formed in the atmosphere, and when
(D) ozone, formed in the atmosphere when
(E) ozone, formed in the atmosphere from

69. Although she had signed a pledge of abstinence <u>while being an adolescent</u>, Frances Willard was 35 years old before she chose to become a temperance activist.

(A) while being an adolescent
(B) while in adolescence
(C) at the time of her being adolescent
(D) as being in adolescence
(E) as an adolescent

70. A President entering the final two years of a second term is <u>likely to be at a severe disadvantage and is often unable to</u> carry out a legislative program.

(A) likely to be at a severe disadvantage and is often unable to
(B) likely severely disadvantaged and often unable to
(C) liable to be severely disadvantaged and cannot often
(D) liable that he or she is at a severe disadvantage and cannot often
(E) at a severe disadvantage, often likely to be unable that he or she can

71. The original building and loan associations were organized as limited life funds, whose members made monthly payments on their share subscriptions, then taking turns drawing on the funds for home mortgages.

(A) subscriptions, then taking turns drawing
(B) subscriptions, and then taking turns drawing
(C) subscriptions and then took turns drawing
(D) subscriptions and then took turns, they drew
(E) subscriptions and then drew, taking turns

72. The number of undergraduate degrees in engineering awarded by colleges and universities in the United States increased by more than twice from 1978 to 1985.

(A) increased by more than twice
(B) increased more than two times
(C) more than doubled
(D) was more than doubled
(E) had more than doubled

73. The British Admiralty and the War Office met in March 1892 to consider a possible Russian attempt to seize Constantinople and how they would have to act militarily to deal with them.

(A) how they would have to act militarily to deal with them
(B) how to deal with them if military action would be necessary
(C) what would be necessary militarily for dealing with such an event
(D) what military action would be necessary in order to deal with such an event
(E) the necessity of what kind of military action in order to take for dealing with it

74. Growing competitive pressures may be encouraging auditors to bend the rules in favor of clients; auditors may, for instance, allow a questionable loan to remain on the books in order to maintain a bank's profits on paper.

(A) clients; auditors may, for instance, allow
(B) clients, as an instance, to allow
(C) clients, like to allow
(D) clients, such as to be allowing
(E) clients; which might, as an instance, be the allowing of

75. If the proposed expenditures for gathering information abroad are reduced even further, international news reports have been and will continue to diminish in number and quality.

(A) have been and will continue to diminish
(B) have and will continue to diminish
(C) will continue to diminish, as they already did,
(D) will continue to diminish, as they have already,
(E) will continue to diminish

76. Gall's hypothesis of there being different mental functions localized in different parts of the brain is widely accepted today.

(A) of there being different mental functions localized in different parts of the brain is widely accepted today
(B) of different mental functions that are localized in different parts of the brain is widely accepted today
(C) that different mental functions are localized in different parts of the brain is widely accepted today
(D) which is that there are different mental functions localized in different parts of the brain is widely accepted today
(E) which is widely accepted today is that there are different mental functions localized in different parts of the brain

77. Though the term "graphic design" may suggest laying out corporate brochures and annual reports, they have come to signify widely ranging work, from package designs and company logotypes to signs, book jackets, computer graphics, and film titles.

(A) suggest laying out corporate brochures and annual reports, they have come to signify widely ranging
(B) suggest laying out corporate brochures and annual reports, it has come to signify a wide range of
(C) suggest corporate brochure and annual report layout, it has signified widely ranging
(D) have suggested corporate brochure and annual report layout, it has signified a wide range of
(E) have suggested laying out corporate brochures and annual reports, they have come to signify widely ranging

78. The root systems of most flowering perennials either become too crowded, which results in loss in vigor, and spread too far outward, producing a bare center.

(A) which results in loss in vigor, and spread
(B) resulting in loss in vigor, or spreading
(C) with the result of loss of vigor, or spreading
(D) resulting in loss of vigor, or spread
(E) with a resulting loss of vigor, and spread

79. George Sand (Aurore Lucile Dupin) was one of the first European writers to consider the rural poor to be legitimate subjects for literature and portray these with sympathy and respect in her novels.

(A) to be legitimate subjects for literature and portray these
(B) should be legitimate subjects for literature and portray these
(C) as being legitimate subjects for literature and portraying them
(D) as if they were legitimate subjects for literature and portray them
(E) legitimate subjects for literature and to portray them

80. Salt deposits and moisture threaten to destroy the Mohenjo-Daro excavation in Pakistan, the site of an ancient civilization that flourished at the same time as the civilizations in the Nile delta and the river valleys of the Tigris and Euphrates.

(A) that flourished at the same time as the civilizations
(B) that had flourished at the same time as had the civilizations
(C) that flourished at the same time those had
(D) flourishing at the same time as those did
(E) flourishing at the same time as those were

81. In 1973 mortgage payments represented twenty-one percent of an average thirty-year-old male's income; and forty-four percent in 1984.

(A) income; and forty-four percent in 1984
(B) income; in 1984 the figure was forty-four percent
(C) income, and in 1984 forty-four percent
(D) income, forty-four percent in 1984 was the figure
(E) income that rose to forty-four percent in 1984

82. In contrast to large steel plants that take iron ore through all the steps needed to produce several different kinds of steel, processing steel scrap into a specialized group of products has enabled small mills to put capital into new technology and remain economically viable.

(A) processing steel scrap into a specialized group of products has enabled small mills to put capital into new technology and remain
(B) processing steel scrap into a specialized group of products has enabled small mills to put capital into new technology, remaining
(C) the processing of steel scrap into a specialized group of products has enabled small mills to put capital into new technology, remaining
(D) small mills, by processing steel scrap into a specialized group of products, have been able to put capital into new technology and remain
(E) small mills, by processing steel scrap into a specialized group of products, have been able to put capital into new technology and remained

83. Any medical test will sometimes fail to detect a condition when it is present and indicate that there is one when it is not.

(A) a condition when it is present and indicate that there is one
(B) when a condition is present and indicate that there is one
(C) a condition when it is present and indicate that it is present
(D) when a condition is present and indicate its presence
(E) the presence of a condition when it is there and indicate its presence

84. One legacy of Madison Avenue's recent campaign to appeal to people fifty years old and over is the realization that as a person ages, their concerns change as well.

(A) the realization that as a person ages, their
(B) the realization that as people age, their
(C) to realize that when a person ages, his or her
(D) to realize that when people age, their
(E) realizing that as people age, their

85. Out of America's fascination with all things antique have grown a market for bygone styles of furniture and fixtures that are bringing back the chaise lounge, the overstuffed sofa, and the claw-footed bathtub.

(A) things antique have grown a market for bygone styles of furniture and fixtures that are bringing

(B) things antique has grown a market for bygone styles of furniture and fixtures that is bringing

(C) things that are antiques has grown a market for bygone styles of furniture and fixtures that bring

(D) antique things have grown a market for bygone styles of furniture and fixtures that are bringing

(E) antique things has grown a market for bygone styles of furniture and fixtures that bring

86. Having the right hand and arm being crippled by a sniper's bullet during the First World War, Horace Pippin, a Black American painter, worked by holding the brush in his right hand and guiding its movements with his left.

(A) Having the right hand and arm being crippled by a sniper's bullet during the First World War

(B) In spite of his right hand and arm being crippled by a sniper's bullet during the First World War

(C) Because there had been a sniper's bullet during the First World War that crippled his right hand and arm

(D) The right hand and arm being crippled by a sniper's bullet during the First World War

(E) His right hand and arm crippled by a sniper's bullet during the First World War

87. Beyond the immediate cash flow crisis that the museum faces, its survival depends on if it can broaden its membership and leave its cramped quarters for a site where it can store and exhibit its more than 12,000 artifacts.

(A) if it can broaden its membership and leave

(B) whether it can broaden its membership and leave

(C) whether or not it has the capability to broaden its membership and can leave

(D) its ability for broadening its membership and leaving

(E) the ability for it to broaden its membership and leave

88. The Emperor Augustus, it appears, commissioned an idealized sculptured portrait, the features of which are so unrealistic as to constitute what one scholar calls an "artificial face."

(A) so unrealistic as to constitute

(B) so unrealistic they constituted

(C) so unrealistic that they have constituted

(D) unrealistic enough so that they constitute

(E) unrealistic enough so as to constitute

89. A recent national study of the public schools shows that there are now one microcomputer for every thirty-two pupils, four times as many than there were four years ago.

(A) there are now one microcomputer for every thirty-two pupils, four times as many than there were

(B) there is now one microcomputer for every thirty-two pupils, four times as many than there were

(C) there is now one microcomputer for every thirty-two pupils, four times as many as there were

(D) every thirty-two pupils now have one microcomputer, four times as many than there were

(E) every thirty-two pupils now has one microcomputer, four times as many as

90. Since 1986, when the Department of Labor began to allow investment officers' fees to be based on how the funds they manage perform, several corporations began paying their investment advisers a small basic fee, with a contract promising higher fees if the managers perform well.

(A) investment officers' fees to be based on how the funds they manage perform, several corporations began

(B) investment officers' fees to be based on the performance of the funds they manage, several corporations began

(C) that fees of investment officers be based on how the funds they manage perform, several corporations have begun

(D) fees of investment officers to be based on the performance of the funds they manage, several corporations have begun

(E) that investment officers' fees be based on the performance of the funds they manage, several corporations began

91. <u>Like</u> many self-taught artists, Perle Hessing did not begin to paint until she was well into middle age.

(A) Like
(B) As have
(C) Just as with
(D) Just like
(E) As did

92. Never before had taxpayers confronted <u>so many changes at once as they had in</u> the Tax Reform Act of 1986.

(A) so many changes at once as they had in
(B) at once as many changes as
(C) at once as many changes that there were with
(D) as many changes at once as they confronted in
(E) so many changes at once that confronted them in

93. It is well known in the supermarket industry that how items are placed on shelves and <u>the frequency of inventory turnovers can be</u> crucial to profits.

(A) the frequency of inventory turnovers can be
(B) the frequency of inventory turnovers is often
(C) the frequency with which the inventory turns over is often
(D) how frequently is the inventory turned over are often
(E) how frequently the inventory turns over can be

94. The psychologist William James believed that facial expressions not only provide a visible sign of an <u>emotion, actually contributing to the feeling itself</u>.

(A) emotion, actually contributing to the feeling itself
(B) emotion but also actually contributing to the feeling itself
(C) emotion but also actually contribute to the feeling itself
(D) emotion; they also actually contribute to the feeling of it
(E) emotion; the feeling itself is also actually contributed to by them

95. Along with the drop in producer prices announced yesterday, the strong retail sales figures released today seem <u>like it is indicative that</u> the economy, although growing slowly, is not nearing a recession.

(A) like it is indicative that
(B) as if to indicate
(C) to indicate that
(D) indicative of
(E) like an indication of

96. The National Transportation Safety Board has recommended the use of fail-safe mechanisms on airliner cargo door latches <u>assuring the doors are properly closed</u> before takeoff and to prevent them from popping open in flight.

(A) assuring the doors are properly closed
(B) for the assurance of proper closing
(C) assuring proper closure
(D) to assure closing the doors properly
(E) to assure that the doors are properly closed

97. Iguanas have been an important food source in Latin America since prehistoric times, and <u>it is still prized as a game animal</u> by the campesinos, who typically cook the meat in a heavily spiced stew.

(A) it is still prized as a game animal
(B) it is still prized as game animals
(C) they are still prized as game animals
(D) they are still prized as being a game animal
(E) being still prized as a game animal

98. The financial crash of October 1987 demonstrated that the world's capital markets are <u>integrated more closely than never before and</u> events in one part of the global village may be transmitted to the rest of the village—almost instantaneously.

(A) integrated more closely than never before and
(B) closely integrated more than ever before so
(C) more closely integrated as never before while
(D) more closely integrated than ever before and that
(E) more than ever before closely integrated as

99. New theories propose that catastrophic impacts of asteroids and comets may have caused reversals in the Earth's magnetic field, the onset of ice ages, <u>splitting apart continents</u> 80 million years ago, and great volcanic eruptions.

(A) splitting apart continents
(B) the splitting apart of continents
(C) split apart continents
(D) continents split apart
(E) continents that were split apart

100. Wisconsin, Illinois, Florida, and Minnesota have begun to enforce statewide bans prohibiting landfills to accept leaves, brush, and grass clippings.

   (A) prohibiting landfills to accept leaves, brush, and grass clippings
   (B) prohibiting that landfills accept leaves, brush, and grass clippings
   (C) prohibiting landfills from accepting leaves, brush, and grass clippings
   (D) that leaves, brush, and grass clippings cannot be accepted in landfills
   (E) that landfills cannot accept leaves, brush, and grass clippings

101. Even though the direct costs of malpractice disputes amounts to a sum lower than one percent of the $541 billion the nation spent on health care last year, doctors say fear of lawsuits plays a major role in health-care inflation.

   (A) amounts to a sum lower
   (B) amounts to less
   (C) amounted to less
   (D) amounted to lower
   (E) amounted to a lower sum

102. Except for a concert performance that the composer himself staged in 1911, Scott Joplin's ragtime opera *Treemonisha* was not produced until 1972, sixty-one years after its completion.

   (A) Except for a concert performance that the composer himself staged
   (B) Except for a concert performance with the composer himself staging it
   (C) Besides a concert performance being staged by the composer himself
   (D) Excepting a concert performance that the composer himself staged
   (E) With the exception of a concert performance with the staging done by the composer himself

103. Students in the metropolitan school district lack math skills to such a large degree as to make it difficult to absorb them into a city economy becoming ever more dependent on information-based industries.

   (A) lack math skills to such a large degree as to make it difficult to absorb them into a city economy becoming
   (B) lack math skills to a large enough degree that they will be difficult to absorb into a city's economy that becomes
   (C) lack of math skills is so large as to be difficult to absorb them into a city's economy that becomes
   (D) are lacking so much in math skills as to be difficult to absorb into a city's economy becoming
   (E) are so lacking in math skills that it will be difficult to absorb them into a city economy becoming

104. The diet of the ordinary Greek in classical times was largely vegetarian—vegetables, fresh cheese, oatmeal, and meal cakes, and meat rarely.

   (A) and meat rarely
   (B) and meat was rare
   (C) with meat as rare
   (D) meat a rarity
   (E) with meat as a rarity

105. An inventory equal to 90 days sales is as much as even the strongest businesses carry, and then only as a way to anticipate higher prices or ensure against shortages.

   (A) as much as even
   (B) so much as even
   (C) even so much as
   (D) even as much that
   (E) even so much that

106. The decision by one of the nation's largest banks to admit to $3 billion in potential losses on foreign loans could mean less lending by commercial banks to developing countries and increasing the pressure on multigovernment lenders to supply the funds.

   (A) increasing the pressure
   (B) the increasing pressure
   (C) increased pressure
   (D) the pressure increased
   (E) the pressure increasing

107. Downzoning, zoning that typically results in the reduction of housing density, allows for more open space in areas where little water or services exist.

(A) little water or services exist
(B) little water or services exists
(C) few services and little water exists
(D) there is little water or services available
(E) there are few services and little available water

108. Reporting that one of its many problems had been the recent extended sales slump in women's apparel, the seven-store retailer said it would start a three-month liquidation sale in all of its stores.

(A) its many problems had been the recent
(B) its many problems has been the recently
(C) its many problems is the recently
(D) their many problems is the recent
(E) their many problems had been the recent

109. Legislation in the Canadian province of Ontario requires of both public and private employers that pay be the same for jobs historically held by women as for jobs requiring comparable skill that are usually held by men.

(A) that pay be the same for jobs historically held by women as for jobs requiring comparable skill that are
(B) that pay for jobs historically held by women should be the same as for a job requiring comparable skills
(C) to pay the same in jobs historically held by women as in jobs of comparable skill that are
(D) to pay the same regardless of whether a job was historically held by women or is one demanding comparable skills
(E) to pay as much for jobs historically held by women as for a job demanding comparable skills

110. It has been estimated that the annual cost to the United States of illiteracy in lost industrial output and tax revenues is at least $20 billion a year.

(A) the annual cost to the United States of illiteracy in lost industrial output and tax revenues is at least $20 billion a year
(B) the annual cost of illiteracy to the United States is at least $20 billion a year because of lost industrial output and tax revenues
(C) illiteracy costs the United States at least $20 billion a year in lost industrial output and tax revenues
(D) $20 billion a year in lost industrial output and tax revenues is the annual cost to the United States of illiteracy
(E) lost industrial output and tax revenues cost the United States at least $20 billion a year because of illiteracy

111. Egyptians are credited as having pioneered embalming methods as long ago as 2650 B.C.

(A) as having
(B) with having
(C) to have
(D) as the ones who
(E) for being the ones who

112. Domestic automobile manufacturers have invested millions of dollars into research to develop cars more gasoline-efficient even than presently on the road.

(A) into research to develop cars more gasoline-efficient even than presently on the road
(B) into research for developing even more gasoline-efficient cars on the road than at present
(C) for research for cars to be developed that are more gasoline-efficient even than presently on the road
(D) in research to develop cars even more gasoline-efficient than those at present on the road
(E) in research for developing cars that are even more gasoline-efficient than presently on the road

113. Visitors to the park have often looked up into the leafy canopy and <u>saw monkeys sleeping on the branches, whose arms and legs hang</u> like socks on a clothesline.

(A) saw monkeys sleeping on the branches, whose arms and legs hang
(B) saw monkeys sleeping on the branches, whose arms and legs were hanging
(C) saw monkeys sleeping on the branches, with arms and legs hanging
(D) seen monkeys sleeping on the branches, with arms and legs hanging
(E) seen monkeys sleeping on the branches, whose arms and legs have hung

114. From the bark of the paper birch tree the Menomini crafted a canoe about twenty feet long and two feet wide, with small ribs and rails of cedar, which could carry four persons or eight hundred pounds of <u>baggage so light</u> that a person could easily portage it around impeding rapids.

(A) baggage so light
(B) baggage being so light
(C) baggage, yet being so light
(D) baggage, and so light
(E) baggage yet was so light

115. From the time of its defeat by the Germans in 1940 until its liberation in 1944, France was a bitter and divided country; a kind of civil war raged in the Vichy government <u>between those who wanted to collaborate with the Nazis with those who opposed</u> them.

(A) between those who wanted to collaborate with the Nazis with those who opposed
(B) between those who wanted to collaborate with the Nazis and those who opposed
(C) between those wanting to collaborate with the Nazis with those opposing
(D) among those who wanted to collaborate with the Nazis and those who opposed
(E) among those wanting to collaborate with the Nazis with those opposing

116. Those who come to church with a predisposition to religious belief will be happy in an auditorium or even a storefront, and there is no doubt that religion is sometimes better served by <u>adapted spaces of this kind instead of by some of the buildings actually designed for it</u>.

(A) adapted spaces of this kind instead of by some of the buildings actually designed for it
(B) adapted spaces like these rather than some of the buildings actually designed for them
(C) these adapted spaces instead of by some of the buildings actually designed for it
(D) such adapted spaces rather than by some of the buildings actually designed for them
(E) such adapted spaces than by some of the buildings actually designed for it

117. A firm that specializes in the analysis of handwriting claims <u>from a one-page writing sample that it can assess</u> more than three hundred personality traits, including enthusiasm, imagination, and ambition.

(A) from a one-page writing sample that it can assess
(B) from a one-page writing sample it has the ability of assessing
(C) the ability, from a one-page writing sample, of assessing
(D) to be able, from a one-page writing sample, to assess
(E) being able to assess, from a one-page writing sample,

118. The question of whether to divest themselves of stock in companies that do business in South Africa is particularly troublesome for the nation's 116 private Black colleges because their economic bases are often more fragile <u>than</u> most predominantly White colleges.

(A) than
(B) than those of
(C) than is so of
(D) compared to
(E) compared to those of

-670-

119. Executives and federal officials say that the use of crack and cocaine is growing rapidly among workers, significantly compounding the effects of drug and alcohol abuse, which already are a cost to business of more than $100 billion a year.

(A) significantly compounding the effects of drug and alcohol abuse, which already are a cost to business of
(B) significantly compounding the effects of drug and alcohol abuse, which already cost business
(C) significantly compounding the effects of drug and alcohol abuse, already with business costs of
(D) significant in compounding the effects of drug and alcohol abuse, and already costing business
(E) significant in compounding the effects of drug and alcohol abuse, and already costs business

120. The Parthenon was a church from 1204 until 1456, when Athens was taken by General Mohammed the Conqueror, the Turkish sultan, who established a mosque in the building and used the Acropolis as a fortress.

(A) who established a mosque in the building and used the Acropolis as
(B) who, establishing a mosque in the building, used the Acropolis like
(C) who, when he had established a mosque in the building, used the Acropolis like
(D) who had established a mosque in the building, using the Acropolis to be
(E) establishing a mosque in the building and using the Acropolis as

121. The concept of the grand jury dates from the twelfth century, when Henry II of England ordered panels of common citizens should prepare lists of who were their communities' suspected criminals.

(A) should prepare lists of who were their communities' suspected criminals
(B) would do the preparation of lists of their communities' suspected criminals
(C) preparing lists of suspected criminals in their communities
(D) the preparing of a list of suspected criminals in their communities
(E) to prepare lists of suspected criminals in their communities

122. Chinese, the most ancient of living writing systems, consists of tens of thousands of ideographic characters, each character a miniature calligraphic composition inside its own square frame.

(A) each character a miniature calligraphic composition inside its
(B) all the characters a miniature calligraphic composition inside their
(C) all the characters a miniature calligraphic composition inside its
(D) every character a miniature calligraphic composition inside their
(E) each character a miniature calligraphic composition inside their

123. In developing new facilities for the incineration of solid wastes, we must avoid the danger of shifting environmental problems from landfills polluting the water to polluting the air with incinerators.

(A) landfills polluting the water to polluting the air with incinerators
(B) landfills polluting the water to the air being polluted with incinerators
(C) the pollution of water by landfills to the pollution of air by incinerators
(D) pollution of the water by landfills to incinerators that pollute the air
(E) water that is polluted by landfills to incinerators that pollute the air

124. During Roosevelt's years in office, Black Americans began voting for Democrats rather than Republicans in national elections, but Black support for Democrats at the state and local levels developed only after when civil rights legislation was supported by Harry Truman.

(A) developed only after when civil rights legislation was supported by Harry Truman
(B) developed only after when Harry Truman supported civil rights legislation
(C) developed only after Harry Truman's support of civil rights legislation
(D) develops only at the time after the supporting of civil rights legislation by Harry Truman
(E) developed only after there being Harry Truman's support of civil rights legislation

125. The winds that howl across the Great Plains not only blow away valuable topsoil, thereby reducing the potential crop yield of a tract of land, <u>and also damage or destroy</u> young plants.

(A) and also damage or destroy
(B) as well as damaging or destroying
(C) but they also cause damage or destroy
(D) but also damage or destroy
(E) but also causing damage or destroying

126. More than thirty years ago Dr. Barbara McClintock, the Nobel Prize winner, reported that genes can "jump," <u>as pearls moving mysteriously from one necklace to another</u>.

(A) as pearls moving mysteriously from one necklace to another
(B) like pearls moving mysteriously from one necklace to another
(C) as pearls do that move mysteriously from one necklace to others
(D) like pearls do that move mysteriously from one necklace to others
(E) as do pearls that move mysteriously from one necklace to some other one

127. In theory, international civil servants at the United Nations are prohibited from continuing to draw salaries from their own governments; in practice, however, some governments merely substitute living allowances <u>for their employees' paychecks, assigned by them</u> to the United Nations.

(A) for their employees' paychecks, assigned by them
(B) for the paychecks of their employees who have been assigned
(C) for the paychecks of their employees, having been assigned
(D) in place of their employees' paychecks, for those of them assigned
(E) in place of the paychecks of their employees to have been assigned by them

128. New hardy varieties of rice show promise of producing high yields without the costly <u>requirements of irrigation and application of commercial fertilizer by earlier high-yielding varieties</u>.

(A) requirements of irrigation and application of commercial fertilizer by earlier high-yielding varieties
(B) requirements by earlier high-yielding varieties of application of commercial fertilizer and irrigation
(C) requirements for application of commercial fertilizer and irrigation of earlier high-yielding varieties
(D) application of commercial fertilizer and irrigation that was required by earlier high-yielding varieties
(E) irrigation and application of commercial fertilizer that were required by earlier high-yielding varieties

129. In an effort to reduce their inventories, Italian vintners have cut prices; their wines <u>have been priced to sell, and they are</u>.

(A) have been priced to sell, and they are
(B) are priced to sell, and they have
(C) are priced to sell, and they do
(D) are being priced to sell, and have
(E) had been priced to sell, and they have

130. In a 5-to-4 decision, the Supreme Court ruled <u>that two upstate New York counties owed restitution to three tribes of Oneida Indians for the unlawful seizure of</u> their ancestral lands in the eighteenth century.

(A) that two upstate New York counties owed restitution to three tribes of Oneida Indians for the unlawful seizure of
(B) that two upstate New York counties owed restitution to three tribes of Oneida Indians because of their unlawful seizure of
(C) two upstate New York counties to owe restitution to three tribes of Oneida Indians for their unlawful seizure of
(D) on two upstate New York counties that owed restitution to three tribes of Oneida Indians because they unlawfully seized
(E) on the restitution that two upstate New York counties owed to three tribes of Oneida Indians for the unlawful seizure of

131. The Commerce Department announced that the economy grew during the second quarter at a 7.5 percent annual rate, while inflation eased when it might have been expected for it to rise.

   (A) it might have been expected for it to rise
   (B) it might have been expected to rise
   (C) it might have been expected that it should rise
   (D) its rise might have been expected
   (E) there might have been an expectation it would rise

132. According to a study by the Carnegie Foundation for the Advancement of Teaching, companies in the United States are providing job training and general education for nearly eight million people, about equivalent to the enrollment of the nation's four-year colleges and universities.

   (A) equivalent to the enrollment of
   (B) the equivalent of those enrolled in
   (C) equal to those who are enrolled in
   (D) as many as the enrollment of
   (E) as many as are enrolled in

133. In Holland, a larger percentage of the gross national product is spent on defense of their coasts from rising seas than is spent on military defense in the United States.

   (A) In Holland, a larger percentage of the gross national product is spent on defense of their coasts from rising seas than is spent on military defense in the United States.
   (B) In Holland they spend a larger percentage of their gross national product on defending their coasts from rising seas than the United States does on military defense.
   (C) A larger percentage of Holland's gross national product is spent on defending their coasts from rising seas than the United States spends on military defense.
   (D) Holland spends a larger percentage of its gross national product defending its coasts from rising seas than the military defense spending of the United States.
   (E) Holland spends a larger percentage of its gross national product on defending its coasts from rising seas than the United States does on military defense.

134. Canadian scientists have calculated that one human being should be struck every nine years by a meteorite, while each year sixteen buildings can be expected to sustain damage from such objects.

   (A) one human being should be struck every nine years by a meteorite
   (B) a human being should be struck by a meteorite once in every nine years
   (C) a meteorite will strike one human being once in every nine years
   (D) every nine years a human being will be struck by a meteorite
   (E) every nine years a human being should be struck by a meteorite

135. Intar, the oldest Hispanic theater company in New York, has moved away from the Spanish classics and now it draws on the works both of contemporary Hispanic authors who live abroad and of those in the United States.

   (A) now it draws on the works both of contemporary Hispanic authors who live abroad and of those
   (B) now draws on the works of contemporary Hispanic authors, both those who live abroad and those who live
   (C) it draws on the works of contemporary Hispanic authors now, both those living abroad and who live
   (D) draws now on the works both of contemporary Hispanic authors living abroad and who are living
   (E) draws on the works now of both contemporary Hispanic authors living abroad and those

136. Although schistosomiasis is not often fatal, it is so debilitating that it has become an economic drain on many developing countries.

   (A) it is so debilitating that it has become an economic
   (B) it is of such debilitation, it has become an economical
   (C) so debilitating is it as to become an economic
   (D) such is its debilitation, it becomes an economical
   (E) there is so much debilitation that it has become an economical

137. In 1982 the median income for married-couple families with a wage-earning wife was $9,000 more than a family where the husband only was employed.

(A) a family where the husband only
(B) of a family where only the husband
(C) that for families in which only the husband
(D) a family in which only the husband
(E) those of families in which the husband only

138. Senator Lasker has proposed legislation requiring that employers should retain all older workers indefinitely or show just cause for dismissal.

(A) that employers should retain all older workers
(B) that all older workers be retained by employers
(C) the retaining by employers of all older workers
(D) employers' retention of all older workers
(E) employers to retain all older workers

139. The extraordinary diary of William Lyon Mackenzie King, prime minister of Canada for over twenty years, revealed that this most bland and circumspect of men was a mystic guided in both public and private life by omens, messages received at séances, and signs from heaven.

(A) that this most bland and circumspect of men was a mystic guided in both public and
(B) that this most bland and circumspect of men was a mystic and also guided both in public as well as
(C) this most bland and circumspect of men was a mystic and that he was guided in both public and
(D) this most bland and circumspect of men was a mystic and that he was guided in both public as well as
(E) this most bland and circumspect of men to have been a mystic and that he guided himself both in public as well as

140. Declining values for farm equipment and land, the collateral against which farmers borrow to get through the harvest season, is going to force many lenders to tighten or deny credit this spring.

(A) the collateral against which farmers borrow to get through the harvest season, is
(B) which farmers use as collateral to borrow against to get through the harvest season, is
(C) the collateral which is borrowed against by farmers to get through the harvest season, is
(D) which farmers use as collateral to borrow against to get through the harvest season, are
(E) the collateral against which farmers borrow to get through the harvest season, are

141. Unlike transplants between identical twins, whose genetic endowment is the same, all patients receiving hearts or other organs must take antirejection drugs for the rest of their lives.

(A) Unlike transplants between identical twins, whose genetic endowment is the same
(B) Besides transplants involving identical twins with the same genetic endowment
(C) Unless the transplant involves identical twins who have the same genetic endowment
(D) Aside from a transplant between identical twins with the same genetic endowment
(E) Other than transplants between identical twins, whose genetic endowment is the same

142. In one of the most stunning reversals in the history of marketing, the Coca-Cola company in July 1985 yielded to thousands of irate consumers demanding that it should bring back the original Coke formula.

(A) demanding that it should
(B) demanding it to
(C) and their demand to
(D) who demanded that it
(E) who demanded it to

143. Recently discovered fossil remains strongly suggest that the Australian egg-laying mammals of today are a branch of the main stem of mammalian evolution rather than developing independently from a common ancestor of mammals more than 220 million years ago.

(A) rather than developing independently from
(B) rather than a type that developed independently from
(C) rather than a type whose development was independent of
(D) instead of developing independently from
(E) instead of a development that was independent of

144. Efforts to equalize the funds available to school districts, a major goal of education reformers and many states in the 1970's, has not significantly reduced the gaps existing between the richest and poorest districts.

(A) has not significantly reduced the gaps existing
(B) has not been significant in reducing the gap that exists
(C) has not made a significant reduction in the gap that exists
(D) have not significantly reduced the gap that exists
(E) have not been significant in a reduction of the gaps existing

145. Most state constitutions now <u>mandate that the state budget be balanced</u> each year.

(A) mandate that the state budget be balanced
(B) mandate the state budget to be balanced
(C) mandate that the state budget will be balanced
(D) have a mandate for a balanced state budget
(E) have a mandate to balance the state budget

146. A patient accusing a doctor of malpractice will find it difficult to prove damage <u>if there is a lack of some other doctor to testify</u> about proper medical procedures.

(A) if there is a lack of some other doctor to testify
(B) unless there will be another doctor to testify
(C) without another doctor's testimony
(D) should there be no testimony from some other doctor
(E) lacking another doctor to testify

147. <u>Samuel Sewall viewed marriage, as other seventeenth-century colonists, like a property arrangement rather than</u> an emotional bond based on romantic love.

(A) Samuel Sewall viewed marriage, as other seventeenth-century colonists, like a property arrangement rather than
(B) As did other seventeenth-century colonists, Samuel Sewall viewed marriage to be a property arrangement rather than viewing it as
(C) Samuel Sewall viewed marriage to be a property arrangement, like other seventeenth-century colonists, rather than viewing it as
(D) Marriage to Samuel Sewall, like other seventeenth-century colonists, was viewed as a property arrangement rather than
(E) Samuel Sewall, like other seventeenth-century colonists, viewed marriage as a property arrangement rather than

148. Under the Safe Drinking Water Act, the Environmental Protection Agency is required either to approve individual state plans for controlling the discharge of wastes into underground water or <u>that they enforce their</u> own plan for states without adequate regulations.

(A) that they enforce their
(B) for enforcing their
(C) they should enforce their
(D) it should enforce its
(E) to enforce its

149. Last year, land values in most parts of the pinelands rose almost <u>so fast, and in some parts even faster than what they did</u> outside the pinelands.

(A) so fast, and in some parts even faster than what they did
(B) so fast, and in some parts even faster than, those
(C) as fast, and in some parts even faster than, those
(D) as fast as, and in some parts even faster than, those
(E) as fast as, and in some parts even faster than what they did

150. In the mid-1960's a newly installed radar warning system mistook the <u>rising of the moon as a massive missile attack by the Soviets</u>.

(A) rising of the moon as a massive missile attack by the Soviets
(B) rising of the moon for a massive Soviet missile attack
(C) moon rising to a massive missile attack by the Soviets
(D) moon as it was rising for a massive Soviet missile attack
(E) rise of the moon as a massive Soviet missile attack

151. <u>If Dr. Wade was right, any apparent connection of the eating of</u> highly processed foods and excelling at sports is purely coincidental.

(A) If Dr. Wade was right, any apparent connection of the eating of
(B) Should Dr. Wade be right, any apparent connection of eating
(C) If Dr. Wade is right, any connection that is apparent between eating of
(D) If Dr. Wade is right, any apparent connection between eating
(E) Should Dr. Wade have been right, any connection apparent between eating

152. When the technique known as gene-splicing was invented in the early 1970's, it was feared that scientists might inadvertently create an "Andromeda strain," a microbe never before seen on Earth that might escape from the laboratory and it would kill vast numbers of humans who would have no natural defenses against it.

   (A) it would kill vast numbers of humans who would have no natural defenses against it
   (B) it might kill vast numbers of humans with no natural defenses against it
   (C) kill vast numbers of humans who would have no natural defenses against it
   (D) kill vast numbers of humans who have no natural defenses against them
   (E) kill vast numbers of humans with no natural defenses against them

153. A recording system was so secretly installed and operated in the Kennedy Oval Office that even Theodore C. Sorensen, the White House counsel, did not know it existed.

   (A) A recording system was so secretly installed and operated in the Kennedy Oval Office that
   (B) So secret was a recording system installation and operation in the Kennedy Oval Office
   (C) It was so secret that a recording system was installed and operated in the Kennedy Oval Office
   (D) A recording system that was so secretly installed and operated in the Kennedy Oval Office
   (E) Installed and operated so secretly in the Kennedy Oval Office was a recording system that

154. In 1791 Robert Carter III, one of the wealthiest plantation owners in Virginia, stunned his family, friends, and neighbors by filing a deed of emancipation, setting free the more than 500 slaves who were legally considered his property.

   (A) setting free the more than 500 slaves who were legally considered
   (B) setting free more than the 500 slaves legally considered as
   (C) and set free more than 500 slaves, who were legally considered as
   (D) and set free more than the 500 slaves who were legally considered
   (E) and he set free the more than 500 slaves who were legally considered as

155. Federal authorities involved in the investigation have found the local witnesses are difficult to locate, reticent, and are suspicious of strangers.

   (A) the local witnesses are difficult to locate, reticent, and are
   (B) local witnesses to be difficult to locate, reticent, and are
   (C) that local witnesses are difficult to locate, reticent, and
   (D) local witnesses are difficult to locate and reticent, and they are
   (E) that local witnesses are difficult to locate and reticent, and they are

156. Dirt roads may evoke the bucolic simplicity of another century, but financially strained townships point out that dirt roads cost twice as much as maintaining paved roads.

   (A) dirt roads cost twice as much as maintaining paved roads
   (B) dirt roads cost twice as much to maintain as paved roads do
   (C) maintaining dirt roads costs twice as much as paved roads do
   (D) maintaining dirt roads costs twice as much as it does for paved roads
   (E) to maintain dirt roads costs twice as much as for paved roads

157. A number of linguists contend that all of the thousands of languages spoken by the world's five billion people can be traced back to a common root language.

   (A) that all of the thousands of languages spoken by the world's five billion people can be traced
   (B) that the world's five billion people speak thousands of languages of which all can be traced
   (C) the world's five billion people speak thousands of languages which are all traceable
   (D) all of the thousands of languages spoken by the world's five billion people to be traceable
   (E) the ability to trace all of the thousands of languages that are spoken by the world's five billion people

158. <u>With</u> only 5 percent of the world's population, United States citizens consume 28 percent of its nonrenewable resources, drive more than one-third of its automobiles, and use 21 times more water per capita than Europeans do.

(A) With
(B) As
(C) Being
(D) Despite having
(E) Although accounting for

159. While depressed property values can hurt some large investors, <u>they are potentially devastating for homeowners, whose</u> equity — in many cases representing a life's savings — can plunge or even disappear.

(A) they are potentially devastating for homeowners, whose
(B) they can potentially devastate homeowners in that their
(C) for homeowners they are potentially devastating, because their
(D) for homeowners, it is potentially devastating in that their
(E) it can potentially devastate homeowners, whose

160. While some propose to combat widespread illegal copying of computer programs by attempting to change people's attitudes toward pirating, others <u>by suggesting reducing software prices to decrease the incentive for pirating, and still others by calling</u> for the prosecution of those who copy software illegally.

(A) by suggesting reducing software prices to decrease the incentive for pirating, and still others by calling
(B) by suggesting the reduction of software prices to decrease the incentive for pirating, and still others call
(C) suggest the reduction of software prices for decreasing the incentive for pirating, and still others call
(D) suggest the reduction of software prices to decrease the incentive for pirating, and still others by calling
(E) suggest reducing software prices to decrease the incentive for pirating, and still others are calling

161. A wildlife expert predicts that the reintroduction of the caribou into northern Minnesota <u>would fail if the density of the timber wolf population in that region is more numerous than</u> one wolf for every 39 square miles.

(A) would fail if the density of the timber wolf population in that region is more numerous than
(B) would fail provided the density of the timber wolf population in that region is more than
(C) should fail if the timber wolf density in that region was greater than
(D) will fail if the density of the timber wolf population in that region is greater than
(E) will fail if the timber wolf density in that region were more numerous than

162. Concerned at the increase in accident fatalities, Tennessee adopted a child-passenger protection law requiring <u>the parents of children under four years of age to be restrained in a child safety seat</u>.

(A) the parents of children under four years of age to be restrained in a child safety seat
(B) the restraint of parents of children under four years of age in a child safety seat
(C) that parents restrain children under four years of age in a child safety seat
(D) that children be restrained under four years of age in a child safety seat by their parents
(E) children to be restrained under four years of age by their parents in a child safety seat

163. Found throughout Central and South America, <u>sloths hang from trees by long rubbery limbs and sleep fifteen hours a day, moving infrequently enough</u> that two species of algae grow on its coat and between its toes.

(A) sloths hang from trees by long rubbery limbs and sleep fifteen hours a day, moving infrequently enough
(B) sloths hang from trees by long rubbery limbs, they sleep fifteen hours a day, and with such infrequent movements
(C) sloths use their long rubbery limbs to hang from trees, sleep fifteen hours a day, and move so infrequently
(D) the sloth hangs from trees by its long rubbery limbs, sleeping fifteen hours a day and moving so infrequently
(E) the sloth hangs from trees by its long rubbery limbs, sleeps fifteen hours a day, and it moves infrequently enough

164. The commission proposed that funding for the park's development, which could be open to the public early next year, is obtained through a local bond issue.

(A) that funding for the park's development, which could be open to the public early next year, is

(B) that funding for development of the park, which could be open to the public early next year, be

(C) funding for the development of the park, perhaps open to the public early next year, to be

(D) funds for the park's development, perhaps open to the public early next year, be

(E) development funding for the park, which could be open to the public early next year, is to be

165. At Shiprock, New Mexico, a perennially powerful girls' high school basketball team has become a path to college for some and a source of pride for a community where the household incomes of 49 percent of them are below the poverty level.

(A) where the household incomes of 49 percent of them are

(B) where they have 49 percent of the household incomes

(C) where 49 percent of the household incomes are

(D) which has 49 percent of the household incomes

(E) in which 49 percent of them have household incomes

166. The prime lending rate is a key rate in the economy: not only are the interest rates on most loans to small and medium-sized businesses tied to the prime, but also on a growing number of consumer loans, including home equity loans.

(A) not only are the interest rates on most loans to small and medium-sized businesses tied to the prime, but also on

(B) tied to the prime are the interest rates not only on most loans to small and medium-sized businesses, but also on

(C) the interest rates not only on most loans to small and medium-sized businesses are tied to the prime, but also

(D) not only the interest rates on most loans to small and medium-sized businesses are tied to the prime, but also on

(E) the interest rates are tied to the prime, not only on most loans to small and medium-sized businesses, but also

167. Neanderthals had a vocal tract that resembled those of the apes and so were probably without language, a shortcoming that may explain why they were supplanted by our own species.

(A) Neanderthals had a vocal tract that resembled those of the apes

(B) Neanderthals had a vocal tract resembling an ape's

(C) The vocal tracts of Neanderthals resembled an ape's

(D) The Neanderthal's vocal tracts resembled the apes'

(E) The vocal tracts of the Neanderthals resembled those of the apes

168. Today, because of improvements in agricultural technology, the same amount of acreage produces double the apples that it has in 1910.

(A) double the apples that it has

(B) twice as many apples as it did

(C) as much as twice the apples it has

(D) two times as many apples as there were

(E) a doubling of the apples that it did

169. Seismologists studying the earthquake that struck northern California in October 1989 are still investigating some of its mysteries: the unexpected power of the seismic waves, the upward thrust that threw one man straight into the air, and the strange electromagnetic signals detected hours before the temblor.

(A) the upward thrust that threw one man straight into the air, and the strange electromagnetic signals detected hours before the temblor

(B) the upward thrust that threw one man straight into the air, and strange electromagnetic signals were detected hours before the temblor

(C) the upward thrust threw one man straight into the air, and hours before the temblor strange electromagnetic signals were detected

(D) one man was thrown straight into the air by the upward thrust, and hours before the temblor strange electromagnetic signals were detected

(E) one man who was thrown straight into the air by the upward thrust, and strange electromagnetic signals that were detected hours before the temblor

170. Although early soap operas <u>were first aired on evening radio in the 1920's, they had moved to the daytime hours of the 1930's</u> when the evening schedule became crowded with comedians and variety shows.

(A) were first aired on evening radio in the 1920's, they had moved to the daytime hours of the 1930's
(B) were first aired on evening radio in the 1920's, they were moved to the daytime hours in the 1930's
(C) were aired first on evening radio in the 1920's, moving to the daytime hours in the 1930's
(D) were aired first in the evening on 1920's radio, they moved to the daytime hours of the 1930's
(E) aired on evening radio first in the 1920's, they were moved to the 1930's in the daytime hours

171. In 1527 King Henry VIII sought to have his marriage to Queen Catherine annulled <u>so as to marry</u> Anne Boleyn.

(A) so as to marry
(B) and so could be married to
(C) to be married to
(D) so that he could marry
(E) in order that he would marry

172. The energy source on *Voyager 2* is not a nuclear reactor, in which atoms are actively broken <u>apart; rather</u> a kind of nuclear battery that uses natural radioactive decay to produce power.

(A) apart; rather
(B) apart, but rather
(C) apart, but rather that of
(D) apart, but that of
(E) apart; it is that of

173. Joan of Arc, a young Frenchwoman who claimed to be divinely inspired, turned the tide of English victories in her country by liberating the city of Orléans and <u>she persuaded Charles VII of France to claim his throne</u>.

(A) she persuaded Charles VII of France to claim his throne
(B) persuaded Charles VII of France in claiming his throne
(C) persuading that the throne be claimed by Charles VII of France
(D) persuaded Charles VII of France to claim his throne
(E) persuading that Charles VII of France should claim the throne

174. <u>A letter by Mark Twain, written in the same year as *The Adventures of Huckleberry Finn* were published,</u> reveals that Twain provided financial assistance to one of the first Black students at Yale Law School.

(A) A letter by Mark Twain, written in the same year as *The Adventures of Huckleberry Finn* were published,
(B) A letter by Mark Twain, written in the same year of publication as *The Adventures of Huckleberry Finn*,
(C) A letter by Mark Twain, written in the same year that *The Adventures of Huckleberry Finn* was published,
(D) Mark Twain wrote a letter in the same year as he published *The Adventures of Huckleberry Finn* that
(E) Mark Twain wrote a letter in the same year of publication as *The Adventures of Huckleberry Finn* that

175. Two new studies indicate that many people become obese more <u>due to the fact that their bodies burn calories too slowly than overeating</u>.

    (A) due to the fact that their bodies burn calories too slowly than overeating

    (B) due to their bodies burning calories too slowly than to eating too much

    (C) because their bodies burn calories too slowly than that they are overeaters

    (D) because their bodies burn calories too slowly than because they eat too much

    (E) because of their bodies burning calories too slowly than because of their eating too much

176. As a result of the ground-breaking work of Barbara McClintock, many scientists now believe that all of the information encoded in <u>50,000 to 100,000 of the different genes found in a human cell are contained in merely</u> three percent of the cell's DNA.

    (A) 50,000 to 100,000 of the different genes found in a human cell are contained in merely

    (B) 50,000 to 100,000 of the human cell's different genes are contained in a mere

    (C) the 50,000 to 100,000 different genes found in human cells are contained in merely

    (D) 50,000 to 100,000 of human cells' different genes is contained in merely

    (E) the 50,000 to 100,000 different genes found in a human cell is contained in a mere

177. <u>So poorly educated and trained are many young recruits to the United States work force that</u> many business executives fear this country will lose its economic preeminence.

    (A) So poorly educated and trained are many young recruits to the United States work force that

    (B) As poorly educated and trained as many young recruits to the United States work force are,

    (C) Because of many young recruits to the United States work force who are so poorly educated and trained,

    (D) That many young recruits to the United States work force are so poorly educated and trained is why

    (E) Many young recruits to the United States work force who are so poorly educated and trained explains why

178. In the last few years, the number of convicted criminals given community service <u>sentences, which allow the criminals to remain unconfined while they perform specific jobs benefiting the public, have</u> risen dramatically.

    (A) sentences, which allow the criminals to remain unconfined while they perform specific jobs benefiting the public, have

    (B) sentences, performing specific jobs that benefit the public while being allowed to remain unconfined, have

    (C) sentences, performing specific jobs beneficial to the public while they are allowed to remain unconfined, have

    (D) sentences which allow them to remain unconfined in their performing of specific jobs beneficial to the public has

    (E) sentences allowing them to remain unconfined while performing specific jobs that benefit the public has

179. During the early years of European settlement on a continent that was viewed as "wilderness" by the newcomers, <u>Native Americans, intimately knowing the ecology of the land, were a help in the rescuing of</u> many Pilgrims and pioneers from hardship, or even death.

    (A) Native Americans, intimately knowing the ecology of the land, were a help in the rescuing of

    (B) Native Americans knew the ecology and the land intimately and this enabled them to help in the rescue of

    (C) Native Americans, with their intimate knowledge of the ecology of the land, helped to rescue

    (D) having intimate knowledge of the ecology of the land, Native Americans helped the rescue of

    (E) knowing intimately the ecology of the land, Native Americans helped to rescue

180. Quasars are so distant that their light has taken billions of years to reach the Earth; consequently, <u>we see them as they were during</u> the formation of the universe.

    (A) we see them as they were during

    (B) we see them as they had been during

    (C) we see them as if during

    (D) they appear to us as they did in

    (E) they appear to us as though in

181. Because of the enormous research and development expenditures required to survive in the electronics industry, an industry marked by rapid innovation and volatile demand, such firms tend to be very large.

(A) to survive
(B) of firms to survive
(C) for surviving
(D) for survival
(E) for firms' survival

182. Consumers may not think of household cleaning products to be hazardous substances, but many of them can be harmful to health, especially if they are used improperly.

(A) Consumers may not think of household cleaning products to be
(B) Consumers may not think of household cleaning products being
(C) A consumer may not think of their household cleaning products being
(D) A consumer may not think of household cleaning products as
(E) Household cleaning products may not be thought of, by consumers, as

183. Archaeologists in Ireland believe that a recently discovered chalice, which dates from the eighth century, was probably buried to keep from being stolen by invaders.

(A) to keep from
(B) to keep it from
(C) to avoid
(D) in order that it would avoid
(E) in order to keep from

184. As measured by the Commerce Department, corporate profits peaked in the fourth quarter of 1988 and have slipped since then, as many companies have been unable to pass on higher costs.

(A) and have slipped since then, as many companies have been unable to pass on higher costs
(B) and have slipped since then, the reason being because many companies have been unable to pass on higher costs
(C) and slipped since then, many companies being unable to pass on higher costs
(D) but, many companies unable to pass on higher costs, they have slipped since then
(E) yet are slipping since then, because many companies were unable to pass on higher costs

185. The recent surge in the number of airplane flights has clogged the nation's air-traffic control system, to lead to 55 percent more delays at airports, and prompts fears among some officials that safety is being compromised.

(A) to lead to 55 percent more delays at airports, and prompts
(B) leading to 55 percent more delay at airports and prompting
(C) to lead to a 55 percent increase in delay at airports and prompt
(D) to lead to an increase of 55 percent in delays at airports, and prompted
(E) leading to a 55-percent increase in delays at airports and prompting

186. Judge Bonham denied a motion to allow members of the jury to go home at the end of each day instead of to confine them to a hotel.

(A) to allow members of the jury to go home at the end of each day instead of to confine them to
(B) that would have allowed members of the jury to go home at the end of each day instead of confined to
(C) under which members of the jury are allowed to go home at the end of each day instead of confining them in
(D) that would allow members of the jury to go home at the end of each day rather than confinement in
(E) to allow members of the jury to go home at the end of each day rather than be confined to

187. In one of the bloodiest battles of the Civil War, fought at Sharpsburg, Maryland, on September 17, 1862, four times as many Americans were killed as would later be killed on the beaches of Normandy during D-Day.

(A) Americans were killed as
(B) Americans were killed than
(C) Americans were killed than those who
(D) more Americans were killed as there
(E) more Americans were killed as those who

188. As a result of medical advances, many people that might at one time have died as children of such infections as diphtheria, pneumonia, or rheumatic fever now live well into old age.

(A) that might at one time have died as children
(B) who might once have died in childhood
(C) that as children might once have died
(D) who in childhood might have at one time died
(E) who, when they were children, might at one time have died

189. Proponents of artificial intelligence say they will be able to make computers that can understand English and other human languages, recognize objects, and reason as an expert does—computers that will be used to diagnose equipment breakdowns, deciding whether to authorize a loan, or other purposes such as these.

(A) as an expert does—computers that will be used to diagnose equipment breakdowns, deciding whether to authorize a loan, or other purposes such as these
(B) as an expert does, which may be used for purposes such as diagnosing equipment breakdowns or deciding whether to authorize a loan
(C) like an expert—computers that will be used for such purposes as diagnosing equipment breakdowns or deciding whether to authorize a loan
(D) like an expert, the use of which would be for purposes like the diagnosis of equipment breakdowns or the decision whether or not a loan should be authorized
(E) like an expert, to be used to diagnose equipment breakdowns, deciding whether to authorize a loan or not, or the like

190. Manifestations of Islamic political militancy in the first period of religious reformism were the rise of the Wahhabis in Arabia, the Sanusi in Cyrenaica, the Fulani in Nigeria, the Mahdi in the Sudan, and the victory of the Usuli "mujtahids" in Shiite Iran and Iraq.

(A) Manifestations of Islamic political militancy in the first period of religious reformism were the rise of the Wahhabis in Arabia, the Sanusi in Cyrenaica, the Fulani in Nigeria, the Mahdi in the Sudan, and
(B) Manifestations of Islamic political militancy in the first period of religious reformism were shown in the rise of the Wahhabis in Arabia, the Sanusi in Cyrenaica, the Fulani in Nigeria, the Mahdi in the Sudan, and also
(C) In the first period of religious reformism, manifestations of Islamic political militancy were the rise of the Wahhabis in Arabia, of the Sanusi in Cyrenaica, the Fulani in Nigeria, the Mahdi in the Sudan, and
(D) In the first period of religious reformism, manifestations of Islamic political militancy were shown in the rise of the Wahhabis in Arabia, the Sanusi in Cyrenaica, the Fulani in Nigeria, the Mahdi in the Sudan, and
(E) In the first period of religious reformism, Islamic political militancy was manifested in the rise of the Wahhabis in Arabia, the Sanusi in Cyrenaica, the Fulani in Nigeria, and the Mahdi in the Sudan, and in

191. Lawmakers are examining measures that would require banks to disclose all fees and account requirements in writing, provide free cashing of government checks, and to create basic savings accounts to carry minimal fees and require minimal initial deposits.

(A) provide free cashing of government checks, and to create basic savings accounts to carry
(B) provide free cashing of government checks, and creating basic savings accounts carrying
(C) to provide free cashing of government checks, and creating basic savings accounts that carry
(D) to provide free cashing of government checks, creating basic savings accounts to carry
(E) to provide free cashing of government checks, and to create basic savings accounts that carry

192. Cajuns speak a dialect brought to southern Louisiana by the four thousand Acadians who migrated there in 1755; their language is basically seventeenth-century French to which has been added English, Spanish, and Italian words.

(A) to which has been added English, Spanish, and Italian words
(B) added to which is English, Spanish, and Italian words
(C) to which English, Spanish, and Italian words have been added
(D) with English, Spanish, and Italian words having been added to it
(E) and, in addition, English, Spanish, and Italian words are added

193. Unlike the United States, where farmers can usually depend on rain or snow all year long, the rains in most parts of Sri Lanka are concentrated in the monsoon months, June to September, and the skies are generally clear for the rest of the year.

(A) Unlike the United States, where farmers can usually depend on rain or snow all year long, the rains in most parts of Sri Lanka
(B) Unlike the United States farmers who can usually depend on rain or snow all year long, the rains in most parts of Sri Lanka
(C) Unlike those of the United States, where farmers can usually depend on rain or snow all year long, most parts of Sri Lanka's rains
(D) In comparison with the United States, whose farmers can usually depend on rain or snow all year long, the rains in most parts of Sri Lanka
(E) In the United States, farmers can usually depend on rain or snow all year long, but in most parts of Sri Lanka the rains

194. Presenters at the seminar, one who is blind, will demonstrate adaptive equipment that allows visually impaired people to use computers.

(A) one who
(B) one of them who
(C) and one of them who
(D) one of whom
(E) one of which

195. Dr. Tonegawa won the Nobel Prize for discovering how the body can constantly change its genes to fashion a seeming unlimited number of antibodies, each specifically targeted at an invading microbe or foreign substance.

(A) seeming unlimited number of antibodies, each specifically targeted at
(B) seeming unlimited number of antibodies, each targeted specifically to
(C) seeming unlimited number of antibodies, all specifically targeted at
(D) seemingly unlimited number of antibodies, all of them targeted specifically to
(E) seemingly unlimited number of antibodies, each targeted specifically at

196. It is possible that Native Americans originally have migrated to the Western Hemisphere over a bridge of land that once existed between Siberia and Alaska.

(A) have migrated to the Western Hemisphere over a bridge of land that once existed
(B) were migrating to the Western Hemisphere over a bridge of land that existed once
(C) migrated over a bridge of land to the Western Hemisphere that once existed
(D) migrated to the Western Hemisphere over a bridge of land that once existed
(E) were migrating to the Western Hemisphere over a bridge of land existing once

197. In the fall of 1985, only 10 percent of the women entering college planned to major in education, while 28 percent chose business, making it the most popular major for women as well as for men.

(A) as well as for men
(B) as well as the men
(C) and men too
(D) and men as well
(E) and also men

198. Although Napoleon's army entered Russia with far more supplies than they had in their previous campaigns, it had provisions for only twenty-four days.

(A) they had in their previous campaigns
(B) their previous campaigns had had
(C) they had for any previous campaign
(D) in their previous campaigns
(E) for any previous campaign

199. Because the Earth's crust is more solid there and thus better able to transmit shock waves, an earthquake of a given magnitude typically devastates an area 100 times greater in the eastern United States than it does in the West.

(A) of a given magnitude typically devastates an area 100 times greater in the eastern United States than it does in the West
(B) of a given magnitude will typically devastate 100 times the area if it occurs in the eastern United States instead of the West
(C) will typically devastate 100 times the area in the eastern United States than one of comparable magnitude occurring in the West
(D) in the eastern United States will typically devastate an area 100 times greater than will a quake of comparable magnitude occurring in the West
(E) that occurs in the eastern United States will typically devastate 100 times more area than if it occurred with comparable magnitude in the West

200. Certain pesticides can become ineffective if used repeatedly in the same place; one reason is suggested by the finding that there are much larger populations of pesticide-degrading microbes in soils with a relatively long history of pesticide use than in soils that are free of such chemicals.

(A) Certain pesticides can become ineffective if used repeatedly in the same place; one reason is suggested by the finding that there are much larger populations of pesticide-degrading microbes in soils with a relatively long history of pesticide use than in soils that are free of such chemicals.
(B) If used repeatedly in the same place, one reason that certain pesticides can become ineffective is suggested by the finding that there are much larger populations of pesticide-degrading microbes in soils with a relatively long history of pesticide use than in soils that are free of such chemicals.
(C) If used repeatedly in the same place, one reason certain pesticides can become ineffective is suggested by the finding that much larger populations of pesticide-degrading microbes are found in soils with a relatively long history of pesticide use than those that are free of such chemicals.
(D) The finding that there are much larger populations of pesticide-degrading microbes in soils with a relatively long history of pesticide use than in soils that are free of such chemicals is suggestive of one reason, if used repeatedly in the same place, certain pesticides can become ineffective.
(E) The finding of much larger populations of pesticide-degrading microbes in soils with a relatively long history of pesticide use than in those that are free of such chemicals suggests one reason certain pesticides can become ineffective if used repeatedly in the same place.

201. One view of the economy contends that a large drop in oil prices should eventually lead to <u>lowering interest rates, as well as lowering fears about inflation,</u> a rally in stocks and bonds, and a weakening of the dollar.

(A) lowering interest rates, as well as lowering fears about inflation,
(B) a lowering of interest rates and of fears about inflation,
(C) a lowering of interest rates, along with fears about inflation,
(D) interest rates being lowered, along with fears about inflation,
(E) interest rates and fears about inflation being lowered, with

202. After the Civil War, contemporaries of Harriet <u>Tubman's maintained that she has</u> all of the qualities of a great leader: coolness in the face of danger, an excellent sense of strategy, and an ability to plan in minute detail.

(A) Tubman's maintained that she has
(B) Tubman's maintain that she had
(C) Tubman's have maintained that she had
(D) Tubman maintained that she had
(E) Tubman had maintained that she has

203. <u>From 1982 to 1987 sales of new small boats increased between five and ten percent annually.</u>

(A) From 1982 to 1987 sales of new small boats increased between five and ten percent annually.
(B) Five to ten percent is the annual increase in sales of new small boats in the years 1982 to 1987.
(C) Sales of new small boats have increased annually five and ten percent in the years 1982 to 1987.
(D) Annually an increase of five to ten percent has occurred between 1982 and 1987 in the sales of new small boats.
(E) Occurring from 1982 to 1987 was an annual increase of five and ten percent in the sales of new small boats.

204. In recent years cattle breeders have increasingly used crossbreeding, <u>in part that their steers should acquire certain characteristics</u> and partly because crossbreeding is said to provide hybrid vigor.

(A) in part that their steers should acquire certain characteristics
(B) in part for the acquisition of certain characteristics in their steers
(C) partly because of their steers acquiring certain characteristics
(D) partly because certain characteristics should be acquired by their steers
(E) partly to acquire certain characteristics in their steers

205. The peaks of a mountain range, acting like rocks in a streambed, produce ripples in the air flowing over them; the resulting flow pattern, with <u>crests and troughs that remain stationary although the air that forms them is moving rapidly, are</u> known as "standing waves."

(A) crests and troughs that remain stationary although the air that forms them is moving rapidly, are
(B) crests and troughs that remain stationary although they are formed by rapidly moving air, are
(C) crests and troughs that remain stationary although the air that forms them is moving rapidly, is
(D) stationary crests and troughs although the air that forms them is moving rapidly, are
(E) stationary crests and troughs although they are formed by rapidly moving air, is

206. <u>Like Auden, the language of James Merrill</u> is chatty, arch, and conversational—given to complex syntactic flights as well as to prosaic free-verse strolls.

(A) Like Auden, the language of James Merrill
(B) Like Auden, James Merrill's language
(C) Like Auden's, James Merrill's language
(D) As with Auden, James Merrill's language
(E) As is Auden's the language of James Merrill

207. In the textbook publishing business, the second quarter is historically weak, because revenues are low and marketing expenses are high as companies prepare for the coming school year.

(A) low and marketing expenses are high as companies prepare
(B) low and their marketing expenses are high as they prepare
(C) low with higher marketing expenses in preparation
(D) low, while marketing expenses are higher to prepare
(E) low, while their marketing expenses are higher in preparation

208. Teratomas are unusual forms of cancer because they are composed of tissues such as tooth and bone not normally found in the organ in which the tumor appears.

(A) because they are composed of tissues such as tooth and bone
(B) because they are composed of tissues like tooth and bone that are
(C) because they are composed of tissues, like tooth and bone, tissues
(D) in that their composition, tissues such as tooth and bone, is
(E) in that they are composed of tissues such as tooth and bone, tissues

209. The Senate approved immigration legislation that would grant permanent residency to millions of aliens currently residing here and if employers hired illegal aliens they would be penalized.

(A) if employers hired illegal aliens they would be penalized
(B) hiring illegal aliens would be a penalty for employers
(C) penalize employers who hire illegal aliens
(D) penalizing employers hiring illegal aliens
(E) employers to be penalized for hiring illegal aliens

210. Scientists have recently discovered what could be the largest and oldest living organism on Earth, a giant fungus that is an interwoven filigree of mushrooms and rootlike tentacles spawned by a single fertilized spore some 10,000 years ago and extending for more than 30 acres in the soil of a Michigan forest.

(A) extending
(B) extends
(C) extended
(D) it extended
(E) is extending

211. The period when the great painted caves at Lascaux and Altamira were occupied by Upper Paleolithic people has been established by carbon-14 dating, but what is much more difficult to determine are the reason for their decoration, the use to which primitive people put the caves, and the meaning of the magnificently depicted animals.

(A) has been established by carbon-14 dating, but what is much more difficult to determine are
(B) has been established by carbon-14 dating, but what is much more difficult to determine is
(C) have been established by carbon-14 dating, but what is much more difficult to determine is
(D) have been established by carbon-14 dating, but what is much more difficult to determine are
(E) are established by carbon-14 dating, but that which is much more difficult to determine is

212. The Baldrick Manufacturing Company has for several years followed a policy aimed at decreasing operating costs and improving the efficiency of its distribution system.

(A) aimed at decreasing operating costs and improving
(B) aimed at the decreasing of operating costs and to improve
(C) aiming at the decreasing of operating costs and improving
(D) the aim of which is the decreasing of operating costs and improving
(E) with the aim to decrease operating costs and to improve

213. *The Federalist* papers, a strong defense of the United States Constitution and important as a body of work in political science as well, represents the handiwork of three different authors.

(A) and important as a body of work in political science as well, represents
(B) as well as an important body of work in political science, represent
(C) and also a body of work of importance in political science is representing
(D) an important body of work in political science and has been representative of
(E) and as political science an important body of work too, represent

214. Although the term "psychopath" is popularly applied to an especially brutal criminal, in psychology it is someone who is apparently incapable of feeling compassion or the pangs of conscience.

(A) it is someone who is
(B) it is a person
(C) they are people who are
(D) it refers to someone who is
(E) it is in reference to people

215. Parliament did not accord full refugee benefits to twelve of the recent immigrants because it believed that to do it rewards them for entering the country illegally.

(A) to do it rewards
(B) doing it rewards
(C) to do this would reward
(D) doing so would reward
(E) to do it would reward

216. Many policy experts say that shifting a portion of health-benefit costs back to the workers helps to control the employer's costs, but also helps to limit medical spending by making patients more careful consumers.

(A) helps to control the employer's costs, but also helps
(B) helps the control of the employer's costs, and also
(C) not only helps to control the employer's costs, but also helps
(D) helps to control not only the employer's costs, but
(E) not only helps to control the employer's costs, and also helps

217. The plot of *The Bostonians* centers on the rivalry between Olive Chancellor, an active feminist, with her charming and cynical cousin, Basil Ransom, when they find themselves drawn to the same radiant young woman whose talent for public speaking has won her an ardent following.

(A) rivalry between Olive Chancellor, an active feminist, with her charming and cynical cousin, Basil Ransom
(B) rivals Olive Chancellor, an active feminist, against her charming and cynical cousin, Basil Ransom
(C) rivalry that develops between Olive Chancellor, an active feminist, and Basil Ransom, her charming and cynical cousin
(D) developing rivalry between Olive Chancellor, an active feminist, with Basil Ransom, her charming and cynical cousin
(E) active feminist, Olive Chancellor, and the rivalry with her charming and cynical cousin Basil Ransom

218. Despite protests from some waste-disposal companies, state health officials have ordered the levels of bacteria in seawater at popular beaches to be measured and that the results be published.

(A) the levels of bacteria in seawater at popular beaches to be measured and that the results be
(B) that seawater at popular beaches should be measured for their levels of bacteria, with the results being
(C) the measure of levels of bacteria in seawater at popular beaches and the results to be
(D) seawater measured at popular beaches for levels of bacteria, with their results
(E) that the levels of bacteria in seawater at popular beaches be measured and the results

219. While larger banks can afford to maintain their own data-processing operations, many smaller regional and community banks are finding that the <u>cost associated with</u> upgrading data-processing equipment and with the development and maintenance of new products and technical staff are prohibitive.

(A) cost associated with
(B) costs associated with
(C) costs arising from
(D) cost of
(E) costs of

220. <u>For almost a hundred years after having its beginning in 1788,</u> England exiled some 160,000 criminals to Australia.

(A) For almost a hundred years after having its beginning in 1788,
(B) Beginning in 1788 for a period of a hundred years,
(C) Beginning a period of almost a hundred years in 1788,
(D) During a hundred years, a period beginning in 1788,
(E) Over a period of a hundred years beginning in 1788,

221. Eating saltwater fish may <u>significantly reduce the risk of heart attacks and also aid for</u> sufferers of rheumatoid arthritis and asthma, according to three research studies published in the *New England Journal of Medicine*.

(A) significantly reduce the risk of heart attacks and also aid for
(B) be significant in reducing the risk of heart attacks and aid for
(C) significantly reduce the risk of heart attacks and aid
(D) cause a significant reduction in the risk of heart attacks and aid to
(E) significantly reduce the risk of heart attacks as well as aiding

222. By a vote of 9 to 0, the Supreme Court awarded the Central Intelligence Agency broad discretionary powers <u>enabling it to withhold from the public</u> the identities of its sources of intelligence information.

(A) enabling it to withhold from the public
(B) for it to withhold from the public
(C) for withholding disclosure to the public of
(D) that enable them to withhold from public disclosure
(E) that they can withhold public disclosure of

223. As business grows more complex, students <u>majoring in specialized areas like those of finance and marketing have been becoming increasingly</u> successful in the job market.

(A) majoring in specialized areas like those of finance and marketing have been becoming increasingly
(B) who major in such specialized areas as finance and marketing are becoming more and more
(C) who majored in specialized areas such as those of finance and marketing are being increasingly
(D) who major in specialized areas like those of finance and marketing have been becoming more and more
(E) having majored in such specialized areas as finance and marketing are being increasingly

224. Inuits of the Bering Sea were <u>in isolation from contact with Europeans longer than</u> Aleuts or Inuits of the North Pacific and northern Alaska.

(A) in isolation from contact with Europeans longer than
(B) isolated from contact with Europeans longer than
(C) in isolation from contact with Europeans longer than were
(D) isolated from contact with Europeans longer than were
(E) in isolation and without contacts with Europeans longer than

225. Minnesota is the only one of the contiguous forty-eight states <u>that still has a sizable wolf population, and where</u> this predator remains the archenemy of cattle and sheep.

(A) that still has a sizable wolf population, and where
(B) that still has a sizable wolf population, where
(C) that still has a sizable population of wolves, and where
(D) where the population of wolves is still sizable;
(E) where there is still a sizable population of wolves and where

226. Pablo Picasso, the late Spanish painter, credited African art <u>with having had</u> a strong influence on his work.

(A) with having had
(B) for its having
(C) to have had
(D) for having
(E) in that it had

227. Judicial rules in many states require that the identities of all prosecution witnesses are made known to defendants so they can attempt to rebut the testimony, but the Constitution explicitly requires only that the defendant have the opportunity to confront an accuser in court.

(A) that the identities of all prosecution witnesses are made known to defendants so they can attempt to rebut
(B) that the identities of all prosecution witnesses be made known to defendants so that they can attempt to rebut
(C) that the defendants should know the identities of all prosecution witnesses so they can attempt a rebuttal of
(D) the identities of all prosecution witnesses should be made known to defendants so they can attempt rebutting
(E) making known to defendants the identities of all prosecution witnesses so that they can attempt to rebut

228. Quasars, at billions of light-years from Earth the most distant observable objects in the universe, believed to be the cores of galaxies in an early stage of development.

(A) believed to be
(B) are believed to be
(C) some believe them to be
(D) some believe they are
(E) it is believed that they are

229. The colorization of black-and-white films by computers is defended by those who own the film rights, for the process can mean increased revenues for them; many others in the film industry, however, contend that the technique degrades major works of art, which they liken to putting lipstick on a Greek statue.

(A) which they liken to putting lipstick on a Greek statue
(B) which they liken to a Greek statue with lipstick put on it
(C) which they liken to lipstick put on a Greek statue
(D) likening it to a Greek statue with lipstick put on it
(E) likening it to putting lipstick on a Greek statue

230. In reference to the current hostility toward smoking, smokers frequently expressed anxiety that their prospects for being hired and promoted are being stunted by their habit.

(A) In reference to the current hostility toward smoking, smokers frequently expressed anxiety that
(B) Referring to the current hostility toward smoking, smokers frequently expressed anxiety about
(C) When referring to the current hostility toward smoking, smokers frequently express anxiety about
(D) With reference to the current hostility toward smoking, smokers frequently expressed anxiety about
(E) Referring to the current hostility toward smoking, smokers frequently express anxiety that

231. Ms. Chambers is among the forecasters who predict that the rate of addition to arable lands will drop while those of loss rise.

(A) those of loss rise
(B) it rises for loss
(C) those of losses rise
(D) the rate of loss rises
(E) there are rises for the rate of loss

232. Unlike auto insurance, the frequency of claims does not affect the premiums for personal property coverage, but if the insurance company is able to prove excessive loss due to owner negligence, it may decline to renew the policy.

(A) Unlike auto insurance, the frequency of claims does not affect the premiums for personal property coverage
(B) Unlike with auto insurance, the frequency of claims do not affect the premiums for personal property coverage
(C) Unlike the frequency of claims for auto insurance, the premiums for personal property coverage are not affected by the frequency of claims
(D) Unlike the premiums for auto insurance, the premiums for personal property coverage are not affected by the frequency of claims
(E) Unlike with the premiums for auto insurance, the premiums for personal property coverage is not affected by the frequency of claims

233. Recently implemented "shift-work equations" based on studies of the human sleep cycle have reduced sickness, sleeping on the job, fatigue among shift workers, and have raised production efficiency in various industries.

(A) fatigue among shift workers, and have raised
(B) fatigue among shift workers, and raised
(C) and fatigue among shift workers while raising
(D) lowered fatigue among shift workers, and raised
(E) and fatigue among shift workers was lowered while raising

234. The physical structure of the human eye enables it to sense light of wavelengths up to 0.0005 millimeters; infrared radiation, however, is invisible because its wavelength—0.1 millimeters—is too long to be registered by the eye.

(A) infrared radiation, however, is invisible because its wavelength—0.1 millimeters—is too long to be registered by the eye
(B) however, the wavelength of infrared radiation—0.1 millimeters—is too long to be registered by the eye making it invisible
(C) infrared radiation, however, is invisible because its wavelength—0.1 millimeters—is too long for the eye to register it
(D) however, because the wavelength of infrared radiation is 0.1 millimeters, it is too long for the eye to register and thus invisible
(E) however, infrared radiation has a wavelength of 0.1 millimeters that is too long for the eye to register, thus making it invisible

235. Spanning more than fifty years, Friedrich Müller began his career in an unpromising apprenticeship as a Sanskrit scholar and culminated in virtually every honor that European governments and learned societies could bestow.

(A) Müller began his career in an unpromising apprenticeship as
(B) Müller's career began in an unpromising apprenticeship as
(C) Müller's career began with the unpromising apprenticeship of being
(D) Müller had begun his career with the unpromising apprenticeship of being
(E) the career of Müller has begun with an unpromising apprenticeship of

236. The Coast Guard is conducting tests to see whether pigeons can be trained to help find survivors of wrecks at sea.

(A) to see whether pigeons can be trained to help find
(B) to see whether pigeons can be trained as help to find
(C) to see if pigeons can be trained for helping to find
(D) that see if pigeons are able to be trained in helping to find
(E) that see whether pigeons are able to be trained for help in finding

237. It seems likely that a number of astronomical phenomena, such as the formation of planetary nebulas, may be caused by the interaction where two stars orbit each other at close range.

(A) may be caused by the interaction where two stars orbit each other
(B) may be caused by the interaction between two stars that each orbit the other
(C) are because of the interaction between two stars that orbit each other
(D) are caused by the interaction of two stars where each is orbiting the other
(E) are caused by the interaction of two stars orbiting each other

238. According to a recent study by Rutgers University, the number of women in state legislatures has grown in every election since 1968.

(A) the number of women in state legislatures has grown
(B) the number of women who are in state legislatures have grown
(C) there has been growth in the number of women in state legislatures
(D) a growing number of women have been in state legislatures
(E) women have been growing in number in state legislatures

239. Organized in 1966 by the Fish and Wildlife Service, the Breeding Bird Survey uses annual roadside counts along established routes for monitoring of population changes of as many as, or of more than 250 bird species, including 180 songbirds.

(A) for monitoring of population changes of as many as, or of
(B) to monitor population changes of as many, or
(C) to monitor changes in the populations of
(D) that monitors population changes of
(E) that monitors changes in populations of as many as, or

240. <u>What brought</u> the automobile company back from the verge of bankruptcy shortly after the Second World War was a special, governmentally sanctioned price increase allowed during a period of wage and price controls.

(A) What brought
(B) The thing that brought
(C) That which brought
(D) Bringing
(E) What has brought

241. <u>As well as heat and light, the Sun is the source of a continuous stream</u> of atomic particles known as the solar wind.

(A) As well as heat and light, the Sun is the source of a continuous stream
(B) Besides heat and light, also the Sun is the source of a continuous stream
(C) Besides heat and light, the Sun is also the source of a continuous streaming
(D) The Sun is the source not only of heat and light, but also of a continuous stream
(E) The Sun is the source of not only heat and light but, as well, of a continuous streaming

242. Even their most ardent champions concede <u>that no less than a technical or scientific breakthrough is necessary</u> before solar cells can meet the goal of providing one percent of the nation's energy needs.

(A) that no less than a technical or scientific breakthrough is necessary
(B) that nothing other than a technical or scientific breakthrough is needed
(C) that a technical or scientific breakthrough is necessary
(D) the necessity for an occurrence of a technical or scientific breakthrough
(E) the necessity for a technical or scientific breakthrough occurring

243. Some scientists have been critical of the laboratory tests conducted by the Federal Drug Administration on the grounds that the amounts of suspected carcinogens fed to animals <u>far exceeds those that humans could consume.</u>

(A) far exceeds those that humans could consume
(B) exceeds by far those humans can consume
(C) far exceeds those humans are able to consume
(D) exceed by far those able to be consumed by humans
(E) far exceed those that humans could consume

244. Like their male counterparts, women scientists are above average in terms of intelligence and creativity, but unlike men of science, <u>their female counterparts have had to work</u> against the grain of occupational stereotyping to enter a "man's world."

(A) their female counterparts have had to work
(B) their problem is working
(C) one thing they have had to do is work
(D) the handicap women of science have had is to work
(E) women of science have had to work

245. Unlike <u>Schoenberg's twelve-tone system that dominated</u> the music of the postwar period, Bartók founded no school and left behind only a handful of disciples.

(A) Schoenberg's twelve-tone system that dominated
(B) Schoenberg and his twelve-tone system which dominated
(C) Schoenberg, whose twelve-tone system dominated
(D) the twelve-tone system of Schoenberg that has dominated
(E) Schoenberg and the twelve-tone system, dominating

246. Joachim Raff and Giacomo Meyerbeer are examples of the kind of composer who receives popular acclaim while living, <u>often goes into decline after death, and never regains popularity again.</u>

(A) often goes into decline after death, and never regains popularity again
(B) whose reputation declines after death and never regains its status again
(C) but whose reputation declines after death and never regains its former status
(D) who declines in reputation after death and who never regained popularity again
(E) then has declined in reputation after death and never regained popularity

247. Faced with an estimated $2 billion budget gap, the city's mayor proposed a nearly 17 percent reduction in the amount allocated the previous year to maintain the city's major cultural institutions and to subsidize hundreds of local arts groups.

(A) proposed a nearly 17 percent reduction in the amount allocated the previous year to maintain the city's major cultural institutions and to subsidize

(B) proposed a reduction from the previous year of nearly 17 percent in the amount it was allocating to maintain the city's major cultural institutions and for subsidizing

(C) proposed to reduce, by nearly 17 percent, the amount from the previous year that was allocated for the maintenance of the city's major cultural institutions and to subsidize

(D) has proposed a reduction from the previous year of nearly 17 percent of the amount it was allocating for maintaining the city's major cultural institutions, and to subsidize

(E) was proposing that the amount they were allocating be reduced by nearly 17 percent from the previous year for maintaining the city's major cultural institutions and for the subsidization

248. By offering lower prices and a menu of personal communications options, such as caller identification and voice mail, the new telecommunications company has not only captured customers from other phone companies but also forced them to offer competitive prices.

(A) has not only captured customers from other phone companies but also forced them

(B) has not only captured customers from other phone companies, but it also forced them

(C) has not only captured customers from other phone companies but also forced these companies

(D) not only has captured customers from other phone companies but also these companies have been forced

(E) not only captured customers from other phone companies, but it also has forced them

249. Bluegrass musician Bill Monroe, whose repertory, views on musical collaboration, and vocal style were influential on generations of bluegrass artists, was also an inspiration to many musicians, that included Elvis Presley and Jerry Garcia, whose music differed significantly from his own.

(A) were influential on generations of bluegrass artists, was also an inspiration to many musicians, that included Elvis Presley and Jerry Garcia, whose music differed significantly from

(B) influenced generations of bluegrass artists, also inspired many musicians, including Elvis Presley and Jerry Garcia, whose music differed significantly from

(C) was influential to generations of bluegrass artists, was also inspirational to many musicians, that included Elvis Presley and Jerry Garcia, whose music was different significantly in comparison to

(D) was influential to generations of bluegrass artists, also inspired many musicians, who included Elvis Presley and Jerry Garcia, the music of whom differed significantly when compared to

(E) were an influence on generations of bluegrass artists, was also an inspiration to many musicians, including Elvis Presley and Jerry Garcia, whose music was significantly different from that of

250. The company announced that its profits declined much less in the second quarter than analysts had expected it to and its business will improve in the second half of the year.

(A) had expected it to and its business will improve

(B) had expected and that its business would improve

(C) expected it would and that it will improve its business

(D) expected them to and its business would improve

(E) expected and that it will have improved its business

251. The gyrfalcon, an Arctic bird of prey, has survived a close brush with extinction; its numbers are now five times greater than when the use of DDT was sharply restricted in the early 1970's.

   (A) extinction; its numbers are now five times greater than
   (B) extinction; its numbers are now five times more than
   (C) extinction, their numbers now fivefold what they were
   (D) extinction, now with fivefold the numbers they had
   (E) extinction, now with numbers five times greater than

252. Three out of every four automobile owners in the United States also own a bicycle.

   (A) Three out of every four automobile owners in the United States also own a bicycle.
   (B) Out of every four, three automobile owners in the United States also owns a bicycle.
   (C) Bicycles are owned by three out of every four owners of automobiles in the United States.
   (D) In the United States, three out of every four automobile owners owns bicycles.
   (E) Out of every four owners of automobiles in the United States, bicycles are also owned by three.

253. Analysts blamed May's sluggish retail sales on unexciting merchandise as well as the weather, colder and wetter than was usual in some regions, which slowed sales of barbecue grills and lawn furniture.

   (A) colder and wetter than was usual in some regions, which slowed
   (B) which was colder and wetter than usual in some regions, slowing
   (C) since it was colder and wetter than usually in some regions, which slowed
   (D) being colder and wetter than usually in some regions, slowing
   (E) having been colder and wetter than was usual in some regions and slowed

254. Balding is much more common among White males than males of other races.

   (A) than
   (B) than among
   (C) than is so of
   (D) compared to
   (E) in comparison with

255. The bank holds $3 billion in loans that are seriously delinquent or in such trouble that they do not expect payments when due.

   (A) they do not expect payments when
   (B) it does not expect payments when it is
   (C) it does not expect payments to be made when they are
   (D) payments are not to be expected to be paid when
   (E) payments are not expected to be paid when they will be

256. The nephew of Pliny the Elder wrote the only eyewitness account of the great eruption of Vesuvius in two letters to the historian Tacitus.

   (A) The nephew of Pliny the Elder wrote the only eyewitness account of the great eruption of Vesuvius in two letters to the historian Tacitus.
   (B) To the historian Tacitus, the nephew of Pliny the Elder wrote two letters, being the only eyewitness accounts of the great eruption of Vesuvius.
   (C) The only eyewitness account is in two letters by the nephew of Pliny the Elder writing to the historian Tacitus an account of the great eruption of Vesuvius.
   (D) Writing the only eyewitness account, Pliny the Elder's nephew accounted for the great eruption of Vesuvius in two letters to the historian Tacitus.
   (E) In two letters to the historian Tacitus, the nephew of Pliny the Elder wrote the only eyewitness account of the great eruption of Vesuvius.

257. The direction in which the Earth and the other solid planets—Mercury, Venus, and Mars—spins were determined from collisions with giant celestial bodies in the early history of the Solar System.

   (A) spins were determined from
   (B) spins were determined because of
   (C) spins was determined through
   (D) spin was determined by
   (E) spin was determined as a result of

258. The British sociologist and activist Barbara Wootton once noted as a humorous example of income maldistribution that the elephant that gave rides to children at the Whipsnade Zoo was earning annually exactly what she then earned as director of adult education for London.

(A) that the elephant that gave rides to children at the Whipsnade Zoo was earning
(B) that the elephant, giving rides to children at the Whipsnade Zoo, had been earning
(C) that there was an elephant giving rides to children at the Whipsnade Zoo, and it earned
(D) the elephant that gave rides to children at the Whipsnade Zoo and was earning
(E) the elephant giving rides to children at the Whipsnade Zoo and that it earned

259. Five fledgling sea eagles left their nests in western Scotland this summer, bringing to 34 the number of wild birds successfully raised since transplants from Norway began in 1975.

(A) bringing
(B) and brings
(C) and it brings
(D) and it brought
(E) and brought

260. According to some economists, the July decrease in unemployment so that it was the lowest in two years suggests that the gradual improvement in the job market is continuing.

(A) so that it was the lowest in two years
(B) so that it was the lowest two-year rate
(C) to what would be the lowest in two years
(D) to a two-year low level
(E) to the lowest level in two years

261. Being a United States citizen since 1988 and born in Calcutta in 1940, author Bharati Mukherjee has lived in England and Canada, and first came to the United States in 1961 to study at the Iowa Writers' Workshop.

(A) Being a United States citizen since 1988 and born in Calcutta in 1940, author Bharati Mukherjee has
(B) Having been a United States citizen since 1988, she was born in Calcutta in 1940; author Bharati Mukherjee
(C) Born in Calcutta in 1940, author Bharati Mukherjee became a United States citizen in 1988; she has
(D) Being born in Calcutta in 1940 and having been a United States citizen since 1988, author Bharati Mukherjee
(E) Having been born in Calcutta in 1940 and being a United States citizen since 1988, author Bharati Mukherjee

262. Initiated five centuries after Europeans arrived in the New World on Columbus Day 1992, Project SETI pledged a $100 million investment in the search for extraterrestrial intelligence.

(A) Initiated five centuries after Europeans arrived in the New World on Columbus Day 1992, Project SETI pledged a $100 million investment in the search for extraterrestrial intelligence.
(B) Initiated on Columbus Day 1992, five centuries after Europeans arrived in the New World, a $100 million investment in the search for extraterrestrial intelligence was pledged by Project SETI.
(C) Initiated on Columbus Day 1992, five centuries after Europeans arrived in the New World, Project SETI pledged a $100 million investment in the search for extraterrestrial intelligence.
(D) Pledging a $100 million investment in the search for extraterrestrial intelligence, the initiation of Project SETI five centuries after Europeans arrived in the New World on Columbus Day 1992.
(E) Pledging a $100 million investment in the search for extraterrestrial intelligence five centuries after Europeans arrived in the New World, on Columbus Day 1992, the initiation of Project SETI took place.

263. In A.D. 391, <u>resulting from the destruction of the largest library of the ancient world at Alexandria,</u> later generations lost all but the *Iliad* and *Odyssey* among Greek epics, most of the poetry of Pindar and Sappho, and dozens of plays by Aeschylus and Euripides.

(A) resulting from the destruction of the largest library of the ancient world at Alexandria,
(B) the destroying of the largest library of the ancient world at Alexandria resulted and
(C) because of the result of the destruction of the library at Alexandria, the largest of the ancient world,
(D) as a result of the destruction of the library at Alexandria, the largest of the ancient world,
(E) Alexandria's largest library of the ancient world was destroyed, and the result was

264. Scientists believe that unlike the males of most species of moth, the male whistling moths of Nambung, Australia, call female moths to them <u>by the use of acoustical signals, but not olfactory ones, and they attract</u> their mates during the day, rather than at night.

(A) by the use of acoustical signals, but not olfactory ones, and they attract
(B) by the use of acoustical signals instead of using olfactory ones, and attracting
(C) by using acoustical signals, not using olfactory ones, and by attracting
(D) using acoustical signals, rather than olfactory ones, and attract
(E) using acoustical signals, but not olfactory ones, and attracting

265. Thomas Eakins' powerful style and his choices of subject—the advances in modern surgery, the discipline of sport, the strains of individuals in tension with society or even with themselves—<u>was as disturbing to his own time as it is</u> compelling for ours.

(A) was as disturbing to his own time as it is
(B) were as disturbing to his own time as they are
(C) has been as disturbing in his own time as they are
(D) had been as disturbing in his own time as it was
(E) have been as disturbing in his own time as

266. In a recent poll, 86 percent of the public favored <u>a Clean Air Act as strong or stronger than</u> the present act.

(A) a Clean Air Act as strong or stronger than
(B) a Clean Air Act that is stronger, or at least so strong as,
(C) at least as strong a Clean Air Act as is
(D) a Clean Air Act as strong or stronger than is
(E) a Clean Air Act at least as strong as

267. <u>Like Rousseau, Tolstoi rebelled</u> against the unnatural complexity of human relations in modern society.

(A) Like Rousseau, Tolstoi rebelled
(B) Like Rousseau, Tolstoi's rebellion was
(C) As Rousseau, Tolstoi rebelled
(D) As did Rousseau, Tolstoi's rebellion was
(E) Tolstoi's rebellion, as Rousseau's, was

268. Ranked as one of the most important of Europe's young playwrights, Franz Xaver Kroetz has written forty plays; his works—translated into over thirty languages—are produced more often <u>than any</u> contemporary German dramatist.

(A) than any
(B) than any other
(C) than are any
(D) than those of any other
(E) as are those of any

Explanatory Material: Sentence Correction

The following discussion is intended to familiarize you with the most efficient and effective approaches to sentence correction questions. The particular questions in this chapter are generally representative of the kinds of questions you will encounter in the GMAT®. Remember that it is the problem-solving strategy that is important, not the specific details of a particular question.

1. The Wallerstein study indicates that even after a decade young men and women still experience some of the effects of a divorce <u>occurring when a child</u>.

   (A) occurring when a child
   (B) occurring when children
   (C) that occurred when a child
   (D) that occurred when they were children
   (E) that has occurred as each was a child

Choice D is best. The phrasing *a divorce that occurred when they were children* correctly uses the relative clause *that occurred* to modify *a divorce* and includes a pronoun and verb (*they were*) that refer unambiguously to their antecedent, *men and women*. Choice A incorrectly introduces the *when . . .* phrase with *occurring,* thus illogically making *divorce* the grammatical referent of *when a child;* furthermore, the singular *child* does not agree with the plural *men and women*. B replaces *child* with *children* but otherwise fails to correct A's errors of structure and logic, and C corrects only the error created by *occurring*. Choice E includes an incorrect verb tense (*has occurred*) and wrongly replaces *when* with *as*. Also, *each was* does not properly refer to *men and women*.

2. Since 1981, when the farm depression began, the number of acres overseen by professional farm-management companies <u>have grown from 48 million to nearly 59 million, an area that is about Colorado's size</u>.

   (A) have grown from 48 million to nearly 59 million, an area that is about Colorado's size
   (B) have grown from 48 million to nearly 59 million, about the size of Colorado
   (C) has grown from 48 million to nearly 59 million, an area about the size of Colorado
   (D) has grown from 48 million up to nearly 59 million, an area about the size of Colorado's
   (E) has grown from 48 million up to nearly 59 million, about Colorado's size

In choice C, the best answer, *an area about the size of Colorado* clearly describes a rough equivalence between the area of Colorado and the area overseen by the companies. In A and B, the plural verb *have* does not agree with the singular subject *number*. Choice A is also wordy, since *that is* can be deleted without loss of clarity. The absence of *an area* in B and E impairs clarity: the phrase beginning with *about* must modify a noun such as *area* that is logically equivalent to the number of acres given. In D and E *up to* is unidiomatic; the correct expression is *from x to y.* In D, *the size of Colorado's* is unidiomatic, since *of Colorado* forms a complete possessive.

3. Some bat caves, like honeybee hives, have residents that take on different duties such as defending the entrance, <u>acting as sentinels and to sound</u> a warning at the approach of danger, and scouting outside the cave for new food and roosting sites.

   (A) acting as sentinels and to sound
   (B) acting as sentinels and sounding
   (C) to act as sentinels and sound
   (D) to act as sentinels and to sound
   (E) to act as a sentinel sounding

Because the verb phrases used to describe the bats' duties are governed by the phrase *different duties such as,* they should each be expressed in the present participial (or "-ing") form to parallel *defending* and *scouting*. Choices A, C, D, and E all violate parallelism by employing infinitives (*to . . .*) in place of participial phrases. In E the singular *sentinel* is not consistent with *residents,* and the omission of *and* distorts the meaning of the original. Only B, the best answer, preserves the sense of the original, uses the correct idiom, and observes the parallelism required among and within the three main verb phrases.

4. The only way for growers to salvage frozen citrus is <u>to process them quickly into juice concentrate before they rot when warmer weather returns</u>.

   (A) to process them quickly into juice concentrate before they rot when warmer weather returns
   (B) if they are quickly processed into juice concentrate before warmer weather returns to rot them
   (C) for them to be processed quickly into juice concentrate before the fruit rots when warmer weather returns
   (D) if the fruit is quickly processed into juice concentrate before they rot when warmer weather returns
   (E) to have it quickly processed into juice concentrate before warmer weather returns and rots the fruit

For parallelism, the linking verb *is* should link two infinitives: *The only way to salvage . . . is to process.* Choice A begins with an infinitive, but the plural pronouns *them* and *they* do not agree with the singular noun *citrus.* Choices B, C, and D do not begin with an infinitive, and all present pronoun errors: the plural pronouns cannot grammatically refer to *citrus* or *fruit,* nor can they refer to *farmers* without absurdity. The best choice, E, has parallel infinitives and uses *fruit* to refer unambiguously to *citrus.* E also expresses the cause-and-effect relationship between the return of warmer weather and the rotting of the fruit; A, C, and D merely describe these events as contemporaneous.

5. Carbon-14 dating reveals that the megalithic monuments in Brittany are nearly 2,000 years <u>as old as any of their supposed</u> Mediterranean predecessors.

(A) as old as any of their supposed
(B) older than any of their supposed
(C) as old as their supposed
(D) older than any of their supposedly
(E) as old as their supposedly

Choices A, C, and E do not state the comparison logically. The expression *as old as* indicates equality of age, but the sentence indicates that the Brittany monuments predate the Mediterranean monuments by 2,000 years. In B, the best choice, *older than* makes this point of comparison clear. B also correctly uses the adjective *supposed,* rather than the adverb *supposedly* used in D and E, to modify the noun phrase *Mediterranean predecessors.*

6. In virtually all types of tissue in every animal species, dioxin induces the production of enzymes that are the organism's <u>trying to metabolize, or render harmless, the chemical that is irritating it</u>.

(A) trying to metabolize, or render harmless, the chemical that is irritating it
(B) trying that it metabolize, or render harmless, the chemical irritant
(C) attempt to try to metabolize, or render harmless, such a chemical irritant
(D) attempt to try and metabolize, or render harmless, the chemical irritating it
(E) attempt to metabolize, or render harmless, the chemical irritant

Although an "-ing" verb such as *trying* can sometimes be used as a noun, the phrase *the organism's trying to metabolize* in A is unidiomatic because *trying* is used as the object of *organism's.* In B, *trying that it metabolize* is ungrammatical. The noun *attempt* could follow *organism's;* also, it would parallel the noun *enzymes,* and parallelism is needed here because the sentence uses the linking verb *are* to equate *enzymes* and *attempt.* In C and D, however, *attempt to try* is redundant. Choice E, which says *attempt to metabolize,* is best. The phrase *the chemical irritant* is also the most concise and precise conclusion for the sentence because it clearly refers to the *dioxin* mentioned earlier.

7. Dr. Hakuta's research among Hispanic children in the United States indicates that the more the children use both Spanish and English, <u>their intellectual advantage is greater in skills underlying reading ability and nonverbal logic</u>.

(A) their intellectual advantage is greater in skills underlying reading ability and nonverbal logic
(B) their intellectual advantage is the greater in skills underlaying reading ability and nonverbal logic
(C) the greater their intellectual advantage in skills underlying reading ability and nonverbal logic
(D) in skills that underlay reading ability and nonverbal logic, their intellectual advantage is the greater
(E) in skills underlying reading ability and nonverbal logic, the greater intellectual advantage is theirs

The best choice is C. The phrase *the more the children* should be completed by a parallel phrase that begins with a comparative adjective and a noun phrase, as in *the greater their . . . advantage.* Only C correctly completes the structure with a parallel phrase. Choices A, B, D, and E present structures that are unwieldy and awkward in addition to being nonparallel, and that state the relationship between language use and skills development less clearly than C does. Also, *underlaying* in B and *underlay* in D are incorrect; the meaning of this sentence requires the present participle of "underlie," *underlying,* as a modifier of *skills.*

8. Lacking information about energy use, people tend to overestimate the amount of energy used by <u>equipment, such as lights, that are visible and must be turned on and off and underestimate that</u> used by unobtrusive equipment, such as water heaters.

(A) equipment, such as lights, that are visible and must be turned on and off and underestimate that
(B) equipment, such as lights, that are visible and must be turned on and off and underestimate it when
(C) equipment, such as lights, that is visible and must be turned on and off and underestimate it when
(D) visible equipment, such as lights, that must be turned on and off and underestimate that
(E) visible equipment, such as lights, that must be turned on and off and underestimate it when

Choices A and B incorrectly use the plural verb *are* with the singular noun *equipment.* In B, C, and E, *when used by* does not parallel *amount . . . used by* and nonsensically suggests that the people are used by the equipment. D, the best choice, correctly parallels *the amount . . . used by* with *that used by,* in which *that* is the pronoun substitute for *amount.* Moreover, D solves the agreement problem of A and B by omitting the *to be* verb used with *visible* and placing *visible* before *equipment*; the phrase *visible equipment* is also parallel with *unobtrusive equipment.*

9. Astronomers at the Palomar Observatory have discovered a distant supernova explosion, one <u>that they believe is</u> a type previously unknown to science.

    (A) that they believe is
    (B) that they believe it to be
    (C) they believe that it is of
    (D) they believe that is
    (E) they believe to be of

Choice E is best. The pronoun *that* in A and B should be deleted, since the pronoun *one* is sufficient to introduce the modifier and the sentence is more fluid without *that*. In B and C, *it* and *that it* are intrusive and ungrammatical: the idiom is "believe x to be y." In the context of this sentence, the infinitive *to be* is more appropriate than the limited present-tense *is* in referring to an event that occurred long ago but has been discovered only recently. Finally, A, B, and D lack *of* and so illogically equate this particular explosion with the whole class of explosions to which it belongs: it is not *a type* but possibly one *of a type*.

10. <u>However much United States voters may agree that</u> there is waste in government and that the government as a whole spends beyond its means, it is difficult to find broad support for a movement toward a minimal state.

    (A) However much United States voters may agree that
    (B) Despite the agreement among United States voters to the fact
    (C) Although United States voters agree
    (D) Even though United States voters may agree
    (E) There is agreement among United States voters that

A is the best choice. Choices B, C, and D incorrectly omit *that* after *agree*; *that* is needed to create the parallel construction *agree that there is waste . . . and that the government . . . spends.* Choice E, though it retains *that,* is grammatically incorrect: because E starts with an independent rather than a subordinate clause and separates its two independent clauses with a comma, it creates a run-on sentence with no logical connection established between the halves. In B, *the agreement . . . to the fact* is unidiomatic, and B, C, and E alter the sense of the original sentence by saying that voters *agree* rather than that they *may agree.*

11. <u>Based on accounts of various ancient writers,</u> scholars have painted a sketchy picture of the activities of an all-female cult that, perhaps as early as the sixth century B.C., worshipped a goddess known in Latin as Bona Dea, "the good goddess."

    (A) Based on accounts of various ancient writers
    (B) Basing it on various ancient writers' accounts
    (C) With accounts of various ancient writers used for a basis
    (D) By the accounts of various ancient writers they used
    (E) Using accounts of various ancient writers

In choice A, the introductory clause beginning *Based on* modifies *scholars,* the noun that immediately follows it: in other words, A says that *scholars* were *based on the accounts of various ancient writers.* Choice B is awkward and imprecise in that the referent for the pronoun *it* is not immediately clear. C and D are also wordy and awkward, and in D *By the accounts . . . they used* is an unidiomatic and roundabout way of saying that scholars used the accounts. E, the best choice, is clear and concise; it correctly uses a present participle (or "-ing" verb) to introduce the modifier describing how the scholars worked.

12. <u>Formulas for cash flow and the ratio of debt to equity do not apply to new small businesses in the same way as they do to established big businesses, because they are growing and are seldom in equilibrium.</u>

    (A) Formulas for cash flow and the ratio of debt to equity do not apply to new small businesses in the same way as they do to established big businesses, because they are growing and are seldom in equilibrium.
    (B) Because they are growing and are seldom in equilibrium, formulas for cash flow and the ratio of debt to equity do not apply to new small businesses in the same way as they do to established big businesses.
    (C) Because they are growing and are seldom in equilibrium, new small businesses are not subject to the same applicability of formulas for cash flow and the ratio of debt to equity as established big businesses.
    (D) Because new small businesses are growing and are seldom in equilibrium, formulas for cash flow and the ratio of debt to equity do not apply to them in the same way as to established big businesses.
    (E) New small businesses are not subject to the applicability of formulas for cash flow and the ratio of debt to equity in the same way as established big businesses, because they are growing and are seldom in equilibrium.

In A, the *they* after *because* is ambiguous; it seems illogically to refer to *Formulas* because *they* and *Formulas* are each the grammatical subject of a clause and because the previous *they* refers to *Formulas*. In A and B, *do not apply to . . . in the same way as they do to* is wordy and awkward. D, the best choice, says more concisely *in the same way as to.* Also in B, because *they* refers *to formulas,* the introductory clause states confusedly that the formulas are growing. In C and E, *subject to the [same] applicability of . . .* is wordy, awkward, and imprecise; furthermore, *are* is preferable either before or after *established big businesses* to complete the comparison. Finally, the referent of *they* is not immediately clear in E.

13. State officials report that soaring rates of liability insurance have risen to force cutbacks in the operations of everything from local governments and school districts to day-care centers and recreational facilities.

(A) rates of liability insurance have risen to force
(B) rates of liability insurance are a force for
(C) rates for liability insurance are forcing
(D) rises in liability insurance rates are forcing
(E) liability insurance rates have risen to force

In choices A and B, *rates of* is incorrect; when *rates* means "prices charged," it should be followed by *for*. Also in B, *are a force for* does not accurately convey the meaning that the soaring rates are actually forcing cutbacks in the present. In A and E, it is redundant to say that soaring rates *have risen*. Similarly, the word *rises* makes D redundant. C, the best choice, is idiomatic and concise, and it correctly uses the progressive verb form *are forcing* to indicate an ongoing situation.

14. Paleontologists believe that fragments of a primate jawbone unearthed in Burma and estimated at 40 to 44 million years old provide evidence of a crucial step along the evolutionary path that led to human beings.

(A) at 40 to 44 million years old provide evidence of
(B) as being 40 to 44 million years old provides evidence of
(C) that it is 40 to 44 million years old provides evidence of what was
(D) to be 40 to 44 million years old provide evidence of
(E) as 40 to 44 million years old provides evidence of what was

D, the best choice, correctly follows *estimated* with *to be*. The other choices present structures that are not idiomatic when used in conjunction with *estimated*. Choices B, C, and E all mismatch the singular verb *provides* with its plural subject, *fragments*, and in choices C and E, *what was* is unnecessary and wordy. In choice C, the use of the verb phrase *estimated that it is* produces an ungrammatical sentence.

15. In his research paper, Dr. Frosh, medical director of the Payne Whitney Clinic, distinguishes mood swings, which may be violent without their being grounded in mental disease, from genuine manic-depressive psychosis.

(A) mood swings, which may be violent without their being grounded in mental disease, from genuine manic-depressive psychosis
(B) mood swings, perhaps violent without being grounded in mental disease, and genuine manic-depressive psychosis
(C) between mood swings, which may be violent without being grounded in mental disease, and genuine manic-depressive psychosis
(D) between mood swings, perhaps violent without being grounded in mental disease, from genuine manic-depressive psychosis
(E) genuine manic-depressive psychosis and mood swings, which may be violent without being grounded in mental disease

The best choice is C because it uses the idiomatically correct expression *distinguishes between* x *and* y and because it provides a structure in which the relative clause beginning *which may be violent* clearly modifies *mood swings*. The other choices use *distinguishes* in unidiomatic constructions. Additionally, *their* in A is intrusive and unnecessary, and the modifier of *mood swings* in B and D (*perhaps violent*) is awkward and less clear than the more developed clause *which may be violent*.

16. Unlike a typical automobile loan, which requires a fifteen- to twenty-percent down payment, the lease-loan buyer is not required to make an initial deposit on the new vehicle.

(A) the lease-loan buyer is not required to make
(B) with lease-loan buying there is no requirement of
(C) lease-loan buyers are not required to make
(D) for the lease-loan buyer there is no requirement of
(E) a lease-loan does not require the buyer to make

Choice E, the best answer, correctly uses a parallel construction to draw a logical comparison: *Unlike a typical automobile loan, . . . a lease-loan . . . .* Choice A illogically compares an *automobile loan*, an inanimate thing, with a *lease-loan buyer*, a person. In choice C, *buyers* makes the comparison inconsistent in number as well as illogical. Choices B and D are syntactically and logically flawed because each attempts to compare the noun *loan* and a prepositional phrase: *with lease-loan buying* in B and *for the lease-loan buyer* in D. Choices B and D are also imprecise and awkward. Finally, choice E is the only option that supplies an active verb form, *does not require*, to parallel *requires*.

17. Native American burial sites dating back 5,000 years indicate that the residents of Maine at that time <u>were part of a widespread culture of Algonquian-speaking people</u>.

    (A)   were part of a widespread culture of Algonquian-speaking people

    (B)   had been part of a widespread culture of people who were Algonquian-speaking

    (C)   were people who were part of a widespread culture that was Algonquian-speaking

    (D)   had been people who were part of a widespread culture that was Algonquian-speaking

    (E)   were a people which had been part of a wide-spread, Algonquian-speaking culture

Choice A is best because it correctly uses the simple past tense, *the residents . . . at that time were*, and because it is the most concise. In B and D, the replacement of *were* with the past perfect *had been* needlessly changes the original meaning by suggesting that the Native Americans had previously ceased to be part of the widespread culture. All of the choices but A are wordy, and in C, D, and E the word *people* redundantly describes *the residents* rather than the larger group to which the residents belonged. These choices are also imprecise because they state that the *culture*, rather than *people*, spoke the Algonquian language. Choice E displays inconsistent tenses and an error of pronoun reference, *people which.*

18. <u>Each of Hemingway's wives—Hadley Richardson, Pauline Pfeiffer, Martha Gelhorn, and Mary Welsh—were strong and interesting women,</u> very different from the often pallid women who populate his novels.

    (A)   Each of Hemingway's wives—Hadley Richardson, Pauline Pfeiffer, Martha Gelhorn, and Mary Welsh—were strong and interesting women,

    (B)   Hadley Richardson, Pauline Pfeiffer, Martha Gelhorn, and Mary Welsh—each of them Hemingway's wives—were strong and interesting women,

    (C)   Hemingway's wives—Hadley Richardson, Pauline Pfeiffer, Martha Gelhorn, and Mary Welsh—were all strong and interesting women,

    (D)   Strong and interesting women—Hadley Richardson, Pauline Pfeiffer, Martha Gelhorn, and Mary Welsh—each a wife of Hemingway, was

    (E)   Strong and interesting women—Hadley Richardson, Pauline Pfeiffer, Martha Gelhorn, and Mary Welsh—every one of Hemingway's wives were

Each choice but C contains errors of agreement. In both A and E, the singular subject (*each* in A, *every one* in E) does not agree with the plural verb *were,* while in D, the plural subject *women* is mismatched with the singular verb *was.* In B, the subject and verb agree, but the descriptive phrase placed between them creates an illogical statement because *each* cannot be *wives*; *each* can be one of the wives, or a wife. The pronoun constructions in A, B, D, and E are wordy; also, B, D, and E are very awkwardly structured and do not convey the point about Hemingway's wives clearly. Choice C correctly links *wives* with *were,* eliminates the unnecessary pronouns, and provides a clearer structure.

19. In addition to having more protein than wheat does, <u>the protein in rice is higher quality than that in</u> wheat, with more of the amino acids essential to the human diet.

    (A)   the protein in rice is higher quality than that in

    (B)   rice has protein of higher quality than that in

    (C)   the protein in rice is higher in quality than it is in

    (D)   rice protein is higher in quality than it is in

    (E)   rice has a protein higher in quality than

In this sentence, the initial clause modifies the nearest noun, identifying it as the thing being compared with *wheat.* By making *protein* the noun modified, choices A, C, and D illogically compare *wheat* with *protein* and claim that the <u>protein</u> in rice has more protein than wheat does. In C and D, the comparative structure *higher in quality than it is in wheat* absurdly suggests that rice protein contains wheat. B, the best choice, logically compares *wheat* to *rice* by placing the noun *rice* immediately after the initial clause. B also uses *that* to refer to *protein* in making the comparison between the proteins of rice and wheat. Choice E needs either *that in* or *does* after *wheat* to make a complete and logical comparison.

20. An array of tax incentives has led to a boom in the construction of new office buildings; <u>so abundant has capital been for commercial real estate that</u> investors regularly scour the country for areas in which to build.

    (A)   so abundant has capital been for commercial real estate that

    (B)   capital has been so abundant for commercial real estate, so that

    (C)   the abundance of capital for commercial real estate has been such,

    (D)   such has the abundance of capital been for commercial real estate that

    (E)   such has been an abundance of capital for commercial real estate,

Choice A is best. The construction *so abundant has capital been . . . that* correctly and clearly expresses the relationship between the abundance and the investors' response. In choice B, the repetition of *so* is illogical and unidiomatic. Choices C, D, and E alter somewhat the intended meaning of the sentence; because of its position in these statements, *such* functions to mean "of a kind" rather than to intensify *abundant.* Choice D awkwardly separates *has* and *been,* and the omission of *that* from C and E makes those choices ungrammatical.

21. Defense attorneys have occasionally argued that their clients' misconduct stemmed from a reaction to something ingested, but in attributing criminal or delinquent behavior to some food allergy, the perpetrators are in effect told that they are not responsible for their actions.

    (A) in attributing criminal or delinquent behavior to some food allergy
    (B) if criminal or delinquent behavior is attributed to an allergy to some food
    (C) in attributing behavior that is criminal or delinquent to an allergy to some food
    (D) if some food allergy is attributed as the cause of criminal or delinquent behavior
    (E) in attributing a food allergy as the cause of criminal or delinquent behavior

In choices A, C, and E, *in attributing . . . behavior* modifies *the perpetrators*, producing the illogical statement that the perpetrators rather than the defense attorneys are attributing behavior to food allergies. Choice C is also wordy, and *attributing . . . as* is unidiomatic in E. In the correct form of the expression, one *attributes* x, an effect, *to* y, a cause; or, if a passive construction is used, x *is attributed to* y. D avoids the initial modification error by using a passive construction (in which the attributors are not identified), but *attributed* x *as the cause of* y is unidiomatic. Choice B is best.

22. The voluminous personal papers of Thomas Alva Edison reveal that his inventions typically sprang to life not in a flash of inspiration but evolved slowly from previous works.

    (A) sprang to life not in a flash of inspiration but evolved slowly
    (B) sprang to life not in a flash of inspiration but were slowly evolved
    (C) did not spring to life in a flash of inspiration but evolved slowly
    (D) did not spring to life in a flash of inspiration but had slowly evolved
    (E) did not spring to life in a flash of inspiration but they were slowly evolved

C, the best choice, places *not* and *but* in such a way that the distinction between springing to life in a flash of inspiration and evolving slowly is logically and idiomatically expressed. A and B are faulty because, for grammatical parallelism, *not in a flash . . .* must be followed by *but in . . .* , not by a conjugated form of the verb. Moreover, *were slowly evolved* is incorrect in B because *evolve,* in this sense of the word, cannot be made passive. Choices C, D, and E all correctly place *not* before *spring.* D, however, contains inconsistent verb tenses; E contains the faulty passive and an intrusive *they.*

23. A Labor Department study states that the numbers of women employed outside the home grew by more than a thirty-five percent increase in the past decade and accounted for more than sixty-two percent of the total growth in the civilian work force.

    (A) numbers of women employed outside the home grew by more than a thirty-five percent increase
    (B) numbers of women employed outside the home grew more than thirty-five percent
    (C) numbers of women employed outside the home were raised by more than thirty-five percent
    (D) number of women employed outside the home increased by more than thirty-five percent
    (E) number of women employed outside the home was raised by more than a thirty-five percent increase

Because a count of women employed outside the home at any given time will be expressed by a single number, the use of the plural noun *numbers* in choices A, B, and C is illogical. In A, the phrase *grew by more than a thirty-five percent increase* is redundant and wordy, since the sense of *increase* is implicit in the verb *grew.* In C and E, the passive verb forms *were raised* and *was raised* are inappropriate because there is no identifiable agent responsible for the raising of the number of women employed. In choice E, *was raised by . . . increase* is redundant. Choice D, which presents the comparison logically and idiomatically, is the best answer.

24. The first decision for most tenants living in a building undergoing being converted to cooperative ownership is if to sign a no-buy pledge with the other tenants.

    (A) being converted to cooperative ownership is if to sign
    (B) being converted to cooperative ownership is whether they should be signing
    (C) being converted to cooperative ownership is whether or not they sign
    (D) conversion to cooperative ownership is if to sign
    (E) conversion to cooperative ownership is whether to sign

In A, B, and C, the phrase *being converted* is awkward and redundant, since the sense of process indicated by *being* has already been conveyed by *undergoing.* A and D can be faulted for saying *if* rather than *whether,* since the sentence poses alternative possibilities, to sign or not to sign. Only E, the best choice, idiomatically completes *whether* with an infinitive, *to sign,* that functions as a noun equivalent of *decision.* Choice E also uses the noun *conversion,* which grammatically completes the phrase begun by *undergoing.*

25. The end of the eighteenth century saw the emergence of prize-stock breeding, with individual bulls and cows receiving awards, fetching unprecedented prices, and <u>excited</u> enormous interest whenever they were put on show.

(A) excited
(B) it excited
(C) exciting
(D) would excite
(E) it had excited

Choice C is best. The third verb phrase in the series describing *bulls and cows* should have the same grammatical form as the first two. Only choice C has a present participle (or "-ing" form) that is parallel with the two preceding verbs, *receiving* and *fetching*. Instead of the present participle, choices A and B use the past tense (*excited*), choice D uses an auxiliary verb (*would excite*), and choice E uses the past perfect tense (*had excited*). Additionally, the incorrect verb tenses in B and E are introduced by a pronoun, *it*, that lacks a logical noun referent.

26. Of all the possible disasters that threaten American agriculture, the possibility of an adverse change in climate <u>is maybe the more difficult for analysis.</u>

(A) is maybe the more difficult for analysis
(B) is probably the most difficult to analyze
(C) is maybe the most difficult for analysis
(D) is probably the more difficult to analyze
(E) is, it may be, the analysis that is most difficult

Choice B is the best answer. The sentence compares one thing, *an adverse change in climate*, to all other things in its class— that is, to *all the possible disasters that threaten American agriculture*; therefore, the sentence requires the superlative form of the adjective, *most difficult*, rather than the comparative form, *more difficult*, which appears in choices A and D. In A and C, the use of *maybe* is unidiomatic, and *difficult* should be completed by the infinitive *to analyze*. Choice E is awkwardly phrased and, when inserted into the sentence, produces an illogical structure: *the possibility . . . is . . . the analysis that*.

27. <u>Published in Harlem, the owner and editor of the *Messenger* were two young journalists, Chandler Owen and A. Philip Randolph, who would later make his reputation as a labor leader.</u>

(A) Published in Harlem, the owner and editor of the *Messenger* were two young journalists, Chandler Owen and A. Philip Randolph, who would later make his reputation as a labor leader.
(B) Published in Harlem, two young journalists, Chandler Owen and A. Philip Randolph, who would later make his reputation as a labor leader, were the owner and editor of the *Messenger*.
(C) Published in Harlem, the *Messenger* was owned and edited by two young journalists, A. Philip Randolph, who would later make his reputation as a labor leader, and Chandler Owen.
(D) The *Messenger* was owned and edited by two young journalists, Chandler Owen and A. Philip Randolph, who would later make his reputation as a labor leader, and published in Harlem.
(E) The owner and editor being two young journalists, Chandler Owen and A. Philip Randolph, who would later make his reputation as a labor leader, the *Messenger* was published in Harlem.

Choices A and B present dangling modifiers that illogically suggest that Owen and Randolph, rather than the *Messenger*, were published in Harlem. In D, the phrase *and published in Harlem* is too remote from *the Messenger* to modify it effectively. In E, *being* produces an awkward construction, and the placement of the main clause at the end of the sentence is confusing. Only in C, the best answer, is *Published in Harlem* followed immediately by *the Messenger*. Also, C makes it clear that the clause beginning *who* refers to Randolph.

28. The rise in the Commerce Department's index of leading economic indicators suggest that the economy should continue its expansion into the coming months, but that the mixed performance of the index's individual components indicates that economic growth will proceed at a more moderate pace than in the first quarter of this year.

(A) suggest that the economy should continue its expansion into the coming months, but that
(B) suggest that the economy is to continue expansion in the coming months, but
(C) suggests that the economy will continue its expanding in the coming months, but that
(D) suggests that the economy is continuing to expand into the coming months, but that
(E) suggests that the economy will continue to expand in the coming months, but

In choices A and B, the verb *suggest* does not agree with its singular subject, *rise*. In context, the phrase *into the coming months* in A and D is not idiomatic; *in the coming months* is preferable. In A, C, and D, the *that* appearing after *but* creates a subordinate clause where an independent clause is needed for the new subject, *mixed performance*. Choice E includes the correct verb form, *suggests*, eliminates *that*, and properly employs the future tense, *will continue to expand*. That this tense is called for is indicated both by the future time to which *the coming months* refers and by the parallel verb form *will proceed* in the nonunderlined part of the sentence. Choice E is best.

29. In three centuries—from 1050 to 1350—several million tons of stone were quarried in France for the building of eighty cathedrals, five hundred large churches, and some tens of thousands of parish churches.

(A) for the building of eighty cathedrals, five hundred large churches, and some
(B) in order that they might build eighty cathedrals, five hundred large churches, and some
(C) so as they might build eighty cathedrals, five hundred large churches, and some
(D) so that there could be built eighty cathedrals, five hundred large churches, and
(E) such that they could build eighty cathedrals, five hundred large churches, and

Choice A is best. The other choices are unidiomatic or unnecessarily wordy, and the pronoun *they*, which appears in B, C, and E, has no grammatical referent.

30. What was as remarkable as the development of the compact disc has been the use of the new technology to revitalize, in better sound than was ever before possible, some of the classic recorded performances of the pre-LP era.

(A) What was as remarkable as the development of the compact disc
(B) The thing that was as remarkable as developing the compact disc
(C) No less remarkable than the development of the compact disc
(D) Developing the compact disc has been none the less remarkable than
(E) Development of the compact disc has been no less remarkable as

Besides being wordy, the clauses beginning *What was* in A and *The thing that was* in B cause inconsistencies in verb tense: *the use of the new technology* cannot logically be described by both the present perfect *has been* and the past *was*. In B and D, *developing the compact disc* is not parallel to *the use of new technology to revitalize . . . performances*; in C, the best answer, the noun *development* is parallel to *use*. The phrases *none the less . . . than* in D and *no less . . . as* in E are unidiomatic; the correct form of expression, *no less . . . than*, appears in C, the best choice.

31. Unlike computer skills or other technical skills, there is a disinclination on the part of many people to recognize the degree to which their analytical skills are weak.

(A) Unlike computer skills or other technical skills, there is a disinclination on the part of many people to recognize the degree to which their analytical skills are weak.
(B) Unlike computer skills or other technical skills, which they admit they lack, many people are disinclined to recognize that their analytical skills are weak.
(C) Unlike computer skills or other technical skills, analytical skills bring out a disinclination in many people to recognize that they are weak to a degree.
(D) Many people, willing to admit that they lack computer skills or other technical skills, are disinclined to recognize that their analytical skills are weak.
(E) Many people have a disinclination to recognize the weakness of their analytical skills while willing to admit their lack of computer skills or other technical skills.

Choice D is best. Choice A illogically compares *skills* to *a disinclination*; choice B compares *skills* to *many people*. Choice C makes the comparison logical by casting *analytical skills* as the subject of the sentence, but it is awkward and unidiomatic to say *skills bring out a disinclination*. Also in C, the referent of *they* is unclear, and *weak to a degree* changes the meaning of the original statement. In E, *have a disinclination . . . while willing* is grammatically incomplete, and *admit their lack* should be *admit to their lack.* By making *people* the subject of the sentence, D best expresses the intended contrast, which pertains not so much to skills as to people's willingness to recognize different areas of weakness.

32. <u>Some buildings that were destroyed and heavily damaged in the earthquake last year were</u> constructed in violation of the city's building code.

   (A) Some buildings that were destroyed and heavily damaged in the earthquake last year were
   (B) Some buildings that were destroyed or heavily damaged in the earthquake last year had been
   (C) Some buildings that the earthquake destroyed and heavily damaged last year have been
   (D) Last year the earthquake destroyed or heavily damaged some buildings that have been
   (E) Last year some of the buildings that were destroyed or heavily damaged in the earthquake had been

Choice B is best. Choices A and C illogically state that some buildings were both destroyed *and* damaged; *or* is needed to indicate that each of the buildings suffered either one fate or the other. In using only one verb tense, *were,* A fails to indicate that the buildings were constructed before the earthquake occurred. Choices C and D use the present perfect tense incorrectly, saying in effect that the buildings *have been constructed* after they were destroyed last year. Choice E suggests that the construction of the buildings, rather than the earthquake, occurred last year, thus making the sequence of events unclear. Only B uses verb tenses correctly to indicate that construction of the buildings was completed prior to the earthquake.

33. From the earliest days of the tribe, kinship determined the way in which the Ojibwa society organized its labor, provided access to its resources, and <u>defined rights and obligations involved in the distribution and consumption of those resources.</u>

   (A) and defined rights and obligations involved in the distribution and consumption of those resources
   (B) defining rights and obligations involved in their distribution and consumption
   (C) and defined rights and obligations as they were involved in its distribution and consumption
   (D) whose rights and obligations were defined in their distribution and consumption
   (E) the distribution and consumption of them defined by rights and obligations

Choice A is best. The activities listed are presented as parallel ideas and should thus be expressed in grammatically parallel structures. Choice A correctly uses the simple past tense *defined* to parallel *organized* and *provided.* Choice A also correctly joins the last two parallel phrases with *and* and clearly expresses the relationship of *rights and obligations* to

resources. Choice C preserves parallelism but is wordy, and *its* has no logical referent. Choices B, D, and E each replace the verb phrase with a subordinate modifier, violating parallelism and making the statements ungrammatical. Furthermore, it is unclear what *defining . . . consumption* in B is intended to modify; in D, *whose* incorrectly attributes *rights and obligations* to *resources*; and E presents *rights and obligations* as defining, rather than as being defined.

34. A report by the American Academy for the Advancement of Science has concluded that <u>much of the currently uncontrolled dioxins to which North Americans are exposed comes</u> from the incineration of wastes.

   (A) much of the currently uncontrolled dioxins to which North Americans are exposed comes
   (B) much of the currently uncontrolled dioxins that North Americans are exposed to come
   (C) much of the dioxins that are currently uncontrolled and that North Americans are exposed to comes
   (D) many of the dioxins that are currently uncontrolled and North Americans are exposed to come
   (E) many of the currently uncontrolled dioxins to which North Americans are exposed come

Choices A, B, and C are flawed because the countable noun *dioxins* should be modified by *many* rather than *much,* which is used with uncountable nouns such as "work" and "happiness." In addition, both A and C incorrectly use the singular verb *comes* with the plural noun *dioxins.* Choices C and D are needlessly wordy, and D requires *that* before *North Americans* to be grammatically complete. Choice E, the best answer, is both grammatically correct and concise.

35. In June of 1987, *The Bridge of Trinquetaille,* Vincent van Gogh's view of an iron bridge over the <u>Rhone sold for $20.2 million and it was</u> the second highest price ever paid for a painting at auction.

   (A) Rhone sold for $20.2 million and it was
   (B) Rhone, which sold for $20.2 million, was
   (C) Rhone, was sold for $20.2 million,
   (D) Rhone was sold for $20.2 million, being
   (E) Rhone, sold for $20.2 million, and was

A comma is needed after *Rhone* in choices A and D to set off the modifying phrase that begins *Vincent . . . ;* without the comma, the phrase appears to be part of the main clause, and it is thus unclear what noun should govern the verb *sold.* Furthermore, *it* in A has no logical referent, and *being* in D is not idiomatic. Choices B and E produce the illogical statement that the painting *was the second highest price.* Choice C, the best answer, avoids this problem by using a noun phrase in which *price* clearly refers to *$20.2 million.* And by using a comma after *Rhone* to set off the phrase that modifies *The Bridge of Trinquetaille,* C makes the painting the subject of *was sold.*

36. *Bufo marinus* toads, fierce predators that will eat frogs, lizards, and even small birds, <u>are native to South America but were introduced into Florida during the 1930's in an attempt to control</u> pests in the state's vast sugarcane fields.

(A) are native to South America but were introduced into Florida during the 1930's in an attempt to control

(B) are native in South America but were introduced into Florida during the 1930's as attempts to control

(C) are natives of South America but were introduced into Florida during the 1930's in an attempt at controlling

(D) had been native to South America but were introduced to Florida during the 1930's as an attempt at controlling

(E) had been natives of South America but were introduced to Florida during the 1930's as attempts at controlling

Choice A is best. The phrasing *are native to* correctly suggests that the toad species is indigenous to, and still exists in, South America. In B, *native in* is unidiomatic; in C and E, *natives of* illogically suggests that each toad now in Florida hails from South America. In D and E, *had been* inaccurately implies that the toads are no longer native, or indigenous, to South America, and *introduced to Florida* is unidiomatic. Both *as attempts* in B and E and *as an attempt* in D are wrong because the attempt consists not of the toads themselves, but of their introduction into the environment. The correct phrase, *in an attempt,* should be completed by an infinitive (here, *to control*), as in A.

37. While some academicians believe that business ethics should be integrated into every business course, others say that students will take ethics seriously <u>only if it would be taught as a separately required course</u>.

(A) only if it would be taught as a separately required course

(B) only if it is taught as a separate, required course

(C) if it is taught only as a course required separately

(D) if it was taught only as a separate and required course

(E) if it would only be taught as a required course, separately

Choice B is best: in sentences expressing a conditional result (*x will happen if y happens*), the verb of the main clause should be in the future tense and the verb of the *if* clause should be in the present indicative. Thus, *is taught* (in B) is consistent with *will take,* whereas *would be taught* (in A and E) and *was taught* (in D) are not. For clarity, *only* in C, D, and E should immediately precede the entire *if* clause that it is meant to modify. Also, the intended meaning is distorted when the adverb *separately* is used to modify *required,* as in A and C, or *taught,* as in E; B correctly uses the adjective *separate* to modify *course.*

38. Scientists have observed large concentrations of heavy-metal deposits in the upper twenty centimeters of <u>Baltic Sea sediments, which are consistent with the growth of industrial activity there</u>.

(A) Baltic Sea sediments, which are consistent with the growth of industrial activity there

(B) Baltic Sea sediments, where the growth of industrial activity is consistent with these findings

(C) Baltic Sea sediments, findings consistent with its growth of industrial activity

(D) sediments from the Baltic Sea, findings consistent with the growth of industrial activity in the area

(E) sediments from the Baltic Sea, consistent with the growth of industrial activity there

All of the choices but D contain ambiguities. In A and B the words *which* and *where* appear to refer to *sediments*, and in E it is not clear what *consistent* describes. In A, C, and E, there is no logical place to which *there* or *its* could refer. In D, the best choice, the phrase *sediments from the Baltic Sea* tells where the sediments originate, *findings* provides a noun for *consistent* to modify, and *in the area* clearly identifies where the industrial activity is growing.

39. For members of the seventeenth-century Ashanti nation in Africa, animal-hide shields with wooden frames were essential items of military equipment, <u>a method to protect</u> warriors against enemy arrows and spears.

(A) a method to protect

(B) as a method protecting

(C) protecting

(D) as a protection of

(E) to protect

Choice C is best because the participle *protecting* begins a phrase that explains what the shields did. Choices A and B awkwardly use the singular word *method* to refer to *items of military equipment* rather than to the <u>use</u> of such items. Also, *a method of protecting* would be more idiomatic than *a method to protect* in A or *a method protecting* in B. In B and D, *as* is incorrect; also, *a protection* in D has no noun for which it can logically substitute. Choice E is incomplete; *used to protect* would have been acceptable.

40. In metalwork one advantage of adhesive-bonding over spot-welding is that the contact, and hence the bonding, is effected continuously over a broad surface <u>instead of</u> a series of regularly spaced points with no bonding in between.

    (A) instead of
    (B) as opposed to
    (C) in contrast with
    (D) rather than at
    (E) as against being at

The corrected sentence must contrast an effect of spot-welding with an effect of adhesive-bonding. To do so logically and grammatically, it must describe the effects in parallel terms. When inserted into the sentence, D produces the parallel construction *over a broad surface rather than at a series*. Having no word such as *over* or *at* indicate location, choices A, B, and C fail to complete the parallel and so illogically draw a contrast between *surface* and *series*. In E, *as against being* is a wordy and unidiomatic way to establish the intended contrast. Choice D is best.

41. Under a provision of the Constitution that <u>was never applied, Congress has been required to call a convention for considering possible amendments to the document when formally asked to do it</u> by the legislatures of two-thirds of the states.

    (A) was never applied, Congress has been required to call a convention for considering possible amendments to the document when formally asked to do it
    (B) was never applied, there has been a requirement that Congress call a convention for consideration of possible amendments to the document when asked to do it formally
    (C) was never applied, whereby Congress is required to call a convention for considering possible amendments to the document when asked to do it formally
    (D) has never been applied, whereby Congress is required to call a convention to consider possible amendments to the document when formally asked to do so
    (E) has never been applied, Congress is required to call a convention to consider possible amendments to the document when formally asked to do so

Choices A, B, C, and D contain tense errors (the use of *was never applied* with *has been required* in A, for example), unidiomatic expressions (*call . . . for considering*), and uses of a pronoun (*it*) with no noun referent. By introducing the subordinating conjunction *whereby*, C and D produce sentence fragments. Only E, the best choice, corrects all of these problems. The predicate *has never been applied* refers to a span of time, from the writing of the Constitution to the present, rather than to a past event (as *was* does), and the

phrase *is required* indicates that the provision still applies. The phrase *call . . . to consider* is idiomatic, and *to do so* can substitute grammatically for it.

42. The current administration, <u>being worried over some foreign trade barriers being removed and our exports failing</u> to increase as a result of deep cuts in the value of the dollar, has formed a group to study ways to sharpen our competitiveness.

    (A) being worried over some foreign trade barriers being removed and our exports failing
    (B) worrying over some foreign trade barriers being removed, also over the failure of our exports
    (C) worried about the removal of some foreign trade barriers and the failure of our exports
    (D) in that they were worried about the removal of some foreign trade barriers and also about the failure of our exports
    (E) because of its worry concerning the removal of some foreign trade barriers, also concerning the failure of our exports

Choice C is best because its phrasing is parallel and concise. A, D, and E begin with unnecessarily wordy phrases. Choice C also uses the idiomatic expression *worried about* rather than *worried over* (as in A) or *worrying over* (as in B); *worried about* is preferable when describing a condition rather than an action. Whereas C uses compact and parallel noun phrases such as *the removal . . . and the failure . . .* , the other choices employ phrases that are wordy, awkward, or nonparallel. D is also flawed in that the plural pronoun *they* does not agree with the singular noun *administration*.

43. In the minds of many people living in England, <u>before Australia was Australia, it was the antipodes</u>, the opposite pole to civilization, an obscure and unimaginable place that was considered the end of the world.

    (A) before Australia was Australia, it was the antipodes
    (B) before there was Australia, it was the antipodes
    (C) it was the antipodes that was Australia
    (D) Australia was what was the antipodes
    (E) Australia was what had been known as the antipodes

Choice A is best, for A alone makes clear that the land now known as Australia was considered the antipodes before it was developed. In B, *it* has no logical referent, because the previous clause describes a time when there was no Australia. Nor does *it* have a referent in C: substituting *Australia* for *it* produces a nonsensical statement. D is wordy, with the unnecessary *what was*, and imprecise in suggesting that Australia was considered the antipodes after it became Australia. E similarly distorts the original meaning, and the past perfect *had been* is inconsistent with the past tense used to establish a time frame for the rest of the sentence.

44. Using a Doppler ultrasound device, fetal heartbeats can be detected by the twelfth week of pregnancy.

(A) Using a Doppler ultrasound device, fetal heartbeats can be detected by the twelfth week of pregnancy.
(B) Fetal heartbeats can be detected by the twelfth week of pregnancy, using a Doppler ultrasound device.
(C) Detecting fetal heartbeats by the twelfth week of pregnancy, a physician can use a Doppler ultrasound device.
(D) By the twelfth week of pregnancy, fetal heartbeats can be detected using a Doppler ultrasound device by a physician.
(E) Using a Doppler ultrasound device, a physician can detect fetal heartbeats by the twelfth week of pregnancy.

Choice A presents a dangling modifier. The phrase beginning the sentence has no noun that it can logically modify and hence cannot fit anywhere in the sentence and make sense. Coming first, it modifies *heartbeats,* the nearest free noun in the main clause; that is, choice A says that the heartbeats are using the Doppler ultrasound device. Choice B contains the same main clause and dangling modifier, now at the end. Contrary to intent, the wording in choice C suggests that physicians can use a Doppler ultrasound device after they detect fetal heartbeats. In choice D the phrase *using . . . device* should follow *physician*, the noun it modifies. Choice E is best.

45. Delighted by the reported earnings for the first quarter of the fiscal year, it was decided by the company manager to give her staff a raise.

(A) It was decided by the company manager to give her staff a raise
(B) the decision of the company manager was to give her staff a raise
(C) the company manager decided to give her staff a raise
(D) the staff was given a raise by the company manager
(E) a raise was given to the staff by the company manager

Grammatically, the participial phrase beginning *delighted* must modify the subject of the main clause. Because it is the manager who was delighted, choice C, in which *the company manager* appears as the subject, is the best answer. Choices A, B, D, and E create illogical statements by using *it, the decision, the staff,* and *a raise*, respectively, as the sentence subject. Use of the passive voice in A, D, and E produces unnecessary wordiness, as does the construction *the decision of the company manager was to* in B.

46. A study commissioned by the Department of Agriculture showed that if calves exercise and associated with other calves, they will require less medication and gain weight quicker than do those raised in confinement.

(A) associated with other calves, they will require less medication and gain weight quicker than do
(B) associated with other calves, they require less medication and gain weight quicker than
(C) associate with other calves, they required less medication and will gain weight quicker than do
(D) associate with other calves, they have required less medication and will gain weight more quickly than do
(E) associate with other calves, they require less medication and gain weight more quickly than

Choice E, the best answer, uses the adverbial phrase *more quickly than* to modify the verb phrase *gain weight*. In A, B, and C, *quicker than* is incorrect because an adjective should not be used to modify a verb phrase. E is also the only choice with consistent verb tenses. The first verb in the clauses introduced by *showed that* is *exercise.* A and B incorrectly compound that present tense verb with a past tense verb, *associated.* C and D correctly use *associate*, but C follows with the past tense *required* and D with the present perfect *have required.* Both C and D incorrectly conclude with the future tense *will gain.*

47. Displays of the aurora borealis, or "northern lights," can heat the atmosphere over the arctic enough to affect the trajectories of ballistic missiles, induce electric currents that can cause blackouts in some areas and corrosion in north-south pipelines.

(A) to affect the trajectories of ballistic missiles, induce
(B) that the trajectories of ballistic missiles are affected, induce
(C) that it affects the trajectories of ballistic missiles, induces
(D) that the trajectories of ballistic missiles are affected and induces
(E) to affect the trajectories of ballistic missiles and induce

The use of the phrasing *can heat . . . enough to affect* in A and E is more idiomatic than the use of the subordinate clause beginning with *that* in B, C, and D. Also, B produces an illogical and ungrammatical statement by making *induce* parallel with the verb *heat* rather than with the appropriate form of the verb *affect*; C lacks agreement in using the singular pronoun *it* to refer to the plural noun *displays*; and D is faulty because *induces* cannot fit grammatically with any noun in the sentence. Choice A incorrectly separates the two infinitives *to affect* and *[to] induce* with a comma when it should compound them with *and*, as does E, the best choice.

48. The golden crab of the Gulf of Mexico has not been fished commercially in great numbers, primarily on account of living at great depths—2,500 to 3,000 feet down.

    (A) on account of living
    (B) on account of their living
    (C) because it lives
    (D) because of living
    (E) being they live

As used in choices A, B, and D, the phrases *on account of* and *because of* are unidiomatic; *because*, which appears in C and E, is preferable here since *because* can introduce a complete subordinate clause explaining the reason why the golden crab has not been fished extensively. B and E also produce agreement errors by using the plural pronouns *their* and *they* to refer to the singular noun *crab*. Choice D, like A, fails to provide a noun or pronoun to perform the action of *living*, but even with *its* the phrases would be more awkward and less clear than *it lives*. C, which uses *because* and *it* as the singular subject of a clause, is the best choice.

49. The cameras of the Voyager II spacecraft detected six small, previously unseen moons circling Uranus, which doubles to twelve the number of satellites now known as orbiting the distant planet.

    (A) which doubles to twelve the number of satellites now known as orbiting
    (B) doubling to twelve the number of satellites now known to orbit
    (C) which doubles to twelve the number of satellites now known in orbit around
    (D) doubling to twelve the number of satellites now known as orbiting
    (E) which doubles to twelve the number of satellites now known that orbit

The pronoun *which* should be used to refer to a previously mentioned noun, not to the idea expressed in an entire clause. In A, C, and E, *which* seems to refer to a vague concept involving the detection of moons, but there is no specific noun, such as *detection*, to which it can refer. Also in E, the use of the phrasing *the number . . . now known that orbit* is ungrammatical and unclear. B and D use the correct participial form, *doubling*, to modify the preceding clause, but D, like A, uses *known as orbiting* rather than *known to orbit*, a phrase that is more idiomatic in context. B, therefore, is the best answer.

50. As a baby emerges from the darkness of the womb with a rudimentary sense of vision, it would be rated about 20/500, or legally blind if it were an adult with such vision.

    (A) As a baby emerges from the darkness of the womb with a rudimentary sense of vision, it would be rated about 20/500, or legally blind if it were an adult with such vision.
    (B) A baby emerges from the darkness of the womb with a rudimentary sense of vision that would be rated about 20/500, or legally blind as an adult.
    (C) As a baby emerges from the darkness of the womb, its rudimentary sense of vision would be rated about 20/500; qualifying it to be legally blind if an adult.
    (D) A baby emerges from the darkness of the womb with a rudimentary sense of vision that would be rated about 20/500; an adult with such vision would be deemed legally blind.
    (E) As a baby emerges from the darkness of the womb, its rudimentary sense of vision, which would deemed legally blind for an adult, would be rated about 20/500.

In choice A, *it*, the subject of the main clause, seems to refer to *baby*, the subject of the subordinate clause; thus, A seems to state that the newborn baby, rather than its sense of vision, would be rated 20/500. Similarly, choices B and E use awkward and ambiguous phrasing that suggests that the *sense of vision*, rather than an adult with 20/500 vision, would be considered legally blind. C incorrectly uses the semicolon, which should separate independent clauses, to set off a verb phrase. The phrase *if an adult* in C is also illogical, since it states that a baby could also be an adult. D is the best choice.

51. While Jackie Robinson was a Brooklyn Dodger, his courage in the face of physical threats and verbal attacks was not unlike that of Rosa Parks, who refused to move to the back of a bus in Montgomery, Alabama.

    (A) not unlike that of Rosa Parks, who refused
    (B) not unlike Rosa Parks, who refused
    (C) like Rosa Parks and her refusal
    (D) like that of Rosa Parks for refusing
    (E) as that of Rosa Parks, who refused

Choices B and C present faulty comparisons: in B, Jackie Robinson's courage is compared to Rosa Parks herself, not to her courage, and in C it is compared to both Rosa Parks and her refusal. Choice D does not make clear whether it was Jackie Robinson or Rosa Parks who showed courage in refusing to move to the back of the bus; in fact, saying *for refusing* rather than *who refused* makes it sound as if *courage* moved to the back of the bus. Choice E incorrectly uses *as* rather than *like* to compare two noun phrases. Choice A is best.

52. The rising of costs of data-processing operations at many financial institutions has created a growing opportunity for independent companies to provide these services more efficiently and at lower cost.

(A) The rising of costs
(B) Rising costs
(C) The rising cost
(D) Because the rising cost
(E) Because of rising costs

C is the best choice. In choice A, *The rising of costs* is unidiomatic, and in B *costs . . . has* lacks subject-verb agreement. Choices D and E produce sentence fragments since *Because* makes the clause subordinate rather than independent.

53. There is no consensus on what role, if any, is played by acid rain in slowing the growth or damaging forests in the eastern United States.

(A) slowing the growth or damaging
(B) the damage or the slowing of the growth of
(C) the damage to or the slowness of the growth of
(D) damaged or slowed growth of
(E) damaging or slowing the growth of

The corrected sentence must make clear that both *damaging* and *slowing the growth of* refer to *forests*. E is the only choice that does so without introducing errors. In choice A, *of* is required after *growth*. In choices B and C, the use of *the damage* instead of *damaging* produces awkward and wordy constructions, and without *to* after *damage*, B is grammatically incomplete. In C, *the slowness of* does not convey the original sense that the rate of growth has been slowed by acid rain. Choice D also changes the meaning of the sentence by making both *damaged* and *slowed* refer to *growth*.

54. Galileo was convinced that natural phenomena, as manifestations of the laws of physics, would appear the same to someone on the deck of a ship moving smoothly and uniformly through the water as a person standing on land.

(A) water as a
(B) water as to a
(C) water; just as it would to a
(D) water, as it would to the
(E) water; just as to the

B, the best choice, uses the idiomatic and grammatically parallel form *the same to X as to Y.* Because A lacks the preposition *to,* it seems to compare the appearance of natural phenomena to that of a person standing on land. C and D unnecessarily repeat *would* and wrongly use the singular *it* to refer to the plural *phenomena.* C and E each contain a faulty semicolon and produce errors in idiom, *the same to X just as [it would] to.* D and E use the definite article *the* where the indefinite article *a* is needed to refer to an unspecified person.

55. A recent study has found that within the past few years, many doctors had elected early retirement rather than face the threats of lawsuits and the rising costs of malpractice insurance.

(A) had elected early retirement rather than face
(B) had elected early retirement instead of facing
(C) have elected retiring early instead of facing
(D) have elected to retire early rather than facing
(E) have elected to retire early rather than face

Because the sentence describes a situation that continues into the present, choices A and B are incorrect in using the past perfect *had elected,* which denotes an action completed at a specific time in the past. Also, alternatives presented in the expressions *x rather than y* and *x instead of y* should be parallel in form, but A and B mismatch the noun *retirement* with the verb forms *face* and *facing.* C is faulty because *have elected,* which is correct in tense, cannot idiomatically be followed by a participle such as *retiring.* D correctly follows *have elected* with an infinitive, *to retire,* but, like A and B, fails to maintain parallelism. Only E, the best choice, uses the correct tense, observes parallelism, and is idiomatic.

56. Architects and stonemasons, huge palace and temple clusters were built by the Maya without benefit of the wheel or animal transport.

(A) huge palace and temple clusters were built by the Maya without benefit of the wheel or animal transport
(B) without the benefits of animal transport or the wheel, huge palace and temple clusters were built by the Maya
(C) the Maya built huge palace and temple clusters without the benefit of animal transport or the wheel
(D) there were built, without the benefit of the wheel or animal transport, huge palace and temple clusters by the Maya
(E) were the Maya who, without the benefit of the wheel or animal transport, built huge palace and temple clusters

A, B, and D illogically suggest that the *palace and temple clusters* were architects and stonemasons. For the modification to be logical, *Architects and stonemasons* must immediately precede *the Maya,* the noun phrase it is meant to modify. A, B, and D also use the passive verb form *were built,* which produces unnecessary awkwardness and wordiness. E is awkwardly phrased and produces a sentence fragment, because the appositive noun phrase *Architects and stonemasons* cannot serve as the subject of *were the Maya.* C, the best answer, places *the Maya* immediately after its modifier and uses the active verb form *built.*

57. In astronomy the term "red shift" denotes the extent to which light from a distant galaxy has been shifted toward the red, or long-wave, end of the light spectrum by the rapid motion of the galaxy away from the Earth.

(A) to which light from a distant galaxy has been shifted
(B) to which light from a distant galaxy has shifted
(C) that light from a distant galaxy has been shifted
(D) of light from a distant galaxy shifting
(E) of the shift of light from a distant galaxy

Choice A is best because it is idiomatic and because its passive verb construction, *has been shifted*, clearly indicates that the *light* has been acted upon *by the rapid motion*. In B, the active verb *has shifted* suggests that the light, not the motion, is the agency of action, but such a construction leaves the phrase *by the rapid motion of the galaxy away from the Earth* without any logical or grammatical function. In C, the construction *the extent that light* is ungrammatical; *denotes the extent* must be completed by *to which*. D incorrectly employs an active verb, *shifting*, and *extent of light* is imprecise and awkward. E is faulty because it contains no verb to express the action performed by the *rapid motion*.

58. William H. Johnson's artistic debt to Scandinavia is evident in paintings that range from sensitive portraits of citizens in his wife's Danish home, Kerteminde, and awe-inspiring views of fjords and mountain peaks in the western and northern regions of Norway.

(A) and
(B) to
(C) and to
(D) with
(E) in addition to

The construction *range from x* must be completed by *to y*, as in choice B, the best answer: Johnson's paintings *range from . . . portraits . . . to . . . views*. Each of the other choices produces an unidiomatic construction.

59. In 1978 only half the women granted child support by a court received the amount awarded; at least as much as a million and more others had not any support agreements whatsoever.

(A) at least as much as a million and more others had not any
(B) at least as much as more than a million others had no
(C) more than a million others had not any
(D) more than a million others had no
(E) there was at least a million or more others without any

D, the best choice, is idiomatic, clear, and concise. Both A and B incorrectly use *much* rather than *many* to describe the countable noun *others*; *much* should be used with uncountable nouns such as "joy" and "labor." Even if this error were

corrected, though, A and B would still be wrong. Because *more than x* necessarily includes the sense of *at least as many as x*, it is redundant and confusing to use elements of both expressions to refer to the same number of women. In A and C, *not any support agreements* is wordy and awkward. Like A and B, E redundantly uses both *at least* and *more*, and it incorrectly links the singular verb *was* with the plural subject *others*.

60. According to a recent poll, owning and living in a freestanding house on its own land is still a goal of a majority of young adults, like that of earlier generations.

(A) like that of earlier generations
(B) as that for earlier generations
(C) just as earlier generations did
(D) as have earlier generations
(E) as it was of earlier generations

The intended comparison should be completed by a clause beginning with *as* and containing a subject and verb that correspond to the subject and verb of the main clause. In E, the best choice, *it* refers unambiguously to the phrasal subject *owning . . . land*, the verb *was* corresponds to *is*, and today's *young adults* are appropriately compared to *earlier generations*. Choices A and B lack a verb corresponding to *is* and a clear referent for *that*. Choices C and D are confusing and illogical because their verbs, *did* and *have*, cannot substitute for *is* in the main clause.

61. The Gorton-Dodd bill requires that a bank disclose to their customers how long they will delay access to funds from deposited checks.

(A) that a bank disclose to their customers how long they will delay access to funds from deposited checks
(B) a bank to disclose to their customers how long they will delay access to funds from a deposited check
(C) that a bank disclose to its customers how long it will delay access to funds from deposited checks
(D) a bank that it should disclose to its customers how long it will delay access to funds from a deposited check
(E) that banks disclose to customers how long access to funds from their deposited check is to be delayed

Choice C is best. In A and B, the plural pronouns *their* and *they* do not agree with the singular noun *bank*. B, like D and E, illogically shifts from the plural *customers* and *funds* to the singular *check*, as if the customers were jointly depositing only one check. In D, *requires a bank that it should* is ungrammatical; *requires that a bank* is the appropriate idiom. In E, the use of the passive construction *is to be delayed* is less informative than the active voice because the passive does not explicitly identify the bank as the agent responsible for the delay.

62. Geologists believe that the warning signs for a major earthquake may include sudden fluctuations in local seismic activity, tilting and other deformations of the Earth's crust, <u>changing the measured strain across a fault zone. and varying</u> the electrical properties of underground rocks.

(A) changing the measured strain across a fault zone and varying

(B) changing measurements of the strain across a fault zone, and varying

(C) changing the strain as measured across a fault zone, and variations of

(D) changes in the measured strain across a fault zone, and variations in

(E) changes in measurements of the strain across a fault zone, and variations among

D, the best choice, describes *the warning signs* in parallel phrases. Despite surface appearances, the nouns *changes* and *variations* are parallel with *tilting*, but the verbal forms *changing* and *varying* in A, B, and C are not: *tilting*, one of the *deformations of the Earth's crust*, is used here as a noun that is parallel *to fluctuations*, whereas *changing* and *varying* are used as verbs indicating some action undertaken. Moreover, these verbs are used incorrectly because the sentence mentions no subject that is performing these actions. B and E illogically state that it is not the *strain* but the *measurements* that portend danger, and *among* in E wrongly suggests a comparison of different electrical properties rather than of different behaviors of the same properties.

63. Health officials estimate that 35 million Africans <u>are in danger of contracting</u> trypanosomiasis, or "African sleeping sickness," a parasitic disease spread by the bites of tsetse flies.

(A) are in danger of contracting
(B) are in danger to contract
(C) have a danger of contracting
(D) are endangered by contraction
(E) have a danger that they will contract

Choice A, which is both idiomatic and concise, is best. In choice B, *to contract* is wrong because the phrase *are in danger* must be followed by *of*, not by an infinitive. The phrase *have a danger* is unidiomatic in C. In D, the phrase *by contraction trypanosomiasis* requires *of* after *contraction*; even if this correction were made, though, the passive construction in D would be unnecessarily wordy and also imprecise, because it is the disease more than the act of contracting it that poses the danger. In E, *have a danger* is again unidiomatic, and the *that* clause following the phrase is, within the structure of the sentence, ungrammatical and awkward.

64. Unlike a funded pension system, in which contributions are invested to pay future beneficiaries, <u>a pay-as-you-go approach is the foundation of Social Security</u>.

(A) a pay-as-you-go approach is the foundation of Social Security

(B) the foundation of Social Security is a pay-as-you-go approach

(C) the approach of Social Security is pay-as-you-go

(D) Social Security's approach is pay-as-you-go

(E) Social Security is founded on a pay-as-you-go approach

In this sentence, the first noun of the main clause grammatically identifies what is being compared with *a funded pension system*; to be logical, the comparison must be made between comparable things. Only E, the best choice, compares one kind of system of providing for retirees, the *funded pension system*, with another such system, *Social Security*. Choices A, C, and D all illogically compare the pension system with the *approach* taken by Social Security itself. In B, the comparison of *pension system* with *foundation* is similarly flawed.

65. Critics of the trend toward privately operated prisons consider corrections facilities <u>to be an integral part of the criminal justice system and question if</u> profits should be made from incarceration.

(A) to be an integral part of the criminal justice system and question if

(B) as an integral part of the criminal justice system and they question if

(C) as being an integral part of the criminal justice system and question whether

(D) an integral part of the criminal justice system and question whether

(E) are an integral part of the criminal justice system, and they question whether

When *consider* means "regard as," as it does in this sentence, its object should be followed immediately by the phrase that identifies or describes that object. Thus, *to be* in A, *as* in B, and *as being* in C produce unidiomatic constructions in the context of the sentence. Also, although *if* and *whether* can be used interchangeably after some verbs, *question if*, which appears in A and B, is unidiomatic, and *they* in B is unnecessary. E also contains the unnecessary *they*, and it uses the ungrammatical construction *consider . . . facilities are*. Grammatically and idiomatically, sound D is the best choice.

66. The Federal Reserve Board's <u>reduction of interest rates on loans to financial institutions is both an acknowledgment of past economic trends and an effort</u> to influence their future direction.

   (A) reduction of interest rates on loans to financial institutions is both an acknowledgment of past economic trends and an effort
   (B) reduction of interest rates on loans to financial institutions is an acknowledgment both of past economic trends as well as an effort
   (C) reduction of interest rates on loans to financial institutions both acknowledge past economic trends and attempt
   (D) reducing interest rates on loans to financial institutions is an acknowledgment both of past economic trends and an effort
   (E) reducing interest rates on loans to financial institutions both acknowledge past economic trends as well as attempt

Choice A is best. In B, *both* must come before *acknowledgment* if it is to link *acknowledgment* and *effort*; as misplaced here, it creates the unfulfilled expectation that the *reduction of interest rates* will be an acknowledgment of two different things. Moreover, *both . . . as well as . . .* is redundant: the correct idiom is *both x and y.* In C, the plural verbs *acknowledge* and *attempt* do not agree with their singular subject, *reduction*; also, it is imprecise to characterize a *reduction* as performing actions such as acknowledging or attempting. In both D and E, the use of the participle *reducing* rather than the noun *reduction is* awkward. Like B, D misplaces *both*, while E repeats both the redundancy of B and the agreement error of C.

67. Congress is debating a bill requiring certain employers <u>provide workers with unpaid leave so as to</u> care for sick or newborn children.

   (A) provide workers with unpaid leave so as to
   (B) to provide workers with unpaid leave so as to
   (C) provide workers with unpaid leave in order that they
   (D) to provide workers with unpaid leave so that they can
   (E) provide workers with unpaid leave and

Choices A, C, and E are ungrammatical because, in this context, *requiring . . . employers* must be followed by an infinitive. These options display additional faults: in A, *so as to* fails to specify that the workers receiving the leave will be the people caring for the infants and children; *in order that they*, as used in C, is imprecise and unidiomatic; and E says that the bill being debated would require the employers themselves to care for the children. Choice B offers the correct infinitive, *to provide*, but contains the faulty *so as to.* Choice D is best.

68. Often visible as smog, <u>ozone is formed in the atmosphere from</u> hydrocarbons and nitrogen oxides, two major pollutants emitted by automobiles, react with sunlight.

   (A) ozone is formed in the atmosphere from
   (B) ozone is formed in the atmosphere when
   (C) ozone is formed in the atmosphere, and when
   (D) ozone, formed in the atmosphere when
   (E) ozone, formed in the atmosphere from

In choice A, the construction from *hydrocarbons and nitrogen oxides . . . react* is ungrammatical. In B, the best choice, the conjunction *when* replaces the preposition *from*, producing a grammatical and logical statement. In choice C, the use of the conjunction *and* results in the illogical assertion that the formation of ozone in the atmosphere happens in addition to, rather than as a result of, its formation when hydrocarbons and nitrogen oxide react with sunlight. Choice D omits the main verb, *is*, leaving a sentence fragment. E compounds the error of D with that of A.

69. Although she had signed a pledge of abstinence <u>while being an adolescent</u>, Frances Willard was 35 years old before she chose to become a temperance activist.

   (A) while being an adolescent
   (B) while in adolescence
   (C) at the time of her being adolescent
   (D) as being in adolescence
   (E) as an adolescent

Choices A, B, and D are unidiomatic. Choice C is awkward and wordy; furthermore, the phrase *at the time of her being adolescent* suggests that Willard's adolescence lasted only for a brief, finite moment rather than for an extended period of time. Choice E, idiomatic and precise, is the best answer.

70. A President entering the final two years of a second term is <u>likely to be at a severe disadvantage and is often unable to</u> carry out a legislative program.

   (A) likely to be at a severe disadvantage and is often unable to
   (B) likely severely disadvantaged and often unable to
   (C) liable to be severely disadvantaged and cannot often
   (D) liable that he or she is at a severe disadvantage and cannot often
   (E) at a severe disadvantage, often likely to be unable that he or she can

Choice A is best. Choice B lacks the necessary infinitive after *likely.* In B and C, *disadvantaged*, which often means "hampered by substandard economic and social conditions," is less precise than *at a disadvantage.* In C and D, *cannot often carry out* suggests that a President with limited time suffers only from an inability to achieve legislative goals frequently, not from a frequent inability to achieve them at all. In C, *liable*, followed by an infinitive, can legitimately be used to express probability with a bad outcome, but C is otherwise flawed as noted. D's *liable* and E's *unable* should be followed by an infinitive rather than by a relative clause beginning with *that.*

71. The original building and loan associations were organized as limited life funds, whose members made monthly payments on their share subscriptions, then taking turns drawing on the funds for home mortgages.

    (A) subscriptions, then taking turns drawing
    (B) subscriptions, and then taking turns drawing
    (C) subscriptions and then took turns drawing
    (D) subscriptions and then took turns, they drew
    (E) ' subscriptions and then drew, taking turns

The sentence speaks of a sequence of actions in the past: shareholders *made* their monthly payments and subsequently *took* turns drawing on the funds. Choice C, the best answer, uses parallel past-tense verb forms to express this sequence. Choices A and B violate parallelism by using *taking* where *took* is required. The wording in D results in a run-on sentence and does not specify what the members took turns doing. Similarly, E does not specify what the members *drew*, and *taking turns* produces nonsense when combined with the rest of the sentence.

72. The number of undergraduate degrees in engineering awarded by colleges and universities in the United States increased by more than twice from 1978 to 1985.

    (A) increased by more than twice
    (B) increased more than two times
    (C) more than doubled
    (D) was more than doubled
    (E) had more than doubled

Choice A is faulty because an adverb such as *twice* cannot function as an object of the preposition *by*. B distorts the sentence's meaning, stating that the number of engineering degrees conferred increased on more than two distinct occasions. D's passive verb *was . . . doubled* suggests without warrant that some unnamed agent increased the number of engineering degrees. The past perfect tense in E, *had . . . doubled*, is inappropriate unless the increase in engineering degrees is specifically being viewed as having occurred further back in the past than some subsequent event. Choice C is best.

73. The British Admiralty and the War Office met in March 1892 to consider a possible Russian attempt to seize Constantinople and how they would have to act militarily to deal with them.

    (A) how they would have to act militarily to deal with them
    (B) how to deal with them if military action would be necessary
    (C) what would be necessary militarily for dealing with such an event
    (D) what military action would be necessary in order to deal with such an event
    (E) the necessity of what kind of military action in order to take for dealing with it

In choices A and B, the pronoun *them* has no antecedent; furthermore, the *if* clause in B must take *should* rather than *would*. In C, *necessary militarily* is awkward and vague. E is wordy and garbles the meaning with incorrect word order. Choice D is best: its phrasing is clear, grammatical, and idiomatic. Moreover, D is the choice that most closely parallels the construction of the nonunderlined portion of the sentence. The sentence states that the Admiralty and the War Office met to consider *x* and *y*, where *x* is the noun phrase *a possible Russian attempt*. D provides a noun phrase, *military action*, that matches the structure of *x* more closely than do the corresponding noun elements in the other choices.

74. Growing competitive pressures may be encouraging auditors to bend the rules in favor of clients; auditors may, for instance, allow a questionable loan to remain on the books in order to maintain a bank's profits on paper.

    (A) clients; auditors may, for instance, allow
    (B) clients, as an instance, to allow
    (C) clients, like to allow
    (D) clients, such as to be allowing
    (E) clients; which might, as an instance, be the allowing of

The first independent clause of the sentence describes a general situation; in A, the best choice, a second independent clause clearly and grammatically presents an example of this circumstance. Choice B uses *as an instance* ungrammatically: *as an instance* requires *of* to form such idiomatic constructions as "She cited x *as an instance of* y." Also, this construction cannot link infinitives such as *to bend* and *to allow*. The infinitive is again incorrect in C and D. C misuses *like*, a comparative preposition, to introduce an example. D requires *by* in place of *to be*. E, aside from being wordy and imprecise, uses the pronoun *which* to refer vaguely to the whole preceding clause rather than to a specific noun referent.

75. If the proposed expenditures for gathering information abroad are reduced even further, international news reports have been and will continue to diminish in number and quality.

    (A) have been and will continue to diminish
    (B) have and will continue to diminish
    (C) will continue to diminish, as they already did,
    (D) will continue to diminish, as they have already,
    (E) will continue to diminish

Choices A and B fail because the logic of the sentence demands that the verb in the main clause be wholly in the future tense: if *x* happens, *y* will happen. To compound the problem, the auxiliary verbs *have been* in A and *have* in B cannot properly be completed by *to diminish*. C, D, and E supply the correct verb form, but C and D conclude with faulty *as* clauses that are awkward and unnecessary, because *will continue* describes an action begun in the past. E is the best choice.

76. Gall's hypothesis <u>of there being different mental functions localized in different parts of the brain is widely accepted today.</u>

   (A) of there being different mental functions localized in different parts of the brain is widely accepted today

   (B) of different mental functions that are localized in different parts of the brain is widely accepted today

   (C) that different mental functions are localized in different parts of the brain is widely accepted today

   (D) which is that there are different mental functions localized in different parts of the brain is widely accepted today

   (E) which is widely accepted today is that there are different mental functions localized in different parts of the brain

Choices A and B are faulty because a relative clause beginning with *that* is needed to state Gall's hypothesis. The phrase *of there being*, as used in A, is wordy and unidiomatic; in B, *of different mental functions* does not convey Gall's point about those functions. Choices D and E are awkward and wordy, and both use *which* where *that* would be the preferred pronoun for introducing a clause that states Gall's point. Further, the phrasing of E misleadingly suggests that a distinction is being made between this hypothesis and others by Gall that are not widely accepted today. Choice C is best.

77. Though the term "graphic design" may <u>suggest laying out corporate brochures and annual reports, they have come to signify widely ranging</u> work, from package designs and company logotypes to signs, book jackets, computer graphics, and film titles.

   (A) suggest laying out corporate brochures and annual reports, they have come to signify widely ranging

   (B) suggest laying out corporate brochures and annual reports, it has come to signify a wide range of

   (C) suggest corporate brochure and annual report layout, it has signified widely ranging

   (D) have suggested corporate brochure and annual report layout, it has signified a wide range of

   (E) have suggested laying out corporate brochures and annual reports, they have come to signify widely ranging

Choice A contains an agreement error: *the term* requires the singular *it has* in place of the plural *they have*. Furthermore, *widely ranging* is imprecise: graphic design work does not range about widely but rather comprises a *wide range* of activities. Choice C contains *widely ranging* and, like D, fails to use a verb form such as *laying out* to define the activities, instead presenting an awkward noun phrase: *corporate brochure and annual report layout*. The present perfect tense is used inappropriately in choices C (*has signified*), D (*have suggested . . . has signified*), and E (*have suggested*) to

indicate recently completed rather than ongoing action. Additionally, E contains the incorrect *they have* and the imprecise *widely ranging*. Choice B is best.

78. The root systems of most flowering perennials either become too crowded, <u>which results in loss in vigor, and spread</u> too far outward, producing a bare center.

   (A) which results in loss in vigor, and spread
   (B) resulting in loss in vigor, or spreading
   (C) with the result of loss of vigor, or spreading
   (D) resulting in loss of vigor, or spread
   (E) with a resulting loss of vigor, and spread

Choice A misuses *which*: as a relative pronoun, *which* should refer to a specific noun rather than to the action of an entire clause. A also produces the unidiomatic and illogical construction *either . . . and*. Choice B properly uses a verb phrase (*resulting . . .*) instead of *which* to modify the action of the first clause and also correctly completes *either* with *or*, but the verbs following *either* and *or* are not parallel: *spreading* must be *spread* to match *become*. Choice C is flawed by the nonparallel verb *spreading* and the wordy phrase that begins *with the result of*. Choice E is similarly wordy and uses *and* where *or* is required. Choice D—concise, idiomatic, and parallel with the rest of the sentence—is best.

79. George Sand (Aurore Lucile Dupin) was one of the first European writers to consider the rural poor <u>to be legitimate subjects for literature and portray these</u> with sympathy and respect in her novels.

   (A) to be legitimate subjects for literature and portray these

   (B) should be legitimate subjects for literature and portray these

   (C) as being legitimate subjects for literature and portraying them

   (D) as if they were legitimate subjects for literature and portray them

   (E) legitimate subjects for literature and to portray them

When the verb *consider* is used to mean "regard" or "deem," it can be used more economically without the *to be* of choice A; *should be* in choice B, *as being* in choice C, and *as if* in choice D are used unidiomatically with this sense of *consider*, and D carries the unwarranted suggestion that Sand is somehow viewing the rural poor hypothetically. Choice E, therefore, is best: each of the other choices inserts an unnecessary, unidiomatic, or misleading phrase before *legitimate subjects*. Moreover, A and B incorrectly use *these* rather than *them* as the pronoun referring to the poor. In C, *portraying* is not parallel with *to consider*. Only E has *to portray*; although not essential, *to* underscores the parallelism of *portray* and *consider*.

80. Salt deposits and moisture threaten to destroy the Mohenjo-Daro excavation in Pakistan, the site of an ancient civilization that flourished at the same time as the civilizations in the Nile delta and the river valleys of the Tigris and Euphrates.

(A) that flourished at the same time as the civilizations
(B) that had flourished at the same time as had the civilizations
(C) that flourished at the same time those had
(D) flourishing at the same time as those did
(E) flourishing at the same time as those were

Choice A, the best answer, uses the simple past tense *flourished* to describe civilizations existing simultaneously in the past. Choice B wrongly uses the past perfect *had flourished*; past perfect tense indicates action that was completed prior to some other event described in the simple past tense: for example, "Mayan civilization *had ceased* to exist by the time Europeans first *reached* the Americas." Choice C lacks *as* after *time.* In choices C, D, and E, the plural pronoun *those* has no plural noun to which it can refer. In C, *had* signals the incorrect past perfect; *did* in D and *were* in E are awkward and unnecessary. D and E also incorrectly use the present participle *flourishing* where *that flourished* is needed.

81. In 1973 mortgage payments represented twenty-one percent of an average thirty-year-old male's income; and forty-four percent in 1984.

(A) income; and forty-four percent in 1984
(B) income; in 1984 the figure was forty-four percent
(C) income, and in 1984 forty-four percent
(D) income, forty-four percent in 1984 was the figure
(E) income that rose to forty-four percent in 1984

To establish the clearest comparison between circumstances in 1973 and those in 1984, a separate clause is needed to describe each year. Choices A and C, in failing to use separate clauses, are too elliptical and therefore unclear. Choice A also incorrectly uses *and* and a semicolon to separate an independent clause and a phrase. Choice D incorrectly separates two independent clauses with a comma; moreover, the placement of *in 1984* is awkward and confusing. In choice E, *that* refers illogically to *income,* thereby producing the misstatement that income rather than mortgage payments rose to forty-four percent in 1984. Choice B is best; two properly constructed clauses that clearly express the comparison are separated by a semicolon.

82. In contrast to large steel plants that take iron ore through all the steps needed to produce several different kinds of steel, processing steel scrap into a specialized group of products has enabled small mills to put capital into new technology and remain economically viable.

(A) processing steel scrap into a specialized group of products has enabled small mills to put capital into new technology and remain
(B) processing steel scrap into a specialized group of products has enabled small mills to put capital into new technology, remaining
(C) the processing of steel scrap into a specialized group of products has enabled small mills to put capital into new technology, remaining
(D) small mills, by processing steel scrap into a specialized group of products, have been able to put capital into new technology and remain
(E) small mills, by processing steel scrap into a specialized group of products, have been able to put capital into new technology and remained

The logical comparison here is between *large steel plants* and *small mills.* Choices A, B, and C illogically contrast *large steel plants* with *[the] processing [of] steel scrap.* Further, in choices B and C *remaining* is not parallel with *put*; consequently, it is not clear exactly what is *remaining economically viable.* The contrast between large plants and small mills is logically phrased in choices D and E, but *remained* in E is not parallel with *put.* Choice D, the best answer, uses parallel verb forms to complete the construction *have been able to put . . . and remain.*

83. Any medical test will sometimes fail to detect a condition when it is present and indicate that there is one when it is not.

(A) a condition when it is present and indicate that there is one
(B) when a condition is present and indicate that there is one
(C) a condition when it is present and indicate that it is present
(D) when a condition is present and indicate its presence
(E) the presence of a condition when it is there and indicate its presence

Only choice C, the best answer, produces a sentence in which every pronoun *it* refers clearly and logically to the noun *condition.* In choices A and B, the phrase *indicate that there is one* does not grammatically fit with *when it is not* because *it* has no referent. Choices B and D are imprecise in saying that a test will fail to detect *when a condition is present,* since the issue is the presence and not the timing of the condition. Further, *its presence* in D leaves the *it* in *when it is not* without a logical referent: *it* must refer to *condition,* not *presence.* Choice E repeats this error; also, *the presence . . . when it is there* is imprecise and redundant.

84. One legacy of Madison Avenue's recent campaign to appeal to people fifty years old and over is the realization that as a person ages, their concerns change as well.

  (A) the realization that as a person ages, their
  (B) the realization that as people age, their
  (C) to realize that when a person ages, his or her
  (D) to realize that when people age, their
  (E) realizing that as people age, their

In choice A, the plural pronoun *their* does not agree in number with the singular noun *person*. Choices C, D, and E can be faulted for failing to complete the construction *One legacy . . . is* with a noun that matches the noun *legacy*; these choices use verb forms—the infinitive *to realize* or the present participle *realizing*—in place of a noun such as *realization*. Further, *when* in C and D is less precise than *as* in characterizing a prolonged and gradual process such as aging. B is the best answer.

85. Out of America's fascination with all things antique have grown a market for bygone styles of furniture and fixtures that are bringing back the chaise lounge, the overstuffed sofa, and the claw-footed bathtub.

  (A) things antique have grown a market for bygone styles of furniture and fixtures that are bringing
  (B) things antique has grown a market for bygone styles of furniture and fixtures that is bringing
  (C) things that are antiques has grown a market for bygone styles of furniture and fixtures that bring
  (D) antique things have grown a market for bygone styles of furniture and fixtures that are bringing
  (E) antique things has grown a market for bygone styles of furniture and fixtures that bring

Choice B is best. In A and D, *have grown* does not agree with the singular noun *market*. In addition, all of the choices except B use plural verbs after *that*, thus illogically stating either that *bygone styles of furniture and fixtures*, or *fixtures* alone, are reviving the particular pieces mentioned; it is instead *the market* for those styles *that is bringing back* such pieces, as B states. Furthermore, choices C and E, by using the verb form *bring*, fail to convey the ongoing nature of the revival properly described by the progressive verb *is bringing*.

86. Having the right hand and arm being crippled by a sniper's bullet during the First World War, Horace Pippin, a Black American painter, worked by holding the brush in his right hand and guiding its movements with his left.

  (A) Having the right hand and arm being crippled by a sniper's bullet during the First World War
  (B) In spite of his right hand and arm being crippled by a sniper's bullet during the First World War
  (C) Because there had been a sniper's bullet during the First World War that crippled his right hand and arm
  (D) The right hand and arm being crippled by a sniper's bullet during the First World War
  (E) His right hand and arm crippled by a sniper's bullet during the First World War

In E, the best answer, the construction *His right hand . . . crippled* clearly and grammatically modifies the subject of the sentence, *Horace Pippin*. In A, the use of the two participles *Having* and *being* is ungrammatical. Choice B is awkward and changes the meaning of the original statement: the point is that Pippin's method of painting arose because of, not *in spite of*, his injury. Choice C is wordy and awkwardly places the clause beginning *that crippled . . .* so that it appears to modify *the First World War* rather than *bullet*. In choice D, *The* should be *His*, and *being* should be omitted.

87. Beyond the immediate cash flow crisis that the museum faces, its survival depends on if it can broaden its membership and leave its cramped quarters for a site where it can store and exhibit its more than 12,000 artifacts.

  (A) if it can broaden its membership and leave
  (B) whether it can broaden its membership and leave
  (C) whether or not it has the capability to broaden its membership and can leave
  (D) its ability for broadening its membership and leaving
  (E) the ability for it to broaden its membership and leave

Choice A is faulty because it uses the unidiomatic construction *depends on if*; *whether* is required to connect *depends on* with the clause beginning *it can . . . .* Choice C uses *whether or not* where only *whether* is needed, includes the awkward and wordy construction *has the capability to*, and unnecessarily repeats the idea of capability with *can*. Choices D and E use unidiomatic constructions where the phrase *its ability to broaden* is required. Choice B—idiomatic, concise, and correct—is best.

88. The Emperor Augustus, it appears, commissioned an idealized sculpture portrait, the features of which are so unrealistic as to constitute what one scholar calls an "artificial face."

  (A) so unrealistic as to constitute
  (B) so unrealistic they constituted
  (C) so unrealistic that they have constituted
  (D) unrealistic enough so that they constitute
  (E) unrealistic enough so as to constitute

The verbs *are* and *calls* indicate that the sculpture is being viewed and judged in the present. Thus, neither the past tense verb *constituted* (in B) nor the present perfect verb *have constituted* (in C) is correct; both suggest that the statue's features once constituted an *artificial face* but no longer do so. Also, B would be better if *that* were inserted after *so unrealistic*, although the omission of *that* is not ungrammatical. Choices D and E use unidiomatic constructions with *enough*: *unrealistic enough to constitute* would be idiomatic, but the use of *enough* is imprecise and awkward in this context. Choice A, which uses the clear, concise, and idiomatic construction *so unrealistic as to constitute*, is best.

89. A recent national study of the public schools shows that <u>there are now one microcomputer for every thirty-two pupils, four times as many than there were</u> four years ago.

(A) there are now one microcomputer for every thirty-two pupils, four times as many than there were

(B) there is now one microcomputer for every thirty-two pupils, four times as many than there were

(C) there is now one microcomputer for every thirty-two pupils, four times as many as there were

(D) every thirty-two pupils now have one microcomputer, four times as many than there were

(E) every thirty-two pupils now has one microcomputer, four times as many as

Choices A, B, and C appropriately use the construction "one X for every thirty-two Y's" to describe the ratio of computers to pupils, but only C, the best answer, is error-free. In A, *are* does not agree with the subject, *one microcomputer*; furthermore, in A, B, and D, *than* is used where *as* is required. Choices D and E reorder and garble the "one X . . ." construction, making *four times as many* refer illogically to *pupils*.

90. Since 1986, when the Department of Labor began to allow <u>investment officers' fees to be based on how the funds they manage perform, several corporations began</u> paying their investment advisers a small basic fee, with a contract promising higher fees if the managers perform well.

(A) investment officers' fees to be based on how the funds they manage perform, several corporations began

(B) investment officers' fees to be based on the performance of the funds they manage, several corporations began

(C) that fees of investment officers be based on how the funds they manage perform, several corporations have begun

(D) fees of investment officers to be based on the performance of the funds they manage, several corporations have begun

(E) that investment officers' fees be based on the performance of the funds they manage, several corporations began

The clause beginning *Since 1986* . . . indicates that the practice described in the second clause continued for some period of time after it began. Choice D, the best answer, supplies the present perfect *have begun*, which conveys this continuity; D also uses a construction that is appropriate when "allow" means "permit": *allow . . . to be based on*. Choices A, B, and E incorrectly use the past tense *began* rather than the present perfect; furthermore, in each of these options, *they* has no referent, since *officers* is a possessive modifier of *fees*. Choices A and C include the awkward phrase *based on how the funds they manage perform*. Choices C and E incorrectly use *allow that . . . fees be based*.

91. <u>Like</u> many self-taught artists, Perle Hessing did not begin to paint until she was well into middle age.

(A) Like
(B) As have
(C) Just as with
(D) Just like
(E) As did

Choice A, the best answer, is concise and grammatically correct, using the comparative preposition *like* to express the comparison between *many self-taught artists* and *Perle Hessing*. Choices B and E, which replace A's prepositional phrase with clauses introduced by *as*, use auxiliary verbs that cannot properly be completed by any part of the verb phrase in the main clause: neither *have . . . did not begin* nor *did . . . did not begin* is logically or grammatically sound. In C and D, *Just as with* and *Just like* are both unnecessarily wordy.

92. Never before had taxpayers confronted <u>so many changes at once as they had in</u> the Tax Reform Act of 1986.

(A) so many changes at once as they had in
(B) at once as many changes as
(C) at once as many changes that there were with
(D) as many changes at once as they confronted in
(E) so many changes at once that confronted them in

Choice D is the best answer, stating grammatically and clearly that, with the 1986 Tax Reform Act, taxpayers confronted more simultaneous changes than ever before. In choice A, the past perfect *had [confronted]* illogically places the 1986 events in the same time frame as *Never before had . . .*; a simple past tense is needed to present the 1986 events as following the earlier ones. Choices B and C awkwardly place *at once* between *confronted* and its direct object, *changes*. Furthermore, B illogically states that the Act itself was *many changes,* when the point is rather that it presented many changes, and *as many . . . that* is an unidiomatic comparison. Choice E, too, presents an unidiomatic comparison with *so many . . . that*.

93. It is well known in the supermarket industry that how items are placed on shelves and <u>the frequency of inventory turnovers can be</u> crucial to profits.

(A) the frequency of inventory turnovers can be
(B) the frequency of inventory turnovers is often
(C) the frequency with which the inventory turns over is often
(D) how frequently is the inventory turned over are often
(E) how frequently the inventory turns over can be

Choice E, the best answer, grammatically and clearly makes the statement "x and y can be crucial," in which x and y are parallel clauses, each introduced by the conjunction *how*. This parallelism is preferable to the use of the noun phrase *the frequency* in A, B, and C. Furthermore, *the frequency of inventory turnovers* in A and B is less clear than *how frequently the inventory turns over*. In B and C *is often* does not agree with the plural compound subject. Choice D ungrammatically reverses the subject-verb order with *is the inventory*.

94. The psychologist William James believed that facial expressions not only provide a visible sign of an <u>emotion, actually contributing to the feeling itself</u>.

   (A) emotion, actually contributing to the feeling itself
   (B) emotion but also actually contributing to the feeling itself
   (C) emotion but also actually contribute to the feeling itself
   (D) emotion; they also actually contribute to the feeling of it
   (E) emotion; the feeling itself is also actually contributed to by them

Only C, the best answer, clearly and correctly states that James believed *facial expressions* perform <u>both</u> functions mentioned: the construction *James believed that facial expressions not only x* is completed by *but also y*, where *x* and *y* are grammatically parallel. In A, the absence of *but also y* results in a sentence fragment. In B, *but also contributing* is not parallel to *not only provide*. Choices D and E again lack *but also y*, instead introducing independent clauses that fail to associate the second part of the belief unequivocally with James. Also, the passive construction *is . . . contributed to by them* in E and the phrase *the feeling of it* in D are awkward in context.

95. Along with the drop in producer prices announced yesterday, the strong retail sales figures released today seem <u>like it is indicative that</u> the economy, although growing slowly, is not nearing a recession.

   (A) like it is indicative that
   (B) as if to indicate
   (C) to indicate that
   (D) indicative of
   (E) like an indication of

Choice C, the best answer, offers a concise and idiomatic grammatical sequence: the main verb *seem* is followed by an infinitive (*to indicate*), which is in turn followed by its direct object, a noun clause introduced by the relative pronoun *that*. In A, *seem* is followed by *like*, a preposition improperly used to introduce a clause. Also, *it* either disagrees in number with *figures* or lacks an antecedent altogether. In B, *as if* is introduced awkwardly and (in context) unidiomatically between *seem* and the infinitive. Also, with *that* omitted, B is ungrammatical. Choices D and E, with *of* substituted for *that*, are likewise ungrammatical: *of*, a preposition, can introduce a phrase, but not a clause.

96. The National Transportation Safety Board has recommended the use of fail-safe mechanisms on airliner cargo door latches <u>assuring the doors are properly closed</u> before takeoff and to prevent them from popping open in flight.

   (A) assuring the doors are properly closed
   (B) for the assurance of proper closing
   (C) assuring proper closure
   (D) to assure closing the doors properly
   (E) to assure that the doors are properly closed

The correct choice will include *to assure*, an infinitive parallel to *to prevent*. Thus, A, B, and C are disqualified. Moreover, the participial phrases in A and C (*assuring . . .*), easily construed as adjectives modifying *latches*, are confusing. Choices B and C are additionally faulty because, in omitting the noun *doors*, they fail both to specify what is being closed and to supply an antecedent for the pronoun *them*. D offers the necessary infinitive, but the gerund phrase *closing . . .* imprecisely refers to the act of closing the doors rather than to the condition of the closed doors. Choice E, with its idiomatic and precise noun clause, is the best answer.

97. Iguanas have been an important food source in Latin America since prehistoric times, and <u>it is still prized as a game animal</u> by the campesinos, who typically cook the meat in a heavily spiced stew.

   (A) it is still prized as a game animal
   (B) it is still prized as game animals
   (C) they are still prized as game animals
   (D) they are still prized as being a game animal
   (E) being still prized as a game animal

All nouns and pronouns grammatically referring back to the plural noun *Iguanas* must be plural. Choices A, B, D, and E all produce agreement problems by using singular forms (*it, animal*), leaving C the best choice. In addition, D is awkward and wordy, and E offers a participial phrase (*being . . .*) where the beginning of an independent clause is required.

98. The financial crash of October 1987 demonstrated that the world's capital markets are <u>integrated more closely than never before and</u> events in one part of the global village may be transmitted to the rest of the village—almost instantaneously.

   (A) integrated more closely than never before and
   (B) closely integrated more than ever before so
   (C) more closely integrated as never before while
   (D) more closely integrated than ever before and that
   (E) more than ever before closely integrated as

Choice D, the best answer, produces a clear sentence in which parallel structure (two clauses introduced by *that*) underscores meaning: *the crash demonstrated [1] that markets are integrated and [2] that events may be transmitted.* The other choices lack this parallel structure and contain additional faults. The phrases *more . . . than never* in A and *more . . . as never* in C are both unidiomatic: the idiom is *more than ever.* Choices B, C, and E end with *so*, *while*, and *as*, respectively: *and that* is needed so that two parallel clauses may be properly joined. Finally, B and E misplace the adverb *more*, which here should come just before *closely*: closer, not more frequent, integration of the world's capital markets is what facilitates the transmission of economic events.

99. New theories propose that catastrophic impacts of asteroids and comets may have caused reversals in the Earth's magnetic field, the onset of ice ages, <u>splitting apart continents</u> 80 million years ago, and great volcanic eruptions.

   (A) splitting apart continents
   (B) the splitting apart of continents
   (C) split apart continents
   (D) continents split apart
   (E) continents that were split apart

The word *splitting* must function as a noun to parallel the other items in the noun series of which it is part: *reversals*, *onset*, and *eruptions*. In B, the best choice, the definite article *the* clearly signifies that *splitting* is to be taken as a noun. In A, *splitting* introduces a verb phrase that breaks the parallelism of the noun series. In C, the verb *split* is similarly disruptive. Choice D, grammatically vague, resembles C if *split* is a verb and E if *split* is an adjective. In E, *continents* illogically replaces *the splitting* in the series: although the *impacts* in question may have caused continents to split, they did not cause those continents that were split apart 80 million years ago to materialize.

100. Wisconsin, Illinois, Florida, and Minnesota have begun to enforce statewide bans <u>prohibiting landfills to accept leaves, brush, and grass clippings</u>.

   (A) prohibiting landfills to accept leaves, brush, and grass clippings
   (B) prohibiting that landfills accept leaves, brush, and grass clippings
   (C) prohibiting landfills from accepting leaves, brush, and grass clippings
   (D) that leaves, brush, and grass clippings cannot be accepted in landfills
   (E) that landfills cannot accept leaves, brush, and grass clippings

Choice C is the best answer. Either of the following constructions would be idiomatic here: *x forbids y to do z* or *x prohibits y from doing z*. Choices A and B violate idiom; D and E introduce constructions that, in context, are faulty. First of all, both *bans that x cannot be done* and *bans that y cannot do x* are unidiomatic formulations. Secondly, the negative *cannot* after *bans* is illogical.

101. Even though the direct costs of malpractice disputes <u>amounts to a sum lower</u> than one percent of the $541 billion the nation spent on health care last year, doctors say fear of lawsuits plays a major role in health-care inflation.

   (A) amounts to a sum lower
   (B) amounts to less
   (C) amounted to less
   (D) amounted to lower
   (E) amounted to a lower sum

The correct choice must feature a verb that agrees with the plural noun *costs* and refers to an action completed *last year* (past tense). The verb *amounts* in A and B fulfills neither condition, and *amounts to a sum* in A is redundant. The same redundancy occurs in E, and the construction *a lower sum than* is awkward and imprecise in the context of the sentence. In D, the adjective *lower* is erroneously used in place of the noun *less* as object of the preposition *to*. Choice C is best.

102. <u>Except for a concert performance that the composer himself staged</u> in 1911, Scott Joplin's ragtime opera *Treemonisha* was not produced until 1972, sixty-one years after its completion.

   (A) Except for a concert performance that the composer himself staged
   (B) Except for a concert performance with the composer himself staging it
   (C) Besides a concert performance being staged by the composer himself
   (D) Excepting a concert performance that the composer himself staged
   (E) With the exception of a concert performance with the staging done by the composer himself

Choice A is best. In B, the participle *staging* inappropriately expresses ongoing rather than completed action, and the prepositional phrase containing this participle (*with . . . it*) is unidiomatic. Likewise, C uses the participle *being* inappropriately. In D, the use of *Excepting* in place of the preposition *Except for* is unidiomatic. Choice E is awkward and wordy.

103. Students in the metropolitan school district <u>lack math skills to such a large degree as to make it difficult to absorb them into a city economy becoming</u> ever more dependent on information-based industries.

   (A) lack math skills to such a large degree as to make it difficult to absorb them into a city economy becoming
   (B) lack math skills to a large enough degree that they will be difficult to absorb into a city's economy that becomes
   (C) lack of math skills is so large as to be difficult to absorb them into a city's economy that becomes
   (D) are lacking so much in math skills as to be difficult to absorb into a city's economy becoming
   (E) are so lacking in math skills that it will be difficult to absorb them into a city economy becoming

In A, *lack* is modified by a wordy and awkward construction, *to such a large degree as to make it difficult to*. B is similarly flawed, and *to a large enough degree that* is unidiomatic. C is ungrammatical because it uses *lack* as a noun rather than as a verb: the phrase beginning *Students . . .* becomes a dangling element, and *them* refers illogically to *skills* rather than *students*. Additionally, A, B, and C fail to use one or both of the "-ing" forms *are lacking* and *becoming*; these forms are preferable to *lack* and *becomes* in describing progressive and ongoing conditions. D uses the "-ing" forms, but *so much . . . as to be difficult to absorb* is an awkward and unidiomatic verbal modifier. Choice E is best.

104. The diet of the ordinary Greek in classical times was largely vegetarian—vegetables, fresh cheese, oatmeal, and meal cakes, and meat rarely.

(A) and meat rarely
(B) and meat was rare
(C) with meat as rare
(D) meat a rarity
(E) with meat as a rarity

The best answer here must qualify the statement made in the main clause, *The diet . . . was largely vegetarian*: it cannot be treated as part of the list of vegetarian foods. In other words, the best answer must logically and grammatically attach to the main clause when the list is omitted. Choice A fails this test: *The diet . . . was largely vegetarian, and meat rarely.* D fails also, because it lacks a function word such as *with* to link it to the main clause. The wording of choice B is imprecise and ambiguous—for example, it could mean that meat was scarce, or that it was not well done or medium. Choice C is unidiomatic. Clearly phrased, grammatically linked, and idiomatically sound, choice E is best.

105. An inventory equal to 90 days sales is as much as even the strongest businesses carry, and then only as a way to anticipate higher prices or ensure against shortages.

(A) as much as even
(B) so much as even
(C) even so much as
(D) even as much that
(E) even so much that

The idiomatic form for this type of comparison is *as much as.* Thus, choice A is best. The phrase *so much as* is used unidiomatically in choices B and C; *so much as* is considered idiomatic if it is preceded by a negative, as in "She left not so much as a trace." In choices C, D, and E, *even* is misplaced so that it no longer clearly modifies *the strongest businesses.* Moreover, the use of *that* rather than *as* is unidiomatic in choices D and E.

106. The decision by one of the nation's largest banks to admit to $3 billion in potential losses on foreign loans could mean less lending by commercial banks to developing countries and increasing the pressure on multigovernment lenders to supply the funds.

(A) increasing the pressure
(B) the increasing pressure
(C) increased pressure
(D) the pressure increased
(E) the pressure increasing

The best answer will complete the phrase *could mean less lending* with a construction that is parallel to *less lending.* Here *less* is an adjective modifying *lending,* which functions as a noun in naming a banking activity. C, the best choice, parallels this *adjective + noun* construction with *increased* [adjective] *pressure* [noun]. Choice A violates parallelism by introducing a phrase in place of the *adjective + noun* construction. Choices D and E also fail to parallel the *adjective + noun* construction. In choice B, the definite article *the* needlessly suggests that some previously mentioned type of pressure is being referred to, and *increasing* implies without warrant that the increase has been continuing for some indefinite period of time, not that it occurs as a consequence of the bank's decision.

107. Downzoning, zoning that typically results in the reduction of housing density, allows for more open space in areas where little water or services exist.

(A) little water or services exist
(B) little water or services exists
(C) few services and little water exists
(D) there is little water or services available
(E) there are few services and little available water

The adjective *little* modifies "mass nouns" (e.g., *water*), which refer to some undifferentiated quantity; the adjective *few* modifies "count nouns" (e.g., *services*), which refer to groups made up of distinct members that can be considered individually. Hence, choices A, B, and D are incorrect because *little* cannot properly modify *services.* Also, since *water* and *services* are being discussed as a pair, they should logically be treated as a compound subject requiring a plural verb; thus, the singular verbs *exists* (in B and C) and *is* (in D) are wrong. Choice E is best: the plural verb *are* is used, and *few* correctly modifies *services.*

108. Reporting that one of its many problems had been the recent extended sales slump in women's apparel, the seven-store retailer said it would start a three-month liquidation sale in all of its stores.

(A) its many problems had been the recent
(B) its many problems has been the recently
(C) its many problems is the recently
(D) their many problems is the recent
(E) their many problems had been the recent

Choice A is best: the singular pronoun *its* agrees in number with the singular noun referent *retailer*; the past perfect verb form *had been* is used appropriately to refer to action completed prior to the action of the simple past tense *said*; and the adjective *recent* correctly modifies the noun phrase *extended sales slump.* The adverb *recently* in choices B and C distorts the meaning of the sentence by illogically suggesting that what was recent was only the extension of the slump, and not the slump itself. In choices D and E, the plural pronoun *their* does not agree with the singular noun *retailer.*

109. Legislation in the Canadian province of Ontario requires of both public and private employers <u>that pay be the same for jobs historically held by women as for jobs requiring comparable skill that are</u> usually held by men.

   (A) that pay be the same for jobs historically held by women as for jobs requiring comparable skill that are

   (B) that pay for jobs historically held by women should be the same as for a job requiring comparable skills

   (C) to pay the same in jobs historically held by women as in jobs of comparable skill that are

   (D) to pay the same regardless of whether a job was historically held by women or is one demanding comparable skills

   (E) to pay as much for jobs historically held by women as for a job demanding comparable skills

Choice A is best. In choice B, *should* is illogical after *requires*, or at least unnecessary, and so is better omitted; in choices B and E, *job* does not agree in number with *jobs*; and in choices B, D, and E, the wording illogically describes the *comparable skills* rather than the *jobs* as being "usually held by men." Choices C, D, and E produce the ungrammatical construction *requires of . . . employers to pay*, in which *of* makes the phrase incorrect. In C, the use of *in* rather than *for* is unidiomatic, and *jobs of comparable skill* confusedly suggests that the jobs rather than the workers possess the skills. In D, the phrase beginning *regardless . . .* is awkward and wordy in addition to being illogical.

110. It has been estimated that <u>the annual cost to the United States of illiteracy in lost industrial output and tax revenues is at least $20 billion a year.</u>

   (A) the annual cost to the United States of illiteracy in lost industrial output and tax revenues is at least $20 billion a year

   (B) the annual cost of illiteracy to the United States is at least $20 billion a year because of lost industrial output and tax revenues

   (C) illiteracy costs the United States at least $20 billion a year in lost industrial output and tax revenues

   (D) $20 billion a year in lost industrial output and tax revenues is the annual cost to the United States of illiteracy

   (E) lost industrial output and tax revenues cost the United States at least $20 billion a year because of illiteracy

In choices A, B, and D, the combined use of *annual* and *a year* is redundant. Choices A, D, and E are awkward and confused because other constructions intrude within the phrase *cost . . . of illiteracy*: for greatest clarity, *cost* should be followed immediately by a phrase (e.g., *of illiteracy*) that identifies the nature of the cost. Choice E is particularly garbled in reversing cause and effect, saying that it is lost output and revenues rather than illiteracy that costs the United States over $20 billion a year. Choice B is wordy and awkward, and idiom requires *in* rather than *because of* to introduce a phrase identifying the constituents of the $20 billion loss. Concise, logically worded, and idiomatic, choice C is best.

111. Egyptians are credited <u>as having</u> pioneered embalming methods as long ago as 2650 B.C.

   (A) as having
   (B) with having
   (C) to have
   (D) as the ones who
   (E) for being the ones who

In English it is idiomatic usage to *credit* someone *with* having done something. Hence, only choice B, the best answer, is idiomatic. The verb *credited* would have to be changed to *regarded* for choices A or D to be idiomatic, to *believed* for choice C to be idiomatic, and to *given credit* for choice E to be idiomatic.

112. Domestic automobile manufacturers have invested millions of dollars <u>into research to develop cars more gasoline-efficient even than presently on the road.</u>

   (A) into research to develop cars more gasoline-efficient even than presently on the road

   (B) into research for developing even more gasoline-efficient cars on the road than at present

   (C) for research for cars to be developed that are more gasoline-efficient even than presently the road

   (D) in research to develop cars even more gasoline-efficient than those at present on the road

   (E) in research for developing cars that are even more gasoline-efficient than presently on the road

Choice D, the best answer, uses the preposition *than* to compare two clearly specified and grammatically parallel terms, the cars the manufacturers hope to develop and *those at present on the road*. In A, the phrase *more gasoline-efficient . . . than presently on the road* does not identify the second term of the comparison. In B, the misuse of modifying phrases produces an ambiguous and awkward statement: *even more gasoline-efficient cars* could refer either to more cars that are efficient or to cars that are more efficient. Choices B, C, and E all use *research for [verb]* where the idiom requires *research to [verb]*. In addition, C awkwardly separates *even* from *more*, and C and E again fail to indicate the second term of the comparison.

113. Visitors to the park have often looked up into the leafy canopy and <u>saw monkeys sleeping on the branches, whose arms and legs hang</u> like socks on a clothesline.

   (A) saw monkeys sleeping on the branches, whose arms and legs hang
   (B) saw monkeys sleeping on the branches, whose arms and legs were hanging
   (C) saw monkeys sleeping on the branches, with arms and legs hanging
   (D) seen monkeys sleeping on the branches, with arms and legs hanging
   (E) seen monkeys sleeping on the branches, whose arms and legs have hung

Choices A, B, and C use *have . . . saw* where *have . . . seen* is required. Choices A, B, and E awkwardly separate the relative clause beginning *whose arms and legs . . .* from *monkeys*, the noun it modifies. Choices A and E also confusingly use the present tense *hang* and the present perfect *have hung*, respectively; neither verb conveys clearly that, at the time the monkeys were spotted sleeping, their arms and legs were hanging in the manner described. Choice D, the best answer, not only forms a correct and clear sentence by supplying the present perfect verb *have . . . seen*, but also solves the problem of the *whose . . .* clause by using the appropriately placed adverbial phrase *with arms and legs hanging . . .* to modify *sleeping*.

114. From the bark of the paper birch tree the Menomini crafted a canoe about twenty feet long and two feet wide, with small ribs and rails of cedar, which could carry four persons or eight hundred pounds of <u>baggage so light</u> that a person could easily portage it around impeding rapids.

   (A) baggage so light
   (B) baggage being so light
   (C) baggage, yet being so light
   (D) baggage, and so light
   (E) baggage yet was so light

Choice E, the best answer, states that although the canoe could transport cargo of considerable weight, it was light: *a canoe . . . which could carry . . . yet was . . . light . . . .* Here, the conjunction *yet* is appropriately and correctly used to link two verb phrases. Choices A and B do not use *yet* with a verb parallel to *could carry* and thus fail to express this contrast. Furthermore, both place adjectival constructions after *baggage*, illogically stating that the *eight hundred pounds of baggage*, rather than the canoe, was light. Choice C supplies *yet* but ungrammatically uses the participle *being* where *was* is required. Similarly, D omits the necessary verb after *and*; and here again, the use of *and* rather than *yet* fails to express the contrast.

115. From the time of its defeat by the Germans in 1940 until its liberation in 1944, France was a bitter and divided country; a kind of civil war raged in the Vichy government <u>between those who wanted to collaborate with the Nazis with those who opposed</u> them.

   (A) between those who wanted to collaborate with the Nazis with those who opposed
   (B) between those who wanted to collaborate with the Nazis and those who opposed
   (C) between those wanting to collaborate with the Nazis with those opposing
   (D) among those who wanted to collaborate with the Nazis and those who opposed
   (E) among those wanting to collaborate with the Nazis with those opposing

Choice B, the best answer, correctly uses the construction *between x and y* to describe the conflict between two opposing groups. Choices A and C each use the ungrammatical *between x with y*. Choices D and E incorrectly use the preposition *among* in place of *between*: *among* is used to describe the relationship of more than two elements, as in "the tension among residents"; *between* is generally used to describe the relationship of two entities. Choice E also repeats the *with* error.

116. Those who come to church with a predisposition to religious belief will be happy in an auditorium or even a storefront, and there is no doubt that religion is sometimes better served by <u>adapted spaces of this kind instead of by some of the buildings actually designed for it.</u>

   (A) adapted spaces of this kind instead of by some of the buildings actually designed for it
   (B) adapted spaces like these rather than some of the buildings actually designed for them
   (C) these adapted spaces instead of by some of the buildings actually designed for it
   (D) such adapted spaces rather than by some of the buildings actually designed for them
   (E) such adapted spaces than by some of the buildings actually designed for it

Choice E, the best answer, correctly uses the construction is *better served by x than by y* and supplies the proper singular pronoun, *it,* to refer to *religion.* Choices A and B complete the construction beginning *better served by x . . .* unidiomatically, with *instead of by y* and *rather than y.* Also in B, *them* does not agree with its logical referent, *religion.* Choice C repeats the unidiomatic *instead* construction; in addition, *such is* preferable to *these* for presenting examples or instances. Choice D repeats the errors with *rather than* and *them.*

117. A firm that specializes in the analysis of handwriting claims <u>from a one-page writing sample that it can assess</u> more than three hundred personality traits, including enthusiasm, imagination, and ambition.

(A) from a one-page writing sample that it can assess
(B) from a one-page writing sample it has the ability of assessing
(C) the ability, from a one-page writing sample, of assessing
(D) to be able, from a one-page writing sample, to assess
(E) being able to assess, from a one-page writing sample,

Choice D, the best answer, correctly uses an infinitive to connect the verb *claims* with the firm's assertion: *claims to be able . . . to assess . . . .* All of the other choices use ungrammatical or unclear constructions after *claims.* Choices A and B present clauses that should be introduced by "claims that." In A, placing *that* after *sample* rather than after *claims* produces the unintended statement that the claim itself is made on the basis of a single *one-page writing sample.* Also, in B, *the ability of assessing* is unidiomatic. Choice C repeats this second fault and uses the unidiomatic *claims the ability.* Choice E uses the ungrammatical *claims being able to assess.*

118. The question of whether to divest themselves of stock in companies that do business in South Africa is particularly troublesome for the nation's 116 private Black colleges because their economic bases are often more fragile <u>than</u> most predominantly White colleges.

(A) than
(B) than those of
(C) than is so of
(D) compared to
(E) compared to those of

Choice B, the best answer, correctly uses the construction *more fragile . . . than* to compare the economic bases of private Black colleges with *those of most predominantly White colleges.* Choice A fails to supply a phrase like *those of,* thus illogically comparing the Black colleges' economic bases to *predominantly White colleges.* Similarly, in C *than is so of* does not clearly identify the second term of the comparison and is unnecessarily wordy. Like A, D makes an illogical comparison between *bases* and *colleges,* and both D and E use the unidiomatic and redundant *more . . . compared to.*

119. Executives and federal officials say that the use of crack and cocaine is growing rapidly among workers, <u>significantly compounding the effects of drug and alcohol abuse, which already are a cost to business of</u> more than $100 billion a year.

(A) significantly compounding the effects of drug and alcohol abuse, which already are a cost to business of
(B) significantly compounding the effects of drug and alcohol abuse, which already cost business
(C) significantly compounding the effects of drug and alcohol abuse, already with business costs of
(D) significant in compounding the effects of drug and alcohol abuse, and already costing business
(E) significant in compounding the effects of drug and alcohol abuse, and already costs business

Choice B, the best answer, uses clear and concise phrasing to state that it is *the effects of drug and alcohol abuse* that *already cost business* the sum mentioned. In A, *to business is* awkwardly and confusingly inserted between *cost* and the prepositional phrase that modifies it, and *are already a cost to business* is wordy and awkward compared to *cost business.* In C, *already with business costs of . . .* is awkward and unclear, failing to specify that those prior *effects* generate the *cost.* Choices D and E produce faulty constructions with the phrase *significant in compounding,* which cannot grammatically modify the verb form *is growing.*

120. The Parthenon was a church from 1204 until 1456, when Athens was taken by General Mohammed the Conqueror, the Turkish sultan, <u>who established a mosque in the building and used the Acropolis as</u> a fortress.

(A) who established a mosque in the building and used the Acropolis as
(B) who, establishing a mosque in the building, used the Acropolis like
(C) who, when he had established a mosque in the building, used the Acropolis like
(D) who had established a mosque in the building, using the Acropolis to be
(E) establishing a mosque in the building and using the Acropolis as

Choice A, the best answer, correctly supplies the past tense verbs *established* and *used* to describe two actions performed in 1456; also, it idiomatically employs the phrase *used the Acropolis as a fortress,* in which *used as* means "employed in the capacity of." Choices B and C incorrectly replace *as* with *like.* Furthermore, in C, *when he had established a mosque* distorts the intended meaning by stating that the first action was completed before the second was begun. Similarly, in D, *had established . . . using* states that Mohammed had already performed the actions before capturing Athens; and in E, *establishing* and *using* modify *Athens,* thus producing an absurd statement. In addition, D includes the unidiomatic construction "using *x* to be *y.*"

121. The concept of the grand jury dates from the twelfth century, when Henry II of England ordered panels of common citizens should prepare lists of who were their communities' suspected criminals.

   (A) should prepare lists of who were their communities' suspected criminals
   (B) would do the preparation of lists of their communities' suspected criminals
   (C) preparing lists of suspected criminals in their communities
   (D) the preparing of a list of suspected criminals in their communities
   (E) to prepare lists of suspected criminals in their communities

Choice E is best: the infinitive *to prepare* follows the verb *ordered*, producing the grammatical and idiomatic sequence *x ordered y to do z.* By contrast, *should prepare* in A and *would do* in B produce ungrammatical sequences: *x ordered y should/would do z.* In C, *preparing . . . communities* functions as a participial phrase modifying *citizens* rather than as a verb phrase describing what the citizens were ordered to do. In D, the construction *ordered panels of common citizens the preparing* is unidiomatic.

122. Chinese, the most ancient of living writing systems, consists of tens of thousands of ideographic characters, each character a miniature calligraphic composition inside its own square frame.

   (A) each character a miniature calligraphic composition inside its
   (B) all the characters a miniature calligraphic composition inside their
   (C) all the characters a miniature calligraphic composition inside its
   (D) every character a miniature calligraphic composition inside their
   (E) each character a miniature calligraphic composition inside their

Choice A is best: the appositive terms *character* and *composition*, both singular, agree in number; both also agree with the singular possessive pronoun *its.* In all the other choices, this three-way agreement in number is violated.

123. In developing new facilities for the incineration of solid wastes, we must avoid the danger of shifting environmental problems from landfills polluting the water to polluting the air with incinerators.

   (A) landfills polluting the water to polluting the air with incinerators
   (B) landfills polluting the water to the air being polluted with incinerators
   (C) the pollution of water by landfills to the pollution of air by incinerators
   (D) pollution of the water by landfills to incinerators that pollute the air
   (E) water that is polluted by landfills to incinerators that pollute the air

The focus here is on the phrases *x* and *y* in the construction *shifting environmental problems from x to y.* In choice C, the best answer, *x* and *y* are parallel not only grammatically but also logically: in each phrase, an environmental problem (*pollution*) affects a substance (*water, air*) and is caused by an agent (*landfills, incinerators*). In choice A the noun *landfills* (agent) is not grammatically or logically parallel with the verb phrase *polluting the air* (environmental problem); in B, *landfills* is not logically parallel with *air* (substance affected). The terms *pollution* (problem) in D and *water* (substance) in E are not logically parallel with *incinerators* (agent).

124. During Roosevelt's years in office, Black Americans began voting for Democrats rather than Republicans in national elections, but Black support for Democrats at the state and local levels developed only after when civil rights legislation was supported by Harry Truman.

   (A) developed only after when civil rights legislation was supported by Harry Truman
   (B) developed only after when Harry Truman supported civil rights legislation
   (C) developed only after Harry Truman's support of civil rights legislation
   (D) develops only at the time after the supporting of civil rights legislation by Harry Truman
   (E) developed only after there being Harry Truman's support of civil rights legislation

In choices A and B, *after when* is unidiomatic: one word or the other can be used to establish temporal sequence, but not both together. In D, the phrase *at the time after* is awkward and temporally confusing; moreover, the present tense *develops* is used incorrectly to describe action completed in the past. In E, the construction *after there being . . . support* is ungrammatical. Choice C, grammatical and idiomatic, is the best answer.

125. The winds that howl across the Great Plains not only blow away valuable topsoil, thereby reducing the potential crop yield of a tract of land, and also damage or destroy young plants.

   (A) and also damage or destroy
   (B) as well as damaging or destroying
   (C) but they also cause damage or destroy
   (D) but also damage or destroy
   (E) but also causing damage or destroying

Choice D, the best answer, correctly employs the correlative construction *not only x but also y,* where *x* and *y* are grammatically parallel and where both *x* and *y* (*damage* and *destroy*) apply to *young plants.* Choices A, (*not only . . . and also*), B (*not only . . . as well as*), and C (*not only . . . but they also*) violate the *not only . . . but also* paradigm. Moreover, B contains terms (*blow . . . damaging*) that are not parallel. In C and E, *damage* is used not as a verb with *young plants* as its direct object but as a noun receiving the action of *cause*; consequently, these choices fail to state explicitly that the damage is done to *young plants.* E also violates parallelism (*not only blow . . . but also causing*).

126. More than thirty years ago Dr. Barbara McClintock, the Nobel Prize winner, reported that genes can "jump," as pearls moving mysteriously from one necklace to another.

(A) as pearls moving mysteriously from one necklace to another
(B) like pearls moving mysteriously from one necklace to another
(C) as pearls do that move mysteriously from one necklace to others
(D) like pearls do that move mysteriously from one necklace to others
(E) as do pearls that move mysteriously from one necklace to some other one

Choice B, the best answer, correctly and idiomatically uses the preposition *like* to introduce a comparison that is expressed in a prepositional phrase. In A, *as* is used unidiomatically; in comparison, *as* is properly employed as a conjunction introducing a subordinate clause. Choices C, D, and E are all faulty because the verb *do* suggests that the migrating pearls are presented as a real phenomenon, not as a figurative illustration. Also, in D, *like* is used ungrammatically to introduce a subordinate clause (*pearls do . . .*); and in E, the phrase *some other one*, substituted for *another*, is awkward and wordy.

127. In theory, international civil servants at the United Nations are prohibited from continuing to draw salaries from their own governments; in practice, however, some governments merely substitute living allowances for their employees' paychecks, assigned by them to the United Nations.

(A) for their employees' paychecks, assigned by them
(B) for the paychecks of their employees who have been assigned
(C) for the paychecks of their employees, having been assigned
(D) in place of their employees' paychecks, for those of them assigned
(E) in place of the paychecks of their employees to have been assigned by them

In choice A, the phrase *assigned by them* modifies the adjacent noun, *paychecks*: the sentence implies that paychecks, rather than employees, work at the United Nations. In C, the phrase *having been assigned . . .* is uncertain in reference, making the sentence unclear. By using *in place of* instead of *for*, choices D and E create the unidiomatic and redundant construction *substitutes x in place of y.* Moreover, D, aside from being wordy, is unclear because the pronoun *them* has no unambiguous antecedent; and in E, *their employees to have been assigned by them* is wordy and awkward. Choice B, the best answer, properly uses the phrase *who have been assigned . . . to the United Nations* to modify *employees*.

128. New hardy varieties of rice show promise of producing high yields without the costly requirements of irrigation and application of commercial fertilizer by earlier high-yielding varieties.

(A) requirements of irrigation and application of commercial fertilizer by earlier high-yielding varieties
(B) requirements by earlier high-yielding varieties of application of commercial fertilizer and irrigation
(C) requirements for application of commercial fertilizer and irrigation of earlier high-yielding varieties
(D) application of commercial fertilizer and irrigation that was required by earlier high-yielding varieties
(E) irrigation and application of commercial fertilizer that were required by earlier high-yielding varieties

Choice E, the best answer, clearly and grammatically expresses the idea that two costly procedures, *irrigation* and the *application of . . . fertilizer*, were required by *earlier high-yielding varieties* of rice. In A, the placement of *by earlier . . . varieties* immediately after *application of fertilizer* suggests that the varieties applied the fertilizer. In B and D, the phrase *application of . . . fertilizer and irrigation is* ambiguous in meaning: it cannot be clearly determined whether applying fertilizer and irrigating are a single operation or two distinct operations. In C, only irrigation—not both irrigation and fertilization—is clearly associated with the *earlier . . . varieties* of rice.

129. In an effort to reduce their inventories, Italian vintners have cut prices; their wines have been priced to sell, and they are.

(A) have been priced to sell, and they are
(B) are priced to sell, and they have
(C) are priced to sell, and they do
(D) are being priced to sell, and have
(E) had been priced to sell, and they have

In choice C, the best answer, *do* is correctly used in place of the full verb *do sell*; in this verb, *do* is a conjugated form and *sell* is in the infinitive form, corresponding to its previous use in the sentence (in the phrase *priced to sell*). In choice A, the omitted word is *selling*; in B, D, and E, it is *sold*. Neither of these forms corresponds properly to *to sell* earlier in the sentence. Also, in E, the past perfect *had been priced* signifies that the wines had been priced to sell before the prices were cut.

130. In a 5-to-4 decision, the Supreme Court ruled <u>that two upstate New York counties owed restitution to three tribes of Oneida Indians for the unlawful seizure of</u> their ancestral lands in the eighteenth century.

(A) that two upstate New York counties owed restitution to three tribes of Oneida Indians for the unlawful seizure of

(B) that two upstate New York counties owed restitution to three tribes of Oneida Indians because of their unlawful seizure of

(C) two upstate New York counties to owe restitution to three tribes of Oneida Indians for their unlawful seizure of

(D) on two upstate New York counties that owed restitution to three tribes of Oneida Indians because they unlawfully seized

(E) on the restitution that two upstate New York counties owed to three tribes of Oneida Indians for the unlawful seizure of

Choice A, the best answer, uses *that* appropriately to introduce a clause that describes the Supreme Court's ruling; A also employs the idiomatic phrase *restitution . . . for.* In choice B, *restitution . . . because of* is not idiomatic. The plural pronouns *their* in B and C and *they* in D are confusing as references to *counties,* especially since *their* refers to the Oneida in the phrase *their ancestral lands.* Choices C, D, and E each fail to use *that* to introduce the clause that explains the Court's ruling; as a result, the phrasing in those choices is awkward, unidiomatic, and imprecise.

131. The Commerce Department announced that the economy grew during the second quarter at a 7.5 percent annual rate, while inflation eased when <u>it might have been expected for it to rise.</u>

(A) it might have been expected for it to rise
(B) it might have been expected to rise
(C) it might have been expected that it should rise
(D) its rise might have been expected
(E) there might have been an expectation it would rise

In English, *x [is] expected to y* is idiomatic usage: *expected for it to* in choice A and *expected that it should* in choice C are thus unidiomatic. Choice D awkwardly substitutes *its rise* for the pronoun *it* as the subject of *might have been expected*; since *it* refers to *inflation,* the subject of the verb *eased, it* is preferable as the subject of *might have been expected,* the verb form corresponding to *eased.* Choice E is needlessly wordy, roundabout, and vague. Choice B is best.

132. According to a study by the Carnegie Foundation for the Advancement of Teaching, companies in the United States are providing job training and general education for nearly eight million people, about <u>equivalent to the enrollment of</u> the nation's four-year colleges and universities.

(A) equivalent to the enrollment of
(B) the equivalent of those enrolled in
(C) equal to those who are enrolled in
(D) as many as the enrollment of
(E) as many as are enrolled in

The phrases *equivalent to* in A, *the equivalent of* in B, and *equal to* in C have too broad a range of meanings to be used precisely here: that is, they can suggest more than merely numerical equality. Also, as quantitative expressions, *equivalent* and *equal* often modify nouns referring to uncountable things, as in "an equivalent amount of resistance" or "a volume of water equal to Lake Michigan." To establish numerical comparability between groups with countable members, the phrase *as many as* is preferable. Choice D, however, uses this phrase improperly in comparing eight million people to *enrollment,* not to other people. The comparison in E, the best choice, is logical because *people* is understood as the subject of *are enrolled.*

133. <u>In Holland, a larger percentage of the gross national product is spent on defense of their coasts from rising seas than is spent on military defense in the United States.</u>

(A) In Holland, a larger percentage of the gross national product is spent on defense of their coasts from rising seas than is spent on military defense in the United States.

(B) In Holland they spend a larger percentage of their gross national product on defending their coasts from rising seas than the United States does on military defense.

(C) A larger percentage of Holland's gross national product is spent on defending their coasts from rising seas than the United States spends on military defense.

(D) Holland spends a larger percentage of its gross national product defending its coasts from rising seas than the military defense spending of the United States.

(E) Holland spends a larger percentage of its gross national product on defending its coasts from rising seas than the United States does on military defense.

In choices A, B, and C, the plural pronouns *their* and *they* have no plural noun for a logical referent. Since *In Holland* modifies all of the sentence that follows, A states confusedly that Holland spends a percentage of its gross national product *on military defense in the United States.* In C, the passive *is spent* is not parallel with the active *spends.* Lack of parallelism in choice D produces an illogical comparison: the *percentage* that *Holland spends* is said to exceed not the percentage that the United States spends but rather its total *military defense spending.* Parallel phrasing allows E, the best choice, to make a logical comparison between what *Holland spends* and what *the United States does* [spend].

134. Canadian scientists have calculated that <u>one human being should be struck every nine years by a meteorite</u>, while each year sixteen buildings can be expected to sustain damage from such objects.

    (A) one human being should be struck every nine years by a meteorite
    (B) a human being should be struck by a meteorite once in every nine years
    (C) a meteorite will strike one human being once in every nine years
    (D) every nine years a human being will be struck by a meteorite
    (E) every nine years a human being should be struck by a meteorite

Choices A, B, and E can be faulted for using *should* in place of *will* to indicate future occurrences: *should* carries the suggestion, especially unwarranted in this context, that the Canadian scientists are describing what <u>ought to</u> happen. The phrase *once in every nine years* is needlessly wordy in B and C. Also, the language of C implies more than can reasonably be maintained: i.e., that a meteorite will strike one person, and no one else, exactly once during every nine-year period. Choice D is best: the phrasing is concise and free of unintended suggestions, and the use of the indefinite article in *a human being* is appropriate for describing what is expected to be true only on the average.

135. Intar, the oldest Hispanic theater company in New York, has moved away from the Spanish classics and <u>now it draws on the works both of contemporary Hispanic authors who live abroad and of those</u> in the United States.

    (A) now it draws on the works both of contemporary Hispanic authors who live abroad and of those
    (B) now draws on the works of contemporary Hispanic authors, both those who live abroad and those who live
    (C) it draws on the works of contemporary Hispanic authors now, both those living abroad and who live
    (D) draws now on the works both of contemporary Hispanic authors living abroad and who are living
    (E) draws on the works now of both contemporary Hispanic authors living abroad and those

In choices A and C, *it* intrudes between the halves of the compound verb *has moved . . . and [now] draws* to introduce a new grammatical subject, thereby creating a run-on sentence: the inclusion of *it* requires a comma after *classics* to set off the new independent clause. The placement of *now* is awkward in C, and the construction *living abroad . . . and who* is not parallel in C and D. Misplacement of words creates ambiguity in E: for example, the positioning of *both* immediately before the phrase describing the authors suggests that there are only two contemporary Hispanic authors living abroad. The logical word placement and parallel phrasing of B, the best choice, resolve such confusions.

136. Although schistosomiasis is not often fatal, <u>it is so debilitating that it has become an economic</u> drain on many developing countries.

    (A) it is so debilitating that it has become an economic
    (B) it is of such debilitation, it has become an economical
    (C) so debilitating is it as to become an economic
    (D) such is its debilitation, it becomes an economical
    (E) there is so much debilitation that it has become an economical

Choice A is best: *is* links the noun *schistosomiasis* with its modifier, *debilitating*, and *so debilitating that* idiomatically introduces a clause that provides a further explanation of *debilitating*. Choices B, D, and E produce awkward, wordy, imprecise, or unidiomatic phrases by substituting the noun *debilitation* for the modifier *debilitating*. Choices B and D fail to introduce the explanatory clause with *that*, and C uses an awkward and wordy construction in place of a *that . . .* clause. Finally, B, D, and E wrongly use *economical* instead of *economic* to mean "pertaining to the economy."

137. In 1982 the median income for married-couple families with a wage-earning wife was $9,000 more than <u>a family where the husband only</u> was employed.

    (A) a family where the husband only
    (B) of a family where only the husband
    (C) that for families in which only the husband
    (D) a family in which only the husband
    (E) those of families in which the husband only

Choices A and D illogically compare *the median income* to *a family* rather than to another median income. Also, *families* would be preferable to *a family* in A, B, and D because the comparison is between groups of families. In A and B, *in which* would be preferable to *where*, since *where* properly refers to location. Choices A and E misplace *only* so that it seems to modify *was employed* rather than *the husband*. In B and E, *of* is less idiomatic than *for*, and the plural pronoun *those* in E does not agree with the singular noun referent *income*. C, the best choice, uses the singular pronoun *that* to stand for *income*, thus establishing a logical comparison.

138. Senator Lasker has proposed legislation requiring <u>that employers should retain all older workers</u> indefinitely or show just cause for dismissal.

    (A) that employers should retain all older workers
    (B) that all older workers be retained by employers
    (C) the retaining by employers of all older workers
    (D) employers' retention of all older workers
    (E) employers to retain all older workers

In English, the idiom is *requiring x to y* or *requiring that x y*, with *x* as the noun subject and *y* the unconjugated form of the verb. Choice E, the best answer, follows the first paradigm. Choice A is less concise and contains the unnecessary *should* before *retain*. In B, the awkward shift to the passive construction makes *workers* the subject of *show*, thus producing the unintended statement that *older workers* [rather than *employers*] are required to *show just cause for dismissal*. Choices C and D are ungrammatical because *the retaining* and *retention* function as nouns, which cannot be joined by *or* to the verb *show*: grammar requires that the compound predicate consist of two verbs, *retain . . . or show.*

139. The extraordinary diary of William Lyon Mackenzie King, prime minister of Canada for over twenty years, revealed <u>that this most bland and circumspect of men was a mystic guided in both public and</u> private life by omens, messages received at séances, and signs from heaven.

    (A) that this most bland and circumspect of men was a mystic guided in both public and
    (B) that this most bland and circumspect of men was a mystic and also guided both in public as well as
    (C) this most bland and circumspect of men was a mystic and that he was guided in both public and
    (D) this most bland and circumspect of men was a mystic and that he was guided in both public as well as
    (E) this most bland and circumspect of men to have been a mystic and that he guided himself both in public as well as

Choice A is best. All of the other choices present errors in coordination or parallelism and also confusingly suggest that King's being *a mystic* and being *guided . . . by omens . . .* were separate matters. In addition, these choices contain errors in grammar and idiom. Choice B ungrammatically uses *and also* to link the noun *mystic* and the past participle *guided*. In choices C and D, *that* is required to introduce the clause *x was a mystic* if *that* introduces the second clause, *he was guided . . . .* In choice E, *to have been* a *mystic* and *that he guided . . .* are not parallel. Finally, B, D, and E use the unidiomatic *both x as well as y* instead of *both x and y.*

140. Declining values for farm equipment and land, <u>the collateral against which farmers borrow to get through the harvest season, is</u> going to force many lenders to tighten or deny credit this spring.

    (A) the collateral against which farmers borrow to get through the harvest season, is
    (B) which farmers use as collateral to borrow against to get through the harvest season, is
    (C) the collateral which is borrowed against by farmers to get through the harvest season, is
    (D) which farmers use as collateral to borrow against to get through the harvest season, are
    (E) the collateral against which farmers borrow to get through the harvest season, are

In choices A, B, and C, the singular verb *is* does not agree with *values*, the subject of the sentence. Choices B, C, and D use awkward and wordy expressions. In B and D, the expression *use as collateral to borrow against to get through . . .* awkwardly juxtaposes two infinitives and is unnecessarily redundant, since *use as* *collateral* and *borrow against* have the same meaning. Choice C presents the wordy expression *the collateral which is borrowed against by farmers to get through . . . ,* in which the passive verb creates an awkward and confusing construction. Choice E, the best answer, succinctly and clearly identifies the *Declining values* as *the collateral against which farmers borrow* and correctly uses the plural verb *are.*

141. <u>Unlike transplants between identical twins, whose genetic endowment is the same</u>, all patients receiving hearts or other organs must take antirejection drugs for the rest of their lives.

    (A) Unlike transplants between identical twins, whose genetic endowment is the same
    (B) Besides transplants involving identical twins with the same genetic endowment
    (C) Unless the transplant involves identical twins who have the same genetic endowment
    (D) Aside from a transplant between identical twins with the same genetic endowment
    (E) Other than transplants between identical twins, whose genetic endowment is the same

In A and B, the phrases beginning *Unlike . . .* and *Besides . . .* modify *patients*, the subject of the main clause; thus A absurdly states that *Unlike transplants . . . , patients . . . must take . . . drugs,* and B that *all patients* except for *transplants . . . must take . . . drugs.* In B and D the expression *identical twins with the same genetic endowment* wrongly suggests that only some identical twin pairs are genetically identical. In E, the construction *Other than transplants . . . , all patients . . . must take . . . drugs* illogically suggests, as in B, that some patients are transplants. Choice C, the best answer, solves these problems by using a clause introduced by *Unless* to describe the exception to the rule and a nonrestrictive clause beginning with *who* to describe the characteristic attributed to all identical twins.

142. In one of the most stunning reversals in the history of marketing, the Coca-Cola company in July 1985 yielded to thousands of irate consumers <u>demanding that it should</u> bring back the original Coke formula.

(A) demanding that it should
(B) demanding it to
(C) and their demand to
(D) who demanded that it
(E) who demanded it to

Choice D, the best answer, uses the grammatically correct expression *demanded that it bring back*, in which *demanded that it* is followed by the subjunctive verb *bring*. Choice A incorrectly uses *should bring* rather than *bring*: *demanding that* already conveys the idea of "should," and at any rate a modal auxiliary verb, such as *should* or *must*, cannot grammatically follow the expression *demanded that*. Similarly, B and E use the ungrammatical expression *demanding/demanded it to*. In C, the expression *yielded to . . . customers and their demand to bring . . .* unnecessarily states that the *company yielded* to the *customers* as well as to their *demand*. This expression also fails to specify that the *company* is expected to bring back the original formula.

143. Recently discovered fossil remains strongly suggest that the Australian egg-laying mammals of today are a branch of the main stem of mammalian evolution <u>rather than developing independently from</u> a common ancestor of mammals more than 220 million years ago.

(A) rather than developing independently from
(B) rather than a type that developed independently from
(C) rather than a type whose development was independent of
(D) instead of developing independently from
(E) instead of a development that was independent of

Choice B, the best answer, correctly uses the construction *mammals . . . are a branch . . . rather than a type*, in which the terms compared by *rather than* are grammatically parallel nouns. Choices A and D fail to parallel *branch* with another noun, instead following *rather than* or *instead of* with the verb phrase *developing independently from . . . .* In C, the expression *a type whose development was independent of a common ancestor* states the opposite of the original point—that the *type* of mammal mentioned was thought to have developed independently of *the main stem of mammalian evolution*, but still to have descended from *a common ancestor.* Choice E repeats the error of C, further straying from the intended meaning by referring to the *type* as a *development.*

144. Efforts to equalize the funds available to school districts, a major goal of education reformers and many states in the 1970's, <u>has not significantly reduced the gaps existing</u> between the richest and poorest districts.

(A) has not significantly reduced the gaps existing
(B) has not been significant in reducing the gap that exists
(C) has not made a significant reduction in the gap that exists
(D) have not significantly reduced the gap that exists
(E) have not been significant in a reduction of the gaps existing

In A, B, and C, the singular auxiliary verb *has* does not agree with the plural subject of the sentence, *Efforts*. In addition, B and C are wordy; *significantly reduced* will suffice here. Choice E uses a similarly wordy expression that changes the meaning of the sentence, stating not that the efforts have significantly reduced the gap but that they failed to play a significant role in some already-existing reduction of several *gaps*. Choice D, the best answer, is grammatically correct, clear, and concise.

145. Most state constitutions now <u>mandate that the state budget be balanced</u> each year.

(A) mandate that the state budget be balanced
(B) mandate the state budget to be balanced
(C) mandate that the state budget will be balanced
(D) have a mandate for a balanced state budget
(E) have a mandate to balance the state budget

When *mandate* is used as a verb to mean "make it mandatory," it must be followed by *that* and a verb in the subjunctive mood, as in A, the best answer: *mandate that x be balanced.* Choice B uses the ungrammatical *mandate x to be balanced.* Choice C inappropriately uses the future indicative, *will be*, rather than the subjunctive. Choices D and E use wordy and imprecise expressions in place of the verb *mandate*: neither *have a mandate for a balanced . . . budget* nor *have a mandate to balance the . . . budget* makes clear that the requirement is made *by* the constitution. It is also unclear in D whether *each year* refers to the mandating or the balancing.

146. A patient accusing a doctor of malpractice will find it difficult to prove damage <u>if there is a lack of some other doctor to testify</u> about proper medical procedures.

(A) if there is a lack of some other doctor to testify
(B) unless there will be another doctor to testify
(C) without another doctor's testimony
(D) should there be no testimony from some other doctor
(E) lacking another doctor to testify

Only C, the best choice, manages to convey the meaning of the sentence efficiently and idiomatically. Choices A and D are plagued by awkwardness and wordiness. Choice A also introduces the unidiomatic phrase *lack of some other doctor.*

Choice B incorrectly uses a future-tense verb (*will be*) in the *if* clause; the *if* clause must use the present tense if it is preceded, as here, by a <u>result</u> clause that uses a future-tense verb (e.g., *will find*). Choice E introduces a dangling modifier: the *lacking . . .* phrase cannot logically modify *damage*, the nearest noun.

147. <u>Samuel Sewall viewed marriage, as other seventeenth-century colonists, like a property arrangement rather than</u> an emotional bond based on romantic love.

(A) Samuel Sewall viewed marriage, as other seventeenth-century colonists, like a property arrangement rather than
(B) As did other seventeenth-century colonists, Samuel Sewall viewed marriage to be a property arrangement rather than viewing it as
(C) Samuel Sewall viewed marriage to be a property arrangement, like other seventeenth-century colonists, rather than viewing it as
(D) Marriage to Samuel Sewall, like other seventeenth-century colonists, was viewed as a property arrangement rather than
(E) Samuel Sewall, like other seventeenth-century colonists, viewed marriage as a property arrangement rather than

In E, the best choice, a modifying phrase begun by *like* immediately follows the name it modifies, *Samuel Sewall*. E also uses the idiomatic construction *viewed marriage as. . . .* Choice A inserts an adverbial modifier, as *other . . . colonists,* without the necessary *did*. It also uses the unidiomatic construction *viewed marriage like . . . .* Both B and C use the unidiomatic construction *viewed marriage to be . . . .* C incorrectly places the adjective phrase *like other . . . colonists* after the word *arrangement*, which it cannot logically modify. D offers a confusing and awkward passive construction *marriage to Samuel Sewall . . . was viewed . . . .*

148. Under the Safe Drinking Water Act, the Environmental Protection Agency is required either to approve individual state plans for controlling the discharge of wastes into underground water or <u>that they enforce their</u> own plan for states without adequate regulations.

(A) that they enforce their
(B) for enforcing their
(C) they should enforce their
(D) it should enforce its
(E) to enforce its

E, the best choice, is the only one that maintains grammatical parallelism by using an infinitive—*to enforce*—to complete the construction *either to approve . . . or . . . .* All of the other choices offer syntactic structures that are not parallel to the infinitive phrase *to approve*. In addition, choices A, B, and C use plural pronouns (*they* and *their*) that have no grammatical referents.

149. Last year, land values in most parts of the pinelands rose almost <u>so fast, and in some parts even faster than what they did</u> outside the pinelands.

(A) so fast, and in some parts even faster than what they did
(B) so fast, and in some parts even faster than, those
(C) as fast, and in some parts even faster than, those
(D) as fast as, and in some parts even faster than, those
(E) as fast as, and in some parts even faster than what they did

The properly completed sentence here must (1) use the proper form of the comparative conjunction, *as fast as*; (2) enclose the parenthetical statement *and . . . even faster than* in commas; and (3) preserve parallel structure, clarity of reference, and economy by using *those* to substitute for *land values* in the completed comparison. D, the best choice, does all these things correctly. A and B use *so* unidiomatically in place of *as*. A and E omit the comma needed after *than* and use the confusing and unparallel *what they did* instead of *those*. C omits the second *as* needed in the comparative conjunction *as fast as*.

150. In the mid-1960's a newly installed radar warning system mistook the <u>rising of the moon as a massive missile attack by the Soviets</u>.

(A) rising of the moon as a massive missile attack by the Soviets
(B) rising of the moon for a massive Soviet missile attack
(C) moon rising to a massive missile attack by the Soviets
(D) moon as it was rising for a massive Soviet missile attack
(E) rise of the moon as a massive Soviet missile attack

Choice B is best because it alone correctly handles the idiom *to mistake x <u>for</u> y*. Though choice D manages the correct preposition, *for*, the phrase the *moon as it was rising for* is less efficient and precise than the phrasing of choice B: since *rising* functions as a verb in D, the phrase *for a massive . . . attack* now seems to modify *rising* rather than *mistook*. Choice C incorrectly uses *mistook . . . to,* and choices A and E incorrectly use *mistake . . . as*. Choice E also employs the nonidiomatic *rise of the moon*.

151. If Dr. Wade was right, any apparent connection of the eating of highly processed foods and excelling at sports is purely coincidental.

(A) If Dr. Wade was right, any apparent connection of the eating of

(B) Should Dr. Wade be right, any apparent connection of eating

(C) If Dr. Wade is right, any connection that is apparent between eating of

(D) If Dr. Wade is right, any apparent connection between eating

(E) Should Dr. Wade have been right, any connection apparent between eating

D, the best choice, deals successfully with four issues. It uses a present indicative verb form in the conditional clause, *If Dr. Wade is right*, in order to agree with the verb in the main clause, *any connection is. . .coincidental.* It uses the idiomatic phrasing *connection between x and y.* It presents the coordinate objects of the preposition *between* (*eating . . .* and *excelling . . .*) in parallel form. Finally, the adjective *apparent* appears in front of its headnoun *connection*, not after. A, B, and E use incorrect verb forms in the conditional clause. A and B use the unidiomatic *connection of x and y.* A and C violate parallelism with *eating of.* C and E incorrectly place *apparent* after its head-word *connection.*

152. When the technique known as gene-splicing was invented in the early 1970's, it was feared that scientists might inadvertently create an "Andromeda strain," a microbe never before seen on Earth that might escape from the laboratory and it would kill vast numbers of humans who would have no natural defenses against it.

(A) it would kill vast numbers of humans who would have no natural defenses against it

(B) it might kill vast numbers of humans with no natural defenses against it

(C) kill vast numbers of humans who would have no natural defenses against it

(D) kill vast numbers of humans who have no natural defenses against them

(E) kill vast numbers of humans with no natural defenses against them

This sentence requires parallel verb forms within the relative clause *that might escape . . . and kill.* C, the best choice, uses parallel verb forms that are followed appropriately by the conditional *would have* in the *who* clause that modifies *humans.* Choices A and B each violate parallel construction by introducing a new independent clause, *it would kill . . .* and *it might kill . . . .* Though choices D and E begin by observing parallelism, the use of *them* at the end of each creates a problem of pronoun reference: *them* cannot refer to the singular *microbe.* In addition, choices B, D, and E lack *would* and thus do not express the conditional.

153. A recording system was so secretly installed and operated in the Kennedy Oval Office that even Theodore C. Sorensen, the White House counsel, did not know it existed.

(A) A recording system was so secretly installed and operated in the Kennedy Oval Office that

(B) So secret was a recording system installation and operation in the Kennedy Oval Office

(C) It was so secret that a recording system was installed and operated in the Kennedy Oval Office

(D) A recording system that was so secretly installed and operated in the Kennedy Oval Office

(E) Installed and operated so secretly in the Kennedy Oval Office was a recording system that

A, the best choice, correctly focuses upon the *recording system* by making it the straightforward subject of the sentence and the logical referent of the pronoun *it* in the last line. B makes *installation and operation* the subject, distorting the focus and leaving *it* without a clear referent. C distorts the focus with an awkward and confusing delayed subject construction. C also omits the conjunction *that* necessary to introduce the clause stating the result (*even Sorenson did not know . . .*). D, a long noun phrase with no finite verb, produces a fragment rather than a complete sentence. E awkwardly inverts the order of the subject and predicate in the main clause and thus cannot be logically connected to the remainder of the sentence.

154. In 1791 Robert Carter III, one of the wealthiest plantation owners in Virginia, stunned his family, friends, and neighbors by filing a deed of emancipation, setting free the more than 500 slaves who were legally considered his property.

(A) setting free the more than 500 slaves who were legally considered

(B) setting free more than the 500 slaves legally considered as

(C) and set free more than 500 slaves, who were legally considered as

(D) and set free more than the 500 slaves who were legally considered

(E) and he set free the more than 500 slaves who were legally considered as

This sentence requires that the participial phrase *setting free . . .* connect to the gerund construction *by filing a deed . . .*; it was the *filing* of a deed that made possible the *setting free . . . .* Choices A and B establish this connection, but only A, the best choice, completes the participial phrase appropriately. In choices B and D the misconstructed phrases *set[ting] free more than the 500 slaves . . .* mistakenly suggest that Carter set free slaves that were not his own. Choices C and D distort meaning by paralleling *stunned* and *set free,* as though these were two separate and independent actions. E begins a second independent clause, which—though grammatically acceptable—again distorts the meaning. In choices B, C, and E, *considered as* is unidiomatic.

155. Federal authorities involved in the investigation have found <u>the local witnesses are difficult to locate, reticent, and are</u> suspicious of strangers.

    (A) the local witnesses are difficult to locate, reticent, and are

    (B) local witnesses to be difficult to locate, reticent, and are

    (C) that local witnesses are difficult to locate, reticent, and

    (D) local witnesses are difficult to locate and reticent, and they are

    (E) that local witnesses are difficult to locate and reticent, and they are

This sentence requires parallelism in the three coordinate complements that form the direct object clause: *local witnesses are* (1) *difficult . . . ,* (2) *reticent*, and (3) *suspicious . . . .* These three elements are logically parallel and must be formally parallel as well. Each must be expressed in an adjective or adjective phrase. C, the best choice, does this clearly and correctly. A, B, D, and E violate the parallelism in one of two ways. A and B convert the third element into a second, coordinate predicate for the object clause by repeating the verb *are*. D and E convert the third element into a second, coordinate object clause by introducing the words *they are*. Moreover, A, B, and D lack the conjunction *that* needed to introduce the direct object clause.

156. Dirt roads may evoke the bucolic simplicity of another century, but financially strained townships point out that <u>dirt roads cost twice as much as maintaining paved roads</u>.

    (A) dirt roads cost twice as much as maintaining paved roads

    (B) dirt roads cost twice as much to maintain as paved roads do

    (C) maintaining dirt roads costs twice as much as paved roads do

    (D) maintaining dirt roads costs twice as much as it does for paved roads

    (E) to maintain dirt roads costs twice as much as for paved roads

This sentence compares the costs required *to maintain* two kinds of roads. B, the best choice, is able to maintain parallelism in the comparison as well. Choice A incorrectly shifts the meaning by comparing the cost of *dirt roads* with the cost of *maintaining paved roads*. Choice C does the opposite: it compares the cost of *maintaining dirt roads* with the cost of *paved roads* themselves. Choice D further confuses the sentence by adding a nonparallel clause, *it does for*, in which *it* has no clear referent. Choice E introduces the infinitive phrase *to maintain . . .* and wrongly attempts to complete the comparison with the nonparallel prepositional phrase *for . . . .*

157. A number of linguists contend <u>that all of the thousands of languages spoken by the world's five billion people can be traced</u> back to a common root language.

    (A) that all of the thousands of languages spoken by the world's five billion people can be traced

    (B) that the world's five billion people speak thousands of languages of which all can be traced

    (C) the world's five billion people speak thousands of languages which are all traceable

    (D) all of the thousands of languages spoken by the world's five billion people to be traceable

    (E) the ability to trace all of the thousands of languages that are spoken by the world's five billion people

A, the best choice, correctly (1) uses a noun clause introduced by *that* after *contend,* (2) keeps the "contention" clear by making *all of the thousands of languages* the subject of the noun clause, and (3) precisely indicates the relationship of the *thousands of languages* to the *common root language* (they *can be traced back to* it). B and C produce convoluted and ill-focused sentences by making *the world's five billion people* the subject of the noun clause. The phrase *of which all* in B is unidiomatic (*all of which* is the idiom). C uses the wordy and indirect *traceable back to*. D incorrectly substitutes an infinitive clause for the "that" noun clause required after *contend*. E, in substituting a noun phrase, becomes incoherent and ungrammatical.

158. <u>With</u> only 5 percent of the world's population, United States citizens consume 28 percent of its nonrenewable resources, drive more than one-third of its automobiles, and use 21 times more water per capita than Europeans do.

    (A) With

    (B) As

    (C) Being

    (D) Despite having

    (E) Although accounting for

The word or phrase that begins this sentence should establish the contrast between the size of the United States population and the activities of its citizens. Choices D and E are the only ones that establish the contrast, and only E, the best choice, expresses meaning accurately with the phrase *Although accounting for.* *With* in choice A and *Despite having* in choice D confusingly suggest that United States citizens somehow possess, rather than constitute, 5 percent of the world's population. Choices B and C lose the contrast between the opening phrase and the main clause, and *As* is unidiomatic in B.

159. While depressed property values can hurt some large investors, they are potentially devastating for homeowners, whose equity—in many cases representing a life's savings—can plunge or even disappear.

(A) they are potentially devastating for homeowners, whose
(B) they can potentially devastate homeowners in that their
(C) for homeowners they are potentially devastating, because their
(D) for homeowners, it is potentially devastating in that their
(E) it can potentially devastate homeowners, whose

Choice A is the best. Its wording is unambiguous and economical. The plural pronoun *they* agrees with its antecedent, *property values*. The pronoun *whose* clearly refers to *homeowners* and efficiently connects them with the idea of lost equity. In B, C, and D, substituting *in that their* or *because their* for *whose* is wordy and confusing since the antecedent of *their* might be *they*, not *homeowners*. Furthermore, *can potentially* is redundant in B and E. Both D and E use the singular pronoun *it*, which does not agree with its logical antecedent, *property values*.

160. While some propose to combat widespread illegal copying of computer programs by attempting to change people's attitudes toward pirating, others by suggesting reducing software prices to decrease the incentive for pirating, and still others by calling for the prosecution of those who copy software illegally.

(A) by suggesting reducing software prices to decrease the incentive for pirating, and still others by calling
(B) by suggesting the reduction of software prices to decrease the incentive for pirating, and still others call
(C) suggest the reduction of software prices for decreasing the incentive for pirating, and still others call
(D) suggest the reduction of software prices to decrease the incentive for pirating, and still others by calling
(E) suggest reducing software prices to decrease the incentive for pirating, and still others are calling

Choice E, the best answer, uses constructions that are parallel to *some propose*: *others suggest . . . , and still others are calling . . . .* Choices A and B immediately lose the parallel construction, and also produce sentence fragments, by shifting to *by suggesting . . .* and *by calling . . . .* Choice B starts like choice A and then shifts back to the verb *call*, losing the parallel with the second part (*by suggesting*). Choices C and D correctly begin the second part of the parallel by using *suggest*. Choice C, however, introduces the nonidiomatic *for decreasing*, which creates some difficulty in meaning. Choice D loses parallel construction in the third part by shifting to *by calling*.

161. A wildlife expert predicts that the reintroduction of the caribou into northern Minnesota would fail if the density of the timber wolf population in that region is more numerous than one wolf for every 39 square miles.

(A) would fail if the density of the timber wolf population in that region is more numerous than
(B) would fail provided the density of the timber wolf population in that region is more than
(C) should fail if the timber wolf density in that region was greater than
(D) will fail if the density of the timber wolf population in that region is greater than
(E) will fail if the timber wolf density in that region were more numerous than

D, the best choice, uses a correct sequence of present and future indicative verb forms—*predicts*, *will fail*, and *is*—in the three related clauses. *Density*, an abstract "mass" noun, is logically construed with *greater than*. In A and B, *would fail* disagrees with the other verbs in tense and mood. Choice A misconstrues *density* with *more numerous than*, and B uses the pretentious and illogical word *provided* for *if* in a conditional clause after a negative idea (*would fail*). C's *should fail* and *was* are confusing and inconsistent with *predicts*. C and E use the absurd phrase *timber wolf density*. (The wolves are not dense; their population is dense.) E also uses an inconsistent subjunctive form, *were*, and misconstrues *density* with *more numerous than*.

162. Concerned at the increase in accident fatalities, Tennessee adopted a child-passenger protection law requiring the parents of children under four years of age to be restrained in a child safety seat.

(A) the parents of children under four years of age to be restrained in a child safety seat
(B) the restraint of parents of children under four years of age in a child safety seat
(C) that parents restrain children under four years of age in a child safety seat
(D) that children be restrained under four years of age in a child safety seat by their parents
(E) children to be restrained under four years of age by their parents in a child safety seat

This question requires the correct placement of sentence parts to achieve accurate meaning and to avoid awkwardness. Choice C most accurately and efficiently expresses the meaning of the Tennessee child-passenger protection law. Choices A and B absurdly indicate that it is the parents, not the children, who are to be restrained. Choices D and E misplace the phrase *under four years of age* so the phrase dangles and seems to modify *restrained* rather than *children*. In addition, E misplaces the phrase *in a child safety seat* to create the idea that the parents are in a child safety seat.

163. **Found throughout Central and South America, <u>sloths hang from trees by long rubbery limbs and sleep fifteen hours a day, moving infrequently enough</u> that two species of algae grow on its coat and between its toes.**

(A) sloths hang from trees by long rubbery limbs and sleep fifteen hours a day, moving infrequently enough

(B) sloths hang from trees by long rubbery limbs, they sleep fifteen hours a day, and with such infrequent movements

(C) sloths use their long rubbery limbs to hang from trees, sleep fifteen hours a day, and move so infrequently

(D) the sloth hangs from trees by its long rubbery limbs, sleeping fifteen hours a day and moving so infrequently

(E) the sloth hangs from trees by its long rubbery limbs, sleeps fifteen hours a day, and it moves infrequently enough

D, the best choice, correctly subordinates *sleeping* and *moving* to *hangs* while using the idiomatically correct phrasing *so* (*infrequently*) *that* . . . . The pronoun *its* shows clearly that the *limbs* belong to the sloth, not the trees. Choice A illogically coordinates *hang* and *sleep* and, like E, uses the unidiomatic expression *infrequently enough that*. B creates an awkward and nonparallel series: *sloths hang* . . . , *they sleep* . . . , *and with* . . . . C creates a confusing and absurd image with *use their* . . . *limbs to hang* . . . , *sleep* . . . , *and move* . . . . A, B, and C all mistakenly use the plural *sloths*, which does not agree with *its coat and* . . . *its toes*. E wrongly coordinates *hangs* and *sleeps* and violates parallelism by inserting *it* before *moves* to create a new independent clause.

164. **The commission proposed <u>that funding for the park's development, which could be open to the public early next year, is</u> obtained through a local bond issue.**

(A) that funding for the park's development, which could be open to the public early next year, is

(B) that funding for development of the park, which could be open to the public early next year, be

(C) funding for the development of the park, perhaps open to the public early next year, to be

(D) funds for the park's development, perhaps open to the public early next year, be

(E) development funding for the park, which could be open to the public early next year, is to be

Choice B is best. Choice A attaches the relative clause *which could be open* . . . to the noun *development*, when, in fact, it is the *park* that could be open. Choice C omits *that*, the object of *proposed* that is needed to introduce the clause describing the proposal. C also uses *to be* unidiomatically where *be* is correct: the commission proposed [that] *funding* . . . *to be obtained* is wrong. Choice D incorrectly uses *perhaps open to*

the public . . . to modify *development*; the phrase should modify *park*. Choice E, which seriously distorts meaning, says that the commission proposed *development funding* and that such funding *could be open to the public* . . . .

165. **At Shiprock, New Mexico, a perennially powerful girls' high school basketball team has become a path to college for some and a source of pride for a community <u>where the household incomes of 49 percent of them are</u> below the poverty level.**

(A) where the household incomes of 49 percent of them are

(B) where they have 49 percent of the household incomes

(C) where 49 percent of the household incomes are

(D) which has 49 percent of the household incomes

(E) in which 49 percent of them have household incomes

C, the best choice, uses a clear, direct, and economical adjective clause to indicate the percentage of household incomes below the poverty line in the community in question. Choices A and E insert the pronoun *them* without a stated antecedent. In addition, the wording of both A and E confuses the percentage of community residents (the implied referent of *them*) with the percentage of households, not the same thing at all. Choice B introduces the pronoun *they* without an antecedent. Furthermore, the use of *have* in B and E and of *has* in D illogically suggests that the community possesses 49% of *all* the household incomes below the poverty line.

166. **The prime lending rate is a key rate in the economy: <u>not only are the interest rates on most loans to small and medium-sized businesses tied to the prime, but also on</u> a growing number of consumer loans, including home equity loans.**

(A) not only are the interest rates on most loans to small and medium-sized businesses tied to the prime, but also on

(B) tied to the prime are the interest rates not only on most loans to small and medium-sized businesses, but also on

(C) the interest rates not only on most loans to small and medium-sized businesses are tied to the prime, but also

(D) not only the interest rates on most loans to small and medium-sized businesses are tied to the prime, but also on

(E) the interest rates are tied to the prime, not only on most loans to small and medium-sized businesses, but also

This sentence uses idiomatic paired coordinators, *not only* . . . , *but also* . . . , to relate two basic kinds of loans to the prime lending rate: (1) loans to small and medium-sized businesses and (2) consumer loans. B, the best choice, is the only one that maintains the necessary parallelism in the phrases following the paired coordinates: *not only on* . . . , *but also on* . . . . Choices C and E omit the *on* after *but also*. Choices A (*not only are . . . , but also on*) and D (*not only the interest rates . . . , but also on*) are not parallel either. Choice D especially garbles the meaning.

167. <u>Neanderthals had a vocal tract that resembled those of the apes</u> and so were probably without language, a shortcoming that may explain why they were supplanted by our own species.

   (A) Neanderthals had a vocal tract that resembled those of the apes
   (B) Neanderthals had a vocal tract resembling an ape's
   (C) The vocal tracts of Neanderthals resembled an ape's
   (D) The Neanderthal's vocal tracts resembled the apes'
   (E) The vocal tracts of the Neanderthals resembled those of the apes

The sentence requires a subject appropriate to both members of a compound predicate, the second member being *and so were probably without language*. B, the best choice, logically uses *Neanderthals* as the subject. Choice A also uses this subject, but the plural pronoun *those* does not agree with its singular antecedent, *a vocal tract*. C, D, and E present the inappropriate subject *vocal tracts,* which cannot logically govern the second member of the predicate (i.e., *vocal tracts* cannot be said to be *without language*). Moreover, it is better to use the singular in referring to an anatomical feature common to an entire species; C, D, and E use the plural *vocal tracts*. D compounds the problem by giving multiple vocal tracts to one Neanderthal.

168. Today, because of improvements in agricultural technology, the same amount of acreage produces <u>double the apples that it has</u> in 1910.

   (A) double the apples that it has
   (B) twice as many apples as it did
   (C) as much as twice the apples it has
   (D) two times as many apples as there were
   (E) a doubling of the apples that it did

Choice B, the best answer, correctly uses the adverbial phrase *twice as many . . .* to modify the verb *produces*; properly employs *many* rather than *much* to describe a quantity made up of countable units (*apples*); and appropriately substitutes *did* for the understood *produced* to express the logically necessary past tense of *produces*. Choice A awkwardly substitutes the adjective *double* for *twice*; uses *that* without a clear referent; and misuses *has* to refer to events occurring in 1910. Choice C employs the incorrect *much* in a wordy construction and also misuses *has*. D is wordy and imprecise; *. . . as there were in 1910* refers to all apples produced in 1910, regardless of location. E is illogical: since *that* refers to *a doubling,* E nonsensically asserts that the doubling occurred in 1910.

169. Seismologists studying the earthquake that struck northern California in October 1989 are still investigating some of its mysteries: the unexpected power of the seismic waves, <u>the upward thrust that threw one man straight into the air, and the strange electromagnetic signals detected hours before the temblor</u>.

   (A) the upward thrust that threw one man straight into the air, and the strange electromagnetic signals detected hours before the temblor
   (B) the upward thrust that threw one man straight into the air, and strange electromagnetic signals were detected hours before the temblor
   (C) the upward thrust threw one man straight into the air, and hours before the temblor strange electromagnetic signals were detected
   (D) one man was thrown straight into the air by the upward thrust, and hours before the temblor strange electromagnetic signals were detected
   (E) one man who was thrown straight into the air by the upward thrust, and strange electromagnetic signals that were detected hours before the temblor

The correct answer will maintain parallelism in a coordinate series. Three *mysteries* are mentioned, and the first establishes the form required for the other two members of the series, a noun phrase introduced by *the* (*the unexpected power . . .*). A, the best choice, correctly uses noun phrases introduced by *the* for the second and third members of the series (*the upward thrust . . .* and *the strange electromagnetic signals . . .*). Choice B substitutes a clause (*strange electromagnetic signals were detected . . .*) for the third noun phrase, and C and D use clauses instead of noun phrases for both additional members of the series. E uses two noun phrases, but they are not introduced by *the*. Furthermore, the phrase *one man who . . .* does not logically identify one of the *mysteries*.

170. Although early soap operas <u>were first aired on evening radio in the 1920's, they had moved to the daytime hours of the 1930's</u> when the evening schedule became crowded with comedians and variety shows.

(A) were first aired on evening radio in the 1920's, they had moved to the daytime hours of the 1930's
(B) were first aired on evening radio in the 1920's, they were moved to the daytime hours in the 1930's
(C) were aired first on evening radio in the 1920's, moving to the daytime hours in the 1930's
(D) were aired first in the evening on 1920's radio, they moved to the daytime hours of the 1930's
(E) aired on evening radio first in the 1920's, they were moved to the 1930's in the daytime hours

Choice B is the best answer. It maintains the passive voice and the past tense (*were . . . aired*) established in the introductory clause. Choice D breaks this parallelism by shifting from passive to active voice (*moved*). Choice A also uses the active voice and inappropriately shifts to the past perfect tense (*had moved*); the past perfect should be used to indicate action completed before, not after, the action of *were aired*. In C, *moving* introduces a dangling participial phrase in place of an independent clause, thus producing a fragment. E drops *were* before *aired* and finishes the sentence with two prepositional phrases that distort the meaning.

171. In 1527 King Henry VIII sought to have his marriage to Queen Catherine annulled <u>so as to marry</u> Anne Boleyn.

(A) so as to marry
(B) and so could be married to
(C) to be married to
(D) so that he could marry
(E) in order that he would marry

The sentence calls for an adverbial clause of purpose to explain why Henry sought the annulment. D, the best choice, does this clearly and correctly. It is introduced by an appropriate conjunction, *so that*, and contains a logically appropriate verb form, *could marry*. Awkward and imprecise, A does not specify who is *to marry* Anne. B substitutes an illogical coordinate predicate for the needed purpose clause; because the annulment had not yet been granted, Henry could not remarry. C lacks an appropriate conjunction, and the infinitive clause *to be married to . . .* makes this choice awkward and unidiomatic. Although E uses an appropriate conjunction, *in order that*, the verb form *would marry* is unidiomatic and illogical (*might marry* would be better).

172. The energy source on *Voyager 2* is not a nuclear reactor, in which atoms are actively broken <u>apart; rather</u> a kind of nuclear battery that uses natural radioactive decay to produce power.

(A) apart; rather
(B) apart, but rather
(C) apart, but rather that of
(D) apart, but that of
(E) apart; it is that of

Choice B, the best answer, follows an idiomatic form of expression for paired coordinates—*not X, but rather Y*; here *rather* is optional but preferable because it helps establish a contrast between the two types of energy source. Choice A incorrectly uses a semicolon rather than a coordinating conjunction (*but*) to connect the coordinate parts; a semicolon should be used to join independent clauses. In choices C, D, and E, *that of* has no grammatical referent and thus produces illogical and incorrect sentences.

173. Joan of Arc, a young Frenchwoman who claimed to be divinely inspired, turned the tide of English victories in her country by liberating the city of Orléans and <u>she persuaded Charles VII of France to claim his throne</u>.

(A) she persuaded Charles VII of France to claim his throne
(B) persuaded Charles VII of France in claiming his throne
(C) persuading that the throne be claimed by Charles VII of France
(D) persuaded Charles VII of France to claim his throne
(E) persuading that Charles VII of France should claim the throne

In choice A, *turned . . . and she persuaded* is needlessly wordy and lacks the compact parallelism of *turned . . . and persuaded*. In choice B, *persuaded . . . in claiming* is unidiomatic; the *form persuaded x to [do] y* is required. In choices C and E, *turned . . . and persuading that* violates parallelism, and the passive construction in C is awkward and unnecessarily wordy. Parallel, idiomatic, and concise, choice D is best.

174. A letter by Mark Twain, written in the same year as *The Adventures of Huckleberry Finn* were published, reveals that Twain provided financial assistance to one of the first Black students at Yale Law School.

(A) A letter by Mark Twain, written in the same year as *The Adventures of Huckleberry Finn* were published,

(B) A letter by Mark Twain, written in the same year of publication as *The Adventures of Huckleberry Finn*,

(C) A letter by Mark Twain, written in the same year that *The Adventures of Huckleberry Finn* was published,

(D) Mark Twain wrote a letter in the same year as he published *The Adventures of Huckleberry Finn* that

(E) Mark Twain wrote a letter in the same year of publication as *The Adventures of Huckleberry Finn* that

In this sentence, the relative pronoun that should introduce the clause *The Adventures* . . . *published* to make a relative clause modifying *year*. Also, the singular title of the novel demands a singular verb: for example, one would say, *"The Adventures of Huckleberry Finn* is (not "are") a great book." Only C, the best choice, satisfies both requirements. Choices A and D incorrectly substitute *as* for *that* to introduce the relative clause. Choice A also mistakes the novel title for a plural (*were published*). B confuses meaning (*written in the same year of publication as*). E creates a similar confusion of meaning, and both D and E are awkward and imprecise because *that* is too far away from its referent (*letter*) to be clear.

175. Two new studies indicate that many people become obese more due to the fact that their bodies burn calories too slowly than overeating.

(A) due to the fact that their bodies burn calories too slowly than overeating

(B) due to their bodies burning calories too slowly than to eating too much

(C) because their bodies burn calories too slowly than that they are overeaters

(D) because their bodies burn calories too slowly than because they eat too much

(E) because of their bodies burning calories too slowly than because of their eating too much

The members of a comparison (*more X than Y*) should be expressed in parallel form. D, the best choice, correctly uses parallel clauses introduced by *because*. The clauses themselves are clear and direct. Choice E uses parallel forms, but the convoluted structures are awkward and wordy. Furthermore, the word *bodies* would need an apostrophe (*bodies'*) since it is the logical subject of the gerund *burning* (that is, it answers the question, "Whose burning?"). A, B, and C do not use parallel forms for the two members of the comparison. In addition, A and B use *due to* unidiomatically to mean *because*; properly used, *due to* is synonymous with *attributable to*.

176. As a result of the ground-breaking work of Barbara McClintock, many scientists now believe that all of the information encoded in 50,000 to 100,000 of the different genes found in a human cell are contained in merely three percent of the cell's DNA.

(A) 50,000 to 100,000 of the different genes found in a human cell are contained in merely

(B) 50,000 to 100,000 of the human cell's different genes are contained in a mere

(C) the 50,000 to 100,000 different genes found in human cells are contained in merely

(D) 50,000 to 100,000 of human cells' different genes is contained in merely

(E) the 50,000 to 100,000 different genes found in a human cell is contained in a mere

This question poses two problems: subject-verb agreement and accuracy of expression. Choice E, the best answer, states the matter clearly and grammatically. The subject, *all of the information*, must be taken as singular because the mass noun *information* is singular. Choices A, B, and C all mistake the number of the subject and incorrectly use the plural verb *are contained*. A, B, and D do not make it clear whether *50,000 to 100,000* represents all or a fraction of the genes in a cell. C and D, by referring to cells in the plural, do not make it clear whether the number mentioned is to be found in each individual cell or in a collection of cells.

177. So poorly educated and trained are many young recruits to the United States work force that many business executives fear this country will lose its economic preeminence.

(A) So poorly educated and trained are many young recruits to the United States work force that

(B) As poorly educated and trained as many young recruits to the United States work force are,

(C) Because of many young recruits to the United States work force who are so poorly educated and trained,

(D) That many young recruits to the United States work force are so poorly educated and trained is why

(E) Many young recruits to the United States work force who are so poorly educated and trained explains why

A, the best choice, uses the idiomatic form *So X that Y* to establish a cause/effect relationship between clauses *X* and *Y*. In B, the subject of the *as . . . as* clause (*young recruits*) should be the subject of the main clause as well (e.g., *they*). Furthermore, main clauses following concessive clauses must express a contrasting notion: for example, "As ill-prepared as they are, they nevertheless find good jobs." C offers a wordy, convoluted *because* clause. In D, the sentence form *X is why* is unidiomatic (*X is the reason why* would be idiomatic but needlessly wordy and awkward). E exhibits subject-verb disagreement: *young recruits . . . explains why*.

178. In the last few years, the number of convicted criminals given community service <u>sentences, which allow the criminals to remain unconfined while they perform specific jobs benefiting the public, have</u> risen dramatically.

(A) sentences, which allow the criminals to remain unconfined while they perform specific jobs benefiting the public, have
(B) sentences, performing specific jobs that benefit the public while being allowed to remain unconfined, have
(C) sentences, performing specific jobs beneficial to the public while they are allowed to remain unconfined, have
(D) sentences which allow them to remain unconfined in their performing of specific jobs beneficial to the public has
(E) sentences allowing them to remain unconfined while performing specific jobs that benefit the public has

At issue in this question is subject-verb agreement; *the number . . . has risen* must be the kernel of the main clause. Choice E, the best answer, uses a singular verb form, *has*, to agree with the singular subject, *the number*. Choices A, B, and C mistake *criminals* for the sentence subject and so incorrectly use the plural verb form *have*. In B and C the verb phrases (*performing . . .*) do not clearly modify *criminals*, because another noun (*sentences*) intrudes, nor do the verb phrases clearly establish temporal relationships among events. D is wordy and imprecise (*in their performing of specific jobs*).

179. During the early years of European settlement on a continent that was viewed as "wilderness" by the newcomers, <u>Native Americans, intimately knowing the ecology of the land, were a help in the rescuing of</u> many Pilgrims and pioneers from hardship, or even death.

(A) Native Americans, intimately knowing the ecology of the land, were a help in the rescuing of
(B) Native Americans knew the ecology and the land intimately and this enabled them to help in the rescue of
(C) Native Americans, with their intimate knowledge of the ecology of the land, helped to rescue
(D) having intimate knowledge of the ecology of the land, Native Americans helped the rescue of
(E) knowing intimately the ecology of the land, Native Americans helped to rescue

Choice A suffers from the wordy and indirect expression *were a help in the rescuing of*. B creates an awkward, redundant, fused sentence in which the first clause has to be repeated in the vague *this* of the second clause; furthermore, the comma required before *and* in larger compound

sentences is omitted. D and E are confusingly worded because they begin with present participles (*having and knowing*) that appear at first to refer to the immediately preceding noun, *newcomers*, rather than to *Native Americans*. D also has the wordy and unidiomatic *helped the rescue of*. Clear, direct, and economical, choice C is best.

180. Quasars are so distant that their light has taken billions of years to reach the Earth; consequently, <u>we see them as they were during</u> the formation of the universe.

(A) we see them as they were during
(B) we see them as they had been during
(C) we see them as if during
(D) they appear to us as they did in
(E) they appear to us as though in

A, the best choice, correctly employs the simple past verb tense to describe a past condition. Choice B inappropriately switches to the past perfect (*had been*); the past perfect properly describes action that is completed prior to some other event described with the simple past tense. Choice C presents a dangling adverbial modifier, *as if during . . .* , that illogically modifies *we see*. D ambiguously suggests that the quasars appeared to us *in the formation of the universe*— that is, as though we were present to view them then. In E, *as though in* distorts the meaning to suggest that we see the quasars in a hypothetical situation— that is, that they may *not* have been involved in the formation of the universe.

181. Because of the enormous research and development expenditures required <u>to survive</u> in the electronics industry, an industry marked by rapid innovation and volatile demand, such firms tend to be very large.

(A) to survive
(B) of firms to survive
(C) for surviving
(D) for survival
(E) for firms' survival

The subject of the main clause (*such firms*) presumes a prior reference to the firms in question. Furthermore, the logical subject of *to survive* and the logical complement of *required* should be made explicit. All three demands are met by B, the best choice. Choices A, C, and D, with no reference to the firms in question, meet none of these demands. In choice E, the illogical and awkward use of a prepositional phrase (*for firms' survival*) buries the needed initial reference to *firms* in a possessive modifier.

182. <u>Consumers may not think of household cleaning products to be</u> hazardous substances, but many of them can be harmful to health, especially if they are used improperly.

(A) Consumers may not think of household cleaning products to be
(B) Consumers may not think of household cleaning products being
(C) A consumer may not think of their household cleaning products being
(D) A consumer may not think of household cleaning products as
(E) Household cleaning products may not be thought of, by consumers, as

A correct sentence will follow the idiomatic form of expression *to think of X as Y*. Only D, the best choice, uses *as* in the comparison. The infinitive *to be* in A and the participle *being* in B and C cannot grammatically and idiomatically connect those choices to the rest of the sentence. Moreover, in C the plural pronoun *their* does not agree with the singular noun referent, *consumer*. E is awkward and wordy in its use of the passive voice.

183. Archaeologists in Ireland believe that a recently discovered chalice, which dates from the eighth century, was probably buried <u>to keep from</u> being stolen by invaders.

(A) to keep from
(B) to keep it from
(C) to avoid
(D) in order that it would avoid
(E) in order to keep from

In choice A, the phrase *from being stolen* lacks the necessary noun or pronoun that specifies what it is that might be stolen. Choice B is best because it provides the pronoun *it*, which refers to *chalice*. Like choice A, choices C and E lack the pronoun. D is wordy and awkward in its use of the passive voice. Moreover, *avoid* is used imprecisely in C and D because it illogically suggests that the chalice is acting to prevent its own theft.

184. As measured by the Commerce Department, corporate profits peaked in the fourth quarter of 1988 <u>and have slipped since then, as many companies have been unable to pass on higher costs.</u>

(A) and have slipped since then, as many companies have been unable to pass on higher costs
(B) and have slipped since then, the reason being because many companies have been unable to pass on higher costs
(C) and slipped since then, many companies being unable to pass on higher costs
(D) but, many companies unable to pass on higher costs, they have slipped since then
(E) yet are slipping since then, because many companies were unable to pass on higher costs

A, the best choice, observes an appropriate sequence of verb tenses—a single act in the past (*peaked*) followed by an extended activity reaching to the present (*have slipped*). The *as* clause states clearly the cause of the slippage. B suffers from the redundant and unidiomatic expression *the reason being because*. In C, the use of the simple past *slipped* with *since then* is unidiomatic because *since then* denotes extended time. In D, the intrusion of the awkward *many . . . costs* causes the antecedent of *they* to become unclear. Furthermore, a comma should precede the *but* since it introduces a second independent clause. In E, *yet* also requires a comma before it, *are slipping* with *since then* is illogical, and *were unable* represents an ungrammatical tense shift.

185. The recent surge in the number of airplane flights has clogged the nation's air-traffic control system, <u>to lead to 55 percent more delays at airports, and prompts</u> fears among some officials that safety is being compromised.

(A) to lead to 55 percent more delays at airports, and prompts
(B) leading to 55 percent more delay at airports and prompting
(C) to lead to a 55 percent increase in delay at airports and prompt
(D) to lead to an increase of 55 percent in delays at airports, and prompted
(E) leading to a 55-percent increase in delays at airports and prompting

This question poses two major problems: parallel structure and precision of expression. In E, the best choice, parallel structure is maintained in the participial phrases introduced by *leading* and *prompting*, and the phrase *55-percent increase in delays* conveys the meaning more accurately than does the phrase *55 percent more delay(s)* in A and B. Also, choice A lacks parallelism. In C and D the infinitive phrase *to lead to . . .* is less idiomatic than the participial phrase *leading to . . .* Choice C uses the singular *delay* where the plural is needed to indicate an increase in the number of delays; the phrase *increase in delay* has no exact meaning.

186. Judge Bonham denied a motion <u>to allow members of the jury to go home at the end of each day instead of to confine them to</u> a hotel.

(A) to allow members of the jury to go home at the end of each day instead of to confine them to
(B) that would have allowed members of the jury to go home at the end of each day instead of confined to
(C) under which members of the jury are allowed to go home at the end of each day instead of confining them in
(D) that would allow members of the jury to go home at the end of each day rather than confinement in
(E) to allow members of the jury to go home at the end of each day rather than be confined to

In this sentence, *members of the jury* are presented with two options: they may (1) *go* home or (2) *be* confined to a hotel. The rejected motion would have allowed them *to do* the first rather than *[to] suffer* the second. *Members of the jury* must be the logical subject of both options, and both must be expressed in parallel form, that is, as infinitive clauses. E, the best choice, observes these requirements. In A and C, the phrase *members of the jury* is not the logical subject of the second option, *to confine them* or *confining them*, since jury members are not doing the confining. In B and D, *confined* and *confinement* are not infinitives and thus do not parallel *to go* in the first option.

187. In one of the bloodiest battles of the Civil War, fought at Sharpsburg, Maryland, on September 17, 1862, four times as many <u>Americans were killed as</u> would later be killed on the beaches of Normandy during D-Day.

(A) Americans were killed as
(B) Americans were killed than
(C) Americans were killed than those who
(D) more Americans were killed as there
(E) more Americans were killed as those who

Choice A, the best answer, is the only option that accurately expresses the comparison by using the idiomatic form *as many . . . as*. In B and C, *as many . . . than* is unidiomatic, and in C and E, *those who* is a wordy intrusion. In D and E, *more* is redundant because the phrase *four times as many* in the original sentence conveys the idea of *more*.

188. As a result of medical advances, many people <u>that might at one time have died as children</u> of such infections as diphtheria, pneumonia, or rheumatic fever now live well into old age.

(A) that might at one time have died as children
(B) who might once have died in childhood
(C) that as children might once have died
(D) who in childhood might have at one time died
(E) who, when they were children, might at one time have died

B, the best choice, uses the preferred relative pronoun, *who*, to refer to *many people*. It observes formal and logical parallelism in the wording of the relative clause and the main clause: first, adverbs (*once* and *now*); second, verbs (*might have died* and *live*); and third, adverbial prepositional phrases (*in childhood* and *into old age*). A and C use the questionable relative pronoun *that* to refer to *many people*. They also violate the parallel structure noted above. D and E, although they use the correct pronoun, *who*, offer convoluted and nonparallel structures for the relative clause.

189. Proponents of artificial intelligence say they will be able to make computers that can understand English and other human languages, recognize objects, and reason <u>as an expert does—computers that will be used to diagnose equipment breakdowns, deciding whether to authorize a loan, or other purposes such as these</u>.

(A) as an expert does—computers that will be used to diagnose equipment breakdowns, deciding whether to authorize a loan, or other purposes such as these
(B) as an expert does, which may be used for purposes such as diagnosing equipment breakdowns or deciding whether to authorize a loan
(C) like an expert—computers that will be used for such purposes as diagnosing equipment breakdowns or deciding whether to authorize a loan
(D) like an expert, the use of which would be for purposes like the diagnosis of equipment breakdowns or the decision whether or not a loan should be authorized
(E) like an expert, to be used to diagnose equipment breakdowns, deciding whether to authorize a loan or not, or the like

A correct sentence must maintain parallel structure. In choice A, the three-part series (*to diagnose . . . , deciding, . . . or other purposes . . .*) lacks parallelism. C, the best choice, replaces A's third element with *for such purposes as*; this phrase functions as a stem for the other two elements, which are recast as two parallel phrases—*diagnosing . . . or deciding . . . .* Thus, choice C not only manages the parallel structure but avoids the less effective *other purposes such as these* at the end of choice A. Choice E uses faulty parallel structure (*to be used...*, *deciding...*, *or the like*). In B and D, *which* and *the use of which* introduce sentence elements that lack antecedents or reference. In addition, D is wordy.

190. Manifestations of Islamic political militancy in the first period of religious reformism were the rise of the Wahhabis in Arabia, the Sanusi in Cyrenaica, the Fulani in Nigeria, the Mahdi in the Sudan, and the victory of the Usuli "mujtahids" in Shiite Iran and Iraq.

   (A) Manifestations of Islamic political militancy in the first period of religious reformism were the rise of the Wahhabis in Arabia, the Sanusi in Cyrenaica, the Fulani in Nigeria, the Mahdi in the Sudan, and

   (B) Manifestations of Islamic political militancy in the first period of religious reformism were shown in the rise of the Wahhabis in Arabia, the Sanusi in Cyrenaica, the Fulani in Nigeria, the Mahdi in the Sudan, and also

   (C) In the first period of religious reformism, manifestations of Islamic political militancy were the rise of the Wahhabis in Arabia, of the Sanusi in Cyrenaica, the Fulani in Nigeria, the Mahdi in the Sudan, and

   (D) In the first period of religious reformism, manifestations of Islamic political militancy were shown in the rise of the Wahhabis in Arabia, the Sanusi in Cyrenaica, the Fulani in Nigeria, the Mahdi in the Sudan, and

   (E) In the first period of religious reformism, Islamic political militancy was manifested in the rise of the Wahhabis in Arabia, the Sanusi in Cyrenaica, the Fulani in Nigeria, and the Mahdi in the Sudan, and in

E, the best choice, uses parallel phrases for the two major coordinate members (*in the rise of... and in the victory of ...*) and also for the series listed in the first of these (*s in t, u in v, w in x, and y in z*). E's placement of the *In... reformism* phrase at the beginning of the sentence is direct and efficient. Choices A, B, C, and D omit *and* before *the Mahdi*, the last element in the first series; thus, they incorrectly merge the second major member (*the victory of*) into the series listed under the first member (*the rise of*). Furthermore, in A and B the *in... reformism* phrase has been awkwardly set between the subject and verb of the sentence.

191. Lawmakers are examining measures that would require banks to disclose all fees and account requirements in writing, provide free cashing of government checks, and to create basic savings accounts to carry minimal fees and require minimal initial deposits.

   (A) provide free cashing of government checks, and to create basic savings accounts to carry

   (B) provide free cashing of government checks, and creating basic savings accounts carrying

   (C) to provide free cashing of government checks, and creating basic savings accounts that carry

   (D) to provide free cashing of government checks, creating basic savings accounts to carry

   (E) to provide free cashing of government checks, and to create basic savings accounts that carry

Choice E, the best answer, is the only choice that maintains parallelism with the infinitive phrases *to disclose...*, [*to*] *provide...*, and *to create....* In A and B, the second element lacks the infinitive marker *to*. Choice C loses parallelism by shifting to a participial phrase, *creating....* Choice D loses parallelism by dropping the conjunction *and*; a modification problem results because the participial phrase *creating...* attaches to the noun *checks*, thus distorting the meaning of the last element of the parallel construction.

192. Cajuns speak a dialect brought to southern Louisiana by the four thousand Acadians who migrated there in 1755; their language is basically seventeenth-century French to which has been added English, Spanish, and Italian words.

   (A) to which has been added English, Spanish, and Italian words

   (B) added to which is English, Spanish, and Italian words

   (C) to which English, Spanish, and Italian words have been added

   (D) with English, Spanish, and Italian words having been added to it

   (E) and, in addition, English, Spanish, and Italian words are added

The underlined section must modify the noun phrase *seventeenth-century French* by noting additions made to French subsequently from foreign vocabularies. C, the best choice, does this clearly, directly, and correctly in the form of a relative clause. Because the subject of this clause is plural (*words*), the verb must also be plural (*have been added*). A and B incorrectly use singular forms *has been added* and *is added*. B also awkwardly inverts and divides the verb phrase (*added... is*). D offers an awkward adverbial construction, which cannot be used to modify nouns. E offers an incoherent and incomplete new clause with the wrong verb tense and no logical complement for *are added*— that is, we are not told to what the words are added.

193. <u>Unlike the United States, where farmers can usually depend on rain or snow all year long, the rains in most parts of Sri Lanka</u> are concentrated in the monsoon months, June to September, and the skies are generally clear for the rest of the year.

   (A) Unlike the United States, where farmers can usually depend on rain or snow all year long, the rains in most parts of Sri Lanka
   (B) Unlike the United States farmers who can usually depend on rain or snow all year long, the rains in most parts of Sri Lanka
   (C) Unlike those of the United States, where farmers can usually depend on rain or snow all year long, most parts of Sri Lanka's rains
   (D) In comparison with the United States, whose farmers can usually depend on rain or snow all year long, the rains in most parts of Sri Lanka
   (E) In the United States, farmers can usually depend on rain or snow all year long, but in most parts of Sri Lanka the rains

In comparative structures *(unlike X, Y . . . ; in comparison with X, Y . . .)* X and Y must be both logically and grammatically parallel. Choices A, B, C, and D all fail to observe logical parallelism: (A) *Unlike the United States, . . . the rains . . . ;* (B) *Unlike the United States farmers . . . , the rains . . . ;* (C) *Unlike those of the United States, . . . most parts of Sri Lanka's rains . . . ;* and (D) *In comparison with the United States, . . . the rains . . . .* C also suffers from the unintelligible *most parts of Sri Lanka's rains.* E, the best choice, avoids the problem by using two independent clauses linked by *but* to present a clear, direct contrast between conditions *in the United States* and those *in most parts of Sri Lanka.*

194. Presenters at the seminar, <u>one who</u> is blind, will demonstrate adaptive equipment that allows visually impaired people to use computers.

   (A) one who
   (B) one of them who
   (C) and one of them who
   (D) one of whom
   (E) one of which

The subject, *presenters*, must be followed by a limiting appositive — such as *one of whom*, that identifies an individual from among a larger group. Choice D is best: *one of whom* best serves an appositive to the subject, *presenters*, because the phrase means "one from among several or many." Choice A, *one who*, is unacceptable because *one who* cannot refer to the plural *presenters*. Choices B and C are ungrammatical because *who* competes with *one* as the subject of *is*. Choice E employs *which*, a relative pronoun that does not refer to people *(presenters),* but only to things.

195. Dr. Tonegawa won the Nobel Prize for discovering how the body can constantly change its genes to fashion a <u>seeming unlimited number of antibodies, each specifically targeted at</u> an invading microbe or foreign substance.

   (A) seeming unlimited number of antibodies, each specifically targeted at
   (B) seeming unlimited number of antibodies, each targeted specifically to
   (C) seeming unlimited number of antibodies, all specifically targeted at
   (D) seemingly unlimited number of antibodies, all of them targeted specifically to
   (E) seemingly unlimited number of antibodies, each targeted specifically at

Choices A, B, and C incorrectly use the adjective form *seeming* to modify the participial adjective *unlimited*. B also uses the unidiomatic preposition *to* instead of the correct *at* after *targeted*, while C violates sense by having *all* the antibodies *specifically* targeted at *an*, that is, *one,* invading microbe or substance. Choice D correctly uses *seemingly,* but it repeats B's incorrect use of *targeted to* and C's illogical *all . . . specifically.* Only E, the best choice, correctly uses the form *seemingly* to modify *unlimited,* the correct preposition, *at,* with *targeted,* and the logically correct *each,* which links the specific antibodies to specific microbes or substances.

196. It is possible that Native Americans originally <u>have migrated to the Western Hemisphere over a bridge of land that once existed</u> between Siberia and Alaska.

   (A) have migrated to the Western Hemisphere over a bridge of land that once existed
   (B) were migrating to the Western Hemisphere over a bridge of land that existed once
   (C) migrated over a bridge of land to the Western Hemisphere that once existed
   (D) migrated to the Western Hemisphere over a bridge of land that once existed
   (E) were migrating to the Western Hemisphere over a bridge of land existing once

Choice D, the best answer, correctly uses the past-tense verb forms *migrated* and *existed* to refer to actions completed in the past. Choices A, B, and E present incorrect verb forms for expressing simple past action, and *existing once* in E is imprecise. Although choice C manages the correct tense, it misplaces the sentence elements so as to suggest that the Western Hemisphere *once existed between Siberia and Alaska.*

197. In the fall of 1985, only 10 percent of the women entering college planned to major in education, while 28 percent chose business, making it the most popular major for women <u>as well as for men</u>.

    (A) as well as for men
    (B) as well as the men
    (C) and men too
    (D) and men as well
    (E) and also men

Two elements connected by a coordinate conjunction should be expressed in parallel form. Only A, the best choice, correctly observes this rule (*the most popular major for women as well as for men*). B, C, D, and E omit the necessary *for* in the second element. In addition, by using the simple coordinate conjunction *and*, C, D, and E create the illogical impression that the decision of 28 percent of the women entering college in 1985 to choose business as a major *also* made the major the most popular among men. The conjunction *as well as* implies that business had already been the most popular major for men and that in 1985, for the first time, it became the most popular major for both sexes.

198. Although Napoleon's army entered Russia with far more supplies than <u>they had in their previous campaigns</u>, it had provisions for only twenty-four days.

    (A) they had in their previous campaigns
    (B) their previous campaigns had had
    (C) they had for any previous campaign
    (D) in their previous campaigns
    (E) for any previous campaign

If *than* is followed by a clause referring to *army*, the subject of that clause must be singular (*it*). Furthermore, the verb of that clause will need to be in the past perfect form (*had had*) because it refers to a time *before* the simple past of *entered*. Finally, the preposition *for* is more precise than *in* because supplies are gathered *for* an upcoming campaign. Choices A and C incorrectly use the plural *they* and the simple past *had*. Moreover, A uses the less precise *in*. Choices D and E wisely dispense with the full clause and use a simple prepositional phrase. D, however, uses the imprecise *in* and the plural *their*. Only E, the best choice, avoids all the errors mentioned above.

199. Because the Earth's crust is more solid there and thus better able to transmit shock waves, an earthquake <u>of a given magnitude typically devastates an area 100 times greater in the eastern United States than it does in the West</u>.

    (A) of a given magnitude typically devastates an area 100 times greater in the eastern United States than it does in the West
    (B) of a given magnitude will typically devastate 100 times the area if it occurs in the eastern United States instead of the West
    (C) will typically devastate 100 times the area in the eastern United States than one of comparable magnitude occurring in the West
    (D) in the eastern United States will typically devastate an area 100 times greater than will a quake of comparable magnitude occurring in the West
    (E) that occurs in the eastern United States will typically devastate 100 times more area than if it occurred with comparable magnitude in the West

At issue is the accurate expression of a complex comparison. Choice D, the best answer, presents the proper form of comparison, *will typically devastate an area 100 times greater than will*; thus, choice D logically indicates that earthquakes in the eastern United States are 100 times more devastating than are western earthquakes. Choices A, B, and E use *it* incorrectly to suggest that the same quake strikes both the eastern and the western United States. In choice C, *100 times the area . . . than* is unidiomatic.

200. <u>Certain pesticides can become ineffective if used repeatedly in the same place; one reason is suggested by the finding that there are much larger populations of pesticide-degrading microbes in soils with a relatively long history of pesticide use than in soils that are free of such chemicals.</u>

(A) Certain pesticides can become ineffective if used repeatedly in the same place; one reason is suggested by the finding that there are much larger populations of pesticide-degrading microbes in soils with a relatively long history of pesticide use than in soils that are free of such chemicals.

(B) If used repeatedly in the same place, one reason that certain pesticides can become ineffective is suggested by the finding that there are much larger populations of pesticide-degrading microbes in soils with a relatively long history of pesticide use than in soils that are free of such chemicals.

(C) If used repeatedly in the same place, one reason certain pesticides can become ineffective is suggested by the finding that much larger populations of pesticide-degrading microbes are found in soils with a relatively long history of pesticide use than those that are free of such chemicals.

(D) The finding that there are much larger populations of pesticide-degrading microbes in soils with a relatively long history of pesticide use than in soils that are free of such chemicals is suggestive of one reason, if used repeatedly in the same place, certain pesticides can become ineffective.

(E) The finding of much larger populations of pesticide-degrading microbes in soils with a relatively long history of pesticide use than in those that are free of such chemicals suggests one reason certain pesticides can become ineffective if used repeatedly in the same place.

Choice A, the best answer, is the only one that manages syntactic control of the sentence. The sentence consists of two independent clauses, beginning *Certain pesticides . . .* and *one reason*, which are connected by a semicolon. Dangling or misplaced modifiers plague choices B, C, and D: in each case, the phrase *if used repeatedly in the same place* illogically modifies *one reason* rather than *certain pesticides*. In choice E, *The finding of much larger populations . . . than in those that* is an improperly constructed comparison.

201. One view of the economy contends that a large drop in oil prices should eventually lead to <u>lowering interest rates, as well as lowering fears about inflation,</u> a rally in stocks and bonds, and a weakening of the dollar.

(A) lowering interest rates, as well as lowering fears about inflation,

(B) a lowering of interest rates and of fears about inflation,

(C) a lowering of interest rates, along with fears about inflation,

(D) interest rates being lowered, along with fears about inflation,

(E) interest rates and fears about inflation being lowered, with

At issue is the need for logical and formal parallelism in a coordinate series. B, the best choice, clearly and correctly uses parallel noun phrases to list three effects of a drop in oil prices: *a lowering of . . . , a rally in . . . , and a weakening of . . . .* In place of the correct *lower* before *fears*, choice A uses an incorrect participial adjective, *lowering,* that could cause confusion by seeming at first to function as a verb. A also violates parallelism. In C and D, the use of *along with* confuses meaning by making *fears about inflation* an independent effect, not an object of *lowering*. D and E violate parallelism by substituting an awkward gerund clause for the first noun phrase.

202. After the Civil War, contemporaries of Harriet <u>Tubman's maintained that she has</u> all of the qualities of a great leader: coolness in the face of danger, an excellent sense of strategy, and an ability to plan in minute detail.

(A) Tubman's maintained that she has
(B) Tubman's maintain that she had
(C) Tubman's have maintained that she had
(D) Tubman maintained that she had
(E) Tubman had maintained that she has

In choice D, the best answer, the phrase *contemporaries of Harriet Tubman* presents a complete possessive without adding an apostrophe (e.g., *Tubman's*). Choices A, B, and C use a redundant possessive: *contemporaries of Harriet Tubman's*. All choices other than D have errors in verb tense. Because the sentence describes essentially simultaneous actions completed in the past, the simple past tense forms *maintained* and *had* are required. Thus, the present tense forms *has* and *maintain* are incorrect in A, B, and E, as are the present perfect *have maintained* in C and the past perfect *had maintained* in E.

203. <u>From 1982 to 1987 sales of new small boats increased between five and ten percent annually.</u>

(A) From 1982 to 1987 sales of new small boats increased between five and ten percent annually.
(B) Five to ten percent is the annual increase in sales of new small boats in the years 1982 to 1987.
(C) Sales of new small boats have increased annually five and ten percent in the years 1982 to 1987.
(D) Annually an increase of five to ten percent has occurred between 1982 and 1987 in the sales of new small boats.
(E) Occurring from 1982 to 1987 was an annual increase of five and ten percent in the sales of new small boats.

A, the best choice, conveys the relevant information clearly and directly. Because the focus of interest is the *sales of new small boats*, that should be the subject of the sentence. Since the period of time covered began and ended in the past, the verb should be in the simple past tense (*increased*). The adverb *annually* fits most logically after the amount of the increases. B, C, D, and E all distort the focus and disrupt the sensible order of ideas. In addition, B, C, and D use incorrect verb tenses to refer to the simple past (*is, have increased,* and *has occurred*). In C, the expression *five and ten percent* makes no sense without the word *between*. Finally, E is especially clumsy and confused.

204. In recent years cattle breeders have increasingly used crossbreeding, <u>in part that their steers should acquire certain characteristics</u> and partly because crossbreeding is said to provide hybrid vigor.

(A) in part that their steers should acquire certain characteristics
(B) in part for the acquisition of certain characteristics in their steers
(C) partly because of their steers acquiring certain characteristics
(D) partly because certain characteristics should be acquired by their steers
(E) partly to acquire certain characteristics in their steers

Choice E is best; it best indicates purpose for crossbreeding— *partly to acquire*. In A, *in part that* does not grammatically connect the underlined portion to the first part of the sentence (the independent clause). In both A and B, *in part* is not parallel with *and partly* in the nonunderlined portion. Choice C causes a misreading, suggesting that the steers' acquisition has *caused* the crossbreeding. D awkwardly and illogically shifts to the passive voice: *certain characteristics should be acquired by their steers*; the steers, however, are not agents in the acquisition.

205. The peaks of a mountain range, acting like rocks in a streambed, produce ripples in the air flowing over them; the resulting flow pattern, with <u>crests and troughs that remain stationary although the air that forms them is moving rapidly, are</u> known as "standing waves."

(A) crests and troughs that remain stationary although the air that forms them is moving rapidly, are
(B) crests and troughs that remain stationary although they are formed by rapidly moving air, are
(C) crests and troughs that remain stationary although the air that forms them is moving rapidly, is
(D) stationary crests and troughs although the air that forms them is moving rapidly, are
(E) stationary crests and troughs although they are formed by rapidly moving air, is

The main challenge in this sentence is to observe the agreement of subject and verb (*the resulting flow pattern . . . is known . . .*) despite the distraction of a complex intervening structure containing several plural elements (*with crests and troughs . . .*). Choices A, B, and D can, therefore, be eliminated because they use an incorrect plural verb form, *are*. Choice E uses the correct verb form, *is*, but it incorrectly introduces a dependent adverbial *although* clause into a prepositional phrase (*with crests . . .*). Choice D also makes this error. Such dependent clauses can only occur in the predicates of full clauses. C, the best choice, uses the correct verb form, *is*, and correctly puts the *although* clause inside the predicate of the relative clause (*that . . . rapidly*).

206. <u>Like Auden, the language of James Merrill</u> is chatty, arch, and conversational—given to complex syntactic flights as well as to prosaic free-verse strolls.

(A) Like Auden, the language of James Merrill
(B) Like Auden, James Merrill's language
(C) Like Auden's, James Merrill's language
(D) As with Auden, James Merrill's language
(E) As is Auden's the language of James Merrill

At issue is a comparison of Auden's language with Merrill's language. Only C, the best choice, uses the elliptical *like Auden's* (*language* being understood), to compare Auden's language with Merrill's language. A, B, and D compare Auden (the person) with Merrill's language. Choice E is awkward and unidiomatic.

207. In the textbook publishing business, the second quarter is historically weak, because revenues are <u>low and marketing expenses are high as companies prepare</u> for the coming school year.

(A) low and marketing expenses are high as companies prepare

(B) low and their marketing expenses are high as they prepare

(C) low with higher marketing expenses in preparation

(D) low, while marketing expenses are higher to prepare

(E) low, while their marketing expenses are higher in preparation

A, the best choice, correctly balances the contrasting terms *low* and *high* in parallel form (adjectives in the positive degree). It also makes clear who, exactly, is preparing for the coming school year (*companies*). B uses the plural pronouns *their* and *they* without an appropriately stated referent. C, D, and E violate the parallelism needed for the contrasting terms by making the second term an adjective in the comparative degree (*higher*). Furthermore, the use of *higher* without a stated point of comparison makes it unclear what the expenses are higher than. E also uses the pronoun *their* without an appropriate referent.

208. Teratomas are unusual forms of cancer <u>because they are composed of tissues such as tooth and bone</u> not normally found in the organ in which the tumor appears.

(A) because they are composed of tissues such as tooth and bone

(B) because they are composed of tissues like tooth and bone that are

(C) because they are composed of tissues, like tooth and bone, tissues

(D) in that their composition, tissues such as tooth and bone, is

(E) in that they are composed of tissues such as tooth and bone, tissues

Only E, the best choice, clearly states that teratomas consist of tissues such as tooth and bone, and that such tissues are not normally found in the organ with the teratoma. Clear statement of this fact requires the repetition of *tissues* to establish the appositive—*tissues normally found* . . . . Without such repetition, A and B imprecisely state that the *tooth and bone*, as opposed to the *tissues*, are not normally found in the affected organ. Choices B and C alter the meaning with the use of *like*; that is, they suggest that the tissues are not tooth and bone, but only *like* them. The confused syntax of D states that *their composition*, not the tissues, *is found in the organ* . . . .

209. The Senate approved immigration legislation that would grant permanent residency to millions of aliens currently residing here and <u>if employers hired illegal aliens they would be penalized</u>.

(A) if employers hired illegal aliens they would be penalized

(B) hiring illegal aliens would be a penalty for employers

(C) penalize employers who hire illegal aliens

(D) penalizing employers hiring illegal aliens

(E) employers to be penalized for hiring illegal aliens

The sentence contains a relative clause (*that . . .*) indicating, in its compound predicate, two effects of the *immigration legislation*: (it) *would grant x and (would) penalize y*. The auxiliary *would* may be omitted before *penalize*, but the main verbs must remain parallel. Only C, the best choice, observes these conditions. A and B produce incoherent, fused sentences in which the two main clauses are not parallel. Furthermore, in A the referent of *they* is unclear, and in B the statement *hiring illegal aliens would be a penalty* makes no sense. D violates parallel structure by substituting a present participle (*penalizing*) for the second main verb. E introduces an incoherent passive infinitive construction that violates sense and parallel structure.

210. Scientists have recently discovered what could be the largest and oldest living organism on Earth, a giant fungus that is an interwoven filigree of mushrooms and rootlike tentacles spawned by a single fertilized spore some 10,000 years ago and <u>extending</u> for more than 30 acres in the soil of a Michigan forest.

(A) extending

(B) extends

(C) extended

(D) it extended

(E) is extending

Choice A, the best answer, preserves grammatical parallelism while allowing for logical expression of temporal relationships; A employs the parallel participial phrases *spawned . . . and extending . . .* to modify *filigree*. Other choices present different grammatical constructions that are not participial modifiers and thus not parallel to *spawned*: *extends* in B is a present-tense verb; *it extended* in D begins a new clause; and *is extending* in E ungrammatically introduces a new predicate. In C, *extended* is nonparallel if it is assumed to be a past tense verb form; if it is assumed to be a past participle, it illogically states, as does D, that the filigree extended only in the past.

211. The period when the great painted caves at Lascaux and Altamira were occupied by Upper Paleolithic people <u>has been established by carbon-14 dating, but what is much more difficult to determine are</u> the reason for their decoration, the use to which primitive people put the caves, and the meaning of the magnificently depicted animals.

(A) has been established by carbon-14 dating, but what is much more difficult to determine are

(B) has been established by carbon-14 dating, but what is much more difficult to determine is

(C) have been established by carbon-14 dating, but what is much more difficult to determine is

(D) have been established by carbon-14 dating, but what is much more difficult to determine are

(E) are established by carbon-14 dating, but that which is much more difficult to determine is

Two instances of subject-verb agreement must be observed in this sentence: *The period . . . has been established* and *what is much more difficult to determine . . . is*. Both clauses have singular subjects and must have singular verbs. Only B, the best choice, observes these requirements. A incorrectly uses the plural form *are* in the second clause. Choices C and D incorrectly use the plural form *have* in the first clause, and D incorrectly uses *are* in the second clause as well. E incorrectly uses the plural form *are* in the first clause. Furthermore, because the date of the period in question was established before the writing of the sentence, the verb of that clause must be in the present perfect form (*has been established*).

212. The Baldrick Manufacturing Company has for several years followed a policy <u>aimed at decreasing operating costs and improving</u> the efficiency of its distribution system.

(A) aimed at decreasing operating costs and improving

(B) aimed at the decreasing of operating costs and to improve

(C) aiming at the decreasing of operating costs and improving

(D) the aim of which is the decreasing of operating costs and improving

(E) with the aim to decrease operating costs and to improve

The best choice, A, offers an adjective phrase unequivocally modifying *policy* and exhibiting grammatical parallelism (*decreasing . . .* and *improving*). In choice B, the gerund *the decreasing* is not grammatically parallel with the infinitive *to improve*. Likewise, in C and D, *the decreasing of . . . costs* is not parallel with *improving the efficiency*. In E, the infinitives *to decrease* and *to improve*, while parallel, are less idiomatic than the prepositional phrase *of decreasing . . . and improving* in modifying the noun *aim*. Also, *with the aim . . . improve* can easily be construed as referring to the Baldrick Manufacturing Company and so does not refer unequivocally to *policy*.

213. *The Federalist* papers, a strong defense of the United States Constitution <u>and important as a body of work in political science as well, represents</u> the handiwork of three different authors.

(A) and important as a body of work in political science as well, represents

(B) as well as an important body of work in political science, represent

(C) and also a body of work of importance in political science is representing

(D) an important body of work in political science and has been representative of

(E) and as political science an important body of work too, represent

Choices A, C, and D contain singular verbs that do not agree in number with the plural subject, *papers*. Furthermore, A violates parallelism by aligning the adjective *important* with the noun *defense*; C, employing the present progressive tense, wrongly suggests that the triple authorship of *The Federalist* papers is a developing situation rather than an accomplished fact; and D, employing the present perfect tense, suggests that the situation of triple authorship is no longer the case. D is also garbled syntactically because the conjunction *and* has been misplaced. In E, the wording is awkward. Choice B is best.

214. Although the term "psychopath" is popularly applied to an especially brutal criminal, in psychology <u>it is someone who is</u> apparently incapable of feeling compassion or the pangs of conscience.

(A) it is someone who is

(B) it is a person

(C) they are people who are

(D) it refers to someone who is

(E) it is in reference to people

In choices A and B, the pronoun *it* simultaneously refers forward to *someone* (or a *person*) and backward to the term "*psychopath*." As a result, the sentence asserts illogically that the term is actually a kind of person rather than a word referring to a kind of person. Choice C repeats this fault and adds an error in agreement: *they* (plural) does not agree in number with *the term* (singular). E omits a main verb, such as *applied*, that, in grammatical context here, is required after *is*. Also, the word *people* incorrectly shifts number from singular to plural. In choice D, the best answer, the verb *refers* is correctly used after *it*, and the alignment of pronouns and antecedents is both logical and grammatical.

215. Parliament did not accord full refugee benefits to twelve of the recent immigrants because it believed that <u>to do it rewards</u> them for entering the country illegally.

(A) to do it rewards
(B) doing it rewards
(C) to do this would reward
(D) doing so would reward
(E) to do it would reward

Choice D, the best answer, appropriately uses the adverb *so* to refer back to the verb *accord*. The other choices inappropriately use pronouns (*it* or *this*) to refer back to the verb. Also, A and B use the indicative verb *rewards*, whereas the logic of the sentence demands the conditional *would reward* (what Parliament believes to be the undue rewarding of illegal immigrants has not actually taken place but is considered only as an outcome of a hypothetical action).

216. Many policy experts say that shifting a portion of health-benefit costs back to the workers <u>helps to control the employer's costs, but also helps</u> to limit medical spending by making patients more careful consumers.

(A) helps to control the employer's costs, but also helps
(B) helps the control of the employer's costs, and also
(C) not only helps to control the employer's costs, but also helps
(D) helps to control not only the employer's costs, but
(E) not only helps to control the employer's costs, and also helps

To convey the idea that shifting a portion of health-benefit costs back to workers has two complementary effects, the correct sentence must link grammatically parallel statements of these effects with *and also* or with *not only . . . but also*. In choice A, *helps . . . but also* undermines the *and also* paradigm, wrongly suggesting a contrast in the effects. In choice E, the unidiomatic *not only . . . and* violates the *not only . . . but also* paradigm. Choices B and D are not parallel. Also, the phrase *helps the control* in B is vague and unidiomatic. Choice C, the best answer, develops the parallel *not only helps to . . . but also helps to*.

217. The plot of *The Bostonians* centers on the <u>rivalry between Olive Chancellor, an active feminist, with her charming and cynical cousin, Basil Ransom,</u> when they find themselves drawn to the same radiant young woman whose talent for public speaking has won her an ardent following.

(A) rivalry between Olive Chancellor, an active feminist, with her charming and cynical cousin, Basil Ransom
(B) rivals Olive Chancellor, an active feminist, against her charming and cynical cousin, Basil Ransom
(C) rivalry that develops between Olive Chancellor, an active feminist, and Basil Ransom, her charming and cynical cousin
(D) developing rivalry between Olive Chancellor, an active feminist, with Basil Ransom, her charming and cynical cousin
(E) active feminist, Olive Chancellor, and the rivalry with her charming and cynical cousin Basil Ransom

The enumeration of the rivals requires the conjunction *and*: either *the rivalry between x and y* or *the rivals x and y*. Choices A and D wrongly substitute *with* for *and* in the first paradigm; choice B wrongly substitutes *against* for *and* in the second. Choice E does not clearly state that Chancellor is party to the rivalry. E also awkwardly pairs *Chancellor* and *rivalry*, not *Chancellor* and *Ransom*, as antecedents of *they*. Choice C, the best answer, correctly uses the *between x and y* paradigm and clearly and unequivocally identifies both parties in the rivalry.

218. Despite protests from some waste-disposal companies, state health officials have ordered <u>the levels of bacteria in seawater at popular beaches to be measured and that the results be</u> published.

(A) the levels of bacteria in seawater at popular beaches to be measured and that the results be
(B) that seawater at popular beaches should be measured for their levels of bacteria, with the results being
(C) the measure of levels of bacteria in seawater at popular beaches and the results to be
(D) seawater measured at popular beaches for levels of bacteria, with their results
(E) that the levels of bacteria in seawater at popular beaches be measured and the results

In this sentence, English idiom requires one of two paradigms: *x ordered y to be z'ed* or *x ordered that y be z'ed*. Choice E, the best answer, employs the second of these paradigms. Choice A mixes the two paradigms (*levels . . . to be measured* and *that the results be published*), producing a sentence that lacks parallelism. C and D use neither paradigm and are thus unidiomatic. Also, in D, the pronoun *their* has no logical and grammatical antecedent. Choice B unidiomatically employs the verb *should* (not in either paradigm); also, the pronoun *their* does not agree in number with *seawater*, its most logical antecedent.

219. While larger banks can afford to maintain their own data-processing operations, many smaller regional and community banks are finding that the cost associated with upgrading data-processing equipment and with the development and maintenance of new products and technical staff are prohibitive.

(A) cost associated with
(B) costs associated with
(C) costs arising from
(D) cost of
(E) costs of

The correct option must offer a noun that agrees in number with the plural verb *are*, the second-to-last word in the sentence, to produce the grammatical sequence *costs . . . are prohibitive*. Also, the best answer will use the preposition *with* to complete the parallel construction *costs associated with upgrading . . . and with the development . . . .* Choice B, the best answer, is the only option that meets both requirements.

220. For almost a hundred years after having its beginning in 1788, England exiled some 160,000 criminals to Australia.

(A) For almost a hundred years after having its beginning in 1788,
(B) Beginning in 1788 for a period of a hundred years,
(C) Beginning a period of almost a hundred years, in 1788
(D) During a hundred years, a period beginning in 1788,
(E) Over a period of a hundred years beginning in 1788,

Aside from being wordy and awkward, choice A is illogical: because *its* refers grammatically to *England*, A states nonsensically that England had *its beginning in 1788*. Choice B is similarly illogical, because the initial verb phrase *Beginning in 1788 . . .* modifies *England*, the subject of the main clause. Choice C is imprecise, saying that England in 1788 was *Beginning a period . . .* but not conveying the sense that anything happened within that period. Choice D is awkward and unidiomatic, and nonsensically suggests that *a hundred years* is defined as *a period beginning in 1788*. Precise and idiomatically phrased, choice E is best.

221. Eating saltwater fish may significantly reduce the risk of heart attacks and also aid for sufferers of rheumatoid arthritis and asthma, according to three research studies published in the *New England Journal of Medicine*.

(A) significantly reduce the risk of heart attacks and also aid for
(B) be significant in reducing the risk of heart attacks and aid for
(C) significantly reduce the risk of heart attacks and aid
(D) cause a significant reduction in the risk of heart attacks and aid to
(E) significantly reduce the risk of heart attacks as well as aiding

Choices A, B, and D each produce a clearly unintended meaning: by using *aid* as a noun rather than a verb, each creates a misleading parallel with the noun *risk* so that the sentences nonsensically state that eating saltwater fish may reduce *aid* as well as *risk*. In addition, B and D are wordy and awkward. Choice C, the best answer, avoids the prepositions *for* (from A and B) and *to* (from D), instead using *aid* as a verb that is parallel with *reduce*. Choice E lacks the grammatical parallelism of *may reduce . . . and aid*, the compound verb in C.

222. By a vote of 9 to 0, the Supreme Court awarded the Central Intelligence Agency broad discretionary powers enabling it to withhold from the public the identities of its sources of intelligence information.

(A) enabling it to withhold from the public
(B) for it to withhold from the public
(C) for withholding disclosure to the public of
(D) that enable them to withhold from public disclosure
(E) that they can withhold public disclosure of

Choice A is best: *enabling . . .* clearly modifies *powers*, *it* refers logically and grammatically to *the Central Intelligence Agency*, and *to withhold from the public* is concisely and idiomatically phrased. In choices B and C, the preposition *for* is used unidiomatically in place of the "-ing" modifier to introduce the phrase describing *powers*. In choices C, D, and E, *withhold(ing) . . . disclosure* is wordy and imprecise, since it is really *the identities* that are to be withheld. The plural pronouns *them* in D and *they* in E do not agree with the singular *Agency*, and *that* in E mistakenly introduces a new independent clause rather than a modifying phrase for *powers*.

223. As business grows more complex, students <u>majoring in specialized areas like those of finance and marketing have been becoming increasingly</u> successful in the job market.

   (A) majoring in specialized areas like those of finance and marketing have been becoming increasingly
   (B) who major in such specialized areas as finance and marketing are becoming more and more
   (C) who majored in specialized areas such as those of finance and marketing are being increasingly
   (D) who major in specialized areas like those of finance and marketing have been becoming more and more
   (E) having majored in such specialized areas as finance and marketing are being increasingly

The phrase *As business grows more complex* introduces an ongoing condition that is leading to consequences described in the rest of the sentence. Those consequences should, like the causal condition, be expressed with simple present-tense or present progressive verb forms. Only choice B, the best answer, consistently employs these forms: *who major . . . and . . . are becoming*. In A and D, the use of *like* rather than *such as* is incorrect: *like* makes a comparison; *such as* introduces examples. In A, C, and D, *those of* is unnecessary verbiage, and *being* in C and E is less precise than *becoming* for describing a pattern of events that is unfolding.

224. Inuits of the Bering Sea were <u>in isolation from contact with Europeans longer than</u> Aleuts or Inuits of the North Pacific and northern Alaska.

   (A) in isolation from contact with Europeans longer than
   (B) isolated from contact with Europeans longer than
   (C) in isolation from contact with Europeans longer than were
   (D) isolated from contact with Europeans longer than were
   (E) in isolation and without contacts with Europeans longer than

The phrasing of the comparisons in choices A, B, and E is incomplete, so the comparisons are ambiguous: because *longer than* could be followed by either *from* or *were*, it is unclear whether Inuits of the Bering Sea were isolated from Europeans longer than from the other Native American groups, or whether they were isolated from Europeans longer than the other groups were. In A and C, *in isolation from contact* is wordy and unidiomatic. The awkward phrasing of E further distorts the sense of the sentence: because *with* cannot idiomatically serve as the preposition for *in isolation*, the sentence suggests that the Bering Sea Inuits were totally isolated. Choice D is best: it employs concise, idiomatic phrasing to express a logically complete comparison.

225. Minnesota is the only one of the contiguous forty-eight states <u>that still has a sizable wolf population, and where</u> this predator remains the archenemy of cattle and sheep.

   (A) that still has a sizable wolf population, and where
   (B) that still has a sizable wolf population, where
   (C) that still has a sizable population of wolves, and where
   (D) where the population of wolves is still sizable;
   (E) where there is still a sizable population of wolves and where

In choices A and C, the construction *that still has . . . , and where* modifies *Minnesota* with clauses that are not grammatically parallel. In choice B, the omission of *and* illogically makes the *where . . .* clause modify *wolf population* rather than *Minnesota*—that is, choice B says in effect that the wolf population is where the wolf remains the archenemy of cattle and sheep. Choice D is grammatically constructed, but it lacks a conjunction that establishes a logical relation between the clauses; since *Minnesota* as a grammatical subject is separated from the clause following the semicolon, the statement there need not even pertain to Minnesota. In E, the best choice, the parallel construction of *where . . . and where . . .* allows both clauses to modify *Minnesota*.

226. Pablo Picasso, the late Spanish painter, credited African art <u>with having had</u> a strong influence on his work.

   (A) with having had
   (B) for its having
   (C) to have had
   (D) for having
   (E) in that it had

Choice A is the best. In this sentence, where *credit(ed)* is used as a verb, the idiom in English is to *credit* something *with* having had some effect. Thus only choice A is idiomatic. Both *for* (in B and D) and *to* (in C) can be used idiomatically when *credit* is a noun, as in "Picasso gave credit to African art for having had a strong influence on his work." The verb form *having had* is used appropriately in choice A to indicate action that occurred prior to action expressed in the simple past tense—that is, to indicate that African art had influenced Picasso before he credited it with having done so.

227. Judicial rules in many states require <u>that the identities of all prosecution witnesses are made known to defendants so they can attempt to rebut</u> the testimony, but the Constitution explicitly requires only that the defendant have the opportunity to confront an accuser in court.

   (A) that the identities of all prosecution witnesses are made known to defendants so they can attempt to rebut
   (B) that the identities of all prosecution witnesses be made known to defendants so that they can attempt to rebut
   (C) that the defendants should know the identities of all prosecution witnesses so they can attempt a rebuttal of
   (D) the identities of all prosecution witnesses should be made known to defendants so they can attempt rebutting
   (E) making known to defendants the identities of all prosecution witnesses so that they can attempt to rebut

In English the subjunctive mood is used to express a wish or requirement that a certain course of action be taken. Such phrasing takes the form *to wish* [or] *require that x be y*, not *that x should be y* or *that x is y*. Choice B, therefore, is best. In place of the subjunctive, A uses the indicative *are* and E uses an awkward gerund, *making*, while C and D contain the unnecessary *should*. A and C also omit *that* after *so*, and D omits *that* after *require*. The phrase *attempt to rebut* is more idiomatic than the phrases that replace it in C and D. Choices C and E awkwardly place the plural noun *witnesses* between the plural pronoun *they* and its referent, *defendants*.

228. Quasars, at billions of light-years from Earth the most distant observable objects in the universe, <u>believed to be</u> the cores of galaxies in an early stage of development.

   (A) believed to be
   (B) are believed to be
   (C) some believe them to be
   (D) some believe they are
   (E) it is believed that they are

Only B, the best answer, supplies a verb that grammatically connects *Quasars* and *cores*: *Quasars . . . are believed to be the cores . . . .* Choice A produces a sentence fragment because it omits the verb *are* and supplies only an adjectival phrase, *believed to be . . . .* Choices C, D, and E all introduce new clauses (*some believe . . . , it is believed . . .*) that cannot grammatically complete the construction begun with *Quasars*.

229. The colorization of black-and-white films by computers is defended by those who own the film rights, for the process can mean increased revenues for them; many others in the film industry, however, contend that the technique degrades major works of art, <u>which they liken to putting lipstick on a Greek statue</u>.

   (A) which they liken to putting lipstick on a Greek statue
   (B) which they liken to a Greek statue with lipstick put on it
   (C) which they liken to lipstick put on a Greek statue
   (D) likening it to a Greek statue with lipstick put on it
   (E) likening it to putting lipstick on a Greek statue

Choice E, the best answer, correctly and logically compares *the technique* of colorization to the act of *putting lipstick on a Greek statue*. In A, B, and C, the relative pronoun *which* refers not to *the technique* but to the noun phrase immediately preceding it, *major works of art*. As a result, these works are compared to *putting lipstick on . . .* in A, to *a Greek statue* in B, and to *lipstick* in C. Choice D corrects this problem by eliminating the *which* construction and supplying the pronoun *it*, thus referring clearly to *the technique*, but it illogically compares *the technique* to *a Greek statue*.

230. <u>In reference to the current hostility toward smoking, smokers frequently expressed anxiety that</u> their prospects for being hired and promoted are being stunted by their habit.

   (A) In reference to the current hostility toward smoking, smokers frequently expressed anxiety that
   (B) Referring to the current hostility toward smoking, smokers frequently expressed anxiety about
   (C) When referring to the current hostility toward smoking, smokers frequently express anxiety about
   (D) With reference to the current hostility toward smoking, smokers frequently expressed anxiety about
   (E) Referring to the current hostility toward smoking, smokers frequently express anxiety that

Choices A, B, and D inappropriately use the past tense verb *expressed*; only the present tense is logical here, since both the *current hostility* to which the *smokers* refer and the anxiety described in the clause *their prospects . . . are being stunted* clearly apply to the present. Furthermore, B, C, and D produce ungrammatical sentences by introducing this clause with the preposition *about*; the conjunction *that* is required to link *anxiety* with the clause that modifies it. Choice E, the best answer, correctly uses both the conjunction *that* and the present-tense verb *express*.

231. Ms. Chambers is among the forecasters who predict that the rate of addition to arable lands will drop while <u>those of loss rise</u>.

    (A) those of loss rise
    (B) it rises for loss
    (C) those of losses rise
    (D) the rate of loss rises
    (E) there are rises for the rate of loss

Choice D, the best answer, uses the idiomatic and clear construction *the rate of addition . . . will drop while the rate of loss rises*. All of the other choices use incorrect, illogical, or imprecise constructions in place of *the rate of loss rises*. In A and C, the plural pronoun *those* has no plural noun to which it can logically refer. In B, *it* refers to *the rate of addition*; consequently, B makes the nonsensical statement that *the rate of addition . . . rises for loss*. Choice E supplies the idiomatic *the rate of loss* but introduces it with the unidiomatic and wordy *there are rises for*.

232. <u>Unlike auto insurance, the frequency of claims does not affect the premiums for personal property coverage</u>, but if the insurance company is able to prove excessive loss due to owner negligence, it may decline to renew the policy.

    (A) Unlike auto insurance, the frequency of claims does not affect the premiums for personal property coverage
    (B) Unlike with auto insurance, the frequency of claims do not affect the premiums for personal property coverage
    (C) Unlike the frequency of claims for auto insurance, the premiums for personal property coverage are not affected by the frequency of claims
    (D) Unlike the premiums for auto insurance, the premiums for personal property coverage are not affected by the frequency of claims
    (E) Unlike with the premiums for auto insurance, the premiums for personal property coverage is not affected by the frequency of claims

Choice D, the best answer, correctly and clearly compares *the premiums for auto insurance* and *the premiums for personal property coverage*. Choices A and C fail to express this comparison: A illogically compares *auto insurance* and *the frequency of claims*, and C illogically compares *the frequency of claims* and *premiums*. *Unlike with* in choices B and E is an unidiomatic form of comparison. In B, the plural *do not affect* fails to agree with *frequency*; in E, the singular *is* does not agree with *premiums*.

233. Recently implemented "shift-work equations" based on studies of the human sleep cycle have reduced sickness, sleeping on the job, <u>fatigue among shift workers, and have raised</u> production efficiency in various industries.

    (A) fatigue among shift workers, and have raised
    (B) fatigue among shift workers, and raised
    (C) and fatigue among shift workers while raising
    (D) lowered fatigue among shift workers, and raised
    (E) and fatigue among shift workers was lowered while raising

The best answer, C, grammatically states that the *equations . . . have reduced x, y, and z* and have raised *efficiency*. Choices A and B fail to use *and* to signal that *fatigue among shift workers* completes the series begun by *have reduced*, and so produce awkward and unclear sentences. Both D and E fail to use *and* to introduce the last item in the list, which is *sleeping* in these constructions. In E, *while raising* has no logical referent, producing only the absurd statement that *fatigue* has raised efficiency.

234. The physical structure of the human eye enables it to sense light of wavelengths up to 0.0005 millimeters; <u>infrared radiation, however, is invisible because its wavelength—0.1 millimeters—is too long to be registered by the eye</u>.

    (A) infrared radiation, however, is invisible because its wavelength—0.1 millimeters—is too long to be registered by the eye
    (B) however, the wavelength of infrared radiation—0.1 millimeters—is too long to be registered by the eye making it invisible
    (C) infrared radiation, however, is invisible because its wavelength—0.1 millimeters—is too long for the eye to register it
    (D) however, because the wavelength of infrared radiation is 0.1 millimeters, it is too long for the eye to register and thus invisible
    (E) however, infrared radiation has a wavelength of 0.1 millimeters that is too long for the eye to register, thus making it invisible

Choice A, the best answer, is clear, idiomatic, and grammatically correct. In B, the misplaced participial phrase *making it invisible* modifies *eye* rather than *wavelength*, thus producing a confusing statement that distorts the meaning. In C, D, and E the use of the second *it* is so imprecise as to be confusing. Furthermore, in D, *and thus invisible* incorrectly modifies wavelength rather than *infrared radiation*. Choice E produces an illogical statement by using a restrictive clause introduced by *that* where a comma followed by the nonrestrictive "which" is required: *a wavelength of 0.1 millimeters that is too long* nonsensically suggests that not all wavelengths *of 0.1 millimeters* are *too long for the eye to register*.

235. Spanning more than fifty years, Friedrich <u>Müller began his career in an unpromising apprenticeship as</u> a Sanskrit scholar and culminated in virtually every honor that European governments and learned societies could bestow.

(A) Müller began his career in an unpromising apprenticeship as
(B) Müller's career began in an unpromising apprenticeship as
(C) Müller's career began with the unpromising apprenticeship of being
(D) Müller had begun his career with the unpromising apprenticeship of being
(E) the career of Müller has begun with an unpromising apprenticeship of

The best answer, B, uses the logical and grammatically correct construction, *Spanning more than fifty years, Friedrich Müller's career began . . . and culminated*. Note that the noun phrase appearing after the comma is modified by *Spanning* and serves as the subject of *began* and *culminated*. Choice A produces an illogical statement by placing *Friedrich Müller* in this subject position. Choice C corrects this error but produces an unidiomatic construction by using *apprenticeship of being* instead of *apprenticeship as*. Choice D repeats both this error and the subject error of A. D and E needlessly change the simple past tense *began* to the past perfect *had begun* and the present perfect *has begun*, respectively, and E uses *apprenticeship of*, which is unidiomatic in this context.

236. The Coast Guard is conducting tests <u>to see whether pigeons can be trained to</u> help find survivors of wrecks at sea.

(A) to see whether pigeons can be trained to help find
(B) to see whether pigeons can be trained as help to find
(C) to see if pigeons can be trained for helping to find
(D) that see if pigeons are able to be trained in helping to find
(E) that see whether pigeons are able to be trained for help in finding

Choice A, the best answer, idiomatically expresses the idea of purpose by using the infinitives *to see* and *to help*: the purpose of the tests is *to see whether pigeons can be trained*, and the purpose of training them is *to help find survivors*. The other choices all produce constructions that are used unidiomatically with *trained*: *as help to find* in B, *for helping to find* in C, *in helping to find* in D, and *for help in finding* in E. In C and D, *whether* would be preferable to *if* in presenting the situation as possible rather than conditional or hypothetical. In D and E, *tests that see* is imprecise, because it is the Coast Guard that will see whether pigeons can be trained.

237. It seems likely that a number of astronomical phenomena, such as the formation of planetary nebulas, <u>may be caused by the interaction where two stars orbit each other</u> at close range.

(A) may be caused by the interaction where two stars orbit each other
(B) may be caused by the interaction between two stars that each orbit the other
(C) are because of the interaction between two stars that orbit each other
(D) are caused by the interaction of two stars where each is orbiting the other
(E) are caused by the interaction of two stars orbiting each other

Choice E, the best answer, avoids redundancy by using *are* rather than *may be*, employs the idiomatic phrase *the interaction of*, and expresses the relationship between the stars in a clear, concise way—*two stars orbiting each other*. In A and B, the use of *may be* is redundant because the beginning phrase *It seems likely that* has already established a degree of uncertainty. In A, the phrase *the interaction where two stars orbit each other* is imprecise and illogical, suggesting that the *interaction* is a place *where* the orbiting occurs. In B, the phrase *two stars that each orbit the other* is both awkward and needlessly wordy. Choice C can be faulted because to form a passive construction, *are* should take a verb form such as *caused* rather than an adverb such as *because*. Also, the phrase *two stars that orbit each other* illogically suggests that there are two particular stars causing all the phenomena in question, rather than various sets of stars in various locations. In D, the word *where* has no clear or logical referent, and *each is orbiting the other* is awkward and unnecessarily wordy; it could be replaced by the clearer and more concise *orbiting each other*.

238. According to a recent study by Rutgers University, <u>the number of women in state legislatures has grown</u> in every election since 1968.

   (A) the number of women in state legislatures has grown

   (B) the number of women who are in state legislatures have grown

   (C) there has been growth in the number of women in state legislatures

   (D) a growing number of women have been in state legislatures

   (E) women have been growing in number in state legislatures

Choice A is best. The singular verb *has* agrees with the subject of the clause, *the number*. Moreover, A conveys the intended meaning concisely and unambiguously. In B, the grammatical subject of the clause is *the number*, not *women*, and so a singular verb is required—*has* rather than *have*. The phrase *who are* is unnecessary; it could be omitted without affecting the meaning of the sentence. In C, the use of the wordy passive construction *there has been growth in* for *has grown* is awkward and does not contribute to the meaning of the sentence. In D, *a . . . number of women* means a group of women, whereas *the . . . number of women* refers to an exact figure; the illogical suggestion is that a group of women has already been in place in every election, rather than that their total has grown as a result of each election. Choice E may be faulted for the awkwardness of *in number in state legislatures in every election*, as well as for weakening clarity by separating the modifying phrase *in state legislatures* from *women*.

239. Organized in 1966 by the Fish and Wildlife Service, the Breeding Bird Survey uses annual roadside counts along established routes <u>for monitoring of population changes of as many as, or of</u> more than 250 bird species, including 180 songbirds.

   (A) for monitoring of population changes of as many as, or of

   (B) to monitor population changes of as many, or

   (C) to monitor changes in the populations of

   (D) that monitors population changes of

   (E) that monitors changes in populations of as many as, or

C is the best choice. The phrase *to monitor changes* is idiomatic as a statement of purpose ([in order] *to monitor*), and the intended meaning is expressed concisely and accurately. Neither A nor B produces the idiomatic phrase ". . . as many as, or more than, 250 . . ."—a phrase that would be needlessly wordy here. Also, *for monitoring of* in A is less concise and idiomatic than *to monitor*, and *population changes* in B is less precise than *changes in population*. In D and E, the pronoun *that* has no singular noun (required by the verb *monitors*) to which it can logically or grammatically refer. *Survey* already has its verb in *uses*, and no other noun can perform the action of *monitors*.

240. <u>What brought</u> the automobile company back from the verge of bankruptcy shortly after the Second World War was a special, governmentally sanctioned price increase allowed during a period of wage and price controls.

   (A) What brought

   (B) The thing that brought

   (C) That which brought

   (D) Bringing

   (E) What has brought

Choice A is best. The verb tense is correct and the pronoun *what* refers most concisely and idiomatically to the noun *increase*. It may help to imagine a simplified version of the sentence and substitute the other answer choices for "The price increase was *what brought* . . ." Both B and C are unnecessarily wordy, and C is awkward and unidiomatic. Both D and E are faulty in tense; *Bringing* suggests an ongoing condition and is incompatible with an action that was completed *shortly after the Second World War*. Similarly, *has brought* indicates action that continues up to the present; the past tense *brought* is needed to parallel *was*.

241. <u>As well as heat and light, the Sun is the source of a continuous stream</u> of atomic particles known as the solar wind.

   (A) As well as heat and light, the Sun is the source of a continuous stream

   (B) Besides heat and light, also the Sun is the source of a continuous stream

   (C) Besides heat and light, the Sun is also the source of a continuous streaming

   (D) The Sun is the source not only of heat and light, but also of a continuous stream

   (E) The Sun is the source of not only heat and light but, as well, of a continuous streaming

Choice D, the best answer, has no modification errors and uses parallel phrases to complete the idiomatic construction *not only . . . but also*. Choices A, B, and C have modification errors: *As well as heat and light* and *Besides heat and light* cannot logically modify *the Sun*, the nearest noun, as grammar requires them to do. This misdirected modification suggests that heat and light are also (in addition to the Sun) a *source* of the solar wind. Choice B may be faulted for the awkward word order of *also the Sun*, while C unnecessarily uses *streaming* rather than the more straightforward *stream*. Choice E fails to use parallel phrases in the idiomatic construction *not only x . . . but [also] y*: *of* should not appear before *not only* if it appears after *but*, and *but also* is preferable to *but*. Finally, the use of the gerund *streaming* rather than the more straightforward noun *stream* is needlessly awkward.

242. Even their most ardent champions concede <u>that no less than a technical or scientific breakthrough is necessary</u> before solar cells can meet the goal of providing one percent of the nation's energy needs.

(A) that no less than a technical or scientific breakthrough is necessary
(B) that nothing other than a technical or scientific breakthrough is needed
(C) that a technical or scientific breakthrough is necessary
(D) the necessity for an occurrence of a technical or scientific breakthrough
(E) the necessity for a technical or scientific breakthrough occurring

C is the best choice. The word *that* functions grammatically to introduce the clause that describes the point that champions of solar cells *concede*. Choices A and B needlessly lengthen the statement by expressing the idea through negation: *no less than* and *nothing other than* could be dropped without loss of meaning. In D and E, the preposition *for* is less idiomatic than *of* in expressing *necessity*. Furthermore, both choices present an awkward and wordy noun-plus-prepositional phrase instead of a *that* clause that would express meaning more exactly and concisely.

243. Some scientists have been critical of the laboratory tests conducted by the Federal Drug Administration on the grounds that the amounts of suspected carcinogens fed to animals far exceeds those that <u>humans could consume</u>.

(A) far exceeds those that humans could consume
(B) exceeds by far those humans can consume
(C) far exceeds those humans are able to consume
(D) exceed by far those able to be consumed by humans
(E) far exceed those that humans could consume

Choice E is best. The plural verb *exceed* agrees in number with its subject, *amounts*, and the phrase *those that humans could consume* conveys the intended meaning clearly and without unnecessary wordiness. In choices A, B, and C, the singular *exceeds* does not agree in number with its plural subject, *amounts*. Choices B and C omit the conjunction *that* —an omission that is grammatically acceptable, but in the case of this sentence diminishes clarity. In D, the use of the passive voice in the phrase *those able to be consumed by humans* is unjustified, as it increases wordiness while stating the meaning less precisely: it is accurate to call *humans* "able," but not to call *those* [amounts] "able."

244. Like their male counterparts, women scientists are above average in terms of intelligence and creativity, but unlike men of science, <u>their female counterparts have had to work</u> against the grain of occupational stereotyping to enter a "man's world."

(A) their female counterparts have had to work
(B) their problem is working
(C) one thing they have had to do is work
(D) the handicap women of science have had is to work
(E) women of science have had to work

E is the best choice. The meaning is clear despite the relative complexity of the sentence, the comparison of *women* with *men* is logical, and parallelism is maintained throughout. In A, the construction *unlike men of science, their female counterparts* violates rules of parallelism and syntax. It would best be rendered as *unlike men of science, women of science . . . .* Choice B incorrectly suggests that a comparison is being made between *men of science* and a *problem* faced by female scientists. In C, the lengthy separation between *women* and *they* makes the pronoun reference vague, and the comparison between *men of science* and *one thing* (rather than *women of science*) is faulty. The phrasing is unnecessarily wordy as well. Choice D introduces unnecessary redundancy and awkwardness with the construction *the handicap women . . . have had is to work*. Choice D also incorrectly compares male scientists with a *handicap* faced by female scientists.

245. Unlike <u>Schoenberg's twelve-tone system that dominated</u> the music of the postwar period, Bartók founded no school and left behind only a handful of disciples.

(A) Schoenberg's twelve-tone system that dominated
(B) Schoenberg and his twelve-tone system which dominated
(C) Schoenberg, whose twelve-tone system dominated
(D) the twelve-tone system of Schoenberg that has dominated
(E) Schoenberg and the twelve-tone system, dominating

C, the best answer, is the only choice that makes a logical comparison: *Unlike Schoenberg, . . . Bartók*. In A, B, and D, Bartók, a person, is compared either to Schoenberg's twelve-tone system or to Schoenberg *and* his twelve-tone system as a unit. Such comparisons are neither logically sound nor semantically parallel. Consequently, A and D illogically suggest that *Schoenberg's twelve-tone system* founded a school and left behind many disciples. Choice B suggests that *Schoenberg and his twelve-tone system* together accomplished these feats. In E, the comparison is illogical and the modification is ambiguous. Schoenberg and his system, as a unit, are not only compared to Bartók, an individual, but also credited with having formed a school. The verb phrase *dominating . . . is* called a "squinting modifier" because it looks in both directions: given the structure of the sentence, it could be meant to modify either *Schoenberg and the twelve-tone system* or *Bartók*.

246. Joachim Raff and Giacomo Meyerbeer are examples of the kind of composer who receives popular acclaim while living, <u>often goes into decline after death, and never regains popularity again</u>.

(A) often goes into decline after death, and never regains popularity again
(B) whose reputation declines after death and never regains its status again
(C) but whose reputation declines after death and never regains its former status
(D) who declines in reputation after death and who never regained popularity again
(E) then has declined in reputation after death and never regained popularity

Choice C, the best answer, maintains parallel structure, keeps verb tense consistent, and contains no redundancies. Choice A illogically suggests that it is the composer who goes into decline after death, rather than the composer's reputation. Choice A may also be faulted for the redundancy of *never regains . . . again*. Choice B is not correct. Grammatically, a coordinating conjunction (e.g., "but") is needed to join the clause *whose reputation declines . . .* with the preceding clause, *who receives popular acclaim . . . .* Furthermore, the phrase *never regains . . . again* suffers from redundancy. Choices D and E suffer from inconsistency in verb tense. To maintain parallelism the verbs must be *receives . . . declines . . . regains.*

247. Faced with an estimated $2 billion budget gap, the city's mayor <u>proposed a nearly 17 percent reduction in the amount allocated the previous year to maintain the city's major cultural institutions and to subsidize</u> hundreds of local arts groups.

(A) proposed a nearly 17 percent reduction in the amount allocated the previous year to maintain the city's major cultural institutions and to subsidize
(B) proposed a reduction from the previous year of nearly 17 percent in the amount it was allocating to maintain the city's major cultural institutions and for subsidizing
(C) proposed to reduce, by nearly 17 percent, the amount from the previous year that was allocated for the maintenance of the city's major cultural institutions and to subsidize
(D) has proposed a reduction from the previous year of nearly 17 percent of the amount it was allocating for maintaining the city's major cultural institutions, and to subsidize
(E) was proposing that the amount they were allocating be reduced by nearly 17 percent from the previous year for maintaining the city's major cultural institutions and for the subsidization

A is the best choice. The construction *the amount allocated . . . to maintain . . . and to subsidize* is parallel, while the phrase *a nearly 17 percent reduction in the amount allocated the previous year* is both clear and concise. In B, the phrase *allocating to maintain . . . and for subsidizing* is not parallel. The construction *a reduction from the previous year of nearly 17 percent in the amount* is awkward, imprecise, and excessively wordy. Furthermore, there is no grammatical referent for *it* in the phrase *it was allocating*. In C, the phrase *proposed to reduce, by nearly 17 percent, the amount from the previous year that was allocated* is unidiomatic and overly wordy. Choice C also violates parallelism with *allocated for the maintenance of . . . and to subsidize*. In D, there is no grammatical referent for *it* in the phrase *it was allocating*: the mayor, not the city, is the subject of the clause. Choice D also violates parallelism with *allocating for maintaining . . . and to subsidize*. In E, the progressive *was proposing* is unnecessary, and there is no grammatical referent for *they* in the phrase *they were allocating*. Furthermore, *for maintaining . . . and for the subsidization* is not parallel.

248. By offering lower prices and a menu of personal communications options, such as caller identification and voice mail, the new telecommunications company <u>has not only captured customers from other phone companies but also forced them</u> to offer competitive prices.

(A) has not only captured customers from other phone companies but also forced them
(B) has not only captured customers from other phone companies, but it also forced them
(C) has not only captured customers from other phone companies but also forced these companies
(D) not only has captured customers from other phone companies but also these companies have been forced
(E) not only captured customers from other phone companies, but it also has forced them

C, the best choice, correctly uses the parallel construction *has not only x'd but also y'd* and avoids ambiguity of reference by using *these companies* rather than *them*. In A, B, and E, the referent of the pronoun *them* is ambiguous; because *them* appears to be parallel to *customers*, the illogical suggestion is that the new telecommunications company has forced *customers* to offer competitive prices. Choices B and E may also be faulted for the improper insertion of *it* to refer redundantly to the new company. Finally, E is not parallel in verb tense with *captured . . . has forced*. Choice D does not maintain parallelism, unnecessarily shifting from active (*company not only has captured*) to passive (*but also these companies have been forced*).

249. Bluegrass musician Bill Monroe, whose repertory, views on musical collaboration, and vocal style <u>were influential on generations of bluegrass artists, was also an inspiration to many musicians, that included Elvis Presley and Jerry Garcia, whose music differed significantly from</u> his own.

(A) were influential on generations of bluegrass artists, was also an inspiration to many musicians, that included Elvis Presley and Jerry Garcia, whose music differed significantly from

(B) influenced generations of bluegrass artists, also inspired many musicians, including Elvis Presley and Jerry Garcia, whose music differed significantly from

(C) was influential to generations of bluegrass artists, was also inspirational to many musicians, that included Elvis Presley and Jerry Garcia, whose music was different significantly in comparison to

(D) was influential to generations of bluegrass artists, also inspired many musicians, who included Elvis Presley and Jerry Garcia, the music of whom differed significantly when compared to

(E) were an influence on generations of bluegrass artists, was also an inspiration to many musicians, including Elvis Presley and Jerry Garcia, whose music was significantly different from that of

B, the best choice, is idiomatic, clear, and without agreement errors or redundancy. In A and E, the phrases *were influential on* and *were an influence on* are not idiomatic and furthermore could be replaced by the more direct *influenced*. In A, *that included Elvis Presley and Jerry Garcia* improperly modifies *many musicians*. In E, the construction *different from that of his own* is confusing since there is no referent for *that*: *different from his own* makes a logical comparison. Both C and D begin with the singular *was*; the compound subject of this verb is plural: *repertory, views on musical collaboration, and vocal style*. Both choices also may be faulted for wordiness and redundancy in their use of *was different significantly in comparison to* and *differed significantly when compared to*. In C, *that included Elvis Presley and Jerry Garcia* improperly modifies *many musicians*. Finally, *the music of whom* in D is cumbersome and stilted.

250. The company announced that its profits declined much less in the second quarter than analysts <u>had expected it to and its business will improve</u> in the second half of the year.

(A) had expected it to and its business will improve

(B) had expected and that its business would improve

(C) expected it would and that it will improve its business

(D) expected them to and its business would improve

(E) expected and that it will have improved its business

B, the best choice, avoids errors of agreement, correctly uses the parallel construction *that x and that y*, and uses *would* rather than *will* to refer to a promised but uncertain future event. In A and C, singular *it* after *expected* has no grammatical referent: its antecedent cannot be *The company*, but rather must be the plural *profits*. Choices A and C also contain errors of verb form, using *will* where *would* is required. Choices A and D fail to maintain parallel structure: properly formed, the construction would have *that* after *expected* to parallel *that* after *announced*. Furthermore, in D, the addition of *them to* is unnecessary. Choice E illogically uses the future perfect *will have improved* to suggest completion of an action that will be continuous *in the second half of the year*.

251. The gyrfalcon, an Arctic bird of prey, has survived a close brush with <u>extinction; its numbers are now five times greater than</u> when the use of DDT was sharply restricted in the early 1970's.

(A) extinction; its numbers are now five times greater than

(B) extinction; its numbers are now five times more than

(C) extinction, their numbers now fivefold what they were

(D) extinction, now with fivefold the numbers they had

(E) extinction, now with numbers five times greater than

A, the best choice, uses a singular pronoun, *its*, to refer to the singular antecedent *The gyrfalcon*, and it properly uses the construction *its numbers are now . . . greater than*. In B, the construction *its numbers are . . . more* is not idiomatic: there are more birds, but not more *numbers*. Choices C and D use a plural pronoun, *their* or *they*, to refer to a grammatically singular antecedent, *The gyrfalcon*. Choices D and E wrongly use a phrase introduced by *now with* to modify *The gyrfalcon*. In both choices, the phrase confusingly seems to parallel *with extinction*; a new clause with a present tense verb is needed to state what the gyrfalcon's numbers are *now*.

252. Three out of every four automobile owners in the United States also own a bicycle.

(A) Three out of every four automobile owners in the United States also own a bicycle.
(B) Out of every four, three automobile owners in the United States also owns a bicycle.
(C) Bicycles are owned by three out of every four owners of automobiles in the United States.
(D) In the United States, three out of every four automobile owners owns bicycles.
(E) Out of every four owners of automobiles in the United States, bicycles are also owned by three.

A, the best choice, is concise, idiomatic, and maintains subject-verb agreement. In B, *Out of every four, three* is unidiomatic. The singular verb *owns* does not agree with its plural subject, *three . . . owners*. The passive construction in C (*Bicycles are owned by*) is cumbersome and does not contribute meaningfully to the sentence. The shift to plural *Bicycles* detracts from clarity by suggesting that multiple bicycles are owned by each person in question. In D, the singular *owns* does not agree with its plural subject *three . . . owners*. Furthermore, the plural *bicycles* detracts from clarity by suggesting that multiple bicycles are owned by each person in question. In E, the phrase beginning *Out of every four . . .* cannot properly modify *bicycles*, and the passive construction (*bicycles are also owned*) is awkward and does not contribute meaningfully to the sentence. The plural nouns *bicycles* and *automobiles* suggest imprecisely that each person owns more than one of each.

253. Analysts blamed May's sluggish retail sales on unexciting merchandise as well as the weather, colder and wetter than was usual in some regions, which slowed sales of barbecue grills and lawn furniture.

(A) colder and wetter than was usual in some regions, which slowed
(B) which was colder and wetter than usual in some regions, slowing
(C) since it was colder and wetter than usually in some regions, which slowed
(D) being colder and wetter than usually in some regions, slowing
(E) having been colder and wetter than was usual in some regions and slowed

Choice B is the best answer. It is concise and idiomatic, and *which* has a clear referent, *the weather*. In A, the insertion of *was* is unnecessary, and the referent of *which* is not clear because *regions*, not *weather*, is the nearest noun. In C, the adjective *usual* is needed in place of the adverb *usually*, and the referent of *which* is unclear because *regions*, not *weather*, is the nearest noun. In D and E, the verb phrases (*being colder . . . , having been colder . . .*) do not refer as clearly to the noun *weather* as the pronoun *which* does. Choice D needs the adjective *usual* in place of the adverb *usually*, while choice E fails to maintain parallelism in verb tense (*having been . . . and slowed*).

254. Balding is much more common among White males than males of other races.

(A) than
(B) than among
(C) than is so of
(D) compared to
(E) in comparison with

B, the best choice, correctly uses the idiomatic construction *more common among x than among y*. In A, the comparison is not parallel and not clear; one illogical but available reading is that balding is more common among White males than are males of other races. To be clear, the sentence should read *more common among White males than among . . . .* In C, the phrase *is so* cannot refer to the process *Balding*, and *more common among . . . than is so* lacks parallelism. In D and E, the phrases *more common . . . compared to* and *more common . . . in comparison with* are redundant and unidiomatic. The correct form is *more common than*.

255. The bank holds $3 billion in loans that are seriously delinquent or in such trouble that they do not expect payments when due.

(A) they do not expect payments when
(B) it does not expect payments when it is
(C) it does not expect payments to be made when they are
(D) payments are not to be expected to be paid when
(E) payments are not expected to be paid when they will be

Choice C, the best answer, expresses its meaning clearly and directly, with subject-verb agreement throughout. Choice A is incorrect: although in some dialects of English a bank is treated as a plural entity, in this case *The bank holds* clearly establishes that *bank* is grammatically singular, and thus it cannot be referred to with the plural pronoun *they*. Furthermore, the structure of *they do not expect payments when due* makes the modification of *due* unclear. In B, *it* correctly refers to the singular *bank*, but *payments when it is due* introduces an agreement error between plural *payments* and singular *it*. In D and E, the use of the passive (*payments are not . . . expected to be paid*) does not contribute meaningfully to the sentence and thus is unwarranted, while *payments . . . to be paid* is redundant and unidiomatic. Also, *are not to be* in D and *will be* in E inappropriately shift action to the future.

256. The nephew of Pliny the Elder wrote the only eyewitness account of the great eruption of Vesuvius in two letters to the historian Tacitus.

(A) The nephew of Pliny the Elder wrote the only eyewitness account of the great eruption of Vesuvius in two letters to the historian Tacitus.

(B) To the historian Tacitus, the nephew of Pliny the Elder wrote two letters, being the only eyewitness accounts of the great eruption of Vesuvius.

(C) The only eyewitness account is in two letters by the nephew of Pliny the Elder writing to the historian Tacitus an account of the great eruption of Vesuvius.

(D) Writing the only eyewitness account, Pliny the Elder's nephew accounted for the great eruption of Vesuvius in two letters to the historian Tacitus.

(E) In two letters to the historian Tacitus, the nephew of Pliny the Elder wrote the only eyewitness account of the great eruption of Vesuvius.

E, the best choice, conveys its meaning clearly, without ambiguity, and uses straightforward syntax. In A, the placement of the phrase *in two letters to the historian Tacitus* generates ambiguity: the nonsensical suggestion is that the eruption of Vesuvius took place in the letters themselves. In B, the verb phrase that begins *being the only eyewitness accounts* modifies the subject of the preceding clause, suggesting nonsensically that the nephew of Pliny the Elder himself was the *eyewitness accounts*. Furthermore, *To the historian Tacitus, the nephew . . . wrote two letters* is unnecessarily clumsy. In C, the meaning of the sentence is unclear (*The only eyewitness account* of what?), the repetition of *account* is clumsy, and the syntax is highly convoluted (. . . *in two letters by the nephew of Pliny the Elder writing to the historian Tacitus an account* . . .). In D, *Writing the only eyewitness account, Pliny the Elder's nephew accounted* is redundant, and the placement of *in two letters to the historian Tacitus* generates ambiguity, suggesting under one available reading that the eruption took place in the letters.

257. The direction in which the Earth and the other solid planets — Mercury, Venus, and Mars — spins were determined from collisions with giant celestial bodies in the early history of the Solar System.

(A) spins were determined from
(B) spins were determined because of
(C) spins was determined through
(D) spin was determined by
(E) spin was determined as a result of

D, the best choice, is clear and concise, and uses correct subject-verb agreement. Choices A, B, and C are incorrect because they use the singular verb *spins* for the plural subject *Earth and the other solid planets—Mercury, Venus, and Mars*. Choices A and B furthermore incorrectly use the plural *were*, which does not agree with the singular subject *The direction*. To express cause, *determined by* is idiomatic; the prepositions *from* and *through* in A and C are not idiomatic. The phrase *determined because of* in B is redundant. In E, the phrase *determined as a result of* is redundant, awkward, and unidiomatic.

258. The British sociologist and activist Barbara Wootton once noted as a humorous example of income maldistribution that the elephant that gave rides to children at the Whipsnade Zoo was earning annually exactly what she then earned as director of adult education for London.

(A) that the elephant that gave rides to children at the Whipsnade Zoo was earning

(B) that the elephant, giving rides to children at the Whipsnade Zoo, had been earning

(C) that there was an elephant giving rides to children at the Whipsnade Zoo, and it earned

(D) the elephant that gave rides to children at the Whipsnade Zoo and was earning

(E) the elephant giving rides to children at the Whipsnade Zoo and that it earned

Choice A, the best answer, uses the idiomatic construction *noted . . . that* and clearly focuses on the salient information— a comparison of annual earnings. In B, the structure of *noted . . . that the elephant, giving rides . . . , had been earning* falsely implies that the reader already knows about the elephant— that is, that the existence of this particular elephant is not new information. Also, the past perfect *had been* improperly places the elephant's *earning* in the past, prior to Wootton's; consistent verb tense is needed to show that the actions are simultaneous. Choice C may be faulted for distortion of meaning and diminished clarity because it suggests that the point of Wootton's example was the elephant's very existence; comparative earnings are presented (after *and*) as incidental detail. Choice D is awkward and inexact; the whole circumstance that Wootton "noted" is best expressed in a clause that begins with *that*. Choice E does not use the idiomatic construction *noted that x*; therefore, *and that it earned* has no parallel construction to which it can be joined.

259. Five fledgling sea eagles left their nests in western Scotland this summer, <u>bringing</u> to 34 the number of wild birds successfully raised since transplants from Norway began in 1975.

    (A) bringing
    (B) and brings
    (C) and it brings
    (D) and it brought
    (E) and brought

Choice A is best. The "-ing" (present participle) form introduces action that is simultaneous with the action of the main clause; i.e., *bringing* indicates that the number of wild birds became 34 when the sea eagles left their nests. In B, there is no subject available for the singular present-tense verb *brings*. The subject cannot be *eagles*, since that noun is plural and the action of its verb *left* is in the past. Neither C nor D contains a grammatical referent for *it*. In E, the use of *and brought* implies two discrete actions on the part of the eagles, and thus lacks the clarity of the best answer, where *bringing* underscores the cause-and-effect nature of the situation.

260. According to some economists, the July decrease in unemployment <u>so that it was the lowest in two years</u> suggests that the gradual improvement in the job market is continuing.

    (A) so that it was the lowest in two years
    (B) so that it was the lowest two-year rate
    (C) to what would be the lowest in two years
    (D) to a two-year low level
    (E) to the lowest level in two years

E, the best choice, employs idiomatic construction and uses the precise *decrease . . . to the lowest level*. Choices A and B are faulty in construction. The adverbial *so that* can modify verbs (e.g., *decreased*) but not nouns (e.g., *the decrease*). The meaning of *lowest two-year rate* in B is unclear; in any event the phrase distorts the intended meaning of *lowest in two years*. In A and B, the referent of *it* is unclear, as the pronoun could refer to either *unemployment* or *decrease*. Choice C improperly uses *would be* to describe a situation that is presented as a current and known fact. Also, there is no noun for *lowest* to modify; clearly "the lowest decrease" is not intended. In D, the phrase *two-year low level* is unidiomatic, as well as unclear in its intended meaning.

261. <u>Being a United States citizen since 1988 and born in Calcutta in 1940, author Bharati Mukherjee has</u> lived in England and Canada, and first came to the United States in 1961 to study at the Iowa Writers' Workshop.

    (A) Being a United States citizen since 1988 and born in Calcutta in 1940, author Bharati Mukherjee has
    (B) Having been a United States citizen since 1988, she was born in Calcutta in 1940; author Bharati Mukherjee
    (C) Born in Calcutta in 1940, author Bharati Mukherjee became a United States citizen in 1988; she has
    (D) Being born in Calcutta in 1940 and having been a United States citizen since 1988, author Bharati Mukherjee
    (E) Having been born in Calcutta in 1940 and being a United States citizen since 1988, author Bharati Mukherjee

C is best. The first clause presents its information clearly and in logical sequence. The use of a semicolon to set apart the remaining information further assists the clarity of the sentence. In A, the phrase *Being . . . and born* violates parallelism and oddly presents its information in reverse chronological order. Choice B illogically suggests that upon her birth in 1940, Mukherjee had already been a United States citizen since 1988. In D and E, the use of progressive forms (*Being born, having been, Having been born,* and *being*) implies continuous action, a notion that is not appropriate to the facts being presented. Also, these forms do not establish a logical time sequence, suggesting, for example, that Mukherjee had been a United States citizen before she lived in England and Canada and first came to the United States.

262. <u>Initiated five centuries after Europeans arrived in the New World on Columbus Day 1992, Project SETI pledged a $100 million investment in the search for extraterrestrial intelligence.</u>

(A) Initiated five centuries after Europeans arrived in the New World on Columbus Day 1992, Project SETI pledged a $100 million investment in the search for extraterrestrial intelligence.
(B) Initiated on Columbus Day 1992, five centuries after Europeans arrived in the New World, a $100 million investment in the search for extraterrestrial intelligence was pledged by Project SETI.
(C) Initiated on Columbus Day 1992, five centuries after Europeans arrived in the New World, Project SETI pledged a $100 million investment in the search for extraterrestrial intelligence.
(D) Pledging a $100 million investment in the search for extraterrestrial intelligence, the initiation of Project SETI five centuries after Europeans arrived in the New World on Columbus Day 1992.
(E) Pledging a $100 million investment in the search for extraterrestrial intelligence five centuries after Europeans arrived in the New World, on Columbus Day 1992, the initiation of Project SETI took place.

Choice C, the best answer, is a complete sentence, and its initial structures correctly modify *Project SETI* so that there is no ambiguity regarding when events took place. Choice A is faulty because its construction illogically suggests that Europeans arrived in the New World on Columbus Day 1992 and that Project SETI was initiated five centuries thereafter. In B, *Initiated on Columbus Day . . .* illogically modifies a *$100 million investment*, suggesting that it was the investment itself, not Project SETI, that was initiated. In D and E, the initial phrase beginning with *Pledging* in both cases illogically modifies *the initiation of Project SETI*; it is not the project's initiation, but the project itself, that pledged a certain investment. Furthermore, D is a sentence fragment, while E may be faulted for ambiguity. The phrase *five centuries after* could modify either *Pledging* or *the search*, and *on Columbus Day 1992* could refer to the date of either the initiation of Project SETI or the arrival of Europeans in the New World.

263. In A.D. 391, <u>resulting from the destruction of the largest library of the ancient world at Alexandria,</u> later generations lost all but the *Iliad* and *Odyssey* among Greek epics, most of the poetry of Pindar and Sappho, and dozens of plays by Aeschylus and Euripides.

(A) resulting from the destruction of the largest library of the ancient world at Alexandria,
(B) the destroying of the largest library of the ancient world at Alexandria resulted and
(C) because of the result of the destruction of the library at Alexandria, the largest of the ancient world,
(D) as a result of the destruction of the library at Alexandria, the largest of the ancient world,
(E) Alexandria's largest library of the ancient world was destroyed, and the result was

D, the best choice, uses the idiomatic *as a result of* and conveys information unambiguously. In A, the phrase that begins *resulting from* cannot properly modify *later generations*. The word order of *the largest library of the ancient world at Alexandria* generates ambiguity: one possible reading is that the ancient world was located at Alexandria. Choice B is incorrect. Although an "-ing" verb such as *destroying* can sometimes act as a noun, in this case the usage is strained. Again, *at Alexandria* is ambiguous (as in choice A). Choice B also uses *resulted* ungrammatically and produces a run-on sentence (*In A.D. 391, the destroying . . . resulted and later generations lost*). In C, the phrase *because of the result of* is unidiomatic as well as redundant. The structure of E illogically suggests that there was more than one *largest library of the ancient world* and that only *Alexandria's* was destroyed. Furthermore, *the result was* should instead be *the result was that*.

264. Scientists believe that unlike the males of most species of moth, the male whistling moths of Nambung, Australia, call female moths to them <u>by the use of acoustical signals, but not olfactory ones, and they attract</u> their mates during the day, rather than at night.

(A) by the use of acoustical signals, but not olfactory ones, and they attract
(B) by the use of acoustical signals instead of using olfactory ones, and attracting
(C) by using acoustical signals, not using olfactory ones, and by attracting
(D) using acoustical signals, rather than olfactory ones, and attract
(E) using acoustical signals, but not olfactory ones, and attracting

Choice D, the best answer, is concise, maintains parallel structure, and clearly conveys the comparisons being made between the two types of moth. In A and E, the comparison between most male moths and the male whistling moth is not clear. The use of *but not* does not clearly convey that most other moths use olfactory signals; *rather than* would be preferable, as well as parallel to *rather than at night*. In A, the phrase *by the use of* is unnecessarily wordy, and the insertion of *they* is not required. In E, the final verb should be *attract* (parallel to *call*), not *attracting* (parallel to *using*). Choice B violates parallelism with *by the use of . . . instead of using*, as well as with *call . . . and attracting*. Choice C distorts the meaning of the original with its suggestion that male whistling moths call female moths to them both by using acoustical signals and by attracting their mates during the day. The insertion of *using* in *not using olfactory ones* is unnecessary.

265. Thomas Eakins' powerful style and his choices of subject — the advances in modern surgery, the discipline of sport, the strains of individuals in tension with society or even with themselves — <u>was as disturbing to his own time as it is</u> compelling for ours.

(A) was as disturbing to his own time as it is
(B) were as disturbing to his own time as they are
(C) has been as disturbing in his own time as they are
(D) had been as disturbing in his own time as it was
(E) have been as disturbing in his own time as

Choice B, the best answer, exhibits correct subject-verb agreement and uses appropriate verb tenses. Choices A, C, and D contain errors of agreement: the compound subject *style and . . . choices of subject* requires a plural verb and should correspond to the plural pronoun *they*, not *it*. Furthermore, C wrongly shifts to the present perfect tense (*has been*) to characterize something that happened in the past, while D uses the past tense *was* to characterize something that is happening in the present. In E, while the plural *have* agrees in number with the compound subject, the use of the present perfect tense (*have been*) is inappropriate for characterizing the effect of Eakins' work in his own time.

266. In a recent poll, 86 percent of the public favored <u>a Clean Air Act as strong or stronger than</u> the present act.

(A) a Clean Air Act as strong or stronger than
(B) a Clean Air Act that is stronger, or at least so strong as,
(C) at least as strong a Clean Air Act as is
(D) a Clean Air Act as strong or stronger than is
(E) a Clean Air Act at least as strong as

E, the best choice, is concise, clear, and idiomatic. Choices A, B, C, and D may be faulted for constructions that are cumbersome, unnecessarily wordy, or unidiomatic. Choices A and D require *as strong as* instead of *as strong*. Similarly, B is missing *than* after *stronger*, and *so* should be *as*. In C and D, *is* should be dropped. Even with revisions, these choices are more wordy and awkward than the best answer.

267. <u>Like Rousseau, Tolstoi rebelled</u> against the unnatural complexity of human relations in modern society.

(A) Like Rousseau, Tolstoi rebelled
(B) Like Rousseau, Tolstoi's rebellion was
(C) As Rousseau, Tolstoi rebelled
(D) As did Rousseau, Tolstoi's rebellion was
(E) Tolstoi's rebellion, as Rousseau's, was

In choice A, the best answer, a clear and logical comparison is made between Rousseau and Tolstoi. Choice B illogically compares a person, Rousseau, to an event, Tolstoi's rebellion. Also, *Tolstoi's rebellion was against* is less direct than *Tolstoi rebelled against*. Inserting *did* after *As* would make C grammatical. Because *As* is a conjunction, it must introduce a clause; hence the noun Rousseau must have a verb. Choice D compares an implied action (*As did Rousseau*) with a noun (*Tolstoi's rebellion*). Choice E is awkwardly formed, and *like* is needed in place of *as* to compare two nouns (*rebellion* is understood after *Rousseau's*). Also, *Tolstoi's rebellion . . . was against* is less direct than *Tolstoi rebelled against.*

268. Ranked as one of the most important of Europe's young playwrights, Franz Xaver Kroetz has written forty plays; his works — translated into over thirty languages — are produced more often <u>than any</u> contemporary German dramatist.

(A) than any
(B) than any other
(C) than are any
(D) than those of any other
(E) as are those of any

Choice D is the best answer. It correctly compares Kroetz's works to the works of other dramatists. Choices A, B, and C illogically compare Kroetz's *works* to *any* (other) *contemporary German dramatist*. In E, the phrase *more often* must be completed by *than* rather than *as*. Also, the comparison is illogical; without *other*, E compares Kroetz's works to a group that includes his works.

9 Analytical Writing Assessment

In these sections of the GMAT®, you are to write a 30-minute response to each of two separate writing tasks. One is called "Analysis of an Issue," and the other is called "Analysis of an Argument." The Analysis of an Issue task requires you to consider a given issue or opinion and then explain your point of view on the subject by citing relevant reasons and/or examples based on your experience, observations, or reading. The Analysis of an Argument task requires you to read a brief argument, analyze the reasoning behind the argument, and then write a critique of the argument. You will write your response on screen using the word-processing functions of the *GMAT* software.

This chapter contains
- test-taking strategies for the Analytical Writing Assessment
- directions for the two types of writing tasks
- scoring guides for the two types of writing tasks
- one sample of each writing task with responses illustrating three selected points on the scoring scale and explanations of why the responses received those scores
- Writing tasks, any of which may appear in your actual *GMAT*

Test-taking Strategies for the Analytical Writing Assessment

General

1. Read the question carefully. Make sure you have taken all parts of a question into account before you begin responding to it.

2. Do not start to write immediately. Take a few minutes to think about the question and plan a response before you begin writing. You may find it helpful to write a brief outline or jot down some ideas on the scratch paper provided. Take care to organize your ideas and develop them fully, but leave time to reread your response and make any revisions that you think would improve it.

Analysis of an Issue

1. Although many "analysis of an issue" questions require you to take a position, you should be careful about the way in which you go about doing so. Do not leap to a position: what is being assessed is your ability to think and write critically. Try to show that you recognize and understand the complexities of an issue or an opinion before you take a position. Consider the issue from different perspectives, and think about your own experiences or reading related to the issue. Work your way to a position rather than simply announcing one.

2. While it is essential to illustrate and develop your ideas by means of examples drawn from your observations, experiences, and reading, it is not a good idea simply to catalogue examples. One or two well-chosen, well-developed examples are much more effective than a long list of them.

Analysis of an Argument

1. Your job here is to analyze and critique a line of thinking or reasoning. Get used to asking yourself questions like the following: What questionable assumptions might underlie the thinking? What alternative explanations might be given? What counterexamples might be raised? What additional evidence might prove useful in fully and fairly evaluating the reasoning?

2. Use the opportunity of discussing alternative explanations or counterexamples to introduce illustrations and examples drawn from your observations, experiences, or reading. Again, do not simply list examples; develop them.

3. Your finished response to this writing task should not read like an outline; it should, rather, read like a discussion with full sentences, a coherent organizational scheme, logical transitions between points, and appropriately introduced and developed examples.

Analysis of an Issue

When finished reading directions click on the icon below

Dismiss Directions

In this section, you will need to analyze the issue presented and explain your views on it. There is no "correct" answer. Instead, you should consider various perspectives as you develop your own position on the issue.

WRITING YOUR RESPONSE: Take a few minutes to think about the issue and plan a response before you begin writing. Be sure to organize your ideas and develop them fully, but leave time to reread your response and make any revisions that you think are necessary.

EVALUATION OF YOUR RESPONSE: College and university faculty members from various subject-matter areas, including management education, will evaluate the overall quality of your thinking and writing. They will consider how well you

- organize, develop, and express your ideas about the issue presented
- provide relevant supporting reasons and examples
- control the elements of standard written English

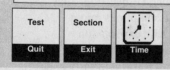

| Test | Section | | | | | ? | Answer | ➡ |
| Quit | Exit | Time | | | | Help | Confirm | Next |

GMAT SCORING GUIDE: ANALYSIS OF AN ISSUE

SCORE

6   OUTSTANDING

A 6 paper presents a cogent, well-articulated analysis of the complexities of the issue and demonstrates mastery of the elements of effective writing.

A typical paper in this category

— explores ideas and develops a position on the issue with insightful reasons and/or persuasive examples
— is clearly well organized
— demonstrates superior control of language, including diction and syntactic variety
— demonstrates superior facility with the conventions (grammar, usage, and mechanics) of standard written English but may have minor flaws

5   STRONG

A 5 paper presents a well-developed analysis of the complexities of the issue and demonstrates a strong control of the elements of effective writing.

A typical paper in this category

— develops a position on the issue with well-chosen reasons and/or cxamples
— is generally well organized
— demonstrates clear control of language, including diction and syntactic variety
— demonstrates facility with the conventions of standard written English but may have minor flaws

4   ADEQUATE

A 4 paper presents a competent analysis of the issue and demonstrates adequate control of the elements of writing.

A typical paper in this category

— develops a position on the issue with relevant reasons and/or examples
— is adequately organized
— demonstrates adequate control of language, including diction and syntax, but may lack syntactic variety
— displays control of the conventions of standard written English but may have some flaws

3   LIMITED

A 3 paper demonstrates some competence in its analysis of the issue and in its control of the elements of writing but is clearly flawed.

A typical paper in this category exhibits *one or more* of the following characteristics:

— is vague or limited in developing a position on the issue
— is poorly organized
— is weak in the use of relevant reasons or examples
— uses language imprecisely and/or lacks sentence variety
— contains occasional major errors or frequent minor errors in grammar, usage, and mechanics

2   SERIOUSLY FLAWED

A 2 paper demonstrates serious weaknesses in analytical writing skills.

A typical paper in this category exhibits *one or more* of the following characteristics:

— is unclear or seriously limited in presenting or developing a position on the issue
— is disorganized
— provides few, if any, relevant reasons or examples
— has serious and frequent problems in the use of language and sentence structure
— contains numerous errors in grammar, usage, or mechanics that interfere with meaning

1   FUNDAMENTALLY DEFICIENT

A 1 paper demonstrates fundamental deficiencies in analytical writing skills.

A typical paper in this category exhibits *one or more* of the following characteristics:

— provides little evidence of the ability to develop or organize a coherent response to the topic
— has severe and persistent errors in language and sentence structure
— contains a pervasive pattern of errors in grammar, usage, and mechanics that severely interferes with meaning

0   Off topic, in a foreign language, merely attempts to copy the topic, or consists only of keystroke characters.

NR   Blank

Read the statement and the instructions that follow it, and then make any notes that will help you plan your response. Begin typing your response in the box at the bottom of the screen.

"People often complain that products are not made to last. They feel that making products that wear out fairly quickly wastes both natural and human resources. What they fail to see, however, is that such manufacturing practices keep costs down for the consumer and stimulate demand."

Which do you find more compelling, the complaint about products that do not last or the response to it? Explain your position using relevant reasons and/or examples from your own experience, observations, or reading.

Cut

Paste

Undo

Test
Quit

Section
Exit

Time

? Help

Answer
Confirm

Next

Many people feel that products are not made to last, and correspondingly, many natural and human resources are wasted. On the other hand, it can be noted that such manufacturing practices keep costs down and hence stimulate demand. In this discussion, I shall present arguments favoring the former statement and refuting the latter statement.

Products that are not made to last waste a great deal of natural and human resources. The exact amount of wasted natural resources depends on the specific product. For example in the automobile industry, the Yugo is the classic example of an underpriced vehicle that was not made to last. Considering that the average Yugo had (not "has" since they are no longer produced!) a life expectancy of two years and 25,000 miles, it was a terrible waste.

Automobile industry standards today create vehicles that are warrantied for about five years and 50,000 miles. By producing cheap Yugos that last less than half as long as most cars are warrantied, the Yugo producer is wasting valuable natural resources. These same resources could be used by Ford or Toyota to produce an Escort or Tercel that will last twice as long, thereby reducing the usage of natural resources by a factor of two.

Human resources in this example are also wasteful. On the production side, manufacturers of a poor quality automobile, like the Yugo, get no personal or profession satisfaction from the fact that their product is the worst automobile in the United States. This knowledge adversely affects the productivity of the Yugo workers.

Conversely, the workers at the Saturn plants constantly receive positive feedback on their successful products. Saturn prides itself with its reputation for quality and innovation — as is seen in its recent massive recall to fix a defect. This recall was handled so well that Saturn's image was actually bolstered. Had a recall occurred at a Yugo plant, the bad situation would have become even worse.

Another factor in the human resources area is the reaction by the consumer. A great deal of human resources have been wasted by Yugo owners waiting for the dreaded tow truck to show up to haul away the Yugo carcass. Any vehicle owner who is uncertain of his/her vehicle's performance at 7 AM as he/she is about to drive to work, senses a great deal of despair. This is a great waste of human resources for the consumer.

While the consumer senses the waste of natural and human resources in a poor quality product, so does the manufacturer. People who argue that low quality manufacturing processes keep costs low for the consumer and hence stimulate demand should look at the Yugo example. In the mid-1980's the Yugo was by far the cheapest car in the United States at $3,995. By 1991, the Yugo was no longer sold here and was synonymous with the word "lemon."

EXPLANATION OF SCORE — 6

The response above is ambitious and somewhat unusual in its focusing on just one example, the lesson of the now defunct Yugo. Responses, especially outstanding ones, typically discuss several different examples that build support for the writer's position on the issue. This sample response, then, should not be taken as necessarily endorsing a one-example writing strategy. What it *does* serve to underscore is how much is to be gained by *developing*, not just *listing*, examples. The strength of the response lies in the organized and thorough way in which it explores the related aspects of the example it cites. The clear organizational scheme (two major points, with the second point subdivided) is readily apparent: Yugo's substandard cars (1) waste natural resources and (2) waste human resources by (a) destroying worker morale and productivity and (b) inconveniencing and upsetting customers. The persuasiveness of the writer's thinking is especially evident in the discussion of the second major point, the waste of human resources. Here the writer not only considers customers as well as workers but also introduces the matter of the Saturn recall in order to show, by contrast with the case of Yugo, how a superior product, satisfied workers, and a company image good for marketing are interrelated.

The response complements its outstanding organizational clarity and thorough development with some syntactic variety and an occasional rhetorical flair (e. g., the image of the despairing Yugo owner waiting for "the dreaded tow truck . . . to haul away the Yugo carcass" in paragraph 6). It is important to point out, however, that the writing is not perfect. For one thing, the opening paragraph is essentially a repeat of the question. In addition, the writing is not — and is not expected to be — entirely free from minor flaws (e. g., "profession satisfaction" [paragraph 4] should obviously be "professional satisfaction," and "Saturn prides itself with" [paragraph 5] should be "Saturn prides itself on"). Nevertheless, these occasional flaws are not serious enough to detract from the general impression that this is an excellent response to the question.

I find the response to the complaint more compelling. Although the complaint is valid, it is most often the case the building a product to last forever will indeed cost more than the average consumer is willing to pay. Creating such a product would require more materials and/or more heavy-duty wear resistant materials which inherently are more expensive. Another factor that would drive costs up is the fact that demand for products would decrease. The demand would decrease since people do not have to replace old products with new product as often. With the increased variable costs for materials combined with a reduction in the production volume associated with lower demand, manufacturers must raise prices to break even or maintain the current level of profits.

Although a few producers may make products to last, it is understandable how these companies can be driven out of existence. If a new competitor enters the market with a similar product that has a shorter life but a substantially lower price, then they will probably steal major portions of the other company's market share. The effects depend heavily upon the consumers' perception of quality and what the customers requirements from the product actually are.

For example, consumers may decide between two types of automobiles. One car may be built to last a long time but may not have the performance or be as comfortable as another car that is cheaper. So most consumers would purchase the cheaper car even though it may not last as long as the heavy-duty car. Consumers may not realize that the more expensive car is of higher quality in the sense that it will last longer and will not be willing to pay the extra cost.

Consumer decisions also depend on what consumers are actually looking for in a product. Consumers typically get tired of driving the same car for many years and want to buy new cars fairly often. This tendency forces producers to keep costs low enough to allow low enough prices for people to buy cars often. People don't want cars to last forever.

In conclusion, producers are in the situation that they're in due to external forces from the consumers. Producers must compete and they have found the best way satisfy the majority of the consumers.

EXPLANATION OF SCORE — 4

This response presents a competent analysis of the issue. It develops its position by explaining some of the ways in which the factors mentioned in the question — manufacturing costs and consumer demand — are affected by making products that do not last very long. By way of illustration, the response cites the example of consumers choosing automobiles. Although this example is relevant, it lacks specificity: no actual types of cars are described in terms of the key issue, durability, and no contrast between more and less durable types is developed to prove a point.

Although the response is competently organized and therefore generally easy to follow in its main lines, its clarity is marred by an awkward transition from the second paragraph to the third. The main idea of the second paragraph is that many consumers will abandon a made-to-last expensive product in favor of a substantially cheaper version with a shorter life. But the last sentence of this paragraph, a sentence that is signally unclear, marks an ill-prepared-for change in the direction of the entire response. "The effects" (the word, used loosely and unclearly, seems to refer to the consumer's final decisions about what to buy) are seen to depend not only upon the simple choice between cost and quality but also upon a complex of new forces — aspects of consumer psychology and "requirements" (consumer needs?) — that now suddenly and puzzlingly face the reader. Although the third and fourth paragraphs go on to develop the writer's views about these new forces, the reader never quite recovers from the sense that the response has abruptly changed course. What is more, the consideration of consumer psychology and "requirements" can cause the writer to stray into side issues. For example, pointing out that customers may choose a car on the basis of performance and comfort rather than durability has no direct bearing on the complaint that products are not made to last.

The wording of this response is generally appropriate, although the language is occasionally awkward, as in "keep costs low enough to allow low enough prices" (paragraph 4) and "producers are in the situation that they're in" (paragraph 5).

I find the response better than the complaint of people. The response seems to originate without much thought involved. It is more of an emotional complaint than one anchored in logic or thought. Yes, it is a waste of human resources but that is without consideration to the benefits: lower costs and stimulated demand. Thus, the response fails to recognize the benefits.

The strength of the response is that it forces the reader to reconsider the complaint. It adds a new dimension to the argument. It, however, fails to address the issue of wasting human resources. Does this mean the responder agrees with the notion of wasting resources.

In all actuality both the response and complaint as ineffective. The complaint doesn't recognize or address the benefits, like the response doesn't address the issue of wasting resources. The response, however, does bring in a new dimension and thus weakens the argument of the complaint.

EXPLANATION OF SCORE — 2

In this piece of writing, the writer's purpose seems to waver between defending "the response" against "the complaint" and weighing the relative strengths and limitations of both. In addition, the writer offers no new reasons or specific examples and so ends up merely repeating assertions made in "the complaint" and "the response."

The writing is marked throughout by vagueness. The writer's decision to adopt the topic's terms "response" and "complaint" as a convenient shorthand for the two positions articulated leads immediately to a confusing lack of specificity, compounded in the first paragraph by the fact that the two terms are mixed up (e.g., "response" in the second and the fifth sentences is meant to refer to "complaint"). The first paragraph is made even more confusing because the pronouns *it* and *that* lack antecedents in the sentence "Yes, it is a waste of human resources but that is without consideration to the benefits."

The general lack of clarity is aggravated by errors in conventional English grammar and usage, most of them concentrated in paragraph 3. The first sentence begins with a unidiomatic phrase ("In all actuality") and lacks a verb ("both the response and complaint as ineffective"). The second sentence incorrectly uses *like* instead of *just as*: "The complaint doesn't recognize or address . . . like the response doesn't address." In short, the writing fits the description of seriously flawed prose in the scoring guide: it displays "serious and frequent problems in the use of language and sentence structure."

Analysis of Issue Questions for the GMAT

In some countries, television and radio programs are carefully censored for offensive language and behavior. In other countries, there is little or no censorship.

In your view, to what extent should government or any other group be able to censor television or radio programs? Explain, giving relevant reasons and/or examples to support your position.

"It is unrealistic to expect individual nations to make, independently, the sacrifices necessary to conserve energy. International leadership and worldwide cooperation are essential if we expect to protect the world's energy resources for future generations."

Discuss the extent to which you agree or disagree with the opinion stated above. Support your views with reasons and/or examples from your own experience, observations, or reading.

"Corporations and other businesses should try to eliminate the many ranks and salary grades that classify employees according to their experience and expertise. A 'flat' organizational structure is more likely to encourage collegiality and cooperation among employees."

Discuss the extent to which you agree or disagree with the opinion stated above. Support your views with reasons and/or examples from your own experience, observations, or reading.

"Of all the manifestations* of power, restraint in the use of that power impresses people most."

*manifestations: apparent signs or indicators

Explain what you think this quotation means and discuss the extent to which you agree or disagree with it. Develop your position with reasons and/or specific examples drawn from history, current events, or your own experience, observations, or reading.

"All groups and organizations should function as teams in which everyone makes decisions and shares responsibilities and duties. Giving one person central authority and responsibility for a project or task is not an effective way to get work done."

To what extent do you agree or disagree with the opinion expressed above? Support your views with reasons and/or specific examples drawn from your own work or school experiences, your observations, or your reading.

"There is only one definition of success — to be able to spend your life in your own way."

To what extent do you agree or disagree with this definition of success? Support your position by using reasons and examples from your reading, your own experience, or your observation of others.

"The best way to give advice to other people is to find out what they want and then advise them how to attain it."

Discuss the extent to which you agree or disagree with the opinion expressed above. Support your point of view with reasons and/or examples from your own experience, observations, or reading.

"For hundreds of years, the monetary system of most countries has been based on the exchange of metal coins and printed pieces of paper. However, because of recent developments in technology, the international community should consider replacing the entire system of coins and paper with a system of electronic accounts of credits and debits."

Discuss the extent to which you agree or disagree with the opinion stated above. Support your views with reasons and/or examples from your own experience, observations, or reading.

"Employees should keep their private lives and personal activities as separate as possible from the workplace."

Discuss the extent to which you agree or disagree with the opinion stated above. Support your views with reasons and/or examples from your own experience, observations, or reading.

"In any enterprise, the process of making or doing something is ultimately more important than the final product."

Discuss the extent to which you agree or disagree with the opinion expressed above. Support your point of view with reasons and/or examples from your own experience, observations, or reading.

Analysis of Issue Questions for the GMAT

"When someone achieves greatness in any field — such as the arts, science, politics, or business — that person's achievements are more important than any of his or her personal faults."

Discuss the extent to which you agree or disagree with the opinion stated above. Support your views with reasons and/or examples from your own experience, observations, or reading.

"Education has become the main provider of individual opportunity in our society. Just as property and money once were the keys to success, education has now become the element that most ensures success in life."

In your opinion, how accurate is the view expressed above? Explain, using reasons and examples based on your own experience, observations, or reading.

"Responsibility for preserving the natural environment ultimately belongs to each individual person, not to government."

Discuss the extent to which you agree or disagree with the opinion stated above. Support your views with reasons and/or examples from your own experience, observations, or reading.

"Organizations should be structured in a clear hierarchy in which the people at each level, from top to bottom, are held accountable for completing a particular component of the work. Any other organizational structure goes against human nature and will ultimately prove fruitless."

Discuss the extent to which you agree or disagree with the opinion expressed above. Support your point of view with reasons and/or examples from your own experience, observations, or reading.

"Nations should cooperate to develop regulations that limit children's access to adult material on the Internet."*

*The Internet is a worldwide computer network.

Discuss the extent to which you agree or disagree with the opinion stated above. Support your views with reasons and/or examples from your own experience, observations, or reading.

"Public buildings reveal much about the attitudes and values of the society that builds them. Today's new schools, courthouses, airports, and libraries, for example, reflect the attitudes and values of today's society."

Discuss the extent to which you agree or disagree with the opinion stated above. Support your views with reasons and/or examples from your own experience, observations, or reading.

"Some people believe that the best approach to effective time management is to make detailed daily and long-term plans and then to adhere to them. However, this highly structured approach to work is counterproductive. Time management needs to be flexible so that employees can respond to unexpected problems as they arise."

Discuss the extent to which you agree or disagree with the opinion expressed above. Support your point of view with reasons and/or examples from your own experience, observations, or reading.

"If the primary duty and concern of a corporation is to make money, then conflict is inevitable when the corporation must also acknowledge a duty to serve society."

From your perspective, how accurate is the above statement? Support your position with reasons and/or examples from your own experience, observations, or reading.

Some employers who recruit recent college graduates for entry-level jobs evaluate applicants only on their performance in business courses such as accounting, marketing, and economics. However, other employers also expect applicants to have a broad background in such courses as history, literature, and philosophy.

Do you think that, in the application process, employers should emphasize one type of background — either specialization in business courses or a more varied academic preparation — over the other? Why or why not? Develop your position by using reasons and/or examples from your own experience, observations, or reading.

Analysis of Issue Questions for the GMAT

"In this age of automation, many people complain that humans are becoming subservient to machines. But, in fact, machines are continually improving our lives."

Discuss the extent to which you agree or disagree with the opinion expressed above. Support your point of view with reasons and/or examples from your own experience, observations, or reading.

"Job security and salary should be based on employee performance, not on years of service. Rewarding employees primarily for years of service discourages people from maintaining consistently high levels of productivity."

Discuss the extent to which you agree or disagree with the opinion stated above. Support your views with reasons and/or examples from your own experience, observations, or reading.

"Clearly, government has a responsibility to support the arts. However, if that support is going to produce anything of value, government must place no restrictions on the art that is produced."

To what extent do you agree or disagree with the opinion expressed above? Develop your position by giving specific reasons and/or examples from your own experience, observations, or reading.

"Schools should be responsible only for teaching academic skills and not for teaching ethical and social values."

Discuss the extent to which you agree or disagree with the opinion expressed above. Support your point of view with reasons and/or examples from your own experience, observations, or reading.

"A powerful business leader has far more opportunity to influence the course of a community or a nation than does any government official."

Discuss the extent to which you agree or disagree with the opinion stated above. Support your views with reasons and/or examples from your own experience, observations, or reading.

"The best strategy for managing a business, or any enterprise, is to find the most capable people and give them as much authority as possible."

Discuss the extent to which you agree or disagree with the opinion stated above. Support your views with reasons and/or examples from your own experience, observations, or reading.

"Location has traditionally been one of the most important determinants of a business's success. The importance of location is not likely to change, no matter how advanced the development of computer communications and others kinds of technology becomes."

Discuss the extent to which you agree or disagree with the opinion stated above. Support your views with reasons and/or examples from your own experience, observations, or reading

---

"A company's long-term success is primarily dependent on the job satisfaction and the job security felt by the company's employees."

Discuss the extent to which you agree or disagree with the opinion stated above. Support your views with reasons and/or examples from your own experience, observations, or reading.

"Because businesses use high-quality advertising to sell low-quality products, schools should give students extensive training in how to make informed decisions before making purchases."

Discuss the extent to which you agree or disagree with the opinion expressed above. Support your point of view with reasons and/or examples from your own experience, observations, or reading.

"Too many people think only about getting results. The key to success, however, is to focus on the specific task at hand and not to worry about results."

What do you think this piece of advice means, and do you think that it is, on the whole, worth following? Support your views with reasons and/or examples drawn from your own experience, observations, or reading.

Analysis of Issue Questions for the GMAT

"Companies benefit when they discourage employees from working extra hours or taking work home. When employees spend their leisure time without 'producing' something for the job, they will be more focused and effective when they return to work."

Discuss the extent to which you agree or disagree with the opinion expressed above. Support your point of view with reasons and/or examples from your own experience, observations, or reading.

"Financial gain should be the most important factor in choosing a career."

Discuss the extent to which you agree or disagree with the opinion stated above. Support your views with reasons and/or examples from your own experience, observations, or reading.

"You can tell the ideas of a nation by its advertisements."

Explain what you think this quotation means and discuss the extent to which you agree or disagree with it. Develop your position with reasons and/or specific examples drawn from history, current events, or your own experience, observations, or reading.

"People are likely to accept as a leader only someone who has demonstrated an ability to perform the same tasks that he or she expects others to perform."

Discuss the extent to which you agree or disagree with the opinion stated above. Support your views with reasons and/or examples from your own experience, observations, or reading.

"All citizens should be required to perform a specified amount of public service. Such service would benefit not only the country as a whole but also the individual participants."

Discuss the extent to which you agree or disagree with the opinion stated above. Support your views with reasons and/or examples from your own experience, observations, or reading.

"Business relations are infected through and through with the disease of short-sighted motives. We are so concerned with immediate results and short-term goals that we fail to look beyond them."

Assuming that the term "business relations" can refer to the decisions and actions of any organization — for instance, a small family business, a community association, or a large international corporation — explain the extent to which you think that this criticism is valid. In your discussion of the issue, use reasons and/or examples from your own experience, your observation of others, or your reading.

"Businesses and other organizations have overemphasized the importance of working as a team. Clearly, in any human group, it is the strong individual, the person with the most commitment and energy, who gets things done."

Discuss the extent to which you agree or disagree with the opinion stated above. Support your views with reasons and/or examples from your own experience, observations, or reading.

"Since science and technology are becoming more and more essential to modern society, schools should devote more time to teaching science and technology and less to teaching the arts and humanities."

Discuss the extent to which you agree or disagree with the opinion stated above. Support your views with reasons and/or examples from your own experience, observations, or reading.

"Courtesy is rapidly disappearing from everyday interactions, and as a result, we are all the poorer for it."

From your perspective, is this an accurate observation? Why or why not? Explain, using reasons and/or examples from your own experience, observations, or reading.

"It is difficult for people to achieve professional success without sacrificing important aspects of a fulfilling personal life."

Discuss the extent to which you agree or disagree with the opinion stated above. Support your views with reasons and/or examples from your own experience, observations, or reading.

Analysis of Issue Questions for the GMAT

"With the increasing emphasis on a global economy and international cooperation, people need to understand that their role as citizens of the world is more important than their role as citizens of a particular country."

Discuss the extent to which you agree or disagree with the opinion stated above. Support your views with reasons and/or examples from your own experience, observations, or reading.

"The best way to preserve the natural environment is to impose penalties — whether fines, imprisonment, or other punishments — on those who are most responsible for polluting or otherwise damaging it."

Discuss the extent to which you agree or disagree with the opinion expressed above. Support your point of view with reasons and/or examples from your own experience, observations, or reading.

"Scientists are continually redefining the standards for what is beneficial or harmful to the environment. Since these standards keep shifting, companies should resist changing their products and processes in response to each new recommendation until those recommendations become government regulations."

Discuss the extent to which you agree or disagree with the opinion stated above. Support your views with reasons and/or examples from your own experience, observations, or reading.

"The most important reason for studying history is not that knowledge of history can make us better people or a better society but that it can provide clues to solving the societal problems that we face today."

Discuss the extent to which you agree or disagree with the opinion expressed above. Support your point of view with reasons and/or examples from your own experience, observations, or reading.

"All companies should invest heavily in advertising because high-quality advertising can sell almost any product or service."

Discuss the extent to which you agree or disagree with the opinion expressed above. Support your point of view with reasons and/or examples from your own experience, observations, or reading.

"The most effective way for a businessperson to maximize profits over a long period of time is to follow the highest standards of ethics."

Discuss the extent to which you agree or disagree with the opinion stated above. Support your views with reasons and/or examples from your own experience, observations, or reading.

Businesses are as likely as are governments to establish large bureaucracies, but bureaucracy is far more damaging to a business than it is to a government.

Discuss the extent to which you agree or disagree with the opinion expressed above. Support your point of view with reasons and/or examples from your own experience, observations, or reading.

The primary responsibility for preventing environmental damage belongs to government, not to individuals or private industry.

Discuss the extent to which you agree or disagree with the opinion expressed above. Support your point of view with reasons and/or examples from your own experience, observations, or reading.

In matching job candidates with job openings, managers must consider not only such variables as previous work experience and educational background but also personality traits and work habits, which are more difficult to judge.

What do you consider essential in an employee or colleague? Explain, using reasons and/or examples from your work or worklike experiences, or from your observations of others.

"Ask most older people to identify the key to success, and they are likely to reply 'hard work.' Yet, I would tell people starting off in a career that work in itself is not the key. In fact, you have to approach work cautiously — too much or too little can be self-defeating."

To what extent do you agree or disagree with this view of work? Develop your position by using reasons and/or examples from your reading, experience, or observations.

Analysis of Issue Questions for the GMAT

How far should a supervisor go in criticizing the performance of a subordinate? Some highly successful managers have been known to rely on verbal abuse and intimidation. Do you think that this is an effective means of communicating expectations? If not, what alternative should a manager use in dealing with someone whose work is less than satisfactory?

Explain your views on this issue. Be sure to support your position with reasons and/or examples from your own experience, observations, or reading.

"The presence of a competitor is always beneficial to a company. Competition forces a company to change itself in ways that improve its practices."

Discuss the extent to which you agree or disagree with the opinion stated above. Support your views with reasons and/or examples from your own experience, observations, or reading.

"Successful individuals typically set their next goal somewhat — but not too much — above their last achievement. In this way, they steadily raise their level of aspiration."

In your opinion, how accurate is this statement? Explain, using specific reasons and examples from your reading, your own experience, or your observation of others.

"The term 'user friendly' is usually applied to the trouble-free way that computer software moves people from screen to screen, function to function. However, the term can also refer to a government office, a library, public transportation, or anything designed to provide information or services in an easy, friendly way. Just as all societies have many striking examples of user-friendly services, so do they abound in examples of user-unfriendly systems."

Identify a system or service that you have found to be either "user-friendly" or "user-unfriendly." Discuss, from the user's perspective, in what way the system either is or is not easy to use and explain the consequences or effect of such a system.

"Popular entertainment is overly influenced by commercial interests. Superficiality, obscenity, and violence characterize films and television today because those qualities are commercially successful."

Discuss the extent to which you agree or disagree with this opinion. To support your position, use reasons and/or examples from your reading, your observations, or your experiences as a consumer of popular entertainment.

"Never tell people how to do things. Tell them what to do, and they will surprise you with their ingenuity."

To what extent do you agree or disagree with the opinion expressed above? Explain your point of view by giving reasons and/or examples from your own experience, observations, or reading.

"The secret of business is to know something that nobody else knows."

Explain what you think the above quotation means and discuss the extent to which you agree or disagree with it. Support your position with relevant reasons and/or examples from your own experience, observations, or reading.

"Everywhere, it seems, there are clear and positive signs that people are becoming more respectful of one another's differences."

In your opinion, how accurate is the view expressed above? Use reasons and/or examples from your own experience, observations, or reading to develop your position.

"What is the final objective of business? It is to make the obtaining of a living — the obtaining of food, clothing, shelter, and a minimum of luxuries — so mechanical and so little time-consuming that people shall have time for other things."
— A business leader, circa 1930

Explain what you think the quotation above means and discuss the extent to which you agree or disagree with the view of business it expresses. Support your views with reasons and/or examples from your own experience, observations, or reading.

"Juvenile crime is a serious social problem, and businesses must become more involved in helping to prevent it."

Discuss the extent to which you agree or disagree with the opinion expressed above. Support your point of view with reasons and/or examples from your own experience, observations, or reading.

Analysis of Issue Questions for the GMAT

"Employers should have no right to obtain information about their employees' health or other aspects of their personal lives without the employees' permission."

Discuss the extent to which you agree or disagree with the opinion stated above. Support your views with reasons and/or examples from your own experience, observations, or reading.

"Even at its best, a government is a tremendous burden to business, though a necessary one."

Discuss the extent to which you agree or disagree with the opinion expressed above. Support your point of view with reasons and/or examples from your own experience, observations, or reading.

"What education fails to teach us is to see the human community as one. Rather than focus on the unique differences that separate one nation from another, education should focus on the similarities among all people and places on Earth."

What do you think of the view of education expressed above? Explain, using reasons and/or specific examples from your own experience, observations, or reading.

"As government bureaucracy increases, citizens become more and more separated from their government."

Discuss the extent to which you agree or disagree with the opinion expressed above. Support your point of view with reasons and/or examples from your own experience, observations, or reading.

"The goal of business should not be to make as big a profit as possible. Instead, business should also concern itself with the well-being of the public."

Discuss the extent to which you agree or disagree with the opinion expressed above. Support your point of view with reasons and/or examples from your own experience, observations, or reading.

"The rise of multinational corporations is leading to global homogeneity*. Because people everywhere are beginning to want the same products and services, regional differences are rapidly disappearing."

* homogeneity: sameness, similarity

Discuss the extent to which you agree or disagree with the opinion expressed above. Support your point of view with reasons and/or examples from your own experience, observations, or reading.

"Manufacturers are responsible for ensuring that their products are safe. If a product injures someone, for whatever reason, the manufacturer should be held legally and financially accountable for the injury."

Discuss the extent to which you agree or disagree with the opinion expressed above. Support your point of view with reasons and/or examples from your own experience, observations, or reading.

"Work greatly influences people's personal lives — their special interests, their leisure activities, even their appearance away from the workplace."

Discuss the extent to which you agree or disagree with the opinion expressed above. Support your point of view with reasons and/or examples from your own experience, observations, or reading.

"Since the physical work environment affects employee productivity and morale, the employees themselves should have the right to decide how their workplace is designed."

Discuss the extent to which you agree or disagree with the opinion stated above. Support your views with reasons and/or examples from your own experience, observations, or reading.

"The most important quality in an employee is not specific knowledge or technical competence. Instead, it is the ability to work well with other employees."

Discuss the extent to which you agree or disagree with the opinion expressed above. Support your point of view with reasons and/or examples from your own experience, observations, or reading.

Analysis of Issue Questions for the GMAT

"So long as no laws are broken, there is nothing unethical about doing whatever you need to do to promote existing products or to create new products."

Discuss the extent to which you agree or disagree with the opinion expressed above. Support your point of view with reasons and/or examples from your own experience, observations, or reading.

"Commercialism has become too widespread. It has even crept into schools and places of worship. Every nation should place limits on what kinds of products, if any, can be sold at certain events or places."

Discuss the extent to which you agree or disagree with the opinion expressed above. Support your point of view with reasons and/or examples from your own experience, observations, or reading.

"Companies should not try to improve employees' performance by giving incentives — for example, awards or gifts. These incentives encourage negative kinds of behavior instead of encouraging a genuine interest in doing the work well."

Discuss the extent to which you agree or disagree with the opinion stated above. Support your views with reasons and/or examples from your own experience, observations, or reading.

People often give the following advice: "Be yourself. Follow your instincts and behave in a way that feels natural."

Do you think that, in general, this is good advice? Why or why not? Develop your point of view by giving reasons and/or examples from your own experience, observations, or reading.

"The people we remember best are the ones who broke the rules."

Discuss the extent to which you agree or disagree with the opinion expressed above. Support your point of view with reasons and/or examples from your own experience, observations, or reading.

"There are essentially two forces that motivate people: self-interest and fear."

Discuss the extent to which you agree or disagree with the opinion stated above. Support your position with reasons and/or examples from your own experience, observations, or reading.

"For a leader there is nothing more difficult, and therefore more important, than to be able to make decisions."

Discuss the extent to which you agree or disagree with the opinion expressed above. Support your point of view with reasons and/or examples from your own experience, observations, or reading.

Although "genius" is difficult to define, one of the qualities of genius is the ability to transcend traditional modes of thought and create new ones.

Explain what you think the above statement means and discuss the extent to which you agree or disagree with this definition of genius. In your discussion, be sure to include at least one example of someone who, in your opinion, exemplifies genius or a particular characteristic of genius.

Most people would agree that buildings represent a valuable record of any society's past, but controversy arises when old buildings stand on ground that modern planners feel could be better used for modern purposes.

In your opinion, which is more important — preserving historic buildings or encouraging modern development? Explain your position, using reasons and examples based on your own experiences, observations, or reading.

"The ability to deal with people is as purchasable a commodity as sugar or coffee, and it is worth more than any other commodity under the sun."

Explain what you think the above quotation means and discuss the extent to which you agree or disagree with it. Support your position with relevant reasons and/or examples from your own experience, observations, or reading.

"As individuals, people save too little and borrow too much."

From your perspective, how accurate is the view expressed above? In your discussion, be sure to consider the conditions under which it is appropriate to save money and the conditions under which it is appropriate to borrow. Develop your position using reasons and/or examples from your own experience, observations, or reading.

Analysis of Issue Questions for the GMAT

"No one can possibly achieve any real and lasting success or 'get rich' in business by conforming to conventional practices or ways of thinking."

Discuss the extent to which you agree or disagree with the opinion stated above. Support your views with reasons and/or examples from your own experience, observations, or reading.

"Business and government must do more, much more, to meet the needs and goals of women in the workplace."

What do you think of the opinion expressed above? In your discussion, be sure to use reasons and/or examples from your own experience, observations, or reading.

"We shape our buildings and afterwards our buildings shape us."

Explain what you think this statement means and discuss the extent to which you do or do not agree with it. Support your views with reasons and/or specific examples from your experience, observations, or reading.

"A business should not be held responsible for providing customers with complete information about its products or services; customers should have the responsibility of gathering information about the products or services they may want to buy."

Discuss the extent to which you agree or disagree with the opinion stated above. Support your views with reasons and/or examples from your own experience, observations, or reading.

"Advertising is the most influential and therefore the most important artistic achievement of the twentieth century."

Discuss the extent to which you agree or disagree with the opinion expressed above. Support your point of view with reasons and/or examples from your own experience, observations, or reading.

"Whether promoting a product, an event, or a person, an advertising campaign is most effective when it appeals to emotion rather than to reason."

Discuss the extent to which you agree or disagree with the opinion expressed above. Support your point of view with reasons and/or examples from your own experience, observations, or reading.

"As technologies and the demand for certain services change, many workers will lose their jobs. The responsibility for those people to adjust to such change should belong to the individual worker, not to government or to business."

Discuss the extent to which you agree or disagree with the opinion stated above. Support your position with specific reasons and/or examples drawn from your reading, your observations, or your own experience.

"Each generation must accept blame not only for the hateful words and actions of some of its members but also for the failure of other members to speak out against those words and actions."

Discuss the extent to which you agree or disagree with the opinion expressed above. Support your point of view with reasons and/or examples from your own experience, observations, or reading.

"The study of history is largely a waste of time because it prevents us from focusing on the challenges of the present."

Discuss the extent to which you agree or disagree with the opinion expressed above. Support your point of view with reasons and/or examples from your own experience, observations, or reading.

"People often complain that products are not made to last. They feel that making products that wear out fairly quickly wastes both natural and human resources. What they fail to see, however, is that such manufacturing practices keep costs down for the consumer and stimulate demand."

Which do you find more compelling: the complaint about products that do not last or the response to it? Explain your position using relevant reasons and/or examples drawn from your own experience, observations, or reading.

"Government should establish regulations to reduce or eliminate any suspected health hazards in the environment, even when the scientific studies of these health hazards are incomplete or contradictory."

Discuss the extent to which you agree or disagree with the opinion stated above. Support your views with reasons and/or examples from your own experience, observations, or reading.

Analysis of Issue Questions for the GMAT

"Employees should show loyalty to their company by fully supporting the company's managers and policies, even when the employees believe that the managers and policies are misguided."

Discuss the extent to which you agree or disagree with the opinion stated above. Support your views with reasons and/or examples from your own experience, observations, or reading.

"To be successful, companies should trust their workers and give them as much freedom as possible. Any company that tries to control employees' behavior through a strict system of rewards and punishments will soon find that such controls have a negative effect on employee morale and, consequently, on the company's success."

Discuss the extent to which you agree or disagree with the opinion stated above. Support your views with reasons and/or examples from your own experience, observations, or reading.

"If parents want to prepare their children to succeed in life, teaching the children self-discipline is more important than teaching them self-esteem."

Discuss the extent to which you agree or disagree with the opinion stated above. Support your views with reasons and/or examples from your own experience, observations, or reading.

"Companies are never justified in employing young children, even if the child's family would benefit from the income."

Discuss the extent to which you agree or disagree with the opinion stated above. Support your views with reasons and/or examples from your own experience, observations, or reading.

"In order to understand a society, we must examine the contents of its museums and the subjects of its memorials. What a society chooses to preserve, display, and commemorate is the truest indicator of what the society values."

Discuss the extent to which you agree or disagree with the opinion stated above. Support your views with reasons and/or examples from your own experience, observations, or reading.

"In business, more than in any other social arena, men and women have learned how to share power effectively."

Discuss the extent to which you agree or disagree with the opinion stated above. Support your views with reasons and/or examples from your own experience, observations, or reading.

"In order to accommodate the increasing number of undergraduate students, colleges and universities should offer most courses through distance learning, such as videotaped instruction that can be accessed through the Internet or cable television. Requiring students to appear at a designated time and place is no longer an effective or efficient way of teaching most undergraduate courses."

Discuss the extent to which you agree or disagree with the opinion stated above. Support your views with reasons and/or examples from your own experience, observations, or reading.

"If a nation is to ensure its own economic success, it must maintain a highly competitive educational system in which students compete among themselves and against students from other countries."

Discuss the extent to which you agree or disagree with the opinion stated above. Support your views with reasons and/or examples from your own experience, observations, or reading.

"In order to force companies to improve policies and practices considered unethical or harmful, society should rely primarily on consumer action — such as refusal to buy products — rather than legislative action."

Discuss the extent to which you agree or disagree with the opinion stated above. Support your views with reasons and/or examples from your own experience, observations, or reading.

"The automobile has caused more problems than it has solved. Most societies would probably be much better off if the automobile had never been invented."

Discuss the extent to which you agree or disagree with the opinion stated above. Support your views with reasons and/or examples from your own experience, observations, or reading.

Analysis of Issue Questions for the GMAT

"An advanced degree may help someone get a particular job. Once a person begins working, however, the advanced degree and the formal education it represents are rarely relevant to success on the job."

Discuss the extent to which you agree or disagree with the opinion stated above. Support your views with reasons and/or examples from your own experience, observations, or reading.

"Most people today place too much emphasis on satisfying their immediate desires. The overall quality of life would be greatly improved if we all focused instead on meeting our long-term needs."

Discuss the extent to which you agree or disagree with the opinion stated above. Support your views with reasons and/or examples from your own experience, observations, or reading.

"The value of any nation should be measured more by its scientific and artistic achievements than by its business successes."

Discuss the extent to which you agree or disagree with the opinion stated above. Support your views with reasons and/or examples from your own experience, observations, or reading.

"All archeological treasures should remain in the country in which they were originally discovered. These works should not be exported, even if museums in other parts of the world are better able to preserve and display them."

Discuss the extent to which you agree or disagree with the opinion stated above. Support your views with reasons and/or examples from your own experience, observations, or reading.

"The most effective way for managers to assign work is to divide complex tasks into their simpler component parts. This way, each worker completes a small portion of the task but contributes to the whole."

Discuss the extent to which you agree or disagree with the opinion stated above. Support your views with reasons and/or examples from your own experience, observations, or reading.

"People are overwhelmed by the increasing amount of information available on the computer. Therefore, the immediate goal of the information technology industry should be to help people learn how to obtain the information they need efficiently and wisely."

Discuss the extent to which you agree or disagree with the opinion stated above. Support your views with reasons and/or examples from your own experience, observations, or reading.

"Employees should not have full access to their own personnel files. If, for example, employees were allowed to see certain confidential materials, the people supplying that information would not be likely to express their opinions candidly."

Discuss the extent to which you agree or disagree with the opinion stated above. Support your views with reasons and/or examples from your own experience, observations, or reading.

"All personnel evaluations at a company should be multi-directional — that is, people at every level of the organization should review not only those working 'under' them but also those working 'over' them."

Discuss the extent to which you agree or disagree with the opinion stated above. Support your views with reasons and/or examples from your own experience, observations, or reading.

"The most effective business leaders are those who maintain the highest ethical standards."

Discuss the extent to which you agree or disagree with the opinion stated above. Support your views with reasons and/or examples from your own experience, observations, or reading.

"Because of recent advancements in business and technology, the overall quality of life in most societies has never been better than at the present time."

Discuss the extent to which you agree or disagree with the opinion stated above. Support your views with reasons and/or examples from your own experience, observations, or reading.

Analysis of Issue Questions for the GMAT

"In most fields — including education, politics, and business — the prevailing philosophy never stays in place very long. This pattern of constantly shifting from one theoretical position to another is an inevitable reflection of human nature: people soon tire of the status quo."

Discuss the extent to which you agree or disagree with the opinion stated above. Support your views with reasons and/or examples from your own experience, observations, or reading.

"It is essential that the nations of the world increase spending on the building of space stations and on the exploration of other planets, even if that means spending less on other government programs."

Discuss the extent to which you agree or disagree with the opinion stated above. Support your views with reasons and/or examples from your own experience, observations, or reading.

"Technology ultimately separates and alienates people more than it serves to bring them together."

Discuss the extent to which you agree or disagree with the opinion stated above. Support your views with reasons and/or examples from your own experience, observations, or reading.

"All employees should help decide how the profits of their company or business should be used."

Discuss the extent to which you agree or disagree with the opinion stated above. Support your views with reasons and/or examples from your own experience, observations, or reading.

"A government should provide funding for the arts, but only for those artistic works that reflect the values and attitudes of the majority of the population."

Discuss the extent to which you agree or disagree with the opinion stated above. Support your views with reasons and/or examples from your own experience, observations, or reading.

"The well-being of a society depends more on the success of small businesses than on the success of a few large, high-profile corporations."

Discuss the extent to which you agree or disagree with the opinion stated above. Support your views with reasons and/or examples from your own experience, observations, or reading.

"People's loyalty to political parties and political leaders significantly hinders their ability to form their own opinions about an issue."

Discuss the extent to which you agree or disagree with the opinion stated above. Support your views with reasons and/or examples from your own experience, observations, or reading.

"It makes no sense for people with strong technological skills to go to college if they know that they can earn a good salary without a college degree."

Discuss the extent to which you agree or disagree with the opinion stated above. Support your views with reasons and/or examples from your own experience, observations, or reading.

"Companies should not allow the trend toward informality in dress and conduct at the workplace to continue; formality in dress and behavior helps create a more disciplined and productive work environment."

Discuss the extent to which you agree or disagree with the opinion stated above. Support your views with reasons and/or examples from your own experience, observations, or reading.

"Whether people accept or reject an idea depends more on the way it is presented to them than on the merits of the idea itself."

Discuss the extent to which you agree or disagree with the opinion stated above. Support your views with reasons and/or examples from your own experience, observations, or reading.

"Schools should not teach specialized information and techniques, which might soon become outdated. Instead, schools should encourage a more general approach to learning."

Discuss the extent to which you agree or disagree with the opinion stated above. Support your views with reasons and/or examples from your own experience, observations, or reading.

Analysis of Issue Questions for the GMAT

"The current trend of moving frequently from company to company has negative consequences: it causes instability in the workplace and, as a result, instability in society. Therefore, companies should require employees to make a long-term commitment to the organization."

Discuss the extent to which you agree or disagree with the opinion stated above. Support your views with reasons and/or examples from your own experience, observations, or reading.

"The most effective leaders are those who can solve complex problems by finding simple, immediate solutions."

Discuss the extent to which you agree or disagree with the opinion stated above. Support your views with reasons and/or examples from your own experience, observations, or reading.

"Formal education should not come to an end when people graduate from college. Instead people should frequently enroll in courses throughout their lives."

Discuss the extent to which you agree or disagree with the opinion stated above. Support your views with reasons and/or examples from your own experience, observations, or reading.

"Laws pertaining to relatively minor crimes must be vigorously enforced if a society hopes to stop more serious crimes."

Discuss the extent to which you agree or disagree with the opinion stated above. Support your views with reasons and/or examples from your own experience, observations, or reading.

"In general, a company's most valuable employees are those who are concerned more with efficiency than with quality."

Discuss the extent to which you agree or disagree with the opinion stated above. Support your views with reasons and/or examples from your own experience, observations, or reading.

"Instead of relying on the advice of outside experts, organizations should place greater value on the advice that can come only from their own highly experienced employees."

Discuss the extent to which you agree or disagree with the opinion stated above. Support your views with reasons and/or examples from your own experience, observations, or reading.

"When judging the qualifications of potential employees, business employers should rely solely on objective information, such as a candidate's résumé and education. Personal interviews are much too subjective and are therefore not a valid basis on which to judge a person's qualifications for a job."

Discuss the extent to which you agree or disagree with the opinion stated above. Support your views with reasons and/or examples from your own experience, observations, or reading.

"We can learn more about a society by observing how its people spend their leisure time than by observing them at work."

Discuss the extent to which you agree or disagree with the opinion stated above. Support your views with reasons and/or examples from your own experience, observations, or reading.

"Governments should not be responsible for regulating businesses and other organizations. Instead, society would benefit if the organizations themselves assumed most of the responsibility for establishing and enforcing their own standards and regulations."

Discuss the extent to which you agree or disagree with the opinion stated above. Support your views with reasons and/or examples from your own experience, observations, or reading.

"In any business or other organization, it is better to have managers with strong leadership skills than managers with expertise and work experience in a particular field."

Discuss the extent to which you agree or disagree with the opinion stated above. Support your views with reasons and/or examples from your own experience, observations, or reading.

Analysis of Issue Questions for the GMAT

"Employees should not be asked to provide formal evaluations of their supervisor because they have little basis for judging or even understanding their supervisor's performance."

Discuss the extent to which you agree or disagree with the opinion stated above. Support your views with reasons and/or examples from your own experience, observations, or reading.

"Although many people object to advertisements and solicitations that intrude into their lives through such means as the telephone, the Internet, and television, companies and organizations must have the right to contact potential customers and donors whenever and however they wish."

Discuss the extent to which you agree or disagree with the opinion stated above. Support your views with reasons and/or examples from your own experience, observations, or reading.

"In business courses, professors should teach only factual information and skills, not ethics."

Discuss the extent to which you agree or disagree with the opinion stated above. Support your views with reasons and/or examples from your own experience, observations, or reading.

In some companies, employees are allowed to express their feelings and opinions about the company by sending electronic messages to everyone in the company. In other companies, this type of communication is strictly prohibited.

What restrictions, if any, do you think companies should place on employees' electronic communications? Support your views with reasons and/or examples from your own experience, observations, or reading.

Some people claim that in order to protect national parks and historical sites, public access to them should be greatly restricted. Others argue that there should be few restrictions, if any, because such places were intended for everyone to use.

Explain your position on this issue. Support your views with reasons and/or examples from your own experience, observations, or reading.

Some people claim that the growth of mass media has stifled intellectual curiosity. Others, however, argue that the availability of so much information and entertainment has encouraged individuals to expand their intellect and creativity.

Explain your position on this issue. Support your views with reasons and/or examples from your own experience, observations, or reading.

Some experts maintain that students learn best in a highly structured environment, one that emphasizes discipline, punctuality, and routine. Others insist that educators, if they are to help students maximize their potential, ought to maintain an atmosphere of relative freedom and spontaneity.

Explain your position on the issue of structure *versus* freedom in an ideal learning environment. Support your views with reasons and/or examples from your own experience, observations, or reading.

Analysis of an Argument

When finished reading directions click on the icon below

Dismiss Directions

In this section, you will be asked to write a critique of the argument presented. *You are NOT being asked to present your own views on the subject.*

WRITING YOUR RESPONSE: Take a few minutes to evaluate the argument and plan a response before you begin writing. Be sure to organize your ideas and develop them fully, but leave time to reread your response and make any revisions that you think are necessary.

EVALUATION OF YOUR RESPONSE: College and university faculty members from various subject-matter areas, including management education, will evaluate the overall quality of your thinking and writing. They will consider how well you

- organize, develop, and express your ideas about the argument presented
- provide relevant supporting reasons and examples
- control the elements of standard written English

Test	Section	Time			?	Answer	→
Quit	Exit				Help	Confirm	Next

GMAT SCORING GUIDE: ANALYSIS OF AN ARGUMENT

SCORE

6   OUTSTANDING

A 6 paper presents a cogent, well-articulated critique of the argument and demonstrates mastery of the elements of effective writing.

A typical paper in this category

— clearly identifies important features of the argument and analyzes them insightfully
— develops ideas cogently, organizes them logically, and connects them with clear transitions
— effectively supports the main points of the critique
— demonstrates control of language, including diction and syntactic variety
— demonstrates facility with the conventions of standard written English but may have minor flaws

---

5   STRONG

A 5 paper presents a well-developed critique of the argument and demonstrates good control of the elements of effective writing.

A typical paper in this category

— clearly identifies important features of the argument and analyzes them in a generally thoughtful way
— develops ideas clearly, organizes them logically, and connects them with appropriate transitions
— sensibly supports the main points of the critique
— demonstrates control of language, including diction and syntactic variety
— demonstrates facility with the conventions of standard written English but may have occasional flaws

---

4   ADEQUATE

A 4 paper presents a competent critique of the argument and demonstrates adequate control of the elements of writing.

A typical paper in this category

— identifies and analyzes important features of the argument
— develops and organizes ideas satisfactorily but may not connect them with transitions
— supports the main points of the critique
— demonstrates sufficient control of language to convey ideas with reasonable clarity
— generally follows the conventions of standard written English but may have some flaws

3   LIMITED

A 3 paper demonstrates some competence in analytical writing skills and in its control of the elements of writing but is plainly flawed.

A typical paper in this category exhibits *one or more* of the following characteristics:

— does not identify or analyze most of the important features of the argument, although some analysis of the argument is present
— mainly analyzes tangential or irrelevant matters, or reasons poorly
— is limited in the logical development and organization of ideas
— offers support of little relevance and value for points of the critique
— does not convey meaning clearly
— contains occasional major errors or frequent minor errors in grammar, usage, and mechanics

2   SERIOUSLY FLAWED

A 2 paper demonstrates serious weaknesses in analytical writing skills.

A typical paper in this category exhibits *one or more* of the following characteristics:

— does not present a critique based on logical analysis, but may instead present the writer's own views on the subject
— does not develop ideas, or is disorganized and illogical
— provides little, if any, relevant or reasonable support
— has serious and frequent problems in the use of language and in sentence structure
— contains numerous errors in grammar, usage, and mechanics that interfere with meaning

1   FUNDAMENTALLY DEFICIENT

A 1 paper demonstrates fundamental deficiencies in analytical writing skills.

A typical paper in this category exhibits *more than one* of the following characteristics:

— provides little evidence of the ability to understand and analyze the argument
— provides little evidence of the ability to develop an organized response
— has severe and persistent errors in language and sentence structure
— contains a pervasive pattern of errors in grammar, usage, and mechanics that results in incoherence

0   Off topic, in a foreign language, merely attempts to copy the topic, or consists only of keystroke characters.

NR   Blank

Read the statement and the instructions that follow it, and then make any notes that will help you plan your response. Begin typing your response in the box at the bottom of the screen.

Beginning

The following appeared as part of an article in a daily newspaper.

"The computerized on-board warning system that will be installed in commercial airliners will virtually solve the problem of midair plane collisions. One plane's warning system can receive signals from another's transponder—a radio set that signals a plane's course—in order to determine the likelihood of a collision and recommend evasive action."

Discuss how well reasoned you find this argument. In your discussion be sure to analyze the line of reasoning and the use of evidence in the argument. For example, you may need to consider what questionable assumptions underline the thinking and what alternative explanations or counterexamples might weaken the conclusion. You can also discuss what sort of evidence would strengthen or refute the argument, what changes in the argument would make it more logically sound, and what, if anything, would help you better evaluate its conclusion.

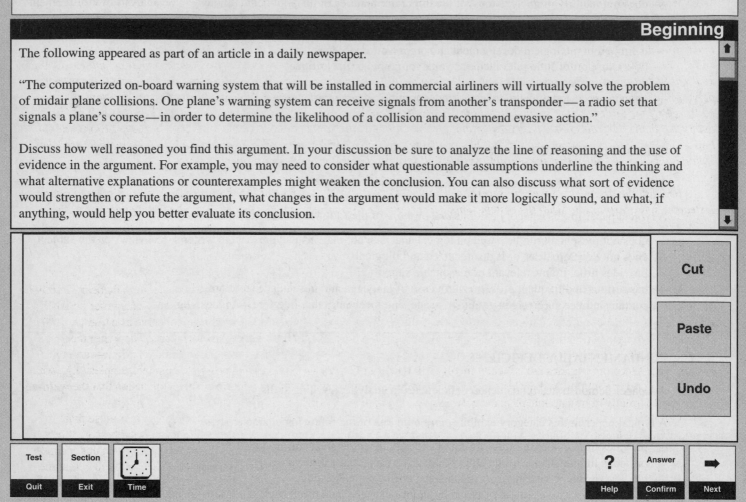

Cut

Paste

Undo

| Test | Section | | | | ? | Answer | ➡ |
| Quit | Exit | Time | | | Help | Confirm | Next |

The argument that this warning system will virtually solve the problem of midair plane collisions omits some important concerns that must be addressed to substantiate the argument. The statement that follows the description of what this warning system will do simply describes the system and how it operates. This alone does not constitute a logical argument in favor of the warning system, and it certainly does not provide support or proof of the main argument.

Most conspicuously, the argument does not address the cause of the problem of midair plane collisions, the use of the system by pilots and flight specialists, or who is involved in the midair plane collisions. First, the argument assumes that the cause of the problem is that the planes' courses, the likelihood of collisions, and actions to avoid collisions are unknown or inaccurate. In a weak attempt to support its claim, the argument describes a system that makes all of these things accurately known. But if the cause of the problem of midair plane collisions is that pilots are not paying attention to their computer systems or flight operations, the warning system will not solve the collision problem. Second, the argument never addresses the interface between individuals and the system and how this will affect the warning system's objective of obliterating the problem of collisions. If the pilot or flight specialist does not conform to what the warning system suggests, midair collisions will not be avoided. Finally, if planes other than commercial airliners are involved in the collisions, the problem of these collisions cannot be solved by a warning system that will not be installed on non-commercial airliners. The argument also does not address what would happen in the event that the warning system collapses, fails, or does not work properly.

Because the argument leaves out several key issues, it is not sound or persuasive. If it included the items discussed above instead of solely explaining what the system supposedly does, the argument would have been more thorough and convincing.

EXPLANATION OF SCORE — 6

This response is, as the scoring guide requires of a 6, "cogent" and "well articulated": all the points made not only bear directly on the argument to be analyzed but also contribute to a single, integrated development of the writer's critique. The writer begins by making the controlling point that a mere *description* of the warning system's mode of operation cannot serve as a true *argument* proving the system's effectiveness, since the description overlooks several major considerations. The writer then identifies these considerations — what causes midair collisions, how pilots will actually use the commercial airline warning system, what kinds of airplanes are typically involved in midair collisions — and, citing appropriate counterexamples (e.g., what if pilots do not pay attention to their instruments?), explains fully how each oversight undermines the conclusion that the warning system will virtually eliminate midair plane collisions.

Throughout, the writer complements the logically organized development of this critique with good, clear prose that demonstrates the ability not only to control language and vary sentence structure but also to express ideas forcibly (e.g., "the argument never addresses the interface between individuals and the system"). Of course, as in any response written under time constraints, occasional minor flaws can be found. For example, "the argument assumes that the cause of the problem is that the planes' courses, the likelihood of collisions, and actions to avoid collisions are unknown or inaccurate" is wordy and imprecise: how can a *course*, a *likelihood*, or *actions* be *inaccurate*? But flaws such as these, minor and infrequent, do not interfere with the overall clarity and forcefulness of this outstanding response.

The argument is not logically convincing. It does not state whether all planes can receive signals from each other. It does not state whether planes constantly receive signals. If they only receive signals once every certain time interval, collisions will not definitely be prevented. Further if they receive a signal right before they are about to crash, they cannot avoid each other.

The main flaw in the argument is that it assumes that the two planes, upon receiving each other's signals, will know which evasive action to take. For example, the two planes could be going towards each other and then receive the signals. If one turns at an angle to the left and the other turns at an angle to the right, the two planes will still crash. Even if they receive an updated signal, they will not have time to avoid each other.

The following argument would be more sound and persuasive. The new warning system will solve the problem of midair plane collisions. Each plane will receive constant, continual signals from each other. If the two planes are headed in a direction where they will crash, the system will coordinate the signals, and tell one plane to go one way, and the other plane to go another way. The new system will ensure that the two planes will turn in different directions so they don't crash by trying to prevent the original crash. In addition, the two planes will be able to see themselves and the other on a computer screen, to aid in the evasive action.

EXPLANATION OF SCORE — 4

This response competently cites a number of deficiencies in the argument presented: the information given about the nature of the signals sent and received and the evasive action recommended does not warrant the conclusion that the onboard warning system "will virtually solve the problem of midair plane collisions." However, in discussing these insufficiencies in the argument, the response reveals an unevenness in the quality of its reasoning. For example, while it is perfectly legitimate to point out that the argument assumes too much and says too little about the evasive action that will be recommended by the warning system, it is farfetched to suggest that the system might be so poorly designed as to route two approaching airplanes to the same spot. Likewise, while it is fair to question the effectiveness of a warning signal about which the argument says so little, it is not reasonable to assume that the system would be designed to space signals so far apart that they would prove useless. Rather than invent implausibly bad versions of the warning system to prove that it might be ineffective, a stronger response would analyze unexplored possibilities inherent in the information that is given — e.g., the possibility that pilots might not be able to respond quickly and effectively to the radio signals the argument says they will receive when the new system is installed. The "more sound and persuasive argument" in the last paragraph, while an improvement on the original, continues to overlook this possibility and also assumes that other types of aircraft without transponders will pose no problems.

The organization of ideas, while generally sound, is sometimes weakened by needless repetition of the same points, as in sentences 4 and 5 of the last paragraph. The writing contains minor instances of awkwardness (e.g., "Each plane will receive constant, continual signals from each other" in paragraph 3), but is free of flaws that make understanding difficult. However, though the writing is generally clean and clear, the syntax does not show much variety. A few sentences begin with "if" clauses, but almost all the rest, even those that begin with a transitional phrase such as "for example" or "in addition," conform to a "subject, verb, complement" pattern. The first paragraph, in which the second and third sentences begin the same way ("It does not state"), is particularly repetitious.

This argument has no information about air collisions. I think most cases happen in new airports because the air traffic is heavy. In this case sound airport control could solve the problem.

I think this argument is logically reasonable. Its assumption is that plane collisions are caused by planes that don't know each others positions. So pilots can do nothing, if they know each others position through the system it will solve the problem.

If it can provide evidence the problem is lack of knowledge of each others positions, it will be more sound and persuasive.

More information about air collisions is helpful, (the reason for air collisions).

EXPLANATION OF SCORE — 2

This response is seriously flawed in several ways. First of all, it has very little substance. The writer appears to make only one point — that while it seems reasonable to assume that midair collisions would be less likely if pilots were sure of each other's positions, readers cannot adequately judge this assumption without more information about where, why, and how such collisions occur. This point, furthermore, is neither explained by a single reason beyond what is given in the topic nor supported by a single example. Legitimate though it is, it cannot, alone and undeveloped, serve as an adequate response to the argument.

Aside from being undeveloped, the response is confusing. At the outset, it seems to be critical of the argument. The writer begins by pointing to the inadequacy of the information given; then speculates, without evidence, that "most cases happen in new airports"; and then suggests that the problem should be addressed by improving "airport control," not (it is implied) by installing onboard warning systems. After criticizing the argument in the first paragraph, the writer confusingly seems to endorse it in the second. Then, in the remainder of the response, the writer returns to a critical stance.

The general lack of coherence is reflected in the serious and frequent writing problems that make meaning hard to determine — e.g., the elliptical and ungrammatical "So pilots can do nothing, if they know each others position through the system it will solve the problem" (paragraph 2) or "If it can provide evidence the problem is lack of knowledge of each others positions, it will be more sound and persuasive" (paragraph 3). The prose suffers from a variety of basic errors in grammar, usage, and mechanics.

Analysis of Argument Questions for the GMAT

The following appeared as part of an annual report sent to stockholders by Olympic Foods, a processor of frozen foods.

"Over time, the costs of processing go down because as organizations learn how to do things better, they become more efficient. In color film processing, for example, the cost of a 3-by-5-inch print fell from 50 cents for five-day service in 1970 to 20 cents for one-day service in 1984. The same principle applies to the processing of food. And since Olympic Foods will soon celebrate its twenty-fifth birthday, we can expect that our long experience will enable us to minimize costs and thus maximize profits."

Discuss how well reasoned you find this argument. In your discussion be sure to analyze the line of reasoning and the use of evidence in the argument. For example, you may need to consider what questionable assumptions underlie the thinking and what alternative explanations or counterexamples might weaken the conclusion. You can also discuss what sort of evidence would strengthen or refute the argument, what changes in the argument would make it more logically sound, and what, if anything, would help you better evaluate its conclusion.

The following appeared in a memorandum from the business department of the Apogee Company.

"When the Apogee Company had all its operations in one location, it was more profitable than it is today. Therefore, the Apogee Company should close down its field offices and conduct all its operations from a single location. Such centralization would improve profitability by cutting costs and helping the company maintain better supervision of all employees."

Discuss how well reasoned . . . etc.

The following appeared in a memorandum issued by a large city's council on the arts.

"In a recent citywide poll, fifteen percent more residents said that they watch television programs about the visual arts than was the case in a poll conducted five years ago. During these past five years, the number of people visiting our city's art museums has increased by a similar percentage. Since the corporate funding that supports public television, where most of the visual arts programs appear, is now being threatened with severe cuts, we can expect that attendance at our city's art museums will also start to decrease. Thus some of the city's funds for supporting the arts should be reallocated to public television."

Discuss how well reasoned . . . etc.

The following appeared in a report presented for discussion at a meeting of the directors of a company that manufactures parts for heavy machinery.

"The falling revenues that the company is experiencing coincide with delays in manufacturing. These delays, in turn, are due in large part to poor planning in purchasing metals. Consider further that the manager of the department that handles purchasing of raw materials has an excellent background in general business, psychology, and sociology, but knows little about the properties of metals. The company should, therefore, move the purchasing manager to the sales department and bring in a scientist from the research division to be manager of the purchasing department."

Discuss how well reasoned . . . etc.

The following appeared in an announcement issued by the publisher of *The Mercury*, a weekly newspaper.

"Since a competing lower-priced newspaper, *The Bugle*, was started five years ago, *The Mercury*'s circulation has declined by 10,000 readers. The best way to get more people to read *The Mercury* is to reduce its price below that of *The Bugle*, at least until circulation increases to former levels. The increased circulation of *The Mercury* will attract more businesses to buy advertising space in the paper."

Discuss how well reasoned . . . etc.

The following appeared as part of an article in a magazine devoted to regional life.

"Corporations should look to the city of Helios when seeking new business opportunities or a new location. Even in the recent recession, Helios's unemployment rate was lower than the regional average. It is the industrial center of the region, and historically it has provided more than its share of the region's manufacturing jobs. In addition, Helios is attempting to expand its economic base by attracting companies that focus on research and development of innovative technologies."

Discuss how well reasoned . . . etc.

The following appeared in the health section of a magazine on trends and lifestyles.

"People who use the artificial sweetener aspartame are better off consuming sugar, since aspartame can actually contribute to weight gain rather than weight loss. For example, high levels of aspartame have been shown to trigger a craving for food by depleting the brain of a chemical that registers satiety, or the sense of being full. Furthermore, studies suggest that sugars, if consumed after at least 45 minutes of continuous exercise, actually enhance the body's ability to burn fat. Consequently, those who drink aspartame-sweetened juices after exercise will also lose this calorie-burning benefit. Thus it appears that people consuming aspartame rather than sugar are unlikely to achieve their dietary goals."

Discuss how well reasoned . . . etc.

Analysis of Argument Questions for the GMAT

The following appeared in the editorial section of a corporate newsletter.

"The common notion that workers are generally apathetic about management issues is false, or at least outdated: a recently published survey indicates that 79 percent of the nearly 1,200 workers who responded to survey questionnaires expressed a high level of interest in the topics of corporate restructuring and redesign of benefits programs."

Discuss how well reasoned . . . *etc.*

The following appeared in the opinion column of a financial magazine.

"On average, middle-aged consumers devote 39 percent of their retail expenditure to department store products and services, while for younger consumers the average is only 25 percent. Since the number of middle-aged people will increase dramatically within the next decade, department stores can expect retail sales to increase significantly during that period. Furthermore, to take advantage of the trend, these stores should begin to replace some of those products intended to attract the younger consumer with products intended to attract the middle-aged consumer."

Discuss how well reasoned . . . *etc.*

The following appeared in the editorial section of a local newspaper.

"This past winter, 200 students from Waymarsh State College traveled to the state capitol building to protest against proposed cuts in funding for various state college programs. The other 12,000 Waymarsh students evidently weren't so concerned about their education: they either stayed on campus or left for winter break. Since the group who did not protest is far more numerous, it is more representative of the state's college students than are the protesters. Therefore the state legislature need not heed the appeals of the protesting students."

Discuss how well reasoned . . . *etc.*

The following appeared in the editorial section of a local newspaper.

"In the first four years that Montoya has served as mayor of the city of San Perdito, the population has decreased and the unemployment rate has increased. Two businesses have closed for each new business that has opened. Under Varro, who served as mayor for four years before Montoya, the unemployment rate decreased and the population increased. Clearly, the residents of San Perdito would be best served if they voted Montoya out of office and reelected Varro."

Discuss how well reasoned . . . *etc.*

The following appeared as part of a promotional campaign to sell advertising space in the *Daily Gazette* to grocery stores in the Marston area.

"Advertising the reduced price of selected grocery items in the *Daily Gazette* will help you increase your sales. Consider the results of a study conducted last month. Thirty sale items from a store in downtown Marston were advertised in the *Gazette* for four days. Each time one or more of the 30 items was purchased, clerks asked whether the shopper had read the ad. Two-thirds of the 200 shoppers asked answered in the affirmative. Furthermore, more than half the customers who answered in the affirmative spent over $100 at the store."

Discuss how well reasoned . . . *etc.*

The following appeared as part of a campaign to sell advertising time on a local radio station to local businesses.

"The Cumquat Cafe began advertising on our local radio station this year and was delighted to see its business increase by 10 percent over last year's totals. Their success shows you how you can use radio advertising to make *your* business more profitable."

Discuss how well reasoned . . . *etc.*

The following appeared as part of a newspaper editorial.

"Two years ago Nova High School began to use interactive computer instruction in three academic subjects. The school dropout rate declined immediately, and last year's graduates have reported some impressive achievements in college. In future budgets the school board should use a greater portion of the available funds to buy more computers, and all schools in the district should adopt interactive computer instruction throughout the curriculum."

Discuss how well reasoned . . . *etc.*

The following appeared as a part of an advertisement for Adams, who is seeking reelection as governor.

"Re-elect Adams, and you will be voting for proven leadership in improving the state's economy. Over the past year alone, seventy percent of the state's workers have had increases in their wages, five thousand new jobs have been created, and six corporations have located their headquarters here. Most of the respondents in a recent poll said they believed that the economy is likely to continue to improve if Adams is reelected. Adams's opponent, Zebulon, would lead our state in the wrong direction, because Zebulon disagrees with many of Adams's economic policies."

Discuss how well reasoned . . . *etc.*

Analysis of Argument Questions for the GMAT

The following appeared as part of an article in the education section of a Waymarsh City newspaper.

"Throughout the last two decades, those who earned graduate degrees found it very difficult to get jobs teaching their academic specialties at the college level. Those with graduate degrees from Waymarsh University had an especially hard time finding such jobs. But better times are coming in the next decade for all academic job seekers, including those from Waymarsh. Demographic trends indicate that an increasing number of people will be reaching college age over the next ten years; consequently, we can expect that the job market will improve dramatically for people seeking college-level teaching positions in their fields."

Discuss how well reasoned . . . *etc*.

The following appeared in an article in a consumer-products magazine.

"Two of today's best-selling brands of full-strength prescription medication for the relief of excess stomach acid, Acid-Ease and Pepticaid, are now available in milder nonprescription forms. Doctors have written 76 million more prescriptions for full-strength Acid-Ease than for full-strength Pepticaid. So people who need an effective but milder nonprescription medication for the relief of excess stomach acid should choose Acid-Ease."

Discuss how well reasoned . . . *etc*.

The following is an excerpt from a memo written by the head of a governmental department.

"Neither stronger ethics regulations nor stronger enforcement mechanisms are necessary to ensure ethical behavior by companies doing business with this department. We already have a code of ethics that companies doing business with this department are urged to abide by, and virtually all of these companies have agreed to follow it. We also know that the code is relevant to the current business environment because it was approved within the last year, and in direct response to specific violations committed by companies with which we were then working — not in abstract anticipation of potential violations, as so many such codes are."

Discuss how well reasoned . . . *etc*.

The following appeared as part of an article in the travel section of a newspaper.

"Over the past decade, the restaurant industry in the country of Spiessa has experienced unprecedented growth. This surge can be expected to continue in the coming years, fueled by recent social changes: personal incomes are rising, more leisure time is available, single-person households are more common, and people have a greater interest in gourmet food, as evidenced by a proliferation of publications on the subject."

Discuss how well reasoned . . . *etc*.

The following appeared in an article in a health and fitness magazine.

"Laboratory studies show that Saluda Natural Spring Water contains several of the minerals necessary for good health and that it is completely free of bacteria. Residents of Saluda, the small town where the water is bottled, are hospitalized less frequently than the national average. Even though Saluda Natural Spring Water may seem expensive, drinking it instead of tap water is a wise investment in good health."

Discuss how well reasoned . . . *etc*.

The following appeared as part of an editorial in an industry newsletter.

"While trucking companies that deliver goods pay only a portion of highway maintenance costs and no property tax on the highways they use, railways spend billions per year maintaining and upgrading their facilities. The government should lower the railroad companies' property taxes, since sending goods by rail is clearly a more appropriate mode of ground transportation than highway shipping. For one thing, trains consume only a third of the fuel a truck would use to carry the same load, making them a more cost-effective and environmentally sound mode of transport. Furthermore, since rail lines already exist, increases in rail traffic would not require building new lines at the expense of taxpaying citizens."

Discuss how well reasoned . . . *etc*.

The following appeared in the editorial section of a newspaper.

"As public concern over drug abuse has increased, authorities have become more vigilant in their efforts to prevent illegal drugs from entering the country. Many drug traffickers have consequently switched from marijuana, which is bulky, or heroin, which has a market too small to justify the risk of severe punishment, to cocaine. Thus enforcement efforts have ironically resulted in an observed increase in the illegal use of cocaine."

Discuss how well reasoned . . . *etc*.

Analysis of Argument Questions for the GMAT

The following appeared in a speech delivered by a member of the city council.

"Twenty years ago, only half of the students who graduated from Einstein High School went on to attend a college or university. Today, two thirds of the students who graduate from Einstein do so. Clearly, Einstein has improved its educational effectiveness over the past two decades. This improvement has occurred despite the fact that the school's funding, when adjusted for inflation, is about the same as it was twenty years ago. Therefore, we do not need to make any substantial increase in the school's funding at this time."

Discuss how well reasoned . . . *etc.*

The following appeared in a memo from the customer service division to the manager of Mammon Savings and Loan.

"We believe that improved customer service is the best way for us to differentiate ourselves from competitors and attract new customers. We can offer our customers better service by reducing waiting time in teller lines from an average of six minutes to an average of three. By opening for business at 8:30 instead of 9:00, and by remaining open for an additional hour beyond our current closing time, we will be better able to accommodate the busy schedules of our customers. These changes will enhance our bank's image as the most customer-friendly bank in town and give us the edge over our competition."

Discuss how well reasoned . . . *etc.*

The following appeared as part of an article in a magazine on lifestyles.

"Two years ago, City L was listed 14th in an annual survey that ranks cities according to the quality of life that can be enjoyed by those living in them. This information will enable people who are moving to the state in which City L is located to confidently identify one place, at least, where schools are good, housing is affordable, people are friendly, the environment is safe, and the arts flourish."

Discuss how well reasoned . . . *etc.*

The following appeared in a memorandum from a member of a financial management and consulting firm.

"We have learned from an employee of Windfall, Ltd., that its accounting department, by checking about ten percent of the last month's purchasing invoices for errors and inconsistencies, saved the company some $10,000 in overpayments. In order to help our clients increase their net gains, we should advise each of them to institute a policy of checking all purchasing invoices for errors. Such a recommendation could also help us get the Windfall account by demonstrating to Windfall the rigorousness of our methods."

Discuss how well reasoned . . . *etc.*

The following appeared in a newspaper editorial.

"As violence in movies increases, so do crime rates in our cities. To combat this problem we must establish a board to censor certain movies, or we must limit admission to persons over 21 years of age. Apparently our legislators are not concerned about this issue since a bill calling for such actions recently failed to receive a majority vote."

Discuss how well reasoned . . . *etc.*

The following appeared in the editorial section of a local newspaper.

"Commuter use of the new subway train is exceeding the transit company's projections. However, commuter use of the shuttle buses that transport people to the subway stations is below the projected volume. If the transit company expects commuters to ride the shuttle buses to the subway rather than drive there, it must either reduce the shuttle bus fares or increase the price of parking at the subway stations."

Discuss how well reasoned . . . *etc.*

The following was excerpted from the speech of a spokesperson for Synthetic Farm Products, Inc.

"Many farmers who invested in the equipment needed to make the switch from synthetic to organic fertilizers and pesticides feel that it would be too expensive to resume synthetic farming at this point. But studies of farmers who switched to organic farming last year indicate that their current crop yields are lower. Hence their purchase of organic farming equipment, a relatively minor investment compared to the losses that would result from continued lower crop yields, cannot justify persisting on an unwise course. And the choice to farm organically *is* financially unwise, given that it was motivated by environmental rather than economic concerns."

Discuss how well reasoned . . . *etc*

Analysis of Argument Questions for the GMAT

The following appeared in a newspaper story giving advice about investments.

"As overall life expectancy continues to rise, the population of our country is growing increasingly older. For example, over twenty percent of the residents of one of our more populated regions are now at least 65 years old, and occupancy rates at resort hotels in that region declined significantly during the past six months. Because of these two related trends, a prudent investor would be well advised to sell interest in hotels and invest in hospitals and nursing homes instead."

Discuss how well reasoned . . . *etc.*

The following appeared as part of the business plan of an investment and financial consulting firm.

"Studies suggest that an average coffee drinker's consumption of coffee increases with age, from age 10 through age 60. Even after age 60, coffee consumption remains high. The average cola drinker's consumption of cola, however, declines with increasing age. Both of these trends have remained stable for the past 40 years. Given that the number of older adults will significantly increase as the population ages over the next 20 years, it follows that the demand for coffee will increase and the demand for cola will decrease during this period. We should, therefore, consider transferring our investments from Cola Loca to Early Bird Coffee."

Discuss how well reasoned . . . *etc.*

The following appeared in the editorial section of a West Cambria newspaper.

"A recent review of the West Cambria volunteer ambulance service revealed a longer average response time to accidents than was reported by a commercial ambulance squad located in East Cambria. In order to provide better patient care for accident victims and to raise revenue for our town by collecting service fees for ambulance use, we should disband our volunteer service and hire a commercial ambulance service."

Discuss how well reasoned . . . *etc.*

The following is part of a business plan being discussed at a board meeting of the Perks Company.

"It is no longer cost-effective for the Perks Company to continue offering its employees a generous package of benefits and incentives year after year. In periods when national unemployment rates are low, Perks may need to offer such a package in order to attract and keep good employees, but since national unemployment rates are now high, Perks does not need to offer the same benefits and incentives. The money thus saved could be better used to replace the existing plant machinery with more technologically sophisticated equipment, or even to build an additional plant."

Discuss how well reasoned . . . *etc.*

The following appeared as part of a plan proposed by an executive of the Easy Credit Company to the president.

"The Easy Credit Company would gain an advantage over competing credit card services if we were to donate a portion of the proceeds from the use of our cards to a well-known environmental organization in exchange for the use of its symbol or logo on our card. Since a recent poll shows that a large percentage of the public is concerned about environmental issues, this policy would attract new customers, increase use among existing customers, and enable us to charge interest rates that are higher than the lowest ones available."

Discuss how well reasoned . . . *etc.*

The following appeared as part of a recommendation from the financial planning office to the administration of Fern Valley University.

"In the past few years, Fern Valley University has suffered from a decline in both enrollments and admissions applications. The reason can be discovered from our students, who most often cite poor teaching and inadequate library resources as their chief sources of dissatisfaction with Fern Valley. Therefore, in order to increase the number of students attending our university, and hence to regain our position as the most prestigious university in the greater Fern Valley metropolitan area, it is necessary to initiate a fund-raising campaign among the alumni that will enable us to expand the range of subjects we teach and to increase the size of our library facilities."

Discuss how well reasoned . . . *etc.*

The following appeared in an article in a college departmental newsletter.

"Professor Taylor of Jones University is promoting a model of foreign language instruction in which students receive ten weeks of intensive training, then go abroad to live with families for ten weeks. The superiority of the model, Professor Taylor contends, is proved by the results of a study in which foreign language tests given to students at 25 other colleges show that first-year foreign language students at Jones speak more fluently after only ten to twenty weeks in the program than do nine out of ten foreign language majors elsewhere at the time of their graduation."

Discuss how well reasoned . . . *etc.*

Analysis of Argument Questions for the GMAT

The following appeared as part of an article in the business section of a local newspaper.

"Motorcycle X has been manufactured in the United States for over 70 years. Although one foreign company has copied the motorcycle and is selling it for less, the company has failed to attract motorcycle X customers — some say because its product lacks the exceptionally loud noise made by motorcycle X. But there must be some other explanation. After all, foreign cars tend to be quieter than similar American-made cars, but they sell at least as well. Also, television advertisements for motorcycle X highlight its durability and sleek lines, not its noisiness, and the ads typically have voice-overs or rock music rather than engine-roar on the sound track."

Discuss how well reasoned . . . *etc.*

The following appeared in the editorial section of a campus newspaper.

"Because occupancy rates for campus housing fell during the last academic year, so did housing revenues. To solve the problem, campus housing officials should reduce the number of available housing units, thereby increasing the occupancy rates. Also, to keep students from choosing to live off campus, housing officials should lower the rents, thereby increasing demand."

Discuss how well reasoned . . . *etc.*

The following appeared in an Avia Airlines departmental memorandum.

"On average, 9 out of every 1,000 passengers who traveled on Avia Airlines last year filed a complaint about our baggage-handling procedures. This means that although some 1 percent of our passengers were unhappy with those procedures, the overwhelming majority were quite satisfied with them; thus it would appear that a review of the procedures is not important to our goal of maintaining or increasing the number of Avia's passengers."

Discuss how well reasoned . . . *etc.*

The following appeared as part of an article in a weekly newsmagazine.

"The country of Sacchar can best solve its current trade deficit problem by lowering the price of sugar, its primary export. Such an action would make Sacchar better able to compete for markets with other sugar-exporting countries. The sale of Sacchar's sugar abroad would increase, and this increase would substantially reduce Sacchar's trade deficit."

Discuss how well reasoned . . . *etc.*

The following appeared as part of an article in a trade publication.

"Stronger laws are needed to protect new kinds of home-security systems from being copied and sold by imitators. With such protection, manufacturers will naturally invest in the development of new home-security products and production technologies. Without stronger laws, therefore, manufacturers will cut back on investment. From this will follow a corresponding decline not only in product quality and marketability, but also in production efficiency, and thus ultimately a loss of manufacturing jobs in the industry."

Discuss how well reasoned . . . *etc.*

The following appeared in the opinion section of a national newsmagazine.

"To reverse the deterioration of the postal service, the government should raise the price of postage stamps. This solution will no doubt prove effective, since the price increase will generate larger revenues and will also reduce the volume of mail, thereby eliminating the strain on the existing system and contributing to improved morale."

Discuss how well reasoned . . . *etc.*

The following appeared in an article in the health section of a newspaper.

"There is a common misconception that university hospitals are better than community or private hospitals. This notion is unfounded, however: the university hospitals in our region employ 15 percent fewer doctors, have a 20 percent lower success rate in treating patients, make far less overall profit, and pay their medical staff considerably less than do private hospitals. Furthermore, many doctors at university hospitals typically divide their time among teaching, conducting research, and treating patients. From this it seems clear that the quality of care at university hospitals is lower than that at other kinds of hospitals."

Discuss how well reasoned . . . *etc.*

Analysis of Argument Questions for the GMAT

The following is part of a business plan created by the management of the Megamart grocery store.

"Our total sales have increased this year by 20 percent since we added a pharmacy section to our grocery store. Clearly, the customer's main concern is the convenience afforded by one-stop shopping. The surest way to increase our profits over the next couple of years, therefore, is to add a clothing department along with an automotive supplies and repair shop. We should also plan to continue adding new departments and services, such as a restaurant and a garden shop, in subsequent years. Being the only store in the area that offers such a range of services will give us a competitive advantage over other local stores."

Discuss how well reasoned . . . *etc.*

The following appeared as part of a column in a popular entertainment magazine.

"The producers of the forthcoming movie *3003* will be most likely to maximize their profits if they are willing to pay Robin Good several million dollars to star in it — even though that amount is far more than any other person involved with the movie will make. After all, Robin has in the past been paid a similar amount to work in several films that were very financially successful."

Discuss how well reasoned . . . *etc.*

The following appeared in a memorandum from the directors of a security and safety consulting service.

"Our research indicates that over the past six years no incidents of employee theft have been reported within ten of the companies that have been our clients. In analyzing the security practices of these ten companies, we have further learned that each of them requires its employees to wear photo identification badges while at work. In the future, therefore, we should recommend the use of such identification badges to all of our clients."

Discuss how well reasoned . . . *etc.*

The following appeared as part of an article in the business section of a local newspaper.

"The owners of the Cumquat Café evidently made a good business decision in moving to a new location, as can be seen from the fact that the Café will soon celebrate its second anniversary there. Moreover, it appears that businesses are not likely to succeed at the old location: since the Café's move, three different businesses — a tanning salon, an antique emporium, and a pet-grooming shop — have occupied its former spot."

Discuss how well reasoned . . . *etc.*

The following appeared in the editorial section of a local newspaper.

"The profitability of Croesus Company, recently restored to private ownership, is a clear indication that businesses fare better under private ownership than under public ownership."

Discuss how well reasoned . . . *etc.*

The following appeared in the editorial section of a local newspaper.

"If the paper from every morning edition of the nation's largest newspaper were collected and rendered into paper pulp that the newspaper could reuse, about 5 million trees would be saved each year. This kind of recycling is unnecessary, however, since the newspaper maintains its own forests to ensure an uninterrupted supply of paper."

Discuss how well reasoned . . . *etc.*

The following appeared as part of a business plan recommended by the new manager of a musical rock group called Zapped.

"To succeed financially, Zapped needs greater name recognition. It should therefore diversify its commercial enterprises. The rock group Zonked plays the same type of music that Zapped plays, but it is much better known than Zapped because in addition to its concert tours and four albums, Zonked has a series of posters, a line of clothing and accessories, and a contract with a major advertising agency to endorse a number of different products."

Discuss how well reasoned . . . *etc.*

The following appeared in a magazine article on trends and lifestyles.

"In general, people are not as concerned as they were a decade ago about regulating their intake of red meat and fatty cheeses. Walk into the Heart's Delight, a store that started selling organic fruits and vegetables and whole-grain flours in the 1960's, and you will also find a wide selection of cheeses made with high butterfat content. Next door, the owners of the Good Earth Café, an old vegetarian restaurant, are still making a modest living, but the owners of the new House of Beef across the street are millionaires."

Discuss how well reasoned . . . *etc.*

Analysis of Argument Questions for the GMAT

The following editorial appeared in the Elm City paper.

"The construction last year of a shopping mall in downtown Oak City was a mistake. Since the mall has opened, a number of local businesses have closed, and the downtown area suffers from an acute parking shortage, and arrests for crime and vagrancy have increased in the nearby Oak City Park. Elm City should pay attention to the example of the Oak City mall and deny the application to build a shopping mall in Elm City."

Discuss how well reasoned . . . etc.

The following appeared as part of an editorial in a weekly newsmagazine.

"Historically, most of this country's engineers have come from our universities; recently, however, our university-age population has begun to shrink, and decreasing enrollments in our high schools clearly show that this drop in numbers will continue throughout the remainder of the decade. Consequently, our nation will soon be facing a shortage of trained engineers. If we are to remain economically competitive in the world marketplace, then, we must increase funding for education — and quickly."

Discuss how well reasoned . . . *etc.*

The following appeared in an Excelsior Company memorandum.

"The Excelsior Company plans to introduce its own brand of coffee. Since coffee is an expensive food item, and since there are already many established brands of coffee, the best way to gain customers for the Excelsior brand is to do what Superior, the leading coffee company, did when it introduced the newest brand in its line of coffees: conduct a temporary sales promotion that offers free samples, price reductions, and discount coupons for the new brand."

Discuss how well reasoned . . . *etc.*

The following appeared as part of an article in a health club trade publication.

"After experiencing a decline in usage by its members, Healthy Heart fitness center built an indoor pool. Since usage did not increase significantly, it appears that health club managers should adopt another approach — lowering membership fees rather than installing expensive new features."

Discuss how well reasoned . . . *etc.*

The following appeared as part of an article in a popular arts and leisure magazine.

"The safety codes governing the construction of public buildings are becoming far too strict. The surest way for architects and builders to prove that they have met the minimum requirements established by these codes is to construct buildings by using the same materials and methods that are currently allowed. But doing so means that there will be very little significant technological innovation within the industry, and hence little evolution of architectural styles and design — merely because of the strictness of these safety codes."

Discuss how well reasoned . . . *etc.*

The following is from a campaign by Big Boards, Inc., to convince companies in River City that their sales will increase if they use Big Boards billboards for advertising their locally manufactured products.

"The potential of Big Boards to increase sales of your products can be seen from an experiment we conducted last year. We increased public awareness of the name of the current national women's marathon champion by publishing her picture and her name on billboards in River City for a period of three months. Before this time, although the champion had just won her title and was receiving extensive national publicity, only five percent of 15,000 randomly surveyed residents of River City could correctly name the champion when shown her picture; after the three-month advertising experiment, 35 percent of respondents from a second survey could supply her name."

Discuss how well reasoned . . . *etc.*

The following appeared as part of an article on government funding of environmental regulatory agencies.

"When scientists finally learn how to create large amounts of copper from other chemical elements, the regulation of copper mining will become unnecessary. For one thing, since the amount of potentially available copper will no longer be limited by the quantity of actual copper deposits, the problem of overmining will quickly be eliminated altogether. For another, manufacturers will not need to use synthetic copper substitutes, the production of which creates pollutants. Thus, since two problems will be settled — overmining and pollution — it makes good sense to reduce funding for mining regulation and either save the money or reallocate it where it is needed more."

Discuss how well reasoned . . . *etc.*

Analysis of Argument Questions for the GMAT

The following appeared as part of an article in a popular science magazine.

"Scientists must typically work 60 to 80 hours a week if they hope to further their careers; consequently, good and affordable all-day child care must be made available to both male and female scientists if they are to advance in their fields. Moreover, requirements for career advancement must be made more flexible so that preschool-age children can spend a significant portion of each day with a parent."

Discuss how well reasoned . . . *etc.*

The following appeared as part of a recommendation by one of the directors of the Beta Company.

"The Alpha Company has just reduced its workforce by laying off fifteen percent of its employees in all divisions and at all levels, and it is encouraging early retirement for other employees. As you know, the Beta Company manufactures some products similar to Alpha's, but our profits have fallen over the last few years. To improve Beta's competitive position, we should try to hire a significant number of Alpha's former workers, since these experienced workers can provide valuable information about Alpha's successful methods, will require little training, and will be particularly motivated to compete against Alpha."

Discuss how well reasoned . . . *etc.*

The following appeared in the letters-to-the-editor section of a local newspaper.

"*Muscle Monthly*, a fitness magazine that regularly features pictures of bodybuilders using state-of-the-art exercise machines, frequently sells out, according to the owner of Skyview Newsstand. To help maximize fitness levels in our town's residents, we should, therefore, equip our new community fitness center with such machines."

Discuss how well reasoned . . . *etc.*

The following appeared as part of an article in the business section of a local newspaper.

"The Cumquat Café made a mistake in moving to a new location. After one year at the new spot, it is doing about the same volume of business as before, but the owners of the RoboWrench plumbing supply wholesale outlet that took over its old location are apparently doing better: RoboWrench is planning to open a store in a neighboring city."

Discuss how well reasoned . . . *etc.*

The following appeared in a memorandum from the Director of Human Resources to the executive officers of Company X.

"Last year, we surveyed our employees on improvements needed at Company X by having them rank, in order of importance, the issues presented in a list of possible improvements. *Improved communications between employees and management* was consistently ranked as the issue of highest importance by the employees who responded to the survey. As you know, we have since instituted regular communications sessions conducted by high-level management, which the employees can attend on a voluntary basis. Therefore, it is likely that most employees at Company X now feel that the improvement most needed at the company has been made."

Discuss how well reasoned . . . *etc.*

The following appeared in a memorandum from the vice president of Road Food, an international chain of fast-food restaurants.

"This past year, we spent almost as much on advertising as did our main competitor, Street Eats, which has fewer restaurants than we do. Although it appeared at first that our advertising agency had created a campaign along the lines we suggested, in fact our total profits were lower than those of Street Eats. In order to motivate our advertising agency to perform better, we should start basing the amount that we pay it on how much total profit we make each year."

Discuss how well reasoned . . . *etc.*

The following appeared in the promotional literature for Cerberus dog food.

"Obesity is a great problem among pet dogs, just as it is among their human owners. Obesity in humans is typically caused by consuming more calories than the body needs. For humans, a proper diet for losing weight is a reduced-calorie diet that is high in fiber and carbohydrates but low in fat. Therefore, the best way for dog owners to help their dogs lose weight in a healthy way is to restrict the dog's diet to Cerberus reduced-calorie dog food, which is high in fiber and carbohydrates but low in fat."

Discuss how well reasoned . . . *etc.*

Analysis of Argument Questions for the GMAT

The following appeared in an article in a travel magazine.

"After the airline industry began requiring airlines to report their on-time rates, Speedee Airlines achieved the number one on-time rate, with over 89 percent of its flights arriving on time each month. And now Speedee is offering more flights to more destinations than ever before. Clearly, Speedee is the best choice for today's business traveler."

Discuss how well reasoned . . . *etc.*

The following appeared in a memorandum to the planning department of an investment firm.

"Costs have begun dropping for several types of equipment currently used to convert solar energy into electricity. Moreover, some exciting new technologies for converting solar energy are now being researched and developed. Hence we can expect that solar energy will soon become more cost efficient and attractive than coal or oil as a source of electrical power. We should, therefore, encourage investment in Solario, a new manufacturer of solar-powered products. After all, Solario's chief executive was once on the financial planning team for Ready-to-Ware, a software engineering firm that has shown remarkable growth since its recent incorporation."

Discuss how well reasoned . . . *etc.*

The following appeared in a memorandum from a company's marketing department.

"Since our company started manufacturing and marketing a deluxe air filter six months ago, sales of our economy filter — and company profits — have decreased significantly. The deluxe air filter sells for 50 percent more than the economy filter, but the economy filter lasts for only one month while the deluxe filter can be used for two months before it must be replaced. To increase repeat sales of our economy filter and maximize profits, we should discontinue the deluxe air filter and concentrate all our advertising efforts on the economy filter."

Discuss how well reasoned . . . *etc.*

The following appeared in a memorandum from the president of a company that makes shampoo.

"A widely publicized study claims that HR2, a chemical compound in our shampoo, can contribute to hair loss after prolonged use. This study, however, involved only 500 subjects. Furthermore, we have received no complaints from our customers during the past year, and some of our competitors actually use more HR2 per bottle of shampoo than we do. Therefore, we do not need to consider replacing the HR2 in our shampoo with a more expensive alternative."

Discuss how well reasoned . . . *etc.*

The following appeared in the editorial section of a local newspaper.

"The tragic crash of a medical helicopter last week points up a situation that needs to be addressed. The medical-helicopter industry supposedly has more stringent guidelines for training pilots and maintaining equipment than do most other airline industries, but these guidelines do not appear to be working: statistics reveal that the rate of medical-helicopter accidents is much higher than the rate of accidents for nonmedical helicopters or commercial airliners."

Discuss how well reasoned . . . *etc.*

The following appeared as part of a recommendation from the business manager of a department store.

"Local clothing stores reported that their profits decreased, on average, for the three-month period between August 1 and October 31. Stores that sell products for the home reported that, on average, their profits increased during this same period. Clearly, consumers are choosing to buy products for their homes instead of clothing. To take advantage of this trend, we should reduce the size of our clothing departments and enlarge our home furnishings and household products departments."

Discuss how well reasoned . . . *etc.*

The following appeared in a letter to the editor of a regional newspaper.

"In response to petitions from the many farmers and rural landowners throughout our region, the legislature has spent valuable time and effort enacting severe laws to deter motorists from picking fruit off the trees, trampling through the fields, and stealing samples of foliage. But how can our local lawmakers occupy themselves with such petty vandalism when crime and violence plague the nation's cities? The fate of apples and leaves is simply too trivial to merit their attention."

Discuss how well reasoned . . . *etc.*

Analysis of Argument Questions for the GMAT

The following appeared as part of an editorial in a campus newspaper.

"With an increasing demand for highly skilled workers, this nation will soon face a serious labor shortage. New positions in technical and professional occupations are increasing rapidly, while at the same time the total labor force is growing slowly. Moreover, the government is proposing to cut funds for aid to education in the near future."

Discuss how well reasoned . . . etc.

The following appeared as part of a memorandum from a government agency.

"Given the limited funding available for the building and repair of roads and bridges, the government should not spend any money this year on fixing the bridge that crosses the Styx River. This bridge is located near a city with a weakening economy, so it is not as important as other bridges; moreover, the city population is small and thus unlikely to contribute a significant enough tax revenue to justify the effort of fixing the bridge."

Discuss how well reasoned . . . etc.

The following appeared as part of an article in an entertainment magazine.

"A series of books based on the characters from a popular movie are consistently bestsellers in local bookstores. Seeking to capitalize on the books' success, Vista Studios is planning to produce a movie sequel based on the books. Due to the success of the books and the original movie, the sequel will undoubtedly be profitable."

Discuss how well reasoned . . . etc.

The following appeared in a letter to the editor of a popular science and technology magazine.

"It is a popular myth that consumers are really benefiting from advances in agricultural technology. Granted — consumers are, on the average, spending a decreasing proportion of their income on food. But consider that the demand for food does not rise in proportion with real income. As real income rises, therefore, consumers can be expected to spend a decreasing proportion of their income on food. Yet agricultural technology is credited with having made our lives better."

Discuss how well reasoned . . . etc.

The following appeared in the editorial section of a local newspaper.

"This city should be able to improve existing services and provide new ones without periodically raising the taxes of the residents. Instead, the city should require that the costs of services be paid for by developers who seek approval for their large new building projects. After all, these projects can be highly profitable to the developers, but they can also raise a city's expenses and increase the demand for its services."

Discuss how well reasoned . . . etc.

The following appeared in the editorial section of a local newspaper.

"In order to avoid the serious health threats associated with many landfills, our municipality should build a plant for burning trash. An incinerator could offer economic as well as ecological advantages over the typical old-fashioned type of landfill: incinerators can be adapted to generate moderate amounts of electricity, and ash residue from some types of trash can be used to condition garden soil."

Discuss how well reasoned . . . etc.

The following appeared in the editorial section of a monthly business newsmagazine.

"Most companies would agree that as the risk of physical injury occurring on the job increases, the wages paid to employees should also increase. Hence it makes financial sense for employers to make the workplace safer: they could thus reduce their payroll expenses and save money."

Discuss how well reasoned . . . etc.

The following appeared as part of a company memorandum.

"Adopting an official code of ethics regarding business practices may in the long run do our company more harm than good in the public eye. When one of our competitors received unfavorable publicity for violating its own code of ethics, it got more attention from the media than it would have if it had had no such code. Rather than adopt an official code of ethics, therefore, we should instead conduct a publicity campaign that stresses the importance of protecting the environment and assisting charitable organizations."

Discuss how well reasoned . . . etc.

Analysis of Argument Questions for the GMAT

The following appeared in the editorial section of a daily newspaper.

"Although forecasts of presidential elections based on opinion polls measure current voter preference, many voters keep changing their minds about whom they prefer until the last few days before the balloting. Some do not even make a final decision until they enter the voting booth. Forecasts based on opinion polls are therefore little better at predicting election outcomes than a random guess would be."

Discuss how well reasoned ... . etc.

The following appeared in the editorial section of a newspaper in the country of West Cambria.

"The practice of officially changing speed limits on the highways — whether by increasing or decreasing them — is a dangerous one. Consider what happened over the past decade whenever neighboring East Cambria changed its speed limits: an average of 3 percent more automobile accidents occurred during the week following the change than had occurred during the week preceding it — even when the speed limit was lowered. This statistic shows that the change in speed limit adversely affected the alertness of drivers."

Discuss how well reasoned . . . etc.

The following appeared as part of a memorandum from the vice president of Nostrum, a large pharmaceutical corporation.

"The proposal to increase the health and retirement benefits that our employees receive should not be implemented at this time. An increase in these benefits is not only financially unjustified, since our last year's profits were lower than those of the preceding year, but also unnecessary, since our chief competitor, Panacea, offers its employees lower health and retirement benefits than we currently offer. We can assume that our employees are reasonably satisfied with the health and retirement benefits that they now have since a recent survey indicated that two-thirds of the respondents viewed them favorably."

Discuss how well reasoned . . . etc.

The following appeared as part of an article on trends in television.

"A recent study of viewers' attitudes toward prime-time television programs shows that many of the programs that were judged by their viewers to be of high quality appeared on (noncommercial) television networks, and that, on commercial television, the most popular shows are typically sponsored by the best-selling products. Thus, it follows that businesses who use commercial television to promote their products will achieve the greatest advertising success by sponsoring only highly-rated programs — and, ideally, programs resembling the highly-rated noncommercial programs on public channels as much as possible."

Discuss how well reasoned . . . etc.

The following appeared as part of an article in the business section of a daily newspaper.

"Company A has a large share of the international market in video-game hardware and software. Company B, the pioneer in these products, was once a $12 billion-a-year giant but collapsed when children became bored with its line of products. Thus Company A can also be expected to fail, especially given the fact that its games are now in so many American homes that the demand for them is nearly exhausted."

Discuss how well reasoned . . . etc.

The following appeared as part of an article in a photography magazine.

"When choosing whether to work in color or in black-and-white, the photographer who wishes to be successful should keep in mind that because color photographs are more true-to-life, magazines use more color photographs than black-and-white ones, and many newspapers are also starting to use color photographs. The realism of color also accounts for the fact that most portrait studios use more color film than black-and-white film. Furthermore, there are more types of color film than black-and-white film available today. Clearly, photographers who work in color have an advantage over those who work in black-and-white."

Discuss how well reasoned . . . etc.

The following appeared as part of a letter to the editor of a local newspaper.

"It makes no sense that in most places fifteen year olds are not eligible for their driver's license while people who are far older can retain all of their driving privileges by simply renewing their license. If older drivers can get these renewals, often without having to pass another driving test, then fifteen year olds should be eligible to get a license. Fifteen year olds typically have much better eyesight, especially at night; much better hand-eye coordination; and much quicker reflexes. They are also less likely to feel confused by unexpected developments or disoriented in unfamiliar surroundings, and they recover from injuries more quickly."

Discuss how well reasoned . . . etc.

Analysis of Argument Questions for the GMAT

The following appeared in an ad for a book titled *How to Write a Screenplay for a Movie*.

"Writers who want to succeed should try to write film screenplays rather than books, since the average film tends to make greater profits than does even a best-selling book. It is true that some books are also made into films. However, our nation's film producers are more likely to produce movies based on original screenplays than to produce films based on books, because in recent years the films that have sold the most tickets have usually been based on original screenplays."

Discuss how well reasoned . . . *etc.*

The following appeared as part of an article in a daily newspaper.

"The computerized onboard warning system that will be installed in commercial airliners will virtually solve the problem of midair plane collisions. One plane's warning system can receive signals from another's transponder — a radio set that signals a plane's course — in order to determine the likelihood of a collision and recommend evasive action."

Discuss how well reasoned . . . *etc.*

The following appeared in a memorandum from the ElectroWares company's marketing department.

"Since our company started manufacturing and marketing a deluxe light bulb six months ago, sales of our economy light bulb — and company profits — have decreased significantly. Although the deluxe light bulb sells for 50 percent more than the economy bulb, it lasts twice as long. Therefore, to increase repeat sales and maximize profits, we should discontinue the deluxe light bulb."

Discuss how well reasoned . . . *etc.*

The following is taken from an editorial in a local newspaper.

"Over the past decade, the price per pound of citrus fruit has increased substantially. Eleven years ago, Megamart charged 15 cents a pound for lemons, but today it commonly charges over a dollar a pound. In only one of these last eleven years was the weather unfavorable for growing citrus crops. Evidently, then, citrus growers have been responsible for the excessive increase in the price of citrus fruit, and strict pricing regulations are needed to prevent them from continuing to inflate prices."

Discuss how well reasoned . . . *etc.*

The following appeared as part of an article in a local newspaper.

"Over the past three years the tartfish industry has changed markedly: fishing technology has improved significantly, and the demand for tartfish has grown in both domestic and foreign markets. As this trend continues, the tartfish industry on Shrimp Island can expect to experience the same over-fishing problems that are already occurring with mainland fishing industries: without restrictions on fishing, fishers see no reason to limit their individual catches. As the catches get bigger, the tartfish population will be dangerously depleted while the surplus of tartfish will devalue the catch for fishers. Government regulation is the only answer: tartfish-fishing should be allowed only during the three-month summer season, when tartfish reproduce and thus are most numerous, rather than throughout the year."

Discuss how well reasoned . . . *etc.*

The following appeared in a proposal from the development office at Platonic University.

"Because Platonic University has had difficulty in meeting its expenses over the past three years, we need to find new ways to increase revenues. We should consider following the example of Greene University, which recently renamed itself after a donor who gave it $100 million. If Platonic University were to advertise to its alumni and other wealthy people that it will rename either individual buildings or the entire university itself after the donors who give the most money, the amount of donations would undoubtedly increase."

Discuss how well reasoned . . . *etc.*

The following appeared as part of an article in the business section of a local newspaper.

"Hippocrene Plumbing Supply recently opened a wholesale outlet in the location once occupied by the Cumquat Café. Hippocrene has apparently been quite successful there because it is planning to open a large outlet in a nearby city. But the Cumquat Café, one year after moving to its new location, has seen its volume of business drop somewhat from the previous year's. Clearly, the former site was the better business location, and the Cumquat Café has made a mistake in moving to its new address."

Discuss how well reasoned . . . *etc.*

Analysis of Argument Questions for the GMAT

The following appeared in the editorial section of a local paper.

"Applications for advertising spots on KMTV, our local cable television channel, decreased last year. Meanwhile a neighboring town's local channel, KOOP, changed its focus to farming issues and reported an increase in advertising applications for the year. To increase applications for advertisement its spots, KMTV should focus its programming on farming issues as well."

Discuss how well reasoned . . . *etc.*

The following appeared as part of an article in a computer magazine.

"A year ago Apex Manufacturing bought its managers computers for their homes and paid for telephone connections so that they could access Apex computers and data files from home after normal business hours. Since last year, productivity at Apex has increased by 15 percent. Other companies can learn from the success at Apex: given home computers and access to company resources, employees will work additional hours at home and thereby increase company profits."

Discuss how well reasoned . . . *etc.*

The following was excerpted from an article in a farming trade publication.

"Farmers who switched from synthetic to organic farming last year have seen their crop yields decline. Many of these farmers feel that it would be too expensive to resume synthetic farming at this point, given the money that they invested in organic farming supplies and equipment. But their investments will be relatively minor compared to the losses from continued lower crop yields. Organic farmers should switch to synthetic farming rather than persist in an unwise course. And the choice to farm organically *is* financially unwise, given that it was motivated by environmental rather than economic concerns."

Discuss how well reasoned . . . *etc.*

The following appeared in a letter to prospective students from the admissions office at Plateau College.

"Every person who earned an advanced degree in science or engineering from Olympus University last year received numerous offers of excellent jobs. Typically, many graduates of Plateau College have gone on to pursue advanced degrees at Olympus. Therefore, enrolling as an undergraduate at Plateau College is a wise choice for students who wish to ensure success in their careers."

Discuss how well reasoned . . . *etc.*

The following appeared in a memorandum sent by a vice-president of the Nadir Company to the company's human resources department.

"Nadir does not need to adopt the costly 'family-friendly' programs that have been proposed, such as part-time work, work at home, and job-sharing. When these programs were made available at the Summit Company, the leader in its industry, only a small percentage of employees participated in them. Rather than adversely affecting our profitability by offering these programs, we should concentrate on offering extensive training that will enable employees to increase their productivity."

Discuss how well reasoned . . . *etc.*

The following appeared as part of an article in a trade magazine for breweries.

"Magic Hat Brewery recently released the results of a survey of visitors to its tasting room last year. Magic Hat reports that the majority of visitors asked to taste its low-calorie beers. To boost sales, other small breweries should brew low-calorie beers as well."

Discuss how well reasoned . . . *etc.*

The following appeared in an editorial from a newspaper serving the town of Saluda.

"The Saluda Consolidated High School offers over 200 different courses from which its students can choose. A much smaller private school down the street offers a basic curriculum of only 80 different courses, but it consistently sends a higher proportion of its graduating seniors on to college than Consolidated does. By eliminating at least half of the courses offered there and focusing on a basic curriculum, we could improve student performance at Consolidated and also save many tax dollars."

Discuss how well reasoned . . . *etc.*

Analysis of Argument Questions for the GMAT

The following appeared as part of an article in the book section of a newspaper.

"Currently more and more books are becoming available in electronic form — either free-of-charge on the Internet or for a very low price-per-book on compact disc.* Thus literary classics are likely to be read more widely than ever before. People who couldn't have purchased these works at bookstore prices will now be able to read them for little or no money; similarly, people who find it inconvenient to visit libraries and wait for books to be returned by other patrons will now have access to whatever classic they choose from their home or work computers. This increase in access to literary classics will radically affect the public taste in reading, creating a far more sophisticated and learned reading audience than has ever existed before."

*A "compact disc" is a small portable disc capable of storing relatively large amounts of data that can be read by a computer.

Discuss how well reasoned . . . *etc.*

The following appeared as an editorial in a magazine concerned with educational issues.

"In our country, the real earnings of men who have only a high-school degree have decreased significantly over the past fifteen years, but those of male college graduates have remained about the same. Therefore, the key to improving the earnings of the next generation of workers is to send all students to college. Our country's most important educational goal, then, should be to establish enough colleges and universities to accommodate all high school graduates."

Discuss how well reasoned . . . *etc.*

The following appeared as part of a business plan created by the management of the Take Heart Fitness Center.

"After opening the new swimming pool early last summer, Take Heart saw a 12 percent increase in the use of the center by its members. Therefore, in order to increase membership in Take Heart, we should continue to add new recreational facilities in subsequent years: for example, a multipurpose game room, a tennis court, and a miniature golf course. Being the only center in the area offering this range of activities would give us a competitive advantage in the health and recreation market."

Discuss how well reasoned . . . *etc.*

The following appeared in a letter from a staff member in the office of admissions at Argent University.

"The most recent nationwide surveys show that undergraduates choose their major field primarily based on their perception of job prospects in that field. At our university, economics is now the most popular major, so students must perceive this field as having the best job prospects. Therefore, we can increase our enrollment if we focus our advertising and recruiting on publicizing the accomplishments of our best-known economics professors and the success of our economics graduates in finding employment."

Discuss how well reasoned . . . *etc.*

The following appeared as part of a memorandum from the loan department of the Frostbite National Bank.

"We should not approve the business loan application of the local group that wants to open a franchise outlet for the Kool Kone chain of ice cream parlors. Frostbite is known for its cold winters, and cold weather can mean slow ice cream sales. For example, even though Frostbite is a town of 10,000 people, it has only one ice cream spot — the Frigid Cow. Despite the lack of competition, the Frigid Cow's net revenues fell by 10 percent last winter."

Discuss how well reasoned . . . *etc.*

The following appeared as part of a letter to the editor of a local newspaper.

"Bayview High School is considering whether to require all of its students to wear uniforms while at school. Students attending Acorn Valley Academy, a private school in town, earn higher grades on average and are more likely to go on to college. Moreover, Acorn Valley reports few instances of tardiness, absenteeism, or discipline problems. Since Acorn Valley requires its students to wear uniforms, Bayview High School would do well to follow suit and require its students to wear uniforms as well."

Discuss how well reasoned . . . *etc.*

The following appeared in a memo to the Saluda town council from the town's business manager.

"Research indicates that those who exercise regularly are hospitalized less than half as often as those who don't exercise. By providing a well-equipped gym for Saluda's municipal employees, we should be able to reduce the cost of our group health insurance coverage by approximately 50% and thereby achieve a balanced town budget."

Discuss how well reasoned . . . *etc.*

Analysis of Argument Questions for the GMAT

The following appeared in a memorandum written by the assistant manager of a store that sells gourmet food items from various countries.

"A local wine store made an interesting discovery last month: it sold more French than Italian wine on days when it played recordings of French accordion music, but it sold more Italian than French wine on days when Italian songs were played. Therefore, I recommend that we put food specialties from one particular country on sale for a week at a time and play only music from that country while the sale is going on. By this means we will increase our profits in the same way that the wine store did, and we will be able to predict more precisely what items we should stock at any given time."

Discuss how well reasoned . . . *etc.*

The following appeared in a memorandum from the director of research and development at Ready-to-Ware, a software engineering firm.

"The package of benefits and incentives that Ready-to-Ware offers to professional staff is too costly. Our quarterly profits have declined since the package was introduced two years ago, at the time of our incorporation. Moreover, the package had little positive effect, as we have had only marginal success in recruiting and training high-quality professional staff. To become more profitable again, Ready-to-Ware should, therefore, offer the reduced benefits package that was in place two years ago and use the savings to fund our current research and development initiatives."

Discuss how well reasoned . . . *etc.*

The following appeared as a memorandum from the vice-president of the Dolci candy company.

"Given the success of our premium and most expensive line of chocolate candies in a recent taste test and the consequent increase in sales, we should shift our business focus to producing additional lines of premium candy rather than our lesser-priced, ordinary candies. When the current economic boom ends and consumers can no longer buy major luxury items, such as cars, they will still want to indulge in small luxuries, such as expensive candies."

Discuss how well reasoned . . . *etc.*

The following appeared in a memorandum from the business office of the Lovin' Cupful, a national restaurant chain.

"The Lovin' Cupful franchises in our northeast region have begun serving customers *AlmosT*, a brand new powdered instant tea, in place of brewed tea. Waiters report that only about 2 percent of the customers have complained, and that customers who want refills typically ask for 'more tea.' It appears, then, that 98 percent of the customers are perfectly happy with the switch, or else they cannot tell powdered instant from brewed tea. Therefore, in order to take advantage of the lower price per pound of *AlmosT*, all of our restaurants should begin substituting it for brewed tea."

Discuss how well reasoned . . . *etc.*

The following appeared in a memorandum from the director of marketing for a pharmaceutical company.

"According to a survey of 5,000 urban residents, the prevalence of stress headaches increases with educational level, so that stress headaches occur most often among people with graduate-school degrees. It is well established that, nationally, higher educational levels usually correspond with higher levels of income. Therefore, in marketing our new pain remedy, Omnilixir, we should send free samples primarily to graduate students and to people with graduate degrees, and we should concentrate on advertising in professional journals rather than in general-interest magazines."

Discuss how well reasoned . . . *etc.*

The following appeared as part of an editorial in the Waymarsh City newspaper.

"Last year the parents of first graders in our school district expressed satisfaction with the reading skills their children developed but complained strongly about their children's math skills. To remedy this serious problem and improve our district's elementary education, everyone in the teacher-training program at Waymarsh University should be required to take more courses in mathematics."

Discuss how well reasoned . . . *etc.*

The following appeared in a letter to the editor of a River City newspaper.

"The Clio Development Group should not be permitted to build a multilevel parking garage on Dock Street since most of the buildings on the block would have to be demolished. Because these buildings were erected decades ago, they have historic significance and must therefore be preserved as economic assets in the effort to revitalize a restored riverfront area. Recall how Lakesburg has benefited from business increases in its historic downtown center. Moreover, there is plenty of vacant land for a parking lot elsewhere in River City."

Discuss how well reasoned . . . *etc.*

Analysis of Argument Questions for the GMAT

The following appeared in a corporate planning memorandum for a company that develops amusement parks.

"Because travel from our country to foreign countries has increased dramatically in recent years, our next project should be a 'World Tour' theme park with replicas of famous foreign buildings, rides that have international themes, and refreshment stands serving only foods from the country represented by the nearest ride. The best location would be near our capital city, which has large percentages of international residents and of children under the age of 16. Given the advantages of this site and the growing interest in foreign countries, the 'World Tour' theme park should be as successful as our space-travel theme park, where attendance has increased tenfold over the past decade."

Discuss how well reasoned . . . *etc.*

The following appeared in a memorandum from the publisher to the staff of *The Clarion*, a large metropolitan newspaper.

"During the recent campaign for mayor, a clear majority of city readers who responded to our survey indicated a desire for more news about city government. To increase circulation, and thus our profits, we should therefore consistently devote a greater proportion of space in all editions of *The Clarion* to coverage of local news."

Discuss how well reasoned . . . *etc.*

The following appeared in a memorandum from the assistant manager of Pageturner Books.

"Over the past two years, Pageturner's profits have decreased by five percent, even though we have added a popular café as well as a music section selling CD's and tapes. At the same time, we have experienced an increase in the theft of merchandise. We should therefore follow the example of Thoreau Books, which increased its profits after putting copies of its most frequently stolen books on a high shelf behind the payment counter. By doing likewise with copies of the titles that our staff reported stolen last year, we too can increase profitability."

Discuss how well reasoned . . . *etc.*

The following appeared in a letter to the editor of a River City newspaper.

"The Clio Development Group's plan for a multilevel parking garage on Dock Street should be approved in order to strengthen the economy of the surrounding area. Although most of the buildings on the block would have to be demolished, they are among the oldest in the city and thus of little current economic value. Those who oppose the project should realize that historic preservation cannot be the only consideration: even Athens or Jerusalem will knock down old buildings to put up new ones that improve the local economy."

Discuss how well reasoned . . . *etc.*

The following appeared in a memorandum from the owner of Carlo's Clothing to the staff.

"Since Disc Depot, the music store on the next block, began a new radio advertising campaign last year, its business has grown dramatically, as evidenced by the large increase in foot traffic into the store. While the Disc Depot's owners have apparently become wealthy enough to retire, profits at Carlo's Clothing have remained stagnant for the past three years. In order to boost our sales and profits, we should therefore switch from newspaper advertising to frequent radio advertisements like those for Disc Depot."

Discuss how well reasoned . . . *etc.*

The following appeared as part of the business plan of the Capital Idea investment firm.

"Across town in the Park Hill district, the Thespian Theater, Pizzazz Pizza, and the Niblick Golf Club have all had business increases over the past two years. Capital Idea should therefore invest in the Roxy Playhouse, the Slice-o'-Pizza, and the Divot Golf Club, three new businesses in the Irongate district. As a condition, we should require them to participate in a special program: Any customer who patronizes two of the businesses will receive a substantial discount at the third. By motivating customers to patronize all three, we will thus contribute to the profitability of each and maximize our return."

Discuss how well reasoned . . . *etc.*

The following appeared as part of an article in a newsletter for farmers.

"Users of Solacium, a medicinal herb now grown mainly in Asia, report that it relieves tension and promotes deep sleep. A recent study indicates that a large number of college students who took pills containing one of the ingredients in Solacium suffered less anxiety. To satisfy the anticipated demands for this very promising therapeutic herb and to reap the financial benefits, farmers in this country should begin growing it."

Discuss how well reasoned . . . *etc.*

Analysis of Argument Questions for the GMAT

The following appeared in a memorandum from the president of Aurora, a company that sells organic milk (milk produced without the use of chemical additives).

"Sales of organic food products in this country have tripled over the past five years. If Aurora is to profit from this continuing trend, we must diversify and start selling products such as organic orange juice and organic eggs in addition to our regular product line. With the recent increase of articles in health magazines questioning the safety of milk and other food products, customers are even more likely to buy our line of organic products. And to help ensure our successful expansion, we should hire the founder of a chain of health-food stores to serve as our vice-president of marketing."

Discuss how well reasoned . . . etc.

The following appeared in a memorandum from the human resources department of Diversified Manufacturing.

"Managers at our central office report that their employees tend to be most productive in the days immediately preceding a vacation. To help counteract our declining market share, we could increase the productivity of our professional staff members, who currently receive four weeks paid vacation a year, by limiting them to a maximum of one week's continuous vacation time. They will thus take more vacation breaks during a year and give us more days of maximum productivity."

Discuss how well reasoned . . . etc.

The following appeared in a memorandum from a regional supervisor of post office operations.

"During a two-week study of postal operations, the Presto City post office handled about twice as many items as the Lento City post office, even though the cities are about the same size. Moreover, customer satisfaction appears to be higher in Presto City, since the study found fewer complaints regarding the Presto City post office. Therefore, the postmasters at these two offices should exchange assignments: the Presto City postmaster will solve the problems of inefficiency and customer dissatisfaction at the Lento City office while the Lento City postmaster learns first-hand the superior methods of Presto City."

Discuss how well reasoned . . . etc.

The following appeared in a memorandum written by the managing director of the Exeunt Theater Company.

"Now that we have moved to a larger theater, we can expect to increase our revenues from ticket sales. To further increase profits, we should start producing the plays that have been most successful when they were performed in our nation's largest cities. In addition, we should hire the Adlib Theater Company's director of fund-raising, since corporate contributions to Adlib have increased significantly over the three years that she has worked for Adlib."

Discuss how well reasoned . . . etc.

The following appeared in a memorandum from the human resources department of HomeStyle, a house remodeling business.

"This year, despite HomeStyle's move to new office space, we have seen a decline in both company morale and productivity, and a corresponding increase in administrative costs. To rectify these problems, we should begin using a newly developed software package for performance appraisal and feedback. Managers will save time by simply choosing comments from a preexisting list; then the software will automatically generate feedback for the employee. The Human Resources department at CounterBalance, the manufacturer of the countertops we install, reports satisfaction with the package."

Discuss how well reasoned . . . etc.

The following appeared as part of an article in a weekly newsmagazine.

"The country of Oleum can best solve the problem of its balance of trade deficit by further increasing the tax on its major import, crude oil. After Oleum increased the tax on imported crude oil four months ago, consumption of gasoline declined by 20 percent. Therefore, by imposing a second and significantly higher tax increase next year, Oleum will dramatically decrease its balance of trade deficit."

Discuss how well reasoned . . . etc.

The following appeared as part of a business plan by the Capital Idea investment firm.

"In recent years the worldwide demand for fish has grown, and improvements in fishing technology have made larger catches and thus increased supply possible: for example, last year's tuna catch was 9 percent greater than the previous year's. To capitalize on these trends, we should therefore invest in the new tartfish processing plant on Tartfish Island, where increasing revenues from tourism indicate a strong local economy."

Discuss how well reasoned . . . etc.

Analysis of Argument Questions for the GMAT

The following appeared in a speech by a stockholder of Consolidated Industries at the company's annual stockholders' meeting.

"In the computer hardware division last year, profits fell significantly below projections, the product line decreased from twenty to only five items, and expenditures for employee benefits increased by 15 percent. Nevertheless, Consolidated's board of directors has approved an annual salary of over one million dollars for our company's chief executive officer. The present board members should be replaced because they are unconcerned about the increasing costs of employee benefits and salaries, in spite of the company's problems generating income."

Discuss how well reasoned . . . *etc.*

The following appeared in a memorandum from the business planning department of Avia Airlines.

"Of all the cities in their region, Beaumont and Fletcher are showing the fastest growth in the number of new businesses. Therefore, Avia should establish a commuter route between them as a means of countering recent losses on its main passenger routes. And to make the commuter route more profitable from the outset, Avia should offer a 1/3 discount on tickets purchased within two days of the flight. Unlike tickets bought earlier, discount tickets will be nonrefundable, and so gain from their sale will be greater."

Discuss how well reasoned . . . *etc.*

The following appeared in a memorandum from the vice-president of Gigantis, a development company that builds and leases retail store facilities.

"Nationwide over the past five years, sales have increased significantly at outlet stores that deal exclusively in reduced-price merchandise. Therefore, we should publicize the new mall that we are building at Pleasantville as a central location for outlet shopping and rent store space only to outlet companies. By taking advantage of the success of outlet stores, this plan should help ensure full occupancy of the mall and enable us to recover quickly the costs of building the mall."

Discuss how well reasoned . . . *etc.*

The following appeared in a memorandum written by the chair of the music department to the president of Omega University.

"Mental health experts have observed that symptoms of mental illness are less pronounced in many patients after group music-therapy sessions, and job openings in the music-therapy field have increased during the past year. Consequently, graduates from our degree program for music therapists should have no trouble finding good positions. To help improve the financial status of Omega University, we should therefore expand our music-therapy degree program by increasing its enrollment targets."

Discuss how well reasoned . . . *etc.*

The following appeared in a memorandum to the work-group supervisors of the GBS Company.

"The CoffeeCart beverage and food service located in the lobby of our main office building is not earning enough in sales to cover its costs, and so the cart may discontinue operating at GBS. Given the low staff morale, as evidenced by the increase in the number of employees leaving the company, the loss of this service could present a problem, especially since the staff morale questionnaire showed widespread dissatisfaction with the snack machines. Therefore, supervisors should remind the employees in their group to patronize the cart—after all, it was leased for their convenience so that they would not have to walk over to the cafeteria on breaks."

Discuss how well reasoned . . . *etc.*

The following appeared as part of an article in a trade magazine.

"During a recent trial period in which government inspections at selected meat-processing plants were more frequent, the amount of bacteria in samples of processed chicken decreased by 50 percent on average from the previous year's level. If the government were to institute more frequent inspections, the incidence of stomach and intestinal infections throughout the country could thus be cut in half. In the meantime, consumers of Excel Meats should be safe from infection because Excel's main processing plant has shown more improvement in eliminating bacterial contamination than any other plant cited in the government report."

Discuss how well reasoned . . . *etc.*

10 Scoring Information

What Are GMAT Scaled Scores?

A scaled score is not simply the number or percentage of questions answered correctly. Instead, it is a score that has been adjusted in such a way that a particular scaled score reflects the same level of ability regardless of the difficulty of the questions or the number or type of questions included in a particular test. GMAT® verbal and quantitative scaled scores range from 0 to 60, although scores below 10 or above 50 are rare. *GMAT* total scaled scores range from 200 to 800 with scores below 250 or above 750 being rare.

How Are GMAT Scores Calculated?

The *GMAT* presents each test taker with an individually selected set of questions. Within each section — verbal and quantitative — the computer selects your questions on the basis of your responses to previous questions. The rule that the computer uses for selecting questions is intended to give you questions that are neither too easy nor too hard for you. When you answer questions correctly, the computer tends to give you harder questions. When you answer incorrectly, it tends to give you easier questions. Your scaled score is determined by a complex mathematical procedure that takes into account the difficulty of the questions that were presented to you. When you answer the easier questions correctly, you get a chance to answer the harder questions that make it possible to earn a high score. After you have completed all of the questions on the test — or when your time is up — the computer will calculate your scaled scores. Your scores on the verbal and quantitative sections are combined to produce your total score. If you have not responded to all of the questions in a section (41 verbal questions or 37 quantitative questions), your score is adjusted using the proportion of questions answered.

Note About the Scoring of the Analytical Writing Assessment

The Analytical Writing Assessment, described in chapter 9 of this book, consists of two writing tasks: Analysis of an Issue and Analysis of an Argument. The responses to each of these tasks are scored on a 6-point scale, with 6 the highest score and 1 the lowest. A score of zero (0) is given to responses that are not written on the assigned topic, that are in a foreign language, or that merely attempt to copy the topic or consist only of keystroke characters. The readers who evaluate the responses are college and university faculty members from various subject matter areas, including management education. These readers read holistically — that is, they respond to the overall quality of your critical thinking and writing. In addition, responses may be scored by e-rater™, an automated scoring program designed to reflect the judgment of expert readers.

To ensure the greatest possible accuracy and consistency in scoring, the readers are required to pass a certification test. Those who qualify are then rigorously trained, using actual candidates' responses that have been annotated by a "chief reader" chosen for his or her expertise in the holistic reading process. In addition, each response is given two independent ratings. If the ratings differ by more than a point, a third reader adjudicates. (Because of ongoing training and monitoring, discrepant ratings are rare.)

Your final score is the average (rounded to the nearest half point) of the four scores independently awarded to your responses — two scores for the Analysis of an Issue and two for the Analysis of an Argument. For example, if you earned scores of 6 and 5 on the Analysis of an Issue and 4 and 4 on the Analysis of an Argument, your final score would be 5: $(6 + 5 + 4 + 4) \div 4 = 4.75$, which rounds up to 5.

Your analytical writing scores are computed and reported separately from the multiple-choice sections of the test and have no effect on your verbal, quantitative, or total scores. The schools that you have designated to receive your scores may choose to receive a copy of your responses to the two writing tasks that comprise the Analytical Writing Assessment. Your own copy of your score report will not include copies of your responses.

Failure to write essays or work on the multiple-choice sections will result in no reportable scores.

What Your Scaled Scores Mean

The following tables contain information that will be of help in understanding your scaled scores. Each table consists of a column marked "Scaled Score" and a column indicating the percentage of test takers in the time period specified who scored below the scores listed. For example, if you earned a total scaled score of about 600 on the GMAT®, the 71 opposite 600 tells you that 71 percent of the 542,575 people taking the test in the 1997-2000 period earned scores lower than that; the remainder earned the same or a higher score. Also given in each table is the mean score of the group tested in the 1997-2000 time period.

Graduate school admissions officers understand the statistical meaning of *GMAT* scores, but each institution uses and interprets the scores according to the needs of its own programs. You should, therefore, consult the schools to which you are applying to learn how they will interpret and use your scores.

Table 1
Percentages of Examinees Tested from April 1997 through March 2000 (including Repeaters) Who Scored below Specified Verbal Scores

Verbal Scaled Score	Percentage Below	Verbal Scaled Score	Percentage Below
46 - 60	99	26	40
45	98	25	35
44	97	24	33
43	97	23	28
42	95	22	26
41	93	21	22
40	90	20	18
39	88	19	15
38	84	18	14
37	82	17	11
36	79	16	8
35	75	15	6
34	70	14	5
33	67	13	4
32	64	12	2
31	59	11	2
30	56	10	1
29	53	9	1
28	48	0 - 8	0
27	43		

Number of Candidates =	542,575
Mean =	27.9
Standard Deviation =	8.7

Table 2
Percentages of Examinees Tested from April 1997 through March 2000 (including Repeaters) Who Scored below Specified Quantitative Scores

Quantitative Scaled Score	Percentage Below	Quantitative Scaled Score	Percentage Below
51 - 60	99	28	25
50	97	27	21
49	93	26	20
48	90	25	16
47	86	24	15
46	84	23	13
45	82	22	11
44	78	21	9
43	75	20	8
42	71	19	7
41	68	18	6
40	66	17	5
39	61	16	4
38	58	15	4
37	56	14	3
36	51	13	2
35	47	12	2
34	44	11	1
33	41	10	1
32	37	9	1
31	33	8	1
30	31	0 - 7	0
29	27		

Number of Candidates =	542,575
Mean =	34.5
Standard Deviation =	10.0

Table 3
Percentages of Examinees Tested from
April 1997 through March 2000 (including Repeaters)
Who Scored below Specified Total Scores

Total Scaled Score	Percentage Below	Total Scaled Score	Percentage Below
750 - 800	99	480	32
740	98	470	29
730	97	460	25
720	96	450	23
710	95	440	21
700	93	430	19
690	92	420	17
680	90	410	15
670	89	400	13
660	87	390	11
650	85	380	10
640	81	370	8
630	80	360	7
620	77	350	6
610	74	340	5
600	71	330	4
590	68	320	3
580	65	310	3
570	62	300	2
560	58	290	2
550	55	280	2
540	51	270	1
530	47	260	1
520	45	250	1
510	42	240	1
500	38	200 - 230	0
490	35		

Number of Candidates =	542,575
Mean =	527
Standard Deviation =	112

Table 4
Percentages of Examinees Tested from
April 1997 through March 2000 (including Repeaters)
Who Scored below Specified AWA Scores

AWA Scaled Score	Percentage Below
6.0	97
5.5	91
5.0	80
4.5	63
4.0	43
3.5	26
3.0	13
2.5	6
2.0	2
1.5	1
1.0	1
0 - 0.5	0

Number of Candidates =	540,017
Mean =	3.9
Standard Deviation =	1.0

Guidelines for Use of
Graduate Management Admission Test Scores

Introduction

These guidelines have been prepared to provide information about appropriate score use for those who interpret scores and set criteria for admission and to protect students from unfair decisions based on inappropriate use of scores.

The guidelines are based on several policy and psychometric considerations.

■ The Graduate Management Admission Council® has an obligation to inform users of the scores' strengths and limitations, and the users have a concomitant obligation to use the scores in an appropriate, rather than the most convenient, manner.

■ The purpose of any testing instrument, including the Graduate Management Admission Test®, is to provide information to assist in making decisions; the test alone should not be presumed to be a decision maker.

■ GMAT® test scores are but one of a number of sources of information and should be used, whenever possible, in combination with other information and, in every case, with full recognition of what the test can and cannot do.

The primary asset of the *GMAT* is that it provides a common measure, administered under standard conditions, with known reliability, validity, and other psychometric qualities, for evaluating the academic skills of many individuals. The *GMAT* has two primary limitations: (1) it cannot and does not measure all the qualities important for graduate study in management and other pursuits; (2) there are psychometric limitations to the test — for example, only score differences of certain magnitudes are reliable indicators of real differences in performance. Such limits should be taken into consideration as *GMAT* scores are used.

Specific Guidelines

1. **In recognition of the test's limitations, use multiple criteria.** The *GMAT* itself does not measure every discipline-related skill necessary for academic work, nor does it measure subjective factors important to academic and career success, such as motivation, creativity, and interpersonal skills. Therefore, all available pertinent information about an applicant must be considered before a selection decision is made, with *GMAT* scores being only one of these criteria.

2. **Interpret the analytical writing score on the basis of the criteria and standards established in the *GMAT* Scoring Guides.** These criteria and standards are the best source for interpreting the analytical writing score. Recognize that the score is based on two 30-minute written responses that represent first-draft writing samples. Each response is evaluated according to the scoring guides, although the average score can result from different combinations of ratings. For example, a test taker whose individual ratings are 5 and 6 on the first topic and 3 and 3 on the second topic for an average score of 4.5 (rounded to the nearest half-point interval) receives the same score as a student whose individual ratings are 5 and 5 on the first topic and 4 and 4 on the second topic.

3. **Establish the relationship between *GMAT* scores and performance in your graduate management school.** It is incumbent on any institution using *GMAT* scores in the admissions process that it demonstrate empirically the relationship between test scores and measures of performance in its academic program. Data should be collected and analyzed to provide information about the predictive validity of *GMAT* scores and their appropriateness for the particular use and in the particular circumstances at the score-using school. In addition, any formula used in the admissions process that combines test scores with other criteria should be validated and reviewed regularly to determine whether the weights attached to the particular measures are appropriate for optimizing the prediction of performance in the program.

4. **Avoid the use of cutoff scores.** The use of arbitrary cut-off scores (below which no applicant will be considered for admission) is strongly discouraged, primarily for the reasons cited in the introduction to these guidelines. Distinctions based on score differences not substantial enough to be reliable should be avoided. (For information about reliability, see the GMAT® *Examinee Score Interpretation Guide.*) Cutoff scores should be used only if there is clear empirical evidence that a large proportion of the applicants scoring below the cutoff scores have substantial difficulty doing satisfactory graduate work. In addition, it is incumbent on the school to demonstrate that the use of cutoff scores does not result in the systematic exclusion of members of either sex, of any age or ethnic groups, or of any other relevant groups in the face of other evidence that would indicate their competence or predict their success.

5. **Do not compare *GMAT* scores with those on other tests.** *GMAT* scores cannot be derived from scores on other tests. The *GMAT* is not intended to be parallel to graduate admission tests offered by other testing programs.

6. **Interpret the scores of persons with disabilities cautiously.** The *GMAT* is offered with reasonable accommodations designed to meet the needs of examinees with documented disabilities. Because nonstandard test administrations are conducted under varying conditions and for only a small number of test takers, the degree of comparability of the resulting scores with those achieved under standard conditions is not known. When extended testing time is approved, a statement is included with the score report indicating that the test was taken under nonstandard testing conditions. Final responsibility for interpreting scores will rest with the score report recipient. Separate percentiles are not available for interpreting the scores of test takers who test under nonstandard conditions.

Normally Appropriate Uses of GMAT Scores

1. **For selection of applicants for graduate study in management.** A person's *GMAT* scores tell how the person performed on a test designed to measure general verbal and quantitative abilities that are associated with success in the first year of study at graduate schools of management and that have been developed over a long period of time. The scores can be used in conjunction with other information to help estimate performance in a graduate management program.

2. **For selection of applicants for financial aid based on academic potential.**

3. **For counseling and guidance.** Undergraduate counselors, if they maintain appropriate records, such as the test scores and undergraduate grade point averages of their students accepted by various graduate management programs, may be able to help students estimate their chances of acceptance at given graduate management schools.

Normally Inappropriate Uses of GMAT Scores

1. **As a requisite for awarding a degree.** The *GMAT* is designed to measure broadly defined verbal and quantitative skills and is primarily useful for predicting success in graduate management schools. The use of the test for anything other than selection for graduate management study, financial aid awards, or counseling and guidance is to be avoided.

2. **As a requirement for employment, for licensing or certification to perform a job, or for job-related rewards (raises, promotions, etc.).** For the reasons listed in number 1 above, the use of the *GMAT* for these purposes is inappropriate. Further, approved score-receiving institutions are not permitted to make score reports available for any of these purposes.

3. **As an achievement test.** The *GMAT* is not designed to assess an applicant's achievement or knowledge in specific subject areas.